Frommer's®
Florida

My Florida

by Lesley Abravanel

I'M NOT A NATIVE FLORIDIAN, ALTHOUGH SOME WOULD SAY OTHERWISE.

The general rule of thumb is that if you live in Florida for more than 10 years, you're a native. I've been here more than fifteen. As a born-and-bred New Yorker, I was reluctant to come at first, but I love it now. It's cool here—even if the temperature and humidity can occasionally make you think you're in purgatory. This state has more personalities than Shirley MacLaine, and contrary to popular belief, Florida is not just for retirees and Jennifer Lopez.

Whether you're into boating, fishing, camping, 'blading, boozing, or doing absolutely nothing, you'll find it down here, along with a fascinating mix of people from all cultures and walks of life. Where else can you go from sipping a fifty-dollar martini with Paris Hilton to sipping a two-dollar beer next to a guy from Paris, Texas—and still get the same tan? Florida has vibrancy, sexiness, sultriness, and, in parts, remnants of the old South. The thing about Florida is that it's not what you think it is. It's antique, modern, English, Spanish, deep South, and...I'll leave the rest for you to discover. It would be impossible to describe every facet of this fascinating state, but the photos on these pages capture some of my favorite Florida moments.

© Timothy O'Keefe/Index Stock

When you wish upon a star . . . dreams come true for kids of all ages in Mickey-land, where spinning in tea cups is just the beginning of the fun at **WALT DISNEY WORLD (left).** But WDW isn't all there is to do in Orlando. World-class hotels (some themed to keep the fantasy going, if you choose), outlet shopping, and, yes, other theme parks, are there in case you want them, too.

Thrill rides, theme rides, animated characters, animals, shows, and so much more are sure to entertain you and yours during your stay in Orlando. Don't miss out on the area's roller coasters—some of the best in the world, including the **INCREDIBLE HULK COASTER (above),** at Universal Orlando's Islands of Adventure.

© Richard Cummins/Lonely Planet Images

At Cape Canaveral and the **JOHN F. KENNEDY SPACE CENTER (left),** you can have lunch with an astronaut, feel a rock from the moon, learn how to get lost in space, eat astronaut ice cream, or, if you're lucky, watch an exhilarating shuttle launch or landing. Just keep your eyes on the sky.

Start your engines and plug your ears, because Daytona's racing culture is loud, not to mention exciting. NASCAR is a way of life in Daytona, as well it should be, but you needn't be a NASCAR fan to appreciate the thrill of speed at the **DAYTONA INTERNATIONAL SPEEDWAY (below).** Hear it, feel it, taste it. Just don't attempt it yourself—unless, of course, you're on one of Daytona's many tracks made just for those of us who don't speed for a living.

© Doug Scott/AGE Fotostock

Johnny Weissmuller swam at the **BILTMORE HOTEL'S POOL (left).** So did Esther Williams. But you don't need to be a swim champ to take a dip in Miami's largest pool, where, at times, it can feel like you're all alone on a deserted island. Peace and quiet abound at this pool, where size, indeed, does matter.

It may not be healthy to smoke, but watching someone hand roll cigars may tempt you to puff on one, if only for the experience. Most **LITTLE HAVANA CIGAR ROLLERS (above)** are authentic, having honed their skills in Cuba, but leaving when things got bad. In Miami, things are good, and there are plenty of reasons to celebrate with a hand-rolled stogie.

First page: top, © Doug Scott/AGE Fotostock; bottom, © J. Miller/Robert Harding Picture Library Ltd./Alamy

© 2005 Dan Vidal

South Florida will never leave you bored at night. Hit the techno-beaten path of celeb-saturated **DANCE CLUBS ON SOUTH BEACH (left).** Imbibe some of Fort Lauderdale's old Florida kitsch—like the **HAWAIIAN-THEMED MAI KAI (below),** where happy hour should be renamed Elation Hour and where drinks are larger than the size of most coconuts. Kick back in flip-flops and a t-shirt at **KEY WEST'S LEGENDARY SLOPPY JOE'S BAR (above right).** Or chug a beer with one of the many **HEMINGWAY DOPPELGANGERS (below right)** down in Margaritaville. While South Beach nightlife is a bit more stringent in terms of dress code and price (those mojito-minty-fresh-Cristal-champagne-infused 'tinis don't come cheap), Fort Lauderdale and the Florida Keys are much more laid back and old school (just order the drink straight up).

© Muñoz Studio Photography/The Mai-Kai Restaurant

SLOPPY
JOE'S
BAR
SLOPPY
JOE'S
BAR
SLOPPY JOE'S BAR
Cocktails
SLOPPY
JOE'S

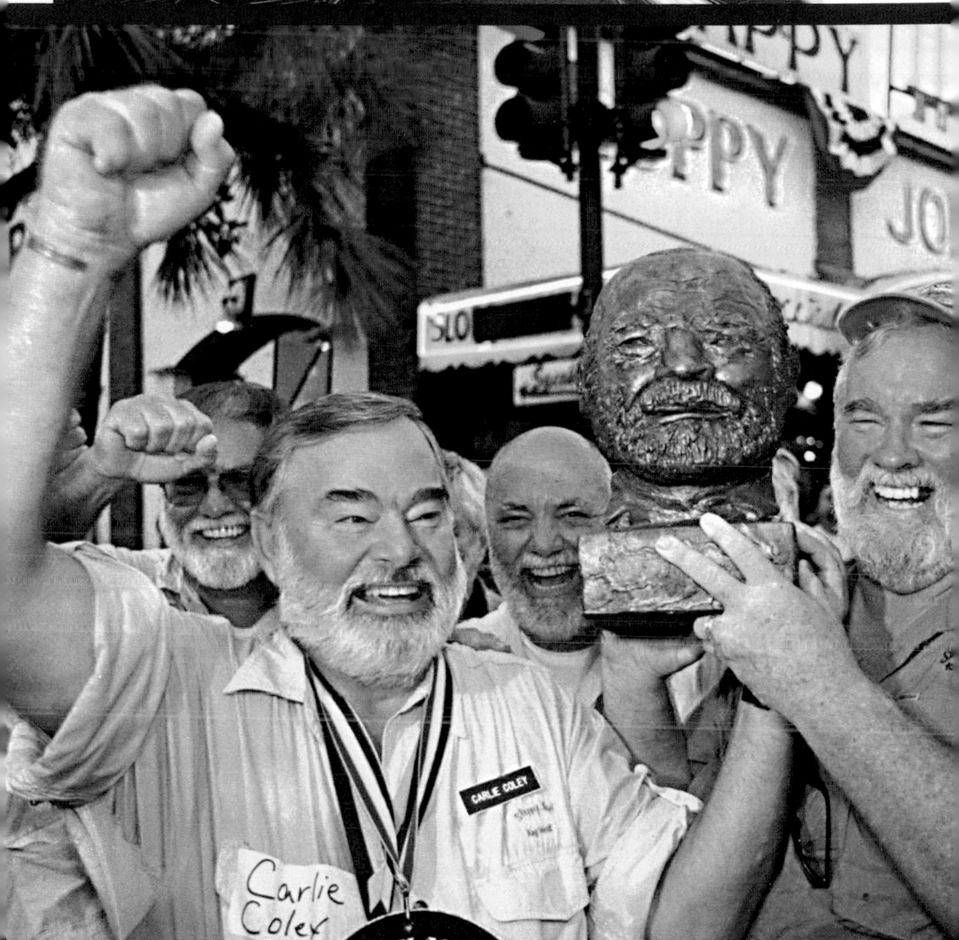

© Solomon's Castle

A long way from czarist Russia, **SOLOMON'S CASTLE (above)** epitomizes the American dream as seen by three generations of a family that escaped Russia in the early 1900s and landed in Ona, Florida. Sculptor and castle-maker Howard Solomon built and resides in this wacky attraction he created mostly from other people's "trash"—the outside of the castle is entirely made of printing plates. Solomon also sculpts, makes other art (a chair made of beer cans, anyone?), creates stained glass, and gives tours of the place. Don't miss this off-the-beaten-track attraction.

Japan is alive and well in South Florida, where the **MORIKAMI MUSEUM AND JAPANESE GARDENS (right)** brings Japanese culture to the state with gardens, a tea house, educational programs, and stunning flora and fauna indigenous to the Yamato Colony, a Japanese farming community that existed in South Florida over 100 years ago.

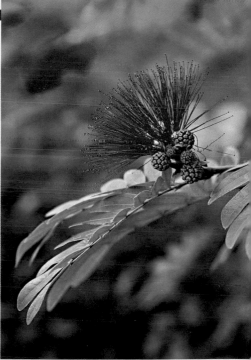

© Michiko Kurisu/Morikami Museum and Japanese Gardens

© S. Grandadam/Robert Harding Picture Library Ltd./Alamy

Don't linger over the state's unnatural wonders of silicone, botox, and saline, because Florida's got way too much natural beauty to be overlooked. First and foremost is the **EVERGLADES,** Florida's River of Grass, which is undeniably beautiful despite its beastly reputation. Take an **AIRBOAT RIDE (left)** to get a good feel for the area.

Although some people think the **MANATEE (below)** looks like a piece of gefilte fish, these endangered gentle giants are cute in their own peaceful way.

Look, but don't even think of touching the **ALLIGATORS (above right)** and crocs you may see across the state.

Under Florida's waters, you'll find a technicolor wonderland that even Mickey can't match. Try **SCUBA DIVING (below right)** and gawk at the coral reefs, neon-colored fish, and other things you'd only expect to see in a Pixar movie. Florida has spectacular scuba spots, both natural and manmade, including Jupiter Beach, where the remains of a Spanish galleon dating back to the 1600s lies in wreck, waiting for you to visit.

© Michael S. Nolan/AGE Fotostock

© Doug Scott/AGE Fotostock

© Stephen Frink/Corbis

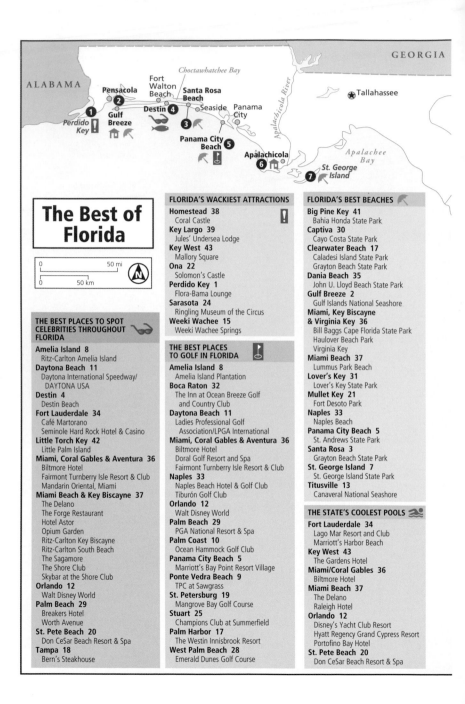

The Best of Florida

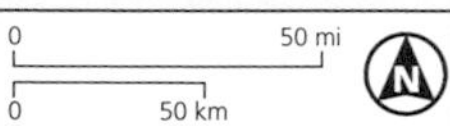

THE BEST PLACES TO SPOT CELEBRITIES THROUGHOUT FLORIDA

Amelia Island 8
Ritz-Carlton Amelia Island
Daytona Beach 11
Daytona International Speedway/ DAYTONA USA
Destin 4
Destin Beach
Fort Lauderdale 34
Café Martorano
Seminole Hard Rock Hotel & Casino
Little Torch Key 42
Little Palm Island
Miami, Coral Gables & Aventura 36
Biltmore Hotel
Fairmont Turnberry Isle Resort & Club
Mandarin Oriental, Miami
Miami Beach & Key Biscayne 37
The Delano
The Forge Restaurant
Hotel Astor
Opium Garden
Ritz-Carlton Key Biscayne
Ritz-Carlton South Beach
The Sagamore
The Shore Club
Skybar at the Shore Club
Orlando 12
Walt Disney World
Palm Beach 29
Breakers Hotel
Worth Avenue
St. Pete Beach 20
Don CeSar Beach Resort & Spa
Tampa 18
Bern's Steakhouse

FLORIDA'S WACKIEST ATTRACTIONS

Homestead 38
Coral Castle
Key Largo 39
Jules' Undersea Lodge
Key West 43
Mallory Square
Ona 22
Solomon's Castle
Perdido Key 1
Flora-Bama Lounge
Sarasota 24
Ringling Museum of the Circus
Weeki Wachee 15
Weeki Wachee Springs

THE BEST PLACES TO GOLF IN FLORIDA

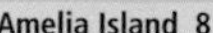

Amelia Island 8
Amelia Island Plantation
Boca Raton 32
The Inn at Ocean Breeze Golf and Country Club
Daytona Beach 11
Ladies Professional Golf Association/LPGA International
Miami, Coral Gables & Aventura 36
Biltmore Hotel
Doral Golf Resort and Spa
Fairmont Turnberry Isle Resort & Club
Naples 33
Naples Beach Hotel & Golf Club
Tiburón Golf Club
Orlando 12
Walt Disney World
Palm Beach 29
PGA National Resort & Spa
Palm Coast 10
Ocean Hammock Golf Club
Panama City Beach 5
Marriott's Bay Point Resort Village
Ponte Vedra Beach 9
TPC at Sawgrass
St. Petersburg 19
Mangrove Bay Golf Course
Stuart 25
Champions Club at Summerfield
Palm Harbor 17
The Westin Innisbrook Resort
West Palm Beach 28
Emerald Dunes Golf Course

FLORIDA'S BEST BEACHES

Big Pine Key 41
Bahia Honda State Park
Captiva 30
Cayo Costa State Park
Clearwater Beach 17
Caladesi Island State Park
Grayton Beach State Park
Dania Beach 35
John U. Lloyd Beach State Park
Gulf Breeze 2
Gulf Islands National Seashore
Miami, Key Biscayne & Virginia Key 36
Bill Baggs Cape Florida State Park
Haulover Beach Park
Virginia Key
Miami Beach 37
Lummus Park Beach
Lover's Key 31
Lover's Key State Park
Mullet Key 21
Fort Desoto Park
Naples 33
Naples Beach
Panama City Beach 5
St. Andrews State Park
Santa Rosa 3
Grayton Beach State Park
St. George Island 7
St. George Island State Park
Titusville 13
Canaveral National Seashore

THE STATE'S COOLEST POOLS

Fort Lauderdale 34
Lago Mar Resort and Club
Marriott's Harbor Beach
Key West 43
The Gardens Hotel
Miami/Coral Gables 36
Biltmore Hotel
Miami Beach 37
The Delano
Raleigh Hotel
Orlando 12
Disney's Yacht Club Resort
Hyatt Regency Grand Cypress Resort
Portofino Bay Hotel
St. Pete Beach 20
Don CeSar Beach Resort & Spa

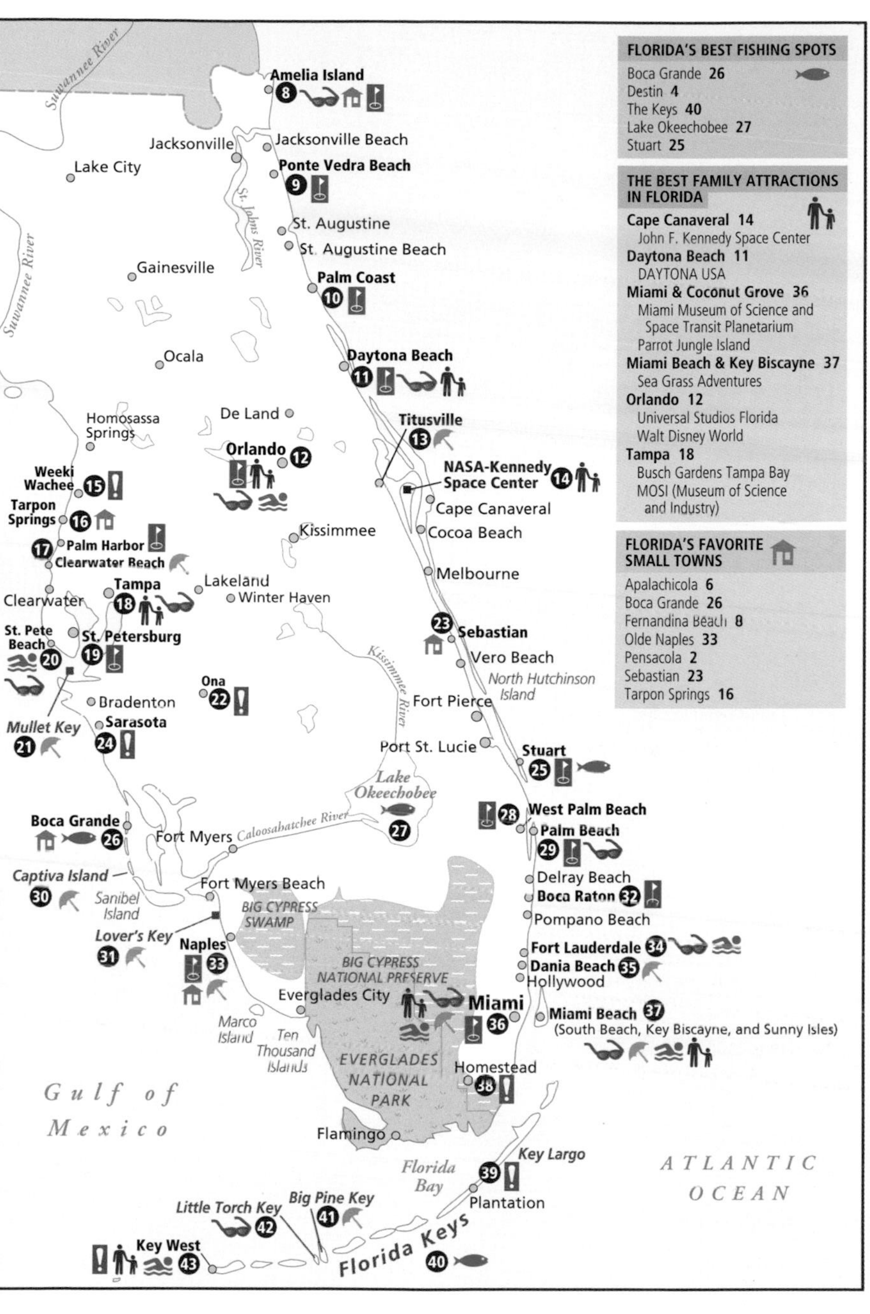

FLORIDA'S BEST FISHING SPOTS
Boca Grande 26
Destin 4
The Keys 40
Lake Okeechobee 27
Stuart 25
THE BEST FAMILY ATTRACTIONS IN FLORIDA
Cape Canaveral 14
John F. Kennedy Space Center
Daytona Beach 11
DAYTONA USA
Miami & Coconut Grove 36
Miami Museum of Science and Space Transit Planetarium
Parrot Jungle Island
Miami Beach & Key Biscayne 37
Sea Grass Adventures
Orlando 12
Universal Studios Florida
Walt Disney World
Tampa 18
Busch Gardens Tampa Bay
MOSI (Museum of Science and Industry)
FLORIDA'S FAVORITE SMALL TOWNS
Apalachicola 6
Boca Grande 26
Fernandina Beach 8
Olde Naples 33
Pensacola 2
Sebastian 23
Tarpon Springs 16
Suwannee River
Amelia Island 8
Jacksonville
Jacksonville Beach
Lake City
Ponte Vedra Beach 9
St. Johns River
St. Augustine
St. Augustine Beach
Gainesville
Palm Coast 10
Ocala
Daytona Beach 11
De Land
Homosassa Springs
Titusville 13
Orlando 12
NASA-Kennedy Space Center 14
Weeki Wachee 15
Tarpon Springs 16
Cape Canaveral
Kissimmee
Cocoa Beach
Palm Harbor 17
Clearwater Beach
Melbourne
Lakeland
Tampa 18
Winter Haven
Clearwater
Sebastian 23
St. Pete Beach 20
St. Petersburg 19
Vero Beach
Kissimmee River
North Hutchinson Island
Ona 22
Bradenton
Fort Pierce
Mullet Key 21
Sarasota 24
Port St. Lucie
Stuart 25
Lake Okeechobee 27
West Palm Beach 28
Boca Grande 26
Fort Myers
Caloosahatchee River
Palm Beach 29
Captiva Island 30
Sanibel Island
Fort Myers Beach
Delray Beach
Boca Raton 32
BIG CYPRESS SWAMP
Pompano Beach
Lover's Key 31
Naples 33
Fort Lauderdale 34
Dania Beach 35
BIG CYPRESS NATIONAL PRESERVE
Hollywood
Everglades City
Miami 36
Miami Beach 37
(South Beach, Key Biscayne, and Sunny Isles)
Marco Island
Ten Thousand Islands
EVERGLADES NATIONAL PARK
Homestead 38
Gulf of Mexico
Flamingo
Key Largo
Florida Bay
39
ATLANTIC OCEAN
Plantation
Little Torch Key 42
Big Pine Key 41
Key West 43
Florida Keys
40

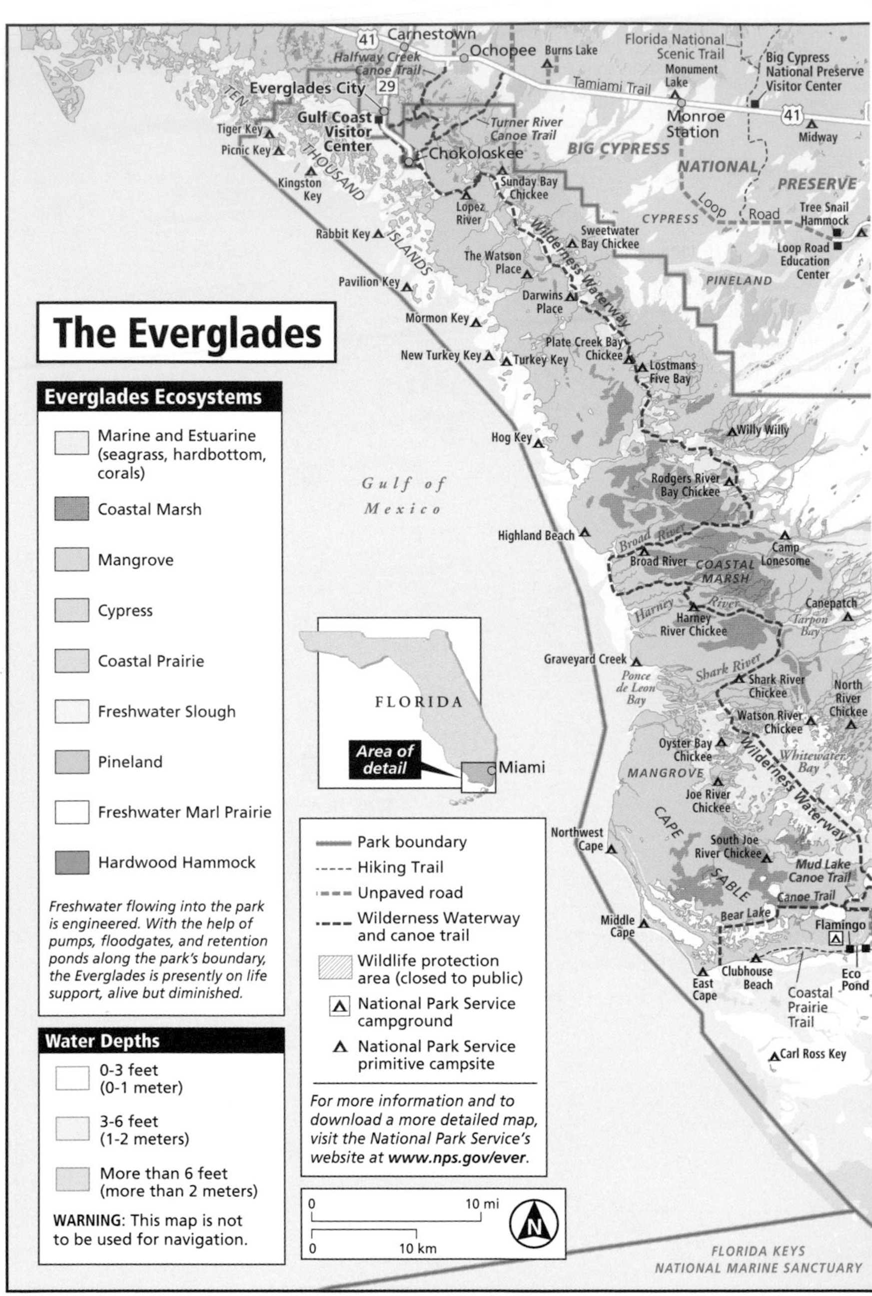

The Everglades
Everglades Ecosystems
Marine and Estuarine (seagrass, hardbottom, corals)
Coastal Marsh
Mangrove
Cypress
Coastal Prairie
Freshwater Slough
Pineland
Freshwater Marl Prairie
Hardwood Hammock
Freshwater flowing into the park is engineered. With the help of pumps, floodgates, and retention ponds along the park's boundary, the Everglades is presently on life support, alive but diminished.
Water Depths
0-3 feet (0-1 meter)
3-6 feet (1-2 meters)
More than 6 feet (more than 2 meters)
WARNING: This map is not to be used for navigation.
Park boundary
Hiking Trail
Unpaved road
Wilderness Waterway and canoe trail
Wildlife protection area (closed to public)
National Park Service campground
National Park Service primitive campsite
For more information and to download a more detailed map, visit the National Park Service's website at www.nps.gov/ever.
0
10 mi
0
10 km
N
FLORIDA
Area of detail
Miami
Gulf of Mexico
41
Carnestown
Ochopee
Burns Lake
Florida National Scenic Trail
Monument Lake
Big Cypress National Preserve Visitor Center
Halfway Creek Canoe Trail
Everglades City
29
Gulf Coast Visitor Center
Tamiami Trail
Monroe Station
41
Midway
Turner River Canoe Trail
Chokoloskee
BIG CYPRESS NATIONAL PRESERVE
TEN THOUSAND ISLANDS
Tiger Key
Picnic Key
Kingston Key
Sunday Bay Chickee
Lopez River
Loop Road
Tree Snail Hammock
CYPRESS
Sweetwater Bay Chickee
Loop Road Education Center
Rabbit Key
The Watson Place
PINELAND
Pavilion Key
Darwins Place
Wilderness Waterway
Mormon Key
Plate Creek Bay Chickee
New Turkey Key
Turkey Key
Lostmans Five Bay
Willy Willy
Hog Key
Rodgers River Bay Chickee
Highland Beach
Broad River
Broad River
Camp Lonesome
COASTAL MARSH
Harney River
Harney River Chickee
Canepatch
Tarpon Bay
Graveyard Creek
Ponce de Leon Bay
Shark River
Shark River Chickee
North River Chickee
Watson River Chickee
Oyster Bay Chickee
Whitewater Bay
MANGROVE
Joe River Chickee
Wilderness Waterway
CAPE SABLE
Northwest Cape
South Joe River Chickee
Mud Lake Canoe Trail
Canoe Trail
Bear Lake
Middle Cape
Flamingo
East Cape
Clubhouse Beach
Eco Pond
Coastal Prairie Trail
Carl Ross Key
FLORIDA KEYS NATIONAL MARINE SANCTUARY

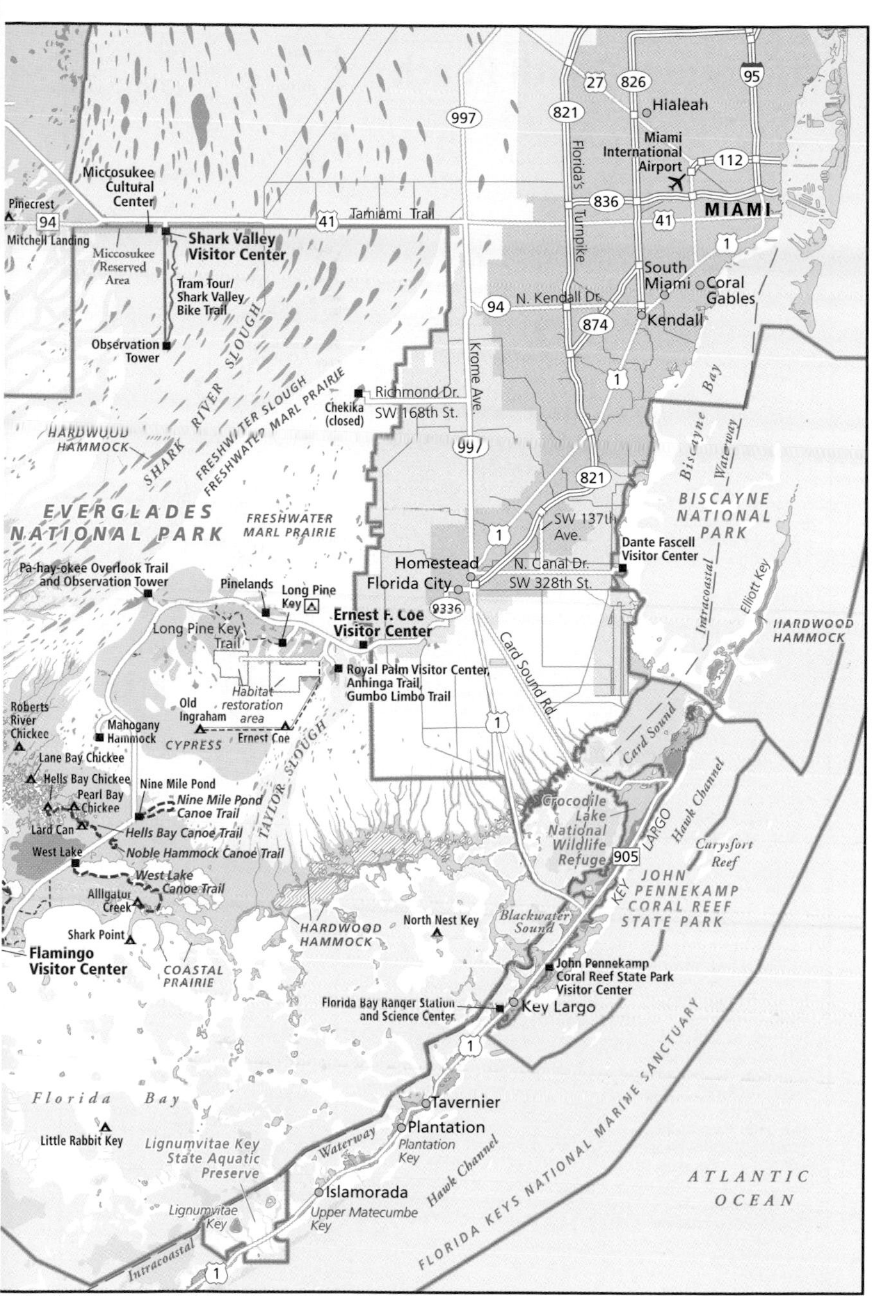

Hialeah
Miami International Airport
MIAMI
Tamiami Trail
Miccosukee Cultural Center
Pinecrest
Mitchell Landing
Miccosukee Reserved Area
Shark Valley Visitor Center
Tram Tour/ Shark Valley Bike Trail
Observation Tower
SHARK RIVER SLOUGH
FRESHWATER SLOUGH
FRESHWATER MARL PRAIRIE
Florida's Turnpike
South Miami
Coral Gables
Kendall
N. Kendall Dr.
Krome Ave.
Richmond Dr.
SW 168th St.
Chekika (closed)
HARDWOOD HAMMOCK
EVERGLADES NATIONAL PARK
FRESHWATER MARL PRAIRIE
Biscayne Bay
Biscayne Waterway
BISCAYNE NATIONAL PARK
SW 137th Ave.
Dante Fascell Visitor Center
Homestead
Florida City
N. Canal Dr.
SW 328th St.
Pa-hay-okee Overlook Trail and Observation Tower
Pinelands
Long Pine Key
Ernest F. Coe Visitor Center
Long Pine Key Trail
Royal Palm Visitor Center, Anhinga Trail, Gumbo Limbo Trail
Habitat restoration area
Card Sound Rd.
Intracoastal
Elliott Key
HARDWOOD HAMMOCK
Roberts River Chickee
Mahogany Hammock
Old Ingraham
Ernest Coe
CYPRESS
TAYLOR SLOUGH
Card Sound
Lane Bay Chickee
Hells Bay Chickee
Pearl Bay Chickee
Nine Mile Pond
Nine Mile Pond Canoe Trail
Lard Can
Hells Bay Canoe Trail
Noble Hammock Canoe Trail
West Lake
West Lake Canoe Trail
Alligator Creek
Crocodile Lake National Wildlife Refuge
KEY LARGO
Hawk Channel
Carysfort Reef
JOHN PENNEKAMP CORAL REEF STATE PARK
Shark Point
Flamingo Visitor Center
COASTAL PRAIRIE
HARDWOOD HAMMOCK
North Nest Key
Blackwater Sound
John Pennekamp Coral Reef State Park Visitor Center
Florida Bay Ranger Station and Science Center
Key Largo
Florida Bay
Little Rabbit Key
Lignumvitae Key State Aquatic Preserve
Tavernier
Plantation
Plantation Key
Waterway
Hawk Channel
FLORIDA KEYS NATIONAL MARINE SANCTUARY
ATLANTIC OCEAN
Islamorada
Upper Matecumbe Key
Lignumvitae Key
Intracoastal

Notorious South Beach

ONLY ON SOUTH BEACH

Hotel Victor 11
P. Diddy hosted this hotel's grand opening and got in trouble by PETA (People for the Ethical Treatment of Animals) for using penguins as props. Also at the Hotel Victor, Shaquille O' Neal's wife Shaunie threw #32 a surprise 33rd birthday party. She got a cake that was a life-sized replica of Shaq— nearly six feet tall and costing $10,000!

Mansion 8
Here, Lindsay Lohan drank "water" all night while her ex-boyfriend Wilmer Valderrama hosted a New Year's party. Britney Spears's ex, Kevin Federline, hosted a party here, too, promoting the release of his new CD. It's also where Jennifer Lopez and Marc Anthony staged a photo-op to prove they were married.

Prime One Twelve 20
Everyone who's anyone has eaten here—from Madonna and Jamie Foxx to the entire Miami Heat team, who closed down the restaurant after winning the 2006 NBA championship.

Raleigh Hotel 3
Madonna, Guy Ritchie, Demi Moore, and boytoy Ashton Kutcher played in the sand here with Madonna's kids while they were all in town for a Kabbalah meeting.

The Setai 1
Beyonce and Jay-Z are almost always hanging out poolside at this homage to Asian swankiness. Rumor has it that Jay-Z may buy the multi-million dollar penthouse here and make it his and Beyonce's permanent home.

Skybar at the Shore Club 2
At Skybar, Jay-Z asked a cocktail waitress if she could get him chicken wings (something that establishment would normally never dream of serving). Nevertheless, the cocktail waitress ran to KFC to accommodate his order.

Versace Mansion 11
The unfortunate spot where fashion designer Gianni Versace was gunned down by an obsessed fan.

FILMED ON SOUTH BEACH

Big Pink 19
In *There's Something About Mary*, Big Pink is where Cameron Diaz and her friends whined and dined. Most recently in 2007, British Prime Minister Tony Blair was captured on film eating a chicken Caesar salad, which he remarked was "massive."

Current site of Johnny Rocket's 16
Remember the brutal chainsaw scene in *Scarface*? The site where that was filmed is now a Johnny Rocket's… Mmm. Pass the ketchup!

Miami Beach Community Church 5
This church was used to simulate California as Cher and Greg Kinnear drank margaritas in *Stuck on You*.

National Hotel 4
This hotel's famous pool was wrongly identified as being the pool from The Delano in the 1999 Sydney Pollack, Harrison Ford film *Random Hearts*.

Nikki Beach Club 20
Justin Guarini and Kelly Clarkson filmed *From Justin to Kelly* here.

South Pointe Park 21
Justin Guarini arrived on the beach at South Pointe via hovercraft in *From Justin to Kelly*.

**You might think that more or better films have been made on South Beach, but the pickings are actually quite slim. Perhaps that's because all the stars, crew, and so forth are so busy partying in South Beach's clubs 24/7 during shooting that nothing ever actually gets done.*

SOUTH BEACH'S BEST ART DECO BUILDINGS

Breakwater Hotel 14
Cardozo Hotel 9
Carlyle Hotel 10
Colony Hotel 16
Essex House 12
Hotel Astor 13
Hotel Chelsea 13
Imperial 17
Leslie 10
Miami Beach Post Office 7
Park Central Hotel 17
Waldorf Towers 15

THE HIPPEST PLACES ON SOUTH BEACH

China Grill 18
Delano 4
Mansion 8
Nikki Beach Club 20
Opium Garden 19
Prime One Twelve 20
The Sagamore 4
Skybar at the Shore Club 2
The Room 19
The Setai 1

THE BEST PLACES TO SPOT CELEBRITIES ON SOUTH BEACH

Delano 4
Hotel Astor 13
Opium Garden 19
Prime One Twelve 20
Ritz-Carlton South Beach 6
The Sagamore 4
The Setai 1
The Shore Club 2
Skybar at the Shore Club 2

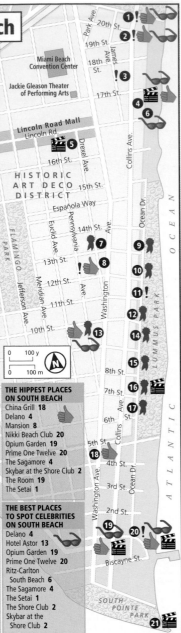

Frommer's®

Florida 2010

by Lesley Abravanel

with Laura Miller

Here's what the critics say about Frommer's:

"Amazingly easy to use. Very portable, very complete."
—BOOKLIST

"Detailed, accurate, and easy-to-read information for all price ranges."
—GLAMOUR MAGAZINE

"Hotel information is close to encyclopedic."
—DES MOINES SUNDAY REGISTER

"Frommer's Guides have a way of giving you a real feel for a place."
—KNIGHT RIDDER NEWSPAPERS

WILEY

Wiley Publishing, Inc.

Published by:

WILEY PUBLISHING, INC.

111 River St.
Hoboken, NJ 07030-5774

ISBN 978-0-470-48216-2

Editor: Stephen Bassman
Production Editor: Jonathan Scott
Cartographer: Andrew Dolan
Photo Editor: Richard Fox
Production by Wiley Indianapolis Composition Services

Front cover photo: Smathers Beach in Key West at dawn. ©Rod McLean/Alamy Images
Back cover photo: Sanibel Island: Roseate Spoonbill walking in shallow water.
©Adam Jones/DanitaDelimont.com/Alamy Images

For information on our other products and services or to obtain technical support, please contact our Customer Care Department within the U.S. at 877/762-2974, outside the U.S. at 317/572-3993 or fax 317/572-4002.

Wiley also publishes its books in a variety of electronic formats. Some content that appears in print may not be available in electronic formats.

Manufactured in the United States of America

5 4 3 2 1

CONTENTS

4 SUGGESTED FLORIDA ITINERARIES 61

5 WHERE TO STAY & DINE IN MIAMI 73

6 WHAT TO SEE & DO IN MIAMI 145

7 THE KEYS & THE DRY TORTUGAS 188

8 THE EVERGLADES & BISCAYNE NATIONAL PARK 246

9 THE GOLD COAST: HALLANDALE TO THE PALM BEACHES 262

10 THE TREASURE COAST: STUART TO SEBASTIAN 309

11 SOUTHWEST FLORIDA 324

12 THE TAMPA BAY AREA 382

13 WALT DISNEY WORLD & ORLANDO 450

14 NORTHEAST FLORIDA 512

15 NORTHWEST FLORIDA: THE PANHANDLE 576

APPENDIX: FAST FACTS, TOLL-FREE NUMBERS & WEBSITES 635

INDEX 643

LIST OF MAPS

ACKNOWLEDGMENTS

To my mother and father, without whose influence, encouragement, and support I never would have ended up in Miami doing what I'm doing. To all the publicists and proprietors for putting up with the endless e-mails, inquiries, and spur-of-the-moment visits, I thank you for your cooperation and eagerness to answer pressing questions about hair dryers, irons, hours, and credit cards. Thanks to all my friends and colleagues who know that I'm more than a party girl and accept my quirkiness, compulsive behavior, and genuine penchant for all things bizarre. A special thanks to my muse Winston for holding it in until I was done. And, last but not at all least, thanks to my husband, Magnus, for putting up with me and my inanity and insanity.

—Lesley Abravanel

ABOUT THE AUTHORS

Lesley Abravanel is a freelance journalist and a graduate of the University of Miami School of Communication. When she isn't combing South Florida for the latest hotels, restaurants, and attractions, she's on the lookout for vacationing celebrities, about whom she writes in her thrice-weekly nightlife and gossip columns and blog, "Scene in the Tropics" and "Velvet Underground," for the *Miami Herald.* She is a contributor to *Time Out* and all three illustrious supermarket tabloids. She is the author of *Frommer's South Florida, Florida For Dummies,* and *Frommer's Portable Miami.*

Laura Miller is a freelance writer based in Orchard Park, New York, though she's spent countless hours scouring Central Florida's theme parks, hotels, and restaurants over the years—with and without the help of her five children. A family travel expert who religiously makes more than just a few trips to the Land the Mouse built, she is also writing a guide and creating a website about Florida just for families.

HOW TO CONTACT US

In researching this book, we discovered many wonderful places—hotels, restaurants, shops, and more. We're sure you'll find others. Please tell us about them, so we can share the information with your fellow travelers in upcoming editions. If you were disappointed with a recommendation, we'd love to know that, too. Please write to:

Frommer's Florida 2010
Wiley Publishing, Inc. • 111 River St. • Hoboken, NJ 07030-5774

AN ADDITIONAL NOTE

Please be advised that travel information is subject to change at any time—and this is especially true of prices. We therefore suggest that you write or call ahead for confirmation when making your travel plans. The authors, editors, and publisher cannot be held responsible for the experiences of readers while traveling. Your safety is important to us, however, so we encourage you to stay alert and be aware of your surroundings. Keep a close eye on cameras, purses, and wallets, all favorite targets of thieves and pickpockets.

FROMMER'S STAR RATINGS, ICONS & ABBREVIATIONS

Every hotel, restaurant, and attraction listing in this guide has been ranked for quality, value, service, amenities, and special features using a **star-rating system.** In country, state, and regional guides, we also rate towns and regions to help you narrow down your choices and budget your time accordingly. Hotels and restaurants are rated on a scale of zero (recommended) to three stars (exceptional). Attractions, shopping, nightlife, towns, and regions are rated according to the following scale: zero stars (recommended), one star (highly recommended), two stars (very highly recommended), and three stars (must-see).

In addition to the star-rating system, we also use **six feature icons** that point you to the great deals, in-the-know advice, and unique experiences that separate travelers from tourists. Throughout the book, look for:

Finds	Special finds—those places only insiders know about
Fun Facts	Fun facts—details that make travelers more informed and their trips more fun
Moments	Special moments—those experiences that memories are made of
Overrated	Places or experiences not worth your time or money
Tips	Insider tips—great ways to save time and money
Value	Great values—where to get the best deals

The following abbreviations are used for credit cards:

AE	American Express	DISC	Discover	V	Visa
DC	Diners Club	MC	MasterCard		

TRAVEL RESOURCES AT FROMMERS.COM

Frommer's travel resources don't end with this guide. Frommer's website, **www.frommers.com**, has travel information on more than 4,000 destinations. We update features regularly, giving you access to the most current trip-planning information and the best airfare, lodging, and car-rental bargains. You can also listen to podcasts, connect with other Frommers.com members through our active-reader forums, share your travel photos, read blogs from guidebook editors and fellow travelers, and much more.

What's New in Florida

Miami Despite the shaky real estate market and predicted bust, the city remains as photogenic as ever. Still beautiful, especially at night and during sunset, the photogenic Miami skyline is peppered with cranes working hard to raise swank, zillion-dollar condos and hotels—or, for the really trendy, condo/hotels for which buyers plunk down millions to live like Eloise in a bona fide hotel. A cash crop of hyperluxe hotels and restaurants have proven that, yes, people will spend thousands of dollars per night on a hotel room and $30 for a drink. Today there's more culture than what is dubiously found inside the city's nightclubs. The nearly $500-million Adrienne Arsht Center for the Performing Arts is in the very fashionable black and ready for its own close-up—despite the fact that, in typical Miami fashion, they forgot to build a parking lot. But that's another story.

Where to Stay in Miami Miami Beach's famed **Eden Roc Resort and Spa** (✆ **305/531-0000**) reopened with $110 million worth of renovations. In the multimillion-dollar makeover, the hotel added a second tower with 283 rooms. See p. 101

Fontainebleau Hotel & Resort (✆ **800/548-8886** or 305/538-2000) debuted its $500-million reconstruction/expansion of the original resort. Gone are most of the Art Deco details and new are 11 restaurants, nightclubs, spa, 825 ultramodern rooms—and a 70% increase on room rates.

Hip has arrived on South Beach's quiet, residential west end in the form of the Morgans Group's terminally trendy **Mondrian,** 1100 West Ave. (✆ **305/672-2662**), a Marcel Wanders designed marvel modeled in the vein of, say, Sleeping Beauty meets South Beach.

The **W Hotel** chain has begun construction on an old Holiday Inn at 2201 Collins and is in the process of turning it into a 25-story condo/hotel with 511 units, trademark Bliss spa, two pools, and a Rande Gerber–owned hip hotel bar. Completion is slated for mid-2010.

Giuseppe Cipriani, of the famous Italian hotel and Harry's Bar, plans to transform the Deco Saxony Hotel into a 170-room luxury condo/hotel. **The Cipriani Resort and Residences South Beach** is expected to open in 2010.

Downtown Miami is still slowly on its way to being a decent place to stay, and Kimpton Hotels hopes to make the area hot with its new **Epic Hotel,** 270 Biscayne Blvd. Way (✆ **305/424-5226**), a modern, 411-room stay with 13,752-square-foot wraparound pool deck with two swimming pools, and fine and casual waterfront dining, including a modern Mediterranean-style restaurant, a waterfront lounge, and a full-service spa and fitness center operated by Exhale.

Across the bridge is the **Viceroy,** 485 Brickell Ave. (✆ **866/720 1991**), a 162-room, Kelly Wearstler–designed resort featuring a sweeping, 15th floor recreation area, hip restaurant, and 28,000-square-foot spa.

Where to Dine in Miami Jonathan Eismann was forced to close his Lincoln Road mainstay, **Pacific Time,** because the rent was too high, but the move into the cheaper, hipper Design District at 35 NE 40th St. (✆ **305/722-7639**) won rave reviews in 2008. Meanwhile occupying the old Lincoln Road Pacific Time is the aptly titled **Meat Market,** 915 Lincoln Rd. (✆ **305/532-0088**), yet another contemporary American steakhouse brought to us by the owners of the now defunct fusion eatery Touch.

China Grill continues to dominate Miami's culinary continent, not just by adding a branch of the Asian-eatery in Fort Lauderdale or with its new zillion-dollar **Kobe Club** at the South Beach China Grill, but with its brand-new Miami branch of **Asia de Cuba** at the hot new Mondrian, 1100 West Ave. (✆ **305/672-2662**).

After moving to its new home at the Hotel Astor, **Maison D'Azur,** 956 Washington Ave. (✆ **305/403-1062**), is *still* where St. Tropez meets South Beach over a flute of champagne and some seriously spectacular seafood. See p. 117.

In other hotel restaurant news, **Philippe,** 2305 Collins Ave. (✆ **305/674-0250**), the high-end (read: pricey) Chinese gourmet spot owned by Philippe Chow opened in the Gansevoort South. Also expected to open there, another steakhouse, this time **STK;** over at the Fontainebleau, another celeb-owned meatery, Alfred Portale's **Gotham Steak,** 4441 Collins Ave. (✆ **305/674-4780**); and high-end N.Y.C. Italian import **Scarpetta,** 4441 Collins Ave. (✆ **305/674-4660**). At the newly renovated Betsy Hotel on Ocean Drive—no joke—another steakhouse, **BLT,** owned by star chef Laurent Tourondel. And just around the corner from bustling Prime 112 in the South of Fifth area of South Beach, **Red The Steakhouse,** 119 Washington Ave. (✆ **305/534-3688**), a Cleveland import housed in a sleek, sexy space and a favorite of basketball legend Michael Jordan.

Nearby in the Design District are star chef Michelle Bernstein's restaurant **Sra. Martinez,** 4000 NE 2nd Ave. (✆ **305/573-5474**), a hip Spanish tapas eatery and brick-walled lounge, and **Fratelli Lyon,** 4141 NE 2nd Ave. (✆ **305/572-2901;** p. 132), a fantastically modern Italian restaurant and wine bar housed in a funky furniture showroom.

After Dark in Miami The masterminds behind Opium, Prive, Mansion, and SET debuted **Louis,** at the Gansevoort South (✆ **305/531-4600**), yet another den of hipster inequity housed behind the hotel's shark tank. See p. 90. **LIV,** a Vegas-style nightclub, has opened at the expanded Fontainebleau Miami Beach. Also at the Fbleau: **Blade,** a subterranean sushi spot and bar located near the resort's pool. The number is the same for both (✆ **305/538-2000**).

THE KEYS The newest luxury resort to hit Key West, **Beachside Resort & Conference Center,** 3841 N. Roosevelt Blvd. (✆ **800/546-0885** or 305/296-8100), is now a Marriott. Apparently luxury still needs a name brand. Official new name: **Key West Marriott Beachside Hotel.** See p. 230. More luxe in Key West can be found nearby at the **Parrot Key Resort,** 2801 N. Roosevelt Blvd. (✆ **305/809-2200**), featuring 74 comfy chic, conch-style beach houses.

THE GOLD COAST While the Gold Coast's beaches remain less congested than those in Miami, the area isn't impervious to development—especially when it comes to resorts, restaurants, and nightlife.

Where to Stay on the Gold Coast Florida's first St. Regis, a $135-million, 23-story luxe property in Fort Lauderdale, with nearly 200 rooms, a gourmet restaurant, an air-conditioned walkway to the beach, a massive spa, and more, couldn't swing it and is now the **Ritz-Carlton Fort Lauderdale** (✆ **800/325-3589**). See p. 274.

The **W Hotel** (✆ **954/525-8133**) is slated to open in the spring of 2009 on Fort Lauderdale Beach. The $220-million boutique-hotel-condominium features the usual W Hotel bells and whistles, including the signature bar and restaurant.

A former Marriott went the boutique route and is now the 589-room **Fort Lauderdale Grande Hotel & Yacht Club** (✆ **954/761-8011**), after a $70-million transformation added a new lobby, redesigned guestrooms and suites, a refurbished swimming pool and tropical deck, and a China Grill restaurant.

Donald Trump is converting a private condo on Fort Lauderdale Beach into the **Trump International Beach Club.** True to Trump's character, some of the 14-story building's suites will be available for purchase. Opening is slated for mid-2009. By the time we go to print, construction should be completed on the **Trump International Hotel & Tower Fort Lauderdale,** a 24-story building designed by world-renowned Michael Graves & Associates. The property will be composed of residences as well as hotel rooms, and its location will afford views of both the Atlantic Ocean and Greater Fort Lauderdale's Intracoastal Waterway. The future of **Trump Las Olas,** a 95 unit resort on Fort Lauderdale beach, is still unclear as we go to print; construction is mostly finished, but Trump says they won't open if fewer than 50 percent of buyers close on their units. Another casualty of the economy?

SOUTHWEST FLORIDA Although Southwest Florida still rests on its natural laurels, it's not impervious to inevitable development, which has taken shape in the form of new museums, shopping centers, and hotels.

The **Children's Museum of Naples** (www.cmon.org) is scheduled to open in spring 2010 with a unique array of quality, interactive educational experiences for children. The museum is located in North Naples Regional Park, a new Collier County public park that will also have a water-park attraction, nature trails, and extensive team sports facilities. See p. 366.

The **Hotel at Naples Bay Resort,** 1500 5th Ave. South (✆ **230/530-1199**), is an 85-room hotel that opened in 2008, part of the new Naples Bay Resort mixed-use development on the Gordon River, with direct access to Naples Bay and the Gulf of Mexico. Naples Bay Resort also includes condos, a spa, vacation cottages, a marina, restaurants, and shopping. See p. 367.

The **Ritz-Carlton, Naples,** 280 Vanderbilt Beach Rd. (✆ **239/598-3300**), opened its state-of-the-art Natures Wonders children's activity center, all themed around the Southwest Florida environment. See p. 370.

Bellasera Hotel, 221 9th St. S. (✆ **239/649-7333**), opened Verde, a new environmentally friendly spa, in April 2008 boasting 100% organic products. See p. 367.

Naples Zoo at Caribbean Gardens, 1590 Goodlette Rd. (✆ **239/262-5409**), is the only zoo in Florida to exhibit the fosa, a rare predator from Madagascar.

Everglades Area Tours (✆ **239/695-9107**) now offers guided half-day kayak eco-tours, customized bird-watching expeditions, as well as bicycle and aerial tours of the Everglades.

A recently added third phase has been opened on the **Great Calusa Blueway** (www.greatcalusablueway.com) through Estero Bay. The third phase leads paddlers to the Caloosahatchee River's creeks and meandering waters.

New on Sanibel Island: **The Sanibel Sea School** (✆ **239/472-8585**), where children and adults learn about marine ecosystems on Sanibel and Captiva islands.

THE TAMPA BAY AREA The **Hyatt Regency Tampa,** 2 Tampa City Center (✆ **813/2254-1234**), has renovated all 521 guest rooms with contemporary furnishings and modern amenities, including the signature Hyatt Grand Bed, 32-inch LCD flatscreen televisions, expanded work stations with oversize desks, and T-Mobile wireless Internet access. The new guest rooms also feature iHome clock radios with an iPod docking station and high-fidelity speakers. The new guest room bathrooms showcase sleek granite countertops and marble floors. See p. 397.

The **Tampa Marriott Waterside Hotel and Marina,** 700 S. Florida Ave. (✆ **813/221-4900**), spent $3 million on renovations to 719 rooms including flatscreen HDTVs and new carpeting.

New in 2009: The **Tampa Bay History Center,** 225 S. Franklin St. (✆ **813/228-0097**), a 60,000-square-foot museum covering everything from Native Americans to tycoons and sports legends who have inhabited Tampa. The museum will feature interactive exhibits, theaters, map gallery, research center, event hall, museum store, and a branch of the internationally acclaimed Columbia Café.

The **Tampa Museum of Art,** 2306 N. Howard Ave. (✆ **813/274-8130**), is constructing a new 66,000-square-foot facility in downtown Tampa. The state-of-the-art museum is scheduled to open in the Fall of 2009 and will provide the region with a variety of world-class traveling exhibitions, a growing collection of contemporary and classical art, expanded educational programs, and access to scenic outdoor events along Tampa's Riverwalk.

WALT DISNEY WORLD (WDW) & ORLANDO Disney has once again revamped their official website—though I have to admit, I'm not convinced that it's for the better. While photos are more plentiful and the graphics more whimsical, the information is presented in a far more round-about (and at times a more generalized) manner. Those having never visited the site before will likely find it inviting—however those who frequently visit the site may find maneuvering it a bit frustrating.

Where to Stay in Disney At press time, the Kidani Village, the second and final phase of Vacation Club villas being added to the lineup at **Disney's Animal Kingdom Lodge** (✆ **407/939-6244**), was making its debut. Built adjacent to the existing lodge, the village features its own full-service restaurant (featuring African-inspired cuisine with an Indian twist), it's own recreational facilities, and an extensively themed pool and water-play area.

The first phase of **Disney's Saratoga Springs Resort and Spa** (✆ **407/827-1100**) opened in May 2004, its final phase (an unanticipated addition)—in 2009. Disney's Treehouse Villas, resurrected and completely redesigned, adds another 60 villas to Disney's lineup of Vacation Club resorts. As the name implies, **Disney's Treehouse Villas** are elevated some 10 feet up off the ground by pedestals and beams and are nestled amid the trees. With room for up to nine, each of the three-bedroom villas features all the comforts of home but with plenty of modern touches (cathedral ceilings, granite countertops, and flatscreen TVs among them).

At press time, construction was wrapping up on the **Contemporary Resort's Bay Lake Tower** (✆ **407/939-6244**)—and the newest member of the Disney Vacation Club resorts. Connected by a sky bridge to the existing resort (its restaurants, shops, and the monorail), the Tower sports a swanky rooftop lounge, a fireworks viewing deck, its own full service restaurant (yet to be named), and a lakeside zero entry pool and water play area. Spacious public areas, accents of modern artwork, trendy suite-style rooms, and an innovative design ensures that the newest addition is Disney chic all the way—and a compliment to the Contemporary's original theme.

Where to Dine in Disney Recent additions to the Orlando Dining scene include **Cuba Libre Restaurant & Rum Bar**

(✆ **407/226-1600**), an exotic addition to the lineup of upscale eateries located at Pointe Orlando, featuring contemporary Cuban cuisine, lively Latin music, professional salsa floor shows, and an open-air tropical ambience with outdoor dining—oh, did I mention the extensive rum selection?

Diners at the **Village Tavern** (✆ **407/581-1740**) will find a varied, wide-ranging menu, unique cocktails, and an award-winning wine list. From bacon-wrapped scallops, 14-ounce rib-eye steak, and 10-spice glazed salmon to braised short ribs, Gruyère and bacon flatbread, and banana crepes, there's something to tempt every diner's palate at this upscale eatery located across from the Mall of Millennia.

At Downtown Disney, the Portobello Yacht Club has undergone a transformation to become **Portobello** (✆ **407/934-8888**). A revamped menu features authentic, regional Italian fare and a reinvigorated wine list, while the atmosphere is now warmer and more inviting with accents of terra-cotta tiles and rustic iron running throughout.

Families may find the **T-REX Café** (✆ **407/828-8739**) more to their liking given its interactive prehistoric environment—think Rainforest Café only a thousand or so years earlier. The menu, while varied, is filled with familiar favorites (rotisserie chicken, ribs, salads, and the like) but with a slightly creative twist. Themes of water, fire, and ice combine with animatronic dinosaurs, bubbling geysers, meteor showers, and a slew of other prehistoric special effects to create an incredibly unique dining environment.

Ocean Prime (✆ **407/363-4801**) is the latest restaurant to open along "Restaurant Row" (on Sand Lake Rd., in the Dr. Phillips district). A welcome addition to the lineup of upscale eateries, this elegant and very sophisticated establishment combines a menu of fresh seafood, sumptuous steaks, an extensive wine list, and an upbeat atmosphere reminiscent of a 1930s supper club (albeit chic and updated). An incredibly knowledgeable and attentive staff top off the exceptional experience—this one should definitely top the list for the discerning diner!

Exploring Walt Disney World Park-goers with aspirations of becoming the world's next singing sensation should head directly to the all new **American Idol Experience** at **Disney's Hollywood Studios,** where they can audition and perform live on stage in an interactive setting (judges and all) that practically replicates the set from the hit TV show of the same name. Other changes include an updated version of the park's ***High School Musical*** street show, which now features songs from all three hit *High School Musical* movies.

At the **Magic Kingdom, Celebrate a Dream Come True Parade** replaces Disney's Dreams Come True Parade—while there are few notable differences, the most predominant are the three stops made along the parade route, the new musical score, and the updated floats. Over in Tomorrowland, **Stitch's Super Sonic Celebration** is a high-energy, retro-futuristic dance party that invites guests to join in on the super-sonic fun with Stitch and troupe of dancers.

Exploring Universal Orlando & SeaWorld **Hollywood Rip, Ride, Rockit,** Universal's newest high-speed thriller, is said to be the most technologically advanced roller coaster in the world, and it's set to debut at **Universal Studios** just as this book goes to print. Word has it that the coaster will cruise through twists, turns, and a record-breaking loop at speeds of up to 65 miles per hour. Add in state-of-the-art special effects, a sophisticated video system, and the hottest music to hit the airwaves and the result is a musically themed multisensory experience like no other.

At **Islands of Adventure, The Wizarding World of Harry Potter** makes its long-awaited debut this year—though few details (other than those released some 2 or so years ago) have been released, keeping fans and park-goers alike on the edge of their seats. **SeaWorld,** unwilling to fall behind, is set to debut its newest thrill ride at roughly the same time. **Manta,** a coaster unlike any other, takes riders soaring up to the sky and swooping to the deepest depths of the sea past underwater habitats filled with hundreds of sharks and rays—all while lying face-down aboard manta-inspired cars.

NORTHEAST FLORIDA **World Golf Village Renaissance Resort,** 500 S. Legacy Trail, St. Augustine, FL 32092 (✆ **888/740-7020**), completed a $10-million renovation to rooms, suites, and technology and also added a new restaurant.

Amelia Island Plantation, 6800 First Coast Hwy. (✆ **888/261-6161**), has earned a lifesaving certification from CR Certification Corporation ("CardioReady"). The organization announced that the Amelia Island Plantation Inn and its Beach Club and Conference centers have met the necessary standards to obtain the CardioReady Certification for cardiac emergency preparedness.

The new **Cumberland Sound Ferry Service** (✆ **877/264-9972;** wwwameliarivercruises.com) runs a minimum of three round-trips per day from Amelia Island, Florida, to St. Marys, Georgia, on Thursday, Friday, and Saturday.

Kayak Amelia ★★ (✆ **888/305-2925** or 904/251-0016; www.kayakamelia.com) is based near Talbot Island State Park (technically in Jacksonville) and offers beginner and advanced-level trips on back bays, creeks, and marshes.

NORTHWEST FLORIDA: THE PANHANDLE New in 2009, in downtown Pensacola: Solé Inn and Suites, opened on Palafox Street in the heart of Downtown Pensacola (✆ **850/470-9298**). Rates at the 1950s-style, retro hotel start at $89 and include complimentary cocktails from 5 to 7pm and breakfast.

If riding the wild surf is a bit too adventurous for you, check out **YOLO Boarding,** 820 N. County Hwy. 393 in Santa Rosa Beach (✆ **850/496-7286**), a new kind of "surfing" that suits those who love the water but not the wave action. YOLO (an acronym for You Only Live Once) involves standing up and paddling on a big, safe, comfortable long-board.

The newest addition to Beaches of South Walton is the 158-acre master planned enclave of **Alys Beach,** which includes 1,500 feet of beach front and a 20-acre nature preserve.

Construction is underway at the new, $330-million **Panama City-Bay County International Airport,** a state-of-the-art international airport that is being built on 1,300 acres of a 4,000-acre site donated by the St. Joe Company. The new airport is expected to open in the first quarter of 2010.

1 The Best of Florida

Although it's the state nickname, describing Florida as the Sunshine State is like calling Martha Stewart "manic." Sure, it's true, but not necessarily all the time—and it doesn't nearly begin to describe the state's other marketable assets. There's a lot more to Florida than just sunshine—and, yes, we get those pesky hurricanes. Weather aside, choosing the best of Florida is by no means simple. While millions of visitors flock here to escape the bleakness of winter and landlocked locations, they don't all come down for sun, fun, and Mickey Mouse. Granted, the promise of (mostly) clear skies and 800 miles of sparkling, sandy beaches is alluring, as are the animatronics and roller coasters in Orlando and Tampa, but there's much more to the state than that. In many ways, Florida is like a beautiful, blond beauty queen who everyone thinks is all fluff—until they find out she's a Rhodes Scholar.

Here you can choose from a colorful, often kitschy assortment of accommodations, from deluxe resorts to the few-and-far-between mom-and-pop motels. You can visit remote little towns such as Apalachicola or a multicultural megalopolis such as Miami. You can devour fresh seafood, from amberjack to oysters—and then work off those calories in such outdoor pursuits as bicycling, golfing, or kayaking. Despite overdevelopment in many parts of the state, Floridians have maintained thousands of acres of wilderness areas, from the little respite of Clam Pass County Park in downtown Naples to the magnificent Everglades National Park that stretches across the state's southern tip.

Choosing the "best" of all this is a daunting task, and the selections in this chapter are only highlights. You'll find numerous other outstanding resorts, hotels, destinations, activities, and attractions described in this book. With an open mind and a sense of adventure, you'll come up with bests of your own.

1 THE BEST BEACHES

- **Virginia Key** (Key Biscayne): The producers of *Survivor* or *Lost* could feasibly shoot their show on this ultrasecluded, picturesque, and deserted key, where people purposely go to not be found. See p. 146.
- **Bill Baggs Cape Florida State Park** (Key Biscayne): The pot of gold at the end of the rainbow, Bill Baggs radiates serenity with $1^{1}/_{4}$ miles of sandy beach, nature trails, and even a historic lighthouse that recalls an era before such pristine places gave way to avaricious developers and pollutants. See p. 155.
- **Lummus Park Beach** (South Beach): This beach is world renowned, not necessarily for its pristine sands, but for its more common name of **South Beach,** on which seeing, being seen, and, at times, the obscene, go hand-in-hand with the sunscreen and beach towels. The 12th Street section is the beach of choice for gay residents and travelers. This beach has had some of the liveliest parties South Beach has ever seen. See p. 145.
- **Haulover Beach** (Miami Beach): Nestled between the Intracoastal Waterway

MISS.
ALA.
G E
MOBILE
Biloxi
Pascagoula
Mobile Bay
Foley
Gulf Shores
Bay Minette
Escambia R.
Pensacola
Gulf Breeze
Santa Rosa I.
Ft. Walton Beach
Destin
Crestview
De Funiak Springs
Marianna
Bainbridge
Thomasville
L. Seminole
Quincy
Tallahassee
APALACHICOLA N.F.
Ochlockonee
Apalachicola R.
Choctawhatchee
Panama City Beach
Panama City
St. Joseph Pt.
Apalachicola
St. George I.
Chandeleur Is.
(Louisiana)
65
98
63
10
59
29
331
85
231
20
319
GULF OF MEXICO
0
100 mi
0
100 km
N

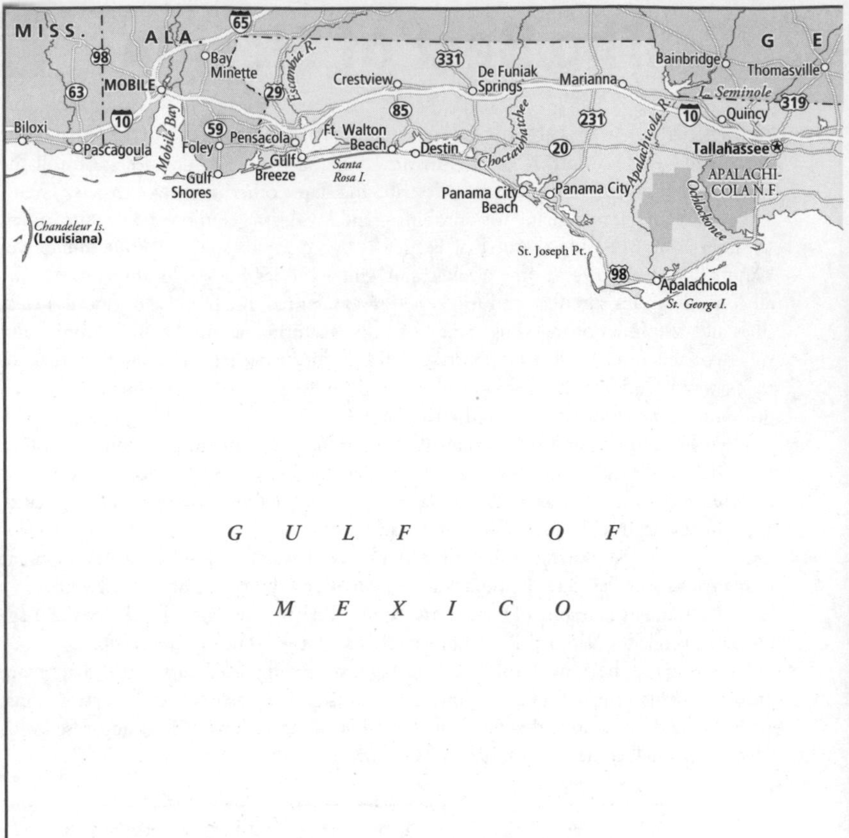

GEORGIA
Valdosta
Brunswick
Cumberland I.
Kingsland
Fernandina Beach
Amelia I.
OKEFENOKEE
St. Mary's
OSCEOLA N.F.
JACKSONVILLE
Jacksonville Beach
Lake City
Perry
Starke
St. John's R.
St. Augustine
ATLANTIC
OCEAN
Suwannee R.
Gainesville
Palatka
Palm Coast
Orange L.
Crescent L.
L. George
OCALA N.F.
Ormond Beach
Daytona Beach
Port Orange
New Smyrna Beach
Ocala
Cedar Key
DeLand
L. Griffin
Deltona
CANAVERAL NATIONAL SEASHORE
Inverness
Homosassa Springs
Tavares
Sanford
Apopka
Altamonte Springs
L. Apopka
Titusville
John F. Kennedy Space Center
C. Canaveral
ORLANDO
Spring Hill
Walt Disney World Resort Complex
Merritt Island
Kissimmee
St. Cloud
Cocoa Beach
L. Tohopekaliga
Tarpon Springs
Palm Harbor
Melbourne
Palm Bay
Plant City
Lakeland
Clearwater
Winter Haven
L. Kissimmee
Largo
TAMPA
Bartow
Sebastian
Pinellas Park
ST. PETERSBURG
Kissimmee
Vero Beach
Mullet Key
Tampa Bay
Ft. Pierce
Bradenton
Sebring
Longboat Key
Sarasota
Peace R.
L. Istokpoga
Port St. Lucie
Hutchinson I.
Okeechobee
Stuart
Siesta Key
Arcadia
Lake Okeechobee
Venice
Port Charlotte
Jupiter
Punta Gorda
Palm Beach Gardens
West Palm Beach
Gasparilla I.
North Ft. Myers
Palm Beach
La Costa I.
Lake Worth
Grand Bahama I.
(Bahamas)
Cape Coral
Ft. Myers
Boynton Beach
Captiva I.
Delray Beach
Sanibel I.
EVERGLADES
Boca Raton
Bonita Springs
Deerfield Beach
Coral Springs
Pompano Beach
BIG CYPRESS NAT'L PRESERVE
Weston
Tamarac
Naples
Davie
FT. LAUDERDALE
Miramar
Hollywood
Marco I.
Miami Gardens
Hallandale Beach
Bimini Is.
(Bahamas)
Everglades City
Hialeah
MIAMI
Miami Beach
Coral Gables
Key Biscayne
Biscayne Bay
Homestead
Elliott Key
BISCAYNE N.P.
EVERGLADES N.P.
Key Largo
C. Sable
Key Largo
Florida Bay
Islamorada
Plantation
Marathon
Florida Keys
DRY TORTUGAS N.P.
Key West
Big Pine Key

and the ocean, especially at the north end, is the place to be for that all-over tan: Haulover is the city's only clothing-optional (that is, nude) beach. See p. 162.

- **Bahia Honda State Park** (Bahia Honda Key): This is one of the nicest and most peaceful beaches in Florida. It's located amid 635 acres of nature trails and a portion of Henry Flagler's railroad. See p. 210.
- **John U. Lloyd Beach State Park** (Dania Beach): Unfettered by high-rise condominiums, T-shirt shops, and hotels, this wonderful beach boasts an untouched shoreline surrounded by a canopy of Australian pine to ensure complete seclusion. See p. 267.
- **Lovers Key State Park** (Fort Myers Beach): You'll have to walk or take a tram through a bird-filled forest of mangroves to this gorgeous, unspoiled beach just a few miles south of busy Fort Myers Beach. Although Sanibel Island gets the accolades, the shelling here is just as good, if not better. See p. 334.
- **Cayo Costa State Park** (off Captiva Island): These days, deserted tropical islands with great beaches are scarce in Florida, but this 2,132-acre barrier strip of sand, pine forest, mangrove swamp, oak hammock, and grassland provides a genuine get-away-from-it-all experience. Access is only by boat from nearby Gasparilla, Pine, and Captiva islands. See p. 358.
- **Naples Beach** (Naples): Many Florida cities and towns have beaches, but few are as lovely as the gorgeous strip that fronts Naples's famous Millionaires' Row. You don't have to be rich to wander its length, peer at the mansions, or stroll on historic Naples Pier to catch a sunset over the Gulf. See p. 365.
- **Barefoot Beach Park** (Bonita Springs): One of the last undeveloped barrier islands on Florida's west coast, this 342-acre natural preserve has an unfettered 8,200 feet of beach and sand dunes and is more than a haven for beach bums—it's the home of the protected gopher tortoise. See www.tinyurl.com/69ppjx.
- **Caladesi Island State Park** (Clearwater Beach): Even though 3½-mile-long Caladesi Island is in the heavily developed Tampa Bay area, it has a lovely, relatively secluded beach with soft sand edged in sea grass and palmettos. In the park itself, there's a nature trail where you might see one of the rattlesnakes, black racers, raccoons, armadillos, or rabbits that live here. The park is accessible only by ferry from Honeymoon Island State Recreation Area, off Dunedin. See p. 418.
- **Fort DeSoto Park** (St. Petersburg): Where else can you get a good tan *and* a history lesson? At Fort DeSoto Park, you have not only 1,136 acres of five interconnected islands and 3 miles of unfettered beaches, but also a fort that's listed on the National Register of Historic Places. There are also nature trails, fishing piers, a 2.25-mile canoe trail, and spectacular views of Tampa Bay and the Gulf. See p. 419.
- **Canaveral National Seashore** (Cape Canaveral): Midway between the crowded attractions at Daytona Beach and Kennedy Space Center is a protected stretch of coastline 24 miles long, backed by cabbage palms, sea grapes, and palmettos. See p. 517.
- **Lighthouse Point Park** (Daytona Beach): With 52 acres of pristine land on the north side of Ponce De León Inlet, the park features fishing, nature trails, an observation deck and tower, swimming, and picnicking. A variety of wildlife also call the park home, including raccoons, possums, skunks, armadillos, shorebirds, and birds of prey. See p. 526.
- **Gulf Islands National Seashore** (Pensacola): All of Northwest Florida's Gulf shore is one of America's great beaches—an almost uninterrupted stretch of pure

white sand that runs the entire length of the Panhandle, from Perdido Key to St. George Island. The Gulf Islands National Seashore preserves much of this natural wonder in its undeveloped state. Countless terns, snowy plovers, black skimmers, and other birds nest along the dunes topped with sea oats. East of the national seashore and equally beautiful are **Grayton Beach State Park,** near Destin; and **St. George Island State Park,** off Apalachicola. See p. 595 and 618.

- **St. Andrews State Park** (Panama City Beach): With more than 1,000 acres of dazzling white sand and dunes, this preserved wilderness demonstrates what Panama City Beach looked like before motels and condominiums lined its shore. Lacy, golden sea oats sway in Gulf breezes and the area is home to foxes and a herd of deer. See p. 610.

2 THE BEST FISHING

- **The Keys:** The Keys boast world-class deep-sea fishing; the prizes are such big-game fish as marlin, sailfish, and tuna. There's reef fishing for "eating fish," such as snapper and grouper, and back-country fishing for bonefish, tarpon, and other "stalking" fish. Dozens of charter-fishing boats operate from Key West marinas and from other, less popular keys. Islamorada, in the Upper Keys, is the sport-fishing capital of the world. Seven-Mile Bridge, linking the Middle and Lower keys, is known as "the longest fishing bridge in the world"; it's also a favorite spot for local fishermen who wait for barracuda and dolphin to bite. See p. 227.
- **Lake Okeechobee:** Many visitors to the Treasure Coast come to fish, and they certainly get their fill from the miles of Atlantic shore and from inland rivers. If you want to fish fresh water and nothing else, head for Lake Okeechobee, the state's largest lake, which is chock-full of good eating fish. It covers more than 467,000 acres—that's more than 730 square miles. At one time, the lake supported an enormous commercial fishing industry. Due to a commercial fishing-net ban, however, much of that industry has died off, leaving the sport fishers all the rich bounty of the lake. ***Note:*** A 2-year drought beginning in 2006 gave way to the quickest rise in lake levels in 77 years of record-keeping. As a result, in 2008, largemouth bass, speckled perch, bluegill, and other species spread out all over the lake, reclaiming habitat that once was dry land. See p. 321.
- **Stuart:** Known as the "Sailfish Capital of the World," Stuart is an angler's haven. The fish bite year-round, but peak months are December through March and June through July. Sailfishing is an art of its own—beginners must learn that exact moment to let the reel drag so the fish run with the lure. See p. 312.
- **Boca Grande:** The deep, shadowy holes of Boca Grande Pass, between Gasparilla and Cayo Costa islands off Fort Myers, harbor the mighty tarpon, the "silver king of the seas." Teddy Roosevelt and his rich buddies used to bag tarpon in these waters, and anglers from around the globe still compete every July in the World's Richest Tarpon Tournament. See p. 324.
- **Destin:** Florida's largest charter-boat fleet, with more than 140 vessels, is based in this Panhandle town, which

calls itself the "World's Luckiest Fishing Village." Anglers here have landed championship catches of grouper, amberjack, snapper, mackerel, cobia, sailfish, wahoo, tuna, and blue marlin. See p. 592.

3 THE BEST SNORKELING & DIVING

- **John Pennekamp Coral Reef State Park** (Key Largo): This is the country's first undersea preserve, with 188 square miles of protected coral reefs. The water throughout much of the park is shallow, so it's an especially great place for snorkelers to see an incredibly vibrant array of coral, including tree-size elkhorn coral and giant brain coral. See p. 196.
- **Looe Key National Marine Sanctuary** (Bahia Honda State Park): With 5 1/3 square miles of gorgeous coral reef, rock ledges up to 35 feet tall, and a colorful and motley marine community, you may never want to come up for air. See p. 212.
- **Florida Keys:** The **Keys Shipwreck Heritage Trail** features nine historic sites from Key Largo to Key West. For each of the nine Shipwreck Trail sites there is an underwater site guide available, who provides the shipwreck and mooring buoy positions, history, and a site map, and identifies marine life you can expect to see. See p. 227.
- **Hutchinson Island:** Three popular artificial reefs off this island provide excellent scenery for divers of any level. The **USS *Rankin,*** sunk in 120 feet of water in 1988, lies 7 miles east–northeast of the St. Lucie Inlet. **Donaldson Reef** consists of a cluster of plumbing fixtures sunk in 58 feet of water. **Ernst Reef,** made from old tires, is a 60-foot dive located 4 1/2 miles east–southeast of the St. Lucie inlet. See chapter 10.

4 THE BEST GOLF COURSES

- **Biltmore Hotel** (Miami): The beautiful, rolling, 18-hole golf course designed by Donald Ross at the majestic Biltmore Hotel in Coral Gables is open to the public, and is a favorite of Bill Clinton's. See p. 164.
- **Doral Golf Resort and Spa** (Miami): Four championship courses make the Doral one of Miami's best golf destinations. The legendary Blue Monster course hosts the annual PGA Ford Championship tourney. See p. 164.
- **Fairmont Turnberry Isle Resort & Club** (Aventura, North Miami Beach): These two 18-hole courses redesigned in 2008 by Raymond Floyd, are open only to guests, but they are among the city's best. See p. 164.
- **PGA National Resort & Spa** (Palm Beach): This rambling resort, the national headquarters of the PGA, is a premier golf destination with five 18-hole courses on more than 2,300 acres. See p. 297.
- **Emerald Dunes Golf Course** (West Palm Beach): This gorgeous Tom Fazio–designed course (featuring 60 acres of water and stunning views of the ocean) is pricey, but it is one of only a few in the area that is open to the public. See www.edgclub.com.
- **Tiburón Golf Club** (Naples): Greg Norman designed this course's 36 championship holes to play like a British Open—but without the thick thatch rough. The course is now home

to the luxurious Ritz-Carlton Golf Resort, Naples. See p. 364.

- **Naples Beach Hotel & Golf Club** (Naples): One of the state's oldest, this resort course is relatively flat, but small greens and masterful bunkers will test your skills. In addition, one of Florida's most charming resort hotels is across the street. See p. 364.
- **Mangrove Bay Golf Course** (St. Petersburg): One of the nation's top 50 municipal courses, the Mangrove Bay course hugs the inlets of Old Tampa Bay and offers 18-hole, par-72 play. Facilities include a driving range; lessons and golf-club rentals are also available. See p. 408.
- **The Innisbrook Resort and Golf Club** (Tarpon Springs): *Golfweek* has called Innisbrook's Copperhead Course, home to the PGA tour every March, number one in Florida. Each year, 1,000 students go through Innisbrook's Golf Institute. Golfers worldwide come here to play the 600 acres of courses. See p. 424.
- **Walt Disney World** (Orlando): The resorts surrounding the theme parks have 99 regulation holes that let you walk in the footsteps (and share the frustrations) of the game's greatest players. Those with a shorter stroke can play the master miniature courses: Fantasia Gardens and Winter Summerland. Call ✆ **407/939-4653** to inquire about golf courses and rates, or try the non-Disney **Golfpac** (✆ **800/486-0948** or 407/260-2288; www.golfpacorlando.com).
- **Hyatt Regency Grand Cypress Resort** (Orlando): No Bermuda shorts are allowed on the four Jack Nicklaus–designed courses, including three 9-hole courses that are played in three 18-hole combinations, and an 18-hole course called the New Course. See p. 468.
- **Ladies Professional Golf Association/LPGA International** (Daytona Beach): This "women-friendly" course has multiple tee settings, unrestricted tee times, a great pro shop, and state-of-the-art facilities. Designed by Rees Jones, the older course here was chosen as one of the "Top Ten You Can Play" by *Golf* magazine. See p. 526.
- **TPC at Sawgrass** (Ponte Vedra Beach, near Jacksonville): With 99 holes, Pete Dye's Tournament Players Club (TPC) at Sawgrass makes top-10 lists everywhere. The 17th hole, on a tricky island, is one of the most photographed holes in the world. See p. 558.
- **Ocean Hammock Golf Club** (Palm Coast, between Daytona Beach and St. Augustine): With 6 of its holes skirting the Atlantic Ocean, the Jack Nicklaus–designed course is the first authentic seaside links built in Florida since the 1920s. Another equally challenging, scenic course was designed by Tom Watson and a third is on the way by Fred Couples. See p. 545.
- **Amelia Island Plantation** (Amelia Island): This exclusive resort has three of the state's best courses. Long Point Club, designed by Tom Fazio, is the most beautiful and challenging. Pete Dye and Bobby Weed's Amelia Links comprises two courses, Oak Marsh and Ocean Links. Each is open only to resort guests. Amelia River, the Tom Jackson–designed course amid a forest of live oaks, sabal palms, and pine trees, is the resort's crown jewel and is open to the public. See p. 571.
- **Marriott's Bay Point Resort Village** (Panama City Beach): Thirty-six holes of championship golf at this Marriott include the Nicklaus-designed Meadows course and Nicklaus Design Course, one of the country's most difficult. See p. 613.

5 THE BEST LUXURY RESORTS

- **The Setai** (South Beach; ✆ **305/520-6000**): Simply put, there is no hotel like this anywhere else in Florida. Rough economy or not, this hotel breaks the bank and takes luxury to a new level, with its imported, not imitated, Asian decor and staff, outstanding Pan-Asian cuisine, and celebrity clientele. Who else can afford these prices? See p. 94.
- **The Ritz-Carlton Key Biscayne** (Key Biscayne; ✆ **800/241-3333** or 305/365-4500): In addition to consistently superior services and amenities, this British colonial–style version of the Ritz rises above its casual Key Biscayne surroundings, with a stellar view of the Atlantic Ocean, not to mention an equally impressive 20,000-square-foot spa. See p. 104.
- **Mandarin Oriental, Miami** (Brickell Key, Miami; ✆ **305/913-8383**): The swank and stunning Mandarin Oriental features a waterfront location, residential-style rooms, superb service, a spa frequented by J-Lo, and several upscale dining and bar facilities. See p. 106.
- **The Ritz-Carlton South Beach** (South Beach; ✆ **800/241-3333** or 786/276-4000): Taking the concept of swanky South Beach to a very literal level, the Ritz-Carlton South Beach may be a landmark building restored to its original 1950s Art Moderne style, but in terms of the hotel's standout service (a tanning butler!), amenities, and ocean frontage, everything else is very much in the immediate present. See p. 93.
- **The Atlantic** (Fort Lauderdale; ✆ **800/325-3589** or 954/567-8020): Set on a golden sand beach, the Mediterranean-style Atlantic brings a fresh sense of modern luxury to Fort Lauderdale, not to mention a fabulous chef hailing from N.Y.C.'s acclaimed Tribeca Grill. See p. 273.
- **The Ritz-Carlton Fort Lauderdale** (Fort Lauderdale; ✆ **800/542-8680** or 954/465-2300): Unparalleled luxury hits Fort Lauderdale beach in the form of this swanky Ritz-Carlton. Formerly and briefly the St. Regis, the Ritz offers everything from beach to butlers. See p. 274.
- **The Breakers** (Palm Beach; ✆ **800/833-3141** or 561/655-6611): This stately, historic hotel epitomizes *la dolce vita,* Palm Beach–style, with an elegant lobby, impeccable service, expansive manicured lawns, and a very scenic golf course that is the state's oldest. See p. 301.
- **Four Seasons Resort Palm Beach** (Palm Beach; ✆ **800/432-2335** or 561/582-2800): "Exquisite" is the adjective most often used to describe this posher-than-posh hotel. Luxurious, but hardly stuffy, the Four Seasons was the stay of choice for the quintessential aging rockers of Aerosmith, who took great advantage of post-concert pampering. See p. 302.
- **LaPlaya Beach & Golf Resort** (Naples; ✆ **800/237-6883** or 239/597-3123): More intimate than the Ritz, the equally luxe LaPlaya Beach & Golf Resort offers spacious rooms, each with a completely private balcony overlooking the pristine waters of the Gulf or Vanderbilt Bay. The resort has four unique pools, two lagoons, an outdoor whirlpool, the Tiki Bar, the 4,500-square-foot SpaTerre, the 2,700-square-foot fitness center, the Gulf-view Baleen restaurant, and a 6,907-yard championship 18-hole golf course designed by Bob Cupp. See p. 368.
- **The Ritz-Carlton Golf Resort, Naples** (Naples; ✆ **888/856-4372** or 239/593-2000): This luxurious Mediterranean-style resort takes full advantage of the Greg Norman–designed Tiburón Golf

Club. Guests here can use the beach and spa at the Ritz-Carlton, Naples, nearby. See p. 371.

- **The Ritz-Carlton, Naples** (Naples; ✆ **888/856-4372** or 239/598-3300): This opulent 14-story Mediterranean-style hotel at Vanderbilt Beach is a favorite of affluent types who like standard Ritz amenities such as imported marble floors, antique art, Oriental rugs, Waterford chandeliers, and afternoon British-style high tea. Guests relax in high-backed rockers on the verandas or unwind by the heated pool set in a landscaped terrace. See p. 370.
- **Don CeSar Beach Resort, A Loews Hotel** (St. Pete Beach; ✆ **866/728-2206** or 727/360-1881): Dating back to 1928 and listed on the National Register of Historic Places, this "Pink Palace" tropical getaway is so romantic, you may bump into six or seven honeymooning couples in 1 weekend. The lobby has classic high windows and archways, crystal chandeliers, marble floors, and original artwork. Most rooms have high ceilings and offer views of the Gulf or Boca Ciega Bay. See p. 421.
- **Disney's Grand Floridian Resort & Spa** (Lake Buena Vista; ✆ **407/934-7639**): This magnificent Victorian inn has a grand five-story lobby topped by an opulent Tiffany-style glass dome. The glass-enclosed brass cage elevator and Chinese Chippendale aviary are examples of the very refined style that runs throughout the entire resort. An orchestra plays big-band music every evening near Victoria & Albert's, the resort's five-star restaurant, and afternoon tea is a daily event. See p. 460.
- **Hyatt Regency Grand Cypress Resort** (Orlando; ✆ **800/233-1234** or 407/239-1234): The impressive facilities at this luxury resort include a half-acre pool with a dozen waterfalls, caves, and grottoes; three spas; 12 tennis courts; four Jack Nicklaus–designed golf courses; a 45-acre nature walk; a private lake with its own stretch of white-sand beach; and some of Orlando's best restaurants. See p. 468.
- **Amelia Island Plantation** (Amelia Island; ✆ **888/261-6161** or 904/261-6161): Set amid magnolias, oak trees, and the Atlantic Ocean, this gracious resort is straight out of the Deep South. It's more rustic than the nearby Ritz, but it has excellent hiking and biking paths, tennis, swimming, horseback riding, and boating. Golfers can enjoy exclusive use of two of Florida's top courses. See p. 571.

6 THE BEST ROMANTIC HIDEAWAYS

- **Hotel St. Michel** (Coral Gables; ✆ **800/848-HOTEL** [4683] or 305/444-1666): This European-style hotel in the heart of Coral Gables is one of the city's most romantic options. The renovated-in-2008 accommodations and hospitality are very Old World European, complete with dark-wood paneled walls, cozy beds, beautiful antiques, and a quiet elegance that seems startlingly out of place in trendy Miami. See p. 111.
- **Hotel Impala** (South Beach; ✆ **800/646-7252** or 305/673-2021): During the heyday of 1990s excess, Miami Beach was known for the fabulous parties thrown by the eclectic designer Gianni Versace. The late Versace desired an intimate European-style guesthouse that would please well-seasoned travelers, and the Impala is the result. His personal touch on this renovated Mediterranean inn is still evident, from the Greco-Roman frescoes and friezes to an

intimate garden perfumed by strategically planted hanging lilies and gardenias. See p. 96.

- **Jules' Undersea Lodge** (Key Largo; ✆ **305/451-2353**): Submerge yourself in this single-room Atlantis-like hotel that offers a surprisingly comfortable suite 30 feet under water. Don't worry; there's plenty of breathing room. See p. 202.
- **Kona Kai Resort & Gallery** (Key Largo; ✆ 800/365-7829 or 305/852-7200): A haven for vacationing adults, Kona Kai features a private beach and highly stylized, modern rooms and suites amid a lush 2-acre property, lined with native vegetation and fruit-bearing trees. See p. 202.
- **Little Palm Island Resort & Spa** (Little Torch Key; ✆ **800/343-8567** or 305/872-2524): Accessible only by boat, this private 5-acre island is not only remote, it's romantic—there are no TVs, telephones, or fax machines in the luxurious thatched cottages. See p. 212.
- **The Moorings Village** (Islamorada; ✆ **305/664-4708**): A former coconut plantation, the Moorings features 18 different cottages on 18 stunning acres of beachfront and lush gardens studded with bougainvillea and coconut palms. See p. 202.
- **Marquesa Hotel** (Key West; ✆ **800/869-4631** or 305/292-1919): Don't be fooled by the Marquesa's location on heavily populated Key West: This charming B&B is in a wonderful world of its own, far enough from the tumult, yet close enough if you want it. See p. 233.
- **The Gardens Hotel** (Key West; ✆ **800/526-2664** or 305/294-2661): A well-kept secret (until now), the Gardens Hotel is an exotic, lush, serene, and sultry escape from the frat-boy madness that ensues on nearby Duval Street. See p. 230.
- **Sundy House** (Delray Beach; ✆ **877/439-9601** or 561/272-5678): With just 11 suites surrounded by more than 5,000 species of exotic plants and flowers, gazebos, and flowing streams, Sundy House is a gorgeous getaway that's close enough to access the beach, but still safely hidden from the mood-ruining madness and conventionality of your typical tourist-class beach hotel. See p. 288.
- **Island's End Resort** (St. Pete Beach; ✆ **727/360-5023**): Sitting right on Pass-a-Grille, where the Gulf of Mexico meets Tampa Bay, this little all-cottage retreat is a great hideaway from the crowds of St. Pete Beach. You won't have an on-site restaurant, bar, or other such amenities, but you can step from your cottage right onto the beach. And if you get the unit with two living rooms, you'll have a whirlpool tub and your own Gulf-side pool. See p. 422.
- **Turtle Beach Resort** (Siesta Key, off Sarasota; ✆ **941/349-4554**): Sitting beside the bay, this intimate little charmer began life years ago as a traditional Old Florida fishing camp, but today it's one of the state's most romantic retreats. It's a tightly packed little place, but high wooden fences surround each unit's private outdoor hot tub, and one-way-mirror walls let you lounge in bed while passersby see only reflections of themselves. See p. 441.
- **Disney's Wilderness Lodge & Villas** (Lake Buena Vista; ✆ **407/934-7639**): This impressive resort is reminiscent of the grand lodge at Yellowstone National Park. The spewing geyser out back, the mammoth stone hearth in the lobby, the Artist's Point 360-degree view of Bay Lake, and the towering forest sheltering the resort from the rest of the world are just a few of the reasons to stay here. Some guest rooms have patios or balconies overlooking the lake, woodlands, or meadow. See p. 463.

- **The Lodge & Club at Ponte Vedra Beach** (Ponte Vedra Beach, near Jacksonville; ✆ **800/243-4304** or 904/273-9500): Every unit in this intimate hotel in upscale Ponte Vedra Beach has a romantic seat built into its oceanview window, plus a big bathroom with a two-person tub and separate shower. Gas fireplaces in most units add even more charm. One of the three pools and whirlpools here is reserved exclusively for couples. You can even get married in the semicircular meeting room overlooking the Atlantic. See p. 562.
- **WaterColor Inn** (near Destin; ✆ **866/426-2656** or 850/534-5000): This David Rockwell–designed beachfront boutique hotel feels more like a private beach house than a hotel. Guest rooms feature a pantry, a walk-in shower with views to the beach, and Adirondack chairs on the balcony. See p. 602.
- **Seaside** (near Destin; ✆ **800/277-8696** or 850/231-1320): If residents of Northwest Florida don't stay at Henderson Park Inn for their getaways, they head for the romantic Gulf-front cottages at Seaside. Built in the 1980s but evoking the 1880s, the Victorian-style village of Seaside (a short drive east of Destin) has several cozy cottages designed especially for honeymooners. See p. 602.

7 THE BEST MODERATELY PRICED ACCOMMODATIONS

- **Chesterfield Hotel, Suites & Day Spa** (South Beach; ✆ **305/673-3767**): A true value, this charismatic and hip sliver of property has won the loyalty of fashion industrialists and romantics alike. Built in 1929 and restored in 1996, the hotel retains many original details such as facades, woodwork, and fireplaces. See p. 98.
- **The Catalina Hotel & Beach Club** (South Beach; ✆ **877/SOBEGRP** [762-3477] or 305/674-1160): Affordable and hip, the Catalina is a retro fab stay with stylish rooms, Swedish Tempur-Pedic mattresses, a hot bar, and VIP hookups at all the clubs in South Beach. See p. 97.
- **Pelican Hotel** (South Beach; ✆ **800/7-PELICAN** or 305/673-3373): Owned by the creative owners of the Diesel jeans company, the Pelican is South Beach's only self-professed "toy-hotel," and each of its 30 rooms and suites is decorated as outrageously as some of the area's more colorful drag queens. See p. 99.
- **Whitelaw Hotel** (South Beach; ✆ **305/398-7000**): With a slogan that reads, "Clean sheets, hot water, and stiff drinks," the Whitelaw stands apart from the other boutique hotels with its fierce sense of humor and happening happy hours. See p. 99.
- **Conch Key Cottages** (Marathon; ✆ **800/330-1577** or 305/289-1377): This oceanfront hideaway offers rustic but immaculate and well-outfitted cottages that are especially popular with families. Each has a hammock, barbecue grill, and kitchen. See p. 203.
- **Courtyard Villa on the Ocean** (Fort Lauderdale; ✆ **800/291-3560** or 954/776-1164): These fabulous, plush accommodations are located right on the beach, but if you prefer to stay off the sand, the heated spa pool is sublime. See p. 276.
- **Hotel Biba** (West Palm Beach; ✆ **561/832-0094**): The mod squad has adopted—and adapted—this '40s-style motel into a futuristic, kitschy, jet-set hangout that provides swank and sleek

shelter from the upper-crust hotels that surround it. See p. 305.

- **Island's End Resort** (St. Pete Beach; ✆ **727/360-5023**): A wonderful respite from the madding crowd and a great bargain to boot, this little all-cottage hideaway sits on the southern tip of St. Pete Beach, smack-dab on Pass-a-Grille, where the Gulf of Mexico meets Tampa Bay. You can step from the six contemporary cottages right onto the beach. One unit even has a private pool. See p. 422.
- **Disney's Port Orleans Resort** (Lake Buena Vista; ✆ **407/934-7639** or 934-5000): With the refined surroundings of the French Quarter, the casual atmosphere of Alligator Bayou, and the stately air of Magnolia Bend (the latter two at Riverside), this resort's Southern charm appeals to all tastes. The French Quarter's pool sports a water slide that curves from the mouth of a colorful sea serpent, while Riverside's Ol' Man Island has a water hole and playground with a very Tom Sawyer–ish feel. See p. 463.
- **Staybridge Suites** (Lake Buena Vista; ✆ **800/866-4549** or 407/238-0777): Close to the action of Downtown Disney and the theme parks, this resort's one- and two-bedroom suites have full kitchens and are larger and more comfortable than most of the competition's. To help you relax, the resort will do your grocery shopping so you don't have to deal with the hassle. See p. 469.
- **Casa Monica Hotel** (St. Augustine; ✆ **800/648-1888** or 904/827-1888): Built in 1888 as a luxury hotel, this Spanish-style building was gutted and restored to its previous elegance in 1998. The most interesting of the guest quarters are suites installed in two tile-topped towers and a fortresslike central turret. One suite in the turret has a half-round living room with gun-port windows overlooking St. Augustine's historic district. See p. 546.
- **Gibson Inn** (Apalachicola; ✆ **850/653-2191**): Built in 1907 as a seamen's hotel and gorgeously restored in 1985, this cupola-topped inn is such a brilliant example of Victorian architecture that it's listed on the National Register of Historic Inns. No two guest rooms are alike (some still have the original sinks in the sleeping areas), but all are richly furnished with period reproductions. Grab a drink from the bar and relax in one of the high-backed rockers on the old-fashioned veranda. See p. 620.

8 THE BEST FAMILY ATTRACTIONS

- **Jungle Island** (Miami): We adults think it's overrated and touristy, but kids love it. You'll need to watch your head, however, because hundreds of parrots, macaws, peacocks, cockatoos, and flamingos are flying above. Continuous suitable, but cheesy, shows star roller-skating cockatoos, card-playing macaws, and numerous stunt-happy parrots. There are also tortoises, iguanas, and a rare albino alligator on exhibit. See p. 168.
- **Miami Children's Museum** (Miami): This museum has hundreds of bilingual, interactive exhibits, along with programs, classes, and learning materials related to arts, culture, community, and communication. It also has a re-creation of the NBC 6 television studio and a working music studio in which aspiring rock stars can lay down tracks and play instruments. See p. 151.

- **Sea Grass Adventures** (Miami): This is not your typical nature tour. With Sea Grass Adventures, you will be able to wade in the water on Key Biscayne with your guide and catch an assortment of sea life in the provided nets. At the end of the program, participants gather on the beach while the guide explains what everyone has just caught, passing the creatures around in miniature viewing tanks. See p. 170.
- **Miami Science Museum** (Miami): The Science Museum features more than 140 hands-on exhibits that explore the mysteries of the universe. Live demonstrations and collections of rare natural-history specimens make a visit here fun and informative. Many of the demos involve audience participation, which can be lots of fun for willing and able kids and adults alike. See p. 151.
- **J. N. "Ding" Darling National Wildlife Refuge** (Sanibel Island): Consisting of more than half of Sanibel Island, this 6,000-plus-acre area of mangrove swamps, winding waterways, and uplands has a 2-mile boardwalk nature trail and a 5-mile, one-way safari-esque **Wildlife Drive** on which you'll view a motley crew of species including alligators, raccoons, birds, and other wildlife. See p. 342.
- **Busch Gardens Africa** (Tampa): Although the thrill rides, live entertainment, shops, restaurants, and games get most of the ink at this 335-acre family theme park, Busch Gardens Africa also ranks among the top zoos in the country, with several thousand animals living in naturalistic environments. If you can get them off the roller coasters, kids can find out what all those wild beasts they've seen on the Discovery Channel look like in person. See p. 387.
- **MOSI (Museum of Science and Industry;** Tampa): One of the largest educational science centers in the Southeast, MOSI has more than 450 interactive exhibits in which the kids can experience hurricane-force winds, defy the laws of gravity, cruise the mysterious world of microbes, explore the human body, and more. They can also watch stunning movies in MOSIMAX, Florida's first IMAX dome theater. See p. 392.
- **Universal Studios Florida** (Orlando): Universal Orlando's original Florida park has many rides based on Hollywood blockbusters or cartoon heroes such as Shrek, Spiderman, Jaws, and Jimmy Neutron's Nicktoon Blast. Kids can get slimed at Nickelodeon Studios or get thrilled by the pint-size roller coaster and other fun in Woody Woodpecker's KidZone. See p. 501.
- **Walt Disney World's Magic Kingdom** (Orlando): You can introduce your wee ones to Disney's many characters at Mickey's Toontown Fair in the Magic Kingdom—Disney's premier park. There's also a ton of fun on rides themed after Winnie the Pooh, Peter Pan, Dumbo, Cinderella, Aladdin, and Buzz Lightyear. Rides such as Splash Mountain, Space Mountain, and Pirates of the Caribbean make sure older guests have fun, too. See p. 477.
- **Kennedy Space Center** (Cape Canaveral): Especially since the recent multimillion-dollar renovation and expansion, this family destination is a must-see. There is plenty to keep kids and parents busy for at least a full day, including interactive computer games, IMAX films, and dozens of informative displays on the space program. Try to schedule a trip during a real launch; there are more than a dozen each year. See p. 515.
- **DAYTONA USA** (Daytona Beach): Opened in late 1996 on Daytona International Speedway grounds, this huge state-of-the-art interactive attraction is an exciting and fast-paced stop even for nonrace fans. Kids can see real stock cars, go-karts, and motorcycles, and even participate in a pit stop on a NASCAR Winston Cup race car. See p. 525.

9 THE BEST OFFBEAT TRAVEL EXPERIENCES

- **Jimbo's** (Miami): Located at the very end of Virginia Key, in Key Biscayne, on the lagoon where they shot *Flipper,* Jimbo's has become the quintessential, albeit hard-to-find, South Florida watering hole, snack bar, and hangout for a wacky assortment of colorful characters, from shrimpers and yachters to politicos. Dollar beers and excellent smoked fish are sold from a cooler, vacant shacks serve as backdrops for films, and visitors are able to test their skills in a game of bocce ball. See p. 138.
- **Alabama Jack's** (Key Largo): En route to the Keys, veer off onto Card Sound Road, once the only way to get down there, and follow the Harley-Davidsons to Alabama Jack's. A waterfront biker bar, restaurant, and live-music joint built on two barges, Alabama Jack's on Sunday is the place to be for country line dancers, many of whom are in full *Hee Haw* regalia; lazy folks whiling away the day over beer, conch fritters, and the best Key lime and peanut butter pie ever; and just good ol', interesting folks passin' through. See p. 190.
- **Columbus Day Regatta** (Biscayne Bay): This unique observation of Columbus Day revolves around a so-called regatta in Biscayne Bay but always ends with participants stripping down to their bare, ahem, necessities and partying at the sandbar in the middle of the bay. There is a boat race at some point of the day, but most people are too preoccupied to notice. See p. 42.
- **People-Watching on South Beach and Worth Avenue** (Miami and Palm Beach): As cliché as the notion of people-watching may seem, it's never the same old scenario on Miami's neon-hued Riviera, where equally colorful locals and luminaries proudly prance as if every day were the Easter parade. See p. 146. In Palm Beach, titled nobility, bejeweled socialites, and an assortment of upper-crust folks put on the ritz along the city's version of Rodeo Drive. See p. 300.
- **Swimming with the Dolphins at the Dolphin Research Center** (Marathon): Of the four such centers in the continental United States, the Dolphin Research Center is the most impressive. With advance reservations, you can splash around with dolphins in their natural lagoon homes. It's an amazing experience. See p. 195.
- **Underwater Stay at Jules' Undersea Lodge** (Key Largo): We give this a vote as one of Florida's most romantic retreats, but this underwater hotel is also, hands down, the most unusual. Where else can you have a pizza delivered via scuba diver? See p. 202.
- **Fantasy Fest** (Key West): Mardi Gras takes a Floridian vacation as the streets of Key West are overtaken by wildly costumed revelers who have no shame and no parental guidance. This week-long, hedonistic, X-rated Halloween party is *not* for children under 18. See p. 43.
- **Babcock Wilderness Adventures** (Fort Myers): Experienced naturalists lead "swamp buggy" tours through the Babcock Ranch, 8000 State Road 31, Punta Gorda (✆ **800/500-5583;** www.babcockwilderness.com), including the mysterious Telegraph Swamp, where alligators lounge in the sun. Although the Babcock Ranch is the largest cattle operation east of the Mississippi (with bison and quarter horses, too), it is also a major wildlife preserve inhabited by countless birds and other creatures.

- **Swimming with the Manatees** (Crystal River, north of Clearwater): Some 360 manatees spend the winter in the Crystal River, and you can swim, snorkel, or scuba with them in the warm-water natural springs of Kings Bay, about 7 miles north of Homosassa Springs. It's not uncommon to be surrounded in the 72°F (22°C) water by 30 to 40 "sea cows" that nudge and caress you as you swim with them. See p. 410.
- **Wrangling an Alligator** (Orlando): Play trainer for a day and meet some of the toothy stars up close and *real* personal at Gatorland. You might even get to be part of the gator show, so hop on and hold on tight. Trainers will snap a quick photo before the gators snap back! See p. 509.
- **Learning to Surf the Big Curls at Cocoa Beach Surfing School** (Cocoa Beach): Even if you don't know how to hang ten, this school will get you riding the waves with the best of them. It provides equipment and lessons for all skill levels—beginner to pro—at the best surf beaches in Florida. See p. 519.

10 THE BEST SPAS

- **Agua Spa at Delano** (Miami; ✆ **800/555-5001** or 305/672-2000): One trip to this sublime, celebrity-saturated rooftop spa in a haute hotel overlooking the Atlantic, and you'll feel like you're in heaven. Try the milk-and-honey massage and you'll understand. See p. 92.
- **The Spa at Mandarin Oriental, Miami** (Miami; ✆ **866/526-6567** or 305/913-8383): If it's good enough for J-Lo, then it must be good enough for the rest of us. But seriously, this star-studded spa isn't the best because of its clientele, but because of its Chinese, Balinese, Indian, and European treatments applied by professionals well versed in the inimitable Mandarin Oriental brand of pampering. See p. 93.
- **The Spa at The Setai** (South Beach; ✆ **305/520-6100**): Nirvana is alive and well at the Spa at the Setai, where the philosophy of relaxation is derived from an ancient Sanskrit legend, natural elixirs, eternal youth, and Asian treatments and ingredients such as green tea. See p. 94.
- **The Spa at The Standard** (South Beach; ✆ **305/673-1717**): What used to be an old-school, Borscht Belt–style Miami Beach health spa is now one of the hottest, trendiest places to take a Turkish bath in a bona fide hammam, let out steam in a cedar sauna, or get spritzed in the hotel's sublime Wall of Sound Shower. See p. 93.
- **The Ritz-Carlton Spa, Key Biscayne** (Key Biscayne; ✆ **305/365-4158**): This spa is a sublime, 20,000-square-foot West Indies colonial-style Eden, where you can indulge in more than 60 treatments, including the Key Lime Coconut Body Scrub and the Everglades Grass Body Wrap in one of 21 treatment rooms. For a real splurge, the Fountain of Youth Balance treatment is a 6-hour indulgence with a facial, massage, manicure, pedicure, shampoo, styling, and lunch served on the oceanfront terrace. See p. 93.
- **ESPA at Acqualina** (Sunny Isles Beach; ✆ **305/918-8000**): The first of its kind in the U.S., ESPA features groundbreaking treatments in a stunning, two-story space overlooking the Atlantic. See p. 108.
- **L'Institut De Guerlain Spa** (Bal Harbour; ✆ **305/866-2121**): The 10,000-square-foot pleasure palace is Miami's first

from the French beauty brand featuring a waterfront hydrotherapy lounge, Vichy body treatments, and, of course, all products for sale. See p. 110.

- **Marriott's Harbor Beach** (Fort Lauderdale; ✆ **800/222-6543** or 954/525-4000): This $8-million, 24,000-square-foot European spa is the first full-service seaside facility of its kind in Fort Lauderdale. See p. 273.
- **PGA National Resort & Spa** (Palm Beach Gardens; ✆ **800/633-9150** or 561/627-2000): This lauded golf resort provides the perfect pampering for sore golfers and bored nongolfers, with its Mediterranean Spa offering just about every treatment imaginable, including special ones for pregnant women. See p. 303.
- **Sanibel Harbour Resort & Spa** (Fort Myers; ✆ **800/767-7777** or 239/466-4000): Many call this high-rise resort overlooking Sanibel Island the best spa value in the country. Regardless of the price, the spa obliges your every whim. Try the amazing Betar Bed, a suspended "bed of music" that floats you to a level where stresses disappear. There are also mud, algae, seaweed, and mineral wraps, along with Swiss showers, paraffin facials, and more. Day packages, makeovers, and men's sports packages are popular. The fitness center is also state of the art. See p. 332.
- **Naples Beach Hotel & Golf Club** (Naples; ✆ **800/237-7600** or 239/261-2222): This modern spa adds complete relaxation to a stay at this venerable hotel, already one of Florida's most relaxing resorts. A deep-body massage followed by a milk-and-honey wrap will leave you on cloud nine, and a special wedding package will have you primed for the big day. See p. 369.
- **The Ritz-Carlton, Naples** (Naples; ✆ **888/856-4372** or 239/598-3300): An impressive, hard-to-leave, full-service spa will leave you thoroughly relaxed before or after your stroll through the mangrove forest to the white-sand beach at one of Florida's finest luxury resorts. See p. 370.
- **Safety Harbor Resort and Spa** (Tampa Bay Area; ✆ **888/237-8772** or 727/726-1161): Tucked away off the beaten track amid moss-draped oaks and cobblestone streets, Safety Harbor is the oldest continually running spa in the United States, and Florida's only spa built around natural healing springs—the feeling is very European. The Phil Green tennis school is also on the grounds, and many tennis programs are available. See p. 413.
- **Amelia Island Plantation** (Amelia Island; ✆ **888/261-6161** or 904/261-6161): Besides a spectacular resort and a stunning spa facility, the Amelia Island Plantation has a dedicated Watsu massage facility on its own island right near the spa. See p. 571.

11 THE BEST SEAFOOD RESTAURANTS

- **Joe's Stone Crab Restaurant** (South Beach; ✆ **305/673-0365**): Open only during stone-crab season (Oct–May), this always-packed Miami institution knows how to reel in the crowds with the freshest, meatiest stone crabs and the side dishes to go with them, from creamed spinach to excellent sweet-potato french fries. See p. 117.
- **Garcia's Seafood Grille & Fish** (Downtown Miami; ✆ **305/375-0765**). We're not sure what's better, the fresh stone

crabs, catches of the day and conch fritters, or the fact that it's all so inexpensive and comes with a fantastic view of the Miami River. See p. 132.

- **Seven Fish** (Key West; ✆ **305/296-2777**): It may be a little tough to find and it doesn't have a water view, but the tiny, hip Seven Fish isn't about the frills. A mostly locals' seafood spot, the motto here is "simple good food." We disagree. The food isn't simple; it's simply the best seafood in town, with fresh catches of the day, phenomenal crab cakes, friendly servers, and a cool, in-the-know crowd. See p. 240.
- **Green Turtle Inn** (Islamorada; ✆ **305/664-2006**). Whether or not you think turtle is a seafood, consider the Green Turtle's conch chowder and braised Florida lobster as some of the best in town. See p. 207.
- **Marker 88** (Islamorada; ✆ **305/852-9315**): Bahamian conch, stone crabs from the Florida Bay, and shrimp from the West Coast are just some of the fresh items, innovatively prepared, at this Upper Keys institution. See p. 207.
- **Rustic Inn Crabhouse** (Fort Lauderdale; ✆ **954/584-1637**): A cacophonous Lauderdale landmark, Rustic Inn is famous for its garlic crabs and equally famous for the symphony of mallets crushing them at the table. Despite the newspaper tablecloths and paper bibs, this place is so good that even diva Barbra Streisand stopped by—though she asked the waiter to shell her crabs, probably so she wouldn't break a fingernail. See p. 281.
- **Sunfish Grill** (Pompano Beach; ✆ **954/788-2434**): Some argue that this is the best seafood restaurant on the entire Gold Coast, and we won't argue against them, thanks to the chef/owner who buys seafood fresh from local fishermen and prepares it with stunning results. See p. 280.
- **Channel Mark** (Fort Myers Beach; ✆ **239/463-9127**): Every table looks out on a maze of channel markers on Hurricane Bay, and a dock with palms growing through it makes the Channel Mark a relaxing place for a waterside lunch. The atmosphere changes dramatically at night, when the relaxed tropical ambience is ideal for kindling romance. Congenial owners Mike McGuigan and Andy Welsh put a creative spin on their seafood dishes, and their delicately seasoned crab cakes are tops. See p. 340.
- **Lobster Pot** (Redington Shores, near St. Pete Beach; ✆ **727/391-8592**): Come here for some of the finest seafood dishes on St. Pete and Clearwater beaches. Among the amazing variety of lobster dishes is one flambéed in brandy with garlic, and the bouillabaisse is as authentic as any you'll find in the South of France. See p. 426.
- **Fulton's Crab House** (Lake Buena Vista; ✆ **407/934-2628**): Located in a riverboat replica, Fulton's has a nostalgic mood and an array of good seafood, though meals can get a bit pricey if you opt for stone or king crab. There's also an excellent wine list. See p. 481.
- **Todd English's bluezoo** (Lake Buena Vista; ✆ **407/934-1111**): This recent addition to the Walt Disney World Dolphin is the hippest dining spot in town. A chic and sophisticated undersea theme combines with a creative menu of fresh seafood and coastal cuisine to make the bluezoo a must for discerning diners. See p. 480.
- **Ted Peters' Famous Smoked Fish** (near St. Pete Beach; ✆ **727/381-7931**): The Peters clan has served mouthwatering meals since 1948, when

they started smoking fish and icing draft beer at the end of the causeway that leads from St. Pete Beach to the St. Petersburg mainland. Options include mullet, mackerel, and salmon, or you can bring your own fish to be smoked over the red oak coals, at $1.50 per pound. See p. 426.

- **Back Porch** (Destin; © **850/837-2022**): The food isn't gourmet at this cedar-shingled shack with a long porch offering glorious beach and Gulf views, but this is where charcoal-grilled amberjack originated. Today, you'll see it on menus throughout Florida. Other fish and seafood, as well as chicken and juicy hamburgers, also are prepared on the coals. See p. 603.
- **Chef Eddie's Magnolia Grill** (Apalachicola; © **850/653-8000**): Chef Eddie Cass's pleasant restaurant occupies a small bungalow, built in the 1880s, that still possesses the original black-cypress paneling in its central hallway. Nightly specials emphasize fresh local seafood and New Orleans–style sauces. Chef Eddie received more than 2,000 orders for his spicy seafood gumbo at a recent Florida Seafood Festival. See p. 621.

12 THE BEST LOCAL DINING EXPERIENCES

- **Blue Door** (South Beach; © **305/674-6400**): While the Delano may rise and fall and rise again on the hipster radar, this Claude Troisgrois restaurant remains one of Miami's best, with sensual French fare and a surreal, stylish setting that gives stiff competition to the beautiful people who frequent here. See p. 115.
- **Prime One Twelve** (South Beach; © **305/532-8112**): This South of Fifth Street steakhouse sizzles with Kobe beef hot dogs, aged and oversize steaks, and an unparalleled celebrity clientele that has everyone begging for reservations up to 2 months in advance. See p. 118.
- **Big Fish** (downtown Miami; © **305/373-1770**): Located on the Miami River across from the spectacular Miami skyline, Big Fish is indeed just that, in a little pond—or river—with scenic value that is priceless. See p. 130.
- **Dogma Grill** (Miami; © **305/759-3433**): A hip hot dog stand on the corner of Biscayne Boulevard's burgeoning Upper East side, Dogma serves more than 20 kinds of hot dogs and has priceless views of urban revitalization in action. See p. 134.
- **Versailles** (Little Havana; © **305/444-0240**): This iconoclastic Cuban diner isn't as swanky as its palatial French namesake, but it is full of mirrors through which you can view the colorful—and audible—Cuban clientele that congregates here for down-home cuisine and hearty conversation. See p. 136.
- **Island Grill** (Islamorada; © **305/664-8400**): Located directly on the water right before a bridge, Island Grill is *the* place locals go to for fresh fish, views, and live music on any given day or night. See p. 208.
- **Islamorada Fish Company** (Islamorada; © **800/258-2559** or 305/664-9271): We're not sure which is better, the view or the seafood—but whichever it is, it's a winning combination. See p. 208.
- **Blue Heaven** (Key West; © **305/296-8666**): What was once a well-kept secret in Key West's Bahama Village is now a popular eatery known for fresh

food (it's some of the best in town) and a motley, bohemian crowd. See p. 240.

- **Cap's Place Island Restaurant** (Lighthouse Point; ✆ **954/941-0418**): The only way to get to this rustic seafood restaurant, the former bootlegging and gambling hangout of Al Capone, is by boat, but don't be dismayed—it's not the least bit Disneyfied. Churchill, Roosevelt, Marilyn Monroe, and Sylvester Stallone have all indulged in this delicious taste of Old Florida. See p. 281.
- **Taverna Opa** (South Beach, Hollywood and Fort Lauderdale; ✆ **305/673-6730**): Don't get nervous if you hear plates breaking when you enter this raucous, authentic Greek taverna situated directly on the Intracoastal Waterway—it's just the restaurant's lively wait staff making sure your experience here is 100% Greek. See p. 177.
- **Farmer's Market Restaurant** (Fort Myers; ✆ **239/334-1687**): The retail Farmers Market next door may be tiny, but the best of the cabbage, okra, green beans, and tomatoes ends up here at this simple eatery, frequented by everyone from business executives to truck drivers. The specialties of the house are such Southern favorites as smoked ham hocks with a bowl of black-eyed peas. See p. 333.
- **Fourth Street Shrimp Store** (St. Petersburg; ✆ **727/822-0325**): The outside of this place looks like it's covered with graffiti, but it's actually a gigantic drawing of people eating. Inside, murals on two walls seem to look out on an early-19th-century seaport (one painted sailor permanently peers in to see what you're eating). This is the best and certainly the most interesting bargain in St. Petersburg. See p. 414.
- **Moore's Stone Crab** (Longboat Key, off Sarasota; ✆ **941/383-1748**): Set in Longbeach, the old fishing village on the north end of Longboat Key, this popular bay-front restaurant still looks a little like a packing house (it's an offshoot of a family seafood business), but the view of the bay (dotted with mangrove islands) makes a fine complement to stone crabs fresh from the family's own traps. See p. 446.
- **Ocean Prime** (Orlando/Dr. Phillips; ✆ **407/363-4801**): This elegant and sophisticated establishment combines a menu of the freshest steaks and seafood with an extensive wine list, and an upbeat atmosphere that's reminiscent of a 1930s supper club (albeit chic and updated). An incredibly knowledgeable and attentive staff top off the exceptional experience—without a doubt among the finest restaurants in Orlando. See p. 484.
- **Singleton's Seafood Shack** (Mayport/Jacksonville; ✆ **904/246-4442**): This rustic Old Florida fish camp has kept up with the times by offering fresh fish in more ways than just battered and fried, yet it has still managed to retain the charming casualness of a riverside fish camp. Even if you don't want seafood, this spot is worth stopping at, if only for a feel of Old Florida. See p. 565.
- **The Boss Oyster** (Apalachicola; ✆ **850/653-9364**): This rustic, dockside eatery is a good place to see if what they say about the aphrodisiac properties of Apalachicola oysters is true. The bivalves are served raw, steamed, or under a dozen toppings ranging from capers to crabmeat. You can even steam three dozen oysters and do the shucking yourself. Dine inside or at picnic tables on a screened dockside porch. See p. 621.

13 THE BEST BARS & NIGHTSPOTS

- **The Room** (South Beach; © **305/531-6061**): This N.Y.C. import exudes that hip Meatpacking District vibe with its simple, yet chic, concept of an impressive international collection of beer and wine only, comfy seats, candlelight only, and a contingency of locals who know about this place and refuse to share it with the other poor souls who don't. See p. 176.
- **Mokai** (South Beach; © **305/531-4166**): A small lounge off the beaten path of South Beach proper, Mokai is reminiscent of an après-ski bar in Aspen—with its brick walls, dim lighting, and comfy leather couches—but quintessentially Miami, with celebrity clientele, star DJs, and astronomical drink prices. See p. 175.
- **Opium/Prive, Mansion,** and **SET** (South Beach; © **305/531-5535**): This trendy troika of nightspots is among the hottest in Miami for dancing, drinking, and slews of celebrity sightings. Friday and Saturday are the hottest nights at any of them, and you're almost guaranteed to spot a celebrity at any given moment. See p. 179.
- **Tobacco Road** (Downtown Miami; © **305/374-1198**): Al Capone used to hang out here when it was a speakeasy. Now locals flock to this road-well-traveled place to hear live, local bands perform, as well as national acts such as George Clinton and the P-Funk All-Stars, Koko Taylor, and the Radiators. It's small, it's gritty, and it's meant to be that way here as it's the proud owner of Miami's very first liquor license. See p. 181.
- **Upstairs at the Van Dyke Cafe** (South Beach; © **305/534-3600**): Even though this jazz bar isn't in a basement, but rather on the second floor of the Van Dyke Cafe, it resembles a classy speakeasy in which local jazz performers play to an intimate, enthusiastic crowd of mostly adults and sophisticated young things who huddle at the small tables often until the wee hours. See p. 181.
- **La Covacha** (West Miami; © **305/594-3717**): This hut, located virtually in the middle of nowhere, is the hottest Latin joint in the entire city. Do not wear silk here, as you *will* sweat. Friday is *the* night, so much so that the owners had to place a red velvet rope out front to maintain some semblance of order. See p. 182.
- **Nikki Beach Club** (South Beach; © **305/538-1111**): What the Playboy Mansion is to Hollywood, the Nikki Beach Club is to South Beach. It's here where *Survivor* meets *The Brady Bunch in Hawaii,* with a bit of St. Tropez thrown in for taste. See p. 179.
- **Automatic Slim's** (South Beach; © **305/695-0795**): Proudly billing itself as a place where "the beautiful people come to get ugly," Automatic Slim's is a good-time bar in which anything goes and pretenses are left at the door. See p. 173.
- **Twist** (South Beach; © **305/538-9478**): South Beach's most popular and long-lasting gay bar, Twist is where the who's who of the gay community convene for cocktails, consorting, and, at times, contorting. See p. 182.
- **Le Tub** (Hollywood; © **954/931-9425**): This former 1959 Sunoco gas station was transformed into a kitschy waterfront oasis whose resplendent scenery is almost secondary to the decor: old toilet bowls, bathtubs, and sinks—seriously. Not the least bit as gross as it sounds, Le Tub also has the best hamburgers, chili, a 4am closing time, and a strict "no children" policy. See p. 283.
- **Duval Street** (Key West): South Florida's own version of Bourbon Street,

Duval Street is party central, with bars galore. See p. 242.

- **Clematis Street** (West Palm Beach): Until recently, nightlife in Palm Beach County was either an oxymoron or reserved for haughty private clubs on the island of Palm Beach. Thanks to a downtown revitalization, downtown West Palm now boasts a strip of its own, with trendy restaurants, clubs, and bars. See p. 308.
- **Las Olas Boulevard/Riverwalk** (Fort Lauderdale): Moving off the beachfront strip and onto the quainter (but no less calm) riverside, Fort Lauderdale now boasts its very own downtown nightlife scene with restaurants, bars, and clubs. See p. 272.
- **Biba Bar** (West Palm Beach; © **561/832-0094**): The harder to find, the hipper it is, so they say, which is why this dimly lit, loungey hotel bar is tucked away in the middle of this mod motor inn (p. 305)—a hangout for in-the-know locals and visitors.
- **The Dock at Crayton Cove** (Naples; © **239/263-9940**): Right on the City Dock, this lively pub is a perfect place for an open-air meal or libation while watching the action on Naples Bay. See p. 373.
- **CityWalk** (Orlando; © **407/363-8000**): This 12-acre entertainment complex is a collection of eateries and nighttime entertainment spots. It's also a haven for theme restaurant aficionados, featuring a Hard Rock Cafe, the NASCAR Grille, a Bubba Gump Shrimp Co., and Jimmy Buffett's Margaritaville. Additionally, you'll find plenty of places to dance the night away to the sounds of jazz, reggae, hip-hop, and pop. See p. 510.
- **Ocean Deck Restaurant & Beach Club** (Daytona Beach; © **386/253-5224**): Reggae rules at this hot, noisy, packed, and always-fun beach bar near Daytona Beach's municipal pier, the town's "happening" district. By contrast, the upstairs restaurant is suitable for children, and it has great ocean views to accompany its fine and inexpensive fare. See p. 532.
- **Seville Quarter** (Pensacola; © **850/434-6211**): In Pensacola's Seville Historic District, this restored antique brick complex with New Orleans–style wrought-iron balconies contains pubs and restaurants whose names capture the ambience: Rosie O'Grady's Goodtime Emporium, Lili Marlene's Aviator's Pub, Apple Annie's Courtyard, End o' the Alley Bar, Phineas Phogg's Balloon Works (a dance hall, not a balloon shop), and Fast Eddie's Billiard Parlor (which has electronic games for kids, too). Live entertainment ranges from Dixieland jazz to country and western. See p. 592.
- **Flora-Bama Lounge** (Perdido Key, near Pensacola; © **850/492-0611**): This slapped-together Gulf-side pub is almost a shrine to country music, with jam sessions from noon until way past midnight on Saturdays and Sundays. Flora-Bama is the prime sponsor and a key venue for the Frank Brown International Songwriters' Festival during the first week of November. Take in the great Gulf views from the Deck Bar, and, if you're coming in late April, don't miss the Interstate Mullet Toss and Beach Party. See p. 591.
- **Shuckums Oyster Pub & Seafood Grill** (Panama City Beach; © **850/235-3214**): "We shuck 'em, you suck 'em" is the motto of this extremely informal pub that became famous when comedian Martin Short tried unsuccessfully to shuck oysters here during the making of an MTV Spring Break special. The original bar is virtually papered over with dollar bills signed by old and young patrons who have been flocking here since 1967. See p. 616.

14 THE REST OF THE BEST

- **Best Driving Route:** A1A, a gorgeous oceanfront route that runs north up Miami Beach, through Sunny Isles and Hollywood into Fort Lauderdale (starting at Ocean Dr. and 1st St. in Miami, and merging onto Collins Ave. before running north), embodies the essence that is Florida. From time-warped hotels steeped in Art Deco kitsch to multimillion-dollar modern high-rises, A1A is one of the most scenic, albeit heavily trafficked, roads in all of Florida.
- **Best Place for People-Watching:** Lunchtime at News Cafe on Ocean Drive is the quintessential South Beach experience—lunching at News Cafe is more of a spectator sport than a dining experience. What the Big Mac is to McDonald's, people-watching is to News Cafe, whose Ocean Drive location is one of the best sidewalk spots from which to observe the wacky, colorful mix of pedestrians on parade. See p. 125.
- **Best Place to Hear a Moonlight Concert:** The Barnacle State Historic Site hosts a once-monthly, on or near the full moon (except July–Aug) concert in the backyard of its charming 1908 Coconut Grove bungalow, built on 5 acres of waterfront property. Listeners are welcome to picnic and bask in this sublime setting for a mere $5. See p. 153.
- **Best Place to Learn the Salsa:** If the only salsa you're familiar with is the kind you put on your tacos, get over to Bongo's Cuban Café, the hottest salsa club north of Havana, where Miami's most talented salsa dancers will teach you how to move your two left feet in the right direction. See p. 178.
- **Best Place to Discover Your Inner Flipper:** The nonprofit Dolphin Research Center in Marathon Key (home to approximately 15 dolphins) will teach you how to communicate with, touch, swim, and play with the mammals. See p. 195.
- **Best Cemetery:** The Key West Cemetery is funky, picturesque, and the epitome of the quirky Key West image, as irreverent as it is humorous. Headstones reflect residents' lighthearted attitudes toward life and death. I TOLD YOU I WAS SICK is one of the more famous epitaphs, as is the tongue-in-cheek widow's inscription AT LEAST I KNOW WHERE HE'S SLEEPING TONIGHT. See p. 221.
- **Best Way to See the Everglades Without Breaking a Sweat:** Airboat rides through the outskirts of the Everglades are particularly wonderful, as the area is unfettered by jet skis, cruise ships, and neon bikinis. The Everglades is Florida's Outback, resplendent in its swampy nature. It is best explored either by slow-moving canoes that really get you acquainted with your surroundings or via an airboat that can quickly navigate its way through the most stubborn of saw grass, providing you with an up-close-and-personal (as well as fun) view of the land's inhabitants, from alligators and manatees to raccoons and Florida panthers. See p. 253.
- **Best Place to Drive on a World Record:** The Sunshine Skyway Bridge crosses Tampa Bay and at 5½ miles in length is the longest cable span bridge in the world.
- **Best Place for a Family Vacation:** With eight theme parks, 80 smaller attractions, and virtually everything with a kid-friendly touch, it's hard to top Orlando and Lake Buena Vista. See chapter 13.
- **Best Blending of Old South with the Modern Era:** There's as much Old South ambience in the state's capital, Tallahassee, as anywhere else in Florida.

Here you'll find 19th-century homes nestled among towering pine trees and sprawling live oaks, historic plantations, ancient Native American settlement sites and mounds, gorgeous gardens, quiet parks with picnic areas, beautiful lakes and streams, and myriad outdoor activities. The state legislature is here, along with two college football teams and all the modern conveniences you could want. See p. 622.

- **Best Place for Sunsets:** Florida's Panhandle is the Land of the Two-Way Sun. It has spectacular sunrises to the east and equally gorgeous sunsets to the west. One of the best viewing places is Bud & Alley's rooftop restaurant in Seaside. See p. 608.

2

Florida in Depth

Although there's no Liberty Bell or hallowed homage to Revolutionary War history, Florida isn't just an American swamp turned condo-canyon with pretty palm trees and beaches. And contrary to popular belief, the state's history is a lot richer than its reputation as a haven for retirees, celebrities, and people in dire need of a thaw out and a deep, dark tan. From its emergence as a prehistoric swamp, a nexus of Native American culture and civilization, and a 16th-century hot spot for treasure-hunting Spanish explorers to a 21st-century destination of development, politics, and pop culture, Florida has experienced more reincarnations than Shirley MacLaine.

1 THE LAND & ITS PEOPLE

Stretching 1,197 miles along the Atlantic Ocean and Gulf of Mexico, Florida—and all its 53,927 square miles of islands, low peninsula, and swampland—is the 22nd largest state in the country. Based on the population growth, however, it's not nearly big enough. Population is expected to grow to 19,920,348 by April 1, 2010 (a 25% increase over 2000). Florida's population is also becoming increasingly Hispanic (persons of Hispanic origin may be any race). In 1980, the Census enumerated 858,158 persons of Hispanic origin (8.8% of the total). The number of Hispanics increased to 1,574,143 in 1990 (12% of the total) and to 2,682,715 in 2000 (17% of the total). The Hispanic population increased by 70% between 1990 and 2000.

There are bigger issues than population growth, however. Scientists have observed changes in Florida consistent with the early effects of global warming: retreating and eroding shorelines, dying coral reefs, saltwater intrusion into inland freshwater aquifers, an upswing in forest fires, and warmer air and sea-surface temperatures. As glaciers melt and warming waters expand, sea levels will rise anywhere from 8 inches to 2½ feet over the next century. In Florida, seawater will advance inland as much as 400 feet in low-lying areas, flooding shoreline homes and hotels, limiting future development, and eroding the state's beloved beaches. People aren't kidding when they say that one day, Florida will be underwater.

On a more positive note, some say this perceived global warming threat has been greatly exaggerated. Though preliminary research raised concerns that warmer ocean temperatures would lead to more frequent hurricanes, scientists now discount this theory. Nevertheless, global warming may increase hurricanes' maximum intensity, which will serve to exacerbate a natural cyclical trend toward more severe storms—a trend likely to persist for the next 25 to 40 years.

2 A LOOK AT THE PAST

PREHISTORIC FLORIDA

Fourteen thousand years ago, Florida would have made an ideal location for the show *Land of the Lost*—that is, if there were actually dinosaurs down here. Not so much. During the age of dinosaurs, the Florida peninsula was underwater and did not exist as a landmass. Therefore, no dinosaur remains were ever deposited in Florida. Paleo-Indians, however, were here, and got here by crossing over to North America from Asia. Most of their activity was around the watering holes, and sinkholes and basins in the beds of modern rivers.

Paleo-Indian culture was eventually replaced by, or evolved into, the Early Archaic culture. There were now more people in Florida, and as they were no longer tied to a few water holes in an arid land, they left their artifacts in many more locations.

The Early Archaic period evolved into the Middle Archaic period around 5000 B.C. People started living in villages near wetlands, and favored sites may have been occupied for multiple generations. The Late Archaic period started around 3000 B.C., when Florida's climate had reached current conditions and the sea had risen close to its present level. People now lived everywhere fresh- or saltwater wetlands were found. Many people lived in large villages with purpose-built mounds. Fired pottery appeared in Florida by 2000 B.C. By about 500 B.C., the Archaic culture that had been fairly uniform across Florida began to fragment into regional cultures.

The post-Archaic cultures of eastern and southern Florida developed in relative isolation, and it is likely that the peoples living in those areas at the time of first European contact were direct descendants of the inhabitants of the areas in late Archaic times. The cultures of the Florida Panhandle and the north and central Gulf coast of the Florida peninsula were strongly influenced by the Mississippian culture, although there is continuity in cultural history, suggesting that the peoples of those cultures were also descended from the inhabitants of the Archaic period. Cultivation of maize was adopted in the Panhandle and the northern part of the peninsula, but was absent or very restricted in the tribes that lived south of the Timucuan-speaking people (that is, south of a line approximately from present-day Daytona Beach to a point on or north of Tampa Bay).

NATIVE AMERICANS Spanish explorers of the early 16th century were likely the first Europeans to interact with the native population of Florida. The first documented encounter of Europeans with Native Americans of the United States came with the first expedition of Juan Ponce de León to Florida in 1513, although he encountered at least one native that spoke Spanish. In 1521, he encountered the Calusa Indians, who established 30 villages in the Everglades, during a failed colonization attempt in which they drove off the Europeans.

The Spanish recorded nearly 100 names of groups they encountered, ranging from organized political entities, such as the Apalachee, with a population of around 50,000, to villages with no known political affiliation. There were an estimated 150,000 speakers of dialects of the Timucua language, but the Timucua were only organized as groups of villages, and did not share a common culture. Other tribes in Florida at the time of first contact included the Ais; Calusa; Jaega; Mayaimi; Tequesta, who lived on the southeast coast of the Everglades; and Tocobaga. All of these tribes diminished in numbers during the period of Spanish control of Florida.

At the beginning of the 18th century, tribes from areas to the north of Florida, supplied, encouraged, and occasionally accompanied by white colonists from the Province of Carolina, raided throughout Florida, burning villages, killing many of the inhabitants, and carrying captives back to Charles Towne to be sold as slaves. Most of the villages in Florida were abandoned, and the survivors sought refuge at St. Augustine or in isolated spots around the state. Some of the Apalachee eventually reached Louisiana, where they survived as a distinct group for at least another century.

The few surviving members of these tribes were evacuated to Cuba when Spain transferred Florida to the British Empire in 1763. The Seminole, originally an offshoot of the Creek people who absorbed other groups, developed as a distinct tribe in Florida during the 18th century, and are now represented in the Seminole Nation of Oklahoma, the Seminole Tribe of Florida, and the Miccosukee Tribe of Indians of Florida.

SPANISH RULE Once Ponce de León laid his eyes on Florida in 1513, a slew of competitive conquistadors made futile efforts to find gold there and colonize the region. The first to establish a fort in Florida were the French, actually, but it was ultimately destroyed by the Spanish, who introduced Christianity, horses, and cattle to the region. Unfortunately they also introduced diseases and conquistador brutality, which ultimately decimated Indian populations. Eager to expand its own American colony collection, Britain led several raids into Florida in the 1700s to overthrow Spanish rule. Among the most notable Spaniards in Florida included the aforementioned de León; Hernando de Soto, the most ruthless of the explorers whose thirst for gold led to the massacre of many Indians; Panfilo de Narvaez, whose quest for El Dorado—the land of gold—landed him in Tampa Bay; and Pedro Menendez de Aviles, who founded St. Augustine after defeating the French.

BRITISH RULE The Brits weren't interested in gold: They were all about Florida's bounty of hides and furs, and they'd stop at nothing to get them. After taking control in 1763, the Brits divided Florida into two. Because Florida was subsidized by the English, Floridians remained loyal to Mother England during the American Revolution—that is, until the Spanish returned and regained West Florida in 1781 and, 2 years later, East Florida. During the Spanish reconquest, American slaves fled to Florida, causing major turmoil between Spain and the U.S. Combined with Indian raids in the north and an Indian alliance with runaway slaves, Florida was, well, a mess, until General Andrew Jackson invaded Spanish Florida, captured Pensacola, and occupied West Florida. Then Florida was a disaster. Jackson's invasion kicked off the First Seminole War in 1817. Finally, to settle Spain's $5-million debt to the U.S., all Spanish lands east of the Mississippi, including Florida, were ceded to the U.S. in 1819.

AMERICAN RULE Florida became an organized territory of the United States on March 30, 1822. The Americans merged East Florida and West Florida (although the majority of West Florida was annexed to Orleans Territory and Mississippi Territory), and established a new capital in Tallahassee, conveniently located halfway between the East Florida capital of St. Augustine and the West Florida capital of Pensacola. The boundaries of Florida's first two counties, Escambia and St. Johns, approximately coincided with the boundaries of West and East Florida respectively.

At this time, the plantation system was adopted by north Florida and because the settlers wanted the best possible land, the Federal government tried moving all Indians west of the Mississippi, resulting in the Second and Third Seminole Wars. When Abraham Lincoln was elected president in

1860, Florida became the third state to secede from the Union. Florida saw little action during the Civil War—its main role was to supply beef and salt to the Confederates. The state got off easy for a change.

After meeting the requirements of Reconstruction, including amendments to the U.S. Constitution, Florida was readmitted to the United States on July 25, 1868.

UNLOCKING THE KEYS No one knows exactly when the first European set foot on one of the Florida Keys, but as exploration and shipping increased, the islands became prominent on nautical maps. The nearby treacherous coral reefs claimed many actual seafaring "martyrs" from the time of early recorded history. The chain was eventually called "keys," also attributed to the Spanish, from *cayos,* meaning "small islands."

In 1763, the Spanish ceded Florida to the British in a trade for the port of Havana. The treaty was unclear as to the status of the Keys. An agent of the King of Spain claimed that the islands, rich in fish, turtles, and mahogany for shipbuilding, were part of Cuba, fearing that the English might build fortresses and dominate the shipping lanes. The British also realized the treaty was ambiguous, but declared that the Keys should be occupied and defended as part of Florida. The British claim was never officially contested. Ironically, the British gave the islands back to Spain in 1783, to keep them out of the hands of the United States, but in 1821 all of Florida, including the necklace of islands, officially became American territory.

Many of the residents of Key West were immigrants from the Bahamas, known as "conchs" (pronounced *conks*), who arrived in increasing numbers after 1830. Many were sons and daughters of Loyalists who fled to the nearest crown soil during the American Revolution.

In the 20th century many residents of Key West started referring to themselves as "conchs," and the term is now generally applied to all residents of Key West. Some residents use the term "conch" to refer to a person born in Key West, while the term "freshwater conch" refers to a resident not born in Key West but who has lived in Key West for 7 years or more.

In 1982, Key West and the rest of the Florida Keys briefly declared its "independence" as the Conch Republic in a protest over a United States Border Patrol blockade. This blockade was set up on U.S. 1, where the northern end of the Overseas Highway meets the mainland at Florida City. This blockade was in response to the Mariel Boatlift. A 17-mile traffic jam ensued while the Border Patrol stopped every car leaving the Keys supposedly searching for illegal aliens attempting to enter the mainland United States. This paralyzed the Florida Keys, which rely heavily on the tourism industry. Flags, T-shirts, and other merchandise representing the Conch Republic are still popular souvenirs for visitors to Key West, and the Conch Republic Independence Celebration—including parades and parties—is celebrated every April 23.

BOOMTOWN, FLORIDA After the Civil War, Florida met its best friend—tourism. Although the state's economy was in the dumps, its warm climate and smallish population called out to investors and developers. Railroad barons Henry Flagler and Henry Plant laid their tracks down the east and west coasts of Florida during the late 1880s, offering tourists a not-so quick escape to paradise, or something close to it. As tourists started pouring down, the economy was stimulated. In February 1888, Florida had a special tourist. President Grover Cleveland, the first lady, and his party visited Florida for a couple of days. He visited the Subtropical Exposition in Jacksonville, where he made a speech supporting tourism to the state;

then, he took a train to St. Augustine, meeting Henry Flagler.

Florida's new railroads opened up large areas to development, spurring the Florida land boom of the 1920s. Investors of all kinds, mostly from outside Florida, raced to buy and sell rapidly appreciating land in newly platted communities such as Miami and Palm Beach. A majority of the people who bought land in Florida were able to do so without stepping foot in the state, by hiring people to speculate and buy the land for them. By 1925, the market ran out of buyers to pay the high prices and soon the boom became a bust. The 1926 Miami Hurricane further depressed the real estate market. The Great Depression arrived in 1929; however, by that time, economic decay already consumed much of Florida from the land boom that collapsed 4 years earlier.

VARIATIONS ON A THEME (PARK)

Florida's first theme parks emerged in the 1930s and include Cypress Gardens (1936), near Winter Haven, and Marineland (1938), near St. Augustine. Walt Disney chose Central Florida as the site of his planned Walt Disney World Resort in the 1960s and began purchasing land. In 1971, the first component of the resort, the Magic Kingdom, opened and began the dramatic transformation of the Orlando area into a major resort destination. More significantly, the Everglades were finally granted National Park status. Thanks to the work of the Everglades' foremost supporter, Ernest F. Coe, Congress passed a park bill in 1934. Dubbed by opponents as the "alligator and snake swamp bill," the legislation stalled during the Great Depression and World War II. Finally, on December 6, 1947, President Harry S Truman dedicated the Everglades National Park.

In that same year, Marjory Stoneman Douglas first published *The Everglades: River of Grass.* She understood its importance as the major watershed for South Florida and as a unique ecosystem.

THE SPACE RACE AND CUBAN INFLUX

With the space race in full blast, Cape Canaveral brought even more of a boom to Florida in the '60s—especially when Buzz Aldrin and Neil Armstrong blasted off from the so-called Florida Space Coast and onto the moon. Sixties Florida also saw another kind of race, as over 300,000 Cubans fled to Florida when Fidel Castro took over Cuba in 1959. Early arrivals landed in Florida via Freedom Flights, but later, refugees risked—and lost—their lives as they made the dangerous 90-mile trip from Cuba to Key West on flimsy rafts. Florida was again in the spotlight in 1962 as the world was on edge during the Cuban Missile Crisis. The large wave of Cubans into South Florida transformed Miami into a major center of commerce, finance, and transportation for all of Latin America. Immigration from Haiti and other Caribbean states continues to the present day.

The plight of Cubans fleeing their native island was highlighted again in 1980 during the Mariel Boatlift, a mass movement of Cubans who departed from Cuba's Mariel Harbor for the United States between April 15 and October 31, 1980. The exodus was ended by mutual agreement between the U.S. and Cuba in October 1980. By that time, up to 125,000 Cubans had made the journey to Florida.

MODERN FLORIDA

Florida today is a fascinating study in, well everything. It seems as if the state is always in the news for *something,* and with this timeline of modern Florida, you'll understand why.

1980 Race riots tear apart Miami. The Mariel boatlift brings 125,000 Cubans to Florida. The Miami Seaquarium celebrates its 25th anniversary. Tampa opens its own $6.2-million water theme park, Adventure Island. A bill raising the drinking age from 18 to 19 is passed; however, all military personnel are excluded.

1981 The first manned space shuttle launches are made from Kennedy Space Center, with launch schedules to increase in the year ahead. Unmanned rockets with payloads are scheduled approximately every month by NASA from the KSC launchpads.

1982 The $800-million EPCOT Center opens at Walt Disney World.

1983 The space shuttle *Challenger* launches its first five-member crew and the first American woman, Sally Ride, into space from Kennedy Space Center. Thirty-eight overseas highway bridges from Key Largo to Key West are completed under the Florida Keys Bridge Replacement Program.

1984 The Sunshine Skyway Bridge over Tampa Bay is under reconstruction. The expected completion date was 1986, at a cost of $215 million. Donald Duck's "50th Anniversary Celebration" is held in June at Walt Disney World. Busch Gardens celebrates its 25th anniversary. The Miami Metro Rail, the only inner-city, elevated rail system in Florida, begins service in May.

1985 Florida's state park system marks its 50th anniversary. Begun during the Depression with nine parks, the system now included 92 park and recreation areas. DeSoto Trail was officially dedicated during May in Inverness. The Kennedy Space Center's Visitor Center is renamed Spaceport USA. Two well-preserved, intact human brains are discovered by Glenn Doran, archaeologist at Florida State University, when he uncovered the 7,000-plus-year-old skulls in the swamps near Titusville.

1986 The Kennedy Space Center witnesses America's worst space tragedy when the space shuttle *Challenger* explodes after takeoff. All seven astronauts aboard are killed. Treasure hunter Mel Fisher continues to salvage vast amounts of gold and silver from his discovery of the Spanish galleon *Nuestra Senora de Atocha,* which sank in 1622 during a hurricane off Key West. The television series *Miami Vice* continues to capture the nation's imagination, revitalizing interest and tourism for South Florida. Walt Disney World breaks ground for a major movie and television production studio to be constructed in Orlando.

1987 Bob Martinez is the first person of Spanish ancestry to become governor of Florida. Calvin Jones, state archaeologist, finds what is believed to be the site of Hernando de Soto's 1539-to-1540 camp in Tallahassee. The U.S. Census Bureau estimates indicate that Florida has surpassed Pennsylvania to become the fourth most populous state in the nation. The ranking will not become official until the Bureau publishes its report in early 1988. It is predicted that Florida will be the third most populous state by the year 2000.

1988 Florida once again becomes the center for America's space program. Regular space shuttle flights resume in October for the first time since the *Challenger* disaster in 1986. Two Republicans capture posts in the Florida Cabinet in the general election. Jim Smith is elected Secretary of State and Tom Gallagher takes over as State Insurance Commissioner. This is the first time since the Reconstruction Era of the 1870s that Republicans have won any statewide office other than governor. Floridians now have a state-operated lottery that gives away some of the largest prizes in the nation. An international team, using experimental technology, completes the world's deepest cave-diving expedition at Wakulla Springs in North Florida.

1989 U.S. Representative Claude Pepper dies in May. Genetic testing reveals that a Wauchula hospital, a decade prior, accidentally switched babies belonging to Sarasota and Pennsylvania couples, setting off a legal battle. A devastating cold front hits the state in December, closing airports and interstates and causing statewide power outages.

1990 Panama's governor Manuel Noriega is brought to Miami in January for trial on drug charges. Joe Robbie, Miami Dolphins founder, dies in January. Flooding Panhandle rivers, in March, force evacuation of 2,000 homes. An owners/players contract dispute delays spring training baseball season. St. Petersburg's Suncoast Dome opens in March. Iraq's invasion of Kuwait in August results in a massive state National Guard and Army Reserve unit call-up. Lotto, in September, awards a record $106-million jackpot. State gasoline prices in September soar to a 7-year high. Democrat Lawton Chiles soundly trounces Republican incumbent Bob Martinez in governor's race. Outgoing Governor Martinez, in November, was named the nation's drug czar. In December, Tampa is awarded a franchise team in the National Hockey League.

1991 Lawton Chiles, in January, is sworn in as the state's 41st governor. Miami-based Eastern Airlines, in January, announces its closure due to financial losses. Former Governor LeRoy Collins, 82, dies in March. U.S. Senator Bruce Smathers, in April, donates record $20 million to University of Florida library system. In May, the Legislature approves a $29.3-billion state budget, including $164 million in new taxes. At Governor Chiles' request, the Legislature, in May, creates the new Department of Elderly Affairs. Also in May, Queen Elizabeth II visits Miami and Tampa, and confers honorary knighthood on Tampa resident Gen. Norman Schwarzkopf. Five Navy bombers found by treasure salvers are determined not to be the "Lost Squadron" of Bermuda Triangle fame that went down in 1945 off the coast of Florida. Miami and Denver are awarded new national major league baseball franchises. The 1990 Federal Census puts Florida's population at 12,937,926, a 34% increase from 1980.

1992 Homestead and adjacent South Florida are devastated on August 24 by the costliest natural disaster in American history, Hurricane Andrew, demanding billions in aid. There are 58 deaths directly or indirectly related to Andrew. The hurricane destroys 25,000 homes and damages 10,000 others. Twenty-two thousand Federal troops are deployed. Shelters house 80,000 persons.

The first elections are held after Florida gained four additional seats in the U.S. House of Representatives; Cubans and African Americans are seated. Lincoln Diaz-Balart (Cuban-born) joins lleana Ros-Lehtinen (the first Cuban elected to the Florida House in 1982, the Florida Senate in 1986, and the U.S. House in 1989). Among African Americans elected to Congress are Carrie Meek of Miami. Sixty-six in 1993, her political career saw her elected first to the Florida House of Representatives, then the Florida Senate, and then to the U.S. House of Representatives.

1993 Janet Reno, State Attorney for Dade County (Miami) for 15 years, is named Attorney General of the U.S. by President Bill Clinton, the first woman to so serve in U.S. history. Although a pro-choice Democrat she managed to win reelection four times in a conservative stronghold, the last time without opposition.

1996 Miami turns 100.

2000 Florida becomes the battleground of the controversial 2000 U.S. presidential election, when a count of the popular votes from Election Day is extremely close and mired in accusations of fraud and manipulation. Subsequent recount efforts degenerate into arguments over mispunched ballots, "hanging chads," and controversial decisions by Florida Secretary of State Katherine Harris and the Florida Supreme Court. Ultimately, the United States Supreme Court ends all recounts and lets stand the official count by Harris, which is accepted by Congress.

2003 The Florida Marlins win the World Series.

2004 George W. Bush wins the presidential election again. His brother, Florida Governor Jeb Bush, celebrates in Florida's State Capitol.

2007 Jeb Bush vacates the governor's office, which is taken over by Florida Governor Charlie Crist.

2008 Florida continues to be one of the fastest growing states in the country. The economy still depends greatly on tourism, but expanding industries in business and manufacturing are strengthening its growth potential. State leaders are working on problems created due to huge population increases and environmental concerns.

2009 Despite the big housing boom that ultimately went bust in 2008, Florida still continues to experience no downturn in the luxury market. That said, economists predict a dismal economic situation throughout the state through 2009. The good news is that those same naysayers predict long-term growth in the state will be positive. At least we have the weather.

3 RECOMMENDED BOOKS & MOVIES

Florida is an author's dream come true. A state of much diversity (read: bizarre characters, to say the least), Florida practically hangs inspiration from the palm trees. If you don't believe us, read the following books. Then you'll get it.

FICTION

- ***The Perez Family*** (W. W. Norton & Co. Inc.), by Christine Bell: Cuban immigrants from the Mariel Boat Lift exchange their talents for an immigration deal in Miami. See below for the film adaptation.
- ***Miami, It's Murder*** (Avon), by Edna Buchannan: Miami's Agatha Christie keeps you in suspense with her reporter protagonist and her life as an investigative crime solver in Miami.
- ***To Have and Have Not*** (Scribner), by Ernest Hemingway: One of the many must-reads by Key West's most famous resident.
- ***Naked Came the Manatee*** (Ballantine Books), by Carl Hiassen: Thirteen *Miami Herald* writers contributed to this hilarious story about the discovery of Castro's head.
- ***Killing Mister Watson*** (Vintage Books USA), by Peter Matthiessen: A fascinating story about the settlement of the Everglades and the problems that ensued.
- ***The Yearling*** (Collier MacMillan Publishers), by Marjorie Kinnan Rawlings: A classic about life in the Florida backwoods.
- ***Seraph on the Suwanee*** (Harper Perennial), by Zora Neale Hurston: A novel about turn-of-the-20th-century Florida "white crackers."
- ***Nine Florida Stories*** (University Press of Florida), by Marjory Stoneman Douglas: The beloved Florida naturalist's fictional take on Florida, set in a scattering of settings (Miami, Fort Lauderdale, the Tamiami Trail, the Keys, the Everglades) and revealing the drama of hurricanes and plane crashes, of kidnappers, escaped convicts, and smugglers.
- ***Swim to Me*** (Algonquin Books), by Betsy Carter: A wacky novel set in Weeki Wachee about a shy teenager who finds her purpose at the mermaid-happy theme park.

NONFICTION

- ***Miami*** (Vintage), by Joan Didion: An intriguing compilation of impressions of the Magic City.

- ***Miami, the Magic City*** (Centennial Press), by Arva Moore Parks: An authoritative history of the city.
- ***The Everglades: River of Grass*** (Pineapple Press) by Marjory Stoneman Douglas: Eco-maniacs will love this personal account of the treasures of Florida's most famous natural resource.
- ***Celebration USA: Living in Disney's Brave New Town*** (Holt Paperbacks), by Douglas Frantz and Catherine Collins: An eye-opening true story about living in Disney's "model town."

MOVIES FILMED IN FLORIDA

- Clarence Brown's ***The Yearling*** (1946), based on the novel by M. K. Rawlings
- John Huston's ***Key Largo*** (1948), based on the novel by Hemingway (gangsters, hurricanes, and Bogey and Bacall)
- Harry Levin's ***Where the Boys Are*** (1960; Spring Break in Fort Lauderdale)
- John Schlesinger's ***Midnight Cowboy*** (1969), based on the novel by James Leo Herlihy
- Ernest Lehman's ***Portnoy's Complaint*** (1972), based on a novel by Philip Roth (Jewish culture)
- Lawrence Kasdan's ***Body Heat*** (1981; crime)
- Ron Howard's ***Cocoon*** (1985), based on a novel by David Saperstein (retirees)
- Tim Burton's ***Edward Scissorhands*** (1990; modern fairy tale filmed in Dade City and Lakeland)
- Mira Nair's ***The Perez Family*** (1995; Cuban culture)
- Mike Nichols's ***The Birdcage*** (1996; South Beach comedy)
- Andrew Bergman's ***Striptease*** (1996), based on the novel by Carl Hiassen
- John Singleton's ***Rosewood*** (1997; African-American culture; based on historic Rosewood massacre)
- Victor Nunez's ***Ulee's Gold*** (1997; Panhandle family drama)
- Peter Weir's ***The Truman Show*** (1998; sci-fi in Seaside)
- Spike Jonze's ***Adaptation*** (2002), loosely based on Susan Orleans's *The Orchid Thief*
- Patty Jenkins's ***Monster*** (2003; biopic of serial killer Aileen Wournos)
- Taylor Hackford's ***Ray*** (2004; biopic of musician Ray Charles, born in Florida)

MUSIC OF FLORIDA

The Miami recording industry did not begin with Gloria Estefan's Miami Sound Machine, contrary to popular belief. In fact, some major rock albums were recorded in Miami's Criteria Studios. Among them: *Rumours* by Fleetwood Mac and *Hotel California* by the Eagles. Longtime local music entrepreneur Henry Stone and his label, TK Records, created the local indie scene in the 1970s. TK Records produced the R&B group KC and the Sunshine Band along with soul singers Betty Wright, George McCrae, and Jimmy "Bo" Horne as well as a number of minor soul and disco hits, many influenced by Caribbean music. In the 1970s and early 1980s, Jacksonville saw a very active music recording scene with Southern rock bands such as Molly Hatchet, the Allman Brothers Band, 38 Special, the Outlaws, and Lynyrd Skynyrd. The Bellamy Brothers also recorded their style of country music in the mid- to late 1970s. They originated from Darby, Florida, just north of Tampa, in Pasco County. Tom Petty is from Gainesville, Florida, while boy band *NSYNC, Britney Spears, Christina Aguilera, and Justin Timberlake were graduates of Orlando's Mickey Mouse Club. In the 2000s, Miami saw an enormous rap boom in the form of Daddy Yankee, Pitbull, Rick Ross, and more.

3

Planning Your Trip to Florida

Whether you plan to spend a day, a week, 2 weeks, or longer in Florida, you'll need to make many "where," "when," and "how" choices before you leave home. This chapter explains how best to plan your trip.

For contact information of any airline, car-rental agency, or other service not listed below, please turn to the "Fast Facts, Toll-Free Numbers & Websites" appendix on p. 635.

1 WHEN TO GO

To a large extent, the timing of your visit will determine how much you'll spend—and how much company you'll have—once you get to Florida. That's because room rates can more than double during high seasons, when countless visitors flock to Florida.

The weather determines the high seasons (see "Climate," below). In subtropical South Florida, high season is in the winter, from mid-December to mid-April. On the other hand, you'll be rewarded with incredible bargains if you can stand the heat and humidity of a South Florida summer between June and early September. In North Florida, the reverse is true: Tourists flock here during the summer, from Memorial Day to Labor Day.

Hurricane season runs from June to November, and, as seen in 2005, the most active hurricane season on record, and in 2007, the quietest, you never know what can happen. Pay close attention to weather forecasts during this season and always be prepared. See "Weather" under "Fast Facts: Florida," p. 638.

Presidents' Day weekend in February, Easter week, Memorial Day weekend at the end of May, the Fourth of July, Labor Day weekend at the start of September, Thanksgiving, Christmas, and New Year's are busy throughout the state, especially at Walt Disney World and the other Orlando-area attractions, which can be packed any time school is out (see chapter 13 for more information on these areas).

Northern and southern Florida share the same shoulder seasons: April through May, and September through November, when the weather is pleasant throughout Florida and hotel rates are considerably lower than during the high season. If price is a consideration, these months of moderate temperatures and fewer tourists are the best times to visit.

See the accommodations sections in the chapters that follow for specifics on the local high, shoulder, and off-seasons.

CLIMATE Northern Florida has a temperate climate, and even in the warmer southern third of the state, it's subtropical, not tropical. Accordingly, Florida sees more extremes of temperatures than, say, the Caribbean islands.

Spring, which runs from late March to May, sees warm temperatures throughout Florida, but it also brings tropical showers.

Summer in Florida extends from May to September, when it's hot and very humid throughout the state. If you're in an inland city during these months, you may not want to do anything too taxing when the sun is at its peak. Coastal areas, however, reap the benefits of sea breezes. Severe afternoon thunderstorms are prevalent during the summer heat (there aren't professional sports teams here named Lightning and Thunder for nothing), so schedule your activities for earlier in the day, and take precautions to avoid being hit by lightning during the storms.

Autumn—about September through November—is a great time to visit, as the hottest days are gone and the crowds have thinned out. Unless a hurricane blows through, November is usually Florida's driest month. June through November is hurricane season here, but even if one threatens, the National Weather Service closely tracks the storms and gives ample warning if there's need to evacuate coastal areas.

Winter can get a bit nippy throughout the state and sometimes downright cold in northern Florida. Although snow is rare, a flake or two has been known to fall as far south as Miami, where those with thin blood have been known to whip out the hats and coats when the temps drop below 80. The "cold snaps" usually last only a few days in the southern half of the state, however, and daytime temperatures quickly return to the 70s (20s Celsius).

For up-to-the-minute weather info, tune in to cable TV's Weather Channel or check out its website at www.weather.com.

Average Temperatures in Select Florida Cities (°F/°C)

	Jan	Feb	Mar	Apr	May	June	July	Aug	Sept	Oct	Nov	Dec
Key West	69/21	72/22	74/23	77/25	80/27	82/28	85/29	85/29	84/29	80/27	74/23	72/22
Miami	69/21	70/21	71/22	74/23	78/26	81/27	82/28	84/29	81/27	78/26	73/23	70/21
Tampa	60/16	61/16	66/19	72/22	77/25	81/27	82/28	82/28	81/27	75/24	67/19	62/17
Orlando	60/16	63/17	66/19	71/22	78/26	82/28	82/28	82/28	81/27	75/24	67/19	61/16
Tallahassee	53/12	56/13	63/17	68/20	72/22	78/26	81/27	81/27	77/25	74/23	66/19	59/15

CALENDAR OF EVENTS

For an exhaustive list of events beyond those listed here, check http://events.frommers.com, where you'll find a searchable, up-to-the-minute roster of what's happening in cities all over the world.

January

FedEx Orange Bowl Championship (✆ **305/341-4700;** www.orangebowl.org), Miami. Football fanatics flock down to the big Orange Bowl game (taking place not at the recently razed Orange Bowl in seedy downtown, but at the much more savory Dolphins Stadium) on New Year's Day, featuring two of the year's best college football teams. Call early if you want tickets; they sell out quickly. First week of January.

Key West Literary Seminar (✆ **888/293-9291;** www.keywestliteraryseminar.org), Key West. Literary types have a good reason to put down their books and head to Key West. This 3-day event features a different theme every year, along with a roster of incredible authors, writers, and other literary types. The event is so popular it sells out well in advance, so call early for tickets. Second week of January.

February

Gasparilla Pirate Fest (✆ **813/353-8108;** www.gasparillapiratefest.com), Tampa. Hundreds of boats and rowdy "pirates" invade the city and then parade along Bayshore Boulevard, showering crowds with beads and coins. Early February.

Everglades City Seafood Festival (✆ **239/695-2561;** www.evergladesseafood.com), Everglades City. What seems like schools of fish-loving people flock down to Everglades City for a 2-day feeding frenzy in which Florida delicacies from stone crab to gator tails are served from shacks and booths on the outskirts of this quaint Old Florida town. Free admission, but you pay for the food you eat, booth by booth. First full weekend in February.

Miami International Film Festival (✆ **877/888-MIFF** [6433]; www.miamifilmfestival.com), Miami. Though not exactly Cannes, the Miami Film Festival, sponsored by the Film Society of America, is an impressive 10-day celluloid celebration, featuring world premieres of Latin American, domestic, and other foreign and independent films. Actors, producers, and directors show up to plug their films and participate in Q&A sessions with the audiences. End of February to early March.

Speedweeks (✆ **386/254-2700;** www.daytonaintlspeedway.com), Daytona. Nineteen days of events, with a series of races that draw the top names in NASCAR stock-car racing, culminate in the **Daytona 500.** All events take place at the Daytona International Speedway. Especially for the Daytona 500, tickets must be purchased as far as a year in advance; they go on sale January 1 of the prior year. First 3 weeks of February.

Miami International Boat Show (✆ **954/441-3231;** www.miamiboatshow.com), Miami Beach. If you don't like crowds, beware, as this show draws a quarter of a million boat enthusiasts to the Miami Beach Convention Center. Some of the world's priciest megayachts, speedboats, sailboats, and schooners are displayed for purchase or for gawking. Mid-February.

South Beach Wine & Food Festival (✆ **877/762-3933;** www.sobewineandfoodfest.com), South Beach. A 3-day celebration featuring some of the Food Network's best chefs, who do their thing in the kitchens of various restaurants and at events around town. In addition, there are tastings, lectures, seminars, and parties that are all open to the public—for a price, of course. Last weekend in February.

March

Bike Week (✆ **800/854-1234;** www.officialbikeweek.com), Daytona Beach. This international gathering of motorcycle enthusiasts draws a crowd of more than 200,000. In addition to major races held at Daytona International Speedway (featuring the world's best road racers, motocrossers, and dirt trackers), there are motorcycle shows, beach parties, and the Annual Motorcycle Parade, with thousands of riders. First week in March.

Winter Party (✆ **305/538-5908;** www.winterparty.com), Miami Beach. Gays and lesbians from around the world book trips to Miami as far as a year in advance to attend this weekend-long series of parties and events benefiting the Dade Human Rights Foundation. Travel arrangements can be made through Different Roads Travel, the event's official travel company, by calling ✆ **888/ROADS-55,** ext. 510. Early March.

Spring Break, Daytona Beach, Miami Beach, Panama City Beach, Key West, and other beaches. College students from all over the United States and Canada flock to Florida for endless partying, wet-T-shirt and bikini contests, free concerts, volleyball tournaments, and more. Three weeks in March.

Calle Ocho Festival (✆ **305/644-8888;** www.carnavalmiami.com), Little Havana. What Carnaval is to Rio, the

Calle Ocho Festival is to Miami. This 10-day extravaganza, also called Carnival Miami, features a lengthy block party spanning 23 blocks, with live salsa music, parades, and, of course, tons of savory Cuban delicacies. Those afraid of mob scenes should avoid this party at all costs. Mid-March.

April

Black College Reunion (✆ **800/854-1234;** www.blackbeachweek.com), Daytona Beach. Some 75,000 students from 115 predominantly African-American universities bring a sometimes-rowdy end to the Spring Break season. Mid-April.

PGA Seniors Golf Championship (✆ **561/624-8400**), Palm Beach Gardens. This is the oldest and most prestigious of the senior golf tournaments, in which aging golfers prove they've still got spunk in their swing. Mid-April.

July

Lower Keys Underwater Music Fest (✆ **800/872-3722**), Looe Key. When you hear the phrase "the music and the madness," you may think of this amusing aural aquatic event in which boaters head out to the underwater reef at the Looe Key Marine Sanctuary, drop speakers into the water, and pipe in all sorts of music, creating a disco-diving spectacular. Considering the heat at this time of year, underwater is probably the coolest place for a concert. Early July.

Blue Angels Air Show (✆ **800/874-1234** or 850/434-1234; www.visitpensacola.com or www.blueangels.navy.mil), Pensacola. World-famous navy pilots do their aerial acrobatics just 33 feet off Pensacola Beach. Early July.

September

NKF Labor Day Pro-Am Surfing Festival (✆ **321/459-2200;** www.spacecoast.com), Cocoa Beach. One of the largest surfing events on the East Coast draws pros and amateurs from around the country. There are also rock-'n-roll bands and swimsuit contests. Labor Day weekend.

October

Biketoberfest (✆ **386/253-RACE;** www.biketoberfest.org), Daytona. Road-racing stars compete at the CCS Motorcycle Championship at Daytona International Speedway. There are parties, parades, concerts, and more. Mid-October.

Clearwater Jazz Holiday (✆ **727/461-5200;** www.clearwaterjazz.com), Clearwater. Top jazz musicians play for 4 days and nights at bayfront Coachman Park in this free musical extravaganza. Mid-October.

Columbus Day Regatta, Miami. On the day that Columbus discovered America, the party-hearty discover their fellow Americans' birthday suits, as this bacchanalia encourages participants in the so-called regatta (there is a boat race at some point during the day, but most people are too preoccupied to notice) to strip down to their bare necessities and party at the sandbar in the middle of Biscayne Bay. You may not need a bathing suit, but you will need a boat to get out to where all the action is. Consider renting one on Key Biscayne, which is the closest to the sandbar. Second weekend of October.

Halloween Horror Nights (✆ **800/837-2273** or 407/363-8000; www.universalorlando.com), Orlando. Universal Studios transforms its grounds for 19 nights into haunted attractions with live bands, a psychopath's maze, special shows, and hundreds of ghouls and goblins roaming the streets. The studio closes at dusk, reopening in a new macabre form at 7pm. Full admission is charged for the event, which is geared toward adults. Mid-October to Halloween.

Mickey's Not-So-Scary Halloween Party (© **407/934-7639;** www.disneyworld.com), Orlando. At Walt Disney World, guests are invited to trick-or-treat in the Magic Kingdom, starting at 7pm. The party includes parades, storytelling, live music, and a bewitching fireworks display. End of October.

Fantasy Fest (© **305/296-1817;** www.fantasyfest.net), Key West. Mardi Gras takes a Floridian holiday as the streets of Key West are overtaken by wildly costumed revelers who have no shame and no parental guidance. This weeklong, hedonistic, X-rated Halloween party is not for children 17 and under. Make reservations in Key West early, as hotels tend to book up quickly during this event. Last week of October.

November

American Sandsculpting Festival (© **239/454-7500;** www.sandfestival.com), Fort Myers Beach. Some 50,000 gather to sculpt and to see the world's finest sand castles. First weekend in November.

Miami Book Fair International (© **305/237-3258**), Miami. Bibliophiles, literati, and some of the world's most prestigious and prolific authors descend upon downtown Miami for a weeklong homage to the written word, which also happens to be the largest book fair in the United States. The weekend street fair is the best attended of the entire event, in which regular folk mix with wordsmiths such as Tom Wolfe, Nora Ephron, Salman Rushdie, and Jane Smiley while indulging in snacks, antiquarian books, and literary gossip. All lectures are free but fill up quickly, so get there early. Mid-November.

Blue Angels Homecoming Air Show (© **800/874-1234** or 850/434-1234; www.visitpensacola.com or www.blueangels.navy.mil), Pensacola. World-famous navy pilots do their aerial acrobatics just 33 feet off the beach. Second weekend in November.

White Party Week, Miami and Fort Lauderdale. This weeklong series of parties to benefit AIDS research is built around the main event, the White Party, which takes place at Villa Vizcaya and sells out as early as a year in advance. Philanthropists and celebrities such as Calvin Klein and David Geffen join thousands of white-clad, mostly gay men (and some women) in what has become one of the world's hottest and hardest-to-score party tickets. Thanksgiving week.

December

Art Basel Miami Beach (www.artbaselmiamibeach.com), Miami Beach/Design District. Switzerland's most exclusive art fair and the world's most prominent collectors fly south for the winter and set up shop on South Beach and in the Design District with thousands of exhibitions, not to mention cocktail parties, concerts, and containers—as in shipping—that are set up on the beach and transformed into makeshift galleries. First or second weekend in December.

Edison & Ford Winter Homes Holiday House (© **239/334-7419;** www.efwefla.org/home.asp), Fort Myers. Christmas music and thousands of lights hail the holiday season here. At the same time, candles create a spectacular Luminary Trail along the full length of Sanibel Island's Periwinkle Way. First week of December.

Christmas at Walt Disney World (www.disneyworld.com), Orlando. As you would imagine, all of the Disney properties get into the holiday spirit. In the Magic Kingdom, Main Street is lavishly decked out with lights and holly and an 80-foot glistening tree. Call © **407/824-4321** for holiday events, or 934-7639 for special travel packages. Throughout December.

British Night Watch & Grand Illumination Ceremony (© **800/OLD-CITY** [653-2489]; www.visitoldcity.com), St. Augustine. A torchlight procession through the Spanish Quarter kicks off a month of Christmas festivities and the "Nights of Lights," in which 1.25 million twinkling bulbs bathe the Old City. First Saturday in December; Nights of Lights until January 31.

Seminole-Hard Rock Winterfest Boat Parade (© **954/767-0686;** www.winterfestparade.com), Fort Lauderdale. People who complain that the holiday season just isn't as festive in South Florida as it is in colder parts of the world haven't been to this spectacular boat parade along the Intracoastal Waterway. Forget decking the halls. At this parade, the decks are decked out in magnificent holiday regalia as they gracefully—and boastfully—glide up and down the water. If you're not on a boat, the best views are from waterfront restaurants or anywhere you can squeeze in along the water. Mid-December.

2 ENTRY REQUIREMENTS

PASSPORTS

Virtually every air traveler entering the U.S. is required to show a passport. All persons, including U.S. citizens, traveling by air between the United States and Canada, Mexico, Central and South America, the Caribbean, and Bermuda are required to present a valid passport. U.S. and Canadian citizens entering the U. S. at land and sea ports of entry from within the western hemisphere will need to present government-issued proof of citizenship, such as a birth certificate, along with a government issued photo ID, such as a driver's license. A passport is not required for U.S. or Canadian citizens entering by land or sea, but it is highly encouraged to carry one.

For information on how to get a passport, go to **"Passports,"** under **"Fast Facts: Florida,"** p. 636—the websites listed provide downloadable passport applications as well as the current fees for processing passport applications. For an up-to-date, country-by-country listing of passport requirements around the world, go to the "Foreign Entry Requirement" Web page of the U.S. Department of State at **http://travel.state.gov**. International visitors can obtain a visa application at the same website. ***Note:*** Children are required to present a passport when entering the United States at airports. More information on obtaining a passport for a minor can be found at http://travel.state.gov.

VISAS

For specifics on how to get a visa, go to **"Visas,"** under **"Fast Facts: Florida,"** p. 637.

The U.S. Department of State has a **Visa Waiver Program (VWP),** allowing citizens of the following countries (at press time) to enter the United States without a visa for stays of up to 90 days: Andorra, Australia, Austria, Belgium, Brunei, Denmark, Finland, France, Germany, Iceland, Ireland, Italy, Japan, Liechtenstein, Luxembourg, Monaco, the Netherlands, New Zealand, Norway, Portugal, San Marino, Singapore, Slovenia, Spain, Sweden, Switzerland, and the United Kingdom. Canadian citizens may enter the United States without visas; they will need to show passports and proof of residence, however. ***Note:*** Any passport issued on or after October 26, 2006, by a VWP country must be an **e-Passport** for VWP travelers to be eligible to enter the U.S. without a visa. Citizens of these nations also need to present a round-trip air or cruise ticket upon arrival. E-Passports contain computer chips capable of storing biometric information, such as the required digital photograph of the holder. (You can identify an e-Passport by the symbol on the bottom center cover of your passport.) If your passport doesn't have this feature, you can still travel without a visa if it is a valid passport issued before October 26, 2005, and includes a machine-readable zone, or issued between October 26, 2005, and October 25, 2006, and includes a digital photograph. For more information, go to **www.travel.state.gov/visa**.

Citizens of all other countries must have (1) a valid passport that expires at least 6 months later than the scheduled end of their visit to the United States and (2) a tourist visa, which may be obtained without charge from any U.S. consulate.

As of January 2004, many international visitors traveling on visas to the United States will be photographed and fingerprinted on arrival at Customs in airports and on cruise ships in a program created by the Department of Homeland Security called **US-VISIT.** Exempt from the extra scrutiny are visitors entering by land or those (mostly from Europe; p. 636) who don't require a visa for short-term visits. For more information, go to the Homeland Security website at **www.dhs.gov/dhspublic**.

CUSTOMS

What You Can Bring Into the U.S.

Every visitor more than 21 years of age may bring in, free of duty, the following: (1) 1 liter of wine or hard liquor; (2) 200 cigarettes, 100 cigars (but not from Cuba), or 3 pounds of smoking tobacco; and (3) $100 worth of gifts. These exemptions are offered to travelers who spend at least 72 hours in the United States and who have not claimed them within the preceding 6 months. It is forbidden to bring into the country almost any meat products (including canned, fresh, and dried meat products such as bouillon, soup mixes, and so on). Generally, condiments including vinegars, oils, spices, coffee, tea, and some cheeses and baked goods are permitted. Avoid rice products, as rice can often harbor insects. Bringing fruits and vegetables is not advised, though not prohibited. Customs will allow produce, depending on where you got it and where you're going after you arrive in the U.S. International visitors may carry in or out up to $10,000 in U.S. or foreign currency with no formalities; larger sums must be declared to U.S. Customs on entering or leaving, which includes filing form CM 4790. For details regarding U.S. Customs and Border Protection, consult your nearest U.S. embassy or consulate, or **U.S. Customs** (www.customs.gov).

What You Can Take Home from Florida:

For information on what you're allowed to bring home, contact one of the following agencies:

Canadian Citizens: Canada Border Services Agency (✆ **800/461-9999** in Canada, or 204/983-3500; www.cbsa-asfc.gc.ca).

U.K. Citizens: HM Customs & Excise at ✆ **0845/010-9000** (from outside the U.K., 020/8929-0152), or consult their website at **www.hmce.gov.uk**.

Australian Citizens: Australian Customs Service at ✆ **1300/363-263,** or log on to **www.customs.gov.au**.

New Zealand Citizens: New Zealand Customs, The Customhouse, 17–21 Whitmore St., Box 2218, Wellington (✆ **04/473-6099** or 0800/428-786; www.customs.govt.nz).

MEDICAL REQUIREMENTS

Unless you're arriving from an area known to be suffering from an epidemic (particularly cholera or yellow fever), inoculations or vaccinations are not required for entry into the United States. If you have a medical condition that requires **syringe-administered medications,** carry a valid signed prescription from your physician; syringes in carry-on baggage will be inspected. Insulin in any form should have the proper pharmaceutical documentation. If you have a disease that requires treatment with **narcotics,** you should also carry documented proof with you—smuggling narcotics aboard a plane carries severe penalties in the U.S.

For **HIV-positive visitors,** requirements for entering the United States are somewhat vague and change frequently. For up-to-the-minute information, contact **AIDSinfo** (© **800/448-0440** or 301/519-6616 outside the U.S.; www.aidsinfo.nih.gov) or the **Gay Men's Health Crisis** (© **212/367-1000;** www.gmhc.org).

3 GETTING THERE & GETTING AROUND

For contact information of any airline or car-rental service listed below, please turn to the "Fast Facts, Toll-Free Numbers & Websites" appendix on p. 635.

GETTING THERE

By Plane

Most major domestic airlines fly to and from many Florida cities. Choose from **American, Continental, Delta, Northwest/KLM, United,** and **US Airways.** Of these, Delta and US Airways have the most extensive network of commuter connections within Florida (see "Getting Around," below).

Several so-called no-frills airlines—with low fares but few, if any, amenities—also fly to Florida. The biggest and best is **Southwest Airlines,** which has flights from many U.S. cities to Fort Lauderdale, Jacksonville, Orlando, and Tampa.

Others flying to Florida include **AirTran; JetBlue; Midwest Airlines;** and **Spirit.**

Internet resources such as **Travelocity** (www.travelocity.com) and **Microsoft Expedia** (www.expedia.com) make it easy to compare prices and purchase tickets.

AIRPORT IMMIGRATION & CUSTOMS CLEARANCE Foreign visitors arriving by air, no matter what the port of entry, should cultivate patience and resignation before setting foot on U.S. soil. U.S. airports have considerably beefed up security clearances in the years since the terrorist attacks of September 11, 2001, and clearing Customs and Immigration can take as long as 2 hours.

People traveling by air from Canada, Bermuda, and certain Caribbean countries can sometimes clear Customs and Immigration at the point of departure, which is much faster.

By Car

Florida is reached by **I-95** along the East Coast, **I-75** from the Central States, and **I-10** from the west. The **Florida Turnpike,** a toll road, links Orlando, West Palm Beach, Fort Lauderdale, and Miami (it's a shortcut from Wildwood on I-75 north of Orlando to Miami). **I-4** cuts across the state from Cape Canaveral through Orlando to Tampa.

See "Getting Around," beginning on p. 47, for more information about driving in Florida and the car-rental firms that operate here.

By Train

Amtrak (© **800/USA-RAIL** [872-7245]; www.amtrak.com) offers train service to Florida from both the East and West coasts. It takes some 26 hours from New York to Miami, and 68 hours from Los Angeles to Miami. Amtrak's fares aren't much less—if not more—than many of the airlines' lowest fares.

Amtrak's ***Silver Meteor*** and ***Silver Star*** both run twice daily between New York and either Miami or Tampa, with intermediate stops along the East Coast and in Florida. Amtrak's Thruway Bus Connections are available from the Fort Lauderdale Amtrak station and Miami International Airport to Key West; from Tampa to St. Petersburg, Treasure Island, Clearwater, Sarasota, Bradenton, and Fort Myers; and from Deland to Daytona Beach. From the West Coast, the ***Sunset Limited*** runs three times weekly between Los Angeles and Orlando. It stops in Pensacola, Crestview (north of Fort Walton Beach and Destin), Chipley (north of Panama City Beach), and Tallahassee. Sleeping accommodations are available for an extra charge.

If you intend to stop along the way, you can save money with Amtrak's **Explore America** (or All Aboard America) fares, which are based on three regions of the country.

Amtrak's **Auto Train** runs daily from Lorton, Virginia (12 miles south of Washington, D.C.), to Sanford, Florida (just northeast of Orlando). You ride in a coach while your car is secured in an enclosed vehicle carrier. Make your train reservations as far in advance as possible.

GETTING AROUND

Having a car is the best and easiest way to see Florida's sights or to get to and from the beach. Public transportation is available only in the cities and larger towns, and even there, it may provide infrequent or inadequate service. When it comes to getting from one city to another, cars and planes are the ways to go.

By Plane

The commuter arms of **Continental, Delta,** and **US Airways** provide extensive service between Florida's major cities and towns. Fares for these short hops tend to be reasonable.

Cape Air flies between Key West and Naples, which means you can avoid backtracking to Miami from Key West if you're touring the state. (You can also take a 3-hour boat ride between Key West and Fort Myers Beach, Naples, or Marco Island during the winter months; see p. 326.) **Collins Aviation** connects Fort Lauderdale with Marathon.

Overseas visitors can take advantage of the APEX (Advance Purchase Excursion) reductions offered by all major U.S. and European carriers. In addition, some large airlines offer transatlantic or transpacific passengers special discount tickets under the name **Visit USA,** which allows mostly one-way travel from one U.S. destination to another at very low prices. Unavailable in the U.S., these discount tickets must be purchased abroad in conjunction with your international fare. This system is the easiest, fastest, and cheapest way to see the country.

By Car

If you're visiting from abroad and plan to rent a car in Florida, keep in mind that foreign driver's licenses are usually recognized in the U.S., but you should get an international one if your home license is not in English.

Jacksonville is about 350 miles north of Miami and 500 miles north of Key West, so don't underestimate how long it will take you to drive all the way down the state. The speed limit is either 65 mph or 70 mph on the rural interstate highways, so you can make good time between cities. Not so on U.S. 1, U.S. 17, U.S. 19, U.S. 41, and U.S. 301; although most have four lanes, these older highways tend to be heavily congested, especially in built-up areas.

Every major car-rental company is represented here, including **Alamo, Avis, Budget, Dollar, Enterprise, Hertz, National,** and **Thrifty.**

State and local **taxes** will add as much as 20% to your final bill. You'll pay an additional $2.05 per day in statewide use tax, and local sales taxes will tack on at least 6% to the total, including the statewide use tax.

Some airports add another 35¢ per day and as much as 10% in "recovery" fees. You can avoid the recovery fee by picking up your car in town rather than at the airport. Budget and Enterprise both have numerous rental locations away from the airports. But be sure to weigh the cost of transportation to and from your hotel against the amount of the fee.

Competition is so fierce among Florida rental firms that most have now stopped charging **drop-off fees** if you pick up a car at one place and leave it at another. Be sure to ask in advance if there's a drop-off fee.

To rent a car, you must have a valid **credit card** (not a debit or check card) in your name, and most companies require you to be at least 25 years old. Some also set maximum ages and may deny cars to anyone with a bad driving record. Ask about requirements and restrictions when you book, in order to avoid problems once you arrive.

By Train

International visitors can buy a **USA Rail Pass,** good for 5, 15, or 30 days of unlimited travel on **Amtrak** (✆ **800/USA-RAIL** [872-7245]; www.amtrak.com). The pass is available online or through many overseas travel agents. See Amtrak's website for the cost of travel within the western, eastern, or northwestern United States. Reservations are generally required and should be made as early as possible. Regional rail passes are also available.

You'll find that train travel isn't terribly feasible within Florida, and it's not significantly less expensive than flying, if at all. See "Getting There," above, for Florida towns served by **Amtrak.**

4 MONEY & COSTS

The easiest way to pay for almost everything in Florida is with a credit card. MasterCard and Visa credit and debit cards are accepted almost everywhere. American Express, Diners Club, and Discover cards are also accepted, although not as widely as MasterCard and Visa.

The best way to get cash while you're traveling in Florida is to use your debit or credit cards at ATMs. Of the big national banks, **First Union Bank** and **Bank of America** have offices with ATMs throughout Florida.

How much money you spend on a Florida vacation will depend on your own desires and choices, when you go, and most definitely *where* you go. The state has a wide range of accommodations, from some of the country's most luxurious and expensive beachfront resorts to no-frills but friendly mom-and-pop motels sitting right by the beach. If you can do without the luxuries, you needn't spend a fortune.

Tourism is Florida's biggest industry, and the economic law of supply and demand dictates that the prices of hotel rooms are highest during the seasons when tourists invade Florida: the winter months in the southern half of the state, the summer months up north.

See "When to Go," earlier in this chapter, for details on Florida's high, low, and in-between seasons.

5 HEALTH & SAFETY

STAYING HEALTHY

Florida doesn't present any unusual health hazards for most people. Folks with certain medical conditions, such as liver disease, diabetes, and stomach ailments, however, should avoid eating raw **oysters,** which can carry a natural bacterium linked to severe diarrhea, vomiting, and even fatal blood poisoning. Cooking kills the bacteria, so if in doubt, order your oysters steamed, broiled, or fried.

Florida has millions of **mosquitoes** and invisible biting **sand flies** (known as "no-see-ums"), especially in the coastal and marshy areas. Fortunately, neither insect carries malaria or other diseases. (Although there were a few cases of mosquitoes carrying West Nile virus in the Panhandle, it's really not a problem in Florida.) Keep these pests at bay with a good insect repellent.

It's especially important to protect yourself against **sunburn.** Don't underestimate the strength of the sun's rays down here, even in the middle of winter. Use a sunscreen with a high protection factor and apply it liberally.

General Availability of Healthcare

Contact the **International Association for Medical Assistance to Travelers (IAMAT; © 716/754-4883** or, in Canada, 416/652-0137; **www.iamat.org**) for tips on travel and health concerns in the countries you're visiting, and for lists of local, English-speaking doctors. The United States **Centers for Disease Control and Prevention** (**© 800/311-3435;** www.cdc.gov) provides up-to-date information on health hazards by region or country and offers tips on food safety. The website **www.tripprep.com**, sponsored by a consortium of travel medicine practitioners, **Travel Health Online,** may also offer helpful advice on traveling abroad. You can find listings of reliable clinics overseas at the **International Society of Travel Medicine** (www.istm.org).

What to Do if You Get Sick Away from Home

We list **hospitals** and **emergency numbers** under "Fast Facts" in chapters throughout this guide.

If you suffer from a chronic illness, consult your doctor before your departure. Pack **prescription medications** in your carry-on luggage, and carry them in their original containers, with pharmacy labels—otherwise they won't make it through airport security. Visitors from outside the U.S. should carry generic names of prescription drugs. For U.S. travelers, most reliable healthcare plans provide coverage if you get sick away from home. Foreign visitors may have to pay all medical costs up front and be reimbursed later.

STAYING SAFE

While tourist areas in Florida are generally safe, you should always stay alert. This is particularly true in the larger cities, such as Miami, Orlando, Tampa, and St. Petersburg. If you're in doubt about which neighborhoods are safe, ask your hotel's front-desk staff or the area's tourist office.

Remember also that hotels are open to the public, and in a large hotel, security may not be able to screen everyone entering. Always lock your room door. Don't assume that, once inside your hotel, you are automatically safe and no longer need to be aware of your surroundings.

6 SPECIALIZED TRAVEL RESOURCES

TRAVELERS WITH DISABILITIES

Most disabilities shouldn't stop anyone from traveling in the U.S. There are more options and resources out there than ever before.

The **American the Beautiful—National Park and Federal Recreational**

General Resources for Green Travel

The following websites provide valuable wide-ranging information on sustainable travel. For a list of even more sustainable resources, as well as tips and explanations on how to travel greener, visit www.frommers.com/planning.

- **Responsible Travel** (www.responsibletravel.com) is a great source of sustainable travel ideas; the site is run by a spokesperson for ethical tourism in the travel industry. **Sustainable Travel International** (www.sustainable travelinternational.org) promotes ethical tourism practices, and manages an extensive directory of sustainable properties and tour operators around the world.
- In the U.K., **Tourism Concern** (www.tourismconcern.org.uk) works to reduce social and environmental problems connected to tourism. The **Association of Independent Tour Operators (AITO;** www.aito.co.uk) is a group of specialist operators leading the field in making holidays sustainable.
- In Canada, **www.greenlivingonline.com** offers extensive content on how to travel sustainably, including a travel and transport section and profiles of the best green shops and services in Toronto, Vancouver, and Calgary.
- **Carbonfund** (www.carbonfund.org), **TerraPass** (www.terrapass.org), and **Carbon Neutral** (www.carbonneutral.org) provide info on "carbon offsetting," or offsetting the greenhouse gas emitted during flights.

Lands Pass—Access Pass (formerly the **Golden Access Passport**) gives visually impaired or permanently disabled persons (regardless of age) free lifetime entrance to federal recreation sites administered by the National Park Service, including the Fish and Wildlife Service, the Forest Service, the Bureau of Land Management, and the Bureau of Reclamation. This may include national parks, monuments, historic sites, recreation areas, and national wildlife refuges.

The American the Beautiful Access Pass can only be obtained in person at any NPS facility that charges an entrance fee. You need to show proof of medically determined disability. Besides free entry, the pass also offers a 50% discount on some federal-use fees charged for such facilities as camping, swimming, parking, boat launching, and tours. For more information, go to www.nps.gov/fees_passes.htm or call ✆ **888/467-2757.**

Organizations that offer a vast range of resources and assistance to travelers with disabilities include **MossRehab** (✆ **800/CALL-MOSS** [225-5667]; www.moss resourcenet.org); the **American Foundation for the Blind (AFB;** ✆ **800/232-5463;** www.afb.org); and **SATH (Society for Accessible Travel & Hospitality;** ✆ **212/447-7284;** www.sath.org). **Air AmbulanceCard.com** is now partnered with SATH and allows you to preselect top-notch hospitals in case of an emergency.

Access-Able Travel Source (✆ **303/232-2979;** www.access-able.com) offers a comprehensive database on travel agencies from around the world with experience in accessible travel; destination-specific access information; and links to such resources as service animals, equipment rentals, and access guides.

Many travel agencies offer customized tours and itineraries for travelers with

- **Greenhotels** (www.greenhotels.com) recommends green-rated member hotels around the world that fulfill the company's stringent environmental requirements. **Environmentally Friendly Hotels** (www.environmentally friendlyhotels.com) offers more green accommodation ratings. The **Hotel Association of Canada** (www.hacgreenhotels.com) has a Green Key Eco-Rating Program, which audits the environmental performance of Canadian hotels, motels, and resorts.
- **Sustain Lane** (www.sustainlane.com) lists sustainable eating and drinking choices around the U.S.; also visit **www.eatwellguide.org** for tips on eating sustainably in the U.S. and Canada.
- For information on animal-friendly issues throughout the world, visit **Tread Lightly** (www.treadlightly.org). For information about the ethics of swimming with dolphins, visit the **Whale and Dolphin Conservation Society** (www.wdcs.org).
- **Volunteer International** (www.volunteerinternational.org) has a list of questions to help you determine the intentions and the nature of a volunteer program. For general info on volunteer travel, visit **www.volunteer abroad.org** and **www.idealist.org**.

disabilities. Among them are **Flying Wheels Travel** (✆ **507/451-5005;** www.flying wheelstravel.com) and **Accessible Journeys** (✆ **800/846-4537** or 610/521-0339; www.disabilitytravel.com).

British travelers should contact **Holiday Care** (✆ **0845/124-9971** in U.K. only; www.holidaycare.org.uk) to access a wide range of travel information and resources for seniors and travelers with disabilities.

GAY & LESBIAN TRAVELERS

The editors of *Out and About,* a gay and lesbian newsletter, have described Miami's **South Beach** as the "hippest, hottest, most happening gay travel destination in the world." Today, however, **Fort Lauderdale**—where gays own more than 20 motels, 40 bars, and numerous other businesses—steals its rainbow-colored crown. For many years, that could also be said of **Key West,** which still is one of the country's most popular destinations for gays.

You can contact the **Gay, Lesbian & Bisexual Community Services of Central Florida,** 946 N. Mills Ave., Orlando, FL 32803 (✆ **407/228-8272;** www.glbcc.org), whose welcome packets usually include the latest issue of the *Triangle,* a quarterly newsletter dedicated to gay and lesbian issues, and a calendar of events pertaining to the gay and lesbian community. Although not a tourist-specific packet, it includes information and ads for the area's gay and lesbian clubs.

Watermark, P.O. Box 533655, Orlando, FL 32853 (✆ **407/481-2243;** fax 407/481-2246; www.watermarkonline.com), is a biweekly tabloid newspaper covering the gay and lesbian scene, including dining and entertainment options, in Orlando, the Tampa Bay area, and Daytona Beach.

The **International Gay and Lesbian Travel Association** (IGLTA; ✆ **800/448-8550** or 954/776-2626; www.iglta.org) is the trade association for the gay and lesbian travel industry, and offers an online directory of gay- and lesbian-friendly travel businesses and tour operators.

SENIOR TRAVEL

With one of the largest retired populations of any state, Florida offers a wide array of activities and benefits for seniors. Don't be shy about asking for discounts, but always carry some kind of identification, such as a driver's license, that shows your date of birth. Mention the fact that you're a senior when you make your travel reservations. In most cities, people over the age of 60 qualify for reduced admission to theaters, museums, and other attractions, as well as discounted fares on public transportation.

Members of **AARP,** 601 E. St. NW, Washington, DC 20049 (✆ **888/687-2277;** www.aarp.org), get discounts on hotels, airfares, and car rentals. Anyone older than 50 can join.

The U.S. National Park Service offers an **America the Beautiful—National Park and Federal Recreational Lands Pass—Senior Pass** (formerly the **Golden Age Passport**), which gives seniors 62 years or older lifetime entrance to all properties administered by the National Park Service—national parks, monuments, historic sites, recreation areas, and national wildlife refuges—for a one-time processing fee of $10. The pass must be purchased in person at any NPS facility that charges an entrance fee. Besides free entry, the American the Beautiful Senior Pass also offers a 50% discount on some federal-use fees charged for such facilities as camping, swimming, parking, boat launching, and tours. For more information, go to www.nps.gov/fees_passes.htm or call ✆ **888/467-2757.**

Many reliable agencies and organizations target the 50-plus market. **Elderhostel** (✆ **800/454-5768;** www.elderhostel.org) arranges worldwide study programs for those ages 55 and older. **ElderTreks** (✆ **800/741-7956** or 416/558-5000 outside North America; www.eldertreks.com) offers small-group tours to off-the-beaten-path or adventure-travel locations, restricted to travelers age 50 and older.

FAMILY TRAVEL

Florida is a great family destination, with Walt Disney World leading the list of theme parks geared to young and old alike. Consequently, most Florida hotels and restaurants are willing, if not eager, to cater to families traveling with children. Many hotels and motels let children age 17 and younger stay free in a parent's room (be sure to ask when you reserve). To locate accommodations, restaurants, and attractions that are particularly kid-friendly, refer to the "Kids" icon throughout this guide.

At the beaches, it's the exception rather than the rule for a resort not to have a children's activities program (some will even mind the youngsters while the parents enjoy a night off!). Even if they don't have a children's program of their own, most will arrange babysitting services.

Recommended family travel websites include **Family Travel Forum** (www.familytravelforum.com), a comprehensive site that offers customized trip planning; **Family Travel Network** (www.familytravelnetwork.com), an online magazine providing travel tips; and **TravelWithYourKids.com** (www.travelwithyourkids.com), a comprehensive site written by parents for parents, offering sound advice for long-distance and international travel with children.

7 SPECIAL-INTEREST TRIPS

Bird-watching, boating and sailing, camping, canoeing and kayaking, fishing, golfing, tennis—you name it, the Sunshine State has it. These and other activities are described in the outdoor-activities sections of the following chapters, but here's a brief overview of some of the best places to move your muscles, with tips on how to get more detailed information.

The **Florida Sports Foundation,** 2390 Kerry Forest Pkwy., Ste. 101, Tallahassee, FL 32309 (✆ **850/488-8347;** fax 850/922-0482; www.flasports.com), publishes free brochures, calendars, schedules, and guides to outdoor pursuits and spectator sports throughout Florida. I've noted some of its specific publications in the sections below.

For excellent color maps of state parks, campgrounds, canoe trails, aquatic preserves, caverns, and more, contact the **Florida Department of Environmental Protection,** Office of Communications, 3900 Commonwealth Blvd., Tallahassee, FL 32399 (✆ **850/245-2118;** www.dep.state.fl.us). Some of the department's publications are mentioned below.

ACTIVITIES A TO Z

BIKING & IN-LINE SKATING Florida's relatively flat terrain makes it ideal for bicycling and in-line skating. You can bike right into **Everglades National Park** along the 38-mile-long Main Park Road, and bike or skate from St. Petersburg to Tarpon Springs on the 47-mile-long converted railroad bed known as the **Pinellas Trail.** Many towns and cities have designated routes for cyclists, skaters, joggers, and walkers, such as the paved pathways running the length of **Sanibel Island,** the lovely Bayshore Boulevard in **Tampa, Ocean Drive** on South Beach, and the bike lanes from downtown **Sarasota** out to St. Armands, Lido, and Longboat keys.

BIRD-WATCHING With hundreds of both land- and sea-based species, Florida is one of America's best places for bird-watching—if you're not careful, pelicans will even steal your picnic lunch on the historic **Naples Pier.** The **J. N. "Ding" Darling National Wildlife Refuge** is great for watching birds, and it shares Sanibel Island with luxury resorts and fine restaurants.

With its northeast Florida section now open, the **Great Florida Birding Trail** will eventually cover some 2,000 miles throughout the state. Fort Clinch State Park, on Amelia Island, and Merritt Island National Wildlife Refuge in Cape Canaveral are gateways to the northeast trail. Information is available from the Birding Trail Coordinator, Florida Fish & Wildlife Conservation Commission, 620 S. Meridian St., Tallahassee, FL 32399-1600 (✆ **850/922-0664;** fax 850/488-1961; www.floridabirdingtrail.com). You can download maps from the website.

Many of the state's wildlife preserves have gift shops that carry books about Florida's birds, including the ***Florida Wildlife Viewing Guide,*** in which authors Susan Cerulean and Ann Morrow profile 96 great parks, refuges, and preserves throughout the state. The guide is also available directly from the publisher, Falcon Press (✆ **888/922-0789;** www.falcbooks.com).

BOATING & SAILING With some 1,350 miles of shoreline, it's not surprising that Florida is a boating and sailing mecca. In fact, you won't be anyplace near the water very long before you see flyers and other advertisements for rental boats and sailboat cruises. Many of them are mentioned in the chapters that follow.

The **Moorings** (✆ **888/952-8420** or 727/530-5651; www.moorings.com), the worldwide sailboat charter company, has its headquarters in Clearwater and its Florida yacht base nearby in St. Petersburg. From St. Pete, experienced sailors can take bareboats as far as the Keys and the Dry Tortugas, out in the Gulf of Mexico.

Key West keeps gaining prominence as a world sailing capital. *Yachting* magazine sponsors the largest winter regatta in America here each January, and smaller events take place regularly.

Even if you've never hauled on a halyard, you can learn the art of sailing at **Steve and Doris Colgate's Offshore Sailing School** (www.offshore-sailing.com), headquartered at the South Seas Plantation Resort & Yacht Harbour on Captiva Island, with an outpost in St. Petersburg. The prestigious **Annapolis Sailing** (www.annapolissailing.com) has bases in St. Petersburg and on Marathon in the Keys.

Florida Boating & Fishing, available for free from the Florida Sports Foundation (see the introduction to this section, above), is a treasure trove of tips on safe boating; state regulations; locations of marinas, hotels, and resorts; marine products and services; and more.

CAMPING Florida is literally dotted with RV parks (if you own such a vehicle, it's the least expensive way to spend your winters here). But for the best tent camping, look to Florida's national preserves and 110 state parks and recreation areas. Options range from luxury sites with hot-water showers and cable TV hookups, to primitive island and beach camping with no facilities whatsoever.

Regular and primitive camping in **St. George Island State Park,** near Apalachicola, is a bird-watcher's dream—plus you'll be on one of the nation's most magnificent beaches. Equally great are the sands at **St. Andrews State Park,** in Panama City Beach (with sites right beside the bay). Other top spots are **Fort DeSoto Park,** in St. Pete Beach (more gorgeous bayside sites); the remarkably preserved **Cayo Costa Island State Park,** between Boca Grande and Captiva Island in Southwest Florida; **Canaveral National Seashore,** near the Kennedy Space Center; **Anastasia State Park,** in St. Augustine; **Fort Clinch State Park,** on Amelia Island; and **Bill Baggs Cape Florida State Park,** on Key Biscayne in Miami. Down in the Keys, the oceanside sites in **Long Key State Park** are about as nice as they get.

In each of these popular campgrounds, reservations are essential, especially during the high season. Each of Florida's state parks take bookings up to 11 months in advance.

The **Florida Department of Environmental Protection,** Division of Recreation and Parks, Mail Station 535, 3900 Commonwealth Blvd., Tallahassee, FL 32399-3000 (✆ **850/245-2118;** www.dep.state.fl.us), publishes an annual guide of tent and RV sites in Florida's state parks and recreation areas.

Pet owners, note: Pets are permitted at some—but not all—state park beaches, campgrounds, and food service areas. Before bringing your animal, check with the department or the individual park to see if your pet will be allowed. And bring your pet's rabies certificate, which is required.

For private campgrounds, the **Florida Association of RV Parks & Campgrounds,** 1340 Vickers Dr., Tallahassee, FL 32303 (✆ **850/562-7151;** fax 850/562-7179; www.floridacamping.com), issues an annual ***Camp Florida*** directory with locator maps and details about its member establishments in the state.

CANOEING & KAYAKING Canoers and kayakers have almost limitless options for discovery here: picturesque rivers, sandy coastlines, marshes, mangroves, and gigantic Lake Okeechobee. Exceptional trails run through several parks and wildlife preserves, including **Everglades National Park,** Sanibel Island's **J. N. "Ding" Darling National Wildlife Refuge,** and **Briggs**

Nature Center, on the edge of the Everglades near Marco Island.

According to the Florida State Legislature, however, the state's official "Canoe Capital" is the Panhandle town of **Milton,** on U.S. 90 near Pensacola. Up here, Blackwater River, Coldwater River, Sweetwater Creek, and Juniper Creek are perfect for tubing, rafting, and paddle boating, as well as canoeing and kayaking.

Another good venue is the waterways winding through the marshes between **Amelia Island** and the mainland.

Many conservation groups throughout the state offer half-day, full-day, and overnight canoe trips. For example, the **Conservancy of Naples** (✆ **239/262-0304;** www.conservancy.org) has a popular series of moonlight canoe trips through the mangroves, among other programs.

Based during the winter at Everglades City, on the park's western border, **North American Canoe Tours, Inc.** (✆ **239/695-3299;** www.evergladesadventures.com), offers weeklong guided canoe expeditions through the Everglades.

Thirty-six creek and river trails, covering 950 miles altogether, are itemized in the excellent free ***Canoe Trails*** booklet published by the Florida Department of Environmental Protection, Office of Communications, 3900 Commonwealth Blvd., Tallahassee, FL 32399 (✆ **850/245-2118;** www.dep.state.fl.us).

Specialized guidebooks include *A Canoeing and Kayaking Guide to the Streams of Florida: Volume 1, North Central Florida and Panhandle,* by Elizabeth F. Carter and John L. Pearce; and *Volume 2, Central and Southern Peninsula,* by Lou Glaros and Doug Sphar. Both are published by Menasha Ridge Press (www.menasharidge.com).

ECO-ADVENTURES If you don't want to do it yourself, you can observe Florida's flora and fauna on guided field expeditions—and contribute to conservation efforts while you're at it.

The **Sierra Club,** the oldest and largest grass-roots environmental organization in the U.S., offers eco-adventures through its Florida chapters. Recent outings have included canoeing or kayaking through the Everglades, hiking the Florida Trail in America's southernmost national forest, camping on a barrier island, and exploring the sinkhole phenomenon in North-Central Florida. You do have to be a Sierra Club member, but you can join at the time of the trip. Contact the club's national outings office at 85 Second St., 2nd Floor, San Francisco, CA 94105-3441 (✆ **415/977-5500;** www.sierraclub.org).

The Florida chapter of the **Nature Conservancy** has protected 578,000 acres of natural lands in Florida and presently owns and manages 36 preserves. For a small fee, you can join one of its field trips or work parties that take place periodically throughout the year; fees vary from year to year and event to event, so call for more information. Participants get a chance to learn about and even participate in the preservation of the ecosystem. For details on all the preserves and adventures, contact the Nature Conservancy, Florida Chapter, 222 S. Westmonte Dr., Ste. 300, Altamonte Springs, FL 32714 (✆ **407/682-3664;** fax 407/682-3077; www.nature.org).

A nonprofit organization dedicated to environmental research, the **Earthwatch Institute,** 3 Clocktower Place, Ste. 100 (P.O. Box 75), Maynard, MA 01754 (✆ **800/776-0188** or 978/461-0081; www.earthwatch.org), has excursions to survey dolphins and manatees around Sarasota and to monitor the well-being of the whooping cranes raised in captivity and released in the wilds of Central Florida.

Another research group, the **Oceanic Society,** Fort Mason Center, Building E, San Francisco, CA 94123 (✆ **800/326-7491** or 415/441-1106; fax 415/474-3395; www.oceanic-society.org), also has Florida trips among its expeditions, including manatee monitoring in the Crystal River area, north of Tampa.

FISHING In addition to the amberjack, bonito, grouper, mackerel, mahimahi, marlin, pompano, redfish, sailfish, snapper, snook, tarpon, tuna, and wahoo running offshore and in inlets, Florida has countless miles of rivers and streams, plus about 30,000 lakes and springs stocked with more than 100 species of freshwater fish. Indeed, Floridians seem to fish everywhere: off canal banks and old bridges, from fishing piers and fishing fleets. You'll even see them standing alongside the Tamiami Trail (U.S. 41) that cuts across the Everglades—one eye on their line, the other watching for alligators.

Anglers 16 and older need a license for any kind of saltwater or freshwater fishing, including lobstering and spearfishing. Licenses are sold at bait-and-tackle shops around the state and online at www.wildlifelicense.com/fl.

The **Florida Department of Environmental Protection,** 3900 Commonwealth Blvd., Tallahassee, FL 32399-3000 (✆ **850/245-2118;** www.dep.state.fl.us), publishes the annual ***Fishing Lines,*** a free magazine with a wealth of information about fishing in Florida, including regulations and licensing requirements. It also distributes free brochures with annual freshwater and saltwater limits. And the Florida Sports Foundation (see the introduction to this section, above) publishes ***Florida Fishing & Boating,*** another treasure trove of information.

GOLF Florida is the unofficial golf capital of the United States—some say the world—because the **World Golf Hall of Fame** is located near St. Augustine. This state-of-the-art museum is worth a visit, even if you're not in love with the game.

One thing is for certain: Florida has more golf courses than any other state—more than 1,150 at last count, and growing. I picked the best for chapter 1, but suffice it to say that you can tee off almost anywhere, anytime there's daylight. The highest concentrations of excellent courses are in Southwest Florida, around Naples and Fort Myers (more than 1,000 holes!); in the Orlando area (Disney alone has 99 holes open to the public); and in the Panhandle, around Destin and Panama City Beach. It's a rare town in Florida that doesn't have a municipal golf course—even Key West has 18 great holes.

Greens fees are usually much lower at the municipal courses than at privately owned clubs. Whether public or private, greens fees tend to vary greatly, depending on the time of year. You could pay $150 or more at a private course during the high season, but less than half that when the tourists are gone. The fee structures vary so much that it's best to call ahead and ask, and always reserve a tee time as far in advance as possible.

You can learn the game or hone your strokes at one of several excellent golf schools in the state. **David Ledbetter** has teaching facilities in Orlando and Naples, **Fred Griffin** is in charge of the Grand Cypress Academy of Golf at Grand Cypress Resort in Orlando, and you'll find **Jimmy Ballard**'s school at the Ocean Reef Club on Key Largo. The Westin Innisbrook Resort at Tarpon Springs has its **Innisbrook Golf Institute,** while Amelia Island (near Jacksonville) is home to the **Amelia Island Plantation Golf School.**

You can get information about most Florida courses, including current greens fees, and reserve tee times through **Tee Times USA,** P.O. Box 641, Flagler Beach, FL 32136 (✆ **888/GOLF-FLO** [465-3356] or 386/439-0001; www.teetimesusa.com), which publishes a vacation guide with many stay-and-play golf packages.

Florida Golf, published by the Florida Sports Foundation (see the introduction to this section, above), lists every course in Florida. It's the state's official golf guide and is available from Visit Florida (www.visitflorida.com).

Golfer's Guide magazine publishes monthly editions covering most of Florida. It is available free at local visitor centers and hotel lobbies, or you can contact the magazine at 2 Park Lane, Ste. E, Hilton Head Island, SC 29928 (© **800/864-6101** or 843/842-7878; fax 843/842-5743; www.golfersguide.com).

Northwest Florida is covered by ***South Coast Golf Guide,*** published by Tee and J's Ent., LLC, P.O. Box 11278, Pensacola, FL 32524-1278 (© **850/505-7553;** fax 850/505-0057; www.southcoastgolfguide.com).

You can also get more information from the **Professional Golfers' Association (PGA),** 400 Ave. of the Champions, Palm Beach Gardens, FL 33418 (© **800/633-9150;** www.pga.com); or from the **Ladies Professional Golf Association (LPGA),** 100 International Golf Dr., Daytona Beach, FL 32124 (© **904/254-6200;** www.lpga.com).

More than 700 courses are profiled in ***Florida Golf Guide,*** by Jimmy Shacky (Open Roads Publishing), available at bookstores for $20.

HIKING Although you won't be climbing any mountains in this relatively flat state, there are thousands of beautiful hiking trails in Florida. The ideal hiking months are October through April, when the weather is cool and dry and mosquitoes are less prominent. Like anywhere else, you'll find trails that are gentle and short, and others that are challenging—some trails in the Everglades require you to wade waist-deep in water!

Most Florida snakes are harmless, but a few have deadly bites, so it's a good idea to avoid them all. If you're venturing into the backcountry, watch out for gators, and don't ever try to feed them (or any wild animal). You risk getting bitten. (They can't tell the difference between the food and your hand.) You're also upsetting the balance of nature, as animals fed by humans lose their ability to find their own food.

The **Florida Trail Association,** 5415 SW 13th St., Gainesville, FL 32608 (© **877/HIKE-FLA** [445-3352] or 352/378-8823; www.florida-trail.org), maintains a large percentage of the public trails in the state and puts out an excellent book packed with maps, details, and color photos.

For a copy of ***Florida Trails,*** which outlines the many options, contact Visit Florida (www.visitflorida.com). Another resource is ***A Guide to Your National Scenic Trails,*** from the Office of Greenways and Trails, Department of Environmental Protection, 3900 Commonwealth Blvd., Tallahassee, FL 32399 (© **850/245-2118;** www.dep.state.fl.us/gwt). You can also contact the office of **National Forests in Florida,** Woodcrest Office Park, 325 John Knox Rd., Ste. F-100, Tallahassee, FL 32303 (© **850/523-8500;** www.southernregion.fs.fed.us/florida). Finally, ***Hiking Florida,*** by M. Timothy O'Keefe (Falcon Press; www.falcbooks.com), details 132 hikes throughout the state, with maps and photos.

SCUBA DIVING & SNORKELING Divers love the Keys, where you can see magnificent formations of tree-size elkhorn coral and giant brain coral, as well as colorful sea fans and dozens of other varieties, sharing space with 300 or more species of rainbow-hued fish. Reef diving is good all the way from Key Largo to Key West, with plenty of tour operators, outfitters, and dive shops along the way. Particularly worthy are **John Pennekamp Coral Reef State Park** in Key Largo, and **Looe Key National Marine Sanctuary** off Big Pine Key. *Skin Diver* magazine picked Looe Key as the number-one dive spot in

North America. Also, the clearest waters in which to view some of the 4,000 sunken ships along Florida's coast are in the Middle Keys and the waters between Key West and the Dry Tortugas. Snorkeling in the Keys is particularly fine between Islamorada and Marathon.

In Northwest Florida, the 100-fathom curve draws closer to the white, sandy Panhandle beaches than to any other spot on the Gulf of Mexico. It's too far north here for coral, but you can see brilliantly colored sponges and fish and, in Timber Hole, discover an undersea "petrified forest" of sunken planes, ships, and even a railroad car. The battleship USS *Massachusetts* lies in 30 feet of water just 3 miles off Pensacola. Every beach town in Northwest Florida has dive shops to outfit, tour, or certify visitors.

In the Crystal River area, north of the St. Petersburg and Clearwater beaches, you can snorkel with the manatees as they bask in the warm spring waters of Kings Bay.

If you want to keep up with what's going on statewide, you can subscribe to the monthly magazine ***Florida Scuba News*** (© **904/783-1610;** www.scubanews.com). You might also want to pick up a specialized guidebook. Some good ones include ***Coral Reefs of Florida,*** by Gilbert L. Voss (Pineapple Press; www.pineapplepress.com); and ***The Diver's Guide to Florida and the Florida Keys,*** by Jim Stachowicz (Windward Publishing).

TENNIS Year-round sunshine makes Florida great for tennis. There are some 7,700 places to play throughout the state, from municipal courts to exclusive resorts. Some municipal facilities—Cambier Park Tennis Center in Naples leaps to mind—equal expensive resorts, except they're free or close to it.

If you can afford it, you can learn from the best in Florida. **Nick Bollettieri** has a sports academy in Bradenton. Safety Harbor Resort and Spa near St. Petersburg hosts the **Phil Green Tennis Program.** Amateurs can hobnob with the superstars at **ATP Tour International Headquarters** in Ponte Vedra Beach, near Jacksonville. **Mary Jo Fernandez** is affiliated with the **Arthur Ashe Tennis Center** at the Doral Golf Resort & Spa in Miami. And **Chris Evert, Robert Seguso,** and **Carling Bassett** have their own center in Boca Raton.

The three hard courts and seven clay courts at the **Key Biscayne Tennis Association,** 6702 Crandon Blvd. (© **305/361-5263**), get crowded on weekends because they're some of Miami's most beautiful. You'll play on the same courts as Lendl, Graf, Evert, McEnroe, and other greats; this is the venue for one of the world's biggest annual tennis events, the NASDAQ 100 Open. There's a pleasant, if limited, pro shop, plus many good pros. Only four courts are lighted at night, but if you reserve at least 48 hours in advance, you can usually take your pick. They cost $6 per person per hour. The courts are open daily from 8am to 9pm.

Famous as the spot where Chris Evert got in her early serves, the **Jimmy Evert Tennis Center,** 701 NE 12th Ave. (off Sunrise Blvd.), Fort Lauderdale (© **954/828-5378**), has 18 clay and three hard courts (15 lighted). Her coach and father, James Evert, still teaches young players here, though he is very picky about whom he'll accept. Nonresidents of Fort Lauderdale pay $6 an hour per person before 5pm and $7 an hour per person after 5pm.

Other top places at which to learn and play are **Amelia Island Plantation,** on Amelia Island; **Colony Beach and Tennis Resort,** on Longboat Key off Sarasota (which *Tennis* magazine picked as the number-two tennis resort in the nation); **Sanibel Harbour Resort & Spa,** in Fort Myers, whose 5,500-seat stadium has hosted Davis Cup matches; **South Seas Resort & Yacht Harbour,** on Captiva Island; and the **Registry Resort,** in Naples.

8 STAYING CONNECTED

TELEPHONES

Generally, hotel surcharges on long-distance and local calls are astronomical, so you're better off using your **cellphone** or a **public pay telephone.** Many convenience groceries and packaging services sell **prepaid calling cards** in denominations up to $50; for international visitors these can be the least expensive way to call home. Many public pay phones at airports now accept American Express, MasterCard, and Visa credit cards. **Local calls** made from pay phones in most locales cost either 25¢ or 35¢ (no pennies, please).

Most long-distance and international calls can be dialed directly from any phone. **For calls within the United States and to Canada,** dial 1 followed by the area code and the seven-digit number. **For other international calls,** dial 011 followed by the country code, city code, and the number you are calling.

Calls to area codes **800, 888, 877,** and **866** are toll free. However, calls to area codes **700** and **900** (chat lines, bulletin boards, "dating" services, and so on) can be very expensive—usually with a charge of 95¢ to $3 or more per minute, and they sometimes have minimum charges that can run as high as $15 or more.

For **reversed-charge or collect calls,** and for person-to-person calls, dial the number 0 then the area code and number; an operator will come on the line, and you should specify whether you are calling collect, person-to-person, or both. If your operator-assisted call is international, ask for the overseas operator.

For **local directory assistance** ("information"), dial 411; for long-distance information, dial 1, then the appropriate area code and 555-1212.

CELLPHONES

Just because your cellphone works at home doesn't mean it'll work everywhere in the U.S. (thanks to our nation's fragmented cellphone system). It's a good bet that your phone will work in major cities, but take a look at your wireless company's coverage map on its website before heading out; T-Mobile, Sprint, and Nextel are particularly weak in rural areas. If you need to stay in touch at a destination where you know your phone won't work, **rent** a phone that does from **InTouch USA** (✆ **800/872-7626;** www.intouchglobal.com) or a rental car location, but beware that you'll pay $1 a minute or more for airtime.

If you're not from the U.S., you'll be appalled at the poor reach of our **GSM (Global System for Mobile Communications) wireless network,** which is used by much of the rest of the world. Your phone will probably work in most major U.S. cities; it definitely won't work in many rural areas. To see where GSM phones work in the U.S., check out www.t-mobile.com/coverage/national_popup.asp. And you may or may not be able to send SMS (text messaging) home.

INTERNET & E-MAIL

Without Your Own Computer

To find cybercafes in your destination, check **www.cybercaptive.com** and **www.cybercafe.com.**

Most major airports have **Internet kiosks** that provide basic Web access for a per-minute fee that's usually higher than cybercafe prices. Check out copy shops such as **Kinko's** (FedEx Kinkos), which offers computer stations with fully loaded software (as well as Wi-Fi).

With Your Own Computer

More and more hotels, resorts, airports, cafes, and retailers are going Wi-Fi (wireless fidelity), becoming "hot spots" that offer free high-speed Wi-Fi access or charge a small fee for usage. Wi-Fi is found in campgrounds, RV parks, and even entire towns. Most laptops sold today have built-in wireless capability. To find public Wi-Fi hot spots at your destination, go to **www.jiwire.com**; its Hotspot Finder holds the world's largest directory of public wireless hot spots.

For dial-up access, most business-class hotels in the U.S. offer dataports for laptop modems, and a few thousand hotels in the U.S. and Europe now offer free high-speed Internet access.

4

Suggested Florida Itineraries

Ask anyone who lives here and they'll tell you: Florida is such a long state. If you drive from Jacksonville to the southernmost point in Key West, it'll take 10 hours at least—without traffic. Same goes for the tedious drive from Miami to the Panhandle. Thankfully, there are flights throughout the state that make exploration much easier. Don't tear your hair out if you can't get from Disney to the Everglades in the same trip. Set your sights on what you want to do and see the most, and simply unwind—this is, after all, a holiday. You can always come back. In fact, return visits are highly encouraged!

The range of possible itineraries is endless; what we've suggested below is a very full program covering Florida over a 2-week period. If possible, you should extend your time—2 weeks is not really enough time if you plan to actually explore the Sunshine State, but if you plan to veg out on a beach, then it's plenty of time—or cut out some of the destinations suggested. You can always tack on one itinerary to the next. We've done our best to keep these itineraries geographically viable and logical. Ideally, you should use the highlights from chapter 1 to work out a route that covers those experiences or sights that really appeal to you. Whatever you finally decide to do, we highly recommend that you at least include a stop at one of Florida's natural wonders, be it the beaches, the Everglades, or the Keys.

Important: Should limited time force you to include only the most obvious stops in your itinerary, you will make contact mainly with those who depend on you to make a living, which regrettably could leave you with a frustrated sense that Florida is one big, long tourist trap. This is why it is so important to *get off the beaten tourist track,* to experience the wacky, the kitschy, the stunning, the baffling, and the fascinating people, places, and things that make this state one of the most popular vacation destinations in the world.

1 THE REGIONS IN BRIEF

Contrary to popular belief, it's not all sun, sea, sand, and butterfly ballots. Here's a brief rundown of the state's regions to help you plan your itinerary.

MIAMI & MIAMI BEACH Sprawling across the southeastern corner of the state, metropolitan Miami is a city that prides itself on benefiting from its multiple, vibrant personalities as well as its no-passport-necessary international flair. Here you will hear a cacophony of Spanish and many other languages, not to mention accents, spoken all around you, for this cosmopolitan area is a melting pot of immigrants from Latin America, the Caribbean, and, undeniably, the northeastern United States in particular. Cross the causeways and you'll come to the sands of Miami Beach, long a resort mecca and home to the hypertrendy South Beach, famous for its Art Deco architecture, electric nightlife, and celebrity sightings. See chapters 5 and 6 for more information on the Miami area; see p. 76 for descriptions of the different districts within Miami.

THE KEYS From the southern tip of the Florida mainland, U.S. 1 travels through a 100-mile-long string of islands stretching from Key Largo to the famous, funky, and laid-back "Conch Republic" of Key West, only 90 miles from Cuba and the southernmost point in the United States (it's always warm down here). While some of the islands are crammed with strip malls and tourist traps, most are dense with unusual species of tropical flora and fauna. The Keys don't have the best beaches in Florida, but the waters here—all in a vast marine preserve—offer the state's best scuba diving and snorkeling, and some of its best deep-sea fishing. See chapter 7 for more information.

EVERGLADES & BISCAYNE NATIONAL PARKS This is not your B-movie swamp. In fact, no excessive Hollywood studio budget could afford to replicate the stunning beauty found in this national landmark. Encompassing more than 2,000 square miles and 1.5 million acres, Everglades National Park covers the entire southern tip of Florida. The park, along with nearby Big Cypress National Preserve, protects a unique and fragile "River of Grass" ecosystem teeming with wildlife that is best seen by canoe, by boat, or on long or short hikes. To the east of the Everglades is Biscayne National Park, which preserves the northernmost living-coral reefs in the continental United States. See chapter 8 for more information.

THE GOLD COAST North of Miami, the Gold Coast is aptly named, for here are booming Hollywood and Fort Lauderdale, ritzy Boca Raton and Palm Beach—the sun-kissed, glitzy, glamorous, and sandy playgrounds of the rich and famous. Beyond its dozens of gorgeous beaches, the area offers fantastic shopping, entertainment, dining, boating, golfing, and tennis, and many places to relax in beautiful settings. With some of the country's most famous golf courses and even more tennis courts, this area also attracts big-name tournaments. See chapter 9 for more information.

THE TREASURE COAST Despite gaining unprecedented numbers of new residents in recent years, the beach communities running from Hobe Sound north to Sebastian Inlet have successfully and blissfully managed to retain their small-town feel. In addition to a vast array of wildlife (not to be mistaken for nightlife, which is intentionally absent from these parts), the area has a rich and colorful history. Its name stems from a violent 1715 hurricane that sank an entire fleet of treasure-laden Spanish ships. The sea around Sebastian Inlet draws surfers to the largest swells in the state, and the area has some great fishing as well. See chapter 10 for more information.

SOUTHWEST FLORIDA Ever since inventor Thomas Alva Edison built a home here in 1885, some of America's wealthiest families have spent their winters along Florida's southwest coast. They're attracted by the area's subtropical climate, shell-strewn beaches, and intricate waterways winding among 10,000-plus islands. Many charming remnants of Old Florida coexist with modern resorts in the sophisticated riverfront towns of Fort Myers and Naples, and on islands such as Gasparilla, Useppa, Sanibel, Captiva, and Marco. Thanks to some timely preservation, the area has many wildlife refuges, including the "back door" to Everglades National Park. See chapter 11 for more information.

THE TAMPA BAY AREA Halfway down the west coast of Florida lies Tampa Bay, one of the state's most densely populated areas. A busy seaport and commercial center, the city of Tampa is home to Busch Gardens Africa, which is both a major theme park and one of the country's largest zoos. Boasting a unique pier and fine museums, St. Petersburg's waterfront downtown is one of Florida's most pleasant. Most visitors elect to stay near the beaches skirting the narrow barrier islands that run some 25 miles between St. Pete Beach and Clearwater Beach. Across the bay to the south lies Sarasota, one of Florida's prime performing-arts venues, the riverfront town of Bradenton, and another string of barrier islands with great beaches and resorts spanning every price range. See chapter 12 for more information.

WALT DISNEY WORLD & ORLANDO Walt Disney announced plans to build the Magic Kingdom in 1965, a year before his death and 6 years before the theme park opened, changing forever what was then a sleepy Southern town. Walt Disney World claims four distinct parks, two entertainment districts, enough hotels and restaurants to fill a small city, and several smaller attractions, including water parks and miniature-golf courses. Then there are the rapidly expanding Universal Studios Orlando and SeaWorld, as well as many more non-Disney attractions. Orlando is Florida's most popular tourist destination, thanks not only to an animated rodent, but also to those enterprising entertainment venues that have risen to the mouse's challenge. See chapter 13 for more information.

NORTHEAST FLORIDA The northeast section of the state contains the oldest permanent settlement in America—St. Augustine, where Spanish colonists arrived and settled more than 4 centuries ago. Today its history comes to life in a quaint historic district. St. Augustine is bordered to the north by Jacksonville, an up-and-coming Sunbelt metropolis with miles of oceanfront beach and beautiful marine views along the St. Johns River. Up on the Georgia border, Amelia Island has two of Florida's finest resorts and its own historic town of Fernandina Beach. To the south of St. Augustine is Daytona Beach, home of the Daytona International Speedway and a maddening spring-break mecca for the MTV generation. Another brand of excitement is offered down at Cape Canaveral, where the Kennedy Space Center launches all manned U.S. space missions. See chapter 14 for more information.

NORTHWEST FLORIDA: THE PANHANDLE Historic roots run deep in Florida's narrow northwest extremity, and Pensacola's historic district, which blends Spanish, French, and British cultures, is a highlight of any visit to today's Panhandle. Despite that, the accents here are decidedly Deep South. So, too, are the powdery, dazzlingly white beaches that stretch for more than 80 miles past the resorts of Pensacola Beach, Fort Walton Beach, Destin, and Panama City Beach. The Gulf Islands National Seashore has preserved much of this beach and its wildlife, and inland are state parks that offer some of the state's best canoeing adventures. All this makes the area a favorite summertime vacation destination for residents of neighboring Georgia and Alabama, with whom Northwest Floridians share many Deep South traditions. Sitting in a pine and oak forest just 30 miles from the Georgia line, the state capital of Tallahassee has a moss-draped, football-loving charm all its own. See chapter 15 for more information.

ALABAMA

GEORGIA

85

10

231

10

Pensacola

98

Destin

Panama City

Tallahassee

19
27

319

98

Panama
City Beach

START: Beachy Keen
Florida in 1 Week

27

Apalachicola

St. George
Island

Apalachee
Bay

Gulf of Mexico

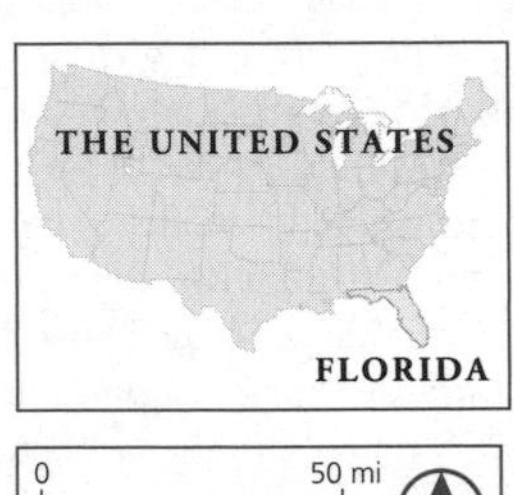

0 50 mi

0 50 km

N

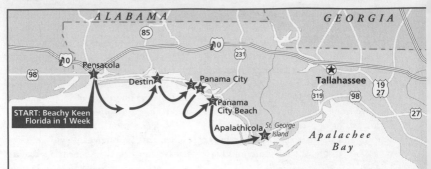

■ START: South Florida in 2 Weeks

▲ START: Florida's Gulf Coast in 1 Week: AKA Relaxing Florida

● START: Florida, Family Style in 1 Week

◆ START: Old Historic Florida in 1 Week

★ START: Beachy Keen Florida in 1 Week

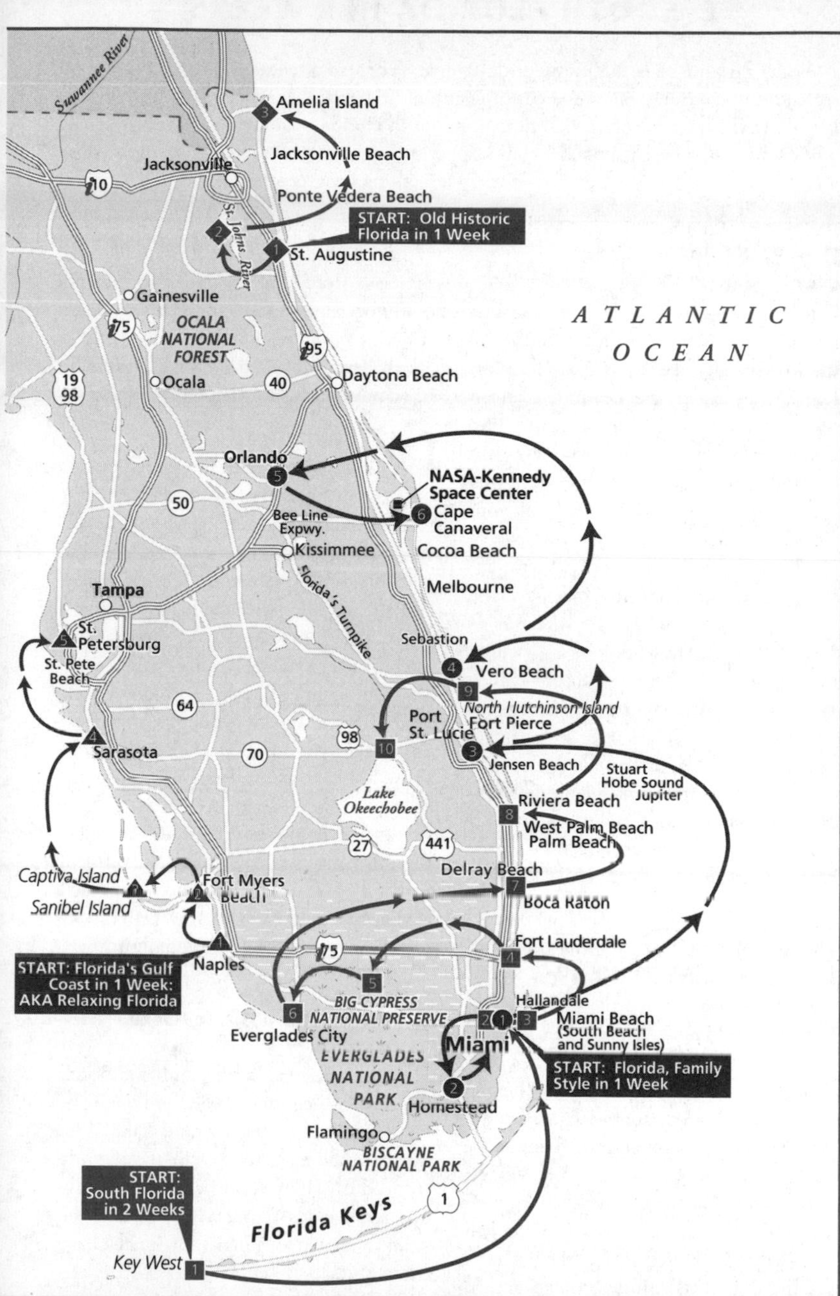
Suwannee River
Amelia Island
Jacksonville Beach
Jacksonville
10
Ponte Vedera Beach
St. Johns River
START: Old Historic Florida in 1 Week
St. Augustine
Gainesville
75
OCALA NATIONAL FOREST
95
ATLANTIC OCEAN
19 98
Ocala
40
Daytona Beach
Orlando
NASA-Kennedy Space Center
50
Bee Line Expwy.
Cape Canaveral
Kissimmee
Cocoa Beach
Florida's Turnpike
Melbourne
Tampa
St. Petersburg
Sebastion
St. Pete Beach
Vero Beach
North Hutchinson Island
64
Port St. Lucie
Fort Pierce
98
Sarasota
70
Jensen Beach
Stuart
Hobe Sound
Jupiter
Lake Okeechobee
Riviera Beach
West Palm Beach
Palm Beach
27
441
Delray Beach
Captiva Island
Fort Myers Beach
Sanibel Island
Boca Raton
Fort Lauderdale
75
START: Florida's Gulf Coast in 1 Week: AKA Relaxing Florida
Naples
BIG CYPRESS NATIONAL PRESERVE
Hallandale
Everglades City
Miami Beach (South Beach and Sunny Isles)
Miami
EVERGLADES NATIONAL PARK
START: Florida, Family Style in 1 Week
Homestead
Flamingo
BISCAYNE NATIONAL PARK
START: South Florida in 2 Weeks
1
Florida Keys
Key West

2 SOUTH FLORIDA IN 2 WEEKS

Consider this tour to be a South Florida sampler. There's not enough time in 2 weeks to see and do everything, but we've custom-built an itinerary that will provide you with a locals'-eye view of some of the best diversions South Florida is known for. Whether you're a beach bum or a beachcomber, a club hopper or someone who prefers to swing a club, a nature lover or a people-watcher—there's something for everyone on this tour.

Days ❶ & ❷: Arrive in Key West ★★★

After arriving in the so-called Conch Republic (or Margaritaville, if you will), plan to spend a day or two at the most here. A full day on the 4×2-mile island is plenty for exploring, but if you're into doing the Duval Bar Crawl, you may want to leave yourself a day to recover from that inevitable hangover. Focus most of your sightseeing energy on Old Town, where you'll see stunning, restored Victorian-style homes, lush, tropical greenery, and the old Bahama Village. Be sure not to miss the sunset celebration at Mallory Square, and, if possible, do dinner at Blue Heaven in Bahama Village. Then hit the Duval Street bars if you're so inclined. Spend the next day either relaxing at your hotel pool—we recommend the Gardens Hotel and Simonton Court for a true Key West experience—or explore the historic seaport and all its shops and Key West kitsch. See chapter 7.

Day ❸: Miami: Coral Gables, Little Havana & South Beach ★★★

Take the 3-hour drive on the Overseas Highway to Miami—one of the most scenic drives you'll ever take, albeit sometimes a boring one. If you've seen it before, just fly. Make a pit stop in Coral Gables, where you can either get a bite to eat at the Latin American Cafeteria or on Miracle Mile, or cool off in the Venetian Pool. If you like what you see, check into the historic Biltmore Hotel. If not, then at least see the hotel and continue on to Southwest 8th Street, otherwise known as Calle Ocho, the heart of Little Havana. Peruse the cigar stores and the old men playing dominoes in Domino Park. Grab a Cuban coffee at Versailles, and then head north to South Beach to spend the night at one of its trendy hotels. See chapters 5 and 6.

Day ❹: South Beach ★★★

Wake up early and catch the sunrise on the beach. Have breakfast at the Front Porch Café. Stake your claim on the sand and spend the morning by the water. Hit Lincoln Road for lunch, and then shop there and along Collins Avenue before having a cocktail at the Rose Bar at the Delano, Skybar at the Shore Club, or the Ritz-Carlton South Beach's DiLido Beach Club. Return to your own hotel for a disco nap; wake up around 9pm. Have dinner at Prime 112 or, for a less pricey, yet still sceney dining experience, the Café at Books and Books, and then hit the clubs: Opium Garden, Prive, Mansion, Cameo, Set, and/or Mokai. Grab a late-night snack at La Sandwicherie, or the 11th Street Diner and then crash at your hotel. See chapters 5 and 6.

Day ❺: From South Beach to Fort Lauderdale ★★

Have breakfast at the Big Pink and watch the club kids coming home from the night before. Get in the car and take A1A north—the scenic route. Hit the recently spruced up Hollywood Beach Boardwalk, our version of Atlantic City, without the casinos. If you're hungry for lunch, have the world's best burger at Le Tub. Continue along A1A until you reach the famous Fort Lauderdale strip. Take a break at the world-famous Elbo Room and watch the action on the beach. Spend the night at the Riverside Hotel on Las Olas Boulevard. See chapters 5 and 6.

Day 6: Sand, Seminoles & Santana ★★

Hit the famous Fort Lauderdale Beach, where Frankie and Annette used to play beach-blanket bingo. Then for a bit of a diversion, head west to the Seminole Hard Rock Hotel and Casino, where you may catch a concert by a *Billboard*-charting artist or even Jerry Seinfeld, hit the jackpot on one of the hundreds of slot machines (the hotel claims it pays out $12.9 million daily!), or relax by the pool. It's almost as nice as, if not nicer than, the one at the Hard Rock Hotel in Vegas. Also check out the Seminole Okalee Indian Village and Museum before heading out to spot signs of real wildlife in the Everglades. See chapters 5 and 6.

Days 7 & 8: Seminole Indian Reservation & Everglades National Park ★★★

Travel 45 minutes west on I-75 to the Seminole Indian Reservation, which encompasses more than 69,000 acres of the Everglades' Big Cypress Swamp. Hop on a swamp buggy at the Billie Swamp Safari to see hogs, bison, gators, and deer. Continue west to Everglades City, check into the Ivey House B&B, and ask owners Sandee and David if they can hook you up with a special, insiders' tour of the 'Glades. See chapter 8.

Days 9 & 10: The Palm Beaches ★★

From one extreme to another, after leaving charming and historic Everglades City, head east and north to charming, historic, and bustling Delray Beach, where the only alligators you'll likely see are on the purses of the ladies who lunch and lounge there. Check into the Sundy House and peruse the hotel's Taru Gardens. The next day, do not miss the Morikami Museum and Japanese Gardens before moving on to West Palm Beach, where you should check into the Hotel Biba and do a little antiques shopping in downtown West Palm. At night, check out the clubs and restaurants in downtown West Palm, on Clematis Street. Be sure to have a beer and enjoy the view at Bradley's. See chapter 9.

Day 11: From Mar-A-Lago to the Moon—or Jupiter, at Least ★★

Spend the morning driving around Palm Beach proper, making sure to stop and catch a glimpse of Donald Trump's palatial Mar-A-Lago that, last we heard, may be up for sale soon, but not before Donald's ex Ivana gets married there—again. Stop by Worth Avenue to see the ladies with little dogs who lunch and shop. It's the Rodeo Drive of South Florida, truly, and you can't miss the people-watching there. For an actual glimpse inside a Palm Beach manse, go to the Flagler Museum, where you can explore Whitehall, Standard Oil tycoon Henry Flagler's wedding present to his third wife. Go back to reality and head toward Jupiter, the home of former resident Burt Reynolds. Check into the PGA National Resort and Spa. See chapter 9.

Days 12 & 13: The Treasure Coast

You may not find gold in your exploration of the Treasure Coast, but you will find Jonathan Dickinson State Park on Hutchinson Island, where you should rent a canoe and explore the plethora of botanical treasures. If you're into snorkeling and diving and feel like delving deeper, check out the most popular artificial reef in the area, the USS *Rankin,* an old World War II ship that was sunk in 1988, located 7 miles east–northeast of the St. Lucie Inlet. Check into the Hutchinson Island Marriott Beach Resort and Marina, and consider taking the *Loxahatchee Queen* for a 2-hour tour of the area. The next day, head to Vero Beach and Sebastian for a taste of Old Florida. Sports fans will want to check out Dodgertown, where the Los Angeles Dodgers used to spend their winters and where the Baltimore Orioles may take up spring training. Check into the completely unique Driftwood Resort or Gloria Estefan's swanky new 94-room boutique hotel Costa D'Este Beach Resort and have dinner at Oriente, a Cuban restaurant with Spanish and Creole accents, if your budget allows. If not, just grab a slice of pizza at Nino's Café. See chapter 10.

Day ⓮: Lake Okeechobee or Bust? If you can't extend your trip to include a side trip to Lake Okeechobee, consider it for next time. In the meantime, fly home out of either Palm Beach International Airport, 35 miles south of Vero Beach, or the Melbourne International Airport, which is less than 35 miles north of Vero Beach. See chapter 10.

3 FLORIDA'S GULF COAST IN 1 WEEK: RELAXING FLORIDA

The beaches on the Gulf Coast are infinitely nicer than those in South Florida, with soft sand, stunning sunsets, and a sense of calm that often evades the hustle and bustle of South Florida. A week on the Gulf is akin to spending a month in a city spa. Refreshing and calming, the Gulf Coast is an ideal spot for those looking to recharge their batteries.

Day ❶: Arrive in Fort Myers Beach ★★

Check into the Edison Beach House All Suite Hotel and take in the panoramic Gulf views. Waste no time making a dinner reservation at the Gulf Shore Grill, where you simply must try shrimp wrapped in bacon and coated with honey. After dinner, consider hitting the rooftop bar at Beached Whale, a locals' favorite. See chapter 11.

Day ❷: Sanibel & Captiva Islands ★★★

Just 14 miles west of Fort Myers are two of Florida's most beautiful islands. Before heading to the wildly kitschy Bubble Room restaurant, be sure to stop at the J. N. "Ding" Darling National Wildlife Refuge, home to alligators, raccoons, otters, and a dazzling array of bird life. Take your car down the Wildlife Drive for a *Cliffs-Notes* version of the park. Then call Captiva Cruises and see if there's room for y'all on the next shuttle out to Boca Grande, sort of the Martha's Vineyard of Florida. After touring Boca Grande, return to Sanibel and check into the Casa Ybel Resort, if your budget allows you to; if not, we highly recommend the Tarpon Tale Inn on Sanibel, or the 'Tween Waters Inn on Captiva. Now you're ready for the Bubble Room or live reggae at Jacaranda! See chapter 11.

Day ❸: To Naples ★★

Wake up early and do not miss breakfast and the biscuits at the Sanibel Café. Drive south for 40 or so miles, and you'll be in swanky, sleepy Naples. Take the Naples Trolley to get a feel for the place and then, without hesitation, hit the beach before sunset. For a ritzy experience, we recommend the Ritz-Carlton, Naples, one of the best in the entire chain. For a flip-flops-and-T-shirt experience with a hopping bar scene at sunset, you'll love the Naples Beach Hotel and Golf Club. Both have fabulous beaches. After the beach, stroll down 5th Avenue, the city's main drag, where you'll find the only real semblance of nightlife, dining, and shopping. The next morning, head 70 miles north to Sarasota. See chapter 11.

Days 4 & 5: Sarasota ★★★

Sarasota's Siesta Key Beach is one of Florida's best. But if culture is your thing, don't miss the Ringling Museum of Art. If you can't stay at the Ritz-Carlton Sarasota, consider the Colony Beach and Tennis Resort on nearby Longboat Key. Do not miss dinner at Euphemia Haye. Just don't. For a fun diversion nearby in Bradenton, stop by the Gamble Plantation and the weird and wacky Solomon's Castle. Before heading to Tampa, have breakfast at the Blue Dolphin Café. See chapter 12.

Days 6 & 7: Tampa Bay, St. Pete & Clearwater ★★

Because this is the relaxing Gulf Coast itinerary, we won't recommend Busch Gardens Africa unless you're really craving roller coasters. The same goes for Ybor City, the hub of Tampa's nightlife. It's rowdy and fun, but hardly relaxing. Therefore, we'd like to send you directly to the Saddlebrook Resort–Tampa, where the likes of Jennifer Capriati play tennis, and aspiring Tiger Woods–types play golf. If you prefer to be on the beach, however, head over to St. Pete Beach and Clearwater, where we recommend either the historic Don CeSar Beach Resort & Spa or the Clearwater Beach Marriott Suites on Sand Key. For arty types, the Salvador Dalí museum in downtown St. Pete is highly recommended. Fly home from Tampa International Airport. See chapter 12.

4 A WEEK IN FLORIDA, FAMILY STYLE

Florida is definitely a kid-friendly destination. Contrary to popular belief, not all diversions are animatronic or even remotely animated. Sure, there are the theme parks, the roller coasters, the talking mouse, and Cinderella Castle. We've got Flipper and Orca and parrots that play poker. Then there's the Playmobil Fun Park. But we've come up with another family-friendly itinerary you may not have experienced yet.

Day 1: Key Biscayne ★★★

The Ritz-Carlton Key Biscayne has fabulous children's programs, not to mention pretty cool diversions for adults. If it's in your budget, spend a day checking out the resort (skip the Miami Seaquarium unless the kids want to swim with the dolphins), and, if not, just spend the day at the Marjory Stoneman Douglas Biscayne Nature Center, where the entire family can explore an ancient fossil tidal pool. If there's time left, check out the Bill Baggs Cape Florida State Park and rent a hydrobike. See chapter 7.

Days 2 & 3: Coral Gables ★★★ & South Miami ★★

Get an early start and head south to Homestead's legendary Coral Castle. When the kids tire of seeing this wacky attraction, grab lunch at the family-friendly, family-run Mexican mainstay, El Toro Taco. On your way to Coral Gables, make a stop at Miami Metrozoo or Monkey Jungle, depending on your preference in animals, and then clean off that stinky animal scent with a splash in Coral Gables's resplendent, refreshing Venetian Pool. If you're up for it, check out Vizcaya Museum and Gardens, and/or the Miami Science Museum. After working up an appetite, take the kids for a big dinner at Rio's Churrascaria, where they'll enjoy holding up signs when they're ready to eat more meat! See chapters 5 and 6.

Day 4: Miami & Port St. Lucie ★★★

Before leaving Miami, be sure to stop at the Miami Children's Museum, where the kids can spend a few hours channeling their inner grown-up in a bona fide TV and recording studio. If the kids are in the mood for animal antics instead, head across the causeway to Jungle Island. Grab a TV dinner at the G-rated Big Pink on South Beach, and then hit the road to Vero Beach. Check into either Disney's Vero Beach Resort or the Club Med Sandpiper on the St. Lucie River, where there are four different children's clubs for ages 4 months all the way up to 13 years old. En route to Vero, you may want to take the kids to West Palm Beach's whimsical Playmobil Fun Park or on a safari through Lion Country Safari, and then grab lunch at Jupiter's legendary Nick's Tomato Pie. See chapters 5, 6, 9, and 10.

Day 5: Vero Beach ★★★

As if Club Med or Disney doesn't have enough for the family to do—or not do—you may want to take the kids out to McLarty Treasure Museum, where they will marvel at pirate's booty, or to one of the beautiful beaches nearby. See chapter 10.

Day 6: Arrive in Lake Buena Vista ★★★

Okay, we lied. Sort of. We're sending you in the environs of Disney and friends, but only to check into the coolest kid-friendly hotel possibly in the entire world. The Nickelodeon Family Suites resort, by Holiday Inn, is the first ever Nickelodeon-branded resort. There are Kid Suites with different themes featuring the kids' favorite Nick characters. I know many a family that has traveled here just so the kids could stay in the hotel. If you choose, you can go to Disney World or one of the theme parks. See chapter 13.

Day 7: Spacing Out at Cape Canaveral ★★★

The John F. Kennedy Space Center is a must-see for everyone, but especially kids. You'll not only see where actual rockets and shuttles are launched, but you can also have lunch with an astronaut! Either spend the night here and fly out of the Melbourne International Airport, or make the 3-hour drive back to Miami International Airport. See chapter 14.

5 FIVE DAYS IN OLD HISTORIC FLORIDA

Many Floridians lament the loss of the days of the plastic pink flamingos, early bird specials, cracker-style homes (as opposed to Cracker Barrel restaurants), and small, quaint towns. The thing is, they still exist! Old Florida begins in St. Augustine and doesn't end there at all. Here's a sample that promises to take you back to a Florida that would even seem ancient to your grandparents.

Day 1: St. Augustine ★★★

The easiest way to hit America's oldest city is to fly into Daytona International Airport. But because this is a tour of Old Florida, we'll have you skip the Daytona spring break and NASCAR scene, and head an hour north into the 17th century.

Everything in St. Augustine claims to be the oldest whatever—and, in most cases, it's true: the Oldest Store, the Oldest Wooden Schoolhouse, the Oldest House, and more. Pop a multivitamin and skip the overrated Fountain of Youth. Instead, hit Anastasia State Park and see what a beach would look like if it were unfettered by modernization. To really keep with the old theme, we suggest a room at the Casablanca Inn on the Bay, a 1914 house listed on the National Register of Historic Places, or for a true Florida experience, spend the night on the SeaClusion, the state's one and only boat and breakfast. See chapter 14.

Days ❷ & ❸: North & South of the St. Johns River ★★

Despite its modern skyline, Jacksonville actually has some serious history. South of the St. Johns River, you will find the Fort Caroline National Memorial, a former 16th-century French Huguenot settlement that was wiped out by the Spanish but preserved in the form of archaeological relics. North of the river is the Zephaniah Kingsley Plantation, or at least the remains of what was once a 19th-century plantation complete with clapboard homes and slave cabins. Check into either the historic House on Cherry Street or, also on the St. Johns, the Inn at Oak Street. See chapter 14.

Days ❹ & ❺: Amelia Island ★★★

With 13 miles of beachfront and bona fide, restored Victorian homes, Amelia Island is worth the 45-minute drive northeast of downtown Jacksonville. It's another world and, for many, out of this world. Also steeped in history, Amelia Island attracted Oprah Winfrey, who has promised to help restore American Beach, the only beach in the 1930s reserved for African Americans. Nearby is Fernandina Beach, which dates back to the post–Civil War period. Here, you'll swear you're somewhere else, with all the Victorian, Queen Anne, and Italianate homes listed on the National Register. Nearby, the Palace Saloon claims to be Florida's oldest watering hole, challenging St. Augustine to an ongoing drinking contest! Check into the Amelia Island Plantation for a posh stay, or consider the Florida House Inn, once again, the oldest operating hotel in the entire state. See chapter 14.

6 BEACHY KEEN FLORIDA IN 1 WEEK

The Panhandle may be known as the Redneck Riviera to some, but to those in the know, the area has some of Florida's best beaches, with undeveloped stretches of powder-white sand that's a hot commodity in the world these days.

Days ❶ & ❷: Gulf Islands National Seashore and Pensacola Beach ★★★

This is, hands down, Florida's best beach. Not only are there 150 miles of protected beach, but there's also a 1,378-acre natural Live Oaks Area full of oaks, pines, and nature trails. Even the Clarion Suites Resort and Convention Center is pretty stunning, with tin-roofed pastel cottages that sit on the sand dunes. Do not leave without hitting the Flora-Bama Lounge, which prides itself on being the "Last Great American Road House." See chapter 15.

Day ❸: Destin Beach ★★

Grayton Beach State Park is a sublime white-sand paradise, with 356 acres of pine forests surrounding a lake. You can camp here to get back to nature, or you can choose to explore Destin's other fabulous beaches, such as Henderson Beach State Park and Fort Walton Beach's Okaloosa Island. You can't really go wrong with any of them. The Sandestin Golf and Beach Resort is good for a longer stay, a community unto itself with restaurants, shops, a private 5-mile beach, and, according to the experts, unparalleled golf. Don't get too marooned because you will want to go off property and check out AJ's Seafood and Oyster Bar, the hottest spot on Destin Harbor, famous for its rooftop bar and live music. See chapter 15.

Days ❹ & ❺: Seaside & Rosemary Beach ★★★

Live *The Truman Show* in this stunning, Victorian-style planned community with old-fashioned beach cottages set upon

South Florida Literary Tour

Pompano Beach: Author Elmore Leonard took his mother to a small motel on Pompano Beach, which some say was his inspiration for the Coconut Palms Resort Apartments, to where George Moran, the main character in Leonard's 1982 book *Cat Chaser,* runs. See p. 265.

Dania Beach Pier: Harry Crews used the Dania Pier as a backdrop for a July 4th fireworks display and beauty contest in *Karate Is a Thing of the Spirit.* See Dania Beach on p. 267.

Bahia Mar Beach Resort: Travis McGee, the protagonist in John D. MacDonald's 21 novels (including *The Deep Blue Goodbye*), lived at this resort, 801 Seabreeze Blvd. (© **888/802-2442;** www.bahiamarhotel.com).

Little Haiti: The place where a no-good former oil-burner repairman wanders, in Russell Banks's *Continental Drift.*

Flagler Street: Where Brett Halliday's private eye, Michael Shayne, kept his office. See p. 171.

Hialeah Race Course: The inspiration for Damon Runyon's short story *Pick the Winner.* Log onto www.tinyurl.com/52552y.

Cardozo Hotel: Elmore Leonard's favorite backdrop—as seen in *Get Shorty, La Brava,* and *Rum Punch*—was this hotel, 1300 Ocean Dr., Miami Beach (© **800/782-6500;** www.cardozohotel.com).

Barnacle State Historic Site: James W. Hall's *Hard Aground* transforms the Barnacle into Mangrove House, a place with a sinister history. See p. 153.

Domino Park: Ana Menendez's *In Cuba I Was a German Shepherd* reminisces about Little Havana's most hopping spot, at the southwest corner of 15th Avenue and 8th Street.

Tobacco Road: Miami's oldest bar gets is name from the 1932 novel by Erskine Caldwell. See p. 181.

unfettered sand dunes. Just 8 miles east of Seaside is Rosemary Beach, a swanky community of Caribbean-style cottages and carriage houses with the most stunning private beach and Kodak-worthy Gulf views. Rent a cottage on the beach and enjoy the views. See chapter 15.

Day 6: Panama City Beach ★★

St. Andrews State Park has 1,000 acres of white sand and dunes, a common theme in the Panhandle. Shell Island is pristine, uninhabited, and known for possessing shells that aren't available for purchase in those touristy souvenir shops. Spend the night at Marriott's Bay Point Village. See chapter 15.

Day 7: Apalachicola ★★

Florida's so-called Last Frontier happens to have one of the country's last amazing beaches, St. George Island State Park. Enjoy the 9 miles of nature before having to go back to reality. Spend your last night at the Apalachicola River Inn, the town's only waterfront stay, and home of the popular Frog Level Oyster Bar and Boss Oyster, where you'll be treated to some of the best crustaceans you've ever had. See chapter 15.

5

Where to Stay & Dine in Miami

A week in Miami is not unlike watching an unbelievable reality show, only this time it's actually *real.* Miami: the city where Jennifer Aniston went "public" with her romance to rocker John Mayer, where troubled British pop star Amy Winehouse married her incarcerated husband, and where the paparazzi camps out for days, hoping to catch a glimpse of something or someone fabulous. It's where former U.S. president Bill Clinton kibitzes with the head of a top modeling agency at a St. Tropez–ish beach club, and where Janet Reno, Ben Affleck, and Matt Damon throw politically driven dance and cocktail parties at a South Beach nightclub. That's just a small sample of the surreal, Fellini-esque world that exists way down here at the bottom of the map. Nothing in Miami is ever what it seems.

What used to be a relatively sleepy beach vacation destination has awakened from its humid slumber, upped its tempo, and finally earned its place in the Blackberries and iPhones of cutting-edge jet-setters worldwide. But don't be fooled by the hipper-than-thou, celebrity-drenched playground known as South Beach. While the chic elite do, indeed, flock to Miami's coolest enclave, it is surprisingly accessible to the average Joe, Jane, or José. For every Philippe Starck–designed, bank account–busting boutique hotel on South Beach, there's a kitschy, candy-coated Art Deco one that's much less taxing on the pockets. For each Pan-Mediterranean-Asian haute cuisine restaurant, there's always the down-home, no-nonsense Cuban bodega offering hearty food at ridiculously cheap prices.

Beyond the whole glitzy, *Entertainment Tonight*–meets-beach-blanket-bacchanalia-as-seen-on-TV, Miami has an endless number of sporting, cultural, and recreational activities to keep you entertained. Its sparkling beaches are beyond compare. Plus, it has excellent shopping and nightlife activities, including ballet, theater, and opera (as well as all the celebrity-saturated hotels, restaurants, bars, and clubs that have helped make Miami so famous).

One thing you'll notice about Miami is the number of construction cranes dotting the skyline, the last remnants of a real estate boom that has since crashed. For now, we take pride in watching the already majestic skyline take a new shape, albeit with multimillion-dollar condos that many describe as soulless.

Leave Miami, be it for the Keys, the Gold Coast, or the Treasure Coast, and you'll expose yourself not only to more UV rays, but to a world of cultural, historical, and sybaritic surprises where you can take in a spring baseball game, walk in the footsteps of Hemingway, get up-close and personal with the area's sea life, soak up the serenity of unspoiled landscapes, catch the filming of *CSI: Miami* or a big-budget Hollywood flick, and much more.

Forget what you've heard about South Florida being "Heaven's Waiting Room." That slogan is as passé as the concept of early-bird dinners (which you can still get—they just no longer define the region). In fact, according to some people, South Florida *is* heaven.

1 ORIENTATION

ARRIVING

Originally carved out of scrubland in 1928 by Pan American Airlines, **Miami International Airport (MIA)** has become second in the United States for international passenger traffic and 10th in the world for total passengers. Despite the heavy traffic, the airport is quite user-friendly and not as much of a hassle as you'd think. You can change money or use your ATM card at Bank of America, located near the exit. Visitor information is available 24 hours a day at the **Miami International Airport Main Visitor Counter,** Concourse E, second level (✆ **305/876-7000**). Information is also available at **www.miami-airport.com**. Because MIA is the busiest airport in South Florida, travelers may want to consider flying into the less crowded **Fort Lauderdale Hollywood International Airport (FLL;** ✆ **954/359-1200)**, which is closer to north Miami than MIA, or the **Palm Beach International Airport (PBI;** ✆ **561/471-7420)**, which is about 1½ hours from Miami.

Getting into Town

Miami International Airport is about 6 miles west of downtown and about 10 miles from the beaches, so it's likely you can get from the plane to your hotel room in less than half an hour. Of course, if you're arriving from an international destination, it will take more time to go through Customs and Immigration.

BY CAR All the major car-rental firms operate off-site branches reached via shuttles from the airline terminals. See the "By Car" section, under "Getting Around," on p. 81, for a list of major rental companies in Miami. Signs at the airport's exit clearly point the way to various parts of the city, but the car-rental firm should also give you directions to your destination. If you're arriving late at night, you might want to take a taxi to your hotel and have the car delivered to you the next day.

BY TAXI Taxis line up in front of a dispatcher's desk outside the airport's arrivals terminals. Most cabs are metered, though some have flat rates to popular destinations. The fare should be about $20 to Coral Gables, $15 to downtown, and $32 to South Beach, plus tip, which should be about 15% (add more for each bag the driver handles). Depending on traffic, the ride to Coral Gables or downtown takes about 15 to 20 minutes, and to South Beach, 20 to 25 minutes.

BY VAN OR LIMO Group limousines (multipassenger vans) circle the arrivals area looking for fares. Destinations are posted on the front of each van, and a flat rate is charged for door-to-door service to the area marked.

SuperShuttle (✆ **305/871-2000;** www.supershuttle.com) is one of the largest airport operators, charging between $10 and $50 per person for a ride within the county. Its vans operate 24 hours a day and accept American Express, MasterCard, and Visa. This is a cheaper alternative to a cab (if you are traveling alone or with one other person), but be prepared to be in the van for quite some time, as you may have to make several stops to drop passengers off before you reach your own destination. SuperShuttle also has begun service from Palm Beach International Airport to the surrounding communities. The door-to-door, shared-ride service operates from the airport to Stuart, Fort Pierce, Palm Beach, and Broward counties.

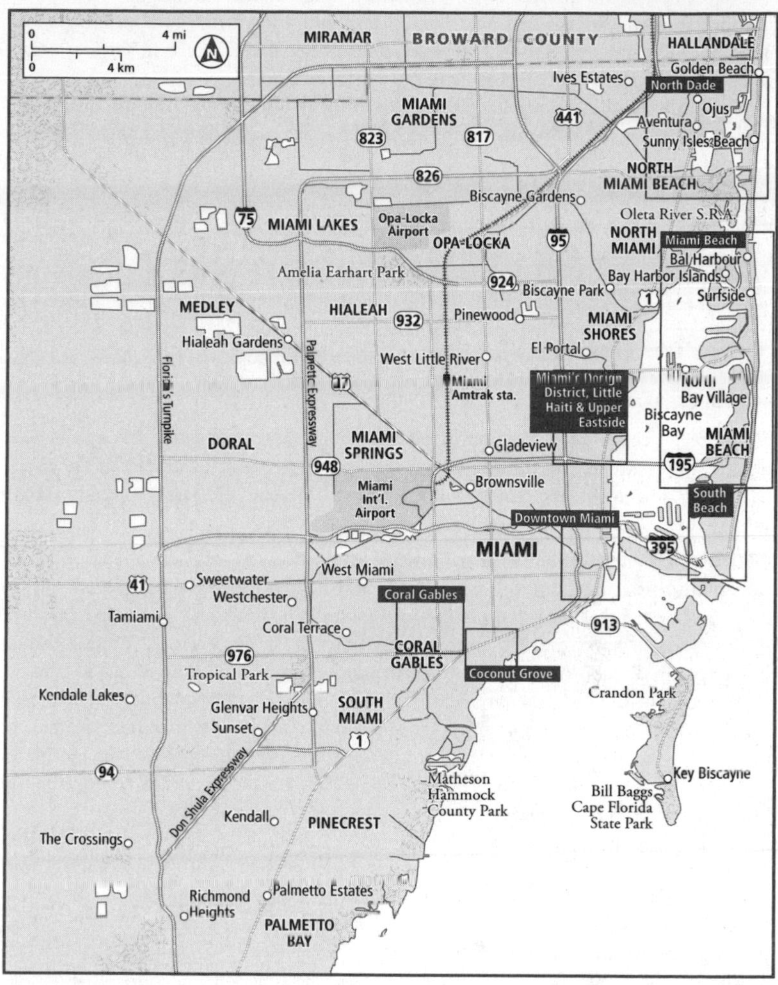

Private limousine arrangements can be made in advance through your local travel agent. A one-way meet-and-greet service should cost about $50. Limo services include **Aventura Limousine** (**© 800/944-9886**) and **Limo Miami** (**© 305/742-5900**).

BY PUBLIC TRANSPORTATION Public transportation in South Florida is a major hassle bordering on a nightmare. Painfully slow and unreliable, buses heading downtown leave the airport only once per hour (from the arrivals level), and connections are spotty, at best. It could take about 1½ hours to get to South Beach via public transportation. Journeys to downtown and Coral Gables, however, are more direct. The fare is $2, plus an additional 50¢ for a transfer.

VISITOR INFORMATION

The most up-to-date information is provided by the **Greater Miami Convention and Visitor's Bureau,** 701 Brickell Ave., Ste. 700, Miami, FL 33131 (✆ **800/933-8448** or 305/539-3000; fax 305/530-3113). Several chambers of commerce in Greater Miami will send out information on their particular neighborhoods.

If you arrive at the Miami International Airport, you can pick up visitor information at the airport's main visitor counter on the second floor of Concourse E. It's open 24 hours a day.

Always check local newspapers for special events during your visit. The city's only daily, the *Miami Herald,* is a good source for current-events listings, particularly the "Weekend" section in Friday's edition. Even better is the free weekly alternative paper the *Miami New Times,* available in bright red boxes throughout the city.

Information on everything from dining to entertainment in Miami is available on the Internet at www.miami.citysearch.com, www.digitalcity.com/southflorida, www.miami newtimes.com, www.miami.com, and www.miamiherald.com.

CITY LAYOUT

Miami seems confusing at first, but quickly becomes easy to navigate. The small cluster of buildings that make up the downtown area is at the geographical heart of the city. In relation to downtown, the airport is northwest, the beaches are east, Coconut Grove is south, Coral Gables is west, and the rest of the city is north.

FINDING AN ADDRESS Miami is divided into dozens of areas with official and unofficial boundaries. Street numbering in the city of Miami is fairly straightforward, but you must first be familiar with the numbering system. The mainland is divided into four sections (NE, NW, SE, and SW) by the intersection of Flagler Street and Miami Avenue. Flagler Street divides Miami from north to south, and Miami Avenue divides the city from east to west. It's helpful to remember that avenues generally run north–south, while streets go east–west. Street numbers (1st St., 2nd St., and so forth) start from here and increase as you go farther out from this intersection, as do numbers of avenues, places, courts, terraces, and lanes. Streets in Hialeah are the exceptions to this pattern; they are listed separately in map indexes.

Getting around the barrier islands that make up Miami Beach is easier than moving around the mainland. Street numbering starts with 1st Street, near Miami Beach's southern tip, and goes up to 192nd Street, in the northern part of Sunny Isles. As in the city of Miami, some streets in Miami Beach have numbers as well as names. When listed in this book, both name and number are given.

The numbered streets in Miami Beach are not the geographical equivalents of those on the mainland, but they are close. For example, the 79th Street Causeway runs into 71st Street on Miami Beach.

STREET MAPS It's easy to get lost in sprawling Miami, so a reliable map is essential. The **Trakker Map of Miami** is a four-color accordion map that encompasses all of Dade County. Some maps of Miami list streets according to area, so you'll have to know which part of the city you are looking for before the street can be found.

THE NEIGHBORHOODS IN BRIEF

South Beach—The Art Deco District South Beach's 10 miles of beach are alive with a frenetic, circuslike atmosphere and are center stage for a motley crew of characters, from eccentric locals, seniors, snowbirds, and college students to gender benders, celebrities, club kids, and curiosity seekers. Individuality is as widely accepted on South Beach as Visa and MasterCard.

Bolstered by a Caribbean-chic cafe society and a sexually charged, tragically hip nightlife, people-watching on South Beach (1st St.–23rd St.) is almost as good as a front-row seat at a Milan fashion show. But although the beautiful people do flock to South Beach, the models aren't the only sights worth drooling over. The thriving Art Deco District within South Beach has the largest concentration of Art Deco architecture in the world (in 1979, much of South Beach was listed in the National Register of Historic Places). The pastel-hued structures are supermodels in their own right—only *these* models improve with age.

Miami Beach In the fabulous '50s, Miami Beach was America's true Riviera. The stomping ground of choice for the Rat Pack and notorious mobsters such as Al Capone, its huge self-contained resort hotels were vacations unto themselves, providing a full day's worth of meals, activities, and entertainment. Then in the 1960s and 1970s, people who fell in love with Miami began to buy apartments rather than rent hotel rooms. Tourism declined, and many area hotels fell into disrepair.

However, since the late 1980s and South Beach's renaissance, Miami Beach has experienced a tide of revitalization. Huge beach hotels, such as the recently renovated and Vegas-esque Fontainebleau and Eden Roc, are finding their niche with new international tourist markets and are attracting large convention crowds. New generations of Americans are quickly rediscovering the qualities that originally made Miami Beach so popular, and they are finding out that the sand and surf now come with a thriving international city.

Before Miami Beach turns into Surfside, there's North Beach, where there are uncrowded beaches, some restaurants, and examples of Miami Modernism architecture. For information on North Beach and its slow renaissance, go to www.gonorthbeach.com.

Surfside, Bal Harbour, and **Sunny Isles** make up the north part of the beach (island). Hotels, motels, restaurants, and beaches line Collins Avenue and, with some outstanding exceptions, the farther north one goes, the cheaper lodging becomes. Excellent prices, location, and facilities make Surfside and Sunny Isles attractive places to stay, although, despite a slow-going renaissance, they are still a little rough around the edges. Revitalization is in the works for these areas, and, while it's highly unlikely they will ever become as chic as South Beach, there is potential for this, especially as South Beach falls prey to the inevitable spoiler: commercialism. Keep in mind that beachfront properties are at a premium, so many of the area's moderately priced hotels have been converted to condominiums, leaving fewer and fewer affordable places to stay.

In exclusive and ritzy Bal Harbour, few hotels besides the swanky Regent and expected-to-open-in-2011 St. Regis, remain amid the many beachfront condominium towers. Instead, fancy homes, tucked away on the bay, hide behind gated communities, and the Rodeo Drive of Miami (known as the Bal Harbour Shops) attracts shoppers who don't flinch at four-, five-, and six-figure price tags.

Note that **North Miami Beach,** a residential area near the Dade-Broward County line (north of 163rd St.; part of N. Dade County), is a misnomer. It is actually northwest of Miami Beach, on the mainland, and has no beaches, though it does have some of Miami's better restaurants and shops. Located within North Miami Beach is the posh residential community of **Aventura,** best known for its high-priced condos, the Fairmont Turnberry Isle Resort, and the Aventura Mall.

Note: South Beach, the historic Art Deco District, is treated as a separate neighborhood from Miami Beach.

Key Biscayne Miami's forested and secluded Key Biscayne is technically a barrier island and is not part of the Florida Keys. This island is nothing like its southern neighbors. Located south of Miami Beach, off the shores of Coconut Grove, Key Biscayne is protected from the troubles of the mainland by the long Rickenbacker Causeway and its $1.25 toll.

Largely an exclusive residential community with million-dollar homes and sweeping water views, Key Biscayne also offers visitors great public beaches, a top (read: pricey) resort hotel, world-class tennis facilities, and a few decent restaurants. Hobie Beach, adjacent to the causeway, is the city's premier spot for windsurfing, sailboarding, and jet-skiing (see "Watersports" in chapter 6). On the island's southern tip, Bill Baggs State Park has great beaches, bike paths, and dense forests for picnicking and partying.

Downtown Miami's downtown boasts one of the world's most beautiful cityscapes. Unfortunately, that's about all it offers—for now. During the day, a vibrant community of students, businesspeople, and merchants makes its way through the bustling streets, where vendors sell fresh-cut pineapples and mangoes while young consumers on shopping sprees lug bags and boxes. However, at night, downtown is mostly desolate (except for NE 11th St., where there is a burgeoning nightlife scene) and not a place where you'd want to get lost. The downtown area does have a mall (Bayside Marketplace, where many cruise passengers come to browse), some culture (Metro-Dade Cultural Center), and a few decent restaurants, as well as the sprawling American Airlines Arena (home to the Miami Heat). A downtown revitalization project in the works promises a cultural arts center, urban-chic dwellings and lofts, and an assortment of hip boutiques, eateries, and bars, all to bring downtown back to a life it never really had. The city has even rebranded the downtown area with a new ad campaign, intentionally misspelling it as DWNTN to inexplicably appeal to hipsters. We don't get it either. The **Downtown Miami Partnership** offers guided historic walking tours daily at 10:30am (✆ **305/379-7070**). For more information on downtown, go to www.downtownmiami.com.

Design District With restaurants springing up between galleries and furniture stores galore, the Design District is, as locals say, the new South Beach, adding a touch of New York's SoHo to an area formerly known as downtown Miami's "Don't Go." The district, which is a hotbed for furniture-import companies, interior designers, architects, and more, has also become a player in Miami's ever-changing nightlife. Its bars, lounges, clubs, and restaurants—including one of Miami's best, Michael's Genuine Food and Drink—ranging from überchic and retro to progressive and indie, have helped the area become hipster central for South Beach expatriates and artsy bohemian types. In anticipation of its growing popularity, the district has also banded together to create an up-to-date website, www.designmiami.com, which includes a calendar of events, such as the internationally lauded Art Basel, which attracts the who's who of the art world. The district is loosely defined as the area bounded by NE 2nd Avenue, NE 5th Avenue East and West, and NW 36th Street to the south.

Biscayne Corridor From downtown, near Bayside, to the 70s (affectionately known as the Upper East Side), where trendy curio shops and upscale restaurants are slowly opening, Biscayne Boulevard is aspiring to reclaim itself as a safe thoroughfare where tourists can wine, dine, and shop. Once known for sketchy, dilapidated 1950s- and 1960s-era hotels that had fallen on hard times, this boulevard is getting a boost from residents fleeing the high prices of the beaches in search of affordable housing. They're renovating Biscayne block by block, trying to make this famous boulevard worthy of a Sunday drive.

Little Havana If you've never been to Cuba, just visit this small section of Miami and you'll come pretty close. The sounds, tastes, and rhythms are very reminiscent of Cuba's capital city, and some say you don't have to speak a word of English to live an independent life here—even street signs are in Spanish and English.

Cuban coffee shops, tailor and furniture stores, and inexpensive restaurants line *Calle Ocho* (pronounced *Ka*-yey *O*-choh), SW 8th Street, the region's main thoroughfare. In Little Havana, salsa and merengue beats ring loudly from old record stores while old men in *guayaberas* (loose-fitting cotton short-sleeved shirts) smoke cigars over their daily game of dominoes. The spotlight focused on the neighborhood during the Elián González situation in 2000, but the area was previously noted for the groups of artists and nocturnal types who had moved their galleries and performance spaces here, sparking culturally charged neobohemian nightlife.

Coral Gables "The City Beautiful," created by George Merrick in the early 1920s, is one of Miami's first planned developments. Houses here were built in a Mediterranean style along lush, tree-lined streets that open onto beautifully carved plazas, many with centerpiece fountains. The best architectural examples of the era have Spanish-style tiled roofs and are built from Miami oolite, native limestone commonly called "coral rock." The Gables's European-flaired shopping and commerce center is home to many thriving corporations. Coral Gables also has landmark hotels, great golfing, upscale shopping to rival Bal Harbour, and some of the city's best restaurants, headed by renowned chefs.

Coconut Grove An arty, hippie hangout in the psychedelic '60s, Coconut Grove once had residents who dressed in swirling tie-dyed garb. Nowadays, they prefer the uniform color schemes of the Gap. Chain stores, theme restaurants, a megaplex, and bars galore make Coconut Grove a commercial success, but this gentrification has pushed most alternative types out. Ritzier types have now resurfaced here, thanks, in part, to the antiboho Ritz-Carlton Coconut Grove (p. 113) and the Mayfair, which is in its umpteenth resurgence as a boutique hotel. The intersection of Grand Avenue, Main Highway, and McFarlane Road pierces the area's heart. Right in the center of it all is CocoWalk, filled with boutiques, eateries, and bars. Sidewalks here are often crowded, especially at night, when University of Miami students come out to play.

Southern Miami–Dade County To locals, South Miami is both a specific area, southwest of Coral Gables, and a general region that encompasses all of southern Dade County, including Kendall, Perrine, Cutler Ridge, and Homestead. For the purposes of clarity, this book has grouped all these southern suburbs under the rubric "Southern

Miami–Dade County." The area is heavily residential and packed with strip malls amid a few remaining plots of farmland. Tourists don't usually stay in these parts, unless they are on their way to the Everglades or the Keys. However, Southern Miami–Dade County contains many of the city's top attractions (see chapter 6), meaning that you're likely to spend at least some of your time in Miami here.

2 GETTING AROUND

Officially, Miami Dade County has opted for a "unified, multimodal transportation network," which basically means you can get around the city by train, bus, and taxi. However, in practice, the network doesn't work very well. Things have improved somewhat thanks to the $17-billion Peoples' Transportation Plan which has offered a full range of transportation services at several community-based centers throughout the county, but, unless you are going from downtown Miami to a not-too-distant spot, you are better off in a rental car or taxi.

With the exception of downtown Coconut Grove and South Beach, Miami is not a walker's city. Because it is so spread out, most attractions are too far apart to make walking between them feasible. In fact, most Miamians are so used to driving that they do so even when going just a few blocks.

BY PUBLIC TRANSPORTATION

BY RAIL Two rail lines, operated by the **Metro-Dade Transit Agency** (✆ **305/770-3131** for information; www.co.miami-dade.fl.us/mdta), run in concert with each other.

Metrorail, the city's modern high-speed commuter train, is a 21-mile elevated line that travels north–south, between downtown Miami and the southern suburbs. Locals like to refer to this semiuseless rail system as Metro*fail.* If you are staying in Coral Gables or Coconut Grove, you can park your car at a nearby station and ride the rails downtown. However, that's about it. There are plans to extend the system to service Miami International Airport, but until those tracks are built, these trains don't go most places tourists go, with the exception of Vizcaya (p. 154) in Coconut Grove. Metrorail operates daily from about 6am to midnight. The fare is $2.

Metromover, a 4½-mile elevated line, circles the downtown area and connects with Metrorail at the Government Center stop. Riding on rubber tires, the single-car train winds past many of the area's most important attractions and its shopping and business districts. You may not go very far on the Metromover, but you will get a beautiful perspective from the towering height of the suspended rails. System hours are daily from about 6am to midnight, and the ride is free.

BY BUS Miami's suburban layout is not conducive to getting around by bus. Lines operate and maps are available, but instead of getting to know the city, you'll find that relying on bus transportation will acquaint you only with how it feels to wait at bus stops. In short, a bus ride in Miami is grueling. You can get a bus map by mail, either from the Greater Miami Convention and Visitor's Bureau (see "Visitor Information," earlier in this chapter) or by writing the Metro-Dade Transit System, 3300 NW 32nd Ave., Miami, FL 33142. In Miami, call ✆ **305/770-3131** for public-transit information. The fare is $2.

BY CAR

Tales circulate about vacationers who have visited Miami without a car, but they are very few indeed. If you are counting on exploring the city, even to a modest degree, a car is essential. Miami's restaurants, hotels, and attractions are far from one another, so any other form of transportation is relatively impractical. You won't need a car, however, if you are spending your entire vacation at a resort, are traveling directly to the Port of Miami for a cruise, or are here for a short stay centered on one area of the city, such as South Beach, where everything is within walking distance and parking is a costly nightmare.

When driving across a causeway or through downtown, allow extra time to reach your destination because of frequent drawbridge openings. Some bridges open about every half-hour for large sailing vessels to make their way through the wide bays and canals that crisscross the city, stalling traffic for several minutes.

RENTALS It seems as though every car-rental company, big and small, has at least one office in Miami. Consequently, the city is one of the cheapest places in the world to rent a car. Many firms regularly advertise prices in the neighborhood of $150 per week for their economy cars. You should also check with your airline: There are often special discounts when you book a flight and reserve your rental car simultaneously. A minimum age, generally 25, is usually required of renters; some rental agencies have also set maximum ages! A national car-rental broker, **Car Rental Referral Service** (© **800/404-4482**), can often find companies willing to rent to drivers between the ages of 21 and 24 and can also get discounts from major companies as well as some regional ones.

National car-rental companies include **Alamo, Avis, Budget, Dollar, Hertz, National,** and **Thrifty.** One excellent company that has offices in every conceivable part of town and offers extremely competitive rates is **Enterprise.** Comparison shop before you make any decisions—car-rental prices can fluctuate more than airfares. For contact information, please see "Appendix: Fast Facts, Toll-Free Numbers & Websites" on p. 638.

Many car-rental companies also offer cellular phones or rentals with GPS. It might be wise to opt for these additional safety features (the phone will definitely come in handy if you get lost), although the cost can be exorbitant.

Finally, think about splurging on a convertible. Not only are convertibles one of the best ways to see the beautiful surroundings, but they're also an ideal way to perfect a tan!

PARKING Always keep plenty of quarters on hand to feed hungry meters, most of which have been removed in favor of those pesky parking payment stations where you feed a machine and get a printed receipt to display on your dash. Or, on Miami Beach, stop by the chamber of commerce at 1920 Meridian Ave. or any Publix grocery store to buy a magnetic **parking card** in denominations of $10, $20, or $25. Parking is usually plentiful (except on South Beach and Coconut Grove), but when it's not, be careful: Fines for illegal parking can be stiff, starting at $18 for an expired meter and going way up from there.

In addition to parking garages, valet services are commonplace and often used. Because parking is such a premium in bustling South Beach as well as in Coconut Grove, prices tend to be jacked up—especially at night and when there are special events (day or night). You can expect to pay an average of $5 to $15 for parking in these areas.

LOCAL DRIVING RULES Florida law allows drivers to make a right turn on a red light after a complete stop, unless otherwise indicated. In addition, all passengers are required to wear seat belts, and children 2 and under must be securely fastened in government-approved car seats.

BY TAXI

If you're not planning on traveling much within the city (and especially if you plan on spending your vacation within the confines of South Beach's Art Deco District), an occasional taxi is a good alternative to renting a car and dealing with the parking hassles that come with renting your own car. Taxi meters start at about $2.50 for the first quarter-mile and cost around $2.40 for each additional mile. You can blame the rate hikes on the gas crunch. There are standard flat-rate charges for frequently traveled routes—for example, Miami Beach's Convention Center to Coconut Grove will cost about $25. During 2008's roller coaster year of insane oil prices, many cabs instituted a fuel surcharge costing $1 extra per person. For specifics on rate increases and surcharges, go to www.taxifarefinder.com.

Major cab companies include **Yellow Cab** (✆ **305/444-4444**) and, on Miami Beach, **Central** (✆ **305/532-5555**).

BY BIKE

Miami is a biker's paradise, especially on Miami Beach, where the hard-packed sand and boardwalks make it an easy and scenic route. However, unless you are a former New York City bike messenger, you won't want to use a bicycle as your main means of transportation.

For more information on bicycles, including where to rent the best ones, see "More Ways to Play, Indoors & Out," in chapter 6.

Fast Facts Miami

Airport See "Orientation," earlier in this chapter.

American Express You'll find American Express offices in downtown Miami at 100 N. Biscayne Blvd. (✆ **305/358-7350;** Mon–Fri 9am–5pm); 9700 Collins Ave., Bal Harbour (✆ **305/865-5959;** Mon–Sat 10am–6pm); and 32 Miracle Mile, Coral Gables (✆ **305/446-3381;** Mon–Fri 9am–5pm and Sat 10am–4pm). To report lost or stolen traveler's checks, call ✆ **800/221-7282.**

Area Code The original area code for Miami and all of Dade County is 305. That is still the code for older phone numbers, but all phone numbers assigned since July 1998 have the area code 786 (SUN). For all local calls, even if you're just calling across the street, you must dial the area code (305 or 786) first. Even though the Keys still share the Dade County area code of 305, calls to there from Miami are considered long distance and must be preceded by 1-305. (Within the Keys, simply dial the seven-digit number.) The area code for Fort Lauderdale is 954; for Palm Beach, Boca Raton, Vero Beach, and Port St. Lucie, it's 561.

Business Hours Banking hours vary, but most banks are open weekdays from 9am to 3pm. Several stay open until 5pm or so at least 1 day during the week, and most banks feature automated teller machines (ATMs) for 24-hour banking. Most stores are open daily from 10am to 6pm; however, there are many exceptions (noted in "Shopping," in chapter 6, beginning on p. 170). As far as business offices are concerned, Miami is generally a 9-to-5 town.

Car Rentals See "Getting Around," above.

Climate See "When to Go," in chapter 3.

Curfew Although not strictly enforced, there is an alleged curfew in effect for minors after 11pm on weeknights and midnight on weekends in all of Miami-Dade County. After those hours, children younger than 17 cannot be out on the streets or driving unless accompanied by a parent or on their way to work. Somehow, however, they still manage to sneak out and congregate in popular areas such as Coconut Grove and South Beach.

Dentists **A&E Dental Associates,** 11400 N. Kendall Dr., Mega Bank Building (✆ **305/271-7777**), offers round-the-clock care and accepts MasterCard and Visa.

Doctors In an emergency, call an ambulance by dialing ✆ **911** (a free call) from any phone. The Dade County Medical Association sponsors a **Physician Referral Service** (✆ **305/324-8717**), weekdays from 9am to 5pm. **Health South Doctors' Hospital,** 5000 University Dr., Coral Gables (✆ **305/666-2111**), is a 285-bed acute-care hospital with a 24-hour physician-staffed emergency department.

Driving Rules See "Getting Around," above.

Drugstores See "Pharmacies," below.

Emergencies To reach the police, an ambulance, or the fire department, dial ✆ **911** from any phone. No coins are needed. Emergency hotlines include **Crisis Intervention** (✆ **305/358-HELP** [4357] or 305/358-4357) and the **Poison Information Center** (✆ **800/222-1222**).

Eyeglasses **Pearle Vision Center,** 7901 Biscayne Blvd. (✆ **305/754-5144**), can usually fill prescriptions in about an hour.

Hospitals See "Doctors," above.

Information See "Visitor Information," earlier in this chapter.

Internet Access Internet access is available at **Kafka's Cyber Cafe,** 1464 Washington Ave., South Beach (✆ **305/673-9669**); the **South Beach Internet Cafe,** 1106 Collins Ave. (✆ **305/532-4331**); and, no joke, the swanky all-in-one **Mobil Station,** at 2500 NW 87th Ave., Doral (✆ **305/477-2501**).

Laundry & Dry Cleaning **Clean Machine Laundry,** 226 12th St., South Beach (✆ **305/534-9429**), is convenient to South Beach's Art Deco hotels and is open 24 hours a day. **Coral Gables Laundry & Dry Cleaning,** 250 Minorca Ave., Coral Gables (✆ **305/446-6458**), has been dry cleaning, altering, and laundering since 1930. It offers a lifesaving same-day service and is open weekdays from 7am to 7pm and Saturday from 8am to 3pm.

Liquor Laws Only adults 21 or older may legally purchase or consume alcohol in the state of Florida. Minors are usually permitted in bars, as long as the bars also serve food. Liquor laws are strictly enforced; if you look young, carry identification. Beer and wine are sold in most supermarkets and convenience stores. The city of Miami's liquor stores are closed on Sunday. Liquor stores in the city of Miami Beach are open daily.

Lost Property If you lost something at the airport, call the **Airport Lost and Found** office (✆ **305/876-7377**). If you lost something on the bus, Metrorail, or Metromover, call **Metro-Dade Transit Agency** (✆ **305/770-3131**). If you lost something anywhere else, phone the **Dade County Police Lost and Found** (✆ **305/375-3366**). You may also want to fill out a police report for insurance purposes.

Luggage Storage & Lockers In addition to the baggage check at Miami International Airport, most hotels offer luggage-storage facilities. If you are taking a cruise from the Port of Miami, bags can be stored in your ship's departure terminal.

Newspapers & Magazines The ***Miami Herald*** is the city's only English-language daily. It is especially known for its extensive Latin American coverage and has a decent Friday "Weekend" entertainment guide. The most respected alternative weekly is the giveaway tabloid called ***New Times,*** which contains up-to-date listings and reviews of food, films, theater, music, and whatever else is happening in town. Also free, if you can find it, is ***Ocean Drive,*** an oversize glossy magazine that's limited on text (no literary value) and heavy on ads and society photos. It's what you should read if you want to know who's who and where to go for fun; it's available at a number of chic South Beach boutiques and restaurants. It is also available at newsstands.

For a large selection of foreign-language newspapers and magazines, check with any of the large bookstores or try **News Cafe,** 800 Ocean Dr., South Beach (✆ **305/538-6397**). Adjacent to the **Van Dyke Cafe,** 846 Lincoln Rd., South Beach (✆ **305/534-3600**), is a fantastic newsstand with magazines and newspapers from all over the world. Also check out **Eddie's News,** 1096 Normandy Dr., Miami Beach (✆ **305/866-2661**), and **Worldwide News,** 1629 NE 163rd St., North Miami Beach (✆ **305/940-4090**).

Pharmacies **Walgreens Pharmacy** has dozens of locations all over town, including 8550 Coral Way (✆ **305/221-9271**), in Coral Gables; 1845 Alton Rd. (✆ **305/531-8868**), in South Beach; and 6700 Collins Ave. (✆ **305/861-6742**), in Miami Beach. The branch at 5731 Bird Rd., at SW 40th Street (✆ **305/666-0757**), is open 24 hours, as is **CVS,** 6460 S. Dixie Hwy., in South Miami (✆ **305/661-0778**).

Photographic Needs Walgreens and CVS (see above, under "Pharmacies") or Eckerd will develop film for the next day for about $10. Both will also print digital photos for less than $0.20 each, usually in under an hour. See www.walgreens.com and www.cvs.com for many locations.

Police For emergencies, dial ✆ **911** from any phone. No coins are needed for this call. For other police matters, call ✆ **305/595-6263.**

Post Office The **Main Post Office,** 2200 Milam Dairy Rd., Miami, FL 33152 (✆ **800/275-8777**), is located west of the Miami International Airport. Conveniently located post offices include 1300 Washington Ave. in South Beach and 3191 Grand Ave. in Coconut Grove. There is one central number for all post offices: ✆ **800/275-8777.**

Radio On the AM dial, 610 (WIOD), 790 (WNWS), 1230 (WJNO), and 1340 (WPBR) are all talk. There is no all-news station in town, although 940 (WINZ) gives traffic updates and headline news in between its talk shows. WDBF (1420) is a good big-band station, and WPBG (1290) features golden oldies. Switching to the FM dial, the two most popular R&B stations are WEDR/99 Jams (99.1) and Hot 105 (105.1). The best rock stations on the FM dial are WPYM/93 Rock (93.1), WBGG/Big 106 (105.9), and the progressive college station WVUM (90.5). WKIS (99.9) is the top country station. Top-40 music can be heard on WHYI (100.3), and hip-hop on Mega 103 (103.5). For more hip-hop and dance music, Power 96 (96.5) WPOW will help you get your groove on. WGTR (97.3) plays easy listening, WDNA (88.9) has the best Latin jazz and multiethnic sounds, and public radio can be heard either on WXEL (90.7) or WLRN (91.3).

Religious Services Miami houses of worship are as varied as the city's population and include St. Patrick Catholic Church, 3716 Garden Ave., Miami Beach (✆ **305/531-1124**); Coral Gables Baptist Church, 5501 Granada Blvd. (✆ **305/665-4072**); Temple Judea, 5500 Granada Blvd., Coral Gables (✆ **305/667-5657**); Coconut Grove United Methodist, 2850 SW 27th Ave. (✆ **305/443-0880**); Christ Episcopal Church, 3481 Hibiscus St., Coconut Grove (✆ **305/442-8542**); Plymouth Congregational Church, 3400 Devon Rd., at Main Highway, Coconut Grove (✆ **305/444-6521**); Masjid Al-Ansar (Muslim), 5245 NW 7th Ave., Miami (✆ **305/757-8741**); and Buddhist Temple of Miami, 15200 SW 240th St., Homestead (✆ **305/245-2702**).

Restrooms Stores rarely let customers use their restrooms, and many restaurants offer their facilities only for their patrons. However, most malls have restrooms, as do many fast-food restaurants. Public beaches and large parks often provide toilets, though in some places you have to pay or tip an attendant. Most large hotels have clean restrooms in their lobbies.

Safety As always, use your common sense and be aware of your surroundings at all times. Don't walk alone at night, and be extra wary when walking or driving though downtown Miami and surrounding areas.

Reacting to several highly publicized crimes against tourists several years ago, local and state governments alike have taken steps to help protect visitors. These measures include special highly visible police units patrolling the airport and surrounding neighborhoods, and better signs on the state's most tourist-traveled routes.

Taxes A 6% state sales tax (plus 1% local tax, for a total of 7% in Miami-Dade County [from Homestead to North Miami Beach]) is added on at the register for all goods and services purchased in Florida. In addition, most municipalities levy special taxes on restaurants and hotels. In Surfside, hotel taxes total 10.5%; in Bal Harbour, 9.5%; in Miami Beach (including South Beach), 11.5%; and in the rest of Dade County, a whopping 12.5%. In Miami Beach, Surfside, and Bal Harbour, the resort (hotel) tax also applies to hotel restaurants and restaurants with liquor licenses.

Taxis See "Getting Around," earlier in this chapter.

Television The local stations are channel 4, WFOR (CBS); channel 6, WTVJ (NBC); channel 7, WSVN (FOX); channel 10, WPLG (ABC); channel 17, WLRN (PBS); channel 23, WLTV (independent); and channel 33, WBFS (independent). Channel 39 is the CW (WBZL), and channel 33 is UPN (WBFS).

Time Zone Miami, like New York, is in the Eastern Standard Time (EST) zone. Between the second Sunday of March and the first Sunday of November, daylight saving time is adopted, and clocks are set 1 hour ahead. America's eastern seaboard is 5 hours behind Greenwich Mean Time. To find out what time it is, call ✆ **305/324-8811.**

Transit Information For Metrorail or Metromover schedule information, phone ✆ **305/770-3131** or surf over to www.co.miami-dade.fl.us/mdta.

Weather Hurricane season in Miami runs June through November. For an up-to-date recording of current weather conditions and forecast reports, call ✆ **305/ 229-4522.** Also see the "When to Go" section in chapter 3 for more information on the weather.

3 WHERE TO STAY IN MIAMI

As much a part of the landscape as the palm trees, many of Miami's hotels are on display as if they were contestants in a beauty pageant. The city's long-lasting status on the destination A-list has given rise to an ever-increasing number of upscale hotels, and no place in Miami has seen a greater increase in construction than Miami Beach. Since the area's renaissance, which began in the late 1980s, the beach has turned what used to be a beachfront retirement community into a sand-swept hot spot for the Gucci and Prada set. Contrary to popular belief, however, the beach does not discriminate, and it's the juxtaposition of the chic elite and the hoi polloi that contributes to its allure.

While the increasing demand for rooms on South Beach means increasing costs, you can still find a decent room at a fair price. In fact, most hotels in the Art Deco District are less Ritz-Carlton than they are Holiday Inn, unless, of course, they've been renovated (many hotels in this area were built in the 1930s for the middle class). Unless you plan your vacation entirely in and around your hotel, most of the cheaper Deco hotels are adequate and a wise choice for those who plan to use the room only to sleep. Smart vacationers can almost name their price if they're willing to live without a few luxuries, such as an oceanfront view.

Many of the old hotels from the 1930s, 1940s, and 1950s have been totally renovated, giving way to dozens of "boutique" (small, swanky, and, for the most part, independently owned) hotels. Keep in mind that when a hotel claims that it was just renovated, it can mean that they've completely gutted the building—or just applied a coat of fresh paint. Always ask what specific changes were made during a renovation, and be sure to ask if a hotel will be undergoing construction while you're there. You should also find out how near your room will be to the center of the nightlife crowd; trying to sleep directly on Ocean Drive or Collins and Washington avenues, especially during the weekend, is next to impossible, unless your lullaby of choice happens to include throbbing salsa and bass beats.

The best hotel options in each price category and those that have been fully upgraded recently are listed below. You should also know that along South Beach's Collins Avenue, there are dozens of hotels and motels—in all price categories—so there's bound to be a vacancy somewhere. If you do try the walk-in routine, don't forget to ask to see a room first. A few dollars extra could mean all the difference between fleabag and fabulous.

While South Beach may be the nucleus of all things hyped and hip, it's not the only place with hotels. The advantage to staying on South Beach as opposed to, say, Coral Gables or Coconut Grove, is that the beaches are within walking distance, the nightlife and restaurant options are aplenty, and, basically, everything you need is right there. However, staying there is definitely not for everyone. If you're wary, don't worry: South Beach is centrally located and only about a 15- to 30-minute drive from most other parts of Miami.

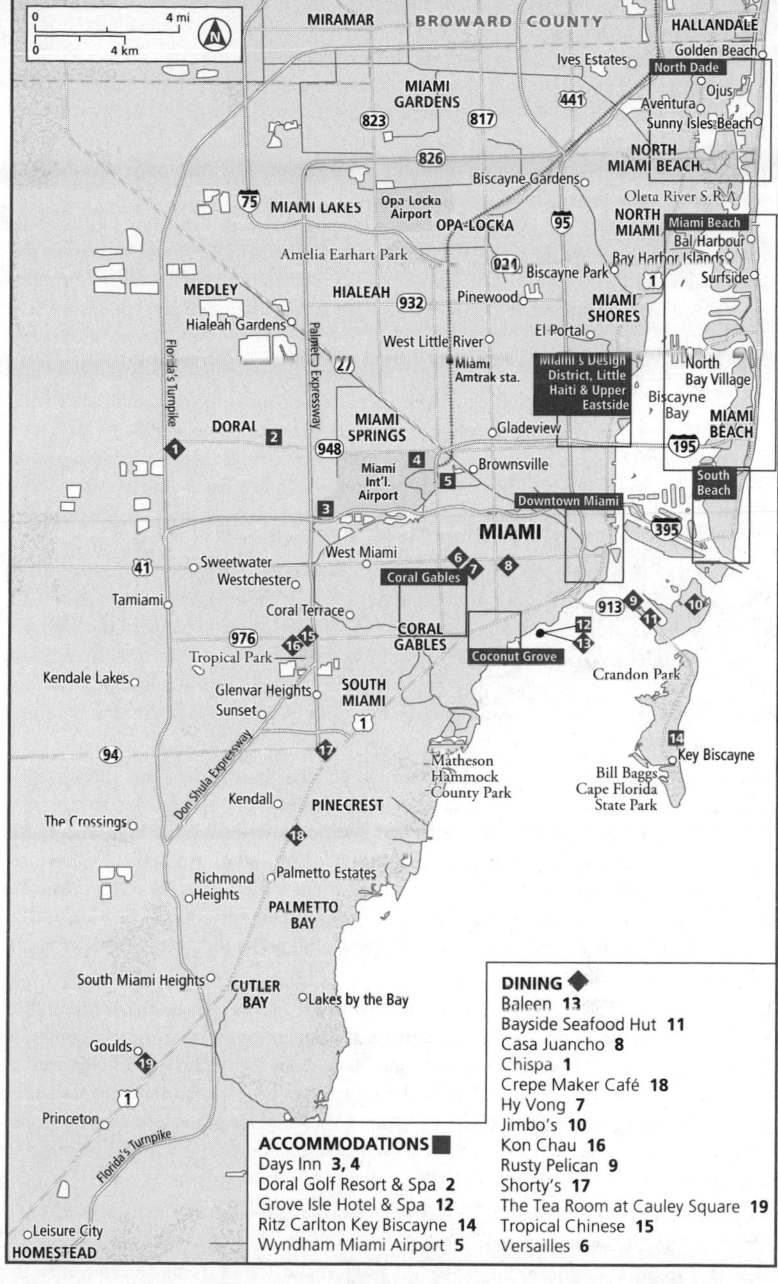
MIRAMAR
BROWARD COUNTY
HALLANDALE
Golden Beach
Ives Estates
North Dade
Ojus
Aventura
Sunny Isles Beach
MIAMI GARDENS
NORTH MIAMI BEACH
Biscayne Gardens
Oleta River S.R.A.
MIAMI LAKES
Opa Locka Airport
OPA-LOCKA
NORTH MIAMI
Miami Beach
Bal Harbour
Amelia Earhart Park
Bay Harbor Islands
Biscayne Park
Surfside
MEDLEY
HIALEAH
Pinewood
MIAMI SHORES
Hialeah Gardens
El Portal
West Little River
Florida's Turnpike
Palmetto Expressway
Miami Amtrak sta.
Miami's Design District, Little Haiti & Upper Eastside
North Bay Village
Biscayne Bay
DORAL
MIAMI SPRINGS
Gladeview
MIAMI BEACH
Brownsville
Miami Int'l. Airport
South Beach
Downtown Miami
MIAMI
Sweetwater
West Miami
Westchester
Coral Gables
Tamiami
Coral Terrace
CORAL GABLES
Tropical Park
Coconut Grove
Crandon Park
Kendale Lakes
Glenvar Heights
SOUTH MIAMI
Sunset
Don Shula Expressway
Key Biscayne
Matheson Hammock County Park
Bill Baggs Cape Florida State Park
Kendall
PINECREST
The Crossings
Richmond Heights
Palmetto Estates
PALMETTO BAY
South Miami Heights
CUTLER BAY
Lakes by the Bay
Goulds
Princeton
Florida's Turnpike
Leisure City
HOMESTEAD
0 4 mi
0 4 km
DINING
Baleen 13
Bayside Seafood Hut 11
Casa Juancho 8
Chispa 1
Crepe Maker Café 18
Hy Vong 7
Jimbo's 10
Kon Chau 16
Rusty Pelican 9
Shorty's 17
The Tea Room at Cauley Square 19
Tropical Chinese 15
Versailles 6
ACCOMMODATIONS
Days Inn 3, 4
Doral Golf Resort & Spa 2
Grove Isle Hotel & Spa 12
Ritz Carlton Key Biscayne 14
Wyndham Miami Airport 5

For a less expensive stay that's only a 10-minute cab ride from South Beach, Miami Beach proper (the area north of 23rd St. and Collins Ave. all the way up to 163rd St. and Collins Ave.) offers a slew of reasonable stays, right on the beach, that won't cost you your kids' college education fund.

What *will* cost you a small fortune are the luxury hotels in the city's financial Brickell Avenue district, the area of choice for expense-account business travelers and camera-shy celebrities trying to avoid the South Beach spotlight.

For a less frenetic, more relaxed, and more tropical experience, the ritzy resort on Key Biscayne exudes an island feel, even though, across the water, a cosmopolitan vibe beckons, thanks to the shimmering, spectacular Miami skyline.

Those who'd rather bag the beach in favor of shopping bags will enjoy North Miami Beach's proximity to the Aventura Mall. For Miami with an Old World European flair, Coral Gables and its charming hotels and exquisite restaurants provide a more prim and proper, well-heeled perspective of Miami than the trendy boutique and condo hotels on South Beach.

SEASONS & RATES South Florida's tourist season is well-defined, beginning in mid-November and lasting until Easter. Hotel prices escalate until about March, after which they begin to decline. During the off-season, hotel rates are typically 30% to 50% lower than their winter highs. But timing isn't everything. Rates also depend on your hotel's proximity to the beach and how much ocean you can see from your window. Small motels a block or two from the water can be up to 40% cheaper than similar properties right on the sand.

The rates listed below are broken down into two broad categories: winter (generally, Thanksgiving through Easter) and off-season (about mid-May through Aug). The months in between, the shoulder season, should fall somewhere in between the highs and lows, while rates always go up on holidays. Remember, too, that state and city taxes can add as much as 12.5% to your bill in some parts of Miami. Some hotels, especially those in South Beach, also tack on additional service charges, and don't forget that parking is a pricey endeavor.

PRICE CATEGORIES The hotels below are divided first by area and then by price (**very expensive, expensive, moderate,** or **inexpensive**). Price categories are based on published rates (or rack rates) for a standard double room during the high season. You should also check with the reservations agent, as many rooms are available above and below the category ranges listed below; and ask about packages, as it's often possible to get a better deal than these "official" rates. Most important, always call the hotel to confirm rates, which may be subject to change without notice because of special events, holidays, or blackout dates.

LONG-TERM STAYS If you plan to visit Miami for a month, a season, or more, think about renting a condominium apartment or a room in a long-term hotel. Long-term accommodations exist in every price category, from budget to deluxe, and in general are extremely reasonable, especially during the off-season. Check with the reservation services below, or write a short note to the chamber of commerce in the area where you plan to stay. In addition, many local real estate agents handle short-term rentals (meaning less than a year).

RESERVATION SERVICES **Central Reservation Service** (© **800/950-0232** or 305/274-6832; www.reservation-services.com) works with many of Miami's hotels and can often secure discounts of up to 40%. It also gives advice on specific locales, especially in Miami Beach and downtown. During holiday time, there may be a 3- to 5-day minimum stay required to use their services. Call for more information.

For bed-and-breakfast information throughout the state, contact **Florida Bed and Breakfast Inns** (✆ **800/524-1880;** www.florida-inns.com). For information on the ubiquitous boutique hotels, check out the **Greater Miami Convention and Visitor's Bureau**'s new website, www.miamiboutiquehotels.com.

SOUTH BEACH

Choosing a hotel on South Beach is similar to deciding whether you'd rather pay $2 for french fries at Denny's or $12 for the same fries—but let's call them *pommes frites,* and add $2 for some fancy salt from a fancy resort town on the Mediterranean—in a pricey haute-cuisine restaurant. It's all about atmosphere. The rooms of some hotels may *look* ultrachic, but they are as comfortable as sleeping on a concrete slab. Once you decide how much atmosphere you want, the choice will be easier. Fortunately, for every chichi hotel in South Beach—and there are many—there are just as many moderately priced, more casual options.

Prices mentioned here are rack rates—that is, the price you would be quoted if you walked up to the front desk and inquired about rates. The actual price you will end up paying will usually be less than this—especially if a travel agent makes the reservations for you. Many hotels on South Beach have chosen to go with a low-to-high rate representing the hotel's complete pricing range. It pays to try to negotiate the price of a room. In some of the trendier hotels, however, negotiating is highly unfashionable and not well regarded. In other words, your attempt at negotiation will either be met with a blank stare or a snippy refusal. It never hurts to try, though.

If status is important to you, as it is to many South Beach visitors, then you will be quite pleased with the number of haute hotels in the area. But the times may be a-changin': **Courtyard by Marriott** (✆ **800/321-2211** or 305/604-8887) maintains a 90-room, moderately priced hotel on a seedy stretch of Washington Avenue, smack in the middle of Clubland, a horror to many a South Beach trend-seeker.

Note: Art Deco hotels, while pleasing to the eye, may be a bit run-down inside. It's par for the course on South Beach, where appearances are, at times, deceiving.

To locate the hotels in this section, see the "South Beach Accommodations & Dining" map (p. 91).

Very Expensive

The Angler's Resort ★ Opened in 2007, the Angler's isn't your typical South Beach boutique hotel in that here, *service*—not surface—is paramount. Located 2 blocks from the beach, the hotel is a unique collection of four very different buildings—two completely restored and two brand new buildings offering a variety of accommodations from suites and duplexes to triplex villas. All rooms feature the typical luxury comforts of Wi-Fi, flatscreen TVs, and iPod. Not so typical: One remote control works on all of these features—even the internal and external lights. An outdoor pool is surrounded by gardens. For those who'd rather do the beach than the pool, stop by the front desk to pick up a beach goodie bag complete with sunscreen, toys, water, snacks, and even the latest best-selling novel. Novel, indeed.

660 Washington Ave., South Beach, FL 33139. ✆ **305/534-9600.** Fax 305/532-3099. www.theanglersresort.com. 46 fully furnished residences, including suites and villas. Winter Studio Suites $225–$495; Duplex Suites $500–$1,200. AE, DISC, MC, V. Valet parking $19 per night. Pets accepted. **Amenities:** Restaurant; poolside dining cabanas; beach concession; pool; indoor and poolside spa services; 24-hr.

concierge service; room service; Wi-Fi; private rooftop terraces and gardens. *In room:* A/C, flatscreen TV/DVD, minibar, hair dryer, safe, iPod docking station.

Delano ★ Though Madonna and Beyoncé may choose the Setai over the Delano these days, it doesn't mean South Beach's original see-and-be-seen hotel is over just yet. The stunning pool area, Rose Bar, Agua Spa, Lenny Kravitz–designed speakeasy The Florida Room, and Blue Door restaurant are still studded with the boldface and the beautiful; but today, the Delano, a place where smiles from staffers were as rare as snow in Miami, is somewhat kinder and gentler. The fact that Delano's parent company, Morgans Hotel Group, scrapped plans to expand the Delano in favor of opening a less expensive Delano-esque hotel across the street speaks volumes. But it certainly is still amusing to look at—with 40-foot sheer white billowing curtains hanging outside, mirrors everywhere, Adirondack chairs, and faux fur–covered beds. Rooms that were once done up sanitarium-style, sterile yet terribly trendy, just received a revamp that boasts a splash of color and reworked bathrooms that went from spartan to spacious.

1685 Collins Ave., South Beach, FL 33139. ✆ **800/555-5001** or 305/672-2000. Fax 305/532-0099. www.delano-hotel.com. 194 units, including 1 penthouse. Winter $475–$825 standard, $1,250–$2,600 suite, $2,200–$3,500 bungalow or 2-bedroom, $4,000–$6,000 penthouse; off-season $425–$745 standard, $1,200–$2,300 suite, $1,700–$3,200 bungalow or 2-bedroom, $4,000–$5,500 penthouse. Additional person $50. AE, DC, DISC, MC, V. Valet parking $37. **Amenities:** 3 restaurants (featuring the acclaimed Blue Door); The Florida Room, Rose Bar, and pool Bar; large outdoor pool; state-of-the-art gym; spa; children's programs; concierge; business center; room service; in-room massage; same-day laundry and dry-cleaning services. *In room:* A/C, TV/DVD, Wi-Fi, minibar, hair dryer, safe, CD player,, Bose iPod docking station.

Gansevoort South ★ One of NYC's hippest hotels opened on South Beach in January 2008 much to the delight of hipsters, jet-setters, and the scene-obsessed. This 334-room hotel features the flagship David Barton Gym and Spa, expansive oceanview rooftop pool and bar, trendy meatery STK, a restaurant by Philippe Chow, and, inexplicably, a shark tank with 27 types of fish and sharks that spans 50 feet of the terminally trendy lobby. A 26,000-square-foot rooftop playground (complete with a 110-ft. elevated swimming pool, Plunge bar, and lounge) offers divine views of the ocean, the bay, and downtown. On the main level is a 40,000-square-foot semicircular oceanfront pool plaza with infinity edge pool, teak decking, and cabanas. Room furniture screams hot pink, magenta, and yellow, set against charcoal-gray suede walls dotted with pictures of '40s pinup girls. Most rooms have balconies overlooking the ocean.

2377 Collins Ave., South Beach, FL 33139. ✆ **305/604-1000.** Fax 305/604-6886. www.gansevoortsouth.com. 334 units. $300–$495 deluxe double or king; $685–$1,000 suite. AE, DC, DISC, MC, V. Valet parking for $15 per night. **Amenities:** 2 restaurants; bar and lounge; beachfront lounge; infinity-edge rooftop pool; fitness center; spa; concierge; salon; 24-hr. room service. *In room:* A/C, TV/DVD, Wi-Fi, minibar, hair dryer, safe, CD player, iPod docking stations.

Hotel Victor ★★ A victory for Ocean Drive, a street that hasn't seen such a swank stay since the Tides, Hotel Victor is a hyperluxe, 88-room boutique see-and-be-seen hotel designed by Parisian Jacques Garcia—this is his first hotel foray in the U.S. Best known for his design work at Paris's tragically hip Hotel Costes and the discriminating Sultan of Brunei, Garcia has lent his exquisite taste to this hotel located on notoriously tacky Ocean Drive. The hotel's cabana-dotted pool and bistro Vix have become command central for hipsters and celebrities—especially on Thursday nights and Saturday afternoons. Directly across from the ocean, Hotel Victor stands apart from the rest of the cookie-cutter minimalist Miami hotels, breaking from bare minimalism and daring to go

South Beach Accommodations & Dining

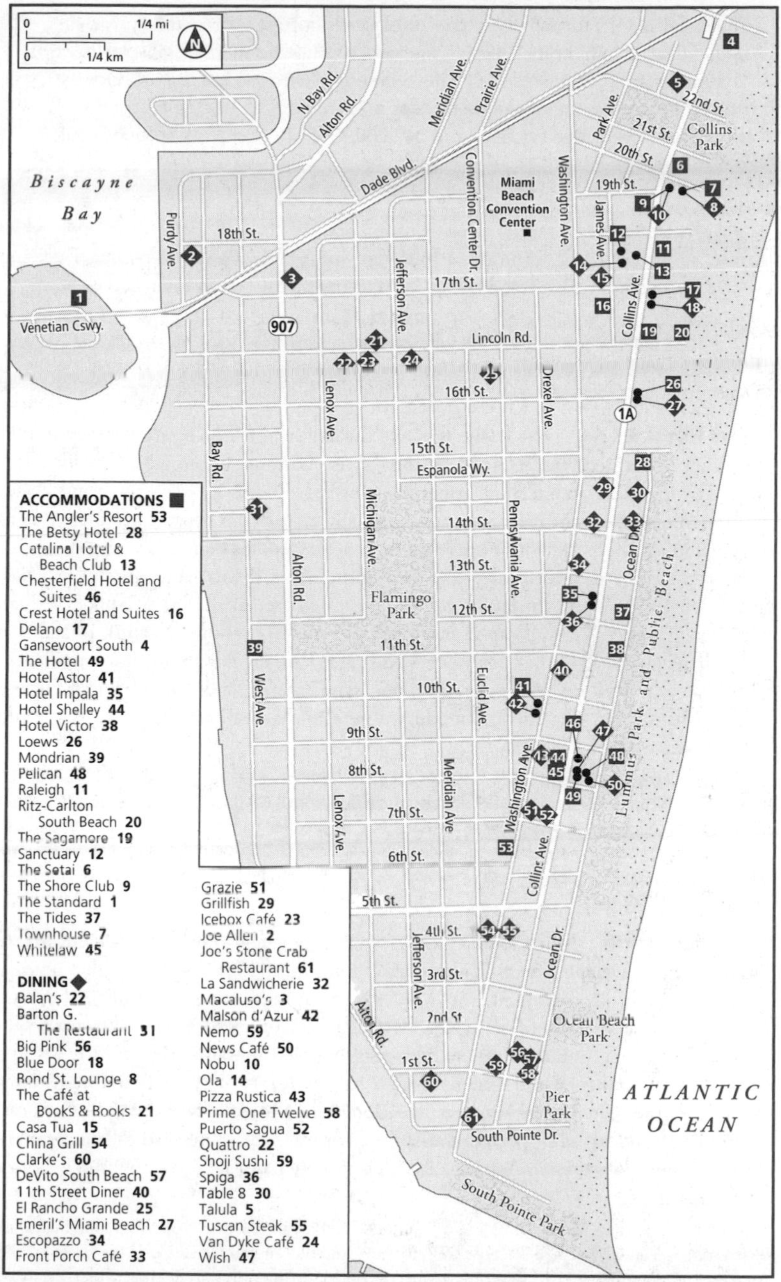

ACCOMMODATIONS ■

- The Angler's Resort **53**
- The Betsy Hotel **28**
- Catalina Hotel & Beach Club **13**
- Chesterfield Hotel and Suites **46**
- Crest Hotel and Suites **16**
- Delano **17**
- Gansevoort South **4**
- The Hotel **49**
- Hotel Astor **41**
- Hotel Impala **35**
- Hotel Shelley **44**
- Hotel Victor **38**
- Loews **26**
- Mondrian **39**
- Pelican **48**
- Raleigh **11**
- Ritz-Carlton South Beach **20**
- The Sagamore **19**
- Sanctuary **12**
- The Setai **6**
- The Shore Club **9**
- The Standard **1**
- The Tides **37**
- Townhouse **7**
- Whitelaw **45**

DINING ◆

- Balan's **22**
- Barton G. The Restaurant **31**
- Big Pink **56**
- Blue Door **18**
- Bond St. Lounge **8**
- The Café at Books & Books **21**
- Casa Tua **15**
- China Grill **54**
- Clarke's **60**
- DeVito South Beach **57**
- 11th Street Diner **40**
- El Rancho Grande **25**
- Emeril's Miami Beach **27**
- Escopazzo **34**
- Front Porch Café **33**
- Grazie **51**
- Grillfish **29**
- Icebox Café **23**
- Joe Allen **2**
- Joe's Stone Crab Restaurant **61**
- La Sandwicherie **32**
- Macaluso's **3**
- Maison d'Azur **42**
- Nemo **59**
- News Café **50**
- Nobu **10**
- Ola **14**
- Pizza Rustica **43**
- Prime One Twelve **58**
- Puerto Sagua **52**
- Quattro **22**
- Shoji Sushi **59**
- Spiga **36**
- Table 8 **30**
- Talula **5**
- Tuscan Steak **55**
- Van Dyke Café **24**
- Wish **47**

A Turkish Spa at the Victor

The Hotel Victor's Turkish-style spa is the hotel's hottest spot—literally, with its large unisex steam room, Turkish hammam, and heated marble slabs. ***Insider tip:*** Shaunie O'Neal, Shaquille's (ex?) wife, teamed up with the spa to introduce its newest treatment, the Miami Heat ritual, a 75-minute full-body massage to relax and restore overactive bodies—and, at $200, to drain your bank account, too!

bold with color and rich fabrics. Deluxe rooms are just that, all with ocean views, white marble, ebony-lacquered furniture, a full—not mini—bar, flatscreen plasma TVs, and massive white-marbled bathrooms with infinity-edge bathtubs and rain showerheads.

1144 Ocean Dr., South Beach, FL 33139. ✆ **305/428-1234.** Fax 305/421-6281. www.hotelvictorsouthbeach.com. 88 units. Winter $470–$1,045 suite; off-season $289–$659 suite. AE, DC, DISC, MC, V. Valet parking $32. **Amenities:** 2 restaurants; 2 bars; outdoor pool; 6,000-sq.-ft. fitness center, spa, and Turkish hammam; concierge; room service. *In room:* A/C, TV/DVD, Wi-Fi, minibar, hair dryer, stereo/CD player.

Loews Hotel ★ Kids The Loews is one of the largest hotels on South Beach, consuming an unprecedented 900 feet of oceanfront. This 790-room behemoth is considered an eyesore by many, an architectural triumph by others. Rooms are a bit boxy and bland, nothing to rave about, but are clean and have new carpets and bedspreads to erase signs of wear and tear from the hotel's heavy traffic. The best rooms do not face very congested Collins Avenue, as rooms that do tend to be quite noisy. If you can steer your way past all the conventioneers in the lobby, you can escape to the equally massive pool (with an undisputedly gorgeous, landscaped entrance that's more Maui than Miami). In addition to children's fare, such as the Loews Loves Kids program, the hotel hosts fun activities for adults, such as Dive in Movies at the pool, salsa lessons, and bingo. Emeril Lagasse opened Miami's first-ever Emeril's restaurant here, and a new sprawling Elemis Spa and Fitness Center debuted in 2007.

1601 Collins Ave., South Beach, FL 33139. ✆ **800/23-LOEWS** (5-6397) or 305/604-1601. www.loewshotels.com. 790 units. Winter from $499 double; off-season from $289 double. AE, DC, DISC, MC, V. Valet parking $30. Pets accepted. **Amenities:** 4 restaurants; 2 bars; coffee bar; sprawling outdoor pool; health club; spa; Jacuzzi; sauna; watersports equipment/rentals; children's programs; concierge; business center; 24-hr. room service; babysitting; dry cleaning. *In room:* A/C, TV, high-speed Internet access, minibar, coffeemaker, hair dryer.

Mondrian ★★★ Much to everyone's surprise, the latest offering from the Morgans Hotel Group of Delano fame isn't just another humdrum, been-there-done-that homage to all things painfully trendy. Sure, it's painfully trendy, but it's also refreshingly different. For one, it's located on the western, residential bay side of South Beach, where its neighbors (and its former incarnation) are high-rise condos. Panoramic views of the bay and skyline are stunning. World-famous design star and *Elle Décor*'s 2006 International Designer of the Year, Marcel Wanders, envisioned the property as Sleeping Beauty's castle, with whimsical adult-playground-style environs. The hotel's so-called "Modern Resort" concept features an Agua spa (of Delano fame) and Jeffrey Chodorow's Asia de Cuba restaurant.

1100 West Ave., Miami Beach, FL 33139. ✆ **305/672-2662.** Fax 305/672-3766. www.mondriansouthbeach.com. 335 units. Winter $645 studio, $2,000 deluxe 2-bedroom suite; off-season $495 studio, $1,595 deluxe 2-bedroom suite. AE, DC, DISC, MC, V. Valet parking $37. **Amenities:** Restaurant; 3 bars; 2 pools (1 for kids); fitness center; Agua spa; watersports equipment/rentals; concierge; 24-hr. room service;

babysitting; dry cleaning; marina and boat slips; banquet/catering; foliage-curtained cabanas; adult sand box; private party rooms. *In room:* A/C, plasma TV, high-speed Internet access, kitchenette, safe.

The Ritz-Carlton South Beach ★★★ Kids Far from ostentatious, the Ritz-Carlton South Beach moves away from gilded opulence in favor of the more soothing pastel-washed touches of Deco. Though South Beach is better known for its trendy boutique hotels, the Ritz-Carlton provides comfort to those who might prefer 100% cotton Frette sheets and goose-down pillows to high-style minimalism. The best rooms, by far, are the 72 poolside and oceanview lanai rooms. There's also a tanning butler who will spritz you with SPF and water whenever you want. With its impeccable service, an elevated pool with unobstructed views of the Atlantic and a weekend DJ, an impressive stretch of sand with a fabulous beach club, and a world-class 13,000-square-foot spa and wellness center, the Ritz-Carlton kicks sand in the faces of some smaller hotels that think they're doing *you* a favor by allowing you to sleep there. Parents love the Ritz Kids program for kids

Hotel Spas

There are a number of great spa packages at some of the ritzier hotels, but those without spas often team up with on-call massage therapists, and your concierge can usually make an appointment for an in-room session. Popular day spas include the **Russian Turkish Baths,** 5445 Collins Ave., at the Castle Hotel (✆ **305/867-8313**), otherwise known as "The Schvitz," where the old guard meets the new in eucalyptus-scented Turkish steam rooms and aroma baths bolstered by marble columns. As far as hotel spas go, these are my three favorites:

The **Spa at Mandarin Oriental** (p. 106) is where the likes of Jennifer Aniston, Jacko, J-Lo, and Diddy are pampered with treatments such as the 4-hour Ultimate Spa Indulgence that includes a welcome foot ritual, purifying herbal linen wrap with hot stones, facial cleanse, body exfoliation, body wrap with fresh algae and nourishing mud, Ayurvedic holistic massage, heated volcanic stones or oil-pouring Shirodhara, herbal tea, two-course lunch, aromatherapy facial, holistic hand and nail treatment, foot and nail treatment, yoga, Oriental bath soak, and choice of Thai massage or shiatsu. You needn't be a celebrity to experience this spa's stellar treatment.

The **Ritz-Carlton, Key Biscayne**'s (p. 104) spa, has 20,000 square feet of space overlooking the Atlantic Ocean. It features unheard-of treatments such as the Rum Molasses Waterfall treatment (a combination massage/hair treatment), the Key Lime Coconut Body Scrub, and the Everglades Grass Body Wrap.

Hip hotelier Andre Balazs pulled out all the stops when renovating the old-school, Borscht Belt–style Lido Spa and transforming it into South Beach's very own branch of L.A.'s hip **Standard Hotel** (p. 97). While Tinseltown's Standards are high, the South Beach version breaks new ground in town as a bona fide spa hotel complete with hundreds of treatments, including an authentic Turkish hammam, the Wall of Sound Shower, a cedar sauna room, and more.

ages 5 through 12; and for gourmands, there's the Ritz's amazing Sunday champagne brunch.

1 Lincoln Rd., South Beach, FL 33139. ✆ **800/241-3333** or 786/276-4000. Fax 786/276-4001. www.ritzcarlton.com. 375 units. Winter $609 double, $1,009 suite; off-season $359 double, $479 suite. AE, DISC, MC, V. Valet parking $36 (overnight), $24 (daily). **Amenities:** 2 restaurants; 2 bars; outdoor heated pool; fitness center; spa; extensive watersports equipment/rentals; children's program; business center; shopping arcade; salon; 24-hr. room service; babysitting; overnight laundry service; beach service. *In room:* A/C, TV, dataport, minibar, hair dryer, iron, safe.

The Sagamore ★★★ Just two doors down from the Delano Hotel is the Sagamore, fabulous in its own right, with an ultramodern lobby-cum-art-gallery-cum-restaurant that's infinitely warmer than your typical pop-art exhibit at the Museum of Modern Art. The hotel doesn't take itself too seriously and boasts a tongue-in-cheek sense of humor that was evidenced when it hosted a Lox and Botox party—no, we're not kidding. Although the lobby and its requisite restaurant, bar, and lounge areas have become command central for the international chic elite and celebrities, the Sagamore's all-suite, apartmentlike rooms are havens from the hype, with all the cushy comforts of home and then some. The sprawling outdoor lawn, dotted with cabanas with plasma TVs screening everything from Japanese anime to digital art, pool, and beachfront makes you realize you're not in Kansas anymore. A new branch of Miami's coiffeur to the stars, Rik Rak, opened in one of the outdoor bungalows; and, in late 2009, a new restaurant, Alchemy, was expected to open by flamboyant caterer/restaurateur Barton G. Weiss.

1671 Collins Ave., South Beach, FL 33139. ✆ **877/SAGAMORE** (724-2667) or 305/535-8088. Fax 305/535-8185. www.sagamorehotel.com. 93 units. Winter $495–$4,500 suite; off-season $245–$3,500 suite. AE, DC, DISC, MC, V. Valet parking $30. **Amenities:** Restaurant; bar; pool bar; pool; fitness center; spa; concierge; salon; room service. *In room:* A/C, TV/VCR/DVD, Wi-Fi, kitchen, minibar, coffeemaker, hair dryer, iron, safe, CD player.

The Sanctuary Hotel of South Beach ★ Set a bit off the beaten path is this modern, all-suite resident hotel (meaning people can actually rent or buy rooms and live here) that takes luxury very seriously, even if it does resemble a souped-up motel, with its ground-floor rooms only accessible from a communal outdoor courtyard area. Flying into town? Let the Sanctuary's Range Rover pick you up at the airport. Soothingly modern, all rooms have full state-of-the-art Italian kitchens, flat plasma-screen televisions, and Wi-Fi. In addition, bathrooms come with Jacuzzi tubs, and in-room fridges are stocked with everything you specify before checking into the hotel. A roof-deck "bedroom" allows you to relax in the sun or slink around in the wading pool. Star chef Douglas Rodriguez recently opened Ola, a fashionable Latin eatery and hot spot situated smack in the middle of the very posh, albeit tiny, lobby.

1745 James Ave., South Beach, FL 33139. ✆ **305/673-5455.** Fax 305/673-3113. www.sanctuarysobe.com. 30 units. Winter $375–$1,500 suite; off-season $215–$1,050 suite. AE, DC, DISC, MC, V. Valet parking $18. **Amenities:** Restaurant; bar; pool bar; rooftop pool; fitness center; spa; concierge; room service. *In room:* A/C, TV/VCR/DVD, Wi-Fi, kitchen, minibar, coffeemaker, hair dryer, iron, safe, CD player.

The Setai ★★★ With bank-busting room rates, dinner tabs coming in at around $200 per person (although 2008 saw the addition of some "recession friendly" prix-fixe menus starting at $55 per person), martinis starting at $15, and a celebrity clientele who doesn't have to ask how much, the Zen-like, Asian-inspired Setai is truly for that 1% of society who can afford it. But if you want to splurge, this is where to do it. All of the suites—some are actually condos participating in the condo-hotel program—are gorgeous apartments with floor-to-ceiling windows, full kitchens, and Jacuzzi bathtubs bigger than a small swimming pool. There are 85 regular hotel rooms that are an average of 600 square feet, compared to the suites' 1,300 to 3,500 square feet. All are adorned in sleek Asian decor with over-the-top comforts, including Lavazza espresso makers, Laura Tonatto bathroom amenities, and washer/dryers. The garden area with reflecting pools is lovely, but not as cool as the pool area with a bar serving $18 burgers to celebrity clientele. The Restaurant, its proper name, is authentically Asian, with stainless-steel tandoori ovens—but with these steep prices and small portions you may as well buy a ticket to Asia.

2001 Collins Ave., South Beach, FL 33139. ✆ **305/520-6000.** Fax 305/520-6600. www.setai.com. 130 units. Winter $1,150 studio suite, $30,000 penthouse; off-season $550 studio suite, price available on request for penthouse. AE, DC, DISC, MC, V. Valet parking $40. **Amenities:** 3 restaurants; 2 bars; 3 pools; fitness center; spa; concierge; 24-hr. room service. *In room:* A/C, TV/DVD, Wi-Fi, kitchen (1-, 2-, and 3-bedroom suites only), minibar, coffeemaker, hair dryer, iron, safe, CD player.

The Shore Club ★ In the fickle world of hot hotels, the Shore Club secures its place at the top, thanks to Florida's only Nobu sushi restaurant and a celebrity clientele that would fill up an entire issue of *Us Weekly*. Because this hotel is infinitely more cavernous than its hipster neighbor, the Delano (see above), publicity-shy celebrities such as Janet Jackson and Denzel Washington have been known to call it their home away from home—there are indeed places for them to hide. An outpost of L.A.'s celebrity-laden SkyBar reigns supreme with a Marrakech-meets-Miami motif that stretches throughout the hotel's sprawling pool, patio, and garden areas. Beware of surly doormen if you're not a hotel guest. There's also a branch of L.A.'s—and Robert De Niro's—pricey pasta spot Ago. Rooms—80% of which have an ocean view—are loaded with state-of-the-art amenities and, frankly, have a bit more personality than those at the Delano.

1901 Collins Ave., Miami Beach, FL 33139. ✆ **877/640-9500** or 305/695-3100. Fax 305/695-3299. www.shoreclub.com. 309 units, including 8 bungalows. Winter $405–$715 double, $825–$1,300 suite, $2,200–$3,500 bungalow; off-season $405–$715 double, $725–$1,125 suite, $1,700–$3,200 bungalow. AE, DC, MC, V. Valet parking $34. **Amenities:** 2 restaurants; 4 bars; 2 outdoor swimming pools; spa; concierge; 24-hr. room service. *In room:* A/C, TV, stereo/CD player, high-speed Internet access, minibar.

The Tides ★★★ This 10-story Art Deco masterpiece reminiscent of a gleaming ocean liner with porthole windows received a massive makeover by trendsetting designer Kelly Wearstler and is now a condo/hotel. Rooms have been newly washed in warm earth tones. Also, all rooms are at least twice the size of a typical South Beach hotel room and have a breathtaking panoramic view of the ocean. The penthouses on the 9th and 10th floors are situated at the highest point on Ocean Drive, allowing for a priceless panoramic view of the ocean, the skyline, and the beach. The hotel's restaurant, La Marea, is located in the lobby, and is good, but very pricey. Located just off the lobby is the new Coral Bar, a small and romantic spot for a cocktail or two with the help of its very own rum sommelier. A full selection of spa services is available in rooms and poolside. Best of all, the Tides has what they call "Pool Personal Assistants" who provide magazines, frozen fruits, and chilled water and will even clean and polish your sunglasses, and "Oceanfront Personal Assistants" who assist in scoring lounges, umbrellas, towels, and picnic baskets if you wish.

1220 Ocean Dr., South Beach, FL 33139. ✆ **800/439-4095** or 305/604-5070. Fax 305/503-3275. www.tidessouthbeach.com. 45 units. Winter $595 studio suites, $1,500–$5,000 penthouse suites; off-season $395 studio suites, $1,000–$4,000 penthouse suites. Extra person $100. AE, DC, DISC, MC, V. Valet parking $32. Pets $150 1-time fee including new "Paws" program. **Amenities:** Restaurant; lounge and bar; outdoor heated pool w/poolside spa cabanas; fitness room; concierge; 24-hr. room service; in-room massage; laundry service; dry cleaning; beach lounge service; 24-hr. Personal Assistant service. *In room:* A/C, TV/VCR, dataport, minibar, hair dryer, safe, stereo/CD player, music- and video-rental library.

Expensive

The Betsy Hotel ★ Listed on the National Register of Historic Places, the Betsy is the lone surviving example of Florida Georgian architecture on the famous byway, Ocean Drive. Behind its plantation-style shutters and columned facade, the Betsy Hotel offers a tropical colonial beachside haven. Each room and suite in the oceanfront hotel is a nod to the stately colonial rooms of yesteryear blended with the modern aesthetic of South Beach. The Betsy boasts the South Florida installment of New York's BLT Steak restaurant by A-list chef Laurent Tourondel; a roof deck solarium with Zen garden for sunning, spa services, drinks, and light fare; a well-heeled lobby bar scene; and a private basement lounge where guests enter by invitation only. While the beach is a few steps away, the hotel also offers a serene outdoor pool scene.

1440 Ocean Dr., Miami Beach, FL 33139. ✆ 305/531-3934 or 866/531-8950. Fax 305/531-9009.www.thebetsyhotel.com. 63 units. Winter $409–$879 double, $979–$4,000 suite; off-season $309–$779 double, $879–$3,500 suite. AE, DC, DISC, MC, V. Valet parking $30. **Amenities:** BLT Steak restaurant; lobby bar; outdoor pool; roof deck solarium with spa services; 24-hr. concierge; 24-hr. room service; babysitting; beach butlers. *In room:* A/C, TV/DVD, Wi-Fi, minibar, coffeemaker, hair dryer, iron, safe, CD player, MP3 docking station, gaming hub.

The Hotel ★ Kitschy fashion designer Todd Oldham whimsically restored this 1939 gem (formerly the Tiffany Hotel) as he would have restored a vintage piece of couture. He laced it with lush, cool colors, hand-cut mirrors, and glass mosaics from his ready-to-wear factory, then added artisan detailing, terrazzo floors, and porthole windows. The small, soundproof rooms are very comfortable and incredibly stylish, though the bathrooms are a bit cramped. Nevertheless, the showers are irresistible, with fantastic rain showerheads. There's no need to pay more for an oceanfront view here—go up to the rooftop, where the hip and funky Spire Bar and pool are located, and you'll have an amazing view of the Atlantic. The hotel's restaurant, Wish (p. 119), is one of South Beach's best.

801 Collins Ave., South Beach, FL 33139. ✆ **877/843-4683** or 305/531-2222. Fax 305/531-3222. www.thehotelofsouthbeach.com. 53 units. Winter $285–$335 double, $525 suite; off-season $205–$265 double, $375 suite. AE, DC, DISC, MC, V. Valet parking $18. **Amenities:** Restaurant; bar; pool bar; small pool; health club; concierge; business center; room service. *In room:* A/C, TV/VCR, dataport, minibar, coffeemaker, hair dryer, stereo system w/CD and cassette players, video library.

Hotel Astor ★ This venerable Deco hotel has been spruced up with highly stylized rooms by designer Sam Robin who added handcrafted furniture, whangee floors, sisal carpets, and blond oak and whangee cabinetry. Other new additions to the hotel include a nightlife butler who will guide you through South Beach's crazy club scene, and an excellent St. Tropez–meets–South Beach seafood spot, Maison D'Azur. No pool here anymore, but it's 2 blocks from the beach.

956 Washington Ave., South Beach, FL 33139. ✆ **800/270-4981** or 305/531-8081. Fax 305/531-3193. www.hotelastor.com. 40 units. Winter $155–$220 double, $340–$700 suite; off-season $125–$170 double, $220–$500 suite. AE, DC, MC, V. Valet parking $20. **Amenities:** Restaurant; 2 bars; pool; access to nearby health club; 24-hr. concierge service; secretarial services; room service; in-room massage; babysitting; laundry service; dry cleaning. *In room:* A/C, TV, dataport, minibar, fridge, hair dryer, safe.

Hotel Impala ★ (Finds) This charming Mediterranean hideaway is one of the area's best, and it's just beautiful, from the Greco-Roman frescoes and friezes to an intimate garden that is perfumed with the scent of hanging lilies and gardenias. Rooms have supercushy sleigh beds, sisal rug floors, wrought-iron fixtures, imported Belgian cotton linens, wood furniture, and fabulous-looking, but also incredibly small, bathrooms done up in stainless steel and coral rock. The two smallest rooms here are nos. 102 and 206; otherwise, the rooms are pretty spacious and cushy. Adjacent to the hotel is Spiga (p. 124), an intimate, excellent Italian restaurant that is reasonably priced. Enclaves like this one are rare on South Beach. Rates include complimentary continental breakfast and access to Nikki Beach Club.

1228 Collins Ave., South Beach, FL 33139. ✆ **800/646-7252** or 305/673-2021. Fax 305/673-5984. www.hotelimpalamiamibeach.com. 17 units. Winter $195–$225 double, $325–$425 suite; off-season $145–$195 double, $250–$325 suite. Rates include continental breakfast. AE, DC, MC, V. Valet parking $20. Small pets permitted. **Amenities:** Restaurant; concierge; room service. *In room:* A/C, TV/VCR, high-speed Internet access, hair dryer, stereo/CD player, video library.

Raleigh Hotel ★★ The Raleigh is quintessential old school Miami Beach with a modern twist. Polished wood, original terrazzo floors, and an intimate martini bar add to the fabulous atmosphere that's favored by fashion photographers, for whom the hotel's fleur-de-lis pool is the favorite subject. In fact, one look at the pool and you'll expect Esther Williams to splash up in a dramatic, aquatic plié. The entire outdoor area is a stunning oasis that elicits oohs and aahs from even the most jaded jet-setters. Thanks to the hotel's owner Andre Balazs (of New York's Mercer and Los Angeles's Chateau Marmont and Standard hotels fame), rooms have been redone with period furnishings, iPod docking stations, gourmet minibars, and terrazzo floors (those overlooking the pool and ocean are the most peaceful). The massive penthouse is a favorite among visiting celebrities and authors. But it's the Raleigh's warm, romantic Deco atmosphere that lures people away from chillier, neighboring boutique hotels.

1775 Collins Ave., Miami Beach, FL 33139. ✆ **800/848-1775** or 305/534-6300. Fax 305/538-8140. www.raleighhotel.com. 104 units. Winter $495–$925 double, $950–$2,750 suite; off-season $225–$700 double, $700–$2,000 suite. AE, DC, DISC, MC, V. Valet parking $30. **Amenities:** Restaurant; bar; coffee bar; fantastic large outdoor pool; concierge; business services; 24-hr. room service; massage; overnight laundry service. *In room:* A/C, TV/VCR, Wi-Fi, minibar, fridge, hair dryer, iron, safe, CD player.

The Standard ★★ The quintessential spa resort, the Standard, owned by Raleigh owner Andre Balazs, is housed in Miami Beach's legendary Lido Spa spot, a place that was swinging back in the days when women still wore bathing caps. Today, the hotel is full of all the modern trappings of a swank spa resort, with a bayfront view and a serene location on the Venetian Causeway—walking distance to all the South Beach craziness. Remnants of the atomic age of the fabulous '50s still exist here—the lobby's white marble walls, terrazzo floors, and stainless-steel elevators. Add to that a touch of Scandinavian retro modernism. Whitewashed guest rooms are serviced by roaming carts offering herbal teas and aromatherapy footbaths. There's a cedar sauna; a Turkish hammam; tongue-in-cheek treatments, such as the cellulite-fighting Standard Spanking; a chlorine-free plunge pool, with a 12-foot-tall waterfall and DJ-spun music piped beneath the water; clothing-optional mud baths; and a waterfront restaurant with glorious waterfront views. Anything but standard.

40 Island Ave., Miami Beach, FL 33139. ✆ **305/673-1717.** Fax 305/673-8181. www.standardhotel.com. 105 units. $165–$1,250 suite. AE, DC, DISC, MC, V. Valet parking $25. **Amenities:** Restaurant; bar; pool; fitness center; spa; sauna; limited room service; concierge. *In room:* A/C, TV/DVD, Wi-Fi, minibar, hair dryer, iron, safe, stereo/CD player.

Moderate

The Catalina Hotel & Beach Club ★★ The Catalina is something straight out of an Austin Powers movie. It's groovy, indeed! So much so that the hotel took over the space next door and added 60 more rooms, a rooftop pool, and a funky sushi restaurant.

Stylish but not at all stuffy, the Catalina is perhaps the only hotel in the area that can pull off using red shag carpeting—though it tends to get a bit mangy. The mod squad lobby decor gives way to rooms glazed in white with hints of bright colors featuring Tempur-Pedic Swedish mattresses, 300-thread-count Mascioni sheets, goose-down comforters and pillows, iPods, and, of course, flatscreen TVs. The hotel has a happening bar and lounge scene with a decidedly European jet-set vibe and a splashy beach club where you can get poolside manicures and pedicures. Free passes to nightclubs and free transportation to and from Miami International are among the many perks here. If Catalina is sold out, check out its sister hotel, the **Metropole Suites,** 635 Collins Ave. (✆ **305/672-0009;** www.metropolesouthbeach.com), another favorite for hipsters and recording artists. Rates there start at $195 in season and $125 off-season.

1732 Collins Ave., South Beach, FL 33139. ✆ **305/674-1160.** Fax 305/672-8216. www.catalinahotel.com. 136 units. Winter $225–$300 double; off-season $125–$250 double. Rates include continental breakfast bar and unlimited happy-hour cocktails daily from 7–8pm. AE, DC, MC, V. Valet parking $30. **Amenities:** 2 restaurants; 3 bars; 2 pools; beach club access; complimentary bike cruisers; laundry services. *In room:* A/C, TV/VCR, Wi-Fi ($15 a day), minibar, hair dryer, iron, safe, CD player.

Chesterfield Hotel, Suites & Day Spa ★ This charismatic sliver of a property has won the loyalty of fashion industrialists and romantics alike. Unfortunately, not everyone loves it. Some complain of the constant construction, apathetic service, and run-down or complete lack of amenities. But if you're in a partying mood, this place is for you. The very central location (1 block from the ocean) is a plus, especially because the hotel lacks a pool. Most of the rooms are immaculate and reminiscent of a loft apartment; large bathrooms with big, deep tubs are especially enticing. However, some rooms are dark and have not had such upgrades (we have gotten complaints), and are to be avoided; do not hesitate to ask for a room change. We've also gotten complaints about the music coming from the hotel next door, but you have to realize that if you're staying on Collins or Washington avenues, you're going to hear noise: South Beach isn't known for its quiet, peaceful demeanor. For R&R, try the hotel's new day spa.

841 Collins Ave., South Beach, FL 33139. ✆ **305/673-3767.** Fax 305/535-9665. www.thechesterfieldhotel.com. 90 units. Winter $175–$245 suite, $395 penthouse; off-season $125–$195 suite, $335 penthouse. Additional person $20. AE, DC, MC, V. Valet parking $30. Well-behaved pets accepted. **Amenities:** Restaurant; 2 bars; reduced rates at local gym; spa; concierge; business services. *In room:* A/C, TV, high-speed Internet access, minibar, hair dryer, safe, CD player.

Crest Hotel Suites ★ (Finds) One of South Beach's best-kept secrets, the Crest Hotel has a quietly fashionable, contemporary, relaxed atmosphere with friendly service. Built in 1939, the Crest was restored to preserve its Art Deco architecture, but the interior of the hotel is thoroughly modern, with rooms resembling cosmopolitan apartments. All suites have a living room/dining room area, kitchenette, and executive work space. An indoor/outdoor cafe with terrace and poolside dining isn't besieged with trendy locals, but does attract a younger crowd. Around the corner from the hotel is Lincoln Road, with its sidewalk cafes, gourmet restaurants, theaters, and galleries. In an effort to expand its quiet trendiness, the Crest opened its second hotel, the **South Beach Hotel,** at 236 21st St., in an area that presently isn't so great (though it's on its way up). Until the neighborhood goes through more of a renaissance, this second hotel should be a last resort if you can't get a room elsewhere.

1670 James Ave., Miami Beach, FL 33139. ✆ **800/531-3880** or 305/531-0321. Fax 305/531-8180. www.crestgrouphotels.com/cresthotelsuites.htm. 64 units. Winter $120–$165 double, $211 suite; off-season $115 double, $175 suite. Packages available and 10% discount offered if booked on website. AE, MC, V.

Amenities: Restaurant; cafe; pool; laundry service; dry cleaning. *In room:* A/C, TV, dataport, kitchenette, fridge, coffeemaker (in select units).

Pelican Hotel ★★ Owned by the same creative folks behind the Diesel Jeans company, the fashionable Pelican is South Beach's only self-professed "toy-hotel," in which each of its 30 rooms and suites is decorated as outrageously as some of the area's more colorful drag queens. Each room has been designed daringly and rather wittily by Swedish interior decorator Magnus Ehrland. Countless trips to antiques markets, combined with his wild imagination, have turned room no. 309, for instance, into the "Psychedelic(ate) Girl"; room no. 201 into the "Executive Fifties" suite; and no. 209 into the "Love, Peace, and Leafforest" room. But the most popular room is the tough-to-score no. 215, or the "Best Whorehouse," which is said to have made even former Hollywood madam Heidi Fleiss red with envy. The Ocean Drive location and the hotel's cafe make the Pelican a very popular people-watching spot.

826 Ocean Dr., Miami Beach, FL 33139. ✆ **800/7-PELICAN** (73-5422) or 305/673-3373. Fax 305/673-3255. www.pelicanhotel.com. 30 units. Winter $280–$450 double, $480–$800 oceanfront suite; off-season $165–$220 double, $330–$540 oceanfront suite. Valet parking $22. AE, DC, MC, V. **Amenities:** Restaurant; bar; access to area gyms; concierge; business services; Wi-Fi; room service; same-day laundry service; dry cleaning. *In room:* A/C, TV, stereo/CD player, fridge with complimentary water, hair dryer, iron, safe.

Townhouse ★★ New York hipster Jonathan Morr felt that Miami Beach had lost touch with the bons vivants who gave the city its original cachet, so he decided to take matters into his own hands. His solution: this 67-room, five-story so-called shabby-chic hotel. The charm of this hotel is in its clean and simple yet chic design with quirky details: exercise equipment that stands alone in the hallways, free laundry machines in the lobby, and a water bed–lined rooftop. Comfortable, shabby-chic rooms boast L-shaped couches for extra guests (for whom you aren't charged). Though the rooms are all pretty much the same, consider the ones with the partial ocean view. The hotel also offers beach access, with chair and umbrella rentals available. The hotel's basement features the hot sushi spot, Bond St. Lounge (p. 122).

150 20th St., South Beach, FL 33139. ✆ **877/534-3800** or 305/534-3800. Fax 305/534-3811. www.townhousehotel.com. 70 units. Winter $240–$450 double, $395–$450 penthouse; off-season $115–$235 double, $395–$450 penthouse. Rates include Parisian-style (coffee and pastry) breakfast. AE, MC, V. Valet parking $25. **Amenities:** Restaurant; bar; workout stations; bike rental; free Wi-Fi; free laundry service; rooftop terrace w/water beds. *In room:* A/C, TV/VCR, dataport, fridge, hair dryer, safe, CD player.

Whitelaw Hotel ★ With a slogan that reads "Clean sheets, hot water, and stiff drinks," the Whitelaw Hotel stands apart from other boutique hotels with its fierce sense of humor. Only half a block from Ocean Drive, this hotel, like its clientele, is full of distinct personalities, pairing such disparate elements as luxurious Belgian sheets with shag carpeting to create an innovative setting. All-white rooms manage to be homey and plush, and not at all antiseptic, but some guests have complained that their rooms looked more like 1950s kitchens with linoleum floors than anything else. Bathrooms are pretty small and not that well stocked, and towels are sometimes in short supply, but those who stay here aren't really looking for luxury—they just want to party. Complimentary cocktails in the lobby every night from 7 to 8pm contribute to a very social atmosphere. In 2008, the owners of the Whitelaw opened a new stay, the **Riviera** (✆ **877/762-3477**), tucked away at 2000 Liberty Ave., on South Beach, featuring imaginatively designed one-bedroom apartmentlike accommodations with full gourmet kitchens; a courtyard pool complete with an outdoor bar, grill, and private cabanas; a lobby lounge; a state-of-the-art spa and yoga room; and a sun deck with sweeping views of the city and ocean. Rates start at $215 in the winter and $145 off-season.

808 Collins Ave., Miami Beach, FL 33139. ✆ **305/398-7000.** Fax 305/398-7010. www.whitelawhotel.com. 49 units. Winter $145–$195 double/king; off-season $95–$145 double/king. Rates subject to change during special events. Rates include complimentary continental breakfast and free cocktails in the lobby (7–8pm daily). AE, DC, MC, V. Parking $30. **Amenities:** Lounge; concierge; business services; free airport pickup (to and from MIA); laundry service; complimentary passes to area nightclubs. *In room:* A/C, TV, Wi-Fi ($15 per day), minibar, hair dryer, safe, CD player.

Inexpensive

Hotel Shelley ★ The renovated Hotel Shelley has a laid-back beach atmosphere, yet cutting-edge style. The architecturally sound boutique hotel built in 1931 in the heart of the Art Deco District of Miami Beach has reinvented itself with a complete $1.5-million renovation of its 49 guest rooms. Complete with Mascioni 300-thread-count linens, goose-down pillows and comforters, LCD plasma TVs, and custom-built cabinetry, the guest rooms at the Shelley allow you to chill out after a long day at the beach or rock out before a big night of partying. The subtle purple hues in the rooms and public areas are in true Art Deco style. The bar in the lobby offers free drinks from 7 to 8pm every night and VIP passes to area nightclubs. Located on Collins and 1 block from Ocean Drive, this hotel allows you to reach beach, shopping, or nightlife within a few minutes' walk.

844 Collins Ave., Miami Beach, FL 33139. ✆ **305/531-3341.** Fax 305/535-9665. www.hotelshelley.com. 49 units. Winter $145–$225 double, $165–$245 king, $165–$300 minisuite; off-season $75–$125 double, $95–$145 king, $115–$165 minisuite. Rates are subject to change for special events and holidays. Rates include free cocktails in the lobby. AE, DC, MC, V. Parking $30. **Amenities:** Lounge; concierge; free airport pickup (to and from MIA); laundry service; complimentary passes to area nightclubs. *In room:* A/C, TV, dataport, minibar, hair dryer, safe, CD player.

MIAMI BEACH: SURFSIDE, BAL HARBOUR, SUNNY ISLES & NORTH BEACH

The area just north of South Beach, known as Miami Beach, encompasses Surfside, Bal Harbour, and Sunny Isles. Unrestricted by zoning codes throughout the 1950s, 1960s, and especially 1970s, area developers went crazy, building ever-bigger and more brazen structures, especially north of 41st Street, known as "Condo Canyon." Consequently, there's now a glut of medium-quality condos, with a few scattered holdouts of older hotels and motels casting shadows over the newer, swankier stays emerging on the beachfront.

To locate the hotels in this section, see the map "Miami Beach Accommodations & Dining" (p. 102).

Very Expensive

Canyon Ranch Miami Beach Opened in late 2008 in the former Carillon Hotel on an unseemly stretch of Collins Avenue, the Miami version of the famous Arizona and Lenox, Massachusetts, spa and wellness hotel is located directly on the beach. If you're looking to drop in excess of, say, $330 for a Japanese bathing ritual, or $350 for an insomnia consultation with a doctor, then this place is for you. The main draw isn't a trendy bar, restaurant, or night club, but a 75,000-square-foot health club that includes a 32-foot-tall climbing wall as well as equipment for testing oxygen saturation and bone density. There's even a $125,000 body scanner that, according to the resort's clinical director, is the best in the world. The resort has a full-time medical staff of 11, including a Chinese medicine specialist, nutritionist, and physical therapist. Because the resort operates as a condo as well, every suite has fine furnishings, top electronics, and a designer kitchen. All have balconies. The oceanfront Canyon Ranch Grill features all healthy fare. In addition to 750 feet of beach, the resort has four pools, a reading garden, and water therapy programs. To preserve the tranquil vibe here, cellphone use is prohibited in many of the hotel's public areas.

6900 Collins Ave., Miami Beach, FL 33140. ✆ **800/742-9000** or 305/514-7000. Fax 305/864-2744. www.canyonranch.com. 150 units. Winter suites from $650; off-season suites from $450. AE, DISC, MC, V. Valet parking $35. **Amenities:** 3 restaurants; juice and smoothie bar; 4 outdoor pools; fitness center; spa; salon; 24-hr. room service; in-room massage; babysitting; laundry service; dry cleaning; rock-climbing arena. *In room:* A/C, TV, dataport, kitchen.

Eden Roc Resort and Spa Just next door to the mammoth Fontainebleau, this Morris Lapidus–designed flamboyant hotel, which opened in 1956, in 2008 received a $190-million face-lift, doubling its size from 349 to 631 rooms and complete with a new 283-room oceanfront tower, 17 bungalow suites, five pools, two restaurants, and a spa. The focal point is now an oasis of pools, water features, and gardens, threaded with walkways and intimate seating areas.

4525 Collins Ave., Miami Beach, FL 33140. ✆ **800/327-8337** or 305/531-0000. Fax 305/674-5555. www.edenrocresort.com. 349 units. Winter $339–$425 double, $394 suite, $2,500 penthouse; off-season $199–$274 double, $239 suite, $1,500 penthouse. Additional person $15. Packages available. AE, DC, DISC, MC, V. Valet parking $24. Pets are accepted for a fee. **Amenities:** 2 restaurants; lounge; bar; 2 outdoor pools; health club; spa; watersports equipment/rentals; concierge; tour desk; car-rental desk; business center; salon; limited room service; in-room massage; babysitting; laundry service; dry cleaning; squash, racquetball, and basketball courts; rock-climbing arena. *In room:* A/C, TV, dataport, kitchenettes (in suites and penthouse), minibar, coffeemaker, hair dryer, safe, VCRs for rent.

Expensive

Fontainebleau Hotel and Resort ★ Big changes—$500 million worth—are afoot at Miami Beach's legendary hotel. Designed by the late Morris Lapidus, this grand monolith symbolized Old Miami decadence. This is where all the greats performed in their prime; but now it's all just nostalgia, as the hotel readies itself for the 21st century with a massive renovation. Reopened in 2008 as a modern Vegas-style hotel, entertainment, and dining complex, the Fontainebleau features all the trappings of a luxury hotel—flatscreen TVs, plush bedding, and, well, you get the idea. Choose from the main property or the modern, brand-new all-suite hotel tower, where rooms are plush and posh. A 40,000-square-foot spa, with mineral-rich water therapies and co-ed swimming pools; a dramatic oceanfront poolscape, featuring "walls of water," intermingled with a free-form, Lapidus-influenced pool; and a sexy, intimate enclave surrounded by cabanas and sun loungers are among the many highlights. The hotel has brought celebrity chefs as well—with Alfred Portale's Gotham Steak, Scott Conant's hot New York Italian outpost Scarpetta, and London's highly rated Chinese restaurant Hakkasan all among the 11 (yes 11) restaurants and lounges. In addition, there are three nightclubs, big-name musical headliners, and other Vegas-style entertainment options. Rates will increase, too—up to 70%. In its infancy in early 2009, we received many complaints about the service, the emptiness—1,500 plus rooms are hard to fill at these prices—and the lack of any sort of vibe, but if you're looking for a one-stop hot spot that you won't likely want to leave, this is the place to be.

4441 Collins Ave., Miami Beach, FL 33140. ✆ **800/548-8886** or 305/538-2000. Fax 305/535-3286. www.fontainebleau.com. 1,504 units. Winter from $399 double, from $509 suite; off-season from $229 double, from $299 suite. AE, DISC, MC, V. Valet parking $32. Pets accepted. **Amenities:** 11 restaurants and lounges; 11 pools with cabanas; fitness center; spa; concierge; full-service salon; room service. *In room:* A/C, TV/DVD, fax, dataport, iMac with high-speed internet, kitchenette (in suites), minibar, hair dryer, iron, safe.

Miami Beach Accommodations & Dining

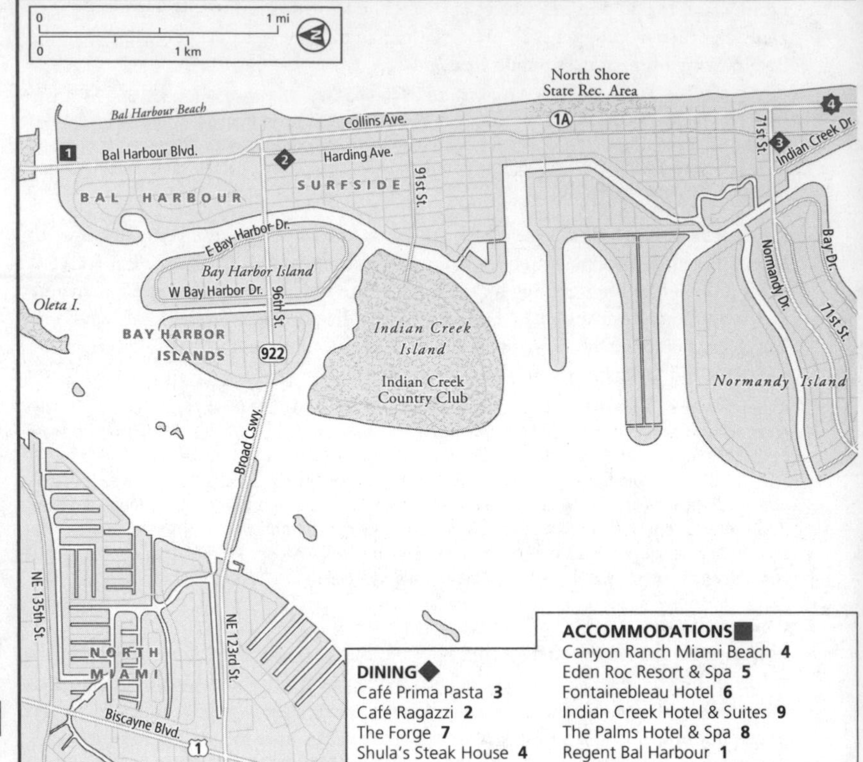

Moderate

Indian Creek Hotel and Suites ★ Finds Located off the beaten path, the Indian Creek Hotel is a meticulously restored 1936 building with one of the first operating elevators in Miami Beach. Because of its location, which faces the Indian Creek waterway, and its lush landscaping, this place feels like an old-fashioned Key West bed-and-breakfast. The revamped rooms are outfitted in Art Deco furnishings, such as antique writing desks, pretty tropical prints, and small but spotless bathrooms. Just 1 block from a good stretch of sand, the hotel also has a landscaped pool area in the back garden. Although one reader who stayed there complained that the staff was surly, the room was dirty, the lush courtyard was overgrown, and he wasn't informed that he needed a parking pass—obtainable at the hotel—the good news is that there is new ownership and things seem to be running smoother. The hotel's restaurant, Creek 28, is one of Miami's best-kept secrets.

2727 Indian Creek Dr. (1 block west of Collins Ave. and the ocean), Miami Beach, FL 33140. ✆ **800/491-2772** or 305/531-2727. Fax 305/531-5651. www.indiancreekhotel.com. 61 units. Winter $149–$199 double, $269–$289 suite; off-season $69–$199 double, $179–$249 suite. Additional person $25. Group packages and summer specials available. AE, DC, DISC, MC, V. **Amenities:** Restaurant; bar; pool; concierge; limited room service. *In room:* A/C, TV/VCR, Wi-Fi, fridge (in suites), hair dryer, CD player (in suites).

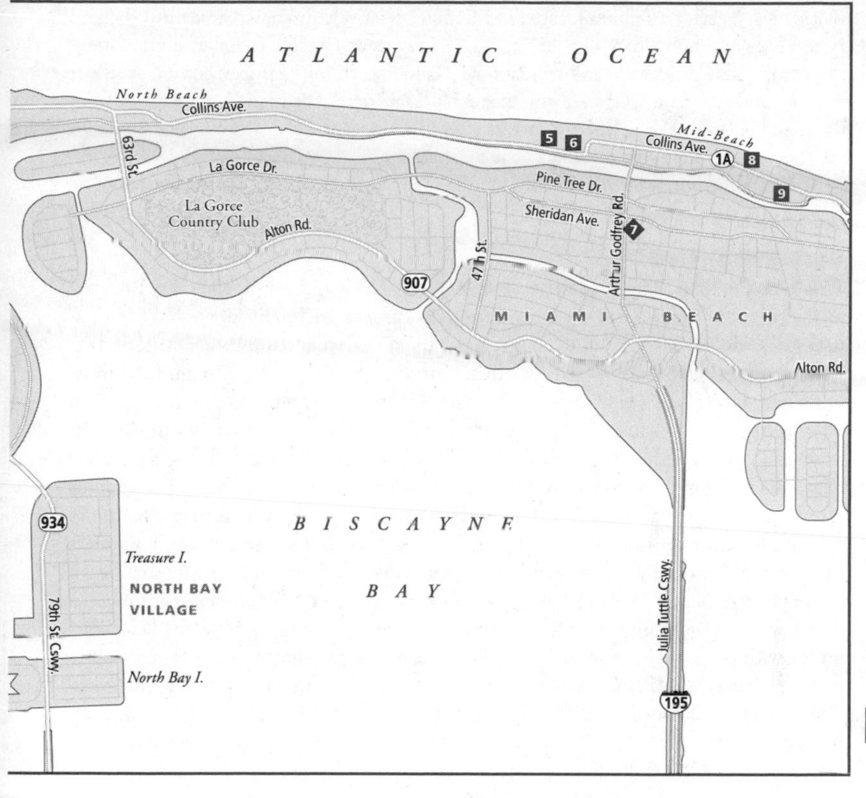

The Palms Hotel & Spa ★ Just a stone's throw away from Miami Beach's entertainment district, the Palms Hotel & Spa is ideally located on the beach on the northern, more tranquil side of South Beach. As a sophisticated yet genuine oceanfront resort, it features lush gardens landscaped with palms and other tropical plants and a large freshwater pool as its centerpiece. Luxurious accommodations as well as warm and caring service are also signature features of this property. The hotel boasts the Palms Spa, South Florida's only Aveda destination spa, offering a highly personalized experience through Aveda's holistic treatments in five multipurpose treatment rooms and four outdoor treatment cabanas, as well as hair, nail, and makeup services. In its quest to provide a natural and wholesome experience for every guest, the hotel also features a new restaurant and lounge—Essensia, the pure essence of taste—with a cuisine that blends the freshness and light nature of the Mediterranean with the liveliness of the Caribbean.

3025 Collins Ave., Miami Beach, FL 33140. ✆ **800/550-0505** or 305/534-0505. Fax 305/534-0515. www.thepalmshotel.com. 243 units. Winter $219–$599 double, $749 suite; off-season $159–$579 double, $549 suite. AE, DC, MC, V. Valet parking around $27. **Amenities:** Restaurant; poolside bar; lounge; heated pool; spa; bike rental; concierge; room service; laundry service; dry cleaning. *In room:* A/C, plasma TV, Wi-Fi, minibar, hair dryer, iron, safe, iPod docking station.

KEY BISCAYNE

Locals call it the Key, and technically, Key Biscayne is the northernmost island in the Florida Keys, even though it's located in Miami. A relatively unknown area until Richard Nixon bought a home here in the '70s, Key Biscayne, at $1^1/_4$ square miles, is an affluent but hardly lively residential and recreational island known for its pricey homes, excellent beaches, and actor Andy Garcia, who makes his home here. The island is far enough from the mainland to make it feel semiprivate, yet close enough to downtown for guests to take advantage of everything Miami has to offer.

To locate the hotels in this section, see the map "Greater Miami Accommodations & Dining" (p. 87).

Very Expensive

The Ritz-Carlton, Key Biscayne ★★★ Kids The Ritz-Carlton takes Key Biscayne to the height of luxury with 44 acres of tropical gardens, a 20,000-square-foot destination spa, and a world-class tennis center under the direction of tennis pro Cliff Drysdale. Decorated in British colonial style, the Ritz-Carlton is straight out of Bermuda, with its impressive flower-laden landscaping. The Ritz Kids programs provide children ages 5 to 12 with fantastic activities, and the 1,200-foot beachfront, named among the Top 10 Beaches in the U.S. by Dr. Stephen "Beach" Leatherman, offers everything from pure relaxation to fishing, boating, or windsurfing. Spacious and luxuriously appointed rooms feature new decor that embodies the resort's island-destination feel and large balconies that overlook the ocean or lush gardens. The oceanfront Italian restaurant Cioppino is excellent for formal dining, or, if you prefer casual dining, the oceanfront Cantina Beach serves great authentic Mexican food and even has a "tequlier"—a sommelier for tequila. The new St. Tropez–inspired Dune Oceanfront Burger Lounge is ideal for lazy afternoons with one of their gourmet burgers and a glass of champagne, while the resort's nighttime spot RUMBAR hearkens back to Old Havana with an impressive rum selection and light Cuban-inspired fare. The hotel's remote location—just a 10-minute drive from the hustle and bustle—makes it a favorite for those (John Travolta, among others) who want to avoid the hubbub.

455 Grand Bay Dr., Key Biscayne, FL 33149. ✆ **800/241-3333** or 305/365-4500. Fax 305/365-4501. www.ritzcarlton.com. 402 units. Winter $629 double, $1,100 suite; off-season $269 double, $525 suite. AE, DC, DISC, MC, V. Valet parking (call for fees). **Amenities:** 4 restaurants; 3 bars; 2 outdoor heated pools; tennis center with lessons available; fitness center; spa; watersports equipment/rentals; children's programs; concierge; business center; shopping arcade; salon; 24-hr. room service; 24-hour laundry service. *In room:* A/C, TV, dataport, minibar, hair dryer, safe.

DOWNTOWN

If you've ever read Tom Wolfe's *Bonfire of the Vanities,* you may understand what downtown Miami is all about. If not, it's this simple: Take a wrong turn and you could find yourself in some serious trouble. Desolate and dangerous at night, downtown is trying to change its image, but it's been a long, tedious process. Recently, however, part of the area has experienced a renaissance in terms of nightlife, with several popular dance clubs and bars opening up in the environs of NE 11th Street, off Biscayne Boulevard. If you're the kind of person who digs an urban setting, you may enjoy downtown, but if you're looking for shiny, happy Miami, you're in the wrong place (for now). As posh, pricey lofts keep going up faster than the nation's deficit, downtown is about to experience the renaissance it has been waiting for. Keep your eye on this area, and remember that you read it here first: Like orange—or pink, or white, or blue—being the new black, downtown Miami will be the new South Beach.

Most downtown hotels cater primarily to business travelers and cruise passengers. Although business hotels can be expensive, quality and service are of a high standard. Look for discounts and packages on weekends, when offices are closed and rooms often go empty.

To locate the hotels in this section, see the map "Greater Miami Accommodations & Dining" (p. 87).

Very Expensive

Epic ★★★ Although it's yet another condo/hotel, the new in 2009 Epic, a Kimpton Hotel, doesn't make you feel like you're intruding on someone's privacy. In fact, it feels as if you are a resident as well in a posh, plush high rise with stunning views of the Miami skyline and Biscayne Bay. The dramatic lobby—separate from the resident lobby—features vaulted ceilings, glass walls, and shimmering pools, not to mention a buzzing two-story lounge and a yet-to-be-announced restaurant from a star chef. The guest rooms and suites are full of open space and light, offering breathtaking views, exceptional Aqua di Parma amenities, and a huge bathroom with open cutout into the bedroom area. Luxury services include an on-site hotel spa as well as in-room spa treatments, multiple swimming pools, and an excellent seafood restaurant/lounge, Area 31, on the 16th floor. The hotel is extremely pet friendly, offering beds, bones, and bottled water for your furry friend. Another perk: a daily wine reception in the lobby, featuring free pours of reds, whites, and bubbly along with some tasty snacks.

270 Biscayne Blvd. Way, Miami, FL 33131. ✆ **305/424-5226.** Fax 305/424-5232. www.epichotel.com. 411 units. Winter $369–$519 double, $519–$619 suite; off-season $229–$379 double, $379–$479 suite. AE, DC, DISC, MC, V. Valet parking $32. **Amenities:** 2 restaurants; waterfront lounge; 2 outdoor pools; fitness center; Exhale spa; concierge; 24-hr. business center; 24-hr. room service; evening wine reception. *In room:* A/C, TV, high-speed Internet access, Wi-Fi, desktop computer, hair dryer, iron, safe, iPod docking station.

The Four Seasons ★★★ (Kids Deciding between the hyperluxe Mandarin Oriental and the equally luxe, albeit somewhat museumlike, Four Seasons is almost like trying to tell the difference between Ava and Zsa Zsa Gabor. There are some obvious differences and some similarities, but they're kind of subtle. While the architecturally striking Mandarin is located on the semiprivate Brickell Key, the 70-story Four Seasons resembles an office building and is smack in the middle of the business district. The rooms and suites are plush, and, like the Mandarin, service is paramount. Most rooms overlook Biscayne Bay, and while all rooms are cushy, thanks to the hotel's signature "untucked" beds, the bland decor leaves a lot to be desired, really. The best rooms are the corner suites with views facing both south and east over the water. There are three gorgeous pools spread out on more than 2 acres with cabanas featuring flatscreen TVs, private bars, and iPod docking stations. Guests at the hotel all have access to and free classes at the Sports Club/LA, a gym popular with visiting celebs.

1435 Brickell Ave., Miami, FL 33131. ✆ **305/358-3535.** Fax 305/358-7758. www.fourseasons.com/miami.com. 260 units. Winter $395–$495 double, $675 suite; off-season $375–$475 double, $575 suite. AE, DC, DISC, MC, V. Valet parking $33. **Amenities:** 2 restaurants; 2 bars; 3 outdoor pools; the Sports Club/LA fitness center; full-service spa; outdoor Jacuzzi; concierge; 24-hr. business center. *In room:* A/C, TV, dataport, high-speed Internet access, Wi-Fi, minibar, hair dryer, iron, safe.

Mandarin Oriental, Miami ★★★ Corporate big shots and celebrities not in the mood for the South Beach spotlight have a high-end luxury hotel to stay in while wheeling and dealing their way through Miami. Catering to business travelers, big-time celebrities (Jennifer Aniston, J-Lo, Jacko, Will Smith, and so on), and the leisure traveler who doesn't mind spending big bucks, the swank Mandarin Oriental features a waterfront location, residential-style rooms with Asian touches (all with balconies), upscale dining, and bathrooms equipped with Aromatherapy Associates products. The waterfront view of the city is the hotel's best asset. The hotel's two restaurants, the high-end Azul (p. 129) and the more casual Café Sambal, are two of Miami's best, as is the 15,000-square-foot spa, in which traditional Thai massages and ayurvedic treatments are the norm. The hotel is also home to a 20,000-foot white-sand beach club with a fabulous Friday night happy hour, complete with beach butlers and beachside cabana treatments, which is nice, considering that the hotel is 15 minutes from the beach. For those who want to venture out, the Mandarin offers the city's only official "nightlife guide" to lead you to the hot spots.

Wanna Be Signin' Something . . .

Celebrity tidbit: The late Michael Jackson signed his name to a painting in the suite he was staying in at the Mandarin Oriental Miami—despite the fact that he didn't paint it. The hotel was amused and decided to keep it.

500 Brickell Key Dr., Miami, FL 33131. ✆ **305/913-8383.** Fax 305/913-8300. www.mandarinoriental.com. 326 units. $435–$900 double; $1,300–$6,500 suite. AE, DC, DISC, MC, V. Valet parking $24. Pets welcome. **Amenities:** 2 restaurants; 3 bars; Oasis Beach Club; infinity pool; nearby golf; nearby tennis; state-of-the-art fitness center; full-service holistic spa; outdoor Jacuzzi; kids' club; concierge; business center; shopping arcade; outdoor jogging trail. *In room:* A/C, TV, dataport, Wi-Fi, minibar, hair dryer, iron, safe.

The Viceroy ★ One of the few condo-hotel combos to make it before the bust, the trendy Kelly Wearstler-designed Viceroy is located on prime real estate on Biscayne Bay between downtown Miami and trendy Brickell Avenue. The hotel itself occupies its own tower within a three-tower structure and is the only facility to house a 162-room hotel in conjunction with residences. All rooms are full of the modern trappings—Wii and PlayStation gaming systems, DVD players, portable printers, 42-inch flatscreen televisions, and hair- and body-care products by Aromapothecary. Residents and guests alike share exclusive access to the 15th-floor outdoor podium's sweeping recreation area—lounge and deck space, sun deck with cabanas, and a 310-foot infinity pool overlooking the bay. As with any new hotel, there's a chic restaurant overlooking the 15th floor pool, with alfresco dining, fireplace, and waterfront views. Even better is Fifty, the upscale rooftop lounge/restaurant right next to the pool on the 50th floor, not to mention a full-service 28,000-square-foot spa at Icon Brickell with treatment rooms that overlook the bay.

485 Brickell Ave., Miami, Florida 33131. ✆ **866/720 1991.** www.viceroymiami.com. 162 units. Winter $400–$500 double; off-season $300 double. AE, DC, DISC, MC, V. Valet parking $35. **Amenities:** Restaurant; lounge; 2 outdoor pools; 500-sq.-ft. state-of-the-art fitness facility; full-service spa; 24-hr. room service. *In room:* A/C, TV, dataport, high-speed Internet access, Wi-Fi, well-equipped kitchen or kitchenette, hair dryer, iron, safe, portable GPS device.

Moderate

Miami River Inn ★★★ Finds The Miami River Inn, listed on the National Register of Historic Places, is a quaint, country-style hideaway (Miami's *only* bed-and-breakfast!), consisting of four cottages smack in the middle of downtown Miami. In fact, it's so hidden that most locals don't even know it exists, which only adds to its panache. Every room has hardwood floors and is uniquely furnished with antiques dating from 1908. In one room, you might find a hand-painted bathtub, a Singer sewing machine, and an armoire from the turn of the 20th century, restored to perfection. Thirty-eight rooms have private bathrooms—four have showers only, six have tubs only, and 28 have splendid tub/shower combinations. One- and two-bedroom apartments are available as well. In the foyer, you can peruse a library filled with books about Old Miami. It's close to public transportation, restaurants, and museums, and only 5 minutes from the business district.

118 SW South River Dr., Miami, FL 33130. ✆ **800/468-3589** or 305/325-0045. Fax 305/325-9227. www.miamiriverinn.com. 38 units. Winter $149–$299 double; off-season $89–$139 double. Rates include continental breakfast and parking. Extra person $15. AE, DC, DISC, MC, V. Free parking. Pets accepted for $25 per night. **Amenities:** Small pool; access to nearby gym facilities; Jacuzzi; babysitting; laundry service; dry cleaning; coin-op washers/dryers. *In room:* A/C, TV, hair dryer (upon request), iron/ironing board (upon request).

WEST MIAMI & AIRPORT AREA

As Miami continues to grow at a rapid pace, expansion has begun westward, where land is plentiful. Several resorts have taken advantage of the space to build world-class tennis and golf courses. While there's no sea to swim in, a plethora of facilities can definitely make up for the lack of an ocean view.

To locate the hotels in this section, see the map "Greater Miami Accommodations & Dining" (p. 87).

Expensive

Doral Golf Resort and Spa ★ Kids This sprawling 650-acre resort in a suburban West Miami enclave is all about golf. Doral is where world-class tournaments and the excruciating Blue Monster course have seen even Tiger frustrated. There's also the Great White Course—the Southeast's first desertscape course, designed by the Shark himself, Greg Norman. Repeat guests usually book the season well in advance. Rooms are spacious, all with private balconies, many overlooking a golf course or garden. Rooms reveal a plantation-style decor with lots of wicker and wood and large marble bathrooms. Enhancements to the golf courses, spa suites, and driving range have also brought the resort up to speed with its competition. There's a phenomenal kids program and the Blue Lagoon water park featuring two 80,000-gallon pools with cascading waterfalls, a rock facade, and a 125-foot water slide. For a spa or golf vacation, the Doral is an ideal choice. Otherwise, consider investing your money in a hotel that's better located.

4400 NW 87th Ave., Miami, FL 33178. ✆ **800/71-DORAL** or 305/592-2000. Fax 305/594-4682. www.doralresort.com. 693 units. Winter $269 double, $370 suite, $420 1-bedroom suite, $500 2-bedroom suite; off-season $119 double, $280 suite, $400 1-bedroom suite, $480 2-bedroom suite. Additional person $35. Golf and spa packages available. AE, DC, DISC, MC, V. Valet parking $17. **Amenities:** 5 restaurants; 6 pools; 5 golf courses; driving range; 10 tennis courts; health club; world-class spa; concierge; business center; room service; babysitting; laundry service; dry cleaning. *In room:* A/C, TV, dataport, minibar, coffeemaker, hair dryer, iron, safe.

Bargain Chains

If you must stay near the airport, consider any of the dozens of moderately priced chain hotels. You'll find one of the cheapest and most recommendable options at either of the **Days Inn** locations at 7250 NW 11th St. and 4767 NW 36th St. (✆ **800/329-7466** for both, or 305/888-3661 or 305/261-4230, respectively), each about 2 miles from the airport. The larger property on 36th Street offers slightly cheaper rates, with singles starting as low as $69. The 11th Street locale may charge more on weekends, but prices usually start at $70. Prices include free transportation from the airport.

A more luxurious option is the **Wyndham Miami Airport,** at 3900 NW 21st St. (✆ **305/871-3800**), with rates from $125 to $225.

NORTH DADE

To locate the hotels in this section, see the map "North Dade Accommodations & Dining" (p. 109).

Very Expensive

Acqualina ★ Some people are still scratching their heads as to why this luxurious resort opened across the street from a Denny's and T-shirt shops, but once you step inside, you forget that you're even in Miami and feel as if you're on the Italian Riviera. On 4½ beachfront acres, with more than 400 feet of Atlantic coastline, Acqualina is a Mediterranean-style resort towering over all the others, with its baroque fountains, 97

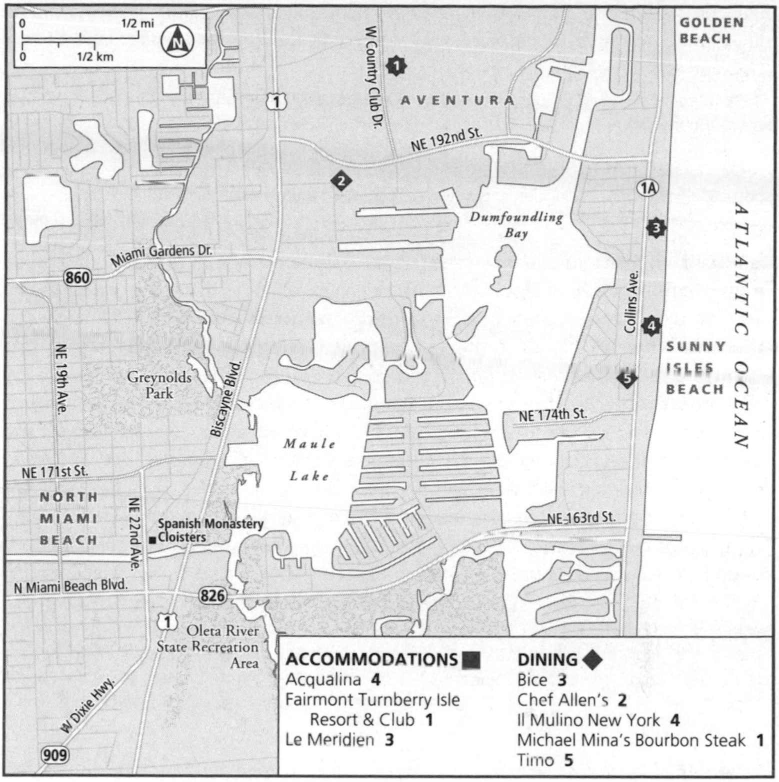

ACCOMMODATIONS ■
Acqualina **4**
Fairmont Turnberry Isle Resort & Club **1**
Le Meridien **3**

DINING ◆
Bice **3**
Chef Allen's **2**
Il Mulino New York **4**
Michael Mina's Bourbon Steak **1**
Timo **5**

impeccably appointed suites, and a branch of NYC's acclaimed Il Mulino restaurant. The ESPA is one of Miami's priciest and poshest spas, and while there are three pools just steps away from the beach, the outdoor area is uninspiring. The hotel's AcquaMarine Program has a splashy array of marine-biology activities for kids and adults. Best of all, the chance of Paris Hilton and Tara Reid partying here is unlikely. In fact, there's really no scene here at all, which for some is just blissful.

17875 Collins Ave., Sunny Isles Beach, FL 33160. ✆ **305/918-8000.** Fax 305/918-8100. www.acqualina.com. 97 units. Winter $850–$1,050 double, $1,600–$3,350 suite; off-season $475–$675 double, $1,025–$2,000 suite. AE, DC, DISC, MC, V. Valet parking $30. **Amenities:** 2 restaurants; bar; 3 outdoor pools; state-of-the-art spa; 24-hr. concierge; 24-hr. room service; babysitting. In room: A/C, TV, fax, Wi-Fi, minibar, coffeemaker, hair dryer, iron, safe, CD player.

Fairmont Turnberry Isle Resort & Club ★★★ One of Miami's classiest—and priciest—resorts (along the lines of the Mandarin Oriental), this gorgeous 300-acre retreat has every possible facility for active guests, particularly golfers. You'll pay a lot to stay here thanks to a $150-million renovation of all guest rooms and suites, golf courses, restaurants, the spa and fitness center, pool, tennis center, and beach club. The main attractions are two Raymond Floyd championship courses, available only to members and guests of the hotel, and Bourbon Steak, a restaurant by star chef Michael Mina. The Willow Stream Spa offers an unabridged menu of treatments. A location in the well-manicured residential and shopping area of Aventura appeals to those who want peace, quiet, and a great mall. A complimentary shuttle bus takes guests to and from the Ocean Club and Aventura Mall.

19999 W. Country Club Dr., Aventura, FL 33180. ✆ **866/612-7739** or 786/279-6770. Fax 305/933-6560. www.fairmont.com/turnberryisle. 392 units. Winter $499–$699 double, $919–$5,500 suite; off-season $199–$299 double, $499–$2,700 suite. AE, DC, DISC, MC, V. Valet parking $30. Amenities: 4 restaurants; 5 bars and lounges; 3 outdoor pools; 2 golf courses; 4 clay hydro tennis courts; state-of-the-art spa; watersports equipment/rentals; concierge; business center; 24-hr. room service; babysitting. *In room:* A/C, TV/VCR, fax, dataport, minibar, fridge (upon request), coffee and tea maker, hair dryer, iron, safe, CD player.

Le Meridien Sunny Isles Beach ★ This all-suite beachfront resort is Le Meridien's first oceanfront resort in the U.S. It brings a nice touch of European-style glitz and glamour to the area and, sorry Donald, it trumps the nearby Trump resort in many ways. All rooms—there are 130 one-bedroom suites and 80 two-bedroom suites—feature king-size beds with Egyptian cotton linens, and the latest in technology, not to mention full-size Italian kitchens, washer/dryers, and spa-quality bathrooms. The gorgeous lobby has a bustling 30-seat bar where people usually hang out when waiting for a table at the delicious Bice Italian restaurant. Service throughout the hotel is impeccable. The hotel's 6,000-square-foot spa is also a hot spot for those seeking pampering, but I prefer the pool area, where an infinity-edged beachfront pool stands out like a supermodel in a crowd of circus clowns. A great spot for families looking for a bit more luxury than usual, Le Meridien has planned activities for kids and adults.

18683 Collins Ave., Miami Beach, FL 33140. ✆ **888/627-8557** or 305/503-6000. Fax 305/503-6001. www.lemeridien.com/miami. 210 units. Winter $319–$459 double, $539–$1,350 suite; off-season $299–$399 double, $439–$619 suite. AE, DC, DISC, MC, V. Valet parking $25. **Amenities:** Restaurant; lounge; bar; outdoor pool; spa; watersports equipment/rentals; 24-hr. concierge; business center; 24-hr. room service; in-room massage; babysitting; laundry service; dry cleaning. *In room:* A/C, TV/DVD, Wi-Fi, kitchen, minibar, coffeemaker, hair dryer, safe.

Regent Bal Harbour ★★★ Proving too swanky even for South Beach, the very regal Regent packed its bags and moved uptown—to a more fitting locale in the chichi shopping hamlet of Bal Harbour. But this is no mall hotel. Until the St. Regis finishes completion in the former Sheraton Bal Harbour, this is the only oceanfront resort in the area, and despite that, there's no competition. The penultimate in luxury, Regent suites are resplendent in mahogany floors, with leather walls, panoramic views of the ocean, and bathrooms with 10-foot floor-to-ceiling windows and, my favorite, a free-standing tub overlooking the ocean. Elevators take you directly into your suite, like a luxury apartment building. A Guerlain spa, butler service, spectacular pool and beach area, and world-class dining helmed by the hotel's brand new executive chef, New World–cuisine pioneer Mark Militello, will cost you a pretty penny; but if you're looking to be doted on hand and foot without lifting a finger—except to pay your bill at the end—this is the place.

10295 Collins Ave., Bal Harbour, FL 33154. ✆ **800/545-4000** or 305/455-5400. Fax 305/866-2419. www.regentbalharbour.com. 124 units. Winter from $600 doubles; off-season from $295 doubles; presidential suite $8,500. AE, MC, V. Valet parking. **Amenities:** Restaurant; bar; outdoor pool; spa; 24-hr. concierge; luxury car service; business center; 24-hr. room service; in-room massage; laundry service; dry cleaning; butler service; private jet/yacht charter. *In room:* A/C, 42-in. flatscreen TV/DVD/CD player, Wi-Fi, minibar, coffeemaker, hair dryer, safe.

CORAL GABLES

Translated appropriately as "City Beautiful," the Gables, as it's affectionately known, was one of Miami's original planned communities and is still among the city's prettiest, most pedestrian-friendly, albeit preservation-obsessed neighborhoods. Pristine with a European flair, Coral Gables is best known for its wide array of excellent upscale restaurants of various ethnicities, as well as a hotly contested (the quiet city didn't want to welcome new traffic) shopping megacomplex, with upscale stores such as Nordstrom.

If you're looking for luxury, Coral Gables has a number of wonderful hotels, but if you're on a tight budget, you may be better off elsewhere. One well-priced chain in the area is the **Holiday Inn,** 1350 S. Dixie Hwy. (✆ **800/HOLIDAY** [465-4329] or 305/667-5611), with rates between $105 and $199. It's directly across the street from the University of Miami and is popular with families and friends of students.

To locate the hotels in this section, see the map "Greater Miami Accommodations & Dining" (p. 87).

Very Expensive

Biltmore Hotel ★★★ A romantic sense of Old World glamour combined with a rich history permeates the Biltmore as much as the pricey perfume of the guests who stay here. Built in 1926, it's the oldest Coral Gables hotel and is a National Historic Landmark—one of only two operating hotels in Florida to receive that designation. Rising above the Spanish-style estate is a majestic 300-foot copper-clad tower, modeled after the Giralda bell tower in Seville and visible throughout the city. Large Moorish-style rooms are decorated with tasteful decor, European feather beds, Egyptian cotton duvets, writing desks, and some high-tech amenities. The landmark 23,000-square-foot winding pool now has the requisite hipster accessories—the private cabana, alfresco bar, and restaurant. Always a popular destination for golfers, including former president Clinton (who stays in the Al Capone suite), the Biltmore is situated on a lush, rolling, 18-hole Donald Ross course that is as challenging as it is beautiful. Sunday brunch is an equal feat—book early.

1200 Anastasia Ave., Coral Gables, FL 33134. ✆ **800/727-1926** or 305/445-1926. Fax 305/442-9496. www.biltmorehotel.com. 276 units. Winter $395–$895 double; off-season $229–$499 double; year-round $659–$6,500 specialty suites. Additional person $20. Special packages available. AE, DC, DISC, MC, V. Valet parking $25; self-parking free. **Amenities:** 4 restaurants; 4 bars; outdoor pool; 18-hole golf course; 10 lit tennis courts; state-of-the-art health club; full-service spa; sauna; concierge; car rental through concierge; elaborate business center; salon; 24-hr. room service; laundry service; dry cleaning; wine cellar. *In room:* A/C, TV, fax, dataport, kitchenette (in tower suites), minibar, hair dryer, iron, safe, VCR (upon request).

Expensive

Hotel St. Michel ★★ This European-style hotel, in the heart of Coral Gables, is one of the city's most romantic options. The accommodations and hospitality are straight out of Old World Europe, complete with dark-wood-paneled walls, cozy beds, beautiful antiques, and a quiet elegance that seems startlingly out of place in trendy Miami. Everything here is charming—from the brass elevator and parquet floors to the paddle fans. One-of-a-kind furnishings make each room special. Of course, the antiquity is countered with modernity in the form of flatscreens in all rooms. Bathrooms are on the smaller side, but are hardly cramped. All have tub/shower combinations except for two, which have one or the other. If you're picky, request your preference. Guests are treated to fresh fruit daily and enjoy seamless service throughout their stay.

162 Alcazar Ave., Coral Gables, FL 33134. ✆ **800/848-HOTEL** (4683) or 305/444-1666. Fax 305/529-0074. www.hotelstmichel.com. 28 units. Winter $249 double, $299 suite; off-season $135 double, $165 suite.

Additional person $10. Rates include continental breakfast and fresh fruit daily. AE, DC, MC, V. Self-parking $9. **Amenities:** Bar; lounge; access to nearby health club; concierge; free Wi-Fi in all public areas; room service; laundry service; dry cleaning. *In room:* A/C, TV, dataport, hair dryer, iron/ironing board (upon request).

COCONUT GROVE

This waterfront village hugs the shores of Biscayne Bay, just south of U.S. 1 and about 10 minutes from the beaches. Once a haven for hippies, head shops, and artsy bohemian characters, the Grove succumbed to the inevitable temptations of commercialism and has become a Gap nation, featuring a host of theme restaurants, bars, a megaplex, and lots of stores. Outside the main shopping area, however, you'll find the beautiful remnants of Old Miami in the form of flora, fauna, and, of course, water.

To locate the hotels in this section, see the map "Greater Miami Accommodations & Dining" (p. 87).

Very Expensive

Grove Isle Hotel and Spa ★ Hidden away in the bougainvillea and lushness of the Grove, the Grove Isle Hotel and Spa is off the beaten path on its own lushly landscaped 20-acre island, just outside the heart of Coconut Grove. The isolated exclusivity of this resort contributes to a country-club vibe, though for the most part, the people here aren't snooty, but just value their privacy and precious relaxation time. Everyone dresses in white and pastels, and if they're not on their way to a set of tennis, they're not in a rush to get anywhere. You'll step into suites that are elegantly furnished, with mosquito-netted canopy beds and a patio overlooking the bay. You'll need to reserve early here—rooms go very fast. Baleen (p. 138), a hit or miss haute-cuisine restaurant, serves fresh seafood and other regional specialties in a spectacular, elegant dining room, or, better yet, outside on the water. The 6,000-square-foot, Indonesian-inspired Spaterre is, er, terre-ific.

4 Grove Isle Dr., Coconut Grove, FL 33133. ✆ **800/884-7683** or 305/858-8300. Fax 305/854-6702. www.groveisle.com. 49 units. Winter $689–$849 double, $839–$949 suite; off-season $379–$549 double, $589–$675 suite. Packages available. AE, DC, MC, V. Valet parking $17. **Amenities:** Restaurant; large outdoor heated pool; 12 tennis courts; full-service spa; concierge; secretarial services; salon; room service; in-room massage; babysitting; laundry service; dry cleaning. *In room:* A/C, TV/VCR, dataport, minibar, hair dryer, iron, safe, CD player.

Mayfair Hotel and Spa ★★ Coconut Grove's hippest new alternative to cookie-cutter hotel brands, the Mayfair Hotel and Spa is an eclectic, Art Deco/Nouveau retreat nestled in Coconut Grove. Complimentary Wi-Fi, terry robes, 300-thread-count sheets, and plasma TVs are in every room of this newly renovated gem. Located on the rooftop is the celebrity-chic Cabana One Rooftop Pool & Lounge featuring a floating cabana roof and planks of teakwood, a serpentine bench built into the parapet which winds around a fire feature, and billowing white curtains surrounding eight private cabanas with L-shaped sofas, flatscreen TVs, Nintendo Wiis, and private safes. The famed New York steakhouse Angelo and Maxie's is also here, as is the Jurlique Spa, which exclusively utilizes its own line of organic products and follows a holistic approach to outer beauty and inner health.

3000 Florida Ave., Coconut Grove, FL 33133. ✆ **800/433-4555** or 305/441-0000. Fax 305/447-9173. www.mayfairhotelandspa.com. 179 units. Winter $279–$679 suite; off-season $149–$579 suite; year-round $3,000 penthouse. Packages available. AE, DC, DISC, MC, V. Valet parking $26. Pets accepted. **Amenities:** Restaurant; rooftop snack bar; outdoor pool; Jacuzzi; concierge; business center; 24-hr. room service; dry cleaning. *In room:* A/C, TV/DVD player, fax, dataport, minibar, coffeemaker, hair dryer, safe, CD player.

The Ritz-Carlton Coconut Grove, Miami The third and smallest of Miami's Ritz-Carlton hotels is, hands down, the most intimate of its properties, surrounded by 2 acres of tropical gardens and overlooking Biscayne Bay and the Miami skyline. Decorated in an Italian Renaissance design, the hotel's understated luxury is a welcome addition to an area known for its gaudiness. A room renovation in 2008 saw the addition of Italian Renaissance damask patterns, Carrara marble bathrooms and dark Emperador marble-topped dressers that create the feeling of being in a luxurious, private villa. That said, this is more of a business hotel than a vacation or resort property. In addition to the usual Ritz-Carlton standard of service and comfort, the hotel has an excellent, extremely elegant Tuscan steakhouse (with footstools for women to put their purses on—how classy!), Bizcaya, and a sophisticated wine-tasting scene at the chic lobby lounge.

3300 SW 27th Ave., Coconut Grove, FL 33133. ✆ **800/241-3333** or 305/644-4680. Fax 305/644-4681. www.ritzcarlton.com. 115 units. Winter $469 double, $569 suite; off-season $249 double, $359 suite. AE, DC, DISC, MC, V. Valet parking $25. **Amenities:** Restaurant; pool grill; 2 bars; outdoor heated pool; fitness center; spa; concierge; business center; shopping arcade; 24-hr. room service; babysitting; 24-hour laundry service. *In room:* A/C, TV, dataport, minibar, hair dryer, safe.

Sonesta Bayfront Hotel Coconut Grove ★ With a great location offering panoramic views of Biscayne Bay, the marina and the Miami skyline, the Sonesta is more than just a chain hotel—it's a condo too! And because of that, it's meticulously maintained and features 225 contemporary styled guest rooms, all with flatscreens and balconies and many with ocean views. The fantastic eighth-floor pool and hot tub overlooks the water and the hustle and bustle down below in the Grove, while the restaurant, Panorama, serves delicious Peruvian cuisine.

2889 McFarlane Rd., Coconut Grove, FL 33133. ✆ **800/SONESTA** (766-3782) or 305/529-2828. Fax 305/529-2008. www.sonesta.com/coconutgrove. 225 units. Winter $469 double, $569 suite; off-season $249 double, $359 suite. AE, DC, DISC, MC, V. Valet parking $25. **Amenities:** Restaurant; pool; outdoor heated pool; 24-hr. room service; babysitting; 24-hour laundry service. *In room:* A/C, TV, dataport, free Wi-Fi, minibar, hair dryer, safe.

4 WHERE TO DINE IN MIAMI

Don't be fooled by the plethora of superlean model types you're likely to see posing throughout Miami. Contrary to popular belief, dining in this city is as much a sport as plastic surgery and in-line skating on Ocean Drive. With more than 6,000 restaurants to choose from, dining out in Miami has become a passionate pastime for locals and visitors alike. Our star chefs have fused Californian-Asian with Caribbean and Latin elements to create a world-class flavor all its own: Floribbean. Think mango chutney splashed over fresh swordfish or a spicy sushi sauce served alongside Peruvian ceviche.

Formerly synonymous with early-bird specials, Miami's new-wave cuisine now rivals that of San Francisco—or even New York. Nouveau Cuban chef Douglas Rodriguez returned to his roots with a fabulous South Beach nouveau Latino eatery. In addition, other stellar chefs—such as Mark Militello, the Food Network's Michelle Bernstein, Allen Susser, Norman Van Aken, Govind Armstrong, and Clay Conley—remain firmly planted in the city's culinary scene, fusing local ingredients into edible masterpieces. Florida foodies are bracing themselves for the arrival of Alain Ducasse—sometime when the construction ends on Biscayne Boulevard—as well as Alfred Portale at the swanky new Fontainebleau, and Laurent Tourondel, who plans to open on the northern end of

Ocean Drive. This New World cuisine is not only high in calories, it's high in price. But if you can manage to splurge at least once, it'll be worth it.

Thanks to a thriving cafe society in both South Beach and Coconut Grove, you can also enjoy a moderately priced meal and linger for hours without having a waiter hover over you. In Little Havana, you can chow down on a meal that serves about six for less than $10. Because seafood is plentiful, it doesn't have to cost you an arm and a leg to enjoy the appendages of a crab or lobster. Don't be put off by the looks of our recommended seafood shacks in places such as Key Biscayne—often, these spots get the best and freshest catches.

Whatever you're craving, Miami's got it—with the exception of decent Chinese food and a New York–style slice of pizza. If you're craving a scene with your steak, then South Beach is the place to be. Like many cities in Europe and Latin America, it is fashionable to dine late in South Beach, preferably after 9pm, sometimes as late as midnight. Service on South Beach is notoriously slow and arrogant, but it comes with the turf. (Of course, it is possible to find restaurants that defy the notoriety and actually pride themselves on friendly service.) On the mainland—especially in Coral Gables and, more recently, downtown and on Brickell Avenue—you can also experience fine dining without the pretense.

The biggest complaint when it comes to Miami dining isn't the haughtiness, but rather the dearth of truly moderately priced restaurants, especially in South Beach and Coral Gables. It's either really cheap or really expensive; the in between somehow gets lost in the culinary shuffle. Quick-service diners don't exist here as they do in other cosmopolitan areas. I've tried to cover a range of cuisine in a range of prices. But with new restaurants opening on a weekly basis, you're bound to find an array of savory dining choices for every budget.

Many restaurants keep extended hours in high season (roughly Dec–Apr) and may close for lunch and/or dinner on Monday, when the traffic is slower. Always call ahead, as schedules do change. During the month of August, many Miami restaurants participate in Miami Spice, where three-course lunches and dinners are served at affordable prices. Check out www.miamirestaurantmonth.com. Also, always look carefully at your bill—many Miami restaurants add a 15% to 18% gratuity to your total due to the enormous influx of European tourists who are not accustomed to tipping. Keep in mind that this amount is the *suggested* amount and can be adjusted, either higher or lower, depending on your assessment of the service provided. Because of this tipping-included policy, South Beach waitstaff are best known for their lax or inattentive service. *Feel free to adjust it* if you feel your server deserves more or less.

SOUTH BEACH

The renaissance of South Beach started in the early '90s and is still continuing as classic cuisine gives in to modern temptation by inevitably fusing with more chic, nouveau developments created by faithful followers and devotees of the Food Network school of cooking. The ultimate result has spawned dozens of first-rate restaurants. In fact, big-name restaurants from across the country have capitalized on South Beach's international appeal and have continued to open branches here with great success. A few old standbys remain from the *Miami Vice* days, but the flock of newcomers dominates the scene, with places going in and out of style as quickly as the tides.

On South Beach, new restaurants are opening and closing as frequently as Emeril says "Bam!" As it's impossible to list them all, I recommend strolling and browsing. Most restaurants post a copy of their menu outside. With very few exceptions, the places on

Ocean Drive are crowded with tourists and priced accordingly. You'll do better to venture a little farther onto the pedestrian-friendly streets just west of Ocean Drive.

To locate the restaurants in this section, see the "South Beach Accommodations & Dining" map (p. 91).

Very Expensive

Blue Door ★★★ FRENCH BRAZILIAN It used to be that the Blue Door's greatest claim to fame was that Madonna was part owner. The food was unremarkable, but the eye candy was sickly sweet. When the Material Girl fled, so did others, leaving the Blue Door wide open for anything, as long as it was as fabulous as the hotel in which it sits. This really is quintessential South Beach dining. The most recent incarnation of the restaurant begs for superlatives more flattering than the standard "fabulous." The eye candy is still here, but now you have good reason to focus your eyes on the food rather than who's eating it. Thanks to award-winning chef Claude Troisgros (rhymes with foie gras)—a star in his own right—the menu frowns upon the ubiquitous fusion moniker in favor of a more classic French approach to tropical spices and ingredients. Caramelized rack of lamb with toasted Moroccan couscous in a mint passion-fruit glaze, and beef tenderloin with Gorgonzola cream sauce, Beaujolais-poached Asian pear, crispy potato, raisins, and green peppercorns are just a few of the Blue Door's tempting offerings, but the menu changes frequently. Service, which used to be snippy, slow, and, at times, downright rude, has improved dramatically. Sunday brunch here is one of the most popular in town.

In the Delano Hotel, 1685 Collins Ave., South Beach. ✆ **305/674-6400.** www.chinagrillmgt.com. Reservations recommended for dinner. Main courses $31–$46. AE, DC, MC, V. Daily 7am–4pm and 7pm–midnight (bar until 3am); Sun brunch 10:30am–2:30pm.

Casa Tua ★★ (Finds) ITALIAN The stunning Casa Tua is a sleek and chic, country Italian–style establishment set in a refurbished 1925 Mediterranean-style house-cum-hotel. It has several dining areas, including a resplendent outdoor garden, comfy Ralph Lauren–esque living room, and a communal eat-in kitchen. The roasted rack of lamb is stratospheric in price—upwards of $50—but sublime in taste, and a bargain compared to the whole branzino served for two at twice that price. Service is, as always with South Beach eateries, inconsistent, ranging from ultraprofessional to absurdly lackadaisical. For these prices, they should be wiping our mouths for us. What used to be a fabulous lounge upstairs is now a members-only club, so don't even try to get in.

1700 James Ave., South Beach. ✆ **305/673-1010.** Reservations required. Main courses $24–$100. AE, DC, MC, V. Mon–Sat 7pm–midnight.

China Grill ★ PAN-ASIAN If ever a restaurant could be as cavernous as, say, the Asian continent, this would be it. Formerly a hub of hype and pompous circumstance, China Grill has calmed on the coolness meter despite the infrequent appearance of the likes of J-Lo and Enrique Iglesias (separately, of course), but its cuisine is still sizzling, if not better than ever. With an incomparable and dizzying array of amply portioned dishes (such as the outrageous crispy spinach, wasabi mashed potatoes, seared rare tuna in spicy Japanese pepper, broccoli rabe dumplings, lobster pancakes, and a sinfully delicious dessert sampler complete with sparklers), this epicurean journey into the world of near-perfect Pan-Asian cuisine is well worth a stop on any foodie's itinerary. Keep in mind that China Grill is a family-style restaurant and dishes are for sharing. For those who can't stay away from sushi, China Grill also has Dragon, a 40-seat "sushi den" in a private back room with such one-of-a-kind rolls as the Havana Roll—yellowtail snapper, rum, coconut, avocado, and red tobiko—and cocktails such as the Lemongrass Saketini. New in 2008, in what was once China Grill's private room, is a South Beach branch of the ultrapricey **Kobe Club** (✆ **305/673-5370**), a 52-seat restaurant devoted to all things meaty, where a "flight" of beef—Kobe, Waygu, American—costs upwards of $350. You really better love meat to spend that money. For those in Fort Lauderdale, there's a China Grill up there now, with water views, at 881 SE 17th St. (✆ **954/759-9950**).

404 Washington Ave., South Beach. ✆ **305/534-2211.** www.chinagrillmgmt.com/chinaMI. Reservations strongly recommended. Main courses $26–$59. AE, DC, MC, V. Mon–Thurs 11:45am–midnight; Fri 11:45am–1am; Sat 6pm–1am; Sun 6pm–midnight.

DeVito South Beach ★ ITALIAN CHOPHOUSE The latest production from actor Danny DeVito (and a few bona fide restaurant professionals), this Italian-style chophouse is a stunning homage to decor—and DeVito. Brick walls and rich, textured bordello-style paneling are adorned with flatscreen TVs playing DeVito's greatest hits, although one weekend night they switched it up with James Bond. An elegant, warm interior is matched by an even more elegant price tag—dinner for two can cost upwards of $200 thanks to a heavily sauced, heavily priced menu of steaks and assorted family-style dishes including Dover sole, Maine lobster risotto, an excellent calamari appetizer, and a gargantuan veal parmigiana that is enough to serve the entire restaurant. The $300 (!) Global Steak Flight is the restaurant's signature dish, with three different kinds of Kobe beef—authentic Japanese Kobe Beef, Australian Wagyu Rollatini, and American Kobe Flat Iron. Order wisely here, and take advantage of the freebies you get when you sit down—homemade popovers and a selection of salumi, cheese, and veggies.

150 Ocean Dr., South Beach. ✆ **305/531-0911.** www.devitosouthbeach.com. Reservations strongly recommended. Main courses $18–$300. AE, DC, MC, V. Daily noon–3pm; Sun–Thurs 5pm–midnight; Fri–Sat 5pm–1am.

Emeril's Miami Beach ★★★ CREOLE This is the real deal. In a city where restaurants pride themselves on celebrity sightings and snooty service, Emeril's is a spicy breath of fresh air. If you've never dined at Emeril's original restaurant(s) in New Orleans and you're craving gourmet Creole cuisine, dine here ASAP. Elaborately designed by David Rockwell, the 8,000-square-foot restaurant is reminiscent of a bustling and cavernous New York City hot spot with chandeliers, massive wine cellars, and a very inviting open kitchen in which Emeril himself sometimes stars. Call the restaurant ahead to find out when he's in town, and book your reservations immediately. Portions are massive, and signature dishes include New Orleans barbecue shrimp with a petite rosemary biscuit; Niman Ranch double-cut pork chop with tamarind glaze, caramelized sweet potatoes, and green chili mole sauce; and banana cream pie with banana crust, caramel sauce, and chocolate shavings. Service is stellar and should serve as an example to other area restaurants. A 3-hour Sunday Jazz Brunch is worth breaking the diet for, too.

In the Loews Hotel, 1601 Collins Ave., South Beach. ✆ **305/695-4550.** www.emerils.com. Reservations required. Main courses $18–$50. AE, MC, V. Sun–Thurs 11:30am–2pm and 5:30–10pm; Fri–Sat 11:30am–2pm and 5:30–11pm.

Escopazzo ★★★ ITALIAN *Escopazzo* means "I'm going crazy" in Italian, but the only sign of insanity in this primo Northern Italian eatery is the fact that it seats only 90 and it's one of the best restaurants in town. The wine bottles have it better—the restaurant's cellar holds 1,000 bottles of various vintages. In 2007, Escopazzo added "Organic Italian Restaurant" to its title. Not necessary, as the ingredients here have always been of the freshest, but for those who need further encouragement, there it is. Should you be so lucky to score a table at this romantic local favorite (choose one in the back dining room that's reminiscent of an Italian courtyard, complete with fountain and faux windows; it's not cheesy at all), you'll have trouble deciding between dishes that will have you swearing off the Olive Garden with your first bite. Standouts are milk and basil dough pasta with baby calamari, chickpeas, tomatoes, and arugula, or grass-fed hanger steak with roasted baby organic veggies in a truffle sauce. The hand-rolled pastas and risotto are near perfection. Eating here is like dining with a big Italian family—it's never boring (the menu changes five or six times a year), the service is excellent, and nobody's happy until you are blissfully full.

1311 Washington Ave., South Beach. ✆ **305/674-9450.** www.escopazzo.com. Reservations required. Main courses $27–$55. AE, MC, V. Mon–Fri 6pm–midnight; Sat 6pm–1am; Sun 6–11pm.

Joe's Stone Crab Restaurant ★ SEAFOOD Unless you grease the palms of one of the stone-faced maitre d's with some stone-cold cash, you'll be waiting for those famous claws for up to 2 hours—if not more. As much a Miami landmark as the beaches themselves, Joe's is a microcosm of the city, attracting everyone from T-shirted locals to a bejeweled Ivana Trump. Whatever you wear, however, will be eclipsed by a kitschy, unglamorous plastic bib that your waiter will tie on you unless you say otherwise. Open only during stone-crab season (Oct–May), Joe's reels in the crowds with the freshest (though some disagree and consider Joe's stash subpar to less-assuming area restaurants), meatiest stone crabs and their essential accouterments: creamed spinach and excellent sweet-potato fries. The claws come in medium, large, and jumbo. Some say size doesn't matter; others swear by the jumbo (and more expensive) ones. Whatever you choose, pair them with a savory mustard sauce (a perfect mix of mayo and mustard) or hot butter. Not feeling crabby? The fried chicken and liver and onions on the regular menu are actually considered by many as far superior—they're definitely far cheaper—to the crabs. Oh yes, and save room for dessert. The Key lime pie here is the best in town. If you don't feel like waiting, try Joe's Takeaway, which is next door to the restaurant—it's a lot quicker and just as tasty.

11 Washington Ave. (at Biscayne St., just south of 1st St.), South Beach. ✆ **305/673-0365** or 673-4611 for takeout. www.joesstonecrab.com. Reservations not accepted. Market price varies but averages $45–$65. AE, DC, DISC, MC, V. Sun 11:30am–2pm and 4–10pm; Mon–Thurs 11:30am–2pm and 5–10pm; Fri–Sat 11:30am–2pm and 5–11pm. Closed mid-May to mid-Oct.

Maison d'Azur ★★★ SEAFOOD A swanky seafood brasserie that moved from the Angler's Hotel up the block to the Astor is where South Beach meets St. Tropez (but owned by a congenial French Canadian turned N.Y.C. restaurateur). Thank goodness the attitude was left back in France and what remains is stellar service and outstanding fresh French fare. The steak frites are among the best in town, if not *the* best, and for high rollers, there's an unabridged list of caviars and wines by the glass. Soothing lighting and modern French brasserie decor makes for an outstanding dining experience, complete with a DJ imported straight from the Riviera, who spins an assortment of dinner music that's unusually soothing and entertaining. An outdoor garden area is perfect for cool nights. The menu changes often; ask for the chef's recommendations. Among ours: the John Dorie, perfectly filleted and served tableside; the seafood platter that's as tall as the Eiffel Tower, full of oysters, caviar, crab, shrimp, and escargot; and for a true indulgence, the foie gras is fantastic. Save room for dessert—the chef makes his own ice cream *and* ice cream cones—don't miss the Nutella-flavored ice cream. *C'est magnifique!*

956 Washington Ave. (btw. 6th and 7th), South Beach. ✆ **305/534-9600.** Reservations suggested. Main courses $26–$65. AE, MC, V. Sun–Wed 7am–1am; Thurs–Sat 7am–4am.

Nobu ★★★ SUSHI When Madonna ate here, no one really noticed. The same thing happened when Justin Timberlake and Cameron Diaz canoodled here. It's not because people were purposely trying not to notice, but because the real star at Nobu is the sushi. The raw facts: Nobu has been hailed as one of the best sushi restaurants in the world, with always-packed eateries in New York, London, and Los Angeles. The Omakase, or Chef's Choice—a multicourse menu entirely up to the chef for $70 per person and up—gets consistent raves. Although you won't wait long for your food to be cooked, you will wait forever to score a table here.

At The Shore Club Hotel, 1901 Collins Ave., South Beach. ✆ **305/695-3232.** Reservations for parties of 6 or more only. Main courses $26 and above. AE, MC, V. Sun 7–11pm; Mon–Thurs 7pm–midnight; Fri–Sat 7pm–1am.

Ola ★★ NUEVO LATINO Star chef Douglas Rodriguez single-handedly created the nouveau Latino and Cubano cuisine in Miami when he founded Lincoln Road's Yuca restaurant in 1989. From there, he skyrocketed to fame (and left Yuca to rot in mediocrity) and became co-owner and executive chef at New York City's lauded Patria (leaving Miami restaurantgoers to wallow in their sorrows). But now Rodriguez is back in full force with Ola, which moved from its larger confines in the Deco landmark, the Savoy, to the smaller, chicer Sanctuary Hotel, serving Spanish tapas and ceviches as well as Rodriguez's very own inimitable culinary concoctions. For those who are addicted to the low-carb craze, you'll find several items on the menu tailored to your diet. But why bother? Latin food is about flavor and carbs, so indulge here (like your wallet will have to).

1745 James Ave., in the Sanctuary Hotel, Miami Beach. ✆ **305/673-5455.** Reservations recommended. Main courses $26–$50. AE, DC, MC, V. Mon–Thurs 5:30–11pm; Fri–Sat 5:30pm–midnight.

Prime One Twelve ★★★ STEAKHOUSE Part of the ever-expanding culinary empire of Nemo, Big Pink, and Shoji Sushi, Prime One Twelve is the media darling of the exclusive group of restaurants in the hot South of Fifth Street area of South Beach, ranking near the top of the list of highest-grossing restaurants in the entire country in 2007 and proving recession proof in 2008, reporting an unheard of *increase* in business and profits. A celebrity-saturated sleek steakhouse ambience and bustling bar (complete with dried strips of bacon in lieu of nuts) play second fiddle to the beef, which is arguably the best in the entire city. The 12-ounce filet mignon is seared to perfection and can be enhanced with optional dipping sauces (for a price)—truffle, garlic herb, foie gras, and chipotle. The 22-ounce bone-in rib-eye is fabulous, as is the gigantic 48-ounce porterhouse. Prime One Twelve also features a $25 Kobe-beef hot dog, Kobe-beef sliders—think White Castle on an expense account ($25)—and a Kobe burger, a $30 version of sheer ecstasy. Fries are extra at $10, as are all the side dishes (the broccoli rabe sautéed in garlic is outstanding, as are the scalloped potatoes)—typical in a steakhouse, but the prices here are hefty. A powerhouse crowd gathers here for lunch and dinner, and reservations are rarer than the yellowfin tuna tartare appetizer, but should you be lucky enough to score such a "prime" reservation, take it without hesitation.

112 Ocean Dr. (in the Browns Hotel), South Beach. ✆ **305/532-8112.** www.prime112.com. Reservations recommended. Main courses $20–$88. AE, DISC, MC, V. Mon–Fri 11:30am–3pm; daily 6:30pm–midnight.

Table 8 ★ CALIFORNIA CUISINE Star chef Govind Armstrong, who got his start at the age of 13 with Wolfgang Puck at L.A.'s legendary Spago, opened a branch of this L.A. hot spot on South Beach. Housed in an Ocean Drive hotel, Table 8, which experienced its fair share of economic troubles in 2008, features 255 seats spread out in a main dining room, a private dining room for celebrity and VIP clientele, and a wine room.

There's also a 40-seat lounge situated beneath the hotel's fabulous glass-bottom pool and featuring a delicious small-plate lounge menu that, in our opinion, is better than the actual menu—try the grilled cheese, and then tell us what you think! Among Chef Armstrong's signature dishes is a salt-roasted porterhouse steak, which the *Robb Report* called the Best of the Best in one of its coveted "best of" issues; it isn't on the menu, so consider that an inside tip.

1458 Ocean Dr., South Beach. ✆ **305/695-4114.** www.table8restaurants.com. Reservations recommended. Main courses $26–$52. AE, DC, DISC, MC, V. Sun–Tues 6–11pm; Wed–Sat 6pm–midnight.

Wish ★★★ ITALIAN Located in the stylish Todd Oldham–designed The Hotel, this is one of the most beautiful, romantic outdoor restaurants in South Beach. Chef Marco Ferraro, who has worked under the toque of Jean-Georges Vongerichten, has taken the restaurant to a new level of taste with a menu he describes as "fresh, seasonal, light, and vibrant." He's putting it mildly. The Maine lobster ravioli is exquisite, as is the oven-roasted Kurobuta pork chop served with a parsley purée and luscious stuffed eggplant. And then there are the "electric cocktails," such as the glowing green-apple martini served with psychedelic ice cubes. The only thing you'll wish for after you leave here is to go back!

801 Collins Ave., South Beach. ✆ **305/531-2222.** Reservations recommended. Main courses $28–$46. AE, DC, MC, V. Mon 11:30am–3pm; Tues–Sun 11:30am–3pm and 6–11pm (Fri–Sat to midnight).

Expensive

Barton G. The Restaurant ★ AMERICAN For those who are jaded by pan-fusion, pan-everything cuisine these days, Barton G. The Restaurant is the culinary antithesis, an homage to gourmet kitsch. Set on a residential block on the west side of South Beach, Barton G., named after its owner, who happens to be one of Miami's best-known, most over-the-top event planners, is a place that looks like a trendy restaurant, but eats like a show. Here, presentation is paramount. Take, for instance, the popcorn shrimp appetizer. This is not your average Red Lobster popcorn shrimp. Served on a plateful of, yes, popcorn, with field greens and the plump, crispy rock shrimp stuffed into an actual popcorn box, this dish is one of many awe-inspiring—and tasty—items you'll find in this unique restaurant in Miami. A grilled sea bass that is light and flavorful is served in a brown paper bag with laundry clips keeping the steam in until your server unclips them and releases the flavor within. Desserts are equally outrageous, including the Chocolate Fun-Do, a mini chocolate fountain overflowing with 4 pounds of Belgian chocolate and tons of dipping delicacies from cake to fruit. A giant plume of cotton candy reminiscent of drag diva Dame Edna's hair is surrounded by three white-, dark-, and milk-chocolate-covered popcorn balls that, when cracked, reveal a sinful chocolate truffle inside. There's nothing ordinary about this seemingly ordinary restaurant, which is why people such as Tom Cruise and Will Smith are regulars. An elegant, well-lit indoor dining room is popular with members of the socialite set, for whom Barton G. has done many an affair, while the bar area and outdoor courtyard is the place to be for younger trend-seekers who appreciate what's on their plates as much as they do who's sitting next to them.

1427 West Ave., South Beach. ✆ **305/672-8881.** www.bartong.com. Reservations suggested. Main courses $10–$50. AE, DC, DISC, MC, V. Daily 6pm–midnight.

Grazie ★★ ITALIAN Owned and operated by an Israeli and a Honduran, Grazie, go figure, is one of Miami's best-loved *Italian* restaurants. The warm and inviting dining room blissfully offsets the surrounding schmaltz of Washington Avenue. The food is authentically Italian, with a variety of carpaccios—yellowtail and beef-cheek carpaccio rock—hot and cold antipasti, including an addictive bruschetta; and, the reason you're here—homemade pastas, from *fusilli alla Bolognese* with homemade sausage to angel hair with fresh garlic and ravioli stuffed with lump crabmeat in a pink lobster sauce. There are not many places to get pasta as good as you'll have it here. Just ask former Miami Heat giant Shaquille O'Neal, who still occasionally eats pasta here.

701 Washington Ave., South Beach. ✆ **305/673-1312.** www.grazieitaliancuisine.com. Reservations recommended. Main courses $17–$45. AE, MC, V. Sun–Thurs 6–11pm; Fri–Sat 6pm–midnight.

Nemo ★ PAN-ASIAN Located in the chic South Beach area known as SoFi ("South of Fifth St."), Nemo is a funky, high-style eatery with an open kitchen and an outdoor courtyard canopied by trees and lined with an eclectic mix of model types and foodies. Among the reasons to eat in this restaurant (whose name is actually *omen* spelled backward): grilled Indian-spiced pork chop; grilled local mahimahi with citrus and grilled sweet-onion salad, kimchi glaze, basil, and crispy potatoes; and an inspired dessert menu that's not for the faint of calories. Seating inside is comfy-cozy, but borders on cramped. On Sunday mornings, the open kitchen is converted into a buffet counter for the restaurant's unparalleled brunch. Be prepared for a wait, however, as the line tends to spill out onto the street.

100 Collins Ave., South Beach. ✆ **305/532-4550.** www.nemorestaurant.com. Reservations recommended. Main courses $26–$48; Sun brunch $34. AE, MC, V. Mon–Sat noon–3pm and 6:30pm–midnight; Sun 11am–3pm and 6pm–midnight. Valet parking $10–$20.

Quattro ★★ ITALIAN Not just another Italian restaurant on Lincoln Road, Quattro is a Northern Italian standout thanks to its chefs—29-year-old twin brothers hailing from the Piedmont region of Italy who barely speak English, but speak pasta fluently. Signature dishes on the menu include homemade fontina ravioli with white truffle oil and veal wraps with melted Parmesan cheese and bread crumbs. The wine list is all Italian and reasonably priced. The room is gorgeous, with dramatic lighting, chandeliers, and an all-glass bar that buzzes with *la dolce vita.* Try the cheese plate if you're not too hungry—it's a meal in itself and features that salami you wished you had smuggled back home the last time you returned from Italy.

1014 Lincoln Rd., South Beach. ✆ **305/531-4833.** www.quattromiami.com. Reservations recommended. Main courses $31–$50. AE, MC, V. Sun–Thurs noon–4pm and 6pm–midnight; Fri–Sat noon–4pm and 6pm–1am.

Shoji Sushi ★ SUSHI Despite the sushi saturation on South Beach, Shoji stands apart from the typical sashimi-and-California-roll routine with expertly prepared, exquisitely fresh, and innovative top-notch rolls. The sleek sister to its next-door neighbor Nemo, Shoji is known for its authentic Japanese box sushi technique, in which the sushi, rice, and ingredients are packed into a tidy, tasty cake that won't crumble into your lap. Among the rolls I can't seem to get enough of here are the *hamachi* jalapeño—cilantro, daikon sprout, asparagus, avocado, and jalapeños—and the spicy lobster roll, which consists of mango, avocado, scallion, *shiso,* salmon egg, and huge chunks of lobster. Wash it all down with a "saketini," or my personal fave, the "gingertini," which is made with ginger, vodka, triple sec, ginger ale, and pickled ginger juice.

100 Collins Ave., South Beach. ✆ **305/532-4245.** www.shojisushi.com. Reservations recommended. Sushi $1–$13; main courses $13–$21. AE, MC, V. Mon–Thurs noon–3pm and 6pm–midnight; Fri noon–3pm and 6pm–1am; Sat–Sun 6pm–1am. Valet parking $10.

Talula ★★★ CONTEMPORARY AMERICAN Take two celebrity chefs and combine their epicurean efforts, and you've got Talula, one of the most creative, refreshing restaurants to come onto the South Beach scene since Barton G. The Restaurant (p. 119).

Anti Social? South Beach Loses a Hot Spot

We didn't see it coming. When China Grill's emperor Jeffrey Chodorow took over the arty lobby of the Sagamore with his ode to fashionable fare, the hotel was overrun by hipsters. Beyond all the glitz, glamour, and celebrity, **Social Miami** was a serious restaurant, with a fantastic, creative menu. And now it's gone. The official statement from China Grill Management: "Due to operational differences with hotel ownership, China Grill Management announces it has ceased operations at Social Miami at Sagamore as of Sunday, July 6, 2008. We look forward to relocating the Social concept to another South Florida location in the near future. No other information (or comment) is available at this time." We'll always have fond memories of the place—its chicken lollipops and deviled eggs especially—a place where lots of big (and not so big) celebs and chefs have passed through. Keep your ears open for news of a reopening, or check Frommers.com for updates.

Owned by husband-and-wife team Andrea Curto-Randazzo and Frank Randazzo, Talula is a blissful marriage of many flavors, as seen in such signature dishes as grilled Canadian foie gras, with caramelized figs, blue-corn pancakes, chili syrup, and candied walnuts; and sausage-and-Vidalia-onion-stuffed grilled center pork chop, with garlic-sautéed broccoli rabe, apple smoke bacon, bean ragout, caramelized Granny Smith apple, and whole-grain mustard sauce. Chef Frank's chophouse specials are also hot-ticket items, including the 14-ounce, 21-day dry-aged rib-eye. Daily specials always include a chopped salad, soup, risotto, and a meat or fish dish. The wine list is well-balanced, featuring 85 vintages from California, Italy, France, Australia, and South America. Wines by the glass are a reasonable, un–South Beach $11 to $20. As to be expected with any restaurant in South Beach, Talula is cool looking, with an unpretentious, warm decor and outdoor garden patio that is a popular spot for the fantastic buffet-style Sunday brunches. An exhibition kitchen is a tempting seating option, with five seats that offer a view of the culinary action.

210 23rd St., South Beach. ✆ **305/672-0778.** www.talulaonline.com. Reservations recommended. Main courses $13–$84. AE, MC, V. Tues–Thurs noon–2:30pm and 6:30–11pm; Fri noon–2:30pm and 6:30–11:30pm; Sat 6:30–11:30pm; Sun 6–10pm. Happy hour Tues–Sun 5–7pm.

Moderate

Balan's ★ MEDITERRANEAN Balan's provides undeniable evidence that the Brits actually do know a thing or two about cuisine. A direct import from London's Soho, Balan's draws inspiration from various Mediterranean and Asian influences, labeling its cuisine "Mediterrasian." With a brightly colored interior straight out of a mod '60s flick, Balan's is a favorite among the gay and arty crowds, especially on weekends during brunch hours. The moderately priced food is rather good here—especially the double-baked cheese soufflé; citrus tossed mixed greens; Thai red curry; and the pan-fried Tilapia with Indian garbanzo bean curry and mint yogurt. When in doubt, the restaurant's signature US1 Burger is always a good choice. Adding to the ambience is the restaurant's people-watching vantage point on Lincoln Road. In 2009, Balan's expanded over the causeway and opened a second location at 901 S. Miami Ave., in the bustling Brickell area. In mid-2009, they were set to open a *third* at Biscayne Boulevard and 67th Street in the Upper East Side neighborhood.

1022 Lincoln Rd. (btw. Lenox and Michigan), South Beach. ✆ **305/534-9191.** www.balans.co.uk. Reservations accepted, except for weekend brunch. Main courses $9–$37 (breakfast and dinner specials Mon–Fri). AE, DISC, MC, V. Sun–Thurs 8am–midnight; Fri–Sat 8am–1am; Sat–Sun brunch noon–3:30pm.

Big Pink ★ (Kids AMERICAN "Real Food for Real People" is the motto to which this restaurant strictly adheres. Set on what used to be a gritty corner of Collins Avenue, Big Pink—owned by the folks at the higher-end Nemo—is quickly identified by a whimsical Pippi Longstocking–type mascot on a sign outside. Scooters and motorcycles line the streets surrounding the place, which is a favorite among beach bums, club kids, and those craving Big Pink's comforting and hugely portioned pizzas, sandwiches, salads, and hamburgers. The fare is above average, at best, and the menu is massive, but it comes with a good dose of kitsch, such as the "gourmet" spin on the classic TV dinner, which is done perfectly, right down to the compartmentalized dessert. Televisions line the bar area, and the family-style table arrangement (there are several booths, too) promotes camaraderie among diners. Outdoor tables are available. Even picky kids will like the food here, and parents can enjoy the family-friendly atmosphere (not the norm for South Beach) without worrying whether their kids are making too much noise.

157 Collins Ave., Miami Beach. ✆ **305/532-4700.** www.bigpinkrestaurant.com. Main courses $9–$20. AE, DC, MC, V. Mon–Wed 8am–midnight; Thurs 8am–2am; Fri–Sat 8am–5am; Sun 8am–2am.

Bond St. Lounge ★ SUSHI A New York City import, the scenеy Bond St. Lounge is in the basement of the shabby-chic Townhouse Hotel and is packing in hipsters as tightly as the crabmeat in a California roll. Despite its tiny size, Bond St. Lounge's super-fresh nigiri and sashimi, and funky sushi rolls such as the sun-dried tomato and avocado or the arugula crispy potato, are worth cramming in here for. As the evening progresses, however, Bond St. becomes more of a bar scene than a restaurant, but sushi is always available at the bar to accompany your sake Bloody Mary.

Townhouse Hotel, 150 20th St., South Beach. ✆ **305/398-1806.** Reservations recommended. Sushi $6–$20. AE, MC, V. Daily 6pm–2am.

The Café at Books & Books ★ AMERICAN Not only does this sidewalk cafe offer some of the best, freshest breakfasts and lunches in town—the egg-and-tuna-salad combo is my favorite, as are the amazing homemade hash browns—but gourmet dinners as well. This is not your chain bookstore's prefab tuna sandwich. Sadly, in 2009, the bookstore became a Diesel store, but the cafe stayed. Chef Bernie Matz gave star chef Douglas Rodriguez his start—enough said. Sandwiches, salads, and burgers are good, but after 5pm the real gourmand comes out in Matz with dishes like a juicy flank steak marinated in espresso and brown sugar, seared, sliced, and served with a pineapple and onion salsa and a pair of plantain nests smothered in garlicky mojo. If you're still inspired to buy a cookbook after your meal, Books & Books set up a small annex in the back of the courtyard.

933 Lincoln Rd., South Beach. ✆ **305/695-8898.** Main courses $5–$25. AE, MC, V. Daily 9am–11pm.

Clarke's ★ IRISH There's more to this neighborhood pub than pints of Guinness. With a warm, inviting ambience and a gorgeously rich wood bar as the focal point, Clarke's is the only true gastropub in Miami, with excellent fare that goes beyond bangers and mash and delicious burgers, and delves into the gourmet. Highlights include olive oil yellowtail poached snapper with mushroom confit, tomato marmalade, and frisée salad; Sazerac House crab cakes, whose secret recipe hails from owner Laura Cullen's father's New York City landmark, the Sazerac House; and Mom's Montauk-style scallops. If you're not in the mood for full fare, my favorite is the New York–style pretzel, served on a spike with mustard on the side. The vibe here is very friendly, which is why everyone from Miami Heat basketball players to South Beach celebrity types choose Clarke's when they want a low-key night with delicious fare—and even more delicious "dish."

840 1st St., South Beach. ✆ **305/538-9885.** www.clarkesmiamibeach.com. Main courses $6–$27. AE, MC, V. Mon–Sat 5pm–midnight; Sun 11am–3pm (brunch) and 4pm–midnight.

El Rancho Grande ★★ MEXICAN Hidden on a side street off of Lincoln Road, El Rancho Grande is a favorite local cantina that has attracted the likes of Cher and Matt Damon, thanks to its ultrafresh fare and unassuming ambience. With a "Pottery Barn meets Acapulco" decor, El Rancho Grande doesn't hold anything back when it comes to the cuisine. The Aztec soup, a hot-and-spicy blend of chicken and tortilla strips, is one of the best I've had. The salsa here is not at all watery and is freshly made—a tongue-tickling blend of spices, cilantro, tomatoes, onions, and peppers—and the Mexican favorites of burritos, enchiladas, and fajitas are all very well represented. All portions are huge and can be shared or taken home for extra meal mileage. Margaritas are a little weak when frozen and better ordered on the rocks. Expect a wait at the small bar for your table, especially on weekends. Limited outdoor seating is also available.

1626 Pennsylvania Ave., South Beach. ✆ **305/673-0480.** Main courses $10–$20. AE, DC, MC, V. Daily 11am–11pm.

Grillfish ★ SEAFOOD The Cher of South Beach seafood spots, Grillfish is one of the city's longest lasting, and, frankly, most well preserved. From the beautiful Byzantine-style mural and the gleaming oak bar, you'd think you were eating in a much more expensive restaurant, but Grillfish manages to pay the exorbitant South Beach rent with the help of a loyal following of locals who come for fresh, simple seafood in a relaxed but upscale atmosphere. The servers are friendly and know the menu well. The barroom seafood chowder is full of chunks of shellfish, as well as some fresh whitefish filets in a tomato broth. The small ear of corn included with each entree is about as close as you'll get to any type of vegetable offering, besides the pedestrian salad. Still, at these prices, it's worth a visit to try some local fare, including mako shark, swordfish, tuna, marlin, and wahoo.

1444 Collins Ave. (corner of Española Way), South Beach. ✆ **305/538-9908.** www.grillfish.com. Reservations accepted for parties of 6 or more only. Main courses $9–$26. AE, DC, DISC, MC, V. Daily 11:30am–4pm and 5:30pm–midnight.

Joe Allen ★ Finds AMERICAN It's hard to compete in a city with haute spots everywhere you look, but Joe Allen, a restaurant that has proven itself in both New York and London, has stood up to the challenge by establishing itself off the beaten path in possibly the only area of South Beach that has remained impervious to trendiness and overdevelopment. Located on the bay side of the beach, Joe Allen is conspicuously devoid of neon lights, valet parkers, and fashionable pedestrians. Inside, however, one discovers a hidden jewel: a stark yet elegant interior and no-nonsense, fairly priced, ample-portioned dishes such as meatloaf, pizza, fresh fish, and salads. The scene has a homey feel favored by locals looking to escape the hype without compromising quality.

1787 Purdy Ave./Sunset Harbor Dr. (3 blocks west of Alton Rd.), South Beach. ✆ **305/531-7007.** Reservations recommended, especially Sat–Sun. Main courses $15–$25. MC, V. Daily 11:30am–11:30pm.

Macaluso's ★★ ITALIAN This restaurant epitomizes the Italians' love for—and mastery of—savory, plentiful, down-home Staten Island–style food. While the storefront restaurant is intimate and demure in nature, there's nothing delicate about the bold mix of flavors in every meat and pasta dish here. Catch the fantastic clam pie when in season—

the portions are huge. Pricier items vary throughout the season but will likely feature fresh fish handpicked by Chef (and owner) Michael, the don of the kitchen, who is so accommodating that he'll take special requests or even bring to your table a complimentary signature meatball. If he doesn't, don't hesitate to ask your waiter for one; he'll be glad to bring it to you. Everyone will recommend favorites such as the rigatoni and broccoli rabe. There are also delicious desserts ranging from homemade anisette cookies to gooey pastries. The wine list is also good. Keep your eyes peeled, as this is a major celeb hot spot, where everyone from Lindsay Lohan to Roger Federer and Billy Joel have been known to eat here and kibitz with the chef in the kitchen.

1747 Alton Rd., Miami Beach. ✆ **305/604-1811.** Main courses $15–$40; pizza $10–$20. MC, V. Tues–Sat 6pm–midnight; Sun 6–11pm. After 10:30pm, only pies are served.

Spiga ★★ (Finds) ITALIAN If you want a side scene with your spaghetti, don't even think of dining at Spiga, a place that's so low-key that many of South Beach's most ostentatious hipsters have never even heard of it. The complimentary bruschetta with grilled eggplant, served to you at one of the few tables inside or out, is the first of many culinary treats. The simple gnocchi with tomato and basil is a garlicky sensation, not to mention a most filling entree. The fresh asparagus baked in Parmesan cheese is so fresh that gourmands insist that Alice Waters, the queen of organic cooking, had something to do with it; and the red snapper with kalamata olives, fresh tomatoes, capers, and onions is a refreshingly simple departure from the fusion variety that can be found in almost any area restaurant. The place is extremely romantic and vaguely reminiscent of a Florentine trattoria.

Hotel Impala, 1228 Collins Ave., South Beach. ✆ **305/534-0079.** www.spigarestaurant.com. Reservations accepted. Main courses $12–$26. AE, DC, MC, V. Daily 6pm–midnight.

Van Dyke Cafe ★ AMERICAN News Cafe's younger, less harried sibling, Van Dyke is a locals' favorite, at which people-watching is also premium, but attitude is practically nonexistent. Like News, the menu here is pretty cut and dried—sandwiches, salads, eggs, and so on, but the Van Dyke's warm, wood-floored interior, upstairs jazz bar, accessible parking, and intense chocolate soufflé make it a less taxing alternative. Also, unlike News, Van Dyke turns into a sizzling nightspot featuring live jazz nearly every night of the week. Outside there's a vast tree-lined seating area that's ideal for people-watching. Those allergic to or afraid of dogs might reconsider eating here, as Van Dyke is also a canine hot spot.

846 Lincoln Rd., South Beach. ✆ **305/534-3600.** www.thevandykecafe.com. Main courses $9–$20. AE, DC, MC, V. Daily 8am–2am.

Inexpensive

11th Street Diner AMERICAN The only real diner on the beach, the 11th Street Diner is the antidote to a late-night run to Denny's. Some of Miami's most colorful characters, especially the drunk ones, convene here at odd hours, and your greasy-spoon experience can quickly turn into a three-ring circus. Uprooted from its 1948 Wilkes-Barre, Pennsylvania, foundation, the actual structure was dismantled and rebuilt on a busy—and colorful (a gay bar is right next door, so be on the lookout for flamboyant drag queens) corner of Washington Avenue. Although it can use a good window cleaning, it remains a popular round-the-clock spot that attracts all walks of life. If you're craving french fries, order them smothered in mozzarella with a side of gravy—a tasty concoction that I call disco fries because of its popularity among starving clubbers.

1065 Washington Ave., South Beach. ✆ **305/534-6373.** Items $8–$15. AE, MC. Daily 24 hr.

Front Porch Café ★ AMERICAN Located in an unassuming, rather dreary-looking Art Deco hotel, the Front Porch Café is a relaxed local hangout known for cheap breakfasts. Some of the servers tend to be a bit attitudinal and lackadaisical (many are bartenders or club kids by night), so this isn't the place to be if you're in a hurry, especially on the weekends, when the place is packed all day long and lines are the norm. Enjoy home-style French toast with bananas and walnuts, omelets, fresh fruit salads, pizzas, and classic breakfast pancakes that put IHOP to shame. If you're looking to avoid the tourists and prefer to dine with the locals, Front Porch is where it's at for breakfast, lunch, and even dinner.

In the Penguin Hotel, 1418 Ocean Dr., South Beach. ✆ **305/531-8300.** Main courses $5–$18. AE, DC, DISC, MC, V. Daily 8am–10:30pm.

Icebox Café ★ AMERICAN Locals love this place for its homey comfort food—tuna melts, potpies, and eggs for breakfast, lunch, and dinner. Oprah Winfrey singled it out for its desserts, which is really why people raid the Icebox whenever that sweet tooth calls. In the Icebox, you'll discover the best chocolate cake, pound cake, and banana cream pies outside of your grandma's kitchen.

1657 Michigan Ave., South Beach. ✆ **305/538-8448.** Main courses and desserts $3–$10. AE, MC, V. Daily 8am–10:30pm.

La Sandwicherie SANDWICHES You can get mustard, mayo, or oil and vinegar on sandwiches elsewhere in town, but you'd be missing out on all the local flavor. This gourmet sandwich bar, open until the crack of dawn, caters to ravenous club kids, biker types, and the body artists who work in the tattoo parlor next door. For many people, in fact, no night of clubbing is complete without capping it off with a turkey sub from La Sandwicherie.

229 14th St. (behind the Amoco station), South Beach. ✆ **305/532-8934.** Sandwiches and salads $6–$12. AE, MC, V. Daily 9am–5am. Delivery 9:30am–11pm.

News Cafe ★ AMERICAN This South Beach cafe-cum-landmark hasn't fallen off the radar as far as buzz and hype are concerned. The quintessential South Beach experience, News is still au courant, albeit swarming with mostly tourists. Unless it's appallingly hot or rainy out, you should wait for an outside table, where you must be to fully appreciate the experience. Service is abysmal and often arrogant (perhaps because the tip is included), but the menu is reliable, running the gamut from sandwiches and salads to pasta dishes and omelets. My favorite here is the Middle Eastern platter, a dip lover's paradise, with hummus, tahini, tabbouleh, baba ghanouj, and fresh pita bread. If it's not too busy, feel free to order just a cappuccino—your server may snarl, but that's what News is all about; creative types like to bring their laptops and sit here all day (or all night—this place is open 24 hr. a day). If you're alone and need something to read, there's an extensive collection of national and international newspapers and magazines at the in-house newsstand.

800 Ocean Dr., South Beach. ✆ **305/538-6397.** Items $5–$20. AE, DC, MC, V. Daily 24 hr.

Puerto Sagua ★ CUBAN/SPANISH This brown-walled diner is one of the only old holdouts on South Beach. Its steady stream of regulars ranges from *abuelitos* (little old grandfathers) and local politicos who meet here every Tuesday morning to hipsters who stop in after clubbing. It has endured because the food is good, if a little greasy. Some of the less heavy dishes are a superchunky fish soup with pieces of whole flaky grouper, chicken, and seafood paella, or marinated kingfish. Also good are most of the shrimp dishes, especially the shrimp in garlic sauce, which is served with white rice and salad.

This is one of the most reasonably priced places left on the beach for simple, hearty fare. Don't be intimidated by the hunched, older waiters in their white button-down shirts and black pants. If you don't speak Spanish, they're usually willing to do charades. Anyway, the extensive menu, which ranges from BLTs to grilled lobsters to yummy fried plantains, is translated into English. Hurry, before another boutique goes up in its place.

700 Collins Ave., South Beach. ✆ **305/673-1115.** Main courses $6–$24; sandwiches and salads $5–$10. AE, DC, MC, V. Daily 7:30am–2am.

MIAMI BEACH, SURFSIDE, BAL HARBOUR & SUNNY ISLES

The area north of the Art Deco District—from about 21st Street to 163rd Street—had its heyday in the 1950s, when huge hotels and gambling halls blocked the view of the ocean. Now many of the old hotels have been converted into condos or budget lodgings, and the bayfront mansions have been renovated by and for wealthy entrepreneurs, families, and speculators. The area has many more residents, albeit seasonal, than visitors. On the culinary front, the result is a handful of superexpensive, traditional establishments as well as a number of value-oriented spots.

To locate the restaurants in this section, see the map "Miami Beach Accommodations & Dining" (p. 102).

Very Expensive

The Forge Restaurant ★★★ STEAK/AMERICAN English oak paneling and Tiffany glass suggest high prices and haute cuisine, and that's exactly what you get at the Forge. Each elegant dining room possesses its own character and features high ceilings, ornate chandeliers, and European artwork. The atmosphere is elegant but not too stuffy. On Wednesday night (the party night here), however, it's pandemonium as the who's who of Miami society gathers for dinner, dancing, and schmoozing. Like the rest of the menu, appetizers are mostly classics, from beluga caviar to baked onion soup to shrimp cocktail and escargot. When they're in season, order the stone crabs. For the main course, any of the seafood, chicken, or veal dishes are recommendable, but the Forge is especially known for its award-winning steaks. Its wine selection is equally lauded—ask for a tour of the cellar. ***Celeb alert:*** None other than Michael Jackson has dined here on numerous occasions and considers the Forge one of his favorite restaurants of all time. Same goes for Sharon Stone, Madonna, Jennifer Lopez, Paris Hilton, Michael Jordan, and, well, you get the picture.

432 Arthur Godfrey Rd. (41st St.), Miami Beach. ✆ **305/538-8533.** Reservations recommended. Main courses $25–$60. AE, DC, MC, V. Sun–Thurs 6pm–midnight; Fri–Sat 6pm–1am.

Expensive

Timo ★★★ ITALIAN/MEDITERRANEAN This hip, haute restaurant is in Sunny Isles, where, not so long ago, Tony Roma's was the hottest eatery. Timo is a stylish Italian/Mediterranean restaurant catering to mostly North Miami Beach locals who have been yearning for something else besides the fabulous Chef Allen's. Among the specialties, try the handcrafted pastas, including foie gras ravioli with wild mushrooms, asparagus, and black truffle jus; sea bass with truffled polenta and roasted wild mushrooms; and a phenomenal veal scaloppini. Less pricey, less heavy items are also available, such as a delicious ricotta-and-fontina wood-fired pizza with white truffle oil—perfect for lunch or a happy-hour snack. At Timo, a cool bistro-meets-lounge atmosphere gives way to a decidedly cool vibe, something that was always conspicuously lacking at Tony Roma's.

17624 Collins Ave., Sunny Isles. ✆ **305/936-1008.** www.timorestaurant.com. Reservations required. Main courses $9–$32. AE, DC, MC, V. Sun–Thurs 11:30am–3pm and 6–10:30pm; Fri–Sat 11:30am–3pm and 6–11pm.

Moderate

Cafe Prima Pasta ★ ITALIAN Once a small, unknown trattoria on a very trafficky, tacky street, Cafe Prima Pasta has expanded into a place to be for excellent Italian food and quite a bit of fanfare, especially when regular customer Matt Damon comes in. Because a massive waiting line always spilled out onto the street, the cafe expanded to include ample outdoor seating that is set back from the street noise and traffic, thanks to some creative landscaping. The pasta here is homemade and the kitchen's choice ingredients include ripe, juicy tomatoes; imported olive oil that would cost you a boatload if you bought it in the store; fresh, drippy mozzarella, and fish that tastes as if it has just been caught right out back. The zesty, spicy garlic and oil that is brought out as dip for the bread should be kept with you during your meal, for it doubles as extra seasoning for your food—not that it's necessary. Though tables are packed in, the atmosphere still manages to be romantic. Due to the chef's fancy for garlic, this is a three-Altoid restaurant, so be prepared to pop a few or request that they go light on the garlic.

414 71st St. (half a block east of the Byron movie theater), Miami Beach. ✆ **305/867-0106.** Reservations accepted for parties of 6 or more. Main courses $10–$28; pastas $12–$20. MC, V. Mon–Thurs noon–midnight; Fri noon–1am; Sat 1pm–1am; Sun 5pm–midnight.

Cafe Ragazzi ★★ ITALIAN This diminutive Italian cafe, with its rustic decor and a swift, knowledgeable waitstaff, enjoys great success for its tasty, simple pastas. The spicy puttanesca sauce with a subtle hint of fish is perfectly prepared. Also recommended is the salmon with radicchio. You can choose from many decent salads and carpaccio, too. Ragazzi has a faithful following of regulars, so be prepared for the crowd spill on the street—especially on weekend nights.

9500 Harding Ave. (on the corner of 95th St.), Surfside. ✆ **305/866-4495.** Reservations accepted for parties of 3 or more. Main courses $10–$25. MC, V. Mon–Fri 11:30am–3pm; daily 5–11:30pm.

NORTH MIAMI BEACH

Although there aren't many hotels in North Dade, the population in the winter months explodes due to the onslaught of seasonal residents from the Northeast. A number of exclusive condominiums and country clubs (including William's Island and Turnberry) breed a demanding clientele, many of whom dine out nightly. That's good news for visitors, who can find superior service and cuisine at value prices.

To locate the restaurants in this section, see the map "Miami Beach Accommodations & Dining" (p. 102).

Very Expensive

Chef Allen's ★★★ NEW WORLD If anyone deserves to have a restaurant named after him, it's Chef Allen Susser, winner of the esteemed James Beard Award for Best American Chef in the Southeast—the Academy Award of cuisine—and practically every other form of praise and honor awarded by the most discriminating palates. Chef Allen, the man, is royalty around here. Chef Allen's, the restaurant, is his province, and foodies are his disciples. His platform? New World cuisine and the harmony of exotic tropical fruits, spices, and vegetables. In 2009, Susser introduced a new bistro concept, focusing on the best locally caught sustainable fish, seafood, and regional produce. It is under Chef Allen's magic that ordinary Key limes and mangoes reappear in the forms of succulent salsas and sauces. Dishes are some of the most innovative in town. For starters, there are reasonably priced "snacks" at $4 to $7, much like the concept made famous by Michael's Genuine Food and Drink. Among them: chicken truffles, mini chicken meatballs in a piquant chili sauce, and devils on horseback (roasted chutney-stuffed dates wrapped in applewood smoked bacon). But don't get too full, as the main courses are just as tempting—a surf-and-turf combo of garlicky guava shrimp and Niman Ranch skirt steak served with crisp yuca fries; blackened red snapper with *platanos maduros* and a cool orange raita; meaty swordfish with wood-grilled pineapple, Thai stir-fry, and tomato salsa; grouper with rock shrimp, leeks, mango, and coconut rum; mahimahi in a savory sofrito with Peruvian lima beans; wild Florida shrimp scampi, with zucchini and ricotta ravioli, shallots, lemon, and caviar. Save room for dessert, because they rock, too. Try the milk chocolate hazelnut "Kit Kat" or the peanut butter mousse bombe. Unlike other restaurants where location is key, the recently renovated 100-seat Chef Allen's, located at the rear of a strip mall, could be in the desert and hordes of people would still make the trek.

19088 NE 29th Ave. (at Biscayne Blvd.), North Miami Beach. ✆ **305/935-2900.** www.chefallens.com. Reservations recommended. Main courses $19–$34. AE, DC, MC, V. Sun–Thurs 6–10pm; Fri–Sat 6–11pm.

Il Mulino New York ★ ITALIAN New York's veritable Greenwich Village Italian hot spot opened in Sunny Isles to mixed reviews. An ornate restaurant located in the even more ornate Acqualina Resort, Il Mulino is a saucy affair with signature dishes such as spaghettini Bolognese, a cartoon-size rack of lamb, veal chop, and more. Service ranges from spotty to spectacular, but there's something about the tuxedoed waiters that makes it all so elegant and romantic. But again, there's that sauce issue. When I ate here, my dish was so covered in sauce I forgot what I had ordered. This restaurant is hit or miss, but when it does hit, it's a fancy Italian pleasure.

17875 Collins Ave. (in Acqualina), Sunny Isles. ✆ **305/466-9191.** Reservations recommended. Main courses $25–$60. AE, MC, V. Mon–Thurs 5–10:30pm; Fri–Sat 5–11:30pm.

Michael Mina's Bourbon Steak ★★ STEAKHOUSE Although there's no shortage of steakhouses in Miami, there's nothing like this one. Reminiscent of something out of Las Vegas, everything here is massive—from the stunning all-glass wine cellar that takes up an entire wall, to the sheer size of the place at 7,600 square feet. And then there are the prices. But if you don't mind splurging, a meal at the star chef's first and only South Florida location is worth it. Start off with some oysters on the half shell—East Coast or West Coast, your choice—and then continue with the all-natural farm-raised angus beef, American Kobe beef, or actual Japanese Kobe beef—where a 6-ounce rib-eye will set you back $190! Side dishes are delicious—jalapeño creamed corn ($9), truffled mac and cheese ($12), and a Bourbon Steak trio of Duck Fat Fries comes complimentary to every table (additional orders are $8 a pop), along with a potato focaccia bread with truffle butter and chives. A scene of well-heeled Aventura residents—including actor James Caan and perma-tanned man George Hamilton—and elegantly dressed hotel guests compose the equally rich crowd.

19999 West Country Club Dr. (in the Fairmont Turnberry Isle Resort & Club), Aventura. ✆ **786/279-6600.** Reservations recommended. Main courses $22–$190. AE, DC, DISC, MC, V. Mon–Thurs 6–10pm; Fri–Sat 6–11pm.

DOWNTOWN

Downtown Miami is a large, sprawling area divided by the Brickell Bridge into two distinct areas: Brickell Avenue and the bayfront area near Biscayne Boulevard. You shouldn't walk from one to the other—it's quite a distance and unsafe at night. Convenient Metromover stops do adjoin the areas, so it's better to hop on the scenic sky tram (it's closed after midnight).

To locate the restaurants in this section, see the map "Greater Miami Accommodations & Dining" (p. 87).

Very Expensive

Azul ★★★ GLOBAL FUSION Azul is one of the most upscale, prettiest—and priciest—waterfront restaurants in town. The views of the city skyline are stunning and rival the food—well, almost. Executive Chef Clay Conley, who honed his skills with star chef Todd English, creates a tour de force of international cuisine, inspired by Asian and Mediterranean flavors. Like a stunning designer gown, the restaurant's decor, with its waterfront view, high ceilings, walls burnished in copper, and silk-covered chairs, is complemented by sparkling jewels—in this case, the food. Among the standouts: Moroccan-inspired lamb; a miso-marinated duck breast; and, my favorite, "A Study in Tuna": raw tuna, tempura avocado, and Asian sauces with osetra caviar. Downstairs is the Mandarin's more casual, less expensive **Café Sambal,** an Asian eatery serving breakfast, lunch, and dinner with the same priceless views and a sushi bar.

At the Mandarin Oriental, 500 Brickell Key Dr., Miami. ✆ **305/913-8538.** Reservations strongly recommended. Main courses $24–$55. AE, DC, DISC, MC, V. Mon–Sat 7–11pm.

Capital Grille ★★ STEAKHOUSE The best of all the chain steakhouses, Capital Grille is a serious power spot. Wine cellars are filled with high-end classics, and the dark-wood paneling, pristine white tablecloths, chandeliers, and marble floors all contribute to the clubby atmosphere. For an appetizer, start with the lobster and crab cakes. If you're not in the mood for beef or lobster, try the pan-seared red snapper and asparagus covered with hollandaise. You're surrounded by wine cellars filled with about 5,000 bottles of wine—too extensive and rare to list. While some people prefer the more stalwart style and service of Morton's up the block, others find Capital to be a bit livelier. The food's pretty much the same between the two, though I find the steaks at Morton's to be a notch better; however, the atmosphere at the Capital Grille is *much* more inviting. Complimentary valet parking here (as opposed to Morton's, which charges a fee) is another reason to visit this carnivorous capital.

444 Brickell Ave., Miami. ✆ **305/374-4500.** www.thecapitalgrille.com. Reservations recommended. Main courses $25–$39. AE, DC, DISC, MC, V. Mon–Thurs 11:30am–3pm and 5–10:30pm; Fri 11:30am–3pm and 5–11pm; Sat 6–11pm; Sun 5–10pm.

Rio's Churrascaria ★ BRAZILIAN The beloved Porcao was taken over by Rio's, and while the name isn't as fun, it's still an excellent Brazilian *churrascaria* (a Brazilian-style restaurant devoted mostly to meat—it's the Portuguese translation of "steakhouse"). For about $45, you can feast on salads and meat *after* you sample the unlimited gourmet buffet, which includes such fillers as pickled quail eggs, marinated onions, and an entire pig. Do not stuff yourself here, as the next step is the meaty part: Choose as much lamb, filet mignon, chicken hearts, and steak as you like, grilled, skewered, and sliced right at your table. Side dishes also come with the meal, ranging from beans and rice to fried yucca.

801 Brickell Bay Dr., Miami. ✆ **305/373-2777.** Reservations accepted. Prix-fixe $45 per adult, $22 per child, all you can eat. AE, DC, MC, V. Daily noon–midnight.

Big Fish ★★ Finds SEAFOOD/ITALIAN This scenic seafood shack on the Miami River is a real catch—if you can find it. Hard to locate but well worth the search, Big Fish's remote locale keeps many people biting. In fact, some Italian options were added to its all-seafood menu in the hopes of luring more people, and that worked, too. Big Fish has a sweeping view of the Miami skyline and some of the freshest catches around. But the spectacular setting may be the real draw, right there on the Miami River where freighters, fishing boats, dinghies, and sometimes yachts slink by to the amusement of faithful diners who no longer have to fish around for a charming, serene seafood restaurant. However, you should beware of Friday nights, when Big Fish turns into a big happy-hour scene.

55 SW Miami Avenue Rd. ✆ **305/373-1770.** Reservations recommended. Main courses $15–$35. AE, DC, MC, V. Mon–Thurs noon–11pm; Fri–Sat noon–midnight. Cross the Brickell Ave. Bridge heading south and take the 1st right on SW 5th St. The road narrows under a bridge. The restaurant is just on the other side.

Grass Restaurant and Lounge ★★ Finds AMERICAN/ASIAN What once used to be a snooty, haughtier-than-thou lounge/restaurant is now a welcoming restaurant/lounge, where the priority is excellent, fresh cuisine, not fresh doormen (who have thankfully been weeded out). Signature dishes include ginger-lime-marinated grilled mahi-mahi, grass-fed grilled and smoked beef rib-eye, and wasabi-and-ginger-crusted wild salmon. The Tiki-chic eatery—surrounded by vines, bamboo, and cozy banquettes—is all outdoors, so it's weather-permitting, but when it's nice out, it's a stunning departure from the rest of Miami's ultramodern restaurants. A soon-to-open indoor dining area and lounge will make this an all-season restaurant—but most importantly, the food's always fresh. After dinner, check out the latest to sprout up on the expanding Grass—the **King Is Dead**—a strangely named, fabulously hip cocktail lounge.

28 NE 40th St. ✆ **305/573-3355.** www.grasslounge.com. Reservations recommended. Main courses $20–$80. AE, DC, MC, V. Wed–Sat 6–11pm; late-night bar menu 11pm–2am.

Michy's ★★ Finds LATIN Star chef Michelle Bernstein left the fancy confines of the Mandarin Oriental Miami's Azul to open her own, homey 50-seat eatery on Miami's burgeoning Upper East Side. If you drive too fast, you'll miss the small storefront restaurant, a deceiving facade for a whimsical retro orange-and-blue interior where stellar small plates such as ham-and-blue-cheese croquettes are consumed in massive quantities because they're that good. There's also a zingy ceviche; braised duck with Jerez and peaches; conch escargot-style in parsley, butter, and garlic; and, for those whose palates can take it, sautéed sweetbreads with bacon and orange juice. There's nothing ordinary about Michy's, except for the fact that a reservation here is nearly impossible to score if not made weeks in advance.

6927 Biscayne Blvd. ✆ **305/759-2001.** Reservations recommended. Main courses $15–$30. AE, DC, MC, V. Tues–Thurs noon–3pm and 6–10:30pm; Fri noon–3pm and 6–11pm; Sat 6–11pm; Sun 6–10:30pm.

Oceanaire Seafood Room ★★ SEAFOOD The first restaurant to open in the Mary Brickell Village, Oceanaire is a pricey ocean-liner-inspired chain seafooder known for fresh-caught fare. The elegant streamlined dining room is always abuzz with power types and foodies looking for the freshest fish dishes in town. This is not always the case, but it's not everywhere in Miami where you can indulge in *guajillo* barbecue salmon with spicy crispy red onions, or order Nairagi marlin for that matter. Chef Sean Bernal is a rare talent, so much so that the folks behind Discovery Channel's hit reality show *The*

Deadliest Catch invited him on board one of the crab vessels in the Bering Sea to exercise his fishing skills. So if you're in the downtown area and in the mood for serious fish dishes, this is the place. If you want stone crabs or something simpler, save your money and check out Garcia's (reviewed below) instead.

900 S. Miami Ave. ✆ **305/372-8862.** Reservations recommended. Main courses $15–$30. AE, DC, MC, V. Sun–Thurs 5–10pm; Fri–Sat 5–11pm.

Provence Grill ★ FRENCH This restaurant serves some of the tastiest French meals this side of Toulouse. The brothers Cormouls-Houles have used their prodigious culinary skills to assemble an affordable menu that allows us to know just how the French really live—and they do it, dare we say, with incredible panache. The grilled specialties, from chicken to salmon, are imbued with only the best seasonings and sauces. Sautéed mussels with garlic and chives are fabulous as a meal and as a dipping sauce for the crusty bread. Duck lovers will enjoy the grilled duck filet in a red port sauce. Real culinary adventurers should try the outstanding steak tartare. A full bar outside brings you back from your French delusions of grandeur to a delightful downtown Miami state of mind and beautiful views of the city skyline.

1001 South Miami Ave., Miami. ✆ **305/373-1940.** Reservations recommended Sat–Sun. Main courses $12–$26. AE, MC, V. Sun 5:30–10:30pm; Mon–Thurs 11am–3pm and 5:30–10:30pm; Fri 11am–3pm and 5:30–11pm; Sat 5:30–11pm.

Rosa Mexicano ★★ MEXICAN Also in the Mary Brickell Village, this upscale chain Mexican is always lively and not just because the frozen pomegranate margaritas pack a major punch. A stunning decor with 15-foot waterfall and a great bar scene are two assets, but Rosa's use of serious spices and tableside guacamole preparation, served in a lava rock bowl with homemade tortillas (they make them right there in the middle of the dining room) make this one of Miami's most talked about in a long time. Among the dishes: Mole de Xico, a Veracruz mole made with mulatto, ancho, and pasilla chilies; Chamorro, a crispy, pork shank, slow-roasted for 6 hours, dipped in the deep-fryer, and served with mushroom-chipotle cream sauce and red bean–chorizo chili. And did we mention the margaritas and the guacamole? *Ole!*

900 S. Miami Ave. ✆ **786/425-1001.** www.rosamexicano.com. Reservations recommended. Main courses $13–$30. AE, DC, MC, V. Mon–Fri 11am–3pm; Sun–Thurs 5–10pm; Fri–Sat 5–11pm.

Sra. Martinez ★★ TAPAS Housed in a historic post office, this upscale tapas joint whose name is short for Senora Martinez, features traditional items and several others with Chef Michelle Bernstein's creative flair. Speaking of flair, the menus come folded up inside envelopes in tribute to the venue's original function. Be careful ordering—if you go nuts, your bill could end up costing $40 to $50 a head excluding tax, tip, and booze. That said, some of the standouts include the pork belly—crispy outside and super tender within—topped with a smear of a not-too-sweet fennel-orange marmalade and accompanied with a small salad; sweetbreads are crispy outside and tender and fluffy inside, served with a pestolike paste of dried red peppers, almonds and garlic, a caper berry, and a lemon wedge; massive head-on Madagascar prawns grilled and served with cloves of confit garlic and a schmear of a smooth chimichurri; and a sea urchin sandwich pressed and grilled with some soy-ginger butter. To wash it all down, try one of the amazingly updated takes on old-school cocktail classics, including the sazerac, pisco sour, and Bloody Mary.

4000 NE 2nd Ave. ✆ **305/573-5474.** Reservations recommended. Tapas $10–$20. AE, DC, MC, V. Mon–Thurs 6–11pm; Fri–Sat 6pm–2am.

Brosia ★★★ Finds MEDITERRANEAN Located on a quiet corner in the normally quiet Design District, Brosia is bringing some much needed life to the area with its outstanding cuisine and spectacular setting. With a chef who schooled under the tutelage of Norman Van Aken's kitchen, Brosia isn't just another trendy bistro; the Mediterranean meze platter with *sopressata,* manchego cheese, and an assortment of olives and fig jams is a great sharing dish as are the sautéed shrimp with garlic sherry wine and the grilled mini lamb chops. Save room for the grilled pork tenderloin with caper berries, cornichons, and grain mustard, with a side of perfectly salted, skinny french fries and roasted garlic asparagus. Seriously out of this world. And it all goes down well with the restaurant's signature sangria—in red or white—we prefer the red, but either one will do. And then there's that courtyard, a serene, spectacular outdoor space with couches, tables, and mosaic tile underneath a large oak tree. There's something about Brosia that's very comforting but you may want to wear comfy pants before you go, because you'll definitely want to eat as much as you can here.

163 NE 39th St., Miami. ✆ **305/572-1400.** www.brosiamiami.com. Reservations recommended. Main courses $18–$29. AE, DC, DISC, MC, V. Mon–Fri 11am–5pm and 5–11pm; Sat–Sun 5–11pm.

Fratelli Lyon ★ Finds ITALIAN We've heard of restaurants housed in markets and even department stores, but this Design District standout appropriately resides in a fabulously industrial modern furniture showroom. And while the not-so-comfy but cool-looking chairs you'll be sitting on may be for sale at an astronomical price, when it comes to the wine and cheese, well, they're bargain basement in comparison. Owned by a former caterer, Fratelli, as its known by locals, offers everything from a multitiered platter of antipasti to pizzas, bruschettas, salads, and main courses that include delicious saffron risotto served with boneless *osso buco.* A popular spot for appetizers and wine, Fratelli's also a top spot for lunches among the arty set who live, work, and play in the Design District.

4141 NE 2nd Ave., Miami. ✆ **305/572-2901.** Reservations recommended. Main courses $8–$25. AE, DC, DISC, MC, V. Mon–Sat 11:30am–2pm; Mon–Thurs 6–10pm; Fri–Sat 6pm–midnight.

Garcia's Seafood Grille & Fish ★ Finds SEAFOOD A good catch on the banks of the Miami River, Garcia's has a great waterfront setting and a fairly simple yet tasty menu of fresh fish cooked in a number of ways—grilled, broiled, fried, or, the best in my opinion, in garlic or green sauce. Meals are quite the deal here, all served with green salad or grouper soup, and yellow rice or french fries. The complimentary fish-spread appetizer is also a nice touch. Because of this, not to mention the great, gritty ambience that takes you away from neon, neo-Miami in favor of the old seafaring days, there's usually a wait for a table. If so, hang out at the bar and order an appetizer of inexpensive stone crabs or famous conch fritters. They also recently opened an upstairs bar and lounge overlooking the river.

398 NW N. River Dr., Miami. ✆ **305/375-0765.** Reservations recommended. Main courses $14–$23. AE, DC, DISC, MC, V. Sun–Thurs 11am–10pm; Fri–Sat 11am–11pm.

Michael's Genuine Food and Drink ★★★ NEW AMERICAN The sleek, yet unassuming dining room and serene courtyard seating are constantly abuzz with Design District hipsters, foodies, and celebrities (Jennifer Aniston had her first public date with John Mayer here in '08) thanks to Chef/owner Michael Schwartz's fresh vision for fabulous food. The food is stellar, a fresh mix of all organic products, some from Schwartz's own stash, including eggs hatched from his own hens. With an emphasis on products sourced from local growers and farmers, the menu, which changes daily, is divided into small, medium, large, and extra large plates, all rather reasonably priced and extremely hard to choose from. There are also excellent pizzas, such as the exotic mushroom pizza with cave-aged Gruyère, caramelized onion, fresh thyme, and truffle oil; a slow-roasted Berkshire pork shoulder with Anson Mills cheese grits, pickled onion, and parsley sauce; and my personal favorite, the $4 to $6 bar menu, featuring crispy hominy with chili and lime, deviled eggs, kimchi, and chicken liver crostini. For a sweet tooth, nobody satisfies it better than pastry genius Hedy Goldsmith, whose candied Granny Smith apple and walnut streusel panini is beyond description. There's something for everyone here—that is except a reservation. Book early for Michael's, as it's always crowded. Genuinely.

130 NE 40th St., Miami. ✆ **305/573-5550.** www.michaelsgenuine.com. Reservations recommended. Main courses $14–$46. AE, DC, DISC, MC, V. Mon–Fri 11:30am–3pm; Mon–Thurs 5:30–11pm; Fri 5:30pm–midnight; Sat 6pm–midnight; Sun 5:30–10pm.

Perricone's Marketplace ★ ITALIAN A large selection of groceries and wine, plus an outdoor porch and patio for dining, makes this one of the most welcoming spots downtown. Its rustic setting in the midst of downtown is a fantastic respite from city life. Sunday offers buffet brunches and all-you-can-eat dinners, too. But the place is most popular on weekdays at noon, when the "suits" show up for delectable sandwiches, quick and delicious pastas, and hearty salads.

15 SE 10th St. (corner of S. Miami Ave.), Miami. ✆ **305/374-9693.** Sandwiches $6 and up; pastas $14 and up. AE, MC, V. Sun–Mon 7am–10pm; Tues–Sat 7am–11pm.

Red Light ★★ CAJUN/CREOLE This one takes the award for the most offbeat location in town, as the on-site restaurant for one of Biscayne Boulevard's grittier motels (which since the restaurant opened is in the process of its own revitalization). If you can ignore the location, not to mention some of the motel's more, uh, colorful clientele, consider Chef Kris Wessell's daring menu instead. Although the place looks like a greasy spoon with vinyl booths and an old diner vibe, this is gourmet fare on the Boulevard at its finest, with southern accents. The BBQ shrimp are outstanding, typically themselves sautéed and served in a pan sauce made by sautéing the shrimp heads with butter, lemon, Worcestershire, and Tabasco—served with bread for dipping in the sauce. For an entree, don't miss the quail. A full order features two birds, deboned except for wings and legs, perfectly roasted, stuffed with cubed brioche and sauced with mushrooms and roasted cherries with a sweet reduction. After dinner, head downstairs and have a cocktail on the shore of the very pungent Little Miami River. It's just par for the offbeat course.

In the Motel Blu, 7700 Biscayne Blvd., Miami. ✆ **305/757-7773.** Reservations recommended on weekends. Main courses $8–$18. AE, DC, MC, V. Tues–Sat 6pm–2am.

River Oyster Bar ★★ SEAFOOD A small, yet always packed seafood hot spot next door to Tobacco Road, River Oyster Bar is a buzzy and unpretentious spot for some of the best oysters in town—shipped fresh from all over the world daily—as well as some delicious dishes, including pan-fried Alaskan halibut with roasted garlic chive and pickled asparagus; monkfish paella with chorizo, roasted peppers, and pigeon peas; and for the land lubber, outstanding braised short ribs with creamy mac and cheese. A great spot for happy hour, River Oyster's bar is a lively one, where you can suck down some oysters with some seriously stiff drinks or excellent wines.

15 SE 10th St. (corner of S. Miami Ave.), Miami. ✆ **305/374-9693.** Oysters $1–$10; main courses $15–$28. AE, MC, V. Mon–Fri 11:30am–5pm; Mon–Thurs 6–10:30pm; Fri 6pm–midnight; Sat 5:30pm–midnight.

Soyka Restaurant & Café ★ AMERICAN Brought to us by the same man who owned the News and Van Dyke cafes in South Beach, Soyka, like its former siblings, was catalyst to the Biscayne Corridor revival. The motif inside is industrial chic, reminiscent of a souped-up warehouse you might find in New York. Lunches focus on burgers, sandwiches, and wood-fired oven pizzas. Dinners include simple fare, such as an excellent, massive Cobb salad, or more elaborate dishes such as the delicious turkey Salisbury steak. The bar area provides a few comfy couches and bar stools and tables at which to dine, if you prefer not to sit in the open dining room. A children's menu is available for both lunch and dinner. A lively crowd of bohemian Design District types, professionals, and singles gather here for a taste of urban life. On weekends, the place is packed and very loud. Do not expect an after-dinner stroll around the neighborhood—it's still too dangerous for pedestrian traffic. Head over the causeway to South Beach and stroll there.

5556 NE 4th Court (Design District, off Biscayne Blvd. and 55th St.), Miami. ✆ **305/759-3117.** Reservations recommended for parties of 8 or more. Main courses $8–$26. AE, MC, V. Sun–Thurs 11am–11pm (bar open until midnight); Fri–Sat 11am–midnight (bar open until 1am). Happy hour Mon–Fri 4–7pm.

Inexpensive

Andiamo Brick Oven Pizza ★ PIZZA Leave it to visionary Mark Soyka (News Cafe, Van Dyke Cafe, Soyka) to turn a retro-style 1960s carwash into one of the city's best pizza places. The brick-oven pizzas are to die for, whether you choose the simple Andiamo pie (tomato sauce, mozzarella, and basil) or the designer combos of pancetta and caramelized onions; hot and sweet sausage with broccoli rabe; or portobello mushrooms with truffle oil and goat cheese. Pizzas come in three sizes—10, 13, and 16 inch. Though the pizza is undeniably delicious here, the most talked-about aspect of Andiamo is the fact that while you're washing down slice after slice, you can get your car washed and detailed at Leo's, the space's original and still-existing occupant out back.

5600 Biscayne Blvd., Miami. ✆ **305/762-5751.** Main courses $3–$15. MC, V. Sun–Thurs 11am–11pm; Fri–Sat 11am–midnight.

Dogma Grill ★★ HOT DOGS A little bit of L.A. comes to a gritty stretch of Biscayne Boulevard in the form of this very tongue-and-cheeky hot-dog stand whose motto is "A Frank Philosophy." The brainchild of a former MTV executive, Dogma will change the way you view hot dogs, offering a plethora of choices, from your typical chili dog to Chicago style, with celery salt, hot peppers, onions, and relish. The tropical version with pineapple is a bit funky but fitting for this stand, which attracts a very colorful, arty crowd from the nearby Design District. The buns here are softer than feather pillows, and the hot dogs are grilled to perfection. Try the garlic fries and the lemonade, too. Two new locations of Dogma opened, one across the street from the Museum of Contemporary Art at 899 NE 125th St., in North Miami.

7030 Biscayne Blvd., Miami. ✆ **305/759-3433.** www.dogmagrill.com. Main courses $3–$4. No credit cards. Daily 11am–9pm.

Jimmy's East Side Diner ★ DINER The only thing wrong with this quintessential, consummate greasy-spoon diner is that it's not open 24 hours. Other than that, for the cheapest breakfasts in town, not to mention lunches and early dinners, Jimmy's is a dream come true. Try the banana pancakes, corned-beef hash, roasted chicken, or Philly cheesesteak. Located on the newly hip Upper East Side of Biscayne Boulevard, Jimmy's is a very neighborhoody place, where late Bee Gee Maurice Gibb used to dine every Sunday. Adding to the aging regulars is a new, eclectic contingency of hung-over hipsters for whom Jimmy's is a sweet—and cheap—morning-after salvation.

7201 Biscayne Blvd., Miami. ✆ **305/759-3433.** Main courses $3–$11. No credit cards. Daily 7am–4pm.

Jumbo's ★★★ Finds SOUL FOOD Open 24 hours daily, this Miami institution is the kind of place where you'll see everyone from Rastafarian musicians and cabdrivers to Lenny Kravitz. It's in a shady neighborhood—Carol City—so if you go there, you're going for only one reason—Jumbo's. Family owned for more than 50 years, Jumbo's is known for its world-famous fried shrimp, fried chicken, catfish fingers, and collard greens. Their motto—"Life is to be enjoyed, not to be endured . . . Making friends is our business" is spot on. The service is friendly and fun, and there's history here, too. Jumbo's is the first restaurant in Miami to integrate in 1966, and the first to hire African-American employees in 1967.

7501 NW 7th Ave., Miami. ✆ **305/751-1127.** Main courses $5–$15. AE, DC, MC, V. Daily 24 hr.

Karma Car Wash ★ Finds TAPAS The funkiest thing to hit Biscayne Boulevard since Dogma, this carwash-cum-tapas-and-wine-bar is a big hit with the locals who love their SUVs as much as their hot spots. Put your car in for a wash and relax on the outdoor patio, reminiscent of your best friend's backyard, where you can sip from an impressive number of micro beers, wines, and coffees, and snack on delicious tapas, from cheese plates to chorizo. DJs and cocktail parties make it a happening spot from Thursday on, and while we don't encourage you to drink and drive, of course, there's never been a better excuse to shine your car (it's pricey, but they do a spotless job!) while waxing social at the same time.

7010 Biscayne Blvd., Miami. ✆ **305/759-1392.** Tapas $5–$15. AE, DC, MC, V. Tapas bar/cafe Wed–Sat 8am–1am. Car wash daily 8am–8pm.

Tobacco Road AMERICAN Miami's oldest bar is a bluesy, Route 66–inspired institution favored by barflies, professionals, and anyone else who wishes to indulge in good and greasy bar fare—chicken wings, nachos, and so on—at reasonable prices in a down-home, gritty-but-charming atmosphere. The burgers are also good—particularly the Death Burger, a deliciously unhealthful combo of choice sirloin topped with grilled onions, jalapeños, and pepper-jack cheese (bring on the Tums!). Also a live-music venue, the Road, as it's known by locals, is well traveled, especially during Friday's happy hour and Tuesday's Lobster Night, when 100 $1^{1}/_{4}$-pound lobsters go for only $12 apiece.

626 S. Miami Ave. ✆ **305/374-1198.** www.tobacco-road.com. Main courses $7–$10; nightly specials $12–$15. AE, DC, MC, V. Mon–Sat 11:30am–5am; Sun noon–5am. Cover $5–$6 Fri–Sat nights.

LITTLE HAVANA

The main artery of Little Havana is a busy commercial strip called SW 8th Street, or Calle Ocho. Auto-body shops, cigar factories, and furniture stores line this street, and on every corner, there seems to be a pass-through window serving superstrong Cuban coffee and snacks. In addition, many of the Cuban, Dominican, Nicaraguan, Peruvian, and other Latin American immigrants have opened full-scale restaurants ranging from intimate candlelit establishments to bustling stand-up lunch counters.

To locate the restaurants in this section, see the map "Greater Miami Accommodations & Dining" (p. 87).

Expensive

Casa Juancho ★★ SPANISH A generous taste of Spain comes to Miami in the form of the cavernous Casa Juancho, which looks like it escaped from a production of *Don Quixote.* The numerous dining rooms are decorated with traditional Spanish furnishings and enlivened nightly by strolling Spanish musicians who tend to be annoying and expect tips—do not encourage them to play at your table; you'll hear them loud and clear from other tables, trust me. Try not to be frustrated with the older staff members who don't speak English or respond quickly to your subtle glance—the food is worth the frustration. Your best bet is to order lots of tapas, small dishes of Spanish finger food. Some of the best include mixed seafood vinaigrette, fresh shrimp in hot garlic sauce, and fried calamari rings. A few entrees stand out, such as roast suckling pig, baby eels in garlic and olive oil, and Iberian-style snapper.

2436 SW 8th St. (just east of SW 27th Ave.), Little Havana. ✆ **305/642-2452.** www.casajuancho.com. Reservations recommended but not accepted Fri–Sat after 8pm. Main courses $25–$42; tapas $6–$30. AE, DC, DISC, MC, V. Sun–Thurs noon–midnight; Fri–Sat noon–1am.

Moderate

Hy-Vong ★★ VIETNAMESE This place is a must in Little Havana, so expect to wait hours for a table and don't even think of mumbling a complaint. This Vietnamese cuisine combines the best of Asian and French cooking with spectacular results. Food at Hy-Vong is elegantly simple and super spicy. Appetizers include small, tightly packed Vietnamese spring rolls, and kimchi, a spicy, fermented cabbage (they ran out of it on my last visit, because I got there too late—so get there early!). Star entrees include pastry-enclosed chicken with watercress cream-cheese sauce and fish in tangy mango sauce. Unfortunately, service here is not at all friendly or stellar—in fact, it borders on abysmal, but once you finally get your food, all will be forgotten.

Enjoy the wait with a traditional Vietnamese beer and lots of company. Outside this tiny storefront restaurant, you'll meet interesting students, musicians, and foodies who come for the large, delicious portions.

3458 SW 8th St. (btw. 34th and 35th aves.), Little Havana. ✆ **305/446-3674.** Reservations accepted for parties of 5 or more. Main courses $7–$20. AE, DISC, MC, V. Sun–Thurs 6–11pm; Fri–Sat 6–11:30pm. Closed 2 weeks in Aug.

Inexpensive

Versailles ★★ CUBAN Versailles is the meeting place of Miami's Cuban power brokers, who meet daily over *café con leche* to discuss the future of the Cuban exiles' fate. A glorified diner, the place sparkles with glass, chandeliers, murals, and mirrors meant to evoke the French palace. There's nothing fancy here—nothing French, either—just straightforward food from the home country. The menu is a veritable survey of Cuban cooking and includes specialties such as Moors and Christians (flavorful black beans with white rice), *ropa vieja* (shredded beef stew), and fried whole fish. Versailles is the place to come for *mucho* helpings of Cuban kitsch. With its late hours, it's also the perfect place to come after spending your night in Little Havana.

3555 SW 8th St., Little Havana. ✆ **305/444-0240.** Main courses $5–$20; soup and salad $2–$10. DC, DISC, MC, V. Mon–Thurs 8am–2am; Fri 8am–3am; Sat 8am–4:30am; Sun 9am–1am.

KEY BISCAYNE

Key Biscayne is home to the Ritz-Carlton and some of the world's nicest beaches and parks, yet it is not known for great food. Locals, or "Key rats," as they're known, tend to go off island for meals or takeout, but here are some of the best on-the-island choices.

To locate the restaurants in this section, see the map "Greater Miami Accommodations & Dining" (p. 87).

Expensive

Rusty Pelican ★ SEAFOOD This is Miami's Tavern on the Green. We give it a star for the views, not the food. The Pelican's private tropical walkway leads over a lush waterfall

into one of the most romantic dining rooms in the city, located right on beautiful blue-green Biscayne Bay. The restaurant's windows look out over the water onto the sparkling stalagmites of Miami's magnificent downtown. Inside, quiet wicker paddle fans whirl overhead and saltwater fish swim in pretty tableside aquariums. The restaurant's surf-and-turf menu features conservatively prepared prime steaks, veal, shrimp, and lobster. The food is so-so, but the atmosphere—the reason why you're here—is even better, especially at sunset, when the view over the city is magical.

3201 Rickenbacker Causeway, Key Biscayne. ✆ **305/361-3818.** Reservations recommended. Main courses $16–$30. AE, DC, MC, V. Sun–Thurs 11:30am–4pm and 5–11pm; Fri–Sat 11:30am–4pm and 5pm–midnight.

Inexpensive

Bayside Seafood Hut ★ Finds SEAFOOD Known by locals as "the Hut," this ramshackle restaurant and bar is a laid-back outdoor Tiki hut and terrace that serves pretty good sandwiches and fish platters on paper plates. A blackboard lists the latest catches, which can be prepared blackened, fried, broiled, or in a garlic sauce. The fish dip is wonderfully smoky and moist, if a little heavy on mayonnaise. Local fishers and yachties share this rustic outpost with equal enthusiasm and loyalty. A completely new, air-conditioned area for those who can't stand the heat is a welcome addition, as is the new deck and the spruced-up decor. But behind it all, it's nothing fancier than a hut—if it were anything else, it wouldn't be nearly as appealing.

3501 Rickenbacker Causeway, Key Biscayne. ✆ **305/361-0808.** Reservations accepted for parties of 15 or more. Appetizers, salads, and sandwiches $5–$15; platters $7–$13. AE, MC, V. Daily 10am until closing (which varies).

Jimbo's Finds SEAFOOD Locals like to keep quiet about Jimbo's, a ramshackle seafood shack that started as a gathering spot for fishermen and has since become the quintessential South Florida watering hole, snack bar, and hangout for those in the know. If ever Miami had a backwoods, this is it, right down to the smoldering garbage can, stray dogs, and chickens. Do *not* get dressed up to come here—you will get dirty. Go to the bathroom before you get here, too, because the porta-potties are absolutely rancid. Grab yourself a dollar can of beer (there's only beer, water, and soda, but you are allowed to bring your own choice of drink if you want) from the cooler and take in the view of the tropical lagoon where they shot *Flipper.* You may even see a manatee or two. Vacant shacks that served as backdrops for films such as *True Lies* surround this hidden enclave, which attracts everyone from shrimpers and politicians to well-oiled beach bums. Oddly enough, there's even a bocce court here, and the owner, Jimbo, may challenge you to a game. Play if you must, but word has it he never loses. Jimbo's smoked fish—marlin or salmon—is the best in town, but ***be forewarned:*** There are no utensils or napkins. When I asked for some, the woman said, "Lady, this is a place where you eat with your hands." I couldn't have said it better.

Off the Rickenbacker Causeway at Sewerline Rd., Virginia Key. ✆ **305/361-7026.** Smoked fish about $8 a pound. No credit cards. Mon–Fri 6am–6:30pm; Sat–Sun 6am–7:30pm. Head south on the main road toward Key Biscayne, make a left just after the MAST Academy (there will be a sign that says VIRGINIA KEY); tell the person in the tollbooth you're going to Jimbo's, and he'll point you in the right direction.

COCONUT GROVE

Coconut Grove was long known as the artists' haven of Miami, but the rush of developers trying to cash in on the laid-back charm of this old settlement has turned it into something of an overgrown mall. Still, there are several great dining spots both inside and outside the confines of Mayfair and CocoWalk.

To locate the restaurants in this section, see the map "Greater Miami Accommodations & Dining" (p. 87).

Very Expensive

Baleen ★★★ SEAFOOD/MEDITERRANEAN While the prices aren't lean, the cuisine here is worth every pricey, precious penny. Oversize crab cakes, oak-smoked diver scallops, and steakhouse-quality meats are among Baleen's excellent offerings. The lobster bisque is the best on Biscayne Bay. Everything here is a la carte, so order wisely, as it tends to add up quicker than you can put your fork down. The restaurant's spectacular waterfront

Coconut Grove Accommodations & Dining

ACCOMMODATIONS
Mayfair Hotel and Spa **3**
Ritz-Carlton Coconut Grove **5**
Sunista Bayfront Hotel **4**

DINING
George's in the Grove **1**
Le Bouchon du Grove **2**

setting makes Baleen a true knockout. Request one of the few tables that are actually on the water's edge; lit with Tiki torches and an illuminated backdrop of Biscayne Bay, Baleen is the kind of restaurant a reality show like *The Bachelor* would use for a scene when the happy couple expresses their love for each other.

4 Grove Isle Dr. (in the Grove Isle Hotel), Coconut Grove. ✆ **305/858-8300.** Reservations recommended. Main courses $18–$50. AE, DC, MC, V. Sun–Wed 7am–10pm; Thurs–Sat 7am–11pm.

Expensive

Le Bouchon du Grove ★ FRENCH This very authentic bistro is French right down to the waitstaff, who may speak only French to you, forgetting they're in the heart of Coconut Grove, U.S.A. But it matters not. The food, prepared by an animated French (what else?) chef, is good. It used to be superb, but it has fallen off a bit. Still, a delicious starter that's always reliable is the *gratinée Lyonnaise* (traditional French onion soup). Fish is brought in fresh daily; try the Chilean sea bass *(filet de loup poele)* when it's in season. Though slightly heavy on the oil, it is delivered with succulent artichokes, tomato confit, and seasoned roasted garlic and it is a gastronomic triumph. The *carre d'agneau roti* (roasted rack of lamb with Provence herbs) is served warm and tender, with a perfect amount of seasoning. There's also an excellent selection of pricey, but drinkable, French and American red and white wines.

3430 Main Hwy., Coconut Grove. ✆ **305/448-6060.** Reservations recommended. Main courses $18–$26. AE, MC, V. Mon–Thurs 10am–3pm and 5–11pm; Fri 10am–3pm and 5pm–midnight; Sat 8am–3pm and 5pm–midnight; Sun 8am–3pm and 5–11pm.

George's in the Grove ★★ FRENCH When the former owner of Le Bouchon du Grove opened his own bistro around the corner, shouts of *"mon Dieu!"* were heard loud and clear. But there's really no comparison. Whereas Le Bouchon is a traditional French bistro, George's is a modern version, with sleek decor and a sleeker champagne-sipping clientele. Entrees range from such classics as ratatouille and steak frites to a very Miami mango tarte tatin. Food is good, but the ambience is better. As the night goes on, music gets louder and a party scene ensues. If you want romance, go to Le Bouchon; if you want a *Sex and the City* scene, George's is *le place.*

3145 Commodore Plaza, Coconut Grove. ✆ **305/444-7878.** Main courses $13–$40. AE, DC, MC, V. Sun and Tues–Wed 6–11pm; Thurs–Sat 6pm–1am.

CORAL GABLES & ENVIRONS

Coral Gables is a foodie's paradise—a city in which you certainly won't go hungry. What Starbucks is to most major cities, excellent gourmet and ethnic restaurants are to Coral Gables, where there's a restaurant on every corner and everywhere in between.

To locate the restaurants in this section, see the map "Greater Miami Accommodations & Dining" (p. 87).

Very Expensive

Christy's ★★ STEAK/AMERICAN Power is palpable at this old-school English-style Miami steakhouse where a rock star can be sitting at one table, an ex-president at another. When we say rock star, we mean aging rock star à la Rod Stewart, though. This isn't your flashy South Beach scenery. But Christy's is the kind of place where conversations are at a hush and no one seems to care whom they're sitting next to. The selling point here, rather, is the broiled lamb chops, prime rib of beef with horseradish sauce, teriyaki-marinated filet mignon, herb-crusted sea bass, crab cakes, and perfectly tossed Caesar salad. Baked sweet potatoes and a sublime blackout cake are also yours for the taking. For a little drama, order the baked Alaska. It livens things up. Just like a fine wine or the typical Christy's customer, the meat here is aged a long time. A landmark since 1978, Christy's has thrived amid the comings and goings of neighboring nouveau Coral Gables restaurants. It's located on a nondescript corner, and you'll know you've arrived at the right place if you can count the Rolls-Royces parked out front.

3101 Ponce de León Blvd., Coral Gables. ✆ **305/446-1400.** www.christysrestaurant.com. Reservations recommended. Main courses $20–$48. AE, DC, MC, V. Mon–Thurs 11:30am–10pm; Fri 11:30am–11pm; Sat 5–11pm; Sun 5–10pm.

Expensive

Caffe Abbracci ★★ ITALIAN You'll understand why this restaurant's name means "hugs" in Italian the moment you enter the dark, romantic enclave: Your appetite will be embraced by the savory scents of fantastic Italian cuisine wafting through the restaurant. The homemade black-and-red ravioli filled with lobster in pink sauce, risotto with porcini

Coral Gables Accommodations & Dining

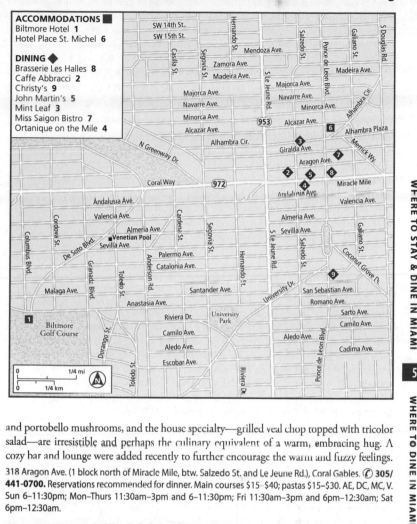

ACCOMMODATIONS ■
Biltmore Hotel **1**
Hotel Place St. Michel **6**

DINING ◆
Brasserie Les Halles **8**
Caffe Abbracci **2**
Christy's **9**
John Martin's **5**
Mint Leaf **3**
Miss Saigon Bistro **7**
Ortanique on the Mile **4**

and portobello mushrooms, and the house specialty—grilled veal chop topped with tricolor salad—are irresistible and perhaps the culinary equivalent of a warm, embracing hug. A cozy bar and lounge were added recently to further encourage the warm and fuzzy feelings. 318 Aragon Ave. (1 block north of Miracle Mile, btw. Salzedo St. and Le Jeune Rd.), Coral Gables. ✆ **305/441-0700.** Reservations recommended for dinner. Main courses $15–$40; pastas $15–$30. AE, DC, MC, V. Sun 6–11:30pm; Mon–Thurs 11:30am–3pm and 6–11:30pm; Fri 11:30am–3pm and 6pm–12:30am; Sat 6pm–12:30am.

Ortanique on the Mile ★★★ NEW WORLD CARIBBEAN You'll be greeted as you enter with soft, spiderlike lights and canopied mosquito netting that will make you wonder whether you're on a secluded island or inside one of King Tut's temples. Chef Cindy Hutson has truly perfected her tantalizing New World Caribbean cuisine that also graces the menus of her two other Ortaniques in Washington, D.C., and Las Vegas. For starters, an absolute must is the pumpkin bisque with a hint of pepper sherry. Afterward, move on to the tropical mango salad with fresh marinated sable hearts of palm, julienne mango, baby field greens, toasted Caribbean candied pecans, and passion-fruit vinaigrette.

For an entree, I recommend the pan-sautéed Bahamian black grouper marinated in teriyaki and sesame oil. It's served with an *ortanique* (an orangelike fruit) orange liqueur sauce and topped with steamed seasoned chayote, zucchini, and carrots on a lemon-orange *boniato*–sweet plantain mash. For dessert, try the chocolate mango tower—layers of brownie, chocolate mango mousse, meringue, and sponge cake, accompanied by mango sorbet and tropical-fruit salsa. Entrees may not be cheap, but they're a lot less than airfare to the islands, which is where most, if not all, of the ingredients hail from.

278 Miracle Mile (next to Actor's Playhouse), Coral Gables. ✆ **305/446-7710.** Reservations requested. Main courses $19–$40. AE, DC, MC, V. Mon–Tues 6–10pm; Wed–Sat 6–11pm; Sun 5:30–9:30pm.

Moderate

John Martin's ★ IRISH PUB Forest-green and dark-wood walls provide a very intimate, publike atmosphere in which local businesspeople and barflies alike come to hoist a pint or two. The menu offers some tasty British specialties (not necessarily an oxymoron!), such as bangers and mash and shepherd's pie, as well as Irish lamb stew and corned beef and cabbage.

Of course, to wash it down, you'll want to try one of the ales on tap or one of the more than 20 single-malt scotches. The crowd is upscale and chatty, as is the young waitstaff. Check out happy hour on weeknights, plus the Sunday brunch with loads of hand-carved meats and seafood.

253 Miracle Mile, Coral Gables. ✆ **305/445-3777.** Reservations recommended on weekends. Main courses $9–$20; sandwiches and salads $5–$16. AE, DC, DISC, MC, V. Sun–Thurs 11:30am–midnight; Fri–Sat 11:30am–2am.

Mint Leaf ★ INDIAN Straight from London is this cozy (read: tiny) modern Indian eatery where Bollywood films play on the flatscreen and the congenial owner runs around making sure everyone's happy. And you will be happy as long as you score a table here—there are only about 15 inside and a miniature bar with two stools. Cuisine is authentic if not particularly spicy (I asked for extra hot sauce on the side but was given a watery concoction instead), with all traditional tandoori favorites, samosas, naans, and *dosas.*

276 Alhambra Circle, Coral Gables. ✆ **305/443-3739.** Reservations strongly recommended. Main courses $16–$20. AE, DC, DISC, MC, V. Daily noon–3pm and 6–10:30pm.

Inexpensive

Miss Saigon Bistro ★★ VIETNAMESE Unlike Alain Boublil and Claude-Michel Schönberg's bombastic Broadway show, this Miss Saigon is small, quiet, and not at all flashy. Servers at this family-run restaurant will graciously recommend dishes or even have something custom-made for you. The menu is varied and reasonably priced, and the portions are huge—large enough to share. Noodle dishes and soup bowls are hearty and flavorful; caramelized prawns are fantastic, as is the whole snapper with lemongrass and ginger sauce. Despite the fact that there are few tables inside and a hungry crowd usually gathers outside in the street, you won't be rushed through your meal, which is worth savoring. There is also a much larger location at 9503 S. Dixie Hwy., in South Miami's Pinecrest (✆ **305/661-2911**).

148 Giralda Ave. (at Ponce de León and 37th Ave.), Coral Gables. ✆ **305/446-8006.** Main courses $10–$22. AE, DC, DISC, MC, V. Mon and Wed–Thurs 11:30am–3pm and 5:30–10pm; Tues 11:30am–3pm and 6:30–10pm; Fri 11:30am–3pm and 5:30–11pm; Sat 5:30–11pm; Sun 5:30–10pm.

SOUTH MIAMI & WEST MIAMI

Though mostly residential, these areas nonetheless have several eating establishments worth the drive.

Expensive

Chispa ★★★ CONTEMPORARY LATIN Simply put, Chispa rocks. The brainchild of star chef Robin Haas (formerly of Baleen), this cavernous, stylish nouveau Latin restaurant will blow you away. If you've ever tasted the delicious, greasy *croquettas* at any Cuban bodega, wait until you try Chispa's gourmet version—a magnificent shrimp-and-black-eyed-pea *croquetta* that renders the greasy ones good for hangovers only. For a real Cuban experience, try Sergio's spit-roasted young suckling pig. A slew of fantastic seafood ceviches, an unparalleled mahimahi with sour orange aioli, and those addictive shrimp-and-black-eyed-pea *croquettas* with wood-roasted mushrooms atop a seared cornmeal stew prove that there is indeed a way to be creative with Cuban food. A 40-foot bar and massive booths seating 8 to 10 people make Chispa a great place for large groups. The acoustics, however, need to be improved, as it's louder than a Celia Cruz tribute in here.

11500 NW 41st St. ✆ **305/591-7166.** www.chisparestaurant.com. Reservations strongly recommended. Main courses $9–$33. AE, DC, MC, V. Sun–Thurs 11:30am–2:30pm and 5:30–10:30pm; Fri–Sat 5:30–11:30pm.

Tropical Chinese ★★ CHINESE This strip-mall restaurant, way out in West Miami–Dade, is hailed as the best Chinese restaurant in the city. While the food is indeed very good—certainly more interesting than at your typical beef-and-broccoli place—it still seems overpriced. Garlic spinach and prawns in a clay pot are delicious, with the perfect mix of garlic cloves, mushrooms, and fresh spinach. But this isn't your typical Chinese takeout. It's not cheap. Unlike most Chinese restaurants, the dishes here are not large enough to share. Sunday-afternoon dim sum is extremely popular, and lines often snake around the shopping center.

7991 Bird Rd., West Miami. ✆ **305/262-7576.** Reservations highly recommended on weekends. Main courses $15–$30. AE, DC, MC, V. Mon–Fri 11:30am–10:30pm; Sat 11am–11:30pm; Sun 10:30am–10pm. Take U.S. 1 to Bird Rd. and go west on Bird, all the way down to 78th Ave. The restaurant is btw. 78th and 79th on the north side of Bird Rd.

Inexpensive

Crepe Maker Café ★ Kids FRENCH Create your own delicious crepes at this little French cafe. You can choose from ham, tuna, black olives, red peppers, capers, artichoke hearts, and pine nuts. Some of the best include a Philly cheesesteak with mushrooms, and a classic chicken *cordon bleu*. Delicious dessert crepes include ice cream, strawberries, peaches, walnuts, and pineapples. Enjoy your crepe fresh off the griddle at the counter or from a bar stool. The soups are delicious. Kids can run around in a small play area.

8269 SW 124th St., South Miami. ✆ **305/233-4458** or 233-1113. www.crepemaker.com. Crepes $1.50–$10. AE, DC, MC, V. Sun–Thurs 11:30am–9:30pm; Fri–Sat 11:30am–10:30pm. Take U.S. 1 south to 124th St. and make a left. The restaurant is on the north side of the street, across from the park.

El Toro Taco Family Restaurant ★★★ Finds MEXICAN Until I discovered this Mexican oasis in the midst of South Florida farmland, I never had a good enough reason to leave my quasi-cosmopolitan confines in Miami for rural Homestead, way down south. I've put major mileage on my car since I first stumbled upon this 96-seat family-run restaurant a few years ago, when I was lost and very hungry. Fabulous (and I mean fabulous) Mexican fare—tacos, enchiladas, and burritos drenched with the freshest and zestiest salsa this side of Baja—is what you'll find here in abundance. It may sound odd to travel from a big city with tons of restaurants to farm country for Mexican food, but trust me: It's so cheap and delicious, it's worth the trip.

1 S. Krome Ave., Homestead. ✆ **305/245-8182.** Main courses $1.75–$12. DISC, MC, V. Tues–Sun 10am–9pm; Fri–Sat 10am–10pm. Take 836 W. (Dolphin Expwy.) toward Miami International Airport. Take Florida

 Turnpike S. ramp toward Florida City/Key West. Take U.S. 41/SW 8th St. exit (exit 25) and turn left onto SW 8th St. Take SW 8th St. to Krome Ave. (1/4 mile) and turn left.

Kon Chau ★ CHINESE/DIM SUM Don't be put off by the rather unappealing shopping center in which this cheap dim-sum place is located. If you want fancy plastic chopsticks and fancy prices, go up the block to Tropical Chinese (see above). If you want delicious dim sum at ridiculously low prices, Kon Chau is where you'll find it. A simple checklist allows you to choose as many items as you want, from savory steamed shrimp dumplings to airy pork buns, for as little as $1 apiece, all day long. There are also regular dishes if you don't want dim sum.

8376 Bird Rd., West Miami. ✆ **305/553-7799.** Items $1 and up. MC, V. Mon–Sat 11am–9:45pm; Sun 10am–9:30pm. Take Bird Rd. west to 83rd St. The restaurant is btw. 83rd and 84th sts., on the south side of the road, in a Dunkin' Donuts shopping center.

Shorty's ★ BARBECUE A Miami tradition since 1951, this honky-tonk of a log cabin still serves some of the best ribs and chicken in South Florida. People line up for the smoke-flavored, slow-cooked meat that's so tender it seems to fall off the bone. The secret, however, is to ask for your order with sweet sauce. The regular stuff tastes bland and bottled. All of the side dishes, including the coleslaw, corn on the cob, and baked beans, look commercial but complete the experience. This is a jeans-and-T-shirt kind of place, but you may want to wear jeans with an elastic waistband, as overeating is not uncommon.

9200 S. Dixie Hwy. (btw. U.S. 1 and Dadeland Blvd.), South Miami. ✆ **305/670-7732.** Main courses $5–$15. DISC, MC, V. Sun–Thurs 11am–10pm; Fri–Sat 11am–11pm.

The Tea Room at Cauley Square ★ ENGLISH TEA Do stop in for a spot of tea at this cozy tearoom in historic Cauley Square, off U.S. 1. The little lace-curtained room is an unusual sight in this heavily industrial area better known for its warehouses than its doilies. Try one of the simple sandwiches, such as the turkey club with potato salad and a small lettuce garnish, or onion soup—rich brown broth and stringy cheese. The ambrosia with finger sandwiches is an interesting choice: a blend of pineapple, mandarin oranges, miniature marshmallows, and sour cream served with finger sandwiches or banana-nut bread. Daily specials (such as spinach-and-mushroom quiche) and delectable desserts are musts before you begin your explorations of the old antiques and art shops in this little enclave of civility down south. Oh, and remember to put your pinky up while sipping your tea.

12310 SW 224th St. (at Cauley Sq.), South Miami. ✆ **305/258-0044.** Sandwiches and salads $7–$12; soups $3–$6. AE, DISC, MC, V. Daily 11am–4pm. Take 836 W. (Dolphin Expwy.) toward Miami International Airport. Take Palmetto Expwy. S. ramp toward Coral Way. Merge onto 826 S. Follow signs to Florida Tpk. toward Homestead. Take the tpk. south and exit at Caribbean Blvd. (exit 12). Go about 1 mile on Caribbean Blvd. and turn left on S. Dixie Hwy. and then right at SW 224th St. Then turn left onto Old Dixie Hwy. and take a slight right onto SW 224th St. The restaurant is at Cauley Square Center.

White Lion Cafe ★ AMERICAN The quintessence of a quaint off-the-beaten-path eatery in not-so-quaint Miami, the White Lion Cafe is a hidden gem serving Southern-style blue-plate specials, including delicious meatloaf and fried chicken. There's also an extensive entertainment calendar here, with everything from live jazz to karaoke. If you're in the Homestead area en route to or coming from the Keys, it's definitely worth a stop here, where time seems to stand still, at least until the band starts playing.

146 NW 7th St., Homestead. ✆ **305/248-1076.** www.whitelioncafe.com. Main courses $10–$22. AE, DISC, MC, V. Daily 5pm until "the fat lady sings." Take the 836 E. to the 826 S., at exit 6 make a left and head West on 8th St. (Campbell Dr.), after crossing Krome Ave. take a left at 1st Ave. (the very next light) and turn right on 7th St. The cafe is on the left.

6

What to See & Do in Miami

If there's one thing Miami doesn't have, it's an identity crisis. Multiple personalities, maybe, but hardly a crisis. In fact, it's the city's vibrant, multifaceted personality that attracts millions each year from all over the world. South Beach may be on the top of many Miami to-do lists, but the rest of the city, a fascinating assemblage of multicultural neighborhoods, should not be overlooked. Once considered "God's Waiting Room," the Magic City now attracts an eclectic mix of old and young, celebs and plebes, American and international, and geek and chic with an equally varied roster of activities.

For starters, Miami boasts some of the world's most natural beauty, with dazzling blue waters, fine sandy beaches, and lush tropical parks. The city's man-made brilliance, in the form of crayon-colored architecture, never seems to fade in Miami's unique Art Deco district. For cultural variation, you can experience the tastes, sounds, and rhythms of Cuba in Little Havana.

As in any metropolis, though, some areas aren't as great as others. Downtown Miami, for instance, is still in the throes of a major, albeit slow, renaissance, in which the sketchier warehouse sections of the city are being transformed into hubs of all things hip. In contrast to this development, however, are the still poverty-stricken areas of downtown such as Overtown, Liberty City, and Little Haiti (though Overtown is striving to transform itself into the Overtown Historic Village, showcasing its landmarks such as the famous Lyric Theater and the home of DA Dorsey, Miami's first African-American millionaire). While I obviously advise you to exercise caution when exploring the less-traveled parts of the city, I would also be remiss in telling you to bypass them completely.

Lose yourself in the city's nature and its neighborhoods and, best of all, its people—a sassy collection of artists and intellectuals, beach bums and international transplants, dolled-up drag queens and bodies beautiful. No wonder celebrities love to vacation here—the spotlight is on the city and its residents. Also, unlike most stars, Miami is always ready for its close-up. With so much to do and see, Miami is a virtual amusement park that's bound to entertain all those who pass through its palm-lined gates.

In this chapter, you'll find a "Miami Area Attractions & Beaches" map on p. 147 and a "South Beach Attractions" map on p. 187.

1 MIAMI'S BEACHES

Perhaps Miami's most popular attraction is its incredible 35-mile stretch of beachfront, which runs from the tip of South Beach north to Sunny Isles, then circles Key Biscayne and numerous other pristine islands dotting the Atlantic. The characteristics of Miami's many beaches are as varied as the city's population: There are beaches for swimming, socializing, or serenity; for family, seniors, or gay singles; some to make you forget you're in the city, others darkened by huge condominiums. Whatever type of beach vacation you're looking for, you'll find it in one of Miami's two distinct beach areas: Miami Beach and Key Biscayne.

MIAMI BEACH'S BEACHES Collins Avenue fronts more than a dozen miles of white-sand beach and blue-green waters from 1st to 192nd streets. Although most of this stretch is lined with a solid wall of hotels and condos, beach access is plentiful. There are lots of public beaches here, wide and well maintained, complete with lifeguards, bathroom facilities, concession stands, and metered parking (bring lots of quarters). Except for a thin strip close to the water, most of the sand is hard packed—the result of a $10-million Army Corps of Engineers Beach Rebuilding Project meant to protect buildings from the effects of eroding sand.

In general, the beaches on this barrier island (all on the eastern, oceanside of the island) become less crowded the farther north you go. A wooden boardwalk runs along the hotel side of the beach from 21st to 46th streets—about 1½ miles—offering a terrific sun-and-surf experience without getting sand in your shoes. Miami's lifeguard-protected public beaches include 21st Street, at the beginning of the boardwalk; 35th Street, popular with an older crowd; 46th Street, next to the Fontainebleau Hotel; 53rd Street, a narrower, more sedate beach; 64th Street, one of the quietest strips around; and 72nd Street, a local old-timers' spot.

KEY BISCAYNE'S BEACHES If Miami Beach doesn't provide the privacy you're looking for, try Virginia Key and Key Biscayne. Crossing the Rickenbacker Causeway ($1 toll), however, can be a lengthy process, especially on weekends, when beach bums and tan-o-rexics flock to the Key. The 5 miles of public beach there, however, are blessed with softer sand and are less developed and more laid-back than the hotel-laden strips to the north. In 2008, Key Biscayne reopened the historic **Virginia Key Beach Park,** 4020 Virginia Beach Dr. (✆ **305/960-4600;** www.virginiakeybeachpark.net), the former "colored only" beach that opened in 1945 and closed in 1982 because of high maintenance costs. After an $11-million renovation, the 83-acre historic site features picnic tables and grills, shoreline renourishment, a new playground for children with special needs, and a miniature railroad. The beach eventually plans to open a civil rights museum as well. Open from sunrise to sunset daily, with free admission.

2 THE ART DECO DISTRICT (SOUTH BEACH)

"You know what they used to say? 'Who's Art?'" recalls Art Deco revivalist Dona Zemo. "You'd say, 'This is an Art Deco building,' and they'd say, 'Really, who is Art?' These people thought 'Art Deco' was some guy's name."

How things have changed. This guy Art has become one of the most popular Florida attractions since, well, that mouse named Mickey. The district is roughly bounded by the Atlantic Ocean on the east, Alton Road on the west, 6th Street to the south, and Dade Boulevard (along the Collins Canal) to the north.

Simply put, Art Deco is a style of architecture that, in its heyday of the 1920s and 1930s, used to be considered ultramodern. Today, fans of the style consider it retro fabulous. But while some people may not consider the style fabulous, it's undoubtedly retro. According to the experts, Art Deco made its debut in 1925 at an exposition in Paris in which it set a stylistic tone, with buildings based on early neoclassical styles with the application of exotic motifs such as flora, fauna, and fountains based on geometric patterns. In Miami, Art Deco is marked by the pastel-hued buildings that line South Beach

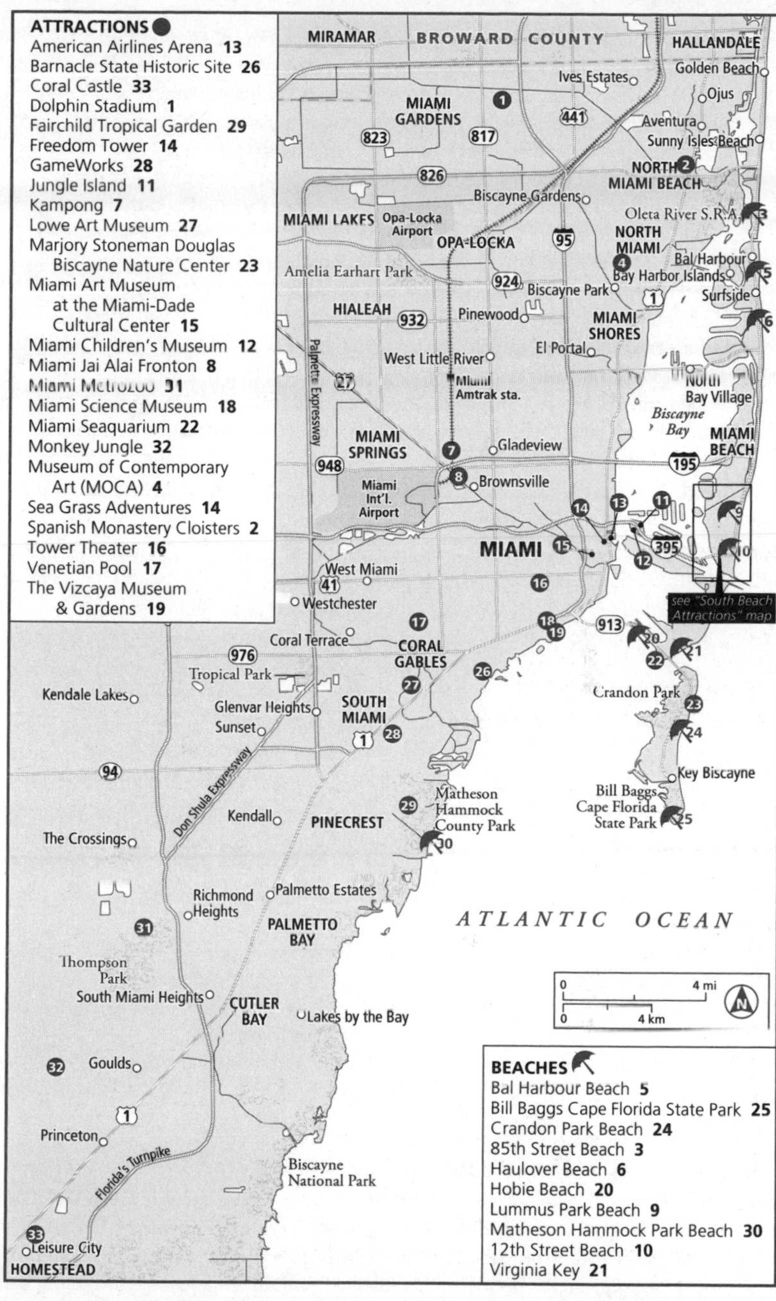
ATTRACTIONS
American Airlines Arena 13
Barnacle State Historic Site 26
Coral Castle 33
Dolphin Stadium 1
Fairchild Tropical Garden 29
Freedom Tower 14
GameWorks 28
Jungle Island 11
Kampong 7
Lowe Art Museum 27
Marjory Stoneman Douglas Biscayne Nature Center 23
Miami Art Museum at the Miami-Dade Cultural Center 15
Miami Children's Museum 12
Miami Jai Alai Fronton 8
Miami Metrozoo 31
Miami Science Museum 18
Miami Seaquarium 22
Monkey Jungle 32
Museum of Contemporary Art (MOCA) 4
Sea Grass Adventures 14
Spanish Monastery Cloisters 2
Tower Theater 16
Venetian Pool 17
The Vizcaya Museum & Gardens 19
BEACHES
Bal Harbour Beach 5
Bill Baggs Cape Florida State Park 25
Crandon Park Beach 24
85th Street Beach 3
Haulover Beach 6
Hobie Beach 20
Lummus Park Beach 9
Matheson Hammock Park Beach 30
12th Street Beach 10
Virginia Key 21
MIRAMAR
BROWARD COUNTY
HALLANDALE
Golden Beach
Ives Estates
Ojus
MIAMI GARDENS
Aventura
Sunny Isles Beach
NORTH MIAMI BEACH
Biscayne Gardens
Oleta River S.R.A.
MIAMI LAKES
Opa-Locka Airport
OPA-LOCKA
NORTH MIAMI
Amelia Earhart Park
Bal Harbour
Bay Harbor Islands
Biscayne Park
Surfside
HIALEAH
Pinewood
MIAMI SHORES
El Portal
West Little River
Palmetto Expressway
Miami Amtrak sta.
North Bay Village
Biscayne Bay
MIAMI SPRINGS
Gladeview
MIAMI BEACH
Brownsville
Miami Int'l. Airport
MIAMI
see "South Beach Attractions" map
West Miami
Westchester
Coral Terrace
CORAL GABLES
Tropical Park
Crandon Park
Kendale Lakes
Glenvar Heights
Sunset
SOUTH MIAMI
Key Biscayne
Don Shula Expressway
Matheson Hammock County Park
Bill Baggs Cape Florida State Park
Kendall
PINECREST
The Crossings
Richmond Heights
Palmetto Estates
ATLANTIC OCEAN
PALMETTO BAY
Thompson Park
South Miami Heights
CUTLER BAY
Lakes by the Bay
0
4 mi
4 km
Goulds
Princeton
Florida's Turnpike
Biscayne National Park
Leisure City
HOMESTEAD

Finds Walking by Design

The Miami Design Preservation League offers several tours of Miami Beach's historic architecture, all of which leave from the Art Deco Welcome Center at 1001 Ocean Dr., in Miami Beach. A self-guided audio tour (available 7 days a week, 10am–4pm) turns the streets into a virtual outdoor museum, taking you through Miami Beach's Art Deco district at your own leisure, with tours in several languages for just $15 for adults, $10 for seniors. Guided tours conducted by local historians and architects offer an in-depth look at the structures and their history. The 90-minute Ocean Drive and Beyond tour (offered every Wed and Sat at 10:30am) takes you through the district, pointing out the differences between Mediterranean Revival and Art Deco for $20 for adults, $15 for seniors. If you're not blinded by neon, the Thursday night Art Deco District Up-to-Date Tour (leaving at 6:30pm) will whisk you around for a 90-minute walk, making note of how certain local hot spots were architecturally famous way before the likes of Madonna and Co. entered the scene. The cost is $20 for adults, $15 for seniors. For more information on tours or reservations, call © **305/672-2014** or log on to www.mdpl.org.

and Miami Beach. But it's a lot more than just color. If you look carefully, you will see the intricacies and impressive craftsmanship that went into each building back in Miami in the '20s, '30s, '40s, and today, thanks to intensive restoration.

Most of the finest examples of the whimsical Art Deco style are concentrated along three parallel streets—Ocean Drive, Collins Avenue, and Washington Avenue—from about 6th to 23rd streets.

After years of neglect and calls for the wholesale demolition of its buildings, South Beach got a new lease on life in 1979. Under the leadership of Barbara Baer Capitman, a dedicated crusader for the Art Deco region, and the Miami Design Preservation League, founded by Baer Capitman and five friends, an area made up of an estimated 800 buildings was granted a listing on the National Register of Historic Places. Designers then began highlighting long-lost architectural details with soft sherbet shades of peach, periwinkle, turquoise, and purple. Developers soon moved in, and the full-scale refurbishment of the area's hotels was underway.

Not everyone was pleased, though. Former Miami Beach commissioner Abe Resnick said, "I love old buildings. But these Art Deco buildings are 40, 50 years old. They aren't historic. They aren't special. We shouldn't be forced to keep them." But Miami Beach kept those buildings, and Resnick lost his seat on the commission.

Today hundreds of new establishments—hotels, restaurants, and nightclubs—have renovated these older, historic buildings, putting South Beach on the cutting edge of Miami's cultural and nightlife scene.

EXPLORING THE AREA

If you're touring this unique neighborhood on your own, start at the **Art Deco Welcome Center,** 1001 Ocean Dr. (© **305/531-3484**), which is run by the Miami Design Preservation League. The only beachside building across from the Clevelander Hotel and bar, the center gives away lots of informational material, including maps and pamphlets, and runs guided tours around the neighborhood. Art Deco books (including *The Art Deco*

Guide, an informative compendium of all the buildings here), T-shirts, postcards, mugs, and other paraphernalia are for sale. It's open daily from 10am to 7:30pm.

Take a stroll along **Ocean Drive** for the best view of sidewalk cafes, bars, colorful hotels, and even more colorful people. Another great place for a walk is **Lincoln Road,** which is lined with boutiques, large chain stores, cafes, and funky art and antiques stores. The Community Church, at the corner of Lincoln Road and Drexel Avenue, was the neighborhood's first church and is one of its oldest surviving buildings, dating from 1921.

Or, if you prefer to cruise South Beach in a tiny yellow buggy—part scooter, part golf cart—consider **GoCar,** 1661 James Ave. (✆ **888/462-2755;** www.gocartours.com), a three-wheeled vehicle for two that comes with a GPS device that not only tracks and tells you where to go, but prompts a recorded tour that kicks on with every site you cruise by. Cost is $49 for the first hour, $39 for the second hour, and $29 for the third hour, or $150 for the entire day.

For a map of these sights see "South Beach Attractions" on p. 187

3 MIAMI'S MUSEUM & ART SCENE

Miami has never been known as a cultural mecca as far as museums are concerned, though its reputation is improving thanks to the international attention brought to the scene by such esteemed fairs as Switzerland's Art Basel, which comes to Miami for a week every December. Though several exhibition spaces have made forays into collecting nationally acclaimed work, limited support and political infighting have made it a difficult proposition. Recently, however, things have changed as museums such as the Wolfsonian, the Museum of Contemporary Art, the Bass Museum of Art, and the Miami Art Museum have gotten on the bandwagon, boasting collections and exhibitions high on the list of art aficionados. It's now safe to say that world-class exhibitions start here. Listed below are the most lauded museums that have become a part of the city's cultural heritage and are as diverse as the city itself. Art lovers should check local listings for periodic gallery walks. Please note that many art museums and galleries are closed in the summer; call ahead so you won't be disappointed.

The focal point of December's enormously popular Art Basel is **Collins Park Cultural Center,** which comprises a trio of arts buildings on Collins Park and Park Avenue (off Collins Ave.), bounded by 21st to 23rd streets—the newly expanded Bass Museum of Art (see below), the new Arquitectonica-designed home of the Miami City Ballet, and the Miami Beach Regional Library, an ultramodern building designed by architect Robert A. M. Stern, with a special focus on the arts. The Library Café is on the library's first floor, serving coffee and pastries and exuding that cafe society ambience. Collins Park, the former site of the Miami Beach Library, returned to its original incarnation as an open space extending to the Atlantic, but it is also now the site of large sculpture installations and cultural activities planned jointly by the organizations that share the space.

ArtCenter/South Florida ★ Not exactly a museum in the classic sense of the word, ArtCenter/South Florida is a multichambered space, where local artists display their works in all media—from photography and sculpture to video and just about anything else that might exemplify their artistic nature. Admission is free, and it's quite fun to mosey through the space viewing the various artists at work in their studios. Of course, all the art is for sale, but there's no pressure to buy. If you call ahead, you can schedule a guided tour of all the studios, which will give you extra insight into the exhibits. Otherwise, just wander and enjoy.

 800–924 Lincoln Rd. (at Meridian Ave.), South Beach. ✆ **305/674-8278.** www.artcentersf.org. Free admission. Daily 11am–10pm.

Bass Museum of Art ★★★ The Bass Museum of Art has expanded and received a dramatically new look, rendering it Miami's most progressive art museum. World-renowned Japanese architect Arata Isozaki designed the magnificent new facility, which has triple the former exhibition space, and added an outdoor sculpture terrace, a museum cafe and courtyard, and a museum shop, among other improvements. In addition to providing space in which to show the permanent collection, exhibitions of a scale and quality not previously seen in Miami will now be featured at the Bass. The museum's permanent collection includes European paintings from the 15th through the early 20th centuries, with special emphasis on northern European art of the Renaissance and baroque periods, including Dutch and Flemish masters. Past exhibitions have included the works of Picasso, Frida Kahlo, and Francois-Marie Banier. The museum also has a lab, the New Information Workshop, making it possible for all aspiring artists to create their own masterpieces on computers for free or a nominal charge.

2121 Park Ave. (1 block west of Collins Ave.), South Beach. ✆ **305/673-7530.** www.bassmuseum.org. Admission $8 adults, $6 students and seniors, free for children 6 and under. Free 2nd Thurs of the month 6–9pm. Tues–Wed and Fri–Sat 10am–5pm; Thurs 10am–9pm; Sun 11am–5pm.

Holocaust Memorial ★★★ This heart-wrenching memorial is hard to miss and would be a shame to overlook. The powerful centerpiece, Kenneth Treister's *A Sculpture of Love and Anguish,* depicts victims of the concentration camps crawling up a giant yearning hand stretching up to the sky, marked with an Auschwitz number tattoo. Along the reflecting pool is the story of the Holocaust, told in cut marble slabs. Inside the center of the memorial is a tableau that is one of the most solemn and moving tributes to the millions of Jews who lost their lives in the Holocaust I've seen. You can walk through an open hallway lined with photographs and the names of concentration camps and their victims. From the street, you'll see the outstretched arm, but do stop and tour the sculpture at ground level.

1933 Meridian Ave. (at Dade Blvd.), South Beach. ✆ **305/538-1663.** www.holocaustmmb.org. Free admission. Daily 9am–9pm.

Lowe Art Museum ★★ Located on the University of Miami campus, the Lowe Art Museum has a dazzling collection of 8,000 works that include American paintings, Latin American art, Navajo and Pueblo Indian textiles, and Renaissance and baroque art. Traveling exhibits, such as *Wine Spectator* magazine's classic posters of the Belle Epoque, also stop here. For the most part, the Lowe is known for its collection of Greek and Roman antiquities, and, as compared to the more modern MOCA, Bass, and Miami Art Museum, features mostly European and international art hailing back to ancient times.

University of Miami, 1301 Stanford Dr. (at Ponce de León Blvd.), Coral Gables. ✆ **305/284-3603.** www.lowemuseum.org. Admission $10 adults, $5 seniors and students with ID. Donation day is 1st Tues of the month. Tues–Wed and Fri–Sat 10am–5pm; Thurs noon–7pm; Sun noon–5pm.

Miami Art Museum ★★★ The Miami Art Museum (MAM) features an eclectic mix of modern and contemporary works by such artists as Eric Fischl, Max Beckmann, Jim Dine, and Stuart Davis. Rotating exhibitions span ages and styles, and often focus on Latin American or Caribbean artists. JAM at MAM is the museum's popular happy hour, which takes place on the third Thursday of the month and is tied in to a particular exhibit. Almost as artistic as the works inside the museum is the composite sketch of the people—young and old—who attend these events.

The Miami-Dade Cultural Center, where the museum is housed, is a fortresslike complex designed by Philip Johnson. In addition to the acclaimed Miami Art Museum, the center houses the main branch of the Miami-Dade Public Library, which sometimes features art and cultural exhibits, and the Historical Museum of Southern Florida, which highlights the fascinating history of the area. Unfortunately, the plaza onto which the complex opens is home to many of those in downtown Miami's homeless population, which makes it a bit off-putting but not dangerous. Work has yet to begin on Museum Park, a $200-plus-million project on an underused 29-acre property on the bay in downtown Miami that will become MAM's new home. The 125,000-square-foot Museum Park will include a sculpture garden and spacious galleries. Estimated completion is sometime in 2012.

101 W. Flagler St., Miami. ✆ **305/375-3000.** www.miamiartmuseum.org. Admission $8 adults, $4 seniors, free for children 11 and under. Tues–Fri 10am–5pm; 3rd Thurs of each month 10am–9pm; Sat–Sun noon–5pm. Closed major holidays. From I-95 south, exit at Orange Bowl–NW 8th St. and continue south to NW 2nd St.; turn left at NW 2nd St. and go 1½ blocks to NW 2nd Ave.; turn right.

Miami Children's Museum ★★ Kids The Children's Museum, located on the MacArthur Causeway, across from Jungle Island, is a modern, albeit odd-looking, 56,500-square-foot facility that includes 14 galleries, classrooms, a parent/teacher resource center, a Kid Smart educational gift shop, a 200-seat auditorium, a Subway restaurant, and an outdoor, interactive play area. The museum offers hundreds of bilingual, interactive exhibits as well as programs, classes, and learning materials related to arts, culture, community, and communication. Even as an adult, I have to say I was tempted to participate in some kids-only activities and exhibitions, such as the miniature Bank of America and Publix Supermarket, and a re-creation of the NBC 6 television studio. There's also a re-creation of a Carnival cruise ship and a gallery of teddy bears from around the world. Perhaps the coolest thing of all is the World Music Studio, in which aspiring rock stars can lay down a few tracks and play instruments.

980 MacArthur Causeway, Miami. ✆ **305/373-5437.** www.miamichildrensmuseum.org. Admission $12 adults and children 13 months and over. Daily 10am–6pm.

Miami Science Museum ★★ Kids The Miami Science Museum features more than 140 hands-on exhibits that explore the mysteries of the universe. Live demonstrations and collections of rare natural history specimens make a visit here fun and informative. Many of the demos involve audience participation, which can be lots of fun for willing and able kids and adults alike. There is also the Wildlife Center, with more than 175 live reptiles and birds of prey. The adjacent Space Transit Planetarium projects astronomy and laser shows as well as interactive demonstrations of upcoming computer technology and cyberspace features. Call or visit the website for a list of upcoming exhibits and laser shows.

3280 S. Miami Ave. (just south of the Rickenbacker Causeway), Coconut Grove. ✆ **305/646-4200.** www.miamisci.org. Admission $18 adults, $16 seniors and students, $13 children 3–12, free for children 2 and under. Daily 10am–6pm; 1st Fri of every month 10am–10pm; call for show times (last show is at 4pm Mon–Fri and 5pm Sat–Sun). Closed Thanksgiving and Christmas.

Museum of Contemporary Art (MOCA) ★★★ MOCA boasts an impressive collection of internationally acclaimed art with a local flavor. It is also known for its forward thinking and ability to discover and highlight new artists. A high-tech screening facility allows for film presentations to complement the exhibitions. You can see works by Jasper Johns, Roy Lichtenstein, Larry Rivers, Duane Michaels, and Claes Oldenburg, plus there are special exhibitions by such artists as Yoko Ono, Sigmar Polke, John Baldessari, and Goya. Guided tours are offered in English, Spanish, French, Creole, Portuguese, German, and Italian. The MOCA Annex at the Goldman Warehouse in the gritty, yet burgeoning Wynwood Arts District, 404 NW 26th St., is used to exhibit portions of the museum's permanent collection and projects by emerging artists.

770 NE 125th St., North Miami. ✆ **305/893-6211.** Fax 305/891-1472. www.mocanomi.org. Admission $5 adults, $3 seniors and students with ID, free for children 12 and under. Tues by donation. Tues–Sat 11am–5pm; Sun noon–5pm. Closed major holidays.

Patricia and Phillip Frost Art Museum ★★ Housed in a $16-million building designed by architect Yann Weymouth, the Patricia and Phillip Frost Art Museum, located on the campus of Florida International University, was closed to the public until 2009. Toady, it is the only art museum in Florida to attempt to exhibit paintings in natural light. The museum has recently begun to present exhibitions in Latin America and is working on future collaborations and partnerships with leading art institutions in these regions. Among the permanent collections is the General Collection, which holds a strong representation of American printmaking from the 1960s and 1970s, photography, pre-Columbian objects dating from A.D. 200 to 500, and a growing number of works by contemporary Caribbean and Latin American artists.

Florida International University, 10975 SW 17th St. ✆ **305/348-2890.** http://thefrost.fiu.edu. Free admission. Tues–Sat 10am–5pm; Sun noon–5pm.

Rubell Family Art Collection ★★★ Finds This impressive collection, owned by the Miami hotelier family the Rubells, is housed in a two-story, 40,000-square-foot, former Drug Enforcement Agency warehouse in a sketchy area north of downtown Miami. The building looks like a fortress, which is fitting: Inside is a priceless collection of more than 1,000 works of contemporary art by the likes of Keith Haring, Damien Hirst, Julian Schnabel, Jean-Michel Basquiat, Paul McCarthy, Charles Ray, and Cindy Sherman. But ***be forewarned:*** Some of the art is extremely graphic and may be off-putting to some. The gallery changes exhibitions twice yearly, and there is a seasonal program of lectures, artists' talks, and performances by prominent artists.

95 NW 29th St. (on the corner of NW 1st Ave. near the Design District), Miami. ✆ **305/573-6090.** www.rubellfamilycollection.com. Admission $10 adults, $5 seniors and students. Wed–Sun 10am–6pm.

Sanford L. Ziff Jewish Museum of Florida ★ Chronicling over 230 years of Jewish heritage and experiences in Florida, the Jewish Museum presents a fascinating look at religion and culture through films, lectures, and exhibits such as Mosaic: Jewish Life in Florida, which features over 500 photos and artifacts documenting the Jewish experience in Florida since 1763. Housed in a former synagogue, the museum also delves into the Jewish roots of Latin America.

301 Washington Ave., South Beach. ✆ **305/672-5044.** www.jewishmuseum.com. Admission $6 adults, $5 seniors and students, $12 families. Free admission Sat. Tues–Sun 10am–5pm. Closed Jewish holidays.

Wolfsonian-Florida International University ★★★ Finds Mitchell Wolfson, Jr., heir to a family fortune built on movie theaters, was known as an eccentric, but I'd call him a pack rat. A premier collector of propaganda and advertising art, Wolfson was spending so much money storing his booty that he decided to buy the warehouse that was housing it. It ultimately held more than 70,000 of his items, from controversial Nazi propaganda to King Farouk of Egypt's match collection. Thrown in the eclectic mix are also zany works from great modernists such as Charles Eames and Marcel Duchamp. He then gave this incredibly diverse collection to Florida International University. The former 1927 storage facility has been transformed into a museum that is the envy of curators around the world. The museum is unquestionably fascinating and hosts lectures and rather swinging events surrounding particular exhibits. The Dynamo, the museum's cafe and shop, is a fun and funky spot serving coffee, wine, beer, and nibbles, whose focal point is a large library shelving system from the late 19th century, donated by Samson Management, designed by Bernard R. Green, and crafted of iron by the Snead & Company Iron Works. The design represents the first modular book-stacking system ever created. Leave it to the Wolfsonian to make even its restaurant a piece of work!

1001 Washington Ave., South Beach. ✆ **305/531-1001.** www.wolfsonian.org. Admission $7 adults; $5 seniors, students with ID, and children 6–12. Mon–Tues and Fri–Sat 11am–6pm; Thurs 11am–9pm; Sun noon–5pm.

The World Erotic Art Museum ★ The Hustler store across the street has nothing on this wacky, X-rated museum. Opened in 2005 by 70-year-old grandmother Naomi Wilzig, the museum features Wilzig's collection of more than 4,000 pieces of erotic art, including Kama Sutra temple carvings from India, peek-a-boo Victorian figurines that flash their booties, and a prop from the sexual thriller *A Clockwork Orange.* The 12,000-square-foot museum is located above Mansion, a club that's no stranger to erotic art—that is, performance art. This is a great place to spend an hour or two on a rainy day, and more than anything, the stuff is more amusing than sexy or racy.

1205 Washington Ave., South Beach. ✆ **305/532-9336.** www.weam.com. Admission $15; under 18 years not admitted. Daily 11am–midnight.

4 HISTORIC HOMES & SITES

South Beach's well-touted Art Deco District is but one of many colorful neighborhoods that can boast dazzling architecture. The rediscovery of the entire Biscayne Corridor (from downtown to about 80th St. and Biscayne Blvd.) has given light to a host of ancillary neighborhoods on either side, which are filled with Mediterranean-style homes and Frank Lloyd Wright gems. Coral Gables is home to many large and beautiful homes, mansions, and churches that reflect architecture from the 1920s, 1930s, and 1940s. Some of the homes, or portions of their structures, have been created from coral rock and shells. The Biltmore Hotel is also filled with history; see p. 158 for information on touring it.

Barnacle State Historic Site ★★ The former home of naval architect and early settler Ralph Middleton Munroe is now a museum in the heart of Coconut Grove. It's the oldest house in Miami and it rests on its original foundation, which sits on 5 acres of natural hardwood forest and landscaped lawns. The house's quiet surroundings, wide porches, and period furnishings illustrate how Miami's first snowbird lived in the days before condomania and luxury hotels. Enthusiastic and knowledgeable state park employees provide a wealth of historical information to those interested in quiet, low-tech attractions such as this one. On Wednesdays from 6 to 7:30pm they have sunset yoga by the sea. Call for details on the fabulous monthly moonlight concerts during which folk, blues, or classical music is presented and picnicking is encouraged.

3485 Main Hwy. (1 block south of Commodore Plaza), Coconut Grove. ✆ **305/448-9445.** Fax 305/448-7484. Admission $1. Concerts $5, free for children 9 and under. Fri–Mon 9am–4pm. Tours Fri–Mon at 10am, 11:30am, 1pm, and 2:30pm. From downtown Miami, take U.S. 1 south to 27th Ave., make a left, and continue to S. Bayshore Dr.; then make a right, follow to the intersection of Main Hwy., and turn left.

Coral Castle ★ Finds There's plenty of competition, but Coral Castle is probably the strangest attraction in Florida. In 1923, the story goes, a 26-year-old crazed Latvian, suffering from the unrequited love of a 16-year-old who left him at the altar, immigrated to South Miami and spent the next 25 years of his life carving huge boulders into a prehistoric-looking roofless "castle." It seems impossible that one rather short man could have done all this, but there are scores of affidavits on display from neighbors who swear it happened. Apparently, experts have studied this phenomenon to help figure out how the great pyramids and Stonehenge were built. Rocker Billy Idol was said to have been inspired by this place to write his song "Sweet 16." An interesting 25-minute audio tour guides you through the spot, now on the National Register of Historic Places. Although Coral Castle is overpriced and undermaintained, it's worth a visit when you're in the area, which is about 37 miles from Miami.

28655 S. Dixie Hwy., Homestead. ✆ **305/248-6345.** www.coralcastle.com. Admission $9.75 adults, $6.50 seniors, $5 children 7–12. Group rates available. Daily 7am–8pm. Take 836 W (Dolphin Expwy.) toward Miami International Airport. Merge onto 826 S (Palmetto Expwy.) and take it to the Florida Tpk. toward Homestead. Take the 288th St. exit (#5) and then take a right on S. Dixie Hwy., a left on SW 157th Ave., and then a sharp left back onto S. Dixie Hwy. Coral Castle is on the left side of the street.

Spanish Monastery Cloisters ★★★ Finds Did you know that the alleged oldest building in the Western Hemisphere dates from 1133 and is located in Miami? The Spanish Monastery Cloisters were first erected in Segovia, Spain. Centuries later, newspaper magnate William Randolph Hearst purchased and brought them to America in pieces. The carefully numbered stones were quarantined for years until they were finally reassembled on the present site in 1954. It has often been used as a backdrop for weddings, movies, and commercials, and is a very popular tourist attraction.

16711 W. Dixie Hwy. (at NE 167th St.), North Miami Beach. ✆ **305/945-1461.** www.spanishmonastery.com. Admission $5 adults, $2.50 seniors and students with ID, $1 children 3–12. Mon–Fri 10am–4pm; Sun 1–5pm. Call ahead because the monastery closes for special events without notice.

Venetian Pool ★★★ Kids Miami's most beautiful and unusual swimming pool, dating from 1924, is hidden behind pastel stucco walls and is honored with a listing in the National Register of Historic Places. Underground artesian wells feed the free-form lagoon, which is shaded by three-story Spanish porticos and has both fountains and waterfalls. It can be cold in the winter months. During summer, the pool's 800,000 gallons of water are drained and refilled nightly, thanks to an underground aquifer, ensuring a cool, *clean* swim. Visitors are free to swim and sunbathe here, just as Esther Williams and Johnny Weissmuller did decades ago. For a modest fee, you or your children can learn to swim during special summer programs.

2701 DeSoto Blvd. (at Toledo St.), Coral Gables. ✆ **305/460-5356.** www.venetianpool.com. Admission Nov–Mar $5.50 for those 13 and older, $3.50 for children 12 and under; Apr–Oct $10 for those 13 and older, $6.75 for children 12 and under. Children must be at least 3 years old and provide proof of age with birth certificate, or 38 in. tall to enter. Daily hours are at least 11am–4:30pm but are often longer. Call for more information.

The Vizcaya Museum and Gardens ★★★ Sometimes referred to as the "Hearst Castle of the East," this magnificent villa is more Gatsby-esque than anything else you'll find in Miami. It was built in 1916 as a winter retreat for James Deering, cofounder and former vice president of International Harvester. The industrialist was fascinated by 16th-century art and architecture, and his ornate mansion, which took 1,000 artisans 5 years to build, became a celebration of that period. If you love antiques, this place is a dream come true, packed with European relics and works of art from the 16th to the 19th centuries. Most of the original furnishings, including dishes and paintings, are still intact. You will see very early versions of a telephone switchboard, central vacuum-cleaning system, elevators, and fire sprinklers. A free guided tour of the 34 furnished rooms on the first floor takes about 45 minutes. The second floor, which consists mostly of bedrooms, is open to tour on your own. The spectacularly opulent villa wraps itself around a central courtyard. Outside, lush formal gardens, accented with statuary, balustrades, and decorative urns, front an enormous swath of Biscayne Bay. Definitely take the tour of the rooms, but immediately thereafter, you will want to wander and get lost in the resplendent gardens.

3251 S. Miami Ave. (just south of Rickenbacker Causeway), North Coconut Grove. ✆ **305/250-9133.** www.vizcayamuseum.com. Admission $15 adults, $10 seniors, $6 children 6–12, free for children 5 and under. Villa daily 9:30am–5pm (ticket booth closes at 4:30pm); gardens daily 9:30am–5:30pm.

5 NATURE PRESERVES, PARKS & GARDENS

The Miami area is a great place for outdoor types, with beaches, parks, nature preserves, and gardens galore. For information on South Florida's two national parks, the Everglades and Biscayne National Park, see chapter 8.

The **Amelia Earhart Park,** 401 E. 65th St., Hialeah (✆ **305/685-8389**), is the only real reason to travel to industrial, traffic-riddled Hialeah. The park has five lakes stocked with bass and bream for fishing, playgrounds, picnic facilities, a skate park, and a big red barn that houses cows, sheep, and goats for petting and ponies for riding. There's also the Bill Graham Farm Village, a re-created Miami-Dade County homestead housing a country store and dozens of old-time farm activities such as horseshoeing, sugar-cane processing, and more. Parking is free on weekdays and $4 per car on weekends. The park is open daily from 9am to sunset, but all the attractions close at about 4pm. To drive here, take I-95 north to the NW 103rd Street exit, go west to East 4th Avenue, and then turn right. Parking is 1½ miles down the street. Depending on traffic, Hialeah is about a half-hour from downtown Miami.

At the historic **Bill Baggs Cape Florida State Park ★**, 1200 Crandon Blvd. (✆ **305/361-5811**), at the southern tip of Key Biscayne about 20 minutes from downtown Miami, you can explore the unfettered wilds and enjoy some of the most secluded beaches in Miami. There's also a historic lighthouse that was built in 1825, which is the oldest lighthouse in South Florida. The lighthouse was damaged during the Second Seminole War (1836) and again in 1861 during the Civil War. Out of commission for a while, it was restored to working lighthouse condition in 1978 by the U.S. Coast Guard. A rental shack leases bikes, hydrobikes, kayaks, and many more water toys. It's a great place to picnic, but there are also two restaurants on-site: the Lighthouse Café, which serves homemade Latin food, including great fish soups and sandwiches, and the Boater's Grill offering casual waterfront dining. Just be careful that the raccoons don't get your lunch—the furry black-eyed beasts are everywhere. Wildlife aside, however, Bill Baggs has been consistently rated as one of the top 10 beaches in the U.S. for its 1¼ miles of wide, sandy beaches and its secluded, serene atmosphere. Admission is $5 per car with up to eight people (or $3 for a car with only one person; $1 to enter by foot or bicycle). Open daily from 8am to sunset. Tours of the lighthouse are available every Thursday through Monday at 10am and 1pm. Arrive at least half an hour early to sign up—there is room for only 10 people on each tour. Take I-95 to the Rickenbacker Causeway and take that all the way to the end.

Fairchild Tropical Garden ★★★, at 10901 Old Cutler Rd., in Coral Gables (✆ **305/667-1651;** www.ftg.org), is the largest of its kind in the continental United States. A veritable rainforest of both rare and exotic plants, as well as 11 lakes and countless meadows, are spread across 83 acres. Palmettos, vine pergola, palm glades, and other unique species create a scenic, lush environment. More than 100 species of birds have been spotted at the garden (ask for a checklist at the front gate), and it's home to a variety of animals. You should not miss the 30-minute narrated tram tour (tours leave on the hour 10am–3pm weekdays and 10am–4pm on weekends) to learn about the various flowers and trees on the grounds. There is also a museum, a cafe, a picnic area, and a gift shop with edible gifts and fantastic books on gardening and cooking. Fairchild often hosts major art exhibits by the likes of Dale Chihuly and Roy Lichtenstein. The 2-acre rainforest exhibit, Windows to the Tropics, will save you a trip to the Amazon. Expect to spend a minimum of 2 hours here.

Admission is $20 for adults, $15 for seniors, $10 for children ages 3 to 12, and free for children 2 and under. Open daily, except Christmas, from 9:30am to 4:30pm. Take I-95 south to U.S. 1, turn left onto Le Jeune Road, and follow it straight to the traffic circle; from there, take Old Cutler Road 2 miles to the park.

On Biscayne Bay in Coconut Grove (4013 Douglas Rd.; www.ntbg.org/gardens/kampong.php), the **Kampong ★★** is a 7-acre botanical garden with a stunning array of flowering trees and tropical fruit trees, including mango, avocado, and pomelos. In the early 1900s, noted plant explorer David Fairchild traveled the world seeking rare plants of economic and aesthetic value that might be cultivated in the United States. In 1928, Fairchild and his wife, Marian—the daughter of Alexander Graham Bell—decided to build a residence here (now listed on the National Register of Historic Places) surrounded by some of his findings, and named it after the Malaysian word *kampong,* meaning "home in a garden." In the 1960s, the Fairchilds sold the Kampong to Catherine Hauberg Sweeney, who donated it to the National Tropical Botanical Garden to promote and preserve this South Florida treasure. It's a must-see for those interested in horticulture. Admission and tours are by appointment only, from Monday to Friday. For tour and price information, call ✆ **305/442-7169** from 9am to 5pm Monday through Friday. Take U.S. 1 to Douglas Road (SW 37th Ave.). Go east on Douglas Road for about a mile. The Kampong will be on your left.

Named after the late champion of the Everglades, the **Marjory Stoneman Douglas Biscayne Nature Center ★**, 6767 Crandon Blvd., Key Biscayne (✆ **305/361-6767;** www.biscaynenaturecenter.org), is housed in a $4-million facility and offers hands-on marine exploration, hikes through coastal hammocks, bike trips, and beach walks. Local environmentalists and historians lead intriguing trips through the local habitat. Call to reserve a spot on a regularly scheduled weekend tour or program. Be sure to wear comfortable, closed-toe shoes for hikes through wet or rocky terrain. Open daily 10am to 4pm. Admission to the park is $4 per person; admission to the nature center is free. Special programs and tours cost $10 per person. Call for weekend programs. To get there, take I-95 to the Rickenbacker Causeway exit (#1) and take the causeway all the way until it becomes Crandon Boulevard. The center is on the east side of the street (the Atlantic Ocean side) and about 25 minutes from downtown Miami.

Because so many people are focused on the beach itself, the **Miami Beach Botanical Garden,** 2000 Convention Center Dr., Miami Beach (✆ **305/673-7256**), remains a secret garden. The lush, tropical 4½-acre garden is a fabulous natural retreat from the hustle and bustle of the silicone-enhanced city. Open Tuesday through Sunday from 9am to 5pm; admission is free.

The **Oleta River State Recreation Area ★★**, 3400 NE 163rd St., North Miami (© **305/919-1846**), consists of 993 acres—the largest urban park in the state—on Biscayne Bay. The beauty of the Oleta River, combined with the fact that you're essentially in the middle of a city, makes this park especially worth visiting. With miles of bicycle and canoe trails, a sandy swimming beach, kayak and mountain bike rental shop, Blue Marlin Fish House Restaurant, shaded picnic pavilions, and a fishing pier, Oleta River State Recreation Area allows for an outstanding outdoor recreational experience cloistered from the confines of the big city. There are 14 air-conditioned cabins on the premises that sleep four people. The cost is $45 per night, and guests are required to bring their own linens. Bathrooms and showers are outside, as is a fire circle with a grill for cooking. For reservations, call © **800/326-3521.** It's open daily from 8am to sunset. Admission for pedestrians and cyclists is $1 per person. By car: Driver plus car costs $3; driver plus one to seven passengers and car costs $5. Take 1-95 to exit 17 (S.R. 826 E.) and go all the way east until just before the causeway. The park entrance is on your right. Driving time from downtown Miami is about a half-hour.

A testament to Miami's unusual climate, the **Preston B. Bird and Mary Heinlein Fruit and Spice Park ★**, 24801 SW 187th Ave., Homestead (© **305/247-5727;** www.fruitandspicepark.org), harbors rare fruit trees that cannot survive elsewhere in the country. If a volunteer is available, you'll learn some fascinating things about this 30-acre living plant museum, where the most exotic varieties of fruits and spices—ackee, mango, Ugli fruits, carambola, and breadfruit—grow on strange-looking trees with unpronounceable names. There are also original coral rock buildings dating back to 1912. The Strawberry Folk Festival in February and an art festival here in January are among the park's most popular—and populated—events. The best part? You're free to take anything that has *naturally* fallen to the ground (no picking here). You'll also find samples of interesting fruits and jellies made from the park's bounty, as well as exotic ingredients and cookbooks in the gift store.

Admission to the spice park is $6 for adults and $1.50 for children 12 and under. It's open daily from 10am to 5pm; closed on Christmas. Tours are included in the price of admission and are offered at 11am, 1:30pm, and 3pm. Take U.S. 1 south, turn right on SW 248th Street, and go straight for 5 miles to SW 187th Avenue. The drive from Miami should take 45 minutes to an hour.

Tropical Park, 7900 SW 40th St. (© **305/226-8315**), is remotely located out in West Miami, but it has lots to offer, especially if its during the holiday season when the place is all decked out in millions of holiday lights, with attractions such as Santa's Enchanted Forest. Enjoy a game of tennis or racquetball for a minimal fee, swim and sun yourself on the secluded little lake, rent bikes, or try horseback riding. You can use the fishing pond for free, and they'll even supply you with the rods and bait. If you catch anything, however, you're on your own. Open daily from 7am to 10pm; admission is free. To get there, go west on Bird Road until you reach the overpass for the Palmetto Expressway (826). The park is on the left side immediately after the overpass.

6 ORGANIZED TOURS

SIGHTSEEING TOURS

Miami Nice Excursion Travel and Service ★ Pick your destination and the Miami Nice tours will take you by bus to the Everglades, Fort Lauderdale, South Beach, the Seaquarium, Key West, Cape Canaveral, or wherever else you desire. The best trip for first-timers is the City Tour, a comprehensive tour of the entire city and its various neighborhoods. If you've got the time, you will definitely want to add on a side trip to the Everglades and/or Key West (though I suggest exploring the Everglades on your own). Included in most Miami trips is a fairly comprehensive city tour narrated by a knowledgeable guide. The company is one of the oldest in town.

18801 Collins Ave., Miami Beach. ✆ **305/949-9180.** www.miaminicetours.com. Tours $25–$70 adults, $25–$62 children 3–9. Mon–Sat 7am–10pm. Call ahead for directions to various pickup areas.

SPECIALIZED TOURS

In addition to tours listed below, a great option for seeing the city is a tour led by **Dr. Paul George.** Dr. George is a history teacher at Miami-Dade Community College and a historian at the Historical Museum of Southern Florida. He also happens to be "Mr. Miami." There's a variety of tours (including the "Mystery, Mayhem and Vice Crime Bus Tour," detailed below), all fascinating to South Florida buffs. Tours focus on such neighborhoods as Little Havana, Brickell Avenue, or Key Biscayne, and on themes such as Miami cemeteries and the Miami River. There are also eco-history coach, walking, and bike tours. The often-long-winded discussions can be a bit much for those who just want a quick look around, but Dr. George certainly knows his stuff. The cost is $5 to $44, and reservations are required (✆ **305/375-1621;** www.hmsf.org/programs-adult.htm). Tours leave from the Historical Museum at 101 W. Flagler St., downtown. Call for a schedule.

Biltmore Hotel Tour ★★★ Value Take advantage of these free, 55-minute Sunday walking tours to enjoy the hotel's history and beautiful grounds. Starting in the upstairs lobby, the tour will even take you to Everglades Suite, when available, home to dignitaries, heads of state, and a sanctuary for celebrities. Call ahead to confirm.

1200 Anastasia Ave., Coral Gables. ✆ **305/445-1926.** www.biltmorehotel.com. Free admission. Tours depart Sun at 1:30, 2:30, and 3:30pm.

Eco-Adventure Tours ★★★ For the eco-conscious traveler, the Miami-Dade Parks and Recreation Department offers guided nature, adventure, and historic tours involving biking, canoeing, snorkeling, hiking, and bird-watching all over the city. Contact them for more information.

✆ **305/365-3018.** www.miamidade.gov/parks/fun-eco_adventures.asp.

Hispanic Heritage Tour This is offered during October only (Hispanic Heritage Month): For those looking to immerse themselves in Miami's rich Latin-American culture, the Herencia Hispana Tour is the ideal way to explore it all. Hop on a bus and zoom past such hotbeds of Latin activity as downtown's Flagler Street, the unavoidable Elián González house, and Little Havana's Domino Park and Tower Theater, among others. Not just a sightseeing tour, this one includes two very knowledgeable, albeit corny, guides who know just when to infuse a necessary dose of humor into the Elián saga, a segment of history that some people may not consider so amusing.

Tours depart from the Steven P. Clark Government Center, 111 NW 1st St. ✆ **305/770-3131.** www.co.miami-dade.fl.us/transit/hispanicher.asp. Tours (in Spanish or English, but you must specify which one you require) are free, but advanced reservations are required. Tours depart at 9, 9:30, and 10am every Sat in Oct.

Little Havana Walking Tour ★★★ Dr. Paul George will guide you through Little Havana, pointing out the significance of South Florida bungalow architecture, the Tower Theater, old-fashioned hand rollers at a cigar factory, and more. Visit Cuban Memorial

Vintage Miami

Although it's hardly Napa Valley, Miami does have an actual winery: **Schnebly Redland's Winery,** 30205 SW 217th Ave., Homestead (✆ **888/717-WINE;** www.schneblywinery.com), in whose $1.5-million tasting room you can sample from various vintages. I've tried some, and while they're too fruity for my taste, it's still worth a trip down just to see the press deck where fruit becomes juice and eventually wine. There's live music and extended hours on Saturday and Sunday, and if you like what you taste, you can buy any four bottles of wine for $65. Open 10am to 5pm Monday to Friday, 10am to 8pm Saturday, and noon to 7pm Sunday.

Boulevard and observe the monuments that speak to the exile presence in Miami. See the home of Miami's first mayor. The tour ends with an optional lunch at the iconic Versailles.

✆ **305/375-1621.** www.hmsf.org. Tour $25.

Miami Design Preservation League ★★ On Thursday evenings and Saturday mornings, the Design Preservation League sponsors walking tours that provide a fascinating inside look at the city's historic Art Deco District. Tourgoers meet for a 1½-hour walk through some of America's most exuberantly "architectured" buildings. The league led the fight to designate this area a National Historic District and is proud to share the splendid locale with visitors. Also see p. 148 for more information.

Art Deco Welcome Center, 1001 Ocean Dr., South Beach. ✆ **305/672-2014.** www.mdpl.org. Walking tours $20 per person. Tours leave Wed and Sat at 10:30am and Thurs at 6:30pm. Self-guided audio tours also available daily for $15. No reservations necessary, but arrive 15 min. early. Call ahead for updated schedules.

Mystery, Mayhem and Vice Crime Bus Tour ★★★ Visit the past by video and bus to Miami-Dade's most celebrated crimes and criminals from the 1800s to the present, including some sites where the '80s TV series *Miami Vice* was filmed. From the murder spree of the Ashley Gang to the most notorious murders and crimes of the last century, including the murder of designer Gianni Versace, historian Paul George conducts a most fascinating 3-hour tour of scandalous proportions.

Leaves from the Dade Cultural Center, 101 W. Flagler St., Miami. Advance reservations required; call ✆ **305/375-1621.** Tickets $44. Held twice a year, usually in Apr and Oct.

Redland Tropical Trail Tours ★★★ Check out South Florida farmlands—yes, they do exist in an area near Homestead called the Redlands—on this tour featuring a circuit of stops, tastings, and sightseeing that will take you from gardens and jungles to an orchid farm, an actual working winery (see below), fruit stand, and more. There's no cost to follow the trail with a map (available on the website) on your own, but call for pricing information for certain attractions found on the trail.

✆ **305/245-9180.** www.redlandtrail.com.

7 WATERSPORTS

There are many ways to get well acquainted with Miami's wet look. Choose your own adventure from the suggestions listed below.

BOATING

Private rental outfits include **Boat Rental Plus,** 2400 Collins Ave., Miami Beach (© **305/534-4307**), where 50-horsepower, 18-foot powerboats rent for some of the best prices on the beach. There's a 2-hour minimum, and rates go from $100 to $500, including taxes and gas. They also have great specials on Sunday. Cruising is permitted only in and around Biscayne Bay (ocean access is prohibited), and renters must be 21 or older to rent a boat. The rental office is at 23rd Street, on the inland waterway in Miami Beach. It's open daily from 10am to sunset. If you want a specific type of boat, call ahead to reserve. Otherwise, show up and take what's available.

Club Nautico, of Coconut Grove, 2560 S. Bayshore Dr. (© **305/858-6258;** www.clubnauticousa.com), rents high-quality powerboats for fishing, water-skiing, diving, and cruising in the bay or ocean. All boats are Coast Guard–equipped, with VHF radios and safety gear. Rates start at $359 for 4 hours and $469 for 8 hours; prices go up as the boats get larger. You can also rent by the hour at $125. Club Nautico is open daily from 8am to 6pm (weather permitting). Other locations include the Crandon Park Marina, 4000 Crandon Blvd., Key Biscayne (© **305/361-9217**), with the same rates and hours as the Coconut Grove location; and the Miami Beach Marina, Pier E, 300 Alton Rd., South Beach (© **305/673-2502**). Nautico, on Miami Beach, is open daily from 9am to 5pm.

JET SKIS/WAVERUNNERS

Don't miss a chance to tour the islands on the back of your own powerful watercraft. Bravery is, however, a prerequisite, as Miami's waterways are full of speeding jet skiers and boaters who think they're in the Indy 500. Many beachfront concessionaires rent a variety of these popular (and loud) water scooters. The latest models are fast and smooth. **American Watersports,** at the Miami Beach Marina, 300 Alton Rd. (© **305/538-7549;** www.jetskiz.com), is the area's most popular spot for jet-ski rental. Rates begin at $75 for a half-hour and $140 for an hour. They also offer fun jet-ski tours past celebrity homes for $160 for the first hour and $80 for the second.

KAYAKING

The **Blue Moon Outdoor Center** rents kayaks at 3400 NE 163rd St., in Oleta River Park (© **305/957-3040;** www.bluemoonmiami.com). The outfitters here give explorers a map to take with them and quick instructions on how to work the paddles and boats. They also operate very scenic 4-hour guided tours through rivers with mangroves and islands—fewer than 10 people on the tour costs $45 per person; more than 10 people costs $35 per person. Their signature tour, a 3-hour kayak and mountain bike tour exploring the park and trails costs $75 for two to four participants, and $65 for five or more. Without the bike tour it's $20 less. These must be booked in advance. Hourly and half-day rentals are available for single, tandem, and canoe. Prices range from $18 to $45. Guided eco-tours are also available with advance reservation for $45 to $55 per person. A full moon kayak tour includes a bonfire on the beach. While you are on the paddling route, make sure to stop at the Blue Marlin Fish House for some smoked fish. They also rent mountain bikes. Open daily from 9am to sunset. Special event tours at night are also available.

SAILING

You can rent sailboats and catamarans through the beachfront concessions desks of several top resorts, such as the Doral Golf Resort and Spa (p. 108).

Aquatic Rental Center, at northern Biscayne Bay in the Pelican Harbor Marina, 1275 NE 79th St. (© **305/751-7514** days, 279-7424 evenings; www.arcmiami.com), can also get you out on the water. A 22-foot sailboat rents for $85 for 2 hours, $150 for a half-day, and $225 for a full day. A Sunfish sailboat for two people rents at $30 per hour. If you've always had a dream to win the America's Cup but can't sail, the able teachers here will get you started. They offer a 10-hour course over 5 days for $350 for one person, or $500 for you and a buddy.

SCUBA DIVING & SNORKELING

In 1981, the U.S. government began a wide-scale project designed to increase the number of habitats available to marine organisms. One of the program's major accomplishments has been the creation of nearby artificial reefs, which have attracted all kinds of tropical plants, fish, and animals. In addition, Biscayne National Park (see the park's section in chapter 8, beginning on p. 258) offers a protected marine environment just south of downtown.

Several dive shops around the city offer organized weekend outings, either to the reefs or to one of more than a dozen old shipwrecks around Miami's shores. Check "Divers" in the Yellow Pages for rental equipment and for a full list of undersea tour operators.

Diver's Paradise, of Key Biscayne, 4000 Crandon Blvd. (© **305/361-3483;** www.keydivers.com), offers one dive expedition per day during the week and two per day on the weekends to the more than 30 wrecks and artificial reefs off the coast of Miami Beach and Key Biscayne. You can take a 3-day certification course for $499, which includes all the dives and gear. If you already have your C-card, a dive trip costs about $100 if you need equipment and $60 if you bring your own gear. It's open Tuesday through Friday from 10am to 6pm and Saturday and Sunday from 8am to 6pm. Call ahead for times and locations of dives. For snorkeling, they will set you up with equipment and maps on where to see the best underwater sights. Rental for mask, fins, and snorkel is $50.

South Beach Divers, 850 Washington Ave., Miami Beach (© **305/531-6110;** www.southbeachdivers.com), will also be happy to tell you where to go under the sea and will provide you with scuba rental equipment as well for $65. You can rent snorkel gear for $20. They also do dive trips to Key Largo three times a week and do dives off Miami on Sunday at $100 for a two-tank dive or $80 if you have your own equipment.

The most amusing and apropos South Beach diving spot has to be the **Jose Cuervo Underwater Bar,** located 150 yards southeast of the Second Street lifeguard station—a 22-ton concrete margarita bar that was sunk on May 5, 2000. Nicknamed "Sinko De Mayo," the site is designed with a dive flag roof, six bar stools, and a protective wall of tetrahedrons.

WINDSURFING

Many hotels rent windsurfers to their guests, but if yours doesn't have a watersports concession stand, head for Key Biscayne. **Sailboards Miami,** Rickenbacker Causeway, Key Biscayne (© **305/361-SAIL** [7245]; www.sailboardsmiami.com), operates out of two big yellow trucks on Windsurfer Beach, the most popular (though our pick for best is Hobie Beach) windsurfing spot in the city. For those who've never ridden a board but want to try it, they offer a 2-hour lesson for $69 that's guaranteed to turn you into a wave warrior, or you get your money back. After that, you can rent a board for $25 to $30 an hour. If you want to make a day of it, a 10-hour prepaid card costs $220. These cards reduce the price by about $70 for the day. You can use the card year-round, until the time on it runs out. Open Tuesday through Sunday from 10am to 5:30pm. Make your first right after the tollbooth (at the beginning of the causeway—you can't miss it) to find the outfitters. They also rent kayaks.

8 MORE WAYS TO PLAY, INDOORS & OUT

BIKING The cement promenade on the southern tip of South Beach is a great place to ride. Biking up the beach (either on the beach or along the beach on a cement pathway—which is a lot easier!) is great for surf, sun, sand, exercise, and people-watching—just be sure to keep your eyes on the road, as the scenery can be most distracting. Most of the big beach hotels rent bicycles, as does the **Miami Beach Bicycle Center,** 601 5th St., South Beach (✆ **305/674-0150;** www.bikemiamibeach.com), which charges $8 per hour or $24 for up to 24 hours. It's open Monday through Saturday from 10am to 7pm, Sunday from 10am to 5pm.

Bikers can also enjoy more than 130 miles of paved paths throughout Miami. The beautiful and quiet streets of Coral Gables and Coconut Grove (several bike trails are spread throughout these neighborhoods) are great for bicyclists, where old trees form canopies over wide, flat roads lined with grand homes and quaint street markers.

The terrain in Key Biscayne is perfect for biking, especially along the park and beach roads. If you don't mind the sound of cars whooshing by your bike lane, **Rickenbacker Causeway** is also fantastic, as it is one of the only bikeable inclines in Miami from which you get fantastic elevated views of the city and waterways. However, be warned that this is a grueling ride, especially going up the causeway. **Key Cycling,** 61 Harbor Dr., Key Biscayne (✆ **305/361-0061;** www.keycycling.com), rents mountain bikes for $15 for 2 hours or $20 a day. It's open Tuesday through Friday from 10am to 7pm, Monday and Saturday from 10am to 6pm, and Sunday from 10am to 3pm.

If you want to avoid the traffic altogether, head out to **Shark Valley** in the Everglades National Park—one of South Florida's most scenic bicycle trails and a favorite haunt of city-weary locals. For more information on Shark Valley and the Everglades, see chapter 8.

For a decent list of trail suggestions throughout South Florida, visit www.geocities.com/floutdoorzone/bike.html. ***Biking note:*** Children 15 and under are required by Florida law to wear a helmet, which can be purchased at any bike store or retail outlet selling biking supplies.

FISHING Fishing licenses are required in Florida. If you go out with one of the fishing charter boats listed below, you are automatically accredited because the companies are. If you go out on your own, however, you must have a Florida fishing license, which costs $17 for 3 days and $30 for a week. Call ✆ **888/FISH-FLO** (347-4356) or visit www.wildlifelicense.com for more information.

Some of the best surf-casting in the city can be had at **Haulover Beach Park** at Collins Avenue and 105th Street, where there's a bait-and-tackle shop right on the pier. **South Pointe Park,** at the southern tip of Miami Beach, is another popular fishing spot and features a long pier, comfortable benches, and a great view of the ships passing through Government Cut, the deep channel made when the port of Miami was dug.

You can also do some deep-sea fishing in the Miami area. One bargain outfitter, the **Kelley Fishing Fleet,** at the Haulover Marina, 10800 Collins Ave. (at 108th St.), Miami

Beach (✆ **305/945-3801;** www.miamibeachfishing.com), has half-day, full-day, and night fishing aboard diesel-powered "party boats." The fleet's emphasis on drifting is geared toward trolling and bottom fishing for snapper, sailfish, and mackerel. Half-day and night-fishing trips are $31 for adults and $22 for children up to 10 years old, and full-day trips are $49 for adults and $39 for children; prices are $5 cheaper if you have your own rod. Daily departures are scheduled at 9am and 1:45 and 8pm; reservations are recommended.

Also at the Haulover Marina is the charter boat ***Helen C*** (10800 Collins Ave.; ✆ **305/947-4081;** www.fishmiamibeach.com). Although there's no shortage of private charter boats here, Captain Dawn Mergelsberg is a good pick, because she puts individuals together to get a full boat. The *Helen C* is a twin-engine 55-footer, equipped for big-game fish such as marlin, tuna, mahimahi, shark, and sailfish. The cost is $150 per person. Private, full day trips are available for groups of six people per vessel and cost $1,350; half-days are $750. Group rates and specials are also available. Trips are scheduled for 8am to noon and 1 to 5pm daily; call for reservations. Beginners and children are always welcomed.

For a serious fishing charter, Captain Charlie Hotchkiss's ***Sea Dancer*** (✆ **305/733-5126;** www.seadancercharter.com) offers a first-class experience on a 38-foot Luhrs boat complete with tuna tower and air-conditioned cabin. If you're all about big game—marlin, dolphin, tuna, wahoo, swordfish, and sailfish—this is the charter for you. Catch and release or fillet your catch to take home. The *Sea Dancer* also offers two fun water adventures, including a 6-hour Bar Cruz, covering the finest watering holes in Miami and Fort Lauderdale, or a Sandbar Cruz, where the boat drops anchor out by Biscayne Bay's historic Stiltsville where you'll swim, bounce on a water trampoline, and play sports—all in the middle of the bay. Auto transportation is available to wherever the boat may be docked. Rates are $700 for a half-day and $1,100 for a full day and $500 for the specialty tours. Tours are also available to Bimini. Call for pricing.

Key Biscayne offers deep-sea fishing to those willing to get their hands dirty and pay a bundle. The competition among the boats is fierce, but the prices are basically the same, no matter which you choose. The going rate is about $400 to $450 for a half-day and $600 to $700 for a full day of fishing. These rates are usually for a party of up to six, and the boats supply you with rods and bait as well as instruction for first-timers. Some will also take you out to the Upper Keys if the fish aren't biting in Miami.

You might also consider the following boats, all of which sail out of the Key Biscayne marina and are in relatively good shape and nicer than most out there: ***Sunny Boy*** (✆ **305/361-2217**), ***Top Hatt*** (✆ **305/361-2528**), and ***L & H*** (✆ **305/361-9318**). Call for reservations.

Bridge fishing in Biscayne Bay is also popular in Miami; you'll see people with poles over almost every waterway. But look carefully for signs telling you whether it's legal to do so wherever you are: Some bridges forbid fishing.

GAMBLING Although gambling is technically illegal in Miami, there are plenty of loopholes that allow all kinds of wagering. Gamblers can try their luck at offshore casinos or on shore at bingo, jai alai, card rooms, horse tracks, dog races, and Native American reservations. You can also drive up to Broward County, where the **Seminole Hard Rock Hotel and Casino** (www.seminolehardrock.com) and the new **Gulfstream Park Casino and Racing** (www.gulfstreampark.com) in Hallandale both offer slots and poker.

Despite the Hard Rock in Hollywood's behemoth presence on the gambling circuit, some people prefer the less flashy **Miccosukee Indian Gaming,** 500 SW 177th Ave. (off

S.R. 41, in West Miami, on the outskirts of the Everglades; ✆ **800/741-4600** or 305/222-4600), where a touch of Vegas meets west Miami. This tacky casino isn't Caesar's Palace, but you can play tab slots, high-speed bingo (watch out for the serious blue-haired players who will scoff if you make too much noise or if you win before they do), and even poker (with more tables added now that they're competing with Seminole Hard Rock; see above). With more than 85,000 square feet of playing space, the complex even provides overnight accommodations for those who can't get enough of the thrill and don't want to make the approximately 1-hour trip back to downtown Miami. Take the Florida Turnpike south toward Florida City/Key West. Take the SW 8th Street exit (#25) and turn left onto SW 8th Street. Drive for about 3½ miles and then turn left onto Krome Avenue, and left again at 177th Street; you can't miss it.

GOLF There are more than 50 private and public golf courses in the Miami area. Contact the **Greater Miami Convention and Visitor's Bureau** (✆ **800/933-8448;** www.miamiandbeaches.com) for a list of courses and costs.

The best hotel courses in Miami are found at the **Doral Golf Resort and Spa** (p. 108), home of the legendary Blue Monster course, as well as the Gold Course, designed by Raymond Floyd; the Great White Shark Course; and the Silver Course, refinished by Jerry Pate.

Other hotels with excellent golf courses include the **Fairmont Turnberry Isle Resort & Club** (p. 109), with two Robert Trent Jones, Sr.–designed courses for guests and members, and the **Biltmore Hotel ★★** (p. 111), which is my pick for best public golf course because of its modest greens fees and an 18-hole par-71 course located on the hotel's spectacular grounds. It must be good: Despite his penchant for privacy, former president Bill Clinton prefers teeing off at this course more than any other in Miami!

Otherwise, the following represent some of the area's best public courses. **Crandon Park Golf Course,** formerly known as the Links, 6700 Crandon Blvd., Key Biscayne (✆ **305/361-9129;** www.crandongolfclub.com), is the number-one-ranked municipal course in the state and one of the top five in the country. The park is situated on 200 bayfront acres and offers a pro shop, rentals, lessons, carts, and a lighted driving range. The course is open daily from dawn to dusk; greens fees (including cart) are $59 for nonresidents and include a cart. Special twilight rates are also available.

One of the most popular courses among real enthusiasts is the **Doral Park Golf and Country Club,** 5001 NW 104th Ave., West Miami (✆ **305/591-8800**); it's not related to the Doral Hotel or spa. Call to book in advance, as this challenging, semiprivate 18-holer is extremely popular with locals. The course is open from 6:30am to 6pm during the winter and until 7pm during the summer. Cart and greens fees vary, so call ✆ **305/592-2000,** ext. 2104, for information.

Known as one of the best in the city, the **Country Club of Miami,** 6801 Miami Gardens Dr., at NW 68th Avenue, North Miami (✆ **305/829-8456;** www.golfmiamicc.com), has three 18-hole courses of varying degrees of difficulty. You'll encounter lush fairways, rolling greens, and some history, to boot. The west course, designed in 1961 by Robert Trent Jones, Sr., and updated in the 1990s by the PGA, was where Jack Nicklaus played his first professional tournament and Lee Trevino won his first professional championship. The course is open daily from 7am to sunset. Cart and greens fees are $23 to $43 depending on season and tee times. Special twilight rates are available.

The recently renovated **Miami Beach Golf Club,** 2301 Alton Rd., South Beach (✆ **305/532-3350;** www.miamibeachgolfclub.com), is a gorgeous, 79-year-old course that, par for the, er, course in Miami Beach, received a $10-million face-lift. Miami Heat players and Matt Damon have been known to tee off here. Greens fees range from $100 to $200 depending on the season.

Golfers looking for some cheap practice time will appreciate **Haulover Beach Park,** 10800 Collins Ave., Miami Beach (✆ **305/940-6719**), in a pretty bayside location. The longest hole on this par-27 course is 125 yards. It's open daily from 7:30am to 6pm during the winter, and until 7:30pm during the summer. Greens fees are $7 per person during the winter and summer.

IN-LINE SKATING Miami's consistently flat terrain makes in-line skating a breeze. Lincoln Road, for example, is a virtual skating rink, as bladers compete with bikers and walkers for a slab of slate. But the city's heavy traffic and construction do make it tough to find long routes suitable for blading.

Because of the popularity of blading and skateboarding, the city passed a law prohibiting skating on the west side (the cafe-lined strip) of Ocean Drive in the evenings, as well as a law that all bladers must skate slowly and safely. Also, if you're going to partake of the sport, remember to keep a pair of sandals or sneakers with you, as many area shops won't allow you inside with skates on.

Despite all the rules, you can still have fun, and the following rental outfit can help chart an interesting course for you and supply you with all the necessary gear. In South Beach, **Fritz's Skate Shop,** 1620 Washington Ave. (✆ **305/532-1954;** www.fritzsmiami beach.com), rents top-quality skates, including safety pads, for $10 per hour, $24 per day, and $69 per week. They provide free lessons at 10:30am on Sunday when you rent equipment, or they can hook you up with an instructor for private lessons. The shop also stocks lots of gear and clothing and rents surfboards and assorted surf-related items as well.

SWIMMING There is no shortage of water in the Miami area. See the Venetian Pool listing (p. 154) and the "Miami's Beaches" section on p. 145 for descriptions of good swimming options.

TENNIS Hundreds of tennis courts in South Florida are open to the public for a minimal fee. Most courts operate on a first-come, first-served basis and are open from sunrise to sunset. For information and directions, call the **City of Miami Beach Recreation, Culture, and Parks Department** (✆ **305/673-7730**) or the **City of Miami Parks and Recreation Department** (✆ **305/575-5256**). Of the 590 public tennis courts throughout Miami, the three hard courts and seven clay courts at the **Crandon Tennis Center,** 6702 Crandon Blvd. (✆ **305/361-5263**), are the best and most beautiful. Because of this, they often get crowded on weekends. You'll play on the same courts as Lendl, Graf, Evert, McEnroe, Federer, the Williams sisters, and other greats; this is also the venue for one of the world's biggest annual tennis events, the Sony Ericsson Open. There's a pleasant, if limited, pro shop, plus many good pros. Only four courts are lit at night, but if you reserve at least 24 to 48 hours in advance, you can usually take your pick. Hard courts cost $3 person per hour during the day, $5 per person per hour at night. Clay courts cost $6 per person per hour during the day. There are no night hours on the clay courts. The courts are open Monday through Friday from 8am to 9pm, Saturday and Sunday until 6pm.

Other courts are pretty run-of-the-mill and can be found in most neighborhoods. I do, however, recommend the **Miami Beach public courts at Flamingo Park,** 1001 12th St., in South Beach (✆ **305/673-7761**), where there are 19 clay courts that cost $4 per person an hour for Miami Beach residents and $8 per person an hour for nonresidents.

It's first-come, first-served. Open 8am to 9pm Monday through Friday, 8am to 8pm Saturday and Sunday.

Hotels with the best tennis facilities are the Biltmore, Fairmont Turnberry Isle Resort and Spa, Doral Resort and Spa, and Inn and Spa at Fisher Island.

9 SPECTATOR SPORTS

Check the *Miami Herald's* sports section for a daily listing of local events and the paper's Friday "Weekend" section for comprehensive coverage and in-depth reports. For last-minute tickets, call the venue directly, as many season ticket holders sell singles and return unused tickets. Expensive tickets are available from brokers or individuals listed in the classified sections of the local papers. Some tickets are also available through **Ticketmaster** (✆ **305/358-5885;** www.ticketmaster.com).

BASEBALL The 2003 World Champion **Florida Marlins** shocked the sports world in 1997 when it became the youngest expansion team to win a World Series, but then floundered as its star players were sold off by former owner Wayne Huizenga. The team shocked the sports world again in 2003 by winning the World Series, and turned many of Miami's apathetic sports fans into major-league ball fans. The Marlins are not as good as they were anymore after trading their best players, and every day there's a new rumor that the team is either looking to move to another state or that they'll move to a proposed brand new baseball stadium in the space formerly known as the Orange Bowl. The Maine Marlins? Sounds fishy. Anyway, if you're interested in catching a game, ***be warned:*** The summer heat in Miami can be unbearable, even in the evenings.

Home games are held at **Dolphin Stadium,** 2269 NW 199th St., North Miami Beach (✆ **305/623-6200**). Tickets cost from $4 to $50. Box office hours are Monday to Friday from 8:30am to 5:30pm and before games; tickets are also available through Ticketmaster. The team currently holds spring training in Melbourne, Florida.

BASKETBALL The **Miami Heat** (✆ **786/777-1000**), once again led by celebrity coach Pat Riley, is one of Miami's hottest tickets, especially since the team won the NBA championship in 2006. Courtside seats are full of visiting celebrities. The season lasts from October to April, with most games beginning at 7:30pm. The team plays in the brand-new waterfront **American Airlines Arena,** downtown on Biscayne Boulevard. Tickets are $10 to $100 or much more. Box office hours are Monday through Friday from 10am to 5pm (until 8pm on game nights); tickets are also available through Ticketmaster (✆ **305/358-5885**).

FOOTBALL Miami's golden boys are the **Miami Dolphins,** the city's most recognizable team, followed by thousands of "dolfans." The team plays at least eight home games during the season, between September and December, at **Dolphin Stadium,** 2269 NW 199th St., North Miami Beach (✆ **305/620-2578**). Tickets cost between $20 and much, much more. The box office is open Monday through Friday from 8:30am to 5:30pm; tickets are also available through Ticketmaster (✆ **305/358-5885;** www.ticketmaster.com).

HORSE RACING Located on the Dade–Broward County border in Hallandale (just north of North Miami Beach/Aventura) is **Gulfstream Racing & Casino,** at U.S. 1 and Hallandale Beach Boulevard (✆ **305/454-7000;** www.gulfstreampark.com), South Florida's very own version of Churchill Downs, but without the hats. This horse track is a haven for serious gamblers and voyeurs alike. Large purses and important races are commonplace at this sprawling suburban course, and the track is typically crowded, especially after receiving a multimillion-dollar face-lift that has added to the park a brand-new flashy casino, nightclubs, and restaurants. Admission and parking are free. January 3 through April 23, post times are 1:15pm Wednesday through Sunday. The track is closed Mondays and Tuesdays, though the casino remains open. If you're hungry, South Florida's venerable Christine Lee's Chinese restaurant is housed here. And while not exactly racing, a newish event that takes place on the sands of South Beach is the **Miami Beach Polo Cup,** featuring hard-core sand-kicking polo matches, a parade of the ponies down the beach, and chic parties. General admission to matches throughout the weekend is free to the public, while VIP tickets are available for those seeking more than a view from the sidelines and for coveted events outside of the arena. Visit www.miamipolo.com.

ICE HOCKEY The **Florida Panthers** (✆ **954/835-7000**) has amassed a legion of loving fans. Much to the disappointment of Miamians, the Panthers moved to a new venue in Sunrise, the next county north of Miami-Dade, more than an hour from downtown Miami. Call for directions and ticket information.

JAI ALAI Jai alai, sort of a Spanish-style indoor lacrosse, was introduced to Miami in 1924 and is regularly played in two Miami-area frontons (the buildings in which jai alai is played). Although the sport has roots stemming from ancient Egypt, the game, as it's now played, was invented by Basque peasants in the Pyrenees Mountains during the 17th century. Players use *cesetas,* curved wicker baskets strapped to their wrists, to hurl balls, called *pelotas,* at speeds that sometimes exceed 170 mph. Spectators, who are protected behind a wall of glass, place bets on the evening's players. The Florida Gaming Corporation owns the jai alai operations throughout the state, making betting on this sport as legal as buying a lottery ticket.

The **Miami Jai Alai Fronton,** 3500 NW 37th Ave., at NW 35th Street (✆ **305/633-6400**), is America's oldest fronton, dating from 1926. It schedules 13 games per night, which typically last 10 to 20 minutes, but can occasionally go much longer. Admission is free. There are year-round games. On Wednesday, Thursday, and Sunday, there are matinees only, which run from noon to 5:30pm. Friday, Saturday, and Monday, there are matinees in addition to evening games, from 7pm to midnight. The fronton is closed on

Jai Alai Explained

Jai alai originated in the Basque country of northern Spain, where players used church walls as their courts. The game looks very much like lacrosse, actually, with rules similar to handball or tennis. The game is played on a court with numbered lines. What makes the game totally unique, however, is the requirement that the ball must be returned in one continuous motion. The server must bounce the ball behind the serving line and, with the basket, must hurl the ball to the front wall, with the aim being that, upon rebound, the ball will bounce between lines four and seven. If it doesn't, it is an under- or overserve and the other team receives a point.

 Tuesday. This is the main location where jai alai is played in Miami. The other South Florida jai alai venue is in Dania, near the Fort Lauderdale–Hollywood International Airport. See p. 269 for more information on **Dania Jai Alai.**

10 ANIMAL PARKS

For a tropical location, Miami's got a lot of nontropical animals to see, and we're not talking about the motorists on I-95. Everything from dolphins and alligators to lions, tigers, and bears call Miami home (most in parks, some in nature). Call the parks to inquire about discount packages or coupons, which may be offered at area retail stores or in local papers.

Jungle Island ★ Kids Not exactly an island and not quite a jungle, Jungle Island is an excellent diversion for the kids and for animal lovers. While the island doubles as a protected bird sanctuary, the very pricey 19-acre park features an Everglades exhibit, a petting zoo, and several theaters, jungle trails, and aviaries. Watch your heads because flying above are hundreds of parrots, macaws, peacocks, cockatoos, and flamingos. Be sure to check out the Crocosaurus, a 20-foot-long saltwater crocodile that hangs out in the park's Serpentarium. Also a pleasant surprise here is the Ichimura Miami Japan Garden (see the "A Japanese Garden" box, below). Continuous shows star roller-skating cockatoos, card-playing macaws, and numerous stunt-happy parrots. Two of the most popular shows are Tale of the Tiger, featuring awesome animals and Gator X-treme, which brings man face-to-face with alligators in a thrilling encounter both in the water and out. Jungle Island also features the only African penguins in South Florida as well as a liger—part lion, part tiger—and endangered baby lemurs. There are also tortoises, iguanas, and a rare albino alligator on exhibit. The park's website sometimes offers downloadable discount coupons, so take a look before you visit because you definitely won't want to pay full price for this park, which has nerve to charge for parking. If you do get your money's worth and see all the shows and exhibits, expect to spend upward of 4 hours here. ***Note:*** The former South Miami site of (Parrot) Jungle Island is now known as **Pinecrest Gardens,** 11000 Red Rd. (© **305/669-6942**), which features a petting zoo, mini water park, lake, natural hammocks, and banyan caves. Open daily from 8am until sunset; admission is free.

1111 Parrot Jungle Trail, Watson Island (on the north side of MacArthur Causeway/I-395). © **305/372-3822.** www.parrotjungle.com. Admission $30 adults, $28 seniors and military, $24 children 3–10. Parking $7 per vehicle. Daily 10am–6pm. From I-95, take I-395 E. (MacArthur Causeway); make a right on Parrot Jungle Trail, which is the 1st exit after the bridge. Follow the road around and under the causeway to the parking garage on the left side.

Miami Metrozoo ★★ Kids This 290-acre complex is quite a distance from Miami proper and the beaches—about 45 minutes—but worth the trip. Isolated and never really crowded, it's also completely cageless—animals are kept at bay by cleverly designed moats. This is a fantastic spot to take younger kids; there are wonderful play areas, safari cycles for rent, and the zoo offers several daily programs designed to educate and entertain like The Wildlife Show and Diego's Discovery Den Show. Mufasa and Simba (of Disney fame) were modeled on a couple of Metrozoo's lions. Other residents include one rare white Bengal tiger, Komodo dragons, koalas, kangaroos, and African meerkats. The air-conditioned monorail and tram tours offer visitors a nice overview of the park. The zoo is always upgrading its facilities, including the impressive aviary, Wings of Asia. Cool

A Japanese Garden

If you ask someone what Japanese influences can be found in Miami, they'll likely point to Nobu, Shoji Sushi, and even Benihana. But back in the '50s, well before sushi became trendy, Kiyoshi Ichimura became obsessed with Miami and started sending people and objects from Tokyo, including carpenters, gardeners, and a landscape architect to design and construct the San-Ai-An Japanese Garden. Originally located in the Jungle Island space, the garden was dismantled during construction and re-created adjacent to the park. The completed 1-acre garden was renamed Ichimura Miami Japan Garden, in honor of its original benefactor, and its sculptures and Japanese artifacts are managed by a coalition of city organizations. Japanese holidays and festivals are celebrated here.

activities include the Samburu Giraffe Feeding Station, where, for $2, you get to feed the giraffes veggies and Humpy's Camel Rides where you can hop on a camel for $5. Opened in December 2008, Amazon & Beyond features jaguars, anacondas, giant river otters, harpy eagles, a stingray touch tank, two interactive water features, the Flooded Forest building with a unique display of a forest before and during flood times, and an indoor Cloud Forest building that houses reptiles. At 27 acres and a cost of $50 million, the exhibit is massive and makes Metrozoo the third zoo in the country to have giant river otters, one of its keystone species. Private tours and overnights are also available for those who really want to commune with nature. ***Note:*** The distance between animal habitats can be great, so you'll do *a lot* of walking here. There are benches, shaded gazebos, cool misters, a water shooting mushroom and two water play areas strategically positioned throughout the zoo so you can escape the heat when you need to. Also, because the zoo can be miserably hot during summer months, plan these visits in the early morning or late afternoon. Expect to spend all day here if you want to see it all.

12400 SW 152nd St., Miami. ✆ **305/251-0400.** www.miamimetrozoo.com. Admission $16 adults, $12 children 3–12. Daily 9:30am–5:30pm (ticket booth closes at 4pm). Free parking. From U.S. 1 south, turn right on SW 152nd St., and follow signs about 3 miles to the entrance. From FL Turnpike South, take exit 16 west to the entrance.

Miami Seaquarium ★ **Kids** **Overrated** If you've been to Orlando's SeaWorld, you may be disappointed with Miami's version, which is considerably smaller and not as well maintained. It's hardly a sprawling Seaquarium, but you will want to arrive early to enjoy the effects of its mild splash. You'll need at least 3 hours to tour the 35-acre oceanarium and see all four daily shows, starring a number of showy ocean mammals. You can cut your visit to 2 hours if you limit your shows to the better, albeit corny, *Flipper Show* and *Killer Whale Show.* The highly regarded Dolphin Encounter allows visitors to touch and swim with dolphins in the Flipper Lagoon. The program costs $139 per person participating, $45 per adult observer, $36 per child observer ages 3 to 9, and is offered daily at 12:15 and 3:15pm. Children must be at least 52 inches tall to participate. Reservations are necessary for this program. Call ✆ 305/365-2501 in advance for reservations. The Seaquarium also debuted a new sea lion show.

4400 Rickenbacker Causeway (south side), en route to Key Biscayne. ✆ **305/361-5705.** www.miami seaquarium.com. Admission $36 adults, $27 children 3–9, free for children 2 and under. Parking $8. Daily 9:30am–6pm (ticket booth closes at 4pm).

Monkey Jungle ★ Personally, I think this place is nasty. It reeks, the monkeys are either sleeping or in heat, and it's really far from the city, even farther than the zoo. But if primates are your thing and you'd rather pass on the zoo, you'll be in paradise. You'll see rare Brazilian golden lion tamarins and Asian macaques. There are no cages to restrain the antics of the monkeys as they swing, chatter, and play their way into your heart. Screened-in trails wind through acres of "jungle," and daily shows feature the talents of the park's most progressive pupils. People who come here are not monkeying around—many of the park's frequent visitors are scientists and anthropologists. In fact, an interesting archaeological exhibition excavated from a Monkey Jungle sinkhole displays 10,000-year-old artifacts, including human teeth and animal bones. A somewhat amusing attraction here, if you can call it that, is the Wild Monkey Swimming Pool, a show in which you get to watch monkeys diving for food. If you can stand the humidity, the smell, and the bugs (flies, mosquitoes, and so on), expect to spend about 2 hours here. The park's website sometimes offers downloadable discount coupons, so if you have Internet access, take a look before you visit.

14805 SW 216th St., South Miami. ✆ **305/235-1611.** www.monkeyjungle.com. Admission $26 adults, $24 seniors and active-duty military, $20 children 4–12. Daily 9:30am–5pm (tickets sold until 4pm). Take U.S. 1 south to SW 216th St., or from Florida Turnpike, take exit 11 and follow the signs.

Sea Grass Adventures ★ (Value) (Kids) Even better than the Seaquarium is Sea Grass Adventures, in which a naturalist from the Marjory Stoneman Douglas Biscayne Nature Center introduces ($10 per person) kids and adults to an amazing variety of creatures that live in the sea grass beds of the Bear Cut Nature Preserve near Crandon Beach on Key Biscayne. You will be able to wade in the water with your guide and catch an assortment of sea life in nets provided by the guides. At the end of the program, participants gather on the beach while the guide explains what everyone has just caught, passing the creatures around in miniature viewing tanks. Call for available dates, times, and reservations.

Marjory Stoneman Douglas Biscayne Nature Center, 6767 Crandon Blvd., Key Biscayne. ✆ **305/361-6767.** Free admission to the center. Daily 10am–4pm.

11 SHOPPING

If you're not into sunbathing and outdoor activities, or you just can't take the heat, you'll be in good company in one of Miami's many malls—and you are not likely to emerge empty-handed. In addition to the strip malls, Miami offers a choice of megamalls, from the upscale Village of Merrick Park and mammoth Aventura Mall to the ritzy Bal Harbour Shops and touristy yet scenic Bayside Marketplace (just to name a few).

Miami also offers more unique shopping spots, such as the up-and-coming Biscayne Corridor, where funky boutiques dare to defy the Gap, and Little Havana, where you can buy hand-rolled cigars and *guayaberas.*

You may want to order the Greater Miami Convention and Visitors Bureau's *Shop Miami: A Guide to a Tropical Shopping Adventure.* Although it is limited to details on the bureau's paying members, it provides some good advice and otherwise unpublished discount offers. The glossy little pamphlet is printed in English, Spanish, and Portuguese, and provides information on transportation from hotels, translation services, and shipping. Call ✆ **800/283-2707** or 305/539-3000 for more information.

SHOPPING HOURS & TAXES

As a general rule, shop hours are Monday through Saturday from 10am to 6pm, and Sunday from noon to 5pm. Many stores stay open late (until 9pm or so) 1 night of the week, usually Thursday. Shops in Coconut Grove are open until 9pm Sunday through Thursday, and even later on Friday and Saturday. South Beach's stores also stay open later—as late as midnight. Department stores and shopping malls keep longer hours as well, with most staying open from 10am to 9 or 10pm Monday through Saturday, noon to 6pm on Sunday. With all these variations, you may want to call specific stores to find out their hours.

The 6.5% state and local sales tax is added to the price of all nonfood purchases. Food and beverage in hotels and restaurants are subject to the resort tax, which is 3% in Miami/South Beach and Bal Harbour, 4% in Surfside, and 2% in the rest of Miami-Dade County.

SHOPPING AREAS

Most of Miami's shopping happens at the many megamalls scattered from one end of the county to the other. However, excellent boutique shopping and browsing can be found in the following areas (see "The Neighborhoods in Brief," on p. 76, for more information):

AVENTURA On Biscayne Boulevard, between Miami Gardens Drive and the county line at Hallandale Beach Boulevard, is a 2-mile stretch of major retail stores including Best Buy; Borders; DSW; Bed, Bath and Beyond; Lochmann's; Linens 'n Things; Marshalls; Sports Authority; and more. Also here is the mammoth Aventura Mall, housing a fabulous collection of shops and restaurants.

CALLE OCHO For a taste of Little Havana, take a walk down 8th Street between SW 27th Avenue and SW 12th Avenue, where you'll find some lively street life and many shops selling cigars, baked goods, shoes, and furniture, as well as record stores specializing in Latin music. For help, take your Spanish dictionary.

COCONUT GROVE Downtown Coconut Grove, centered on Main Highway and Grand Avenue, and branching onto the adjoining streets, is one of Miami's most pedestrian-friendly zones. The Grove's wide sidewalks, lined with cafes and boutiques, can provide hours of browsing pleasure. Coconut Grove is best known for its chain stores (Gap, Victoria's Secret, and so on) and some funky holdovers from the days when the Grove was a bit more bohemian, plus excellent sidewalk cafes centered on CocoWalk and the Streets of Mayfair.

MIRACLE MILE (CORAL GABLES) Actually only a half-mile long, this central shopping street was an integral part of George Merrick's original city plan. Today the strip still enjoys popularity, especially for its bridal stores, ladies' shops, haberdashers, and gift shops. Recently, newer chain stores, such as Barnes & Noble, Old Navy, and Starbucks, have been appearing on the Mile. The hyperupscale **Village of Merrick Park,** a mammoth, 850,000-square-foot outdoor shopping complex between Ponce de León Boulevard and Le Jeune Road, just off the Mile, houses Nordstrom, Neiman Marcus, Armani, Gucci, Jimmy Choo, and Yves St. Laurent, to name a few.

DOWNTOWN MIAMI If you're looking for discounts on all types of goods—especially watches, fabric, buttons, lace, shoes, luggage, and leather—Flagler Street, just west of Biscayne Boulevard, is the best place to start. I wouldn't necessarily recommend buying expensive items here, as many stores seem to be on the shady side and do not understand the word *warranty.* However, you can still have fun here as long as you are a savvy shopper and don't mind haggling. Most signs are printed in English, Spanish, and Portuguese; however, many shopkeepers may not be entirely fluent in English. Mary Brickell Village, a 192,000-square-foot urban entertainment center west of Brickell Avenue and straddling South Miami Avenue between 9th and 10th streets downtown, opened in 2006. Although there were still a slew of empty stores as of this writing, the $80-million complex aspires to consist of a slew of trendy restaurants, boutiques to exist amidst the already open restaurants, and the requisite Starbucks—a sure sign that a neighborhood has been revitalized.

BISCAYNE CORRIDOR ★ Amid the ramshackle old motels of yesteryear exist several funky, kitschy, and arty boutiques along the stretch of Biscayne Boulevard from 50th Street to about 79th Street, known as the Biscayne Corridor. Everything from hand-painted tank tops to expensive Juicy Couture sweat suits can be found here, but it's not just about fashion: Several furniture stores selling antiques and modern pieces exist along here as well, so look carefully, as you may find something here that would cause the appraisers on *Antiques Road Show* to lose their wigs. For more mainstream creature comforts—Target, PetSmart, Loehmann's, Marshalls, and West Elm—a new complex called the Shops at Midtown Miami has opened on a gritty (watch your bags), yet developing street at North Miami Avenue and NE 36th Street.

SOUTH BEACH ★ Slowly but surely, South Beach has come into its own as far as shopping is concerned. While the requisite stores such as Gap and Banana Republic have anchored here, several higher-end stores have also opened on the southern blocks of Collins Avenue, which has become the Madison Avenue of Miami. For the hippest clothing boutiques (including Armani Exchange, Ralph Lauren, Versace, Benetton, Levi's, Barneys Co-Op, Diesel, Guess, Club Monaco, Kenneth Cole, and Nicole Miller, among others), stroll along this pretty strip of the Art Deco District.

For those who are interested in a little more fun with their shopping, consider South Beach's legendary Lincoln Road. This pedestrian mall, originally designed in 1957 by Morris Lapidus, recently underwent a multimillion-dollar renovation, restoring it to its former glory. Here shoppers find an array of clothing, books, tchotchkes, and art, as well as a menagerie of sidewalk cafes flanked on one end by a multiplex movie theater and, at the other, by the Atlantic Ocean.

12 MIAMI AFTER DARK

With all the hype, you'd expect Miami to have long outlived its 15 minutes of fame by now. But you'd be wrong. Miami's nightlife, in South Beach *and,* slowly but surely, downtown, is hotter than ever before—and still getting hotter. Practically every club in the area has installed closely guarded velvet ropes to create an air of exclusivity. Don't be fooled or intimidated by them—*anyone* can go clubbing in the Magic City, and throughout this section, I've provided tips to ensure that you gain entry to your desired venue.

South Beach is certainly Miami's uncontested nocturnal nucleus, but more and more diverse areas, such as the Design District, South Miami, and even Little Havana, are increasingly providing fun alternatives without the ludicrous cover charges, "fashionably late" hours of operation (things don't typically get started on South Beach until after 11pm), lack of sufficient self-parking, and outrageous drink prices that are standard in South Beach.

While South Beach dances to a more electronic beat, other parts of Miami dance to a Latin beat—from salsa and merengue to tango and cha-cha. However, if you're looking for a less frenetic good time, Miami's bar scene has something for everyone, from haute hotel bars to sleek, loungey watering holes.

Parts of downtown, such as the Biscayne Corridor, the Miami River, and the Design District, are undergoing a trendy makeover à la New York City's Meatpacking District. Cool lounges, bars, and clubs are popping up and providing the "in" crowds with a newer, more urban-chic nocturnal pasture.

But if the possibility of a celebrity sighting in one of the city's lounges, bars, or clubs doesn't fulfill your cultural needs, Miami also provides a variety of first-rate diversions in theater, music, and dance, including a world-class ballet (under the aegis of Edward Villella), a recognized symphony, and a talented opera company. The new Cesar Pelli–designed, $446-million Adrienne Arsht Center for the Performing Arts is the focal point for the arts, created to prove to the world that Miami isn't as shallow and devoid of culture as people once thought.

For up-to-date listing information, and to make sure the club of the moment hasn't expired, check the *Miami Herald's* "Weekend" section, which runs on Friday, or the more comprehensive listings in *New Times,* Miami's free alternative weekly, available each Wednesday; or visit www.miami.com online.

BARS & LOUNGES

There are countless bars and lounges in and around Miami (most require proof that you are 21 or older to enter), with the highest concentration on trendy South Beach. The selection here is a mere sample. Keep in mind that many of the popular bars—and the easiest to get into—are in hotels (with a few notable exceptions—see below). For a clubbier scene, if you don't mind making your way through hordes of inebriated club kids, a stroll on Washington Avenue will provide you with ample insight into what's hot and what's not. Just hold on to your bags. It's not dangerous, but, occasionally, a few shady types manage to slip into the crowd. Another very important tip when in a club: *Never put your drink down out of your sight*—there have been unfortunate incidents in which drinks have been spiked with illegal chemical substances. For a less hard-core, more collegiate nightlife, head to Coconut Grove. Oh, yes, and when going out in South Beach, make sure to take a so-called disco nap, as things don't get going until at least 11pm. If you go earlier, be prepared to face an empty bar or club. Off of South Beach and in hotel bars in general, the hours are fashionably earlier, with the action starting as early as, say, 7pm.

The Abbey Dark, dank, and hard to find, this local microbrewery is a favorite for locals looking to escape the $20 candy-flavored martini scene. Best of all, there's never a cover and it's always open until 5am, perfect for those pesky and insatiable hops cravings that pop up at 3 or 4am. 1115 16th St., South Beach. ✆ **305/538-8110.**

Automatic Slim's This is *the* bar where Ozzie and Harriet types become more like Ozzy and Sharon. As South Beach's most popular unpretentious bar, Automatic Slim's is indeed a slim space of bar, but it packs people in, thanks to an exhaustive list of cheap(er) drinks, lack of attitude, great rock music, and a decor that can only be described as white trash–chic. 1216 Washington Ave., South Beach. ✆ **305/695-0795.**

Badrutt's Place Owned by the same family that owns Switzerland's ritzy resort of the same name, this high-energy, high-style lounge and restaurant complete with cozy velvet couches and an expansive outdoor terrace is the place to be for champagne, foie gras, and a well heeled crowd of Europeans, jet-setters, and scene shakers. 1250 S. Miami Ave., Downtown. ✆ **305/415-0700.**

Impressions

There are two shifts in South Beach. There's 9 to 5. And then there's 9 to 5.

—South Beach artist Stewart Stewart

Blue A very laid-back, very local scene set to a sultry soundtrack of deep soul and house music has Miami's hipsters feeling the blues here on a nightly basis from 10pm to 5am. Before you whip out the St. John's wort, dive into this so-not-trendy-it's-trendy lounge, in which the pervasive color blue will actually heighten your spirits as an eclectic haze of models, locals, and lounge lizards gather to commiserate over their dreaded trendy status. 222 Española Way (btw. Washington and Collins aves.), South Beach. ✆ **305/534-1009.**

Clarke's This classy, brassy, and sassy Irish pub and restaurant in the chichi South of Fifth Street area of South Beach has become command central for everyone from *Burn Notice* star Jeffrey Donovan, Miami Heat players, and the Miami Beach police chief to local moguls and club kids looking for cold beer and, surprisingly, a gourmet menu consisting of shepherd's pie, seared scallops, and the best burger in the 'hood. My personal favorite, however, is the New York–style pretzel served on a spike with a side of mustard. 840 1st St., South Beach. ✆ **305/538-9885.**

Clevelander If wet-T-shirt contests and a fraternity party atmosphere are your thing, then this Ocean Drive mainstay is your kind of place. Popular with tourists and locals who like to pretend they're tourists, the Clevelander, which was still closed at the time of this writing, in the throes of much needed renovations, attracts a lively, sporty crowd of only adults (the burly bouncers *will* confiscate fake IDs) who have no interest in being part of a scene, but, rather, like to take in the very revealing scenery. A great time to check out the Clevelander is on a weekend afternoon, when beach Barbies and Kens line the bar for a post-tanning beer or frozen cocktail. 1020 Ocean Dr., South Beach. ✆ **305/531-3485.**

Cozy A very French, very expensive piano bar in the South of Fifth neighborhood right next door to the zillion-dollar Apogee condo, where the likes of actor Michael Caine and basketball's Pat Riley call home, Cozy lives up to its name in ambience with blood-red walls and chandeliers; but when it comes to the check, there's nothing cozy about it, with a cheese plate coming in at a whopping $50 and glasses of wine starting at $20. But if you're in the mood for a nightcap—and we mean just one—and some great live piano and surprise celebrity musicians (the Gypsy Kings love dropping in and jamming out here when in town), Cozy, or Sarkozy as we like to call it, is entirely worth the splurge. 500 South Pointe Drive., South Beach. ✆ **305/532-2699.**

The Florida Room The Florida Room is a dimly chandelier-lit den of old school Florida decor meets swanky cruise ship lounge—a place of 200 maximum capacity—where everyone from young hipsters and swanky sophisticates to the Golden Girls would go for a fancy night out, where Rue McClanahan's feisty, randy Blanche would climb atop the Lucite piano channeling Michelle Pfeiffer in *The Fabulous Baker Boys.* Designed by rocker Lenny Kravitz, the interior of this subterranean speakeasy is the antithesis of the sleek, stark hotel in which it resides, and for that, we love it. 1685 Collins Ave. (in the Delano), South Beach. ✆ **305/672-2000.**

Forge The Forge bar hosts an unusual mix of the uptight and those who wear their clothes too tight. It's also where surgically altered ladies look for their cigar-chomping sugar daddies in a setting that somehow reminds me of *Dynasty.* Call well in advance if you want to watch the parade of characters from a dinner table (p. 126). The Forge owners also own **Glass,** a ritzier nightclub attached to the restaurant (they say it's a private club, but if you dine at the restaurant or are acquainted with someone in the know, you can get in; dress up and you should have no problem). 432 41st St., Miami Beach. ✆ **305/538-8533.**

Mac's Club Deuce Standing amid an oasis of trendiness, Mac's Club Deuce is the quintessential dive bar, with cheap drinks and a cast of characters ranging from your typical barfly to your atypical drag queen. It's got a well-stocked jukebox, friendly bartenders, and a pool table. Best of all, it's an insomniac's dream, open daily from 8am to 5am. 222 14th St., South Beach. ✆ **305/673-9537.**

Mokai Trendy, yes, but tragically so? Not at all. This chic, cozy lounge is the brainchild of several South Beach nightlife impresarios who know how to attract the A-list. Reminiscent of an après-ski bar in Aspen, Mokai's stone walls, dim lighting, and plush leather couches are upscale reminders that elegant slumming doesn't come cheap. Drink prices are expectedly high, but it's the price you pay for hanging out with celebrities, such as the stars of *Entourage* who hang out here to jam, or the visiting DJs who spin everything from bar mitzvah kitsch to deep house. 235 23rd St., South Beach. ✆ **305/531-4166.** www.mokaimiami.com.

Mynt A massive 6,000-square-foot place, Mynt is nothing more than a huge living room in which models, celebrities, and assorted hangers-on bask in the green glow to the beat of very loud lounge and dance music. If you want to dance—or move, for that matter—this is not the place in which to do so. It's all about striking a pose in here. Unless you know the person at the door, be prepared to be ridiculed, emasculated, and socially shattered, as you may be forced to wait outside upward of an hour. If that's the case, forget it; it's not worth it. Wait next door at the Greek place for a celebrity sighting, as you'll have a better chance of seeing people from there instead of just waiting in the melee at the door. 1921 Collins Ave., South Beach. ✆ **786/276-6132.** Cover $10–$20.

Playwright Irish Pub Bono came here once when U2 was in town, not because it's such an authentic Irish pub, but because the bar was showing some European soccer match—and serves pints of Guinness. A great pre- or postclub spot, Playwright is one of the few places in town that also features live music from time to time. 1265 Washington Ave., South Beach. ✆ **305/534-0667.**

Plunge Possibly the best thing about the Gansevoort South, Plunge is the hotel's rockin' rooftop pool lounge, where on any given day or night, scantily clad scene- (and bikini-) chasers can be found either in or out of the water, sipping colorful cocktails to the tune of DJ-spun music. 2399 Collins Ave., South Beach. ✆ **305/604-1000.**

Moments **Stargazing**

The most popular places for celebrity sightings include Mynt, Opium Garden, Skybar, poolside at the Shore Club or the Delano, and, when it comes to J-Lo, somewhere on the beach around 20th Street. Miami Heat basketball games are also star magnets.

The Purdy Lounge With the exception of a wall of lava lamps, Purdy is not unlike your best friend's basement, featuring a pool table and a slew of board games such as Operation to keep the attention-deficit-disordered from getting bored. It even has a bingo and spelling-bee night! Because it's a no-nonsense bar with relatively cheap cocktails (by South Beach standards), Purdy gets away with not having a star DJ or fancy bass-heavy Bose sound system. A CD player somehow does the trick. With no cover and no attitude, a line is inevitable (it gets crowded inside), so be prepared to wait. Saturday night has become the preferred night for locals, while Friday night's happy hour draws a young professional crowd on the prowl. 1811 Purdy Ave. at Sunset Harbor, South Beach. ✆ **305/531-4622.**

Rok Bar Larger-than-life rocker Tommy Lee has assembled a motley Miami crew at this paradox of a bar that combines down-'n'-dirty rock 'n' roll with the swank comforts of a chic lounge. The place is claustrophobic, with limited seating (unless you're Pamela Anderson, forget about scoring a table), high-priced drinks, and an oxymoronic soundtrack of Lynyrd Skynyrd, Michael Jackson, and Kid Rock. 1905 Collins Ave., South Beach. ✆ **305/538-7171.**

The Room It's beer and wine only at this South of Fifth hideaway, where locals and N.Y. expats (there are a few Rooms in N.Y.C.) come to get away from the insanity just a few blocks away. The beer selection is comprehensive with brews from almost everywhere in the world. The wine is not so great, but there's no whining here at this tiny, industrial-style, candlelit spot that doesn't have a DJ—just a CD player spinning indie tunes—or those pesky Paris Hilton sightings. 100 Collins Ave., South Beach. ✆ **305/531-6061.**

Rose Bar at the Delano If every rose has its thorn, the thorn at this painfully chic hotel bar is the excruciatingly high price of cocktails. Otherwise, the crowd here is full of the so-called glitterati and other assorted poseurs who view life through (Italian-made) rose-colored glasses. 1685 Collins Ave., South Beach. ✆ **305/672-2000.**

Segafredo Espresso Although Segafredo is technically a cafe, it has become an integral part of Miami's nightlife as command central for Euros who miss that very special brand of European cafe society. Not in the mood for a club or bar, but want to hear great music, sip a few cocktails, snack on delicious sandwiches and pizza, and sit outside and people-watch? This is the place. European lounge music, tons of outdoor tables on a prime corner of Lincoln Road, and always a mob scene make 'Fredo one of my—and many other Miamians'—favorite nocturnal diversions. Although South Beach boasts the original, another Segafredo, with different owners, a larger food menu, and separate nightclub is open in the Brickell Area, at 1421 S. Miami Ave., and another cafe opened at 124 Collins Ave., in the South of Fifth area. 1040 Lincoln Rd., South Beach. ✆ **305/673-0047.**

Skybar at The Shore Club Skybar lives up to its name in terms of loftiness; something this place has perfected better than anyone else, whether at its original L.A. location or the sprawling South Beach location at the Shore Club. If you're not a hotel guest, not Beyoncé, or not on the "list," or if you're a guy with several other guys and no girls, forget about it. For those of you who can't get in, the Skybar is basically the entire backyard area of the Shore Club, consisting of several areas, including the Moroccan-themed garden area, the hip-hop-themed indoor Red Room, the Sand Bar by the beach, and the Rum Bar by the pool. Sunday afternoon pool parties are a magnet for celebs and locals alike. Popular on any given night, Skybar is yet another brilliant example of how hotelier

Ian Schrager has managed to control the hipsters in a most Pavlovian way. At The Shore Club, 1901 Collins Ave., South Beach. ✆ **305/695-3100.**

Taverna Opa Although this Greek taverna (also located in Hollywood and Fort Lauderdale) calls itself a restaurant, I consider it more of a raucous dance club that just happens to serve excellent Greek food. How many restaurants do you know of that allow patrons to dance suggestively with waiters on tables, throw napkins in the air as if they were confetti, and guzzle ouzo straight from the bottle, all to the tune of some very loud, jazzed-up Greek dance music? Get here early, as the place is always packed—and I mean *packed* as in standing room only. Although there is an outdoor bar, the real fun and scenery are indoors in the dining room, where the tables double as dance floors and some very animated characters channel their best Zorbas. Be prepared for a big, fat Greek hangover the next day. 36 Ocean Dr., South Beach. ✆ **305/673-6730.**

Transit Lounge It's hard to locate, but once you do find Transit Lounge, you'll be happy you did. Reminiscent of what locals describe as "a real big-city lounge," Transit is cavernous, featuring a huge bar, tons of cozy couches and tables, board games, a funky crowd, and, hallelujah, live music. 1729 SW 1st Ave., Miami. ✆ **305/377-4628.**

Wet Willie's With such telling drinks as Call a Cab, this beachfront oasis is not the place to go if you have a long drive ahead of you. A well-liked pre- and postbeach hangout, Wet Willie's inspires serious drinking. Popular with the Harley-Davidson set, tourists, and beachcombers, this bar is best known for its rooftop patio (get there early if you plan to get a seat) and its half-nude bikini beauties. 760 Ocean Dr., South Beach. ✆ **305/532-5650.**

DANCE CLUBS

Clubs are as much a cottage industry in Miami as is, say, cheese in Wisconsin. Clubland, as it is known, is a way of life for some. On any given night in Miami, there's something going on—no excuses are needed to throw a party here. Short of throwing a glamorous event for the grand opening of a new gas station, Miami is very party hearty, celebrating everything from the fact that it's Tuesday night to the debut of a hot new DJ. Within this very bizarre after-dark community, a colorful assortment of characters emerges, from (a) typical 9-to-5ers to shady characters who have reinvented themselves as hot shots on the club circuit. While this see-and-be-seen scene may not be your cup of Absolut, it's certainly never boring.

The club music played on Miami's ever-evolving social circuit is good enough to get even the most rhythmically challenged wallflowers dancing. For aspiring DJs, a branch of the renowned **Scratch DJ Academy,** 642 6th St. (✆ **305/535-2599**), opened; for $300 a session, you, too, can become a master of the turntables.

To keep things fresh in Clubland, local promoters throw one-nighters, which are essentially parties with various themes or motifs, from funk to fashion. Because these change so often, we can't possibly list them here. Word of mouth, local advertising, and listings in the free weekly *New Times,* www.miami.citysearch.com, or the "Weekend" section of the *Miami Herald* are the best ways to find out about these ever-changing events.

Before you get all decked out to hit the town as soon as the sun sets, consider the fact that Miami is a very late town. Things generally don't get started here before 11pm. The Catch-22 is that if you don't arrive on South Beach early enough, you may find yourself driving around aimlessly for parking, as it is very limited outside of absurd $20 valet charges. Municipal lots fill up quickly, so your best bet is to arrive on South Beach somewhat early and kill time by strolling around, having something to eat, or sipping a

Tips Ground Rules: Stepping Out in Miami

- Nightlife on South Beach doesn't really get going until after 11pm. As a result, you may want to consider taking what is known as a disco nap so that you'll be fully charged until the wee hours.
- If you're unsure of what to wear out on South Beach, your safest bet is anything black.
- Do not try to tip the doormen manning the velvet ropes. That will only make you look desperate, and you'll find yourself standing outside for what will seem like an ungodly amount of time. Instead, try to land your name on the ever-present guest list by calling the club early in the day yourself or, better yet, having the concierge at your hotel do it for you. If you don't have connections and you find yourself without a concierge, then act assertive, not surly, at the velvet rope, and your patience will usually be rewarded with admittance. If all else fails—for men, especially—surround yourself with a few leggy model types and you'll be noticed quicker.
- If you are a man going out with a group of men, unless you're going to a gay bar, you will most likely not get into any South Beach hot spot unless you are with women.
- Finally, have fun. It may look like serious business when you're on the outside, but once you're in, it's another story. Attacking Clubland with a sense of humor is the best approach to a successful, memorable evening out.

cocktail in a hotel bar. Another advantage of arriving a bit earlier than the crowds is that some clubs don't charge a cover before 11pm or midnight, which could save you a wad of cash over time. Most clubs are open every night of the week, though some are open only Thursday to Sunday and others are open only Monday through Saturday. Call ahead to get the most up-to-date information possible: Things change very quickly around here, and a call in advance can help you make sure that the dance club you're planning to go to hasn't become a video arcade. Cover charges are very haphazard, too. If you're not on the ubiquitous guest list (ask your concierge to put you on the list—he or she usually has the ability to do so, which won't help you with the wait to get in, but will eliminate the cover charge), you may have to fork over a ridiculous $20 to walk past the ropes. Don't fret, though. There are many clubs and bars that have no cover charge—they just make up for it by charging $15 for a martini!

Bongo's Cuban Café Gloria Estefan's latest hit in the restaurant business pays homage to the sights, sounds, and cuisine of pre-Castro Cuba. Bongo's is a mammoth restaurant attached to the American Airlines Arena in downtown Miami. On Friday after 11pm and Saturday after 11:30pm, it's transformed from a friendly family restaurant into the city's hottest 21-and-over salsa nightclub. Cover charges can be hefty, but consider it your ticket to an astounding show of some of the best salsa dancers in the city. Prepare yourself for standing room only. Salsa lessons are also available for those with two left feet. At the American Airlines Arena, 601 Biscayne Blvd., Downtown Miami. ✆ **786/777-2100.** Cover Fri $10 for guys only; Sat $20 for all.

Cameo ★ Still haunted by the ghost of clubs past, the space formerly known as crobar has undergone much-needed renovations and reopened as Cameo, its original incarnation. Though not as see-and-be-seen as it used to be, it still boasts a supersonic sound system, star DJs, and plenty of VIP seating. Cameo also has a club-within-a-club upstairs known as Vice. Open Thursday through Monday from 10pm to 5am. 1445 Washington Ave., South Beach. ✆ **305/531-8225.** Cover Thurs, Sun, Mon $20; Fri–Sat $25.

Club Space ★ Clubland hits the mainland with this cavernous downtown warehouse of a club. With more than 30,000 square feet of dance space, you can spin around à la Stevie Nicks (albeit to a techno beat) without having to worry about banging into someone. On Saturday and Sunday nights, the party usually extends to the next morning, sometimes as late as 10am. It's quite a sight to see club kids rushing off to work straight from Space on a Monday morning. Known as the venue of choice for world-renowned DJs, Club Space sometimes charges ludicrous admission fees to cover its hefty price tags. ***Note:*** Club Space doesn't really get going until around 3am. Call for more information, as it doesn't have a concrete schedule. 34 NE 11th St., Miami. ✆ **305/372-9378.** www.clubspace.com. Cover up to $20.

LIV and Blade The latest in Miami's celebrity saturated nightlife, LIV (as in, "celebrities live for LIV") and Blade are the recently revamped Fontainebleau's dance club and subterranean lounge slash pool bar, respectively. Because they're new, they're at the top of the A-list. 4441 Collins Ave., South Beach. ✆ **305/538-2000.** www.fontainebleau.com. Cover $10–$50.

Mansion A product of the same team behind the utterly addictive Opium Garden (see below), this place is a massive multilevel lounge that, according to the owners and promoters, is entirely "VIP," meaning you'd best know someone to get in or else you'll be among the masses outside and not even close to the manse. Live DJs, models, and celebrities galore—ubiquitous Paris Hilton, Britney Spears, Lindsay Lohan, Justin Timberlake, Beyoncé, Jay Z, and more—not to mention high ceilings, wood floors, brick walls, and a decidedly nonsmoky interior—make this Mansion, despite its cheesy name, a *must* on the list of see-and-be-scenesters. Open Tuesday through Sunday from 11pm to 5am. 1235 Washington Ave., South Beach. ✆ **305/531-5535.** www.theopiumgroup.com. Cover $10–$40.

Nikki Beach Club What the Playboy Mansion is to L.A., the Nikki Beach Club is to South Beach—but if you want a locals scene, you won't find it here. The allure is mostly for visiting tourists who love to gawk at their fellow half naked ladies and men actually venturing into the daylight on Sunday (around 4pm, which is ungodly in this town) to see, be seen, and, at times, be obscene. At night, it's very "Brady Bunch goes to Hawaii," with a sexy Tiki hut/Polynesian theme style, albeit rated R. Also located within this bastion of hedonism is the second-floor Club Nikki (formerly Pearl restaurant), for those who want to dance on an actual dance floor and not sand. 101 Ocean Dr., South Beach. ✆ **305/538-1111.** www.nikkibeach.com. Cover $10–$20.

Opium Garden Housed in a massive open-air space, Opium Garden is a highly addictive nocturnal habit for those looking for a combination of sexy dance music; scantily clad dancers; celebrities such as J-Lo, Janet Jackson, Lenny Kravitz, and Diddy; and, for the masochists out there, an oppressive door policy and two sets of velvet ropes set up to keep those deemed unworthy out of this see-and-be-sceney den of iniquity. Opium has an ultra-VIP, celeb-saturated lounge, Prive, whose separate door policy makes the aforementioned seem like a romp in the sand. 136 Collins Ave., South Beach. ✆ **305/531-5535.** www.theopiumgroup.com. Cover $20.

Winter Music Conference

Every March, Miami is besieged by the most unconventional conventioneers the city has ever seen. These fiercely dedicated souls descend upon the city in a very audible way, with dark circles under their eyes and bleeps, blips, and scratches that can wake the dead. No, we're not talking about a Star Trek convention, but, rather, the Winter Music Conference (WMC), the world's biggest and most important gathering of DJs, remixers, agents, artists, and pretty much anyone who makes a dime off of the booming electronic music industry hailing from more than 60 countries from all over the world. But unlike most conventions, this one is completely interactive and open to the paying public as South Beach and Miami's hottest clubs transform into showcases for the various audio wares. For 5 consecutive days and nights, DJs, artists, and software producers play for audiences comprised of A&R reps, talent scouts, and locals just along for the ride. Parties take place everywhere, from hotel pools to street corners. There's always something going on every hour on the hour, and most people who really get into the throes of the WMC get little or no sleep. Energy drinks become more important than water, and, for the most part, if you see people popping pills, they're not likely to be vitamins. At any rate, the WMC is worth checking out if you get ecstatic over names such as Hex Hector, Paul Oakenfold, Ultra Naté, Chris Cox, and Mark Ronson, among many, many others. For more information on WMC events, go to www.wmcon.com. And for those who just yearn to be the next big DJ, the **Scratch DJ Academy,** 642 6th St., South Beach (✆ **305/535-2599;** www.scratch.com), is now open and ready to teach you the turntables for a whopping $300 per 70-minute course. But just think, top DJs these days make in excess of $300,000 per gig, so it may be worth the investment!

Parkwest Nightclub A 6,000-foot dance and lounge palace, Parkwest features the usual top-of-the-line sound system and an unusual LED wall, the only one of its size in South Florida. With five bars—two of the most popular are Stero and Rehab, the club's indie-rock inspired dance lounge featuring antique gas pumps, celebrity mug shots, three bars, two levels, and 2,500 square feet—VIP areas and lounge seating throughout the space, Parkwest is for the hard-core clubgoer. 30 NE 11th St., Downtown. ✆ **305/350-7444.** www.stereomiami.com. Cover $20.

SET The Opium Group's undisputed "it" child, SET is *the* place to be, at least at the time of this writing. A luxurious lounge with chandeliers and design mag–worthy decor is always full of trendsetters, celebs, and wannabes. Where you really want to be, however, is upstairs, in the private VIP room, where Britney Spears was seen downing purple hooter shots. A classy place that doesn't designate the behavior of its patrons, SET is also known for a ruthless door policy. Ask your hotel concierge to get you in or else you may find yourself standing on the wrong side of the velvet ropes wasting precious vacation time. 320 Lincoln Rd., South Beach. ✆ **305/531-2800.** www.setmiami.com. Cover $20.

The White Room (Finds) Yet another cavernous, warehousey cocktail hall featuring 6,000 square feet of outdoor space and 4,500 square feet of indoor space where the long-running Brit-pop, hipster-happy one-nighter Pop Life takes up residence every Saturday. 1306 N. Miami Ave., Downtown. ✆ **305/995-5050.** www.whiteroommiami.com. Cover up to $10.

Impressions

Working the door teaches you a lot about human nature.

—A former South Beach doorman

LIVE MUSIC

Unfortunately, Miami's live music scene is not thriving. Instead of local bands garnering devoted fans, local DJs are more admired, skyrocketing much more easily to fame—thanks to the city's lauded dance-club scene. However, there are still several places that strive to bring Miami up to speed as far as live music is concerned. You just have to look—and listen—for it a bit more carefully. The following is a list of places where you can, from time to time, catch some live acts.

Churchill's Hideaway (Finds) British expatriate Dave Daniels couldn't live in Miami without a true English-style pub, so he opened Churchill's Hideaway, the city's premier space for live rock music. Filthy and located in a rather unsavory neighborhood, Churchill's is committed to promoting and extending the lifeline of the lagging local music scene. A fun no-frills crowd hangs out here. Bring earplugs with you, as it is deafening once the music starts. Monday is open-mic night, while Wednesday is reserved for ladies' wrestling. 5501 NE 2nd Ave., Little Haiti. ✆ **305/757-1807.** www.churchillspub.com. Cover up to $6.

Jazid (Finds) Smoky, sultry, and illuminated by flickering candelabras, Jazid is the kind of place where you'd expect to hear Sade's "Smooth Operator" on constant rotation. Instead, however, you'll hear live jazz (sometimes acid jazz), soul, and funk. An eclectic mix of mellow folk convenes here for a much-needed respite from the surrounding Washington Avenue mayhem. 1342 Washington Ave., South Beach. ✆ **305/673-9372.** www.jazid.net. Cover $10.

Tobacco Road Al Capone used to hang out here when it was a speakeasy. Now locals flock here to see local bands perform, as well as national acts such as George Clinton and the P-Funk All-Stars, Koko Taylor, and the Radiators. Tobacco Road (the proud owner of Miami's very first liquor license) is small and gritty, and meant to be that way. Escape the smoke and sweat in the backyard patio, where air is a welcome commodity. The downright cheap nightly specials, such as the $11 lobster on Tuesday, are quite good and served until 2am; the bar is open until 5am. 626 S. Miami Ave. (over the Miami Ave. Bridge, near Brickell Ave.), Downtown. ✆ **305/374-1198.** www.tobacco-road.com. Cover Thurs–Sat $5–$10.

Upstairs at the Van Dyke Cafe (Finds) The cafe's jazz bar, located on the second floor, resembles a classy speak-easy in which local jazz performers play to an intimate, enthusiastic crowd of mostly adults and sophisticated young things, who often huddle at the small tables until the wee hours. 846 Lincoln Rd., South Beach. ✆ **305/534-3600.** www.thevandykecafe.com. Cover Sun–Thurs $5, Fri–Sat $10 for a seat; no cover at the bar.

THE GAY & LESBIAN SCENE

Miami and the beaches have long been host to what is called a "first-tier" gay community. Similar to the Big Apple, the Bay Area, or LaLa land, Miami has had a large alternative community since the days when Anita Bryant used her citrus power to boycott the rise in political activism in the early '70s. Well, things have changed and Miami-Dade now has a gay-rights ordinance.

Newcomers intending to party in any bar, whether downtown or certainly on the beach, will want to check ahead for the schedule, as all clubs must have a gay or lesbian night to pay their rent. Miami Beach, in fact, is a capital of the gay circuit party scene, rivaling San Francisco, Palm Springs, and even the mighty Sydney, Australia, for tourist dollars. However, ever since South Beach got bit by the hip-hop bug, many of Miami's gays have been crossing county lines into Fort Lauderdale, where there are, surprisingly, many more gay establishments.

Score There's a reason this Lincoln Road hotbed of gay activity is called Score. In addition to the huge pickup scene, Score offers a multitude of bars, dance floors, lounge areas, and outdoor tables, in case you need to come up for air. Sunday afternoon tea dances are legendary. 727 Lincoln Rd., South Beach. ✆ **305/535-1111.** www.scorebar.net.

Twist One of the most popular bars (and hideaways) on South Beach, this recently expanded bar (which is literally right across the street from the police station) has a casual yet lively atmosphere. 1057 Washington Ave., South Beach. ✆ **305/538-9478.** www.twistsobe.com.

LATIN CLUBS

Considering that Hispanics make up a large part of Miami's population and that there's a huge influx of Spanish-speaking visitors, it's no surprise that there are some great Latin nightclubs in the city. Plus, with the meteoric rise of the international music scene based in Miami, many international stars come through the offices of MTV Latino, SONY International, and a multitude of Latin TV studios based in Miami—and they're all looking for a good club scene on weekends. Most of the Anglo clubs also reserve at least 1 night a week for Latin rhythms.

Casa Panza *Finds* This *casa* is one of Little Havana's liveliest and most popular nightspots. Every Tuesday, Thursday, and Saturday night, Casa Panza, in the heart of Little Havana, becomes the House of Flamenco, with shows at 8 and 11pm. You can either enjoy a flamenco show or strap on your own dancing shoes and participate in the celebration. Enjoy a fantastic Spanish meal before the show, or just a glass of sangria before you start stomping. Open until 4am, Casa Panza is a hot spot for young Latin club kids and, occasionally, a few older folks who are so taken by the music and the scene that they've failed to realize it's well past their bedtime. 1620 SW 8th St. (Calle Ocho), Little Havana. ✆ **305/643-5343.** www.casapanza.com.

Hoy Como Ayer Formerly known as Cafe Nostalgia, the Little Havana hangout dedicated to reminiscing about Old Cuba, Hoy Como Ayer is like the Brady Bunch of Latin hangouts—while it was extremely popular with old-timers in its Cafe Nostalgia incarnation, it is now experiencing a resurgence among the younger generation seeking its own brand of nostalgia. Its Thursday night party, Fuacata (slang for "Pow!"), is a magnet for Latin hipsters, featuring classic Cuban music mixed in with modern DJ-spun sound effects. Open Thursday to Sunday from 9pm to 4am. 2212 SW 8th St. (Calle Ocho), Little Havana. ✆ **305/541-2631.** Cover Thurs–Sun $10.

La Covacha *Finds* This hut, located virtually in the middle of nowhere (West Miami), is the hottest Latin joint in the entire city. Sunday features the best in Latin rock, with local and international acts. But the shack is really jumping on weekend nights, when the place is open until 5am. Friday is *the* night here, so much so that the owners had to place a red velvet rope out front to maintain some semblance of order. It's an

The Rhythm Is Gonna Get You

Are you feeling shy about hitting a Latin club because you fear your two left feet will stand out? Then take a few lessons from one of the following dance companies or dance teachers. They offer individual and group lessons to dancers of any origin who are willing to learn. These folks have made it their mission to teach merengue and flamenco to non-Latinos and Latino left-foots, and are among the most reliable, consistent, and popular ones in Miami. So what are you waiting for?

Thursday and Friday nights at **Bongo's Cuban Café** (American Airlines Arena, 601 Biscayne Blvd., Downtown; © **786/777-2100**) are amazing showcases for some of the city's best salsa dancers, but amateurs need not be intimidated, thanks to the instructors from Latin Groove Dance Studios, who are on hand to help you with your two left feet. Lessons are free.

At **Ballet Flamenco La Rosa** (in the Performing Arts Network [PAN] building, 13126 W. Dixie Hwy., North Miami; © **305/899-7730**), you can learn to flamenco, salsa, or merengue. This is the only professional flamenco company in the area. They charge $15 per class.

Nobody teaches salsa like **Luz Pinto** (© **305/868-9418**). She teaches 7 days a week and, trust me, with her, you'll learn cool turns easily. She charges $50 for a private lesson for up to four people, and $10 per person for a group lesson. She also teaches group classes at PAN on Miami Beach. Although she teaches everything from classic to hip wedding dances to ballroom and merengue, her specialty is Casino style salsa, popularized in the 1950s in Cuba, Luz's homeland. You will be impressed with how well and quickly Luz can teach you to have fun and feel great dancing. Call her for more information.

Angel Arroyo has been teaching salsa to the clueless out of his home (at 16467 NE 27th Ave., North Miami Beach; © **305/949-7799**) for the past 10 years. Just $10 will buy you an hour's time. He traditionally teaches Monday and Wednesday nights, but call ahead to check for any schedule and rate changes.

amusing sight—a velvet rope guarding a shack—but once you get in, you'll understand the need for it. Do not wear silk here, as you *will* sweat. 10730 NW 25th St. (at NW 107th Ave.), West Miami. © **305/594-3717.** www.lacovacha.com. Cover up to $10.

Mango's Tropical Café Claustrophobic types do not want to go near Mango's—ever. One of the most popular spots on Ocean Drive, this outdoor enclave of Latin liveliness shakes with the intensity of a Richter-busting earthquake. Mango's is *Cabaret,* Latin style. Nightly live Brazilian and other Latin music, not to mention scantily clad male and female dancers, draws huge gawking crowds in from the sidewalk. But pay attention to the music, if you can: Incognito international musicians often lose their anonymity and jam with the house band on stage. Open daily from 11am to 5am. 900 Ocean Dr., South Beach. © **305/673-4422.** www.mangostropicalcafe.com. Cover $5–$15.

Highbrows and culture vultures complain that there is a dearth of decent cultural offerings in Miami. What do locals tell them? Go back to New York! In all seriousness, however, in recent years, Miami's performing arts scene has improved greatly. The city's Broadway Series features Tony Award–winning shows (the touring versions, of course), which aren't always Broadway caliber, but usually pretty good and not nearly as pricey. Local arts groups such as the Miami Light Project, a not-for-profit cultural organization that presents live performances by innovative dance, music, and theater artists, have had huge success in attracting big-name artists such as Nina Simone and Philip Glass to Miami. Also, a burgeoning bohemian movement in Little Havana has given way to performance spaces that are nightclubs in their own right.

Theater

The **Actors' Playhouse,** a musical theater at the newly restored Miracle Theater at 280 Miracle Mile, Coral Gables (✆ **305/444-9293;** www.actorsplayhouse.org), is a grand 1948 Art Deco movie palace with a 600-seat main theater and a smaller theater/rehearsal hall that hosts a number of excellent musicals for children throughout the year. In addition to these two theaters, the Playhouse recently added a 300-seat children's balcony theater. Tickets run from $27 to $40.

The **Gables Stage,** at the Biltmore Hotel (p. 111), Anastasia Avenue, Coral Gables (✆ **305/445-1119**), stages at least one Shakespearean play, one classic, and one contemporary piece a year. This well-regarded theater usually tries to secure the rights to a national or local premiere as well. Tickets cost $35 for adults, and $15 and $32, respectively, for students and seniors.

The **Jerry Herman Ring Theatre** is on the main campus of the University of Miami in Coral Gables (✆ **305/284-3355**). The University's Department of Theater Arts uses this stage for advanced-student productions of comedies, dramas, and musicals. Faculty and guest actors are regularly featured, as are contemporary works by local playwrights. Performances are usually scheduled Tuesday through Saturday during the academic year. In the summer, don't miss "Summer Shorts," a selection of superb one acts. Tickets sell for $14 to $16.

The **New Theatre,** 4120 Laguna St., Coral Gables (✆ **305/443-5909;** www.newtheatre.org), prides itself on showing renowned works from America and Europe. As the name implies, you'll find mostly contemporary plays, with a few classics thrown in. Performances are staged Thursday through Sunday year-round. Tickets are $35 on Thursday, $40 on Friday and Saturday, and $35 to $40 on Sunday. If tickets are available on the day of the performance—and they usually are—students pay half-price.

Classical Music

In addition to a number of local orchestras and operas (see below), which regularly offer quality music and world-renowned guest artists, each year brings a slew of classical-music special events and touring artists to Miami. The **Concert Association of Florida** (**CAF;** ✆ **877/433-3200**) produces one of the most important and longest-running series. Known for more than a quarter of a century for its high-caliber, star-packed schedules, CAF regularly arranges the best "serious" music concerts for the city. Season after season, the schedules are punctuated by world-renowned dance companies and seasoned virtuosi such as Itzhak Perlman, Andre Watts, and Kathleen Battle. Because CAF does not have its own space, performances are usually scheduled in the Miami-Dade County Auditorium or the Jackie Gleason Theater of the Performing Arts (see the "Major Venues" section below). The season lasts October through April, and ticket prices range from $20 to $70.

Miami Chamber Symphony This professional orchestra is a small, subscription-series orchestra that's not affiliated with any major arts organizations and is therefore an inexpensive alternative to the high-priced classical venues. Renowned international soloists perform regularly here. The season runs October to May, and most concerts are held in the Gusman Concert Hall, on the University of Miami campus. 5690 N. Kendall Dr., Kendall. ✆ **305/284-6477.** Tickets $12–$30.

New World Symphony This organization, led by artistic director Michael Tilson Thomas, is a stepping stone for gifted young musicians seeking professional careers. The orchestra specializes in innovative, energetic performances, and often features renowned guest soloists and conductors. The season lasts from October to May, during which time there are many free concerts. 541 Lincoln Rd., South Beach. ✆ **305/673-3331.** www.nws.org. Tickets free–$50. Rush tickets (remaining tickets sold 1 hr. before performance) $20. Students $10 (1 hr. before concerts; limited seating).

Opera

Florida Grand Opera Around for more than 60 years, this company regularly features singers from top houses in both America and Europe. All productions are sung in their original language and staged with projected English supertitles. Tickets become scarce when Placido Domingo comes to town. The season runs roughly from November to April, with five performances each week. In 2007, the opera moved into more upscale headquarters in the Sanford and Dolores Ziff Ballet Opera House at the Arsht (formerly Carnival Center) Center for the Performing Arts. Box office: 1300 Biscayne Blvd. Miami. ✆ **305/949-6722.** www.fgo.org. Tickets $24–$125. Student discounts available.

Dance

Several local dance companies train and perform in the Greater Miami area. In addition, top traveling troupes regularly stop at the venues listed below. Keep your eyes open for special events and guest artists.

Ballet Flamenco La Rosa For a taste of local Latin flavor, see this lively troupe perform impressive flamenco and other styles of Latin dance on Miami stages. (They also teach Latin dancing—see the "The Rhythm Is Gonna Get You" box above.) 13126 W. Dixie Hwy., North Miami. ✆ **305/899-7729.** www.panmiami.org. Tickets $25 at door; $20 in advance; $18 for students and seniors.

Miami City Ballet This artistically acclaimed and innovative company, directed by Edward Villella, features a repertoire of more than 60 ballets, many by George Balanchine, and has had more than 20 world premieres. The company's three-story center features eight rehearsal rooms, a ballet school, a boutique, and ticket offices. The City Ballet season runs from September to April. Ophelia and Juan Jr. Roca Center, Collins Ave. and 22nd St., South Beach. ✆ **305/929-7000,** or 929-7010 for box office. Tickets $17–$50.

MAJOR VENUES

The **Colony Theater,** 1040 Lincoln Rd. in South Beach (✆ **305/674-1040**), which has become an architectural showpiece of the Art Deco District, opened in 2006 after a $4.3-million renovation that added wing and fly space, improved access for those with disabilities, and restored the lobby to its original Art Deco look.

At the **Miami-Dade County Auditorium,** West Flagler Street at 29th Avenue, Southwest Miami (✆ **305/547-5414**), performers gripe about the lack of space, and for patrons, this 2,430-seat auditorium was once the only Miami space in which you can hear the opera (not any more; see the Arsht Center below). The Auditorium is home to the city's Florida Grand Opera, and it also stages productions by the Concert Association of Florida, many programs in Spanish, and a variety of other shows.

At the 1,700-seat **Gusman Center for the Performing Arts,** 174 E. Flagler St., downtown Miami (✆ **305/372-0925**), seating is tight, and so is funding, but the sound is superb. In addition to hosting the Miami Film Festival, the elegant Gusman Center features pop concerts, plays, film screenings, and special events. The auditorium was built as the Olympia Theater in 1926, and its ornate palace interior is typical of that era, complete with fancy columns, a huge pipe organ, and twinkling "stars" on the ceiling.

Not to be confused with the Gusman Center (above), the **Gusman Concert Hall,** 1314 Miller Dr., at 14th Street, Coral Gables (✆ **305/284-6477**), is a roomy 600-seat hall that gives a stage to the Miami Chamber Symphony and a varied program of university recitals.

The newly revamped **Fillmore Miami Beach at the Jackie Gleason Theater,** located in South Beach at Washington Avenue and 17th Street (✆ **305/673-7300**), may be a mouthful, but when it comes to live music, it truly rocks. In addition to its very modern Hard Rock–meets–Miami Beach decor, complete with requisite bars, chandeliers, and an homage to the original legendary Fillmore in San Francisco, Fillmore, which was taken over by Live Nation, brings major talent to the beach, from Kid Rock and Fall Out Boy to comediennes Sarah Silverman and Lisa Lampanelli. Fillmore also hosts various awards shows, from the Food Network Awards to the Fox Sports Awards.

Last, but definitely not least, the **Adrienne Arsht Center for the Performing Arts,** 1300 Biscayne Blvd. (✆ **786/468-2000**), opened in late 2006 after a whopping $446-million tab. In 2008, philanthropist Adrienne Arsht donated $30 million to the financially troubled center, renaming it the Adrienne Arsht Center for the Performing Arts of Miami-Dade County (or the Arsht Center, for short). Included: The 2,400-seat **Sanford and Dolores Ziff Ballet Opera House** and the 2,200-seat **Knight Concert Hall** are Miami venues for the **Concert Association of Florida, Florida Grand Opera, Miami City Ballet,** and **New World Symphony,** as well as premier venues for a wide array of local, national, and international performances, ranging from Broadway musicals and visiting classical artists to world and urban music, Latin concerts, and popular entertainment from many cultures. The **Studio Theater,** a flexible black-box space designed for up to 200 seats, hosts intimate performances of contemporary theater, dance, music, cabaret, and other entertainment. The **Peacock Education Center** acts as a catalyst for arts education and enrichment programs for children and adults. Finally, the **Plaza for the Arts** is a magnificent setting for outdoor entertainment, social celebrations, and informal community gatherings.

Designed by world-renowned architect Cesar Pelli, the Carnival Center is the focal point of a planned Arts, Media, and Entertainment District in mid-Miami. The complex is wrapped in limestone, slate, decorative stone, stainless steel, glass curtain walls, and tropical landscaping, and was completed in mid-2006. The biggest joke in town, however, is that after spending all that money, the planners forgot to include parking facilities. As a result, valet parking is available for $10 to $20 or you can park at the Marriott nearby, but it's truly a pain, so to make things easy, just take a cab. It'll cost you the same and you won't have to deal with traipsing across Biscayne Boulevard in your fine theater threads. For more information, check out the website at www.arshtcenter.org.

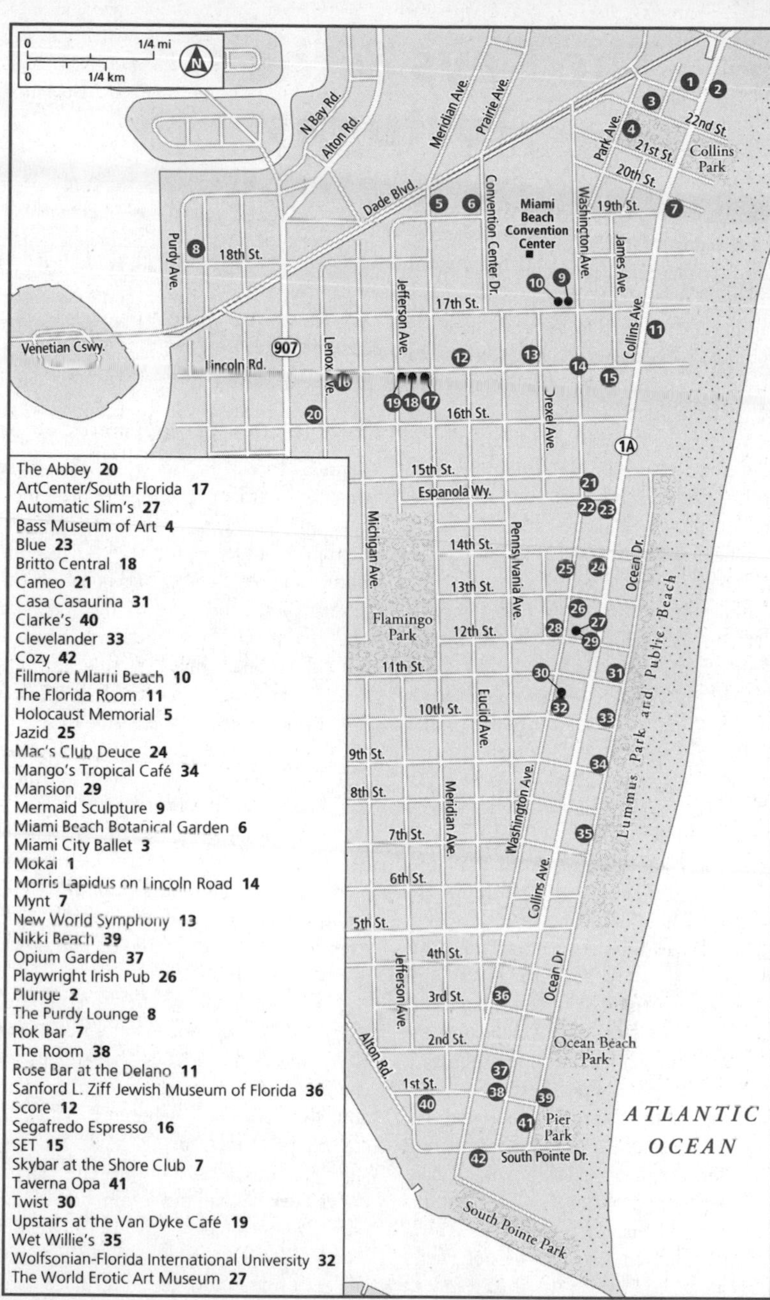

The Abbey **20**
ArtCenter/South Florida **17**
Automatic Slim's **27**
Bass Museum of Art **4**
Blue **23**
Britto Central **18**
Cameo **21**
Casa Casaurina **31**
Clarke's **40**
Clevelander **33**
Cozy **42**
Fillmore Miami Beach **10**
The Florida Room **11**
Holocaust Memorial **5**
Jazid **25**
Mac's Club Deuce **24**
Mango's Tropical Café **34**
Mansion **29**
Mermaid Sculpture **9**
Miami Beach Botanical Garden **6**
Miami City Ballet **3**
Mokai **1**
Morris Lapidus on Lincoln Road **14**
Mynt **7**
New World Symphony **13**
Nikki Beach **39**
Opium Garden **37**
Playwright Irish Pub **26**
Plunge **2**
The Purdy Lounge **8**
Rok Bar **7**
The Room **38**
Rose Bar at the Delano **11**
Sanford L. Ziff Jewish Museum of Florida **36**
Score **12**
Segafredo Espresso **16**
SET **15**
Skybar at the Shore Club **7**
Taverna Opa **41**
Twist **30**
Upstairs at the Van Dyke Café **19**
Wet Willie's **35**
Wolfsonian-Florida International University **32**
The World Erotic Art Museum **27**

7

The Keys & the Dry Tortugas

The drive from Miami to the Keys is a slow descent into an unusual but breathtaking American ecosystem: On either side of you, for miles ahead, lies nothing but emerald waters. (On weekends, however, you will also see plenty of traffic.) Strung out across the Atlantic Ocean like loose strands of cultured pearls, more than 400 islands make up this 150-mile-long necklace.

Despite the usually calm landscape, these rocky islands can be treacherous, as tropical storms, hurricanes, and tornadoes are always possibilities. The exposed coast poses dangers to those on land as well as at sea.

When Spanish explorers Juan Ponce de León and Antonio de Herrera sailed amid these craggy, dangerous rocks in 1513, they and their men dubbed the string of islands "Los Martires" (The Martyrs) because they thought the rocks looked like men suffering in the surf. It wasn't until the early 1800s that rugged and ambitious pioneers, who amassed great wealth by salvaging cargo from ships sunk nearby, settled the larger islands (legend has it that these shipwrecks were sometimes caused by "wreckers," who removed navigational markers from the shallows to lure unwitting captains aground). At the height of the salvaging mania (in the 1830s), Key West boasted the highest per-capita income in the country.

However, wars, fires, hurricanes, mosquitoes, and the Depression took their toll on these resilient islands in the early part of the 20th century, causing wild swings between fortune and poverty. In 1938, the spectacular Overseas Highway (U.S. 1) was finally completed atop the ruins of Henry Flagler's railroad (which was destroyed by a hurricane in 1935, leaving only bits and pieces still found today), opening the region to tourists, who had never before been able to drive to this sea-bound destination. These days, the highway connects more than 30 of the populated islands in the Keys. The hundreds of small, undeveloped islands that surround these "mainline" keys are known locally as the "backcountry" and are home to dozens of exotic animals and plants. Therein lie some of the most renowned outdoor sporting opportunities, from bonefishing to spearfishing and—at appropriate times of the year—diving for lobsters and stone crabs. To get to the backcountry, you must take to the water—a vital part of any trip to the Keys. Whether you fish, snorkel, dive, or cruise, include some time on a boat in your itinerary; otherwise, you haven't truly seen the Keys.

Of course, people go to the Keys for the peaceful waters and year-round warmth, but the sea and the teeming life beneath and around it are the main attractions here: Countless species of brilliantly colored fish can be found swimming above the ocean's floor, and you'll discover a stunning abundance of tropical and exotic plants, birds, and reptiles.

The warm, shallow waters (deeper and rougher on the eastern/Atlantic side of the Keys) nurture living coral that supports a complex, delicate ecosystem of plants and animals—sponges, anemones, jellyfish, crabs, rays, sharks, turtles, snails, lobsters, and thousands of types of fish. This vibrant underwater habitat thrives on one of the only living tropical reefs on the entire North American continent. As a result, anglers, divers, snorkelers, and watersports enthusiasts of all kinds come to explore.

Heavy traffic has taken its toll on this fragile eco-scape, but conservation efforts are underway (traffic laws are strictly enforced on Deer Key, for example, due to deer crossings that have been contained, thanks to newly installed fences). In fact, environmental efforts in the Keys exceed those in many other high-traffic visitor destinations.

Although the atmosphere throughout the Keys is that of a laid-back beach town, don't expect many impressive beaches here, especially after the damaging effects of recent hurricane seasons. Nice beaches are mostly found in a few private resorts, though there are some small, sandy strips in John Pennekamp Coral Reef State Park, Bahia Honda State Park, and Key West. One great exception is Sombrero Beach, in Marathon (p. 193), which is well maintained by Monroe County and is larger and considerably nicer than other beaches in the Keys. Sombrero Beach has a beachfront park, picnic facilities, a playground, and a protected cove for children.

The Keys are divided into three sections, both geographically and in this chapter. The Upper and Middle Keys are closest to the Florida mainland, so they are popular with weekend warriors who come by boat or car to fish or relax in such towns as Key Largo, Islamorada, and Marathon. Farther on, just beyond the impressive Seven-Mile Bridge (which actually measures $6^1/_2$ miles), are the Lower Keys, a small, unspoiled swath of islands teeming with wildlife. Here, in the protected regions of the Lower Keys, is where you're most likely to catch sight of the area's many endangered animals—with patience, you may spot the rare eagle, egret, or Key deer. You should also keep an eye out for alligators, turtles, rabbits, and a huge variety of birds.

Key West, the most renowned—and last—island in the Lower Keys, is literally at the end of the road. The southernmost point in the continental United States (made famous by Ernest Hemingway), this tiny island is the most popular destination in the Florida Keys, overrun with cruise-ship passengers and day-trippers, as well as franchises and T-shirt shops. More than 1.6 million visitors pass through it each year. Still, this "Conch Republic" has a tightly knit community of permanent residents who cling fiercely to their live-and-let-live attitude—an atmosphere that has made Key West famously popular with painters, writers, and free spirits, despite the recent influx of money-hungry developers who want to turn Key West into Palm Beach south.

The last section in this chapter is devoted to the Dry Tortugas, a national park located 68 nautical miles from Key West.

EXPLORING THE KEYS BY CAR

After you've left the Florida Turnpike and landed on U.S. 1, which is also known as the Overseas Highway (see "Getting There" under "Essentials," below), you'll have no

Don't Be Fooled

Avoid the many "tourist information centers" that dot the main highway. Most are private companies hired to lure visitors to specific lodgings or outfitters. (Anything that says FREE DISNEY TICKETS or something like that is probably a scam or time-share racket.) You're better off sticking with the official, not-for-profit centers (the legit ones usually don't advertise on the turnpike), which are extremely well located and staffed.

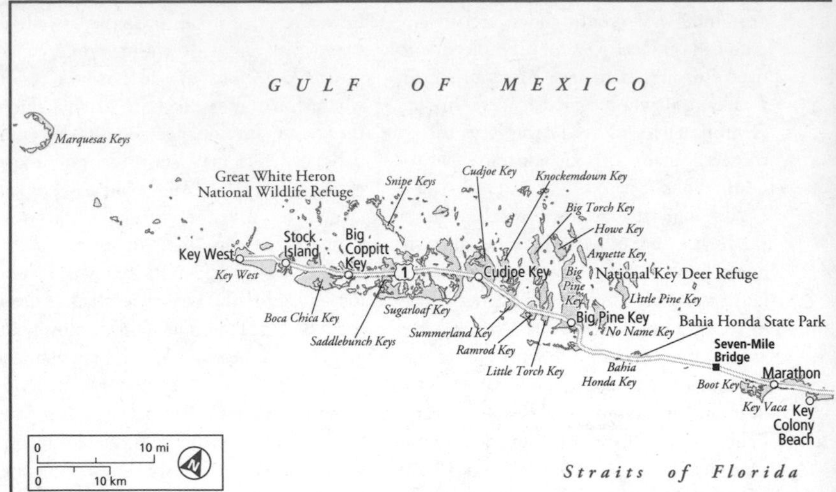

trouble negotiating these narrow islands, as only one main road connects the Keys. The scenic, lazy drive from Miami can be very enjoyable if you have the patience to linger and explore the diverse towns and islands along the way. If you have the time, I recommend allowing at least 2 days to work your way down to Key West, and 3 or more days once there.

Most of U.S. 1 is a narrow two-lane highway, with some wider passing zones along the way. The speed limit is usually 55 mph (35–45 mph on Big Pine Key and in some commercial areas). Despite the protests of island residents, there has been talk of expanding the highway, but plans have not been finalized. Even on the narrow road, you can usually get from downtown Miami to Key Largo in just over an hour. If you're determined to drive straight through to Key West, allow at least 3½ hours. Weekend travel is another

Moments No Place Like Card Sound

On its own, there's not much to the waterfront shack that is **Alabama Jack's,** 5800 Card Sound Rd., Card Sound (✆ **305/248-8741**). The bar serves beer and wine only, and the restaurant specializes in delicious, albeit greasy, bar fare. But this quintessential Old Floridian dive, located in a historic fishing village called Card Sound between Homestead and Key Largo, is a colorful must on the drive south, especially on Sunday, when bikers mix with barflies, anglers, line dancers, and Southern belles who look as if they just got off the *Hee Haw* set in all their fabulous frills. Live country music resurrects the legendary Johnny Cash and Co. Pull up a bar stool, order a cold one, and take in the sights—in the bay and at the bar. The views of the mangroves are spectacular. To get here, pick up Card Sound Road (the old Rte. 1) a few miles after you pass Homestead, heading toward Key Largo. Alabama Jack's is on the right side and can't be missed.

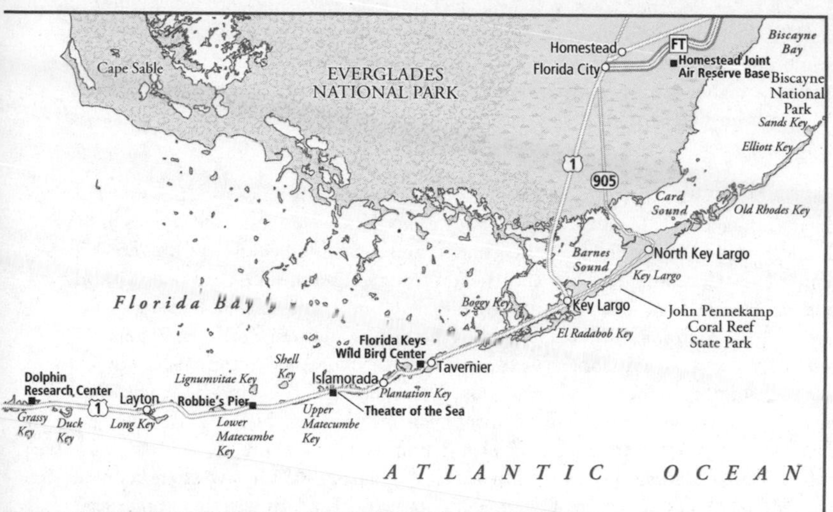

matter entirely: When the roads are jammed with travelers from the mainland, the trip can take upward of 5 to 6 hours (when there's an accident, traffic is at an absolute standstill). If at all possible, I strongly urge you to avoid driving anywhere in the Keys on Friday afternoon or Sunday evening.

To find an address in the Keys, don't bother looking for building numbers; most addresses (except in Key West and parts of Marathon) are delineated by mile markers (MM), small green signs on the roadside that announce the distance from Key West. The markers start at no. 127, just south of the Florida mainland. The zero marker is in Key West, at the corner of Whitehead and Fleming streets. Addresses in this chapter are accompanied by a mile marker (MM) designation when appropriate.

1 THE UPPER & MIDDLE KEYS

58 miles SW of Miami

The Upper Keys are a popular year-round refuge for South Floridians, who take advantage of the islands' proximity to the mainland. This is the fishing and diving capital of America, and the swarms of outfitters and billboards never let you forget it.

Key Largo, once called Rock Harbor but renamed to capitalize on the success of the 1948 Humphrey Bogart film (which wasn't actually filmed here), is the largest key and is more developed than its neighbors to the south. Dozens of chain hotels, restaurants, and tourist information centers service the water enthusiasts who come to explore the nation's first underwater state park, **John Pennekamp Coral Reef State Park,** and its adjacent marine sanctuary. **Islamorada,** the unofficial capital of the Upper Keys, has the area's best atmosphere, food, fishing, entertainment, and lodging. It's an unofficial "party capital" for mainlanders seeking a quick tropical excursion. Here (Islamorada is actually composed of four islands), nature lovers can enjoy walking trails, historic exploration, and big-purse fishing tournaments. For a more tranquil, less party-hearty Keys experience, all other keys besides Key West and Islamorada are better choices. **Marathon,** smack in the middle of the Florida Keys, is known as the heart of the Keys and is one of the most populated. It is part fishing village, part tourist center, and part nature preserve. This area's highly developed infrastructure includes resort hotels, a commercial airport, and a highway that expands to four lanes.

ESSENTIALS

GETTING THERE From Miami International Airport (there is also an airport in Marathon), take Le Jeune Road (NW 42nd Ave.) to Route 836 West. Follow signs to the Florida Turnpike South, about 7 miles. The turnpike extension connects with U.S. 1 in Florida City. Continue south on U.S. 1. For a scenic option, take Card Sound Road, south of Florida City, a backcountry drive that reconnects with U.S. 1 in upper Key Largo. The view from Card Sound Bridge is spectacular and well worth the $1 toll.

If you're coming from Florida's west coast, take Alligator Alley to the Miami exit and then turn south onto the turnpike extension. The turnpike ends in Florida City, at which time you will be dumped directly onto the two-lane U.S. 1, which leads to the Keys. Have plenty of quarters (at least $10 worth, round-trip) for the tolls.

The **TransFloridian** luxury motorcoach (✆ **954/523-0859;** www.transfloridian.com) will take you down to the Keys in a 26-foot luxury car with reclining leather seats, plenty of legroom, wireless Internet service, in-seat power ports for electronic devices, personal headphone jacks, multichannel audio entertainment, overhead DVD monitors, and service by onboard attendants. Transportation from Miami, Fort Lauderdale, or Orlando to and from the Florida Keys ranges from $45 to $260.

Greyhound (✆ **800/231-2222;** www.greyhound.com) has three buses leaving Miami for Key West every day, with stops in Key Largo, Tavernier, Islamorada, Marathon, Big Pine Key, Cudjoe Key, Sugarloaf, and Big Coppit on the way south. Prices range from $13 to $46 one-way and $26 to $88 round-trip; the trip takes from 1 hour and 40 minutes to 4 hours and 40 minutes, depending on how far south you're going. Seats fill quickly in season, so come early. It's first-come, first-served.

Once you've arrived in the Keys, let **Scenic Helicopters** (✆ **866/596-7006;** www.scenic-helicopters.com) take you on 10- to 20-minute helicopter tours of the Middle Keys and Marathon areas, departing from Florida Keys Marathon Airport, MM (mile marker) 52.2 bay side. Up to three passengers can be accommodated on each tour, depending on weight. Cost is $150 to $250 for two, $195 to $300 for three.

VISITOR INFORMATION Make sure you get your information from an official not-for-profit center. The **Key Largo Chamber of Commerce,** U.S. 1 at MM 106, Key Largo, FL 33037 (✆ **800/822-1088** or 305/451-1414; fax 305/451-4726; www.keylargo.org), runs an excellent facility, with free direct-dial phones and plenty of brochures. Headquartered in a handsome clapboard house, the chamber operates as an information clearinghouse for all of the Keys and is open daily from 9am to 6pm.

The **Islamorada Chamber of Commerce,** housed in a little red caboose, U.S. 1 at MM 82.5, P.O. Box 915, Islamorada, FL 33036 (✆ **800/322-5397** or 305/664-4503; fax 305/664-4289; www.islamoradachamber.com), offers maps and literature on the Upper Keys.

You can't miss the big, blue visitor center at MM 53.5, **Greater Marathon Chamber of Commerce,** 12222 Overseas Hwy., Marathon, FL 33050 (✆ **800/262-7284** or 305/743-5417; fax 305/289-0183; www.floridakeysmarathon.com). Here you can receive free information on local events, festivals, attractions, dining, and lodging.

OUTDOOR SIGHTS & ACTIVITIES

Anne's Beach (MM 73.5, on Lower Matecumbe Key, at the southwest end of Islamorada) is really more picnic spot than full-fledged beach, but die-hard tanners still congregate on this lovely but tiny strip of coarse sand that was damaged beyond recognition during the series of storms in 1998. The place has been spruced up a bit, but the public bathrooms there are rancid and need some attention.

A better choice for real beaching is **Sombrero Beach ★★**, in Marathon, at the end of Sombrero Beach Road (near MM 50). This wide swath of uncluttered beachfront actually benefited from Hurricane George in 1998, with generous deposits of extra sand and a face-lift courtesy of the Monroe County Tourist Development Council. More than 90 feet of sand is dotted with palms, Australian pines, and royal poincianas, as well as with grills, clean restrooms, and Tiki huts for relaxing in the shade. It's also a popular nesting spot for turtles that lay their eggs at night.

If you're interested in seeing the Keys in their natural, pre-modern development state, you must venture off the highway and take to the water. Two backcountry islands that offer a glimpse of the "real" Keys are **Indian Key** and **Lignumvitae Key ★★★**. Visitors come here to relax and enjoy the islands' colorful birds and lush hammocks (elevated pieces of land above a marsh).

Named for the lignum vitae ("wood of life") trees found there, Lignumvitae Key supports a virgin tropical forest, the kind that once thrived on most of the Upper Keys. Over the years, human settlers imported "exotic" plants and animals to the Keys, irrevocably changing the botanical makeup of many backcountry islands and threatening much of the indigenous wildlife. Over the past 25 years, however, the Florida Department of Natural Resources has successfully removed most of the exotic vegetation from this key, leaving the 280-acre site much as it existed in the 18th century. The island also holds the Matheson House, a historic structure built in 1919 that has survived numerous hurricanes. You can go inside, but it's interesting only if you appreciate the coral rock of which the house is made. It's now a museum dedicated to the history, nature, and topography of the area. More interesting are the Botanical Gardens, which surround the house and are a state preserve. Lignumvitae Key has a visitor center at MM 88.5 (✆ **305/664-2540**).

Indian Key, a much smaller island on the Atlantic side of Islamorada, was occupied by Native Americans for thousands of years before European settlers arrived. The 10-acre historic site was also the original seat of Dade County before the Civil War. Interestingly, from an archaeological standpoint, you can see the ruins of the previous settlement and tour the lush grounds on well-marked trails (off Indian Key Fill, Overseas Hwy., MM 79). For more information on Indian Key, call the Florida Park Service (✆ **305/664-4815**) or check out www.abfla.com/parks/indiankey/indiankey.html.

If you want to see both islands, plan to spend at least half a day. You can rent your own powerboat from **Robbie's Rent-A-Boat,** U.S. 1 at MM 77.5 (on the bay side), on Islamorada. It's then a $1 admission fee to each island, which includes an informative hour-long guided tour by park rangers. This is a good option if you're a confident boater. I also recommend Robbie's **ferry service.** A visit to Lignumvitae Key costs $20 for adults and $12 for kids 12 and under, which includes the $1 park admission. The ferry goes to Indian Key, too. (A trip to both islands costs $25.) The ferry is a more economical, easier way to enjoy the beauty of the islands when you aren't negotiating the shallow reefs along the way. The runabouts, which carry up to six people, depart from Robbie's Pier (p. 196) Thursday through Monday at 10am and 2pm for Lignumvitae Key. In high season, you may need to book 2 days before departure. Robbie's also does eco-tours, 2-hour trips through passages among the sea grass beds that rim the many protected shallow bays. You'll get to cruise among the hundreds of small, uninhabited mangrove and hardwood hammock islands, which host an amazing variety of wildlife and create the island network of the Florida Bay. Call ✆ **305/664-4815** for information from the park service; or call ✆ **305/664-9814,** or visit www.robbies.com for Robbie's.

Crane Point Hammock ★★ Finds Kids Crane Point Hammock is a little-known but worthwhile stop, especially for those interested in the rich botanical and archaeological history of the Keys. This privately owned, 64-acre nature area is considered one of the most important historic sites in the Keys. It contains what is probably the last virgin thatch-palm hammock in North America, as well as a rainforest exhibit and an archaeological site with prehistoric Indian and Bahamian artifacts.

Also headquarters for the Florida Keys Land and Sea Trust, the hammock's impressive nature museum has simple, informative displays of the Keys' wildlife, including a walk-through replica of a coral-reef cave and life-size dioramas with tropical birds and Key deer. Kids can participate in art projects, see 6-foot-long iguanas, climb through a scaled-down pirate ship, and touch a variety of indigenous aquatic and landlubber creatures.

5550 Overseas Hwy. (MM 50), Marathon. ✆ **305/743-9100.** www.cranepoint.net. Admission $8 adults, $7 seniors 66 and over, $5 students, free for children 5 and under. Mon–Sat 9am–5pm; Sun noon–5pm.

Pigeon Key ★★ At the curve of the old bridge on Pigeon Key is an intriguing historic site that has been under renovation since late 1993. This 5-acre island once had the camp for the crew that built the old railway in the early 20th century, which later served as housing for the bridge builders. From here, the vista includes the vestiges of Henry Flagler's old Seven-Mile Bridge and the one on which traffic presently soars, as well as many old wooden cottages and a truly tranquil stretch of lush foliage and sea. If you miss the shuttle tour from the Pigeon Key visitor center or would rather walk or bike to the site, it's about 2½ miles. Either way, you may want to bring a picnic to enjoy after a brief self-guided walking tour of the Key and a museum visit to what has become an homage to Flagler's railroad, featuring artifacts and photographs of the old bridge. An informative 28-minute video of the island's history is shown every hour starting at 10am. Parking is available at the Knight's Key end of the bridge, at MM 48, or at the visitor center at MM 47, on the ocean side.

East end of the Seven-Mile Bridge near MM 47, Marathon. ✆ **305/743-5999.** www.pigeonkey.net. Admission $11 adults, $8.50 children 12 and under. Prices include shuttle transportation from the visitor center. Daily 10am–3pm; shuttle tours run hourly 10am–4pm.

Seven-Mile Bridge ★★★ A stop at the Seven-Mile Bridge is a rewarding and relaxing break on the drive south. Built alongside the ruins of oil magnate Henry Flagler's incredible Overseas Railroad, the "new" bridge (btw. MMs 40 and 47) is considered an architectural feat. The apex of the wide-arched span, completed in 1985 at a cost of more than $45 million, is the highest point in the Keys. The new bridge and its now-defunct neighbor provide excellent vantage points from which to view the stunning waters of the Keys. In the daytime, you may want to walk, jog, or bike along the scenic 4-mile stretch of old bridge. Or you may join local anglers, who catch barracuda, yellowtail, and dolphin (the fish, not the mammal) on what is known as "the longest fishing pier in the world." Parking is available on both sides of the bridge.

Btw. MMs 40 and 47 on U.S. 1. ✆ **305/289-0025.**

Fun Facts Bridge Mix

The Seven-Mile Bridge is the longest fragmented (unconnected pieces) bridge in the world. Completed in 1985, it was constructed parallel to the original bridge, part of Henry Flagler's Florida East Coast Railroad, which served as the original link to the Lower Keys. Some people may recognize the remnants of the old bridge from the Arnold Schwarzenegger movie *True Lies.* Others fearfully contemplate a wrong turn leading them to the old bridge instead of the new one. Not to worry: The old bridge is closed to cars and has been transformed into the world's longest fishing pier.

VISITING WITH THE ANIMALS

Dolphin Research Center ★★★ Kids If you've always wanted to touch, swim, or play with dolphins, this is the place to do it. Of the several such centers in the continental United States (all located in the Keys), the Dolphin Research Center is a nonprofit facility and one of the most organized and informative. Although some people argue that training dolphins is cruel and selfish, this is one of the most respected of the institutions that study and protect the mammals. Knowledgeable trainers at the center will also tell you that the dolphins need stimulation and enjoy human contact. They certainly seem to. They nuzzle and seem to smile and kiss the lucky people who get to interact with them in daily interactive programs. The "family" of 19 dolphins swims in a 90,000-square-foot natural saltwater pool carved out of the shoreline. If you can't get into an interactive program, you can watch the frequent sessions that cover a variety of topics from fun facts about dolphins, to therapeutic qualities of dolphins, to research projects in progress. Because the Dolphin Encounter swimming program is the most popular, advanced reservations are required and can be made up to 6 months in advance. The cost is $180 per person. If you're not brave enough to swim with the dolphins or if you have a child under 5 (not permitted to swim with dolphins), try the Dolphin Dip program, in which participants stand on a submerged platform from which they can "meet and greet" the critters. A participating adult must hold children younger than 5. Cost for this program is $100 per person (free for children 4 and under).

Note: Swimming with dolphins has both its critics and its supporters. You may want to visit the Whale and Dolphin Conservation Society's website at www.wdcs.org. For more information about responsible travel in general, check out www.treadlightly.org and www.ecotourism.org.

U.S. 1 at MM 59 (on the bay side), Marathon. ✆ **305/289-1121.** www.dolphins.org. Admission $20 adults, $17 seniors, $15 children 4–12. Daily 9am–4:30pm. Narrated behavior sessions with Atlantic bottlenose dolphins and California sea lions as well as educational presentations roughly every half-hour throughout the day.

Florida Keys Wild Bird Center ★ Wander through lush canopies of mangroves on wooden walkways to see some of the Keys' most famous residents—the large variety of native birds, including broad-wing hawks, great blue and white herons, roseate spoonbills, cattle egrets, and pelicans. This not-for-profit center operates as a hospital for the many birds that have been injured by accident or disease. In 2002, the World Parrot Mission was established here, focusing on caring for parrots and educating the public about the birds. Visit at feeding time, usually about 3:30pm, when you can watch the dedicated staff feed the hundreds of hungry birds.

U.S. 1 at MM 93.6 (bay side), Tavernier. © **305/852-4486.** www.fkwbc.org. Donations suggested. Daily 8:30am–6pm.

Robbie's Pier ★★★ (Value) One of the best and definitely one of the cheapest attractions in the Upper Keys is the famed Robbie's Pier. Here the fierce steely tarpons, a prized catch for backcountry anglers, have been gathering for the past 20 years. You may recognize these prehistoric-looking giants that grow up to 200 pounds; many are displayed as trophies and mounted on local restaurant walls. To see them live, head to Robbie's Pier, where tens and sometimes hundreds of these behemoths circle the shallow waters waiting for you to feed them. Robbie's Pier also offers ranger-led boat tours and guided kayak tours to Indian Key, where you can go snorkeling or just bask in the glory of your surroundings.

U.S. 1 at MM 77.5, Islamorada. © **305/664-9814.** www.robbies.com. Admission $1. Bucket of fish $2. Daily 8am–5pm. Make a hard right U-turn off the highway, then it's a short drive before you'll see a HUNGRY TARPON restaurant sign. Robbie's driveway is just before the restaurant.

Theater of the Sea ★ (Kids) Established in 1946, the Theater of the Sea is one of the world's oldest marine zoos. Recently refurbished, the park's dolphin and sea-lion shows are entertaining and informative, especially for children. If you want to swim with dolphins and haven't booked well in advance, you may be able to get into this place with just a few hours' notice, as opposed to the more rigid Dolphin Research Center in Marathon (see above). While the Dolphin Research Center is a legitimate, scientific establishment, Theater of the Sea is more like a theme-park attraction. That's not to say the dolphins are mistreated, but it's not as educational and professional as the Dolphin Research Center. Theater of the Sea also permits you to swim with sea lions. (Children 4 and under cannot participate.) There are twice-daily 4-hour adventure and snorkel cruises that cost $69 for adults and $45 for children ages 3 to 12, during which you can learn about the history and ecology of the marine environment.

U.S. 1 at MM 84.5, Islamorada. © **305/664-2431.** www.theaterofthesea.com. Admission $26 adults, $19 children 3–12. Dolphin swim $175; sea-lion swim $135. Reservations are a must. Daily 10am–5pm (ticket office closes at 4pm).

TWO EXCEPTIONAL STATE PARKS

One of the best places to discover the diverse ecosystem of the Upper Keys is its most famous park, **John Pennekamp Coral Reef State Park** ★★★, located on U.S. 1 at MM 102.5, in Key Largo (© **305/451-6300;** www.pennekamppark.com). Named for a former *Miami Herald* editor and conservationist, the 188-square-mile park is the nation's first undersea preserve: It's a sanctuary for part of the only living coral reef in the continental United States. The original plans for Everglades National Park included this part of the reef within its boundaries, but opposition from local homeowners made its inclusion politically impossible.

Because the water is extremely shallow, the 40 species of coral and more than 650 species of fish here are accessible to divers, snorkelers, and glass-bottom boat passengers. To experience this park, visitors must get in the water—you can't see the reef from the shore. Your first stop should be the visitor center, which has a mammoth 30,000-gallon saltwater aquarium that re-creates a reef ecosystem. At the adjacent dive shop, you can rent snorkeling and diving equipment and join one of the boat trips that depart for the reef throughout the day. Visitors can also rent motorboats, sailboats, sailboards, and canoes. The 2½-hour glass-bottom boat tour is the best way to see the coral reefs if you don't want to get wet. Watch for the lobsters and other sea life residing in the fairly shallow ridge walls beneath the coastal waters. ***Remember:*** These are protected waters, so you can't remove anything from them.

Canoeing around the park's narrow mangrove channels and tidal creeks is also popular. You can go on your own in a rented canoe or, in winter, sign up for a tour led by a local naturalist. Hikers have two short trails from which to choose: a boardwalk through the mangroves, and a dirt trail through a tropical hardwood hammock. Ranger-led walks are usually scheduled daily from the end of November to April. Call © **305/451-1202** for schedule information and reservations.

Park admission is $5 per vehicle, plus 50¢ per passenger. Pedestrians and bicyclists pay $1.50 each. On busy weekends, there's often a line of cars waiting to get into the park. On your way in, ask the ranger for a map. Glass-bottom boat tours cost $24 for adults and $17 for children 11 and under. Tours depart three times daily, at 9:15am, 12:15pm, and 3pm. Snorkeling tours are $30 for adults and $25 for children 17 and under; masks, fins, and snorkels cost $5 and the snorkel is yours to keep. Canoes rent for $12 per hour; kayaks are $12 per hour for a single, $17 per hour for a double. For experienced boaters only, four different sizes of reef boats (powerboats) rent for $160 to $210 for 4 hours, and $259 to $359 for a full day; call © **305/451-6325** for information. Fishing boats range from $135 to $359. A minimum $400 deposit (or more, depending on boat size) is required. The park's boat-rental office is open daily from 8am to 5pm (last boat rented at 3pm); phone for tour and dive times. Reservations are recommended for all of the above. Also see below for more options on diving, fishing, and snorkeling off these reefs.

Long Key State Recreation Area ★★★, U.S. 1 at MM 68, Long Key (© **305/664-4815;** www.abfla.com/parks/longkey/longkey.html), is one of the best places in the Middle Keys for hiking, camping, snorkeling, and canoeing. This 965-acre site is situated atop the remains of an ancient coral reef. At the entrance gate, ask for a free flyer describing the local trails and wildlife.

Three nature trails can be explored via foot or canoe. The Golden Orb Trail is a 40 minute walk through mostly plants; the Layton Trail is a 15-minute walk along the bay; and the Long Key Canoe Trail glides along a shallow-water lagoon. The excellent 1.5-mile canoe trail is short and sweet, allowing visitors to loop around the mangroves in about an hour. Long Key is also a great spot to stop for a picnic if you get hungry on your way to Key West. Campsites are available along the Atlantic Ocean. The swimming and saltwater fishing (license required) are top-notch here, as is the snorkeling, which is shallow and on the shoreline of the Atlantic. For novices, educational programs on the aforementioned are available, too.

Railroad builder Henry Flagler created the Long Key Fishing Club here in 1906, and the waters surrounding the park are still popular with game fishers. In summer, sea turtles lumber onto the protected coast to lay their eggs. Educational programs are available to view this phenomenon.

Admission is $4 per car, plus 50¢ per person (except for the Layton Trail, which is free). The recreation area is open daily from 8am to sunset. You can rent canoes at the trail head for about $5 per hour or $10 a day. The nearest place to rent snorkel equipment is **Holiday Isle,** 84001 U.S. 1, Islamorada (© **800/327-7070**).

The 10 "Keymandments"

The Keys have always attracted independent spirits, from Ernest Hemingway and Tennessee Williams to Jimmy Buffett, Zane Grey, and local hero Mel Fisher. Writers, artists, and freethinkers have long drifted down here to escape.

Although you'll generally find a very laid-back and tolerant code of behavior in the Keys, some rules do exist. Be sure to respect the 10 "Keymandments" while you're here, or suffer the consequences.

- Don't anchor on a reef. (Reefs are alive.)
- Don't feed the animals. (They'll want to follow you home.)
- Don't trash our place (or we'll send Bubba to trash yours).
- Don't touch the coral. (After all, you don't even know them. Some pose a mild risk of injury to you as well.)
- Don't speed (especially on Big Pine Key, where deer reside and tar-and-feathering is still practiced).
- Don't catch more fish than you can eat. (Better yet, let them go. Some of them support schools.)
- Don't collect conch. (This species is protected by Bubba.)
- Don't disturb the birds' nests. (They find it very annoying.)
- Don't damage the sea grass (and don't even think about making a skirt out of it).
- Don't drink and drive on land or sea. (There's nothing funny about it.)

WATERSPORTS FROM A TO Z

There are literally hundreds of outfitters in the Keys who will arrange all kinds of water activities, from cave dives to parasailing. If those recommended below are booked up or unreachable, ask the local chamber of commerce for a list of qualified members.

BOATING In addition to the rental shops in the state parks, you'll find dozens of outfitters along U.S. 1 offering a range of runabouts and skiffs for boaters of any experience level. **Captain Pip's,** U.S. 1 at MM 47.5, Marathon (✆ **800/707-1692** or 305/743-4403; www.captainpips.com), charges $145 to $300 per day. Overnight accommodations are available and include a free boat rental: 2-night minimum $250 to $450 in season and $225 to $415 off-season; weekly $1,185 to $2,595. Rooms are Key West comfortable and charming, with ceiling fans, tile floors, and pine paneling. But the best part is that every room comes with an 18- to 21-foot boat for your use during your stay. **Robbie's Rent-a-Boat,** U.S. 1 at MM 77.5, Islamorada (✆ **305/664-9814;** www.robbies.com), rents 18- to 26-foot motorboats with engines ranging from 60 to 130 horsepower. Boat rentals are $135 to $185 for a half-day and $185 to $235 for a full day.

CANOEING & KAYAKING I can think of no better way to explore the uninhabited backcountry on the Gulf side of the Keys than by kayak or canoe, as you can reach places that big boats just can't get to because of their large draft. Manatees will sometimes cuddle up to the boats, thinking them to be another friendly species.

Many area hotels rent kayaks and canoes to guests, as do the outfitters listed here. **Florida Bay Outfitters,** U.S. 1 at MM 104, Key Largo (✆ **305/451-3018;** www.kayak

floridakeys.com), rents canoes and sea kayaks for use in and around John Pennekamp Coral Reef State Park for $40 to $75 for a half-day, $50 to $90 for a full day. At **Coral Reef Park Co.,** U.S. 1 at MM 102.5, Key Largo (✆ **305/451-1621**), you can rent canoes and kayaks for $12 per hour; most canoes are sit-on-tops. **Florida Keys Kayak and Sail,** U.S. 1 at MM 75.5, Islamorada (✆ **305/664-4878;** www.floridakeyskayakandski.com), at Robbie's Pier, offers backcountry tours, botanical-preserve tours of Lignumvitae Key, historic-site tours of Indian Key, and sunset tours through the mangrove tunnels and saltwater flats. Tour rates are from $39 to $49; rental rates range from $15 per hour to $45 per day for a single kayak, and $20 per hour to $60 per day for a double kayak. **Reflections Nature Tours** (✆ **305/872-4668;** www.floridakeyskayaktours.com) is a small mobile company that specializes in kayak tours through the Lower Keys. Guided kayak excursions cost $50 per person for a 3-hour tour, $40 per person for a 2-hour full-moon tour. The 3-hour custom tours start at $125 for one person and $195 for two people. All tours are by appointment only. Nature lovers can slip through the silent backcountry waters off Key West and the Lower Keys in a kayak, discovering the flora and fauna that make up the unique Keys ecosystem, on **Blue Planet Kayak Tours'** (✆ **305/294-8087;** www.blue-planet-kayak.com) starlight tour. All excursions are led by an environmental scientist. The starlight tours last between 2½ and 3 hours. No previous kayaking experience is necessary. Cost for the guided kayak adventure is $50 per person.

DIVING & SNORKELING Just 6 miles off Key Largo is a U.S. Navy Landing Ship Dock, the latest artificial wreck site to hit the Keys—or, rather, to be submerged 130 feet *below* the Keys.

The **Florida Keys Dive Center,** U.S. 1 at MM 90.5, Tavernier (✆ **305/852-4599;** www.floridakeysdivectr.com), takes snorkelers and divers to the reefs of John Pennekamp Coral Reef State Park and environs every day. PADI (Professional Association of Diving Instructors) training courses are available for the uninitiated. While some people have complained that employees are rude here, others disagree; I suggest you decide for yourself. Tours leave at 8am and 12:30pm; the cost is $35 per person to snorkel (plus $10 rental fee for mask, snorkel, and fins), and $50 per person to dive (plus an extra $24 if you need to rent all the gear).

At **Hall's Dive Center & Career Institute,** U.S. 1 at MM 48.5, Marathon (✆ **305/743-5929;** www.hallsdiving.com), snorkelers and divers can dive at Looe Key, Sombrero Reef, Delta Shoal, Content Key, or Coffins Patch. Tours are scheduled daily at 9am and 1pm. You'll spend 1 hour at each of two sites per tour. It's $50 per person to snorkel (gear included) and $60 per person to dive (tanks $9 each).

Acquaint Yourself

Fans of stone crabs can get further acquainted with the seasonal crustaceans on 3-hour tours offered by **Keys Fisheries,** aboard 40- to 50-foot vessels that leave from Marathon. The tour includes views of fishermen as they collect crabs from traps and process their claws. The $450 cost includes up to six passengers and up to 6 pounds of fresh claws iced for travel or prepared at a dockside restaurant. Stone-crab season is October 15 to May 15. Call ✆ **305/743-4353** or check www.keysfisheries.com for more information.

 Robbie's Partyboats & Charters, U.S. 1 at MM 77.5, Islamorada (✆ **305/664-8070** or 664-8498; www.robbies.com), located at Robbie's Marina on Lower Matecumbe Key, offers day and night deep-sea and reef-fishing trips aboard a 65-foot party boat. Big-game fishing charters are also available, and "splits" are arranged for solo fishers. Party-boat fishing costs about $35 for a half-day morning tour ($3 for rod and reel rental); it's $20 extra if you want to go back out on an afternoon tour. Charters run about $700 for a half-day, $900 for a full day; splits begin at $120 per person. Phone for information and reservations.

Bud n' Mary's Fishing Marina, U.S. 1 at MM 79.8, Islamorada (✆ **800/742-7945** or 305/664-2461; www.budnmarys.com), one of the largest marinas between Miami and Key West, is packed with sailors offering backcountry fishing charters. This is the place to go if you want to stalk tarpon, bonefish, and snapper. If the seas are not too rough, deep-sea and coral fishing trips can also be arranged. Charters cost $400 to $550 for a half-day, $500 to $650 for a full day; splits begin at $125 per person.

WHERE TO STAY

U.S. 1 is lined with chain hotels in all price ranges. In the Upper Keys, the best moderately priced option is the **Key Largo Ramada,** off U.S. 1 at MM 100, Key Largo (✆ **800/THE-KEYS** [843-5397] or 305/451-3939), which has three pools and a casino boat, and is just 3 miles from John Pennekamp Coral Reef State Park. Another good Upper Keys option is **Days Inn Oceanfront Resort,** U.S. 1 at MM 82.5 (✆ **800/DAYS-INN** [329-7466] or 305/664-3681). In the Middle Keys, the **Wellesley Inn,** 13351 Overseas Hwy., MM 54 in Marathon (✆ **305/743-8550**), offers reasonably priced oceanside rooms.

Because the real beauty of the Keys lies mostly beyond the highways, there is no better way to see this area than by boat. So why not stay in a floating hotel? Especially if you're traveling with a group, houseboats can be economical. To rent a houseboat, contact **Houseboat Vacations,** 85944 Overseas Hwy., Islamorada (✆ **305/664-4009;** www.thefloridakeys.com/houseboats). Rates are from $847 to $1,012 for 3 nights. Boats accommodate up to eight people.

For land options, consider the recommendations below.

Very Expensive

Cheeca Lodge & Spa ★★★ (Kids Located on 27 lush acres of beachfront, this rambling resort sports one of the only golf courses in the Upper Keys. Rooms have the amenities of a world-class resort in a very laid-back setting. You may not feel compelled to leave the sprawling grounds, but it's good to know that the hotel is conveniently situated near excellent restaurants and colorful nightlife. Most of the guest rooms and suites feature luxurious West Indies–style decor, marble baths, fine linens, plasma TVs, and wireless DSL. The Spa at Cheeca offers a variety of massage therapies, skincare, signature body treatments, fitness room, fitness classes, and butler-serviced poolside cabanas. Cheeca's culinary team dishes up unique regional fare with a focus on fresh seafood, served indoors or al fresco. The resort's newest edition is Nikai, where the sake is flowing and guests enjoy Asian-inspired cuisine and the Keys freshest sushi. For recreation, Cheeca offers tennis, a 9-hole golf course, eco-tours, sunset cruises, snorkel excursions to America's only living coral barrier reef, and much more. The $39 daily resort fee may seem steep at first, but it's worth it, including unlimited tennis, golf, fishing rods, bicycles, beach shade cabanas, sea kayaks, valet parking, wireless Internet access, exercise classes, in-room Starbucks coffee service and bottled water, housekeeping gratuity, local calls, daily newspaper, and fax services. ***Note:*** A December 2008 fire destroyed many of the rooms in the hotel's main building and as of press time, the entire resort was closed for repairs.

U.S. 1 at MM 82 (P.O. Box 527), Islamorada, FL 33036. ✆ **305/664-4651.** Fax 305/664-2893. www.cheeca.com. 199 units. Winter $319–$369 deluxe double, $529–$848 deluxe suite; off-season $269–$369 deluxe double, $479–$748 deluxe suite. AE, DC, DISC, MC, V. **Amenities:** Restaurant; sushi bar; 2 lounges (1 poolside); 2 outdoor heated pools; saltwater lagoon; 9-hole golf course; 6 lighted hard tennis courts; full-service spa; 5 Jacuzzis; watersports equipment/rentals; bike rental; children's nature programs; concierge; limited room service; in-room massage; babysitting; laundry services; dry cleaning. *In room:* A/C, TV/DVD, dataport, kitchenette (in suites), minibar, coffeemaker, hair dryer, iron, CD player, robe.

Hawk's Cay Resort ★★★ Kids Set on its own 60-acre island in the Middle Keys, when it comes to activities, this resort is far superior to Cheeca Lodge. In addition to sailing, fishing, snorkeling, and water-skiing, guests have the unique opportunity to interact directly with dolphins in the resort's natural saltwater lagoon. (You'll need to reserve a spot well in advance for this.) Guest rooms are large, with spacious bathrooms, island-style furniture, and private balconies with ocean or tropical views. There are also 225 hyperposh villas modeled after the kitschy 1950s concept of the "boatel," the recipients of a sophisticated redesign. The 7,000-square-foot Calm Waters Spa provides stellar treatments. Organized children's activities include marine- and ecology-inspired programs. A $35-million renovation in 2008 included a veranda and a new lobby incorporating direct water views, a bar and lounge, as well as a vastly expanded main resort pool featuring new landscaping, multitiered sun terrace, and private butlered cabanas. Fine dining options include a Nuevo-Latino restaurant and bar featuring hard-to-find rums.

61 Hawk's Cay Blvd., at MM 61, Duck Key, FL 33050. ✆ **888/814-9104** or 305/743-7000. Fax 305/743-5215. www.hawkscay.com. 402 units, including 225 2- and 3-bedroom villas. Winter $329–$539 double, $549–$1,300 suite, $519–$1,400 villa; off-season $279–$459 double, $479–$900 suite, $449–$1,000 villa. Packages available. AE, DC, DISC, MC, V. **Amenities:** 5 restaurants; lounge; 5 outdoor heated pools; adults-only private pool; nearby golf course (transportation available); 8 tennis courts (6 hard, 2 clay, 2 lighted); exercise room; full-service spa; Jacuzzi; watersports equipment/rentals; bike rental; children's programs ($28–$35 per child); game room; concierge; room service; full-service marina. *In room:* A/C, TV/VCR, DVD (in villas), fridge, coffeemaker, hair dryer, iron.

Expensive

Casa Morada ★★ Finds The closest thing to a boutique hotel in the Florida Keys, Casa Morada is the brainchild of a trio of New York women who used to work for hip hotelier Ian Schrager. This 16-suite property is a hipster haven tucked away off a sleepy street and radiates serenity and style in an area where serenity is aplenty, but style is elusive. Sitting on 1¾ acres of prime bayfront, the hotel features a limestone grotto, freshwater pool, and poolside beverage service. Each of the cool rooms has either a private garden or a terrace—request the one with the open-air Jacuzzi that faces the bay. While the decor is decidedly island, think St. Barts rather than, say, Gilligan's. There's no on-site restaurant, a complimentary breakfast is served daily, and there's free yoga Wednesday to Sunday at 8:30am. Enjoy free use of bikes, bocce balls, and board games. Despite the games, this place is not recommended for kids.

136 Madeira Rd., Islamorada, FL 33036. ✆ **888/881-3030** or 305/664-0044. Fax 305/664-0674. www.casamorada.com. 16 units. Winter $329–$659 double; off-season $249–$509 double. Rates include continental breakfast. AE, DISC, MC, V. From U.S. 1 S., at MM 82.2, turn right onto Madeira Rd. and continue to the end of the street. The hotel is on the right. Friendly pets are welcome. **Amenities:** Freshwater pool; complimentary bike use; bocce ball. *In room:* A/C, TV/DVD, minibar, hair dryer, safe, CD player.

Jules' Undersea Lodge ★★★ (Finds) Staying here is certainly an experience of a lifetime—if you're brave enough to take the plunge. Originally built as a research lab, this small underwater compartment, which rests on pillars on the ocean floor, now operates as a two-room hotel. As expensive as it is unusual, Jules' is most popular with diving honeymooners. To get inside, guests swim 21 feet under the structure and pop up into the unit through a 4×6-foot "moon pool" that gurgles soothingly all night long. The 30-foot-deep underwater suite consists of two separate bedrooms that share a common living area. Room service will deliver your meals, daily newspapers, and even a late-night pizza in waterproof containers, at no extra charge. If you don't have time or a desire to spend the night, you can hang out and explore the lodge for 3 hours for $125 to $165 per person.

51 Shoreland Dr., Key Largo, FL 33037. ✆ **305/451-2353.** Fax 305/451-4789. www.jul.com. 2 units. $375–$475 per person. Rates include breakfast and dinner, as well as all equipment and unlimited scuba diving in the lagoon for certified divers. Packages available. AE, DISC, MC, V. From U.S. 1 S., at MM 103.2, turn left onto Transylvania Ave., across from the Central Plaza shopping mall. **Amenities:** Entertainment center; dining area. *In room:* A/C, kitchenette.

Kona Kai Resort & Gallery ★★★ (Finds) This little haven is an exquisite, adults-only waterfront property right on Florida Bay—a choice location that offers a stunning sunset view overlooking Everglades National Park. Highly stylized, modern rooms and suites dot the lush 2-acre property, brimming with native vegetation and fruit-bearing trees from which you're free to sample. An orchid house has more than 350 flowers. Lounge chairs, hammocks, a beachfront freshwater pool (heated in winter and cooled in summer), complimentary bottled water and fresh fruit poolside, a Jacuzzi, and one of the largest private beaches on the island make Kona Kai perfect for relaxation. For the more adventurous, Kona Kai's complimentary concierge services will organize excursions to the Everglades and the backcountry as well as fishing, snorkeling, diving, and more. Kayaks, paddleboats, tennis, Wi-Fi, and CD/DVD libraries are included at no extra charge. In-room massage and private yoga are available. For meals, three restaurants are within walking distance and the exceptional staff will give you insider tips—and discounts—to their favorite local eateries and watering holes. A fine art gallery doubles as the lobby.

97802 Overseas Hwy. (U.S. 1 at MM 97.8), Key Largo, FL 33037. ✆ 800/365-7829 or 305/852-7200. Fax 305/852-4629. www.konakairesort.com. 11 units. Winter $308–$561 double and 1-bedroom suite, $736–$940 2-bedroom suite; off-season $211–$454 double and 1-bedroom suite, $552–$656 2-bedroom suite. AE, DISC, MC, V. Closed Sept. Children 15 and under not permitted. Amenities: Beachfront heated/cooled pool; lighted tennis court; Jacuzzi; watersports equipment/rentals; concierge; Wi-Fi; in-room massage and facials; beachside Ping-Pong; shuffleboard; boat dockage. In room: A/C, TV/DVD, full kitchen (suites only), fridge, coffee/tea maker, hair dryer, CD player w/selection of CDs by local recording artists, DVD library, daily newspaper, no phone.

The Moorings ★★★ (Finds) You'll never see another soul on this 18-acre resort, a former coconut plantation, if you choose not to. There isn't even maid service unless you request it. The romantic whitewashed units, from cozy cottages to three-bedroom houses, are spacious with fully equipped kitchens and rustic, yet modern, decor. Most have washers and dryers, and all have CD players and DVD players; ask when you book. The real reason to come to this resort is to relax on the 1,000-plus-foot beach (one of the only real beaches around). You'll also find a great pool, hard tennis court, and a few kayaks and sailboards, but no motorized water vehicles in the waters surrounding the hotel, making it completely tranquil. There's no room service or restaurant, but Morada Bay and Pierres across the street are excellent. This is a place for people who like each other a lot. Leave the kids at home unless they're extremely well-behaved and not easily bored.

123 Beach Rd., near MM 81.5, on the ocean side, Islamorada, FL 33036. ✆ **305/664-4708.** Fax 305/664-4242. www.mooringsvillage.com. 18 units. Winter $325 small cottage, $650 1-bedroom house, $4,550–$10,500 weekly oceanfront house; off-season $250 small cottage, $450 1-bedroom house, $3,150–$7,700 weekly oceanfront house. 2-night minimum for smaller cottages; 1-week minimum for larger cottages and oceanfront house. AE, MC, V. **Amenities:** Large outdoor heated pool; tennis court; spa; watersports equipment; private beach. *In room:* A/C, TV/DVD, kitchen, coffeemaker, hair dryer, CD player, microwave, washer/dryer.

Tranquility Bay Beach House Resort ★★★ Kids The newest luxury resort in the mid Keys, Tranquility Bay sits on a tropically landscaped 12 acres on the Gulf of Mexico. You'll feel like you're in your own beach house—literally, with gorgeous two- and three-bedroom homes all with water views. All of the subtly decorated beach houses come equipped with everything a techno-savvy beach bum needs—even washers and dryers. Best of all, every beach house has spacious porches with French doors, wooden deck chairs, and 180-degree views of the water. The restaurant, Butterfly Café, is just as fine, with seasonal seafood menus. A private spa, Island Spice, helps you relax, but, really, this is one of the most relaxing resorts in all the Keys. Grounds sport lagoon pools, gazebos, a great lawn, and a beachfront Tiki bar. There are also activities, from adventure fishing and snorkeling to an adventure kids' program. ***Note:*** This is a nonsmoking resort. Smoking isn't even permitted on porches, only in designated areas.

2600 Overseas Hwy., Marathon, FL 33036. ✆ **305/259-0888.** Fax 305/289-0667. www.tranquilitybay.com. 87 units. Winter $399–$539 doubles; off-season $279–$509 doubles. AE, DC, MC, V. **Amenities:** Large outdoor heated pool; fitness center; spa; watersports equipment/rentals. *In room:* A/C, TV/DVD, Wi-Fi, kitchen, coffeemaker, hair dryer, CD player, microwave.

Moderate

Banana Bay Resort & Marina ★★ Finds It doesn't look like much from the sign-cluttered Overseas Highway, but once you enter the lush grounds of Banana Bay, you'll realize you're in one of the most bucolic and best-run properties in the Upper Keys. The resort is a beachfront maze of two-story buildings hidden among banyans and palms, with moderately sized rooms, many with private balconies. A recreational activity area has horseshoe pits, a bocce court, barbecue grills, and a giant lawn chessboard. The kitschy restaurant serves three meals a day, indoors and poolside. The hotel also rents bikes, boats, WaveRunners, kayaks, day-sailing dinghies, and bait and tackle. Another surprising amenity is Pretty Joe Rock, the hotel's private island, available for long weekends and weekly rentals. On it is a two-bedroom, two-bathroom cottage that's ideal for romantic escapes. Banana Bay is family friendly, but for an adults-only resort, there's **Banana Bay Resort,** at 2319 N. Roosevelt Blvd., in Key West (✆ **305/296-6925**), which doesn't allow children.

U.S. 1 at MM 49.5, Marathon, FL 33050. ✆ **800/BANANA-1** or 305/743-3500. Fax 305/743-2670. www.bananabay.com. 60 units. Winter $185–$245 double; off-season $105–$225 double. Rates include continental breakfast. 3- and 7-night honeymoon and wedding packages available. AE, DC, DISC, MC, V. **Amenities:** Restaurant; bar; pool; tennis courts; Jacuzzi; watersports equipment/rentals; bicycle rentals; self-service laundry; small beach; marina; fishing charters; barbecue pit; snorkeling area. *In room:* A/C, TV, fridge, hair dryer, iron.

Conch Key Cottages ★ Finds Here's your chance to play castaway in the Keys. Occupying its own private microisland just off U.S. 1, Conch Key Cottages is a comfortable hideaway, a place to get away from it all. The cottages offer solitude, with the exception of one or two interesting eateries. The units, which were built at different times over the past 40 years, overlook their own stretch of natural, but very small, private beach. They have screened-in porches, cozy bedrooms, bathrooms, hammocks, barbecue grills, and two-person kayaks. The two-bedroom cottages are the most spacious and are well designed, practically tailor-made for couples or families. On the other side of the pool is a handful of efficiency apartments that are similarly outfitted but don't enjoy beach frontage.

Private Island off U.S. 1 at MM 62.3, Marathon, FL 33050. ✆ **800/330-1577** or 305/289-1377. Fax 305/743-8661. www.conchkeycottages.com. 12 cottages. Dec 15–Sept 7 $139–$349 for up to 6 people; Sept 8–Dec 14 $85–$199 for up to 4 people. AE, DISC, MC, V. **Amenities:** Pool; Internet; sandy beach; dockage; complimentary kayaks. *In room:* A/C, TV, full kitchen, no phone.

Holiday Isle Beach Resort & Marina Holiday Isle attracts a Spring Break kind of crowd year-round, a crowd that tends not to care about the rooms themselves—and has no qualms cramming an entire fraternity into a single unit for budget reasons. The famous Tiki Bar claims to have invented the Rum Runner drink (151-proof rum, blackberry brandy, banana liqueur, grenadine, and lime juice), and there's no reason to doubt it. It's the Tiki Bar that brings the people, really. Hordes of partyers are attracted to the resort's nonstop merrymaking, live music, and beachfront bars. As a result, some of the accommodations can be noisy. Rooms are bare-bones; despite the ocean views, they're pretty awful and need a good scrub down—especially the units that lead to the filthy, sandy Tiki Bar. But, really, isn't that why you're here in the first place?

U.S. 1 at MM 84, Islamorada, FL 33036. ✆ **800/327-7070** or 305/664-2321. Fax 305/664-2703. www.holidayisle.com. 178 units. Winter $144–$294 double, $274–$450 suite; off-season $119–$199 double, $245–$425 suite. AE, DISC, MC, V. **Amenities:** 5 restaurants; 12 bars; 3 outdoor heated pools; kids' pool; Jacuzzi; watersports equipment/rentals; kids' programs; laundry facilities. *In room:* A/C, TV, fridge, hair dryer.

Lime Tree Bay Resort Motel The only place to stay in the tiny town of Layton (pop. 183), Lime Tree is midway between Islamorada and Marathon and is situated on a pretty piece of waterfront graced with hundreds of mature palm trees and tropical foliage. It prides itself on its promise of no hustle, no valets, and, most amusingly, no bartenders in Hawaiian shirts! Motel rooms and efficiencies have tiny bathrooms with showers, but are clean and well maintained. The best deal is the two-bedroom bay-view suite: A spacious living area with new furnishings leads to a large private deck overlooking the Gulf. There's also a full kitchen and two full bathrooms. Fifteen efficiencies and suites have kitchenettes. Pretty cool in its own right is the Zane Grey Suite (named after the famous author and screenwriter, who lived right around the corner), a two-bedroom, one-bathroom unit with the best views and a second-story location with private stairs.

U.S. 1 at MM 68.5, Layton, Long Key, FL 33001. ✆ **800/723-4519** or 305/664-4740. Fax 305/664-0750. www.limetreebayresort.com. 36 units. Winter $117–$375 double; summer $100–$320 double; off-season $89–$290 double. AE, DC, DISC, MC, V. **Amenities:** Restaurant; small outdoor pool; tennis court; Jacuzzi; Wi-Fi in business center. *In room:* A/C, TV, kitchenette (in some), fridge, coffeemaker.

Pines and Palms ★★★ (Finds Looking for a beachfront cottage or, better yet, an oceanfront villa, but don't want to spend your (future) child's college fund? This is the place. Cheery, cozy cottages, Atlantic views, and a private beachfront with hammocks and a pool give way to a relaxed, tropical paradise. Service is friendly and accommodating. All rooms and cottages have full kitchens and balconies, and are ideal for extended stays. Although there's no restaurant on-site, the staff will be happy to bring a Weber barbecue to your patio so you can grill out by the beach. Because of its popularity, Pines and Palms usually has a 2-night minimum.

MM 80.4 (ocean side), Islamorada, FL 33036. ✆ **800/624-0964** or 305/664-4343. www.pinesandpalms.com. 25 units. $89–$219 double; $129–$299 suite; $159–$459 cottage; $399–$579 villa. AE, MC, V. **Amenities:** Oceanfront heated freshwater pool; watersports equipment/rentals; bike rental; coin-op washer/dryer. *In room:* A/C, kitchen (in most), fridge, coffeemaker.

Inexpensive

Ragged Edge Resort ★★ This small oceanfront property's Tahitian-style units are spread along more than half a dozen gorgeous, grassy waterfront acres. All are immaculately clean and comfortable, and most are outfitted with full kitchens and tasteful furnishings. There's no bar, restaurant, or staff to speak of, but the retreat's affable owner is happy to lend bicycles and give advice on the area's offerings. A large dock attracts boaters and a variety of local and migratory birds. An outdoor heated freshwater pool is a bonus for those months when the temperature gets a bit chilly.

243 Treasure Harbor Rd. (near MM 86.5), Islamorada, FL 33036. ✆ **800/436-2023** or 305/852-5389. www.ragged-edge.com. 11 units. $69–$99 double; $100–$259 suite. AE, MC, V. **Amenities:** Outdoor pool; free use of bikes; coin-op washer/dryer. *In room:* A/C, kitchen (in most), fridge, coffeemaker.

Camping

John Pennekamp Coral Reef State Park ★★ One of Florida's best parks (p. 196), Pennekamp has 47 well-separated campsites, half of which are available by advance reservation. The tent sites are small but equipped with restrooms, hot water, and showers. Note that the local environment provides fertile breeding grounds for insects, particularly in late summer, so bring repellent. Two man-made beaches and a small lagoon nearby attract many large wading birds. Reservations are held until 5pm; the park must be notified of late arrival by phone on the check-in date. Pennekamp opens at 8am and closes around sundown.

U.S. 1 at MM 102.5 (P.O. Box 487), Key Largo, FL 33037. ✆ **305/451-1202.** www.pennekamppark.com. Reservations can be made in advance by calling Reserve America (✆ 800/326-3521). 47 campsites. $26–$32 (with electricity) per site. Park entry $5 per vehicle with driver (50¢ for each additional person). Yearly permits and passes available. AE, DISC, MC, V. No pets.

Long Key State Park ★ The Upper Keys' other main state park is more secluded than its northern neighbor—and more popular. All sites are located ocean side and surrounded by narrow rows of trees and nearby restroom facilities. Reserve well in advance, especially in winter.

U.S. 1 at MM 67.5 (P.O. Box 776), Long Key, FL 33001. ✆ **305/664-4815.** www.abfla.com/parks/longkey/longkey.html. 60 sites. $26 per site for 1–4 people; $3.25 per vehicle. AE, DISC, MC, V. No pets.

WHERE TO DINE

Although not known as a culinary hot spot (though always improving), the Upper and Middle Keys do have some excellent restaurants, most of which specialize in seafood. The landmark **Green Turtle Inn** (below) is alive and well, featuring classic and contemporary Florida cuisine by star chef Andy Niedenthal, a full bar and tasting station, custom catering, gourmet to go, and a Green Turtle product line, all in a beautiful, laid-back rustic environment. The restaurant is flanked by an art gallery and sport-fishing outfitter, making it a one-stop shop for locals and fun-loving tourists who have put Islamorada on the map.

Often, visitors (especially those who fish) take advantage of accommodations that have kitchen facilities and cook their own meals. Some restaurants will even clean and cook your catch, for a fee.

Very Expensive

Kaiyo ★★★ JAPANESE/SUSHI This funky, colorful restaurant looks out of place in an area where most eateries are housed in shanty shacks, and its exquisite, modern sushi is a first for Islamorada—but the food is so good, people from all over South Florida plan trips around a meal at Kaiyo. It's not your typical sushi restaurant, but rather one that fuses Florida's fine ingredients with some of the freshest raw fish this side of Tokyo. Signature sushi items, such as the spicy volcano conch roll and the Key lime lobster roll, are outstanding, as are the farm-raised raw oysters and farmed baby-conch tempura. A hip, modern interior is an amusing contrast to the casually dressed, Key-ed up diners, and service here is of five-star caliber—something not typically found in the laid-back Keys. Before you say that you came to the Keys not for trendy sushi, but for fresh fish and conch fritters, do have a meal at Kaiyo. It may change the way you view Keys cuisine.

81701 Old Hwy., U.S. 1 at MM 82, Islamorada. ✆ **305/664-5556.** www.kaiyokeys.com. Reservations recommended. Main courses $12–$36; sushi $7.50–$16. AE, DC, MC, V. Mon–Sat noon–10pm.

Pierre's ★★★ FRENCH The two-story British West Indies–style plantation home that houses this exquisite French restaurant is only part of the dramatic effect of a memorable dinner at Pierre's. Inside, you'll find more design drama—in a good way, of course—in the form of an eclectic mix of Moroccan, Indian, and African artifacts. Lighting is dim, with candlelight and Tiki torches outside, and it's completely romantic—especially outdoors on the second-floor veranda overlooking the water. The food challenges the setting, with amazing flavors and gorgeous presentation. The tempura lobster tail with hearts of palm hash, soy glaze, and wasabi crème fraîche, and the Florida Keys Hogfish Meunière with roasted creamer potatoes, pattypan squash, and baby zucchini are to die for. Desserts are equally divine, and if you can't decide what to have, order the Valrhona Chocolate Fondue with biscotti, pâté a choux, lemon sugar cookies, strawberries, and mandarin oranges. After dinner, head downstairs to the Green Flash Lounge, where you'll find a laid-back cocktail scene, with locals and visitors marveling at the exquisite, priceless setting. Pierre's also hosts a fabulous, monthly Full Moon Party with its casual dining sister, Morada Bay Beach Café.

U.S. 1 at MM 81.6 (bay side), Islamorada. ✆ **305/664-3225.** www.pierres-restaurant.com. Main courses $35–$42. AE, MC, V. Sun–Thurs 6–10pm; Fri–Sat 6–11pm. Lounge open at 5pm daily. Restaurant closed on Tues during summer.

Expensive

Barracuda Grill ★★ SEAFOOD Owned by Lance Hill and his wife, Jan, a former sous-chef at Little Palm Island (p. 214), this small, casual spot serves excellent seafood, steaks, and chops. Some favorites here are the Caicos gold conch, braised pork shank, and mangrove snapper and mango. Try the appetizer of tipsy olives, marinated in gin or vodka, to kick-start your meal. For fans of spicy food, go for the red-hot calamari. Decorated with barracuda-themed art, the restaurant also features a well-priced American wine list with lots of California vintages.

U.S. 1 at MM 49.5 (bay side), Marathon. ✆ **305/743-3314.** Main courses $15–$30. AE, MC, V. Wed–Sat 6–10pm.

Butterfly Café ★★★ SEAFOOD Housed in the stunning Tranquility Bay resort, Butterfly Café is the newest gourmet hot spot in the Middle Keys, with water views and a stellar menu of fresh local seafood. Among the dishes not to miss: sugar-cane-spiced glazed dolphin with mango-ginger salsa; Cuban-spiced, grilled double-cut pork chops with mango-lime mojo and spiced macadamia basmati rice. Service is very friendly and knowledgeable, and desserts are to die for. Save room for the sticky toffee pudding and nutty-crust Key lime pie with white chocolate mousse. Open for breakfast, lunch, and dinner, but Sunday brunch is especially spectacular. Don't miss the tropical French toast.

2600 Overseas Hwy., in the Tranquility Bay Resort, Marathon. ✆ **305/289-0888.** www.tranquilitybay.com. Main courses $18–$37. AE, MC, V. Daily 7–10am and 11:30am–10pm; Sun brunch 10:30am–2:30pm.

Green Turtle Inn ★★★ SEAFOOD The legend is back, but this time with a gourmet market and cuisine cooked with locally farmed vegetables and microgreens. While it may not be a throwback to the old Florida Keys, Green Turtle, reopened by Dawn Sieber, who subsequently left "for a change of scenery," and now helmed by star chef Andy Niedenthal, remains a must stop for anyone looking for a fabulous dining experience. Some old menu items remain—the famous turtle chowder with pepper sherry, and luscious conch chowder. But the new menu items are nothing to sneer at either. Small plates, including pan-seared scallops with goat cheese–whipped potatoes, sherry vinegar brown butter, white truffle oil, and sizzled leeks make for satisfying main courses, but don't miss entrees such as Snapper En Papillote in ginger, cilantro, and Key lime. And whatever you do, do not pass up the chocolate bombe. After dinner, check out the art gallery and gourmet shop.

81219 Overseas Hwy., at MM 81.2, Islamorada. ✆ **305/664-2006.** www.greenturtlekeys.com. Main courses $20–$38. AE, MC, V. Daily 7–10am and 11:30am–10pm.

Marker 88 ★★★ SEAFOOD An institution in the Upper Keys, Marker 88 has been pleasing locals and visitors since it opened in the 1970s. New chefs and owners have infused a new life into the place and the menu, which still utilizes fresh fruits, local ingredients, and fish caught in the Keys' waters. Among the menu highlights are the yellowtail Rangoon, sautéed and topped with black currant gelée and cinnamon, and served with fresh tropical fruits; and yellowtail Martinique, sautéed and topped with sweet basil, grilled bananas, and garlic butter. The waitresses, who are pleasant enough, require a bit of patience, but the food—not to mention the spectacular Gulf views—is worth it.

U.S. 1 at MM 88 (bay side), Islamorada. ✆ **305/852-9315.** www.marker88.info. Reservations suggested. Main courses $20–$39. AE, DC, DISC, MC, V. Tues–Sun 5–11pm. Closed Sept.

Moderate

Lorelei Restaurant and Cabana Bar ★ SEAFOOD/BAR FARE Don't resist the siren call of the enormous roadside mermaid—you won't be dashed onto the rocks. This big old fish house and bar, with excellent views of the bay, is a great place for a snack, a meal, or a beer. A good-value menu focuses mainly on seafood; in season, lobster is the way to go. Other fare includes the standard clam chowder, fried shrimp, and doughy conch fritters. Salads and soups are hearty and satisfying. For those tired of fish, the menu offers a few beef options. The outside bar has live music every evening, and you can order snacks and light meals from a limited menu.

U.S. 1 at MM 82, Islamorada. ✆ **305/664-4656.** Reservations not usually required. Main courses $10–$26. AE, DC, DISC, MC, V. Daily 7am–10:30pm. Outside bar serves breakfast 7–11am; lunch/appetizer menu 11am–9pm. Bar closes at midnight.

Inexpensive

Calypso's Seafood Grill ★★ (Finds) SEAFOOD With a motto proudly declaring "Yes, we know the music is loud and the food is spicy. That's the way we like it!" you know you're in a typical Keys eatery. Thankfully the food is anything but, with inventive seafood dishes in a casual and rustic waterside setting. Among the house specialties is cracked conch and superb steamed clams; but if you're not too hot out there, try the She-Crab soup. It's exceptional. The prices are surprisingly reasonable, but the service may be a bit more laid-back than you're used to. And don't be dismayed by the paper plates—Calypso's is one of Key Largo's most exceptional restaurants, so much so that owner/chef Todd Lollis has opened a second restaurant in the area, Big Fish, 99010 Overseas Hwy. (✆ **305/453-0820**), which is a bit easier to find but no less stellar.

1 Seagate Blvd. (near MM 99.5), Key Largo. ✆ **305/451-0600.** Main courses $10–$20. No credit cards. Wed–Thurs and Sun–Mon 11:30am–10pm; Fri–Sat 11:30am–11pm. From the south, turn right at the blinking yellow lights near MM 99.5 to Ocean Bay Dr. and then turn right. Look for the blue vinyl-sided building on the left.

Harriette's Restaurant ★ BREAKFAST/BRUNCH This little yellow shack packs in a major crowd for breakfast, thanks to friendly service, old school greasy spoon–style fare, and colossal homemade biscuits and muffins. Despite the grease factor, Harriette's realizes some people want to eat healthy—you're in the Keys, though, go nuts—and offers South Beach Diet and Atkins menu items as well.

MM 95.7, Key Largo. ✆ **305/852-8689.** Breakfast $5–$7. No credit cards. Daily 6am–2pm.

Islamorada Fish Company ★★ SEAFOOD Pick up a cooler of stone crab claws in season (mid-Oct to Apr), or try the great fried-fish sandwiches. A few hundred yards up the road (at MM 81.6) is Islamorada Fish Company Restaurant & Bakery, the newer establishment, which looks like an average diner but has fantastic seafood, pastas, and breakfasts. Locals gather here for politics and gossip as well as delicious grits, oatmeal, omelets, and pastries. Keep your eyes open while dining outside—the last time I was here, baby manatees were floating around, waiting for their close-ups.

U.S. 1 at MM 81.5 (up the street from Cheeca Lodge), Islamorada. ✆ **800/258-2559** or 305/664-9271. www.islamoradafishco.com. Reservations not accepted. Main courses $10–$37. DISC, MC, V. Sun–Thurs 11am–9pm; Fri–Sat 11am–10pm.

Island Grill ★ SEAFOOD If you drive too fast over Snake Creek Bridge, you may miss one of the best Keys' dining experiences around. Located just under the bridge and on the bay, Island Grill is a locals' favorite, with an expansive outdoor deck and bar and cozy waterfront dining room serving some fresh fare, including their famous tuna nachos, guava barbecued shrimp, and graham cracker–dusted calamari. There are also salads, sandwiches—try the lobster roll—and entrees, including a whole yellowtail snapper with Thai sweet chili sauce that's out of this world. Bring your own catch, and they'll cook and prepare it for you—served family style with veggies and rice for only $12. Live entertainment almost every night brings in a great, colorful Keys crowd. Although they serve breakfast, too, we say skip the food and just stick to the Bloody Marys.

MM 88.5 (ocean side at Snake Creek Bridge), Islamorada. ✆ **305/664-8400.** www.keysislandgrill.com. Reservations not necessary. Main courses $8–$25. Sun–Thurs 11am–10pm; Fri–Sat 11am–11pm.

Key Largo Conch House Restaurant & Coffee Bar ★★ AMERICAN A funky, cozy, and off-the-beaten-path hot spot for breakfast, lunch, and dinner, Key Largo Conch House is exactly that—a house set amid lush foliage, complete with resident dog, parrot, wraparound veranda for outdoor dining, and a warm and inviting indoor dining room reminiscent of your grandma's. Food is fresh and fabulously priced—from the heaping $13 plate of Mom's Lasagna, to $8-to-$13 twists on the usual eggs Benedict, including my favorite, the crab cakes Benedict. Featured on the Food Network, Conch

House should be a feature on everyone's trip down to the Keys, if not just for a cup of excellent coffee and a slice of homemade Key lime pie. It's also one of the few pet-friendly restaurants in the area.

U.S. 1 at MM 100, Key Largo. ✆ **305/453-4844.** www.keylargocoffeehouse.com. Reservations recommended. Main courses $8–$21. AE, DC, DISC, MC, V. Daily 7am–10pm.

Snapper's ★ SEAFOOD A locals' waterfront favorite, Snapper's serves fresh seafood caught by local fishermen—or by you, if you dare! The blackened mahimahi is exceptional and a bargain, complete with salad, vegetable, and choice of starch. There's also live music nightly and a lively, colorful—and deliciously casual—crowd.

139 Seaside Ave., at MM 94.5, Key Largo. ✆ **305/852-5956.** www.snapperskeylargo.com. Main courses $10–$25. DISC, MC, V. Sun–Thurs 11am–9pm; Fri–Sat 11am–10pm.

THE UPPER & MIDDLE KEYS AFTER DARK

Nightlife in the Upper Keys tends to start before the sun goes down, often at noon, as most people—visitors and locals alike—are on vacation. Also, many anglers and sports-minded folk go to bed early.

Hog Heaven, MM 85.3, just off the main road on the ocean side, Islamorada (✆ **305/664-9669**), opened in the early 1990s, the joint venture of young locals tired of tourist traps. This whitewashed biker bar is a welcome respite from the neon-colored cocktail circuit. It has a waterside view and diversions such as big-screen TVs and video games. The food isn't bad, either. The atmosphere is cliquish because most patrons are regulars, so start up a game of pool to break the ice. Open daily from 11am to 4am.

No trip to the Keys is complete without a stop at the **Tiki Bar at the Holiday Isle Resort** (p. 204), U.S. 1 at MM 84, Islamorada (✆ **305/664-2321**). Hundreds of revelers visit this oceanside spot for drinks and dancing at any time of day, but the live rock starts at 8:30pm. The thatched-roof Tiki Bar draws a mix of thirsty people, all in pursuit of a good time. In the afternoon and early evening (when everyone is either sunburned, drunk, or just happy to be dancing to live reggae), head for **Kokomo's,** next door. It often closes at 7:30pm on weekends (5:30pm on weekdays), so arrive early. For information, call the Holiday Isle Resort. Rumor has it that greedy developers are going to raze the Tiki Bar to make way for million-dollar condos, but loyal boozehounds are raising hell over it, and some are even trying to have the Tiki Bar declared a Florida landmark! Stay tuned.

Locals and tourists mingle at the outdoor cabana bar at **Lorelei** (see "Where to Dine," above). Most evenings after 5pm, you'll find local bands playing on a thatched-roof stage—mainly rock or reggae, and sometimes blues.

Woody's Saloon and Restaurant, U.S. 1 at MM 82, Islamorada (✆ **305/664-4335**), is a lively, wacky, loud, raunchy, local legend of a place serving up mediocre pizzas, buck-naked strippers, and live bands almost every night. The house band, Big Dick and the Extenders, showcases a 300-pound Native American who does a lewd, rude, and crude routine of politically incorrect jokes and songs starting at 9pm Tuesday through Sunday. He is a legend. By the way, don't think you're lucky if you're offered the front table: It's the target seat for Big Dick's haranguing. Avoid the lame karaoke performance on Sunday and Monday evenings. There's a small cover on most nights. Drink specials, contests, and the legendary Big Dick keep this place packed until 4am almost every night. ***Note:*** This place is not for the faint of heart, but more for those from the Howard Stern school of nightlife.

For a more subdued atmosphere, try the handsome stained-glass and mahogany-wood bar and club at **Zane Grey's,** on the second floor of World Wide Sportsman, MM 81.5 (✆ **305/664-4244**). Outside, enjoy a view of the calm waters of the bay; inside, soak up the history of real longtime anglers. It's open from 11am to at least 11pm (later on weekends). Call to find out who's playing on Friday and Saturday nights, when there's live entertainment and no cover.

2 THE LOWER KEYS

128 miles SW of Miami

Unlike their neighbors to the north and south, the Lower Keys (including **Big Pine**, **Sugarloaf**, and **Summerland**) are devoid of rowdy Spring Break crowds, boast few T-shirt and trinket shops, and have almost no late-night bars. What they do offer are the very best opportunities to enjoy the vast natural resources on land and water that make the area so rich. Stay overnight in the Lower Keys, rent a boat, and explore the reefs—it might be the most memorable part of your trip.

ESSENTIALS

GETTING THERE See "Essentials" for the Upper and Middle Keys (p. 192) and continue south on U.S. 1. The Lower Keys start at the end of the Seven-Mile Bridge. There are also airports in Marathon and Key West.

VISITOR INFORMATION **Big Pine and Lower Keys Chamber of Commerce,** ocean side of U.S. 1 at MM 31 (P.O. Box 430511), Big Pine Key, FL 33043 (✆ **800/872-3722** or 305/872-2411; fax 305/872-0752; www.lowerkeyschamber.com), is open Monday through Friday from 9am to 5pm, and Saturday from 9am to 3pm. The pleasant staff will help with anything a traveler may need. Call, write, or stop in for a comprehensive, detailed information packet.

WHAT TO SEE & DO

Once the centerpiece (these days, it's Big Pine Key) of the Lower Keys and still a great asset is **Bahia Honda State Park** ★, U.S. 1 at MM 37.5, Big Pine Key (✆ **305/872-2353;** www.bahiahondapark.com), which, even after the violent storms of 2005, has one of the most beautiful coastlines in South Florida. Bahia (pronounced *Bah*-ya) Honda is a great place for hiking, bird-watching, swimming, snorkeling, and fishing. The 524-acre park encompasses a wide variety of ecosystems, including coastal mangroves, beach dunes, and tropical hammocks. There are miles of trails packed with unusual plants and animals, plus a small white-sand beach. Shaded seaside picnic areas are fitted with tables and grills. Although the beach is never wider than 5 feet, even at low tide, this is the Lower Keys' best beach area.

True to its name (Spanish for "deep bay"), the park has relatively deep waters close to shore—perfect for snorkeling and diving. Easy offshore snorkeling here gives even novices a chance to lie suspended in warm water and simply observe diverse marine life passing by. Or else head to the stunning reefs at Looe Key, where the coral and fish are more vibrant than anywhere else in the United States. Snorkeling trips go from the Bahia Honda concessions to Looe Key National Marine Sanctuary (4 miles offshore). They depart twice daily March through September and cost $30 for adults, $25 for children 6 to 14, and $8 for equipment rental. Call ✆ **305/872-3210** for a schedule.

Entry to the park is $5 per vehicle (plus 50¢ per person), $1.50 per pedestrian or bicyclist, free for children 5 and under. If you're alone in a car, you'll pay only $2.50. Open daily from 8am to sunset.

The most famous residents of the Lower Keys are the tiny Key deer. Of the estimated 300 existing in the world, two-thirds live on Big Pine Key's **National Key Deer Refuge ★**. To get your bearings, stop by the rangers' office at the Winn-Dixie Shopping Plaza, near MM 30.5 off U.S. 1. They'll give you an informative brochure and map of the area. The refuge is open Monday through Friday from 8am to 5pm.

If the office is closed, head out to the **Blue Hole,** a former rock quarry now filled with the fresh water that's vital to the deer's survival. To get there, turn right at Big Pine Key's only traffic light at Key Deer Boulevard (take the left fork immediately after the turn) and continue 1½ miles to the observation-site parking lot, on your left. The .5-mile **Watson Hammock Trail,** about one-third mile past the Blue Hole, is the refuge's only marked footpath. The deer are more active in cool hours, so try coming out to the path in the early morning or late evening to catch a glimpse of these gentle dog-size creatures. There is an observation deck from which you can watch and photograph the protected species. Refuge lands are open daily from a half-hour before sunrise to a half-hour after sunset. Don't be surprised to see a lazy alligator warming itself in the sun, particularly in outlying areas around the Blue Hole. If you do see a gator, do not go near it, do not touch it, and do not provoke it. Keep your distance; if you must get a photo, use a zoom lens. Also, whatever you do, do not feed the deer—it will threaten their survival. Call the **park office** (**© 305/872-2239**) to find out about the infrequent free tours of the refuge, scheduled throughout the year.

OUTDOOR ACTIVITIES

BIKING The Lower Keys are a great place to get off busy U.S. 1 to explore the beautiful back roads. On Big Pine Key, cruise along Key Deer Boulevard (at MM 30). Those with fat tires can ride into the National Key Deer Refuge. Many lodgings offer bike rentals.

BIRD-WATCHING A stopping point for migratory birds on the Eastern Flyway, the Lower Keys are populated with many West Indian bird species, especially in spring and fall. The small, vegetated islands of the Keys are the only nesting sites in the U.S. for the white-crowned pigeon. They're also some of the few breeding places for the reddish egret, roseate spoonbill, mangrove cuckoo, and black whiskered vireo. Look for them on Bahia Honda Key and the many uninhabited islands nearby.

BOATING Dozens of shops rent powerboats for fishing and reef exploring. Most also rent tackle, sell bait, and have charter captains available. For instance, **Florida Keys Boat Rental** (**© 305/664-2003**; www.keysboat.com) offers an impressive selection of boats from $125 to $450 for a half-day and $105 to $650 for a full day. They also offer kayaks and paddle boats for eco-tours.

CANOEING & KAYAKING The Overseas Highway (U.S. 1) touches on only a few dozen of the many hundreds of islands that make up the Keys. To really see the Lower Keys, rent a kayak or canoe—perfect for these shallow waters. **Reflections Kayak Nature Tours,** operating out of the Old Wooden Bridge Fishing Camp, 1791 Bogie Dr., MM 30, Big Pine Key (**© 305/872-4668;** www.floridakeyskayaktours.com), offers fully outfitted backcountry wildlife tours, either on your own or with an expert. The expert, U.S.C.G.-licensed Captain Bill Keogh, literally wrote the book on the subject. *The Florida Keys Paddling Guide* (Countryman Press), written by Bill in 2004, covers all the unique ecosystems and inhabitants as well as launches and favorite routes from Key

Biscayne to the Dry Tortugas National Park. The 3-hour kayak tours cost $50 per person. An extended 4-hour backcountry tour for two to six people costs $125 per person and uses a mother ship to ferry kayaks and paddlers to the remote reaches of the refuge. Reservations required.

FISHING A day spent fishing, either in the shallow backcountry or in the deep sea, is a great way to ensure a fresh-fish dinner, or you can release your catch and just appreciate the challenge. Whichever you choose, **Strike Zone Charters,** U.S. 1 at MM 29.5, Big Pine Key (© **305/872-9863**), is the charter service to call. Prices for fishing boats start at $500 for a half-day and $650 for a full day with a $50 fuel surcharge added to the cost. If you have enough anglers to share the price (they take up to six people), it isn't too steep. The outfitter may also be able to match you with other interested visitors. Strike Zone also offers daily trips to Looe Key National Marine Sanctuary on a glass-bottom boat. The 2-hour trip costs $25 for viewing, $30 for snorkeling, and $40 for scuba diving. Strike Zone's 5-hour **Eco Island** excursion offers a vivid history of the Keys from the glass-bottom boat. The tour stops for snorkeling and light tackle fishing and eventually docks at an island for their famous island fish cookout. Cost is $49 per person plus an additional $4 surcharge for fuel, including mask, snorkel, fins, vests, rods, reel, bait, fishing licenses, food, and all soft drinks.

HIKING You can hike throughout the flat, marshy Keys on both marked trails and meandering coastlines. The best places to trek through nature are **Bahia Honda State Park,** at MM 29.5, and **National Key Deer Refuge,** at MM 30 (for more information on both, see "What to See & Do," above). Bahia Honda Park has a free brochure describing an excellent self-guided tour along the Silver Palm Nature Trail. You'll traverse hammocks, mangroves, and sand dunes, and cross a lagoon. The walk (less than a mile) explores a great cross section of the natural habitat in the Lower Keys and can be done in less than half an hour.

SNORKELING & SCUBA DIVING Snorkelers and divers should not miss the Keys' most dramatic reefs at the **Looe Key National Marine Sanctuary.** Here you'll see more than 150 varieties of hard and soft coral—some centuries old—as well as every type of tropical fish, including gold and blue parrotfish, moray eels, barracudas, French angels, and tarpon. **Looe Key Dive Center,** U.S. 1 at MM 27.5, Ramrod Key (© **305/872-2215;** www.diveflakeys.com), offers a mind-blowing 5-hour tour aboard a 45-foot catamaran with two shallow 1-hour dives for snorkelers and scuba divers. Snorkelers pay $40; divers pay $80. Equipment is available for rental for $10. On Wednesday and Saturday, you can do a fascinating dive to the *Adolphus Busch, Sr.,* a shipwreck off Looe Key in 100 feet of water, for $80. (See "What to See & Do," above, for other diving options.)

WHERE TO STAY

There are a number of cheap, fairly unappealing fish shacks along the highway for those who want bare-bones accommodations. So far, there are no national hotel chains in the Lower Keys. For information on lodging in cabins or trailers at local campgrounds, see "Camping," below.

Very Expensive

Little Palm Island Resort & Spa ★★★ This exclusive island escape—host to presidents, royalty, and even Howard Stern—is not just a place to stay while in the Lower Keys; it is a destination all its own. Built on a private 5½-acre island, it's accessible only by boat or seaplane. Guests stay in thatched-roof duplexes amid lush foliage and flowering tropical plants—and gentle Key deer, which are to this island what cats are to Key West. Many villas have ocean views and private decks with hammocks. Inside, the romantic suites have all the comforts of a swank beach cottage, but without phones, TVs, or alarm clocks. Mosquitoes can be a problem, even in winter. (Bring spray and lightweight, long-sleeved clothing.) Known for a stellar spa and innovative and pricey food, Little Palm also hosts visitors just for dinner, brunch, or lunch. If you're staying on the island, opt for the full American plan, which includes three meals a day.

Launch is on the ocean side of U.S. 1 at MM 28.5, Little Torch Key, FL 33042. ✆ **800/343-8567** or 305/872-2524. Fax 305/872-4843. www.littlepalmisland.com. 30 units. Winter $840–$1,695 double; off-season $640–$1,595 double. Rates include transportation to and from the island and unlimited (nonmotorized) watersports. Meal plans include 2 meals daily for $125 per person per day, 3 meals at $140 per person. AE, DC, DISC, MC, V. No children 15 and under. **Amenities:** Restaurant; bar; 2 pools (1 outdoor w/small waterfall, 1 indoor); health club; spa; extensive watersports equipment/rentals; concierge; courtesy van from Key West or Marathon airport; ferry service to and from the mainland; limited room service; in-room massage; laundry service; dry cleaning; jogging trail. *In room:* A/C, dataport, minibar, coffeemaker, hair dryer, Jacuzzi, no phone.

Inexpensive

Parmer's Resort ★ Parmer's, a fixture here for more than 20 years, is well known for its charming hospitality and helpful staff. This downscale resort offers modest but comfortable cottages, each of them unique. Some are waterfront, many have kitchenettes, and others are just a bedroom. The Wahoo room (no. 26), a one-bedroom efficiency, is especially nice, with a small sitting area that faces the water. All units have been recently updated and are very clean. Many can be combined to accommodate families. The hotel's waterfront location, not to mention the fact that it's only a half-hour from lively Key West, almost makes up for the fact that you must pay extra for maid service.

565 Barry Ave. (P.O. Box 430665), near MM 28.5, Little Torch Key, FL 33043. ✆ **305/872-2157.** Fax 305/872-2014. www.parmersresort.com. 45 units. Winter $134–$194 double, from $174 efficiency; off-season $99–$129 double, from $129 efficiency. Rates include continental breakfast. AE, DISC, MC, V. From U.S. 1, turn right onto Barry Ave. Resort is 1/2 mile down on the right. **Amenities:** Heated pool; kayak rental; bike rental; coin-op washer/dryer; boat ramp. *In room:* A/C, TV.

Camping

Bahia Honda State Park ★★★ (✆ **800/326-3521;** www.abfla.com/parks/bahiahonda/bahiahonda.html) offers some of the best camping in the Keys. It is as loaded with facilities and activities as it is with campers. But don't be discouraged by its popularity—this park encompasses more than 500 acres of land, 80 campsites spread throughout three areas, and three spacious and comfortable duplex cabins. Cabins hold up to eight guests each and come complete with linens, kitchenettes, wraparound terraces, barbecue pits, and rocking chairs. For one to four people, camping costs about $26 per site. Depending on the season, cabin prices range from $75 to $120.

Another excellent value can be found at the **KOA Sugarloaf Key Resort ★★**, near MM 20. This oceanside facility has 200 fully equipped sites, with water, electricity, and sewer, which rent for about $94 a night (no-hookup sites cost about $84). Or you can pitch a tent on the 5 acres of waterfront property. This place is especially nice because of its private beaches and access to diving, snorkeling, and boating; its grounds are also well maintained. In addition, the resort rents travel trailers: The 25-foot Dutchman sleeps six and costs about $120 a day. For details, contact the resort at P.O. Box 420469, Summerland Key, FL 33042 (✆ **800/562-7731** or 305/745-3549; fax 305/745-9889; www.koa.com).

WHERE TO DINE

There aren't many fine-dining options in the Lower Keys, with the exception of the **Dining Room at Little Palm Island,** MM 285, Little Torch Key (✆ **305/872-2551**), where you'll be wowed with gourmet French Caribbean fare that looks like a meal but tastes like a vacation (see p. 212 for the hotel listing). You need to take a ferry to this chichi private island, where you can indulge at the exquisite oceanside restaurant even if you're not staying over.

Moderate

Mangrove Mama's Restaurant SEAFOOD/CARIBBEAN As the dedicated locals who come daily for happy hour will tell you, this is a true Lower Keys institution and a dive in the best sense of the word (the restaurant is a shack that used to have a gas pump as well as a grill). Guests share the property with stray cats and some miniature horses out back. It's run-down, but in a charming Keys sort of way—they serve beer in a jelly glass. A handful of simple tables, inside and out, are shaded by banana trees and palm fronds. Fish is the menu's mainstay, although soups, salads, sandwiches, and omelets are also good. Grilled-chicken and club sandwiches are tasty alternatives to fish, as are meatless chef's salads and spicy barbecued baby back ribs. The restaurant is under new ownership, which some say has let the place slip a bit, though they still rock their Sunday brunch with amazing crab Benedict.

U.S. 1 at MM 20, Sugarloaf Key. ✆ **305/745-3030.** Main courses $10–$20; lunch $6–$10; brunch $5–$15. MC, V. Daily 11am–3pm and 5:30–10pm.

Inexpensive

Coco's Kitchen ★ CUBAN/AMERICAN This tiny storefront has been dishing out black beans, rice, and shredded beef for more than 10 years. The owners, who are actually from Nicaragua, cook not only superior Cuban food, but local specialties, Italian dishes, and Caribbean choices. Specialties include fried shrimp, whole fried yellowtail, and Cuban-style roast pork (available only on Sat). The best bet is the daily special, which may be roasted pork or fresh grouper, served with rice and beans or salad and crispy fries. Top off the huge, cheap meal with a rich caramel-soaked flan.

283 Key Deer Blvd. (in the Winn-Dixie Shopping Center), Big Pine Key. ✆ **305/872-4495.** Main courses $6–$15; breakfast $2–$10. MC, V. Mon–Sat 7am–7:30pm. Turn right at the traffic light near MM 30.5; stay in the left lane.

No Name Pub PUB FARE/PIZZA This funky old bar out in the boondocks serves snacks and sandwiches until 11pm on most nights, and drinks until midnight. Pizzas are tasty—try one topped with local shrimp. Or consider a bowl of chili with all the fixings. Everything is served on paper plates. Locals hang out at the rustic bar, one of the Keys' oldest bars, drinking beer and listening to a jukebox heavy with 1980s tunes.

1/4 mile south of No Name Bridge on N. Watson Blvd., Big Pine Key. ✆ **305/872-9115.** Pizzas $6–$18; subs $5. MC, V. Daily 11am–11pm. Turn right at Big Pine's only traffic light (near MM 30.5) onto Key Deer Blvd. Turn right on Watson Blvd. At the stop sign, turn left. Look for a small wooden sign on the left marking the spot.

THE LOWER KEYS AFTER DARK

Although the mellow islands of the Lower Keys aren't exactly known for wild nightlife, there are some friendly bars and restaurants where locals and tourists gather to hang out and drink. One of the most scenic is **Paradise Waterfont,** Barry Avenue near MM 28.5 (✆ **305/872-9989**), the only waterfront restaurant between Key West and Marathon.

The place is enclosed with windows looking out onto the water where there's a shark pond for those who are curious. Delicious food is served from 10:30am until 10pm, and the bar closes around midnight. The place even has its own brand of wine, which is currently being marketed in France, of all places. Paradise attracts an odd mix of bikers and blue-hairs daily, and is a great place to overhear local gossip and colorful metaphors. Pool tables are the main attraction, but there's also live music some nights. The drinks are reasonably priced, and the food isn't too bad, either. For another fun bar scene, see the **No Name Pub,** listed above in "Where to Dine."

3 KEY WEST ★★★

159 miles SW of Miami

There are two schools of thought on Key West—one is that it has become way too commercial, and the other is that it's still a place where you don't have to worry about being prim, proper, or even well-groomed. I think it's a bizarre fusion of both—a fascinating look at small-town America where people truly live by the (off) beat of their own drum, albeit one with a Coach outlet, Banana Republic, Starbucks, and, most recently, a handful of multimillion-dollar condo developments, thrown in to bring you back to reality. The locals, or "conchs" (pronounced *conks*), and the developers here have been at odds for years. This once low-key island has been thoroughly commercialized—there's a Hard Rock Cafe smack in the middle of Duval Street, and thousands of cruise-ship passengers descend on Mallory Square each day. It's definitely not the seedy town Hemingway and his cronies once called their own. Or is it?

Laid-back Key West still exists, but it's now found in different places: the backyard of a popular guesthouse, for example, or an art gallery, a secret garden, a clothing-optional bar, or the hip hangouts of Bahama Village. Fortunately, there are plenty of these, and Key West's greatest historical charm is found just off the beaten path. Don't be afraid to explore these residential areas, as conchs are notoriously friendly. In fact, exploring the side streets always seems to yield a new discovery. Of course, there are always the calm waters of the Atlantic and the Gulf of Mexico all around.

The heart of town offers party people a good time—that is, if your idea of a good time is the smell of stale beer, loud music, and hardly shy revelers. Here you'll find good restaurants, fun bars, live music, rickshaw rides, and lots of shopping. Key West is still very gay-centric, except during Spring Break. Same-sex couples that walk hand in hand are the norm here; if you're not open-minded and prefer to avoid this scene, look for the ubiquitous rainbow flag hanging outside gay establishments and you'll know what to expect. For the most part, however, the scene is extremely mixed and colorful. If partying isn't your thing, then avoid Duval Street—the Bourbon Street of South Florida—at all costs. Instead, take in the scenery at a dockside bar or oceanside Jacuzzi. Whatever you do, don't bother with a watch or tie—this is the home of the perennial vacation.

ESSENTIALS

GETTING THERE For directions by car, see "Essentials" (p. 192) for the Upper and Middle Keys and continue south on U.S. 1. When entering Key West, stay in the far-right lane onto North Roosevelt Boulevard, which becomes Truman Avenue in Old Town. Continue for a few blocks and you'll find yourself on **Duval Street ★**, in the heart of the city. If you stay to the left, you'll also reach the city center after passing the airport

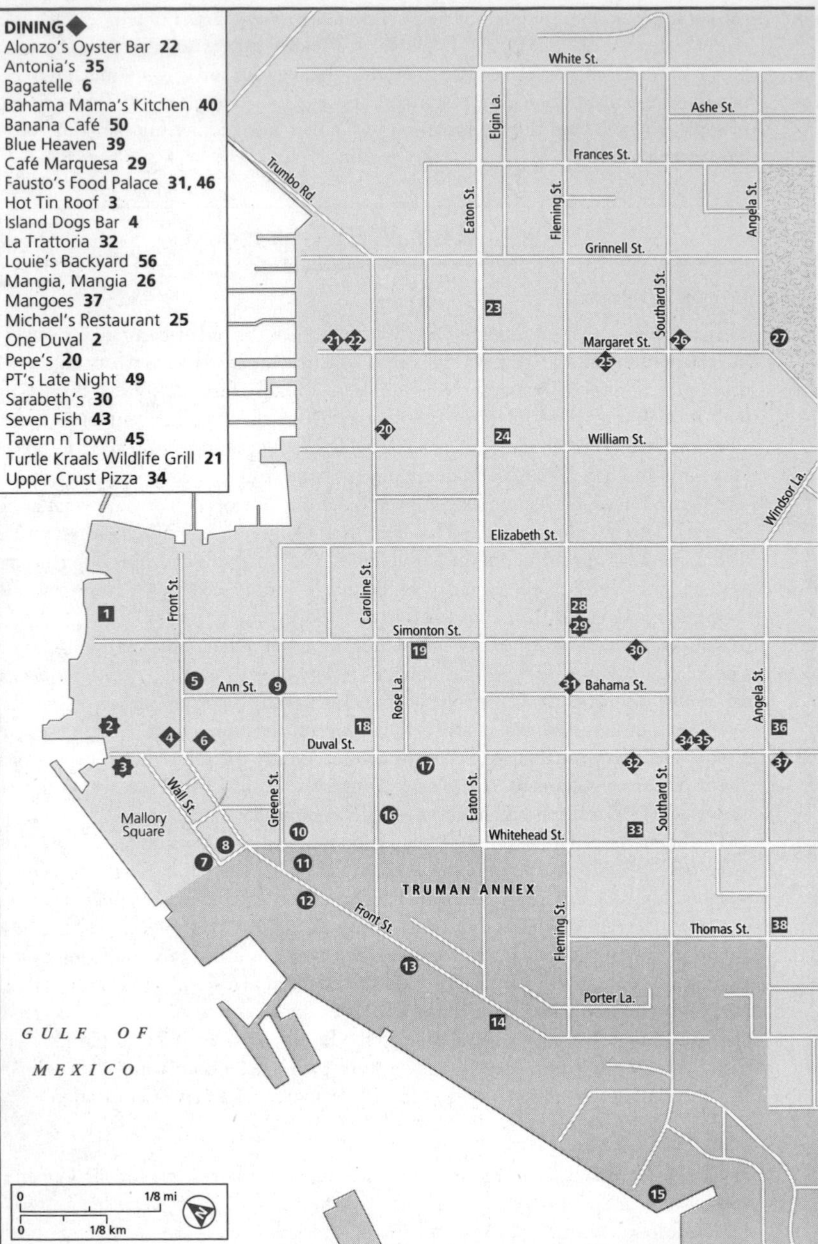

DINING
Alonzo's Oyster Bar 22
Antonia's 35
Bagatelle 6
Bahama Mama's Kitchen 40
Banana Café 50
Blue Heaven 39
Café Marquesa 29
Fausto's Food Palace 31, 46
Hot Tin Roof 3
Island Dogs Bar 4
La Trattoria 32
Louie's Backyard 56
Mangia, Mangia 26
Mangoes 37
Michael's Restaurant 25
One Duval 2
Pepe's 20
PT's Late Night 49
Sarabeth's 30
Seven Fish 43
Tavern n Town 45
Turtle Kraals Wildlife Grill 21
Upper Crust Pizza 34
White St.
Ashe St.
Elgin La.
Frances St.
Trumbo Rd.
Eaton St.
Fleming St.
Angela St.
Grinnell St.
Southard St.
Margaret St.
William St.
Windsor La.
Elizabeth St.
Front St.
Caroline St.
Simonton St.
Ann St.
Bahama St.
Rose La.
Duval St.
Wall St.
Greene St.
Mallory Square
Whitehead St.
TRUMAN ANNEX
Front St.
Thomas St.
Porter La.
GULF OF MEXICO
0 1/8 mi
0 1/8 km

ACCOMMODATIONS ■

Ambrosia Key West **28**
Angelina Guest House **38**
Big Ruby's **33**
Casa Marina Resort & Beach Club **57**
Curry Mansion Inn **18**
Doubletree Grand Key Resort **45**
The Gardens Hotel **36**
The Grand **47**
Hyatt Key West Resort & Marina **1**
Island City House Hotel **24**
Key West International Hostel & Seashell Motel **55**
Key West Marriott Beachside Hotel **45**
La Pensione **44**
Marquesa Hotel **29**
Ocean Key Resort & Spa **3**
Parrot Key Resort **45**
Pearl's Rainbow **51**
Pier House Resort & Caribbean Spa **2**
Reach Resort **54**
Simonton Court **19**
Southernmost Point Guest House **53**
Weatherstation Inn **14**
Westin Key West Resort & Marina **11**
Westwinds Inn **23**

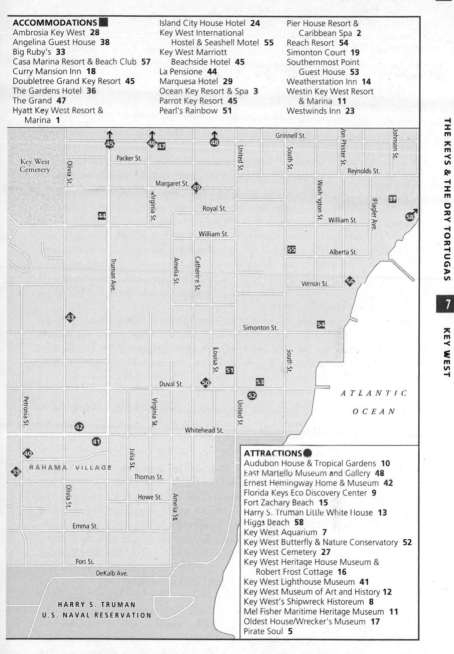

ATTRACTIONS ●

Audubon House & Tropical Gardens **10**
East Martello Museum and Gallery **48**
Ernest Hemingway Home & Museum **42**
Florida Keys Eco Discovery Center **9**
Fort Zachary Beach **15**
Harry S. Truman Little White House **13**
Higgs Beach **58**
Key West Aquarium **7**
Key West Butterfly & Nature Conservatory **52**
Key West Cemetery **27**
Key West Heritage House Museum & Robert Frost Cottage **16**
Key West Lighthouse Museum **41**
Key West Museum of Art and History **12**
Key West's Shipwreck Historeum **8**
Mel Fisher Maritime Heritage Museum **11**
Oldest House/Wrecker's Museum **17**
Pirate Soul **5**

and the remnants of historic houseboat row, where a motley collection of boats once made up one of Key West's most interesting neighborhoods.

Several regional airlines fly nonstop (about 55 min.) from Miami to Key West; fares are about $120 to $300 round-trip. **American Eagle** (✆ **800/433-7300**), **Continental** (✆ **800/525-0280**), **Delta** (✆ **800/221-1212**), and **US Airways Express** (✆ **800/428-4322**) land at **Key West International Airport,** South Roosevelt Boulevard (✆ **305/296-5439**), on the southeastern corner of the island.

Greyhound (✆ **800/231-2222;** www.greyhound.com) has buses leaving Miami for Key West every day for about $45 one-way and $80 round-trip. Seats fill up in season, so come early. The ride takes about 4½ hours.

You can also get to Key West from Ft. Myers or Marco Island via the **Key West Express** (✆ **866/KW-FERRY** [593-3779]), a 155-foot-long catamaran that travels to Key West at 40 mph. The Big Cat features two enclosed cabins, sun seated deck, observation deck, satellite TV, and full galley and bar. Prices range from $73 to $85 one-way and $119 to $130 round-trip per person.

GETTING AROUND Old Town Key West has limited parking, narrow streets, and congested traffic, so driving is more of a pain than a convenience. Unless you're staying in one of the more remote accommodations, consider trading in your car for a bicycle. The island is small and flat as a board, which makes it easy to negotiate, especially away from the crowded downtown area. Many tourists choose to cruise by moped, an option that can make navigating the streets risky, especially because there are no helmet laws in Key West. Hundreds of visitors are seriously injured each year, so be careful and spend the extra few bucks to rent a helmet.

Rates for simple one-speed cruisers start at about $10 per day. Mopeds start at about $20 for 2 hours, $35 per day, and $100 per week. The best shops include the **Bicycle Center,** 523 Truman Ave. (✆ **305/294-4556**); the **Moped Hospital,** 601 Truman Ave. (✆ **305/296-3344**); and **Tropical Bicycles & Scooter Rentals,** 1300 Duval St. (✆ **305/294-8136**). The **Bike Shop,** 1110 Truman Ave. (✆ **305/294-1073**), rents cruisers for $12 per day, $60 per week; a $150 deposit is required.

PARKING Parking in Key West's Old Town is particularly limited, but there is a well-placed **municipal parking lot** at Simonton and Angela streets, just behind the firehouse and police station. If you've brought a car, you may want to stash it here while you enjoy the very walkable downtown part of Key West.

VISITOR INFORMATION The **Key West Chamber of Commerce,** 402 Wall St., Key West, FL 33040 (✆ **800/527-8539** or 305/294-2587; www.keywestchamber.com), provides both general and specialized information. The lobby is open daily from 8:30am to 6pm; phones are answered from 8am to 8pm. The **Key West Visitor Center** (✆ **800/LAST-KEY** [527-8539]) is the area's best for information on accommodations, goings-on, and restaurants; it's open Monday through Friday from 8am to 5:30pm, Saturday and Sunday from 8:30am to 5pm. Gay travelers may want to call the **Key West Business Guild** (✆ **305/294-4603**), which represents more than 50 guesthouses and B&Bs, as well as many other gay-owned businesses (ask for its color brochure).

While you're in one of the above offices, be sure to pick up a free copy of *Sharon Wells' Walking & Biking Guide to Historic Key West.* Though I still couldn't find all the spots I wanted to in the Key West Cemetery (p. 221) while using the guide, it was helpful for historic descriptions throughout town. Sharon Wells also leads guided walking tours around the island. For information, call her at ✆ **305/294-8380** or go to www.seekeywest.com.

ORIENTATION A mere 2×4-mile island, Key West is simple to navigate, even though there's no real order to the arrangement of streets and avenues. As you enter town on U.S. 1 (Roosevelt Blvd.), you will see most of the moderate chain hotels and fast-food restaurants. The better restaurants, shops, and outfitters are crammed onto Duval Street, the main thoroughfare of Key West's Old Town. On surrounding streets, many inns and lodges are set in picturesque Victorian/Bahamian homes. On the southern side of the island are the coral-beach area and some of the larger resort hotels.

The area called Bahama Village is the furthest thing from a tourist trap, but can be a bit spotty at night if you aren't familiar with the area. With several newly opened, trendy restaurants and guesthouses, this hippie-ish neighborhood, complete with street-roaming chickens and cats, is the roughest and most urban you'll find in the Keys. You might see a few drug deals happening on street corners, but they're nothing to be overly concerned about: It looks worse than it is, and resident business owners tend to keep a vigilant eye on the neighborhood. The area is actually quite funky and should be a welcome diversion from the Duvalian mainstream.

SEEING THE SIGHTS

Key West's greenest attraction, the **Florida Keys Eco-Discovery Center,** opened in early 2007. Overlooking the waterfront at the Truman Annex (35 E. Quay Rd., © **305/809-4750**), the Center features 6,000 square feet of interactive exhibits depicting Florida Keys underwater and upland habitats—with emphasis on the ecosystem of North America's only living contiguous barrier coral reef, which parallels the Keys. Kids dig the interactive yellow submarine while adults seem to get into the cinematic depiction of an underwater abyss. Free admission. Open 9am to 4pm daily except Sunday and Monday.

Before shelling out big bucks for any of the dozens of worthwhile attractions in Key West, I recommend getting an overview on either of the two comprehensive island tours, the **Conch Tour Train** or the **Old Town Trolley** (p. 223 for both). There are simply too many attractions and historic houses to list. I've highlighted my favorites below, but I encourage you to seek out others.

Audubon House & Tropical Gardens ★★ This well-preserved 19th-century home stands as a prime example of early Key West architecture. Named after renowned painter and bird expert John James Audubon, who is said to have visited the house in 1832, the graceful two-story structure is a peaceful retreat from the bustle of Old Town. Included in the price of admission is a self-guided, half-hour audio tour that spotlights rare Audubon prints, gorgeous antiques, historical photos, and lush tropical gardens. With voices of several characters from the house's past, the tour never gets boring—though it is a bit hokey at times. Even if you don't want to explore the grounds and home, check out the impressive gift shop, which sells a variety of fine mementos at reasonable prices. Expect to spend 30 minutes to an hour.

205 Whitehead St. (btw. Greene and Caroline sts.). © **305/294-2116.** www.audubonhouse.com. Admission $11 adults, $5 children 6–12, $6.50 children 13–17. Daily 9:30am–5pm (last entry at 4:30pm).

East Martello Museum and Gallery Adjacent to the airport, the East Martello Museum is in a Civil War–era brick fort that itself is worth a visit. The museum contains a bizarre variety of exhibits that collectively do a thorough job of interpreting the city's intriguing past. Historic artifacts include model ships, a deep-sea diver's wooden air pump, a crude raft from a Cuban "boat lift," a supposedly haunted doll, and a horse-drawn hearse. Exhibits illustrate the Keys' history of salvaging, sponging, and cigar making. After seeing the galleries (which should take 45–60 min.), climb a steep spiral staircase to the top of the lookout tower for good views over the island and ocean. A member of the Key West Art and Historical Society, East Martello has two cousins: the **Key West Museum of Art and History,** 281 Front St. (✆ **305/295-6616**), and the **Key West Lighthouse Museum** (p. 221). Expect to spend 1 to 2 hours.

3501 S. Roosevelt Blvd. ✆ **305/296-3913.** www.kwahs.com/martello.htm. Admission $6 adults, $5 seniors, $3 children 8–12. Daily 9:30am–4:30pm (last entry at 4pm).

Ernest Hemingway Home and Museum ★ Hemingway's particularly handsome stone Spanish colonial house, built in 1851, was one of the first on the island to be fitted with indoor plumbing and a built-in fireplace. It also has the first swimming pool built on Key West (look for the penny that Hemingway pressed into the cement near the pool). The author owned the home from 1931 until his death in 1961, and lived here with about 50 cats, whose descendants, including the famed six-toed felines, still roam the premises. It was during those years that the Nobel Prize–winning author wrote some of his most famous works, including *For Whom the Bell Tolls, A Farewell to Arms,* and *The Snows of Kilimanjaro.* Fans may want to take the optional half-hour house tour to see his study as well as rooms with glass cabinets that store certain artifacts, books, and pieces of mail addressed to him. It's interesting (to an extent) and included in the price of admission. If you don't take the tour or have no interest in Hemingway, the price of admission is really a waste of money, except for the lovely architecture and garden. If you're feline phobic, beware: There are cats everywhere. Guided tours are given every 15 minutes, and expect to spend an hour on the property.

907 Whitehead St. (btw. Truman Ave. and Olivia St.). ✆ **305/294-1136.** Fax 305/294-2755. www.hemingwayhome.com. Admission $11 adults, $6 children. Daily 9am–5pm. Limited parking.

Harry S Truman Little White House ★★ President Truman used to refer to the White House as the "Great White Jail." On temporary leave from the Big House, Truman discovered the serenity of Key West and made his escape to what became known as the Little White House, which is open to the public for touring. The house is fully restored; the exhibits document Truman's time in the Keys. Tours run every 15 minutes and last between 45 and 50 minutes, so plan to spend more than an hour here. For fans of all things Oval Office–related, there's a presidential gift shop on the premises.

Impressions

I've a notion to move the Capitol to Key West and just stay.

—President Harry S Truman

111 Front St. ✆ **305/294-9911.** www.trumanlittlewhitehouse.com. Admission $12 adults, $6 children 11 and under. Daily 9am–4:30pm.

Key West Aquarium ★★ Kids The oldest attraction on the island, the Key West Aquarium is a modest but fascinating place. A long hallway of eye-level displays showcases dozens of varieties of fish and crustaceans. Kids can touch sea cucumbers and sea anemones in a shallow tank. If possible, catch one of the free guided tours—you can witness the dramatic feeding frenzy of the sharks, tarpon, barracudas, stingrays, and turtles. Expect to spend 1 to 1½ hours here.

1 Whitehead St. (at Mallory Sq.). ✆ **305/296-2051.** www.keywestaquarium.com. Admission $12 adults, $5 children 4–12. Website offers tickets for $1 cheaper. Tickets good for 2 consecutive days. Look for discount coupons at local hotels, at Duval St. kiosks, and from trolley and train tours. Daily 10am–6pm; tours at 11am and 1, 3, and 4pm.

Key West Butterfly & Nature Conservatory ★★ Kids Housed in a 13,000-square-foot pavilion, this attraction has nature lovers flitting with excitement, thanks to the 5,000-square-foot, glass-enclosed butterfly aviary as well as a gallery, learning center, and gift shop exploring all aspects of the butterfly world. Inside, more than 1,500 butterflies and 3,500 plants, including rare orchids, and even fish and turtles coexist in a controlled climate. You'll walk freely among the butterflies, so if you have even the slightest fear of the creatures, consider twice before entering. Expect to spend about an hour inside.

1316 Duval St. ✆ **305/296-2988.** www.keywestbutterfly.com. Admission $10 adults, $8.50 seniors, $7.50 children 4–12. Daily 9am–5pm; last ticket sold at 4:30pm.

Key West Cemetery ★★★ Finds This funky cemetery is the epitome of quirky Key West: irreverent and humorous. Many tombs are stacked several high, condominium style, because the rocky soil made digging 6 feet under nearly impossible for early settlers. Epitaphs reflect residents' lighthearted attitudes toward life and death. I TOLD YOU I WAS SICK is one of the more famous, as is the tongue in cheek widow's inscription AT LEAST I KNOW WHERE HE'S SLEEPING TONIGHT. Pick up a copy of *Sharon Wells' Walking & Biking Guide to Historic Key West* (p. 218). Some of the inscriptions are hard to find even with the free walking-tour guide, but this place is fun to explore. Plan to spend 30 minutes to an hour or more depending on how morbid your curiosity is.

Entrance at the corner of Margaret and Angela sts. Free admission. Daily dawn–dusk.

Key West Heritage House For a glimpse into one of the oldest houses in Key West, check out the Heritage House Museum, the former 1834 home of Jessie Porter, a Key West preservationist who hosted the likes of Robert Frost, Tennessee Williams, Ernest Hemingway, Gloria Swanson, and Tallulah Bankhead. Furnished with 19th-century antiques, the house is a fascinating look at 19th- and early-20th-century Key West. Guided tours are informative and entertaining, sort of an antique version of an *E! True Hollywood Story.* Expect to spend 30 minutes to an hour.

410 Caroline St. ✆ **305/296-3573.** www.heritagehousemuseum.org. Guided tour $7, self-guided tour $5. Mon–Sat 10am–4pm.

Key West Lighthouse Museum ★ When the Key West Lighthouse opened in 1848, it signaled the end of a profitable era for the pirate salvagers who looted reef-stricken ships. The story of this and other area lighthouses is illustrated in a small museum that was formerly the keeper's quarters. It's worth mustering the energy to climb the 88 claustrophobic steps to the top, where you'll be rewarded with magnificent panoramic views of Key West and the ocean. Expect to spend 30 minutes to an hour.

938 Whitehead St. ✆ **305/295-6616.** www.kwahs.com Admission $10 adults, $9 seniors and locals, $5 children 7–12. Daily 9:30am–4:30pm.

Key West's Shipwreck Historeum You'll see more impressive artifacts at nearby Mel Fisher's museum, but for the morbidly curious, shipwrecks should rank right up there with car wrecks. For those of you who can't help but look, this museum is the place to be for everything you ever wanted to know about shipwrecks and more. See movies, artifacts, and a real-life wrecker, who will be more than happy to indulge your curiosity about the wrecking industry that preoccupied the early pioneers of Key West. Depending on your level of interest, you can expect to spend up to 2 hours here.

1 Whitehead St. (at Mallory Sq.). ✆ **305/292-8990.** Fax 305/292-5536. www.shipwreckhistoreum.com. Admission $12 adults, $5 children 4–12. Website sells tickets for $1 cheaper. Shows daily every half-hour 9:45am–4:45pm.

Going, Going, Gone: Where to Catch the Famous Key West Sunset

A tradition in Key West, the Sunset Celebration can be relaxing or overwhelming, depending on your vantage point. If you're in town, you must check out this ritual at least once. Every evening, locals and visitors gather at the docks behind Mallory Square (at the westernmost end of Whitehead St.) to celebrate the day gone by. Secure a spot on the docks early to experience the carnival of portrait artists, acrobats, food vendors, animal acts, and other performers trading on the island's bohemian image. But the carnival atmosphere isn't for everyone: In season, the crowd can be overwhelming, especially when the cruise ships are in port. Also, hold on to your bags and wallets, as the tight crowds make Mallory Square at sunset prime pickpocketing territory.

A more refined choice is the Westin's **Sunset Deck** (✆ **305/294-4000**), a luxurious second-floor bar on Front Street, right next door to Mallory Square. From the civilized calm of a casual bar, you can look down on the mayhem with a drink in hand.

Also near the Mallory madness is the bar at the **Ocean Key Resort,** at the very tip of Duval Street (✆ **800/328-9815** or 305/296-7701). This long open-air pier serves drinks and decent bar food against a dramatic pink-and-yellow-streaked sky.

For the very best potent cocktails and great bar food on an outside patio or enclosed lounge, try **Pier House Resort and Caribbean Spa's Havana Docks,** 1 Duval St. (✆ **305/296-4600**). There's usually live music and a lively gathering of visitors enjoying this island's bounty. The bar is right on the water and makes a prime sunset-viewing spot.

Mel Fisher Maritime Heritage Museum ★★ This museum honors local hero Mel Fisher, whose death in 1998 was mourned throughout South Florida and who, along with a crew of other salvagers, found a multimillion-dollar treasure trove in 1985 aboard the wreck of the Spanish galleon *Nuestra Señora de Atocha.* If you're into diving, pirates, and sunken treasures, check out this small museum, full of doubloons, pieces of eight, emeralds, and solid-gold bars (one of them you can lift!). A 1700 English merchant slave ship, the only tangible evidence of the transatlantic slave trade, is on view on the museum's second floor. An exhibition telling the story of more than 1,400 African slaves captured in Cuban waters and brought to Key West for sanctuary is the museum's latest, most fascinating exhibit to date. Expect to spend 1 to 3 hours.

200 Greene St. ✆ **305/294-2633.** www.melfisher.org. Admission $12 adults, $11 students and seniors, $6 children 6–12. Daily 9:30am–5pm. Take U.S. 1 to Whitehead St. and turn left on Greene.

Oldest House/Wrecker's Museum ★ Dating from 1829, this old New England Bahama House has survived pirates, hurricanes, fires, warfare, and economic ups and downs. The one-and-a-half-story home was designed by a ship's carpenter and incorporates many features from maritime architecture, including portholes and a ship's hatch designed for ventilation before the advent of air-conditioning. Especially interesting is

Moments **A Great Escape**

Many people complain that Key West's quirky, quaint panache has been lost to the vulture of capitalism, evidenced by the glut of T-shirt shops and tacky bars. But that's not entirely so. For a quiet respite, visit the **Key West Tropical Forest Botanical Gardens** (© **305/296-1504;** www.keywestbotanicalgarden.org), a little-known slice of serenity tucked between the Aqueduct Authority plant and the Key West Golf Course. The 11-acre gardens—maintained by volunteers and funded by donations—contain the last hardwood hammock in Key West, plus a colorful representation of wildflowers, butterflies, and birds. Over 60 endangered botanical species are alive and well here. A genetically cloned tree is one of the many sites at "the only frost-free tropical moist garden in the continental United States." Located at Botanical Garden Way and College Road, Stock Island. Free admission but a donation of $5 is suggested. Open daily from 8am to sunset. Follow College Road; then turn right just past Bayshore Manor.

the detached kitchen building outfitted with a brick "beehive" oven and vintage cooking utensils. Although not a must-see on the Key West tour, history and architecture buffs will appreciate the finely preserved details and the glimpse of a slower, easier time in the island's life. Plan to spend 30 minutes to an hour.

322 Duval St. © **305/294-9501.** Free admission. Daily 10am–4pm.

Pirate Soul ★ Kids Thanks to Johnny Depp and Disney's *Pirates of the Caribbean,* pirates have never been hotter. This museum is dedicated to everything about the legendary seafaring rogues, featuring more than 500 artifacts from the golden age of piracy, as well as animatronics and interactive exhibits. Among the highlights are the only authentic pirate treasure chest in America, originally belonging to Captain Thomas Tew, and Blackbeard's original blunderbuss. As with any kitschy museum, there's a store where you can buy all sorts of gear, from eye patches to bath products sporting the Jolly Roger. If you find yourself thirsty or hungry, Rum Barrel is the museum's homage to grub and grog. Plan to spend 30 minutes to an arrrrrrrgh, I mean hour.

524 Front St. © **305/292-1113.** www.piratesoul.com. Admission $15 adults, $9 children 6–12. Tickets are cheaper on the website. Daily 9am–7pm.

ORGANIZED TOURS

BY TRAM & TROLLEY-BUS Yes, it's more than a bit hokey to sit on this 60-foot tram of yellow cars, but it's worth it—at least once. The city's whole story is packed into a neat, 90-minute package on the **Conch Tour Train,** which covers the island and all its rich, raunchy history. In operation since 1958, the cars are open-air, which can make the ride uncomfortable in bad weather. The engine of the "train" is a propane-powered jeep disguised as a locomotive. Tours depart from both Mallory Square and the Welcome Center, near where U.S. 1 becomes North Roosevelt Boulevard, on the less-developed side of the island. For information, call © **305/294-5161** or go to www.conchtourtrain.com. The cost is $29 for adults, $14 for children 4 to 12. Tickets are cheaper on the website. Daily departures are every half-hour from 9am to 4:30pm.

The **Old Town Trolley** is the choice in bad weather or if you're staying at one of the hotels on its route. Humorous drivers maintain a running commentary as the enclosed

Literary Key West

Counting Ernest Hemingway and Tennessee Williams among your denizens would give any city the right to call itself a literary mecca. But over the years, tiny Key West has been home—or at least home away from home—to dozens of literary types who are drawn to some combination of its gentle pace, tropical atmosphere, and lighthearted mood (not to mention its lingering reputation for an oft-ribald lifestyle). Writers have long known that more than a few muses prowl the tree-laden streets of Key West.

Robert Frost first visited Key West in 1934 and wintered here for the remainder of his life. In the early–20th century, writers such as John Dewey, Archibald MacLeish, John Dos Passos, Wallace Stevens, and S. J. Perelman were drawn to the island. Even as Key West boomed and busted and boomed again, and despite the island's growing popularity with world travelers, writers continued to move to Key West or to visit it with such regularity that they were deemed honorary "conchs." Novelists Phil Caputo, Tom McGuane, Jim Harrison, John Hershey, Alison Lurie, and Robert Stone were among these.

Of course, one of Key West's favorite sons also earned a spot in the annals of local literary history. Famous for his good-time, tropical-laced music, Jimmy Buffett was also a surprisingly well-received novelist in the 1990s. Although Buffett now makes the infinitely ritzier Palm Beach his Florida home, his presence is still felt in virtually every corner of Key West.

But it is Nobel Prize–winner and avid outdoorsman Ernest Hemingway who is most identified with Key West. Much of the island has changed since he lived here from 1931 to 1961. Even the famous Sloppy Joe's bar, which Hemingway frequented mostly from 1933 to 1937, has changed locations (reportedly without closing—customers picked up their drinks and whatever else they could carry from the bar and brought it all down the block to the new location, and service resumed with barely a blink!). Fortunately, the Ernest Hemingway Home and Museum (p. 220) has been lovingly preserved. But to get the best feel for what Hemingway loved most about Key West, visit the docks at Garrison Bight. It is from here that Hemingway and his many famous (and infamous) friends and contemporaries departed for Caribbean ports of call and for sport upon the sea.

Key West pays homage to its literary legacy with the annual Key West Literary Seminar in January. For information, call ✆ **888/293-9291** or visit www.keywestliteraryseminar.org.

trolley loops around the island's streets past all the major sights. Trolley buses depart from Mallory Square and other points around the island, including many area hotels. For details, call ✆ **305/296-6688** or visit www.trolleytours.com. Tours are $29 for adults, $14 for children 4 to 12. Tickets are cheaper on the website. Departures are daily every half-hour (though not always on the half-hour) from 9am to 4:30pm.

Whichever you choose, both of these historic, trivia-packed tours are well worth the price of tickets.

BY AIR Proclaimed by the mayor as "the official air force of the Conch Republic," **Island Airplane Tours,** at Key West Airport, 3469 S. Roosevelt Blvd. (✆ **305/294-8687**), offers windy rides in its open-cockpit 1940 Waco biplanes that take you over the reefs and around the islands. Thrill-seekers will also enjoy a spin in the company's S2-B aerobatics airplane, which does loops, rolls, and sideways figure eights. Company owner Fred Cabanas was decorated in 1991, after he spotted a Cuban airman defecting to the United States in a Russian-built MIG fighter. Sightseeing flights cost $60 to $245 for two people, depending on duration.

BY BOAT The catamaran ***The Pride of Key West*** and the glass-bottom boat ***Fireball,*** both at Zero Duval St. (✆ **305/296-6293;** www.keywestattractions.org/pride of key west.php), depart on daytime coral-reef tours and evening sunset cruises (call for times). Reef trips cost $35 per person; sunset cruises are $37 per person. Kids ages 5 through 12 sail on all cruises for $15.

The schooner ***Western Union*** (✆ **305/292-9830;** www.schoonerwesternunion.com) was built in 1939 and served as a cable-repair vessel until it was designated the flagship of the city of Key West and began day, sunset, and charter sailings. Sunset sailings are especially memorable and include entertainment, cocktails, and a cannon fire. Prices vary; inquire for details.

A new boat tour combines Florida Keys sunsets with delectable Keys cuisine. **Sunset Culinaire Tours** (✆ **305/296-0982;** www.sunsetculinaire.com) is a cruise aboard the vessel *RB's Lady* and includes a tour of Key West harbor as the sun sinks below the horizon, and a gourmet dinner prepared by Chef Brian Kirkpatrick. The vessel departs from Sunset Marina, off U.S. 1 at 5555 College Rd., at 5:30pm nightly. Boarding time is 5pm and the cost is $75 per person.

OTHER TOURS **Sharon Wells** (✆ **305/294-8380;** www.seekeywest.com) leads a slew of great tours throughout the island, focusing on things as diverse as literature, architecture, and places connected with the island's gay and lesbian culture.

For a lively look at Key West, try the **Key West Pub Crawl** (✆ **305/744-9804;** www.keywestwalkingtours.com), a tour of the island's most famous bars. It's given on Tuesday and Friday nights at 8pm, lasts 2½ hours, costs $30, and includes five (!) drinks. Another fun option is the 1-mile, 90-minute **ghost tour** (✆ **305/294-WALK** [294-9255]; www.hauntedtours.com), leaving daily at 8pm from the Holiday Inn La Concha, 430 Duval St. Cost is $15 for adults and $10 for children 11 and under. This spooky and interesting tour gives participants insight into many old island legends.

Key West's **Ghosts and Legends Tour** (✆ **866/622-4467** or 305/294-1713) is a fun, 90-minute narrated tour of the island and spirits that don't come in a plastic cup or mug. You'll walk through the shadowy streets and lanes of Old Town, stopping at allegedly haunted Victorian mansions, and learning about fascinating island pirate lore, voodoo superstitions and rituals, a Count who lived with the corpse of his beloved, and other bizarre yet true aspects of this eerie place. Tours depart nightly from the Porter Mansion on the corner of Duval and Caroline Street. Space is limited and reservations are required. Tickets are usually $18, but with a mention of Frommer's it's $15.

Since the early 1940s, Key West has been a haven for gay luminaries such as Tennessee Williams and Broadway legend Jerry Herman. A trolley tour of **Gay Key West,** created by the Key West Business Guild, showcases the history, contributions, and landmarks associated with the island's flourishing gay and lesbian culture. Highlights include Williams's house, the art gallery owned by Key West's first gay mayor, and a variety of guesthouses whose gay owners fueled the island's architectural-restoration movement. The

Parrotheads on Parade

For Jimmy Buffett fans, or "parrotheads," as they're also known, **Trails and Tales of Key West** (✆ **305/292-2040;** www.trailsandtalesofkeywest.com) is an amusing, 2-hour guided walking tour in which Key West's finest storytellers share tales of Jimmy Buffett, Captain Tony, Ernest Hemingway, Mel Fisher, and more. The informative and often hilarious guides lead you past the hangouts and other high points of these colorful characters' Key West. Visit legendary pubs and the historic seaport; plus, hear fascinating stories about the Conch Republic and get some insider tips to the secrets of Key West. This 2-hour tour departs daily at 4pm from **Captain Tony's Saloon,** 428 Greene St., where Buffett used to hang out and perform, and ends at—you guessed it—**Margaritaville Cafe,** on Duval Street. The tour conveniently goes during happy hour. Tickets are $20 for adults, and $10 for children 6 to 12. Bring cash or traveler's checks; no credit cards are accepted. Reservations are required.

70-minute tour takes place Saturday at 11am, starting and ending at City of Key West parking lot, corner of Simonton Street and Angela Street. Look for the trolley with the rainbow flags. The cost is $25. Call ✆ **305/294-4603.**

OUTDOOR ACTIVITIES

BEACHES Unlike the rest of the Keys, Key West actually has a few small beaches, although they don't compare with the state's wide natural wonders up the coast; the Keys' beaches are typically narrow and rocky. Here are your options: Smathers Beach, off South Roosevelt Boulevard, west of the airport; Higgs Beach, along Atlantic Boulevard, between White Street and Reynolds Road; and Fort Zachary Beach, located off the western end of Southard Boulevard.

A magnet for partying teenagers, **Smathers Beach** is Key West's largest and most overpopulated. Despite the number of rowdy teens, the beach is actually quite clean and looks lovely since its renovation in the spring of 2000. If you go early enough in the morning, you may notice people sleeping on the beach from the night before.

Higgs Beach is a favorite among Key West's gay crowds, but what many people don't know is that beneath the sand is an unmarked cemetery of African slaves who died while waiting for freedom. Higgs has a playground and tennis courts, and is near the minute Rest Beach, which is actually hidden by the White Street pier.

Although there is an entrance fee ($3.50 per car, plus more for each passenger), I recommend **Fort Zachary Beach,** as it has a great historic fort, a Civil War museum, and a large picnic area with tables, barbecue grills, restrooms, and showers. Large trees scattered across 87 acres provide shade for those who are reluctant to bake in the sun.

BIKING & MOPEDING A popular mode of transportation for locals and visitors, bikes and mopeds are available at many rental outlets in the city. Escape the hectic downtown scene and explore the island's scenic side streets by heading away from Duval Street toward South Roosevelt Boulevard and the beachside enclaves along the way.

DIVING One of the area's largest scuba schools, **Dive Key West, Inc.,** 3128 N. Roosevelt Blvd. (✆ **800/426-0707** or 305/296-3823; www.divekeywest.com), offers instruction at all levels; its dive boats take participants to scuba and snorkel sites on nearby reefs.

Key West Marine Park (✆ **305/294-3100**), the newest dive park along the island's Atlantic shore, incorporates no-motor "swim-only" lanes marked by buoys, providing swimmers and snorkelers with a safe way to explore the waters around Key West. The park's boundaries stretch from the foot of Duval Street to Higgs Beach.

Wreck dives and night dives are two of the special offerings of **Lost Reef Adventures,** 261 Margaret St. (✆ **800/952-2749** or 305/296-9737). Regularly scheduled runs and private charters can be arranged. Phone for departure information.

For a map of the Florida **Keys Shipwreck Heritage Trail,** an entire network of wrecks from Key Largo to Key West, go to http://floridakeys.noaa.gov/sanctuary_resources/shipwreck_trail/welcome.html.

Also see **Mosquito Coast Outfitters,** under "Kayaking," below.

FISHING As any angler will tell you, there's no fishing like Keys fishing. Key West has it all: bonefish, tarpon, dolphin, tuna, grouper, cobia, and more—sharks, too.

Step aboard a small exposed skiff for an incredibly diverse day of fishing. In the morning, you can head offshore for sailfish or dolphin (the fish, not the mammal), and then by afternoon get closer to land for a shot at tarpon, permit, grouper, or snapper. Here in Key West, you can probably pick up more cobia—one of the best fighting and eating fish around—than anywhere else in the world. For a real fight, ask your skipper to go for the tarpon—the greatest fighting fish there is, famous for its dramatic "tail walk" on the water after it's hooked. Shark fishing is also popular.

You'll find plenty of competition among the charter-fishing boats in and around Mallory Square. You can negotiate a good deal at **Charter Boat Row,** 1801 N. Roosevelt Ave. (across from the Shell station), home to more than 30 charter-fishing and party boats. Just show up to arrange your outing, or call **Garrison Bight Marina** (✆ **305/292-8167**) for details.

The advantage of the smaller, more expensive charter boats is that you can call the shots. They'll take you where you want to go, to fish for what you want to catch. These "light tackles" are also easier to maneuver, which means you can go to backcountry spots for tarpon and bonefish, as well as out to the open ocean for tuna and dolphinfish. You'll really be able to feel the fish, and you'll get some good fights, too. Larger boats, for up to six or seven people, are cheaper and are best for kingfish, billfish, and sailfish. Consider Capt. Vinnie Argiro's **Heavy Hitters Charters** (✆ **305/745-6665**) if you want a light-tackle experience. For a larger boat, try Capt. Henry Otto's 44-foot ***Sunday,*** docked at the Hyatt in Key West (✆ **305/294-7052**).

Reel Deals

When looking for the best deals on fishing excursions, know that the bookers from the kiosks in town generally take 20% of a captain's fee in addition to an extra monthly fee. You can usually save yourself money by booking directly with a captain or by going straight to one of the docks.

The huge commercial party boats are more for sightseeing than serious angling, though you can be lucky enough to get a few bites at one of the fishing holes. One especially good deal is the ***Gulfstream III*** (✆ **305/296-8494;** www.keywestpartyboat.com), an all-day charter that goes out daily from 11am to 4:30pm. You'll pay $55 for adults, $35 for kids 11 and under, and the price includes rod, bait, tackle, and license. This 65-foot party boat usually has at least 30 other anglers. Bring your own cooler or buy snacks onboard. Beer and wine are allowed.

Serious anglers should consider the light-tackle boats that leave from **Oceanside Marina,** on Stock Island at 5950 Peninsula Ave., 1½ miles off U.S. 1 (© **305/294-4676**). It's a 20-minute drive from Old Town on the Atlantic side. There are more than 30 light-tackle guides, which range from flatbed, backcountry skiffs to 28-foot open boats. There are also a few larger charters and a party boat that goes to the Dry Tortugas. Call for details.

For a light-tackle outing with a very colorful Key West flair, call **Capt. Bruce Cronin** (© **305/294-4929;** www.fishbruce.com) or **Capt. Kenny Harris** (© **305/294-8843**), two of the more famous (and pricey) captains working these docks for more than 20 years. You'll pay from $750 for a full day, usually about 8am to 4pm, and from $500 for a half-day.

GOLF A relative newcomer in terms of local recreation, golf is gaining in popularity here, as it is in many visitor destinations. The area's only public golf club is **Key West Golf Club** (© **305/294-5232;** www.keywestgolf.com), an 18-hole course at the entrance to the island of Key West at MM 4.5 (turn onto College Rd. to the course entrance). Designed by Rees Jones, the course, which was renovated in 2008, has plenty of mangroves and water hazards on its 6,526 yards. It's open to the public and has a new pro shop. Call ahead for tee-time reservations. Rates are $95 per player during off-season and $165 in season, or $70 off-season and $95 in season after 2:30pm, including cart.

KAYAKING Housed in a woodsy wine bar, **Mosquito Coast Outfitters,** 1017 Duval St. (© **305/294-7178;** www.mosquitocoast.net), operates a first-rate kayaking and snorkeling tour every day as long as the weather is mild. The tours depart at 9am sharp and return around 3pm. Included in the $60 price are snacks, soft drinks, and a guided tour of the mangrove-studded islands of Sugar Key or Geiger Key, just north of Key West. The tour is primarily for kayaking, but you'll have the opportunity to get in the water for snorkeling, if you're interested. A new 2-hour tour called the Doggie Paddle Tour allows you to bring your furry friend along.

SHOPPING

You'll find all kinds of unique gifts and souvenirs in Key West, from coconut postcards to Key lime pies. On Duval Street, T-shirt shops outnumber almost any other business. If you must get a wearable memento, be careful of unscrupulous salespeople. Despite efforts to curtail the practice, many shops have been known to rip off unwitting shoppers. It pays to check the prices and the exchange rate before signing any sales slips. You are entitled to a written estimate of any T-shirt work before you pay for it.

At Mallory Square, you'll find the **Clinton Street Market,** an overly air-conditioned mall of kiosks and stalls designed for the many cruise-ship passengers who never venture beyond this super-commercial zone. There are some delicious coffee and candy shops, and some high-priced hats and shoes. There's also a free and clean restroom.

Once the main industry of Key West, cigar making is enjoying renewed success at the handful of factories that survived the slow years. Stroll through **Cigar Alley** (while on Greene St., go 2 blocks west and you'll hit Cigar Alley, also known as Pirate's Alley), where you will find *viejitos* (little old men) rolling fat stogies just as they used to do in their homeland across the Florida Straits. Stop at the **Conch Republic Cigar Factory,** 512 Greene St. (© **305/295-9036**), for an excellent selection of imported and locally rolled smokes, including the famous El Hemingway. Remember, buying or selling Cuban-made cigars is illegal. Shops advertising "Cuban cigars" are usually referring to domestic cigars made from tobacco grown from seeds that were brought from Cuba decades ago. To be fair, though, many premium cigars today are grown from Cuban seed tobacco—only it is grown in Latin America and the Caribbean, not Cuba.

If you're looking for local or Caribbean art, you'll find nearly a dozen galleries and shops clustered on Duval Street between Catherine and Fleming streets. There are also some excellent shops scattered on the side streets. One worth seeking out is the **Haitian Art Co.,** 600 Frances St. (© **305/296-8932**), where you can browse through room upon room of original paintings from well-known and obscure Haitian artists, in a range of prices from a few dollars to a few thousand. Also check out **Cuba, Cuba!** at 814 Duval St. (© **305/295-9442;** www.cubacubastore.com), where you'll see paintings, sculpture, and photos by Cuban artists, as well as books and art from the island.

From sweet to spicy, **Peppers of Key West,** 602 Greene St. (© **305/295-9333;** www.peppersofkeywest.com), is a hot-sauce-lover's heaven, with hundreds of variations, from mild to brutally spicy. Grab a seat at the tasting bar and be prepared to let your taste buds sizzle. ***Tip:*** Bring beer, and they'll let you taste some of their secret sauces!

Literature and music buffs will appreciate the many bookshops and record stores on the island. **Key West Island Bookstore,** 513 Fleming St. (© **305/294-2904**), carries new, used, and rare books, and specializes in fiction by residents of the Keys, including Ernest Hemingway, Tennessee Williams, Shel Silverstein, Ann Beattie, Richard Wilbur, and John Hersey. The bookstore is open daily from 10am to 9pm.

For anything else, from bed linens to candlesticks to clothing, go to downtown's oldest and most renowned department store, **Fast Buck Freddie's,** 500 Duval St. (© **305/294-2007**). For the same merchandise at reduced prices, try **Half Buck Freddie's** ★, 726 Caroline St. (© **305/294-2007**), where you can shop for out-of-season bargains and "rejects" from the main store.

Also check out **KW Light Gallery,** 534 Fleming St. (© **305/294-0566**), for high-quality contemporary photography as well as historic images and other artwork relating to the Keys or to the concept of light and its varied interpretations. The gallery is open Thursday through Tuesday from 10am to 6pm (10am–4pm in summer).

WHERE TO STAY

You'll find a wide variety of places to stay in Key West, from resorts with all the amenities to seaside motels, quaint bed-and-breakfasts, and clothing-optional guesthouses. Unless you're in town during Key West's most popular holidays—Fantasy Fest (around Halloween), where Mardi Gras meets South Florida for the NC-17 set and most hotels have outrageous rates and 5-night minimums; Hemingway Days (in July), where Papa is seemingly and eerily alive and well; and Christmas and New Year's—or for a big fishing tournament (many are held Oct–Dec) or a boat-racing tourney, you can almost always find a place to stay at the last minute. However, you may want to book early, especially in winter, when prime properties fill up and many require 2- or 3-night minimum stays. Prices at these times are extremely high. Finding a decent room for less than $100 a night is a real trick.

Another suggestion, and my recommendation, is to call **Vacation Key West** (© **800/595-5397** or 305/295-9500; www.vacationkw.com), a wholesaler that offers discounts of 20% to 30% and is skilled at finding last-minute deals. It represents mostly larger hotels and motels, but can also place visitors in guesthouses. The phones are answered Monday through Friday from 9am to 6pm, and Saturday from 11am to 2pm. **Key West Innkeepers Association** (© **800/492-1911** or 305/292-3600) can also help you find lodging in any price range from among its members and affiliates.

Gay travelers may want to call the **Key West Business Guild** (✆ **305/294-4603**), which represents more than 50 guesthouses and B&Bs in town, as well as many other gay-owned businesses. Be advised that most gay guesthouses have a clothing-optional policy. One of the most elegant and popular is **Big Ruby's,** 409 Applerouth Lane (✆ **800/477-7829** or 305/296-2323; www.bigrubys.com), located on a little alley just off Duval Street. Rates start at $173 double in peak season and $125 off-season. A low cluster of buildings surrounds a lush courtyard where a hearty breakfast is served each morning and wine is poured at dusk. The all-male guests hang out by the pool, tanning in the buff.

For women only, **Pearl's Rainbow,** 525 United St. (✆ **800/74-WOMYN** [9-6696] or 305/292-1450; www.pearlsrainbow.com), is a large, fairly well-maintained guesthouse with lots of privacy and amenities, including two pools and two hot tubs. Rates range from $89 to $369.

Very Expensive

The Gardens Hotel ★★★ *Finds* At last, the true Garden of Eden has been located—and it's on Angela Street in Key West. Once a private residence, the Gardens Hotel (whose main house is listed on the National Register of Historic Places) is hidden amid exotic botanical gardens. Behind the greenery is a Bahamian-style hideaway with luxuriously appointed rooms in the main house, garden and courtyard rooms in the carriage house, and one ultrasecluded cottage. Though the place is within walking distance of frenetic Duval Street, you may not want to leave. A pretty free-form pool is centered in the courtyard, where a Tiki bar serves libations. The Jacuzzi is hidden behind foliage. Guest rooms have hardwood floors, plantation beds with Tempurpedic mattresses, and marble bathrooms. Winding brick pathways leading to secluded seating areas in the private gardens make for an idyllic getaway. On Sunday afternoons the hotel features live jazz in the gardens. ***Note:*** If you plan to party, do not stay here—guests tend to be on the quieter, more sophisticated side.

526 Angela St., Key West, FL 33040. ✆ **800/526-2664** or 305/294-2661. Fax 305/292-1007. www.gardenshotel.com. 17 units. Winter $300–$415 double, $495–$620 suite; off-season $175–$325 double, $225–$395 suite. Rates include continental breakfast. AE, DC, MC, V. **Amenities:** Bar; pool. *In room:* A/C, TV, hair dryer, safe.

Key West Marriott Beachside Hotel ★★★ Key West's newest luxury resort, this one is right at the entrance to Key West, overlooking the Gulf of Mexico and the only one in town to boast a helicopter pad on the roof for some of the resort's more boldface names. The resort has hyperluxe one-, two-, and three-bedroom suites as well as king bedrooms, all adorned with oversize balconies with waterfront views, open gourmet

It's Not Easy Being a Green Hotel

The **Gardens** is one of the first **"Florida Green Lodging Hotels"** in the Keys, meaning the hotel has installed energy-efficient light bulbs throughout the property, uses all "green" cleaning products, eliminated plastics and Styrofoam use, educates staff and guests of the importance of recycling, and raises room temperatures to 78°F (26°C) when not in use, among other eco-friendly efforts. For more info on the organization and participating hotels, see www.floridagreenlodging.org.

kitchens, marble Jacuzzi tubs, and, on the third floor, private sun decks. Tavern N Town Restaurant, Key West's culinary destination, features a theater kitchen and a gourmet menu of tapas, pizzas, fantastic steaks, and taste of the island seafood, and a private dining room for up to 16 guests. At the tropical waterfront pool, you'll find available private cabanas, a private tanning beach, and the Blue Bar, a casual dining oasis with always a generous splash of island geniality. Although the resort is located on busy Roosevelt Boulevard, home to chain motels and restaurants, you'll feel like you're in another world once you enter the premises.

3841 N. Roosevelt Blvd., Key West, FL 33040. ✆ **800/546-0885** or 305/296-8100. Fax 305/293-0205. www.beachsidekeywest.com. 222 units. Winter $539 double, $739–$1,889 suite; off-season $299 double, $499–$1,649 suite. AE, DC, MC, V. Valet parking $20 per day. **Amenities:** 2 restaurants; 2 bars; heated pool; water-view fitness center; watersports equipment/rentals; moped/bike rental; 24-hr. concierge that can facilitate almost anything; transportation to and from downtown Key West; business center; Wi-Fi in common areas; in-room massage; babysitting; dry-cleaning services; private helicopter pad; private cabanas; private beach on the Gulf; bell service. *In room:* A/C, LCD flatscreen TV w/satellite, Internet access, full gourmet kitchen (in suites) that can be stocked w/personal preferences, coffeemaker, hair dryer, iron, washer/dryer (in suites).

Ocean Key Resort and Spa ★ You can't beat the location of this 100-room resort, at the foot of Mallory Square, the epicenter of the sunset ritual. Ocean Key also features a Gulf-side heated pool and the lively Sunset Pier, where guests can wind down with cocktails and live music. Guest rooms are huge and luxuriously appointed, with living and dining areas, oversize Jacuzzis, and views of the Gulf, the harbor, or Mallory Square and Duval Street. The two-bedroom suite is 1,200 square feet and has a full kitchen, three beds, and a large private balcony. The property is adorned in classic Key West decor, from the tile floors and hand-painted furniture to the pastel art. The Indonesian-inspired Spa Terre is perhaps the best in town. The resort's restaurant, Hot Tin Roof (p. 238), is one of Key West's best.

Zero Duval St. (near Mallory Docks), Key West, FL 33040. ✆ **800/328-9815** or 305/296-7701. Fax 305/292-2198. www.oceankey.com. 100 units. Winter $379–$679 double, $479–$1,149 suite; off-season $239–$439 double, $319–$639 suite. AE, DC, MC, V. **Amenities:** 2 restaurants; 3 bars; heated pool; watersports equipment/rentals; moped/bike rental; concierge; room service; in-room massage; babysitting; laundry services. *In room:* A/C, TV, Wi-Fi, minibar, coffeemaker, hair dryer, iron.

Westin Key West Resort & Marina ★★ Ideally situated in the heart of Old Town, the Westin Key West Resort & Marina is next to Mallory Square and within walking distance of famous Duval Street. Featuring large well-appointed rooms with all the modern conveniences and the signature Westin Heavenly Bed, most of the 178 rooms and suites have ocean views and balconies. Bistro 245 serves ample breakfasts and a huge Sunday brunch. Visit the Westin Sunset Pier for the nightly Sunset Celebration, with live performers and outdoor dining. The Westin's sister property, **Sunset Key Guest Cottages, A Westin Resort ★★★** (✆ **888/477-7SUN** [7786] or 305/292-5300; fax 305/292-5395; www.sunsetkeyisland.com), features 37 luxurious cottages just 10 minutes by boat from Key West. Check in at the Westin Key West Resort & Marina and take a 10-minute launch ride to the secluded island of Sunset Key, where there is a white sandy beach, free-form pool with whirlpool jets, two tennis courts, and Latitudes Beach Cafe. Cottages are equipped with full kitchens, high-tech entertainment centers, and one, two, or three bedrooms. Private chef and grocery shopping services available upon request. Guests at Sunset Key have access to all the amenities at the Westin Key West Resort & Marina. For a nominal fee, guests of the Westin Key West Resort & Marina can enjoy the beach on Sunset Key, however, access is limited and on a first-come, first-served basis.

245 Front St. (at the end of Duval St.), Key West, FL 33040. ✆ **800/221-2424** or 305/294-4000. Fax 305/294-4086. www.westin.com/keywest. 215 units, including cottages. Winter $399–$550 double, $469–$1,149 suite, $595–$2,225 Sunset Key Cottage, up to 5 people; off-season $229–$459 double, $359–$949 suite, $595–$1,345 Sunset Key Cottage, up to 5 people. AE, DC, DISC, MC, V. Valet parking $20; self-parking $6/hr. ($24 per day). Pets up to 40 lbs. allowed. **Amenities:** 5 restaurants; 3 bars; outdoor heated pool; health club; Jacuzzi; watersports equipment/rentals; bike rental; concierge; business center; limited room service; in-room massage; self-service laundry; dry cleaning; full-service marina. *In room/cottages:* A/C, TV, Wi-Fi, dataport, coffeemaker, refreshment center, hair dryer, iron/ironing board.

Expensive

Casa Marina Resort & Beach Club ★ (Kids) This resort has completed a dramatic $43-million renovation to offer a pleasing mix of historic architecture and modern Key West vibe. Supremely located on the south side of the island, spanning more than 1,000 feet of private beach, the Casa Marina features sweeping lawns, a grand veranda, and a new "water walk" leading from the historic lobby to the water's edge. Newly designed rooms have a fresh, softer look than before, with vibrant pastel walls, tropical-print furnishings, crown molding, and soft carpets over chic tiles or hardwood floors. One- and two-bedroom oceanview suites have stellar views and separate living areas. In addition to the beach itself, there are also two outdoor pools, a full-service spa, and an outdoor restaurant. Nightly movies shown at the pool with free popcorn and snacks cater to families with kids.

1500 Reynolds St., Key West, FL 33040. ✆ **866/397-6342** or 305/296-3535. Fax 305/296-3008. www.casamarinaresort.com. 311 units. Winter $249–$499 double, $349–$799 suite; off-season $149–$399 double, $249–$699 suite. AE, DC, MC, V. **Amenities:** Restaurant; bar; 2 pools; nearby tennis and golf; fitness center; spa; watersports equipment/rentals; bike/scooter rental; concierge; business services; 24-hr. room service; dry cleaning. *In room:* A/C, TV, high-speed Internet, minibar, coffeemaker; hair dryer, iron, safe.

Curry Mansion Inn ★★ (Finds) This charismatic inn is the former home of the island's first millionaire, a once-penniless Bahamian immigrant who made a fortune as a pirate. Owned today by Al and Edith Amsterdam, the Curry Mansion is now on the National Register of Historic Places, but you won't feel like you're staying in a museum—it's rather like a wonderfully warm home. Rooms are very sparsely decorated, with wicker furniture, four-poster beds, and pink walls—call it Key West minimalism meets Victorian. The dining room is reminiscent of a Victorian dollhouse, with elegant table settings and rich wood floors and furnishings. Every morning, there's a delicious European-style breakfast buffet; at night, cocktail parties are held. There's also a really nice patio, on which, from time to time, there's live entertainment.

511 Caroline St., Key West, FL 33040. ✆ **800/253-3466** or 305/294-5349. Fax 305/294-4093. www.currymansion.com. 28 units. Winter $240–$300 double, $315–$365 suite; off-season $195–$235 double, $260–$285 suite. Rates include breakfast buffet. AE, DC, MC, V. No children 11 and under. **Amenities:** Dining room; pool; bike rental; concierge. *In room:* A/C, TV, minibar.

Hyatt Key West Resort & Marina ★ After a $9-million renovation, the Hyatt is now up to speed with other luxe resorts in the area. Ideally situated on the bay, the Hyatt features a waterfront pool, small beach area, and guest rooms with white porcelain tile floors, flatscreen TVs, and fabulous bathrooms. New spa cabanas allow for outdoor treatments, and a restaurant overlooking the water is great for dinner but spotty on breakfast service. Located right near Duval Street and next door to several lively bars, the Hyatt offers the best of both worlds when it comes to Key West relaxation—and partying.

601 Front St., Key West, FL 33040. ✆ **800/55-HYATT** (4-9288) or 305/809-1234. Fax 305/809-4050. www.keywest.hyatt.com. 118 rooms. Winter $485–$550 double; off-season $335–$450 double. AE, DC, DISC,

MC, V. **Amenities:** Restaurant; bar; pool; fitness center; spa; watersports equipment/rentals; meeting and conference space; private sailboat; private sunbathing beach. *In room:* A/C, plasma TV, dataport, Wi-Fi, minibar, coffeemaker, hair dryer, safe.

Island City House Hotel ★★ The oldest running B&B in Key West, the Island City House consists of three separate buildings that share a common junglelike patio and pool. The first building is a historic three-story wooden structure with wraparound verandas on every floor. The warmly outfitted interiors here include wood floors and many antiques. The tile bathrooms could use more counter space, but eccentricities are part of this hotel's charm. The unpainted wooden Cigar House has particularly large bedrooms, similar in ambience to those in the Island City House. The Arch House has newly renovated floors and features six airy Caribbean-style suites. Built of Dade County pine, this house's cozy bedrooms are furnished in wicker and rattan, and come with small kitchens and bathrooms. A shaded brick courtyard and pretty pool are surrounded by lush gardens where, every morning, a delicious continental breakfast is served. ***Note:*** For those who have a fear or dislike of cats, there are several friendly "resident" felines who call Island City House home.

411 William St., Key West, FL 33040. Ⓒ **800/634-8230** or 305/294-5702. Fax 305/294-1289. www.islandcityhouse.com. 24 units. Winter $250–$420 double; off-season $150–$300 double. Rates include breakfast. AE, DC, DISC, MC, V. **Amenities:** Outdoor heated pool; access to nearby health club; Jacuzzi; bike rental; concierge; in-room massage; babysitting; laundry service; dry cleaning; self-service laundry. *In room:* A/C, TV, kitchen, coffeemaker, hair dryer.

Marquesa Hotel ★★★ (Finds) The exquisite Marquesa offers the charm of a small historic hotel coupled with the amenities of a large resort. It encompasses four buildings, two pools, and a three-stage waterfall that cascades into a lily pond. Two of the hotel's buildings are luxuriously restored Victorian homes outfitted with plush antiques and contemporary furniture. The rooms in the two newly constructed buildings are even more opulent; many have four-poster wrought-iron beds with bright floral spreads. The bathrooms in the new buildings are lush and spacious; those in the older buildings are also nice, but not nearly as huge and luxe. The decor is simple, elegant, and spotless. The hotel also boasts one of Key West's most elegant restaurants, Café Marquesa.

600 Fleming St. (at Simonton St.), Key West, FL 33040. Ⓒ **800/869-4631** or 305/292-1919. Fax 305/294-2121. www.marquesa.com. 27 units. Winter $330–$395 double, $495–$520 suite; off-season $220–$290 double, $270–$330 suite. AE, DC, MC, V. No children 11 and under. **Amenities:** Restaurant; 2 outdoor pools (1 heated); access to nearby health club; bike rental; concierge; limited room service. *In room:* A/C, TV, dataport, minibar, hair dryer, iron, safe, CD player.

Parrot Key Resort ★★★ Brand new in 2008, Parrot Key's 74 conch-style beach homes are the epitome of beachy luxury, with gourmet kitchens, first and second level private porches with waterfront views, 42-inch plasma TVs in the living rooms, premium cable service, DVD/stereo systems, and are all smoke-free. Situated on 5 acres of lush tropical landscaping, the resort has four private pools, each in its own garden setting, and private white sand sunbathing terraces surrounding two sides of the resort. Minutes from the action on Duval Street, Parrot Key is an idyllic retreat from the neighboring madness. There's also a poolside cafe and Tiki bar.

2801 N. Roosevelt Blvd., Key West, FL 33040. Ⓒ **305/809-2200.** Fax 305/292-3322. www.parrotkeyresort.com. 74 units. Winter $319–$489 double; off-season $189–$389 double. AE, DC, DISC, MC, V. **Amenities:** 2 restaurants; bar; outdoor heated pool; nearby tennis and golf; health club; spa; watersports equipment rental; bike rental; concierge; tour desk; business center; salon; 24-hr. room service; in-room massage; babysitting; dry cleaning. *In room:* A/C, TV, dataport, minibar, fridge, coffeemaker, hair dryer, iron.

Pier House Resort and Caribbean Spa ★ If you're looking for something a bit more intimate than the Reach Resort (see below), Pier House is an ideal choice. Its location—at the foot of Duval Street and just steps from Mallory Docks—is the envy of every hotel on the island. Set back from the busy street, on a short strip of private beach, this place is a welcome oasis of calm. The accommodations vary tremendously, from simple business-style rooms to romantic quarters complete with stereos and whirlpool tubs. Although every unit has either a balcony or a patio, not all overlook the water. My favorites, in the two-story spa building, don't have any view at all. But what they lack in scenery, they make up for in opulence: Each well-appointed spa room has a sitting area and a huge Jacuzzi bathroom.

1 Duval St. (near Mallory Docks), Key West, FL 33040. ✆ **800/327-8340** or 305/296-4600. Fax 305/296-9085. www.pierhouse.com. 142 units. Winter $309–$529 double, $479–$3,000 suite; off-season $229–$369 double, $389–$2,000 suite. AE, DC, MC, V. **Amenities:** 3 restaurants; 3 bars; heated pool; full-service spa and fitness center; 2 Jacuzzis; sauna; watersports equipment/rentals; moped/bike rental; concierge; limited room service; in-room massage; babysitting; laundry services. *In room:* A/C, TV, dataport, minibar, coffeemaker, hair dryer, iron.

The Reach Resort ★★★ Fresh from a $37-million renovation, the boutique-style Reach Resort features gingerbread balconies, tin roof accents, and shaded Spanish walkways characteristic of historic Key West. Newly refurbished guest rooms are large, with modernized decor and custom furnishings that are vibrant and crisp. Every room features comfortable sectional sofas and sliding glass doors that open onto balconies, some with ocean views. Sixty-eight boutique and 10 executive suites are also available. A new pool deck and 450-foot natural sand beach are the perfect settings to enjoy a massive array of watersports, available right on the premises. The resort is also home to the Manhattan-based Strip House restaurant, which is as delicious as it is gorgeous. Unlike most area resorts which are small-ish, this one seems infinitely larger and, in many ways, worlds away from the rest of Key West.

1435 Simonton St., Key West, FL 33040. ✆ **866/397-6427** or 305/296-5000 for reservations. Fax 305/296-3008. www.reachresort.com. 150 units. Winter $249–$499 double, $299–$549 suite; off-season $149–$399 double, $199–$449 suite. AE, DC, DISC, MC, V. **Amenities:** 2 restaurants; bar; outdoor heated pool; nearby tennis and golf; spa; watersports equipment/rentals; bike rental; concierge; tour desk; business services; salon; 24-hr. room service; in-room massage; dry cleaning. *In room:* A/C, TV, high-speed Internet; minibar, minifridge, coffeemaker, hair dryer, iron.

Simonton Court ★★★ (Finds) This is my favorite stay in Key West—too bad it's always booked. Once a cigar factory, Simonton Court features meticulously appointed restored historic cottages and suites amid sparkling pools and luxuriant private gardens. There are several options to choose from: bed-and-breakfast, cottages, guesthouse, mansion, and inn. Some cottages even have their own pools. There's no restaurant here, but the well-informed concierge will help you with reservations anywhere no matter what you crave. What I really crave, however, is a standing reservation here. People love the place so much, they book years in advance. Once you stay here, if you're lucky, you'll understand why.

320 Simonton St., Key West, FL 33040. ✆ **800/944-2687** or 305/294-6386. Fax 305/293-8446. www.simontoncourt.com. 30 units. Winter $195–$395 double in mansion, $275–$495 cottage, $195–$395 inn, $285–$425 manor house, $200–$515 town house; off-season $145–$265 double in mansion, $155–$375 cottage, $145–$265 inn, $215–$315 manor house, $155–$395 town house. Rates include continental breakfast. AE, DISC, MC, V. **Amenities:** Outdoor pool; concierge. *In room:* A/C, TV/VCR, hair dryer.

Weatherstation Inn ★ (Finds) Originally built in 1912 as a weather station, this beautifully restored, meticulously maintained, Renaissance-style inn is just 2 blocks from

Duval Street but seems worlds away. It's situated on the tropical grounds of the former Old Navy Yard, now an exclusive and private gated community. Presidents Truman, Eisenhower, and JFK all visited the station. Spacious and uncluttered, each guest room is uniquely furnished to complement the interior architecture: hardwood floors, tall sash windows, and high ceilings. The large, modern bathrooms are especially appealing. The staff is both friendly and accommodating.

57 Front St., Key West, FL 33040. ✆ **800/815-2707** or 305/294-7277. Fax 305/294-0544. www.weatherstationinn.com. 8 units. Winter $235–$335 double; off-season $180–$245 double. Rates include continental breakfast. AE, DISC, MC, V. **Amenities:** Outdoor pool; concierge. *In room:* A/C, TV/VCR, hair dryer.

Moderate

Ambrosia Key West ★★ (Finds Despite countless visits each year to the tiny island of Key West, I discover yet another hidden treasure every time I go back. Ambrosia is one of them, a private compound set on 2 lush acres just a block from Duval Street. Three lagoon-style pools, suites, town houses, and a cottage are spread around the grounds. Town houses have living rooms, kitchens, and spiral staircases leading to master suites with vaulted ceilings and private decks. The cottage, overlooking a dip pool, is a perfect family retreat, with two bedrooms, two bathrooms, a living room, and a kitchen. All rooms, several which recently received major renovations, have private entrances, most with French doors opening onto a variety of intimate outdoor spaces, including private verandas, patios, and gardens with sculptures, fountains, and pools. The breakfast buffet rocks, with eggs, biscuits, gravy, bacon, sausage, and pretty much anything you'd want. Fantastic service, bolstered by the philosophy that it's better to have high occupancy than high rates, explains why Ambrosia has a 90% year-round occupancy—a record in seasonal Key West.

622 Fleming St., Key West, FL 33040. ✆ **800/535-9838** or 305/296-9838. Fax 305/296-2425. www.ambrosiakeywest.com. 20 units. Winter $279–$609 suite; off-season $179–$389 suite. Rates include breakfast buffet. AE, DISC, MC, V. Off- and on-street parking. Pets accepted. **Amenities:** 3 outdoor heated pools. *In room:* A/C, TV, Wi-Fi, kitchen (in some), fridge, coffeemaker, hair dryer, iron, microwave, CD player.

Doubletree Grand Key Resort ★ (Finds If you don't mind staying on the quiet "other" side of the island, a 10-minute cab ride away from Duval Street, the Doubletree is an excellent choice, not to mention excellent value. An ecologically conscious resort, the hotel has been renovated with eco-sensitive materials as well as an interior created to conserve energy, reduce waste, and preserve the area's natural resources. Rooms are clean and comfortable, with some looking onto the spacious pool area, which is surrounded by an unsightly empty lot of mangroves and marshes. Best of all, there's a free shuttle to transport guests to and from Duval Street, which is a considerable walk or cab ride from here.

3990 S. Roosevelt Blvd., Key West, FL 33040. ✆ **888/310-1540** or 305/293-1818. Fax 305/296-6962. www.doubletreekeywest.com. 216 units. Winter $255–$279 double, $295–$495 suite; off-season $189–$198 double, $239–$379 suite. AE, DISC, MC, V. Valet or self-parking $10. **Amenities:** Restaurant; Tiki bar and lounge; pool; gym; concierge; limited room service; meeting rooms. *In room:* A/C, TV/WebTV, Internet access, minibar, coffeemaker, hair dryer, iron, safe.

La Pensione ★★ This classic B&B, set in a stunning 1891 home, is a total charmer. The comfortable rooms all have air-conditioning, ceiling fans, and king-size beds. Many also have French doors opening onto spacious verandas. Although the rooms have no TVs, the distractions of Duval Street, only steps away, should keep you adequately occupied. Breakfast, which includes Belgian waffles, fresh fruit, and a variety of breads or muffins, can be taken on the wraparound porch or at the communal dining table. Recent guests, however, have informed us that service here is not as friendly as it used to be and that the inn's location on U.S. 1 isn't so hot when it comes to the noise and traffic levels.

809 Truman Ave. (btw. Windsor and Margaret sts.), Key West, FL 33040. ✆ **800/893-1193** or 305/292-9923. Fax 305/296-6509. www.lapensione.com. 9 units. Winter $168–$328 double; off-season $118–$168 double. Rates include breakfast. Discount of 10% for readers who mention this book. AE, DC, DISC, MC, V. No children. **Amenities:** Outdoor pool; bike rental; Wi-Fi. *In room:* A/C.

Southernmost Point Guest House ★★ Finds Kids One of the few inns that actually welcomes children and pets, this romantic guesthouse is a real find. The antiseptically clean rooms are not as fancy as the house's ornate 1885 exterior, but each is unique and includes some combination of basic beds and a hodgepodge of furnishings, such as futon couches and high-back wicker chairs. Room no. 5 is best, with a private porch, ocean view, and windows that let in lots of light. Every unit comes with fresh flowers, wine, and a full decanter of sherry. Mona Santiago, the kind, laid-back owner, provides chairs and towels for the beach, which is just a block away. Guests can help themselves to free wine as they soak in the 14-seat hot tub. Kids will enjoy the backyard swings and the pet rabbits.

1327 Duval St., Key West, FL 33040. ✆ **305/294-0715.** Fax 305/296-0641. www.southernmostpoint.com. 6 units. Winter $125–$200 double, $260–$285 suite; off-season $75–$120 double, $165–$175 suite. Rates include breakfast. AE, MC, V. Pets accepted ($5 in summer, $10 in winter). **Amenities:** Garden pool; hot tub; laundry facilities; barbecue grills. *In room:* A/C, TV/VCR, fridge, coffeemaker, hair dryer, iron.

Westwinds Inn ★ A close second to staying in your own private 19th-century, tin-roofed clapboard house is this tranquil inn, just 4 blocks from Duval Street in the historic seaport district. Lush landscaping keeps the place extremely private and secluded; at times, you'll feel as if you're alone. Two pools, one heated in winter, are offset by alcoves, fountains, and the well-maintained whitewashed inn, which is actually composed of five separate buildings. Rooms are Key West comfortable, with private bathrooms, wicker furnishings, and fans. All rooms are nonsmoking.

914 Eaton St., Key West, FL 33040. ✆ **800/788-4150** or 305/296-4440. Fax 305/293-0931. www.westwindskeywest.com. 22 units. Winter $185–$220 double, $225–$275 suite; off-season $90–$180 double, $140–$195 suite. Rates include continental breakfast. DISC, MC, V. No children 11 and under. **Amenities:** 2 pools (1 heated); bike rental; self-service laundry. *In room:* A/C, TV (in some), kitchenette (in some).

Inexpensive

Angelina Guest House ★★ This former bordello and gambling-hall-turned-youth-hostel-type guesthouse is one of the cheapest in town—and it's conveniently located near a hot hippie restaurant called Blue Heaven (p. 240). Though the neighborhood is definitely urban, it's generally safe and full of character. Accommodations are furnished uniquely in a modest style. Two rooms have full kitchens, one has a microwave and small fridge, and all but three have private bathrooms. A gorgeous lagoon-style heated pool, with waterfall and tropical landscaping, is an excellent addition. Even better are the poolside hammocks—get out there early, as they go quickly! Even though the Angelina is sparse (perfect for bohemian types who don't mind a little grit), it's a great place to crash if you're traveling on the cheap.

302 Angela St. (at Thomas St.), Key West, FL 33040. ✆ **888/303-4480** or 305/294-4480. Fax 305/272-0681. www.angelinaguesthouse.com. 13 units. Winter $99–$199 double; off-season $69–$139 double. Rates include continental breakfast. DISC, MC, V. **Amenities:** Outdoor heated pool; concierge. *In room:* A/C, no phone.

The Grand ★★ *Finds* Don't expect cabbies or locals to know about this well-kept secret, located in a modest residential section of Old Town, about 5 blocks from Duval Street. It's got almost everything you could want, including a very moderate price tag. Proprietors Jim Brown and Jeffrey Daubman provide any and all services for their appreciative guests. All units have private bathrooms, air-conditioning, and private entrances. The best deal is room no. 2; it's small and lacks a closet, but it has a porch and the most privacy. Suites are a real steal, too: The large two-room units come with kitchenettes. This place is undoubtedly the best bargain in town.

1116 Grinnell St. (btw. Virginia and Catherine sts.), Key West, FL 33040. ✆ **888/947-2630** or 305/294-0590. Fax 305/294-0477. www.thegrandguesthouse.com. 10 units. Winter $168–$208 double, $228–$268 suite; off-season $98 $148 double, $128–$188 suite. Rates include expanded continental breakfast. DISC, MC, V. Free parking. **Amenities:** Bike/scooter rental; full concierge. *In room:* A/C and ceiling fans, TV, Wi-Fi, fridge.

Key West International Hostel & Seashell Motel This well-run hostel is a 3-minute walk to the beach and Old Town. Very busy with European backpackers, it's a great place to meet people. The dorm rooms are dark, grimy, and sparse, but livable if you're desperate for a cheap stay. There are all-male, all-female, and co-ed dorm rooms for couples. The higher-priced private motel rooms are a good deal, especially those equipped with kitchens. Amenities include a pool table under a Tiki roof; bike rentals; cheap food at breakfast, lunch, and dinner; and discounted prices for snorkeling, diving, and sunset cruises. There's also free wireless Internet access throughout the property.

718 South St., Key West, FL 33040. ✆ **800/51-HOSTEL** or 305/296-5719. Fax 305/296 0672. www.keywesthostel.com. 92 dorm beds, 10 motel rooms. Year-round $34 dorm room. Winter $75–$105 motel room; off-season $55–$85 motel room. MC, V. Free parking. **Amenities:** Bike rental; kitchen. *In room:* Motel rooms have A/C, TV, fridge, coffeemaker, hair dryer; dorm rooms have A/C only.

WHERE TO DINE

With its share of the usual drive-through fast-food franchises—mostly up on Roosevelt Boulevard—and Duval Street succumbing to the lure of a Hard Rock Cafe and Starbucks, you might be surprised to learn that, over the years, an upscale and high-quality dining scene has begun to thrive in Key West. Just wander Old Town or the newly spruced-up Bahama Village and browse menus after you've exhausted my list of picks below.

If you're staying in a condominium or efficiency, you may want to stock your fridge with groceries, beer, wine, and snacks from the area's oldest grocer, **Fausto's Food Palace.** Open since 1926, Fausto's has two locations: 1105 White St. and 522 Fleming St. The Fleming Street location will deliver with a $25-minimum order (✆ **305/294-5221** or 305/296-5663).

Very Expensive

Café Marquesa ★★★ CONTEMPORARY AMERICAN If you're looking for fabulous dining (and service) in Key West, this is the place. The intimate, 50-seat restaurant is something to look at, but it's really the food that you'll want to admire. Specialties include macadamia-crusted yellowtail snapper, prosciutto-wrapped black Angus filet, and roast duck breast with red curry coconut sauce. If you're looking to splurge, this is the place.

In the Marquesa Hotel, 600 Fleming St. ✆ **305/292-1919.** Reservations highly recommended. Main courses $25–$38. AE, DC, MC, V. Summer daily 7–11pm; winter daily 6–11pm.

Hot Tin Roof ★★★ FUSION SEAFOOD Ever hear of conch fusion cuisine? Neither did I, until I experienced it firsthand at Hot Tin Roof, Ocean Key Resort's chichi restaurant which transforms South American, Asian, French, and Keys cuisine into an experience unlike any other in this part of the world. The vibrant 3,000-square-foot space features both indoor and outdoor deck seating overlooking the harbor. Live jazz/fusion adds to the stunning environment—it's the epitome of casual elegance. Signature dishes include an irresistible lobster with garlic, chilies, and Cuban mojo sauce; macadamia-crusted grouper with yellow curry sauce; and chocolate-lava cake that makes this tin roof very hot, to say the least, especially for Key West. Last time I ate here, Meryl Streep was sitting next to me with her family, looking as impressed as she was impressive.

In the Ocean Key Resort, Zero Duval St. ✆ **305/296-7701.** Reservations highly recommended. Main courses $20–$40. AE, DC, MC, V. Daily 7:30–11am and 5–10pm.

Louie's Backyard ★★ CARIBBEAN Nestled amid blooming bougainvillea on a lush slice of the Gulf, Louie's remains one of the most romantic restaurants on earth. It's off the beaten path, which makes it even more romantic. Famed chef Norman Van Aken, of Norman's in Miami, brought his talents farther south and started what has become one of the finest dining spots in the Keys. As a result, this is one of the hardest places to score a reservation: Either call way in advance or hope that your hotel concierge has some pull. Try the sweet-and-sour sweetbreads with sticky rice, or the grilled chili-rubbed Berkshire pork chop that is to die for. After dinner, sit at the dockside bar and watch the waves crash, almost touching your feet, while enjoying a cocktail at sunset. You can't go wrong with the fresh catch of the day, or any seafood dish, for that matter. The weekend brunches are also great. And a ritual for many in Key West are sunset cocktails at the oceanfront Tiki bar. If you can't stay for dinner, go for lunch; this is one dining experience you won't want to miss.

700 Waddell Ave. ✆ **305/294-1061.** www.louiesbackyard.com. Reservations highly recommended. Main courses $25–$35; lunch $10–$20. AE, DC, MC, V. Daily 11:30am–3pm and 6–10:30pm.

One Duval ★★★ CARIBBEAN The waterfront setting of this restaurant at the Pier House Resort is beautiful, but you may be too distracted to notice the views when you taste the food. One of the best restaurants in Key West, One Duval blends the ingredients of the Caribbean and Florida with an innovative twist. For starters, the crabmeat stuffed in phyllo is outstanding, and the goat-cheese soufflé is incredibly hedonistic. For main courses, try the macadamia-nut-crusted mahimahi or the lobster thermidor stuffed with crabmeat. The Key lime pie with meringue is a must-have. Service is friendly and professional; this is not the kind of restaurant where waiters will rush you. Eat first, then sit back and digest the views so you don't miss any of this fine restaurant's offerings.

In the Pier House Resort, 1 Duval St. ✆ **305/296-4600.** Reservations highly recommended. Main courses $25–$36. AE, DC, MC, V. Daily 6–10:30pm.

Tavern N Town ★ FLORIBBEAN Tavern and Town are two separate eateries within a bi-level space—superstar chef Norman Van Aken, who left here (but left some of his Floribbean influences) in 2008, called it a hyphenated restaurant, with Tavern featuring tapas and small plates and Town a more world-class dining experience, but both equally good. An open theater kitchen shows action, but the real show is on your plate. At Tavern, try the tempura short rib cake with wasabi *crema.* Over at Town, black grouper in a miso ginger or pan-cooked filet of yellowtail are a far cry from Duval Street's chicken fingers and conch fritters. Although it's not as good as when Van Aken was here, it's still worth a splurge.

In the Beachside Resort, 3841 N. Roosevelt Blvd. ✆ **305/296-8100.** Reservations highly recommended. Main courses $19–$32. AE, DC, MC, V. Tavern daily 8am–10:30pm. Town daily 6–11pm.

Expensive

Antonia's ★★ REGIONAL ITALIAN The food is great, but the atmosphere a bit fussy for Key West. If you don't have a reservation in season, don't even bother. Still, if you don't mind paying high prices for dishes that go for much less elsewhere, try this old favorite. From the perfectly seasoned homemade focaccia to an exemplary crème brûlée, this elegant little standout is amazingly consistent. The menu includes a small selection of classics, linguine with shrimp, delicious, pillowy gnocchi, *zuppa di pesce* (fish soup), and veal Marsala. And don't miss the outstanding warm goat cheese soufflé served with pan-seared asparagus, baby green beans, carrots, and Belgian endive over a roasted tomato vinaigrette. You can't go wrong with any of the handmade pastas. And the owners, Antonia Berto and Phillip Smith, travel to Italy every year to research recipes, so you can be sure you're getting an authentic taste of Italy in small-town Key West.

615 Duval St. ✆ **305/294-6565.** Fax 305/294-3888. www.antoniaskeywest.com. Reservations suggested. Main courses $20–$30; pastas $15–$30. AE, DC, MC, V. Daily 6–11pm.

Bagatelle ★★★ SEAFOOD/TROPICAL Reserve a seat at the elegant second-floor veranda overlooking Duval Street's mayhem. From the calm above, you may want to start your meal with the zingy conch ceviche or the sashimi-like seared sesame tuna rolled in black peppercorns. The best chicken and beef dishes are given a tropical treatment: grilled with papaya, ginger, and soy. The Jamaican curry chicken is a favorite.

115 Duval St. ✆ **305/296-6609.** Reservations recommended. Main courses $15–$25; lunch $5–$15. AE, DISC, MC, V. Sun–Thurs 11:30am–10pm; Fri–Sat 11:30am–11pm.

La Trattoria ★ ITALIAN Have a true Italian feast in a relaxed atmosphere. Each dish here is prepared and presented according to old Italian tradition. Try the delicious breadcrumb-stuffed mushroom caps; they're firm yet tender. The stuffed eggplant with ricotta and roasted peppers is light and flavorful. Or have the seafood salad of shrimp, calamari, and mussels, which is fish-market fresh and tasty. The pasta dishes are also great—go for the penne Venezia, with mushrooms, sun-dried tomatoes, and crabmeat. For dessert, don't skip the homemade tiramisu; it's light yet full-flavored. The dining room is spacious but still intimate, and the waiters are friendly. Before you leave, visit Virgilio's, the restaurant's resplendent indoor/outdoor cocktail lounge with live jazz until 2am.

524 Duval St. ✆ **305/296-1075.** www.latrattoria.us. Main courses $16–$40; pasta $14–$26. AE, DC, DISC, MC, V. Daily 5:30–11pm.

Mangoes ★★★ FLORIBBEAN This restaurant's large brick patio, shaded by overgrown banyan trees, is so alluring to passersby that it's packed almost every night of the week. Many people don't realize how pricey the meals can be here because, upon first glance, it looks like a casual Duval Street cafe. Appetizers include grilled shrimp cocktail with spicy mango chutney. Crispy curried chicken and local snapper with passion-fruit sauce are typical among the entrees, but the garlic and lime pinks—a half-pound of Key West pink shrimp seasoned and grilled with a roasted garlic and Key lime glaze—is the menu's best offering by far. Even though it's right on touristy Duval Street, Mangoes enjoys a good reputation among locals and stands out from the rest of the places offering greasy bar fare. For a cool, locals loungey scene, check out the speakeasy-esque back bar inside.

700 Duval St. (at Angela St.). ✆ **305/292-4606.** Reservations recommended for parties of 6 or more. Main courses $15–$30; pizzas $10–$15; lunch $7–$18. AE, DC, DISC, MC, V. Daily 11am–midnight; pizza until 1am.

Michael's ★★★ Finds STEAKHOUSE Tucked away in a residential neighborhood, Michael's is a meaty oasis in a big sea of fish. With steaks flown in daily from Chicago, this is *the* steakhouse for when you're craving meat, from New York strip to porterhouse. Unlike most steakhouses, Michael's exudes a relaxed, tropical ambience with a fabulous indoor/outdoor setting that's romantic but not stuffy. A fantastic fondue menu makes for a tasty snack or even a meal, complemented by an excellent, reasonably priced wine list. Sure, Michael's is on the pricier side, but it's not every day that you can enjoy slabs of beef from Chicago in a warm, tropical setting.

532 Margaret St. ✆ **305/295-1300.** www.michaelskeywest.com. Reservations recommended. Main courses $15–$40. AE, DC, DISC, MC, V. Daily 5–11pm.

Seven Fish ★★★ Finds SEAFOOD "Simple, good food" is Seven Fish's motto, but this hidden little secret is much more than simple. One of the most popular restaurants with locals, Seven Fish is a chic seafood spot serving some of the best fish dishes on the island. Crab and shiitake-mushroom pasta, fish of the day, and gnocchi with blue cheese and sautéed fish are among the dishes to choose from. For dessert, do not miss the Key lime cake over tart lime curd with fresh berries.

632 Olivia St. ✆ **305/296-2777.** www.7fish.com. Reservations recommended. Main courses $15–$26. AE, MC, V. Wed–Mon 6–10pm.

Moderate

Alonzo's Oyster Bar ★ SEAFOOD Alonzo's serves good seafood in a casual setting. It's on the ground floor of the A&B Lobster House, at the end of Front Street in the marina; if you want to dress up, go upstairs for the "fine dining." To start your meal, try the steamed beer shrimp—tantalizingly fresh jumbo shrimp in a sauce of garlic, Old Bay seasoning, beer, and cayenne pepper. A house specialty is white-clam chili, a delicious mix of tender clams, white beans, and potatoes served with a dollop of sour cream. The staff is cheerful and informative, and the service is very good.

700 Front St. ✆ **305/294-5880.** www.alonzosoysterbar.com. Main courses $11–$17; appetizers $5–$8. MC, V. Daily 11am–11pm.

Banana Café ★★★ Finds FRENCH Banana Café benefits from a French-country-cafe look and feel. The upscale local eatery discovered by savvy visitors on the less-congested end of Duval Street has retained its loyal clientele with affordable prices and delightful, light preparations. The crepes are legendary on the island, for breakfast or lunch; the fresh ingredients and French-themed menu bring daytime diners back for the casual, classy, tropical-influenced dinner menu. There's live jazz every Thursday night.

1211 Duval St. ✆ **305/294-7227.** Main courses $5–$25; breakfast and lunch $2–$10. AE, DC, MC, V. Daily 8am–11pm.

Blue Heaven ★★★ Finds SEAFOOD/AMERICAN/NATURAL This hippie-run restaurant has become the place to be in Key West—and with good reason. Be prepared to wait in line. The food here is some of the best in town—especially at breakfast, which features homemade granola, tropical-fruit pancakes, and seafood Benedict. Dinners are just as good and run the gamut from fresh-caught fish and Jamaican jerk chicken to curried soups and vegetarian stews. Some people are put off by the dirt floors and roaming cats and birds, but frankly, it adds to the charm. The building used to be a bordello, where Hemingway was said to hang out watching cockfights. It's still lively here, but not *that* lively!

305 Petronia St. ✆ **305/296-8666.** Main courses $10–$30; lunch $6–$14; breakfast $5–$11. DISC, MC, V. Daily 8–11:30am, noon–3pm, and 6–10:30pm; Sun brunch 8am–1pm. Closed mid-Sept to early Oct.

Mangia, Mangia ★ Value ITALIAN/AMERICAN Locals appreciate that they can get good, inexpensive food here in a town filled with tourist traps. Off the beaten track, this great Chicago-style pasta place has some of the best Italian food in the Keys. The family-run restaurant serves superb homemade pastas of every description, including one of the tastiest marinara sauces around. The simple grilled chicken breast brushed with olive oil and sprinkled with pepper is another good choice. You wouldn't know it from the front, but there's a fantastic little patio dotted with twinkling pepper lights and lots of plants. While you wait for your table, relax out back with a glass of wine—this place is said to have the largest selection in the Keys—or homemade beer.

900 Southard St. (at Margaret St.). ✆ **305/294-2469.** Reservations not accepted. Main courses $9–$15. AE, MC, V. Daily 5:30–10pm.

Pepe's ★ Finds AMERICAN This old dive has been serving good, basic food for nearly a century. Steaks and Apalachicola Bay oysters are the big draws for regulars, who appreciate the rustic barroom setting and historical photos on the walls. Look for original scenes of Key West in 1909, when Pepe's first opened. If the weather is nice, choose a seat on the patio under a stunning mahogany tree. Burgers, fish sandwiches, and standard chili satisfy hearty eaters. Buttery sautéed mushrooms and rich mashed potatoes are the best comfort foods in Key West. There's always a wait, so stop by early for breakfast, when you can get old-fashioned chipped beef on toast and all the usual egg dishes. In the evening, reasonably priced cocktails are served on the deck.

806 Caroline St. (btw. Margaret and Williams sts.). ✆ **305/294-7192.** Main courses $15–$25; breakfast $2–$10; lunch $5–$10. DISC, MC, V. Daily 6:30am–10:30pm.

Sarabeth's ★★ Finds AMERICAN An offshoot of the popular New York City breakfast hot spot, Sarabeth's brings a much-needed shot of cosmopolitan comfort food to Key West in the form of delicious breakfasts with Sarabeth's signature homemade jams and jellies. Choose from buttermilk to lemon ricotta pancakes or almond-crusted cinnamon French toast. For lunch, the traditional Caesar salad, burger, or Key West pinks shrimp roll with avocado are all excellent choices. Dinner is simple, but savory, with top-notch dishes from chicken potpie and meatloaf to a divine green-chili-pepper macaroni with three cheeses or meaty shrimp-and-crabmeat cakes. The dining room is cozy and intimate, and it feels like you're eating in someone's house; a few tables are on a small outdoor patio.

530 Simonton St. ✆ **305/293-8181.** Main courses $13–$20, breakfast $5.50–$10, lunch $5.75–$14. MC, V. Mon 8am–3pm; Wed–Sun 8am–3pm and 6–10pm.

Turtle Kraals Wildlife Grill ★ Finds Kids SOUTHWESTERN/SEAFOOD You'll join lots of locals in this out-of-the-way converted warehouse with indoor and dockside seating, which serves innovative seafood at great prices. Try the twin lobster tails stuffed with mango and crabmeat, stone crabs when in season (Oct–May), or any of the big quesadillas or fajitas. Kids will like the wildlife exhibits, the turtle cannery, and the very cheesy menu. Blues bands play most nights.

213 Margaret St. (at Caroline St.). ✆ **305/294-2640.** Main courses $10–$20. DISC, MC, V. Mon–Thurs 11am–10:30pm; Fri–Sat 11am–11pm; Sun noon–10:30pm. Bar closes at midnight.

Inexpensive

Bahama Mama's Kitchen ★ BAHAMIAN Sit outside under an umbrella and enjoy the authentic Bahamian fare made from recipes that have been handed down for the past 150 years. Try the coconut shrimp: butterflied, soaked in coconut oil, battered with egg, then rolled in fresh shredded coconut and deep-fried. The fresh catch comes blackened, broiled, or fried, and is served with island plantains, shrimp hash cakes, and crab rice. The service is good and the staff is friendly.

In the Bahama Village Market, 324 Petronia St. ✆ **305/294-3355.** Main courses $10–$15; appetizers $4–$10. MC, V. Daily 11am–10pm.

Island Dogs Bar ★ AMERICAN This islandy, Tommy Bahama–esque bar is a cool spot to throw back a few while catching a game or a live band. But more importantly is the fare—not your typical bar fare, but delicious burgers, chicken fingers, chicken wings, and, well, you get the picture. Sit at the bar or at one of the few outdoor tables ideally placed for watching the crowds stumble—literally—off Duval Street.

505 Front St. ✆ **305/295-0501.** Main courses $5–$10. AE, DISC, MC, V. Daily 11am–2am.

Upper Crust Pizza ★★ PIZZA There's nothing better after a day or night of drinking rum runners than chasing them down with a slice or three of this heavenly pizza. The owner hails from Boston and won't tell us his secret to the perfectly crisp, garlicky crust, but as long as he keeps up the good work, we won't bother him for it. All sorts of varieties, from cheese to spinach with goat cheese, are available until the wee hours of the night.

611 Duval St. ✆ **305/293-8890.** www.uppercrustkeywest.com. Pizza $5 slice, $13–$16 pie. AE, DISC, MC, V. Daily 11am–2am.

KEY WEST AFTER DARK

Duval Street is the Bourbon Street of Florida. Amid the T-shirt shops and clothing boutiques, you'll find bar after bar serving neon-colored frozen drinks to revelers who bounce from bar to bar from noon until dawn. Bands and crowds vary from night to night and season to season. Your best bet is to start at Truman Avenue and head up Duval to check them out for yourself. Cover charges are rare, except in gay clubs (see "The Gay Scene," below), so stop into a dozen and see which you like. For the most part, Key West is a late-night town, and bars and clubs don't close until around 3 or 4am.

Captain Tony's Saloon Just around the corner from Duval's beaten path, this smoky old bar is about as authentic as you'll find. It comes complete with old-time regulars who remember the island before cruise ships docked here; they say Hemingway drank, caroused, and even wrote here. The late owner, Capt. Tony Tarracino, was a former controversial Key West mayor—immortalized in Jimmy Buffett's "Last Mango in Paris." 428 Greene St. ✆ **305/294-1838.** www.capttonyssaloon.com.

Durty Harry's This large complex features live rock bands almost every night. You can wander to one of the many outdoor bars or head to Upstairs at Rick's, an indoor/outdoor dance club that gets going late. For racy singles or couples, there is the Red Garter, a pocket-size strip club. The hawker outside reminds couples, in case they've forgotten, that "the family that strips together, sticks together." 208 Duval St. ✆ **305/296-4890.** www.ricksanddurtyharrys.com.

Sloppy Joe's You'll have to stop in here just to say you did. Scholars and drunks debate whether this is the same Sloppy Joe's that Hemingway wrote about, but there's no argument that this classic bar's early-20th-century wooden ceiling and cracked-tile floors are Key West originals. There's live music nightly, as well as a cigar room and martini bar. 201 Duval St. ✆ **305/294-5717,** ext. 10. www.sloppyjoes.com.

THE GAY SCENE

Key West's bohemian live-and-let-live atmosphere extends to its thriving and quirky gay community. Before and after Tennessee Williams, Key West has provided the perfect backdrop to a gay scene unlike that of many large urban areas. Seamlessly blended with the prevailing culture, there is no "gay ghetto" in Key West, where alternative lifestyles are embraced and even celebrated.

Although restaurants and businesses welcome visitors without discrimination, nightlife *is* inevitably nightlife. In Key West, the best music and dancing can be found at the predominantly gay clubs. While many of the area's other hot spots are geared toward tourists who like to imbibe, the gay clubs are for those who want to rave, gay or not. Covers vary, but are rarely more than $10.

Two popular adjacent late-night spots are the **801 Bourbon Bar/One Saloon** (801 Duval St. and 514 Petronia St.; ✆ **305/294-9349** for both), featuring great drag and lots more disco. A mostly male clientele frequents this hot spot from 9pm until 4am. Another Duval Street favorite is **Aqua,** 711 Duval St. (✆ **305/292-8500**), where you might catch drag queens belting out torch songs or judges voting on the best package in the wet-jockey-shorts contest.

Sunday nights are fun at La-Te-Da, proper name: **La Terraza de Martí,** 1125 Duval St. (✆ **305/296-6706**), the former Key West home of Cuban exile José Martí. This is a great spot to gather poolside for the best martini in town—but don't bother with the food. Just upstairs is the **Crystal Room** (✆ **305/296-6706**), with a high-caliber cabaret performance featuring the popular Randy Roberts in winter.

4 THE DRY TORTUGAS ★★

70 miles W of Key West

Few people realize that the Florida Keys don't end at Key West, as about 70 miles west is a chain of seven small islands known as the Dry Tortugas. Because you've come this far, you might wish to visit them, especially if you're into bird-watching, their primary draw.

Ponce de León, who discovered this far-flung cluster of coral keys in 1513, named them Las Tortugas because of the many sea turtles, which still flock to the area during nesting season in the warm summer months. Oceanic charts later carried the preface "dry" to warn mariners that fresh water was unavailable here. Modern intervention has made drinking water available, but little else.

These undeveloped islands make a great day trip for travelers interested in seeing the natural anomalies of the Florida Keys—especially the birds. The Dry Tortugas are nesting grounds and roosting sites for thousands of tropical and subtropical oceanic birds. Visitors will also find a historic fort, good fishing, and terrific snorkeling around shallow reefs.

GETTING THERE

BY BOAT The **Yankee Fleet,** based in Key West (✆ **800/634-0939** or 305/294-7009; www.yankeefleet.com/keywest.cfm), offers day trips from Key West for sightseeing, snorkeling, or both. Cruises leave daily at 7:30am for the 3-hour journey from Land's End Marina at Margaret Street to Garden Key. Breakfast is served onboard. Once on the island, you can join a guided tour of Fort Jefferson or explore it on your own. Boats return to Key West by 7pm. Tours cost $164 for adults; $154 for seniors, students, and military personnel; and $119 for children 16 and under. Prices include breakfast, lunch, dinner, and snorkeling equipment. Call for reservations.

Sunny Days Catamarans (✆ **800/236-7937** or 305/292-6100; www.sunnydayskeywest.com) operates the *Fast Cat,* which is faster, quieter, and more high-tech than the loud Yankee fleet, as well as a better value. The round-trip fare ($145 for adults, $135 for seniors, $100 for children) includes a continental breakfast; a buffet lunch with cold cuts, fresh veggies, fruits, salads, and unlimited sodas and water; an island tour; and a snorkeling excursion to a shipwreck in 5 to 20 feet of water. The high-speed catamaran leaves Key West for Garden Key at 8am and returns by 6pm.

BY PLANE **Seaplanes of Key West,** based at Key West Airport (✆ **800/950-2-FLY** [2359] or 305/294-0709; www.seaplanesofkeywest.com), offers daily excursions. Weather permitting, flights depart at 8am, 10am, noon, and 2pm. The 40-minute trip at about 500 feet offers a great introduction to the Dry Tortugas. Fares include snorkeling equipment and a cooler for use on the island. A half-day costs $229 for adults, $179 for kids 7 to 12, and $149 for kids 6 and under; a full day costs $405 for adults, $325 for kids 7 to 12, and $270 for kids 6 and under. Bring a bathing suit and snacks to enjoy on these remote and beautiful islands.

EXPLORING THE DRY TORTUGAS

Of the seven islands that make up the Dry Tortugas, Garden Key is the most visited because it is where Fort Jefferson and the visitor center are located. Loggerhead Key, Middle Key, and East Key are open only during the day and are for hiking. Bush Key is for the birds—literally! It's a nesting area for birds only, though it is open from October to January for special excursions. Hospital and Long keys are closed to the public.

Fort Jefferson, a huge six-sided, 19th-century fortress, is set almost at the water's edge of Garden Key, so it appears to float in the middle of the sea. The monumental structure is surrounded by formidable 8-foot-thick walls that rise from the sand to a height of nearly 50 feet. Impressive archways, stonework, and parapets make this 150-year-old monument a grand sight. With the invention of the rifled cannon, the fort's masonry construction became obsolete and the building was never completed. For 10 years, however, from 1863 to 1873, Fort Jefferson served as a prison, a kind of "Alcatraz East." Among its prisoners were four of the "Lincoln Conspirators," including Samuel A. Mudd, the doctor who set the broken leg of fugitive assassin John Wilkes Booth. In 1935, Fort Jefferson became a national monument administered by the National Park Service. Today, however, Fort Jefferson is struggling to resist erosion from the salt and sea, as iron used in the gun openings and the shutters in the fort's walls has accelerated the deterioration, and the structure's openings need to be rebricked. As a result, the National Park Service has designated the fort as the recipient of a $15-million face-lift, a project that may take up to a decade to complete.

For more information on Fort Jefferson and the Dry Tortugas, call the **Everglades National Park Service** (✆ **305/242-7700**) or visit www.fortjefferson.com. Fort Jefferson is open during daylight hours. A self-guided tour describes the history of the human presence in the Dry Tortugas while leading visitors through the fort.

OUTDOOR ACTIVITIES

BIRD-WATCHING Bring your binoculars and your bird books: Bird-watching is *the* reason to visit this little cluster of tropical islands. The Dry Tortugas, uniquely situated in the middle of the migration flyway between North and South America, serve as an important rest stop for the more than 200 winged varieties that pass through here annually. The season peaks from mid-March to mid-May, when thousands of birds show up, but many species from the West Indies can be found here year-round.

DIVING & SNORKELING The warm, clear, shallow waters of the Dry Tortugas produce optimum conditions for snorkeling and scuba diving. Four endangered species of sea turtles—green, leatherback, Atlantic Ridley, and hawksbill—can be found here, along with myriad marine species. The region just outside the seawall of Fort Jefferson is excellent for underwater touring; an abundant variety of fish, coral, and more live in just 3 to 4 feet of water.

FISHING In July 2001, a federal law closed off all fishing in a 90-square-mile tract of open ocean called the Tortugas North and a 61-square-mile tract of open ocean called the Tortugas South. It basically prohibits all fishing in order to preserve the dwindling population of fish (a result of commercial fishing and environmental factors). Instead, head to Key West.

CAMPING

The rustic beauty of tiny Garden Key (the only island of the Dry Tortugas where campers are allowed to pitch tents) is a camper's dream. Don't worry about sharing your site with noisy RVs or motor homes; they can't get here. The abundance of birds doesn't make it quiet, but the camping—a stone's throw from the water—is as picturesque as it gets. Picnic tables, cooking grills, and toilets are provided, but there are no showers. All supplies must be packed in and out. Sites are $3 per person per night and are available on a first-come, first-served basis. The 10 sites book up fast. For more information, call the **National Park Service** (✆ **305/242-7700**).

8

The Everglades & Biscayne National Park

President Harry S Truman once declared the Everglades "an irreplaceable primitive area." While those words don't exactly do justice to the Everglades and the surrounding Biscayne National Park, he clarified what he said: "Here are no lofty peaks seeking the sky, no mighty glaciers or rushing streams wearing away the uplifted land. Here is land, tranquil in its quiet beauty, serving not as the source of water, but as the last receiver of it. To its natural abundance, we owe the spectacular plant and animal life that distinguishes this place from all others in our country."

There's no better reality show than the one that exists in the Everglades. Up-close-and-personal views of alligators, crocodiles, and bona fide wildlife—not the kind you'd find on, say, South Beach, after midnight—make for an interesting, photo-opportunistic experience that's worthy of a show on Animal Planet.

Tourists in South Florida shouldn't leave the area without taking time to see some of the wild plant and animal life in the swampy Everglades and the underwater treasures of Biscayne National Park.

1 A GLIMPSE OF EVERGLADES NATIONAL PARK ★★

35 miles SW of Miami

Before visiting it, my conception of the Everglades was that it was one big swamp swarming with ominous creatures, like something from the programming geeks at the Sci Fi Channel. For someone who'd rather endure an endless series of root canals than audition for a role on *Survivor* (the closest I'd ever been to nature was sleep-away camp), the Everglades might as well have been the *Never*glades—that is, until I finally decided to venture there. To my surprise, and contrary to popular belief, the Everglades isn't really a swamp at all, but one of the country's most fascinating natural resources.

For first-timers or those with dubious athletic skills, the best way to see the 'Glades is probably via airboats, which aren't actually allowed in the park proper, but cut through the saw grass on the park's outskirts, taking you past countless birds, alligators, crocodiles, deer, and raccoons. A walk on one of the park's many trails will provide you with a different vantage point: up-close interaction with an assortment of tame wildlife. But the absolute best way to see the 'Glades is via canoe, which allows you to get incredibly close to nature. Whichever method you choose, I guarantee that you will marvel at the sheer beauty of the Everglades. Despite the multitude of mosquito bites (the bugs seem to be immune to repellent—wear long pants and cover your arms), an Everglades experience will definitely contribute to a newfound appreciation for Florida's natural (and beautiful) wonderland.

This vast and unusual ecosystem is actually a shallow, 40-mile-wide, slow-moving river. Rarely more than knee-deep, the water is the lifeblood of this wilderness, and the subtle shifts in water level dictate the life cycles of the native plants and animals. In 1947, 1.5 million acres—less than 20% of the Everglades' wilderness—were established as Everglades National Park. At that time, few lawmakers understood how neighboring ecosystems relate to each other. Consequently, the park is heavily affected by surrounding territories and is at the butt end of every environmental insult that occurs upstream in Miami.

While there has been a marked decrease in the indigenous wildlife here, Everglades National Park nevertheless remains one of the few places where you can see dozens of endangered species in their natural habitat, including the swallowtail butterfly, American crocodile, leatherback turtle, southern bald eagle, West Indian manatee, and Florida panther.

Take your time on the trails, and a hypnotic beauty begins to unfold. Follow the rustling of a bush, and you might see a small green tree frog or tiny brown anole lizard, with its bright-red spotted throat. Crane your neck to see around a bend, and discover a delicate, brightly painted mule-ear orchid.

Lazy River

It takes a month for 1 gallon of water to move through Everglades National Park.

The slow and subtle splendor of this exotic land may not be immediately appealing to kids raised on video games and rapid-fire commercials, but they'll certainly remember the experience and thank you for it later. Your kids will find plenty of dramatic fun around the park, such as airboat rides, hiking, and biking, to keep them satisfied for at least a day.

JUST THE FACTS

GETTING THERE & ACCESS POINTS Although the Everglades may seem overwhelmingly large and unapproachable, it's easy to get to the park's two main areas—the northern section, accessible via Shark Valley and Everglades City, and the southern section, accessible through the Ernest F. Coe Visitor Center, near Homestead and Florida City.

NORTHERN ENTRANCES A popular day trip for Miamians, **Shark Valley,** a 15-mile paved loop road (with an observation tower in the middle of the loop) overlooking the pulsating heart of the Everglades, is the easiest and most scenic way to explore the national park. Just 25 miles west of the Florida Turnpike, Shark Valley is best reached via the Tamiami Trail, South Florida's preturnpike, two-lane road, which cuts across the southern part of the state along the park's northern border. Roadside attractions (boat rides and alligator farms, for example) along the Tamiami Trail are operated by the Miccosukee Indian Village and are worth a quick, fun stop. An excellent tram tour (leaving from the Shark Valley Visitor Center) goes deep into the park along a trail that's also terrific for biking. Shark Valley is about an hour's drive from Miami.

A little less than 10 miles west along the Tamiami Trail from Shark Valley, you'll discover **Big Cypress National Preserve,** in which stretches of vibrant green cypress and pine trees make for a fabulous Kodak moment. If you pick up S.R. 29 and head south from the Tamiami Trail, you'll hit a modified version of civilization in the form of Everglades City (where the Everglades meet the Gulf of Mexico), where there's another entrance to the park and the **Gulf Coast Visitor Center.** From Miami to Shark Valley: Go west on I-395 to S.R. 821 South (the Florida Tpk.). Take the U.S. 41/Southwest 8th Street (Tamiami Trail) exit. The Shark Valley entrance is just 25 miles west. To get to Everglades City, continue west on the Tamiami Trail and head south on S.R. 29. Everglades

City is approximately a 2½-hour drive from Miami, but because it is scenic, it may take longer if you stop or slow down to view your surroundings.

SOUTHERN ENTRANCE (VIA HOMESTEAD & FLORIDA CITY) If you're in a rush to hit the 'Glades and don't care about the scenic route, this is your best bet. Just southeast of Homestead and Florida City, off S.R. 9336, the southern access to the park will bring you directly to the Ernest F. Coe Visitor Center. Right inside the park, 4 miles beyond the Ernest F. Coe Visitor Center, is the Royal Palm Visitor Center, which is the starting point for the two most popular walking trails, Gumbo Limbo and Anhinga, where you'll witness a plethora of birds and wildlife roaming freely, unperturbed by human voyeurs. Thirteen miles west of the Ernest F. Coe Visitor Center, you'll hit Pa-hay-okee Overlook Trail, which is worth a trek across the boardwalk to reach the observation tower, over which vultures and hawks hover protectively amid a resplendent, picturesque, bird's-eye view of the Everglades. From Miami to the southern entrance: Go west on I-395 to S.R. 821 South (Florida Turnpike), which will end in Florida City. Take the first right through the center of town (you can't miss it) and follow signs to the park entrance on S.R. 9336. The Ernest F. Coe Visitor Center is about 1½ hours from Miami.

VISITOR CENTERS & INFORMATION General inquiries and specific questions should be directed to **Everglades National Park Headquarters,** 40001 S.R. 9336, Homestead, FL 33034 (© **305/242-7700**). Ask for a copy of *Parks and Preserves,* a free newspaper that's filled with up-to-date information about goings-on in the Everglades. Headquarters is staffed by helpful phone operators daily from 8:30am to 4:30pm. You can also try www.nps.gov/ever.

Note that all hours listed are for the high season, generally November through May. During the slow summer months, many offices and outfitters keep abbreviated hours. Always call ahead to confirm hours of operation.

The **Ernest F. Coe Visitor Center,** located at the Park Headquarters entrance, west of Homestead and Florida City, is the best place to gather information for your trip. In addition to details on tours and boat rentals, and free brochures outlining trails, wildlife, and activities, you will find state-of-the-art educational displays, films, and interactive exhibits. A gift shop sells postcards, film, an impressive selection of books about the Everglades, unusual gift items, and a supply of your most important gear: insect repellent. The shop is open daily from 8am to 5pm.

The **Royal Palm Visitor Center,** a small nature museum located 3 miles past the park's main entrance, is a smaller information center. The museum is not great (its displays are equipped with recordings about the park's ecosystem), but the center is the departure point for the popular Anhinga and Gumbo Limbo trails. The center is open daily from 8am to 4pm.

'Glades in the Spotlight

ABC's canceled television series Invasion may have been shot mostly on a set in Los Angeles, but its creator, Shaun Cassidy, a Florida resident and, yes, that Shaun Cassidy, has been to the Everglades and is as intrigued as the rest of us. "It's a very primordial place," Cassidy said in a magazine interview. "There are a lot of species that have existed there that have not existed anywhere else. It's a place that was cut off from the rest of the world for a very long time."

Would You Like Some More Mercury with Your Bass?

Warning: High levels of mercury have been found in Everglades' bass and in some fish species in northern Florida Bay. Do not eat bass caught north of the Main Park Road. Do not eat bass caught south of the Main Park Road more than once a week. Children and pregnant women should not eat any bass. The following saltwater species caught in northern Florida Bay should not be consumed more than once per week by adults or once per month by women of child-bearing age and children: spotted sea trout, gaff-topsail, catfish, bluefish, jack crevalle, or ladyfish.

Knowledgeable rangers, who provide brochures and personal insight into the park's activities, also staff the **Flamingo Visitor Center,** 38 miles from the main entrance, at the park's southern access, with natural-history exhibits and information on visitor services, and the **Shark Valley Visitor Center,** at the park's northern entrance. Both are open daily from 8:30am to 5pm.

ENTRANCE FEES, PERMITS & REGULATIONS Permits and passes can be purchased only at the main park or Shark Valley entrance station. Even if you are just visiting the park for an afternoon, you'll need to buy a 7-day permit, which costs $10 per vehicle. Pedestrians and cyclists are charged $5 each. An Everglades Park Pass, valid for a year's worth of unlimited admissions, is available for $25. You may also purchase a 12-month America the Beautiful National Parks and Federal Recreation Lands Pass–Annual Pass for $50, which is valid for entrance into any U.S. national park. U.S. citizens ages 62 and older pay only $10 for a America the Beautiful National Parks and Federal Recreation Lands Pass–Senior Pass that's valid for life. A America the Beautiful National Parks and Federal Recreation Lands Pass–Access Pass is available free to U.S. citizens with disabilities.

Permits are required for campers to stay overnight either in the backcountry or at the primitive campsites. See "Camping in the Everglades," on p. 255.

Those who want to fish without a charter captain must obtain a standard State of Florida saltwater fishing license. These are available in the park at Flamingo Lodge or at any tackle shop or sporting goods store nearby. Nonresidents pay $30 for a 7-day license or $17 for a 3-day license. Florida residents pay $17 for an annual fishing license. Snook and crawfish licenses must be purchased separately at a cost of $2 each.

Charter captains carry vessel licenses that cover all paying passengers, but ask to be sure. Freshwater fishing licenses are available at various bait-and-tackle stores outside the park at the same rates as those offered inside the park. A good one nearby is **Don's Bait & Tackle,** 30710 S. Federal Hwy., right on U.S. 1 in Homestead (✆ **305/247-6616**). ***Note:*** Most of the area's freshwater fishing, limited to murky canals and artificial lakes near housing developments, is hardly worth the trouble when so much good saltwater fishing is available.

SEASONS There are two distinct seasons in the Everglades: high season and mosquito season. High season is also dry season and lasts from late November to May. Most winters here are warm, sunny, and breezy—a good combination for keeping the bugs away. This is the best time to visit because low water levels attract the largest variety of wading birds and their predators. As the dry season wanes, wildlife follows the receding water; by the end of May, the only living things you are sure to spot will make you itch. The worst, called "no-see-ums," are not even swattable. If you choose to visit during the buggy season, be vigilant in applying bug spray. Also, realize that many establishments and operators either close or curtail offerings in summer, so always call ahead to check schedules.

RANGER PROGRAMS More than 50 ranger programs, free with entry, are offered each month during high season and give visitors an opportunity to gain an expert's perspective. Ranger-led walks and talks are offered year-round from Royal Palm Visitor Center, and at the Flamingo and Gulf Coast visitor centers, as well as Shark Valley Visitor Center during winter months. Park rangers tend to be helpful, well informed, and good humored. Some programs occur regularly, such as Royal Palm Visitor Center's Glade Glimpses, a walking tour on which rangers point out flora and fauna, and discuss issues affecting the Everglades' survival. Tours are scheduled at 1:30pm daily. The Anhinga Amble, a similar program that takes place on the Anhinga Trail, starts at 10:30am daily. Because times, programs, and locations vary from month to month, check the schedule, available at any of the visitor centers.

SAFETY There are many dangers inherent in this vast wilderness area. *Always* let someone know your itinerary before you set out on an extended hike. It's mandatory that you file an itinerary when camping overnight in the backcountry (which you can do when you apply for your overnight permit at either the Flamingo Visitor Center or the Gulf Coast Visitor Center). When you're on the water, watch for weather changes; severe thunderstorms and high winds often develop rapidly. Swimming is not recommended because of the presence of alligators, sharks, and barracudas. Watch out for the region's four indigenous poisonous snakes: diamondback and pygmy rattlesnakes, coral snakes (identifiable by their colorful rings), and water moccasins (which swim on the surface of the water). Bring insect repellent to ward off mosquitoes and biting flies. First aid is available from park rangers. The nearest hospital is in Homestead, 10 miles from the park's main entrance.

SEEING THE HIGHLIGHTS

Shark Valley, a 15-mile paved road (ideal for biking) through the Everglades, provides a fine introduction to the wonders of the park, but don't plan on spending more than a few hours here. Bicycling and taking a guided tram tour (p. 254) are fantastic ways to cover the highlights.

If you want to see a greater array of plant and animal life, make sure that you venture into the park through the main entrance, pick up a trail map, and dedicate at least a day to exploring from there.

Stop first along the Anhinga and Gumbo Limbo trails, which start right next to each other, 3 miles from the park's main entrance. These trails provide a thorough introduction to Everglades' flora and fauna and are highly recommended to first-time visitors. Each is a .5-mile round-trip. **Gumbo Limbo Trail** (my pick for best walking trail in the Everglades) meanders through a gorgeous, shaded, junglelike hammock of gumbo-limbo trees, royal palms, ferns, orchids, air plants, and a general blanket of vegetation, though it doesn't put you in close contact with much wildlife. **Anhinga Trail** is one of the most popular trails in the park because of its abundance of wildlife: There's more water and wildlife in this area than in most parts of the Everglades, especially during dry season. Alligators, lizards, turtles, river otters, herons, egrets, and other animals abound, making this one of the best trails for seeing wildlife. Arrive early to spot the widest selection of exotic birds, such as the Anhinga bird, the trail's namesake, a large black fishing bird so accustomed to humans that many of them build their nests in plain view. Take your time—at least an hour is recommended for each trail. Both are wheelchair accessible. If you treat the trails and modern boardwalk as pathways to get through quickly, rather than destinations to experience and savor, you'll miss out on the still beauty and hidden treasures that await you.

To get closer to nature, a few hours in a canoe along any of the trails allows paddlers the chance to sense the park's fluid motion and to become a part of the ecosphere. Visitors who choose this option end up feeling more like explorers than observers. (See "Sports & Outdoor Activities," below.)

No matter which option you choose (and there are many), I strongly recommend staying for the 7pm program, available during high season at the Long Pine Key Amphitheater. This ranger-led talk and slide show will give you a detailed overview of the park's history, natural resources, wildlife, and threats to its survival.

SPORTS & OUTDOOR ACTIVITIES

BIKING The relatively flat, 38-mile paved **Main Park Road** is great for biking because of the multitude of hardwood hammocks (treelike islands or dense stands of hardwood trees that grow only a few inches above land) and a dwarf cypress forest (stunted and thinly distributed cypress trees, which grow in poor soil on drier land).

Shark Valley, however, is the best biking trail by far. If the park isn't flooded from excess rain (which it often is, especially in spring), this is South Florida's most scenic bicycle trail. Many locals haul their bikes out to the 'Glades for a relaxing day of wilderness-trail riding. You'll share the flat, paved road only with other bikers, trams, and a menagerie of wildlife. (Don't be surprised to see a gator lounging in the sun or a deer munching on some grass. Otters, turtles, alligators, and snakes are common companions in the Shark Valley area.) There are no shortcuts, so if you become tired or are unable to complete the entire 15-mile trip, turn around and return on the same road. Allow 2 to 3 hours to bike the entire loop.

Those who love to mountain-bike and who prefer solitude might check out the **Southern Glades Trail,** a 14-mile unpaved trail lined with native trees and teeming with wildlife, such as deer, alligators, and the occasional snake. The remote trail runs along the C-111 canal, off S.R. 9336 and Southwest 217th Street.

Bicycles are available from **Shark Valley Tram Tours,** at the park's Shark Valley entrance (**© 305/221-8455;** www.sharkvalleytramtours.com), for $6.50 per hour; rentals can be picked up anytime between 8:30am and 3pm and must be returned by 4pm.

BIRD-WATCHING More than 350 species of birds make their home in the Everglades. Tropical birds from the Caribbean and temperate species from North America can be found here, along with exotics that have flown in from more distant regions. Eco and Mrazek ponds, located near Flamingo, are two of the best places for birding, especially in early morning or late afternoon in the dry winter months. Pick up a free birding checklist from one of the visitor centers (p. 248) and inquire about what's been spotted in recent days.

CANOEING Canoeing through the Everglades may be one of the most serene, surprisingly diverse adventures you'll ever have. From a canoe (where you're incredibly close to the water level), your vantage point is priceless. Canoers in the 'Glades can coexist with the gators and birds in a way no one else can; the creatures behave as if you're part of the ecosystem—something that won't happen on an airboat. A ranger-guided boat tour is your best bet and oftentimes they are either free or very inexpensive at around $7 to $12 per person. As always, a ranger will help you understand the surroundings and what you're seeing. They don't take reservations, but for more information on the various boat tours, call ✆ **239/695-3311.**

Everglades National Park's longest "trails" are designed for boat and canoe travel, and many are marked as clearly as walking trails. The **Noble Hammock Canoe Trail,** a 2-mile loop, takes 1 to 2 hours and is recommended for beginners. The **Hell's Bay Canoe Trail,** a 3- to 6-mile course for hardier paddlers, takes 2 to 6 hours, depending on how far you choose to go. Fans of this trail like to say, "It's hell to get in and hell to get out." Park rangers can recommend other trails that best suit your abilities, time limitations, and interests.

You can rent a canoe at the **Ivey House B&B** (✆ **877/577-0679;** www.evergladesadventures.com; p. 255) for $50 for 24 hours, $35 per full day (any 8-hr. period), or for $25 per half-day (1–5pm only). Kayaks and tandem kayaks are also available. The rental agent will shuttle your party to the trail head of your choice and pick you up afterward. Rental facilities are open daily from 8am to 5pm.

Overnight canoe rentals are available for $50 to $60. During ideal weather conditions (stay away during bug season!), you can paddle right out to the Gulf and camp on the beach. However, Gulf waters at beach sites can be extremely rough, and people in small watercraft such as a canoe should exercise caution.

You can also take a canoe tour from the Parks Docks on Chokoloskee Causeway on S.R. 29, 1/2 mile south of the traffic circle at the ranger station in Everglades City. Call **Everglades National Park Boat Tours** (✆ **800/445-7724**) for information. And for an eco-tour of the 'Glades, **Everglades Area Tours** (✆ **239/695-9107;** www.evergladesareatours.com) not only offers guided kayak fishing, but also guided half-day kayak eco-tours, customized bird-watching expeditions, as well as bicycle and aerial tours of the Everglades. Capt. Charles Wright can put six kayaks and six passengers into the Yak Attack shuttle motorboat for the trip out to the Wilderness Waterway, deep within Everglades National Park's Ten Thousand Islands, where you will paddle in the absolute wilderness, spotting birds, dolphins, manatees, sea turtles, and perhaps even the elusive American crocodile. The shuttle then brings you back to Everglades City. The trip costs $195 per angler and includes transportation, guide services, outfitted kayaks, and all safety equipment.

FISHING About a third of Everglades National Park is open water. Freshwater fishing is popular in brackish **Nine-Mile Pond** (25 miles from the main entrance) and other spots along the Main Park Road, but because of the high mercury levels found in the Everglades, freshwater fishers are warned not to eat their catch (see "Would You Like Some Mercury with Your Bass" box, above). Before casting, check in at a visitor center, as many of the park's lakes are preserved for observation only. Fishing licenses are required; see p. 249 for more information.

Saltwater anglers will find snapper and sea trout plentiful. Charter boats and guides are available at Flamingo Lodge, Marina, and Outpost Resort (see below). Phone for information and reservations.

MOTORBOATING Motorboating around the Everglades seems like a great way to see plants and animals in remote habitats, and, indeed, it's an interesting and fulfilling experience as you throttle into nature. However, environmentalists are taking stock of the damage inflicted by motorboats (especially airboats) on the delicate ecosystem. If you choose to motor, remember that most of the areas near land are "no wake" zones and that, for the protection of nesting birds, landing is prohibited on most of the little mangrove islands. Motorboating is allowed in certain areas, such as Florida Bay, the backcountry toward Everglades City, and the Ten Thousand Islands area. In all the freshwater lakes, however, motorboats are prohibited if they're above 5 horsepower. There's a long list of restrictions and restricted areas, so get a copy of the park's boating rules from Park Headquarters before setting out.

The Everglades' only marina—accommodating about 50 boats with electric and water hookups—is **Flamingo Lodge, Marina, and Outpost Resort,** 1 Flamingo Lodge Hwy., Everglades City (✆ **239/695-3101**). This place, which suffered terrible damage from Hurricanes Katrina and Wilma in 2005, is most likely going to be demolished and rebuilt sometime in 2009. As of this writing, they were still renting boats, but only from May through October. The well-marked channel to the Flamingo is accessible to boats with a maximum 4-foot draft and is open year-round. Reservations can be made through the marina store (✆ **239/695-3101**). Skiffs with 15-horsepower motors are available for rent. These low-power boats cost about $155 per day, $100 per half-day. A $100 deposit is required.

ORGANIZED TOURS

AIRBOAT TOURS Shallow-draft, fan-powered airboats were invented in the Everglades by frog hunters who were tired of poling through the brushes. Airboats cut through the saw grass and are sort of like hydraulic boats; at high-enough speeds, a boat actually rises above the saw grass and into the air. Even though airboats are the most efficient (not to mention fast and fun!) way to get around, they are not permitted in the park—these shallow-bottom runabouts tend to inflict severe damage on animals and plants. Just outside the boundaries of the Everglades, however, you'll find a number of outfitters offering rides. ***Tip:*** Consider bringing earplugs, as these high-speed boats are loud. Sometimes they give you plugs, but bring a pair just in case.

One of the best airboat outfitters is **Gator Park,** 12 miles west of the Florida Turnpike at 24050 SW Eighth St. (✆ **305/559-2255;** www.gatorpark.com), which, despite its touristy name, happens to be one of the most informative and entertaining airboat-tour operators around, not to mention the only one to give out free earplugs. Some of the guides deserve a medal for getting into the water and poking around a massive alligator, even though they're not really supposed to. After the boat ride, there's a free interactive wildlife show that features alligator wrestling and several other frightening acts involving scorpions. Take note of the gorgeous peacocks that live in the trees here. Admission for the boat ride and show is $21 for adults, $11 for children 6 to 11; prices are cheaper if you purchase tickets online. Airboats depart every 20 minutes. Gator Park is open daily from 9am to 7pm.

Another outfitter I recommend is **Coopertown Airboat Tours** (✆ **305/226-6048;** www.coopertownairboats.com), located about 11 miles west of the Florida Turnpike on the Tamiami Trail (U.S. 41), in a town that boasts a total population of eight humans! The super-friendly staff has helped the company garner the title of "Florida's Best" by the *Miami Herald* for 40 years in a row. You never know what you're going to see, but with great guides, you're sure to see *something* of interest on the 40-minute, 8-mile round-trip tours. There's also a restaurant and a small gator farm on the premises. Airboat rides cost $21 for adults, $10 for children 7 to 11. Private airboat tours are $85 per hour, per person. The company is open daily from 8am to 6pm; tours leave frequently.

Thirty-minute airboat rides are also offered at the **Miccosukee Indian Village,** just west of the Shark Valley entrance on U.S. 41/Tamiami Trail and MM 70 (✆ **305/223-8380;** www.miccosukeetours.com). The price is $10 per person, with cheaper rates online. However, ***be warned and advised:*** I am not recommending this particular outfit over others—it's merely the one closest to the Shark Valley entrance. As always, the quality of your tour is only as good as the quality of your tour guide, and, unfortunately, I've gotten some complaints about the Miccosukee tours.

The **Everglades Alligator Farm,** 4 miles south of Palm Drive on Southwest 192nd Avenue (© **305/247-2628;** www.everglades.com), offers half-hour guided airboat tours daily from 9am until 6pm. The price, which includes admission to the park, is $23 for adults and $16 for children 4 to 11.

Another reputable company is **Captain Doug's,** located 35 miles south of Naples and 1 mile past the bridge in Everglades City (© **800/282-9194**).

CANOE TOURS A fabulous way to explore the Everglades backcountry is via canoe. Slink through the mangroves, slide across saw-grass prairies, and even walk the sands of the unfettered Ten Thousand Islands. Expert guides will lead you in the right direction. Contact **Everglades Adventures** (© **877/567-0679;** www.evergladesadventures.com) at the Ivey House B&B (p. 255).

ECO-TOURS Although it's fascinating to explore on your own, it would be a shame for you to tour the Everglades without a clue about what you're seeing. It's a lot more than saw grass and alligators in the backcountry, which is why **Everglades Adventures** (© **877/567-0679;** www.evergladesadventures.com), located within the Ivey House B&B (p. 255), is there to guide and entertain you, as well as explain such key issues as the differences between alligators and crocodiles, or between swamps and the Everglades.

MOTORBOAT TOURS Both Florida Bay and backcountry tours are offered Thursday to Monday at the **Flamingo Lodge, Marina, and Outpost Resort** (see "Motorboating" above). Florida Bay tours cruise nearby estuaries and sandbars, while six-passenger backcountry boats visit smaller sloughs. Passengers can expect to see birds and a variety of other animals (I once saw a raccoon and some wild pigs). Both are available in 1½- and 2-hour versions that cost $12 or $18 for adults, $7 or $12 for children 6 to 13. Tours depart throughout the day; reservations are recommended. Charter-fishing and sightseeing boats can also be booked through the resort's main reservation number (© **239/695-3101**).

TRAM TOURS At the park's Shark Valley entrance, open-air tram buses take visitors on 2-hour naturalist-led tours that delve 7½ miles into the wilderness and are the best quick introduction you can get to the Everglades. At the trail's midsection, passengers can disembark and climb a 65-foot observation tower with good views of the 'Glades (though the tower on the Pa-hay-okee Trail is better). Visitors will see plenty of wildlife and endless acres of saw grass. Tours run December through April, daily on the hour between 9am and 4pm, and May through November at 9:30am, 11am, 1pm, and 3pm. They're sometimes stalled by flooding or particularly heavy mosquito infestation. Reservations are recommended from December to March. The cost is $15 for adults, $14 for seniors, and $9.25 for children 12 and under. For further information, contact **Shark Valley Tram Tours** (© **305/221-8455;** www.sharkvalleytramtours.com).

WHERE TO STAY

The only lodging in the park proper is Flamingo Lodge (see "Motorboating" above). At the time of this writing, however, Flamingo Lodge's overnight facilities were closed for business after taking a walloping in 2005 from Hurricanes Katrina and Wilma. A 2008 *Miami Herald* article reported that the lodge was being demolished and redone. "Under the best case scenarios, it's probably going to be another 3 to 5 years for any kind of permanent facility," said park planner Fred Herling. The National Park Service, however, ruled out building a new, large hotel unless private interests chip in. Until they all agree on what to do with the rebuilding, however, Flamingo Lodge remains closed to sleepovers. However, a few accommodations just outside the park are even cheaper. A $45-million casino hotel, **Miccosukee Resort** (✆ **877/242-6464;** www.miccosukee.com), is adjacent to the Miccosukee bingo and gaming hall on the northern edge of the park. Although bugs can be a major nuisance, especially in the warm months, camping (the best way to fully experience South Florida's wilderness) is really the way to go in this very primitive environment.

Camping in the Everglades

Campgrounds are available year-round in Flamingo and Long Pine Key. Both have drinking water, picnic tables, charcoal grills, restrooms, and tent and trailer pads, and welcome RVs (Flamingo allows up to 40-ft. vehicles, while Long Pine Key accepts up to 60-footers), though there are no electrical hookups. Flamingo has cold-water showers; Long Pine Key does not have showers or hookups for showers. Private ground fires are not permitted, but supervised campfire programs are conducted during winter months. Long Pine Key and Flamingo are popular and require reservations in advance, which can be made through the National Park Reservations Service (✆ **800/365-CAMP;** www.nps.gov). Campsites are $14 per night, and during winter season (Nov–Apr), there's a 14-day consecutive-stay limit, and a maximum of 30 days a year.

Camping is also available year-round in the **backcountry** (those remote areas accessible only by boat, foot, or canoe—basically most of the park), on a first-come, first-served basis. Campers must register with park rangers and get a free permit in person or by phone no less than 24 hours before the start of their trip. For more information, contact the **Gulf Coast Visitor Center** (✆ **239/695-3311**) or the **Flamingo Visitor Center** (✆ **239/695-2945**), which are the only two places that give out these permits. Once you have one, camping sites cost $14 (with a maximum of eight people per site), or $28 for a group site (maximum of 15 people). Campers can use only designated campsites, which are plentiful and well marked on visitor maps.

Many backcountry sites are **chickee huts**—covered wooden platforms (with toilets) on stilts. They're accessible only by canoe and can accommodate free-standing tents (without stakes). Ground sites are located along interior bays and rivers, and beach camping is also popular. In summer especially, mosquito repellent is necessary gear.

Lodging in Everglades City

As Everglades City is 35 miles southeast of Naples and 83 miles west of Miami, many visitors choose to explore this western entrance to Everglades National Park, located off the Tamiami Trail, on S.R. 29. An annual seafood festival held the first weekend in February is a major event that draws hordes of people. Everglades City (the gateway to the Ten Thousand Islands), where the 'Glades meet the Gulf of Mexico, is the closest thing you'll get to civilization in South Florida's swampy frontier, with a few tourist traps—er, shops—a restaurant, and one bed-and-breakfast.

Ivey House B&B ★★ Finds The first certified Green Lodging in Collier County, the Ivey House offers a variety of accommodations: the Ivey House Inn, featuring spacious rooms with private bathrooms, TVs, phones, and a view of the courtyard pool and waterfall; the Ivey House Lodge, housed in what used to be a recreational center for the men who built the Tamiami Trail, featuring 10 small rooms with communal bathrooms (one each for women and men), no TVs or phones; and the Ivey House Cottage, with two bedrooms, a full kitchen, a private bathroom, and a screened-in porch. Owners Sandee and David Harraden are extremely knowledgeable about the Everglades and assist guests providing a variety of daily excursions. Rates include a Continental breakfast, served from 6:30 to 10am. A full hot breakfast is provided during peak season. Box lunches are available year-round for $11. ***Note:*** There is no smoking in any of the buildings.

107 Camellia St., Everglades City, FL 34139. ✆ **877/567-0679** or 239/695-3299. Fax 239/695-4155. www.iveyhouse.com. 28 units. Winter $100–$200 in Inn, $60–$105 in Lodge, $175–$235 in Cottage; off-season $75–$85 in Inn, $60–$65 in Lodge, $135 in Cottage. 2-night minimum in all facilities during Everglades Seafood Festival in Feb. MC, V. **Amenities:** Restaurant; pool; Wi-Fi; Everglades excursions. *In room:* A/C, TV, kitchen (in cottages), fridge (in inn and cottages).

Rod & Gun Lodge ★ Set on the banks of the sleepy Baron River, this rustic, old white-clapboard house has plenty of history and all kinds of activities for sports enthusiasts, including a pool, bike rentals, a tennis center, and nearby boat rentals and private fishing guides. Hoover vacationed here after his 1928 election victory, and Truman flew in to sign Everglades National Park into existence in 1947 and stayed over as well. Other guests have included Richard Nixon, Burt Reynolds, and Mick Jagger. The public rooms are beautifully paneled and hung with tarpon, wild boar, deer antlers, and other trophies. Guest rooms in this single-story building are unfussy but perfectly comfortable. All have porches looking out on the river. Out by the pool, a screened veranda with ceiling fans is a pleasant place for a libation. The excellent seafood restaurant serves breakfast, lunch, and dinner. The entire property is nonsmoking.

Riverside Dr. and Broadway (P.O. Box 190), Everglades City, FL 34139. ✆ **239/695-2101.** www.evergladesrodandgun.com 17 units. Winter $110–$140 double; off-season $95 double. No credit cards. Closed after July 4 for the summer. **Amenities:** Restaurant; pool; tennis courts; bike rental. *In room:* A/C, TV.

Lodging in Homestead & Florida City

Homestead and Florida City, two adjacent towns that were almost blown off the map by Hurricane Andrew in 1992, have come back better than before. About 10 miles from the park's main entrance, along U.S. 1, 35 miles south of Miami, these somewhat rural towns offer several budget options, including chain hotels. There is a **Days Inn** (✆ **305/245-1260**) in Homestead and a **Hampton Inn** (✆ **800/426-7866** or 305/247-8833) right off the turnpike in Florida City. The best options are listed below.

Best Western Gateway to the Keys This standard two-story motel provides contemporary style and comfort about 10 miles from the park's main entrance. A decent-size pool and a small spa make it attractive to some. Each standard room has bright, tropical bedspreads and oversize picture windows. The suites have convenient extras such as microwaves, coffeemakers, extra sinks, and small fridges. Clean and conveniently located, the only drawback is that, in season, there is often a 3-day minimum-stay requirement. You would do best to call the local reservation line instead of the toll-free number—on several occasions, the hotel has made an exception to the rule, while the central reservation line could not.

411 S. Krome Ave. (U.S. 1), Florida City, FL 33034. ✆ **800/528-1234** or 305/246-5100. Fax 305/242-0056. www.bestwestern.com. 114 units. $100–$150 double. Rates include continental breakfast. During races and the very high season, there may be a 3-night minimum stay. AE, DC, DISC, MC, V. **Amenities:** Pool; spa; laundry service; dry cleaning. *In room:* A/C, TV, dataport, fridge, coffeemaker, hair dryer.

Everglades International Hostel ★ This is what a hostel *should* be. Sure, I've seen cleaner, more modern ones, but the feeling of camaraderie here is what hostels are all about. Located in a 1930s boardinghouse, this hostel has dorm rooms as well as doubles (all with shared bathrooms), a great kitchen, a washer/dryer, high-speed Internet access, bike rentals, and a garden (with tents, forts, and an outdoor chess board). The friendly, amazingly accommodating staff here provides tons of helpful information and runs sightseeing/canoe trips to the Everglades. ***Note:*** Some rooms here are cheaper than the rates listed below, but do not have air-conditioning.

20 SW 2nd Ave., Florida City, FL 33034. ✆ **800/372-3874** or 305/248-1122. www.evergladeshostel.com. $25–$28 dorm bed; $75 private double; $55 semi-private room; $18 per person garden camping. MC, V. **Amenities:** Bike rental; tours; Internet access; laundry facilities; kitchen. *In room:* A/C (in some).

WHERE TO DINE IN & AROUND THE PARK

You won't find fancy nouvelle cuisine in this suburbanized farm country, but there are plenty of fast-food chains along U.S. 1 and a few old favorites worth a taste.

Here for nearly a quarter of a century, **El Toro Taco Family Restaurant,** 1 S. Krome Ave., near Mowry and Campbell drives, Homestead (✆ **305/245-8182**), opens daily at 9:30am and stays crowded until at least 9pm most days. The fresh grilled meats, tacos, burritos, salsas, guacamole, and stews are all mild and delicious. No matter how big your appetite, it's hard to spend more than $15 per person at this Mexican outpost. Bring your own beer or wine.

Housed in a one-story, windowless building that looks something like a medieval fort, the **Capri Restaurant,** 935 N. Krome Ave., Florida City (✆ **305/247-1542**), has been serving hearty Italian-American fare since 1958. Great pastas and salads complement a menu of meat and fish dishes; portions are big. Lunch and dinner are served Monday through Friday until 9:30pm and Saturday until 10:30pm. The **White Lion Café,** 146 NW 7th St., Homestead (✆ **305/248-1076**), is a quaint home-and-gardens-cum-cafe with live blues, jazz, and swing music at night, and a menu with such items as Dirty Little Shrimp and Poor Man's Steak, which is actually delicious meatloaf with mushrooms, gravy, mashed potatoes, and veggies for just $11. Dinner is served Tuesday through Saturday from 5pm until "the fat lady sings."

The **Miccosukee Restaurant,** just west of the Shark Valley entrance on the Tamiami Trail/U.S. 41 (✆ **305/223-8380**), serves authentic pumpkin bread, fry bread, and fish, and not-so-authentic Native American interpretations of tacos and fried chicken. It's worth a stop for brunch, lunch, or dinner.

Near the Miccosukee reservation is the **Pit Bar-B-Q,** 16400 SW 8th St. (✆ **305/226-2272**), a total pit of a place known for some of the best smoked ribs, barbecued chicken, and corn bread this side of the Deep South. It's open daily from 11am to 8pm.

In Everglades City, the **Oyster House,** on Chokoloskee Causeway, S.R. (the locals call it Hwy.) 29 South (✆ **239/695-2073**), is a large but homey seafood restaurant with modest prices, excellent service, and a fantastic view of the Ten Thousand Islands. Try the hush puppies. For more authentic local flavor, try the **Camellia Street Grill,** 208 Camellia St. (✆ **239/695-2003**), an off-the-beaten-path, rust waterfront fish joint fusing Southern hospitality with outstanding seafood served with a gourmet twist. An on-site herb and veggie garden provides the freshest ingredients and stellar salads. Some say the oysters here are among the best they've ever had. Everything is homemade, including the Key lime pie and there's live music on Fridays and Saturdays.

2 BISCAYNE NATIONAL PARK ★

35 miles S of Miami; 21 miles E of Everglades National Park

With only about 500,000 visitors each year (mostly boaters and divers), the unusual Biscayne National Park is one of the least-crowded parks in the country. Perhaps that's because the park is a little more difficult than most to access—more than 95% of its 181,500 acres is under water.

The park's significance was first formally acknowledged in 1968 when, in an unprecedented move (and despite intense pressure from developers), President Lyndon B. Johnson signed a bill to conserve the barrier islands off South Florida's east coast as a national monument—a protected status just a rung below national park. After being twice enlarged, once in 1974 and again in 1980, the waters and land surrounding the northernmost coral reef in North America became a full-fledged national park—the largest of its kind in the country.

To be fully appreciated, Biscayne National Park should be thought of as more preserve than destination. Use your time here to explore underwater life, but also to relax. The park's small mainland mangrove shoreline and keys are best explored by boat. Its extensive reef system is renowned by divers and snorkelers worldwide.

The park consists of 44 islands, but only a few of them are open to visitors. The most popular is **Elliott Key,** which has campsites and a visitor center, plus freshwater showers (cold water only), restrooms, trails, and a buoyed swim area. It's about 9 miles from **Convoy Point,** the park's official headquarters on land. During Columbus Day weekend, there is a very popular regatta for which a lively crowd of party people gathers—sometimes in the nude—to celebrate the long weekend. If you'd prefer to rough it a little more, the 29-acre island known as **Boca Chita Key,** once an exclusive haven for yachters, has now become a popular spot for all manner of boaters. Visitors can camp and tour the island's restored historic buildings, including the county's second-largest lighthouse and a tiny chapel.

JUST THE FACTS

GETTING THERE & ACCESS POINTS Convoy Point, the park's mainland entrance, is 9 miles east of Homestead. To reach the park from Miami, take the Florida Turnpike to the Tallahassee Road (SW 137th Ave.) exit. Turn left, then left again at North Canal Drive (SW 328th St.), and follow signs to the park. Another option is to rent a speedboat in Miami and cruise south for about 1½ hours. If you're coming from U.S. 1, whether you're heading north or south, turn east at North Canal Drive (SW 328th St.). The entrance is approximately 9 miles away. The rest of the park is accessible only by boat.

Because most of Biscayne National Park is accessible only to boaters, mooring buoys abound, as it is illegal to anchor on coral. When no buoys are available, boaters must anchor on sand or on the docks surrounding the small harbor off Boca Chita. Boats can also dock here overnight for $20. Even the most experienced boaters should carry updated nautical charts of the area, which are available at Convoy Point's Dante Fascell Visitor Center. The waters are often murky, making the abundant reefs and sandbars difficult to detect—and there are more interesting ways to spend a day than waiting for the tide to rise. There's a boat launch at adjacent Homestead Bayfront Park and 66 slips on Elliott Key, available free on a first-come, first-served basis.

Round-trip transportation to and from the visitor center to Elliott Key costs $35 (plus tax) round-trip per person and takes about an hour. This is a convenient option, ensuring that you don't get lost on some deserted island by boating there yourself. Call ✆ **305/230-1100** for the seasonal schedule.

VISITOR CENTERS & INFORMATION **Dante Fascell Visitor Center,** often referred to by its older name, **Convoy Point Visitor Center,** 9700 SW 328th St., Homestead, FL 33033-5634, at the park's main entrance (✆ **305/230-7275;** fax 305/230-1190; www.nps.gov/bisc), is the natural starting point for any venture into the park without a boat. It provides comprehensive information about the park; on request, rangers will show you a short video on the park, its natural surroundings, and what you may see. The center is open daily from 9am to 5pm.

For information on transportation, glass-bottom boat tours, and snorkeling and scuba-diving expeditions, contact the park concessionaire, **Biscayne National Underwater Park, Inc.,** P.O. Box 1270, Homestead, FL 33030 (✆ **305/230-1100;** fax 305/230-1120; www.nps.gov/bisc). It's open daily from 8:30am to 5pm.

ENTRANCE FEES & PERMITS Entering Biscayne National Park is free. There is a $20 overnight docking fee at both Boca Chita Key Harbor and Elliott Key Harbor, which includes a campsite. Campsites are $15 for those staying without a boat. Group camping costs $30 a day and covers up to six tents and 25 people. See p. 249 for information on fishing permits. Backcountry camping permits are free and can be picked up from the Dante Fascell Visitor Center. For more information on fees and permits, call the park ranger at ✆ **305/230-1144.**

SEEING THE HIGHLIGHTS

Because the park is primarily underwater, the only way to truly experience it is with snorkel or scuba gear. Beneath the surface of Biscayne National Park, the aquatic universe pulses with multicolored life: abounding bright parrotfish and angelfish, gently rocking sea fans, and coral labyrinths. (See the "Snorkeling & Scuba Diving" section below for more information.) Afterward, take a picnic out to Elliott Key and taste the crisp salt air blowing off the Atlantic. Or head to Boca Chita, an intriguing island that was once the private playground of wealthy yachters.

SPORTS & OUTDOOR ACTIVITIES

CANOEING & KAYAKING Biscayne National Park affords excellent canoeing, both along the coast and across the open water to nearby mangroves and artificial islands dotting the longest uninterrupted shoreline in the state of Florida. Because tides can be strong, only experienced canoeists should attempt to paddle far from shore. If you do plan to go far, first obtain a tide table from the visitor center and paddle with the current. Free ranger-led canoe tours are scheduled from 9am to noon on the second and fourth Saturdays of the month between January 10 and April 24; phone for information. You can rent a canoe at the park's concession stand for $12 an hour. Two-person kayaks go for $16 an hour. Call ✆ **305/230-1100** for reservations, information, ranger tours, and boat rentals.

FISHING Ocean fishing is excellent year-round at Biscayne National Park; many people cast their lines from the breakwater jetty at Convoy Point. A fishing license is required. (See p. 249 for more information.) Bait is not available in Biscayne National Park, but it is sold in adjacent Homestead Bayfront Park. Stone crabs and Florida lobsters can be found here, but you're allowed to catch these only on the ocean side when they're in season. There are strict limits on size, season, number, and method of take (including spearfishing) for both freshwater and saltwater fishing. The latest regulations are available at most marinas, bait-and-tackle shops, and the park's visitor centers; or you can contact the **Florida Fish and Wildlife Conservation Commission,** Bryant Building, 620 S. Meridian St., Tallahassee, FL 32399-1600 (✆ **850/488-0331**).

HIKING & EXPLORING As the majority of this park is underwater, hiking is not the main attraction here, but there are some interesting sights and trails nonetheless. At Convoy Point, you can walk along the 370-foot boardwalk and along the half-mile jetty that serves as a breakwater for the park's harbor. From here, you can usually see brown pelicans, little blue herons, snowy egrets, and a few exotic fish.

Elliott Key is accessible only by boat, but once you're there, you have two good trail options. True to its name, the Loop Trail makes a 1.5-mile circle from the bayside visitor center, through a hardwood hammock and mangroves, to an elevated oceanside boardwalk. You'll likely see land crabs scurrying around the mangrove roots.

Reopened in 1998, Boca Chita Key was once a playground for wealthy tycoons, and it still has the peaceful beauty that attracted elite anglers from cold climates. Many of the historic buildings are still intact, including an ornamental lighthouse that was never put to use. Take advantage of the tours, usually led by a park ranger and available every Sunday in winter only at 1:30pm. The tour, including the boat trip, takes about 3 hours. The price is $25 for adults, $20 for seniors, and $17 for children 11 and under. However, call in advance to see if the sea is calm enough for the trip—the boats won't run in rough waters. See "Glass-Bottom Boat Tours," below, for information about the daily 10am excursions.

SNORKELING & SCUBA DIVING The clear, warm waters of Biscayne National Park are packed with colorful tropical fish that swim in the offshore reefs. If you don't have your own gear, or if you don't want to lug it to the park, you can rent or buy snorkeling and scuba gear at the full-service dive shop at Convoy Point. Rates are in line with those at mainland dive shops.

The best way to see the park from under water is to take a snorkeling or diving tour operated by **Biscayne National Underwater Park, Inc.** (✆ **305/230-1100;** www.nps.gov/bisc). Snorkeling tours depart at 1:30pm daily, last about 3 hours, and cost $38 per adult and $30 per child, including equipment. There are also weekend two-tank dives for certified divers; the price is $75, including two tanks and weights. Make your reservations in advance. The shop is open daily from 9am to 5pm.

Before entering the water, be sure to apply waterproof sun block—once you begin to explore, it's easy to lose track of time, and the Florida sun is brutal, even during winter.

SWIMMING You can swim off the protected beaches of Elliott Key, Boca Chita Key, and adjacent Homestead Bayfront Park, but none of these match the width or softness of other South Florida beaches. Check the water conditions before heading into the sea: The strong currents that make this a popular destination for windsurfers and sailors can be dangerous, even for strong swimmers. Homestead Bayfront Park is really just a marina next to Biscayne National Park, but it does have a beach and picnic facilities, as well as fishing areas and a playground. It's located at Convoy Point, 9698 SW 328th St., Homestead (✆ **305/230-3034**).

GLASS-BOTTOM BOAT TOURS

If you prefer not to dive, the best way to see the sights is on a glass-bottom boat. **Biscayne National Underwater Park, Inc.** (✆ **305/230-1100;** www.nps.gov/bisc), has daily trips to view some of the country's most beautiful coral reefs and tropical fish. Boats depart year-round from Convoy Point at 10am and stay out for about 3 hours. At $25 for adults, $20 for seniors, and $17 for children 12 and under, the scenic and informative tours are well worth the price. Boats carry fewer than 50 passengers; reservations are almost always necessary.

WHERE TO STAY

Besides campsites, there are no facilities available for overnight guests to this watery park. Most noncamping visitors come for an afternoon, on their way to the Keys, and stay overnight in nearby Homestead, where there are many national chain hotels and other affordable lodgings; see p. 256 for more information.

Although you won't find hotels or lodges in Biscayne National Park, it does have some of the state's most pristine campsites. Because they are inaccessible by motor vehicle, you'll be sure to avoid the mass of RVs so prevalent in many of the state's other campgrounds. The sites on Elliott Key and Boca Chita can be reached only by boat. If you don't have your own boat, call ✆ **305/230-1100** to arrange a drop-off. Transportation to Elliott Key from the visitor center costs $35 (plus tax). They do not provide transportation to Boca Chita, so you'll have to rent a boat. Boca Chita has only saltwater toilets (no showers or sinks); Elliot Key has freshwater, cold-water showers and toilets, but is otherwise no less primitive. If you didn't pay for the overnight docking fee, campsites are $10.

With a backcountry permit, available free from the visitor center, you can pitch your tent somewhere even more private. Ask for a map and be sure to bring plenty of bug spray. Sites cost $10 a night for up to six persons staying in one or two tents. Backcountry camping is allowed only on Elliott Key, which is a very popular spot (accessible only by boat) for boaters and campers. It is approximately 9 miles from the Dante Fascell Visitor Center and offers hiking trails, fresh water, boat slips, showers, and restrooms. While there, don't miss the Old Road, a 7-mile tropical hammock trail that runs the length of Elliott Key. This trail is one of the few places left in the world to see the highly endangered Schaus swallowtail butterfly, recognizable by its black wings with diagonal yellow bands. These butterflies are usually out from late April to July.

9

The Gold Coast: Hallandale to the Palm Beaches

Named not for the sun-kissed skin of the area's residents, but for the gold salvaged from shipwrecks off its coastline, the Gold Coast embraces more than 60 miles of beautiful Atlantic shoreline—from the pristine sands of Palm Beach to the legendary strip of beaches in Fort Lauderdale.

If you haven't visited the cities along Florida's southeastern coast in the last few years, you'll be amazed at how much has changed. Miles of sprawling grassland and empty lots have been replaced with luxurious resorts and high-rise condominiums. Taking advantage of their proximity to Miami, the cities that make up the Gold Coast have attracted millions of people looking to escape crowded sidewalks, traffic jams, and the everyday routines of life.

Fortunately, amid all the building, much of the natural treasure of the Gold Coast remains. There are 300 miles of Intracoastal Waterway, not to mention Fort Lauderdale's Venetian-inspired canals, and the unspoiled splendor of the Everglades is just a few miles inland.

The most popular areas in the Gold Coast are Fort Lauderdale, Boca Raton, and Palm Beach. While Fort Lauderdale is a favored beachfront destination, Boca Raton and Palm Beach are better known for their country-club lifestyles and excellent shopping. Farther north is the quietly popular Jupiter, best known for spring training at the Roger Dean Stadium and for former resident Burt Reynolds. In between these better-traveled destinations are a few things worth stopping for, but not much. Driving north along the coastline is one of the best ways to fully appreciate what the Gold Coast is all about—it's a perspective you certainly won't find in a shopping mall.

Tourists come here by the droves, but they aren't the only people coming; thousands of transplants, fleeing the increasing population influx in Miami and the frigid winters up north, have made this area their home. As a result, there was a brief construction boom in the existing cities and even westward, into the swampy areas of the Everglades. The boom is at a standstill now, obviously, though you'll still see construction on some homes contracted before the recession, in Broward County, for instance. There has also been a great revitalization of several downtown areas, including Hollywood, Fort Lauderdale, and West Palm Beach. These once-desolate urban centers have been spruced up and now attract more young travelers and families than ever.

Unfortunately, like its neighbors to the south, the Gold Coast can be prohibitively hot and buggy in summer. The good news is that bargains are plentiful from May through October, when many locals take advantage of package deals and uncrowded resorts.

For the purposes of this chapter, the Gold Coast will consist of the towns of Hallandale, Hollywood, Pompano Beach, Fort Lauderdale, Dania, Deerfield, Boca Raton, Delray Beach, Boynton Beach, and Palm Beach.

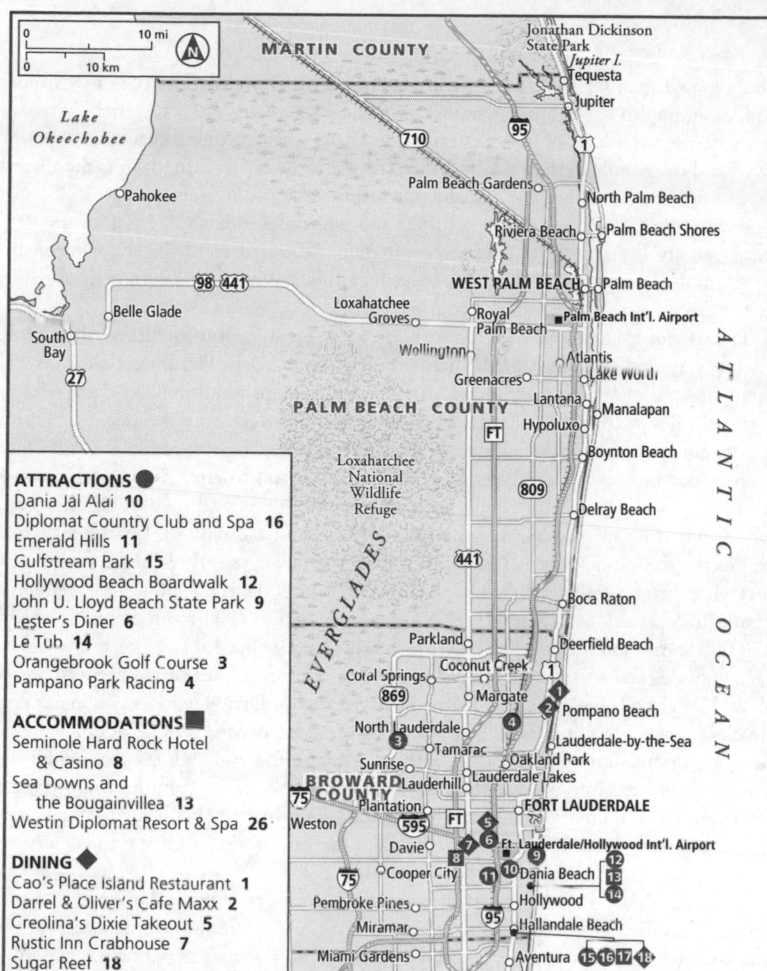

EXPLORING THE GOLD COAST BY CAR

Like most of South Florida, the Gold Coast consists of a mainland and adjacent barrier islands. You'll have to check maps to keep track of the many bridges that allow access to the islands where most tourist activity is centered. Interstate 95, which runs north–south, is the area's main highway. Farther west is the Florida Turnpike, a toll road that can be worth the expense, as the speed limit is higher and it's often less congested than I-95. Also on the mainland is U.S. 1, which generally runs parallel to I-95 (to the east) and is a narrower thoroughfare that is mostly crowded with strip malls and seedy hotels.

I recommend taking Florida A1A, a slow oceanside road that connects the long, thin islands of Florida's entire east coast. Although the road is narrow, it is the most scenic and, thus, ushers you into the relaxed atmosphere of these resort towns.

1 BROWARD COUNTY

23 miles N of Miami

Less exposed than highly hyped Miami-Dade County, Broward County is a lot calmer and, according to some, a lot friendlier than the Magic City. In fact, a friendly rivalry exists between residents of both counties. Miamians consider themselves more sophisticated and cosmopolitan than their northern neighbors, who, in turn, dismiss the alleged sophistication as snobbery and actually prefer their own county's gentler pace.

With more than 23 miles of beachfront and 300 miles of navigable waterways, Broward County is also a great outdoor destination. Scattered amid the shopping malls, condominiums, and tourist traps is a beautiful landscape lined with hundreds of parks, golf courses, tennis courts, and, of course, beaches.

The City of Hallandale Beach is a small, peaceful oceanfront town just north of Dade County's Aventura. Condos are the predominant landmarks in Hallandale, which is still pretty much a retirement community, although the revamped multimillion-dollar Westin Diplomat Resort (p. 275) is slowly trying to revitalize and liven up the area.

Just north of Hallandale is the more energetic, burgeoning city of Hollywood. Once a sleepy community wedged between Fort Lauderdale and Miami, Hollywood is now a bustling area of 1.5 million people with an array of ethnic and racial identities: from white and African American to Jamaican, Chinese, and Dominican. (*Money* magazine trumpeted the self-described "City of the Future" as having an ethnic makeup that mirrors what the U.S. will look like by the year 2022.) In 2004, the $300-million Seminole Hard Rock Hotel & Casino (p. 277) debuted, with a 500-room hotel, spa, and 130,000-square-foot casino. This was exactly what the city needed to kick its slow renaissance up a notch. A spate of redevelopment has made the pedestrian-friendly center along Hollywood Boulevard and Harrison Street, east of Dixie Highway, a popular destination for travelers and locals alike. Some predict Hollywood will be South Florida's next big destination—South Beach without the attitude and traffic jams. While the prediction is a dubious one, Hollywood is definitely awakening from its long slumber. Prices are a fraction of those at other tourist areas, and a quasi-bohemian vibe is apparent in the galleries, clubs, and restaurants that dot the new "strip." Its gritty undercurrent, however, prevents it from becoming too trendy.

Fort Lauderdale, with its well-known strip of beaches, restaurants, bars, and souvenir shops, has really undergone a major transformation. Once famous (or infamous) for the annual mayhem it hosted during Spring Break, this area is now attracting a more affluent, better-behaved yachting crowd. The *Miami Herald* business section discussed the changes in a 2006 article, "Upscale Inn Crowd," which agreed that "the city once famous for Spring Break antics undergoes a broad upgrade of its hotel stock." In fact, Starwood's new W Fort Lauderdale, a 346-room boutique hotel, opened at the end of 2008, as did the swanky Ritz-Carlton.

In addition to beautiful wide beaches, Fort Lauderdale, known as the Venice of America, has more than 300 miles of navigable waterways and innumerable canals, which permit thousands of residents to anchor boats in their backyards. Boating is not just a hobby here; it's a lifestyle. Visitors can easily get on the water, too, by renting a boat or by hailing a moderately priced water taxi.

Huge cruise ships also take advantage of Florida's deepest harbor, Port Everglades. The seaport is on the southeastern coast of the Florida peninsula, near the Fort Lauderdale Hollywood International Airport on the outskirts of Hollywood and Dania Beach. Port

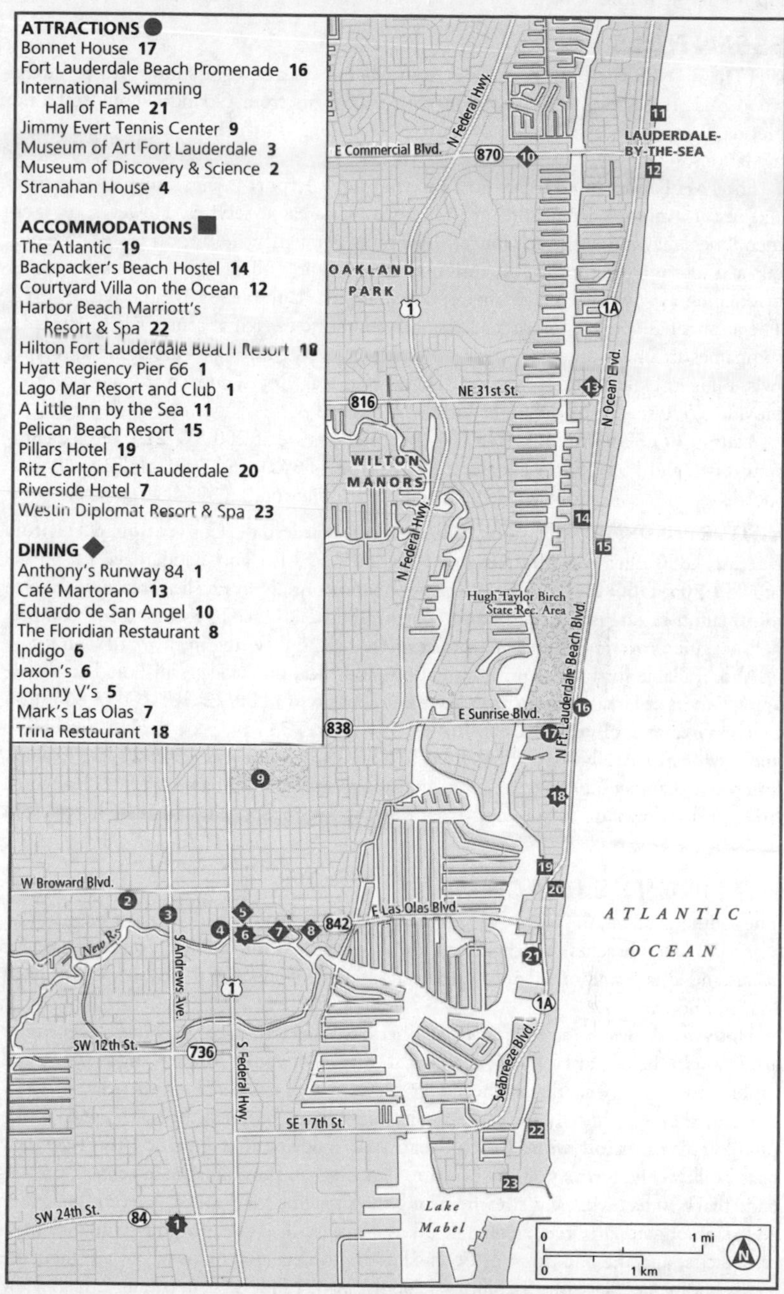
ATTRACTIONS
Bonnet House 17
Fort Lauderdale Beach Promenade 16
International Swimming Hall of Fame 21
Jimmy Evert Tennis Center 9
Museum of Art Fort Lauderdale 3
Museum of Discovery & Science 2
Stranahan House 4
ACCOMMODATIONS
The Atlantic 19
Backpacker's Beach Hostel 14
Courtyard Villa on the Ocean 12
Harbor Beach Marriott's Resort & Spa 22
Hilton Fort Lauderdale Beach Resort 18
Hyatt Regiency Pier 66 1
Lago Mar Resort and Club 1
A Little Inn by the Sea 11
Pelican Beach Resort 15
Pillars Hotel 19
Ritz Carlton Fort Lauderdale 20
Riverside Hotel 7
Westin Diplomat Resort & Spa 23
DINING
Anthony's Runway 84 1
Café Martorano 13
Eduardo de San Angel 10
The Floridian Restaurant 8
Indigo 6
Jaxon's 6
Johnny V's 5
Mark's Las Olas 7
Trina Restaurant 18
N Federal Hwy.
E Commercial Blvd.
870
LAUDERDALE-BY-THE-SEA
OAKLAND PARK
1
1A
NE 31st St.
816
N Ocean Blvd.
WILTON MANORS
Hugh Taylor Birch State Rec. Area
N Ft. Lauderdale Beach Blvd.
E Sunrise Blvd.
838
W Broward Blvd.
E Las Olas Blvd.
842
New R.
S Andrews Ave.
ATLANTIC OCEAN
SW 12th St.
736
S Federal Hwy.
Seabreeze Blvd.
SE 17th St.
Lake Mabel
SW 24th St.
84
0
1 mi
1 km
N

Everglades is the second-busiest cruise-ship base in Florida, after Miami, and one of the top five in the world.

ESSENTIALS

GETTING THERE If you're driving from Miami, it's a straight shot north to Hollywood or Fort Lauderdale. Visitors on their way to or from Orlando should take the Florida Turnpike to exit 53, 54, 58, or 62, depending on the location of your accommodations.

The **Fort Lauderdale Hollywood International Airport** is small, easy to negotiate, and just 15 minutes from both of the downtown areas it services. However, its user-friendliness may not last much longer: Due to its popularity, the airport is still undergoing a $700-million runway expansion and renovation that often renders it just as maddening as any other major metropolitan airport. Completion is expected in 2012. The airport has wireless Internet access and a fantastic car-rental center where 10 rental companies are under one roof—very convenient. Levels 1 through 4 are home to Alamo, Avis, Budget, Dollar, Enterprise, E-Z, Hertz, National, Royal, and Thrifty. Levels 5 to 9 provide 5,500 spaces for public parking.

Amtrak (✆ **800/USA-RAIL** [872-7245]) stations are at 200 SW 21st Terrace (Broward Blvd. and I-95), Fort Lauderdale (✆ **954/587-6692**), and 3001 Hollywood Blvd. (northwest corner of Hollywood Blvd. and I-95, Hollywood; ✆ **954/921-4517**).

VISITOR INFORMATION The **Greater Fort Lauderdale Convention & Visitors Bureau,** 1850 Eller Dr., Ste. 303 (off I-95 and I-595 E), Fort Lauderdale, FL 33316 (✆ **954/765-4466;** fax 954/765-4467; www.sunny.org), is an excellent resource for area information in English, Spanish, and French. Call in advance to request a free comprehensive guide covering events, accommodations, and sightseeing in Broward County.

Also available for brochures, information, and vacation packages in Fort Lauderdale are operators at **Greater Than Ever Fort Lauderdale** (✆ **800/22-SUNNY** [7-8669]).

The **Greater Hollywood Chamber of Commerce,** 330 N. Federal Hwy. (at U.S. 1 and Taylor St.), Hollywood, FL 33020 (✆ **954/923-4000;** fax 954/923-8737; www.hollywoodchamber.org), is open Monday through Friday from 9am to 5pm. Here you'll find the lowdown on all of Hollywood's events, attractions, restaurants, hotels, and tours.

HITTING THE BEACH

The southern part of the Gold Coast, Broward County, has the region's most popular and amenities-laden beaches, which stretch for more than 23 miles. Most do not charge for access and all are well maintained. Here's a selection of some of the county's best, from south to north:

Hollywood Beach, stretching from Sheridan Street to Georgia Street, is a major attraction in the city of Hollywood, a virtual carnival of young hipsters, big families, and sunburned French Canadians who dodge bicyclers and skaters along the rows of tacky souvenir shops, T-shirt shops, game rooms, snack bars, beer stands, hotels, and miniature-golf courses. **Hollywood Beach Broadwalk,** modeled after Atlantic City's legendary boardwalk, is the town's popular beachfront pedestrian thoroughfare, a cement promenade that's 30 feet wide and stretches along the shoreline for 3 miles. A recent makeover added, among other things, a concrete bike path, a crushed-shell jogging path, new trash receptacles, and the relocation of beach showers to each street end (all of are them are accessible for people with disabilities). Popular with runners, skaters, and cruisers, the

Turtle Trail

In June and July, the John U. Lloyd Beach is crawling with nature lovers who come for the spectacular **Sea Turtle Awareness Program.** Park rangers begin the evening with a lecture and slide show, while scouts search the beach for nesting loggerhead sea turtles. If a turtle is located—plenty of them usually are—a beach walk allows participants to see the turtles nest and, sometimes, their eggs hatch. The program begins at 9pm on Wednesday and Friday from mid-May to mid-July. Call © **954/923-2833** for reservations. Walks last between 1 and 3 hours. Comfortable walking shoes and insect repellent are necessary. The park entrance fee of $3 to $5 per carload applies.

Broadwalk is also renowned as a hangout for thousands of retirement-age snowbirds who get together for frequent dances and shows at a faded outdoor amphitheater. Despite efforts to clear out a seedy element, the area remains a haven for drunks and scammers, so keep alert.

If you tire of the hectic diversity that defines Hollywood's Broadwalk, enjoy the natural beauty of the beach itself, which is wide and clean. There are lifeguards, showers, restroom facilities, and public areas for picnics and parties.

The **Fort Lauderdale Beach Promenade,** along the beach, underwent a $26-million renovation and looks fantastic. It's especially peaceful in the mornings, when there's just a smattering of joggers and walkers; but even at its most crowded on weekends, the expansive promenade provides room for everyone. Note, however, that the beach is hardly pristine; it is across the street from an uninterrupted stretch of hotels, bars, and retail outlets. Also nearby is a retail-and-dining megacomplex, Beach Place (p. 272), in the throes of its own renovation that will add newer, hipper stores, bars, and restaurants, on Florida A1A, midway between Las Olas and Sunrise boulevards.

On the sand just across the road, most days you'll find hard-core volleyball players who always welcome anyone with a good spike, and you'll find an inviting ocean for swimmers of any level. The unusually clear waters are under the careful watch of some of Florida's best-looking lifeguards. Freshen up afterward in the clean showers and restrooms conveniently located along the strip. Pets have been banned from most of the beach in order to maintain the impressive cleanliness; a designated area for pets exists away from the main sunbathing areas.

Especially on weekends, parking at the oceanside meters is nearly impossible. Try biking, skating, or hitching a ride on the water taxi instead. The strip is located on Florida A1A, between SE 17th Street and Sunrise Boulevard.

Dania Beach's **John U. Lloyd Beach State Park,** 6503 N. Ocean Dr., Dania (© **954/923-2833**), consists of 251 acres of barrier island, situated between the Atlantic Ocean and the Intracoastal Waterway, from Port Everglades on the north to Dania on the south. Its natural setting contrasts sharply with the urban development of Fort Lauderdale. Lloyd Beach, one of Broward County's most important nesting beaches for sea turtles, produces some 10,000 hatchlings a year. The park's broad, flat beach is popular for both swimming and sunning. Self-guided nature trails are great for those too restless to sunbathe. The park and beach received significant damage during 2005's Hurricane Wilma, but you'd never know it. All is restored back to its pristine condition.

BOATING Often called the "yachting capital of the world," Fort Lauderdale provides ample opportunity for visitors to get out on the water, either along the Intracoastal Waterway or on the open ocean. If your hotel doesn't rent boats, try **Aloha Watersports,** Marriott's Harbor Beach Resort, 3030 Holiday Dr., Fort Lauderdale (✆ **954/462-7245;** www.alohawatersports.com). It can outfit you with a variety of craft, including jet skis, WaveRunners, and catamarans. Rates start at $65 per half-hour for WaveRunners ($15 each additional rider; doubles and triples available), $70 to $125 for sailboats, $60 to $70 for catamarans, $20 per person per hour for ocean kayaks, and $75 per person for a 15-minute parasailing ride. Aloha also offers a Surfing School ($40—though the waves are hardly rippin' here!) and a Coast Guard class (9am daily), through which adults can obtain their Florida Boaters License for $3. And for the treasure hunters, you can rent a metal detector for $20 per hour.

FISHING The **IGFA** (International Game Fish Association) **World Fishing Center,** 300 Gulf Stream Way, Dania Beach (✆ **954/922-4212;** www.igfa.org), is an angler's paradise. One of the highlights of this museum, library, and park is the virtual-reality fishing simulator that allows visitors to actually reel in their own computer-generated catch. Also included in the 3-acre park are displays of antique fishing gear, record catches, famous anglers, various vessels, and a wetlands lab. To get a list of local captains and guides, call **IGFA headquarters** (✆ **954/927-2628**) and ask for the librarian. Admission is $6 for adults, $5 for seniors and children 3 to 16. The museum and library are open daily from 10am to 6pm. On the grounds is also **Bass Pro Shops Outdoor World,** a huge retail complex set on a 3-acre lake.

GOLF More than 50 golf courses in all price ranges compete for players. Among the best is **Emerald Hills,** 4100 N. Hills Dr., Hollywood (✆ **954/961-4000;** www.theclubatemeraldhills.com), just west of I-95 between Sterling Road and Sheridan Street. This beauty consistently lands on the "best of" lists of golf writers nationwide. The 18th hole, on a two-tier green, is the course's signature; it's surrounded by water and is more than a bit rough. The course is pricey—Friday through Sunday, greens fees start at $150 for tee times after 1pm, and $175 for tee times before noon during high season; Monday through Friday, the fees are $125 before noon and $110 after 1pm. Rates are cheaper during the brutally hot summers.

The **Diplomat Golf Resort and Spa,** 501 Diplomat Pkwy., Hallandale Beach (✆ **954/602-6000;** www.diplomatgolfresortandspa.com), is across the Intracoastal from the Westin Diplomat Resort. It has fabulous golf facilities, with 8 acres of lakes and rolling fairways, plus a fantastic delivery service that brings lunch and drinks to your cart. You pay for the services, however, with greens fees of about $215 during high season and $95 to $169 off-season. Twilight fees at 2pm cost from $35 to $95.

For one of Broward's best municipal challenges, try the 18-holer at the **Orangebrook Golf Course,** 400 Entrada Dr., Hollywood (✆ **954/967-GOLF** [4653]). Built in 1937, this is one of the state's oldest courses and one of the area's best bargains. Morning and noon rates are $17 to $23. After 3pm, you can play for about $13, including a cart. Men must wear collared shirts to play here, and no spikes are allowed.

SCUBA DIVING In Broward County, the best dive wreck is the *Mercedes I,* a 197-foot freighter that washed up in the backyard of a Palm Beach socialite in 1984 and was sunk for divers the following year off Pompano Beach. The artificial reef, filled with colorful sponges, spiny lobsters, and barracudas, is 97 feet below the surface, a mile offshore between Oakland Park and Sunrise boulevards. Dozens of reputable dive shops line the beach. Ask at your hotel for a nearby recommendation, or contact **Neil Watson's Undersea Adventures,** 1525 S. Andrews Ave., Fort Lauderdale (© **954/462-3400;** www.nealwatson.com).

SPECTATOR SPORTS Baseball fans can get their fix at the **Fort Lauderdale Stadium,** 5301 NW 12th Ave. (© **954/828-4980**), where the Baltimore Orioles (who have recently been asked to take over Vero Beach's Dodgertown) play spring-training exhibition games starting in early March; call © **954/776-1921** for tickets. General admission is $10, a spot in the grandstand $14, and box seats $20; admission for kids 14 and under is $4. During the season, the Florida Marlins play just south of Hallandale at **Dolphin Stadium,** near the Dade–Broward County line. Tickets go on sale in January for $4 to $100; call **Ticketmaster** (© **305/358-5885;** www.ticketmaster.com) to purchase them.

Pompano Park Racing, 1800 SW 3rd St., Pompano Beach (© **954/972-2000**), has parimutuel harness racing from October to early August. Admission is free to both grandstand and clubhouse.

Wrapped around an artificial lake, **Gulfstream Park Racing and Casino,** at U.S. 1 and Hallandale Beach Boulevard, Hallandale (© **954/454-7000;** www.gulfstreampark.com), is pretty and popular, especially after its multimillion-dollar renovation, with a spanking-new casino and restaurants. Large purses and important horse races are commonplace at this recently refurbished suburban course, and the track is often crowded. The most recent renovation has transformed it into a world-class, state-of-the-art facility with four higher-end restaurants, 20 luxury suites, private accommodations for top players, and more. It hosts the Florida Derby each March. Call for schedules. Admission and parking are free. From January 3 to April 25, post times are 1:15pm Wednesday through Sunday, and the doors open at 11:30am.

Jai alai, a sort of Spanish-style indoor lacrosse, was introduced to Florida in 1924 and still draws big crowds that bet on the fast-paced action. Broward's only fronton, **Dania Jai Alai,** 301 E. Dania Beach Blvd., at Florida A1A and U.S. 1 (© **954/920-1511**), is a great place to spend an afternoon or evening.

In the sport of ice hockey, the young **Florida Panthers** (© **954/835-7000**) play in Sunrise at the **BankAtlantic Center,** 2555 NW 137th Way (© **954/835-8000**). Tickets range from $15 to $100. Call for directions and ticket information.

TENNIS There are hundreds of courts in Broward County, and plenty are accessible to the public. Many are at resorts and hotels. If yours has none, try the **Jimmy Evert Tennis Center,** 701 NE 12th Ave. (off Sunrise Blvd.), Fort Lauderdale (© **954/828-5378**), famous as the spot where Chris Evert trained (see p. 58). There are 18 lighted clay courts and three hard courts here. Nonresidents of Fort Lauderdale pay $6 per hour before 4pm and $7 after. Reservations are accepted after 2pm for the following day, but cost an extra $3.

SEEING THE SIGHTS

Billie Swamp Safari ★ Billie Swamp Safari is an up-close-and-personal view of the Seminole Indians' 2,200-acre Big Cypress Reservation. There are daily tours into reservation wetlands, hardwood hammocks, and areas where wildlife (seemingly strategically placed deer, water buffalo, bison, wild hogs, ornery ostriches, rare birds, and alligators) reside. Tours are provided aboard swamp buggies, customized motorized vehicles specially designed to provide visitors with an elevated view of the frontier while they comfortably ride through the wetlands and cypress heads. The more adventurous may want

One If by Land, Taxi If by Sea

Plan to spend at least an afternoon or evening cruising Fort Lauderdale's 300 miles of waterways the only way you can: by boat. The **Water Bus of Fort Lauderdale** (✆ **954/467-6677;** www.watertaxi.com) is one of the greatest innovations for water lovers since those cool Velcro sandals. A trusty fleet of older port boats serves the dual purpose of transporting and entertaining visitors as they cruise through the "Venice of America." Because of its popularity, the water taxi fleet has welcomed several sleek, 70-passenger "water buses" (featuring indoor and outdoor seating with an atriumlike roof).

Taxis operate on demand and also along a fairly regular route, carrying up to 48 passengers to 20 stops. If you're staying at a hotel on the route, you can be picked up there, usually within 15 minutes of calling, and then be shuttled to any of the dozens of restaurants, bars, and attractions on or near the waterfront. If you aren't sure where you want to go, ask one of the personable captains, who can point out historic and fun spots along the way.

Starting daily at 8am, boats run until midnight 7 days a week, depending on the weather. Check the website for exact times of pickup. The cost is $13 for an all-day pass with unlimited stops on and off. If you want to go to South Beach, it's $23 plus a $1 fuel charge. Tickets are available onboard; no credit cards are accepted.

to take a fast-moving airboat ride or trek a nature trail. Airboat rides run about 20 minutes, while swamp-buggy tours last about an hour. A stop at an alligator farm reeks of Disney, but the kids won't care. You can stay overnight in a native Tiki hut for $35 per night if you're really looking to immerse yourself in the culture.

Big Cypress Seminole Reservation, 1½-hr. drive west of Fort Lauderdale. ✆ **800/949-6101.** www.semtribe.com/safari. Free admission. Swamp-buggy tours $25 adults, $23 seniors 62 and over, $15 children 4–12; airboat tours $15 for all ages. Daily 8:30am–6pm. Airboats depart every 30 min. from 9:30am to 4:30pm. Swamp-buggy tours leave on the hour btw. 10am and 5pm. Reptile and Critter Shows daily. Day and overnight packages available.

Bonnet House ★★★ This historic 35-acre plantation home and estate, accessible by guided tour only, will provide you with a fantastic glimpse of Old Florida. Built in 1921, the sprawling two-story waterfront home (surrounded by formal tropical gardens) is really the backdrop of a love story, which the very chatty volunteer guides will share with you if you ask. Some have actually lunched with the former resident of the house, the late Evelyn Bartlett, wife of world-acclaimed artist Frederic Clay Bartlett. The worthwhile 1¼-hour tour introduces you to quirky people, whimsical artwork, lush grounds, and interesting design.

900 N. Birch Rd. (1 block west of the ocean, south of Sunrise Blvd.), Fort Lauderdale. ✆ **954/563-5393.** www.bonnethouse.org. Admission $20 adults, $18 seniors, $16 students 18 and under, free for children 6 and under. Call for hours and tour times.

International Swimming Hall of Fame (ISHOF) ★★★ Any aspiring Michael Phelps (who may or may not donate one of his million gold medals to the museum) or those who appreciate the sport will love this splashy homage to the best backstrokers, front crawlers, and divers in the world. The museum houses the world's largest collection of aquatic memorabilia and is the single largest source of aquatic books, manuscripts, and literature. Among the highlights are Johnny Weissmuller's Olympic medals, Mark Spitz's starting block used to win six of his seven 1972 Olympic gold medals, and more than 60 Olympic, national, and club uniforms, warm-ups, and swimsuits. For those who don't mind getting their feet wet, the ISHOF Aquatic Complex is the only one of its kind in the world with two 50m (164-ft.) pools, a diving well, and a swimming flume.

1 Hall of Fame Dr., Fort Lauderdale. ✆ **954/462-6536.** www.ishof.org. Admission $8 adults, $6 seniors, $4 children 12 and over. Call for hours and tour times.

Museum of Art Fort Lauderdale ★ (Kids A fantastic modern-art facility, the Museum of Art Fort Lauderdale has permanent collections, including those from William Glackens; the CoBrA Movement in Copenhagen, Brussels, and Amsterdam, with more than 200 paintings; 50 sculptures; 1,200 works on paper from 1948 to 1951, including the largest repository of Asger Jorn graphics outside the Silkeborg Kunstmuseum in Denmark; stunning Picasso ceramics; and contemporary works from more than 90 Cuban artists in exile around the world. Traveling exhibits and continuing art classes make the museum a great place to spend a rainy day—or night, on Thursdays, the cafe and wine bar have happy hour from 5 to 7pm.

1 E. Las Olas Blvd., Fort Lauderdale. ✆ **954/525-5500.** www.moafl.org. Admission $10 adults, $7 seniors and children 6–17, free for children 5 and under. Oct–May daily 11am–5pm, Thurs until 8pm; June–Sept Mon and Wed–Sun 11am–5pm.

Museum of Discovery & Science ★★ (Kids This museum's high-tech, interactive approach to education proves that science can equal fun. Adults won't feel as if they're in a kiddie museum, either. Kids ages 7 and under enjoy navigating their way through the excellent explorations in the Discovery Center. Florida Ecoscapes is particularly interesting, with a living coral reef, bees, bats, frogs, turtles, and alligators. Most weekend nights, you'll find a diverse crowd ranging from hip high-school kids to 30-somethings enjoying a rock film in the IMAX theater, which also shows short, science-related films daily. Out front in the atrium, see the 52-foot-tall *Great Gravity Clock,* the largest kinetic-energy sculpture in the state.

401 SW 2nd St., Fort Lauderdale. ✆ **954/467-6637.** www.mods.org. Admission (includes IMAX film) $15 adults, $14 seniors, $12 children 2–12; without IMAX film $10 adults, $9 seniors, $8 children 2–12. Mon–Sat 10am–5pm; Sun noon–6pm. Movie theater closes later. From I-95, exit on Broward Blvd. E. Continue to SW 5th Ave., turn right; garage is on the right.

Stranahan House ★★★ In a town where nothing appears to date back earlier than 1940, visitors may want to take a minute to see Fort Lauderdale's very oldest standing structure and a prime example of classic "Florida Frontier" architecture. Built in 1901 by the "father of Fort Lauderdale," Frank Stranahan, this house once served as a trading post for Seminole trappers who came here to sell pelts. It's been a post office, town hall, and general store, and now serves as a worthwhile little museum of South Florida pioneer life, containing turn-of-the-20th-century furnishings and historical photos of the area. It is also the site of occasional concerts and social functions; call for details.

335 SE 6th Ave. (Las Olas Blvd. at the New River Tunnel), Fort Lauderdale. ✆ **954/524-4736.** www.stranahanhouse.org. Admission $12 adults, $11 seniors, $7 students and children. Wed–Sat 10am–3pm; Sun 1–3pm. Tours are on the hour; last tour at 3pm. Accessible by water taxi.

SHOPPING

It's all about malls in Broward County and, while most of the best shopping is within Fort Lauderdale proper, other areas are also worth browsing.

Dania is known as the antiques capital of the South because within 1 square mile of Federal Highway, the city has more than 100 dealers selling everything from small collectibles to fine antiques. Parking is best along Federal Highway, on the "row," where Federal Highway meets U.S. 1. For information on "Antique Row," call © **954/924-3627.** Also in Dania is the **Design Center of the Americas (DCOTA),** at the intersection of I-95 and Griffin Road (© **954/920-7997;** www.designcenteroftheamericas.com), a 775,000-square-foot interior-design center with furniture showrooms (featuring everything from ultramod to classic), designer studios, and, from time to time, fabulous sample sales. Last time we visited Dania, Matt Damon and his then-fiancée (now wife) were there furnishing their zillion-dollar Miami Beach manse.

For bargain mavens, there's a strip of "fashion" stores on Hallandale Beach Boulevard's "Schmatta Row," east of Dixie Highway and the railroad tracks, where off-brand shoes, bags, and jewelry are sold at deep discounts. Hollywood Boulevard also has some interesting shops, with everything from Indonesian artifacts to used and rare books, leather bustiers, and handmade hats. Dozens of shops line the pedestrian-friendly strip just west of Young Circle. The art galleries are clustered along Harrison Street, just east of Dixie Highway.

The area's only beachfront mall, the **Gallery at Beach Place,** is in Fort Lauderdale on Florida A1A just north of Las Olas Boulevard. This 100,000-square-foot giant sports the usual chains, such as Sunglass Hut, as well as chain bars and restaurants such as Hooter's. While it was once all the rage with the Spring Break set, Beach Place is now aiming for a much more upscale clientele, adding many new higher-end stores and restaurants. Still, we think it's just one big tourist trap.

Other more traditional malls include the upscale **Galleria,** at Sunrise Boulevard near the Fort Lauderdale Beach, and **Broward Mall,** west of I-95 on Broward Boulevard, in Plantation.

If you're looking for unusual boutiques, especially art galleries, head to quaint **Las Olas Boulevard ★**, located west of A1A and a block east of Federal Highway/U.S. 1, off SE 8th Street, where there are hundreds of shops with alluring window decorations (like kitchen utensils posing as modern-art sculptures) and intriguing merchandise such as mural-size oil paintings. On the edge of the Arts and Science District is **Las Olas Riverfront,** a retail complex on the water with a few restaurants, nightclubs, bars, and boutiques. While it's not worth a trip on its own, if you're in the area, you may want to take a quick stroll there.

For bargains, there's no better place than **Sawgrass Mills,** 12801 W. Sunrise Blvd. (© **954/846-0179**), featuring over 350 name brand outlets such as Off Fifth and Nordstrom Rack. Nearby is Florida's first ever **Ikea,** 151 NW 136th Ave. (© **954/838-9292;** www.ikea.com), purveyor of all things sleek and Swedish—everything from furniture to meatballs.

WHERE TO STAY

The Fort Lauderdale beach has a hotel or motel on nearly every block, ranging from run-down to luxurious. **Fort Lauderdale Beach Resort Hotel and Suites,** 4221 N. Ocean Blvd. (© **800/329-7466** or 954/563-2521), has clean oceanside rooms starting at about $65. For a cushier stay, look into the **Ritz-Carlton Fort Lauderdale** resort (see below), which opened in May 2007 as a St. Regis and was quickly taken over by the Ritz (see below). Projected to open in the fall of 2009 is the $220-million **W Fort Lauderdale Hotel & Residences** (✆ **954/525-8133**), a boutique-hotel-slash-condominium with ocean views and a very hip and happening bar.

In Hollywood, where prices are generally cheaper, the **Ramada Hollywood Beach Resort,** 101 N. Ocean Dr. (✆ **954/921-0990;** www.ramadahbr.com), operates a full-service hotel right on the ocean. With prices starting at around $79 in season and discounts for AAA members, it's a great deal. **Marriott Hollywood Oceanfront,** 2501 N. Ocean Dr. (I-95 to Sheridan St. E. to Fla. A1A S.; ✆ **866/306-5453** or 954/924-2202), is a recently renovated beach resort with a fantastic location right on the beach.

Extended Stay America/Crossland Economy Studios (✆ **800/398-7829;** www.extendedstayhotels.com) has four super-clean properties in Fort Lauderdale and offers year-round rates as low as $49 a night and $159 per week. The studios are designed with business travelers in mind: Each includes free local calls, a dataport, a kitchenette, and a well-lit desk.

For rentals for a few weeks or months, call **Florida Sunbreak** (✆ **800/SUNBREAK** [786-2732]) or check the annual list of small lodgings compiled by the **Greater Fort Lauderdale Convention & Visitors Bureau** (✆ **954/765-4466**). The latter is especially helpful if you're looking for privately owned, charming, affordable lodgings.

Very Expensive

The Atlantic ★★★ Sitting on 23 miles of white sand, the Atlantic is a study in minimal modernity—soothing colors and comfortable, stylish decor. Besides the usual high-tech amenities found in all rooms of this category—flatscreen TVs, wireless Internet—the Atlantic boasts something other hotels do not: a star chef hailing from New York City's Tribeca Grill and a five-star restaurant. Trina Restaurant and Lounge comes to Fort Lauderdale, thanks to celebrated restaurateurs Don Pintabona, former executive chef of Tribeca Grill, and Nick Mautone, former managing partner of Gramercy Tavern. The 6,000-square-foot spa isn't too shabby, either. Service is usually stellar, though we've had some complaints of a bit of attitude, but for some die-hard New Yorkers who stay here, that's a plus!

601 N. Fort Lauderdale Beach Blvd., Fort Lauderdale, FL 33304. ✆ **866/837-4274** or 954/567-8020. Fax 954/567-8040. www.starwoodhotels.com or www.luxurycollection.com/atlantic. 124 units. Winter $389–$619 double, $969–$999 suite; off-season $219–$529 double, $789 suite. AF, DC, DISC, MC, V. Valet parking $28. **Amenities:** 2 restaurants; bar; outdoor heated pool; spa; watersports equipment/rentals; bike rentals; concierge; business center; salon; 24-hr. room service; laundry service; dry cleaning. *In room:* A/C, TV, Wi-Fi, minibar, coffeemaker, hair dryer, iron, safe, microwave.

Harbor Beach Marriott Resort & Spa ★★ (Kids Harbor Beach is loaded with the same amenities as Pier 66 (below), but has a more secluded setting on 16 oceanfront acres just south of Fort Lauderdale's "strip." Everything in this place is huge—from the quarter-mile of private beach to the 8,000-square-foot pool and the $8-million, 22,000-square-foot European spa. Accommodations feature pillow-top bedding, marble, crown molding, and bathrooms with granite vanities, marble flooring, designer lighting, and wraparound mirrors. Most units open onto private balconies overlooking the pool, the city, the ocean, or the Intracoastal Waterway. The hotel's 3030 Ocean is an excellent seafood restaurant and raw bar; the Riva, a Mediterranean-style oceanfront eatery, is also top-notch. Return guests include many convention groups and families who enjoy the space and great location. The hotel's Beachside Buddies kids' program, $45 half-day and $80 full day, including lunch, provides arts and crafts, watersports, and games to keep the young 'uns happily occupied. Speaking of watersports, this hotel has the most comprehensive list, from surfing to parasailing.

3030 Holiday Dr., Fort Lauderdale, FL 33316. ✆ **800/222-6543** or 954/525-4000. Fax 954/766-6152. www.marriottharborbeach.com. 650 units. Winter $439–$699 double; off-season $269–$649 double; year-round from $850 suite. AE, DC, DISC, MC, V. Valet parking $27; self-parking $22. From I-95, exit on I-595 E. to U.S. 1 N.; proceed to SE 17th St.; make a right and go over the Intracoastal Bridge past 3 traffic lights to Holiday Dr.; turn right. **Amenities:** 3 restaurants; 2 bars; outdoor heated pool; 4 clay tennis courts; health club; European-style spa; extensive watersports equipment/rentals; bike rentals; children's center and programs; game room; concierge; business center; salon; 24-hr. room service; in-room massage; babysitting can be arranged; laundry service; self-service laundry; basketball court. *In room:* A/C, TV, dataport, minibar, coffeemaker, hair dryer, iron, safe, PlayStation capability.

Hilton Fort Lauderdale Beach Resort ★★★ The Hilton Fort Lauderdale Beach Resort is a 25-story landmark property located on the shoreline of Fort Lauderdale's exclusive North Beach between the palm-shaded boulevards of Sunrise and Las Olas. Guests enter the resort through a gracious porte-cochere into a dramatic two-story lobby offering unobstructed views of the Atlantic Ocean. The sixth floor Sunrise Terrace features a zero-entry pool and private cabanas and is reminiscent of the deck of a luxury yacht. The resort's commitment to personal service can be experienced through a dedicated beach concierge, kids program, premium transfer service, and deluxe turndown service. Each of the 374 studios and suites is outfitted with a separate shower and soaking tub, high-definition flatscreen television, and private oceanview balcony with expansive views of the Atlantic. The resort features the Spa Q and two distinct dining options including ilios—an upscale signature restaurant of contemporary Mediterranean cuisine.

505 N. Fort Lauderdale Beach Blvd., Fort Lauderdale, FL 33404. ✆ 800/HILTONS (445-8667) or 954/414-2222. Fax 954/414-2612. www.fortlauderdalebeachresort.hilton.com. 374 units. Seasonal from $400 double. AE, DISC, MC, V. **Amenities:** 2 restaurants; pool; spa; concierge; business center; high-speed Internet access; 24-hr. room service. *In room:* A/C, TV, fridge, microwave.

Hyatt Regency Pier 66 ★★ Set on 22 tropical acres on the Intracoastal Waterway, this resort is best known for its world-class marina and a rooftop lounge that spins every 66 minutes. If you experience vertigo after sitting in the revolving lounge, an invigorating treatment at the hotel's exquisite Spa 66 will help relocate your sense of balance. Equally invigorating are the recreational amenities, which include a three-pool complex with a 40-person hydrotherapy pool, tennis courts, and an aquatic center with watersports. Grille 66 and Bar, a classy, upscale steakhouse, is a welcome addition. A $25-million refurbishment has transformed the lobby, lawn, and remaining guest rooms with a retro modern decor. New lanai guest rooms have cherrywood furnishings and bathrooms with marble floors and granite vanities. All units have flatscreen televisions, wireless Internet access, and balconies with views of the Intracoastal Waterway and the hotel's lushly landscaped gardens.

2301 SE 17th St. Causeway, Fort Lauderdale, FL 33316. ✆ **800/233-1234** or 954/525-6666. Fax 954/728-3541. www.pier66.com. 380 units. Winter $289–$409 double; off-season $160–$280 double; year-round from $1,000 suite. Rates are cheaper on the hotel's website. AE, DC, DISC, MC, V. Valet parking $25; self-parking $20. **Amenities:** 5 restaurants; 2 bars; 3 pools; 2 lighted clay tennis courts; spa; watersports equipment/rentals; bike rentals; concierge; business center; salon; 24-hr. room service; laundry service; dry cleaning; self-service laundry. *In room:* A/C, TV, dataport, Wi-Fi, minibar, coffeemaker, hair dryer, iron, safe.

The Ritz-Carlton Fort Lauderdale ★★★ The first and only five-star hotel on Fort Lauderdale Beach, this $160-million property formerly run by St. Regis and now a Ritz-Carlton has elevated the strip to an entirely new level of luxury. The 183 rooms, including 28 private residences and 34 hotel condominiums, all feature views of the Atlantic or the Intracoastal Waterway, have Wi-Fi Internet access, a state-of-the-art DVD theater entertainment system with a 32-inch LCD panel TV, a 13-inch LCD panel TV in each bathroom, Italian linens, designer bath amenities, and a refrigerated minicellar of refreshments. We particularly like chef Toby Joseph's Cero Restaurant, a stellar seafooder, and the 1,500-bottle wine bar. The oceanfront pool is nice, yet understated, and the spa is sublime. Some people have complained that service is snooty while others deem it refined and top-notch. What's universal is that this is a welcome departure from the norm for the area. Inside tip: All rooms ending in 10 offer floor-to-ceiling windows and spectacular views!

1 N. Fort Lauderdale Beach Blvd., Fort Lauderdale, FL 33316. ✆ **800/325-3589** or 954/465-2300. Fax 954/766-6193. www.ritzcarlton.com. 183 units. Winter from $649 double; off-season from $359 double; year-round from $600 suite. AE, DC, DISC, MC, V. Valet parking $27; self-parking $22. From I-95, exit on I-595 E. to U.S. 1 N.; proceed to SE 17th St.; make a right and go over the Intracoastal Bridge past 3 traffic lights to Holiday Dr.; turn right. **Amenities:** 3 restaurants; 2 bars; outdoor heated pool; health club; European-style spa; children's programs; concierge; business center; 24-hr. room service; in-room massage; laundry service. *In room:* A/C, TV/DVD, dataport, Wi-Fi, minibar, coffeemaker, hair dryer, iron, safe.

Westin Diplomat Resort & Spa The Diplomat is a 1,060-room, full-service beach resort—the only one of its kind in the somewhat desolate area—loaded with amenities. The main building is a 39-story oceanfront tower surrounded by 8 acres of man-made lakes. A gorgeous bridged, glass-bottom pool with waterfalls, private cabanas, and a slew of watersports, adds a tropical touch. Rooms are a cross between those in a subtle boutique hotel and in an Art Deco throwback, with dark woods, hand-cut marble, and the 10-layer Heavenly Bed, a Westin trademark, with custom-designed pillow-top mattresses and very cushy down blankets. Dining options are aplenty, from the fine-dining steakhouse to several more-casual places. Diplomat Landing, the hotel's shopping-and-entertainment complex across the street, features shops and an offshoot of South Beach's Nikki Beach Club. The resort's golf resort and spa is located across the Intracoastal, featuring 60 luxurious guest rooms, yacht slips, a 155-acre golf course, and a world-class spa and tennis club.

3555 S. Ocean Dr. (Fla. A1A), Hollywood, FL 33019. ✆ **888/627-9057** or 954/602-6000. Fax 954/602-7000. www.diplomatresort.com. 998 units. Winter $305–$515 double, $675–$875 suite; off-season $220–$340 double, $475–$675 suite. AE, DC, DISC, MC, V. Valet parking $22. **Amenities:** 8 restaurants; 3 lounges; 2 pools; golf course; 10 clay tennis courts; health club; spa; watersports equipment/rentals; 24-hr. room service. *In room:* A/C, TV/WebTV, fax, dataport, minibar, coffeemaker, hair dryer.

Expensive

Lago Mar Resort and Club ★★ Kids A charming lobby with a rock fireplace and saltwater aquarium sets the tone of this utterly inviting resort, a casually elegant piece of Old Florida that occupies its own little island between Lake Mayan and the Atlantic. Guests have access to the broadest and best strip of 500-feet of private beach in the entire city, not to mention a wonderful bougainvillea-lined, 9,000-square-foot swimming lagoon. Lago Mar is very family oriented, with many facilities and supervised activities for children. Service is spectacular. The plush rooms and suites have Mediterranean or Key West influences. A full-service spa offers a wide array of treatments, while the 1,000-square-foot exercise facility may come in handy after you indulge in the hotel's Northern Italian restaurant, Acquario, which is worth a visit even if you don't stay here. A new $15-million six-story wing of one- and two-bedroom oceanfront suites with individual balconies and larger luxurious bathrooms includes a deck of native tropical landscaping and a 5,000-square-foot saltwater lagoon.

1700 S. Ocean Lane, Fort Lauderdale, FL 33316. ✆ **800/524-6627** or 954/523-6511. Fax 954/524-6627. www.lagomar.com. 212 units. Winter $295 double, from $365 suite; off-season $175 double, from $200 suite. AE, DC, MC, V. Free valet parking. From Federal Hwy. (U.S. 1), turn east onto SE 17th St. Causeway; turn right onto Mayan Dr.; turn right again onto S. Ocean Dr.; turn left onto Grace Dr.; then turn left again onto S. Ocean Lane to the hotel. **Amenities:** 4 restaurants; bar; wine room; outdoor pool and lagoon; 2 tennis courts; exercise room; watersports equipment/rentals; children's programs during holiday periods; game room; concierge; tour desk; business center; 24-hr. room service; laundry service; dry cleaning. *In room:* A/C, TV, dataport, kitchenette, coffeemaker (in some), hair dryer.

Pillars Hotel ★ Finds It took me awhile to discover this hotel—and apparently that's exactly the point. One of Fort Lauderdale's best-kept secrets, the Pillars transports you from the neon-hued flash and splash of Fort Lauderdale's strip and takes you to a two-story British colonial, Caribbean-style retreat tucked away on the bustling Intracoastal Waterway. Because it has just 22 rooms, you'll feel as if you have the grand house all to yourself—albeit a house with white-tablecloth room service, an Edenistic courtyard with a free-form pool, lush landscaping, access to a water taxi, and a private chef. Rooms are luxurious and loaded with amenities such as flatscreen TVs, DVD players, private-label bath products, ultraplush bedding, and, if you're so inclined, a private masseuse to iron out your personal kinks. The hotel's private restaurant, the Secret Garden, is open only to guests providing gourmet dinner served under the stars and overlooking the Intracoastal. A library area (with over 500 books) is at your disposal, as is pretty much anything else you request here. Not everyone agrees. One reader complained that her room was small, musty, and far from luxurious.

111 N. Birch Rd., Fort Lauderdale, FL 33304. ✆ **954/467-9639.** Fax 954/763-2845. www.pillarshotel.com. 22 units. Winter $285–$355 double, $399–$575 suite; off-season $195–$235 double, $275–$469 suite. AE, DC, DISC, MC, V. Free off-street parking. **Amenities:** Restaurant; waterfront pool; 24-hr. concierge; business services; free Wi-Fi; 24-hr. room service; same-day laundry service; water-taxi service. *In room:* A/C, TV/DVD, dataport, minibar, hair dryer, iron, safe.

Riverside Hotel ★★ A touch of New Orleans hits Fort Lauderdale's popular Las Olas Boulevard in the form of this charming, six-story 1936 hotel. There's no beach here, but the hotel is set on the sleepy and scenic New River, capturing the essence of that ever-elusive Old Florida. Guest rooms, outfitted in Mexican tile and wicker furnishings, are spacious and well maintained. Such details as intricately tiled bathrooms and old-style furniture enhance the charm of the otherwise stark building. The best units face the river, but it's hard to see the water past the parking lot and trees. Twelve rooms offer king-size beds with mirrored canopies and flowing drapes. There are also seven elegantly decorated suites with wet bars and French doors that lead to private balconies. The hotel has two restaurants worth trying: Indigo, a fantastic seafood spot (p. 281), and the Grill Room, for Old World elegance.

620 E. Las Olas Blvd., Fort Lauderdale, FL 33301. ✆ **800/325-3280** or 954/467-0671. Fax 954/462-2148. www.riversidehotel.com. 217 units. Winter $229–$279 suite; off-season $139–$185 suite. Special packages available. Online discounts available. AE, DC, MC, V. Valet parking $8–$10. From I-95, exit onto Broward Blvd.; turn right onto Federal Hwy. (U.S. 1); turn left onto Las Olas Blvd. **Amenities:** 2 restaurants; outdoor pool; concierge; secretarial services; limited room service; laundry service; dry cleaning. *In room:* A/C, TV, dataport, minibar, fridge, coffeemaker, hair dryer, iron.

Moderate

Courtyard Villa on the Ocean ★ Nestled between a bunch of larger hotels, this small historic hotel is a romantic getaway right on the beach. Courtyard Villa has spacious oceanfront efficiencies with private balconies, larger suites overlooking the pool, and full two-bedroom apartments. Accommodations are plush, with chenille bedspreads and carved four-poster beds; fully equipped kitchenettes are an added convenience. The tiled bathrooms have strong, hot showers to wash off the beach sand. Room no. 8 is especially nice, with French doors that open to a private balcony overlooking the ocean. Relax in the hotel's unique heated pool/spa or on the second-floor sun deck. You can also swim from the beach to a living reef just 50 feet offshore.

4312 El Mar Dr., Lauderdale-by-the-Sea, FL 33308. ✆ **800/291-3560** or 954/776-1164. Fax 954/491-0768. www.courtyardvilla.com. 10 units. Winter $159–$359; off-season $109–$225. Rates include full breakfast. AE, MC, V. Pets less than 35 lb. accepted with a $200 deposit; must be caged while outside; no pit bulls, Dobermans, or Rottweilers. **Amenities:** Outdoor heated pool; Jacuzzi; free use of bikes; free laptop use w/Internet access; limited room service; scuba instruction. *In room:* A/C, TV/VCR, kitchenette, coffeemaker, hair dryer.

Pelican Grand Beach Resort ★ Kids The Pelican Beach Resort sits on a 500-foot private beach, with 159 oversize accommodations, oceanfront suites with balconies, and a sublimely relaxing, wraparound oceanfront veranda and sun deck with rocking chairs. What also rocks about this place is the zero-entry pool and the Lazy River tubing ride. This is a great, low-key luxury resort, especially for families looking for a relaxing vacation, with all the amenities of a more harried chain resort overwrought with slews of people. The resort is also completely nonsmoking.

2000 N. Ocean Blvd., Fort Lauderdale, FL 33305. ✆ **800/525-OCEAN** (6232) or 954/568-9431. Fax 954/565-2662. www.pelicanbeach.com. 159 units. Winter $299–$349 double, $520 suite; off-season $220–$270 double, $420 suite. AE, DC, MC, V. Parking $24. **Amenities:** Restaurant; bar; ice cream parlor; zero-entry pool; fitness center; sun deck. *In room:* A/C, TV, high-speed Internet, fridge, coffeemaker, hair dryer, microwave.

Seminole Hard Rock Hotel & Casino ★★★ The Seminole Indians have created a miniature Vegas within Hollywood, Florida, and it's doing a booming business. Although the massive, 130,000 square foot casino doesn't have typical bet-against-the-house Vegas games (such as blackjack, roulette, or craps), it does have thousands of Vegas-style slot machines, baccarat, and all kinds of poker tables that are always packed. The main draw here is the casino, but the guest rooms are surprisingly cushy and swank, with flatscreen TVs, Egyptian-cotton linens, and big bathrooms with massive shower heads; the suites are hyperluxurious. Equally impressive is the 4½-acre lagoon-style pool that's very similar to the one at the Hard Rock in Vegas, with waterfalls, hot tubs, wireless Internet access, and, of course, a bar. There are lots of bars here, especially at the attached entertainment complex, with two clubs open 24/7, as well as restaurants and stores. There's also a food court, or you can choose from several on-site, full-service restaurants, including a swanky steakhouse. There's also a massive spa.

1 Seminole Way, Hollywood, FL 33314. ✆ **800/937-0010** or 954/327-7625. Fax 954/327-7655. www.seminolehardrockhollywood.com. 481 units. $189–$259 double; $279 luxury room; $650–$2,000 suite. AE, DC, DISC, MC, V. **Amenities:** 16 restaurants; 10 nightclubs and lounges; pool; spa; Jacuzzi; luxury/

Anna Nicole & "Room 607"

Anna Nicole Smith died tragically in Room 607 at the **Seminole Hard Rock Hotel** on February 8, 2007. Because the hotel didn't want to create a macabre tourist attraction, they took the room number "out of inventory," meaning the room is still there, but the number has been changed.

exotic car rentals; extensive shopping arcade; 24-hr. room service; casino; car wash. *In room:* A/C, TV, high-speed Internet access, coffeemaker, hair dryer, Tivoli sound system w/CD player.

Inexpensive

Backpacker's Beach Hostel For the young, or for backpackers on a budget, this hostel is a great option, with both dorm beds and private rooms at bargain-basement prices. Clean and conveniently located, the hostel is just 654 feet from the ocean. It features free parking, free phones, free food for self-cooking, free breakfast buffet, and, if you're lucky, free use of the surfboards or in-line skates lying around.

2115 N. Ocean Blvd., Fort Lauderdale, FL 33305. ✆ **954/567-7275.** www.fortlauderdalehostel.com. 12 units. Dorm beds $20 per night, $145 per week; private rooms $55 double. Rates include breakfast buffet. MC, V. **Amenities:** Ping-Pong; kiosk with free Internet access; sundeck; garden. *In room:* A/C, TV, iron.

A Little Inn by the Sea ★ It's not fancy, but A Little Inn by the Sea sits on a primo piece of oceanfront, and most rooms have private balconies overlooking the ocean. There's also 300 feet of private, palm-tree-lined beach. The accommodations are hardly worthy of a spread in an interior-design magazine, but the views make up for the lackluster decor. A free breakfast buffet, a rooftop terrace, and a heated freshwater pool are lovely perks.

4546 El Mar Dr., Lauderdale-by-the-Sea, FL 33308. ✆ **800/492-0311** or 954/772-2450. Fax 954/938-9354. www.alittleinn.com. 29 units. Winter $159–$169 double, $209–$239 suite, $398 2-bedroom apt; off-season $109–$129 double, $129–$169 suite, $179–$298 2-bedroom apt. MC, V. Free parking. **Amenities:** Heated pool; access to nearby tennis court; nearby children's playground; coin-op laundry. *In room:* A/C, TV.

Sea Downs (and the Bougainvillea) ★★ This bargain lodging is often booked months in advance by return guests (mostly Europeans) who want to be directly on the beach without paying a fortune. The hosts of this super-clean 1950s motel, Claudia and Karl Herzog, live on the premises and keep things running smoothly. All rooms have fully equipped kitchens with fridges, stoves, utensils, and glassware and have been redecorated here and at the Herzogs' other, even less expensive property next door, the 11-unit Bougainvillea. Guests at both hotels share the Sea Downs' pool. All rooms are now nonsmoking.

2900 N. Surf Rd., Hollywood, FL 33019. ✆ **954/923-4968.** Fax 954/923-8747. www.seadowns.com or www.bougainvilleahollywood.com. 12 units. Winter $111–$168 studio, $127–$198 1-bedroom apt; off-season $88–$144 studio, $106–$144 1-bedroom apt. Weekly discounted rates available. No credit cards. From I-95, exit Sheridan St. E to Fla. A1A and go south; drive 1/2 mile to Coolidge St.; turn left. **Amenities:** Freshwater outdoor pool; concierge; laundry facilities. *In room:* A/C, TV, dataport, fully equipped kitchen, fridge, coffeemaker.

WHERE TO DINE

It took awhile for a more sophisticated, varied epicurean scene to reach these shores, but Fort Lauderdale—and, to some extent, Hollywood—finally has several fine restaurants. Increasingly, ethnic options are joining the legions of surf-and-turferies that have dominated the area for so long. **Las Olas Boulevard** has so many eateries that the city has put a moratorium on the opening of new restaurants on the 2-mile street.

Very Expensive

Café Martorano ★★ ITALIAN This small storefront eatery doesn't win any awards for decor or location, but when it comes to food that's good enough for an entire Italian family, Café Martorano, which recently opened to rave reviews in Las Vegas, is one of the best. People wait for a table for upward of 2 hours because the restaurant accepts no reservations and can get away with it. An almost-offensive sound system (playing disco tunes and Sinatra) has a tendency to turn off many a diner, but you don't go to Café Martorano for an intimate dinner. Dining here is like being at a big, fat, Italian wedding, where eating, drinking, and dancing are paramount. The menu changes daily, but regulars can request special off-the-menu items. If you don't ask, you don't get, so open your mouth. Also keep your eyes wide open for such celebrities as Liza Minnelli, James Gandolfini, and Steven Van Zandt, among others, who make it a point to stop here for a meal while in town.

3343 E. Oakland Park Blvd., Fort Lauderdale. ✆ **954/561-2554.** www.cafemartorano.com. Reservations not accepted. Main courses $18–$36. MC, V. Daily 5–11pm.

Darrel & Oliver's Cafe Maxx ★★ FLORIBBEAN/NEW WORLD Despite its bleak location in an unassuming storefront, Darrel & Oliver's Cafe Maxx is one of the best restaurants in Broward County. When it opened in 1984, it was the first restaurant to have an open kitchen, and what a stir that caused! Now, instead of the kitchen, the marvel is what comes out of it. Consider cumin-lime-seared jumbo sea scallops; lemon-pepper-roasted mahimahi; or New Zealand venison chop with smoky mountain plum glaze. Yum. But save room for dessert—the honey-roasted peanut butter and banana bread pudding or El Rey Milk Chocolate Pot du Creme are just two of many diet- and mind-blowing options.

2601 E. Atlantic Blvd., Pompano Beach. ✆ **954/782-0606.** Fax 954/782-0648. www.cafemaxx.com. Reservations recommended. Main courses $10–$57. AE, DC, DISC, MC, V. Mon–Thurs 5:30–10:30pm; Fri–Sat 5:30–11pm; Sun 5:30–10pm. From I-95, exit at Atlantic Blvd. E. The restaurant is 3 lights east of Federal Hwy.

Expensive

Anthony's Runway 84 ★★★ ITALIAN Meet Anthony, the gregarious owner of this Fort Lauderdale restaurant with an interior all about jet-setting—albeit in the mid- to late '70s—and a bar crafted out of a plane fuselage. Once you meet him, he will introduce your server, whose name is likely to be Tony. Same goes for the bartender. The quintessential, convivial Italian vibe in here (think Travolta in *Saturday Night Fever*) is conducive to one of the most enjoyable meals you'll ever have. The best way to go is—what else?—family-style, in which you'll be able to share lots of dishes such as mussels marinara, fried clams, roasted red peppers in garlic, shrimp parmigiana, an out-of-this-world rigatoni with cauliflower (although it sounds boring, order it no matter what!), and stellar meat and poultry dishes that frequent fliers to Anthony's rave about each time, as if it were their last meal. For the best pizza, try nearby **Anthony's Coal Fired Pizza,** 2203 S. Federal Hwy. (✆ **954/462-5555**).

330 S.R. 84, Fort Lauderdale. ✆ **954/467-8484.** Reservations strongly recommended. Main courses $15–$50. AE, DC, DISC, MC, V. Tues–Thurs and Sun noon–10pm; Fri–Sat 5–11pm.

Eduardo De San Angel ★★★ MEXICAN Gourmet Mexican is *not* an oxymoron, and for those who don't believe that, take one meal at the sublime Eduardo De San Angel and you'll see how true it is. Chef Eduardo Pria has a masterful way with food, as seen in dishes such as *jaibas rellenas* (fresh Florida blue crab, plum tomatoes, onions, jalapeños, and Spanish green olives baked in a shell with melted jack cheese au gratin and mole poblano). Fresh flowers and candlelight, not to mention the fact that the restaurant resembles an intimate hacienda, also drive home the fact that this isn't your mom's Old El Paso taco dinner. Beer and wine only.

2822 E. Commercial Blvd., Fort Lauderdale. ✆ **954/772-4731.** www.eduardodesanangel.com. Reservations essential. Main courses $24–$32. AE, DC, DISC, MC, V. Mon–Thurs 11:30am–10:30pm; Fri–Sat 5:30–10:30pm.

Himmarshee Bar & Grille ★ AMERICAN Located on a popular street of bars frequented by Fort Lauderdale's young professionals, Himmarshee Bar & Grille is known for its scene and cuisine. A mezzanine bar upstairs is ideal for people-watching; outdoor tables are tight, but strategically situated in front of all the street's action. On weekend nights, in particular, it's difficult to get a table. However, if you can deal with cramming into the bar, it's worth a cocktail or two. The wine list is impressive, and the grilled chili–dusted pork chop with boniato-stuffed poblano chili, Monterey Jack cheese, and creamy, spicy corn sauce is to die for. Also try the chorizo taquitos as an appetizer. Check out Side Bar, the restaurant's very ski-lodgey bar next door featuring live music and a bustling crowd of young hipsters.

210 SW 2nd St. (south of Broward Blvd., west of U.S. 1), Fort Lauderdale. ✆ **954/524-1818.** www.himmarshee.com. Reservations recommended. Main courses $22–$36. AE, MC, V. Mon–Thurs 11:30am–2:30pm and 6–10:30pm; Fri 11:30am–2:30pm and 6–11:30pm; Sat 6–11:30pm; Sun 6–10:30pm.

Johnny V's ★★★ SOUTHWESTERN South Florida's favorite so-called Caribbean Cowboy, Chef Johnny Vinczencz, has moved around quite a bit—from South Beach's Hotel Astor (twice!) to Delray Beach's Sundy House. But this Las Olas hot spot looks to be his final stop, and that's good news to all Johnny V's faithful foodies who will travel to the end of the earth to sample some of his barbecue and Caribbean-inspired contemporary cuisine. What that means is, smoked pheasant nachos, sage-grilled Florida dolphinfish with lobster pan gravy served atop rock shrimp plantain stuffing with cranberry mango chutney, and a slew of dishes you've likely never seen before. Once you've tasted his fare, you'll understand why a herd of hungry folks are extremely happy to have a place to satisfy their cravings for such gourmet grub. Barbra Streisand dined here while in town for her sold-out concerts in 2006 and couldn't stop singing the praises of Johnny V—onstage during her show! She—and Johnny—were *verklempt* (falling over themselves with delight)! Chef Johnny has also opened a new, inexpensive eatery where nothing is over $20, including a delicious Philly cheesesteak sandwich with shaved rib-eye for $11. **Smith & Jones Bar and Grill,** 1313 Las Olas Blvd., will also feature live jazz and blues nightly.

625 E. Las Olas Blvd. ✆ **954/761-7920.** www.johnnyvlasolas.com. Reservations suggested. Main courses $19–$38. AE, DC, MC, V. Mon–Thurs 11:30am–2:30pm and 5:30–11pm; Fri 11:30am–2:30pm and 5:30pm–midnight; Sat 5:30pm–midnight; Sun 5:30–11pm.

Sunfish Grill ★★★ SEAFOOD Unlike its fellow contemporary seafood restaurants, the Sunfish Grill chooses to focus on fish, not fusion. Chef Anthony Sindaco is content to leave the spotlight on his fantastic fish dishes, which are possibly the freshest in town, thanks to the fact that he buys his fish at local markets and often from well-known fishermen who appear at his back door with their catches of the day. Chef Tony's tuna tartare is legendary and the shrimp bisque cappuccino is a deliciously rich soup served in a demitasse cup—because it's that rich. Conch fritters are purely spectacular and not full of filler. Chilean sea bass, expertly cooked with roasted fennel, saffron potatoes, and a caramelized-onion broth, is wonderful. The best dish, in my opinion, is the seared tuna resting on a bed of mushroom and oxtail ragout with garlic mashed potatoes. In fact, almost everything at the Sunfish Grill is better than at most seafood restaurants.

2761 E. Oakland Park Blvd., Pompano Beach. ✆ **954/788-2434.** www.sunfishgrill.com. Reservations recommended. Main courses $28–$38. AE, MC, V. Mon–Thurs 6–9:30pm; Fri–Sat 6–10:30pm.

Trina Restaurant ★★★ MEDITERRANEAN A bona fide dining hot spot like this is a novelty to the area because restaurants this hot usually open in Miami, not Fort

Lauderdale. Thanks to the collaborative efforts of Don Pintabona, former executive chef of Tribeca Grill in New York City and Nick Mautone, formerly of Gramercy Tavern, Miami has some competition. Yes, it's expensive, but the Mediterranean-infused seafood dishes are worth every penny. Try the skewers of diver scallops and braised short ribs with summer truffle reduction and truffled cauliflower. Reservations here are hard to come by, especially in season, but the Trina Lounge is also a great option, offering lighter—and cheaper—fare with high-style ambience. Although we love the buzz of the indoor dining room, request a table outside overlooking the ocean.

601 N. Fort Lauderdale Beach Blvd., Fort Lauderdale. ✆ **954/567-8070.** www.trinarestaurantandlounge.com. Reservations recommended. Main courses $22–$42. AE, DC, DISC, MC, V. Sun–Thurs 5:30–10pm; Fri–Sat 5:30–10:30pm. Lounge open later.

Moderate

Cap's Place Island Restaurant ★ Finds SEAFOOD Opened in 1928 by a bootlegger who ran in the same circles as gangster Meyer Lansky, this barge-turned-restaurant is one of the area's best-kept secrets. Although it's no longer a rum-running restaurant and casino, its illustrious past (FDR and Winston Churchill dined here together) landed it a spot on the National Register of Historic Places. To get here, you have to take a ferryboat, provided by the restaurant. The short ride across the Intracoastal definitely adds to the Cap's Place experience. The food is good, not great. Traditional seafood dishes such as Florida or Maine lobster, clams casino, and oysters Rockefeller will take you back to the days when a soprano was just an opera singer.

2765 NE 28th Court, Lighthouse Point. ✆ **954/941-0418.** www.capsplace.com. Reservations recommended. Main courses $14–$32. MC, V. Daily 5:30pm–midnight. To get to Cap's Place, motor-launch from I-95, exit at Copan's Rd. and go east to U.S. 1 (Federal Hwy.). At NE 24th St., turn right and follow the double lines and signs to the Lighthouse Point Yacht Basin and Marina (8 miles north of Fort Lauderdale). From here, follow the CAP'S PLACE sign pointing you to the shuttle.

Creolina's Dixie Takeout ★ CREOLE You'll find authentic Louisiana Creole cuisine at this small but very popular restaurant that moved from the Riverwalk area in 2008 to nearby suburb Davie when the landlord decided to expand the neighboring bar into the restaurant. Though the new strip mall locale is hardly idyllic, the prices are–gumbo is offered all day at just $7. In addition to Creole, the chef has added Southern classics including country fried steak, chicken and dumplings, pulled pork, and country-style ribs. Sides include corn bread, greens, black-eyed peas, as well macaroni and cheese. There is also a terrific New Orleans Sunday brunch. Ask to sit in sassy Rosie's section.

13150 W. State Road 84, Fort Lauderdale. ✆ **954/524-2003.** Main courses $5–$20. AE, MC, V. Mon 11am–2:30pm and 5–9pm; Tues–Thurs 11am–2:30pm and 5–10pm; Fri 11am–2:30pm and 5–11pm; Sat 5–11pm; Sun 5–9pm.

Indigo ★ SEAFOOD A popular people-watching spot, Indigo is a reliable seafood restaurant housed in the New Orleans–style Riverside Hotel. The dining room is nice enough, but sit outside and watch the pedestrian parade that is Las Olas Boulevard. Among the menu highlights: pan-roasted Florida snapper, citrus-crusted Florida grouper, and chargrilled pork loin.

In the Riverside Hotel, 620 E. Las Olas Blvd., Fort Lauderdale. ✆ **954/467-0671.** Reservations accepted for parties of 6 or more. Main courses $10–$36. AE, DC, DISC, MC, V. Daily 7am–9:45pm.

Rustic Inn Crabhouse ★★ SEAFOOD A Fort Lauderdale rough-and-tumble landmark for more than 50 years, Rustic Inn isn't the place for a romantic, intimate, quiet dinner. The minute you walk in, you're assaulted by a cacophonous banging—a symphony from a packed house of happy diners cracking their crabs with wooden mallets. Although you don't *have* to crack your own crabs—diva Barbra Streisand didn't when she dined here (she requested them already cracked—god forbid she should break a nail!)—it's all part of the experience. Newspaper lines the tables, so prepare to get your hands dirty. Although the restaurant is known for its "world-famous garlic crabs" (and we think they are totally deserving of that lofty tagline), you can also order lobster, pasta, and all sorts of fried fish—even fried alligator (it's chewier than chicken!). The fried clams are especially good, but if you want to gorge yourself, try the Reef Raft, a basket of fried oysters, fried scallops, and fried fish. Dress very casual and prepare to wait awhile for a table; but trust me, it's worth it.

4331 Ravenswood Rd., Fort Lauderdale. ✆ **954/584-1637.** Reservations not accepted. Main courses $10–$20; crabs are market price. AE, DC, DISC, MC, V. Mon–Sat 11:30am–10:45pm; Sun 2–9:45pm.

Sugar Reef ★★ FRENCH CARIBBEAN I could go on about this restaurant's priceless ocean view, but the menu of Mediterranean, Caribbean, and French dishes is just as outstanding. A pleasant tropical decor is bolstered by fresh air wafting in from the Atlantic. Seafood bouillabaisse in green curry and coconut broth and Sugar Reef *pho*—a Vietnamese noodle dish with chicken, shrimp, ginger, and spices—are among the restaurant's most popular dishes. The kitchen puts a savory spin on duck, roasted and topped with sweet-chili-and-papaya salsa. This is not a place you'd expect to find on a beach boardwalk, which makes it all the more delightful.

600 N. Surf Rd. (on the Broadwalk, just north of Hollywood Blvd.), Hollywood. ✆ **954/922-1119.** www.sugarreefgrill.com. Reservations accepted for parties of 6 or more. Main courses $10–$28. AE, DISC, MC, V. Mon 4–10:30pm; Tues–Thurs 11am–10:30pm; Fri–Sun 11am–11pm (sometimes later in winter).

Inexpensive

The Floridian Restaurant ★ (Value) AMERICAN/DINER The Floridian, affectionately known as "The Flo" has been filling South Florida's diner void for more than 63 years, serving breakfast, lunch, and dinner, 24/7. It's especially busy on weekend mornings when locals and tourists come in for huge omelets, fresh oatmeal, sausage, and biscuits. Just to prove it's up to par with swanky Fort Lauderdale, the Floridian offers a $300 Fat Cat meal for two that includes steak, eggs, and a bottle of Dom Perignon! While some say the place needs a major cleaning, others insist that the grit and grime are part of the greasy spoon's charm.

1410 E. Las Olas Blvd., Fort Lauderdale. ✆ **954/463-4041.** Fax 954/761-3930. Sandwiches $3–$7; breakfast combos $3.50–$8; hot platters $7–$14. No credit cards. Daily 24 hr.

Jaxon's ★ (Kids) ICE CREAM South Florida's best and only authentic old-fashioned ice-cream parlor and country store attracts those with sweet tooths from all over the area. Their cravings are satisfied with an unabridged assortment of homemade ice cream served any which way. Kids love the candy store in the front of the restaurant, and adults love the pre–Ben & Jerry's authenticity. For the calorie-conscious, the sugar-free and fat-free versions are pretty good. Jaxon's most famous everything-but-the-kitchen-sink sundae has countless scoops and endless toppings.

128 S. Federal Hwy., Dania Beach. ✆ **954/923-4445.** Sundaes $2.75–$7.95. AE, DISC, MC, V. Mon–Thurs 11:30am–11pm; Fri–Sat 11:30am–midnight; Sun noon–11pm.

Lester's Diner ★ AMERICAN Since 1968, Lester's Diner has been serving swarms of South Floridians large portions of great greasy-spoon fare until the wee hours. Try the eggs Benedict and the 14-ounce "cup" of classic coffee, or sample one of Lester's many homemade desserts. The place serves breakfast 24 hours a day and is a Fort Lauderdale institution that attracts locals, club crowds, city officials, and a generally motley, friendly crew of hungry people craving no-nonsense food served by seasoned waitresses with beehive hairdos that contribute to the campy atmosphere.

250 S.R. 84, Fort Lauderdale. ✆ **954/525-5641.** Main courses $5–$12. AE, MC, V. Daily 24 hr.

Le Tub ★★ Finds AMERICAN Hands down, this is one of the coolest, most unpretentious, quintessential pre–swanky South Florida restaurants, if not one of the coolest restaurants, period. Established in 1959 as a Sunoco gas station, Le Tub was purchased in 1974 by a man who personally transformed the place into this waterfront restaurant, made out of flotsam, jetsam, and ocean-bone treasures gathered over 4 years of jogging on Hollywood Beach. But the waterfront location and unique building aren't the only things to marvel at. As you walk in, take note of the hand-painted bathtubs and toilet bowls (it's not at all gross; they're used as planters) lining the walkway. Inside is a divey bar complete with pool table and jukebox; outside seating on the deck is the real gem. Le Tub is famous for its burgers (which *Esquire* magazine and Oprah have declared the country's best, thereby increasing the masses who flock here a million fold), chili, and seafood, but more appealing than the food is the peaceful, easy feeling exuded by the place.

1100 N. Ocean Dr., Hollywood. ✆ **954/931-9425.** Main courses $6–$17. No credit cards. Daily 10:30am–4am.

2 BOCA RATON ★★ & DELRAY BEACH ★

26 miles S of Palm Beach; 40 miles N of Miami; 21 miles N of Fort Lauderdale

Boca Raton is one of South Florida's most expensive, well-maintained cities—home to ladies who lunch and SUV-driving yuppies. The city's name literally translates as "rat's mouth," but you'd be hard-pressed to find rodents in this area's fancy digs.

If you're looking for funky, wacky, and eclectic, look elsewhere. Boca is a luxurious resort community and, for some, the only place worth staying in South Florida. Although Jerry Seinfeld's TV parents retired to the fictional Del Boca Vista, Boca is just too pricey to be a retirement community. With minimal nightlife, entertainment in Boca is restricted to leisure sports, excellent dining, and upscale shopping. The city's residents and vacationers happily comply.

Delray Beach, named after a suburb of Detroit, is a sleepy-yet-starting-to-awaken beachfront community that grew up completely separate from its southern neighbor. Because of their proximity, Boca and Delray can easily be explored together. Budget-conscious travelers would do well to eat and sleep in Delray and dip into Boca for sightseeing and beaching only. The 2-mile stretch of beach here is well maintained and crowded, though not mobbed. Delray's "downtown" area is confined to Atlantic Avenue, which is known for restaurants from casual to chic, quaint shops, and art galleries. During the day, Delray is slumbering, but thanks to the recent addition of trendy restaurants and bars, nighttime is a much more animated hotbed of hipster activity. Still, compared to Boca, Delray is much more laid-back, hardly as chichi, and more cute little beach town than sprawling, swanky, suburban Boca.

ESSENTIALS

GETTING THERE Like the rest of the cities on the Gold Coast, Boca Raton and Delray are easily reached from I-95 or the Florida Turnpike. Both the Fort Lauderdale Hollywood International Airport and the Palm Beach International Airport are about 20

minutes away. **Amtrak** (✆ **800/USA-RAIL** [872-7245]; www.amtrak.com) trains make stops in Delray Beach at an unattended station at 345 S. Congress Ave.

VISITOR INFORMATION Contact or stop by the **Palm Beach County Convention and Visitors Bureau,** 1555 Palm Beach Lakes Blvd., Ste. 800, West Palm Beach, FL 33401 (✆ **800/554-PALM** [7256] or 561/233-3000; fax 561/471-3990; www.palmbeachfl.com). It's open Monday through Friday from 8:30am to 5:30pm and has excellent coupons and discounts. Monday through Friday from 8:30am until at least 4pm, stop by the **Greater Boca Raton Chamber of Commerce,** 1800 N. Dixie Hwy., 4 blocks north of Glades Road, Boca Raton, FL 33432 (✆ **561/395-4433;** fax 561/392-3780; www.bocaratonchamber.com), for information on attractions, accommodations, and events in the area. You can also try the **Greater Delray Beach Chamber of Commerce,** 64 SE 5th Ave., half a block south of Atlantic Avenue on U.S. 1, Delray Beach, FL 33483 (✆ **561/278-0424;** fax 561/278-0555; www.delraybeach.com), but I recommend the Palm Beach County Convention and Visitors Bureau as it has information on the entire county.

BEACHES & OUTDOOR ACTIVITIES

BEACHES Thankfully, Florida had the foresight to set aside some of its most beautiful coastal areas for the public's enjoyment. Many of the area's best beaches are located in state parks and are free to pedestrians and bikers, though most do charge for parking. Among the beaches I recommend are Delray Beach's **Atlantic Dunes Beach,** 1600 S. Ocean Blvd., which charges no admission to access a 7-acre developed beach with lifeguards, restrooms, changing rooms, and a family park area; and Boca Raton's **South Beach Park,** 400 N. Ocean Blvd., with 1,670 feet of beach, 25 acres, lifeguards, picnic areas, restrooms, showers, and 955 feet of developed beach south of the Boca Inlet, accessible for an admission charge of $15 Monday through Friday, and $17 Saturday and Sunday. The two beaches below are also very popular.

Delray Beach, on Ocean Boulevard at the east end of Atlantic Avenue, is one of the area's most popular hangouts. Weekends especially attract a young and good-looking crowd of active locals and tourists. Refreshments, snack shops, bars, and restaurants are just across the street. Families enjoy the protection of lifeguards on the clean, wide strip. Gentle waters make it a good swimming beach, too. Restrooms and showers are available, and there's limited parking at meters along Ocean Boulevard.

Spanish River Park Beach, on North Ocean Boulevard (Fla. A1A), 2 miles north of Palmetto Park Road in Boca Raton, is a huge 95-acre oceanfront park with a half-mile-long beach with lifeguards as well as a large grassy area, making it one of the best choices for picnicking. Facilities include picnic tables, grills, restrooms, showers, and a 40-foot observation tower. You can walk through tunnels under the highway to access nature trails that wind through fertile grasslands. Volleyball nets always have at least one game going on. The park is open from 8am to 8pm. Admission is $16 for vehicles Monday through Friday; $18 on Saturday, Sunday, and major holidays.

Also see the description of **Red Reef Park** under "Scuba Diving & Snorkeling," below.

GOLF This area has plenty of good courses. The best ones that are not in a gated community are **Boca Raton Resort & Club** (p. 288) and the **Inn at Ocean Breeze Golf and Country Club** (p. 289), formerly known as the Inn at Boca Teeca. Another great place to swing clubs is at the **Deer Creek Golf Club,** 2801 Country Club Blvd., Deerfield Beach (✆ **954/421-5550;** www.deercreekflorida.com), a 300-plus-yard driving range

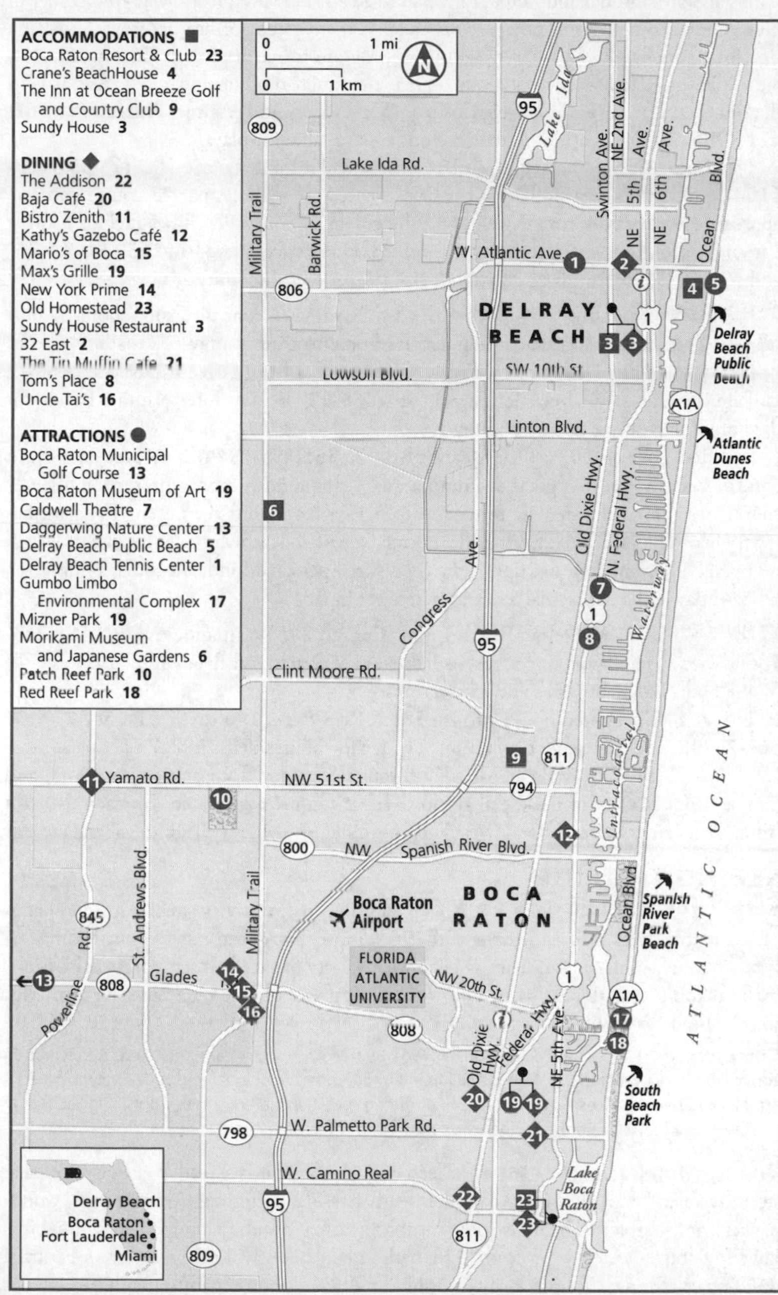
ACCOMMODATIONS
Boca Raton Resort & Club 23
Crane's BeachHouse 4
The Inn at Ocean Breeze Golf and Country Club 9
Sundy House 3
DINING
The Addison 22
Baja Café 20
Bistro Zenith 11
Kathy's Gazebo Café 12
Mario's of Boca 15
Max's Grille 19
New York Prime 14
Old Homestead 23
Sundy House Restaurant 3
32 East 2
The Tin Muffin Cafe 21
Tom's Place 8
Uncle Tai's 16
ATTRACTIONS
Boca Raton Municipal Golf Course 13
Boca Raton Museum of Art 19
Caldwell Theatre 7
Daggerwing Nature Center 13
Delray Beach Public Beach 5
Delray Beach Tennis Center 1
Gumbo Limbo Environmental Complex 17
Mizner Park 19
Morikami Museum and Japanese Gardens 6
Patch Reef Park 10
Red Reef Park 18
0 1 mi
0 1 km
N
DELRAY BEACH
BOCA RATON
Lake Ida
Lake Ida Rd.
W. Atlantic Ave.
Lowson Blvd.
SW 10th St.
Linton Blvd.
Military Trail
Barwick Rd.
Swinton Ave.
NE 2nd Ave.
NE 5th Ave.
NE 6th Ave.
Ocean Blvd.
Old Dixie Hwy.
N. Federal Hwy.
Congress Ave.
Clint Moore Rd.
Yamato Rd.
NW 51st St.
NW Spanish River Blvd.
St. Andrews Blvd.
Powerline Rd.
Glades
NW 20th St.
Federal Hwy.
NE 5th Ave.
W. Palmetto Park Rd.
W. Camino Real
Intracoastal Waterway
ATLANTIC OCEAN
Delray Beach Public Beach
Atlantic Dunes Beach
Spanish River Park Beach
South Beach Park
Boca Raton Airport
FLORIDA ATLANTIC UNIVERSITY
Lake Boca Raton
Delray Beach
Boca Raton
Fort Lauderdale
Miami

where a large bucket of balls costs $9 and a small one costs $5. Rates at the Deer Creek Golf Club are seasonal and range from $45 to $135. However, from May to October or November, about a dozen private courses open their greens to visitors staying in Palm Beach County hotels. This "Golf-A-Round" program is free or severely discounted (carts are additional), and reservations can be made through most major hotels. Ask at your hotel or contact the **Palm Beach County Convention and Visitors Bureau** (✆ **561/471-3995**) for information on which clubs are available for play.

The **Boca Raton Municipal Golf Course,** 8111 Golf Course Rd. (✆ **561/483-6100**), is the area's best public golf course. There's an 18-hole, par-72 course covering approximately 6,200 yards, as well as a 9-hole, par-30 course. Facilities include a snack bar and a pro shop where clubs can be rented. Greens fees are $16 to $32 for 9 holes, and $24 to $56 for 18 holes. Ask about special summer discounts.

SCUBA DIVING & SNORKELING **Moray Bend,** a 58-foot dive spot about 3/4 mile off Boca Inlet, is the area's most popular. It's home to three moray eels that are used to being fed by scuba divers. The reef is accessible by boat from **Force E Dive Center,** 877 E. Palmetto Park Rd., Boca Raton (✆ **561/368-0555;** www.force-e.com). Phone for dive times. Dives cost $55 to $65 per person.

Red Reef Park, 1400 N. Ocean Park Blvd. (✆ **561/393-7974**), a 67-acre oceanfront park in Boca Raton, has good swimming and year-round lifeguard protection. There's snorkeling around the shallow rocks and reefs that lie just off the beach. The park has restrooms and a picnic area with grills. Located a half-mile north of Palmetto Park Road, it's open daily from 8am to 10pm. The cost is $16 per car Monday through Friday, $18 on Saturday and Sunday; walkers and bikers get in free.

TENNIS The snazzy **Delray Beach Tennis Center,** 201 W. Atlantic Ave. (✆ **561/243-7360;** www.delraytennis.com), has 14 lighted clay courts and five hard courts available by the hour. Phone for rates and reservations.

The 17 public lighted hard courts at **Patch Reef Park,** 2000 NW 51st St. (✆ **561/367-7090**), are available by reservation. The fee for nonresidents is $5.75 per person per 1 1/2 hours. Courts are available Monday through Saturday from 7:30am to 10pm, and Sunday from 7:30am to dusk; call ahead to see if a court is available. To reach the park from I-95, exit at Yamato Road West and continue past Military Trail to the park.

SEEING THE SIGHTS

Boca Raton Museum of Art ★★ In addition to a relatively small but well-chosen permanent collection that's strongest in 19th-century European oils (Degas, Klee, Matisse, Picasso, Seurat), the museum stages a wide variety of excellent temporary exhibitions by local and international artists. Lectures and films are offered on a fairly regular basis, so call ahead for details.

Mizner Park, 501 Plaza Real, Boca Raton. ✆ **561/392-2500.** www.bocamuseum.org. Admission $8 adults, $6 seniors, $4 students, free for children 11 and under. Additional fees may apply for special exhibits and performances. Free on Wed except during special exhibitions. Tues, Thurs, and Sat 10am–5pm; Wed and Fri 10am–9pm; Sun noon–5pm.

Daggerwing Nature Center ★ Seen enough snowbirds? Head over to this 39-acre swampy splendor where birds of another feather reside, including herons, egrets, woodpeckers, and warblers. The trails come complete with a soundtrack provided by songbirds hovering above (watch your head). The park's night hikes will take you on a nocturnal wake-up call for owls at 6pm. Bring a flashlight. A $2-million expansion in 2007 includes a 3,000-square-foot exhibit hall, a laboratory classroom, and exciting wet forest and conservation exhibits. Completion was expected spring of 2008.

South County Regional Park, 11200 Park Access Rd., Boca Raton. © **561/488-9953.** Free admission. Tues–Fri 1–4:30pm; Sat 9am–4:30pm. Call for tour and activity schedule.

Gumbo Limbo Environmental Complex ★★★ If manicured lawns and golf courses aren't your idea of communing with nature, then head to Gumbo Limbo. Named for an indigenous hardwood tree, the 20-acre complex protects one of the few surviving coastal hammocks, or forest islands, in South Florida. Walk through the hammock on a half-mile-long boardwalk that ends at a 40-foot observation tower, from which you can see the Atlantic Ocean, the Intracoastal Waterway, and much of Boca Raton. From mid-April to September, sea turtles come ashore here to lay eggs.

1801 N. Ocean Blvd. (on Fla. A1A btw. Spanish River Blvd. and Palmetto Park Rd.), Boca Raton. © **561/338-1473.** www.gumbolimbo.org. Free admission ($3 donation suggested). Mon–Sat 9am–4pm; Sun noon–4pm.

Morikami Museum and Japanese Gardens ★★★ Slip off your shoes and enter a serene Japanese garden that dates from 1905, when an entrepreneurial farmer, Jo Sakai, came to Boca Raton to build a tropical agricultural community. The Yamato Colony, as it was known, was short-lived; by the 1920s, only one tenacious colonist remained: George Sukeji Morikami. But Morikami was quite successful, eventually running one of the largest pineapple plantations in the area. The 200-acre Morikami Museum and Japanese Gardens, which opened to the public in 1977, was Morikami's gift to Palm Beach County and the state of Florida. A stroll through the garden is almost a mile long. An artificial waterfall that cascades into a koi- and carp-filled moat; a small rock garden for meditation; and a large bonsai collection with miniature maple, buttonwood, juniper, and Australian pine trees are all worth contemplation. There's also a cafe with an Asian-inspired menu if you want to stay for lunch.

4000 Morikami Park Rd., Delray Beach. © **561/495-0233.** www.morikami.org. Museum $10 adults, $9 seniors, $6 children 6–18. Museum Tues–Sun 10am–5pm; gardens Tues–Sat 10am–5pm. Closed major holidays.

SHOPPING

Even if you don't plan to buy anything, a trip to Boca Raton's **Mizner Park** is essential for capturing the essence of the city. Mizner is the place to see and be seen, where Rolls-Royces and Ferraris are parked curbside, freshly coiffed women sit amid shopping bags at outdoor cafes, and young movers and shakers chat on their constantly buzzing cellphones. Beyond the human scenery, however, Mizner Park is scenic in its own right, with beautiful landscaping. It's really an outdoor mall, with 45 specialty shops, seven good restaurants, and a multiplex. Each shop front faces a grassy island with gazebos, potted plants, and garden benches. Mizner Park is on Federal Highway, between Palmetto Park and Glades roads (© **561/362-0606**).

Boca's **Town Center Mall,** on the south side of Glades Road, just west of I-95, has seven huge department stores, including Nordstrom, Bloomingdale's, Burdines, Lord & Taylor, and Saks Fifth Avenue. Add hundreds of specialty shops, an extensive food court, and a range of other restaurants, and you have the area's most comprehensive shopping center.

On Delray Beach's Atlantic Avenue, especially east of Swinton Avenue, you'll find a few antiques shops, clothing stores, and galleries shaded by palm trees and colorful awnings. Pick up the *Downtown Delray Beach* map and guide at almost any of the stores on this strip, or call © **561/278-0424** for more information.

A number of national chain hotels worth considering include the moderately priced **Holiday Inn Highland Beach Oceanside,** 2809 S. Ocean Blvd., on Florida A1A, southeast of Linton Boulevard (✆ **800/234-6835** or 561/278-6241). Although you won't find rows of cheap hotels as in Fort Lauderdale and Hollywood, a handful of mom-and-pop motels have survived along Florida A1A between the towering condominiums of Delray Beach. Look along the beach just south of Atlantic Boulevard. Especially noteworthy is the pleasant little two-story, shingle-roofed **Bermuda Inn,** 64 S. Ocean Blvd. (✆ **561/276-5288**).

Even more economical options can be found in Deerfield Beach, Boca's neighbor, south of the county line. A number of beachfront efficiencies offer great deals, even in the winter months. Try the **Panther Motel and Apartments,** 715 S. A1A (✆ **954/427-0700**), a clean and convenient motel with rates starting as low as $49 (in season, you may have to book for a week at a time; rates then start at $250).

Very Expensive

Boca Raton Resort & Club ★★ Kids This landmark resort is a sprawling 350-acre collection of posh, yet oddly matched buildings: the original Cloister; the drab pink 27-story Tower; the renovated Beach Club and Pool Oasis, accessible by water shuttle and featuring three redesigned swimming pools, oceanfront bar, beach access, cabana, and sunning terraces; a Yacht Club, a Venetian-style wing of 112 luxury rooms and suites. Fans of the old-school resort should feel right at home as Old World blends beautifully with New World, modern twists. Everything at this resort, which straddles the Intracoastal, is at your fingertips, but may sometimes require some effort to reach. Thankfully the resort provides transportation shuttles every 10 minutes. Amenities include the grand Spa Palazzo, two 18-hole championship golf courses, a $10-million tennis and fitness center, a 25-slip marina, and a private beach with watersports equipment. Extensive resort renovations include public spaces, remodeled bungalows, an entirely redesigned Boca Beach Club, and a restored Palm Court reminiscent of an Italian piazza. The resort's also foodie heaven, with a choice of 10 places to dine including N.Y.C.'s Old Homestead steakhouse, Morimoto, and Gordon Ramsay's Cielo. Newly opened as we go to print: a branch of N.Y.C.'s venerable Serendipity ice cream parlor.

501 E. Camino Real (P.O. Box 5025), Boca Raton, FL 33432. ✆ **888/495-BOCA** or 561/447-3000. Fax 561/447-3183. www.bocaresort.com. 1,047 units. Winter $259–$760 double; off-season $169–$329 double. Seasonal packages available. AE, DC, DISC, MC, V. From I-95 N., exit onto Palmetto Park Rd. E. Turn right onto Federal Hwy. (U.S. 1), then left onto Camino Real. **Amenities:** 10 restaurants; 5 bars; 4 pools; 2 18-hole championship golf courses; 30 hydrogrid tennis courts; 2 fitness centers; Mediterranean spa; watersports equipment/rentals; extensive children's programs; concierge; business center; 24-hr. room service; laundry service; 32-slip marina; indoor basketball court. *In room:* A/C, TV, minibar, hair dryer.

Sundy House ★★★ The oldest residence in Delray Beach, Sundy House is a bona fide 1902 Queen Anne that has been restored to its Victorian glory—on the outside, at least. Inside, the four one- and two-bedroom apartments are in a style best described as Caribbean funky, adorned in brilliant colors and outfitted with state-of-the-art electronics, full modern kitchens, and laundry facilities. Six guest rooms known as the Stables are equestrian chic, with rustic appointments in dark woods. While the rooms here are outstanding, it's the surrounding property that garners the most oohs and aahs. Set on an acre of lush gardens, the Sundy House is surrounded by more than 5,000 species of exotic plants, streams, and parrots, making an escape here seem more Hawaii than Florida. You can even swim with fish in the hotel's swimming pond! The on-site restaurant features exquisite New Florida cuisine, often using fresh fruits and herbs straight from Sundy House's botanical Taru Garden.

106 S. Swinton Ave., Delray Beach, FL 33444. ✆ **877/439-9601** or 561/272-5678. Fax 561/272-1115. www.sundyhouse.com. 11 units. Winter $349–$669 1- or 2-bedroom or cottage; off-season $169–$559 1- or 2-bedroom or cottage. AE, DC, DISC, MC, V. **Amenities:** Restaurant; bar; swimming pond; limited room service. *In room:* A/C, TV/DVD, kitchen, coffeemaker, hair dryer, safe, CD player, washer/dryer.

Expensive

Crane's BeachHouse ★★ If you can't afford your own South Florida beach house—and why bother with all the maintenance, anyway?—Crane's BeachHouse, meticulously run and maintained by husband and wife Michael and Cheryl Crane, is a haven away from home, located just 1 block from the beach and right in the middle of historic Delray Beach. The main draws here are the whimsical, tropical suites, in which every piece of furniture and bric-a-brac is completely original and often crafted by local artists. Although each unit has its own theme—Hawaii, Amazon, Anacapri, and Capetown, for instance—the beds are all the same, in that they are downright heavenly. Lush gardens, a Tiki bar, and a swimming pool leave you with little reason to flee the premises, but when you do, you'll want to return as quickly as possible.

82 Gleason St., Delray Beach, FL 33483. ✆ **866/372-7263** or 561/278-1700. Fax 561/278-7826. www.cranesbeachhouse.com. 27 units. Winter $189–$239 double, $289–$499 suite; off-season $139–$169 double, $199–$299 suite. AE, DC, DISC, V. Free parking. **Amenities:** 2 small outdoor pools. *In room:* A/C, TV/VCR, dataport, minibar, full kitchen, coffeemaker, hair dryer, iron, safe.

Inexpensive

The Inn at Ocean Breeze Golf and Country Club ★ For more than 3 decades, this lodging has attracted golf fanatics who couldn't care less about the small but comfortable rooms, because they're too busy out on the superb 27-hole golf course, open only to members and guests. For the golf widow(er)s, most of the rooms in this three-story motel-style building have balconies or patios from which to watch or signal to their significant others that it's time for dinner.

5800 NW 2nd Ave., Boca Raton, FL 33487. ✆ **561/994-0400.** Fax 561/998-8279. www.theinnatoceanbreeze.com. 46 units. Winter from $119 double; off-season from $59 double. AE, DC, MC, V. **Amenities:** Restaurant; small pool; golf course; 6 tennis courts; fitness center. *In room:* A/C, TV, free Wi-Fi.

WHERE TO DINE

Boca Raton and its surrounding area is the kind of place where you discuss dinner plans at the breakfast table. Nightlife in Boca means going out to a restaurant. But who cares? This is some of the best dining in South Florida.

Very Expensive

The Addison ★★★ CONTINENTAL Located in Addison Mizner's 1925 office building near his famous Boca Raton Resort, the Addison is one of Boca's most popular—and romantic—restaurants, with a stunning courtyard and a setting straight out of a swank Spanish village. The menu ranges from comfort food, including such dishes as fried chicken and barbecued beef short ribs, steaks, and chops, to more nouveau dishes such as corn-crusted soft-shell crab with roasted garlic mash and fennel salad. Service is swift and professional, but people really come here for the ambience.

2 East Camino Real, Boca Raton. ✆ **561/395-9335.** www.theaddison.com. Reservations recommended. Main courses $16–$34. AE, DC, DISC, MC, V. Sun–Thurs 5–10pm; Fri–Sat 5–11pm.

Kathy's Gazebo Cafe ★★★ CONTINENTAL An elegant, old school Continental restaurant with chandeliers and white linen tablecloths, Kathy's white-glove restaurant is an ideal spot for special occasions or culinary nostalgia. The food is superb—the Dover sole is flown in from Holland and prepared with nothing fancier than an almandine or meunière sauce; chateaubriand is also spectacular and, in a city smitten by plain ol' steak and sushi, it's a delicious throwback to simpler, delicious days. Fresh homemade pastries and peach Melba are among the desserts. While jackets aren't commonly required at restaurants in South Florida, you'll want to wear one here just to fit in with the dapper moneyed types who frequent the place.

4199 N. Federal Hwy., Boca Raton. ✆ **561/395-6033.** www.kathysgazebo.com. Reservations required. Main courses $11–$50. AE, MC, V. Daily 5:30–10pm.

New York Prime ★ STEAKHOUSE This South Florida outpost of a South Carolina–based chain is the prime spot for carnivores looking to satisfy their cravings for big, succulent steaks. Fish dishes are also available, including lobsters ranging from 3 to 13 pounds. But excess does not come cheap. In fact, the restaurant brazenly states its case on the menu: "We strive to be the Mercedes of steakhouses by offering the very best . . . but you can't drive a Mercedes for the same price as a Buick." Cute motto, but in terms of consistency, New York Prime is a Pinto. On one night, the food and service are exquisite, while on another, abysmal. Take your chances, though, because if you do hit it on a good night, you won't be disappointed.

2350 Executive Center Dr., Boca Raton. ✆ **561/998-3881.** www.newyorkprime.com. Reservations recommended. Main courses $20–$79. AE, MC, V. Daily 5–11pm.

Old Homestead ★★★ STEAKHOUSE If you're homesick for New York, this branch of New York's oldest meatery is the place to cure your yearnings, especially if money is no object. The 48-ounce Meatpacking District long-bone rib steak for two at $40 per person is pricey, but cheaper than a plane ticket to Gotham—and it's worth it. The meat here is divine. Sides are a la carte and outstanding. The hash-brown potato pie and buttermilk onion rings are my favorites, but all sorts of starches and veggies are available at steep prices from $8 to $12 per dish. Seafood is also aplenty, from fresh shucked oysters to Maine lobsters; and for diners who just can't seem to find the ideal chopped salad, the hand-chopped version of blue cheese, olives, mushrooms, bacon bits, eggs, and hearts of palm is a meal in itself. The restaurant also made news when it decided to charge a whopping $100 for its tri-beef burger, a meaty mixture of Kobe, American, and Argentinean beef, with $10 of its hefty price going to the Make-A-Wish Foundation. After creating a stir regardless of the charity tie-in, the burger was reduced to $37.

501 E. Camino Real (in the Boca Raton Resort), Boca Raton. ✆ **561/447-3640.** www.bocaresort.com. Reservations required. Main courses $28–$47. AE, MC, V. Sun–Wed 5–10pm; Thurs–Sat 5–11pm.

Expensive

Max's Grille ★ AMERICAN Max's Grille is a very popular, very good option in Mizner Park, but you'll have to wait to be seated. An exhibition kitchen occupies the back wall of the restaurant, so those diners lucky enough to score a table can watch as their yellowfin tuna steak or filet mignon is seared on a flaming oak grill. There's also a large selection of chicken, meatloaf, pastas, and main-course salads.

404 Plaza Real, in Mizner Park, Boca Raton. ✆ **561/368-0080.** Reservations accepted for parties of 6 or more. Main courses $11–$30. AE, DC, DISC, MC, V. Mon–Thurs 11:30am–3pm and 5–10:30pm; Fri–Sat 11:30am–3pm and 5–11pm; Sun 11:30am–10pm.

Sundy House Restaurant ★★ FLORIBBEAN This restaurant is a stunning place that combines elegant indoor dining and lush tropical outdoor settings with a gastronomic wizardry of fresh fruits, vegetables, and spices grown on the Sundy House's 5-acre farm. Each dish is prepared with palpable precision. Consider the following: herb-seared Chilean sea bass with truffle oil and chive risotto, or the mojo-glazed Caribbean spiced pork tenderloin with cabernet sauce, chive sour cream, and buttered asparagus. Save room for dessert, including a decadent Earl Grey crème brûlée and mandarin orange chocolate torte. A decadent Sunday brunch buffet makes the day before you return to work infinitely more bearable. On the negative side, the service here can be surly and spotty.

In the Sundy House, 106 S. Swinton Ave., Delray Beach. ✆ **561/272-5678.** www.sundyhouse.com. Reservations essential. Main courses $26–$35. AE, DC, DISC, MC, V. Daily 11:30am–2:30pm and 6–10pm; Sun brunch 10:30am–2:30pm.

32 East ★★ NEW AMERICAN The menu changes every day at this popular people-watching outpost of tasty, contemporary American food, which has added hipness to the Delray Beach scene. Among the standouts are sauté of Gulf Coast grouper with hedgehog mushrooms, Cipollini onions, and white beans in butternut squash sherry broth; and grilled duck breast and radicchio with parsnip-yam purée and pomegranate-Saba brown butter. The buzzing ambience makes 32 East a popular hangout spot for the cocktail set.

32 E. Atlantic Ave., Delray Beach. ✆ **561/276-7868.** www.32east.com. Reservations recommended. Main courses $18–$37. AE, DC, MC, V. Sun–Thurs 5:30–10pm; Fri–Sat 5:30–11pm. Bar until 2am.

Uncle Tai's ★★★ CHINESE Not your average egg-roll-and-lo-mein place, Uncle Tai's, Boca's best upscale Chinese restaurant, offers a savory spin on classics such as garlic chicken and duck with plum sauce. A family-run restaurant, Uncle Tai's is the product of Wen Dah Tai, who studied with master chefs in China, Japan, and the Philippines. Tai wants to make sure you emerge from his restaurant satisfied, and he'll go the extra mile to discourage you from ordering a dish that's less suited to Western palates because it was specially created for the restaurant's many Chinese diners.

5250 Town Center Circle (btw. Glades and Palmetto Park roads), Boca Raton. ✆ **561/368-8806.** www.uncle-tais.com. Reservations suggested. Main courses $11–$52. AE, DISC, MC, V. Sun–Thurs 11:30am–2:30pm and 5–10pm; Fri–Sat 11:30am–2:30pm and 5–10:30pm.

Moderate

Bistro Zenith ★ NEW AMERICAN At the height of innovative cuisine, Bistro Zenith's consistently changing menu keeps local foodies coming back for its tasty traditional American dishes graced with Asian, Mediterranean, or Southwestern influences. The pineapple jerk marinated skirt steak with chipotle corn, jicama salsa, fried plantains with yellow rice, and black beans is my favorite. At press time, the restaurant was closed for "renovation" and "vacation" according to a phone recording, so hopefully this Zenith hasn't reached its nadir.

In the Regency Court, 3011 Yamato Rd., Boca Raton. ✆ **561/997-2570.** Reservations recommended. Main courses $12–$30. AE, MC, V. Mon–Thurs 11:30am–2:30pm and 5:30–10pm; Fri 11:30am–2:30pm and 5:30–11pm; Sat 5:30–11pm; Sun 5:30–10pm.

Mario's of Boca ★ ITALIAN This extremely popular, bustling Italian bistro keeps Boca's biggest mouths busy with massive portions of great homemade Italian food. The garlic rolls and the pizza are especially worth piping down for. If you're really hungry, an all-you-can-eat buffet is available 7 days a week.

1901 N. Military Trail (at the Holiday Inn, opposite Kings Market), Boca Raton. ✆ **561/392-5595.** www.mariosofboca.com. Reservations not accepted. Main courses $11–$22. AE, MC, V. Daily 7–10:30am; Mon–Thurs 11:30am–10pm; Fri–Sat 11:30am–11pm; Sun noon–9:30pm.

Inexpensive

Baja Cafe ★ MEXICAN A jeans-and-T-shirt kind of place with wooden tables, Baja Cafe serves fantastic Mexican food at even better prices. Although the salsa borders on somewhat sweet, they do have the hottest sauces; if you like spicy, they will be happy to slap plenty on your meal if you request it. This place is located right by the Florida East Coast Railway tracks, so don't be surprised if you feel a little rattling. Live music and entertainment make this place a hot spot for an unpretentious crowd.

201 NW 1st Ave., Boca Raton. ✆ **561/394-5449.** Reservations not accepted. Main courses $6–$12. No credit cards. Mon–Thurs 11:30am–10pm; Fri–Sat 11:30am–11pm; Sun 5–10pm.

The Tin Muffin Cafe ★ BAKERY/SANDWICH SHOP Popular with the downtown lunch crowd, this excellent storefront bakery keeps folks lining up for big sandwiches on fresh bread, plus muffins, quiches, and good homemade soups such as split pea or lentil. The curried-chicken sandwich is stuffed with chunks of white meat doused in a creamy curry dressing and fruit. There are a few cafe tables inside and even one outside on a tiny patio. Be warned, however, that service is forgivably slow and parking is a nightmare. Try looking for a spot a few blocks away at a meter.

364 E. Palmetto Park Rd. (btw. Federal Hwy. and the Intracoastal Bridge), Boca Raton. ✆ **561/392-9446.** Sandwiches and salads $6.50–$11. No credit cards. Mon–Fri 11am–5pm; Sat 11am–4pm.

BOCA RATON & DELRAY BEACH AFTER DARK

The Bar, Club & Music Scene

Atlantic Avenue in Delray Beach has finally gotten quite hip to nightlife and is now lined with sleek and chic restaurants, lounges, and bars that attract the Palm Beach County "in crowd," along with a few random patrons such as Yanni, who has a house nearby. Although it's hardly South Beach or Fort Lauderdale's Las Olas and Riverfront, Atlantic Avenue holds its own as far as a vibrant nightlife is concerned. In Boca Raton, **Mizner Park** is the nucleus of nightlife, with restaurants masking themselves as nightclubs or, at the very least, sceney bars, such as **Gigi's Tavern,** 346 Plaza Real (✆ **561/368-4488**), and **Dubliner Irish Pub,** 433 Plaza Real (✆ **561/620-2540**).

Boston's on the Beach This is a family restaurant with a somewhat lively bar scene. It's a good choice for post-sunbathing, super-casual happy hours Monday through Friday from 4 to 8pm, or live reggae on Monday. With two decks overlooking the ocean, Boston's is an ideal place to mellow out and take in the scenery. Open daily from 7am to 2am. 40 S. Ocean Blvd., Delray Beach. ✆ **561/278-3364.**

Dada Dada is a nocturnal outpost of food, drink, music, art, culture, and history. In other words, here you can expect to find neobohemian, arty types lingering in their dark glasses and berets on one of the living room's cozy couches, listening to music, poetry, or dissertations on life. Live music, great food, a bar, an outdoor patio area, and a very eclectic crowd make Dada the coolest hangout in Delray. Open daily from 5:30pm to 2am. 52 N. Swinton Ave., Delray Beach. ✆ **561/330-DADA** (3232).

Delux Believe it or not, this red-hued dance club on Atlantic Avenue is cooler than some of South Beach's big-shot clubs, thanks to a soundtrack of sexy house music, bed-like seating, and a beautiful crowd in which someone as striking as past patron Gwen

Stefani can actually blend in without being noticed. Open Wednesday through Sunday from 7pm to 2am. 16 E. Atlantic Ave., Delray Beach. ✆ **561/279-4792.**

Elwood's Over the train tracks, just steps from the chic bars and restaurants on Atlantic Avenue, is this fabulous, blues-themed biker bar housed in a former gas station and garage. No fancy martinis here, just cold beer and good tunes. Open Monday through Friday from 5pm to 2am, Saturday from 11am to 2am, and Sunday from 11am to midnight. 301 E. Atlantic Ave., Delray Beach. ✆ **561/272-7427.**

Falcon House A cozy wine and tapas bar on a side street off the Atlantic Avenue bustle, Falcon House is reminiscent of a bar you'd find in Napa Valley, with an impressive selection of wine and a hip, well-heeled crowd. It's a haven for those who are over the whole hip-hop scene on Atlantic Avenue. Open Monday through Saturday from 5pm to 2am. 116 NE 6th Ave., Delray Beach. ✆ **561/243-9499.**

Gatsby's This always-busy bar is singles central, featuring big-screen TVs, microbrews, and martinis. Thursday college nights are especially popular, as are Friday happy hours. Open Monday, Tuesday, and Thursday from 4pm to 2am; Wednesday from 4pm to 3am; Friday from 4pm to 4am; Saturday from 6pm to 4am; and Sunday from 4pm to 3am. 5970 SW 18th St., Boca Raton. ✆ **561/393-3900.**

The Performing Arts

For details on upcoming events, check the *Boca News* or the *Sun-Sentinel,* or call the **Palm Beach County Cultural Council** information line at ✆ **800/882-ARTS** (2787). During business hours, a staffer can give details on current performances. After hours, a recorded message describes the week's events.

For live concerts, featuring everyone from Dolly Parton to Kelly Clarkson, the **Mizner Park Amphitheater** (✆ **866/571-ARTS** [2787]) is the place to see them in an open-air format, under the stars, and, at times, rain. If you're not that big a fan, you'll still hear the concerts from Mizner Park!

The **Florida Symphonic Pops,** a 70-piece professional orchestra, performs jazz, swing, rock, big-band, and classical music throughout Boca Raton. This musical force has entertained audiences for nearly 50 years. Call ✆ **561/393-7677** for a schedule.

Boca's best theater company is the **Caldwell Theatre,** and it's worth checking out. Located in a strip shopping center at 7873 N. Federal Hwy., this equity showcase does well-known dramas, comedies, classics, off-Broadway hits, and new works throughout the year. Ticket prices are reasonable—usually $36 to $42. Full-time students with ID will be especially interested in the little-advertised student rush. When available, tickets are sold for $5 if you arrive at least an hour early. Call ✆ **561/241-7432** for details.

3 PALM BEACH ★★ & WEST PALM BEACH ★

65 miles N of Miami; 193 miles E of Tampa; 45 miles N of Fort Lauderdale

Palm Beach County encompasses cities from Boca Raton in the south to Jupiter and Tequesta in the north. But it is Palm Beach, the small island town across the Intracoastal Waterway, that has been the traditional winter home of America's aristocracy—the Kennedys, the Rockefellers, the Pulitzers, the Trumps, titled socialites, and plenty of CEOs. For a perspective on what it means to put on the ritz, there is no better place than Palm Beach, where teenagers cruise around in their parents' Rolls-Royces while socialites seem to jump out of the glossy pages of society magazines and into an even glitzier real life. It's something to be seen, despite the fact that some may consider it all over the top and, frankly, obscene. But this is not just a city of upscale resorts and chic boutiques. In fact, Palm Beach holds some surprises, from a world-class art museum to one of the top bird-watching areas in the state.

Across the water from Palm Beach proper, or the "island" as locals call it, is downtown West Palm Beach, which is where everybody else lives. Clematis Street is the area's nightlife hub, with a great selection of bars, clubs, and restaurants. City Place is West Palm's version of Mizner Park; shops, restaurants, and other entertainment options liven up this once-dead area. In addition to good beaching, boating, and diving, you'll find great golf and tennis throughout the county. ***Note:*** Palm Beach's population swells from 20,000 in the summer to 40,000 in the winter. Book early if you plan to visit during the winter months.

ESSENTIALS

GETTING THERE If you're driving up or down the Florida coast, you'll probably reach the Palm Beach area by way of I-95. Exit at Belvedere Road or Okeechobee Boulevard, and head east to reach the most central part of Palm Beach.

Visitors on their way to or from Orlando or Miami should take the Florida Turnpike, a toll road with a speed limit of 65 mph. Tolls are pricey, though; you may pay upward of $9 from Orlando and $4 from Miami. If you're coming from Florida's west coast, you can take either S.R. 70, which runs north of Lake Okeechobee to Fort Pierce, or S.R. 80, which runs south of the lake to Palm Beach.

All major airlines fly to the **Palm Beach International Airport,** at Congress Avenue and Belvedere Road (✆ **561/471-7400**). **Amtrak** (✆ **800/USA-RAIL** [872-7245]; www.amtrak.com) has a terminal in West Palm Beach, at 201 S. Tamarind Ave. (✆ **561/832-6169**).

GETTING AROUND Although a car is almost a necessity in this area, a recently revamped public transportation system is extremely convenient for getting to some attractions in both West Palm and Palm Beach. **Palm Tran** (www.palmtran.org) covers 32 routes with more than 140 buses. The fare is $1.50 for adults, 75¢ for children 3 to 18, seniors, and riders with disabilities. Free route maps are available by calling ✆ **561/233-4-BUS** (4287). Information operators are available Monday through Saturday from 6am to 7pm.

In downtown West Palm, free shuttles from City Place to Clematis Street operate Monday through Friday from 9am until 4pm, with plans to expand operations to evenings and weekends, too. Allegedly, the shuttles come every 5 minutes, but I'd count on them taking longer. Look for the bubblegum-pink minibuses throughout downtown. Call ✆ **561/833-8873** for details.

For a more nostalgic route, consider the stately wicker chariots that run in the downtown area, especially on weekends and during special events. Rates vary according to the time of day, but average $1 to $2 per block, plus a per-person charge of $1. Call ✆ **561/835-8922** for pickup or information.

VISITOR INFORMATION The **Palm Beach County Convention and Visitors Bureau,** 1555 Palm Beach Lakes Blvd., Ste. 204, West Palm Beach, FL 33401 (✆ **800/554-PALM** [7256] or 561/471-3995; www.palmbeachfl.com), distributes an informative brochure and answers questions about visiting the Palm Beaches. Ask for a map as well as a copy of the *Arts and Attractions Calendar,* a day-to-day guide to art, music, stage, and other events in the county.

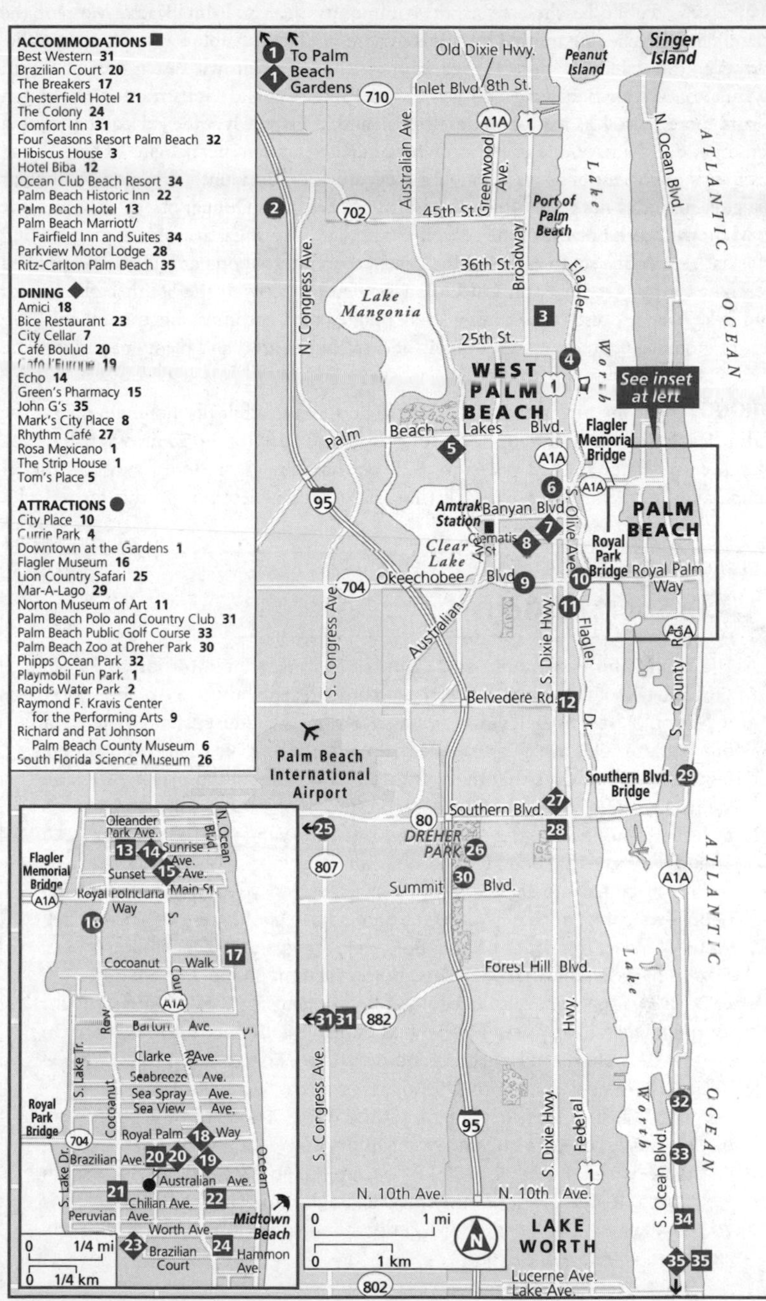
ACCOMMODATIONS
Best Western 31
Brazilian Court 20
The Breakers 17
Chesterfield Hotel 21
The Colony 24
Comfort Inn 31
Four Seasons Resort Palm Beach 32
Hibiscus House 3
Hotel Biba 12
Ocean Club Beach Resort 34
Palm Beach Historic Inn 22
Palm Beach Hotel 13
Palm Beach Marriott/ Fairfield Inn and Suites 34
Parkview Motor Lodge 28
Ritz-Carlton Palm Beach 35
DINING
Amici 18
Bice Restaurant 23
City Cellar 7
Café Boulud 20
Café l'Europe 19
Echo 14
Green's Pharmacy 15
John G's 35
Mark's City Place 8
Rhythm Café 27
Rosa Mexicano 1
The Strip House 1
Tom's Place 5
ATTRACTIONS
City Place 10
Currie Park 4
Downtown at the Gardens 1
Flagler Museum 16
Lion Country Safari 25
Mar-A-Lago 29
Norton Museum of Art 11
Palm Beach Polo and Country Club 31
Palm Beach Public Golf Course 33
Palm Beach Zoo at Dreher Park 30
Phipps Ocean Park 32
Playmobil Fun Park 1
Rapids Water Park 2
Raymond F. Kravis Center for the Performing Arts 9
Richard and Pat Johnson Palm Beach County Museum 6
South Florida Science Museum 26
To Palm Beach Gardens
Old Dixie Hwy.
Inlet Blvd.
8th St.
Peanut Island
Singer Island
Australian Ave.
Greenwood Ave.
45th St.
Port of Palm Beach
N. Ocean Blvd.
ATLANTIC OCEAN
N. Congress Ave.
Lake Mangonia
36th St.
Broadway
Flagler
Lake Worth
25th St.
WEST PALM BEACH
See inset at left
Palm Beach Lakes Blvd.
Flagler Memorial Bridge
Amtrak Station
Banyan Blvd
Clematis St
Clear Lake
S. Olive Ave.
PALM BEACH
Royal Park Bridge
Royal Palm Way
Okeechobee Blvd
S. Congress Ave.
Australian
S. Dixie Hwy.
Flagler Dr.
S. County Rd.
Belvedere Rd.
Palm Beach International Airport
Southern Blvd. Bridge
Southern Blvd.
DREHER PARK
Summit Blvd.
Forest Hill Blvd.
Hwy.
Federal
N. 10th Ave.
LAKE WORTH
Lucerne Ave.
Lake Ave.
S. Ocean Blvd.
0 1 mi
0 1 km
Oleander Park Ave.
Sunrise Ave.
Sunset Ave.
Main St.
Royal Poinciana Way
Cocoanut Row
Walk
S. County Rd
Barton Ave.
Clarke Ave.
Seabreeze Ave.
Sea Spray Ave.
Sea View Ave.
S. Lake Tr.
Royal Palm Way
Brazilian Ave.
Australian Ave.
S. Lake Dr.
Chilian Ave.
Peruvian Ave.
Worth Ave.
Brazilian Court
Hammon Ave.
Midtown Beach
Ocean
0 1/4 mi
0 1/4 km

BEACHES Public beaches are a rare commodity here in Palm Beach. Most of the island's best beaches are fronted by private estates and inaccessible to the general public. However, there are a few notable exceptions, including **Midtown Beach,** east of Worth Avenue, on Ocean Boulevard between Royal Palm Way and Gulfstream Road, which boasts more than 100 feet of undeveloped sand. This newly widened coast is now a centerpiece and a natural oasis in a town dominated by commercial glitz. There are no restrooms or concessions here, though a lifeguard is on duty until sundown. A popular hangout for locals lies about 1½ miles north of here, near Dunbar Street; they prefer it to Midtown Beach because of the relaxed atmosphere. Parking is available at meters along Florida A1A. At the south end of Palm Beach, there's a less-popular but better-equipped beach at **Phipps Ocean Park.** On Ocean Boulevard, between the Southern Boulevard and Lake Avenue causeways, there's a lively public beach encompassing more than 1,300 feet of groomed oceanfront. With picnic and recreation areas and plenty of parking, the area is especially good for families.

BIKING Rent anything from an English single-speed to a full-tilt mountain bike at the **Palm Beach Bicycle Trail Shop,** 223 Sunrise Ave. (✆ **561/659-4583;** www.palmbeachbicycle.com). Rates are $12 per hour, $29 per half-day (9am–5pm), and $39 for 24 hours, and include a basket and lock (not that a lock is necessary in this fortress of a

The Sport of Kings

The posh **Palm Beach Polo and Country Club** and the **International Polo Club** are two of the world's premier polo grounds and host some of the sport's top-rated players. Even if you're not a sports fan, you must attend a match at one of these fields, which are on the mainland in a rural area called Wellington. Rest assured, however, that the spectators, and many of the players, are pure Palm Beach. After all, a day at the pony grounds is one of the only good reasons to leave Palm Beach proper. You need not be a Vanderbilt or a Kennedy to attend—matches are open to the public and are surprisingly affordable.

Even if you haven't a clue how the game is played, you can spend your time people-watching. In recent years, stargazers have spotted Prince Charles, Sylvester Stallone, Tommy Lee Jones, Bo Derek, and Ivana Trump, among others. Dozens of lesser-known royalty keep box seats right on the grounds.

Dress is casual; a navy or tweed blazer over jeans or khakis is the standard for men, while neat-looking jeans or a pantsuit is the norm for women. On warmer days, shorts and, of course, polo shirts are fine, too.

General admission is $15 to $45; box seats cost $75 to $100 but are for members only. Matches are held throughout the week. Schedules vary, but the big names usually compete on Sunday at 3:30pm from January to April.

The fields are located at 11809 Polo Club Rd. and 3667 120th Ave., South Wellington, 10 miles west of the Forest Hill Boulevard exit off I-95. Call ✆ **561/793-1440** or 204-5687, or visit www.internationalpoloclub.com for tickets and a detailed schedule of events.

town). The most scenic route is called the Lake Trail, running the length of the island along the Intracoastal Waterway. On it, you'll see some of the most magnificent mansions and grounds, and enjoy the views of downtown West Palm Beach as well as some great wildlife.

GOLF There's good golfing in the Palm Beaches, but many private-club courses are maintained exclusively for members' use. Ask at your hotel or contact the **Palm Beach County Convention and Visitors Bureau** (© **561/471-3995**) for information on which clubs are available for play. In the off-season, some private courses open to visitors staying in Palm Beach County hotels. This "Golf-A-Round" program boasts no greens fees; reservations can be made through most major hotels.

The best hotel for golf in the area is the **PGA National Resort & Spa** (p. 303; © **800/633-9150**), which features a whopping 90 holes of golf.

The **Palm Beach Public Golf Course,** 2345 S. Ocean Blvd. (© **561/547-0598;** www.golfontheocean.com), a popular public 18-hole course, is a par-3. The course opens at 8am on a first-come, first-served basis. Club rentals are available. Greens fees start at $17 to $47 per person.

SCUBA DIVING Year-round warm waters, barrier reefs, and plenty of wrecks make South Florida one of the world's most popular places for diving. One of the best-known artificial reefs in this area is a vintage Rolls-Royce Silver Shadow, which was sunk offshore in 1985. Nature has taken its toll, however, and divers can no longer sit in the car, which has been ravaged by time and salt water. For gear and excursions, call **Jim Abernaethy's Scuba Adventures,** 2116 Ave. B, Riviera Beach (© **561/691-5808**).

TENNIS There are hundreds of tennis courts in Palm Beach County. Wherever you are staying, you're bound to be within walking distance of one. In addition to the many hotel tennis courts (see "Where to Stay," below), you can play at **Currie Park,** 2400 N. Flagler Dr., West Palm Beach (© **561/835-7025**), a public park with three lighted hard courts. They're free and available on a first-come, first-served basis.

WATERSPORTS Call the **Seaside Activities Station** (© **561/835-8922**) to arrange sailboat, jet-ski, bicycle, kayak, water-ski, and parasail rentals.

SEEING THE SIGHTS

Flagler Museum ★★★ The Gilded Age is preserved in this luxurious mansion commissioned by Standard Oil tycoon Henry Flagler as a wedding present to his third wife. Whitehall, also known as the Taj Mahal of North America, is a classic Edwardian-style mansion containing 55 rooms, including a Louis XIV music room and art gallery, a Louis XV ballroom, and 14 guest suites outfitted with original antique European furnishings. Out back, you can climb aboard the *Rambler,* Mr. Flagler's private restored railroad car. Allow at least 1½ hours to tour the stunning grounds and interior. Group tours are available, but for the most part, this is a self-guided museum.

1 Whitehall Way (at Cocoanut Row and Whitehall Way), Palm Beach. © **561/655-2833.** www.flagler museum.us. Admission $15 adults, $8 ages 13–18, $3 children 6–12. Tues–Sat 10am–5pm; Sun noon–5pm.

Norton Museum of Art ★★★ The Norton is world famous for its prestigious permanent collection and top temporary exhibitions. The museum's major collections are divided geographically. The American galleries contain major works by Hopper, O'Keeffe, and Pollock. The French collection contains Impressionist and post-Impressionist paintings by Cézanne, Degas, Gauguin, Matisse, Monet, Picasso, Pissarro, and Renoir. The Chinese collection contains more than 200 bronzes, jades, and ceramics, as

Unreal Estate

No trip to Palm Beach is complete without at least a glimpse of **Mar-A-Lago,** the stately residence of Donald Trump, the 21st century's answer to Jay Gatsby. In 1985, Trump purchased the estate of cereal heiress Marjorie Merriweather Post for a meager $8 million (for a fully furnished beachfront property of this stature, it was a relative bargain), to the great consternation of locals, who feared that he would turn the place into a casino. Instead, Trump, who sometimes resides in a portion of the palace, opened the house to the public—for a price, of course—as a tony country club (membership fee: $100,000). Rumor has it Trump is selling the place. In the meantime, he continues to make his presence loudly known in Palm Beach.

While there are currently no tours open to the public, you can glimpse the gorgeous manse as you cross the bridge from West Palm Beach into Palm Beach. It's located at 1100 S. Ocean Blvd., Palm Beach.

well as monumental Buddhist sculptures. Allow about 2 hours to see this museum, depending on your level of interest.

1451 S. Olive Ave., West Palm Beach. ✆ **561/832-5196.** Fax 561/659-4689. www.norton.org. Admission $8 adults, $3 ages 13–21. Mon–Sat 10am–5pm; Sun 1–5pm. Closed Mon May–Oct and all major holidays. Take I-95 to exit 52 (Okeechobee Blvd. E.). Travel east on Okeechobee to Dixie Hwy., then south 1/2 mile to the Norton. Access parking through entrances on Dixie Hwy. and S. Olive Ave.

Playmobil Fun Park ★★ Kids For a child, it doesn't get any better than this. The 17,000-square-foot Playmobil Fun Park is housed in a replica castle and loaded with themed areas for imaginative play: a medieval village, a Western town, a fantasy dollhouse, and more. Kids can play with the Playmobil boats on two water-filled tables. Tech-minded youths may get bored, but tots up to age 5 or so will love this place. You *could* spend hours here and not spend a penny, but parents, beware: Everything is available for purchase. There's another Playmobil park in Orlando.

8031 N. Military Trail, Palm Beach Gardens. ✆ **800/351-8697** or 561/691-9880. Fax 561/691-9517. www.playmobil.com. Admission $1. Mon–Sat 10am–6pm; Sun noon–5pm. From I-95, go north to Palm Beach Lakes Blvd., then west to Military Trail. Turn left; the park is about a mile down on the right.

NATURE PRESERVES & ATTRACTIONS

Lion Country Safari ★★ Kids More than 1,300 animals on this 500-acre preserve (the nation's first cageless drive-through safari) are divided into their indigenous regions, from the East African preserve of the Serengeti to the American West. Elephants, lions, wildebeest, ostriches, American bison, buffalo, watusi, pink flamingos, and many other unusual species roam the preserve. When I visited, most of the lions were asleep; when awake, they travel freely throughout the cageless grassy landscape (this can be very scary). In fact, you're the one who's confined in your own car without an escort (no convertibles allowed). You're given a detailed pamphlet with photos and descriptions, and are instructed to obey the 15 mph speed limit—unless you see the rhinos charge (a rare occasion), in which case you're encouraged to floor it. Driving the loop takes slightly more than an hour, though you could make a day of just watching the chimpanzees play on their secluded islands. Included in the admission is Safari World, an amusement park with paddle boats, a carousel, miniature golf, and a baby animal nursery. Picnics are encouraged, and camping is available. The best time to go is late afternoon, right before the park closes; it's much cooler then, so the lions are more active. Though some may consider this a tourist trap, I had a great time.

Southern Blvd. W. at S.R. 80, West Palm Beach. ✆ **561/793-1084,** or 793-9797 for camping reservations. www.lioncountrysafari.com. Admission $24 adults, $22 seniors, $18 children 3–9. Van rental $10 per hour. Daily 9:30am–5:30pm (last vehicle admitted at 4:30pm). From I-95, exit on Southern Blvd. Go west for about 18 miles.

Palm Beach Zoo at Dreher Park ★ If you want animals, go to Lion Country Safari (above). Unlike big-city zoos, this intimate 23-acre attraction is more like a stroll in the park than an all-day excursion. It features about 500 animals representing more than 100 different species. The monkey exhibit and petting zoo are favorites with kids. Stroller and wagon rentals are available. The newest attraction is the Tropics of the Americas, a 3-acre jungle path and complex that immerses guests in the animals, plants, and culture of a New World rainforest. You'll encounter animals such as jaguars, monkeys, giant anteaters, tapirs, bats, birds, snakes, and more. A new Siamang Habitat opened in 2005; it is currently home to a pair of primates known to be the largest species of lesser apes in the world. There are two Malayan tigers at the zoo now—there are only 47 in North America. A baby jaguar cub was born in October of 2008. Mom is one of the zoo's endangered jags. Allow at least 2 hours to see all of the sights here.

1301 Summit Blvd. (east of I-95 btw. Southern and Forest Hill boulevards). ✆ **561/547-WILD** (9453). www.palmbeachzoo.org. Admission $13 adults, $10 seniors, $9 children 3–12. Daily 9am–5pm. Closed Thanksgiving.

Rapids Water Park ★ Kids It may not be on the same grand scale as the theme parks in Orlando, but Rapids is a great way to cool off on a hot day. There are 12 acres of water rides, including a children's area and miniature golf course. A few new attractions opened in 2007, including the Black Thunder, involving a huge dark funnel and water; a Raging Rapids ride; and an aquatic obstacle course. Check out the Superbowl, a tubeless water ride that spins and swirls before dumping you into the pool below, and the Big Thunder, a giant funnel that plunges you down 50 feet in a four-person tube. Claustrophobia, anyone?

6566 N. Military Trail, West Palm Beach (1 mile west of I-95 on Military, btw. 45th St./exit 54 and Blue Heron Blvd./exit 55 in West Palm Beach). ✆ **561/842-8756.** www.rapidswaterpark.com. Admission $32 plus tax; free for children 2 and under. Parking $5. Mid-Mar to Sept Mon–Fri 10am–5pm; Sat–Sun 10am–6pm.

Richard and Pat Johnson Palm Beach County Museum ★ There's more to Palm Beach history than Donald Trump and well-preserved octogenarians. Opened to the public in March 2008 within the historic 1916 Courthouse in downtown West Palm Beach, the museum has two permanent exhibits—the People Gallery, a tribute to approximately 100 individuals and families who have contributed to the growth of Palm Beach County, and the Place Gallery, featuring models and photographs exploring Palm Beach county's natural environment and the animals and ecology that make it unique.

300 N. Dixie Hwy., West Palm Beach. Entrance is on 2nd floor of courthouse. ✆ **561/832-4164.** www.historicalsocietypbc.org. Free admission. Tues–Sat 10am–5pm; Sun 1–5pm.

South Florida Science Museum ★ Kids It's hands on at this veteran West Palm science museum, boasting a planetarium, aquarium, interactive galleries, and traveling exhibitions. But the museum got a big boost in 2009 when its Marvin Dekelboum Planetarium became one of only a handful of planetariums in the country to showcase state-of-the-art, full-dome digital projection capability that allows visitors to take a virtual space walk or to explore the realms of the sea. Upgrades also include a new, programmable laser system to continue the popular laser concerts, LED lighting, and Blu-ray high-definition video technology.

4801 Dreher Trail North, West Palm Beach (at the north end of Dreher Park). ✆ **561/832-1988.** www.sfsm.org. Admission $9 adults, $7.50 seniors, $6 children. Planetarium shows $4 adults, $2 children in addition to museum admission. Laser shows $5 per person. Mon–Fri 10am–5pm; Sat 10am–6pm; Sun noon–6pm.

SHOPPING

No matter what your budget, be sure to take a stroll down Worth Avenue, the "Rodeo Drive of the South" and a window-shopper's dream. Between South Ocean Boulevard and Cocoanut Row, there are more than 200 boutiques, posh shops, art galleries, and upscale restaurants. If you want to fit in, dress as if you are going to an elegant luncheon, not the mall down the street.

You'd never know there was ever a recession based on the swarms of shoppers armed with bags from **Gucci, Chanel, Armani, Hermès,** and **Louis Vuitton,** among others. And besides the boldface collection of couturiers there are also a good number of unique, independent boutiques. **History Buff,** 32 Via Mizner (✆ **561/366-8255**), is a virtual museum selling every genre of original historic autographs, some dating back to the 1600s, as well as vintage signed photos, first-edition books, and memorabilia. For privileged feet, **Stubbs & Wooton,** 4 Via Parigi (✆ **561/655-4105**), sells velvet slippers that are a favorite of the loofahed locals. For rare and estate jewelry, **Richter's of Palm Beach,** 224 Worth Ave. (✆ **561/655-0774**), has been specializing in priceless gems since 1893. Just off Worth Avenue is the **Church Mouse,** 374 S. County Rd. (✆ **561/659-2154**), a great consignment/thrift shop with antique furnishings and tableware, as well as lots of good castoff clothing and shoes from socialites who've moved on to the next designers or, worse than that, to the big gala in the sky. This shop usually closes for 2 months during the summer; call to be sure.

City Place, Okeechobee Road (at I-95), West Palm Beach (✆ **561/820-9716**), is a $550-million, Mediterranean-style shopping, dining, and entertainment complex that's responsible for revitalizing what was once a lifeless downtown West Palm Beach. Among the 78 mostly chain stores are **Macy's, Barnes & Noble, Banana Republic, Armani Exchange, Pottery Barn,** and **SEE** eyewear. Restaurants include a Ghirardelli ice-cream shop; Legal Seafoods; the legendary Tampa-based Cuban restaurant Columbia; Miami Beach, Fort Lauderdale, and Hollywood's Taverna Opa; City Cellar Wine Bar and Grill; and Cheesecake Factory. Best of all is the Muvico Parisian, a 20-screen movie theater where you can wine and dine while watching a feature.

WHERE TO STAY

The island of Palm Beach is the epitome of *Lifestyles of the Rich and Famous,* oozing with glitz, glamour, and the occasional scandal. Royalty and celebrities come to winter here, and there are plenty of lavishly priced options to accommodate them. Happily, there are also a few special inns that offer reasonably priced rooms in elegant settings. But most of the more modest places to lay your straw hat surround the island.

A few of the larger hotel chains operating in Palm Beach include the **Palm Beach Fairfield Inn and Suites,** 2870 S. Ocean Blvd. (✆ **800/228-2800** or 561/582-2581), across the street from the beach. Also beachside is the pricey **Ocean Club Beach Resort,** 2842 S. Ocean Blvd. (✆ **561/586-6542;** theocbeachresort.com), which underwent a massive renovation and reopened in early 2009. In West Palm Beach, chain hotels are mostly on the main arteries close to the highways and a short drive from downtown. They include **Best Western,** 1800 Palm Beach Lakes Blvd. (✆ **800/331-9569** or 561/683-8810), and, just down the road, **Comfort Inn,** 1901 Palm Beach Lakes Blvd. (✆ **800/221-2222** or 561/689-6100). Farther south is **Parkview Motor Lodge,** 4710 S. Dixie Hwy., just south of Southern Boulevard (✆ **561/833-4644**). This 28-room motel is the best of many along Dixie Highway (U.S. 1). With rates starting at about $75 for a room with TV, air-conditioning, and phone (don't laugh, some don't have any), you can't ask for more.

For other options, contact **Palm Beach Accommodations** (✆ **800/543-SWIM** [7946]).

Very Expensive

Brazilian Court ★★★ This elegant, Old World, Mediterranean-style hotel dates from the 1920s and almost looks like a Beverly Hills bungalow. Much like Palm Beach residents, the hotel debuted a new youthful glow after a remake in 2008 by owner/designer Leslie Schlesinger, who spruced up the signature Mediterranean Revival and historic Dutch Colonial styles of legendary architects Maurice Fatio and Rosario Candela. The 80 custom-redesigned suites all feature mahogany case goods and crown molding, Provence-style wood shutters, and king-size beds topped with imported linens. Pampered pets under 20 lbs. (you know the type: held hostage in Mummy's Gucci bag) receive gift bags full of treats for a (required) one-time $100 pet fee. A large hotel by Palm Beach standards (the Breakers notwithstanding), Brazilian Court sprawls over half a block and features fountains and private courtyards. Celebrity stylist Frederic Fekkai offers the hotel's premier salon and spa. With the addition of renowned chef Daniel Boulud's hauter-than-thou Café Boulud (which provides stellar room service), Brazilian Court is Palm Beach's number-one place to see and be seen.

301 Australian Ave., Palm Beach, FL 33480. ✆ 800/552-0335 or 561/655-7740. Fax 561/655-0801. www.thebraziliancourt.com. 80 units. From $550 studio; from $950 1-bedroom suite; from $1,145 2-bedroom suite. Special packages available. AE, DC, DISC, MC, V. Pampered pet fee $100. Amenities: Restaurant; heated outdoor pool; exercise room; spa treatments; concierge; salon; room service; library. In room: A/C, TV, Wi-Fi, minibar, coffeemaker, hair dryer, iron.

The Breakers Palm Beach ★★★ Kids This 140-acre beachfront hotel is quintessential Palm Beach, where old money mixes with new money, and the Old World gives way, albeit reluctantly, to a bit of modernity. The seven-story building is a marvel, with a frescoed lobby and long, palatial hallways. Plush rooms feature huge bathrooms and views of the ocean or the magnificently manicured grounds. The Mediterranean-style Beach Club features magnificent vistas of the ocean and is reminiscent of a panoramic island escape. After a $15-million beachfront redevelopment project, the Beach Club now features five pools, four whirlpool spas, expansive pool decks, lush tropical landscaping, and lawn space; a 6,000-square-foot rooftop terrace, 20 private, luxury beach bungalows, and 10 pool cabanas for daytime rental, with a dedicated staff of concierges; a beach gazebo; and two restaurants. The 20,000-square-foot oceanfront spa features 17 private treatment rooms for a variety of massages, body wraps, scrubs, and Guerlain skin care treatments and steam and sauna. Spa treatments fill a 16-page book! A revamp of Florida's oldest existing golf course transformed the Ocean Course into a 6,100-yard, championship-level par-70, and the Breakers Rees Jones Course underwent a $6-million redesign and reconstruction in 2004. Kids aren't neglected either at the impressive Family Entertainment Center, a 6,160-square-foot space that includes an arcade, toddler's playroom, arts-and-crafts area, children's movie theater, and video game room all filled with the latest in high-tech toys and games. All nine distinct restaurants are fantastic, but don't miss the remarkable Sunday brunch.

1 S. County Rd., Palm Beach, FL 33480. ✆ **1-888-BREAKERS** (273-2537) or 561/655-6611. Fax 561/659-8403. www.thebreakers.com. 540 units. Winter $550–$1,340 double, $1,310–$6,100 suite; during the summer season, rooms start as low as $249 based on stays of 5 nights or longer. AE, DC, DISC, MC, V. Valet parking $25. From I-95, exit Okeechobee Blvd. E., head east to S. County Rd., and turn left. **Amenities:** 9 restaurants; 5 bars; 5 outdoor pools; 2 championship golf courses; 10 Har-Tru tennis courts; 2 fitness centers; indoor/outdoor spa; 4 whirlpool spas; watersports equipment/rentals; bike rentals; children's programs; concierge; business center; shopping arcade; salon; 24-hr. room service; in-room massage; babysitting; laundry service; dry cleaning. *In room:* A/C, flatscreen TV/DVD/CD player, dataports, high-speed Internet access, Wi-Fi, minibar, hair dryer, private electronic safe, iPod docking station, wireless keyboard , PlayStation.

Four Seasons Resort Palm Beach ★★ Kids Situated on the pristine Palm Beach oceanfront, Four Seasons is a quiet retreat from Worth Avenue—a pricey cab ride from the hotel. Guest rooms are spacious, with private balconies and lavish bathrooms. The full-service spa is excellent and brand new at 9,000 square feet, featuring nine treatment rooms including a "Man Room," a wet room, spa suite, and full-service salon. The main dining room, known simply as the Restaurant, features the Southeastern regional cuisine of Executive Chef Hubert Des Marais. Two other less-formal restaurants, the Ocean Bistro—which is sub par for this kind of hotel—and the Atlantic Bar & Grill, round out the dining options. The resort offers a complimentary kids program, and teens will enjoy the game room with Xbox, a pool table, and a large-screen TV. Meanwhile, parents can entertain themselves in the Living Room, a swank lounge featuring live jazz on weekends.

2800 S. Ocean Blvd., Palm Beach, FL 33480. ✆ **800/432-2335** or 561/582-2800. Fax 561/547-1557. www.fourseasons.com/palmbeach. 210 units. Winter $429–$745 double, from $2,150 1-bedroom suite, from $3,850 2-bedroom suite; off-season $299–$599 double, $1,250 1-bedroom suite, $3,050 2-bedroom suite. AE, DC, DISC, MC, V. Valet parking $23. From I-95, take the 6th Ave. exit east and turn left onto Dixie Hwy. Turn east onto Lake Ave. and north onto A1A (S. Ocean Blvd.); the resort is just ahead on your right. Pets less than 20 lbs. accepted. **Amenities:** 3 restaurants; lounge/outdoor patio; outdoor heated pool; 2 tennis courts; fitness center; spa; whirlpool; watersports equipment/rentals; children's programs; concierge; business center; salon; 24-hr. room service; in-room massage; babysitting; laundry service; dry cleaning. *In room:* A/C, TV/DVD/VCR, high-speed Internet access, minibar, fridge, hair dryer, iron, safe, CD/MP3 player.

The Omphoy Ocean Resort Not yet open at press time, this 134-room waterfront boutique hotel is the first new resort to open in Palm Beach in 18 years and is owned by the same company that owns the fabulous Brazilian Court. Featuring an open lobby and a minimalist South Beach modern vibe, the Omphoy aspires to be the island's least pretentious hotel. Rooms will offer panoramic ocean or Intracoastal views. The resort will also feature surfside cuisine, by Miami's star chef Michelle Bernstein, and New York–based Exhale Spa, with 5,000 square feet of dedicated spa space with indoor and outdoor treatments and a 1,000-square-foot yoga studio featuring its signature "core fusion yoga." The spa will also offer Eliza, of Eliza's Eyes of New York, known for its eyebrow shaping/sculpting services, part of the year.

2842 S. Ocean Blvd., Palm Beach, FL 33480. www.omphoy.com. 134 units. Winter $450–$700 suite; off-season $279–$450 suite. **Amenities:** 2 restaurants; 2 bars; pool; spa; watersports equipment/rentals; free Wi-Fi in business center. *In room:* A/C, TV/DVD.

PGA National Resort & Spa ★★★ This expansive Northern Palm Beach resort is a premier golf-vacation spot, but its top-rated European spa could be a destination in itself. With five 18-hole championship courses on more than 2,300 acres, golfers and other sports-minded travelers will find plenty to keep them occupied—such as croquet, tennis, swimming, a complete health and fitness center, and that sublime spa. The par-72 Champion Course, redesigned in 1990 by Jack Nicklaus and upgraded again in 2007 and 2008, is the resort's most valuable asset and home to the PGA Tour's Honda Classic. Guest rooms are spacious and comfortable, bordering on residential, with immense bathrooms and private terrace or patio. Club cottages are especially convenient, offering great privacy and serenity. In 2008, the resort completed a $65-million renovation including extensive renovations to the resort's public spaces, a new lobby and restaurant, a lush new resort pool, and a complete renovation of the Palmer course. This is not a beach resort, however; multiple resort pools including a lap pool, main pool, soothing whirlpools, and a collection of outdoor therapy pools create a true oasis. The new Ironwood Grille has quickly become a popular dining destination in Palm Beach Gardens. Offering fresh seafood and juicy steaks, Ironwood Grille and the accompanying iBar are comfortable spots to see and be seen.

400 Ave. of the Champions, Palm Beach Gardens, FL 33418. ✆ **800/633-9150** or 561/627-2000. Fax 561/225-2595. www.pgaresort.com. 398 units. Winter $299–$339 double, $369–$829 suite; off-season $144–$169 double, $174–$659 suite. Children 16 and under stay free in parent's room. Special packages available. AE, DC, DISC, MC, V. From I-95, take exit 57B (PGA Blvd.) going west and continue for approximately 2 miles to the resort entrance on the left. **Amenities:** 7 restaurants and lounges; 9 pools; 5 18-hole tournament courses plus the PGA National Golf Academy; 19 Har-Tru clay tennis courts; aerobics studio; European spa; watersports equipment/rentals; concierge; car-rental desk; Wi-Fi; salon; room service; babysitting; laundry service; 5 tournament croquet lawns; 5 indoor racquetball courts. *In room:* A/C, TV, dataport, minibar, hair dryer, safe.

The Ritz-Carlton Palm Beach ★★★ Kids If the Breakers is too mammoth for your taste, consider the Ritz. A lot warmer than the Four Seasons, the Ritz, located on a beautiful beach in a tiny town about 8 miles from Worth Avenue, lacks pretension and feels more like a boutique hotel. A $100-million renovation in 2007 added flatscreen HDTVs, bedside electronic control "pamper panels," and Italian custom mahogany furniture. New oceanfront suites have oceanview stone soaking tubs, a sofa sleeper, two-line phones, and two HDTVs. Two pools are perfect for families and/or ideal for relaxation. The 41,000-square-foot Eau Spa debuted in spring 2009, complete with a custom Scrub and Polish Bar, Spa Villas with outdoor verdant gardens, and the Self-Centered Garden featuring water massage benches. The signature restaurant, Angle, is open for dinner only; a casual oceanfront all-day restaurant called Temple Orange features Italian/Mediterranean fare with fresh seafood. Stir Bar serves muddled, stirred, or mixed cocktails and light bites. There's also Breeze, a poolside cafe and bar.

100 S. Ocean Blvd., Manalapan, FL 33462. ✆ **800/241-3333** or 561/533-6000. Fax 561/588-4202. www.ritzcarlton.com. 310 units. Winter $449–$949 double, $699–$1,649 suite, $6,000 presidential suite; off-season $239–$389 double, $469–$749 suite, $4,000 presidential suite. AE, DISC, MC, V. Valet parking $25. From I-95, take exit for Lantana Rd., heading east. After 1 mile, turn right onto Federal Hwy. (U.S. 1/Dixie). Continue south to the next light and turn left onto Ocean Ave. Cross the Intracoastal Waterway and turn right onto Fla. A1A. **Amenities:** 3 restaurants; bar; 2 outdoor pools; fitness center; spa; Jacuzzi; watersports equipment/rentals; bike rental; AquaNuts children's programs and Coast teen's programs; concierge; business lounge; salon; 24-hr. room service; laundry service; dry cleaning; oceanfront cabanas; poolside business cabanas. *In room:* A/C, flatscreen HDTV/DVD, Wi-Fi, minibar, hair dryer, iron, safe.

Expensive

Chesterfield Hotel ★★★ Reminiscent of an English country manor, the Chesterfield in all its flowery, Laura Ashley–inspired glory is a magnificent, charming hotel with exceptional service. Warm and inviting, the Chesterfield is one of the only places in South Florida where the idea of a fireplace (there's one in the hotel's library) doesn't seem ridiculous. Traditional English tea is served every afternoon, including fresh-baked scones, petit fours, and sandwiches. Rooms are decorated with antiques and with bright fabrics and wallpaper. The roomy marble bathrooms are stocked with an array of luxurious toiletries. A small heated pool and courtyard are nice, and the beach is only 3 blocks away, but the real action is inside: The hotel's retro-elegant Leopard Lounge serves decent Continental cuisine, but is better as a late-night hangout for live music, schmoozing, and staring at the local cognoscenti.

363 Cocoanut Row, Palm Beach, FL 33480. ✆ **800/243-7871** or 561/659-5800. Fax 561/659-6707. www.chesterfieldpb.com. 52 units. Winter $395–$465 queen, $495–$570 king, $675–$1,585 suite; off-season $175–$249 queen, $259–$319 king, $339–$719 suite. Rollaway bed $15. Packages available. AE, DC, DISC, MC, V. Free valet parking. From I-95, exit onto Okeechobee Blvd. E., cross the Intracoastal Waterway, and turn right onto Cocoanut Row. **Amenities:** Restaurant; lounge; heated pool and hot tub spa; access to nearby health club; concierge; business center; Wi-Fi; 24-hr. room service; in-room massage; dry cleaning; library. *In room:* A/C, flat-panel TV, entertainment center w/DVD/CD (in kings/suites only), high-speed Internet access, fridge (in kings/suites only), hair dryer, iron, safe.

Moderate

The Colony ★★ The sign outside this Palm Beach mainstay should read ROXANNE PULITZER SLEPT HERE. She did, actually, for quite a while after her 7-week marriage went bust. For years, the Colony has been a favorite hangout—hide-out, perhaps—for old-timers, socialites, and mysterious luminaries. Beyond that, this Georgian-style hotel is known for its attentive staff, floral-decorated guest rooms, and, unfortunately, really small bathrooms. The 39 suites and apartments, not to mention the seven two-bedroom villas with Jacuzzis, are much more lavish—and lavishly priced.

155 Hammon Ave., Palm Beach, FL 33480. ✆ **800/521-5525** or 561/655-5430. Fax 561/659-8104. www.thecolonypalmbeach.com. 92 units. Winter $310–$335 double, $405–$460 suite; off-season $190–$215 double, $270–$365 suite. AE, DC, MC, V. From I-95, exit onto Okeechobee Blvd. E. and cross the Intracoastal Waterway. Turn right on S. County Rd. and then left onto Hammon Ave. **Amenities:** Restaurant; bar; heated Florida-shaped pool; spa; concierge; limited seasonal room service. *In room:* A/C, TV, dataport, hair dryer, iron.

Palm Beach Historic Inn ★★ Built in 1923, the Palm Beach Historic Inn is an area landmark within a block's walking distance of the beach (chairs and towels are provided for guests of the hotel), Worth Avenue, and several good restaurants. The small lobby is filled with antiques, books, magazines, and an old-fashioned umbrella stand, all of which add to the homey feel of this intimate B&B. In-room wine, fruit, snacks, tea, and cookies ensure that you won't go hungry—never mind the excellent continental breakfast that is brought to you daily. All bedrooms are uniquely decorated and have hardwood floors, down comforters, Egyptian-cotton linens, fluffy bathrobes, and plenty of good-smelling toiletries. Here you'll find a casual elegance that's comfortable for everyone. In addition, a baby grand piano and guitars for the musically inclined, as well as videotapes to keep the kids entertained, have been added to the hotel's amenities. ***Note:*** Smoking is not permitted.

365 S. County Rd., Palm Beach, FL 33480. ✆ **561/832-4009.** Fax 561/832-6255. www.palmbeachhistoricinn.com. 13 units. Winter $185–$345 double, $345–$395 suite; off-season $145–$175 double, $225 suite.

Rates include breakfast. Children stay free in parent's room. AE, MC, V. Small pets accepted. *In room:* A/C, TV/VCR, fridge, hair dryer, iron.

Inexpensive

Hibiscus House ★★ Finds Inexpensive bed-and-breakfasts are rare in Southeast Florida, making the Hibiscus House, one of the area's first, a true find. Located a few miles from the coast in a quiet residential neighborhood, this 1920s-era B&B is filled with handsome antiques and tapestries. Every room has a private terrace or balcony. The Red Room has a fabulous bathroom with Jacuzzi. The peaceful backyard retreat has been transformed into a tropical garden, with a heated pool and lounge chairs. There are pretty indoor areas for guests to enjoy; one little sitting room is wrapped in glass and is stocked with playing cards and board games. Huge gourmet breakfast portions are as filling as they are beautiful. Make any special requests in advance; owners Raleigh Hill and Colin Rayer will be happy to oblige.

501 30th St., West Palm Beach, FL 33407. ✆ **800/203-4927** or 561/863-5633. Fax 561/863-5633. www.hibiscushouse.com. 8 units. Winter $125–$210 double; off-season $100–$150 double. Rates include breakfast. AE, DC, DISC, MC, V. From I-95, exit onto Palm Beach Lakes Blvd. E. and continue 4 miles. Turn left onto Flagler Dr. and continue for about 1/2 mile; then turn left onto 30th St. Pets accepted. **Amenities:** Heated pool; concierge. *In room:* A/C, TV, hair dryer.

Hotel Biba ★★ Finds Located in the historic El Cid neighborhood, just 1 mile from City Place and Clematis Street, the very cool Biba answers the call for an inexpensive, chic hotel that young hipsters can call their own. Housed in a renovated Colonial-style 1940s motor lodge, Biba has been remarkably updated by de rigueur designer Barbara Hulanicki and features a sleek lobby with the hip hotel bar, and a gorgeously landscaped outdoor pool area with Asian-inspired gardens. Guest rooms are shabby chic, with private patios, mosaic-tile floors, custom-made mahogany furniture, Egyptian-cotton linens, down pillows, and flatscreen TVs. The bold color schemes mix nicely with the high-fashion crowd that convenes here. ***A word of advice:*** This place is not exactly soundproof. Rooms may be cloistered by fence and gardens, but they're still extremely close to a major thoroughfare. Ask for a room that's on the quieter Belvedere Road, as opposed to those facing South Olive Avenue.

320 Belvedere Rd., West Palm Beach, FL 33405. ✆ **561/832-0094.** Fax 561/833-7848. www.hotelbiba.com. 41 units. $110–$215 double; $200–$300 suite. Rates include breakfast. Online discounts available. AE, MC, V. **Amenities:** Lounge; outdoor pool; concierge. *In room:* A/C, TV, free Wi-Fi, hair dryer, CD player.

WHERE TO DINE

Palm Beach has some of the area's swankiest restaurants. Thanks to the development of downtown West Palm Beach, however, there is also a great selection of trendier, less expensive spots. Dress here is slightly more formal than in most other areas of Florida: Men wear blazers, and women generally put on modest dresses or chic suits when they dine out, even on the oppressively hot days of summer.

Very Expensive

Café Boulud ★★★ FRENCH Snowbird socialites rejoiced over the opening of star chef Daniel Boulud's eponymous restaurant in the Brazilian Court hotel. Nonsocialites said, "Figures, another restaurant where we can't afford even a bread crumb." If you're out to splurge, Boulud is ideal, with an exquisite menu divided into four sections—La Tradition (French and American classics), La Saison (seasonal dishes), Le Potager (dishes inspired by the vegetable market), and Le Voyage (world cuisine). The roasted barramundi with squash, pomegranate, and brown butter is superb. There's also a light and somewhat reasonably priced menu offering salads, sandwiches—including possibly the best I've ever had, the BLT with smoked beef brisket, lettuce slaw, Creole mustard, fried green tomatoes, and homemade pickles—and even a cheeseburger if you prefer; try the chickpea fries with *piquillo* pepper ketchup. If star chefs, stuffy socialites, and froufrou cuisine aren't your thing, don't even bother.

In the Brazilian Court, 301 Australian Ave., Palm Beach. ✆ **561/655-6060.** www.danielnyc.com. Reservations essential. Main courses $30–$50. AE, DC, MC, V. Daily 9am–10pm.

Cafe l'Europe ★★★ CONTINENTAL One of Palm Beach's finest and most popular spots, this award-winning, romantic, and formal restaurant gives you a good reason to get dressed up. The enticing appetizers served by a superb staff might include Chinese spring rolls, baked-goat-cheese salad with raspberry-walnut dressing, poached salmon, or chilled gazpacho with avocado. Main courses run the gamut from wiener schnitzel with herbed spaetzle to sautéed potato-crusted Florida snapper to roasted rack of lamb. Seafood dishes and steaks in sumptuous but light sauces are always exceptional.

331 S. County Rd. (at Brazilian Ave.), Palm Beach. ✆ **561/655-4020.** www.cafeleurope.com. Reservations recommended. Main courses $29–$40. AE, DC, DISC, MC, V. Tues–Sat noon–3pm and 6–10pm; Sun 6–10pm.

Echo ★★★ ASIAN This hyperstylish, sleek eatery is the Breakers hotel's homage to young and hip. The hotel runs the restaurant, even though it's off premises, and it's worth leaving the comfy, upper-crust confines of the Breakers for this resounding Echo. The menu is broken down into categories: earth, wind, fire, water, and flavor, which doesn't do the food any real justice. Sushi bar specialties, such as the *hamachi kama,* grilled *hamachi,* Asian greens, and citrus soy, and the outstanding echo roll with shrimp tempura, cucumber, avocado, and tobiko in a sesame soy sheet with superspicy *sriracha* sauce, are two of my favorites. But it's not all sushi. There are Chinese dim sum specialties, too. The dim sum sampler, at $26, feeds two and is an ideal starter or full-blown meal. Then there's the Thai roast duck, and the open-flame wok specialties. There's too much to choose from, but it's all good. Be sure to check out the restaurant's Dragonfly Lounge after dinner. It's a hopping scene, especially by Palm Beach standards.

230 Sunrise Ave., Palm Beach. ✆ **561/802-4222.** www.echopalmbeach.com. Reservations essential. Main courses $18–$60. AE, DC, MC, V. Tues–Sun 5:30–9:30pm.

The Strip House ★★★ STEAKHOUSE Yet another New York–based steakhouse has opened in Palm Beach County and, like the others (Old Homestead), this one has opened to rave reviews. The a la carte menu offers impressive porterhouses, but according to some diners, even more impressive are the photos of exotic dancers (hence the restaurant's name) that line the walls. It's a bit of camp with your meat, especially with the bordello-red booths; but that's okay, because once you start slicing into the perfectly prepared steaks here, all memories of scantily clad women as wallpaper may remain just that—scant.

11708 Lake Victoria Gardens Ave. (Downtown at the Gardens), Palm Beach Gardens. ✆ **561/296-4900.** www.theglaziergroup.com. Reservations recommended. Main courses $15–$46. AE, DC, MC, V. Mon–Thurs 11am–10pm; Fri 11am–11:30pm; Sat 4–11:30pm; Sun 4–10pm.

Expensive

Amici ★ **Overrated** ITALIAN This is one of those restaurants whose scene is tastier than its cuisine. An upper-crusty Palm Beach set convenes here and consistently raves about above-average, overpriced Italian food. The best item on the menu is gnocchi with white truffle oil, fontina cheese, and spinach. Everything else is fairly standard: grilled sandwiches, pastas with rustic sauces, pizzas, grilled shrimp, and fish. Despite its less-than-stellar food, Amici is always crowded and very noisy.

288 S. County Rd. (at Royal Palm Way), Palm Beach. ✆ **561/832-0201.** www.amicipalmbeach.com. Reservations strongly recommended on weekends. Main courses $26–$44; pizzas $14–$18. AE, DC, MC, V. Mon–Thurs 11:30am–3pm and 5:30–10:30pm; Fri–Sat 11:30am–3pm and 5:30–11pm; Sun 5:30–10:30pm.

Bice Restaurant ★★ NORTHERN ITALIAN Bice's Milanese cuisine far surpasses that of Amici's, but as far as atmosphere, the air in here is a bit haughty, bordering on rude. Servers and diners alike have attitudes, but you'll forget all that with one bite of the juicy veal cutlet with tomato salad or the *pasta e fagioli* (pasta with beans).

313½ Worth Ave., Palm Beach. ✆ **561/835-1600.** Reservations essential. Main courses $20–$40. AE, DC, MC, V. Daily noon–10pm.

Moderate

City Cellar ★★ AMERICAN If the Palm Beach–proper dining scene is too stuffy, head over to City Place to find this yuppie brick-and-pressed-tin enclave where people-watching is at a premium. Despite its all-American appearance, City Cellar offers a varied menu, from pizzas and pastas to steak and sea bass. We love the onion and mushroom soup with Pinot Grigio and the twin 7-ounce pork chops with potato purée, sweet-and-sour shallots, and a sherry mustard butter. The place is mobbed on weekends, so plan for a long wait that's best spent at the action-packed bar.

700 S. Rosemary Ave., West Palm Beach. ✆ **561/659-1853.** Reservations suggested. Main courses $11–$32. AE, MC, V. Sun–Wed 11:30am–10:30pm (bar until 1am); Thurs–Sat 11:30am–11pm (bar until 2am).

Rhythm Café ★ (Finds) ECLECTIC AMERICAN This funky hole-in-the-wall is where those in the know come to eat some of West Palm Beach's most laid-back gourmet food. On the handwritten, photocopied menu (which changes daily), you'll always find a fish specialty accompanied by a hefty dose of greens and garnishes. Reliably outstanding is the pork tenderloin with mango chutney. Salads and soups are a great bargain, as portions are relatively large. The kitschy decor of this tiny cafe comes complete with vinyl tablecloths and a changing display of paintings by local amateurs. Young, handsome waiters are attentive, but not solicitous. The old drugstore where the restaurant recently relocated features an original 1950s lunch counter and stools.

3800 S. Dixie Hwy., West Palm Beach. ✆ **561/833-3406.** www.rhythmcafe.cc. Reservations recommended Sat–Sun. Main courses $13–$24. AE, DISC, MC, V. Tues–Sat 6–10pm; Sun (Dec–Mar) 5:30–9pm. Closed in early Sept. From I-95, exit east on Southern Blvd. Go 1 block north of Southern Blvd.; restaurant is on the right.

Inexpensive

Green's Pharmacy ★ (Value) AMERICAN This neighborhood pharmacy offers one of the best meal deals in Palm Beach. Both breakfast and lunch are served coffee-shop style, either at a Formica bar or at tables on a black-and-white checkerboard floor. Breakfast specials include eggs and omelets served with home fries and bacon, sausage, or corned-beef hash. The grill serves burgers and sandwiches, as well as ice-cream sodas and milkshakes, to a loyal crowd of pastel-clad Palm Beachers.

151 N. County Rd., Palm Beach. ✆ **561/832-0304.** Fax 561/832-6502. Breakfast $2–$6; burgers and sandwiches $3–$8; soups and salads $2–$8. AE, DISC, MC, V. Mon–Sat 7am–5pm; Sun 7am–3pm.

Palm Beach Nightlife Is Not an Oxymoron

In 2008, Clematis Street, West Palm Beach's hub of nightlife, also known as the Clematis District, celebrated an immense resurgence, with a slew of new dining destinations, retailers, and nightspots. Among them, celebrity-driven restaurants and nightlife destinations, including **Dr. Feelgood's Rock Bar and Grill,** 219 Clematis St. (© **561/833-6500;** www.drfeelgoodsbar.com), co-owned by Mötley Crüe's Vince Neil, and **Forte di Asprinio,** 225 Clematis St. (© **561/833-3936**), a modern chic, Italian-inspired restaurant and lounge by Stephen Asprinio, star of Bravo network's *Top Chef* and a Palm Beach County native.

John G's ★ AMERICAN This coffee shop is the most popular in the county. For decades, John G's has been attracting huge breakfast crowds; lines run out the door (on weekends, all the way down the block). Stop in for good, greasy-spoon food served in heaping portions right on the beachfront. This place is known for fresh and tasty fish and chips, and its selection of creative omelets and grill specials.

10 S. Ocean Blvd., Lake Worth. © **561/585-9860.** www.johngs.com. Reservations not accepted. Breakfast $3–$10; lunch $4–$15. No credit cards. Daily 7am–3pm. From the Florida Tpk., take the Lake Worth exit and head toward the ocean.

Tom's Place for Ribs ★★ Finds BARBECUE There are two important factors in a successful barbecue: the cooking and the sauce. Tom and Helen Wright's no-nonsense shack wins on both counts, offering flawlessly grilled meats paired with well-spiced sauces. Beef, chicken, pork, and fish are served soul-food style, with corn bread and your choice of sides such as rice with gravy, collard greens, black-eyed peas, coleslaw, or mashed potatoes. There's another very popular branch of Tom's in Boca Raton, at 7251 N. Federal Hwy. (© **561/997-0920**).

1225 Palm Beach Lakes Blvd., West Palm Beach. © **561/832-8774.** Reservations not accepted. Main courses $8–$15; sandwiches $5–$6. AE, MC, V. Tues–Thurs 11:30am–10:30pm; Fri 11:30am–10pm; Sat noon–10pm.

10

The Treasure Coast: Stuart to Sebastian

The area north of Palm Beach is known as the Treasure Coast for the same reason that the area from Fort Lauderdale to Palm Beach is known as the Gold Coast—it was the site of a number of shipwrecks that date back more than 300 years, which led to the discovery of priceless treasures in the water (some historians believe that treasures *still* lie buried deep beneath the ocean floor).

The difference, however, is that while the Gold Coast is a bit, well, tarnished as far as development is concerned, the Treasure Coast remains, for the most part, an unspoiled, quiet natural jewel. Miles of uninterrupted beaches and aquamarine waters attract swimmers, boaters, divers, anglers, and sun worshipers. If you love the great outdoors and prefer a more understated environment than hyperdeveloped Miami and Fort Lauderdale, the Treasure Coast is a real find.

For hundreds of years, Florida's east coast was a popular stopover for European explorers, many of whom arrived from Spain with full coffers of gold and silver. Rough weather and poor navigation often took a toll on their ships, but in 1715, a violent hurricane stunned the northeast coast and sank an entire fleet of Spanish ships laden with gold. Although Spanish salvagers worked for years to collect the lost treasure, much of it remained buried beneath the shifting sand. Workers hired to excavate the area in the 1950s and 1960s discovered centuries-old coins under their tractors.

Today you can still see shipwrecks and incredible barrier reefs in St. Lucie County, which can be reached from the beaches of Fort Pierce and Hutchinson Island. On these same beaches, you'll also find an occasional treasure hunter trolling the sand with a metal detector, alongside swimmers and sunbathers who come to enjoy the stretches of beach that extend into the horizon. The sea, especially around Sebastian Inlet, is a mecca for surfers, who find some of the largest swells in the state.

Along with the pleasures of the talcum-powder sands, the Treasure Coast has good shopping and sports, and numerous other opportunities to take a reprieve from the hubbub of the rat race. Visitors to this part of South Florida should not miss the extensive array of wildlife, which includes the endangered West Indian manatee, loggerhead and leatherback turtles, tropical fish, alligators, deer, and exotic birds. Sports enthusiasts will find boundless opportunities here—from golf and tennis to polo, motorcar racing, the New York Mets during spring training, and the best freshwater fishing around.

The downtown areas of the Treasure Coast have been experiencing a very slow rebirth in the past few years, along with an unprecedented influx of new residents. Fortunately, growth has occurred at a reasonable pace, allowing the neighborhoods to retain their small-town feel. The result is a batch of freshly spruced-up accommodations, shops, and restaurants from Stuart to Sebastian.

While the Treasure Coast took a major hit during the brutal 2005 hurricane season, all is still golden here.

For the purposes of this chapter, the Treasure Coast runs roughly from Hobe Sound in the south to Sebastian Inlet in the north, encompassing some of Martin, St. Lucie, and Indian River counties, and all of Hutchinson Island.

TREASURE COAST ESSENTIALS

Getting There

Because virtually every town described in this chapter runs along a straight route by the Atlantic Ocean, I've given all directions below.

BY PLANE The **Palm Beach International Airport** (© **561/471-7420**), about 35 miles south of Stuart, is the closest gateway to this region if you're flying. See the "Getting There" section on Palm Beach, on p. 294, for complete information. If you're traveling to the northern part of the Treasure Coast, **Melbourne International Airport,** off U.S. 1 in Melbourne (© **321/723-6227**), is less than 25 miles north of Sebastian and about 35 miles north of Vero Beach.

BY CAR If you're driving up or down the Florida coast, you'll probably reach the Treasure Coast via I-95. If you're heading to Stuart or Jensen Beach, take exit 61 (Rte. 76/Tanner Hwy.) or 62 (Rte. 714); to Port St. Lucie or Fort Pierce, take exit 63 or 64 (Okeechobee Rd.); to Vero Beach, take exit 68 (S.R. 60); to Sebastian, take exit 69 (County Rd.). You can also take the Florida Turnpike; this toll road is the fastest (but not the most scenic) route, especially if you're coming from Orlando. If you're heading to Stuart or Jensen Beach, take exit 133; to Fort Pierce, take exit 152 (Okeechobee Rd.); to Port St. Lucie, take exit 142 or 152; to Vero Beach, take exit 193 (S.R. 60); to Sebastian, take exit 193 to S.R. 60 east and connect to I-95 N.

If you're staying in Hutchinson Island, which runs almost the entire length of the Treasure Coast, you should check with your hotel or see the listings below to find the best route to take.

Finally, if you're coming directly from the west coast, you'll probably take S.R. 70, which runs north of Lake Okeechobee to Fort Pierce, up the road from Stuart.

BY RAIL **Amtrak** (© **800/USA-RAIL** [872-7245]; www.amtrak.com) stops in West Palm Beach, at 201 S. Tamarind Ave.; and in Okeechobee, at 801 N. Parrot Ave., off U.S. 441 N.

BY BUS **Greyhound** (© **800/231-2222;** www.greyhound.com) serves the area with bus terminals in Stuart, at 1308 S. Federal Hwy.; in Fort Pierce, at 7005 Okeechobee Rd. (© **772/461-3299**); and in Vero Beach, at U.S. 1 and S.R. 60 (© **772/562-6588**).

Getting Around

A car is a necessity in this large and rural region. Although heavy traffic is not usually a problem here, on the smaller coastal roads, such as A1A, expect to travel at a slow pace, usually between 25 and 40 mph.

1 PORT ST. LUCIE & FORT PIERCE

Port St. Lucie: 120 miles N of Miami; 120 miles S of Orlando

Port St. Lucie and Fort Pierce are two true Old Florida towns—reminiscent of the pre-neon, pre-condomaniacal Florida, a sleepy world apart from the Gold Coast and Miami. Both towns thrive on sport fishing, and a seemingly endless row of piers juts out along

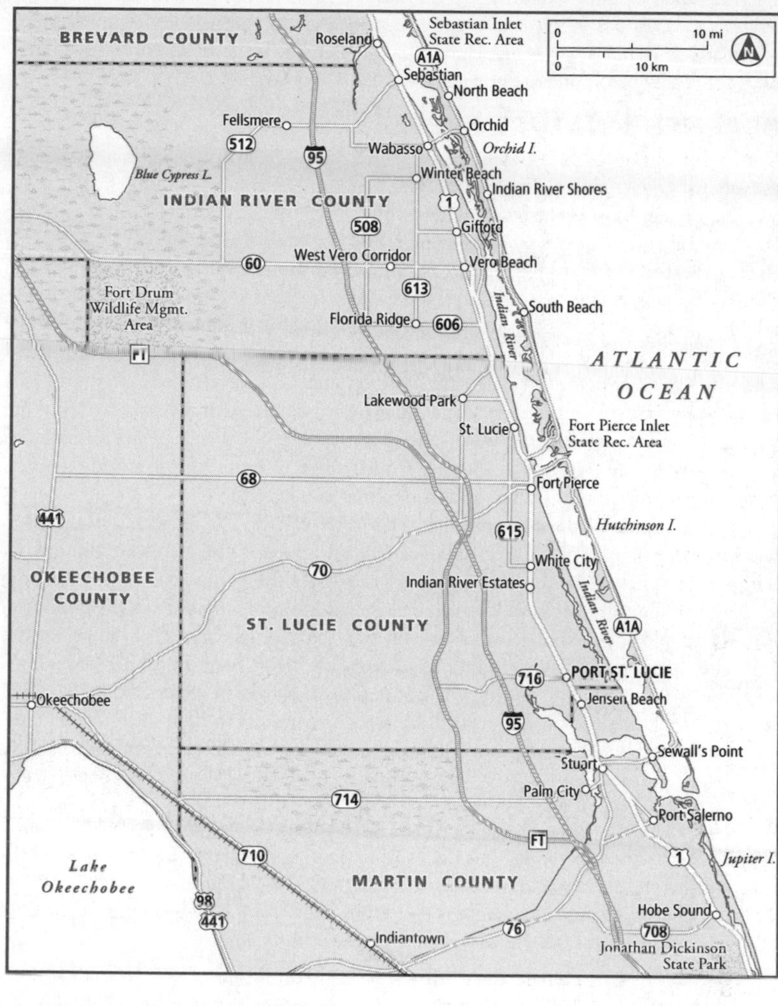

the Intracoastal Waterway and the Fort Pierce Inlet for both river and ocean runs. Visitors can dive, snorkel, beachcomb, and sunbathe in an area left untouched by the overdevelopment that has altered its neighbors to the south and north.

Most sightseeing takes place along the main beach road (the strip across from the ocean/A1A). Driving along Florida A1A on Hutchinson Island, you'll discover several secluded beach clubs interspersed with 1950s-style homes, a few small inns, grungy raw bars, and a few high-rise condominiums. Much of this island is government-owned and kept undeveloped for the public's enjoyment.

ESSENTIALS

The **St. Lucie County Chamber of Commerce,** 2200 Virginia Ave., Fort Pierce, FL 34982 (✆ **772/595-9999;** www.stluciechamber.org), is the region's main source of information. There's another branch at 1626 SE Port St. Lucie Blvd., in Port St. Lucie. Both spots are open Monday through Friday from 9am to 5pm.

BEACHES & NATURE PRESERVES

North Hutchinson Island's beaches are the most pristine in this area. You won't find restaurants, hotels, or shopping; instead, you'll spend your time swimming, surfing, fishing, and diving. Most of the beaches along this stretch of the Atlantic Ocean are private, but thankfully the state has set aside some of the best areas for the public.

Fort Pierce Inlet State Recreation Area (✆ **772/468-3985**) is a stunning 340-acre park with almost 4,000 feet of sandy shores that were once the training ground for the original navy frogmen. A short nature trail leads through a canopy of live oaks, cabbage palms, sea grapes, and strangler figs. The western side of the area has swamps of red mangroves that are home to fiddler crabs, osprey, and a multitude of wading birds. Jack Island State Preserve, in the state recreation area, is popular with bird-watchers and has hiking trails. Jutting into the Indian River, the mangrove-covered peninsula contains several marked trails, varying in distance from .5 mile to more than 4 miles. The trails through mangrove forests lead to a short observation tower.

The best beach in the state recreation area, **Jetty Park,** lies in the northern part. Families will enjoy the picnic areas and barbecue grills here. There are also restrooms and outdoor showers, and lifeguards look after swimmers. In 2008, the park was the recipient of a $1.2-million makeover which included the addition of a wildlife observation area, fitness trail, picnic pavilion, game tables, and an area designated for, of all things, Frisbee golf. The park is at 905 Shorewinds Dr., north of Fort Pierce Inlet. To get here from I-95, take exit 66 East (Rte. 68) and turn left onto U.S. 1 North; in about 2 miles, you will see signs to Florida A1A and the North Bridge Causeway. Turn right on A1A and cross over to North Hutchinson Island. Admission is $4 per vehicle; the park is open daily from 8am to sunset.

SPECTATOR SPORTS & OUTDOOR PURSUITS

BASEBALL The **New York Mets** hold spring training in Port St. Lucie from late February to the end of March at **Tradition Field,** 525 NW Peacock Blvd. (✆ **772/871-2115**). Tickets for games and practices cost $6 to $25. From April to August, their farm team, the Vero Beach Dodgers, plays home games in the stadium.

FISHING The **Fort Pierce City Marina,** 1 Ave. A, Fort Pierce (✆ **772/464-1245**), has more than a dozen charter captains who keep their motors running for anglers anxious to catch a few. Brochures available at the marina list all of the privately owned charter operators, who organize trips on an as-desired basis. The price usually starts at $150 per person for half-day tours, depending on the season.

GOLF The most notable courses in Port St. Lucie are at the **PGA Golf Club,** 1916 Perfect Dr. (✆ **772/467-1300**). The club's first of three 18-hole public golf courses opened in 1996 and was designed by Tom Fazio; another course was designed by Pete Dye. The South Course, a classic Old Florida–style course, is set on wetlands, affords views of native wildlife, and is the most popular. The center also provides lessons for amateurs. The club is open daily from 7am to 6pm. Greens fees are usually $55 to $65, but after 2pm they go down to $39. Reserve at least 9 days in advance.

Harbor Branch Oceanographic Institution ★★ Harbor Branch is a working nonprofit scientific institute that studies oceanic resources and welcomes visitors on scheduled tours. Stops include the J. Seward Johnson Marine Education Center, which houses submersibles used to conduct research at depths of up to 3,000 feet. A video details current projects, and several large aquariums simulate the environments of the Indian River Lagoon and a saltwater reef. Visitors see the Aqua-Culture Farming Center, a research facility that contains tanks growing seaweed and other oceanic plants. The 90-minute Lagoon Wildlife Tour examines the Indian River Lagoon from a pontoon boat. The boat tours are offered Monday through Saturday at 10am and 1 and 3pm; the cost is $17 for adults, $12 for children 6 to 12. The bus tour of the 600-acre campus costs $10 and leaves Monday through Saturday at 10am, noon, and 2pm.

5600 U.S. 1 N., Fort Pierce. ✆ **772/465-2400.** www.hboi.edu. Admission $10 adults, $6 children 6–12. Mon–Fri 8am–5pm; visitor center gift shop Mon–Sat 9am–5pm. Arrive at least 20 min. before tour.

Savannahs Recreation Area ★★★ Finds A 550-acre former reservoir, Savannahs is one of the most interesting places in these parts—it's a veritable wilderness, with botanical gardens, nature trails, campsites, a petting zoo, and scenery reminiscent of the Florida Everglades, but in a much more contained environment.

1400 E. Midway Rd., Fort Pierce. ✆ **772/464-7855.** Admission $1 per car. Daily 8am–6pm.

UDT-SEAL Museum (Underwater Demolition Team Museum) Florida is full of unique museums, but none more curious than the UDT-SEAL Museum, an interesting tribute to the secret forces of the U.S. Navy frogmen and their successors, the SEAL teams. Chronological displays trace the history of these clandestine divers and detail their most important achievements. The best exhibits are those on the intricately detailed equipment used by the navy's most elite members. Expect to spend about an hour here, depending on your interests.

3300 N. S.R. A1A, Fort Pierce. ✆ **772/595-5845.** www.navysealmuseum.com. Admission $6 adults, $3 children 6–12. Mon 10am–4pm (Jan–Apr only); Tues–Sat 10am–4pm; Sun noon–4pm. off-season.

WHERE TO STAY

The Port St. Lucie mainland is pretty run-down, but there are a number of inexpensive hotel options on scenic Hutchinson Island that are charming and well priced. Probably the best choice is the **Hampton Inn,** 2831 Reynolds Dr. (✆ **800/426-7866** or 772/828-4100), which is beautifully maintained.

Expensive

Club Med Sandpiper ★★ Kids This 400-acre, all inclusive resort isn't your typical bacchanalian Club Med, but rather a fabulous getaway for families with kids. The hotel markets itself to families looking for a Florida getaway. They come in droves (Americans, Canadians, and a handful of Europeans) with all the kids and nannies for an active vacation with lavish meals, from buffets to sit-downs, for a package price. Thanks to tailored programs for kids—there's Baby Club Med, Petit Club Med, Mini Club Med, and Junior's Club Med—the resort is all about families with kids. Rooms are currently so-so and retro, but the resort company recently announced a full renovation of Sandpiper to be complete by early 2010. However, there's so much to do that you really won't be spending much time inside anyway. The drawback is that guests are 20 minutes from the nearest beach. The buildings could use an overhaul, but there are plenty of diversions on-site, such as golf, tennis, bocce ball, volleyball, water-skiing, sailing, and boating on the Indian River, and even a circus school!

4500 SE Pine Valley, Port St. Lucie, FL 34952. ✆ **800/CLUB-MED** (258-2633) or 772/398-5100. Fax 772/398-5101. www.clubmed.us. 337 units. Winter $800–$2,320 per week per adult; off-season $700–$2,180 per week per adult (reduced rates are offered for children). Rates include all meals; unlimited wine, beer, and soft drinks with snacks, breakfast, lunch, and dinner; sports equipment and instruction; and nightly entertainment. Transportation from your city of departure to the village, as well as transfers to and from the village, is available. AE, MC, V. Closed Nov–Mar. From U.S. 1 S., turn left onto Westmoreland Blvd. Make another left onto Pine Valley Rd.; the resort entrance is straight ahead. **Amenities:** 2 restaurants; bar; 4 pools; 3 golf courses; 19 tennis courts (9 lighted); fitness center; watersports equipment; game rooms; coin-op washers/dryers. *In room:* A/C, TV, hair dryer.

Moderate

Dockside Inn and Resort ★ Fronting the Intracoastal Waterway, the Dockside Inn is an ideal choice for boating and fishing enthusiasts, with 15 boat slips and two private fishing piers. The hotel itself carries on the nautical theme with pierlike wooden stairs and rope railings. While not exactly captain's quarters, the rooms (straight out of Rooms to Go, albeit with a bit of a nautical flair) are attractive enough. Higher-priced units have either waterfront balconies or small kitchenettes.

1160 Seaway Dr., S. Hutchinson Island, FL 34949. ✆ **800/286-1745** or 772/468-3555. Fax 772/489-9848. www.docksideinn.com. 64 units. Winter $79 standard, $95–$130 efficiency, $130–$155 suite; off-season $70–$105 standard or efficiency, $119–$145 suite. AE, DISC, MC, V. **Amenities:** 2 outdoor heated pools; self-service laundry; 5 lighted fishing docks; boat dockage; grilling areas. *In room:* A/C, TV, dataport, kitchenette (in higher-priced rooms), minibar, coffeemaker.

WHERE TO DINE

Fort Pierce and St. Lucie aren't exactly gourmet destinations, but there are a few good restaurants.

Moderate

Mangrove Mattie's ★★ SEAFOOD A rustic restaurant on the Fort Pierce Inlet, Mangrove Mattie's is the best place for outdoor dining, thanks to both its priceless location—right on the inlet, affording panoramic views of the Atlantic—and its excellent fresh seafood. Happy hours, Monday through Friday from 4 to 7pm, are especially popular and feature a free buffet.

1640 Seaway Dr., Fort Pierce. ✆ **772/466-1044.** Main courses $11–$20. AE, DISC, MC, V. Daily 11:30am–10pm.

Tiki Bar & Restaurant ★ SEAFOOD With waterfront dining on the Indian River, the thatched roof, open air Tiki Bar & Restaurant (don't worry, there's also indoor dining, but why bother?) is a great spot for a sunset cocktail and some nibbles from the raw bar. The menu features sandwiches, salads, burgers, and catches of the day, but the best catch here is the view. Popular daily happy hours from 4 to 7pm and live entertainment are a major lure for locals and visitors alike.

2 Ave. A at the Fort Pierce Marina, Fort Pierce. ✆ **772/461-0880.** www.originaltikibar.com. Main courses $6–$22. AE, DISC, MC, V. Daily 11:30am–11pm.

PORT ST. LUCIE & FORT PIERCE AFTER DARK

An event to showcase the galleries, restaurants, and shops of Fort Pierce, **2nd Wednesday Art Walk,** is held the second Wednesday of every month from 5 to 8pm and costs $5 per person. It begins in front of the Sunrise Theater (✆ **772/466-3880**). All galleries are usually open for this event, and they supply free beverages and cheese. The free **Friday Fest Street Festival** (www.mainstreetfortpierce.org), on the first Friday of every month at the Historic Downtown Riverfront, has live music and refreshments for sale. **Whiskey Jay's,** 338 Port St. Lucie Blvd. (✆ **772/873-1111**), has jazz, blues, and rock music Monday through Sunday nights; reservations are recommended.

2 VERO BEACH ★ & SEBASTIAN ★★

Vero Beach: 87 miles S of Orlando; 95 miles N of Fort Lauderdale

Old Florida is thriving in these remote and tranquil villages. Vero Beach, known for its exclusive and affluent winter population, and Sebastian, known as one of the last remaining fishing villages, are set at the northern tip of the Treasure Coast region in Indian River County. These two beach towns are populated with folks who appreciate the area's small-town feel, and that's exactly the appeal for visitors: a laid-back atmosphere, friendly people, and friendlier prices.

A crowd of well-tanned surfers from all over the state descends on the region, especially the Sebastian Inlet, to catch some of the state's biggest waves. Other watersports enthusiasts enjoy the area's fine diving and windsurfing. Anglers are also in heaven here. In spring, baseball buffs may still be able to catch some action as it's rumored the Baltimore Orioles may be taking over Dodgertown—left vacant by the L.A. team that moved to Arizona—for training in exhibition games.

ESSENTIALS

The **Indian River County Tourist Council,** 1216 21st St., Vero Beach, FL 32961 (✆ **772/567-3491;** fax 772/778-3181; www.indianriverchamber.com), will send visitors a detailed information packet on the county (which includes Vero Beach and Sebastian), with a full-color map, a list of upcoming events, a hotel guide, and more.

BEACHES & OUTDOOR ACTIVITIES

BEACHES You'll find plenty of free and open beachfront along the coast—most areas are uncrowded and are open from 7am until 10pm.

South Beach Park, on South Ocean Drive, at the end of Marigold Lane, is a busy, developed, lifeguarded beach with picnic tables, restrooms, and showers. It's known as one of the best swimming beaches in Vero Beach and attracts a young crowd that plays volleyball in a tranquil setting. A nature walk takes you onto beautiful secluded trails.

At the very north tip of the island, **Sebastian Inlet State Park** ★, 9700 S. Fla. A1A, Melbourne (✆ **321/984-4852**), has flat, sandy beaches with lots of facilities, including kayak, paddle-boat, and canoe rentals; a well-stocked surf shop; picnic tables; and a snack shop. The winds seem to stir up the surf with no jetty to stop the swells, to the delight of surfers and boarders who come here to catch the big waves. Campers enjoy fully equipped sites in a woody area. At press time, the park was readying itself for the arrival of cozy, 1,150- to 1,600-square-foot cabins with high-tech amenities, such as Internet access, as well as woodsy amenities, such as rocking chairs, porches, and fireplaces. According to one park official, however, it's not happening anytime soon, but rather, "in the distant future." Stay tuned. Entry fees to the park are $5 per car and $1 for those who walk or bike in.

FISHING Capt. Terry Lamielle has been fishing the area for more than 40 years and will teach you all about fly-fishing for red fish, snook, and tarpon. His **Easy Days Fishing** (✆ **321/537-5346;** www.easydaysfishing.com) takes anglers on his *Sterling Flats* fishing boat for private river excursions. Half-day jaunts on the Indian River cost $300 for one or two people (the minimum required for a charter), tackle, rigs, and everything included; it's $50 extra for a third person.

Many other charters, guides, party boats, and tackle shops operate in this area. Consult your hotel for suggestions, or call the **Vero Beach Chamber of Commerce** (✆ **772/567-3491**). You can also contact **Captain Hiram's** (✆ **772/589-4345;** www.hirams.com), a restaurant/bar/hotel/marina that houses many charter boats.

GOLF Hard-core golfers insist that of the dozens of courses in the area, only a handful are worth their plots of grass. Set on rolling hills with uncluttered views of sand dunes and sky, the **Sandridge Golf Club,** 5300 73rd St., Vero Beach (✆ **772/770-5000;** www.sandridgegc.com), offers two par-72 18-holers. The Dunes is a long course with rolling fairways, while the newer Lakes course has lots of water. Both charge $28 to $49, including cart. Reservations are recommended and are taken 2 days in advance.

Although less challenging, the **Sebastian Municipal Golf Course,** 1010 E. Airport Dr. (✆ **772/589-6801;** www.sebastiangolfcourse.org), is a good 18-hole par-72 course. It's scenic, well maintained, and a relative bargain. Greens fees are $18 to $44 per player, with cart.

Golfers who are also baseball fans will be pleased to know there are two golf courses at **Dodgertown** (p. 317).

TENNIS Many of the tennis courts around Vero Beach and Sebastian are at hotels and resorts, and are thus closed to nonguests. Try **Riverside Racquet Complex,** 350 Dahlia Lane, at Royal Palm Boulevard, at the east end of Barber Bridge, Vero Beach (✆ **772/231-4787**). This popular park has 10 hard courts (six lighted) that can be rented for $3 per person per hour if you're a county resident, and $5 if not. Reservations are accepted up to 24 hours in advance.

SEEING THE SIGHTS

Environmental Learning Center ★★ Kids The Indian River is not really a river at all, but a large, brackish lagoon that's home to a greater variety of species than any other estuary in North America—it has thousands of species of plants, animals, fish, and birds, including 36 species on the endangered list. The privately funded Environmental Learning Center was created to educate visitors about the Indian River area's environment. Situated on 51 island acres, the center features a 600-foot boardwalk through the mangroves and dozens of hands-on exhibits that are geared to both children and adults. There are touch tanks, exhibits, and microscopes for viewing the smallest sea life up close. The best thing to do is join one of the center's field excursion programs, from guided nature walks and stargazing to river cruise adventures. Best of all, prices range from free to $15 for adults and $7 for children.

255 Live Oak Dr. (just off the 510 Causeway), Wabasso Island (a 51-acre island in the Indian River Lagoon). ✆ **772/589-5050.** www.elcweb.org. Free admission. Tues–Fri 10am–4pm; Sat 9am–noon; Sun 1–4pm.

Indian River Citrus Museum The tiny Indian River Citrus Museum exhibits artifacts relating to the history of the citrus industry, from its initial boom in the late 1800s to the present; a small grove displays several varieties. The gift shop sells citrus-themed items along with, of course, ready-to-ship fruit.

2140 14th Ave., Vero Beach. ✆ **772/770-2263.** Admission $1 donation. Tues–Fri 10am–4pm.

McKee Botanical Garden ★★ This impressive 18-acre attraction was originally opened in 1932 and featured a virtual jungle of orchids, exotic and native trees, monkeys, and birds. After years of neglect, it was placed on the National Register of Historic Places in 1998 and renovated; you can now again experience the full charms of this little Eden.

350 U.S. 1, Vero Beach. ✆ **772/794-0601.** www.mckeegarden.org. Admission $6 adults, $5 seniors, $3.50 children 5–12. Tues–Sat 10am–5pm; Sun noon–5pm.

McLarty Treasure Museum ★ If you're unsure of why this area is called the Treasure Coast, then this is a must-see. Built on the site of a salvage camp from a 1715 shipwreck, this little museum is full of interesting history. It may not have the treasures of the nearby Mel Fisher museum, but it shows an engaging 45-minute video describing the many aspects of treasure hunting. You'll also see household items salvaged from the Spanish fleet and dioramas of life in the 18th century.

13180 N. Fla. A1A, Sebastian Inlet State Recreation Area, Vero Beach. ✆ **772/589-2147.** Admission $1, free for children 5 and under. Daily 10am–4:30pm

DODGERTOWN

Vero was, for 61 years, the winter home of the **Los Angeles Dodgers.** In 2008, the Dodgers pulled a Brooklyn and abandoned Vero Beach for Arizona. At the time of this writing, ball fans were eagerly awaiting the decision of the Baltimore Orioles, who were offered the sprawling compound as their new spring training grounds. If they accept, their move will also include upgrades to Dodgertown as well as a parcel of the Dodgertown golf course, which the team wants to use for a baseball-themed restaurant. Currently, the 450-acre compound, **Dodgertown,** at 3901 26th St. (✆ **772/569-4900**), encompasses spring-training camp, two golf courses, a conference center, a country club, a movie theater, a recreation room, citrus groves, and a residential community. It is a city unto its own for baseball fanatics, though critics say it's not exactly state-of-the-art and is, well, a bit long in the tooth. The Dodgers' farm team, the Vero Beach Devil Rays, has a full season of minor-league baseball in summer. Admission to the complex is free; tickets to games are about $15 for a reserved seat. The complex is open daily from 9am to 5pm, with game time usually at 1pm. From I-95, take the exit for S.R. 60 East to 43rd Avenue and turn left; continue to 26th Street and turn right.

SHOPPING

Ocean Boulevard and Cardinal Drive are Vero's two main shopping streets. Both are near the beach and lined with boutiques, including antiques and home-decor shops.

If you want to send fruit back home, the local source is **Hale Indian River Groves,** 615 Beachland Blvd. (✆ **800/562-4502;** www.halegroves.com), a shipper of local citrus and jams since 1947, with four locations in Vero Beach. The grove is closed 2 to 3 months a year, usually from summer to early fall, depending on the crops; the season generally runs from November to Easter.

The **Horizon Outlet Center,** at S.R. 60 and I-95, Vero Beach (✆ **877/GO-OUTLET** [466-8853] or 772/770-6171), contains more than 80 discount stores selling name-brand shoes, kitchenware, clothing, and more. The center is open Monday through Saturday from 9am to 8pm, and Sunday from 11am to 6pm.

Indian River Mall, 6200 20th St. (S.R. 60), about 5 miles east of I-95 (✆ **772/770-6255**), is a monster mall, with all the big chains and several department stores. It's open Monday through Saturday from 10am to 9pm, and Sunday from noon to 6pm.

WHERE TO STAY

You can choose to stay on the mainland or on the beach. As you might expect, the beachfront accommodations are a bit more expensive—but, I think, worth it. Thanks to the arrival of a couple new luxury beachfront hotels, what was once known as Zero Beach is now worthy of its proper name. A great spot to know, especially if you're planning to fish, is the **Key West Inn at Captain Hiram's,** 1580 U.S. Hwy. 1, Sebastian (✆ 772/388-8588; www.hirams.com), where 70 rooms are available adjacent to the restaurant and overlooking the water. (Also see "Fishing," above, and "Vero Beach & Sebastian After Dark," below.)

Comfortable and inexpensive chain options near the Horizon Outlet Center, off S.R. 60, include **Holiday Inn Express** (✆ **800/465-4329** or 772/567-2500) and **Hampton Inn** (✆ **800/426-7866** or 772/770-4299). Rates for both run between $99 and $120, and include breakfast and local calls.

Expensive

Costa d'Este Beach Resort ★★★ Pop star Gloria Estefan owns this fabulous luxury hotel, but thankfully she left the flash and glitz of her Sound Machine back in Miami. Chic is an understatement here, which Estefan prefers to call a "personal luxury resort," rather than a boutique hotel. Each guest room features modern teak furnishings, flat-panel televisions, and complimentary Wi-Fi. Bathrooms feature tumbled limestone-tile showers with dual shower heads, and beds have buttery soft Egyptian cotton linens. Choose from an oceanview suite or a studio. Although there's beach access, we love the infinity-edge pool. A fantastic spa and sleek Oriente restaurant—Cuban cuisine with Spanish and Creole accents—are also on the premises giving you no reason to really want to leave. Ever.

3244 Ocean Dr., Vero Beach, FL 32963. ✆ **877/562-9919** or 772/562-9919. Fax 772/562-9225. www.costadeste.com. 94 units. Winter from $249 doubles and suites; off-season from $169 doubles and suites. AE, MC, V. **Amenities:** Oceanfront restaurant; pool bar and grill; heated oceanfront pool; golf privileges at local clubs; fitness center; spa; concierge; room service. *In room:* A/C, TV, Wi-Fi, MP3 docking station.

Vero Beach Hotel & Spa, A Kimpton Hotel ★★★ Located on Vero Beach's famed Ocean Drive along one of the country's most exclusive and pristine beaches, the Vero Beach Hotel & Spa is a West Indies–inspired boutique hotel offering 113 designer guest rooms, including one-, two-, and three-bedroom suites that feature dark mahogany woods, Jerusalem stone flooring, granite countertops, flatscreen televisions, sumptuous bedding, and spacious balconies overlooking the spectacular Atlantic Ocean and unspoiled Treasure Coast beaches. The AAA four-diamond award-winning hotel offers such amenities as the oceanfront Indigo Grill restaurant and lounge and Heaton's Reef Bar & Grill. A full-service on-site spa was scheduled for completion in the fall of 2009. Until then, guests may enjoy Kimpton's signature in-room spa services, including massage and body and facial treatments.

3500 Ocean Dr., Vero Beach, FL 32963. ✆ **866/602-VERO** [8376] or 772/231-5666. Fax 772/234-4866. www.verobeachhotelandspa.com. 113 guest rooms. Doubles from $179; suites from $399. AE, MC, V. Valet parking $10 per day. **Amenities:** Oceanfront restaurant; poolside bar and grill; heated oceanfront pool; golf privileges at private clubs; fitness center; spa; concierge; business center services; room service; laundry service. *In room:* A/C, TV/DVD/MP3 player, minibar, fridge, microwave.

Moderate

The Caribbean Court Boutique Hotel ★★ Finds The Caribbean Court is an intimate 18-room island-style hotel, with a heated pool, private beach access, the excellent on-site French restaurant, Maison Martinique, and Havana Nights Piano Bar, featuring spirits, tropical-lite cuisine, and entertainment (see below in "Where to Dine"). Rooms are nicely furnished with four-poster beds, antique furniture, original Caribbean artwork, French country–style bathrooms with ceramic wash basins, and kitchenettes. Most rooms have balconies or patios. More for couples looking for romance than the area's other beachy keen hotels, the Caribbean Court has a beautiful honeymoon suite, too. It's popular with business travelers during the week.

1601 Ocean Dr., Vero Beach, FL 32963. ✆ **772/231-7211.** www.thecaribbeancourt.com. 18 units. Winter $239–$299 double; off-season $139–$199 double. AE, MC, V. Pets accepted. **Amenities:** Restaurant; piano bar; heated pool; private beach access. *In room:* A/C, TV/DVD, high-speed Internet, kitchenette, fridge, coffeemaker, hair dryer, safe, microwave.

Driftwood Resort ★★ Finds Originally planned in the 1930s as a private estate by eccentric entrepreneur Waldo Sexton, the Driftwood was opened to the public in the late '30s. As it was the largest property in Vero Beach, people assumed it was an attraction or, at least, a hotel. All of the guest rooms were renovated in 2000, and each is unique. Some have terra-cotta floors and lighter furniture, while others have a more rustic feel with hardwoods and antiques. Some of the rooms contain Jacuzzis, all are equipped with full kitchens, and all sleep at least four. Two of the best units: the Captain's Quarters, which overlooks the ocean with a private staircase to the pool; and the town house in the breezeway building, featuring a spiral staircase as well as living room and bedroom views of the ocean. The resort is listed on the National Register of Historic Places and, to say the least, has lots of quirky charm.

3150 Ocean Dr., Vero Beach, FL 32963. ✆ **772/231-0550.** Fax 772/234-1981. www.thedriftwood.com. 100 units. Winter $130–$190 double, $200–$310 apt; off-season $100–$130 double, $140–$270 apt. AE, DISC, MC, V. **Amenities:** Restaurant; 2 outdoor heated pools; dry cleaning. *In room:* A/C, TV, full or partial kitchen, Jacuzzi (in some).

Islander Inn ★ This is one of the most comfortable and welcoming inns in the area. Well located in downtown Vero Beach, the small, quaint Key West–meets–Old Florida–style motel is just a short walk to the beach, restaurants, and shops. Every breezy guest room has a small refrigerator, either a king-size bed or two double beds, paddle fans, wicker furniture, and vaulted ceilings. Rooms open onto a pretty courtyard and sparkling pool. Efficiencies have full kitchens.

3101 Ocean Dr., Vero Beach, FL 32963. ✆ **800/952-5886** or 772/231-4431. 16 units. Winter $155–$185 double; off-season $89–$109 double. Efficiencies cost $10 extra. AE, MC, V. **Amenities:** Cafe; pool. *In room:* A/C, TV, fridge.

Sea Turtle Inn & Apartments ★ This two-part, smoke-free property offers the best value on the beach (just 2 blocks from the ocean). The 1950s motel and an adjacent apartment building have been fully renovated and outfitted with understated yet efficient furnishings. You won't find any fancy amenities, but the price and location make up for what the place lacks in frills. The properties share a small pool and sun deck. Book early, especially in season, as they fill up quickly with long-term visitors.

835 Azalea Lane, Vero Beach, FL 32963. ✆ **877/998-8785** or 772/234-0788. www.seaturtleinn.net. 20 units. $99–$145 double; $135–$215 apt. Weekly and monthly rates available. MC, V. From I-95, go east on S.R. 60; it's about 10 miles to Cardinal Dr. Turn right onto Azalea Lane. **Amenities:** Small pool; bike rental; laundry facilities. *In room:* A/C, TV, minifridge, coffeemaker.

Camping

The Vero Beach and Sebastian areas of the Treasure Coast are popular with campers, who choose from nearly a dozen camping locations. If you aren't camping at the scenic and popular **Sebastian Inlet State Park** (p. 315), then try the **Vero Beach Kamp RV Park,** 8850 U.S. 1, Wabasso (✆ **772/589-5665**). This 120-site campground is 2 miles from the ocean and the Intracoastal Waterway, and a quarter-mile from the Indian River, a big draw for fishing fanatics. There's access to running water and electricity, as well as showers, a shop, and hookups for RVs. Rates are $46 per site and $29 for tents. To get here, take I-95 to exit 69 East; at U.S. 1, turn left.

WHERE TO DINE

Expensive

Maison Martinique ★★★ FRENCH/CONTINENTAL Exquisite country French cooking, a comprehensive wine list, and white-glove service complement the fine linens and imported china at this romantic standout owned and operated by Yannick Martin. Formerly known as Café du Soir, Maison Martinique is in the charming waterfront Caribbean Court Hotel. Excellent starters include Louisiana sausage with sautéed apples, foie gras with caramelized raisins, and exceptional escargot. Main courses include sautéed Dover sole and filet mignon stuffed with Roquefort cheese. Desserts might include raspberry and strawberry Napoleons and country apple tarts.

1605 Ocean Dr., Vero Beach. ✆ **772/231-7299.** www.thecaribbeancourt.com. Reservations recommended. Main courses $15–$40. AE, MC, V. Mon–Sat from 6pm; closing time varies based on last reservation.

Moderate

Ocean Grill ★★ Finds STEAKS/SEAFOOD The Ocean Grill attracts faithful devotees with its simple but rich cooking and its stunning locale, right on the ocean's edge; ask for a table along the wall of windows that open onto the sea. Built more than 60 years ago by Vero Beach eccentric Waldo Sexton, the restaurant was once an officers' club for residents of the nearby naval airbase during World War II. All fish can be prepared Cajun-style, wood grilled, or deep-fried. Indian River crab cakes make for a memorable meal, deep-fried with fresh backfin and claw meat rolled in cracker meal. Try stone crab claws when they're in season, or the house shrimp scampi baked in butter and herbs and served with a tangy mustard sauce, or any of the big servings of meats. I especially recommend the Cajun rib-eye, featuring a béarnaise sauce that's delightfully jolting to the taste buds. Dinners are uniformly good here; the only tacky element of this place is the gift shop.

1050 Sexton Plaza (by the ocean at the end of S.R. 60), Vero Beach. ✆ **772/231-5409.** www.ocean-grill.com. Reservations accepted only for parties of 5 or more. Main courses $20–$35. AE, DC, DISC, MC, V. Mon–Fri 11:30am–2:30pm and 5:30–10pm; Sat–Sun 5:30–10pm. Closed Thanksgiving, Super Bowl Sun, and July 4.

Inexpensive

Nino's Cafe ★ ITALIAN This little beachside cafe looks like a stereotypical pizza joint, complete with fake brick walls, murals of the Italian countryside, and red-and-white-checked tablecloths. The atmosphere is pure cheese and so is much of the food—pizza and parmigiana dishes are smothered in the stuff. Still, the thin crust and fresh toppings make pizzas here a cut above the rest—just ask the New York transplants who live for the place. Entrees and pastas are also tasty.

1006 Easter Lily Lane (off Ocean Dr., next to Humiston Park), Vero Beach. ✆ **772/231-9311.** Main courses $9–$15. No credit cards. Mon–Thurs 11am–9pm; Fri–Sat 11am–10pm; Sun 4–9pm.

VERO BEACH & SEBASTIAN AFTER DARK

More than half of the residents in this area are retirees, so it shouldn't be a surprise that, even on weekends, this town retires early. Hotel lounges often have live music and a good bar scene, however, especially in high season, and sometimes stay open as late as 1am, if you're lucky. For beachside drinks, go to the **Driftwood Resort** (p. 319).

Vero Beach is also known as an artsy enclave, hosting galleries such as the **Admiralty Gallery,** 3315 Ocean Dr., Vero Beach (© **772/231-3178**). The **Civic Arts Center,** at Riverside Park, is a hub of culture; it includes the **Riverside Theatre** (© **772/231-6990**), the **Agnes Wahlstrom Youth Playhouse** (© **772/234-8052**), and the **Center for the Arts** (© **772/231-0707**), known for films and an excellent lecture series.

In Sebastian, you'll find live music every weekend (and daily in season) at **Captain Hiram's,** 1606 N. Indian River Dr. (© **772/589-4345**), a salty outdoor restaurant and bar on the Intracoastal Waterway that locals and tourists love at all hours of the day and night (well, until it closes at 11pm, that is). The feel is tacky Key West, complete with a sand floor and thatched-roof bar.

North of the inlet, head for the tried-and-true **Sebastian Beach Inn** (SBI to locals), 7035 S. Fla. A1A (© **321/728-4311**), for live music on weekends. Jazz, blues, or sometimes rock 'n' roll starts at 9pm on Friday and Saturday. On Sunday, it's old-style reggae after 2pm. The inn is open daily for drinks from 11am until anytime between midnight and 2am.

3 A SIDE TRIP INLAND: FISHING AT LAKE OKEECHOBEE ★★★

60 miles SW of West Palm Beach

Many visitors to the Treasure Coast come to fish, and they certainly get their fill off the miles of Atlantic shore and on the inland rivers. But if you want to fish freshwater and nothing else, head for "The Lake"—**Lake Okeechobee,** that is. The state's largest, it's chock-full of good eating fish. Only about a 1[bf]1/2-hour drive from the coast, it is located in what is known as the Freshwater Frontier and makes a great day or weekend excursion.

ESSENTIALS

GETTING THERE From Palm Beach, take I-95 S. to Southern Boulevard (U.S. 98 W.) in West Palm Beach, which merges with S.R. 80 and S.R. 441. Follow signs for S.R. 80 West through Belle Glade to South Bay. In South Bay, turn right onto U.S. 27 North, which leads directly to Clewiston.

VISITOR INFORMATION Contact the **Clewiston Chamber of Commerce,** 544 W. Sugarland Hwy., Clewiston, FL 33440 (© **863/983-7979;** www.clewiston.org), for maps, business directories, and the names of numerous fishing guides throughout the area. In addition, you might contact the **Pahokee Chamber of Commerce,** 115 E. Main St., Pahokee, FL 33476 (© **772/924-5579;** fax 772/924-8116; www.pahokee.com), which will send a complete package of magazines, guides, and accommodations listings.

OUTDOOR ACTIVITIES

BOATING Head out on the Lake with **Big O Airboat Tours,** 920 East Del Monte, at Roland and Mary Ann Martin's Marina (© **863/983-2037;** www.bigofishing.com), and catch a fast glimpse of osprey, roseate spoonbills, bald eagles, and dozens of alligators.

Going After the Big One

Fishing on Lake Okeechobee is a year-round affair, though the fish tend to bite a little better in the winter, perhaps for the benefit of the many snowbirds who flock here (especially Feb–Mar). RV camps are mobbed almost year-round with fish-frenzied anglers who come down for weeks at a time for a decent catch.

You'll need a fishing license to go out with a rod and reel. It's a simple matter to apply. The chamber of commerce and most fishing shops can sign you up on the spot. The cost for non-Florida residents is $17 for 7 days or $47 for the year.

You can rent, charter, or bring your own boat to Clewiston; just be sure to schedule your trip in advance. You don't want to show up during one of the frequent fishing tournaments only to find you can't get a room, campsite, or fishing boat. All tournaments are held at Roland Martin's marina (see below). For more information on tournaments, check out www.rolandmartinmarina.com.

There are several marinas where you can rent or charter boats. If it's your first time on the lake, I suggest chartering a boat with a guide who can show you the most fertile spots and help you handle your tackle. **Roland Martin,** 920 E. Del Monte (✆ **863/983-3151;** www.rolandmartinmarina.com), is the one-stop spot to find a guide, tackle, rods, bait, coolers, picnic supplies, and a choice of boats. Rates for a guided fishing tour are $250 for a half-day and $350 for a full day, for one or two people. You need a fishing license, which is available here for $17. There are also boat rentals: A 16-foot johnboat goes for $40 half-day and $60 full day, with a $40 deposit. Rentals for a 14-footer start at $60 for a half-day, for a maximum of four people. A full day costs $80. If you want a guide, rates start at $250 (for two people) for a half-day, though in the summer (June–Oct), when it's slow, you can get a cheaper deal.

FISHING See "Going After the Big One," below.

SKY DIVING Besides fishing, the biggest sport in Clewiston is jumping out of planes, due to the area's limited air traffic and vast areas of flat, undeveloped land. **Air Adventures** (✆ **800/533-6151** or 863/983-6151; www.skydivefl.com) operates a year-round program from the Airglades Airport. If you've never jumped before, you can go on a tandem dive, where you'll be attached to a "jumpmaster." For the first 60 seconds, the two of you free-fall from about 12,500 feet. Then a quick pull of the chute turns your rapid descent into a gentle, balletlike cruise to the ground, with time to see the whole majestic lake from a privileged perspective. Dive packages range from $170 to $195 depending on how many people are jumping. (***Note:*** You must be 18 or older and less than 240 lb.)

WHERE TO STAY

If you aren't camping, book a room at the **Clewiston Inn** ★★, 108 Royal Palm Ave., Clewiston (✆ **800/749-4466** or 863/983-8151; www.clewistoninn.com). Built in 1938, this allegedly haunted, Southern plantation–inspired hotel is the oldest in the Lake

Okeechobee region. Rumor has it that a very friendly, pretty female ghost roams the halls at night. Its 52 rooms are simply decorated and nondescript. The lounge area sports a 1945 mural depicting the animals of the region. Double rooms start at $99 a night; suites begin at $129. All have air-conditioning and TVs.

Another choice, especially if you're here to fish, is **Roland Martin,** 920 E. Del Monte (✆ **800/473-6766** or 863/983-3151; www.rolandmartinmarina.com), the "Disney of fishing." This RV park (no tent sites) has modest motel rooms, efficiencies, condominiums, apartments, RV hookups, and trailers, with two heated pools, gift and marina shops, and a restaurant. The modern complex, dotted with prefab buildings, is clean and well manicured. Rooms rent from $68 to $95; efficiencies cost from $88 to $105. Condominiums are about $150 to $185 a night, with a 3-night minimum. One- or two-bedroom trailers with full kitchen and living room are $65 to $105. Full-hookup RV sites are $30 a night and include power, water, sewage, and cable TV.

Camping

During the winter, campers own the Clewiston area. Campsites are jammed with regulars who come year after year for the simple pleasures of the lake and, of course, the warm weather. Every manner of RV, from simple pop-top Volkswagens to Winnebagos to fully decked-out mobile homes, finds its way to a lakeside campsite.

Okeechobee Landings, U.S. 27 E. (✆ **863/983-4144;** www.okeechobeelandingsrv.com), is one of the best; it has every conceivable amenity included in the price of a site. More than 250 sites are situated around a lake, clubhouse, *pétanque* courts, pool, Jacuzzi, horseshoe pit, shuffleboard court, and tennis court. Full hookup includes a sewage connection, which is not the case throughout the county. Rates start at $39 a day or $193 a week, plus tax, including hookup. Also see **Roland Martin,** described above.

WHERE TO DINE

If you aren't frying up your own catch for dinner, you may want to reconsider it, as dining options here are few and far between. Thank goodness for the **Clewiston Inn** (see "Where to Stay," above), where you can get catfish, beef stroganoff, ham hocks, fried chicken, and liver and onions in a setting as Southern as the food. The dining room is open daily from 6am to 2pm and 5 to 9pm; entrees cost $10 to $18. Sunday brunch is served from 11:30am to 3pm, and a new lunch buffet served Monday through Friday features traditional Southern foods, a salad bar, dessert assortment, and beverage for $8.95. **Lightsey's,** 1040 Rte. 78 (✆ **863/763-4276**), housed in a lodge, started as a fish company and has expanded to a full-service restaurant. Any catch of the day can be broiled, fried, grilled, or steamed. Try the frogs' legs, gator, and catfish. Entrees are less than $10. Open daily from 11am to 9pm. **Flora & Ella's Restaurant and Country Store,** 550 State Highway 80 (✆ **863/675-2891**), is renowned for its pies (about $3 a slice) and old fashioned Southern cookin' ($5–$15).

11

Southwest Florida

Although there are no adobe houses, cacti, or deserts, and, as far as we know, no extra sensory mystics hawking crystals here, Southwest Florida is definitely the Southwest in terms of serenity, golf, retirees, and expensive homes. While the area itself may be staid, and the ride here, through the Everglades, may be the only adventure you'll have in this neck of the woods, it's definitely an area worth exploring.

As primitive as it gets, Alligator Alley (I-75) is the closest thing to a dirt road in South Florida. Once a desolate two-lane road connecting Southeast Florida with the Gulf Coast, Alligator Alley is still pretty quiet, but hardly lifeless, thanks to the presence of the egrets, wood storks, owls, herons, osprey, red-shouldered hawks, belted kingfishers, and, of course, alligators that call the area behind the fenced-in, protected shoulders home. As you go through Alligator Alley, en route to or from Southwest Florida, your cellphone will not work and your only option for refueling will be at the Miccosukee Indian Reservation. Driving through Alligator Alley is like entering a time warp. When you reach the end, you will enter another world, where million-dollar mansions, posh resorts, golf courses, and all the signs of the good life are juxtaposed with nature.

Bordered on the east and south by the Everglades and on the west by an intriguing island-studded coast, Southwest Florida traces its nature-loving roots to inventor and amateur botanist Thomas A. Edison, who was so enamored of it that he spent his last 46 winters in Fort Myers. His friend Henry Ford liked it, too, and built his own winter home next door. The world's best tarpon fishing lured President Theodore Roosevelt and his buddies to the 10,000 or so islands dotting this coast. Some of the planet's best shelling helped entice the du Ponts of Delaware to Gasparilla Island, where they founded the village of Boca Grande. The unspoiled beauty of Sanibel and Captiva islands so entranced Pulitzer Prize–winning political cartoonist J. N. "Ding" Darling that he campaigned to preserve much of those islands in their natural states. Finally, the millionaires who built Naples made their town one of the most alluring—and expensive—in Florida.

Southwest Florida International Airport, on the eastern outskirts of Fort Myers, is this region's major airport (see "Essentials," in section 1, below). From here it's only 20 miles to Sanibel Island, 35 miles to Naples, and 46 miles to Marco Island. If you have a car, you can see the area's sights and participate in most of its activities easily from one base of operations.

EXCURSIONS TO THE EVERGLADES & KEY WEST You won't be in Southwest Florida for long before you see advertisements for excursions to the Everglades. Naples is only 36 miles from Everglades City, the "back door" to wild and wonderful Everglades National Park, so it's easy to combine a visit to the national park with your stay in Southwest Florida. See chapter 8 for full details on the Everglades.

From Southwest Florida, you can also easily make a day trip to Key West by air or sea. **Cape Air** (**© 800/352-0714;** www.flycapeair.com) shuttles its small planes (and Continental Connection planes) several times a day between Key West and both Southwest Florida International Airport and the Naples Municipal Airport. The same-day round-trip fare rate starts at

ATTRACTIONS

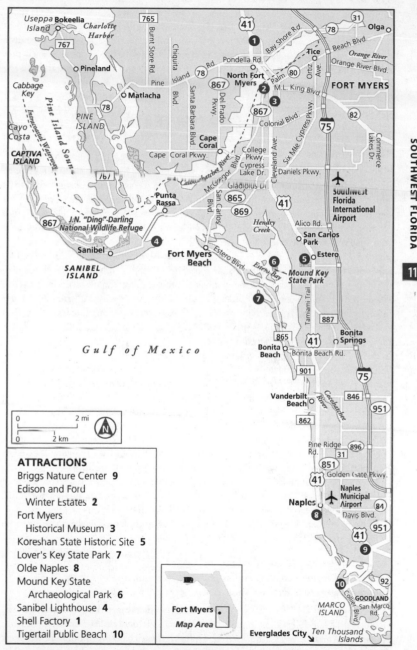

Briggs Nature Center 9
Edison and Ford Winter Estates 2
Fort Myers Historical Museum 3
Koreshan State Historic Site 5
Lover's Key State Park 7
Olde Naples 8
Mound Key State Archaeological Park 6
Sanibel Lighthouse 4
Shell Factory 1
Tigertail Public Beach 10

$209. The **Key West Shuttle** (✆ **888/539-2628** or 239/732-7744; www.keywestshuttle.com) runs to Key West from both Fort Myers Beach and Marco Island between November and May, departing in the morning, arriving in Key West about midday, and beginning the return voyage about 5pm. That gives you about 5 hours in Key West, so you may want to stay there overnight in order to more thoroughly explore the town. Round-trip fare is about $129 for adults, $119 for seniors, and $50 for children 6 to 12. Contact the shuttle for schedules and reservations. See chapter 7 for full details on Key West and the rest of the Keys.

1 FORT MYERS

148 miles NW of Miami; 142 miles S of Tampa; 42 miles N of Naples

Historic Fort Myers has a dual mindset that perhaps can be likened to the two schools of martini drinkers—one has students who consider themselves shaken-not-stirred purists and the other has students who believe in candy-colored cocktails, the brighter and sweeter, the better. The purists usually shudder at the candy-cocktailers, and vice versa. Now replace those opposing martini camps with fans of technological progress and those who believe things were just fine the way they were, and you'll understand the dual mindset of Fort Myers. You see, inventor Thomas Alva Edison came here in 1885 to regain his health after years of incessant toil and the death of his first wife. But unlike most new arrivals, he didn't just merge quietly into the population. Rather, his presence turned the city into one big light bulb: The cows didn't know what hit 'em. Some regret the light bulb ever making its way into Fort Myers. Others couldn't care less.

Today, however, the debate is moot, and the city's prime attractions are the homes built by Edison and Henry Ford on the banks of the Caloosahatchee. Edison planted lush tropical gardens around the two homes and royal palms in front of the properties along McGregor Boulevard, once a cow trail leading from town to the docks at Punta Rassa. If Edison and Ford had never showed up, Fort Myers would probably have been yet another Denny's-lined truck stop. Instead, trees now line McGregor Boulevard for miles and give Fort Myers its nickname: the City of Palms.

> **Impressions**
>
> *There is only one Fort Myers, and 90 million people are going to find out.*
>
> —Thomas Edison

After you've seen the Edison and Ford homes, you'll want to hightail it to the sands of nearby Fort Myers Beach or Sanibel or Captiva islands (see sections 2 and 3, later in this chapter). You also can venture inland and observe incredible amounts of wildlife in river and swamp habitats, including those at the Babcock Ranch, largest of the surviving cattle producers and now a major game preserve.

ESSENTIALS

For the contact information of airline and car services, please see "Appendix: Fast Facts, Toll-Free Numbers & Websites" on p. 638.

GETTING THERE This entire region is served by **Southwest Florida International Airport,** off Daniels Parkway, east of I-75. You can get here on **Air Canada, AirTran, American, America West, Continental, Delta, JetBlue, LTU International, Midwest Airlines, Northwest/KLM, Royal, Spirit, Sun Country, United,** and **US Airways.** The two baggage-claim areas have information booths (with maps) and free phones to various hotels in the region.

Alamo, Avis, Budget, Dollar, Enterprise, Hertz, National, and **Thrifty** have rental cars here.

Vans and **taxis** are available at a booth across the street from baggage claim. The maximum fares for one to three passengers are about $31 to downtown Fort Myers, $45 to Fort Myers Beach, $52 to $70 to Sanibel Island, $75 to Captiva Island, $56 to $85 to Naples, and $85 to Marco Island. It's a dollar more for each additional passenger.

Amtrak (✆ **800/USA-RAIL** [872-7245]; www.amtrak.com) provides bus connections between Fort Myers and its nearest station, in Tampa. The Amtrak buses arrive at and depart from **Greyhound/Trailways** (✆ **800/231-2222;** www.greyhound.com) bus station, at 2275 Cleveland Ave.

VISITOR INFORMATION For advance information on Fort Myers, Fort Myers Beach, and Sanibel and Captiva islands, contact the **Lee Island Coast Visitor and Convention Bureau,** 2180 W. 1st St., Ste. 100, Fort Myers, FL 33901 (✆ **800/237-6444** or 239/338-3500; fax 239/334-1106; www.leeislandcoast.com).

Volunteers staff information booths in the baggage-claim areas at Southwest Florida International Airport. Once you're in town, drop by the **Greater Fort Myers Chamber of Commerce** (✆ **800/366-3622** outside Florida, or 239/332-3624; fax 239/332-7276; www.fortmyers.org), which has a walk-in visitor center at Edwards Drive and Lee Street, on the waterfront. It's open Monday through Friday from 9am to 4:30pm. There's also an information booth at the Edison and Ford Winter Estates (see "Exploring the Area," below).

GETTING AROUND **LeeTran** (✆ **239/275-8726;** www.rideleetran.com) operates public buses. System maps are available from the Greater Fort Myers Chamber of Commerce (see above). There's no public bus service to Sanibel and Captiva islands, but you can connect to the **Fort Myers Beach Trolleys** (p. 334).

For a taxi, call **Yellow Cab** (✆ **239/332-1055**), **Bluebird Taxi** (✆ **239/275-8294**), or **Admiralty Taxi** (✆ **239/275-7000**).

EXPLORING THE AREA

Touring the Estates

Edison and Ford Winter Estates ★★ Thomas Edison and his second wife Mina brought their family to this Victorian retreat—they called it Seminole Lodge—in 1886 and wintered here until the inventor's death, in 1931. Mrs. Edison gave the 14-acre estate to the city of Fort Myers in 1947, and today it's Southwest Florida's top historic attraction. It looks exactly as it did during Edison's lifetime. Costumed actors portraying the Edisons, the Fords, and their friends, such as Harvey S. Firestone, give living-history accounts of how the wealthy lived in those days.

An avid amateur botanist, Edison experimented with the exotic foliage he planted in the lush tropical gardens surrounding the mansion (he turned goldenrod into rubber and used bamboo for light bulb filaments). Some of his light bulbs dating from the 1920s still burn in the laboratory where he and his staff worked on some of his 1,093 inventions. The monstrous banyan tree that shades the laboratory was 4 feet tall when Firestone presented it to Edison in 1925; today, it's the largest specimen in Florida. A museum displays some of Edison's inventions as well as his unique Model-T Ford, a gift from friend Henry Ford.

In 1916, Ford and his wife Clara built Mangoes, the bungalow-style house next door, so they could winter with the Edisons. Like Seminole Lodge, Mangoes is furnished as it appeared in the 1920s. The Fords' home is not as interesting as the Edisons', but when you go to the Edison House, you go through the Ford House, too, as the only way to see either one is on a guided tour that includes both.

2350 McGregor Blvd. ✆ **239/334-7419.** www.efwefla.org. Tour of the homes and gardens $20 adults, $11 children 6–12; tour of botanical gardens only $24 adults, $10 children; for laboratory and museum only $12 adults, $6 children. Daily 9am–5:30pm. (1½-hr. guided and audio tours depart continuously; last tour departs at 4pm daily). Boat rides Mon–Fri 9am–3pm (weather permitting). Closed Thanksgiving and Christmas Day.

Other Downtown Attractions

A good way to explore downtown Fort Myers during the winter season is on a leisurely, 2-hour guided walking tour hosted by the **Southwest Florida Museum of History,** 2300 Peck St., at Jackson Street (✆ **239/321-7430;** www.swflmuseumofhistory.com). The tours are held on Wednesday from 10am to noon and cost $5 for adults, $3 for children. Reservations are required.

The museum itself is housed in the restored Spanish-style depot served by the Atlantic Coast Line from 1924 to 1971. Inside you'll see exhibits depicting the city's history from the ancient Calusa peoples and the Spanish conquistadors to the first settlers. The remains of a P-39 Aircobra helps explain the town's role in training fighter pilots in World War II. Outside stands a replica of an 1800s "cracker" home and the *Esperanza,* the longest and one of the last of the plush Pullman private cars. Admission is $9.50 for adults, $8.50 for seniors, and $5 for children 3 to 12. Open Tuesday through Saturday from 10am to 5pm.

The Georgian Revival **Burroughs Home,** 2505 1st St., at Fowler Street (✆ **239/337-9505;** www.cityftmyers.com/attractions/burroughs.aspx), was built on the banks of the Caloosahatchee River in 1901 by cattleman John Murphy and later sold to the Burroughs family. The home is reserved solely for weddings and events but open to the public for guided tours by appointment only.

To avoid the kids going batty on a rainy day, head for the **Imaginarium,** 2000 Cranford Ave., at Martin Luther King, Jr., Boulevard (✆ **239/337-3332;** www.imaginarium fortmyers.com), a hands-on museum in the old city water plant. A host of toylike exhibits explain basic scientific principles such as gravity and the weather. Admission is $8 for adults, $7 for seniors, and $5 for children 3 to 12. Open Monday through Saturday from 10am to 5pm, Sunday noon to 5pm. Closed Thanksgiving, Christmas, and Easter.

A Nearby Historic Attraction

Koreshan State Historic Site Worth a 15-mile drive south of downtown Fort Myers if you're into canoeing or quirky gurus, these 300 acres on the narrow Estero River were home to the Koreshan Unity Movement (pronounced Ko-*resh*-en), a sect led by Chicagoan Cyrus Reed Teed. The Koreshans—who should not be confused with the late, disturbing Branch Davidian leader David Koresh—believed that humans lived *inside* the earth and—ahead of their time—that women should have equal rights. They established a self-sufficient settlement here in 1894. You can visit their garden and several of their buildings, plus view photos from the archives.

Canoeists will find marked trails winding down the slow-flowing river to **Mound Key,** an islet made of the shells discarded by the Calusa Indians (see "Canoeing & Kayaking" under "Outdoor Activities & Spectator Sports," below). There's also a picnic and camping

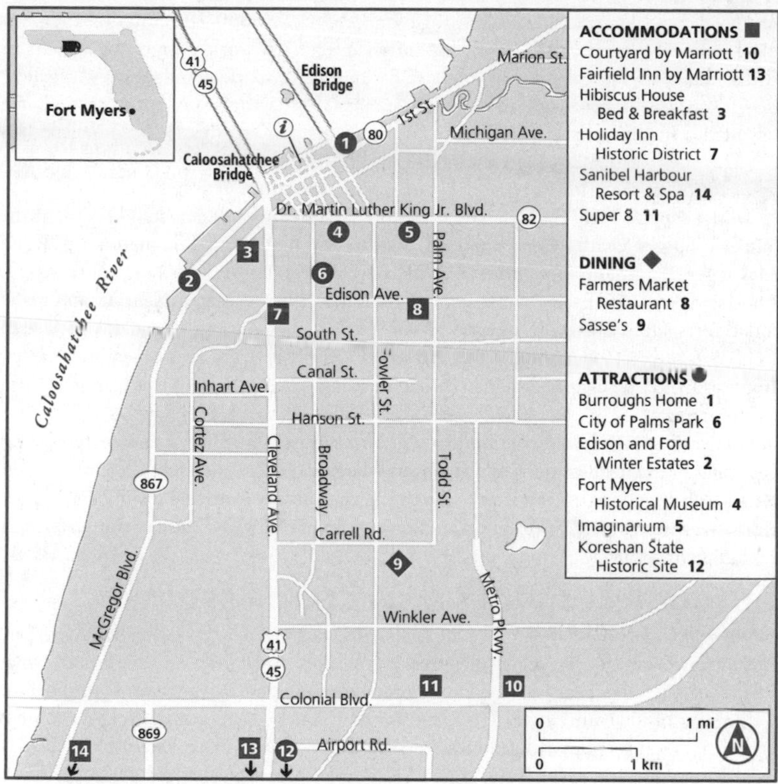

area with 60 wooded sites for tents and RVs. For information, contact the park superintendent at 3800 Corkscrew Rd., Estero, FL 33928.

U.S. 41 at Corkscrew Rd., Estero (15 miles south of downtown Fort Myers). ✆ **239/992-0311.** www.floridastateparks.org/koreshan. Admission $4 per vehicle for up to 8 people, $3 for a single-occupant vehicle, $1 per pedestrian or biker; tours $2 adults, $1 children 6–12. Canoes $5.30 per hour, $27 per day. Camping $22. Park daily 8am–sunset; settlement buildings daily 8am–5pm; 1-hr. tours Sat–Sun 1pm. From I-75, take Corkscrew Rd. (exit 19), go 2 miles west, and cross U.S. 41 into the site.

An Old-Fashioned Train Ride

For those who claim there's little excitement or intrigue to be had in these parts, consider a ride on the **Seminole Gulf Railway** (✆ **800/736-4853** or 239/275-8487; www.semgulf.com), the original railroad that ran between Fort Myers and Naples. Today it chugs on daytime sightseeing trips and evening dinner/murder-mystery excursions south to Bonita Springs and north across the river. Call for the schedule and reservations, which are required for the dinner trips. The trains depart Fort Myers from its Colonial Station, a small, coral-colored building on Colonial Boulevard at Metro Parkway. The Bonita Springs station is on Old U.S. 41 at Pennsylvania Avenue.

SHOPPING

A kitschy (read: tacky) tourist attraction, the **Shell Factory and Nature Park,** 5 miles north of the Caloosahatchee River Bridge on U.S. 41 (© **800/282-5805** or 239/995-2141; www.shellfactory.com), not only carries one of the world's largest collections of shells, corals, sponges, and fossils, but also has bumper-boat rides, a light show, a gallery of African art, a small zoo, and two restaurants. Inside the store, entire sections are devoted to shell jewelry and shell lamps; many items cost less than $10, some less than $1. The Shell Factory is good for a rainy day, but if it's sunny, why pay for shells when you can collect them for free on the beach? Open daily from 9am to 9pm.

Outlet shoppers will find a large Levi's store, among other major-brand shops, at the **Sanibel Tanger Outlet Center,** on the way to the beaches at Summerlin Road and McGregor Boulevard (© **888/471-3939** or 239/454-1974; www.tangeroutlet.com). Another Levi's, plus Brooks Brothers, Donna Karan, Nike, Reebok, Nautica, and many more stores, are at the much larger **Miromar Outlets,** on Corkscrew Road at I-75, Estero (© **239/948-3766;** www.miromar.com), about halfway between Fort Myers and Naples. Both outlet malls are open Monday through Saturday from 10am to 9pm, Sunday from 11am to 6pm.

A once sleepy bedroom community near Fort Myers, Cape Coral now features great shopping in the form of the **Cape Harbour Marina** (5703 Cape Harbour Dr.; © **239/945-6116;** www.capeharbour.com), a yachting community featuring quaint shops, boutiques, and restaurants, including **Rumrunners** (© **239/542-0200**), a fun waterfront restaurant and bar.

OUTDOOR ACTIVITIES & SPECTATOR SPORTS

CANOEING & KAYAKING The area's slow-moving rivers and quiet, island-speckled inland waters are fine for canoe and kayak adventures; you'll visit with birds and manatees along the way. Two popular local venues are the winding waterways around Pine Island west of town and the Estero River south of Fort Myers. The Estero River route is an official Florida canoe trail and leads 3.5 miles from U.S. 41 to Estero Bay, which is itself a state aquatic preserve (p. 334). The whole trail is part of the 190-mile Great Calusa Blueway (www.calusablueway.com). Near the mouth of the river lies **Mound Key State Archaeological Park,** one of the largest Calusa shell middens. Scholars believe that this mostly artificial island dates back some 2,000 years and was the capital of the Calusa chief who ruled all of South Florida when the Spanish arrived. There's no park ranger on the Key, but signs explain its history.

Koreshan State Historic Site, a half-mile south of the bridge at the intersection of U.S. 41 and Corkscrew Road (© **239/992-0311**), has canoe rentals (see "A Nearby Historic Attraction," above). Less than a mile from the site, at the Estero River bridge, **Estero River Tackle & Canoe Outfitters,** 20991 S. Tamiami Trail (U.S. 41), Estero (© **239/992-4050;** www.esteroriveroutfitters.com), offers guided historic and nature tours (call for schedule and prices) and rents canoes and kayaks from 7am to 5pm for $17 to $50 a day. Open daily from 7am to 6pm. Boats must be back by 5pm.

Tropic Star Cruises, based at Pineland Marina, 3921 Waterfront Dr., Pineland on Pine Island (© **239/283-0015;** www.tropicstarcruises.com), rents kayaks and has guided tours over 18 miles of paddling trails. Rentals cost $40 a day for single-seaters, $50 for doubles. Call for schedules and prices of guided tours. The company also has a ferry service to Cayo Costa State Park, where it rents kayaks (p. 359).

GOLF & TENNIS For an excellent rundown of Southwest Florida golf courses, pick up a free copy of *Golfer's Guide,* available at the visitor centers and many hotel lobbies, as well as online at www.golfersguide.com. See p. 57 for information on subscribing or ordering the current edition. Don't forget that you can call **Tee Times USA** (✆ **800/374-8633** or 888/465-3356; www.teetimesusa.com) to book starting times at Florida courses.

Although it looks like an exclusive private enclave, the **Fort Myers Country Club,** McGregor Boulevard at Hill Avenue (✆ **239/321-7489;** www.cityftmyers.com/Attractions/FortMyersCountryClub/tabid/115/Default.aspx), is a municipal course. Designed in 1917 by Donald Ross, it's flat and uninteresting by today's standards, but it's right in town. A steak-and-seafood restaurant now occupies the fine old clubhouse. The municipal course is the more challenging **Eastwood Golf Club,** on Ortiz Avenue between Colonial Boulevard and Dr. Martin Luther King, Jr., Boulevard (✆ **239/321-7487;** www.cityftmyers.com/attractions/golf/eastwood.aspx), in the eastern suburbs. Eastwood received a major renovation in 2007. Greens fees at both courses range from $25 to $45. Nonresidents must book tee times 24 hours in advance.

Other area courses open to the public include a signature Jack Nicklaus, Audubon-certified, standalone course, **Old Corkscrew Golf Course** (✆ **239/949-4700**), just east of I-75 off Corkscrew Road. Over in Bonita Springs is the **Raptor Bay Golf Club** (✆ **239/390-4600**), a par 71, 18-hole course measuring 6,702 yards.

SPECTATOR SPORTS While many baseball teams have jumped around Florida for spring training, the Red Sox and the Twins have worked out in Fort Myers for years. The **Boston Red Sox** play at the 6,990-seat **City of Palms Park,** Edison Avenue and Broadway (✆ **877/733-7699** or 239/334-4799; www.redsox.mlb.com). Tickets range from $10 to $50. The **Minnesota Twins** work out at the 7,500-seat **Bill Hammond Stadium** in the Lee County Sports Complex, on Six Mile Cypress Parkway, between Daniels Parkway and Metro Parkway (✆ **800/338-9467** or 239/768-4200; www.twins.mlb.com). The Twins' minor-league affiliate, the **Fort Myers Miracle** (✆ **239/768-4210;** www.miraclebaseball.com), play in the stadium April through August. Ticket prices range from $5 to $8.

The **Florida Everblades** (✆ **239/948-7825;** www.floridaeverblades.com) play minor-league professional hockey October through April at **Germain Arena,** at exit 19 off I-75 in Estero. Tickets range from $12 to $34.

WHERE TO STAY

If you're looking for a stay in a hotel with personality in Fort Myers proper, you're not going to find it. For that, you'll have to head to Fort Myers Beach (p. 333). But if you're looking for bargains and don't mind driving to the beach, Fort Myers has just about every chain hotel imaginable. Most are quite clean and reliable.

As in the rest of South Florida, winter room rates here are highest, and reservations essential, from mid-December to April. Even the chain hotels and motels along U.S. 41 in Fort Myers—most brands are represented along this thoroughfare—charge premium rates then. During the off-season, however, prices drop by as much as 50% or more.

If you can't get a room at the properties mentioned below, the **Lee Island Coast Visitor and Convention Bureau** operates a free reservations service (✆ **800/733-7935**), covering many more accommodations in Fort Myers, Fort Myers Beach, and Sanibel and Captiva islands.

A few blocks from the Edison and Ford homes, the **Hibiscus House Bed & Breakfast,** 2135 McGregor Blvd., at Clifford Street (✆ **239/332-2651;** fax 239/332-8922; www.thehibiscushouse.net), is a must-stay for B&B fans, with five comfortable rooms, each with private bathroom, in a charming, nearly 100-year-old wooden house. The building was later split in two, floated across the river, and nailed back together. The inn's owners, Leslie and Bill Seiden, bring 20-plus years of culinary experience (as the former owner of haute caterer A Moveable Feast in New York's tony Hamptons). Rates are $119 to $169.

Chain lodgings in the area include **Courtyard by Marriott,** 4455 Metro Pkwy., at Colonial Boulevard (© **800/321-2211** or 239/275-8600; www.marriott.com); **Fairfield Inn by Marriott,** 7090 Cypress Terrace, off U.S. 41, a block south of Daniels Parkway (© **800/228-2800** or 239/437-5600; www.marriott.com); and **Super 8,** 2717 Colonial Blvd. (© **800/800-8000** or 239/275-3500; www.super8.com).

Many business travelers opt for the Art Deco **Holiday Inn Historic District,** 2431 Cleveland Ave. (U.S. 41), at Edison Avenue (© **239/332-3232**). Its location, a 2-block walk to the Red Sox training facility and a short drive to the Edison and Ford homes, is a plus for vacationers, too. Minor-league hopefuls stay here during spring training, so you could meet a future major-leaguer.

All hotel bills in Southwest Florida are subject to an 11% tax.

The only campground with tent sites near here is **Koreshan State Historic Site** (p. 328).

Sanibel Harbour Resort & Spa ★★★ Kids This seaside resort is nestled on a tranquil 85-acre peninsula overlooking San Carlos Bay and Sanibel Island (a resort shuttle provides guests complimentary transportation daily to the island's beaches and to a bike-rental shop). The resort's 400 units are in the hotel tower, the concierge-style **Grande Bay at Sanibel Harbour,** and two condominium towers, all modern and luxurious. All have balconies with water and island views. Five outdoor pools and a bayside beach offer relaxing sunning areas. The spa features over 60 treatments, including the incredible and almost indescribable BETAR bed, one of only 16 such systems in the world, in which the body is bathed in sound waves to create a state of total relaxation. There's also a world-class fitness center, five clay tennis courts, and an assortment of classes and clinics daily. The resort is a fabulous vacation destination for families.

17260 Harbour Pointe Rd., Fort Myers, FL 33908. © **800/767-7777** or 239/466-4000. Fax 239/466-2150. www.sanibel-resort.com. 400 units, including 53 condo apts. Winter $269–$509 double, $429–$569 suite, $529–$729 condo apt; off-season $169–$449 double, $229–$519 suite, $329–$499 condo apt. Daily resort fee is $15 per unit, per day. Packages available. AE, DC, DISC, MC, V. Valet parking $20; self-parking free. Take the last exit off Summerlin Rd. before the Sanibel Causeway toll plaza. **Amenities:** 6 restaurants and lounges; 6 pools (1 indoor); 5 clay tennis courts; health club; spa; watersports equipment/rentals; concierge; children's programs; activities desk; business center; room service; laundry service; dry cleaning. *In room:* A/C, TV, high-speed Internet access, kitchen (in condos), minibar (in hotel tower rooms), minifridge (in Grande Bay building), coffeemaker, hair dryer, iron, safe.

WHERE TO DINE

Fort Myers's main commercial strip, Cleveland Avenue (U.S. 41), is where you'll find most of the national fast-food and family chain restaurants, especially near College Parkway.

Moderate

Sasse's ★★ Finds CONTINENTAL/ITALIAN In a small shopping strip north of the Edison Mall, this informal, often-noisy spot (pronounced sassy, people refer to it as Sassy's) affords one of the area's most unusual and reasonably priced dining experiences. Aromas waft from the wood-fired oven in the open kitchen, from which come enormous slabs of pizzalike bread (served with seasoned olive oil for dipping). The selections change daily, though you can usually count on braised lamb shank served over polenta, as well as veal scaloppini stuffed with prosciutto, roasted peppers, and mozzarella. It's all of a quality rarely found at these prices, and the portions are so huge that most patrons carry home doggie bags. Note that reservations are not accepted (and preference is sometimes given to regulars), so be prepared to wait for a table, especially on weekends. I've gotten complaints about the service here, though I've never personally had a bad experience. Be sure to ask about the restaurant's wine cellar, the Barrel Room, where they offer wine tastings and classes.

3651 Evans Ave., in Carrell Corner shopping center (btw. Carrell Rd. and Winkler Ave.). ✆ **239/278-5544.** Main courses $12–$22. No credit cards. Tues–Sat 5:30–8:30pm; Tues–Fri 11:30am–1:30pm.

Inexpensive

Farmer's Market Restaurant ★★ Finds SOUTHERN Cabbage, okra, green beans, and tomatoes at the retail Farmers Market next door provide fodder for some of Florida's best country-style cooking at this plain and simple restaurant, frequented by everyone from business executives to truck drivers. Specialties are beef and pork barbecue from the tin smokehouse out by Edison Avenue, plus other Southern favorites such as country-fried steak, fried chicken livers and gizzards, fried Lake Okeechobee catfish, and smoked ham hocks with a bowl of lima beans. Yankees can order fried chicken, roast beef, or pork chops, and hash browns instead of grits with the big breakfast. But forget about Southern Comfort: No alcohol is served.

2736 Edison Ave. (at Cranford Ave.). ✆ **239/334-1687.** www.farmersmarketrestaurant.com. Breakfast $3–$10; sandwiches $3–$10; main courses $6–$12. No credit cards. Mon–Sat 6am–8pm; Sun 6am–7pm.

FORT MYERS AFTER DARK

For the most part, Fort Myers shuts down after dark, and the pay-per-view on your hotel room's TV may be your best bet for entertainment. But some activities do take place when the sun goes down. For entertainment ideas and schedules, consult the daily *News-Press* (www.news-press.com), especially Friday's "Gulf Coasting" section. Also be on the lookout for *Happenings,* a tabloid-size entertainment guide distributed free at the visitor centers and in some hotel lobbies. Tickets for most events are available from **Ticketmaster** (✆ **239/334-3309;** www.ticketmaster.com).

The city's showcase performing-arts venue is the **Barbara B. Mann Performing Arts Hall** ★, 8099 College Pkwy., at Summerlin Road (✆ **800/440-7469,** or 239/481-4849 for tickets; www.bbmannpah.com), on the campus of Edison State College. It features world-famous performers and Broadway plays.

Originally a downtown vaudeville playhouse, the 1908-vintage **Arcade Theater,** 2267 1st St., between Bay and Hendry streets (✆ **239/332-4488**), presents a variety of performances. The **Broadway Palm Dinner Theatre,** 1380 Colonial Blvd. (✆ **239/278-4422**), is a popular dinner buffet and show venue.

2 FORT MYERS BEACH ★★

13 miles S of Fort Myers; 28 miles N of Naples; 12 miles E of Sanibel Island

Often overshadowed by trendy Sanibel and Captiva islands to the northwest and by ritzy Naples to the south, down-to-earth Fort Myers Beach, which occupies all of skinny Estero Island, has just as much sun and sand as its affluent neighbors, both a half-hour drive away, but more moderate prices. In fact, if you're looking for that Jimmy Buffet–style of slacking, Fort Myers Beach is where it's at.

Droves of families and young singles flock to the busy intersection of San Carlos Boulevard and Estero Boulevard, an area so packed with bars, beach-apparel shops, restaurants, and motels that the locals call it "Times Square." That Coney Island image certainly doesn't apply to the rest of Estero Island, where old-fashioned beach cottages, manicured condominiums, and quiet motels beckon couples and families in search of more sedate vacations. In fact, promoters of the southern end of the island don't even say they're in Fort Myers Beach; rather, they're on Estero Island. It's their way of distinguishing their part of town from congested Times Square.

Narrow Matanzas Pass leads into broad Estero Bay, which separates the island from the mainland. While the pass is the area's largest commercial fishing port (when they say "fresh off the boat" here, they aren't kidding), the bay is an official state aquatic preserve inhabited by a host of birds as well as manatees, dolphins, and other sea life. Nature cruises go forth onto this lovely protected bay, which is dotted with islands.

A few miles south of Fort Myers Beach, a chain of pristine barrier islands includes unspoiled Lovers Key, a state park where a tractor-pulled tram runs through a mangrove forest to one of Florida's best beaches.

ESSENTIALS

GETTING THERE See section 1 on Fort Myers, beginning on p. 326, for information about Southwest Florida International Airport, car-rental firms, Amtrak trains, and Greyhound/Trailways bus service to the area.

VISITOR INFORMATION You can get advance information from the **Lee County Visitor and Convention Bureau** (p. 327) and from the **Fort Myers Beach Chamber of Commerce,** 17200 San Carlos Blvd., Fort Myers Beach, FL 33931 (© **800/782-9283** or 239/454-7500; fax 239/454-7910; www.fortmyersbeach.org), which also sells a detailed street map ($2) and operates a visitor center on the mainland portion of San Carlos Boulevard, just south of Summerlin Road. The chamber is open Monday through Friday from 9am to 5pm, Saturday from 10am to 5pm, and Sunday from 11am to 5pm.

GETTING AROUND Estero Island is absolutely inundated with traffic during the peak winter months, but you can get around on the **Beach Trolley,** which runs every hour, daily from 6:10am to 8:10pm, along the length of Estero Boulevard from Bowditch Regional Park at the north end south to Lovers Key. In winter, the **Beach Park & Ride Trolley** runs daily from 6:10am to 8:10pm between Summerlin Square Shopping Center, on the mainland at Summerlin Road and San Carlos Boulevard, to Bowditch Regional Park. Both trolleys cost 50¢ per person. Ask your hotel staff or call **LeeTran** (© **239/275-8726;** www.rideleetran.com) for more info.

For a cab, call **Local Motion Taxi** (© **239/463-4111**).

There are no bike paths, per se, although many folks ride along the paved shoulders of Estero Boulevard. A variety of rental bikes, scooters, and in-line skates are available at **Fun Rentals,** 1901 Estero Blvd., at Ohio Avenue (© **239/463-8844;** www.funrentals.org). Rates start at $55 a day for one-passenger scooters, $18 a day for bikes.

HITTING THE BEACH

A prime attraction for beachgoers and nature lovers alike is the gorgeous **Lovers Key State Park ★★★**, 8700 Estero Blvd. (© **239/463-4588;** www.floridastateparks.org/loverskey), on the totally preserved Lovers Key, south of Estero Island. Although the highway runs down the center of the island, access to this unspoiled beach from the parking lot is restricted to footpaths and a tractor-pulled tram through a bird-filled forest

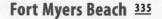

of mangroves. The beach itself is known for its multitude of shells. Facilities include a snack shop and bathhouses with outdoor showers. The park is open daily from 8am to sunset. Admission is $5 per vehicle with two to eight occupants, $3 for vehicles with a single occupant, and $1 for pedestrians and bicyclists. No alcohol is allowed, nor are pets permitted on the beach or in the water (you must keep them on a leash elsewhere in the park).

On Estero Island, **Lynn Hall Memorial Park** has a fishing pier and beach in the middle of Times Square. It has changing rooms, restrooms, and one of the few public parking lots in the area; the meter costs $1 hour, so keep it fed. At the island's north end, **Bowditch Regional Park** has picnic tables, showers, and changing rooms. Parking is only for drivers with disabilities permits, but the park is also the turnaround point for the Beach Connection Trolley.

Several beach locations are hotbeds of parasailing, jet-skiing, sailboating, and other beach activities. **Times Square,** at San Carlos and Estero boulevards, and the **Best Western Beach Resort,** about a quarter-mile north, are popular spots on Estero's busy north end. Other hot spots are **Diamond Head Beach Resort** (p. 337), just south of Times

 Square, and the **Junkanoo Beach Bar** (p. 341), in the midbeach area. Down south, activities are centered on the **Outrigger Beach Resort** (p. 338).

OUTDOOR ACTIVITIES

BOATING & BOAT RENTALS Powerboats are available from the **Snook Bight Marina** (✆ **239/765-4371**), the **Fort Myers Beach Marina** (✆ **239/463-9552**), the **Fish Tale Marina** (✆ **239/463-3600**), and **Salty Sam's Marina** (✆ **239/463-7333;** www.saltysamsmarina.com). **Holiday Watersports** (✆ **239/765-4386;** www.holidaywatersportsfmb.com) rents brand-new boats at the Pink Shell Beach Resort, on Estero Island's northern end. Boat rental costs about $130 for a half-day, $200 to $600 for a full day.

For canoers and kayakers, the big news is that the beaches of Fort Myers and Sanibel have rolled out the **Great Calusa Blueway** (www.greatcalusablueway.com), a new 40-mile paddling trail that covers the waters of Lovers Key State Recreation Area; Mound Key State Archaeological Site; Koreshan State Historic Site; Fort Myers Beach; and Sanibel, Captiva, and Pine islands, ending at Cayo Costa. Even cooler, the Blueway utilizes GPS technology, marking key points along the trail to aid navigation. **Kayak Excursions** (✆ **239/297-7011;** www.kayak-excursions.com) offers rentals; guided tours including wildlife, manatee, and full moon tours; and kayak classes.

For an action-packed thrill ride in a cigarette-style, 14-passenger speedboat, check out **Sea Rocket USA** (✆ **239/233-1578;** www.searocketusa.com), 1030 Estero Blvd., which whisks passengers up to 70 mph and then slows down so you can catch a glimpse of dolphins. Cost is $35 per person for 75 minutes and $500 per person for 4 hours.

The **Key West Express** (✆ **239/463-5733**) offers daily boat service from Fort Myers Beach to Key West for $129 per person round-trip. The boat leaves from Salty Sam's Marina, 2200 Main St.

FISHING You can surf-cast, throw your line off the pier at Times Square, or venture offshore on a number of charter-fishing boats here. The staff at **Getaway Marina,** 18400 San Carlos Blvd., about a half-mile north of the Sky Bridge (✆ **239/466-3600;** www.getawaymarina.com), is adept at matching clients with skilled charter-boat skippers. Expect to spend about $175 per person for a full day's fishing for up to six persons, $55 for a half-day.

No reservations are required on party boats that take groups out. Operating year-round, the ***Great Getaway*** and ***Great Getaway II*** (✆ **239/466-3600**) sail from the Getaway Marina, about a half-mile north of the bridge. Boats depart between 9am and 3pm; cost $55 per adult, $30 for kids, and $25 for those who don't fish; and have air-conditioned lounges with bars. Call for details and reservations.

SCUBA DIVING & SNORKELING Scuba diving is available at **Seahorse Scuba,** 15600 San Carlos Blvd. (✆ **239/872-6295;** www.seahorsescubaftmyers.com). Two-tank dives start at $75. In business since 1989, the company also teaches diver-certification courses.

Playing in the Sand

At the **American Sandsculpting Festival,** held each November on Fort Myers Beach, sand sculptors from around the world compete for prize money in two competitions, one for amateurs and one for pros.

The liveaboard dive boat ***Ultimate Getaway,*** based at Rick's Marina, 18450 San Carlos Blvd. (✆ **239/466-0466;** www.ultimategetaway.net), makes 4- and 5-day voyages to the Dry Tortugas (70 miles west of Key West). This 100-foot vessel carries a maximum of 20 divers and is equipped with a dive platform, chase boat, and TV/DVD. Price varies and includes tanks, weights, belt, food, and soft drinks. Reservations are essential.

SHOPPING

A swank shopping center, the **Shops at Coconut Point,** 7996 Mediterranean Dr. (✆ **239/992-4259**), opened in Estero in late 2006. It has 135 shops and restaurants, including bebe, Coldwater Creek, Guess, J. Crew, Lucky Brand Jeans, Marciano, Sigrid Olsen, Talbots, Tommy Bahama, Bice Grand Cafe, Blue Water Bistro, the Grillroom, California Pizza Kitchen, the Grape, and Ruth's Chris Steak House.

WHERE TO STAY

The **Hyatt Regency Coconut Point Resort & Spa,** 5001 Coconut Rd., Bonita Springs (✆ **239/444-1234;** www.coconutpoint.hyatt.com), opened in 2006, featuring 454 guest rooms, tropical gardens, water views, multiple swimming pools, and a convenient location right next to the Shops at Coconut Point (see above). Rates are $229 to $339 in high season and $149 to $299 in off-season.

The hostelries recommended below are removed from the crowds of Times Square, but some chain motels provide comfortable accommodations close to the center of the action: The best one, the midrise **Best Western Beach Resort** (✆ **800/336-4045** or 239/463-6000), is a quarter-mile north, just far enough to escape the noise but still have a lively beach.

Sunstream Resorts, 6640 Estero Blvd., Fort Myers Beach (✆ **800/625-4111;** www.sunstream.com), manages "condominium hotels" that include the plush **Casa Playa,** 510 Estero Blvd. (✆ **800/569-4876** or 239/765-0510; www.casaplayaresort.com), and the **Lovers Key Beach Club & Resort,** 8771 Estero Blvd. (✆ **877/798-4879** or 239/765-1040; www.loverskey.com). The latter is on the north end of Lovers Key. The 60 spacious apartments in the older, 16-story **Pointe Estero Island Resort,** 6640 Estero Blvd. (✆ **239/765-1155**), all have whirlpool tubs and screened balconies with gorgeous Gulf or bay views. The less expensive **Santa Maria,** 7317 Estero Blvd. (✆ **239/765-6700**), is on the bay side of the island.

For campers, the somewhat-cramped **Red Coconut RV Resort,** 3001 Estero Blvd. (✆ **239/463-7200;** fax 239/463-2609; www.redcoconut.com), has sites for RVs and tents both on the Gulf side of the road and right on the beach. Rates range from $75 to $103.

Expensive

Diamond Head Beach Resort ★ This luxurious 12-story beachside building sports large, comfortable one-bedroom apartments. Sliding-glass doors lead from both the living quarters and bedrooms to screened balconies. The beachfront apartments are the most appealing, but every unit has a view (spectacular from the upper floors). Each room was renovated in 2006 and has a private 700-square-foot balcony, a sleeper sofa, two TVs, and a kitchen area. There's a full-service restaurant indoors, and Cabana's Beach Bar provides libation and light lunches beside the pool. During the winter season, evidence of nightlife can be found at the hotel's lounge, which has live music. If it's summer, however, you're on your own.

 2000 Estero Blvd. (at Palm Ave.), Fort Myers Beach, FL 33931. ✆ **888/765-5002** or 239/765-1694. Fax 239/765-1694. www.diamondheadfl.com. 124 units. Winter $225–$355 suite; off-season $189–$229 suite. AE, DISC, MC, V. **Amenities:** 2 restaurants; 2 bars; heated outdoor pool; exercise room; Jacuzzi; watersports equipment/rental; children's programs; limited room service; laundry service; coin-op washers/dryers. *In room:* A/C, TV, dataport, kitchen, fridge, coffeemaker, hair dryer, iron, microwave.

Edison Beach House All Suites Hotel ★★ No standardized list of amenities does justice to this obsessive-compulsively clean, intimate, five-story, nonsmoking beachside inn; when owner Larry Yax built it in 1999, he equipped every unit as if he were going to live in it. Each of the light and airy rooms has a balcony, ceiling fan, fully equipped kitchen (look for your complimentary bag of popcorn in the microwave oven), writing desk stocked with office supplies, and linen closet packed with extra towels. Also, 47-inch HDTVs and high-speed Internet access have been added to every room. Most of the bathrooms also have washer/dryers. The freshly laundered bedspreads provided to each new guest are but one example of the premium Larry puts on cleanliness. The beachfront units have the best views, but much more romantic are the "A" suites, whose queen-size beds are almost surrounded by windows formed by a turret on one corner of the building—you'll wake up to a panoramic view.

830 Estero Blvd., Fort Myers Beach, FL 33931. ✆ **800/399-2511** or 239/463-1530. Fax 239/765-9430. www.edisonbeachhouse.com. 24 units. Winter $140–$395 double; off-season $125–$195 double. AE, DISC, MC, V. **Amenities:** Heated outdoor pool; laundry service. *In room:* A/C, TV, dataport, high-speed Internet access, kitchen, coffeemaker, hair dryer, iron, washers/dryers (in most units).

Pink Shell Beach Resort & Spa ★★ Kids Nestled at the tip of Estero Island between trendy Naples and laid-back Sanibel and Captiva islands, the 12-acre Pink Shell features deluxe studio and villa-style accommodations all overlooking the beach. Located along a quarter-mile stretch of sugar-white sands along the Gulf of Mexico, the resort offers an array of activities, including various watersports. In addition, guests will experience a broad range of facilities and amenities including sailing with Colgate Offshore Sailing School or a dolphin-sightseeing tour on a WaveRunner. Sip cocktails poolside at Bongo's or enjoy waterfront dining at JoJo's. The new, 6,000-square-foot Aquagēne Spa offers a slew of relaxing treatments. The kids will love Octopool, an undersea fantasy pool, or spending a day of adventure with the Kidds Kampp crew. There's also a new state-of-the-art gym for workout fiends.

275 Estero Blvd., Fort Myers Beach, FL 33931. ✆ **800/237-5786** or 239/463-6181. Fax 239/463-1229. www.pinkshell.com. 225 units. Winter $359–$619 villas or studios; off-season $259–$519 villas or studios. Packages are available. AE, DC, DISC, MC, V. **Amenities:** 3 restaurants (1 closed in off-season); 3 bars; 4 heated outdoor pools; 1 kid's wading pool; watersports equipment/rentals; bike rentals; children's programs; dry cleaning; laundry facilities. *In room:* A/C, TV, high-speed Internet, kitchen, fridge, coffeemaker, hair dryer, iron, safe, microwave.

Moderate

Outrigger Beach Resort Well known for its beachside Tiki bar, this clean, pleasant motel has been owned and operated by the same family since 1965. The "garden efficiencies" in the original building have the feel of small cottages, with excellent ventilation through both front and rear windows, and doors opening to backyard decks. Other buildings here are two-story blocks containing motel-style rooms and efficiencies with views of the large parking lot. The beachside bar is one of the best places in Fort Myers Beach to watch the sun set.

6200 Estero Blvd., Fort Myers Beach, FL 33931. ✆ **800/749-3131** or 239/463-3131. Fax 239/463-6577. www.outriggerfmb.com. 144 units. Winter $200–$310 double; off-season $160–$195 double. AE, MC, V.

Amenities: Restaurant; bar; heated outdoor pool; exercise room; game room; coin-op washers/dryers. *In room:* A/C, TV, dataport, kitchen (in efficiencies), fridge, coffeemaker (in efficiencies), hair dryer, safe.

Sandpiper Gulf Resort Reminiscent of a private condo right on Fort Myers Beach, the Sandpiper Gulf Resort comprises two low-rise buildings, both with front-row access to the beach and the tropical garden courtyards, in case the sand should get too hot. Suites are the beachfront apartments you always wanted to own, but could never afford, and, much to our delight, brand-new suites were introduced in 2006 and feature DIRECTV, DVD players, and wireless Internet access. Shuffleboard courts are delightfully retro, as are the guests (who tend to be on the retired side).

5550 Estero Blvd., Fort Myers Beach, FL 33931. ✆ **800/584-1449** or 239/463-5721. Fax 239/765-0039. www.sandpipergulfresort.com. 63 units. Winter $100–$175 double; off-season $90–$125 double. Additional person $8. AE, DC, DISC, MC, V. **Amenities:** 2 heated pools; Jacuzzi. *In room:* A/C, TV/DVD, dataport, Wi-Fi, kitchen, coffeemaker.

Inexpensive

Edgewater Inn ★ **Value** Located on the quiet, north end of Estero Island right on the bay, the three-story Edgewater Inn has two one-bedroom and four two-bedroom apartments, all with screened lanais. They're available on a weekly basis in winter and for 3-day minimum stays off-season and are closed from July to September. Free beach chairs, bicycles, and barbecue grills are available for guests' use. Just 300 feet from the beach, Edgewater is an ideal spot for peace, quiet, location, and value.

781 Estero Blvd., Fort Myers Beach, FL 33931. ✆ **800/951-9975** or 239/765-5959. Fax 239/765-0090. www.edgewaterinnfmb.com. 6 units. Winter $900–$1,700 apt per week; off-season $450–$950 apt per week. MC, V. **Amenities:** Heated outdoor pool; access to nearby health club; free laundry facilities. *In room:* A/C, TV, full kitchen, hair dryer, iron.

Palm Terrace Apartments ★ **Value** Many European guests stay in these comfortable apartments about midway down the beach. In fact, between them, husband-and-wife owners Peter Piazza and Deborah Bowers speak fluent German and French and passable Italian. Their smaller, less-expensive units are on the ground level, with sliding-glass doors opening to a grassy yard, but even these rooms have full kitchens with dishwashers. Larger units are upstairs, with screened porches or decks overlooking a courtyard with a heated pool, a shuffleboard court, and a charcoal grill for barbecuing. Public access to the beach is across Estero Boulevard. There's no daily maid service, but you'll have an ample supply of clean linens.

3333 Estero Blvd., Fort Myers Beach, FL 33931. ✆ **800/320-5783** or 239/765-5783. Fax 239/765-5783. www.palm-terrace.com. 8 units. Winter $111–$167 double; off-season $62–$102 double. 3-day minimum stay required in winter. Weekly rates available. AE, DISC, MC, V. **Amenities:** Heated outdoor pool; access to nearby health club; coin-op washers/dryers. *In room:* A/C, TV/VCR, Wi-Fi, kitchen, coffeemaker.

WHERE TO DINE

The busy area around Times Square has fast-food joints to augment several local restaurants catering to the beach crowd. The best of these is the **Beach Pierside Grill,** directly on the beach at the foot of Lynn Hall Memorial Pier (✆ **239/765-7800**), a lively pub with blond-wood trim and vivid colors reminiscent of establishments in Miami's South Beach. It opens onto a large beachside patio with dining at umbrella tables, outstanding sunsets, and live bands playing at night. The reasonably priced fare is a catch-all of conch fritters, shrimp and fish baskets, burgers, and seafood main courses. Reservations are accepted; food is served daily from 11am to 11pm.

Moderate

Channel Mark ★★ SEAFOOD The crab cakes, delicately seasoned with Old Bay spice in true Maryland fashion, are enough to make this the beach's best place for seafood. Nestled by the "Little Bridge" leading onto San Carlos Island's northern end, the restaurant has tables that look out on a maze of channel markers on Hurricane Bay. A dock with palms growing through it makes this a tranquil place for a waterside lunch. At night, a relaxed tropical ambience is ideal for kindling romance. The adjacent lounge offers the same menu and has live entertainment on weekends. Ask for the complete dinner specials starting at $7.95.

19001 San Carlos Blvd. (at north end of San Carlos Island). ✆ **239/463-9127.** www.channelmark.com. Reservations recommended on major holidays; not accepted other times. Main courses $8–$20. AE, DISC, MC, V. Sun–Thurs 11am–10pm; Fri–Sat 11am–11pm.

Gulf Shore Grill SEAFOOD/AMERICAN On the southern fringes of Times Square, this old clapboard building has splendid views of the Gulf and the beach. It began life in the 1920s as the Crescent Beach Casino and has seen various incarnations as a bathhouse, gambling casino, dance hall, and rooming house. Traditional Florida-style main courses include baked grouper imperial, grilled mahimahi, and shrimp wrapped in bacon and coated with honey. This is one of the best breakfast spots on the beach, with items ranging from biscuits and gravy to eggs on a muffin with Alaskan crabmeat and a charon (tomato-hollandaise) sauce. The kitchen also provides the pub fare for the **Cottage Bar,** an open-air drinking establishment next door, with daily hours from 11am to 2am.

1270 Estero Blvd. (on the beach at Ave. A). ✆ **239/765-5440.** www.gulfshoregrill.com. Reservations recommended for dinner. Main courses $15–$33; breakfast $5–$15; sandwiches and burgers $9–$13. AE, DISC, MC, V. Daily 8am–3pm and 5–10pm.

Inexpensive

Castaways Bar & Grill AMERICAN Formerly known as Loggerheads, this is the best bet on the island's south end. Charter-boat captains and other locals congregate around a big square bar on one side of the knotty pine–accented dining room. The new menu offers ribs, lasagna, spaghetti and meatballs, and meatloaf. There's also some seriously excellent pizza. The new owners, New Jersey expats, added pool tables, dart board, juke box, and video games. They even host free Texas Hold 'em Sundays at 7pm and there's live entertainment 5 nights a week.

In Santini Marina Plaza, 7205 Estero Blvd. (at Lennel Rd.). ✆ **239/463-4644.** www.loggerheadsfmbeach.com. Reservations recommended on weekends. Main courses $10–$15. AE, DISC, MC, V. Daily 11am–2am.

The Fish House SEAFOOD You'll find the beach's least-expensive outdoor dining at the dockside tables of this friendly, no-frills pub. You'll also see charter-boat skippers slaking their thirst at a large wooden bar occupying about half the open-air screened dining room. Go for the fried or grilled grouper and other fish that the captains have just landed. Sandwiches are available all day, including a tasty grouper version. On Sundays, they offer dollar draft beers and 35¢ oysters.

7225 Estero Blvd. (at Fish Tale Marina, behind Santini Marina Plaza). ✆ **239/765-6766.** Main courses $12–$24; sandwiches $7–$10. AE, DISC, MC, V. Winter daily 11am–11pm; off-season daily 11am–10pm. Closed Thanksgiving and Christmas.

Francesco's Italian Deli & Pizzeria ★ ITALIAN Wonderful aromas of baking pizzas, cannoli, breads, cookies, and fabulous calzones waft from this New York–style

Italian deli. Order at the counter over a chiller packed with fresh deli meats, Italian sausage, and cheeses; then devour your goodies at tables inside or out on the covered walkway, or picnic on the beach. You can also take "heat-and-eat" meals of spaghetti, lasagna, eggplant parmigiana, manicotti, and ravioli to your hotel or condominium oven. The shelves are loaded with Italian wines, pastas, cookies, and anisette toast.

In Santini Marina Plaza, 7205 Estero Blvd. (at Lennel Rd.). ✆ **239/463-5634.** Subs and sandwiches $6–$8; pizzas $12–$14; ready-to-cook meals $9–$11. No credit cards. Mon–Sat 8am–7pm.

FORT MYERS BEACH AFTER DARK

To find out what's going on during your stay, pick up a copy of the daily *News-Press* (www.news-press.com). The two local tabloids, *Beach Bulletin* and *Fort Myers Beach Observer,* are available at the chamber of commerce (p. 334).

The area around Times Square is always active, every day in winter and on weekends in the off-season. At the foot of Lynn Hall Memorial Pier, the **Beach Pierside Grill,** 1000 Estero Blvd. (✆ **239/765-7800;** www.piersidegrill.com), has live entertainment on its beachside patio. It's not directly on the beach, but locals in the know head for the rooftop bar at **Beached Whale,** 1249 Estero Blvd. (✆ **239/463-5505;** www.thebeachedwhale.com), which supplies free chicken wings during its nightly happy hour. Rock and reggae music are played downstairs for dancing. And as mentioned above, **Castaway's Bar & Grill** (✆ **239/463-4644**) features live entertainment 5 nights a week as well as free Texas Hold 'em every Sunday night at 7pm.

Away from the crowds in the "middle beach" area, the **Junkanoo Beach Bar,** under Anthony's on the Gulf, 3040 Estero Blvd. (✆ **239/463-2600;** www.junkanoo-anthonys.com), attracts a more affluent crowd for its bohemian-style parties that run from 11:30am to 1:30am daily. Live bands here specialize in reggae and other island music. On the menu are inexpensive subs, sandwiches, burgers, and pizzas, and a concessionaire rents beach cabanas and watersports toys, making it a good place for a lively day at the beach.

On Sunday afternoons, revelers jam the docks for the famous outdoor reggae parties at the **Bridge Waterfront Restaurant,** 708 Fisherman's Wharf (✆ **239/765-0050;** www.thebridgerestaurant.com), which is under the Sky Bridge on San Carlos Island.

3 SANIBEL & CAPTIVA ISLANDS ★★★

14 miles W of Fort Myers; 40 miles N of Naples

Sanibel and Captiva are Florida's unfussy cousins. They don't need lip gloss and eye shadow to make them pretty. Leave the clown makeup for Miami and Orlando. Here you'll find none of the neon signs, amusement parks, or high-rise condominiums that clutter most beach resorts in the state. Indeed, Sanibel's main drag, Periwinkle Way, runs under a canopy of whispery pines and gnarled oaks so thick they almost obscure the small signs for chic shops and restaurants. This wooded ambience is the work of local voters, who have saved their trees and tropical foliage, limited the size and appearance of signs, permitted no building higher than the tallest palm, and allowed no WaveRunner or other noisy beach toy within 300 yards of their gorgeous, shell-strewn beaches. Although they haven't yet banned cacophonous cellphones, don't be surprised if they eventually do. It's *that* peaceful here.

Nevertheless, the islands have wildlife: More than half of Sanibel Island is preserved in its natural state as a wildlife refuge. You can ride, walk, bike, canoe, or kayak through the J. N. "Ding" Darling National Wildlife Refuge, one of Florida's best.

Legend says that Ponce de León named the larger of these two barrier islands San Ybel, after Queen Isabella of Spain. Another legend claims that Captiva's name comes from the captured women kept here by the pirate Jose Gaspar. The modern era of the islands dates from 1892, when a few farmers settled here. One of them, Clarence Chadwick, started an unsuccessful Key lime and copra plantation on Captiva; many of his towering coconut palms still stand, adding to the little island's tropical luster.

ESSENTIALS

GETTING THERE See section 1 on Fort Myers, beginning on p. 326, for information on air, train, bus, and rental-car services. The Amoco station at 1015 Periwinkle Way, at Causeway Road, is the Sanibel agent for **Hertz** (© **239/472-2125**).

VISITOR INFORMATION The **Sanibel & Captiva Islands Chamber of Commerce,** 1159 Causeway Rd., Sanibel Island, FL 33957 (© **239/472-1080;** fax 239/472-1070; www.sanibel-captiva.org), maintains a visitor center on Causeway Road, as you drive onto Sanibel from Fort Myers. The chamber gives away an island guide and sells a detailed street map for $5. Also for sale are books, such as a comprehensive shelling guide and a helpful collection of menus from the islands' restaurants. Phones are available for making hotel and condominium reservations; check the brochure racks for discounts in summer and the month of December. It's open Monday through Sunday from 9am to 5pm. Another great resource for area information is www.fortmyerssanibel.com.

GETTING AROUND Neither Sanibel nor Captiva has public transportation. No parking is permitted on any street or road on Sanibel. Free beach parking is available on the Sanibel Causeway. Other municipal lots either are reserved for local residents or have a $2 hourly fee. Accordingly, many residents and visitors get around by bicycle (see "More Ways to Enjoy the Outdoors," below). If you need a cab, call **Sanibel Taxi** (© **239/472-4160**).

PARKS & NATURE PRESERVES

Named for the *Des Moines Register* cartoonist who was a frequent visitor here and who started the federal Duck Stamp program, the outstanding **J. N. "Ding" Darling National Wildlife Refuge ★★★** (www.fws.gov/dingdarling), on Sanibel-Captiva Road, is home to alligators, raccoons, otters, and hundreds of species of birds. Occupying more than half of Sanibel Island, this 6,000-plus-acre area of mangrove swamps, winding waterways, and uplands has a 2-mile boardwalk nature trail and a 5-mile, one-way **Wildlife Drive.** The visitor center shows brief videos on the refuge's inhabitants every half-hour and sells a map keyed to numbered stops along the Wildlife Drive. The best times for viewing wildlife are early morning, late afternoon, and at low tide (tables are posted at the visitor center and available at the chamber of commerce). Mosquitoes and "no-see-ums" (tiny, biting sand flies) are especially prevalent at dawn and dusk, so bring repellent.

Admission to the visitor center is free. The Wildlife Drive costs $5 per vehicle, $1 for hikers and bicyclists (free to holders of current federal Duck Stamps and National Park Service access passports). The visitor center is open January through April, daily from 9am to 5pm; off-season, daily from 9am to 4pm. It's open on federal holidays January through April, but closed on holidays the rest of the year. The Wildlife Drive is open year-round Saturday through Thursday, from 1 hour after sunrise to 1 hour before sunset. For more information, contact the refuge at 1 Wildlife Dr., Sanibel Island, FL 33957 (© **239/472-1100**).

You'll get a lot more from your visit by taking a naturalist-narrated tram tour operated by **Tarpon Bay Explorers,** at the north end of Tarpon Bay Road (**✆ 239/472-8900;** www.tarponbayexplorers.com). The tours last 1½ hours and cost $13 for adults, $8 for children 12 and under. Schedules are seasonal, so call ahead.

Tarpon Bay Explorers also offers a variety of guided **canoe and kayak tours,** $30 adults, $20 kids, with an emphasis on the historical, cultural, and environmental aspects of the refuge (call for schedule and reservations, which are required). It also rents canoes, kayaks, and small boats with electric trolling motors (see "More Ways to Enjoy the Outdoors," below).

A short drive from the visitor center, the nonprofit **Sanibel/Captiva Conservation Foundation,** 3333 Sanibel-Captiva Rd. (**✆ 239/472-2329;** www.sccf.org), maintains a nature center, a native-plant nursery, and 4.5 miles of nature trails on 1,100 acres of wetlands along the Sanibel River. You can learn more about the islands' unusual ecosystems through environmental workshops, guided 1½-hour trail walks, beach walks, and a 2-hour natural-history boat cruise (call for seasonal schedules and reservations). Various items are for sale, including native plants and publications on the islands' birds and other wildlife. Admission is $3 for adults, free for children 16 and under. The nature center is

Fun Facts **Did You Know?**

Captiva Island was the inspiration for the best-selling book *A Gift from the Sea,* by Anne Morrow Lindbergh, wife of the famous aviator. She describes in detail the stunning island but never reveals its name.

open from year-round, Monday through Friday from 8:30am to 4pm, Saturday from 10am to 3pm.

Also nearby, the **Clinic for the Rehabilitation of Wildlife (C.R.O.W.),** 3883 Sanibel-Captiva Rd. (✆ **239/472-3644;** www.crowclinic.org), is dedicated to the care of sick, injured, and orphaned wildlife. CROW debuted its new Visitor Education Center in December 2008, open Tuesday through Sunday from 10am to 4pm. This interactive exhibit building replaces their previous daily program and tours. The admission is $5 for adults and children 4 and older.

HITTING THE BEACH

BEACHES Sanibel has four public beach-access areas with metered parking: the eastern point around **Sanibel Lighthouse,** which has a fishing pier; **Gulfside City Park,** at the end of Algiers Lane, off Casa Ybel Road; **Tarpon Bay Road Beach,** at the south end of Tarpon Bay Road; and **Bowman's Beach,** off Sanibel-Captiva Road. **Turner Beach,** at Blind Pass between Sanibel and Captiva, is highly popular at sunset because it faces due west; there's a small free parking lot on the Captiva side, but parking on the Sanibel side is limited to holders of local permits. All except Tarpon Bay Road Beach have restrooms. ***Be forewarned:*** Although nude bathing is illegal, the north end of Bowman's Beach often sees more than its share of bare straight and gay bodies.

Another popular beach on Captiva is at the end of Andy Rosse Lane in front of the Mucky Duck Restaurant. It's the one place here where you can rent motorized watersports equipment (see "More Ways to Enjoy the Outdoors," below), but you'll have to use the Mucky Duck's restrooms if you need to go. There's limited free parking just north of here, at the end of Captiva Drive (go past the entrance to South Seas Resort to the end of the road).

SHELLING Sanibel and Captiva are famous for their seashells, and local residents and visitors alike can be seen in the "Sanibel stoop" or the "Captiva crouch" while searching for some 200 species. Only if you're a hard-core shell fanatic should you check out the **Bailey-Matthews Shell Museum ★★**, 3075 Sanibel-Captiva Rd. (✆ **888/679-6450** or 239/395-2233; www.shellmuseum.org), the only museum in the United States devoted solely to saltwater, freshwater, and land shells (yes, snails are included). The museum is a far cry from the tourist-trap shell factories you'll see throughout the state. Shells from as far away as South Africa surround a 6-foot globe in the middle of the main exhibit hall, thus showing their geographic origins. A spinning wheel–shaped case identifies shells likely to wash up on Sanibel. Other exhibits are devoted to shells in tribal art, fossil shells found in Florida, medicinal qualities of various mollusks, the endangered Florida tree snail, and "sailor's valentines"—shell crafts made by natives of Barbados for sailors to bring home to their loved ones. The library attracts serious malacologists—for the uninitiated, those who study mollusks—and a shop has clever shell-themed gifts. The museum is open daily from 10am to 5pm; admission is $7 for adults and $4 for children 5 to 16.

Tips Don't Take Live Shells

Florida law prohibits taking live shells (those with living creatures inside them) from the beaches, and federal regulations prevent them from being removed from the J. N. "Ding" Darling National Wildlife Refuge.

The months from February to April, or after any storm, are prime times of the year to look for whelks, olives, scallops, sand dollars, conch, and many other varieties of shells. Low tide is the best time of day. The shells can be sharp, so wear Aqua Socks or old running shoes whenever you go walking on the beach.

MORE WAYS TO ENJOY THE OUTDOORS

BIKING, WALKING, JOGGING & IN-LINE SKATING On Sanibel, paved bike paths run alongside most roads, including the length of Periwinkle Way and along Sanibel-Captiva Road to Blind Pass, making the island a paradise for cyclists, walkers, joggers, and in-line skaters. You can also walk or bike the 5-mile, one-way nature trail through the J. N. "Ding" Darling National Wildlife Refuge. There are no bike paths on Captiva, where trees next to the narrow roads can make for dangerous riding.

The chamber of commerce's visitor center has bike maps, as do Sanibel's rental outlets: **Finnimore's Cycle Shop,** 2353 Periwinkle Way (✆ 239/472-5577); **Billy's Rentals,** 1470 Periwinkle Way (✆ 239/472-5248; www.sanibelsegway.com); and **Tarpon Bay Explorers,** at the north end of Tarpon Bay Road (✆ 239/472-8900). On Captiva, **Jim's Bike & Scooter Rentals,** on Andy Rosse Lane (✆ 239/472-1296), rents bikes and beach equipment. Bike rates range from about $10 to $16 for 4 hours to $15 to $25 a day for basic models. Both Finnimore's and Jim's also rent in-line skates. Billy's rents Segways and conducts Wildlife-Eco tours on Segways. Call ✆ **239/472-3620** for pricing.

BOATING & FISHING On Sanibel, rental boats and charter-fishing excursions are available at the **Boat House,** at the Sanibel Marina, North Yachtsman Drive (✆ **239/472-2531**), off Periwinkle Way east of Causeway Road. **Tarpon Bay Explorers,** at the north end of Tarpon Bay Road (✆ **239/472-8900**), rents boats with electric trolling motors and tackle for fishing.

On Captiva, check with **Sweet Water Rentals,** at the 'Tween Waters Inn Marina (✆ **239/472-6336**); **Jensen's Twin Palms Marina** (✆ **239/472-5800;** www.jensen-captiva.com); and **McCarthy's Marina** (✆ **239/472-5200;** www.mccarthysmarina.com), all on Captiva Road. Rental boats cost about $165 for a half-day, $280 for a full day.

Many charter-fishing captains have boats docked at these marinas. Half-day rates are about $300 for up to four people. The skippers leave free brochures at the chamber of commerce's visitor center (p. 342), and they're also listed in the free tourist publications found there.

CANOEING & KAYAKING As noted under "Parks & Nature Preserves," above, **Tarpon Bay Explorers** (✆ **239/472-8900;** www.tarponbayexplorers.com) has guided canoe and kayak trips in the J. N. "Ding" Darling National Wildlife Refuge. Do-it-yourselfers can rent canoes and kayaks here. They cost $20 for the first 2 hours, $10 for each additional hour. **Captiva Kayak Co./WildSide Adventures,** at McCarthy's Marina (✆ **877/395-2925** or 239/395-2925; www.captivakayaks.com), rents canoes and kayaks on Captiva for $15 per hour, $35 for a half-day, and $50 overnight, as does **'Tween Waters Inn**

Don't Take the Bait: Fishing Dos and Don'ts

If you plan on fishing, keep the following information in mind:

- Fees start at about $200 for a half-day (4-hr.) trip; 6-hour and 8-hour trips are also available.
- The guide will provide the boat, license, fishing gear, equipment, and bait.
- Many guides will clean and fillet the catches, and can recommend places that will mount the big ones.
- Licensed guides are required to know CPR and first aid, and are periodically retested.
- Virtually all guides have ship-to-shore radios on their boats in the event of an emergency.
- If a meal is planned at a restaurant after the trip, usually the client buys the guide's lunch.
- Clients usually tip guides after a successful fishing experience, ranging from $20 to $50 per trip.

Marina (✆ **239/472-5161;** www.tween-waters.com) for $20 per 2 hours and $5 to $10 per additional hour.

Tarpon Bay Explorers also offer naturalist-led kayaking trips through the mangrove forest along the Commodore Creek water trail. Learn about the rich back-bay ecosystem and the wildlife that lives there. You'll be surrounded by red mangroves, wading birds, and more for $30 per adult and $20 per children (✆ **239/472-8900**). **Captiva Kayak Co./WildSide Adventures,** based at McCarthy's Marina, on Captiva (✆ **877/395-2925** or 239/395-2925; www.captivakayaks.com), has day and night back-bay ecology trips for $35 for adults, $25 for teens, and $20 for children (add $10 to each price for night trips). The company will customize tours, including camping on Cayo Costa (see "Nearby Island Hopping," beginning on p. 357) for advanced kayakers. Reservations are essential for all operators. **Adventure in Paradise** (✆ **239/472-9443;** www.adventureinparadise inc.com) offers eco-nature canoe and kayak tours through the wildlife-studded Engine Trail and Ibis Isle. Cost is $30 adults, $15 children.

For information on the new 40-mile **Great Calusa Blueway** paddling trail, see p. 336.

GOLF & TENNIS Golfers may view a gallery of wild animals while playing the 5,600-yard, par-70, 18-hole course at the **Dunes Golf and Tennis Club,** 949 Sandcastle Rd., Sanibel (✆ **239/472-2535;** www.dunesgolfsanibel.com), whose back 9 runs across a wildlife preserve. Call a day in advance for seasonal greens fees and a tee time. The Dunes also has seven tennis courts.

You can also play 18 water-bordered holes at **Beachview Golf Club,** 1100 Par View Dr., Sanibel (✆ **239/472-2626**).

The **South Seas Island Resort,** on Captiva (p. 351), has tennis courts and a 9-hole golf course, but they're for guests only.

SAILING If you want to learn how to sail or simply polish your skills, noted yachters Steve and Doris Colgate have a branch of their **Offshore Sailing School** at the South

Seas Island Resort on Captiva (✆ **800/221-4326** or 239/454-1700; www.offshore-sailing.com). Clinics range from a half-day to a full week. Also ask about the popular women-only, father-son, and mother-daughter programs.

Also based on Captiva are two sailboats that take guests out on the waters of Pine Island Sound: the 30-foot ***Adventure*** (✆ **239/472-5300;** www.captivacruises.com), a sailing sloop carrying up to six guests, at $125 per hour with a 2-hour minimum; and the ***New Moon*** (✆ **239/395-1782;** www.newmoonsailing.com), a 40-foot sloop carrying up to 40 passengers from the 'Tween Waters Marina, on 3-hour half-day and 7-hour full-day and sunset charters. Half-day and sunset trips for up to six people cost $385; full-day trips are $770. Reservations are required well in advance, but Captain Mick Gurley tells us "don't be afraid to try last minute."

Do-it-yourselfers can rent small sailboats from **Captiva Kayak Co./WildSide Adventures,** based at McCarthy's Marina (✆ **877/395-2925** or 239/395-2925; www.captivakayaks.com). Prices range from $25 to $35 an hour and $100 for a half-day, depending on the size of the craft.

WATERSPORTS Sanibel may prohibit motorized watersports equipment on its beaches, but Captiva doesn't. **Yolo Watersports** (✆ **239/472-9656;** www.yolo-jims.com) offers parasailing and WaveRunner rentals on the beach in front of the Mucky Duck Restaurant, at the Gulf end of Andy Rosse Lane.

MORE TO SEE & DO

Worth a brief stop after you've done everything else here, the **Sanibel Historical Village & Museum,** 950 Dunlop Rd. (✆ **239/472-4648**), includes the 1913-vintage Rutland home and the 1926 versions of Bailey's General Store (complete with Red Crown gasoline pumps), the post office, and Miss Charlotta's Tea Room. Displays highlight the islands' prehistoric Calusa peoples, as well as old photos from pioneer days, turn-of-the-20th-century clothing, and a variety of memorabilia. It's open from November to May, Wednesday through Saturday from 10am to 4pm; from June to mid-August, Wednesday through Saturday from 10am to 1pm. Admission is by $3 donation.

At the east end of Periwinkle Way, the **Sanibel Lighthouse** has marked the entrance to San Carlos Bay since 1884. The lighthouse keepers used to live in the cottages at the base of the 94-foot tower. The now-automatic lighthouse makes for a lovely Kodak moment, but it isn't open to visitors, though the grounds and beach are.

In addition to its other trips, **Captiva Cruises** (✆ **239/472-5300;** www.captivacruises.com) goes on daily sunset cruises from South Seas Island Resort, on Captiva. The cruise costs $25 adults, $15 children 6 to 12. Call for times and reservations.

SHOPPING

Most shops are open Monday through Saturday from 9am to 6pm, Sunday from noon to 5pm. You can burn up a rainy day and lots of credit at Sanibel's numerous upscale boutiques carrying expensive jewelry, apparel, and gifts. Many are in **Periwinkle Place**—such as **Pandora's Box** (✆ **239/472-6263**), a treasure trove of great vintage jewelry, fabulous cards, beautiful art, and gorgeous children's toys and books, and **Sanibel Day Spa** (✆ **239/395-2220;** www.sanibeldayspa.com), where you can get massages; pedis; manis; and a slew of body, hair, and skin care products—and **Tahitian Gardens,** the main shopping centers along Periwinkle Way. The larger Periwinkle Place sports mostly high-end men's and women's clothiers, while Tahitian Gardens has some excellent gift shops.

More than a dozen Sanibel galleries feature original works of art; pick up a gallery guide at the chamber of commerce's visitor center (p. 342). On Captiva, the treehouse-like **Jungle Drums,** on Andy Rosse Lane (✆ **239/395-2266**), has the area's most unique collection of wildlife art.

Founded in 1899, **Bailey's General Store,** Periwinkle Way and Tarpon Bay Road (✆ **239/472-1516**), is still going strong, with a supermarket, deli, salad bar, hardware store, beach shop, shoe repair, and Western Union all under one roof. Bailey's is open daily from 7am to 9pm.

WHERE TO STAY

Sanibel & Captiva Central Reservations, Inc. (✆ **800/325-1352** or 239/405-7848; fax 239/405-7847; www.rescen.com) and **Reservation Central** (✆ **800/290-6920**) are reservations services that can book you into most condominiums and cottages here.

In general, Sanibel and Captiva room and condominium rates are highest during the shelling season, February through April. January is usually somewhat less expensive. But note that most rates fall drastically during the off-season; don't hesitate to ask for a discount or special deal then. Because most properties on the islands are geared to 1-week vacations, you can save by purchasing a package for stays of 7 nights or longer.

The islands' sole campground, the **Periwinkle Trailer Park,** 1119 Periwinkle Way, Sanibel Island (✆ **239/472-1433**), is so popular it doesn't even advertise. No other camping is permitted on either Sanibel or Captiva.

Sanibel Island

Very Expensive

Casa Ybel Resort ★★★ One of the best resorts on Sanibel, this all-condo property sits on 23 acres beside the beach on the historic site of the island's first beachfront hotel, the Thistle Lodge. The present-day Casa Ybel's turn-of-the-20th-century main building houses a restaurant named Thistle Lodge as a nostalgic reminder of that first hotel, where both guests and other island visitors can enjoy wonderful cuisine—butter-poached lobster tail, pan-steamed Maine lobster, crackling coconut prawns with Thai orange-chili sauce—and magnificent Gulf views. The swimming pool in front of the restaurant is one of Florida's most picturesque. There are also 14 miles of seashell-studded white sand. This is bliss. The spacious one- and two-bedroom condominiums, housed in beach-washed four-story buildings on the island's most beautifully landscaped grounds, all have screened porches (complete with outdoor gas grills facing the Gulf). With upstairs bedrooms, the town house–style units provide more privacy than most condominiums on Sanibel.

2255 W. Gulf Dr., Sanibel Island, FL 33957. ✆ **800/276-4753** or 239/472-3145. Fax 239/472-2109. www.casaybelresort.com. 114 suites. Winter $339–$649 condo; off-season $289–$349 condo. Packages and weekly rates available. AE, DISC, MC, V. **Amenities:** Restaurant; pool bar; heated outdoor pool; tennis courts; Jacuzzi; watersports equipment/rentals; bike rental; children's programs; concierge; in-suite massage; babysitting; laundry service. *In room:* A/C, TV/DVD, high-speed Internet, kitchen, coffeemaker, hair dryer, iron.

Sundial Beach and Golf Resort ★★ Kids The largest resort on Sanibel, this condominium complex lacks intimacy, but it has lots to keep families occupied (even jogging strollers are provided, so you don't have to schlep your own), from a palm-studded, beachside pool area to a free marine-biology program and a small ecology center with touch tank. The one-, two-, and three-bedroom condominiums are housed in two- and three-story buildings (as high as they get on Sanibel) and have screened balconies overlooking the beach or landscaped gardens. Rooms have gone from pleasantly decorated in a *Golden Girls* kind of way to a more tropical, modern vibe. Guests have access to the nearby Dunes Championship Golf Course.

Among several dining options here, overlooking the pool and the Gulf, the relaxing **Beaches Grill & Bar** is popular at sunset and has nightly entertainment. Off-site is **Ellington's Jazz Bar and Restaurant,** serving steaks, seafood, pasta, and Sunday brunch.

1451 Middle Gulf Dr., Sanibel Island, FL 33957. ✆ **800/237-4184** or 239/481-3636. Fax 239/481-4947. www.sundialresort.com. 270 units. Rates from $140–$180 per night or $750–$1,850 per week condo apt. Packages available. AE, DC, DISC, MC, V. **Amenities:** 4 restaurants; 2 bars; 5 heated outdoor pools; 12 tennis courts; exercise room; Jacuzzi; watersports equipment/rentals; bike rental; children's programs; game room; concierge; activities desk; business center; limited room service; massage; babysitting; laundry service; coin-op washers/dryers. *In room:* A/C, TV/VCR, kitchen, coffeemaker, hair dryer, iron.

Moderate

Island Inn ★★ It's difficult to get accommodations here during the winter season, but it's worth trying because this classic beach resort on 550 feet of Gulf beach has been in business for more than a century. Its original central building houses a genteel dining room (closed Sept 3–Nov 15), a spacious lounge, and a library brightly furnished with old-style bentwood and wicker sofas and chairs. This is the kind of place where guests dress for dinner—jackets aren't required but collared shirts are (and ties recommended) for men at dinner—and seating is assigned (some guests have had the same table for years). Don't oversleep and miss the sticky buns served at breakfast. You will thank me for this later (although your waistline won't). Motel rooms (with or without kitchens) are fine, and most have screened porches or balconies, but I say go for a private cottage. They aren't luxurious, but are certainly private and give off that beach-house vibe.

3111 W. Gulf Dr., Sanibel Island, FL 33957. ✆ **800/851-5088** or 239/472-1561. Fax 239/472-0051. www.islandinnsanibel.com. 57 units, including 9 cottages. Winter $165–$560 double, $195–$435 cottage; off-season $150–$300 double, $150–$320 cottage. Winter rates include breakfast and dinner. AE, DISC, MC, V. **Amenities:** Restaurant (seasonal); bar; small heated outdoor pool; tennis court; coin-op washers/dryers; croquet area. *In room:* A/C, TV, kitchen (in some), fridge, coffeemaker, hair dryer, iron.

Sanibel Inn ★ Kids A back-to-nature theme prevails at this beachside inn, in both the room decor and the grounds planted with native Florida foliage specifically designed to attract butterflies and hummingbirds. In fact, back-to-nature children's programs make this a great choice for eco-friendly families. Kids can go on shell safaris, nature walks, and dolphin watches. The hotel rooms and fully equipped two-bedroom, two-bathroom condominium apartments (the latter are some of Sanibel's most luxurious) have been renovated to look like a modern—but warm—beach house with bamboo floors, wicker furnishing, and great lighting. All units have screened porches to keep the relentless mosquitoes out. The award-winning Ellington's Jazz Bar and Restaurant offers seafood, steaks, pasta, and live music.

937 E. Gulf Dr., Sanibel Island, FL 33957. ✆ **800/237-1491** or 239/472-3181. Fax 239/472-5234. www.sanibelcollection.com. 94 units. Winter $155–$200 double, $175–$311 suite; off-season $144–$184 double, $158–$249 suite. Packages available. AE, DC, DISC, MC, V. **Amenities:** Restaurant; bar; heated outdoor pool; tennis courts; access to nearby health club; watersports equipment/rentals; bike rental; children's programs; limited room service; babysitting; laundry service. *In room:* A/C, TV, dataport, kitchen, fridge, coffeemaker, hair dryer, iron.

Sanibel's Seaside Inn ★★ This comfortable, friendly Key West–style establishment enjoys a tranquil location near the island's southeastern tip. The 1960s-style, fully renovated cottage duplexes are spacious, brightly furnished one-bedroom apartments decorated in what I like to call retro-cal—a combo of '50s retro and tropical, but if you can do without a kitchen, the choice units here are the beachfront hotel rooms with screened porches facing the Gulf. The cozy seaside cottages are the nicest, with deck porches and full dining areas. All units have ceiling fans and open-air balconies or decks. No smoking is permitted indoors. Guests receive special privileges at the nearby Dunes Golf and Tennis Club.

541 E. Gulf Dr., Sanibel Island, FL 33957. ✆ **800/831-7384** or 239/472-1400. Fax 239/472-6518. www.seasideinn.com. 32 units. Winter $150–$250 double, $255–$319 suite or cottage; off-season $140–$199 double, $240–$299 suite or cottage. Rates include continental breakfast. Packages available. AE, DC, DISC, MC, V. **Amenities:** Heated outdoor pool; access to nearby health club; free use of bikes; babysitting; coin-op washers/dryers. *In room:* A/C, TV/DVD, Wi-Fi, kitchen (in some), fridge, coffeemaker, hair dryer, iron.

Song of the Sea ★★ Popular with Europeans, this beachside inn has efficiencies and one-bedroom suites with plantation-style shutters behind sliding-glass doors opening to screened porches. Don't expect a lot of extra space in the suites, with bedrooms barely large enough to hold their king-size beds (with 300-thread-count linens); still, the decor is quite lovely. Furnished in French-country style (the hotel calls it West Indies style, so consider it a cross btw. the two), the rooms have oak tables and chairs, and pine Bahamian shutters on patio doors and windows. A pathway leads to the next-door Sanibel Inn (see above), where guests can use the facilities. An extensive continental breakfast is served in the public building and eaten at umbrella tables on a brick patio. Guests get discounts on the facilities at Sundial Beach Resort (see below).

863 E. Gulf Dr., Sanibel Island, FL 33957. ✆ **800/231-1045** or 239/472-2220. Fax 239/472-8569. www.sanibelcollection.com. 30 units. Winter $174–$192 double, $264–$277 suite; off-season $140–$179 double, $209–$219 suite. Rates include continental breakfast. Packages available. AE, DC, DISC, MC, V. **Amenities:** Heated outdoor pool; access to nearby health club; Jacuzzi; free use of bikes; babysitting; coin-op washers/dryers. *In room:* A/C, TV, fax, Wi-Fi, kitchen, fridge, coffeemaker, hair dryer, iron, safe.

Tarpon Tale Inn ★ Finds Owners Dawn and Joe Ramsey preside over this low-slung gray building in Sanibel's Old Town, the island's first settlement, where the ferries from Fort Myers used to dock near the lighthouse. White walls and tile floors make the comfortable units bright; French doors lead to gardens dense with sea grape, palm, and ficus trees, which provide privacy for a large outdoor hot tub. Three of the five units (which are attached yet completely private bungalows hidden amid palms, bougainvillea, hibiscus, ferns, sea grape, gumbo-limbo, and Key lime) have separate bedrooms, while two other "deluxe studios" are actually two-bedroom suites. All units have shower-only bathrooms. The makings for a continental breakfast are delivered the night before. Smoking is not permitted inside the inn's rooms. There is no daily maid service, though towels and linens are exchanged every 3 days or as needed.

367 Periwinkle Way, Sanibel Island, FL 33957. ✆ **888/345-0939** or 239/472-0939. Fax 239/472-6202. www.tarpontale.com. 5 units. Winter $189–$220 double; off-season $109–$149 double. Rates include continental breakfast. AE, DC, DISC, MC, V. Some pets accepted for a fee; call first. **Amenities:** Jacuzzi; free use of bikes; coin-op washers/dryers. *In room:* A/C, TV/VCR, kitchen, coffeemaker, hair dryer (upon request), iron (upon request), CD player, no phone.

Inexpensive

Palm View Motel In a quiet residential area, this little property is one of Sanibel's few inexpensive motels. The best choices here are the spacious, well-ventilated one- and two-bedroom apartments, but even the smaller efficiencies have kitchens and separate living and sleeping areas. There's a hot tub in the backyard, plus fire pits and barbecues, and pets are allowed.

706 Donax St., Sanibel Island, FL 33957. ✆ **239/472-1606.** Fax 239/472-6733. www.palmviewsanibel.com. 5 units. Winter $145–$185 efficiency or apt; off-season $85–$135 efficiency or apt. Weekly rates available. MC, V. Pets accepted ($10 per day). **Amenities:** Jacuzzi; free loan of bikes, beach chairs, and umbrellas; free laundry facilities. *In room:* A/C, TV/VCR, kitchen, coffeemaker, hair dryer, iron, microwave.

Captiva Island

Expensive

South Seas Island Resort ★★ Kids A former Key-lime plantation, this family-friendly "resort town" is located on the eco-balanced island of Captiva and uniquely manages the natural habitat with resort amenities and programs. Occupying 335 acres—all of Captiva's northern third—the resort sits on 2½ miles of gorgeous beach world renowned for shelling, sunsets, and the resident dolphins and manatees. It's so spread out that a free trolley shuttles back and forth through the mangrove forests. Its Gulf-side golf course is one of the most picturesque 9-holers anywhere, and its two marinas host multiple fishing charter boats and guides. Rooms—from standard hotel rooms to one-, two-, and three-bedroom beach condos (they call them villas, but they're more like someone's grandma's apartment which, for some is a good thing, for others like myself, not so much) and private homes—shine in a soothingly swank West Indies decor. If you want new and modern, request to stay by the marina where rooms are redone in a Caribbean chic decor. There's also a fantastic pool complex that overlooks Pine Island Sound with three pools, one with kid's water slides and another with private cabanas. Activities include tennis, golf, a children's camp, and day cruises to Cabbage Key and Useppa. Several restaurants and a Starbucks will keep you well-fed and energized on the property.

540 Plantation Rd., Captiva Island, FL 33924. ✆ 866/565-5089 or 239/432-6760. Fax 239/472-7541. www.southseas.com. 470 units. Winter $369–$587 double, $350–$1,800 condo or house; off-season $182–$259 double, $165–$1,300 condo or house. $14 resort fee per person per day added to room bills, 18%–20% to food and bar bills, in lieu of tipping. Packages available. AE, DC, DISC, MC, V. Amenities: 4 restaurants; 2 bars; 18 heated outdoor pools; 9-hole golf course; 19 tennis courts; health club; Jacuzzis; watersports equipment/rentals; bike rental; children's programs; game room; concierge; activities desk; business center; shopping arcade; micro spa and salon; limited room service; babysitting; laundry service; coin-op washers/dryers. In room: A/C, TV, dataport, Wi-Fi, kitchen (in larger units), coffeemaker, hair dryer, iron.

Moderate

Captiva Island Inn Bed & Breakfast ★ This B&B complex sits virtually surrounded by restaurants, art galleries, and boutiques along Captiva's block-long commercial street. Two suites in the Key West–style main building open to porches overlooking the lane, while four Dutch clapboard cottages sit out back on the fringes of a gravel parking lot (you get just enough yard here for hammocks and a gas grill). The ceiling in one cottage that once housed aviator Charles Lindbergh has clouds painted against a blue sky. All units have ceiling fans, kitchens, large bathrooms, queen size sofa beds in the living rooms, cool tile floors, and designer bed linens (including down comforters for the occasional chilly night). Some rooms have shower-only bathrooms. Guests get free use of towels and chairs for the beach (a block away), as well as a complimentary full breakfast at RC Otters or the **Keylime Bistro,** which has good American-style food and superb Key lime cheesecake; it's open daily from 8am to 10pm.

11509 Andy Rosse Lane (P.O. Box 848), Captiva Island, FL 33924. ✆ **800/454-9898** or 239/395-0882. Fax 239/395-0862. www.captivaislandinn.com. 18 units, including 1 5-bedroom house. Winter $255–$300 double; off-season $99–$180 double. Rates include full breakfast. AE, MC, V. **Amenities:** Pool. *In room:* A/C, TV, fridge, coffeemaker.

'Tween Waters Inn Island Resort ★★ Wedged between the Gulf beach and the bay on the narrowest part of Captiva, this venerable establishment was the regular haunt of cartoonist J. N. "Ding" Darling. Anne Morrow Lindbergh also dined here often while writing *A Gift from the Sea.* Situated in a sandy palm grove, these pink cottages have been upgraded, but still capture that Old Florida spirit. Some face the Gulf, others the bay. Themed to honor famous guests, they range in size from the honeymoon cottage, with barely enough room for its king-size bed and a tiny kitchen, to the three-bedroom, two-bathroom house. The spacious hotel rooms and apartments are in three modern buildings on stilts; all have screened balconies facing the Gulf or the bay. The Old Captiva House restaurant appears very much as it did in Ding Darling's days (note his cartoons adorning the dining-room walls). Charter captains dock at the full-service marina here.

15951 Captiva Rd., Captiva Island, FL 33924. ✆ **800/223-5865** or 239/472-5161. Fax 239/472-0249. www.tween-waters.com. 138 units. Winter $215–$295 double, $280–$620 suite, $300–$630 cottage; off-season $195–$215 double, $255–$470 suite, $215–$510 cottage. Rates include continental breakfast. Packages available. AE, DC, MC, V. Pets accepted in some units ($15 per day). **Amenities:** 2 restaurants; 2 bars; outdoor pool; 3 tennis courts; exercise room; Jacuzzi; watersports equipment/rentals; bike rental; massage; coin-op washers/dryers. *In room:* A/C, TV, dataport, Wi-Fi, kitchen (in suites and cottages), fridge, coffeemaker, hair dryer, iron (in suites), safe.

Cottages

The islands have several Old Florida–style cottages that are charming, often affordable alternatives to hotels and condos. Some of the best are members of the **Sanibel-Captiva Small Inns & Cottages Association.** Contact the association (via its website only) at www.sanibelsmallinns.com for a listing of properties.

Sitting between two condominium complexes off Middle Gulf Drive, **Gulf Breeze Cottages ★★**, 1081 Shell Basket Lane, Sanibel (✆ **800/388-2842** or 239/472-1626; www.gbreeze.com), is a collection of clapboard cottages separated from the beach by a lawn with a covered picnic area and outdoor shower. One two-story building is divided into four efficiencies (the pick is no. 7, with a view of the Gulf from its big picture windows). Rates are $240 to $395 per day in winter, $140 to $295 off-season.

Barely updated since the 1950s are the 32 pink-clapboard structures at **Beachview Cottages,** 3325 W. Gulf Dr., Sanibel (✆ **800/860-0532** or 239/472-1202; fax 239/472-4720; www.beachviewsanibel.com). None of the cottages has a phone, and some have shower-only bathrooms. The outdoor pool is heated. Rates are $189 to $315 in winter, $155 to $225 during the off-season.

On Captiva, **Jensen's on the Gulf,** 15300 Captiva Dr. (✆ **239/472-4684;** www.jensen-captiva.com), rents homes and cottages year-round from $325 to $700 and Gulf- and garden-view suites from $165 to $465. **Jensen's Twin Palm Resort & Marina** (✆ **239/472-5800;** www.jensen-captiva.com), on the bay near Andy Rosse Lane, has cottages ranging from $180 to $285 in winter and from $145 to $190 off-season.

WHERE TO DINE

No restaurant can survive on these affluent islands without serving good food, so you're assured of getting a fine meal wherever you go. Oddly, only a handful of establishments offer dining with water views.

Sanibel Island

Much of the "help" on this affluent island dines at **Jerry's Family Restaurant,** 1700 Periwinkle Way, at Casa Ybel Road (✆ **239/472-9300**), which serves wholesome and inexpensive diner fare (ingredients come fresh from the adjacent Jerry's Supermarket).

Both the restaurant and supermarket are open daily from 6am to 11pm. Breakfast is served from 6am to 4pm, and you can usually get a table quickly here (which can't be said of Sanibel's other popular breakfast spots).

You'll find very reasonably priced pub fare at Sanibel's sports bars, such as the **Lazy Flamingo II** (below) and **Sanibel Grill,** 703 Tarpon Bay Rd., near Palm Ridge Road (✆ **239/472-3128**), which actually serves as the bar for **Timbers** (p. 354), the fine seafood restaurant next door.

For picnics at Sanibel's beaches or on a canoe, the deli and bakery in **Bailey's General Store,** at Periwinkle Way and Tarpon Bay Road (✆ **239/472-1516**), carries a gourmet selection of breads, cheeses, and meats. **Huxter's Deli and Market,** 1203 Periwinkle Way, east of Donax Street (✆ **239/472-6988**), has sandwich fixings and "beach box" lunches to go.

Very Expensive

Chip's Sanibel Steakhouse ★ STEAKHOUSE Carb-cutting islanders love Chip's for its filet mignon, NY strip, cowboy steak, porterhouse, and T-bones. For those who don't do steak, fret not—they also have duck a l'orange, meaty crab cakes, blackened ahi tuna, shrimp tempura, and broiled Florida lobster tail.

1473 Periwinkle Way. ✆ **239/472-5700.** Reservations highly recommended. www.thesanibelsteakhouse.com. Main courses $32–$70. AE, MC, V. Daily 5–10pm.

Ellington's Jazz Bar and Restaurant ★ SEAFOOD With live jazz 7 nights a week, this Sanibel hepcat serves equally jazzy cuisine, from the Gillespie's Red Eye Pork Shank with wild mushroom risotto to Dizzy's Swingin' Steak Tartar. Be sure to try the Bourbon Street escargot, which are made with artichoke, sweet tomatoes, and garlic. The Duke would be proud.

937 E. Gulf Dr. ✆ **239/472-0494.** www.ellingtonsjazz.com. Reservations highly recommended. Main courses $22–$45. AE, MC, V. Daily 5–11pm.

Mad Hatter ★★ ECLECTIC One of Sanibel's best choices for a romantic waterfront dinner, this New American Gulf-front restaurant has only 12 tables, but each has a view that's perfect at sunset. The ever-changing menu features flavors from around the world, such as grilled sake miso–glazed Gulf shrimp with chayote vegetables ceviche, basmati rice cake, and shiitake mushroom cilantro sauce; and a marinated grilled pork chop with melted Taleggio cheese, rosemary-infused potato tower, and spinach gratin.

6467 Sanibel-Captiva Rd., at Blind Pass. ✆ **239/472-0033.** Reservations highly recommended. Main courses $26–$37. AE, MC, V. Tues–Sun 5–9:30pm.

Moderate

Jacaranda SEAFOOD/PASTA/STEAKS This friendly and casual restaurant (named for the purple-flowered jacaranda tree) attracts an affluent over 40 crowd for its nightly live music at the Patio Lounge. (After midnight, a 20-something crowd which lovingly refers to the place as the Jacko sweeps in.) Although the Jacaranda is best known as a local gathering spot, it has also received several dining awards. Fish is well prepared here, or you can choose steaks or prime rib. The linguine with a dozen littleneck clams tossed in a piquant red or white clam sauce is excellent. For dessert, the turtle pie—ice cream, caramel, fudge sauce, chopped nuts, and whipped cream—will send you away stuffed.

1223 Periwinkle Way (east of Donax St.). ✆ **239/472-1771.** Reservations recommended. Main courses $18–$35. AE, MC, V. Daily 5–10pm. Lounge daily 4pm–2:30am.

Deals on Meals

Local restaurants often run advertisements containing discount coupons in the *Sanibel-Captiva Shopper's Guide,* a free publication available at the chamber of commerce's visitor center.

McT's Shrimp House & Tavern SEAFOOD Shrimp reigns at this casual Old Florida–style establishment, where at 4pm you'll see a line of people waiting outside for the early-bird specials served to the first 100 in the door. Shrimp here is prepared in at least a dozen ways, from steamed to fried in a coconut-and-almond batter. There is also grouper and swordfish, plus steaks and chicken for the land-minded, but I recommend sticking to the shrimp here. (The Timbers Restaurant & Fish Market, described below, does a much better job of cooking fish.) McT's Tavern has an extensive choice of appetizers and light dinners. All-you-can-eat peel-and-eat shrimp and stone crabs are available nightly, though if it's not stone-crab season (Oct–May), the crab will likely be frozen.

1523 Periwinkle Way (at Fitzhugh St.). ✆ **239/472-3161.** www.eatmoreshrimp.com. Main courses $17–$22. AE, DC, DISC, MC, V. Shrimp House daily 4–9pm. McT's Tavern daily 4pm–close. Closed Christmas.

The Timbers Restaurant & Fish Market ★★ SEAFOOD/STEAK This casual upstairs restaurant, with bamboo railings, oversize canvas umbrellas, and paintings of tropical scenes through faux windows, is consistently Sanibel's best place for fresh fish and aged beef hot off the charcoal grill. It's true what they say—"We serve it fresh or we don't serve it at all." In the fish market out front, you can view the catch and have the chef chargrill or blacken it to order. The steaks, cut on the premises, are the island's best. You can order a drink from the adjoining Sanibel Grill sports bar and wait for a table out on the shopping center's porch.

703 Tarpon Bay Rd. (btw. Periwinkle Way and Palm Ridge Rd.). ✆ **239/472-3128.** www.prawnbroker.com. Main courses $15–$30. AE, MC, V. Winter daily 4:30–9:30pm; off-season daily 5–9:30pm.

Inexpensive

Grandma Dot's Seaside Saloon SEAFOOD One of Sanibel's most popular lunch spots, this open-air but screened cafe on the docks of Sanibel Marina has excellent salads (try the seafood Caesar) and fine sandwiches, plus, for dinner, a few main courses led by broiled grouper, in a sauce of lemon, dill, butter, and white wine, and a surf and turf for $29.

At Sanibel Marina, 634 N. Yachtsman Dr. ✆ **239/472-8138.** Main courses $17–$29; salads and sandwiches $9–$15. MC, V. Daily 11:30am–8pm.

Hungry Heron ★★ Kids AMERICAN This tropically decorated eatery is Sanibel's most popular family restaurant. There's something for everyone on the huge, tabloid-size menu—from hot and cold appetizers and overstuffed "seawiches" to pasta and steamed shellfish. If the 280 regular items aren't enough, there's a list of nightly specials. Seafood, steaks, and stir-fries from a sizzling skillet are popular with local residents, who bring the kids here for fun and the children's menu.

In Palm Ridge Place, 2330 Palm Ridge Rd. (at Periwinkle Way). ✆ **239/395-2300.** Call for preferred seating. Main courses $11–$23; sandwiches, burgers, and snacks $7–$12. AE, DISC, MC, V. Daily 11am–9pm.

The Island Cow ★ Kids AMERICAN A fun, albeit bovine-themed, restaurant, Island Cow has a great raw bar, not to mention an unabridged menu of burgers, sandwiches, wraps, quesadillas, and, of course, seafood. Fried is the theme here, but kids love the cow motif. They also serve old-fashioned egg creams!

2163 Periwinkle Way. ✆ **239/472-0606.** www.islandcow.com. Main courses $10–$17; sandwiches, burgers, and snacks $7–$12. AE, DISC, MC, V. Daily 8am–8pm (breakfast served daily until 11am and noon Sun).

The Lazy Flamingo II Value SEAFOOD/PUB FARE The Lazy Flamingo is a down-homey type of place where the food is consistently good. Locals and visitors alike become repeat customers, flocking here for the reasonably priced food, a wide choice of beers iced down in a huge box behind the bar, and the sports TVs. Some of that beer is used to steam shrimp and a collection of oysters, clams, and spices known as "The Pot." Best pick, however, is grouper from the charcoals, as either a main course or a sandwich. The flamingo-pink menu has sandwiches, burgers, fish platters, and atomically spicy Dead Parrot Wings (they're so hot they can raise the dead). Fillet your own catch, and the chef will cook it to order for you. Happy-hour prices prevail whenever football games are on.

A sister institution, the **Lazy Flamingo I,** 6520-C Pine Ave., at Sanibel-Captiva Road, a quarter-mile south of Blind Pass (✆ **239/472-5353**), has the same menu and hours.

1036 Periwinkle Way, west of Causeway Blvd. ✆ **239/472-6939.** www.lazyflamingo.com. Main courses $11–$16; sandwiches and snacks $5–$10. Cook your catch $9. AE, DISC, MC, V. Daily 11:30am–midnight.

Lighthouse Cafe ★ Value AMERICAN This casual storefront establishment dishes up breakfast omelets that are meals in themselves, especially the ocean frittata containing delicately seasoned scallops, crabmeat, shrimp, broccoli, and mushrooms, and crowned with an artichoke-heart-and-creamy-Alfredo sauce. Seafood Benedict is one of the more decadent offerings. For the light(er) eater, a slew of creative sandwiches is served after 11am. Reasonably priced, cafe-style dinners are served during winter only. For the best pancakes ever, the Lighthouse Cafe has cornered the market, using a special recipe that draws up to 700 people a day in season. For just $5, go nuts on malted-blueberry or banana pancakes, or pretend to be healthy with granola-nut whole-wheat hot cakes with sliced bananas.

In Seahorse Shops, 362 Periwinkle Way (at Buttonwood Lane, east of Causeway Rd.). ✆ **239/472-0303.** www.lighthousecafe.com. Call ahead for preferred seating. Main courses $10–$15; breakfast $5–$9; sandwiches and salads $5–$11. MC, V. Daily 7am–3pm.

Sanibel Cafe ★ Value AMERICAN Seashells are the not-so-original theme at this locals' favorite, whose tables are museumlike glass cases containing delicate fossilized specimens from the Miocene and Pliocene epochs. Lunch is really dinner, and it's served all day here. Fresh-squeezed orange and grapefruit juice, Danish havarti omelets, and homemade muffins and biscuits highlight the breakfast menu. Lunch features everything from country-fried steak, meatloaf, and surf and turf to specialty sandwiches and shrimp, Greek, and chicken-and-grape salads made with a light, fat-free dressing. Fatten up on homemade red-raspberry jam, apple or cherry crisp, and terrific Key lime pie.

In the Tahitian Gardens, 2007 Periwinkle Way. ✆ **239/472-5323.** www.sanibelcafe.com. Call ahead for preferred seating. Main courses $9–$15; breakfast $6–$11; salads, sandwiches, and burgers $6–$13. MC, V. Daily 7am–3pm.

Captiva Island

Sandwiches and picnic fare are available at the **Captiva Island Store,** Captiva Road at Andy Rosse Lane (✆ **239/472-2374**). The beach is a block from here.

 See the review for the Captiva Island Inn Bed & Breakfast (p. 351) for information on the **Keylime Bistro.**

Moderate

The Bubble Room ★ Kids STEAK/SEAFOOD Imagine Walt Disney on acid, and you'll understand where the Bubble Room is coming from. The kitschiest restaurant you'll probably ever find, the Bubble Room has tongue-in-cheek American cuisine complemented by a decor filled with Christmas and Hollywood memorabilia from the '30s, '40s, and '50s. Distracting, to say the least—but in a very good way—the Bubble Room makes it hard to decide which is more amusing, the name of the dishes on the menu—Porky Pig a la Bobby Phillips and the Eddie Fisherman—or the thousands of movie stills, puppets, antique jukeboxes, and toy trains. ***Note:*** I've gotten complaints about the "awful" food here, but I still think the Bubble Room is fun, with good (though admittedly not fabulous) food and a great atmosphere.

15001 Captiva Rd. (at Andy Rosse Lane). ✆ **239/472-5558.** www.bubbleroomrestaurant.com. Call ahead for preferred seating. Main courses $20–$35. AE, DC, DISC, MC, V. Daily 11:30am–3pm; Fri–Sat 4:30–9:30pm; Sun–Thurs 4:30–9pm. Closed Christmas.

The Green Flash ★ SEAFOOD You can't miss this restaurant, which sits at the infamous "curve" where Captiva Road takes a sharp turn to the north. You won't see the real "green flash" as the sun sets here because this modern building looks eastward across Pine Island Sound, but it does make for a nice view at lunch. Seeing the full moon turn the Sound into glistening silver is worth having at least an evening drink here. The quality of the cuisine is very good, and the prices reasonable for Captiva. Start with oysters Rockefeller or shrimp bisque. Both are house specialties, as is the garlicky grouper "café de Paris" and the salmon with a dill-accented béarnaise sauce.

15183 Captiva Rd. ✆ **239/472-3337.** www.greenflashcaptiva.com. Reservations recommended. Main courses $17–$45. AE, DC, DISC, MC, V. Daily 11:30am–3:30pm and 5:30–9:30pm. Bar daily 11:30am–9:30pm.

Inexpensive

The Cabbage Key Restaurant ★★★ AMERICAN You can get here only by boat, but there are constant shuttles from Captiva, so get onboard and experience the true meaning of cheeseburgers in paradise. Jimmy Buffet allegedly wrote his famous song here, and when you arrive, you'll understand why. The cheeseburgers rock, the setting is sublime, and there are no fried foods or microwaves in sight. It's a place rich in history, and in money: Thousands of dollar bills are signed and stuck to the walls and ceiling with masking tape.

Intracoastal Water Marker 60, N. Fort Myers. ✆ **239/283-2278.** Main courses $5–$15. MC, V. Daily 7:30am–9pm.

Mucky Duck ★ SEAFOOD/PUB FARE A Captiva institution since 1976, this lively, British-style pub, named after a pub of the same name in Shakespeare's Stratford-upon-Avon in the U.K., is the only place on either island where you can dine right by the beach. If you don't get a seat with this great view, the humorous staff will gladly roll over a fake window to appease you. The menu offers a selection of fresh seafood items, plus English fish and chips, steak-and-sausage pie, and a ploughman's lunch. Shrimp fried in beer batter is my favorite. There's also a vegetarian platter. You can't make a reservation, but you can order drinks, listen to live music (Mon–Sat), and bide your time at beachside picnic tables out front (come early for sunset).

Andy Rosse Lane (on the Gulf). © **239/472-3434.** www.muckyduck.com. Main courses $4–$18 lunch, $18–$38 dinner. AE, DC, DISC, MC, V. Mon–Sat 11am–3pm and 5–9:30pm.

R. C. Otter's Island Eats ★★ Value AMERICAN Occupying an old clapboard-sided island cottage, this Key West–style cafe brings informality and good, inexpensive food to Captiva. In contrast to the island's 15 or so formal restaurants, you can dine here in your bare feet and not spend a fortune for an excellent breakfast, snack, lunch, or full meal. The choice seats are under ceiling fans on the front porch or umbrellas on the brick patio. In hot weather, opt for the air-conditioned dining room. The wide-ranging menu includes salads, hot dogs, burgers, sandwiches, meatloaf, country-fried steak, fish, plus delicious nightly specials. The island's best breakfasts are equally varied, from bacon and eggs to a seafood quesadilla. Musicians perform out in the yard every day—you might find yourself dancing on the front porch.

11506 Andy Rosse Lane. © **239/395-1142.** Call ahead for preferred seating. Main courses $10–$20; breakfast $6–$12; salads, sandwiches, and burgers $6–$12. AE, DISC, MC, V. Daily 8–10pm (breakfast to 11am).

SANIBEL & CAPTIVA ISLANDS AFTER DARK

You won't find glitzy nightclubs on these family-oriented islands, but night owls do have places to roost at the resorts and restaurants listed above. Here's a brief recap:

SANIBEL ISLAND The **Patio Lounge,** in the Jacaranda, 1223 Periwinkle Way (© **239/472-1771**), attracts an affluent crowd of everyone from 20-somethings to seniors to its live music every evening. **McT's Tavern,** 1523 Periwinkle Way (© **239/472-3161**), has a large-screen TV for sports fans. Other popular sports bars are the **Sanibel Grill,** 703 Tarpon Bay Rd. (© **239/472-4453**), and the two **Lazy Flamingo** branches, at 1036 Periwinkle Way (© **239/472-6939**) and 6520-C Pine Ave. (© **239/472-5353**).

A group of professional actors perform Broadway dramas and comedies from October to August in Sanibel's state-of-the-art, 150-seat **Schoolhouse Theater,** 2200 Periwinkle Way (© **239/472-6862;** www.theschoolhousetheater.com).

CAPTIVA ISLAND Local songwriters perform their works nightly at **R. C. Otter's Island Eats,** 11500 Andy Rosse Lane (© **239/395-1142**). The **Crow's Nest Lounge,** in the 'Tween Waters Inn on Captiva Road (© **239/472-5161**), is Captiva's top nightspot for dancing. My favorite, however, is the **Keylime Bistro** (© **239/395-4000**), where the musicians performing on the restaurant's resplendent outdoor patio aren't just your local garage band—last time I was there, one of Aaron Neville's band members showed up and played an extra long set. Best of all, there's no cover and entertainment is almost on a nightly basis. Call ahead for schedules.

NEARBY ISLAND HOPPING

Sanibel and Captiva are jumping-off points for island-hopping boat trips to barrier islands and Keys teeming with ancient legends and *Robinson Crusoe*–style beaches. You don't have to get completely lost out here, however, because several islets have comfortable inns and restaurants. The trip itself across shallow Pine Island Sound is a sightseeing adventure, with playful dolphins surfing on the boat's wake and a variety of cormorants, egrets, frigate birds, and (in winter) rare white pelicans flying above.

Captiva Cruises (© **239/472-5300;** www.captivacruises.com) makes daily trips from the South Seas Island Resort on Captiva Island. One vessel goes to Cabbage Key, departing at 10am and returning at 3pm. It stops at Useppa Island, going and coming, daily. Another vessel goes to Boca Grande by way of Cayo Costa State Park, departing daily at

Fun Facts **Where Chocolate Grows on Trees**

From December to February, the area's Black Sapote trees bear a most interesting fruit. Known as the "chocolate pudding fruit," it is round with thin olive-green skin and contains a mass of glossy, chocolate-colored pulp that's soft, sweet, and mild, very much like pudding. It makes a tasty and healthy dessert, a delicious pie filling, or an exotic tropical beverage when mixed with pineapple juice. The **Sunburst Tropical Fruit Company,** on Pine Island (© **239/283-1200**), has the fruit for sale, so you needn't pick from the trees.

10am and returning at 4pm. These day trips cost $45 for adults, $35 for children 6 to 12 to Cabbage Key or Useppa; $35 for adults, $20 for children 6 to 12 to Boca Grande or Cayo Costa. Reservations are required.

From Pine Island off Fort Myers, **Tropic Star Cruises** (© **239/283-0015;** www.tropicstarcruises.com) operates daily ferry service to Cayo Costa (p. 330).

Cabbage Key ★★

You never know who's going to get off a boat at 100-acre Cabbage Key and walk unannounced into the funky **Cabbage Key Inn** ★★, a rustic house built in 1938. Ernest Hemingway liked to hang out here in the early days, and novelist John D. MacDonald was a frequent guest 30 years later. Today, you could find yourself rubbing elbows at the bar with the likes of Walter Cronkite, Ted Koppel, Sean Connery, or Julia Roberts. Singer and avid yachtie Jimmy Buffett likes Cabbage Key so much that it inspired his hit song "Cheeseburger in Paradise."

A path leads from the tiny marina across a lawn dotted with coconut palms to this white-clapboard house that sits atop an ancient Calusa shell mound. Guests dine in the comfort of two screened porches and seek libations in the library-turned-bar, its pine-paneled walls now plastered with dollar bills left by visitors. The straight-back chairs and painted wooden tables show their age, but that's part of Cabbage Key's laid-back, don't-give-a-you-know-what charm.

In addition to the famous thick, juicy cheeseburgers so loved by Jimmy Buffett, the house specialties are fresh broiled fish and shrimp steamed in beer. Lunches range from $5 to $10; main courses at dinner are $15 to $25.

Most visitors come out here for the day, but if you want to stay overnight, the Cabbage Key Inn has six rooms and six cottages. The more expensive cottages, four of which have kitchens, are preferable to the rooms. Although the units have private bathrooms and air conditioners, they are very basic by today's standards, and some of their original 1920s furnishings have seen better days. Service for overnight guests can leave a lot to be desired, and there's no place on the islet to buy snacks or sundries. If you do decide to rough it, rates are $99 to $139 single or double for rooms, $145 to $389 for cottages. For information and reservations, contact Cabbage Key Inn, P.O. Box 200, Pineland, FL 33945 (© **239/283-2278;** fax 239/283-1384; www.cabbage-key.com).

Cayo Costa ★★★

Short of Tom Hanks in *Castaway,* you can't get any more deserted than at **Cayo Costa State Park** ★★★ (pronounced *Cay*-oh *Cos*-tah), which occupies a 2,132-acre, completely unspoiled barrier island with miles of white-sand beaches, pine forests, mangrove swamps, oak-palm hammocks, and grasslands. Other than natural wildlife, the only permanent residents here are park rangers.

Day-trippers can bring their own supplies and use a picnic area with pavilions. A free tram carries visitors from the dock on the sound side to the Gulf beach. The state maintains 12 very basic cabins and a primitive campground on the northern end of the island near Johnson Shoals, where the shelling is spectacular. Cabins cost $27 a day, and campsites are $16 a day year-round. For camping or cabin reservations, call © **800/326-3521** or go to www.reserveamerica.com. There's running water on the island, but no electricity.

The park is open daily from 8am to sundown. There's a $1-per-person honor-system admission fee for day visitors. You can rent single-seat kayaks for $40 a day, two-seaters for $50 a day; for reservations, call **Tropic Star Cruises,** on Pine Island (© **239/283-0015;** www.tropicstarcruises.com).

For more information, contact **Cayo Costa State Park,** P.O. Box 1150, Boca Grande, FL 33921 (© **941/964-0375;** www.floridastateparks.org/cayocosta). Office hours are Monday through Friday from 8am to 5pm.

Upper (North) Captiva

Cut off by a pass from Captiva, its northern barrier-island sibling is occupied by the upscale resort of **North Captiva Island Club,** P.O. Box 1000, Pineland, FL 33945 (© **800/576-7343** or 239/395-1001; fax 239/472-5836; www.northcaptiva.com). Despite the development, however, about 750 of the island's 1,000 acres are included in a state preserve. The club rents accommodations ranging from efficiencies to luxury homes. There's scheduled water-taxi service with **Island Girl Charters** (© **239/633-8142;** www.islandgirlcharters.org). Call for rates, as they change often.

Useppa Island

Useppa was a refuge of President Theodore Roosevelt and his tarpon-loving industrialist friends at the turn of the 20th century. New York advertising magnate Barron G. Collier

Bokeeli-huh?

In Spanish, it means "little mouth," but in terms of traveling through Southwest Florida, *Bokeelia* means "heaven." West of Fort Myers on the northern tip of Charlotte Harbor, Bokeelia joins Pine Island and St. James City as peaceful places where they've yet to pave paradise and put up a Starbucks. The **Bokeelia Tarpon Inn,** 8241 Main St. (© **866/TARPON-2** [827-7662] or 239/283-8961; www.tarponinn.com), is set in the historic Poe Johnson House. Johnson's lineage dates back to 1914. Revamped as an inn, without ruining its historical charm, the six-room house has pine floors and walls, a fireplace, Indonesian wicker furniture, and spacious rooms with louvered shutters and plush queen-size beds. Because the waters around here are swimming with tarpon, among other fish, the inn has a fly-tying room where a local fisherman demonstrates the finer points of fly-fishing. The inn can also arrange boat charters. Complimentary breakfast, wine, and hors d'oeuvres, as well as stunning views of Boca Grande and Charlotte Harbor, mean there's absolutely no reason to leave this unfettered little piece of Starbucks-free paradise.

bought the island in 1906 and built a lovely wooden home overlooking Pine Island Sound. His mansion is now the **Collier Inn,** where day-trippers and overnight guests can partake of lunches and seafood dinners in a place with country-club ambience. You can also visit the **Useppa Museum** (© **239/283-1061;** www.useppa.com/society.html), which explains the island's history and displays 4,000-year-old Calusa artifacts. Admission is by $5 donation.

The Collier Inn is the centerpiece of the **Useppa Island Club** (© **239/283-1061;** www.useppa.com), an exclusive development with more than 100 luxury homes, all in the clapboard-sided, tin-roofed style of Old Florida. For information, rates, and reservations, contact **Collier Inn & Cottages,** P.O. Box 640, Bokeelia, FL 33922 (© **888/735-6335** or 239/283-1061; fax 239/283-0290; www.useppa.com).

4 NAPLES ★★★

42 miles S of Fort Myers; 106 miles W of Miami; 185 miles S of Tampa

Ah, sleepy, swanky Naples. A place that may have defined the meaning of R & R, considering the fact that there's not much to do here besides linger on the beach, play golf, and dream that this isn't a vacation but a way of life. Naples is also easily Southwest Florida's most sophisticated city. But while Naples has its requisite waterfront mansions, sprawling country-club fairways, and a thoroughfare of pricey boutiques and restaurants, it's not nearly as upper-crust as, say, Palm Beach or Beverly Hills. Although the people are indeed very Ralph Lauren types, heavy on the starch, the snobbery factor and upper-tax-bracket lockjaw are conspicuously absent here—unlike the east coast of Florida, which is just as moneyed, but nowhere near as friendly or laid-back.

Don't even think of thumbing your nose at the long-bearded man dressed in ratty shorts and a Hawaiian T-shirt until you make sure he doesn't hop into a Bentley or zillion-dollar yacht. Therein lies the beauty of Naples. People are wealthy here, but have no need to flaunt it—what they do flaunt are St. Tropez tans and a general *joie de vivre.* Leave the kids at home—even though there's a zoo here, it's not a place where the little ones will have fun. Your relaxation *will* be disturbed when little Johnny and Jane start tugging at your shirt whining of boredom. Naples is a romantic spot for couples; it's not a swinging singles scene whatsoever. In fact, this is the kind of city where young singles need to try out for reality shows in order to find a mate. But you never know if the Mr. or Ms. Howell sitting at the bar is recently divorced and looking for a companion with whom to share their wealth. The median age in Naples can't be much lower than 45, but Naples itself isn't a spring chicken, either.

Naples was born in 1886, when a group of 12 Kentuckians and Ohioans bought 8,700 acres fronted by a gorgeous beach, laid out a town, and started selling lots. They built a pier and the 16-room Naples Hotel, whose first guest was President Grover Cleveland's sister Rose. She and other notables soon built a line of beach homes known as "Millionaires' Row." Today the area is known as Olde Naples and is carefully protected by its modern residents. Despite a building boom that expanded the city, the original settlement still retains the air of that time a century ago.

Although high-rise buildings now line the beaches north of the old town, the newer sections of Naples still have their charm, thanks to Ohio manufacturer Henry B. Watkins, Sr. In 1946, Watkins and his partners bought the old hotel and all the town's undeveloped land, and laid out the Naples Plan, which created the very wealthy, but environmentally conscious city you see today.

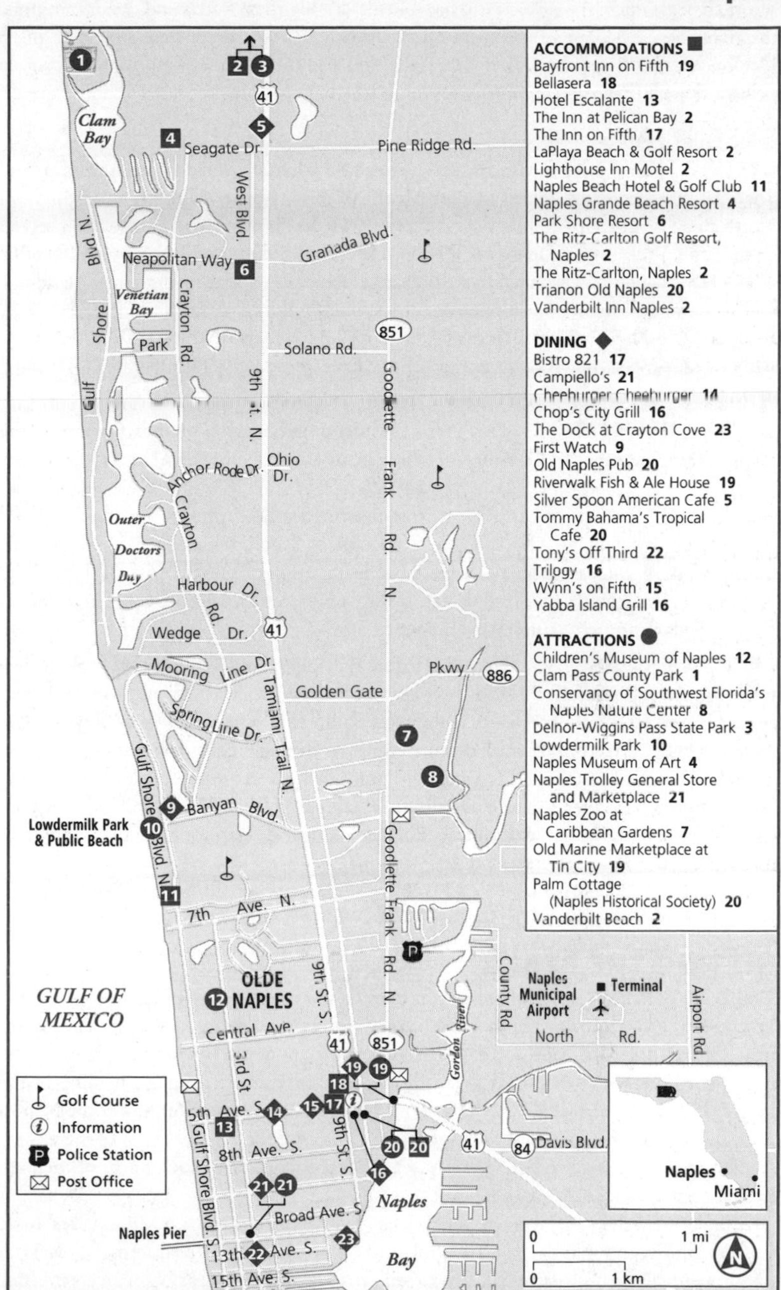
ACCOMMODATIONS
Bayfront Inn on Fifth 19
Bellasera 18
Hotel Escalante 13
The Inn at Pelican Bay 2
The Inn on Fifth 17
LaPlaya Beach & Golf Resort 2
Lighthouse Inn Motel 2
Naples Beach Hotel & Golf Club 11
Naples Grande Beach Resort 4
Park Shore Resort 6
The Ritz-Carlton Golf Resort, Naples 2
The Ritz-Carlton, Naples 2
Trianon Old Naples 20
Vanderbilt Inn Naples 2
DINING
Bistro 821 17
Campiello's 21
Cheeburger Cheeburger 14
Chop's City Grill 16
The Dock at Crayton Cove 23
First Watch 9
Old Naples Pub 20
Riverwalk Fish & Ale House 19
Silver Spoon American Cafe 5
Tommy Bahama's Tropical Cafe 20
Tony's Off Third 22
Trilogy 16
Wynn's on Fifth 15
Yabba Island Grill 16
ATTRACTIONS
Children's Museum of Naples 12
Clam Pass County Park 1
Conservancy of Southwest Florida's Naples Nature Center 8
Delnor-Wiggins Pass State Park 3
Lowdermilk Park 10
Naples Museum of Art 4
Naples Trolley General Store and Marketplace 21
Naples Zoo at Caribbean Gardens 7
Old Marine Marketplace at Tin City 19
Palm Cottage (Naples Historical Society) 20
Vanderbilt Beach 2
Clam Bay
Seagate Dr.
Pine Ridge Rd.
West Blvd.
Granada Blvd.
Neapolitan Way
Venetian Bay
Gulf Shore Blvd. N.
Park
Crayton Rd.
Solano Rd.
9th St. N.
Goodlette Frank Rd. N.
Anchor Rode Dr.
Ohio Dr.
Outer Doctors Bay
Harbour Dr.
Wedge Dr.
Mooring Line Dr.
Golden Gate Pkwy
Spring Line Dr.
Tamiami Trail N.
Gulf Shore Blvd. N.
Banyan Blvd.
Lowdermilk Park & Public Beach
7th Ave. N.
OLDE NAPLES
GULF OF MEXICO
9th St. S.
Central Ave.
County Rd
Naples Municipal Airport
Terminal
North Rd.
Airport Rd.
Gordon River
3rd St
5th Ave. S.
8th Ave. S.
Gulf Shore Blvd. S.
Davis Blvd.
Broad Ave. S.
Naples Bay
Naples Pier
13th Ave. S.
15th Ave. S.
Golf Course
Information
Police Station
Post Office
Naples
Miami
0 1 mi
0 1 km
N

About 4 miles north of Olde Naples, Vanderbilt Beach has a more traditional beach-resort character than the historic district. Lined with high-rise hotels and condominiums, the main beach here sits like an island of development between two preserved areas: Delnor-Wiggins Pass State Park to the north, and a county reserve fronting the expensive Pelican Bay golf-course community to the south.

ESSENTIALS

GETTING THERE Most visitors arrive at the **Southwest Florida International Airport,** 35 miles north of Naples in Fort Myers (p. 326). **Naples Municipal Airport,** on North Road off Airport-Pulling Road (© **239/643-6875;** www.flynaples.com), is served by the commuter arms of **American** (© **800/433-7300**) and **United/US Airways** (© **800/428-4322**), which means you'll have to change planes in Miami, Tampa, or Orlando.

Taxis await all flights outside the small terminal building. **Avis** (© **800/331-1212**), **Budget** (© **800/527-0700**), **Hertz** (© **800/654-3131**), and **National** (© **800/CAR-RENT** [227-7368]) have booths at the airport. **Enterprise** (© **800/325-8007**) is located in town.

VISITOR INFORMATION The most comprehensive source of information is the **Naples Area Chamber of Commerce,** which maintains a visitor center at 895 Fifth Ave. S. (at U.S. 41), Naples, FL 34102 (© **239/262-6141;** fax 239/435-9910; www.napleschamber.org). The center has a lot of free information and phones for making hotel reservations. By mail, it will send you a free list of accommodations and other basic information, or you can order a complete Naples vacation packet for $6 (but don't waste your money, request the *free* one, which is the same minus a street map). The center is open Monday through Saturday from 9am to 5pm.

GETTING AROUND The **Naples Trolley** (© **239/262-7300;** www.naplestrolleytours.com) clangs around 25 stops between the Naples Trolley General Store and Welcome Center, 1010 6th Ave. S., at 10th Street South (2 blocks west of Tin City in Olde Naples), and Vanderbilt Beach. It runs Monday through Saturday from 8:30am to 5:15pm, and Sunday from 10:15am to 5:15pm. Daily fares are $24 for adults and $12 for children 4 to 12, with free reboarding. Schedules are available in brochure racks in the lobbies of most hotels and motels. The drivers provide narration, so the entire loop makes a good 2-hour sightseeing tour.

For a taxi, call **Yellow Cab** (© **239/262-1312**), **Checker Cab** (© **239/455-5555**), **Maxi Taxi** (© **239/262-8977**), or **Naples Taxi** (© **239/775-0505**).

HITTING THE BEACH

Unlike many Florida cities, where you have to drive over to a barrier island to reach the beach, this city's beach is right in Olde Naples. Rather than being fronted by tall condominium buildings, the backdrop here is all the mansions along Millionaires' Row. Access to the gorgeous white sand is at the Gulf end of each avenue, although parking in the neighborhood can be brutal. Try the metered lots on 12th Avenue South near the **Naples Pier,** the town's most popular beach spot (see "Exploring the Town," below), where there are also restrooms and food concessions. Families gather on the beach north of the pier, while bored local teens congregate on the south side.

Also popular, the very Norman Rockwellian **Lowdermilk Park,** on Millionaires' Row, at Gulf Shore and North Banyan boulevards, has a pavilion, restrooms, showers, a refreshment counter, professional-quality volleyball courts (the area's best players practice here), a duck pond, and picnic tables. There's also metered parking, so bring quarters. A few blocks farther north is another metered parking lot with beach access, beside the Naples Beach Hotel & Golf Resort, 851 Gulf Shore Blvd. N., at Golf Drive.

Nature lovers head to the Pelican Bay development north of the historic district and the popular, 35-acre **Clam Pass County Park ★★** (✆ **239/353-0404**). A free tram takes you along a 3,000-foot boardwalk winding through mangrove swamps and across a back bay to a beach of fine white sand. It's strange to see high-rise condominiums standing beyond the mangrove-bordered backwaters, but this is actually a miniature wilderness. Some 6 miles of canoe and kayak trails—with multitudes of birds and an occasional alligator—run from Clam Pass into the winding streams. The beach pavilion here has a bar (drinking is a sport in Naples), restrooms with foot showers only, picnic tables, and beach equipment rentals, including one- and two-person kayaks and 12-foot canoes. Entry is from a metered parking lot beside the Naples Grande Beach Resort, at the end of Seagate Drive. There's a $6-per-vehicle parking fee. You can push, but not ride, bicycles on the boardwalk.

At Vanderbilt Beach, about 4 miles north of Olde Naples, the **Delnor-Wiggins Pass State Park ★★★**, at the west end of Bluebill Avenue–111th Avenue North (✆ **239/597-6196;** www.floridastateparks.org/delnor-wiggins), has been listed among America's top 10 stretches of sand. It has bathhouses, a boat ramp, and the area's best picnic facilities. A concessionaire sells hot dogs, sandwiches, and ice cream, and rents beach chairs, umbrellas, kayaks, canoes, and snorkeling gear. Fish viewing is great over a small reef under 12 feet of water about 150 feet offshore. Fishing from the beach is excellent, too. Rangers provide nature tours throughout the year, with the most interesting during the loggerhead-turtle nesting season from June to October (call or check the park's website for the schedule). After a dredging of the beach in 2007, the sand has expanded to 150 feet and is an ideal spot for shellers. The park is open daily from 8am to sunset. Admission is $3 per vehicle with one occupant, $5 per vehicle with two to eight occupants, and $1 per pedestrian or biker. To get here from Olde Naples, go north on U.S. 41 about 4 miles and take a left onto 111th Avenue, which turns into Bluebill Avenue before it reaches the beach. Note that 111th Avenue is known as Immokalee Road east of U.S. 41.

OUTDOOR ACTIVITIES

BOATING Powerboat and WaveRunner rentals are available from **Club Nautico,** at the Boat Haven Marina, 1484 E. Tamiami Trail (✆ **239/417-3474**), on the east bank of the Gordon River behind Kelly's Fish House; and from **Port-O-Call Marina,** also behind Kelly's Fish House (✆ **239/774-0479**).

CRUISES Day Star Charters features the double-decked ***Double Sunshine*** (✆ **239/263-4949;** www.tincityboats.com), which sallies forth onto the river and bay daily from Tin City, where it has a ticket office. The 1½-hour cruises leave at 10am, noon, 2pm, and an hour before sunset. They cost $30 for adults and $20 for children 11 and under.

The ***Sweet Liberty*** (✆ **239/793-3525;** www.sweetliberty.com), a 53-foot sailing catamaran, makes 3-hour morning shelling cruises to Keewaydin Island. The vessel then spends the afternoon on 2-hour sightseeing cruises (you'll usually see dolphins playing in the river on this one) and 2-hour sunset cruises on Naples Bay before docking at Naples City Dock, 880 12th Ave. S. Shelling cruises cost $40 for adults, $15 for children 12 and under; sightseeing and sunset cruises cost $30 for adults, $15 for children 12 and under.

For a good deal more luxury, the 83-foot ***Naples Princess*** (✆ **800/728-2970** or 239/649-2275; www.naplesprincesscruises.com) has narrated breakfast, lunch, and sunset dinner cruises from Port-O-Call Marina, on the eastern shore of the Gordon River.

With their extensive buffets, the sightseeing, sunset, and shelling cruises are good values, ranging from $28 to $55 per person. Prices for children 12 and under vary on all cruises. Call for schedules and reservations.

FISHING The locals like to fish from the **Naples Pier** (see "Exploring the Town," below). The pier has tables on which to clean your catch, but watch out for the ever-present pelicans, which are master thieves. You can buy tackle and bait from the local marinas (see "Boating," above). The pier is open round-the-clock, and admission is free. No fishing license is required.

The least expensive way for singles, couples, and small families to fish without paying for an entire boat is on the 45-foot ***Lady Brett*** (✆ **239/263-4949;** www.tincityboats.com), which makes two daily half-day trips from Tin City for $75 for adults, $60 for kids 11 and under. Rod, reel, bait, and fishing license are included, but bring your own drinks and lunch. Its sister boat, the ***Captain Paul,*** goes on half-day backcountry fishing trips, departing daily at 9am. These cost $75 for adults, $60 for kids 12 and under.

A number of charter boats are based at the marinas mentioned under "Boating," above; call or visit them for booking information and prices.

GOLF For a city its size, Naples has an extraordinary number of fine golf courses. Most are out in the suburbs, though not the flat but challenging 18 holes at the **Naples Beach Hotel & Golf Club ★★** (p. 369), right in the middle of town. Nonguests can play here, but should call ahead for a tee time.

Two of the best-known courses are the **Lely Flamingo Island Club ★★** and the **Lely Mustang Golf Club,** both on U.S. 41 between Naples and Marco Island (✆ **800/388-GOLF** [4653] or 239/793-2223; www.lely-resort.net). Robert Trent Jones, Sr., designed the Lely Flamingo course; its hourglass fairways and fingerlike bunkers present many challenges. The Lee Trevino–designed Lely Mustang course is more forgiving, but still fun. Former PGA Tour player Paul Trittler has his golf school at these courses. You'll pay a price here in winter, when 18-hole fees are about $145 at Lely Flamingo and $165 at Lely Mustang, including cart and range balls, but they drop progressively after Easter to about $79 in the muggy summer months.

Eagle Lakes Golf Club, on U.S. 41 between Fla. 931 and Fla. 92 (✆ **239/732-5108;** www.eaglelakesgolfclub.com), is another winner, with lots of wildlife inhabiting its many lakes (a 16-ft. alligator reportedly resides near the 17th hole). On-site is a driving range, a practice facility, and a restaurant; instruction is available. Wintertime fees are about $99, but in the off-season they drop to $29 or less. Tee times are taken up to 4 days in advance.

Another local favorite is the player-friendly **Hibiscus Golf Club,** a half-mile east of U.S. 41 off Rattlesnake Hammock Road, East Naples (✆ **239/774-0088;** www.hibiscusgolf.com). A pro shop and teaching professional are available. Fees are about $70 to $85 in winter, cart included, and drop to about $35 in summer.

At the intersection of Vanderbilt Beach and Airport-Pulling roads, the Greg Norman–designed 27 championship holes at the **Tiburón Golf Club ★★**, 2620 Tiburón Dr. (✆ **877/WCI-PLAY** [924-7529] or 239/594-2040; www.tiburongolf.com), play like a British Open course—but without the thick-thatch rough. Greens fees have been dramatically reduced in recent years, starting as low as $47 for 18 holes, with cart, on a weekend day. The course is home to the **Rick Smith Golf Academy** (✆ **877/464-6531** or 239/593-1111) and the **Ritz-Carlton Golf Resort** (p. 371).

The area also has several other courses worth playing, most described in the Naples–Fort Myers edition of the *Golfer's Guide,* available at the chamber of commerce's visitor center (or check the magazine's website at www.golfersguide.com). Online, www.naples golf.com is also a good source of information about area courses.

SCUBA DIVING Kevin Sweeney's **SCUBAdventures,** 971 Creech Rd., at Tamiami Trail (© **239/434-7477**), which also has a base on Marco Island (see section 5, later in this chapter), teaches diver-certification courses, and rents watersports equipment.

TENNIS In Olde Naples, the city's **Cambier Park Tennis Center** ★★, 755 8th Ave. S., at 9th Street South (© **239/213-3060**), is one of the country's finest municipal facilities. In fact, it matches those found at many luxury resorts. To play on its 12 lighted clay courts, it costs $25 an hour. Book at the pro shop in the modern building, which has restrooms but no showers. The shop is open Monday through Friday from 8am to 9pm, Saturday and Sunday from 8am to 5pm.

WATERSPORTS **Naples Watersports,** 550 Port A Call Way (© **239/774-0479**), will hook you up with WaveRunners, jet skis, and the requisite water toys. Hobie Cats and windsurfers can also be rented on the beach at the **Naples Beach Hotel & Golf Club,** 851 Gulf Shore Blvd. N. (© **239/261-2222**); and at **Clam Pass County Park,** at the end of Seagate Drive (© **239/353-0404**). See p. 363 for more about Clam Pass.

EXPLORING THE TOWN

Olde Naples ★★★

Its history may go back only to 1886, but the beach skirting **Olde Naples** still has the charm of that Victorian era. The heart of the district lies south of 5th Avenue South (that's where U.S. 41 takes a 45-degree turn). The town docks are on the bay side, the stunning **Naples Beach** along the Gulf. Laid out on a grid, the tree-lined streets run between many houses, some dating from the town's beginning, and along Millionaires' Row between Gulf Shore Boulevard and the beach. With these gorgeous homes virtually hidden in the palms and casuarinas, Naples Beach seems a century removed from the high-rise condominiums farther north.

The **Naples Pier,** at the Gulf end of 12th Avenue South, is a focal point of the neighborhood. Built in 1888 to let steamers land potential real-estate customers, the original 600-foot-long, T-shape structure was destroyed by hurricanes and damaged by fire. Local residents have rebuilt it because they like strolling its length to catch fantastic Gulf sunsets—and to get a glimpse of Millionaires' Row from the Gulf side. The pier is now a state historic site. It's open 24 hours a day, but parking in the nearby lots is restricted between 11pm and 7am.

Nearby **Palm Cottage,** 137 12th Ave. S., between 1st Street and Gordon Drive (© **239/261-8164**), was built in 1885 by one of Naples's founders, *Louisville Courier-Journal* publisher Walter Haldeman, as a winter retreat for his chief editorial writer. After World War II, its socialite owners hosted many galas attended by Hollywood stars such as Hedy Lamarr, Gary Cooper, and Robert Montgomery. One of the few remaining Southwest Florida houses built of tabby mortar (made by burning shells), Palm Cottage today is the home of the Naples Historical Society, which maintains it as a museum filled with authentic furniture, paintings, photographs, and other memorabilia. Tours are given in winter Monday through Friday from 1 to 3:30pm. Admission is $8 for adults, $5 for children 12 and under.

Near the Gordon River Bridge on 5th Avenue South, the old corrugated waterfront warehouses are now a shopping-and-dining complex known as the **Old Marine Marketplace at Tin City,** to which tourists throng and which local residents assiduously avoid. It does, however, look cool from the outside.

Museums & Zoos

Children's Museum of Naples ★★ When it opens in the spring of 2010, this museum, the first of its kind in Southwest Florida, will feature 10 intricately designed, child-scaled exhibits, from a working art studio and grocery store, to re-creations of space, the Everglades, and the beach. At the heart of the exhibits is the Banyan Tree and Tree House, a soaring, two-story banyan tree with cubbies nestled in vertical prop roots, a lookout platform, and crawling branches that lead to the fascinating treehouse at the top, inspiring children's imaginations as well as body coordination.

North Naples Regional Park, 15000 Livingston Rd. ✆ **239/597-1900.** www.cmon.org. Admission and hours of operation not currently available.

Naples Museum of Art ★★ The first full-scale art museum in Southwest Florida, the Naples Museum of Art has an impressive 15 galleries highlighting paintings, sculptures, and drawings, with major permanent collections concentrating on both the American Modern and Ancient Chinese genres. Touring shows and exhibitions bring a welcome element of eclecticism to the museum, whose very structure, including a 90×45-foot glass dome and 14-foot-high entrance gates, is a dramatic work of art on its own. October through May, free guided tours are given at 11am and 2pm Tuesday through Saturday.

5833 Pelican Bay Blvd. (at West Blvd.). ✆ **239/597-1900.** www.thephil.org. Admission $8 adults, $4 students. Tues–Sat 10am–4pm; Sun noon–4pm. Closed Memorial Day, July 4, Thanksgiving, Christmas Eve, Christmas Day, New Year's Eve, New Year's Day, and Aug 1 to Labor Day.

Naples Zoo at Caribbean Gardens ★ (Kids) The only zoo in Florida to have rare, Indochinese tigers and a supporting cast of lions, leopards, spotted hyenas, and African wild dogs, Caribbean Gardens is an oasis of animal activity. In addition to the standard caged animals, the zoo has boat rides, primate islands, a large display of flora, and close encounters with kangaroos, alligators, and pythons. You can see them on a boat safari that slinks through spectacular tropical gardens and the islands of Lake Victoria, which monkeys, lemurs, and apes call home. The Safari Canyon presentation is a cool multimedia combination of video, music, and live animals that swim, leap, stalk, and slither around the natural rock-work theater that's only a splash away from the audience. The zoo's newest exhibit showcases the fosa, Madagascar's massive carnivore, which feasts on poor lemurs. You will easily fill 3 to 4 hours here. If you have kids along, you may want to divide the zoo into several days of sightseeing so you have something to do when they get antsy after swimming at the beach or pool. Should all this animal activity make you hungry, a Subway branch sells sandwiches, and there are picnic facilities on the premises.

1590 Goodlette-Frank Rd. (at Fleischmann Blvd.). ✆ **239/262-5409.** www.napleszoo.com. Admission $19 adults, $18 seniors, $11 children 4–15. Daily 9:30am–5:30pm. Closed Easter, Thanksgiving, and Christmas.

A Nature Preserve

You can experience Southwest Florida's abundant natural life—and we don't mean those without silicone—without leaving town at the **Conservancy of Southwest Florida's Naples Nature Center ★**, 14th Avenue North, east of Goodlette-Frank Road (✆ **239/262-0304;** www.conservancy.org), one of two preserves operated by the Conservancy. Here, you'll find nature trails and an aviary (with bald eagles and other birds). You can take guided boat rides on the hour, between 10am and 3pm, weather permitting. The naturalist guides will explain the vegetation along the Gordon River, which isn't all that interesting unless you're a plant fanatic. However, the wildlife is interesting—including an occasional monkey escapee from the Naples Zoo next door (see "Museums & Zoos," above). You can also rent a canoe or kayak and see the area by yourself. An excellent nature store carries gift items. A 2007 renovation added a new multimedia exhibit dedicated to the imperiled Florida panther, showcasing the Florida panther in its natural environment, and a new "touch tank" with even more plants, animals, and marine life on display. Admission fees of $9 for adults and $4 for children 3 to 12 include the boat rides. Canoes and kayaks cost $15 for 2 hours, $7 for each additional hour. The center is open year-round Monday through Saturday from 9am to 4:30pm; February through April, it's also open Sunday from 1 to 5pm. Closed July 4, Labor Day, Thanksgiving, Christmas Eve, and Christmas Day.

SHOPPING

A 2-block stretch of **3rd Street South** ★★, at Broad Avenue, aspires to be the Rodeo Drive of Naples, but with the conspicuous absence of Gucci, Prada, and Tiffany, it remains an ordinary (albeit lovely), pricey place for browsing. This collection of jewelers, clothiers, and galleries may be too rich for many wallets, but the window-shopping here is unmatched. Pick up a free brochure from the chamber of commerce's visitor center (p. 362); it lists the merchants and has a map of the area.

Nearby, the **5th Avenue South** ★ shopping area, between 3rd and 9th streets south, is Naples's hottest wining-and-dining spot, complete with the requisite Starbucks. The avenue is longer and a bit less chic than 3rd Street South, with its stock brokerages and real-estate offices thrown into the mix of boutiques and antiques dealers.

Also in Olde Naples, the rustic, tacky **Old Marine Marketplace at Tin City,** 1200 Fifth Ave. S., at the Gordon River (✆ **239/262-4200**), has 50 boutiques selling everything from souvenirs to avant-garde resort wear and imported statuary. There are more boutiques in the **Dockside Boardwalk,** a half-block west on 6th Avenue South.

WHERE TO STAY

Branches of most chain hotels sit along U.S. 41, but these tend to be of higher quality and better value than their counterparts elsewhere in Southwest Florida.

One of the most reasonably priced condominium complexes, **Park Shore Resort,** 600 Neapolitan Way, Naples (✆ **800/548-2077** or 239/263-2222; fax 239/263-0946; www.parkshorefl.com), has 156 attractive one- and two-bedroom condominiums surrounding an artificial lagoon with waterfalls cascading on its own island. Guests can walk across a bridge to the artificial island, where they can swim in the heated pool, barbecue on gas grills, or order a meal from the restaurant or a drink from the bar. There's also once-a-day (11am) complimentary transport to the beach. (To return from the beach, make a reservation at the front desk to catch a ride back at 2pm.) The condominiums range from $130 to $175 in winter, and $100 to $150 during the off-season.

One of the biggest condominium-rental agents here is **Bluebill Properties,** 26201 Hickory Blvd., Bonita Springs (✆ **800/237-2010** or 239/992-6620).

And new to the Naples hotel scene is the **Hotel at Naples Bay Resort,** 1500 5th Ave. S. (✆ **230/530-1199;** www.naplesbayresort.com), an 85-room condo hotel on sceney 5th Avenue South, with rates ranging from $189 to $459.

The accommodations below are organized geographically in Olde Naples and north of the historic district, including Vanderbilt Beach.

In Olde Naples

Very Expensive

Bellasera ★★★ The newest luxury property to hit Naples, Bellasera is the quintessence of swank. Inspired by the villas of Tuscany, the hotel's rooms are all suites that feature crown molding, gorgeous bathrooms with marble tubs, Kiehl's products, granite counters, and beds you may never want to leave. An outdoor heated pool has private cabanas, as well as an Italian-style courtyard with fountain. ZiZi Restaurant and Lounge serves excellent Tuscan fare. Although the hotel is not on the beach, judging by the service here, they'd probably bring the beach to you if you asked. A new spa, Verde, offers organic products and massage services, including Swedish Massage, Bamboosage, Hot Stones, Ashiatsu Oriental Bar Therapy, and Thai Yoga Massage. The top-notch service makes this one of Naples's best hotels, so it's worth having to take a short walk to the beach (or the complimentary beach shuttle).

221 9th St. S., Naples, FL 34102. ✆ **888/612-1115** or 239/649-7333. Fax 239/649-6233. www.bellaseranaples.com. 100 units. Winter $207–$695 double; off-season $124–$225 double. AE, DC, DISC, MC, V. **Amenities:** Restaurant; heated outdoor pool; fitness center; spa; Jacuzzi; limited room service. *In room:* A/C, TV, dataport, minibar, fridge, coffeemaker, hair dryer, iron.

Hotel Escalante ★★ On the quiet end of the 5th Avenue shopping district and 1½ blocks from the beach, this romantic 10-suite boutique hotel is perfect for couples who want convenience, no crowds, and a bit of pampering. The Mediterranean villa–style hotel is ensconced in 4 acres of private gardens with more than 300 species of plant s, walkways of old brick from Chicago, and fountains from France. All units are luxuriously appointed, and the bathrooms come with two hand basins, ample vanity space, and big shower heads (the majority of bathrooms have walk-in showers as opposed to tubs). Special services include a day spa, lunch served on the beach, an evening wine reception, and an honor bar and complimentary cookies in the library. There is also a restaurant, Fonteneda's Grill, which can cater to your every need.

290 5th Ave. S., Naples, FL 34102. ✆ **239/659-3466.** Fax 239/262-8748. www.hotelescalante.com. 10 units. Winter $285–$895 suite; off-season $195–$595 suite. Rates include continental breakfast. AE, MC, V. **Amenities:** Bar; heated outdoor pool; exercise room; day spa; Jacuzzi; laundry service. *In room:* A/C, TV, minibar, hair dryer, iron.

The Inn on Fifth ★ This former bank building still exudes that old-money, Old World European charm—from the outside, at least. Ideally located on the closest thing to "happening" 5th Avenue South, the Inn has large guest rooms, some more elegantly decorated than others, which are a half a step up from a chain hotel, frankly. French doors opening onto a balcony or terrace may not reveal the ocean, but you will see either the pool or the action on the Avenue. McCabe's Irish Pub downstairs is a hotbed of activity, featuring live music, a fabulous beer selection, and a youngish contingency of revelers. There's also an Asian spa and an excellent seafood and steak restaurant on the premises. That aside, it's a mostly quiet (the third-floor rooms facing the street can get a tad noisy btw. 8 and 11pm), ideally located spot—the only hotel in the midst of the downtown Naples bustle.

699 5th Ave. S., Naples, FL 34102. ✆ **888/403-8778** or 239/403-8777. Fax 239/403-8778. www.innonfifth.com. 87 units. Winter $329–$500 double; off-season $150–$359 double. AE, DC, DISC, MC, V. **Amenities:** 2 restaurants; bar; heated outdoor pool; fitness center; spa; Jacuzzi; concierge; business services; room service; laundry service. *In room:* A/C, TV, dataport, free Wi-Fi, coffeemaker, hair dryer, iron, safe, iPod docking station.

LaPlaya Beach & Golf Resort ★★★ There's no dearth of beach resorts in Naples, but what *has* been missing—that is, until now—is a more intimate resort directly on the beach, where you don't feel underdressed or socially inappropriate when walking through the lobby in a bathing-suit cover-up. Located on pristine Vanderbilt Beach, this resort filled the void with plush, beautifully decorated rooms overlooking the Gulf and bay

An Open-Air Bar

Because the **Naples Beach Hotel** predates the city's strict historic-district zoning laws, it also has Olde Naples's only restaurants and bar directly on the beach. Of these, the **Sunset Beach Bar** is one of the region's most famous beachside open-air bars; it's always crammed as the sun sets over the Gulf, with nightly live bands and a very popular Sunday evening pool party.

(each with private balcony), a spectacular 4,500-square-foot spa, gourmet seafood restaurant Baleen, and a sprawling, scenic, and challenging Bob Cupp–designed golf club and the David Leadbetter Golf Academy. But back to the rooms. The French-country decor and goose-down pillows are hardly what you'd expect at a beach resort, but there's the rub! You'll find none of that cookie-cutter, as-seen-in-*Martha-Stewart-Living* stuff here. Big bathrooms are luxurious, decked out in marble. Everything has a distinct personality, especially the impressive staff that will go to any lengths to accommodate you, without being overly doting.

9891 Gulf Shore Dr., Naples, FL 34108. ✆ **800/237-6883** or 239/597-3123. Fax 239/597-6278. www.laplayaresort.com. 189 units. Winter $519–$789 double, $1,300–$1,500 suite; off-season $229–$399 double, $419–$900 suite. AE, DC, DISC, MC, V. Valet parking only $18. **Amenities:** Restaurant; bar; pool bar; 4 outdoor pools; golf course; spa; watersports equipment/rentals (parasailing, kayaking, paddleboats, jet skis); concierge; room service. *In room:* A/C, TV, dataport, minibar, coffeemaker, hair dryer, iron, safe, CD player.

Naples Beach Hotel & Golf Club ★★★ Kids Compared to the Ritz-Carlton and the Naples Grande (see below for both), which could be anywhere, this beachy-keen retro-resort definitely belongs in Olde Naples. It's also Southwest Florida's only resort with its own 18-hole golf course, tennis center, and full-service spa right on the premises. The least expensive rooms are in the Florida Wing, a two-story relic from 1948, with updated units opening to a long porch with views of the pool and Gulf. Tower units are over the main dining room and directly across the boulevard from the golf course. Suites in the Cabana Wing boast redesigned, large bathrooms. The Watkins Wing houses the most spacious suites. Rooms in the Penthouse Wing, removed from the action at the north end of the property, directly face the beach and are the best choice for couples, especially during holidays and summer, when many families stay here—the excellent Beach Klub 4 Kids is *free.* All rooms at the resort were remodeled, with the multimillion-dollar project completed in January 2008. Guest rooms and suites now feature new bedding and fabrics, flat-panel televisions, and accents in calming tropical shades. In addition, the resort is doing a multimillion-dollar remodeling of the bathrooms in all guest rooms. The project is now underway, with many rooms already complete, and all rooms will be done by summer 2009.

851 Gulf Shore Blvd. North, Naples, FL 34102. ✆ **800/237-7600** or 239/261-2222. Fax 239/261-7380. www.naplesbeachhotel.com. 318 units. Winter $335–$615 double, $450–$825 suite; off-season $190–$325 double, $285–$500 suite. Packages available. AE, DC, DISC, MC, V. Free valet parking. **Amenities**: 4 restaurants; 4 bars; heated outdoor pool; 18-hole golf course; 6 tennis courts; fitness center; full-service spa; watersports equipment/rentals; bike rental; children's programs; game room; concierge; activities desk; shopping arcade; salon; room service; massage; babysitting; laundry service. *In room:* A/C, TV, Wi-Fi, fridge, hair dryer, iron, safe.

Expensive

Bayfront Inn on Fifth ★★★ Naples's only downtown waterfront boutique hotel, Bayfront Inn is a Caribbean chic lodging within walking distance to shopping, dining, and, best of all, the waterfront. A heated waterfall pool and spa and waterfront restaurant with live entertainment keep guests happily ensconced here, with no real reason to leave. Guest rooms are plush and posh, with luxe linens, pillow-top mattresses, and the most sublime Trillium gel pillows you've ever laid your head on. Rooms overlook the water and, in season, you can even charter or rent a boat to ride along the bay front. If you're debating between the similarly named, yet worlds apart Inn on Fifth and this place, there's no contest.

1221 5th Ave. S., Naples, FL 34102. ✆ **239/649-5800.** Fax 239/649-0523. www.bayfrontinnnaples.com. 98 units. Winter $210–$310 double, $285–$595 suite; off-season $95–$155 double, $145–$395 suite. AE, DC, DISC, MC, V. **Amenities:** Restaurant; heated outdoor pool; watersports equipment/rentals; concierge; seasonal room service. *In room:* A/C, TV/DVD, high-speed Internet, fridge (in some), coffeemaker, hair dryer, iron, safe.

Trianon Old Naples ★ Located in a quiet (read: no activity) residential neighborhood, this elegant Mediterranean-style building with a classical European interior offers convenience and comfort without a lot of frills. The spacious rooms are equipped with Ritz-Carlton–quality furniture, including mahogany armoires, chairs, and writing desks. All have Tempurpedic mattresses, seating areas, and extra-large bathrooms. Some units have balconies spacious enough for chairs, but others are for standing only. There's no restaurant, but continental breakfast is served on silver in a refined lounge. Wine, beer, champagne, and ports are served at a wine bar in the evenings.

955 7th Ave. S., Naples, FL 34102. ✆ **877/482-5228** or 239/435-9600. Fax 239/261-0025. www.trianon.com. 58 units. Winter $199–$285 double, $380–$425 suite; off-season $95–$205 double, $185–$295 suite. Rates include continental breakfast. AE, DC, DISC, MC, V. **Amenities:** Heated outdoor pool; laundry service. *In room:* A/C, TV, dataport, Wi-Fi, fridge (in some), coffeemaker, hair dryer, iron, safe.

North of Olde Naples

Very Expensive

The Ritz-Carlton, Naples ★★★ Kids This opulent Mediterranean-style resort, one of Florida's finest, is a favorite among affluent guests who like standard Ritz amenities—marble floors, Waterford-crystal chandeliers, British-style afternoon tea, and a staff that starts fawning over you from the moment you arrive. Still, it lacks the wonderful, nonfabricated Old Florida charm of the Naples Beach Hotel & Golf Club (see above). Nor is it as close to the beach—you have to walk through a narrow mangrove forest to reach the sands. The beach here is part of a public park, but hotel staff is out there to answer phones, deliver drinks and snacks, and rent cabanas, boats, and other toys (only towels, chairs, and ice water are complimentary). The plush guest rooms and suites overlook the Gulf, but not all have balconies. A $50-million full-service spa is bliss. Guests here can play the golf course and use the other amenities at the Ritz-Carlton Golf Resort, Naples (see below).

280 Vanderbilt Beach Rd., Naples, FL 34108. ✆ **888/856-4372** or 239/598-3300. Fax 239/598-6690. www.ritzcarlton.com. 450 units. Winter $499–$899 double, $1,395–$4,999 suite; off-season $189–$499 double, $559–$1,219 suite. AE, DC, DISC, MC, V. Valet parking $23. From Olde Naples, go north 3½ miles on U.S. 41. Turn left on Vanderbilt Beach Rd. (C.R. 862) to hotel on the left. **Amenities:** 7 restaurants; 3 bars; 2 heated outdoor pools and children's play pool; access to golf course; 4 tennis courts; full-service spa; Jacuzzi; sauna; watersports equipment/rentals; children's programs; interactive entertainment lounge; concierge; business center; salon; 24-hr. room service; massage; babysitting; laundry service; concierge-level rooms. *In room:* A/C, TV/DVD/CD player, dataport, minibar, coffeemaker, hair dryer, iron, safe.

The Ritz-Carlton Golf Resort, Naples ★★ This Mediterranean-style resort opened in 2002 at the 36-hole (two 18-hole courses), Greg Norman–designed Tiburón Golf Club, in an exclusive residential enclave at the intersection of Vanderbilt Beach and Airport-Pulling roads. This is a golf-lover's version of its sister resort, the Ritz-Carlton, Naples (see above), and guests here can use the spa, beach, and other facilities at its older sibling, a 5-minute drive away. Each of the spacious, luxuriously appointed guest units has a private balcony overlooking the gorgeously landscaped course. Complimentary shuttle service is provided daily from 6:30am to 11:30pm between the resorts. Guests are encouraged to enjoy the services and amenities at both the Ritz-Carlton Resorts of Naples.

2600 Tiburón Dr., Naples, FL 34109. ✆ **888/856-4372** or 239/593-2000. Fax 239/254-3300. www.ritzcarlton.com. 295 units. Winter $309–$699 double, $649–$2,300 suite; off-season $159–$299 double, $299–$2,200 suite. Packages available. AE, DC, DISC, MC, V. From Olde Naples, go north 3½ miles on U.S. 41. Turn right on Vanderbilt Beach Rd. (C.R. 862) to Airport-Pulling Rd. Hotel is on the left. Amenities: 4 restaurants; 2 bars; heated outdoor pool; 2 golf courses; 4 tennis courts; health club; Jacuzzi; sauna; children's programs; games room (billiards, cards); concierge; business center; 24-hr. room service; massage; babysitting; laundry service, concierge-level rooms. *In room:* A/C, TV/DVD/CD player, dataport, minibar, coffeemaker, hair dryer, iron, safe.

Expensive/Moderate

The Inn at Pelican Bay ★ Just 1 mile away from the sands and waters of the Gulf of Mexico, this charming inn features 100 newly renovated guest rooms in the upscale North Naples neighborhood of Pelican Bay. It's quiet and not unlike staying in someone's apartment, only this time you don't have to make the bed. Decor is Mediterranean meets Old World with dark-wood furniture, but amenities are totally New World with LCD TVs, complimentary wireless Internet access, and, in some rooms (request these), bathrooms have a jetted tub, separate shower, and huge vanity area. A complimentary deluxe continental breakfast is offered, as is afternoon tea. The lobby bar overlooks a fountain-filled lake. It's very peaceful and quiet here.

800 Vanderbilt Beach Rd., Naples, FL 34108. ✆ **800/597-8770** or 239/597-8777. Fax 239/597-8012. www.innatpelicanbay.com. 147 units. Winter $139–$179 double; off-season $119–$149 double. Weekly rates available. AE, DC, DISC, MC, V. **Amenities:** Restaurant; bar; heated outdoor pool; business center. *In room:* A/C, TV, Wi-Fi, coffeemaker, hair dryer, iron, safe, microwave.

The Naples Grande Beach Resort ★★ Kids This luxury boutique high-rise is not directly on the beach: Guests must ride the free Clam Pass County Park tram (p. 363) to the Gulf. To compensate, the resort has a big outdoor complex with three pools, a water slide, and cabanas. There's also a 15-Har-Tru-court tennis center and superb Golden Door Spa complete with plunge pools and multisensory massages. The Naples Grande radiates a more relaxed ambience than the traditional Ritz-Carlton, but none of the Old Florida charm of its other chief rival, the Naples Beach Hotel & Golf Club (see above). However, thanks to a complete revamp, the lobby and rooms are now on par with trendy boutique hotels that use 300-thread-count linens, backlit headboards, and sleek furniture. Bungalow suites, 50 of them, are incredible, with plush mattresses and stunning bathrooms with rain showerheads—only 25 have tubs. Kids' programs are impressive, and the little ones (and their parents) will love the pool's 100-foot water slide. A branch of the **Strip House,** the chain steakhouse known for its racy decor (and excellent steaks), debuted in 2007.

475 Seagate Dr., Naples, FL 34103. ✆ **888/422-6177** or 239/597-3232. Fax 239/597-3147. www.naplesgranderesort.com. 474 units. Winter $135–$179 double, $225–$329 suite, $899 grand suite; off-season $150–$209 double, $297–$429 suite, $1,170–$1,299 grand suite. Amenities fee $20 per day. Packages

available. AE, DC, DISC, MC, V. From Olde Naples, go about 1½ miles north on U.S. 41 and turn left on Seagate Dr. Hotel is on the right. **Amenities:** 4 restaurants; 2 bars; 3 heated outdoor pools; access to golf course; 15 tennis courts; fitness center; Golden Door Spa; watersports equipment/rentals; bike rental; children's programs; game room; concierge; business center; 24-hr. room service; massage; babysitting; laundry service. *In room:* A/C, TV, Wi-Fi, coffeemaker, hair dryer, iron, safe.

Inexpensive

Lighthouse Inn Motel A relic from decades gone by, this no-frills but spotlessly clean motel sits across the street from other, more expensive Gulf-side properties on Vanderbilt Beach and within walking distance of the Ritz-Carlton, Naples. The efficiencies and apartments are simple, with cinder-block walls and small kitchens. The one kitchenless room has a small fridge and coffeemaker, but note that no units have phones, and four have shower-only bathrooms. Most guests take advantage of weekly and monthly rates in winter, when the motel is heavily booked. The hotel also operates Buzz's Lighthouse Cafe next door, a pleasant place for an inexpensive dockside breakfast, lunch, or dinner.

9140 Gulf Shore Dr. N., Naples, FL 34108. ✆ **239/597-3345.** Fax 239/597-5541. 15 units. Winter $130 double, $150 suite; off-season $65–$85 double. MC, V. From Olde Naples, go 3½ miles north on U.S. 41; take a left on Vanderbilt Beach Rd. (C.R. 862). Turn right on Gulf Shore Dr. to hotel on the right. **Amenities:** Restaurant; bar; heated outdoor pool. *In room:* A/C, TV, kitchen, fridge, coffeemaker, no phone.

WHERE TO DINE

Naples's beaches are ideal for picnics. In Olde Naples, you can get freshly baked breads and pastries, gourmet sandwiches, and fruit plates at **Tony's Off Third,** 1300 3rd St. S. (✆ **239/262-7999**). Stop by **Wynn's on Fifth,** 745 5th Ave. S., between 8th and Park streets (✆ **239/261-0901**), for high-quality deli items, sandwiches, salads, takeout meals, and gourmet pastries at very reasonable prices. Both have a few sidewalk tables and are fine places for coffee or a snack while window-shopping on 3rd and 5th avenues South.

In Olde Naples

Expensive

Campiello's ★★ ITALIAN It's not about the homemade pasta at this see-and-be-seen spot in Naples, where the open-air bar is command central for local Naples luminaries and suntanned socialites. Par for the Naples course, the martini menu is impressive, featuring more than 20 creative concoctions. The Gulf yellowtail snapper with escarole and Tuscan white-bean *crema* and the homemade linguine with shrimp, garlic, and zucchini are just two of many difficult choices. Daily specials are the most interesting here: There's a slew of fabulous wood-oven pizzas and delicious pastas that you've never heard of before.

1177 3rd St. (at Broad Ave.). ✆ **239/435-1166.** www.campiello.damico.com. Reservations recommended. Main courses $18–$44. AE, DC, DISC, MC, V. Sun–Thurs 11:30am–2:30pm and 5–10:30pm; Fri–Sat 11:30am–2:30pm and 5–11pm.

Chop's City Grill ★★ STEAK/SEAFOOD The smells of steak and money waft through this urbane bistro that's more Miami hip than Naples nautical. Aged, top-quality steaks and lamb chops are the house specialties, either chargrilled to perfection and served with thick onion rings and mashed potatoes, or peppered and served with a blackberry-and-cabernet-wine sauce. Fresh fish from the grill is another good choice. Asian influences appear here, too, such as spiced Yellowfin tuna with mango-chili glaze and served with a "sexy" sweet pepper–coriander sauce, wasabi whipped potatoes, and sesame "chop sticks."

837 5th Ave. S. (btw. 8th and 9th sts. S.). ✆ **239/262-4677.** Reservations recommended. www.chopscitygrill.com. Main courses $18–$40. AE, DC, DISC, MC, V. Mon–Sun 5pm–closing.

Trilogy ★★ FUSION SEAFOOD Global fusion has come to Naples in the form of this fine new (in 2008) eatery, whose lite bites menu—"Not Your Momma's Meatloaf" for $9, among other things—offers a tempting and reasonably priced diversion from its main plates, among which include Tokyo-style grilled salmon with Sunomono cucumbers and sesame miso drizzle and a fantastic hickory-smoked duck breast with crisp potato cake, vanilla bean, and bourbon demi. As with most trendy restaurants, there's also a full sushi bar and an impressive list of wines. Although steaks are tempting here, skip 'em and stick with the specials and the other entrees.

720 5th Ave. S. (btw. 7th and 8th sts. S.). ✆ **239/261-1221.** Reservations recommended. www.trilogyofnaples.com. Lite menu and sushi $6–$17; main courses $24–$59. AE, DC, DISC, MC, V. Sun–Thurs 5–10pm; Fri–Sat 5–11pm.

Moderate

Bistro 821 ★ MEDITERRANEAN FUSION This South Beachy bistro is an excellent choice for Mediterranean-influenced fusion cuisine. Although the quarters are too close for private conversations, small ceiling spotlights romantically illuminate each table. The house specialty is rotisserie chicken, and a daily risotto leads a menu featuring penne in vodka sauce and a seasonal vegetable plate with herb couscous. But in my opinion, the best dishes on the menu are the miso sake–roasted sea bass with roast shallot mashed potatoes, and the coconut, ginger, and lemongrass encrusted snapper with Gulf shrimp and stir-fry veggies in spicy Thai chili peanut sauce. Dishes are huge, but you can order many of them in either full or half portions. There's sidewalk dining here, too.

821 5th Ave. S. (btw. 8th and 9th sts. S.). ✆ **239/261-5821.** www.bistro821.com. Reservations recommended. Main courses $11–$60. AE, DC, MC, V. Daily 5–10pm.

The Dock at Crayton Cove ★★ (Finds) SEAFOOD Located right on the City Dock, this locals' hangout is the best place in town for a supercasual open-air meal or a cool drink while watching the boats go back and forth across Naples Bay. Servers are friendly and conversational. The chow ranges from hearty chowders by the mug to seafood with a Floribbean fare, with Jamaican-style jerk shrimp thrown in for spice; main courses are moderately priced. Grilled seafood, Caesar salad, and a good selection of sandwiches, hot dogs, and other pub-style fare also appear on the menu. "Margarita Madness" happy hour and a half-price raw bar (don't miss the steamed mussels with French bread for dipping into the garlic sauce) run daily from 9:30 to 11:30pm. The Great Dock Canoe Race draws thousands on the second Saturday in May.

12th Ave. S. (at the City Dock in Olde Naples). ✆ **239/263-9940.** Main courses $11–$30; sandwiches $10–$15. AE, DISC, MC, V. Daily 11am–midnight.

Tommy Bahama's Tropical Cafe ★★ CARIBBEAN Walk through a thatch gateway into this lively, island-style watering hole (or upscale Margaritaville, if you will)—an incongruous sight in the middle of the staid 3rd Street South shopping enclave. If they're not wearing Tommy Bahama's Indiana Jones–meets–Florida threads, diners look as if they've stepped right out of a Ralph Lauren or Abercrombie catalog. They gather on a large front patio under shade trees, where a musician performs, or inside, where a large back-wall mural depicts a Polynesian scene. An open kitchen is on one side of the dining room, a bar dispensing drinks on the other. In between, cane chairs and classic ceiling fans add to the exotic mood. Although the Jamaican pork, salmon St. Croix, and other

Caribbean-style cuisine don't quite live up to the ambience, you'll have too much fun here to care whether it's gourmet—and the huge portions will satisfy any appetite. Sandwiches don't appear on the dinner menu, but are served if you request them.

1220 3rd St. S. (btw. 12th and 13th aves. S.). ✆ **239/643-6889.** www.tommybahama.com. Reservations recommended. Main courses $25–$37; sandwiches $11–$18. AE, MC, V. Daily 11am–10pm.

Yabba Island Grill ★ Value CARIBBEAN Perhaps the noisiest, most crowded spot on Fifth Avenue, Yabba Island Grill attempts to channel the Caribbean with loud music, a massive bar, and a tropical decor—and does a very decent job. The food makes as loud a statement as Yabba's pastel color scheme, with most items providing a riot of flavors from across the Caribbean. If the party-hearty crowd that convenes here isn't enough to entice you, consider the jerk-spiced shrimp marinated in Red Stripe beer with fire-roasted peppers and tomatoes, served with chipotle-smoked Gouda polenta cake. If you're looking for a peaceful and quiet meal, get here superearly—in fact, at 4:30pm, right at opening time—before the antsy vacationers start piling in.

711 5th Ave. S. (btw. 8th St. S. and Park Ave. S.). ✆ **239/262-5787.** www.yabbaislandgrill.com. Reservations recommended. Main courses $25–$33; sandwiches $8–$10. AE, DISC, MC, V. Daily 4:30–11pm (bar to 2am Fri–Sat).

Inexpensive

Cheeburger Cheeburger ★ AMERICAN Though this is a chain restaurant, with no decor to speak of, when you're hankering for a good—no, make that great—burger with a side of fries or onion rings and a milkshake, this is definitely the place to go. Choose the size you want (5 oz.–1 lb.!) and any of more than a dozen toppings, and enjoy. There are also salads for those who want to be healthy.

505 5th Ave. S. (btw. 5th and 6th sts.). ✆ **239/435-9796.** Burgers $5–$10. AE, DISC, MC, V. Daily 11am–9pm.

First Watch Value AMERICAN Just like its siblings elsewhere in Florida, this diner is a favorite local haunt for breakfast, brunch, or a midday meal. You may have to wait for a table, but once you're seated, a young staff will provide quick and friendly service. The menu leans heavily on healthful selections, but you can still get your cholesterol from a sizzling skillet of fried eggs served over potatoes, vegetables, and melted cheese. Lunch features large salads, sandwiches, and quesadillas. In addition to the dining room, there's more seating at umbrella tables in the courtyard.

In Gulf Shore Sq., 1400 Gulf Shore Blvd. (at Banyan Rd.). ✆ **239/434-0005.** Most items $4–$10. AE, DISC, MC, V. Daily 7am–2:30pm. Closed Christmas.

Old Naples Pub ★★ Value AMERICAN/PUB FARE You would never guess that the person sitting next to you at the bar here is a mogul of some sort, so relaxed is this small, somewhat-cramped pub near the fabulous 3rd Street South shops. Diners fortunately find more room at tables on the shopping center's patio. The menu features very good pub fare (and at extraordinarily inexpensive prices for Olde Naples), including homemade soups, nachos, burgers, and sandwiches ranging from chargrilled bratwurst to fried grouper. Platters include fish and chips, New York strip steak, grilled tuna, the catch of the day, fried grouper or clam strips, and baby back ribs. Best bets are the chicken salad with grapes and walnuts, along with the burgers, steaks, and fish from the charcoal grill. You can catch live entertainment here nightly during winter, Wednesday through Saturday during off-season.

255 13th Ave. S. (btw. 3rd and 4th sts. S.). ✆ **239/649-8200.** www.oldnaplespub.com. Main courses $12–$20; salads, sandwiches, and burgers $6–$10. AE, DISC, MC, V. Mon–Sat 11am–10pm; Sun noon–9pm.

North of Olde Naples

Silver Spoon American Cafe Value AMERICAN/ITALIAN/SOUTHWEST Even though this member of the American Cafe chain is in the Waterside Shops complex and immediately screams TGI Friday's, it happens to be one of Naples's best dining bargains and makes the perfect spot for lunch. The food is high-quality chain-restaurant cuisine. Thick sandwiches are served with fries, spicy pecan rice, or black beans. The tomato-basil soup is worth a try, and the bruschetta appetizer—served on toasted French bread—is nearly a meal in itself. Gourmet pizzas and pasta dishes are also popular, especially with the after-theater crowds from the nearby Philharmonic Center for the Arts. Main courses, such as Cajun or herb-grilled chicken, are both tasty and an excellent value. Shoppers love to lunch here, so come early or be prepared for a wait.

In the Waterside Shops at Pelican Bay, 5395 N. Tamiami Trail (at Seagate Dr.). © **239/591-2123.** Call ahead for preferred seating. Main courses $10–$15; pizza and pasta $8–$15; soups, salads, and sandwiches $7–$10. AE, DC, DISC, MC, V. Sun–Thurs 11am–10pm; Fri–Sat 11am–11pm. From Olde Naples, go north on U.S. 41 and left on Seagate Dr. right into the shopping center. Proceed right at the dead end, to the restaurant on the left.

NAPLES AFTER DARK

For entertainment ideas, check the *Naples Daily News* (www.naplesnews.com), especially the "Neapolitan" section in Friday's edition.

THE PERFORMING ARTS Known locally as "The Phil," the impressive **Philharmonic Center for the Arts ★★**, 5833 Pelican Bay Blvd., at West Boulevard (© **800/597-1900** or 239/597-1900; www.thephil.org), is the home of the Naples Philharmonic, but its year-round schedule is also filled with cultural events, concerts by celebrated artists and internationally known orchestras, and Broadway plays and shows aimed at families. Call or check the website for the seasonal calendar.

A fine local theater group, the **Naples Players,** holds its winter-season performances in the new Sugden Community Theatre, 701 5th Ave. S. (© **239/263-7990**). Tickets can be hard to get, so call well in advance.

THE CLUB & BAR SCENE Remember: Naples is not South Beach, nor does it pretend to be. It does, however, realize that some people like to party well past early-bird hours, and, as a result, there are a few good spots here to get your groove on.

The restaurants and bistros along 5th Avenue South are popular watering holes, especially for young professional singles who make the area a meat market on Friday nights. **McCabe's Irish Pub,** 699 5th Ave. S. (© **239/403-7170**), features traditional Irish music nightly. For a lot of camp with your cabaret, the **Ridgway Bar and Grill,** 3rd Street South and 13th Avenue (© **239/262-5500**), is a hot spot, thanks to pianist Jim Badger, whose bawdy shows bring in crowds of all ages (not recommended for those under 18).

In the 3rd Street South shopping area, **Old Naples Pub,** 255 13th Ave. S. (© **239/649-8200;** p. 374), has live music nightly during winter, Wednesday through Saturday nights during the off-season.

The touristy **Old Marine Marketplace at Tin City,** which comprises the restored waterfront warehouses on 5th Avenue South on the west side of the Gordon River, comes alive in winter, when visitors flock to its shops and the **Riverwalk Fish & Ale House** (© **239/262-2734**), which has live entertainment during the high season.

The beachside chickee-hut bar at the **Naples Beach Hotel & Golf Club** (**© 239/261-2222**) is always popular, has live entertainment many nights, and is *the* place to go on Sunday afternoon and early evening. So is the beachside bar at the **Vanderbilt Inn Naples** (**© 239/597-3151**).

5 MARCO ISLAND

15 miles SE of Naples; 53 miles S of Fort Myers; 100 miles W of Miami

Marco Island is reminiscent of a sleepy, albeit swanky, beachfront retirement community. When the sun goes down, you can hear a pin drop, though. Which is how the locals prefer it. There's some nightlife here—a new comedy club for the night owls and some local watering holes; but if you're looking for a club scene, Marco isn't for you. That said, Capt. William Collier would still hardly recognize Marco Island if he were to come back from the grave today. No relation to Collier County founder Barron Collier, the captain settled his family on the north end of this island, the largest of Florida's Ten Thousand Islands, back in 1871. He traded pelts with the Native Americans, caught and smoked fish to sell to Key West and Cuba, and charged fishermen and other guests $2 a day for a room in his home. A few turn-of-the-20th-century buildings still stand here, but Collier would be shocked to come across the high-rise bridge to the island and see it now sliced by man-made canals and virtually covered by resorts, condominiums, shops, restaurants, and winter homes. These are the products of an extensive real-estate development begun in 1965, which means that Marco lacks any of the charm found in Naples and on Sanibel and Captiva islands. Much of the sales effort here was aimed at the northeastern states, so the island smacks more of New York and Massachusetts than of the laid-back Midwestern style of its neighbors. Marco's only real attractions are its crescent-shaped beach and access to the nearby waterways running through a maze of small islands, its excellent boating and fishing, and the island's proximity to acres of wildlife preserves.

ESSENTIALS

GETTING THERE See p. 326 and 362, respectively, for information on the **Southwest Florida International Airport** and the **Naples Municipal Airport.** Also see p. 327 for details on Amtrak train service and Greyhound/Trailways bus service to Fort Myers.

VISITOR INFORMATION The **Marco Island Area Chamber of Commerce,** 1102 N. Collier Blvd., Marco Island, FL 34145 (© **800/788-6272** or 239/394-7549; fax 239/394-3061; www.marcoislandchamber.org), provides free information on the island. A message board and a phone are located outside the office for making hotel reservations even outside of operating hours. In winter, the chamber is open Monday through Friday from 9am to 5pm, and Saturday from 10am to 3pm. You can also get a free visitor's guide by contacting the **Naples, Marco Island, Everglades Convention and Visitor's Bureau** at © **800/688-3600,** or via their website at www.paradisecoast.com.

GETTING AROUND **Enterprise Rent-a-Car** (© 800/325-8007 or 239/642-4488) has an office here. For a cab, call **A-Action Taxi** (© 239/394-4400), **Classic Taxi** (© 239/394-1888), or **A-Okay Taxi** (© 239/394-1113).

Depending on the type, rental bicycles cost from $5 an hour to $65 a week at **Scootertown,** 845 Bald Eagle Dr. (© **239/394-8400;** www.islandbikeshops.com), north of North Collier Boulevard, near Olde Marco. Scooters go for about $70 for 24 hours.

HITTING THE BEACH

The sugar-white **Crescent Beach** curves for 3½ miles down the entire western shore of Marco Island. Its southern 2 miles are fronted by an unending row of high-rise condominiums and hotels, but the northern 1½ miles are preserved in **Tigertail Beach** (✆ **239/252-4000**), at the end of Hernando Drive. Restrooms, cold-water outdoor showers, a children's playground, watersports rentals, and a snack bar are available here. The park is open daily from dawn to dusk. There's no admission charge for the beach, but parking in the lot costs $8 per vehicle. The beaches in front of the Marriott, Hilton, and Radisson resorts have parasailing, windsurfing, and other watersports activities, all for a fee.

If you're not staying at the big resorts, Collier County maintains an $8-per-vehicle parking lot and access to the developed beach on the southern end of the island, on Swallow Avenue at South Collier Boulevard.

OUTDOOR ACTIVITIES

Marco River Marina, 951 Bald Eagle Dr. (✆ **239/394-2502;** www.marcoriver.com), is the center for boat rentals, fishing, and cruises. Operating from a booth on the marina's dock, **Sunshine Tours** (✆ **239/642-5415;** www.sunshinetoursmarcoisland.com) will book offshore fishing charters and arrange back-bay fishing ($59 for adults, $49 for children 9 and under), shelling excursions to the small islands ($49 adults, $39 children 9 and under), sunset cruises ($28–$42 adults, $24–$27 children), and dinner cruises ($49–$52 per person). The back-bay fishing trips go at high tide, the shelling trips at low tide; call for the schedule and reservations.

Sea Excursions (✆ **239/642-6400;** www.seaexcursions.com) also has a booth at the marina and books fishing, boating, and shelling cruises on the ***Dolphin Explorer*** (www.dolphin-explorer.com).

SCUBAdventures, based at 845 Bald Eagle Dr., Olde Marco (✆ **239/389-7889;** www.scubamarco.com), charges $75 to $95 for two-tank dives, depending on the distance offshore.

The closest public golf course is **Marriott's The Rookery at Marco** (✆ **239/353-7061**), both in the marshlands off Fla. 951 north of the island. A sign at the Marriott's course ominously warns: PLEASE DON'T DISTURB THE ALLIGATORS. Fees range from as much as $219 in winter down to $89 in summer.

A NATURE PRESERVE

The **Rookery Bay National Estuarine Research Reserve,** 300 Tower Rd. (✆ **239/417-6310;** www.rookerybay.org), operates boat trips out of the now-closed Briggs Nature Center, on Shell Island Road, off Fla. 951 between U.S. 41 and Marco Island. Join a Rookery Bay naturalist for a 2-hour guided exploration of the bays and mangrove forests of Rookery Bay. Discover the unique plants and animals that make this coastal ecosystem so valuable. Tours are offered Wednesdays and Saturdays from 10am to noon. The trip is limited to 10 participants ages 12 and up. Cost is $35. For information, contact the **Conservancy of Southwest Florida,** 1450 Merrihue Dr., Naples, FL 34102 (✆ **239/262-0304;** www.conservancy.org).

WHERE TO STAY

There are no chain hotels on Marco Island other than the large Marriott and Hilton properties (some listed below), which stand in a row along Crescent Beach on the island's southwestern corner. **Century 21 First Southern Trust** (✆ **800/523-0069** or 239/394-7653; fax 239/394-8048; www.c21marco.com) is one of the largest agents representing rental-property owners.

As elsewhere in South Florida, the high season here is from mid-December to mid-April. Rates drop precipitously in the off-season.

Expensive

Marco Beach Ocean Resort ★★ Making up for the lack of a Ritz-y resort on Marco Island is this posh, all-suite place with a full-service spa. The suites are comfy, complete with full kitchens and patios overlooking the Gulf. Bathrooms are large and have delicious Molton Brown bath products. Although the marble lobby is mausoleum-like, with little or no activity, it is a sight to see. After a recent $1-million renovation to landscaping, suites, and other areas, the owners decided to add a new lobby seating area, so you can actually sit and enjoy the scenery. While the pool has private cabanas and great butlers, the beach and the service there is what really matters. There's also a rooftop pool, where you can enjoy massages, butler service, and luxe rental cabanas. The restaurant, Sale e Pepe, features an award-winning Italian-born chef whipping up exquisite northern Italian cuisine with French influences.

480 S. Collier Blvd., Marco Island, FL 34145. ✆ **800/260-5089** or 239/393-1400. Fax 239/393-1401. www.marcoresort.com. 98 units. Winter $339–$419 double, $650–$800 suite; off-season $189–$209 double, $220–$279 suite. Valet parking only $15. AE, DC, DISC, MC, V. **Amenities:** 4 restaurants; 2 bars; heated outdoor pool; golf and tennis at nearby facilities; fitness center; spa; Jacuzzi; sauna; watersports equipment/rentals; concierge; business center; sundry shop; 24-hr. room service; massage; laundry service. *In room:* A/C, TV, dataport, kitchen, fridge, coffeemaker, hair dryer, iron, safe.

Moderate

Boat House Motel (Value) One of the best bargains in these parts, this pleasant little motel is a throwback to the '50s and sits beside the Marco River in Olde Marco, on the island's northern end. The rooms are in an old school, a two-story, lime-green-and-white building that ends at a wooden dock with a small heated pool, lounge furniture, picnic tables, and barbecue grills. Two rooms on the end have their own decks, and all open to tiny courtyards. Bright paint, ceiling fans, and louvered shutters add a tropical ambience throughout. The one-bedroom condominiums next door open onto a riverside dock, upon which is built a two-bedroom cottage named the Gazebo, which has a peaked roof supported by umbrellalike spokes from a central pole.

1180 Edington Place, Marco Island, FL 34148. ✆ **800/528-6345** or 239/642-2400. Fax 239/642-2435. www.theboathousemotel.com. 25 units. Winter $109–$139 double, $129–$290 apt or cottage; off-season $78–$105 double, $100–$220 apt or cottage. MC, V. Pets accepted ($15 fee plus $5 per day). **Amenities:** Heated outdoor pool; coin-op washers/dryers. *In room:* A/C, TV, fridge, iron.

Marco Island Hilton Beach Resort and Spa ★★ About half the size of the nearby Marco Island Marriott Beach Resort & Golf Club (see below), but nevertheless a group-oriented resort, this 11-story beachside tower overlooks the Gulf and a courtyard with a multiangled pool wrapped around four coconut palms. The spacious units have curved balconies angled to give water views. This resort has completed a major upgrade and renovation of its meeting space, lobby, and restaurant areas. New features include floor-to-ceiling windows in the main entrance lobby of the resort and a revamped menu at the Paradise Café. Guest-room and penthouse renovations round out the $15-million project. A new 10,000-square-foot spa with 10 treatment rooms opened in December

2008. Sandcastles Lounge has a piano bar with nightly entertainment. ***Note:*** The hotel is 100% nonsmoking.

560 S. Collier Blvd., Marco Island, FL 34145. ✆ **800/HILTONS** or 239/394-5000. Fax 239/394-8410. www.hiltonmarcoisland.com. 265 units. Year-round $149–$449 double. Packages available. AE, DC, DISC, MC, V. Valet parking $14; self-parking $10. **Amenities:** 2 restaurants; 2 bars; heated outdoor pool; 2 tennis courts; state-of-the-art fitness center; full-service spa; whirlpool; sauna; watersports equipment/rental; children's programs; concierge; activities desk; business center; Wi-Fi; room service; babysitting; laundry service. *In room:* A/C, TV, dataport, fridge, coffeemaker, hair dryer, iron, safe.

Marco Island Marriott Beach Resort, Golf Club & Spa ★★ Kids Marco Island is far from Disney World, so if you plan to bring the kids while you experience the utmost in R & R, the sprawling Marco Island Marriott will make sure they're entertained with activities, from watersports and Everglades excursions to Guitar Hero on the beach, Dance Dance Revolution, and dive-in movies, where families can enjoy a movie while floating or lounging poolside. Parents can play, too, or simply sign up children for the resort's daily kids' camp, Tiki Tribe, which is now available in the evenings too. A $225-million renovation has refreshed all the guest rooms and suites, redesigned the Quinn's Pool and kid-friendly Tiki Pool with water slide, added two restaurants (Pazzi's oven-fired pizzas and the Rookery Steakhouse), renovated the golf clubhouse and 18-hole resort-private golf club just 7 minutes away, and built a 24,000-square-foot Balinese spa with private pool. Luxuriously furnished and decorated, the spacious accommodations range from hotel rooms to two-bedroom suites. All have balconies or patios with indirect views of the Gulf. If you don't want to be bored during your Marco Island sojourn (a common affliction after too much of the pool or beach), definitely stay here, where there actually are things to do off—and on—the beach.

400 S. Collier Blvd., Marco Island, FL 34145. ✆ **800/438-4373** or 239/394-2511. Fax 239/642-2672. www.marcoislandmarriott.com. 732 units. Winter $275–$395 double, from $530 suite; off-season $159–$340 double, from $320 suite. Packages available. AE, DC, DISC, MC, V. Valet parking $11; self-parking free. **Amenities:** 5 restaurants; 4 bars; 3 heated outdoor pools; golf course; tennis court; exercise room; Jacuzzi; watersports equipment/rentals; children's programs; game room; concierge; activities desk; car-rental desk; business center; shopping arcade; salon; limited room service; massage; babysitting; laundry service; concierge-level rooms. *In room:* A/C, TV, dataport, minibar, fridge, coffeemaker, hair dryer, iron, safe.

Olde Marco Island Inn & Suites ★★★ Considered by many to be one of Florida's most romantic resorts, the Victorian-style Olde Marco Island Inn & Suites dates from 1883, when Capt. Bill Collier built it on the Calusa Indian Grounds. While maintaining its historical charm, the place has been remodeled and updated, and now has 51 one- and two-bedroom, two-bathroom suites decorated with a tropical flair. Six large penthouses on the fifth floor overlooking the Gulf are worth the splurge. In addition to stellar service, the inn has two of the area's nicest restaurants, including Cafe de Marco (see below). But the best amenity, hands down, is the private 38-foot catamaran that sails guests to serene, unspoiled beaches on and around Marco Island. These trips are complimentary and include beach chairs and towels. Evening cruises with wine, beer, soft drinks, and appetizers are also available, but for a nominal fee. Couples looking for a first, second, or third honeymoon should stay here, without question.

100 Palm St., Marco Island, FL 34145. ✆ **877/475-3466.** Fax 239/394-4485. www.oldemarcoinn.com. 329 units. Winter $129–$289 1- and 2-bedroom suites, $400–$3,500 penthouse; off-season $119–$159 1-bedroom, $149–$189 2-bedroom, $400–$3,500 penthouse. AE, DC, DISC, MC, V. **Amenities:** 2 restaurants; bar; outdoor pool; fitness center; spa; concierge; limited room service. *In room:* A/C, TV, VCR, dataport, full kitchen, hair dryer, iron.

Signs of Nightlife in Marco Island

Not everyone goes to bed at 7pm here. Thanks to the brand-new-in-2008 **Off the Hook Comedy Club at Capt. Brien's Seafood & Raw Bar,** 599 S. Collier Blvd. (✆ **239/389-6900;** www.offthehookcomedy.com), you can get dinner, a comedy show, music, and dancing until the wee hour of 2am. And it's not just any stand-up, either. Major national acts come here, probably for some R & R, including Tommy Davidson, Robert Schimmel, and Mitch Fatel. Shows average $20.

On the pub scene, **Cathy O'Clarke's Irish Pub & Grill,** 591 S. Collier Blvd. (✆ **239/642-9709**), offers live entertainment Wednesday through Sunday, not to mention all-you-can-eat stone crabs nightly (in season). For the best happy hour in town, **CJ's on the Bay,** 740 N. Collier (✆ **239/389-4511**), features spectacular bay views and amazing drink specials daily from 4 to 7pm from its lively gazebo bar.

And for an authentic taste—and sip—of Old Florida, don't miss **Stan's** in downtown Goodland (✆ **239/394-3041**), an old fishing village that, while reminiscent of, say, a town in *Deliverance,* is a friendly old-school sea shanty of an area, where live music, fantastic seafood, and entertainment reign 6 nights a week until 10pm. Sunday is the best day to check out Stan's, when the house band, the King Buzzard and Live Band, plays from 11am to 6pm; and, if you're lucky, Stan himself will hit the stage with some seriously funny comedy.

WHERE TO DINE

Moderate

Cafe de Marco ★★ SEAFOOD Purveyor of some of the island's finest cuisine, this homelike establishment at the Marco Village shops was originally constructed as housing for maids at Capt. William Collier's Olde Marco Inn. The chef specializes in excellent treatments of fresh seafood, from your choice of shrimp or baked fish with mushrooms, seasoned shallots, and garlic butter, to his own luscious creation of seafood and vegetables combined in a lobster sauce and served over linguine. If your waistline can stand it, finish with homemade Key lime pie. You can dine inside or on a screened patio. For steak Diane and chateaubriand, check out its sister restaurant, Capt. Collier's Steak Room (✆ **239/394-3131**), at the Olde Marco Inn and Suites.

244 Palm St., Olde Marco. ✆ **239/394-6262.** www.cafedemarco.com. Reservations recommended. Main courses $20–$30. AE, MC, V. Winter daily 5–10pm; off-season Mon–Sat 5–10pm. Early-bird specials 5–6pm.

Kretch's ★★ Value SEAFOOD/CONTINENTAL Noted pastry chef Bruce Kretschmer rules this shopping-center roost, Marco's best all-around restaurant. Bruce has created a sinfully rich seafood strudel by combining shrimp, crab, scallops, cheeses, cream, and broccoli in a flaky Bavarian pastry and serving it all under a lobster sauce. It's available as either an appetizer or an entree. Cholesterol-counters can choose from broiled or chargrilled fish, while the rest of us can indulge in shrimp, Florida lobster tail, steaks, or lamb chops. Bruce's popular Mexican Friday lunches feature delicious tacos and other inexpensive south-of-the-border selections. In winter, Sunday is home-cooking night, with chicken and dumplings, Yankee pot roast, and braised lamb shanks.

527 Bald Eagle Dr. (south of N. Collier Blvd.). ✆ **239/394-3433.** www.kretchs.com. Reservations recommended in winter. Main courses $14–$32. DISC, MC, V. Mon–Fri 11am–3pm and 5–9pm; Sat–Sun 5–9pm. Closed Sun off-season and Easter, July 4, Thanksgiving, Christmas Eve, and Christmas Day.

Snook Inn SEAFOOD The choice dinner seats at this Old Florida establishment are in an enclosed dock right beside the scenic Marco River, but for lunch or libation (such as a fabulous Bloody Mary with pickled okra), head to the dockside Chickee Bar, a fun place anytime, but especially at sunset. The new garden courtyard isn't a bad place to be, either, as long as it's not mosquito season, in which case you should avoid all outdoor areas unless you've covered in repellent. There's live entertainment both day and night during the winter season, and nightly the rest of the year. Although seafood is the specialty, tasty steaks, chicken, burgers, and sandwiches are among the choices. Even the sandwiches come with a trip to the salad bar at dinner, making them a fine bargain. Bring a filet of that fish you caught, and the chef will cook it up for you. Call A-Okay Taxi (p. 376) for a free ride from anywhere on Marco Island to Snook Inn.

1215 Bald Eagle Dr. (at Palm St.), Olde Marco. ✆ **239/394-3313.** www.snookinn.com. Main courses $10–$27; sandwiches $8–$11; cook-your-catch $9.50. AE, DC, DISC, MC, V. Daily 11am–4pm and 4:30–10pm. Closed Thanksgiving and Christmas.

12 The Tampa Bay Area

When some people hear the word *Tampa,* they typically think of Busch Gardens and never even mention Tampa's bay area. They're missing out: Tampa is a stunning, picturesque city, and while it may not have a red bridge, such as San Francisco's bay area, it does have a sparkling array of colors reflecting off its waters. If you haven't had a chance to explore Florida's bay area, do so now. There's so much more to the Tampa Bay area than beer and amusement parks. Sure, you can chug as much Busch beer as you want, but you can also do (and see, eat, and experience) much more here.

As Florida's very own city by the bay, Tampa has its own vibrant culture, with roots firmly planted in Cuban and American history.

The city of Tampa is the commercial center of Florida's west coast—a growing seaport and center of banking and high-tech manufacturing. You can come downtown during the day to observe the sea life at the Florida Aquarium and stroll through the Henry B. Plant Museum, housed in an ornate, Moorish-style hotel built more than a century ago to lure tourists to the city. A short trolley ride will take you from downtown Tampa to Ybor City, the historic Cuban enclave, now a bustling, often rowdy nightlife and dining hot spot.

Two bridges and a causeway will whisk you west across Old Tampa Bay to St. Petersburg, Pinellas Park, Clearwater, Dunedin, Tarpon Springs, and other cities on the Pinellas Peninsula, one of Florida's most densely packed urban areas. Over here on the bay, photo-ready downtown St. Petersburg is famous for wintering seniors, a shopping and dining complex built on a pier, and, surprisingly, the world's largest collection of Salvador Dalí's surrealist paintings.

Keep driving west and you'll come to a line of barrier islands, where St. Pete Beach, Clearwater Beach, and other Gulf-side communities boast 28 miles of sunshine, surf, and white sand.

Heading south, I-275 will take you across the mouth of Tampa Bay to Sarasota and another chain of barrier islands that stretches 42 miles along the coast south of Tampa Bay. One of Florida's cultural centers, affluent Sarasota is the gateway to St. Armands and Longboat keys, two playgrounds of the rich and famous, and to Lido and Siesta keys, both attractive to families of more modest means.

1 TAMPA

200 miles SW of Jacksonville; 85 miles SW of Orlando; 254 miles NW of Miami

Even if you stay on the beaches 20 miles to the west, you should consider driving into Tampa for a mild taste of metropolis. If you have children in tow, they may *demand* that you go into the city so they can enjoy the rides and see the animals at Busch Gardens Tampa Bay. Once there, you can also educate them (and yourself) at the Florida Aquarium and the city's other fine museums. Additionally, historic Ybor City has the bay area's liveliest and hottest nightlife.

Tampa was a sleepy little port when Cuban immigrants founded Ybor City's cigar industry in the 1880s. A few years later, Henry B. Plant put Tampa on the tourist map by building a railroad that ran into town and by constructing bulbous minarets atop his garish Tampa Bay Hotel, now a museum named in his honor. During the Spanish-American War, Teddy Roosevelt trained his Rough Riders here and walked the Ybor City streets with Cuban revolutionary José Martí. A land boom in the 1920s gave the city its charming, Victorian-style Hyde Park suburb, now a gentrified redoubt for the baby boomers just across the Hillsborough River from downtown.

Today's downtown skyline is the product of the 1980s and 1990s booms, when banks built skyscrapers and the city put up an expansive convention center, a performing-arts center, and the St. Pete Times Forum (formerly the Ice Palace), a 20,000-seat bayfront arena that is home to professional hockey's Tampa Bay Lightning. The renaissance hasn't been as rapid as planned, given the recent economic recession, but it is continuing into the 21st century with redevelopment of the seaport area east of downtown. There, the existing Florida Aquarium and the Garrison Seaport Center (a major home port for cruise ships bound for Mexico and the Caribbean) are joined by office buildings, apartment complexes, and a major shopping-and-dining center known as Channelside (in the Channel District) at Garrison Seaport.

You won't want to spend your entire Florida vacation in Tampa, but it offers a lot as a somewhat fast-paced, modern city on the go.

ESSENTIALS

For the contact information of airlines and car services, please see "Appendix: Fast Facts, Toll-Free Numbers & Websites" on p. 638.

GETTING THERE **Tampa International Airport** (© **813/870-8770;** www.tampaairport.com), 5 miles northwest of downtown Tampa, is the major air gateway to this area (**St. Petersburg–Clearwater International Airport** has limited service; see section 2, "St. Petersburg," later in this chapter). Most major and many no-frills airlines serve Tampa International, including **Air Canada, AirTran, American, America West, British Airways, Continental, Delta, JetBlue, Lufthansa, MetroJet, Midway, Midwest Airlines, Northwest, Southwest, Spirit, United,** and **US Airways.**

Alamo, Avis, Budget, Dollar, Enterprise, Hertz, National, and **Thrifty** all have rental-car operations here.

The **Limo/SuperShuttle** (© **800/282-6817** or 727/527-1111; www.supershuttle.com) operates van services between the airport and hotels throughout the Tampa Bay area. Fares for one person range from $36 to $50 round-trip, depending on your destination. **Taxis** are plentiful at the airport; the ride to downtown Tampa takes about 15 minutes and costs $15 to $25.

Amtrak trains arrive downtown at the **Tampa Amtrak Station,** 601 Nebraska Ave. N. (© **800/872-7245;** www.amtrak.com).

VISITOR INFORMATION Contact the **Tampa Bay Convention & Visitors Bureau,** 400 N. Tampa St., Tampa, FL 33602-4706 (© **800/448-2672,** 800/368-2672, or 813/223-2752; www.visittampabay.com), for advance information. If you're downtown, you can head to the bureau's **visitor information center** at 400 N. Tampa St. (Channelside), Ste. 2800 (© **813/223-1111**). It's open Monday through Saturday from 9:30am to 5:30pm.

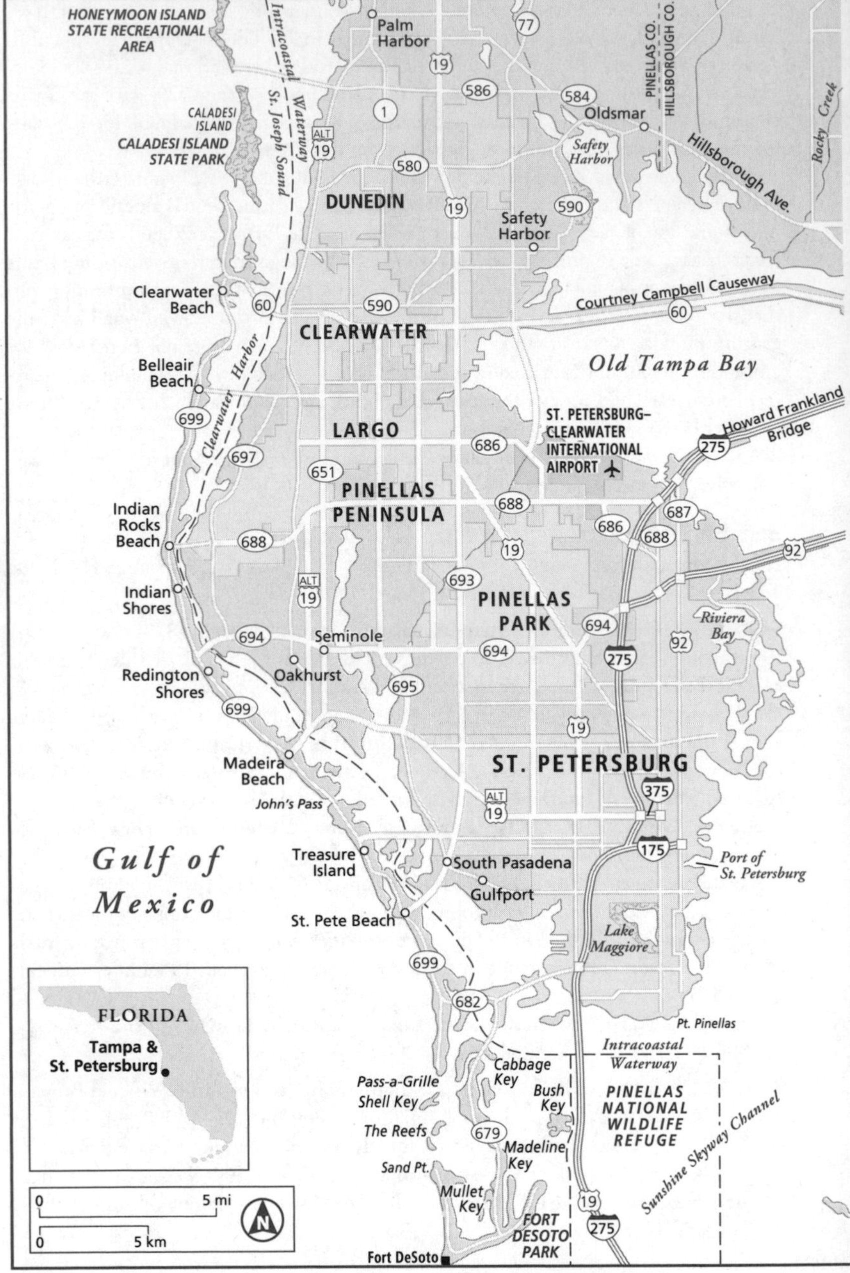
HONEYMOON ISLAND STATE RECREATIONAL AREA
Palm Harbor
Intracoastal Waterway
St. Joseph Sound
PINELLAS CO.
HILLSBOROUGH CO.
Oldsmar
Safety Harbor
Hillsborough Ave.
Rocky Creek
CALADESI ISLAND
CALADESI ISLAND STATE PARK
DUNEDIN
Safety Harbor
Clearwater Beach
Courtney Campbell Causeway
CLEARWATER
Old Tampa Bay
Belleair Beach
Clearwater Harbor
ST. PETERSBURG–CLEARWATER INTERNATIONAL AIRPORT
Howard Frankland Bridge
LARGO
PINELLAS PENINSULA
Indian Rocks Beach
Indian Shores
PINELLAS PARK
Riviera Bay
Seminole
Oakhurst
Redington Shores
Madeira Beach
ST. PETERSBURG
John's Pass
Gulf of Mexico
Treasure Island
South Pasadena
Port of St. Petersburg
Gulfport
St. Pete Beach
Lake Maggiore
Pt. Pinellas
Intracoastal Waterway
FLORIDA
Tampa & St. Petersburg
Cabbage Key
Pass-a-Grille
Shell Key
Bush Key
PINELLAS NATIONAL WILDLIFE REFUGE
The Reefs
Madeline Key
Sunshine Skyway Channel
Sand Pt.
Mullet Key
FORT DESOTO PARK
Fort DeSoto
0 5 mi
0 5 km
N

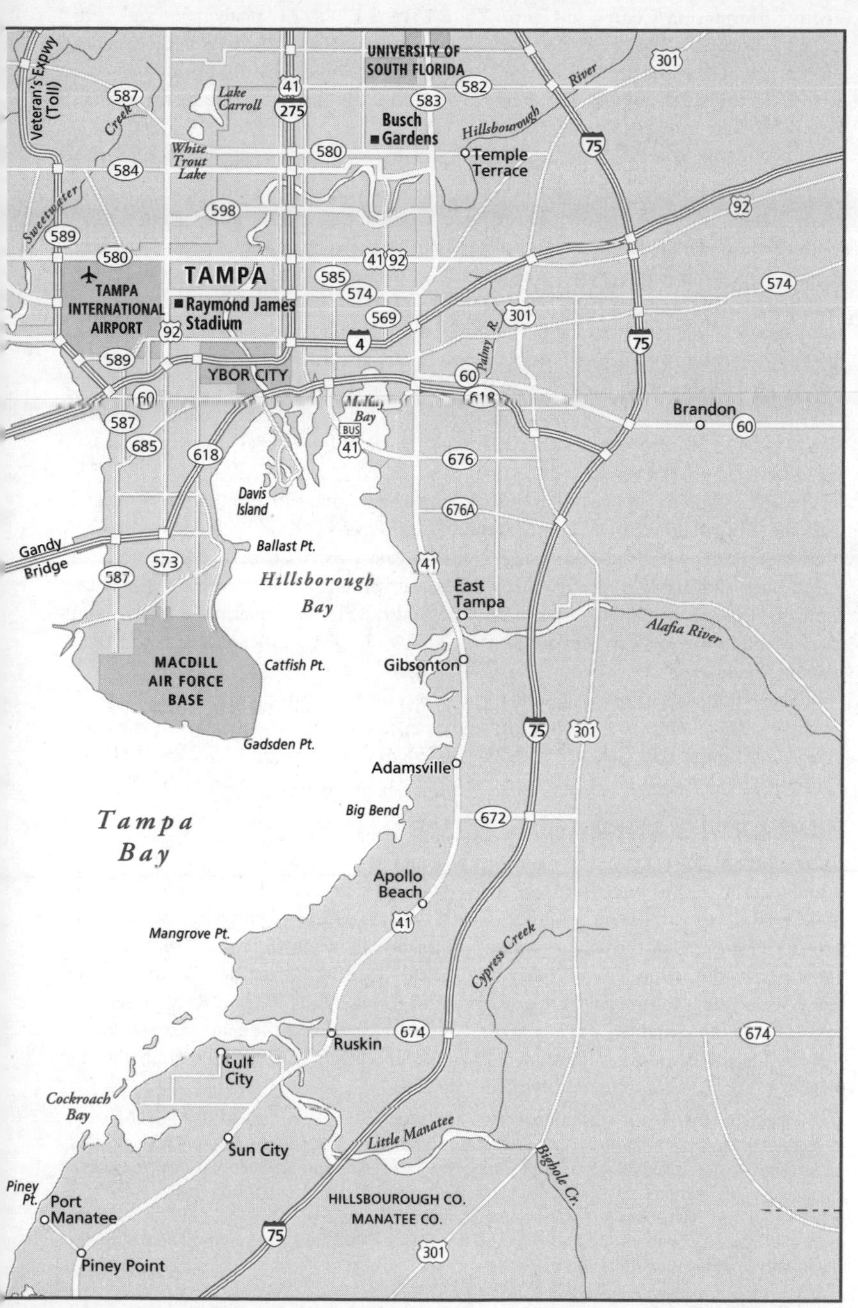
UNIVERSITY OF SOUTH FLORIDA
Busch Gardens
Temple Terrace
Hillsborough River
Veteran's Expwy (Toll)
Lake Carroll
White Trout Lake
Sweetwater Creek
TAMPA
TAMPA INTERNATIONAL AIRPORT
Raymond James Stadium
YBOR CITY
Palmy R.
Brandon
McKay Bay
Davis Island
Ballast Pt.
Gandy Bridge
Hillsborough Bay
East Tampa
Alafia River
MACDILL AIR FORCE BASE
Catfish Pt.
Gibsonton
Gadsden Pt.
Adamsville
Big Bend
Tampa Bay
Apollo Beach
Mangrove Pt.
Cypress Creek
Ruskin
Gulf City
Cockroach Bay
Sun City
Little Manatee
Bighole Cr.
Piney Pt.
Port Manatee
Piney Point
HILLSBOUROUGH CO.
MANATEE CO.

Operated by the Ybor City Chamber of Commerce, the **Centro Ybor Museum and Visitor Information Center,** in Centro Ybor, 1514½ E. 8th Ave. (btw. 15th and 16th sts. E.), Tampa, FL 33605 (✆ **813/248-3712;** www.ybor.org), distributes information and has exhibits on the area's history. A 7-minute video will orient you to this area—an 8-block stretch of 7th Avenue. The center is open Monday through Saturday from 10am to 6pm, Sunday from noon to 6pm.

GETTING AROUND Like most other Florida destinations, it's virtually impossible to see Tampa's major sights and enjoy its best restaurants without a car. You can get around downtown via the free **Uptown-Downtown Connector Trolley,** which runs north–south between Harbor Island and the city's North Terminal bus station on Marion Street at I-275. The trolleys run every 10 minutes from 6am to 6pm Monday through Friday. Southbound, they follow Tampa Street between Tyler and Whiting streets, and Franklin Street between Whiting Street and Harbor Island. Northbound trolleys follow Florida Avenue from the St. Pete Times Forum to Cass Street. The trolleys cost 50¢ and are operated by the **Hillsborough Area Regional Transit/HARTline** (✆ **813/254-4278;** www.hartline.org), the area's transportation authority, which also provides scheduled **bus service** ($1.75–$3.50) between downtown Tampa and the suburbs. Pick up a route map at the visitor center (see above).

The transportation situation has gotten somewhat better, not to mention nostalgic, with the **TECO Line Street Car System** (✆ **813/254-HART** [4278]; www.tecolinestreetcar.org), a new but old-fashioned 2⅓-mile streetcar system, complete with overhead power lines, that hauls passengers between downtown and Ybor City via the St. Pete Times Forum, Channelside, Garrison Seaport, and the Florida Aquarium. The cars run every 30 minutes; one-way fares are $2.50. Check with the visitor center or call HARTline for schedules.

Taxis in Tampa don't normally cruise the streets for fares, but they do line up at public places, such as hotels, the performing arts center, and bus and train depots. If you need a taxi, call **Tampa Bay Cab** (✆ **813/251-5555**), **Yellow Cab** (✆ **813/253-0121**), or **United Cab** (✆ **813/253-2424**). Fares are $2 at flag fall, plus $2.25 for each mile.

EXPLORING ANIMAL & THEME PARKS

Adventure Island Kids If the summer heat gets to you before one of Tampa's famous thunderstorms brings late-afternoon relief, you can take a waterlogged break at this 30-acre outdoor water theme park near Busch Gardens Tampa Bay (see below). You can also frolic here during the cooler days of spring and fall, when the water is heated. The Key West Rapids, Riptide, Gulf Scream, and other exciting water rides will drench the teens, while other, calmer rides are geared toward younger kids. Wahoo Run plunges up to five riders more than 15 feet per second as the half-enclosed tunnel corkscrews more than 600 feet to a waiting splash pool. There are also places to picnic and sunbathe, an arcade, a volleyball complex, and two outdoor cafes.

10001 Malcolm McKinley Dr. (btw. Busch Blvd. and Bougainvillea Ave.). ✆ **813/987-5600.** www.adventureisland.com. Admission at least $40 adults, $36 children 3–9, plus tax; free for children 2 and under. Pick Two tickets with Busch Gardens Tampa Bay (1 day admission per park) $80, free for children 2 and under. Website sometimes offers discounts. Parking $10. Mid-Mar to Labor Day daily 10am–5pm; Sept–Oct Fri–Sun 10am–5pm (extended hours on holidays). Closed Nov–late Feb. Check website for exact opening dates. Take exit 50 off I-275 and go east on Busch Blvd. for 2 miles. Turn left onto McKinley Dr. (N. 40th St.); entry is on the right.

Big Cat Rescue Kids Not your typical animal theme park, this one bills itself as an educational sanctuary in which visitors can get up close and "purrsonal" (groan) with more than 150 big wild cats. The world's largest accredited sanctuary for exotic cats, this one is definitely a unique experience for animal lovers because not only can you view and visit with bobcats and tigers, but you can also feed them, take photo safaris, and even spend a night in one of the sanctuary's cabins. Something different, for sure.

12802 Easy St. ✆ **813/920-4130.** www.bigcatrescue.org. Day tours for ages 10 and over $25 per person Mon–Fri 9am–3pm; special kids tour for all ages $15 per person Sat 9am; night tour for ages 18 and over $50 per person, last Fri of the month at dusk; feeding tours for ages 18 and over $50 per person, reservations required; Keeper for a Day tour for ages 18 and over $100 per person, reservations required. Take Busch Blvd. exit west off I-275 for 9 miles. (It becomes Gunn Hwy.) Watch for the dirt road near the McDonald's.

Busch Gardens Tampa Bay ★★ Kids Although its heart-stopping thrill rides get much of the ink, this venerable theme park (it predates Disney World) ranks among the largest zoos in the country. It's a don't-miss attraction for children and adults who can see, in person, all those wild beasts they've watched on Animal Planet—and they'll get better views of them here than at Disney's Animal Kingdom in Orlando (p. 497). Busch Gardens Tampa Bay has thousands of animals living in natural environments that help carry out the park's overall African theme. Most authentic is the 65-acre plain, reminiscent of the real Serengeti of Tanzania and Kenya, upon which zebras, giraffes, and other animals graze. Unlike the animals on the real Serengeti, however, these grazing creatures have nothing to fear from lions, hyenas, crocodiles, and other predators, which are confined to enclosures—as are the hippos and elephants. The park's seventh roller coaster, SheiKra (see below), was the nation's first dive coaster, carrying riders up 200 feet at 45 degrees and then hurtling them 70 mph back at a 90-degree angle. Yikes.

The park has eight areas, each with its own theme, animals, live entertainment, thrill rides, kiddie attractions, dining, and shopping. A Skyride cable car soars over the park, offering a bird's-eye view of it all. Turn right after the main gate and head to **Morocco,** a walled city with exotic architecture, crafts demonstrations, and an exhibit featuring alligators and turtles. The Moorish-style Moroccan Palace Theater features KaTonga, a Broadway-style musical show featuring original music, dance and puppetry that many families consider to be the park's best entertainment for both adults and children. You can also attend a song-and-dance show in the Marrakech Theater. Overlooking it all is the Crown Colony Restaurant, the park's largest.

Over in **Egypt,** you can visit King Tut's tomb, with its replicas, and youngsters can dig for their own ancient treasures in a sand area. Adults and kids 54 inches or taller can ride Montu, the tallest and longest inverted roller coaster in the world, with seven upside-down loops. Your feet dangle loose on Montu, so make sure your shoes are tied tightly and your lunch has had time to digest.

From Egypt, walk to the **Edge of Africa,** the most unique of the park's eight areas, and home to most of the large animals. Go immediately to the Adventure Tours tent and see if you can get on one of the park's zoologist-led wildlife tours.

Next stop is **Nairobi,** the most beautiful part of the park, where you can see gorillas and chimpanzees in their lush rainforest habitat in the Myombe Reserve. Nairobi also has Jambo Junction—which the park's Animal Ambassadors call home—turtle and reptile displays, an elephant exhibit, and Curiosity Caverns (with bats, reptiles, and other small mammals that dwell in dark places). The entry to Rhino Rally, the park's safari adventure, is at the western end of Nairobi.

Now head to the **Congo,** where the highlights are the rare white Bengal tigers that live in Jungala, the park's newest, 4-acre attraction within the Congo featuring a colorful village hidden deep in the jungle, up-close animal interactions, multistory family play

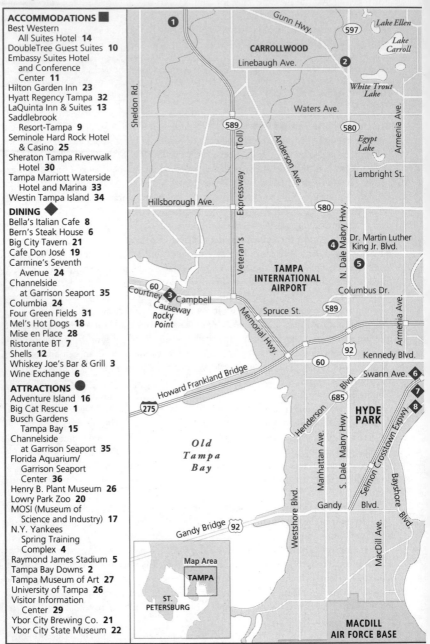

ACCOMMODATIONS ■
Best Western All Suites Hotel **14**
DoubleTree Guest Suites **10**
Embassy Suites Hotel and Conference Center **11**
Hilton Garden Inn **23**
Hyatt Regency Tampa **32**
LaQuinta Inn & Suites **13**
Saddlebrook Resort-Tampa **9**
Seminole Hard Rock Hotel & Casino **25**
Sheraton Tampa Riverwalk Hotel **30**
Tampa Marriott Waterside Hotel and Marina **33**
Westin Tampa Island **34**

DINING ◆
Bella's Italian Cafe **8**
Bern's Steak House **6**
Big City Tavern **21**
Cafe Don José **19**
Carmine's Seventh Avenue **24**
Channelside at Garrison Seaport **35**
Columbia **24**
Four Green Fields **31**
Mel's Hot Dogs **18**
Mise en Place **28**
Ristorante BT **7**
Shells **12**
Whiskey Joe's Bar & Grill **3**
Wine Exchange **6**

ATTRACTIONS ●
Adventure Island **16**
Big Cat Rescue **1**
Busch Gardens Tampa Bay **15**
Channelside at Garrison Seaport **35**
Florida Aquarium/ Garrison Seaport Center **36**
Henry B. Plant Museum **26**
Lowry Park Zoo **20**
MOSI (Museum of Science and Industry) **17**
N.Y. Yankees Spring Training Complex **4**
Raymond James Stadium **5**
Tampa Bay Downs **2**
Tampa Museum of Art **27**
University of Tampa **26**
Visitor Information Center **29**
Ybor City Brewing Co. **21**
Ybor City State Museum **22**

Gunn Hwy.
Lake Ellen
597
Lake Carroll
CARROLLWOOD
Linebaugh Ave.
White Trout Lake
Sheldon Rd.
Waters Ave.
589
(Toll)
580
Egypt Lake
Anderson Ave.
Armenia Ave.
Lambright St.
Hillsborough Ave.
580
Veteran's Expressway
N. Dale Mabry Hwy.
Dr. Martin Luther King Jr. Blvd.
TAMPA INTERNATIONAL AIRPORT
60
Courtney Campbell Causeway
Rocky Point
Columbus Dr.
Memorial Hwy.
Spruce St.
589
Armenia Ave.
92
Kennedy Blvd.
60
Howard Frankland Bridge
Swann Ave.
Henderson Blvd.
685
275
HYDE PARK
Selmon Crosstown Expwy.
Old Tampa Bay
Manhattan Ave.
S. Dale Mabry Hwy.
Bayshore Blvd.
Westshore Blvd.
Gandy Blvd.
Gandy Bridge
92
MacDill Ave.
Map Area
TAMPA
ST. PETERSBURG
MACDILL AIR FORCE BASE

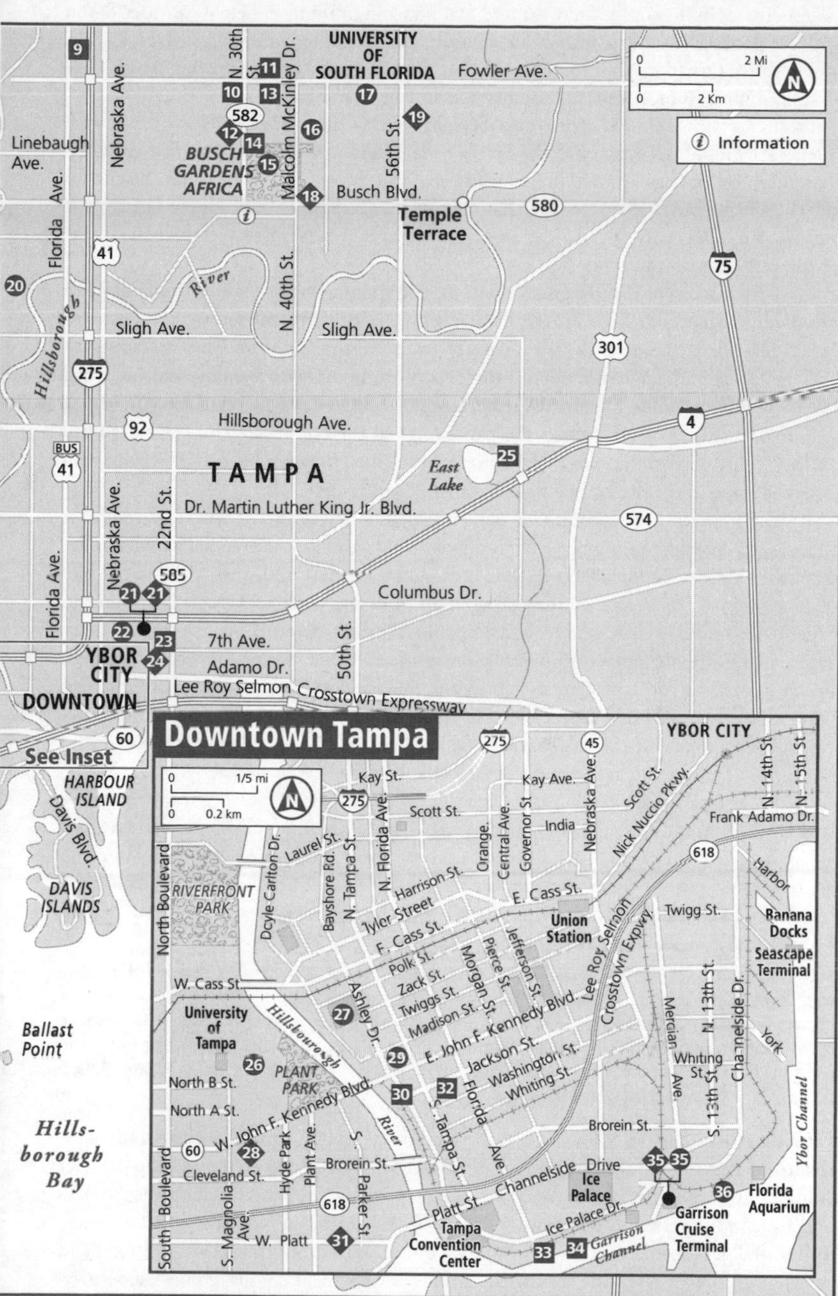

UNIVERSITY OF SOUTH FLORIDA
Fowler Ave.
Linebaugh Ave.
Nebraska Ave.
N. 30th St.
Malcolm McKinley Dr.
56th St.
BUSCH GARDENS AFRICA
Busch Blvd.
Temple Terrace
Florida Ave.
Hillsborough River
N. 40th St.
Sligh Ave.
Hillsborough Ave.
TAMPA
East Lake
Dr. Martin Luther King Jr. Blvd.
22nd St.
Columbus Dr.
50th St.
7th Ave.
Adamo Dr.
YBOR CITY
DOWNTOWN
See Inset
Lee Roy Selmon Crosstown Expressway
HARBOUR ISLAND
Davis Blvd.
DAVIS ISLANDS
Ballast Point
Hillsborough Bay
Information
Downtown Tampa
YBOR CITY
Kay St.
Kay Ave.
Scott St.
India
Nick Nuccio Pkwy.
Frank Adamo Dr.
N. 14th St.
N. 15th St.
Laurel St.
North Boulevard
RIVERFRONT PARK
Dcyle Carlton Dr.
Bayshore Rd.
N. Tampa St.
N. Florida Ave.
Orange
Central Ave.
Governor St.
Nebraska Ave.
Harrison St.
Tyler Street
E. Cass St.
Union Station
Twigg St.
Harbor
Banana Docks
Seascape Terminal
W. Cass St.
Polk St.
Zack St.
Twiggs St.
Madison St.
Morgan St.
Pierce St.
Jefferson St.
E. John F. Kennedy Blvd.
Lee Roy Selmon Crosstown Expwy.
Mercian Ave.
N. 13th St.
Channelside Dr.
York
University of Tampa
Ashley Dr.
Jackson St.
Washington St.
Whiting St.
PLANT PARK
North B St.
North A St.
W. John F. Kennedy Blvd.
S. Tampa St.
Florida Ave.
Ybor Channel
Brorein St.
S. 13th St.
Cleveland St.
Hyde Park Ave.
Plant Ave.
S. Parker St.
Channelside Drive
Ice Palace
Florida Aquarium
South Boulevard
S. Magnolia Ave.
W. Platt
Platt St.
Tampa Convention Center
Ice Palace Dr.
Garrison Channel
Garrison Cruise Terminal

areas, rides, and live entertainment. The Congo is also home to Kumba, the largest and fastest coaster in the southeastern United States (54-in. minimum height for riders). You will get drenched—and refreshed on a hot day—by riding the Congo River Rapids, where you're turned loose in round boats that float down the swiftly flowing "river" (42-in. minimum). Bumper cars and kiddie rides can be found here, too.

From the Congo, walk south into **Stanleyville,** a prototype African village, with SheiKra a shopping bazaar, and the Stanleyville Theater, featuring shows for children. Two more water rides here are the Tanganyika Tidal Wave (48-in. minimum height for riders), where you'll come to a very damp end, and the Stanley Falls Flume (an aquatic version of a roller coaster). Also, the Zambia Smokehouse serves ribs and chicken—some of the best chow in the park.

Up next is **Land of the Dragons,** the most entertaining area for small children. They can spend the day enjoying a variety of entertainment in a fairy-tale setting, plus just-for-kids rides. The area is dominated by Dumphrey, a whimsical dragon who interacts with visitors and guides children around a three-story treehouse with winding stairways, tall towers, stepping stones, illuminated water geysers, and an echo chamber.

The next stop is **Bird Gardens,** the park's original core, offering rich foliage, lagoons, and a free-flight aviary for hundreds of exotic birds, including golden and American bald eagles. Be sure to see the Florida flamingos while you're here.

If your stomach can take another hair-raising ride, try **Gwazi** (48-in. minimum for riders), an adrenaline-pumping attraction in which a pair of old-fashioned wooden roller coasters (named the Lion and the Tiger) start simultaneously and whiz within a few feet of each other six times as they roar along at 50 mph and rise to 90 feet. If you want to experience the park's fifth roller coaster, head to **Timbuktu** and climb aboard the **Scorpion,** a high-speed number with a 60-foot drop and 360-degree loop (42-in. height minimum). Or if you're really crazy, check out the floorless **SheiKra,** where for 200 feet up and 90 degrees straight down, you can view the world—from a floorless perspective. For visual amusement, there's ***Pirates 4-D,*** an animated 4-D special effects movie and theater production starring comedic actor Leslie Nielsen.

Added attractions are a 6-hour zookeeper-for-a-day program and a nighttime safari by lantern-light. You can exchange foreign currency in the park, and interpreters are available. ***Note:*** You can get to Busch Gardens from Orlando via shuttle buses, which pick up at area hotels between 8 and 10:15am for the 1½- to 2-hour ride, with return trips starting at 5pm and continuing until the park closes. Round-trip fares are $10 per person. Call ✆ **800/511-2450** for schedules, pickup locations, and reservations.

3000 E. Busch Blvd. (at McKinley Dr./N. 40th St.). ✆ **888/800-5447** or 813/987-5283. www.buschgardens.com. ***Note:*** Admission prices and hours vary, so call ahead, check website, or get brochure at visitor centers. Admission single-day ticket $70 adults, $60 children 3–9, plus tax; free for children 2 and under. Daily 10am–6pm (to 7 and 8pm in summer and on holidays). Parking $11 for cars; $13 for trucks and campers. Take I-275 north of downtown to Busch Blvd. (exit 50) and go east 2 miles. From I-75, take Fowler Ave. (exit 54) and follow the signs west.

Florida Aquarium ★★ (Kids) See the more than 20,000 aquatic animals and plants that call Florida home at this entertaining attraction. The exhibits follow a drop of water from the springs of the Florida Wetlands Gallery, through a mangrove forest in the Bays and Beaches Gallery, and out onto the Coral Reefs, where an impressive 43-foot-wide, 14-foot-tall panoramic window lets you look out at schools of fish and lots of sharks and stingrays. Also worth visiting are the educational Explore a Shore playground, a deepwater exhibit, and a tank housing moray eels. You can look for birds and sea life on 90-minute Eco Tour cruises in the *Bay Spirit,* a 64-foot catamaran. The aquarium also offers a

Dive with the Sharks program (✆ **813/367-4005**) that gives certified divers the chance to swim with blacktip, sand tiger, and nurse sharks for 30 minutes. Don't be surprised if you come face to face with the 250-pound Goliath Grouper during the dive. The $150 price tag includes a souvenir photo and T-shirt. The Penguin promenade allows you to get up close and personal with the cute creatures in the open Penguin Promenade. Also quite popular and interactive is Ocean Commotion, the most high-tech gallery found in any aquarium in the country, utilizing state of the art technology like "smart Wi-Fi," floor to ceiling interactive displays, virtual dolphins and whales, animation and multimedia presentations. Guests can even upload their own videos to become part of the exhibit. Expect to spend 3-4 hours here.

701 Channelside Dr. ✆ **813/273-4000.** www.flaquarium.org. Admission $20 adults, $17 seniors, $15 children 3–11, free for children 2 and under. Eco Tour $22 adults, $20 seniors, $18 children 3–11, free for children 2 and under. Combination aquarium admission and Eco Tour $33 adults, $30 seniors, $23 children 3–11, free for children 2 and under. Website sometimes offers discounts. Parking $5. Daily 9:30am–5pm. Dolphin Quest Mon–Fri 2pm; Sat–Sun 1 and 3pm. Eco Tour Sun–Fri 2 and 4pm; Sat noon, 2, and 4pm. Closed Thanksgiving and Christmas.

Lowry Park Zoo ★ (Kids) The opportunity to watch 3,000-pound manatees, Komodo dragons, Persian leopards, and rare red pandas makes this a worthwhile excursion after the kids have seen the plains of Africa at Busch Gardens. With lots of greenery, bubbling brooks, and waterfalls, this 24-acre zoo displays animals in settings similar to their natural habitats. Exhibits include the Florida wildlife display, Asian Domain, Primate World, Aquatic Center, free-flight aviary with a birds-of-prey show, hands-on Discovery Center, and endangered-species carousel ride. The Wallaroo Station has kids' rides, a small water park, a kangaroo walk-about, and a petting zoo. Lowry Park has one of Florida's three manatee hospitals and rehabilitation centers. The Eco Tour is very popular, featuring a cruise on the Hillsborough River, where you'll see turtles, herons, and manatees. The cost is $14 for adults, $13 for seniors, and $10 for children 3 to 11 (zoo and Eco Tour Package costs $29 for adults, $27 for seniors, and $21 for children 3–11). The zoo is also a sanctuary for Florida panthers and red wolves. There's also a rare African shoebill stork; an African safari tram-style tour; and a restaurant, the Garden Grille, inside the zoo's front gate.

1101 W. Sligh Ave. ✆ **813/935-8552** or 932-0245 for recorded information. www.lowryparkzoo.com. Admission $19 adults, $18 seniors, $15 children 3–11, free for children 2 and under. Daily 9:30am–5pm. Closed Thanksgiving and Christmas. Take I-275 to Sligh Ave. (exit 48) and follow the signs.

VISITING THE MUSEUMS

Henry B. Plant Museum Originally built in 1891 by railroad tycoon Henry B. Plant as the super-chichi 511-room Tampa Bay Hotel, this ornate building is worth a short trip across the river from downtown to the University of Tampa campus. Its 13 silver minarets and distinctive Moorish architecture, modeled after the Alhambra in Spain, make this National Historic Landmark a focal point of the Tampa skyline. Although the building is the highlight of a visit, don't skip its contents: art and furnishings from Europe and Asia, plus exhibits that explain the history of the original railroad resort, Florida's early tourist industry, and the hotel's role as a staging point for Theodore Roosevelt's Rough Riders during the Spanish-American War.

401 W. Kennedy Blvd. (btw. Hyde Park and Magnolia aves.). ✆ **813/254-1891.** www.plantmuseum.com. Free admission; suggested donation $5 adults, $2 children 12 and under. Tues–Sat 10am–4pm; Sun noon–4pm. Closed Thanksgiving, Christmas Eve, and Christmas Day. Take Kennedy Blvd. (Fla. 60) across the Hillsborough River.

MOSI (Museum of Science and Industry) ★★ Kids A great place to take the kids, MOSI is the largest science center in the Southeast, with more than 450 interactive exhibits. Step into the Gulf Hurricane to experience 74 mph winds, explore the human body in The Amazing You, and, if your heart is up to it, ride a bicycle across a 98-foot-long cable suspended 30 feet above the lobby (don't worry: you'll be harnessed to the bike). You can also watch stunning movies in Florida's first IMAX dome theater. Outside, trails wind through a nature preserve with a butterfly garden. The museum is one of very few in the world to feature the articulated remains of a Sauropod dinosaur.

4801 E. Fowler Ave. (at N. 50th St.). ✆ **813/987-6100.** www.mosi.org. Admission $21 adults, $19 seniors, $17 children 2–12, free for children 1 and under. Admission includes IMAX movies. Daily 9am–5pm or later. From downtown, take I-275 N. to Fowler Ave. E., exit 51. Take this 2 miles east to museum on right.

Tampa Bay History Center ★ Kids Opened in early 2009, this brand-new 60,000-square-foot museum covers everything from Native Americans to tycoons and sports legends who have inhabited Tampa. The museum features interactive exhibits, theaters, map gallery, research center, event hall, museum store, and a branch of the internationally acclaimed Columbia Café. The permanent exhibits explore approximately 500 years of recorded history and 12,000 years of human habitation in the region.

225 S. Franklin St. ✆ **813/228-0097.** www.tampabayhistorycenter.org. Free admission. Mon–Fri 9am–5pm.

Tampa Museum of Art Located on the east bank of the Hillsborough River, next to the round Bank of America building (locals facetiously call it the Beer Can), this fine-arts complex has eight galleries with changing exhibits ranging from classical antiquities to contemporary Floridian art. There's also a 7-acre riverfront park and sculpture garden. Call or check the website for the schedule of temporary exhibits. However, if you have time for only one art museum on your trip, skip this one and head to St. Petersburg for the more innovative Salvador Dalí Museum. In 2008, the museum moved to a temporary location at 2306 Howard while the original Ashley Drive location was being revamped into a 66,000-square-foot museum with state-of-the-art gallery spaces featuring innovative translucent ceilings and polished stone floors. In addition there will be five expansive interior galleries, one exterior sculpture gallery, and an educational classroom equipped with the latest technology. Completion is expected in November 2009. Admission at the temporary location on Howard is free.

600 N. Ashley Dr. (at Twiggs St.), downtown. ✆ **813/274-8130.** www.tampamuseum.com. Admission $8 adults, $6 seniors, $3 children 6–18 and students with ID, free for children 5 and under; by donation Thurs 5–8pm and Sat 10am–noon. Tues–Wed and Fri–Sat 10am–5pm; Thurs 10am–8pm; Sun 11am–5pm. Parking 90¢ per hour. Take I-275 to exit 44 (Ashley Dr.).

YBOR CITY

Northeast of downtown, the city's historic Latin district takes its name from Don Vicente Martinez Ybor (*Eeee*-bore), a Spanish cigar maker who arrived here in 1886 via Cuba and Key West. Soon, his factory and other ones in Tampa were producing more than 300,000 hand-rolled stogies a day.

It may not be the cigar capital of the world anymore, but Ybor is still a smokin' part of Tampa, and it's one of the best places in Florida to buy hand-rolled cigars. It's not on par with New Orleans's Bourbon Street, Washington's Georgetown, or Miami's South Beach, but good food and great music dominate the scene, especially on weekends when the streets bustle until 4am (note to claustrophobes: avoid it at all costs then). Live-music offerings run the gamut from jazz and blues to rock.

At the heart of it all is **Centro Ybor,** a dining-shopping-entertainment complex that sprawls between 7th and 8th avenues and 16th and 17th streets (© **813/242-4660;** www.centroybor.com). Here you'll find a multiscreen cinema, a comedy club, several restaurants, and a large open-air bar. The Ybor City Chamber of Commerce has its visitor center here (see "Essentials," earlier in this chapter), and the Ybor City State Museum's gift shop is here as well (see below).

Check with the visitor center about walking tours of the historic district. **Ybor City Ghost Walks** (© **813/242-9255**) will take you to the spookier parts of the area. The tours cost $11 for adults, or $7.50 for children 3 to 12, by reservation only, and they last 75 minutes. **Tampa Bay Ghost Tours** (© **727/398-5200;** www.allthebesthaunts.com) offers the ultimate in morbid curiosity—a $32 for adults, $19 for kids, 3-hour ghost tour of the Tampa Bay area—in a customized Cadillac hearse limo! For those who enjoy an even darker side, **Secret Ybor: Scandals, Crimes, and Shady Ladies,** explores the more scandalous side of the city. Tours depart at various times from **Gaspar's Grotto,** 1805 E. 7th Ave. (© **813/831-5214;** www.historicguides.com), a wacky, pirate-themed entertainment venue, bar, and restaurant. Cost is $15 per person.

Even if you're not a cigar smoker, you'll enjoy a stroll through the **Ybor City State Museum** ★, 1818 9th Ave., between 18th and 19th streets (© **813/247-6323;** www.ybormuseum.org), housed in the former Ferlita Bakery (1896–1973). You can take a self-guided tour to see the collection of cigar labels, cigar memorabilia, and works by local artisans. Admission is $3. Walking tours of Ybor City are every Saturday morning at 10:30am, cost $6, and start at the Ybor City Museum State Park. Depending on the availability of volunteer docents, admission includes a 15-minute guided tour of **La Casita,** a renovated cigar worker's cottage adjacent to the museum; it's furnished as it was at the turn of the 20th century. The museum is open daily from 9am to 5pm, but you have the best chance for the guided tour if you visit between 11am and 3pm. Better yet, plan to catch a cigar-rolling demonstration (ongoing; no specific schedule), held Friday through Sunday from 10am to 3pm.

Like any area with trendy bars and restaurants, things are always changing, opening, and going out of business, so you may want to check www.ybortimes.com for the latest in Ybor City.

ORGANIZED TOURS

When in the Tampa area, be sure to check out the **Tampa Bay Visitor Information Center,** 3601 E. Busch Blvd. (© **813/985-3601**), opposite Busch Gardens, which operates guided bus tours of Tampa, Ybor City, and environs. Tampa native Jim Boggs will guide you through the city on 4-hour tours, which are given from 10am to 3pm daily, with a stop for lunch at the Columbia Restaurant in Ybor City. The tour costs $45 for adults and $40 for children 12 and under. The full-day tours (10am–5pm) of both Tampa and St. Petersburg give a good overview of the two cities and the beaches; this tour costs $75 for adults and $65 for children. Reservations are required at least 24 hours in advance; passengers are picked up at major hotels and various other points in the Tampa/St. Petersburg area. The company also books bus tours to Orlando, Sarasota, Bradenton, and other regional destinations (call for schedules, prices, and reservations). The center is located on the ground floor of Boggs's bed-and-breakfast, the **Swiss Chalet Bed and Breakfast,** which has been refurbished and enjoyed by many repeat customers. The scrumptious breakfasts are delicious, a major draw in addition to the fact that guests who stay in the B&B may purchase a special ticket that gives them unlimited access to Busch Gardens and Adventure Island during their entire stay. Rates range from $179 to

$199 a night, with 10% discounts to seniors and veterans. Transfers to and from Tampa International Airport can also be arranged, therefore eliminating a rental car and parking charges.

OUTDOOR ACTIVITIES & SPECTATOR SPORTS

BIKING, IN-LINE SKATING & JOGGING Bayshore Boulevard, a 7-mile-long promenade, is famous for its sidewalk right on the shores of Hillsborough Bay and is a favorite with runners, walkers, and in-line skaters. The route goes from the western edge of downtown in a southward direction, passing stately old homes in Hyde Park, a few high-rise condominiums, retirement communities, and houses of worship, ending at Ballast Point Park. The view from the promenade across the bay to the downtown skyline is matchless. (Bayshore Blvd. is also great for a drive.)

FISHING For charters, try **Captain Jim's Inshore Sportfishing Charters,** 512 Palm Ave., Palm Harbor (✆ **727/439-9017;** www.captainhud.com), which offers private sport-fishing trips for tarpon, redfish, trout, and snook. Rates are $350 to $625 for two anglers. Call for schedule and reservations. Rave reviews have come in for **Capt. Gus's Crabby Adventures** (✆ **813/645-6578;** www.crabbyadventures.com), whose 4-hour boating, eating, and eco-experience includes interaction with live blue crabs, stone crabs, and all the living creatures of the bay including manatees, dolphins, laughing gulls, pelicans, herons, egrets, and osprey. Gus instructs guests on how crab traps are pulled and baited. Guests also learn to grade, clean, steam, and eat blue crabs and stone crabs at the Bay Chop Villa, an open-air, waterfront shack and gazebo overlooking a Zen rock garden. Parties of two cost $300; additional passengers are $50 each. The boat leaves at 8am and 2pm.

GOLF Tampa has three municipal golf courses where you can play for about $30 to $35, a relative pittance compared to fees at privately owned courses here and elsewhere in Florida. The **Babe Zaharias Municipal Golf Course,** 11412 Forest Hills Dr., north of Lowry Park (✆ **813/631-4374**), is an 18-hole, par-70 course with a pro shop, putting greens, and a driving range. It is the shortest of the municipal courses, but its small greens and narrow fairways present ample challenges. Water provides obstacles on 12 of the 18 holes at **Rocky Point Golf Course,** 4151 Dana Shores Dr. (✆ **813/673-4316**), located between the airport and the bay. It's a par-71 course with a pro shop, practice range, and putting greens. On the Hillsborough River in north Tampa, the **Rogers Park Golf Course,** 7910 N. 30th St. (✆ **813/673-4396**), is an 18-hole, par-72 championship course with a lighted driving and practice range. All of the courses are open daily from 7am to dusk, and lessons and club rentals are available.

You can book starting times and get information about these and the area's other courses by calling **Tee Times USA** (✆ **800/374-8633;** www.teetimesusa.com).

If you want to do some serious work on your game, the **Arnold Palmer Golf Academy World Headquarters** is at Saddlebrook Resort, 5700 Saddlebrook Way, Wesley Chapel, 12 miles north of Tampa (✆ **800/729-8383** or 813/973-1111; www.saddlebrookresort.com). Half-day and hourly instruction is available, as well as 2-, 3-, and 5-day programs for adults and juniors. You have to stay at the resort or enroll in the golf program to play at Saddlebrook. See p. 399 for more information.

For course information online, go to www.golf.com or www.floridagolfing.com; or call the **Florida Sports Foundation** (✆ **850/488-8347**) or **Florida Golfing** (✆ **866/833-2663**).

SPECTATOR SPORTS Major-league baseball fans were thrilled when the **Tampa Bay Devil Rays** made it to the World Series against Philly in 2008. Although they lost, the games remain a hugely popular draw for sports fans flocking to Tropicana Field, 1 Tropicana Drive, St. Petersburg (© **727/825-3250**). Tickets range from as low as $10 to as high as in the hundreds, depending on how good their season is. In 2009, the Rays moved to a new spring trailing facility in Port Charlotte.

New York Yankees fans can watch the Bronx Bombers during baseball's spring training, from mid-February to the end of March, at **George Steinbrenner Field** (© **813/879-2244** or 875-7753; www.steinbrennerfield.com), opposite Raymond James Stadium. This scaled-down replica of Yankee Stadium is the largest spring-training facility in Florida, with a 10,000-seat capacity. Tickets are $10 to $20. The club's minor-league team, the **Tampa Yankees** (same contact info), plays at Legends Field April through August.

National Football League fans can catch the **Tampa Bay Buccaneers** at the modern, 66,000-seat Raymond James Stadium, 4201 N. Dale Mabry Hwy., at Dr. Martin Luther King, Jr., Boulevard (© **813/879-2827;** www.buccaneers.com), August through December. Single-game tickets are very hard to come by, as they are usually sold out to the plethora of season-ticket holders. This is a huge football city!

The National Hockey League's **Tampa Bay Lightning,** winners of the 2004 Stanley Cup, play in the St. Pete Times Forum starting in October (© **813/301-6500;** www.tampabaylightning.com). You can usually get single-game tickets ($19–$349) on game day.

The only thoroughbred racetrack on Florida's west coast is **Tampa Bay Downs,** 11225 Racetrack Rd., Oldsmar (© **800/200-4434** in Florida, or 813/855-4401; www.tampadowns.com), home of the Tampa Bay Derby. Races are held from December to May ($2 general admission, $3 clubhouse), and the track presents simulcasts year-round. Call for post times.

TENNIS Sharpen your game at the **Hopman Tennis Program,** at the Saddlebrook Resort (p. 399). You must be a member or a guest to play here.

SHOPPING

Hyde Park and Ybor City are two areas of Tampa worth some window-shopping, perhaps sandwiched around lunch at one of the fine restaurants (see "Where to Dine," below).

On the mall front, there's the upscale **International Plaza** (© **813/342-3790;** www.shopinternationalplaza.com), near Tampa International Airport, where the headliners include Neiman Marcus and Nordstrom.

CIGARS Ybor City is no longer a major producer of hand-rolled cigars, but you can still watch artisans making stogies at the **Gonzalez y Martinez Cigar Factory** (www.gonzalezymartinez.com), 2025 7th Ave., in the Columbia Restaurant building (© **813/247-2469**). Gonzalez and Martinez don't speak English, but the staff does at the adjoining **Columbia Cigar Store** (it's best to enter here). Rollers are on duty Monday through Saturday from 10am to 6pm. You can stock up on fine domestic and imported cigars at **El Sol,** 1728 E. 7th Ave. (© **813/247-5554**), the city's oldest cigar store; **King Corona Cigar Factory,** 1523 E. 7th Ave. (© **813/241-9109**); and **Metropolitan Cigars & Wine,** 2014 E. 7th Ave. (© **813/248-3304**).

SHOPPING CENTERS **Old Hyde Park Village,** 1507 W. Swann Ave., at South Dakota Avenue (© **813/251-3500**), is a terrific alternative to cookie-cutter suburban malls. Walk around the little boutiques in the sunshine and simultaneously check out Hyde Park, one of the city's most historic neighborhoods. The cluster of 50 upscale shops is set in a village layout. The selection includes Williams-Sonoma, Pottery Barn, Restoration Hardware, Brooks Brothers, Crabtree & Evelyn, and Godiva, to name a few. There

Fun Facts "Tanpa" + Sloppy Handwriting = "Tampa"

Tampa used to be called Tanpa. No, this is not a spelling error. In the early days, when the place was an Indian fishing village, that's what it was called. Loosely translated, *Tanpa* means "land by the water." Early explorers had illegibly written Tanpa on the maps. In 1539, gold-searching explorers mistakenly changed the name to Tampa.

are also several restaurants there, including the Wine Exchange, Timpano Italian Chophouse, and our favorite, Restaurant BT (see below). There's a free parking garage on South Oregon Avenue behind Jacobson's department store. Most shops are open Monday through Saturday from 10am to 7pm and Sunday from noon to 5pm. A farmers' market (at Swan and Dakota aves.) is held every Saturday from 9am to 2pm, offering local produce, seafood, and assorted tchotchkes.

The centerpiece of the downtown seaport renovation is the massive tourist trap known as **Channelside at Garrison Seaport,** on Channelside Drive between the Garrison Seaport and the Florida Aquarium (✆ **813/223-4250**). It has stores, restaurants, a dance club, and a multiscreen cinema with an IMAX screen.

In Ybor City, **Centro Ybor,** on 7th Avenue East at 16th Street (✆ **813/242-4660;** www.centroybor.com), is primarily a dining and entertainment complex, but you'll find a few chains here, such as American Eagle, Urban Outfitters, and Victoria's Secret.

WHERE TO STAY

The listings below are organized into three geographic areas: near Busch Gardens Tampa Bay, downtown, and Ybor City. If you're going to Busch Gardens, Adventure Island, Lowry Park Zoo, or the Museum of Science and Industry (MOSI), the motels near Busch Gardens are much more convenient than those downtown, about 7 miles to the south. The downtown hotels are geared to business travelers, but staying there will put you near the Florida Aquarium, the Tampa Museum of Art, the Henry B. Plant Museum, the Tampa Bay Performing Arts Center, scenic Bayshore Boulevard, and the dining and shopping opportunities in the Channelside and Hyde Park districts. Staying in Ybor City will put you within walking distance of numerous restaurants and the city's hottest nightspots.

The Westshore area, near the bay, west of downtown, and south of Tampa International Airport, is another commercial center, with a wide range of chain hotels catering to business travelers and conventioneers. It's not far from Raymond James Stadium and the New York Yankees' spring-training complex. Check with your favorite chain for a Westshore-Airport location.

Room rates at most hotels in Tampa vary little from season to season. This is especially true downtown, where the hotels do a brisk convention business year-round. Hillsborough County adds 13% tax to your hotel bill.

Near Busch Gardens Tampa Bay

The nearest chain motel to the park is the **Rodeway Inn,** 4139 E. Busch Blvd. (✆ **813/386-1000**), a motor lodge with very cheap rooms. It's 1½ blocks east of the main entrance. A bit farther away, the 500-room **Embassy Suites Hotel and Conference Center,** 3705 Spectrum Blvd., facing Fowler Avenue (✆ **800/362-2779** or 813/977-7066), is the plushest and most expensive establishment near the park. Almost across the avenue stands **LaQuinta Inn & Suites,** 3701 E. Fowler Ave. (✆ **800/687-6667** or 813/910-7500). Just south of Fowler Avenue are side-by-side branches of **Hyatt Place,** 11408 N. 30th St. (✆ **813/979-1922**), and **Grand Suites Tampa Bay,** 11310 N. 30th St. (✆ **813/971-7690**).

Best Western All Suites Hotel ★ Value This three-story all-suite hotel is the most beachlike vacation venue you'll find close to the park. Whimsical signs lead you around a lush tropical courtyard with a heated pool, hot tub, and lively, sports-oriented Tiki bar. Bathrooms were renovated in 2007. The bar can get noisy before closing at 9pm, and ground-level units are musty, so ask for an upstairs suite away from the action. Suite living rooms are well equipped; the separate bedrooms have narrow screened patios or balconies.

Behind Busch Gardens Tampa Bay, 3001 University Center Dr. (faces N. 30th St., btw. Busch Blvd. and Fowler Ave.), Tampa, FL 33612. ✆ **800/786-7446** or 813/971-8930. Fax 813/971-8935. www.bestwestern.com. 150 units. Winter $99–$189 suite for 2; off-season $99–$109 suite for 2. Rates include hot and cold breakfast buffet. AE, DC, DISC, MC, V. **Amenities:** Restaurant (breakfast and dinner only); bar; heated outdoor pool; access to nearby health club; Jacuzzi; game room; limited room service; laundry service; coin-op washers/dryers. *In room:* A/C, TV, dataport, fridge, coffeemaker, hair dryer, iron.

Downtown Tampa

Hyatt Regency Tampa ★ Just off the Franklin Street pedestrian mall, and in the heart of the business district, the Hyatt attracts a mostly corporate crowd. The spacious, recently renovated contemporary rooms have lots of amenities—iPod docking stations, flatscreen TVs, wireless Internet, and new granite and marble bathrooms—but lack balconies, and the higher office towers that now surround the hotel restrict views from the windows. That said, the heated outdoor pool and rooftop sun deck with whirlpool on the fifth floor is quite nice and resorty. Office workers congregate at the Avanzare restaurant for inexpensive light lunches.

2 Tampa City Center (corner of Tampa and E. Jackson sts.), Tampa, FL 33602. ✆ **813/225-1234.** Fax 813/273-0234. www.tamparegency.hyatt.com. 521 units. $159–$219 double. Weekend packages available in summer. AE, DC, DISC, MC, V. Valet parking $18, self-parking $10. **Amenities:** 2 restaurants; bar; heated outdoor pool; exercise room; Jacuzzi; concierge; business center; limited room service; laundry service; coin-op washers/dryers; concierge-level rooms. *In room:* A/C, TV, dataport, Wi-Fi, coffeemaker, hair dryer, iron.

Sheraton Tampa Riverwalk Hotel ★ Set on the east bank of the Hillsborough River, this six-story hotel remains one of Tampa's better lodgings. Half the rooms face west and have lovely views from their (unlighted) balconies of the Arabesque minarets atop the Henry B. Plant Museum and the University of Tampa across the river—quite a scene at sunset. These rooms cost more but are preferable to units on the east side of the building, which face downtown's skyscrapers and lack balconies. Rooms were newly renovated in 2008 and feature Sweet Sleeper beds. Set beside the river, the Ashley Street Grille serves indoor-outdoor breakfasts and lunches, then offers fine dining in the evenings.

Tips Discount Packages

Many Tampa hotels combine tickets to such major attractions as Busch Gardens Tampa Bay in their packages, so always ask about special deals.

There's also wireless Internet in all public spaces of the hotel. Unless you're here on business or are intent on staying downtown to be close to a specific attraction, such as the performing-arts center, there's not much here to entice a mainstream traveler. The hotel is also completely smoke free.

200 N. Ashley Dr. (at Jackson St.), Tampa, FL 33602. ✆ **800/333-3333** or 813/223-2222. Fax 813/221-5929. 277 units. Winter $175–$209 double; off-season $149–$339 double. Pets up to 80 lbs accepted. AE, DC, DISC, MC, V. Valet parking $16. **Amenities:** 2 restaurants; bar; heated outdoor pool; exercise room; access to nearby health club; sauna; concierge; Wi-Fi; limited room service; laundry service; coin-op washers/dryers; concierge-level rooms. *In room:* A/C, TV, dataport, coffeemaker, hair dryer, iron.

Tampa Marriott Waterside Hotel and Marina ★★ This luxurious 22-story hotel occupies downtown's most strategic location in the area's emerging Channel District—beside the river and between the Tampa Convention Center and the St. Pete Times Forum. Opening onto a riverfront promenade, the towering three-story lobby is large enough to accommodate the many conventioneers drawn to the two neighboring venues and to the hotel's own 50,000 square feet of meeting space. The third floor has a fully equipped spa, modern exercise facility, and outdoor heated pool. About half of the guest quarters have balconies overlooking the bay or city (choice views are high up on the south side). Although spacious, the regular rooms are dwarfed by the 720-square-foot suites. For those interested in boating the bay, there's also a 32-slip marina.

700 S. Florida Ave. (at St. Pete Times Forum Dr.), Tampa, FL 33602. ✆ **800/228-9290** or 813/221-4900. Fax 813/221-0923. www.tampamarriottwaterside.com. 717 units. Winter $259–$285 double, $399–$575 suite; off-season $179–$259 double, $350–$500 suite. Weekend rates available. AE, DC, DISC, MC, V. Valet parking $20 only. **Amenities:** 3 restaurants; 3 bars; heated outdoor pool; health club; spa; Jacuzzi; concierge; activities desk; car-rental desk; business center; salon; limited room service; massage; babysitting; laundry service; coin-op washers/dryers; concierge-level rooms. *In room:* A/C, TV, fax, dataport, high-speed Internet access, fridge, coffeemaker, hair dryer, iron.

The Westin Tampa Harbour Island ★★★ Close enough to downtown but still worlds away on its own 177-acre island, this renovated-in-2008 hotel insists that you're here on vacation and not stuck in some insipid downtown convention hotel. Rooms overlook the harbor and are hypercomfortable, with pillow-top mattresses and large bathrooms featuring dual shower heads, a heavenly signature on par with the hotel's Heavenly Bed. There's also an elegant waterfront restaurant, 725 South, that's popular for business dinners and power lunches. A Reebok gym is a highlight for those into working out. Stroll the boardwalk to fully appreciate your surroundings.

725 S. Harbour Island Blvd., Tampa, FL 33602. ✆ **877/999-3223** or 813/229-5000. Fax 813/229-5322. www.starwoodhotels.com. 299 units. $249–$399 double; $495–$895 suite. Weekend rates available. AE, DC, DISC, MC, V. Valet parking $16; self-parking $14. **Amenities:** Restaurant; 3 bars; heated outdoor pool; access to nearby health club; access to spa; Jacuzzi; concierge; activities desk; car-rental desk; business center; salon; limited room service; massage; babysitting; laundry service. *In room:* A/C, TV, fax, high-speed Internet access, coffeemaker, hair dryer, iron.

Ybor City

Hilton Garden Inn ★ This modern, four-story hotel stands just 2 blocks north of the heart of Ybor City's dining and entertainment district. A one-story brick structure in front houses the bright lobby, a comfy relaxation area with a fireplace, a dining area providing cooked and continental breakfasts, and a small 24-hour pantry selling beer, wine, soft drinks, and frozen dinners. You can heat up the dinners in your comfortable guest room's microwave or store them in your fridge. Because Hilton's Garden hotels are aimed primarily at business travelers, your room will also have a large desk and two phones. If you opt for a suite, you'll get a separate living room and a larger bathroom.

1700 E. 9th Ave. (btw. 17th and 18th sts.), Tampa, FL 33605. © **800/445-8667** or 813/769-9267. Fax 813/769-3299. www.hiltongardeninn.com. 95 units. $149–$299 double. AE, DC, DISC, MC, V. **Amenities:** Restaurant (breakfast only); heated outdoor pool; exercise room; Jacuzzi; business center; laundry service; coin-op washers/dryers. *In room:* A/C, TV, dataport, high-speed Internet access, fridge, coffeemaker, hair dryer, iron.

Seminole Hard Rock Hotel & Casino ★ Despite its location in a somewhat run-down part of town, Tampa's Seminole Hard Rock Hotel & Casino is full of nonstop action. The 12-story building has 250 rooms, each with modern amenities and large bathrooms with excellent lighting. The casino has 90,000 square feet of Vegas-style slots as well as the newly added blackjack, baccarat, Pai Gow poker, Asia poker, Let It Ride poker, Texas Hold 'em, and minibaccarat. Several restaurants and bars keep the nongamblers entertained. The pool area is fine, but not as nice as those at the Hard Rock in Vegas or in Hollywood, Florida. The fitness center is top-notch and even does outdoor treatments in its Zen garden. The first phase of a $120-million construction project unveiled a major casino expansion and the opening of the swanky Council Oak Steaks & Seafood. New in 2009, a new restaurant with a live-action show kitchen.

5223 Orient Rd., Tampa, FL 33605. © **866/502-PLAY** (7529) or 813/627-7625. Fax 813/623-6862. www.seminolehardrocktampa.com. 250 units. Winter $169–$329 double; off-season $219–$309 double. AE, DC, DISC, MC, V. **Amenities:** 5 restaurants; 5 bars; heated outdoor pool; full-service spa; Jacuzzi. *In room:* A/C, TV, dataport, high-speed Internet access, fridge, hair dryer, iron, CD player.

A Nearby Spa & Sports Resort

Saddlebrook Resort–Tampa ★★ Kids Set on 480 rolling acres of priceless countryside, Saddlebrook is a landlocked condominium development off the beaten path (30 min. north of Tampa International Airport). But if you're interested in spas, tennis, or golf, we recommend this resort, which offers complete spa treatments, the Hopman Tennis Program (Jennifer Capriati pitches a tent here), and the Arnold Palmer Golf Academy (see "Outdoor Activities & Spectator Sports," earlier in this chapter). Guests are housed in hotel rooms with Tommy Bahama–esque decor, or one-, two-, or three-bedroom suites. Much more appealing than the rooms, the suites come with a kitchen and either a patio or balcony overlooking lagoons, cypress and palm trees, and the resort's two 18-hole championship golf courses. There are shops, restaurants, a stunning pool, and a kids' club with supervised activities.

5700 Saddlebrook Way, Wesley Chapel, FL 33543. © **800/729-8383** or 813/973-1111. Fax 813/973-4504. www.saddlebrookresort.com. 800 units. Winter $275–$420 suite; off-season $135–$230 suite. Packages available. AE, DC, DISC, MC, V. Valet parking $10. **Amenities:** 4 restaurants; 3 bars; heated outdoor pool; 2 golf courses; 45 grass, clay, and hard tennis courts; health club; spa; Jacuzzi; sauna; bike rental; children's activities program; concierge; activities desk; car-rental desk; business center; limited room service; massage; laundry service; coin-op washers/dryers. *In room:* A/C, TV, dataport, kitchen, minibar, fridge, coffeemaker, hair dryer, iron.

WHERE TO DINE

The restaurants that follow are organized by geographic area: near Busch Gardens, in or near Hyde Park (across the Hillsborough River from downtown), and in Ybor City. Although Ybor City is better known, Tampa's trendiest dining scene is along South Howard Avenue—"SoHo" to the locals—between West Kennedy Boulevard and the bay in affluent Hyde Park.

Near Busch Gardens

You'll find the national fast-food and family restaurants east of I-275 on Busch Boulevard and Fowler Avenue.

Moderate

Cafe Don José SPANISH/AMERICAN It's not nearly on a par with the Columbia in Ybor City (see below), but this Spanish-themed restaurant is among the best within a short drive of Busch Gardens. High-back chairs, dark-wood floors, and Spanish posters and paintings set an appropriate scene for the house specialties of traditional paella (allow 30 min. for preparation) and Valencia-style rice dishes. Don José also offers non-Spanish fare such as red snapper baked in parchment.

11009 N. 56th St. (in Sherwood Forest Shopping Center, 1/4-mile south of Fowler Ave.). ✆ **813/985-2392.** www.cafedonjose.com. Main courses $15–$60. AE, DC, MC, V. Mon–Fri 11:30am–4:30pm and 5–10pm; Sat 5–9pm.

Inexpensive

Mel's Hot Dogs (Kids) AMERICAN Catering to everyone from businesspeople to hungry families craving all-beef hot dogs, Mel Lohn's red-and-white cottage offers everything from traditional Chicago-style and "bagel-dogs" to bacon/cheddar Reuben-style hot dogs. All choices are served on poppy-seed buns and can be ordered with fries and a choice of coleslaw or baked beans. Even the decor is dedicated to wieners: The walls and windows are lined with hot-dog memorabilia, and a wiener-mobile is usually parked out front. Mel's chili is outstanding, too. And just in case hot-dog mania hasn't won you over, there are a few alternatives (chicken, beef, and veggie burgers, and terrific onion rings).

4136 E. Busch Blvd., at 42nd St. ✆ **813/985-8000.** www.melshotdogs.com. Most items $2.75–$11. No credit cards (but there's an ATM on the premises). Sun–Thurs 11am–8pm; Fri–Sat 11am–9pm.

Hyde Park

Expensive

Bern's SteakHouse ★★ STEAKHOUSE The exterior of this famous steakhouse looks like a factory. Inside, however, some say it looks like a brothel, containing eight ornate dining rooms with themes such as Rhône, Burgundy, and Irish Rebellion. However you perceive the decor, this is a carnivore's paradise, and I actually drove from Miami and back just for dinner. Was it worth it? Sort of, but I wouldn't make a special trip just for Bern's again. I would, however, eat there without question if I was in town. At Bern's, you order and pay for grilled steaks of perfectly aged beef according to the thickness and weight (the 60-oz., 3-in.-thick porterhouse can feed four adults). The phone book–size wine list—one of the restaurant's most famous attributes—has more than 7,000 selections, many available by the glass. Ask your server for a sampling before you purchase a bottle. Upstairs, the restaurant's other most famous attribute—the dessert quarters—has 50 romantic booths paneled in aged California redwood; each can privately seat from 2 to 12 guests. All of these little chambers are equipped with phones for placing your order and closed-circuit TVs for watching and listening to a resident pianist. The dessert menu has almost 100 selections, plus some 1,400 after-dinner drinks. It's possible to reserve a booth for dessert only, but preference is given to those who dine.

The big secret here is that steak sandwiches are available at the bar but are not mentioned on the menu. Smaller versions of the chargrilled steaks served in the dining rooms, they come with a choice of french fries or crispy onion rings. Add a salad, and you have a terrific meal for about half the price of the least-expensive main course.

Sidebern's, 2208 W. Morrison Ave., at South Howard Avenue (✆ **813/258-2233**), is the restaurant's New American offshoot. It's also quite good, but choose the original: Missing Bern's would be like watching the remake of *Psycho* without ever seeing the original. And in 2007, plans were announced for Bern's very own hotel, the **Epicurean Hotel,** a 75-room boutique condo/hotel with a new Bern's restaurant, wine shop, culinary

Dining on the Bay

One of the newest additions to Tampa's dining scene is the 180-foot-long ***StarShip* Dining Yacht** (✆ **877/744-7999** or 813/223-7999; www.starshipdining.com), which makes 2-hour lunch, brunch, and dinner cruises from the Channelside out onto Tampa Bay. The ship's four dining rooms serve exceptional cruise fare. A house band plays during dinner and then moves to the top deck for dancing under the stars. Lunch cruises cost $60 per person for adults, $40 for kids. Dinner cruises cost $90 for adults, $60 for kids. There's also a Sunday brunch for $60 for adults, $40 for kids. Call for the schedule.

school, and day spa located right next door to the original restaurant. Completion was expected in mid-2009.

1208 S. Howard Ave. (at Marjory Ave.). ✆ **813/251-2421.** www.bernssteakhouse.com. Reservations recommended. Main courses $17–$60; sandwiches $9–$15. AE, DC, DISC, MC, V. Daily 5–11pm. Closed Christmas. Valet parking $5.

Restaurant BT ★★★ VIETNAMESE I live in Miami and when I heard about this restaurant, I drove the 5 hours to Tampa to see what all the hype was about. It was worth every service plaza, toll fare, and then some! One reviewer called it one of the hippest, most innovative Vietnamese restaurants in the United States. Chef Trina Nguyen-Batley is a genius, creating a chic, sophisticated, stylish oasis of French Vietnamese fare that's as gorgeous as it is delicious. An appetizer of roast sea eel with *ponzu* sauce, rice vinegar, and sesame seeds on chilled cucumber salad prepares the palate for an outstanding onslaught of flavors and textures to come. Baby lamb spareribs braised in star anise, garlic, rice wine, and tamarind are equally spectacular, but if you like spicy, and I do, the spicy prawns in chili, ginger, and garlic sauce over steamed rice is the way to go. Come to think of it, you can't go wrong with anything here. It's authentic, awe-inspiring, and, yes, even worth a 5-hour drive, more so than Bern's, actually.

1633 W. Snow Ave. ✆ **813/258-1916.** www.restaurantbt.com. Reservations recommended. Main courses $18–$29. AE, DC, DISC, MC, V. Mon–Thurs 11:30am–2:30pm and 5:30–9:30pm; Fri–Sat 11:30am–2:30pm and 5:30–10:30pm.

Moderate

Mise en Place ★★ CONTEMPORARY AMERICAN Look around at all those happy, stylish people soaking up the trendy ambience, and you'll know why Chef Marty Blitz and his wife Maryann have been among the culinary darlings of Tampa since 1986. They present the freshest of ingredients in a creative, award-winning menu that changes weekly. Main courses often include such choices as grainy mustard pecan crusted rack of lamb, bourbon shallot demi glace, cayenne onion rings, and tarragon white cheddar grits; or ancho-spiced pan-seared venison rack with pork belly, mushroom ragout, and avocado-lime butter. The tasting menu, with wine, is listed on the menu under "Get Blitzed." They may cook serious food, but at least they have a sense of humor, too!

In Grand Central Place, 442 W. Kennedy Blvd. (at S. Magnolia Ave., opposite the University of Tampa). ✆ **813/254-5373.** www.miseonline.com. Reservations recommended. Main courses $19–$33; tasting menu $69 with wine, $49 without. AE, DC, DISC, MC, V. Tues–Thurs 11:30am–2:30pm and 5:30–10pm; Fri 11:30am–2:30pm and 5:30–11pm; Sat 5–11pm.

Whiskey Joe's Bar & Grill ★ BARBECUE Gorgeous ocean views trump the bar menu at Whiskey Joe's (formerly known as Castaway), where pan-seared grouper, whole snapper, po' boy sandwiches, fried chicken, and barbecue ribs reel in a steady crowd of locals and visitors alike. Insist on sitting on the deck and time your meal around sundown; the vantage point for sunsets here makes developers drool. Live reggae on Sunday and daily happy hours make Whiskey Joe's a popular gathering spot for locals.

7720 Courtney Campbell Causeway. ✆ **813/281-0770.** www.whiskeyjoestampa.com. Reservations recommended. Main courses $10–$20. AE, DC, DISC, MC, V. Daily 11am–11pm.

Wine Exchange ★★ MEDITERRANEAN This Tampa hot spot is an oenophile's dream come true, as each dish is paired with a particular wine available by the bottle or the glass. The menu is rather simple, featuring pizzas, pastas, salads, and sandwiches, but daily specials are more elaborate, including grilled Delmonico steak, blackened pork tenderloin, or Dijon-crusted salmon. The outdoor patio is a great place to sit. There's almost always a wait at this buzz-worthy eatery.

1611 W. Swan Ave. ✆ **813/254-9463.** Main courses $10–$24. AE, DC, DISC, MC, V. Mon–Fri 11:30am–10pm; Sat 11am–11pm; Sun 11am–9pm; brunch Sat–Sun 11am–3pm.

Inexpensive

Bella's Italian Cafe ★ ITALIAN While trendy restaurants in this area come and go, Bella's has been open for more than 20 years and for good reason. A casual, rustic ambience with a wood-fired oven and indoor and outdoor seating attract a sophisticated crowd of foodies of all ages. The restaurant's authentic Italian fare is delicious, from the paper-thin carpaccio with garlic, olives, capers, and basil, to the old-fashioned spaghetti and meatballs. You can also create your own combination of pasta and sauce, choosing from a large list of options, or just order a pizza cooked in the oak-burning oven. Executive chef and co-owner Joanie Corneil studied cooking in Italy, and you can tell. For those who like a strong drink with their dinner, the Bellarita is a popular potion of Conmemorativo tequila and Grand Marnier. On second thought, save that for after dinner so you can at least appreciate your meal as it's going down!

1413 S. Howard Ave. ✆ **813/254-3355.** www.bellasitaliancafe.com. Reservations recommended. Main courses $8–$20; pizza $9–$12. AE, DC, DISC, MC, V. Mon–Wed 11:30am–11:30pm; Thurs 11:30am–12:30am; Fri 11:30am–1:30am; Sat 4pm–1:30am; Sun 4–11:30pm.

Four Green Fields IRISH/AMERICAN Just across the bridge from the downtown convention center, this thatched-roof Irish pub may be surrounded by palm trees instead of potato fields, but it still offers the ambience and tastes of Ireland. Staffed by Irish immigrants, the large room with a square bar in the center smells of Bass and Harp ales. The Gaelic stew is predictably bland, but the salads and sandwiches are passable. Fish and chips are a good bet here, especially with a pint of Guinness. The live Irish music Thursday through Saturday nights and Sunday afternoon draws a fun crowd, ranging from post-college to early retirees.

205 W. Platt St. (btw. Parker St. and Plant Ave.). ✆ **813/254-4444.** www.fourgreenfields.com. Main courses $11–$13; sandwiches $6–$7. AE, MC, V. Daily 11am–3am.

Ybor City

Moderate

Columbia ★★★ SPANISH Columbia celebrated 100 years in 2005. Its tile building occupies an entire city block in the heart of Ybor City. Tourists flock here to soak up the ambience, and so do the locals because it's so much fun to clap along during the fire-belching Spanish flamenco floor shows Monday through Saturday evenings ($6 per person additional charge besides dinner charge). You can't help coming back time after time for the famous Spanish bean soup and original "1905" salad. The *paella a la Valencia* is outstanding, with more than a dozen ingredients ranging from Gulf grouper and Gulf pink shrimp to calamari, mussels, clams, chicken, and pork. Another favorite is *boliche* (eye of round stuffed with chorizo), accompanied by plantains and black beans and rice. Entrees come with a crispy hunk of Cuban bread with butter. Lighter appetites can choose from a limited menu of tapas, including "Cuban caviar" (a spicy black-bean dip). The decor throughout is graced with hand-painted tiles, wrought-iron chandeliers, dark woods, rich red fabrics, and stained-glass windows.

2117 E. 7th Ave. (btw. 21st and 22nd sts.). ✆ **813/248-4961.** www.columbiarestaurant.com. Reservations recommended, especially for flamenco shows. Main courses $15–$30. AE, DC, DISC, MC, V. Mon–Thurs 11am–10pm; Fri–Sat 11am–11pm; Sun noon–9pm.

Inexpensive

Carmine's Seventh Avenue ★ CUBAN/ITALIAN/AMERICAN Bright blue poles hold up an ancient pressed-tin ceiling above this noisy corner cafe. It's not the cleanest joint in town, but a great variety of loyal local patrons gather here for genuine Cuban sandwiches—smoked ham, roast pork, Genoa salami, Swiss cheese, pickles, salad dressing, mustard, lettuce, and tomato on crispy Cuban bread. There's a vegetarian version, too. The combination of a half-sandwich and choice of black beans and rice or a bowl of Spanish soup made with sausages, potatoes, and garbanzo beans is a filling meal just by itself. Main courses are led by Cuban-style roast pork, thin-cut pork chops with mushroom sauce, spaghetti with a blue-crab tomato sauce, and a few seafood and chicken platters.

1802 E. 7th Ave. (at 18th St.). ✆ **813/248-3834.** Main courses $10–$20; sandwiches $5–$10. AE, MC, V. Mon–Tues 11am–11pm; Wed–Thurs 11am–1am; Fri–Sat 11am–3am; Sun 11am–6pm.

TAMPA AFTER DARK

The Tampa/Hillsborough Arts Council maintains an **Artsline** (✆ **813/229-2787**), a 24-hour information service providing the latest on current and upcoming cultural events. Racks in many restaurants and bars have copies of *Creative Loafing Tampa* (www.tampa.creativeloafing.com), and *Accent on Tampa Bay* (www.ampubs.com), two free publications detailing what's going on in the entire bay area. You can also check the "BayLife" and "Friday Extra" sections of the *Tampa Tribune* (www.tampatrib.com), as well as the Thursday "Weekend" section of the *St. Petersburg Times* (www.sptimes.com). The visitor center usually has copies of the week's newspaper sections (see "Essentials," earlier in this chapter).

THE CLUB & MUSIC SCENE Ybor City is Tampa's favorite nighttime venue. All you have to do is stroll along 7th Avenue East between 15th and 20th streets, and you'll hear music blaring from the clubs. On Friday and Saturday, from 9pm to 3am, the avenue is packed with people, the majority high-school kids and early-20-somethings; but you'll

The Hub of Tampa's Bar Scene

Ybor City and Bern's SteakHouse are command central for the boozy sophisticates of Tampa, but if you go downtown, you'll find the true hub of Tampa's bar scene in the form of, well, the **Hub,** 719 N. Franklin St. (✆ **813/229-1553**). It's a classic dive bar in which judges, lawyers, and the over-21 set shake and stir over-stiff libations and a fabulous jukebox.

Tips Careful Where You Park

Parking can be scarce at night in Ybor City, and the area has seen an occasional robbery in the late hours. Play it safe and use the municipal parking lots behind the shops on 8th Avenue East, or the new parking garages near Centro Ybor, on 7th Avenue East at 16th Street.

also find something going on Tuesday through Thursday, and even on Sunday. The clubs change names frequently, so you don't need names, addresses, or phone numbers; your ears will guide you along 7th Avenue East. With all of the sidewalk seating, it's easy to judge what the clientele is like and make your choice from there. Another hipster haven is the Hyde Park area of town, where restaurant bars buzz with late-night activity.

The center of the action these days is **Centro Ybor,** on 7th Avenue East at 16th Street (✆ **813/242-4660;** www.centroybor.com), the district's large dining-and-entertainment complex. The restaurants and pubs in this family-oriented center tend to be tamer than many of those along 7th Avenue, at least on nonweekend nights. You don't have to pay to listen to live music in the center's patio on weekend afternoons.

THE PERFORMING ARTS With a prime downtown location on 9 acres along the east bank of the Hillsborough River, the huge **Tampa Bay Performing Arts Center** ★, 1010 N. MacInnes Place, next to the Tampa Museum of Art (✆ **800/955-1045** or 813/229-7827; www.tampacenter.com), is the largest performing-arts venue south of the Kennedy Center in Washington, D.C. Accordingly, this four-theater complex is the focal point of Tampa's performing-arts scene, presenting a wide range of Broadway plays, classical and pop concerts, operas, improvisation, and special events.

A sightseeing attraction in its own right, the restored **Tampa Theatre,** 711 Franklin St., between Zack and Polk streets (✆ **813/274-8286;** www.tampatheatre.org), dates from 1926 and is on the National Register of Historic Places. It presents a varied program of classic, foreign, and alternative films, as well as concerts and special events (and it's said to be haunted!).

The 66,321-seat **Raymond James Stadium,** 4201 N. Dale Mabry Hwy. (✆ **813/673-4300;** www.raymondjames.com/stadium), is sometimes the site of headliner concerts. The **USF Sun Dome,** 4202 E. Fowler Ave. (✆ **813/974-3111;** www.sundome.org), on the University of South Florida campus, hosts major concerts by touring pop stars, rock bands, jazz groups, and other contemporary artists.

One of the busiest spots in town for live music, rustic-style, is **Skipper's Smokehouse,** 910 Skipper Rd. (✆ **813/971-0666;** www.skipperssmokehouse.com), a Key West–style former smokehouse turned blues, jazz, zydeco, ska, and reggae hot spot.

Ticketmaster (✆ **813/287-8844;** www.ticketmaster.com) sells tickets to most events and shows.

2 ST. PETERSBURG ★

20 miles SW of Tampa; 289 miles NW of Miami; 84 miles SW of Orlando

On the western shore of the bay, St. Petersburg stands in contrast to Tampa, much as San Francisco compares to Oakland in California. Whereas Tampa is the area's business,

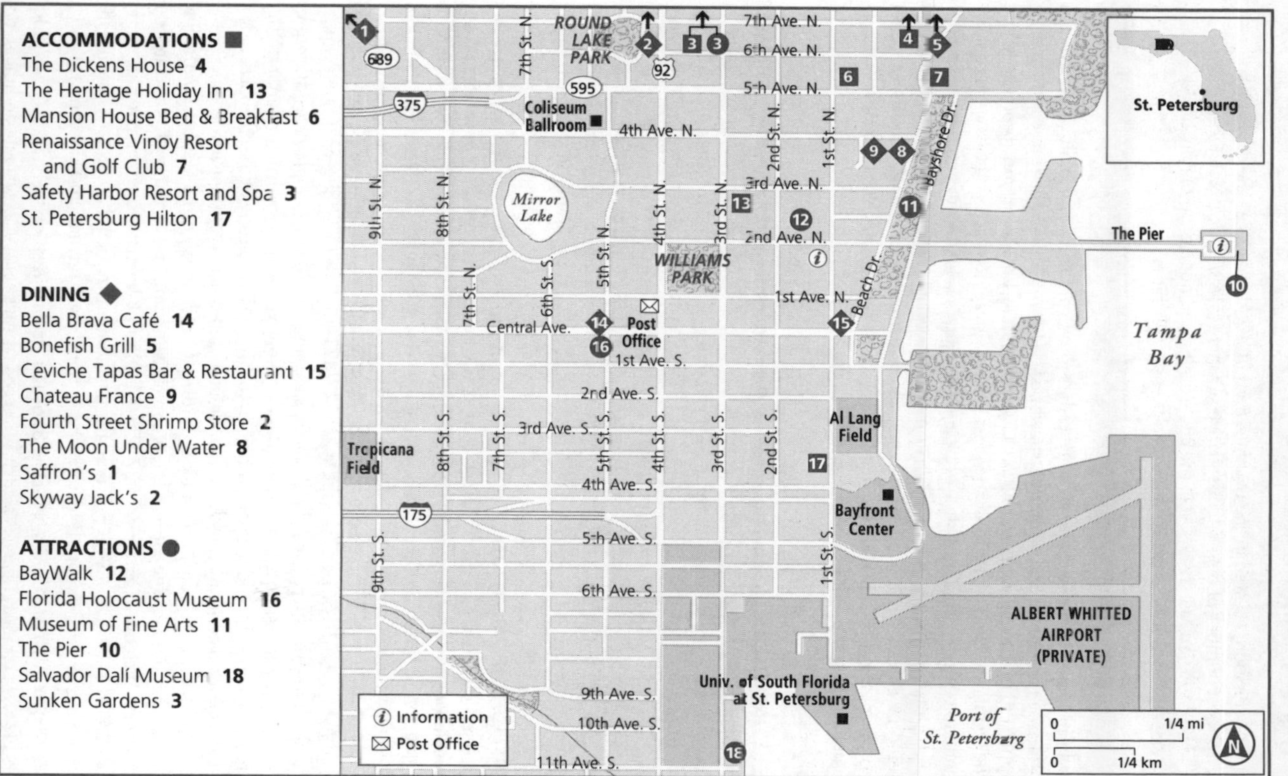
ACCOMMODATIONS
The Dickens House 4
The Heritage Holiday Inn 13
Mansion House Bed & Breakfast 6
Renaissance Vinoy Resort and Golf Club 7
Safety Harbor Resort and Spa 3
St. Petersburg Hilton 17
DINING
Bella Brava Café 14
Bonefish Grill 5
Ceviche Tapas Bar & Restaurant 15
Chateau France 9
Fourth Street Shrimp Store 2
The Moon Under Water 8
Saffron's 1
Skyway Jack's 2
ATTRACTIONS
BayWalk 12
Florida Holocaust Museum 16
Museum of Fine Arts 11
The Pier 10
Salvador Dalí Museum 18
Sunken Gardens 3
ROUND LAKE PARK
Coliseum Ballroom
Mirror Lake
WILLIAMS PARK
Post Office
Tropicana Field
Al Lang Field
Bayfront Center
The Pier
Tampa Bay
ALBERT WHITTED AIRPORT (PRIVATE)
Univ. of South Florida at St. Petersburg
Port of St. Petersburg
St. Petersburg
7th Ave. N.
6th Ave. N.
5th Ave. N.
4th Ave. N.
3rd Ave. N.
2nd Ave. N.
1st Ave. N.
Central Ave.
1st Ave. S.
2nd Ave. S.
3rd Ave. S.
4th Ave. S.
5th Ave. S.
6th Ave. S.
9th Ave. S.
10th Ave. S.
11th Ave. S.
9th St. N.
8th St. N.
7th St. N.
6th St. S.
5th St. N.
4th St. N.
3rd St. N.
2nd St. N.
1st St. N.
8th St. S.
7th St. S.
5th St. S.
4th St. S.
3rd St. S.
2nd St. S.
1st St. S.
9th St. S.
Bayshore Dr.
Beach Dr.
689
375
595
92
175
Information
Post Office
0 1/4 mi
0 1/4 km
N

Fun Facts Sunny Days

St. Petersburg is listed in the *Guinness Book of World Records* as the city with the longest number of days of consecutive sunshine—768, to be exact. From February 9, 1967, to March 17, 1969, the city experienced not a drop of rain, no clouds—just pure, unadulterated, tan-friendly sunshine!

industrial, and shipping center, St. Petersburg was conceived and built a century ago primarily for tourists and wintering snowbirds. Here you'll find one of the most picturesque and pleasant downtowns of any city in Florida, with a waterfront promenade and the famous inverted pyramid–shaped Pier offering great views across the bay, plus quality museums, interesting shops, and a few good restaurants. Thanks to an urban redevelopment program, St. Pete has awoken from its slumber and actually resembles a city that could be considered hip, with renewed, restored streetscapes full of punk'd-out skateboarders, clubs, bars, and a vibrancy that goes well beyond the excitement surrounding bingo night at the "adult" communities in town.

ESSENTIALS

GETTING THERE **Tampa International Airport,** approximately 16 miles northeast of St. Petersburg, is the prime gateway to the area (see "Essentials" in section 1, earlier in this chapter). The primary carrier at **St. Petersburg–Clearwater International Airport,** on Roosevelt Boulevard (Fla. 686), about 10 miles north of downtown St. Petersburg (✆ **727/453-7800;** www.fly2pie.com), is **Allegiant;** other carriers during the winter months include Canadian **Air Transat** (✆ **877/872-6728;** www.airtransat.com). **Amtrak** (✆ **800/USA-RAIL** [872-7245]; www.amtrak.com) has bus connections from its Tampa station to downtown St. Petersburg. (See "Getting There" in section 1, earlier in this chapter.)

VISITOR INFORMATION For advance information on St. Petersburg and the beaches (see section 3, later in this chapter), contact the **St. Petersburg/Clearwater Area Convention & Visitors Bureau,** 14450 46th St. N., Clearwater, FL 34622 (✆ **800/345-6710,** or 727/464-7200 for hotel reservations; fax 727/464-7222; www.floridasbeach.com for information specific to the beaches).

After you arrive, you can head to the **St. Petersburg Area Chamber of Commerce,** 100 2nd Ave. N. (at 1st St.), St. Petersburg (✆ **727/821-4069;** fax 727/895-6326; www.stpete.com). Across the street from the BayWalk shopping-and-dining complex, this downtown main office and visitor center is open Monday through Friday from 8am to 5pm, Saturday from 10am to 4pm, and Sunday from noon to 4pm. Ask for a copy of the chamber's visitor guide, which lists hotels, motels, condominiums, and other accommodations.

Also downtown, you'll find walk-in **information centers** on the first level of the Pier and in the lobby of the Florida International Museum. The chamber also operates the **Suncoast Welcome Center** (✆ **727/573-1449**), on Ulmerton Road, at exit 31B southbound off I-275 (there's no exit here for northbound traffic). The center is open daily from 9am to 5pm except New Year's Day, Easter, Thanksgiving, and Christmas.

GETTING AROUND The **Pinellas Suncoast Transit Authority/PSTA** (✆ **727/530-9911;** www.psta.net) operates regular bus service throughout St. Petersburg and the rest of the Pinellas Peninsula. Rides cost $1.75 for adults, 85¢ for seniors, and $1 for students.

If you need a cab, call **Yellow Cab** (✆ **727/821-7777**) or **Independent Cab** (✆ **727/327-3444**). Fares are $2.25 at flag fall, plus $2.50 for each additional mile.

SEEING THE TOP ATTRACTIONS

Florida Holocaust Museum ★ This thought-provoking museum (the fourth-largest such museum in the U.S.) has exhibits about the Holocaust (Jewish life before the Holocaust, the rise of the Nazi party, and so on), including a boxcar used to transport human cargo to Auschwitz and a gallery of art relating to the Holocaust. Its main focus, however, is to promote tolerance and understanding in the present. It was founded by Walter P. Loebenberg, a local businessman who escaped Nazi Germany in 1939 and fought with the U.S. Army in World War II.

55 5th St. S. (btw. Central Ave. and 1st Ave. S.). ✆ **800/960-7448** or 727/820-0100. www.flholocaustmuseum.org. Admission $12 adults, $10 seniors and college students, $9 children 6–18, free for kids 5 and under. Mon–Fri 10am–5pm; Sat–Sun noon–5pm (last admission at 4pm). Closed Easter, Rosh Hashanah, Yom Kippur, Thanksgiving, and Christmas.

Museum of Fine Arts ★★ Resembling a Mediterranean villa on the waterfront, this museum houses an excellent collection of European, American, pre-Columbian, and Far Eastern art, with works by such artists as Fragonard, Monet, Renoir, Cézanne, and Gauguin. Other highlights include period rooms with antique furnishings, plus a gallery of Steuben crystal, a new decorative-arts gallery, and world-class rotating exhibits. The best way to see it all is on a guided tour, which takes about 1 hour. Ask about classical-music performances from October to April.

255 Beach Dr. NE (at 3rd Ave. N.). ✆ **727/896-2667.** www.fine-arts.org. Admission $12 adults, $10 seniors 65 and over, $6 students with ID, free for children 5 and under (special exhibits cost extra). Admission includes guided tour. Tues–Sat 10am–5pm; Sun 1–5pm. Guided tours Tues–Sat 11am and 1, 2, and 3pm; Sun 1 and 2pm. Closed New Year's Day, Martin Luther King Jr. Day, Thanksgiving, and Christmas.

The Pier (Kids) The Pier is a tourist-trapped waterfront dining-and-shopping complex overlooking Tampa Bay. Originally built as a railroad pier in 1889, today it's capped by a spaceshiplike inverted pyramid offering five levels of shops, three restaurants, a tourist information desk, an observation deck, catwalks for fishing, boat docks, miniature golf, boat and watersports rentals, sightseeing boats, a food court, plus an aquarium. Cruise boats often operate from the Pier during the winter months, and you can rent fishing gear and drop your line into the bay year-round. There's valet parking at the end of the Pier, or you can park on land and ride a free trolley out to the complex.

800 2nd Ave. NE. ✆ **727/821-6443.** www.stpete-pier.com. Free admission to all public areas and decks; donations welcome at the Pier Aquarium. Valet parking $4; self-parking $3. Pier Mon–Thurs 10am–9pm; Fri–Sat 10am–10pm; Sun 11am–7pm. Aquarium Mon–Sat 10am–8pm; Sun 11am–6pm.

Salvador Dali Museum ★★★ This starkly modern museum houses the world's most comprehensive (and most valuable, at $125 million) collection of works by the

Fun Facts Open-Air Mail

St. Petersburg residents don't have to go inside to get mail out of their boxes at St. Petersburg's open-air **post office,** at the corner of 1st Avenue North and 4th Street North. Built in 1917, this granite, arcaded Spanish Colonial structure is a popular local landmark and is often photographed by those enchanted by its charm.

Tips Car Smarts

You can spend a small fortune in a parking garage or by feeding the meters in St. Petersburg, or you can cut costs substantially by parking at the **Pier** ($3 all day) and taking the **Looper,** the city's trolley service, which operates between the Pier and all major downtown attractions.

renowned Spanish surrealist—and for art lovers is reason enough to visit downtown St. Petersburg. Housing six of the artist's masterworks, the museum was given three stars by the Michelin Guide—the highest-ranked museum in the entire South. It includes oil paintings, watercolors, drawings, and more than 1,000 graphics, plus posters, photos, sculptures, objets d'art, and a 5,000-volume library on Dalí and surrealism. Take one of the free docent-led tours to get the most out of the museum.

1000 3rd St. S. (near 11th Ave. S.). © **727/823-3767.** www.salvadordalimuseum.org. Admission $15 adults, $14 seniors, $10 students, $4 children 5–9, free for children 4 and under; $5 for all Thurs 5–8pm. Mon–Wed and Fri–Sat 9:30am–5:30pm; Thurs 9:30am–8pm; Sun noon–5:30pm. Closed Thanksgiving and Christmas.

Sunken Gardens Dating from 1935, this former tourist attraction is now operated as a 7-acre botanical garden by the city of St. Petersburg. It contains a vast array of 5,000 plants, flowers, and trees; a butterfly aviary; a display of snakes, spiders, and scorpions; and a rainforest information center. There's also a daily wildlife show. Call for a schedule of exhibits and tours.

1825 4th St. N. (btw. 18th and 19th aves. NE). © **727/551-3102.** www.stpete.org/sunken/index.asp. Admission $8 adults, $6 seniors, $4 children 3–16, free for children 2 and under. Mon–Sat 10am–4:30pm; Sun noon–4:30pm.

OUTDOOR ACTIVITIES & SPECTATOR SPORTS

BIKING, IN-LINE SKATING & HIKING With miles of flat terrain, the St. Petersburg area is ideal for bikers, in-line skaters, and hikers. The **Pinellas Trail** is especially good, as it follows an abandoned railroad bed 47 miles from St. Petersburg north to Tarpon Springs (© **727/464-8201;** www.pinellascounty.org/trailgd). The **St. Pete trail head** is on 34th Street South (U.S. 19), between 8th and Fairfield avenues south. It's packed on weekends. Free maps of the trail are available at the St. Petersburg Area Chamber of Commerce (see "Visitor Information," above). The 2½-mile-long **Friendship Trail-Bridge,** linking Tampa and St. Petersburg, is another popular venue for hikers, bikers, bicyclists, anglers, and in-line skaters, but be careful going up and down the steep center span, especially if you're on skates.

GOLF One of the nation's top 50 municipal courses, the **Mangrove Bay Golf Course ★★**, 875 62nd Ave. NE (© **727/893-7800**), hugs Old Tampa Bay and offers 18-hole, par-72 play. Facilities include a driving range. Lessons and golf-club rental are also available. Fees are about $30 in winter, slightly lower during off-season.

In Largo, the **Bardmoor Golf & Tennis Club,** 8001 Cumberland Rd. (© **727/392-1234**), is often the venue for major tournaments. Lakes punctuate 17 of the 18 holes on this par-72 championship course. Lessons and rental clubs are available, as is a Tom Fazio–designed practice range. Call the clubhouse for seasonal greens fees. The course is open daily from 7am to dusk.

Call **Tee Times USA** (✆ **800/374-8633;** www.teetimesusa.com) to reserve times at these and other area courses.

For course information online, go to www.golf.com or www.floridagolfing.com; or call the **Florida Sports Foundation** (✆ **850/488-8347**) or **Florida Golfing** (✆ **866/833-2663**).

SAILING Both Steve and Doris Colgate's **Offshore Sailing School** (✆ **888/454-8002** or 239/454-1700; www.offshore-sailing.com) and the **Annapolis Sailing School** (✆ **800/638-9192** or 727/867-8102; www.annapolissailing.com) have operations here. Various courses, lasting from 2 days to a week, are offered. Contact the schools for prices and schedules.

SPECTATOR SPORTS St. Petersburg has always been a baseball town, and **Tropicana Field,** a 45,000-seat domed stadium alongside I-175 between 9th and 16th streets (✆ **727/825-3100**), is the home of the American League's **Tampa Bay Devil Rays** (✆ **888/326-7297** or 727/825-3137; www.devilrays.mlb.com). Baseball season runs from April through October. Single-game tickets are $3 to $75 and are usually available on game days. Call or check the website for the schedule. The Devil Rays move outdoors to a new facility in Port Charlotte in 2009 for spring-training workouts and games from mid-February through March. See the team's website for more information.

The **Philadelphia Phillies** now play their spring-training season in new digs in Clearwater, at Bright House Networks Field, 601 Old Coachman Rd. (✆ **727/442-8496**). Their minor-league affiliate, the **Clearwater Threshers** (✆ **727/441-8638;** www.threshersbaseball.com; $4–$9), plays in the stadium from April through August. The **Toronto Blue Jays** do their spring thing at Knology Park, 311 Douglas Ave., in Dunedin (✆ **800/707-8269** or 813/733-9302; www.bluejays.mlb.com; $13–$24), which is also home to their minor-league affiliate, the **Dunedin Blue Jays** (✆ **727/733-9302;** www.dunedinbluejays.com), April through August.

TENNIS You can learn to play or hone your game at the **Phil Green Tennis Academy,** at Safety Harbor Resort and Spa (p. 413).

SHOPPING

The **Pier,** at the end of 2nd Avenue Northeast (see "Seeing the Top Attractions," above), houses more than a dozen boutiques and crafts shops; but nearby **Beach Drive,** running along the waterfront, is one of the most fashionable downtown strolling and shopping venues. Here you'll find the **Glass Canvas Gallery,** at 4th Avenue NE (✆ **727/821-6767**), featuring a dazzling array of glass sculpture, tableware, art, and crafts items by local, national, and international artists. **Red Cloud,** between 1st and 2nd avenues (✆ **727/821-5824**), is an oasis for Native American crafts, including jewelry, headdresses, and art.

Downtown's commercial showplace is **BayWalk** (✆ **727/895-9277;** www.yourbaywalk.com), an open-air shopping, dining, and entertainment complex bordered by 1st and 2nd streets and 2nd and 3rd avenues north. It has a branch of Ann Taylor, Chico's, Sunglass Hut, some smaller boutiques, and a 20-screen Muvico theater.

Haslam's Book Store, 2025 Central Ave. (✆ **727/822-8616;** www.haslams.com), is a favorite place to browse. Dating from 1933, its collection holds more than 350,000 volumes, making it Florida's largest bookstore. (As a perk, it is said to be haunted.)

Central Avenue is another shopping area, featuring the **Gas Plant Antique Arcade,** between 12th and 13th streets (✆ **727/895-0368;** www.gasplantantique.com), the largest antiques mall on Florida's west coast, with more than 100 dealers displaying their

Ancient Burial Mounds & Manatees

Drive north of St. Petersburg for an hour on congested U.S. 19, and you'll come to one of Florida's original tourist attractions, the famous **Weeki Wachee Springs** (✆ **877/469-3354** or 352/596-2062; www.weekiwachee.com). "Mermaids" have been putting on acrobatic swimming shows here every day since 1947. It's a sight to see them doing their dances in waters that come from one of America's most prolific freshwater springs, pouring some 170 million gallons of 72°F (22°C) water each day into the river. There's more than mermaids here; you can also take a Wilderness River Cruise across the Weeki Wachee River and send the kids on the flume ride at Buccaneer Bay, the water-park part of the attraction. Admission is $14 for adults, $11 for children 3 to 10. Weeki Wachee Springs is open Monday through Thursday from 10am to 3pm, Friday through Sunday from 10am to 4pm. Buccaneer Bay water park is open only on Friday from 10am to 4pm, Saturday and Sunday from 10am to 5pm. Parking is $3.

You can rent kayaks on the Weeki Wachee River for $37 for a one-person kayak and $52 for a two-person kayak per day (✆ **352/597-0360;** www.floridacanoe.com).

From Weeki Wachee, travel 21 miles north to the **Homosassa Springs Wildlife State Park,** 4150 S. Suncoast Blvd. (U.S. 19), in Homosassa Springs (✆ **352/628-5343;** www.floridastateparks.org/homosassasprings). The highlight here is a floating observatory where visitors can "walk" under water and watch manatees in a rehabilitation facility, as well as see thousands of fresh- and saltwater fish. You'll also spot deer, bear, bobcats, otters, egrets, and flamingos along unspoiled nature trails. The park is open daily from 9am to 5:30pm (last tickets sold at 4pm). There are also very educational, entertaining wildlife programs including the alligator and hippo program and the manatee program. Admission is $9 for adults and $5 for children 3 to 12; it includes a 20-minute narrated boat ride.

About 7 miles north of Homosassa Springs, more than 300 manatees spend the winter in Crystal River. You can **swim or snorkel with the manatees ★★** in the warm-water natural spring of Kings Bay. **American Pro Diving Center,** 821 SE Hwy. 19, Crystal River (✆ **800/291-3483** or 352/563-0041; www.americanprodive.com), offers daily swimming and snorkel tours. Early morning is the best time to see the manatees, so try to take the 6:30am departure. The trips range from $30 to $50 per person. Call for schedule and reservations. American Pro Diving also rents cottages on the Homosassa River.

wares. (Downtown has several antiques-and-collectibles dealers; get a list and map from the chamber of commerce.) The **Florida Craftsmen Gallery,** at 5th Street (✆ **727/821-7391;** www.floridacraftsmen.net), is a showcase for the works of more than 150 Florida artisans and craftspeople specializing in jewelry, ceramics, woodwork, fiber work, glassware, paper creations, and metalwork.

Tour the Crystal River with Captain Russ Holliday's **Native Sun Tours** (✆ **352/212-6142**) via a three-tiered airboat that glides over the shallow water. For a sublime stay, the **Blue Moon Bed & Breakfast** (✆ **352/621-1960;** www.thebluemoonbb.com), located amid the thick forest along the Homosassa River, offers elegantly themed rooms and a lodgelike lobby with fireplace from $155. Don't miss an afternoon in Heritage Village in downtown Crystal River, with delicious cafes including **Café on the Avenue** (✆ **352/795-3656;** www.dineontheavenue.com), known for the best three-layer banana-pineapple-pecan cake in the South, and **Back Porch Garden & Tea Bar** (✆ **352/564-1555**), where you can sip an iced tea under an oak tree.

Also check out the **Weedon Island Preserve,** 4801 37th St. S. (✆ **727/893-2627**), located in the upper Tampa Bay waters of Pinellas County, on the western shore of the entrance to Old Tampa Bay and directly west of Port Tampa. The island was named for Dr. Leslie Weedon, a renowned authority on yellow fever, who acquired the 1,250-acre island in 1898 in what is now north St. Petersburg. Weedon had a fascination with Indian culture and developed a weekend retreat on the island, from which he began excavations that first revealed the importance of the site as an Indian burial mound. A Smithsonian expedition to the island in 1923 and 1924 further documented the importance of the site, which is now managed as a county preserve. Today it's home to an assortment of fish, snakes, raccoons, and dolphins. Rent a canoe to explore, and find yourself easily "becoming one" with nature.

Baseball fans won't want to miss the **Ted Williams Museum & Hitters Hall of Fame,** Tropicana Field, One Tropicana Dr., St. Pete (✆ **352/527-6566;** www.twmuseum.com). The museum holds the great hitter's personal memorabilia, including his two Triple Crown batting titles. The museum opens 2 hours before home games, and stays open through the last inning. Admission is exclusive to fans attending games at the stadium.

For more information about the area, contact the **Citrus County Chamber of Commerce,** 28 NW Hwy. 19, Crystal River, FL 34428 (✆ **352/795-3149;** fax 352/795-4260; www.citruscountychamber.com). The chamber's visitor center is open Monday through Friday from 8:30am to 4:30pm, Saturday from 9am to 1pm.

WHERE TO STAY

The **St. Petersburg/Clearwater Area Convention & Visitors Bureau** (see "Essentials," earlier in this section) operates a free **reservations service** (✆ **800/345-6710**), through which you can book rooms at most hotels and motels in St. Petersburg and at the beaches. The bureau also publishes a brochure that lists members of its Superior Small Lodgings program; these establishments have fewer than 50 rooms and have been inspected and certified for cleanliness and value.

Other than the Renaissance Vinoy Resort and Golf Club (see below), the only chain hotel downtown is the **Hilton St. Petersburg Bayfront,** 333 1st St. S., between 3rd and 4th avenues south (✆ **800/445-8667** or 727/894-5000; fax 727/823-4797), a 15-story convention hotel within steps of the Salvador Dalí Museum, Florida Power Park at Al Lang Field, and the Bayfront Center's theaters. Otherwise, views from the upper-floor rooms are the main draws for leisure travelers.

Note: Sales and hotel taxes will add 12% to your bill.

Expensive

Renaissance Vinoy Resort and Golf Club ★★★ For the swankiest digs in the area, the Renaissance Vinoy is it. Built in 1925, this elegant Spanish-style establishment has hosted everyone from Jimmy Stewart to Bill Clinton, and is on the National Register of Historic Places after a total and meticulous $93-million restoration that made it once again the city's finest hotel. Dominating the northern part of downtown, it overlooks Tampa Bay and is within walking distance of the Pier, Central Avenue, and other attractions. All guest rooms, many with views of the bay, offer the utmost in comfort and include three phones, an additional TV in the bathroom, and bath scales. Some rooms in the original building have standing-room-only balconies; if you need enough room to sit outside, request a balconied unit in the new Tower Wing. Overlooking the bay, **Marchand's Grill** is the city's most elegant chophouse. The Vinoy also has 12 tennis courts and an 18-hole golf course. The hotel is nonsmoking.

501 5th Ave. NE (at Beach Dr.), St. Petersburg, FL 33701. ✆ **800/468-3571** or 727/894-1000. Fax 727/822-2785. www.renaissancehotels.com. 360 units. Winter $259–$525 double; off-season $199–$329 double. Packages available. AE, DC, DISC, MC, V. Valet parking $13; self-parking $9. **Amenities:** 4 restaurants; 2 bars; 2 heated outdoor pools (connected by a waterfall); golf course; 12 tennis courts; health club; spa; Jacuzzi; concierge; activities desk; car-rental desk; business center; salon; 24-hr. room service; massage; laundry service; coin-op washers/dryers; concierge-level rooms. *In room:* A/C, TV, dataport, minibar, coffeemaker, hair dryer, iron.

Moderate

The Dickens House ★★★ No relation to British author Charles Dickens, this Dickens House once belonged to Henry and Sadie Dickens, early St. Pete settlers. Purchased in 1995 by mural artist Ed Caldwell, a graduate of the prestigious Rhode Island School of Design, the Dickens House was restored to its original Craftsman-style architecture. The charming inn has five guest rooms: The Cracker Suite has a custom-made bent-willow queen bed and a twin bed. The Orange Blossom Room, while the smallest in the house, nevertheless has a queen bed and a tiny bathroom with a whirlpool. My personal fave, however, is the second-floor Cottage Suite, which resembles a Victorian-age beach cottage with white wicker, sea-grass carpet, roll-up awnings, and nightstands displaying shells. It also sleeps three. Don't miss complimentary snacks and wine every afternoon in the house's living room.

335 8th Ave. NE, St. Petersburg, FL 33701. ✆ **727/822-8622.** www.dickenshouse.com. 5 units. Winter $169–$299 double; off-season $139–$239 double. Rates include full breakfast. AE, DISC, MC, V. **Amenities:** Internet free in guest library; beach supplies. *In room:* A/C, TV, VCR, high-speed wireless and wired Internet access, fridge, hair dryer, iron, voice mail.

The Heritage Hotel ★ This former Holiday Inn has been transformed into the Holiday Inn's hip alter ego, the Indigo, receiving a complete renovation, featuring 76 high-tech rooms with high-definition TVs and "invigorating showers." The hotel's Grab and Go Phi Café serves Starbucks coffee, among other things, and there's also a cool lobby bar, heated pool, and Jacuzzi. Conveniently located within walking distance to restaurants, theaters, museums, and nightlife.

234 3rd Ave. N. (btw. 2nd and 3rd sts.), St. Petersburg, FL 33701. ✆ **800/283-7829** or 727/822-4814. Fax 727/823-1644. 76 units. $134–$152 double. AE, DC, DISC, MC, V. **Amenities:** Restaurant; bar; heated outdoor pool; Jacuzzi; business center; free high-speed Internet; limited room service; laundry service. *In room:* A/C, TV, dataport, coffeemaker, hair dryer, iron.

Mansion House Bed & Breakfast ★★ Mirror images of each other, the two houses of Mansion House are separated by a landscaped courtyard and were built between 1901 and 1912. The comfortable living room in the main house, which has 6 of the 13 units, opens to a sunroom, off which a small screened porch provides mosquito-free lounging. Both houses have upstairs front parlors with TVs, DVDs, and libraries. Tall, old-fashioned windows let lots of light into the attractive guest rooms. The pick of the litter is the Pembroke Room, upstairs over the carriage house. It has a four-poster bed with mosquito netting, along with its own whirlpool tub in an outdoor screened hut. The brick courtyard garden between the two houses (there's a heated pool and Jacuzzi out there) is a popular spot for weddings and receptions. The rates include "wine time, with snacks and homemade cookies galore," says owner Kathy. There's a full-size heated pool and on-site massage therapist and spa.

105 5th Ave. NE (at 1st St. NE), St. Petersburg, FL 33701. ✆ **800/274-7520** or 727/821-9391. Fax 727/821-6909. www.mansionbandb.com. 12 units. $129–$250 double. Rates include full breakfast. AE, DC, DISC, MC, V. **Amenities:** Heated outdoor pool; Jacuzzi; bicycle rentals. *In room:* A/C, TV, Wi-Fi, hair dryer.

A Nearby Spa

Safety Harbor Resort and Spa ★★ (Value) Hernando de Soto thought he found Ponce de León's fabled Fountain of Youth when, in 1539, he happened upon five mineral springs in what is now Safety Harbor on the western shore of Old Tampa Bay (see the "Tampa & St. Petersburg" map on p. 384). You may not recover your youth at this venerable, 50,000-square-foot spa, the recipient of a multimillion-dollar renovation, but you will be rejuvenated. The healing mineral springs are the site of acclaimed water-fitness programs. There's also a tennis academy. The complex of beige-stucco buildings with Spanish-tile roofs offers upgraded rooms with new furniture and understated, yet crisp, soothing shades of tropical earth tones. It sits on 22 waterfront acres in the sleepy town of Safety Harbor, north of St. Petersburg, with a number of shops and restaurants just steps away.

105 N. Bayshore Dr., Safety Harbor, FL 34695. ✆ **888/237-8772** or 727/726 1161. Fax 727/724-7749. www.safetyharborresort.com. 175 units. Winter $169–$359 double; off-season $149–$259 double; year-round from $345 suite. Packages available. AE, DC, DISC, MC, V. Valet parking $12; self-parking free. **Amenities:** 2 restaurants; lobby cocktail lounge; 3 indoor/outdoor pools; 9 tennis courts; 50,000-sq.-ft. spa; fitness center (with classes); free bicycles; room service; laundry service; coin-op washers/dryers. *In room:* A/C, TV, dataport, high-speed Internet access, coffeemaker, hair dryer, iron/ironing board.

WHERE TO DINE

Don't overlook the food court at the **Pier,** where the inexpensive chow is accompanied by a very rich, but quite free, view of the bay. Among the Pier's restaurants is a branch of Tampa's famous **Columbia** (✆ **727/822-8000;** p. 402).

Expensive

Chateau France ★★ CLASSICAL FRENCH Chef Antoine Louro provides St. Petersburg's most romantic setting in this cozy, charming Victorian house built in 1910. He specializes in French classics such as homemade pâté, Dover sole meunière, filet mignon *au poivre,* coq au vin, and rich seafood bouillabaisse. The wine list is excellent, as are the bananas flambé and crêpes suzette.

136 4th Ave. N. (btw. Bayshore Dr. and 1st St. N.). ✆ **727/894-7163.** www.chateaufrancecuisine.com. Reservations recommended. Main courses $24–$39. AE, DC, DISC, MC, V. Daily 5–11pm.

Moderate

Bonefish Grill ★ SEAFOOD Although this noisy seafood spot has become part of the Outback Steakhouse family, it hardly resembles a chain, with its fresh-fish dishes served in massive portions, not to mention a very happening martini bar. Swordfish with spinach and feta cheese is a favorite, but feel free to mix and match from five choices of fish and three sauces. The rock shrimp appetizer is delicious—South Beach's swank sushi spot to the stars, Nobu, has the same dish for about five times the price. Because of this, expect long lines.

5901 4th St. N. ✆ **727/521-3434.** Main courses $13–$20. AE, MC, V. Mon–Thurs 4–10:30pm; Fri–Sat 4–11:30pm; Sun 4–10pm.

Ceviche Tapas Bar & Restaurant ★★ TAPAS A bustling spot in downtown St. Pete, Ceviche is a hot spot thanks to pitchers of the area's best sangria and a selection of 45 tapas for all taste buds, reflecting traditional dishes from the small tapas bars in old Spain. All contain the purest sherry, almonds, tomatoes, garlic, olive oil, olives, Spanish ham, cheeses, great mussels, sea bass, pork, and quail. There's also live flamenco and late-night dining, making it a haven for area hipsters. A Tampa outpost is at 2109 Bayshore Blvd. (✆ **813/250-0134**).

95 Central Ave. ✆ **727/209-2302.** www.cevichetapas.com. Reservations recommended. Tapas $7–$15. AE, DC, DISC, MC, V. Tues–Sat 5pm–2am (tapas served until 12:30am); Sun 5–10pm.

Inexpensive

Bella Brava Café ★ ITALIAN This cafe, popular with the business set by day and trendy barflies on weekend nights, features an excellent assortment of Tuscan fare, from gourmet cheeses to pizzas with crackerlike crusts. Chef Mario Luigi Maggi was born in Florence and trained in the kitchens of Milan, so he knows what he's doing. This isn't your neighborhood pizza joint. Presentations are gorgeous and worthy of a food magazine photo spread. But don't stare too long. Dig into specialties such as fresh basil roasted salmon with ratatouille and roasted garlic potato. Delicious!

515 Central Ave. ✆ **727/895-5515.** www.bellabrava.net. Reservations strongly recommended Fri–Sat. Main courses $11–$30; pizza $11–$13. AE, DC, DISC, MC, V. Mon–Fri 11am–11pm; Sat 5–11pm; Sun 5–10pm.

Fourth Street Shrimp Store ★★ Value SEAFOOD If you're anywhere in the area, at least drive by to see the colorful, cartoonlike mural on the outside of this eclectic and casual establishment just north of downtown. On first impression, it looks like graffiti, but it's actually a gigantic drawing of people eating. Inside it gets even better, with paraphernalia and murals on two walls that make the main dining room seem like a warehouse with windows that look onto an early-19th-century seaport (one painted sailor permanently peers in to see what you're eating). You'll pass a seafood market counter when you enter, from which comes the fresh namesake shrimp, the star here. You can also pick from grouper, clam strips, catfish, or oysters fried, broiled, or steamed, all served in heaping portions. This is the best and certainly the most interesting bargain in town. There's limited outdoor seating.

1006 4th St. N. (at 10th Ave. N.). ✆ **727/822-0325.** Main courses $5–$15; sandwiches $4–$10. MC, V. Daily 11am–9pm.

The Moon Under Water ★ ASIAN/BRITISH/MIDDLE EASTERN/AMERICAN Tables on the veranda or sidewalk in front of this waterfront pub are a great place to take a break during your downtown stroll. The British Raj rules supreme inside the dark-paneled dining room with its slowly twirling ceiling fans and colonial artifacts, including obligatory pith helmets. Your taste buds are in for a treat here. The bill of fare covers a number of former British outposts, including America (burgers and Philly cheesesteaks), but the emphasis is on mild, medium, or blazing-hot Indian curries—with a recommended Irish, British, or Australian beer to slake the resulting thirst. For lighter fare, consider Middle Eastern tabbouleh. There's live music on weekends.

332 Beach Dr. NE (btw. 3rd and 4th aves.). ✆ **727/896-6160.** Main courses $8–$20; sandwiches and salads $6–$10. AE, DC, DISC, MC, V. Sun–Thurs 11:30am–11pm; Fri–Sat 11:30am–midnight. Closed New Year's Day, Thanksgiving, and Christmas.

Skyway Jack's ★ BREAKFAST This is the restaurant that Cracker Barrel aspires to be, a down-home country kitchen with kitsch *and* outstanding breakfast fare. Start the day off with eggs Florentine, stuffed French toast, even sweetbreads and eggs, or go old school with eggs, grits, hash browns, and biscuits 'n' gravy. For early risers or late-night partyers, Skyway Jack's greases its griddle starting at 5am.

2795 34th St. S. ✆ **727/867-1907.** Main courses $3–$7. No credit cards (but there's an ATM on the premises). Daily 5am–3pm.

ST. PETERSBURG AFTER DARK

Good sources of nightlife information are the Thursday "Weekend" section of the *St. Petersburg Times* (www.sptimes.com), the "BayLife" and "Friday Extra" sections of the *Tampa Tribune* (www.tampatrib.com), and *Creative Loafing Tampa* (www.tampa.creative loafing.com), a tabloid available at visitor centers and in many hotel and restaurant lobbies.

The heart of downtown's nighttime scene is **BayWalk** (✆ **727/895-9277;** www.yourbaywalk.com), the shopping-dining-entertainment complex bordered by 1st and 2nd streets and 2nd and 3rd avenues north. Its 20-screen cinema and several restaurants and bars will keep you busy.

THE BAR, CLUB & MUSIC SCENE Ever since St. Pete started upping its hipster quotient, cool bars began appearing as quickly as Britney Spears changes her wigs. Among them are **A Taste for Wine,** 241 Central Ave. (✆ **727/895-1623;** www.tastefor wine.net), an upscale spot with polished woods and a granite bar offering terrific by-the-glass vintages, appetizers, and a gorgeous outdoor balcony; the **Haymarket Pub,** 8308 4th St. N. (✆ **727/577-9621**), the gay-friendly "Cheers" of St. Pete, where audible conversation and reasonably priced drinks aren't implausible demands; **Janus Landing Courtyard,** 16 2nd St. (✆ **727/896-2276;** www.januslandingconcerts.com), a fantastic outdoor concert venue and bar where mostly alternative and rock bands perform; **Ringside Cafe,** 2742 4th St. N. (✆ **727/894-8465**), a laid-back jazz and blues bar; and **Martini Bar,** 131 2nd Ave. N. (✆ **727/895-8558**), where a crowd that looks as if it stepped off the set of *Grey's Anatomy* convenes for serious seeing and being seen.

A historic attraction, the Moorish-style **Coliseum Ballroom,** 535 4th Ave. N. (✆ **727/892-5202;** www.stpete.org/coliseum), has been hosting dancing, big bands, boxing, and other events since 1924 (it even made an appearance in the 1985 movie *Cocoon*). Come out and watch the town's many seniors jitterbug as if it were 1945 again! Call for schedule and prices.

THE PERFORMING ARTS The **Bayfront Center,** 400 1st St. S. (✆ **727/892-5767,** or 892-5700 for information), houses the 8,100-seat Bayfront Arena and the 2,000-seat

 Mahaffey Theater (www.mahaffeytheater.com). The schedule includes a variety of concerts, Broadway shows, big bands, ice shows, and circus performances. **Ticketmaster** (© **813/287-8844**) sells tickets to most events and shows.

Tropicana Field, 1 Stadium Dr. (© **727/825-3100**), has a capacity of 50,000, but it also hosts a variety of smaller events when the Devil Rays aren't playing baseball.

3 ST. PETE & CLEARWATER BEACHES ★★

St. Pete: 20 miles SW of Tampa; 289 miles NW of Miami; 84 miles SW of Orlando. Clearwater Beach: 90 miles W of Orlando; 20 miles W of Tampa; and 20 miles N of St. Petersburg.

If you're looking for sun and sand, you'll find plenty of both on the 28 miles of slim barrier islands that skirt the Gulf shore of the Pinellas Peninsula. With some one million visitors coming here every year, don't be surprised if you have lots of company. But you'll also discover quieter neighborhoods and some of the nation's finest beaches, among them ones protected from development by parks and nature preserves.

At the southern end of the strip, St. Pete Beach is the granddaddy of the area's resorts: Visitors started coming here a century ago, and they haven't quit. Today St. Pete Beach is heavily developed and often overcrowded during the winter season. If you like high-rises and mile-a-minute action (albeit before 9pm, when things start to slow down a bit), St. Pete Beach is for you. But even here, Pass-a-Grille, on the island's southern end, is a quiet residential enclave with eclectic shops and a fine, though crowded, public beach.

A more gentle lifestyle begins just to the north on the 3½-mile-long Treasure Island. From here, you cross famous John's Pass to Sand Key, a 12-mile-long island occupied primarily by residential Madeira Beach, Redington Shores, Indian Shores, Indian Rocks Beach, and Belleair Beach. Finally, the road crosses a soaring bridge to Clearwater Beach, whose silky sands attract active families and couples.

If you like your great outdoors unfettered by development, the jewels here are Fort Desoto Park, south of St. Pete Beach at the mouth of Tampa Bay, and Caladesi Island State Park, north of Clearwater Beach. They are consistently rated among America's top beaches. Sand Key Park, on the southern shores of Little Pass (which separates Clearwater Beach from Belleair Beach), is one of Florida's finest local beach parks.

ESSENTIALS

GETTING THERE See "Getting There" in section 1 (p. 383) for information on getting to the beaches.

VISITOR INFORMATION See "Visitor Information" in section 2 (p. 403) for the St. Petersburg/Clearwater Area Convention & Visitors Bureau and the St. Petersburg Area Chamber of Commerce. The visitors bureau's website, at www.floridasbeach.com, has information specific to the beaches.

Once you're here, you can get beach information at the **Gulf Beaches of Tampa Bay Chamber of Commerce,** 6990 Gulf Blvd. (at 70th Ave.), St. Pete Beach (© **800/944-1847** or 727/360-6957; fax 727/360-2233; www.tampabaybeaches.com). It's open Monday through Friday from 9am to 5pm.

For advance information on Clearwater Beach, contact the **Clearwater Regional Chamber of Commerce,** 1130 Cleveland St., Clearwater, FL 33755 (© **727/461-0011;** fax 727/449-2889; www.clearwaterflorida.org). You can also walk into the **Clearwater Visitor Information Center,** on Causeway Boulevard in the lobby of the Clearwater

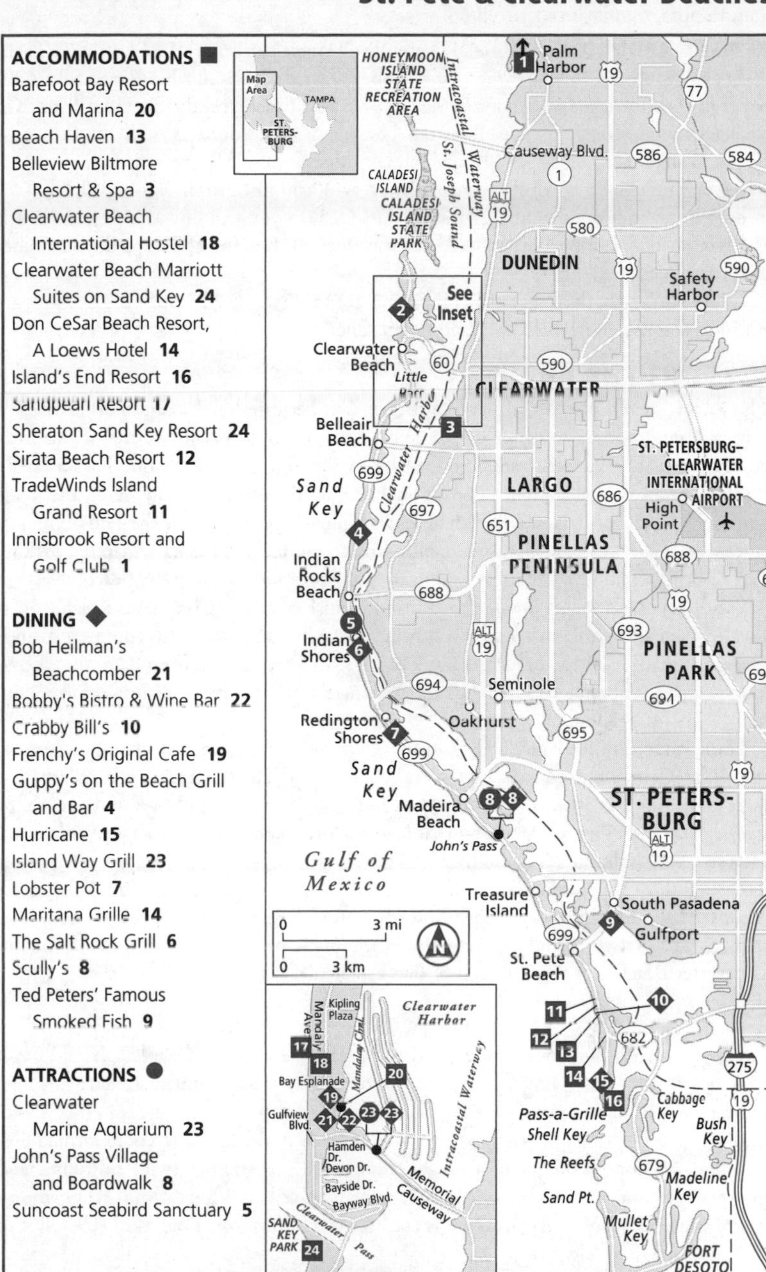
ACCOMMODATIONS
Barefoot Bay Resort and Marina 20
Beach Haven 13
Belleview Biltmore Resort & Spa 3
Clearwater Beach International Hostel 18
Clearwater Beach Marriott Suites on Sand Key 24
Don CeSar Beach Resort, A Loews Hotel 14
Island's End Resort 16
Sandpearl Resort 17
Sheraton Sand Key Resort 24
Sirata Beach Resort 12
TradeWinds Island Grand Resort 11
Innisbrook Resort and Golf Club 1
DINING
Bob Heilman's Beachcomber 21
Bobby's Bistro & Wine Bar 22
Crabby Bill's 10
Frenchy's Original Cafe 19
Guppy's on the Beach Grill and Bar 4
Hurricane 15
Island Way Grill 23
Lobster Pot 7
Maritana Grille 14
The Salt Rock Grill 6
Scully's 8
Ted Peters' Famous Smoked Fish 9
ATTRACTIONS
Clearwater Marine Aquarium 23
John's Pass Village and Boardwalk 8
Suncoast Seabird Sanctuary 5
Map Area
TAMPA
ST. PETERSBURG
HONEYMOON ISLAND STATE RECREATION AREA
Intracoastal Waterway
St. Joseph Sound
Palm Harbor
Causeway Blvd.
CALADESI ISLAND
CALADESI ISLAND STATE PARK
DUNEDIN
Safety Harbor
See Inset
Clearwater Beach
Little Harbor
CLEARWATER
Belleair Beach
Clearwater Harbor
Sand Key
LARGO
ST. PETERSBURG–CLEARWATER INTERNATIONAL AIRPORT
High Point
PINELLAS PENINSULA
Indian Rocks Beach
Indian Shores
PINELLAS PARK
Seminole
Oakhurst
Redington Shores
Madeira Beach
John's Pass
ST. PETERSBURG
Gulf of Mexico
Treasure Island
South Pasadena
Gulfport
St. Pete Beach
0 3 mi
0 3 km
N
Pass-a-Grille
Shell Key
The Reefs
Sand Pt.
Cabbage Key
Bush Key
Madeline Key
Mullet Key
FORT DESOTO PARK
Fort DeSoto
Kipling Plaza
Mandalay Ave.
Mandalay Chnl.
Clearwater Harbor
Bay Esplanade
Gulfview Blvd.
Hamden Dr.
Devon Dr.
Bayside Dr.
Bayway Blvd.
Memorial Causeway
Intracoastal Waterway
Clearwater Pass
SAND KEY PARK
Clearwater Beach

 Beach Marina Building (✆ **727/462-6531**). It's open Monday through Saturday from 9am to 5pm, Sunday from 1 to 5pm.

GETTING AROUND The **Pinellas Suncoast Transit Authority/PSTA** (✆ **727/530-9911;** www.psta.net) operates motorized trolley service along Gulf Boulevard (Fla. 699) between the Hurricane restaurant (p. 426) in St. Pete Beach and the Sheraton Sand Key Resort (the one-way trip takes about an hour), where it connects with the **Suncoast Beach Trolley** (✆ **727/445-1200**), which continues on Gulf Boulevard through Clearwater Beach. The PSTA trolley runs daily, every 20 minutes from 5am to 10pm, until midnight on Friday and Saturday. Rides cost $1.75, or you can buy a daily pass for $4. Call for schedules, or pick up printed copies at the Gulf Beaches of Tampa Bay Chamber of Commerce.

Along the beach, the major cab company is **BATS Taxi** (✆ **727/367-3702**). Fares are $2.50 at flag fall, plus $2.40 each additional mile.

HITTING THE BEACH

This entire stretch of coast is one long beach, but because hotels, condominiums, and private homes occupy much of it, you may want to sun and swim at one of the area's public parks. The very best are described below, but there's also the fine **Pass-a-Grille Public Beach,** on the southern end of St. Pete Beach, where you can watch the boats going in and out of Pass-a-Grille Channel and quench your thirst at the Hurricane restaurant (p. 426). This and all other Pinellas County public beaches have metered parking lots, so bring a supply of quarters. There are public restrooms along the beach.

Sand Key Park ★, on the northern tip of Sand Key facing Clearwater Beach, sports a wide beach and gentle surf, and is relatively off the beaten path in this commercial area. It's a great place to go for a morning walk or jog. The park is open from 8am to dark and has restrooms. Admission is free, but the parking lot has meters. For more information, call ✆ **727/464-3347.**

Clearwater Public Beach (also known as Pier 60) has beach volleyball, watersports rentals, lifeguards, restrooms, showers, and concessions. The swimming is excellent, and there's a fishing pier with a bait-and-tackle shop, plus a children's playground and a now legendary nightly sunset celebration that features local merchants, musicians, and artists. There's a 50¢ walk-on admission fee. Daily fishing fees are $6.30 for adults, $5.25 for seniors, and $5 for children 11 and under. There's metered parking in lots right across the street from the Clearwater Beach Marina, a prime base for boating, cruises, and other water activities (see "Outdoor Activities," below). A somewhat less crowded spot in Clearwater Beach is at the Gulf end of Bay Esplanade.

Caladesi Island State Park ★★★

Occupying a 3½-mile-long island north of Clearwater Beach, **Caladesi Island State Park** boasts one of Florida's top beaches—a lovely, relatively secluded stretch with fine, soft sand edged in sea grass and palmettos. Dolphins often cavort in the waters offshore. In the park itself is a nature trail, where you might see rattlesnakes, raccoons, armadillos, or rabbits. A concession stand, a ranger station, and bathhouses (with restrooms and showers) are available. Caladesi Island is accessible only by ferry from **Honeymoon Island State Recreation Area,** which is connected by Causeway Boulevard (Fla. 586) to Dunedin, north of Clearwater.

You'll first have to pay the admission to Honeymoon Island: $5 per vehicle with two to eight occupants, $3 per single-occupant vehicle, $1 for a pedestrian or bicyclist.

Beginning daily at 10am, the ferry (✆ **727/734-5263**) departs Honeymoon Island every hour. Round-trip rides cost $10 for adults, $6 for kids ages 4 to 12.

Neither Caladesi nor Honeymoon allows camping, but pets are permitted in the inland and on South Beach (bring a leash and use it at all times). The two parks are open daily from 8am to sunset and are administered by Gulf Islands Geopark, 1 Causeway Blvd., Dunedin, FL 34698 (✆ **727/469-5918;** www.floridastateparks.org/caladesiisland and www.floridastateparks.org/honeymoonisland).

Fort DeSoto Park ★★

South of St. Pete Beach at the very mouth of Tampa Bay, **Fort DeSoto Park** encompasses all of Mullet Key, set aside by Pinellas County as a 900-acre bird, animal, and plant sanctuary. Besides the stunning white-sugar sand, it is best known for a Spanish-American War–era fort, which has a museum that's open daily from 9am to 4pm. Other diversions include fishing from piers, large playgrounds for kids, and 4 miles of trails winding through the park for in-line skaters, bicyclists, and joggers. Park rangers conduct nature and history tours, and you can rent canoes and kayaks to explore the winding mangrove channels along the island's bay side. The park has changing rooms and restrooms as well.

Sitting by itself on a heavily forested island, the park's **campground** ★★ is one of Florida's most picturesque (many sites are beside the bay). It's such great camping that the 233 tent and RV sites usually are sold out, especially on weekends, so it's best to reserve well in advance. But there are a few catches: You must appear in person no more than 30 days in advance at the campground office, at 631 Chestnut St. in Clearwater, or at 150 5th St. N. in downtown St. Petersburg. You must pay when you make your reservation, in cash or by traveler's check (no credit cards or personal checks). And you must reserve for at least 2 nights, but you can stay no more than 14 nights in any 30-day period. Sites cost $34 to $39. All sites have water and electricity hookups.

Entry to the park is free. It's open daily from 8am to dusk, although campers and persons fishing from the piers can stay later. To get here, take the Pinellas Byway (50¢ toll) east from St. Pete Beach and follow Florida 679 (35¢ toll) and the signs south to the park. For more information, contact the park at 3500 Pinellas Byway, Tierra Verde, FL 33715 (✆ **727/582-2267;** www.pinellascounty.org/park/05_Ft_DeSoto.htm).

OUTDOOR ACTIVITIES

BOATING, FISHING & OTHER WATERSPORTS You can indulge in parasailing, boating, deep-sea fishing, wave running, sightseeing, dolphin watching, water-skiing, and just about any other waterborne diversion your heart could desire in the St. Pete and Clearwater beaches area. All you have to do is head to one of two beach locations: **Hubbard's Marina,** at John's Pass Village and Boardwalk (✆ **800/755-0677** or 727/393-1947; www.hubbardsmarina.com), in Madeira Beach on the southern tip of Sand Key; or **Clearwater Beach Marina,** at Coronado Drive and Causeway Boulevard (✆ **800/772-4479** or 727/461-3133), which is at the beach end of the causeway leading to downtown Clearwater. Agents in booths there will give you the schedules and prices (expect to pay $35–$65 for a half-day of fishing on a large party boat, $65–$100 for a full day), answer any questions you have, and make reservations, if necessary.

SCUBA DIVING You can dive on reefs and wrecks with **Dive Clearwater** (✆ **800/875-3483** or 727/443-6731; www.divingclearwater.com), which also operates the live-aboard boat *Plunger V.* Call for schedules and prices.

Clearwater Marine Aquarium ★★ Kids This little jewel of an aquarium on Clearwater Harbor is very low-key and friendly; it's dedicated to the rescue and rehabilitation of marine mammals and sea turtles. Exhibits include otters, sea turtles, sharks, stingrays, mangroves, and sea grass. There's a slew of impressive education programs, too, from dolphin encounters to trainer-for-a-day programs.

249 Windward Passage, Clearwater Beach. ✆ **888/239-9414** or 727/441-1790. Admission $11 adults, $9 seniors, $7.50 children 3–11, free for children 2 and under. Mon–Thurs 9am–5pm; Fri–Sat 9am–8pm; Sun 10am–5pm. The aquarium is off the causeway btw. Clearwater and Clearwater Beach; follow the signs.

John's Pass Village and Boardwalk Casual and charming, albeit too touristy, this Old Florida, turn-of-the-20th-century fishing village on John's Pass consists of a string of simple wooden structures topped by tin roofs and connected by a 1,000-foot boardwalk. Most buildings have been converted into shops, art galleries, restaurants, and saloons. The focal points are the boardwalk and marina, where many watersports are available for visitors (see "Outdoor Activities," above). If you don't go out on the water, this is a great place to enjoy an alfresco lunch—**Scully's** (✆ **727/393-7749**) is the best restaurant here—and watch the boats go in and out of the pass.

12901 Gulf Blvd. (at John's Pass), Madeira Beach. ✆ **800/944-1847** or 727/394-0756. www.johnspass.com. Free admission. Shops and activities daily 9am–6pm or later.

Suncoast Seabird Sanctuary ★ At any one time, there are usually more than 500 sea and land birds living at this sanctuary, from cormorants, white herons, and birds of prey to the ubiquitous brown pelican. The nation's largest wild-bird hospital, dedicated to the rescue, medical care, recuperation, and release of sick and injured wild birds, is also here.

18328 Gulf Blvd., Indian Shores. ✆ **727/391-6211.** www.seabirdsanctuary.com. Free admission; donations welcome. Daily 9am–sunset. Free tours Wed and Sun 2pm.

SHOPPING

John's Pass Village and Boardwalk, on John's Pass in Madeira Beach (see "Attractions on Land," above), has an unremarkable collection of beach souvenir shops, but the atmosphere makes it worth a stroll. The pick of the lot is the **Bronze Lady** (✆ **727/398-5994;** www.bronzelady2000.com), featuring a collection of works by the late comedian/artist Red Skelton, best known for his numerous clown paintings. The shops are open daily from 9am to 6pm or later.

If you're in the market for one-of-a-kind jewelry, try **Evander Preston Contemporary Jewelry,** 106 8th Ave., Pass-a-Grille (✆ **800/586-EVAN** [3826] or 727/367-7894; www.evanderpreston.com), a gallery/workshop housed in a 75-year-old building in Pass-a-Grille's block-long 8th Avenue business district. It's open Monday through Saturday from 10am to 5:30pm. There's a branch at TradeWinds Island Grand Resort (see "Where to Stay," below), too.

Among the shops in St. Pete Beach's Corey Landings area, the town's original business strip along 75th Street, east of Gulf Boulevard, the **Shell Store** (✆ **727/360-0586;** www.theshellstore.com) specializes in corals and shells, with an on-premises minimuseum illustrating how they live and grow. There's a good selection of shell home decorations, hobbyist supplies, art, planters, and jewelry. The store is open Monday through Saturday from 10am to 6pm.

WHERE TO STAY

St. Pete Beach and Clearwater Beach have national chain hotels and motels of every name and description. You can also use the St. Petersburg/Clearwater Convention & Visitors Bureau's free **reservations service** (✆ **800/345-6710**) to book rooms at most of them. The **St. Petersburg Area Chamber of Commerce** (p. 406) lists a wide range of hotels, motels, condominiums, and other accommodations in its annual visitor guide, and also publishes a brochure listing members of its Superior Small Lodgings program.

As is the case throughout Florida, there are more short- and long-term rental condominiums than hotel rooms here. Many of them are in high-rise buildings right on the beach. Among local rental agents, **JC Resort Management,** 17200 Gulf Blvd., North Redington Beach, FL 33708 (✆ **800/535-7776** or 727/397-0441; fax 727/397-8894; www.jcresort.com), has many from which to choose.

St. Pete Beach

Very Expensive

Don CeSar Beach Resort, A Loews Hotel ★★★ Kids This Moorish-style "Pink Palace" on the National Register of Historic Places has a rich history and appeals to groups, families, and couples. Sitting majestically on 7½ acres of beachfront, this landmark sports a lobby of classic high windows and archways, crystal chandeliers, marble floors, and original artwork. Some of the 275 rooms under the minarets of the original building may seem small, but they do have high windows and offer views of the Gulf or Boca Ciega Bay. Some have balconies. If you want more space but less charm, go for one of the resort's 70 spacious luxury condominiums in the Don CeSar Beach House, a midrise building ¾ mile to the north (there's 24-hr. complimentary transportation btw. the two). An excellent kids' program features supervised activities, including etiquette classes that instruct kids *and* adults on which fork to use (comes in handy in the hotel's swanky, stuffy restaurant). A new spa debuted in 2007.

3400 Gulf Blvd. (at 34th Ave./Pinellas Byway), St. Pete Beach, FL 33706. ✆ **866/728-2206** or 727/360-1881. Fax 727/367-6952. www.doncesar.com. 277 units. Winter $279–$541 double, $393–$3,000 suite; off-season $189–$429 double, $299–$2,000 suite. $10 per person per day resort fee. Packages available. AE, DC, DISC, MC, V. Valet parking $20 overnight, $13–$18 day; self-parking free. Pet friendly. **Amenities:** 4 restaurants; 4 bars; 2 heated outdoor pools; exercise room; spa; Jacuzzi; watersports equipment/rentals; children's programs; game room; concierge; business center; shopping arcade; salon; 24-hr. room service; massage; babysitting; laundry service; coin-op washers/dryers. *In room:* A/C, TV, Wi-Fi, dataport, minibar, coffeemaker, hair dryer, iron.

Expensive

Sirata Beach Resort ★ A ton of money was spent a few years ago to completely renovate this older property and bring it up to second-tier status, on par with its former sister hotel, the TradeWinds Island Grand Resort, but well below that of Don CeSar Beach Resort & Spa. A yellow-and-green Old Florida–style facade now disguises the eight-story main building, which houses (all nonsmoking) hotel rooms and one-bedroom suites upstairs (upper-level units have nice views), and a convention center. Some guest rooms in this two-story building face the courtyard, but the choice quarters are the Gulf-side rooms, the only units with patios or balconies opening directly onto the beach. The most spacious units are efficiencies and one-bedroom suites in two-story buildings; they all have kitchenettes, but they look out primarily on parking lots. Sirata was recently awarded a Green Lodging certification, too.

5300 Gulf Blvd. (at 53rd Ave.), St. Pete Beach, FL 33706. ✆ **727/363-5100.** Fax 727/363-5195. www.sirata.com. 380 units, including 170 suites. Summer, fall, winter $134–$224 double, $164–$444 suite; spring

$199–$269 double, $229–$489 suite. Optional Resort fee of $15 per day per unit, covers most activities. AE, DC, DISC, MC, V. **Amenities:** 2 restaurants; 4 bars; 3 heated outdoor pools; exercise room; watersports equipment/rentals; game room; concierge; business center; room service; laundry service; coin-op washers/dryers. *In room:* A/C, TV, Wi-Fi, kitchen, fridge, coffeemaker, hair dryer, iron/ironing board, safe.

TradeWinds Island Grand Resort ★ Kids Don't be dismayed by the outward appearance of this six- and seven-story concrete-and-steel monstrosity, for underneath and beside it runs a maze of brick walkways, patios, and lily ponds connected by a quarter-mile of streams. Many of the guest units, which look out on the Gulf or the 18 acres of grounds, have up-to-date kitchens or kitchenettes, and most have private balconies. Choice units directly face the Gulf, but this hotel has a variety of accommodations, so consult the reservations clerk when booking. Although the resort draws large meetings and conventions, it's a big hit with families, too. It's not a fancy place, but when it comes to beach hotels, this one's location can't be beaten. One of the four heated pools is reserved for adults, and there's lots more to keep grown-ups busy. For a quieter experience, check out the resort's sister property, **TradeWinds Sandpiper,** 6000 Gulf Blvd. (✆ **800/360-4016**), where winter rates go from $269 to $323 double, $373 to $409 suite, and off-season $195 to $246 double and $296 to $308 suite.

5500 Gulf Blvd. (at 55th Ave.), St. Pete Beach, FL 33706. ✆ **800/360-4016** or 727/363-2212. Fax 727/363-2222. www.justletgo.com. 584 units. Winter $269–$409 double, $366–$528 suite; off-season $195–$329 double, $287–$421 suite. Resort amenities fee of $25 per day per unit covers most activities. Packages available summer and fall. AE, DC, DISC, MC, V. Valet parking $8; self-parking free. **Amenities:** 7 restaurants; 3 lounges; 4 heated outdoor pools; minigolf; 2 tennis courts; fitness center; spa services; Jacuzzi; sauna; watersports equipment/rentals; children's programs; concierge; activities desk; car-rental agency; resort transportation on-site; business center; Wi-Fi; shopping arcade; salon; room service; laundry service; coin-op washers/dryers. *In room:* A/C, TV, Wi-Fi, fridge, coffeemaker, hair dryer, iron, safe, microwave, toaster, dishware.

Moderate

Island's End Resort ★★★ Value A wonderful respite from the crowds, and a great bargain to boot, this little all-cottage hideaway sits right on the southern tip of St. Pete Beach, smack-dab on Pass-a-Grille, where the Gulf of Mexico meets Tampa Bay. Because the island curves sharply here, nothing will block your view of the emerald bay. Strong currents run through the pass, but you can safely swim in the Gulf or grab a brilliant sunset at the Pass-a-Grille's public beach, just one door removed. Linked to one another by boardwalks, the comfortable one- and three-bedroom cottages have dining areas, living rooms, VCRs and DVD players, and fully equipped kitchens. You will love the one monstrous unit with two living rooms (one can be converted to sleeping quarters), two bathrooms (one with a whirlpool tub and separate shower), and private bayside swimming pool. Maid service is available on request.

1 Pass-a-Grille Way (at 1st Ave.), St. Pete Beach, FL 33706. ✆ **727/360-5023.** Fax 727/367-7890. www.islandsend.com. 6 units. Winter $175–$325 cottage; off-season $145–$325 cottage. Weekly rates available. Complimentary breakfast served Tues, Thurs, and Sat. MC, V. **Amenities:** Free Wi-Fi; coin-op washers/dryers. *In room:* A/C, TV/DVD/VCR, Wi-Fi, kitchen, coffeemaker, hair dryer, iron.

Inexpensive

Beach Haven ★ Value Nestled on the beach between two high-rise condominiums, these low-slung, pink-with-white-trim structures look from the outside like the early 1950s motel they once were. The former owners (who still own Island's End) replaced the innards and installed bright tile floors, vertical blinds, pastel tropical furniture, and many modern amenities, including DVDs and refrigerators. Five of the original quarters remain motel rooms (with shower-only bathrooms), but the others are linked to make 12 one-bedroom units and one two-bedroom unit, all with kitchens. The top choice is the one-bedroom suite with sliding-glass doors opening onto a tiled patio beside an outdoor heated pool. There's also a sunning deck with lounge furniture by the beach. The 1950s rooms are smallish, but every unit is bright, airy, and comfortable. Beach Haven's sister motel, the **Miramar Resort,** 4200 Gulf Blvd. (✆ **727/367-2311;** www.miramarbeachresort.com), is nearby, also on the Gulf, with rates from $85 to $250.

4980 Gulf Blvd. (at 50th Ave.), St. Pete Beach, FL 33706. ✆ **727/367-8642.** Fax 727/360-8202. www.beachhavenvillas.com. 18 units. Winter $85–$180 double; off-season $75–$125 double. AE, DISC, MC, V. **Amenities:** Heated outdoor pool; coin-op washers/dryers; concierge-level rooms. *In room:* A/C, TV, dataport, free Wi-Fi, kitchen, coffeemaker, hair dryer, iron.

Clearwater Beach

Very Expensive

Sandpearl Resort ★★★ When the Clearwater Beach Hotel was razed to make way for this multimillion-dollar luxury resort, many people balked. But when it comes to high-end resorts, there's nothing to complain about. Opened in 2007, the resort sits on 700 feet of beachfront. Rooms are open and airy with balconies and high ceilings. The Sandpearl Spa is swank, with treatments focusing on ocean therapy. A lagoon-style beachfront pool is the way to go for the day, unless, of course you want to dip into Sandpearl's life-enriching programs that take you on guided kayaking tours, naturalist tours of Caladesi Island, behind-the-scenes tours of Clearwater Marine Aquarium, and more. A unique Sunset Celebration invites a chosen guest to ring the dinner bell salvaged from the old Clearwater Beach Resort. Tradition is still here, albeit with a more 21st-century twist. Fine dining options are aplenty. Camp Ridley is for children, and it offers campfire storytelling, sing-alongs, and more. Wait, where do we sign up?

500 Mandalay Ave., Clearwater Beach, FL 33767. ✆ **877/726-3111** or 727/441-2425. Fax 727/449-9024. www.sandpearl.com. 253 units, including 52 suites. Guest rooms, including Gulf Front Junior Suites, off-season $169–$299 double, peak season $289–$509 double; 1- and 2-bedroom suites off-season $289–$659, peak season $479–$1,189. Resort fee $15 per day per unit covers numerous amenities. AE, DC, DISC, MC, V. **Amenities:** 2 restaurants; 2 bars; coffee bar; 1 Gulf-front lagoon-style pool w/private poolside cabanas; fitness center; full-service spa; 2 hot tubs; watersports equipment/rentals; children's programs; concierge; business center; 24-hr. room service. *In room:* A/C, flatscreen TV, free Internet access, fridge, coffeemaker, hair dryer, iron, safe, minibar.

Moderate

Clearwater Beach Marriott Suites on Sand Key ★ Kids You'll see the beauty of Sand Key Island from the suites in this boomerang-shaped, 10-story, all-suite hotel across the boulevard from the Sheraton Sand Key Resort (see below). Although the resort sits on the bay and not the Gulf, it has a large swimming-pool complex next to the water, and the beach and beautiful Sand Key Park are just a short walk or trolley ride away. The resort has a good children's program, and the whole family will enjoy exploring the adjacent boardwalk's 25 shops and restaurants, including a branch of Ybor City's excellent Columbia (p. 402). Each suite has a bedroom with a balcony offering water views, as well as a living room with sofa bed, wet bar, and entertainment unit. The gorgeous heated pool with cascading waterfalls is reminiscent of an exotic resort in Mexico, Hawaii, or even Las Vegas.

1201 Gulf Blvd., Clearwater Beach, FL 33767. ✆ **800/228-9290** or 727/596-1100. Fax 727/595-4292. www.clearwaterbeachmarriottsuites.com. 220 units. Winter $199–$289 suite; off-season $199–$259 suite. Packages available. AE, DC, DISC, MC, V. **Amenities:** 2 restaurants; 2 bars; heated outdoor pool; golf course; exercise room; Jacuzzi; sauna; children's programs; game room; car-rental desk; business center; shopping arcade; limited room service; massage; babysitting; laundry service; coin-op washers/dryers. *In room:* A/C, TV, dataport, minibar, coffeemaker, hair dryer, iron.

Sheraton Sand Key Resort ★ Set on 10 acres next to Sand Key Park, away from the honky-tonk of Clearwater, this nine-story Spanish-style hotel is a big favorite with groups and watersports enthusiasts. It's only a 450-foot walk across the broad beach in front of the hotel to the water's edge. The moderately spacious guest rooms here all have traditional dark-wood furniture and balconies or patios with views of the Gulf or the bay. The exercise room is on the top floor, affording great workout views. For those who love a little scandal, room no. 538 was the one where infamous former Praise The Lord Ministry leader Jim Bakker was busted with his then-assistant Jessica Hahn.

1160 Gulf Blvd., Clearwater Beach, FL 33767. ✆ **800/325-3535** or 727/595-1611. Fax 727/596-1117. www.sheratonsandkey.com. 390 units. Winter $175–$356 double; off-season $155–$269 double. AE, DC, DISC, MC, V. **Amenities:** 2 restaurants; 2 bars; heated outdoor pool; 3 tennis courts; exercise room; Jacuzzi; sauna; watersports equipment/rentals; children's programs (summer only); concierge; business center; 24-hr. convenience store; limited room service; babysitting; laundry service; concierge-level rooms. *In room:* A/C, TV, dataport, coffeemaker, hair dryer, iron, safe.

Inexpensive

Barefoot Bay Resort and Marina ★ A small family-owned-and-operated motel on the bay, Barefoot Bay offers clean, comfortable apartmentlike accommodations at great prices. There are four types of rooms to choose from, including a two-bedroom apartment with full kitchen. But the best part about the place, besides its location, is its backyard pool deck, complete with tropical landscaping and heated pool. It's actually more like hanging out at a friend's house than a motel. Even better, the beach is directly across the street.

401 E. Shore Dr., Clearwater Beach, FL 33767. ✆ **866/447-3316** or 727/447-3316. Fax 727/447-1016. www.barefootbayresort.com. 10 units. Winter $75–$200 double; off-season $65–$170 double. AE, DC, MC, V. **Amenities:** Heated pool; laundry service. *In room:* A/C, TV, fridge, coffeemaker, microwave.

Two Nearby Golf Resorts

Belleview Biltmore Resort & Spa ★ The Gulf Coast's oldest operating tourist hotel, this gabled clapboard structure was built in 1896 by Henry B. Plant as the Hotel Belleview to attract customers to his Orange Belt Railroad. Sited on a bluff overlooking the bay, it's the largest occupied wooden structure in the world. Today it attracts mostly groups and serious golfers (guests play at the adjoining Belleview Country Club), but there's no denying its Victorian charm and old-fashioned ambience—once you get past the out-of-place glass-and-steel foyer added by more recent owners. Historic tours are given daily ($5 adults, $3 kids 12–17). There's also a ghost tour given every Saturday night at 8pm and 10:15pm ($25 adults, $15 kids 7–12). The creaky hallways lead to several shops and a museum explaining the establishment's history. The hotel provides complimentary shuttle service to the country club and to Clearwater Beach, and features a new beach club on nearby Sand Key.

25 Belleview Blvd., Clearwater, FL 33756. ✆ **800/237-8947** or 727/373-3000. Fax 727/441-4173 or 443-6361. www.belleviewbiltmore.com. 226 units. Winter $109–$325 double and suite; off-season $79–$225 double and suite. AE, DC, DISC, MC, V. Valet parking $5; self-parking free. Resort is 1 mile south of downtown on Belleview Blvd., off Alt. U.S. 19. **Amenities:** 3 restaurants; ice cream/coffee parlor; 4 bars; 3 pools; golf course; 4 clay tennis courts; fitness center; spa; business center; resort shop; salon; room service; laundry service. *In room:* A/C, TV, hair dryer, iron.

Innisbrook Resort and Golf Club ★★ *Golf Digest, Golf,* and others pick this as one of the country's best places to play golf. Situated between Palm Harbor and Tarpon Springs, this 1,000-acre, all-condominium resort has 90 holes on championship courses

B&B on the Rocks

The **Laughing Lizard B&B,** located on Indian Rocks Beach, was built in 2005 and is billed as a contemporary throwback to island-style architecture. Inside the three-story Key West–style home, you'll find the antithesis of quaint B&Bs with an elevator, 42 windows all with a view of the Gulf and of Gulf Boulevard, and guest rooms with private bathrooms and kitschy names such as Nautical Newt, Crimson Chameleon, and Gallivanting Gecko. Owner Jan Ockunzzi is artist in residence, with a studio on the first floor, and her husband Bill is the mayor of Indian Rocks Beach. A nightly happy hour features homemade sangria, crackers, and dip; and for those looking for lizards, the only ones you'll find are in Jan's collection consisting of clay, cloth, glass, wood, and plastic versions. Rates are $130 to $170. Head to 2211 Gulf Blvd., Indian Rocks Beach (✆ **727/595-7006;** www.laughinglizardbandb.com).

that are more like the rolling links of the Carolinas than the usually flat courses found in Florida. Some pros think the **Copperhead Course ★★** is number one in Florida. If you want to learn, Innisbrook has the largest resort-owned-and-operated golf school in North America. In addition, it boasts a tennis center with instruction. It's similar to the sports-oriented Saddlebrook Resort near Tampa (p. 399), except that the courses are more challenging here and you're much closer to the beach. A free shuttle runs around the property, and another goes to the beach three times a day. Ranging in size from suites to two-bedroom models, the quarters are privately owned condos spread all over the premises.

36750 U.S. 19 N., Palm Harbor, FL 34684. ✆ **877/752-1480** or 727/942-2000. Fax 727/942-5576. www.innisbrookgolfresort.com. 700 units. Winter $229–$485 suite; off-season $155–$289 suite. Golf packages available. AE, DC, DISC, MC, V. **Amenities:** 7 restaurants; 7 bars; heated outdoor pools; 4 golf courses; 15 tennis courts; health club; Jacuzzis; sauna; children's programs; concierge; activities desk; car-rental desk; limited room service; massage; babysitting; laundry service; coin-op washers/dryers. *In room:* A/C, TV, dataport, kitchen, minibar, coffeemaker, hair dryer, iron.

WHERE TO DINE

The restaurants here are grouped by geographic location: St. Pete Beach, including Pass-a-Grille; Indian Rocks Beach, including Madeira Beach, Redington Beach, North Redington Beach, Redington Shores, and Indian Shores; and Clearwater Beach.

St. Pete Beach

Crabby Bill's Kids SEAFOOD This member of a small local chain sits right on the beach in the heart of the hotel district. It has an open-air rooftop bar, as well as a large dining room enclosed by big glass windows. There are fine water views from picnic tables equipped with rolls of paper towels and buckets of saltine crackers, the better with which to eat the blue, Alaskan, snow, and stone crabs that are the big draws here. The crustaceans fall into the moderate price category or higher, but most other main courses, such as fried fish or shrimp, are inexpensive—and they aren't overcooked or overbreaded. This is a very good place to feed the family.

5300 Gulf Blvd. (at 53rd Ave.), St. Pete Beach. ✆ **727/360-8858.** www.crabbybills.com. Main courses $10–$28; market price for lobster and stone-crab claws; sandwiches $6–$10. AE, MC, V. Mon–Thurs 11:30am–10pm; Fri–Sat 11:30am–11pm; Sun noon–10pm.

Hurricane SEAFOOD A longtime institution, across the street from Pass-a-Grille Public Beach, this three-level gray Victorian building with white gingerbread trim is a great place to toast the sunset, especially from the rooftop bar. It's more beach pub than restaurant, but the grouper sandwiches are excellent, and there's always fresh fish. A blackened, broiled, or deep-fried catfish dinner, served with french fries and coleslaw, goes for a bargain $8. Downstairs, you can dine inside the knotty-pine-paneled dining room or on the sidewalk terrace, where bathers from across Gulf Way are welcome (there's a walk-up bar for beach libation). You must be at least 21 to go up to the Hurricane Watch rooftop bar or to join the revelry when the second level turns into Stormy's Nightclub, at 10pm Wednesday through Saturday.

807 Gulf Way (at 9th Ave.), Pass-a-Grille. ✆ **727/360-9558.** www.thehurricane.com. Main courses $8–$30; sandwiches $4–$14. AE, MC, V. Daily 8am–1am.

Maritana Grille ★★ SEAFOOD/FLORIBBEAN If you're not staying at Don CeSar Resort, at least consider eating there, at this bastion of fabulous Floribbean cuisine. It's known for elegant dinners of steaks and seafood, but even more so for its spectacular Sunday brunch. The dining room is adorned with 1,500 gallons of saltwater aquariums and Florida fish. A specialty that's one of the most innovative dishes I've ever had is the orange habanero barbecued grouper with warm pineapple, vanilla-bean stew, glazed banana, and rum pepper sauce. The chef's table is a degustation that takes place in the kitchen, at a private table from which guests are able to interact directly with the chef and observe him in action.

At Don CeSar Resort, 3400 Gulf Blvd. (at 9th Ave.), St. Pete Beach. ✆ **727/360-1882.** Reservations recommended. Main courses $29–$35. AE, MC, V. Sun brunch 10:30am–2:30pm. Sun–Thurs 5:30–10pm; Fri–Sat 5:30–11pm.

Ted Peters' Famous Smoked Fish ★ (Value) SEAFOOD This open-air eatery is an institution in these parts: Ted's has been around since the '50s. Some folks bring their catches for the staff to smoke, while others figure fishing is a waste of time and come right to Ted's for mullet, mackerel, salmon, and other fish slowly cooked over red oak. Enjoy the aroma and sip a cold one while you wait for your order.

1530 Pasadena Ave. (just across St. Pete Beach Causeway), Pasadena. ✆ **727/381-7931.** Main courses $8–$20. No credit cards. Wed–Mon 11:30am–7:30pm.

Indian Rocks Beach Area

Guppy's on the Beach Grill & Bar ★★ SEAFOOD Locals love this small bar and grill across from Indian Rocks Public Beach because they know they'll always get terrific chow. You won't forget the salmon coated with potatoes and lightly fried, then baked with a creamy leek-and-garlic sauce; it's fattening, yes, but delicious. Another good choice is the lightly cooked tuna with a peppercorn sauce. The atmosphere is casual beach-friendly, with a fun bar in the middle of it all. Try the upside-down apple-walnut pie topped with ice cream. You can dine outside on a patio beside the main road.

1701 Gulf Blvd. (at 17th Ave.), Indian Rocks Beach. ✆ **727/593-2032.** www.3bestchefs.com/guppys. Main courses $12–$40; sandwiches $6–$10. AE, DC, DISC, MC, V. Sun–Thurs 11:30am–10:30pm; Fri–Sat 11:30am–11pm.

Lobster Pot ★★★ SEAFOOD/STEAK Step into this weathered-looking restaurant near the beach and experience some of the finest seafood in the area. The prices are high, but the variety of Maine lobster dishes is amazing. The pan-seared lobster with sweet corn sauté and gazpacho sauce is baked to succulent perfection. In addition to lobster, there's a wide selection of grouper, snapper, salmon, shrimp, scallops, crab, and steaks, most prepared with elaborate sauces. The children's menu here is definitely out of the ordinary: It features half a Maine lobster and a petite filet mignon.

17814 Gulf Blvd. (at 178th Ave.), Redington Shores. ✆ **727/391-8592.** www.lobsterpotrestaurant.com. Reservations recommended. Main courses $20–$45. AE, DC, MC, V. Daily 4:30–10pm.

The Salt Rock Grill ★★ SEAFOOD/STEAK Affluent professionals and the so-called beautiful people pack this waterfront restaurant, making it *the* place to see and be seen on the beaches. The big dining room is built on three levels, thus affording every table a view over the creeklike waterway out back. In fair weather, you can dine out by the dock or slake your thirst at the lively Tiki bar (bands play Sat–Sun during the summer). Thick, aged steaks are the house specialties. Pan-seared peppered tuna and salmon cooked on a cedar board lead the seafood. Avoid spending a fortune by showing up for the early-bird specials, or by ordering the meatloaf topped with mashed potatoes and onion straws ($9.90) or the half-pound sirloin steak ($13).

19325 Gulf Blvd. (north of 193rd Ave.), Indian Shores. ✆ **727/593-7625.** www.saltrockgrill.com. Reservations strongly advised. Main courses $8–$40; early-bird specials $8–$10. AE, DC, DISC, MC, V. Sun–Thurs 4–10pm; Fri–Sat 4–11pm; early-bird specials daily 4–5:30pm. Tiki bar Sat 2pm–midnight (or later); Sun 2–10pm.

Clearwater Beach

Bobby's Bistro & Wine Bar ★★ AMERICAN Son of Bob Heilman's Beachcomber (see below), this chic bistro draws a more urbane crowd than its parent. A wine-cellar theme is amply justified by the real thing: a walk-in closet with several thousand bottles kept at a constant 55°F (13°C). Walk through and pick your vintage, then listen to jazz while you dine inside at tall, bar-height tables or outside on a covered patio. The chef specializes in gourmet pizzas with homemade focaccia crusts, plus chargrilled lamb chops, filet mignon, fresh fish, and monstrous pork chops with caramelized Granny Smith apples and a Mount Vernon mustard sauce. Everything's served a la carte here, so watch your wallet. There's a less expensive sandwich menu featuring bronzed grouper and chicken with a spicy Jack cheese.

447 Mandalay Ave. (at Papaya St., behind Bob Heilman's Beachcomber). ✆ **727/446-9463.** www.bobbysbistro.com. Reservations recommended. Main courses $11–$29; sandwiches and pizzas $6–$13. AE, DC, DISC, MC, V. Sun–Thurs 5–11pm; Fri–Sat 5pm–midnight (bar open later).

Bob Heilman's Beachcomber ★ AMERICAN In a row of restaurants, bars, and T-shirt shops, this establishment has been popular with the locals since 1948. Each dining room here is unique: Large models of sailing crafts create a nautical theme in one, a pianist makes music in a second, works of art create a gallery in the third, and booths and a fireplace make for a cozy fourth. The menu presents a variety of well-prepared fresh seafood and beef, veal, and lamb selections. If you tire of fruits-of-the-sea, the "back to the farm" fried chicken—from an original 1910 Heilman family recipe—is incredible. The Beachcomber shares valet parking and an extensive wine collection with Bobby's Bistro & Wine Bar (see above).

447 Mandalay Ave. (at Papaya St.). ✆ **727/442-4144.** www.heilmansbeachcomber.com. Reservations recommended. Main courses $16–$40. AE, DC, DISC, MC, V. Mon–Sat 11:30am–11pm; Sun noon–10pm.

Frenchy's Original Cafe SEAFOOD Popular with locals and visitors in the know since 1981, this casual pub makes the best grouper sandwiches in the area and has all the awards to prove it. The sandwiches are fresh, thick, juicy, and delicious. The atmosphere is pure Florida casual. There can be a wait during winter and on weekends year-round.

The Sponge Capital of the World

One of Florida's most fascinating small towns and a fine day trip from Tampa, St. Petersburg, or the beaches (30 miles north of St. Petersburg, 23 miles west of Tampa, and 13 miles north of Clearwater), **Tarpon Springs** calls itself the "Sponge Capital of the World." Greek immigrants from the Dodecanese Islands settled here in the late 19th century to harvest sponges, which grew in abundance offshore. By the 1930s, Tarpon Springs was producing more sponges than any other place in the world. A blight ruined the business in the 1940s, but the descendants of those early immigrants stayed on. Today they compose about a third of the population, making Tarpon Springs a center of transplanted Greek culture.

Sponges still arrive at the historic **Sponge Docks,** on Dodecanese Boulevard. With a lively, carnival-like atmosphere, the docks are a great place to spend an afternoon or early evening, poking your head into shops selling sponges and other souvenirs while Greek music comes from the dozen or so family restaurants purveying authentic Aegean cuisine. You can also venture offshore from here: Booths on the docks hawk sightseeing and fishing cruises. Make your reservations as soon as you get here; then go sightseeing ashore or grab a meal at one of the multitudinous Greek restaurants and bakeries.

You also can visit **Spongeorama** (510 Dodecanese Blvd.; ✆ **727/943-2164;** www.spongeorama.com; daily 10am–5pm), a museum dedicated to sponges and sponge divers that sells a wide variety of sponges and shows a 30-minute video on sponge diving several times a day. Admission is free. A scuba diver feeds sharks in the **Konger Tarpon Springs Aquarium** (850 Dodecanese Blvd.; ✆ **727/938-5378;** www.tarponspringsaquarium.com; Mon–Sat 10am–5pm,

For a similarly relaxed setting, directly on the beach, **Frenchy's Rockaway Grill,** at 7 Rockaway St. (✆ **727/446-4844**), has a wonderful outdoor setting and keeps a charcoal grill going to cook fresh fish.

41 Baymont St. ✆ **727/446-3607.** www.frenchysonline.com. Sandwiches and burgers $6–$11. AE, MC, V. Mon–Thurs 11:30am–11pm; Fri–Sat 11:30am–midnight; Sun noon–11pm.

Island Way Grill ★★ SEAFOOD/SUSHI Not your ordinary waterfront seafood shanty, the glass-encased and wood-enhanced sleek Island Way Grill prepares the daily catch Pan-Asian style in its open kitchen. Everything here is delicious, from the resulting fish to the sushi. Even the meatloaf is gourmet, with wasabi mashed potatoes and tumbleweed onions—a bargain at $11. There's also a full sushi bar. The wine list is also superb. Sit out on the patio and then gravitate toward the outdoor bar, where the fabulous people—like members and owners of the Tampa Bay Buccaneers—hang out, talk shop, and scope the scene.

20 Island Way. ✆ **727/461-6617.** www.islandwaygrill.com. Main courses $11–$40. AE, MC, V. Sun–Thurs 4–10pm; Fri–Sat 4–11pm.

Sun noon–5pm), at the western end of the boulevard. Admission is $5.75 for adults, $5 for seniors, and $3.75 for children 3 to 11.

South of the docks, the **Downtown Historic District** sports turn-of-the-20th-century commercial buildings along Tarpon and Pinellas avenues (Alt. U.S. 19). On Tarpon Avenue, west of Pinellas Avenue, you'll come to the Victorian homes overlooking **Spring Bayou.** This creekside area makes for a delightfully picturesque stroll.

For those who enjoy a serious bike ride, one of the best is the Pinellas Bike Trail—a 34-mile ride from Tarpon Springs to southern St. Pete. Rent a bike from **Neptune Lounge & Cyclery** (✆ **727/943-5805;** www.theneptunelounge.com)—an oddly combined live music bar, lounge, and bike rental—for $15 per half-day, $25 per full day, and then hit the trail, which is right outside the front door. You'll pass by unbelievable scenery.

The **Tarpon Springs Chamber of Commerce,** 11 E. Orange St., Tarpon Springs, FL 34689 (✆ **727/937-6109;** fax 727/937-2879; www.tarponsprings.com), has an information office on Dodecanese Boulevard at the Sponge Docks; it's open Tuesday through Sunday from 10:30am to 4:30pm.

To get to Tarpon Springs from Tampa or St. Petersburg, take U.S. 19 N. and turn left on Tarpon Avenue (C.R. 582). From Clearwater Beach, take Alt. U.S. 19 N. through Dunedin. The center of the historic downtown district is at the intersection of Pinellas Avenue (Alt. U.S. 19) and Tarpon Avenue. To reach the Sponge Docks, go 10 blocks north on Pinellas Avenue and turn left at Pappas' Restaurant onto Dodecanese Boulevard.

THE BEACHES AFTER DARK

If you haven't already found it during your sightseeing and shopping excursions, the restored fishing community of **John's Pass Village and Boardwalk,** on Gulf Boulevard at John's Pass in Madeira Beach, has plenty of restaurants, bars, and shops to keep you occupied after the sun sets. Elsewhere, the nightlife scene at the beach revolves around rocking bars that pump out music until 2am. All of the places listed in this section are bars that feature live music.

Pass-a-Grille has the popular, always-lively lounge at **Hurricane,** on Gulf Way at Ninth Avenue, opposite the public beach (p. 426). Up on the northern tip of Treasure Island, **Gators on the Pass** (✆ **727/367-8951**) claims to have the world's longest waterfront bar, with a huge deck overlooking the waters of John's Pass. The complex also has a nonsmoking sports bar and a three-story tower with a top-level observation deck for panoramic views of the Gulf of Mexico. Live music, from acoustic to blues to rock, is featured most nights.

In Clearwater Beach, the **Palm Pavilion Grill & Bar,** on the beach at 18 Bay Esplanade (✆ **727/446-6777**), has live music Tuesday through Sunday nights in winter and on weekends in the off-season. Nearby, **Frenchy's Rockaway Grill,** at 7 Rockaway St. (✆ **727/446-4844;** www.frenchysonline.com/rock_index.html), is another popular hangout.

If you're into laughs, **Coconuts Comedy Club,** at the Tradewinds Sandpiper, 6000 Gulf Blvd., at 61st Avenue in St. Pete Beach (© **727/360-5653;** www.coconutscomedy clubs.com), has an ever-changing program of live stand-up, funny men and women. Call for the schedules and prices.

For a more highbrow evening, go to the Clearwater mainland and the 2,200-seat **Ruth Eckerd Hall,** 1111 McMullen-Booth Rd. (© **727/791-7400;** www.rutheckerdhall.com), which hosts a varied program of Broadway shows, ballet, drama, symphonic works, popular music, jazz, and country music.

4 SARASOTA ★★★

52 miles S of Tampa; 150 miles SW of Orlando; 225 miles NW of Miami

Far enough away from Tampa Bay to have an identity very much its own, Sarasota is, surprisingly, one of Florida's cultural centers. In fact, many retirees spend their winters here because there's so much to keep them entertained and stimulated, including the Van Wezel Performing Arts Hall and the FSU Center for the Performing Arts, home of the annual Asolo Theatre Festival. Sarasota also has an extensive array of first-class resorts, restaurants, and upscale boutiques.

Offshore, more than 40 miles of gloriously white beaches fringe a chain of long, narrow barrier islands stretching from Tampa Bay to Sarasota. To the south, **Siesta Key** is a residential enclave popular with artisans and writers, and is home to Siesta Village, this area's funky, laid-back, and often noisy beach hangout. Shielded from the Gulf by **Lido Key,** which has a string of affordable hotels attractive to family vacationers, **St. Armands Key** sports a quaint and lively shopping and dining district, while adjacent **Longboat Key** is one of the country's swankiest islands.

ESSENTIALS

GETTING THERE You'll probably find a less-expensive airfare by flying into **Tampa International Airport** (p. 383), an hour's drive north of Sarasota, and you can save even more because Tampa's rental-car agencies usually offer some of the best deals in Florida. If you don't rent a car, **Sarasota-Tampa Express** (© **800/326-2800** or 941/727-1344; www.stexps.com) provides bus connections for $40 for adults, $20 for children 4 to 12. Call in advance for a schedule and pickup locations.

If you fly directly here, **Sarasota-Bradenton International Airport** (© 941/359-2770; www.srq-airport.com), north of downtown, off University Parkway between U.S. 41 and U.S. 301, is served by **Continental, Delta, Northwest,** and **US Airways.**

Alamo, Avis, Budget, Dollar, Hertz, and **National** all have car-rental offices here. See "Appendix: Fast Facts, Toll-Free Numbers & Websites," p. 638, for airline and car services contact information.

Diplomat Taxi (© **941/355-5155;** www.srqtaxi.com) has a monopoly on service from the airport to hotels in Sarasota and Bradenton. Look for the cabs outside baggage claim. Fares are all metered at $2.25 at flag fall and $2.15 per additional mile.

Amtrak has bus connections to Sarasota from its Tampa station (© **800/872-7245;** www.amtrak.com).

VISITOR INFORMATION Contact the **Sarasota Convention and Visitors Bureau,** 655 N. Tamiami Trail (U.S. 41), Sarasota, FL 34236 (© **800/522-9799** or 941/957-1877; fax 941/951-2956; www.sarasotafl.org). The bureau and its helpful visitor center

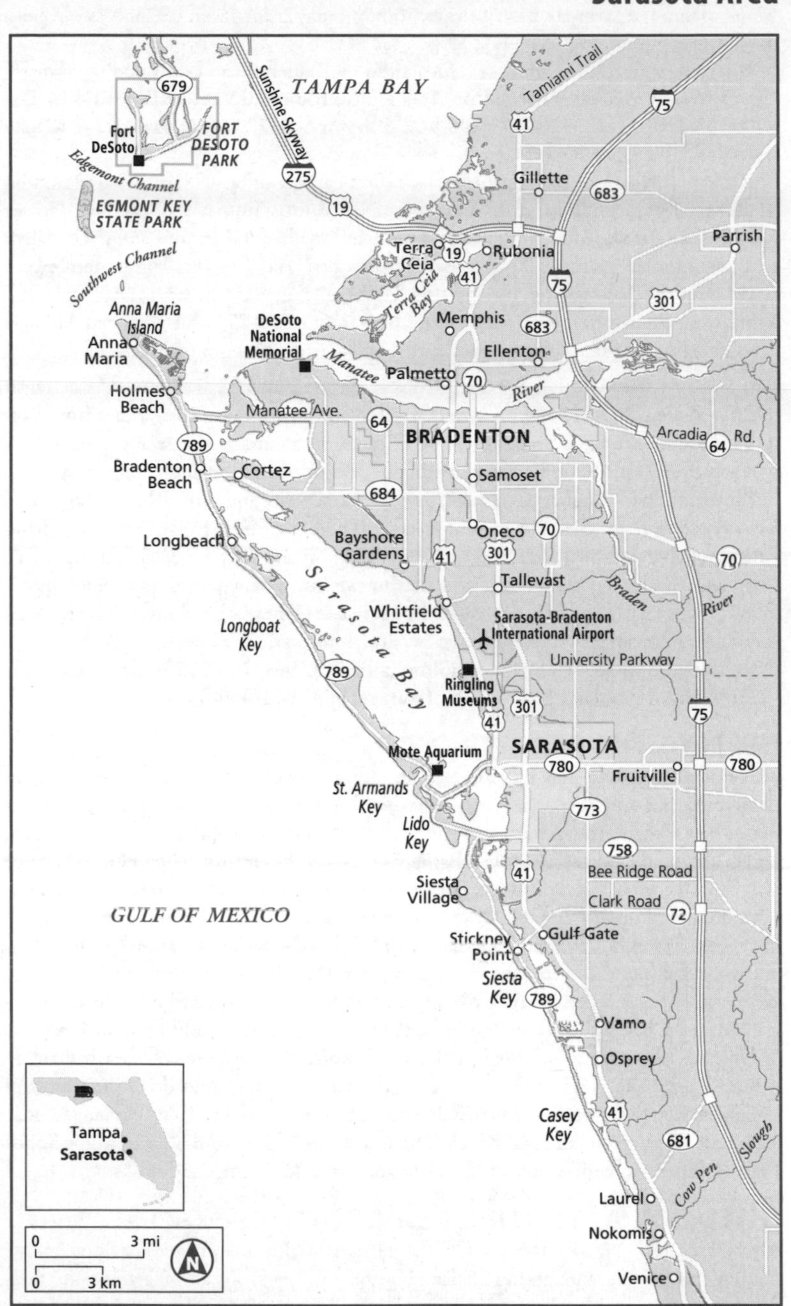
TAMPA BAY
Sunshine Skyway
Tamiami Trail
Fort DeSoto
FORT DESOTO PARK
Edgemont Channel
EGMONT KEY STATE PARK
Southwest Channel
Anna Maria Island
Anna Maria
Holmes Beach
Bradenton Beach
Cortez
Longbeach
DeSoto National Memorial
Manatee River
Manatee Ave.
Terra Ceia
Terra Ceia Bay
Rubonia
Gillette
Parrish
Memphis
Ellenton
Palmetto
BRADENTON
Arcadia Rd.
Samoset
Oneco
Bayshore Gardens
Tallevast
Braden River
Whitfield Estates
Sarasota-Bradenton International Airport
University Parkway
Longboat Key
Sarasota Bay
Ringling Museums
SARASOTA
Mote Aquarium
Fruitville
St. Armands Key
Lido Key
Bee Ridge Road
Clark Road
Siesta Village
GULF OF MEXICO
Gulf Gate
Stickney Point
Siesta Key
Vamo
Osprey
Casey Key
Cow Pen Slough
Laurel
Nokomis
Venice
Tampa
Sarasota
0 3 mi
0 3 km
N

are in a blue pagoda-shaped building on Tamiami Trail (U.S. 41) at 6th Street. Hours are Monday through Saturday from 9am to 5pm, Sunday from 11am to 3pm; closed holidays.

You can get a packet of advance information on Bradenton and surrounding Manatee County from the **Greater Bradenton Area Convention and Visitors Bureau,** P.O. Box 1000, Bradenton, FL 34206 (© **800/462-6283** or 941/729-9177; fax 941/729-1820; www.floridaislandbeaches.org).

If you're driving from the north via I-75, you can get off at U.S. 301 (exit 224) and head west if you want to go to the **Manatee County Tourist Information Center** (© **941/729-7040**), where volunteers are on hand to answer questions and sell excellent road maps for less than you'll pay elsewhere. It's open daily from 8:30am to 5pm except Easter Sunday, Thanksgiving, the day after Thanksgiving, and Christmas Day. The office also has an information kiosk at **Prime Outlets,** across I-75, which is open Monday through Saturday from 10am to 6pm, and Sunday from 11am to 6pm.

GETTING AROUND The **Sarasota Trolley,** operated by Sarasota County Area Transit (**SCAT;** © **941/861-1234;** www.sarasotatrolley.com), runs every 20 minutes from 9am to 5pm Monday through Friday, every 40 minutes on Saturday. The Scenic Loop Trolley operates from Island Park, Bayfront at Ringling Boulevard, through downtown Sarasota, north to the FSU Ringling Center for the Cultural Arts, and out to St. Armands and Lido keys (but not to Siesta or Longboat keys). The Main Street Trolley goes from Island Park through downtown and eastward along Main Street. Fares are $1.50 on the Scenic Loop and 75¢ on the Main Street line, or you can buy a daily pass to both lines for $3. SCAT also operates regularly scheduled bus service. The Sarasota Convention and Visitors Bureau distributes route maps (see "Visitor Information," above).

Sarasota taxi companies include **Diplomat Taxi** (© **941/355-5155**), **Green Cab Taxi** (© **941/922-6666**), and **Yellow Cab of Sarasota** (© **941/955-3341**).

HITTING THE BEACH

Many of the area's 40-plus miles of beaches are occupied by hotels and condominium complexes, but there are excellent public beaches as well. The area's most popular is **Siesta Key Public Beach,** with a picnic area, a 700-car parking lot, crowds of families, and quartz sand reminiscent of the blazingly white beaches in Northwest Florida. There's also beach access at **Siesta Village,** which has a plethora of casual restaurants and pubs with outdoor seating (see the "Where to Dine" section later). The more secluded and quiet **Turtle Beach** is at Siesta Key's south end. It has shelters, boat ramps, picnic tables, and volleyball nets. Both beaches have bathroom facilities. New to the area is **Passage Key,** a nude beach accessible only by boat and located on a protected bird sanctuary. It's located in the bay between the Rod 'n' Reel Pier on Anna Maria and Egmont Key.

Unless you're staying on Longboat Key, you won't be able to hit the beach there, as private houses and condos block access to the Gulf. However, do drive the length of Longboat Key and admire the luxury homes. Then take a right off St. Armands Circle onto Lido Key and **North Lido Beach.** The south end of the island is occupied by **South Lido Beach Park,** with plenty of shade—a good spot for picnics and walks.

OUTDOOR ACTIVITIES & SPECTATOR SPORTS

BIKING & IN-LINE SKATING The flat terrain in this area makes for good in-line skating and for fine, though not challenging, bike riding. You can bike and skate from downtown Sarasota to Lido and Longboat keys, because paved walkways/bike paths run alongside the John Ringling Causeway and then up Longboat Key. **Siesta Sports Rentals,**

6551 Midnight Pass Rd., in the Southbridge Mall, just south of Stickney Point Bridge on Siesta Key (✆ **941/346-1797;** www.siestasportsrentals.com), rents bikes of various sizes (including trail attachments for kids), plus motor scooters, kayaks, and beach chairs and umbrellas. They can even arrange kayak tours, if you wish. Bike rentals range from about $15 a day to $45 a week; scooters go for $45 for a half-day or $60 for a full day. They also rent three-wheeled scooter cars. The shop is open daily from 9am to 5pm.

BOAT RENTALS **All Watersports,** in the Boatyard Shopping Village, on the mainland end of Stickney Point Bridge (✆ **941/921-2754**), rents personal watercraft such as jet skis, speedboats, runabouts, and bow riders. At the island end of the bridge, **C. B.'s Saltwater Outfitters,** 1249 Stickney Point Rd. (✆ **941/349-4400**), and **Dockside Marine,** 1265 Old Stickney Point Rd. (✆ **941/349-8880**), both rent runabouts, pontoon boats, and other craft. Bait and tackle are available at the marinas.

CRUISES The area's best nature cruises depart from Mote Aquarium (see "Exploring the Area," below).

FISHING Charter fishing boats dock at most marinas here; check out **www.sarasota boating.com** for a list. In downtown Sarasota, the **Flying Fish Fleet,** at Marina Jack's Marina, U.S. 41 at Island Park Circle (✆ **941/366-3373;** www.flyingfishfleet.com), offers party-boat charter-fishing excursions, with bait and tackle furnished. Prices for half-day trips are $55 for adults, $50 for seniors, and $45 for kids 4 to 12. All-day voyages cost $86, $80, and $76, respectively. Call for the schedule. Other charter boats also line up along the dock here.

GOLF The **Bobby Jones Golf Complex** ★, 1000 Circus Blvd. (✆ **941/365-4653;** www.bobbyjonesgolfclub.com), is Sarasota's only municipal facility. It has two 18-hole championship layouts—the American (par 71) and British (par 72) courses—and the 9-hole Gillespie executive course (par 30). Tee times are assigned 3 days in advance. Greens fees range from $11 to $51 including cart rental.

The semiprivate **Rolling Green Golf Club,** 4501 Tuttle Ave. (✆ **941/355-6620;** www.rollinggreengc.com), is an 18-hole, par-72 course. Facilities include a driving range, rental clubs, and lessons. Tee times are assigned 2 days in advance. Prices, including cart, are about $15 to $55. Also semiprivate, the **Sarasota Golf Club,** 7820 N. Leewynn Dr. (✆ **941/371-2431;** www.sarasotagc.com), is an 18-hole, par-72 course. Facilities include a driving range, lessons, club rentals, a restaurant, a lounge, and a golf shop. Fees, including cart, are $15 to $28.

If you have reciprocal privileges, **University Park Country Club,** west of I-75 on University Parkway (✆ **941/359-9999;** www.universitypark-fl.com), is Sarasota's only nationally ranked course. Fees, including cart, are about $50 to $70.

Bradenton is home to the well-known **David Leadbetter Golf Academy,** 1414 69th Ave., at U.S. 41 (✆ **800/872-6425** or 941/755-1000; www.leadbetter.com), a part of the Nick Bollettieri Tennis Academy (see "Tennis," below). Presided over by one of golf's leading instructors, this facility offers practice tee instruction, video analysis, scoring strategy, and more.

For course information online, go to www.golf.com or www.floridagolfing.com; or call the **Florida Sports Foundation** (✆ **850/488-8347**) or **Florida Golfing** (✆ **866/833-2663**).

KAYAKING Based at Mote Aquarium (see the "Exploring the Area" section below), **Sarasota Bay Explorers** ★★ (✆ **941/388-4200;** www.sarasotabayexplorers.com) uses a 38-foot pontoon boat to ferry novice and experienced kayakers and their craft to a marine sanctuary, where everyone paddles through tunnels formed by mangroves. The paddling is easy and the waters are shallow. Experienced naturalists serve as guides. Wear a swimsuit and tennis shoes or rubber-soled booties, and bring a towel and lunch. The 3-hour trip is $55 for adults, $45 for children 5 to 17, and free for kids 4 and under (seats are provided for the youngsters). Reservations are required.

SAILING Take a leisurely cruise on the waters of Sarasota Bay and the Gulf of Mexico aboard the 41-foot, 12-passenger ***Enterprise,*** docked at Marina Jack's Marina, U.S. 41 at Island Park Circle (✆ **888/232-7768** or 941/951-1833; www.sarasotasailing.com). Cruises range from 2 hours for $40 per person to 4 hours for $70 a head, while 2-hour sunset excursions cost $45 per person. Departure times vary, and reservations are required. **Siesta Key Sailing,** 1219 Southport Dr. (✆ **941/346-7245;** www.siestakeysailing.com), charges about the same for cruises in a 42-foot Morgan Outlander sloop. Call for rates and reservations.

You can also get to historic Egmont Key, 3 miles off the northern end of Anna Maria Island at the mouth of Tampa Bay, on a 30-foot sloop-rigged sailboat with **Spice Sailing Charters** (✆ **941/778-3240;** http://charters2.tripod.com), based at the Galati Yacht Basin on Bay Boulevard on northern Anna Maria Island. Rates start at $25 per person for a 2½-hour sail to $40 per person for a 4-hour sail. The company has sunset cruises as well. Call for the schedule and reservations.

SPECTATOR SPORTS **Ed Smith Stadium,** 2700 12th St., at Tuttle Avenue, east of downtown Sarasota (✆ **941/954-4464**), is the winter home of the **Cincinnati Reds** (✆ **941/955-6501;** www.cincinnatireds.com), who hold spring training here in February and March. Game tickets are $7 to $15. From April to August, the stadium is home to the **Sarasota Reds** (✆ **941/365-4460;** www.sarasotareds.com), a Class A minor-league affiliate of the Cincinnati Reds. Tickets are $5 to $6.

The **Pittsburgh Pirates** (✆ **941/748-4610;** www.pirateball.com) do their February through March spring training at 6,562-seat McKechnie Field, 9th Street West and 17th Avenue West, south of downtown Bradenton. Tickets are $9 to $18.

The **Sarasota Polo Club,** 8201 Polo Club Lane (✆ **941/907-0000;** www.sarasotapolo.com), at Lakewood Ranch, a planned community midway between Sarasota and Bradenton, is the site of Sunday-afternoon polo matches from mid-December to early April. General admission is $10 for adults, free for children 12 and under. Call for the schedule.

TENNIS The **Nick Bollettieri Tennis Academy,** 5500 34th St. W., Bradenton (✆ **800/872-6425** or 941/755-1000; www.imgacademies.com), is one of the world's largest tennis training facilities, with more than 70 championship grass, clay, and hard courts, and a pro shop. It's open year-round; reservations are required for all activities.

WATERSPORTS You'll find watersports activities in front of the major hotels on the keys (see "Where to Stay," beginning on p. 438). **Siesta Sports Rentals,** 6551 Midnight Pass Rd., on Siesta Key (✆ **813/346-1797;** www.siestasportsrentals.com), rents kayaks and sailboats, plus beach chairs and umbrellas.

EXPLORING THE AREA

In Sarasota

Art Center Sarasota In addition to the marvelous John and Mable Ringling Museum of Art (see below), Sarasota is home to more than 40 galleries and exhibition spaces, all open to the public. A convenient starting point is this downtown community art center, next to the Sarasota Convention and Visitors Bureau. It contains three galleries and a small sculpture garden, presenting the area's largest display of works by national and local artists, ranging from paintings and pottery to sculpture, cartoons, jewelry, and enamelware. There are also art demonstrations and special events.

707 N. Tamiami Trail (at 6th St.). ✆ **941/365-2032.** www.artsarasota.org. Free admission ($2 suggested donation). Tues–Sat 10am–4pm; Sun noon–4pm.

Florida Ever-Glides, Inc. ★★ Ride the future (and get some history at the same time) when you take a tour with this great company, the first in the U.S. to offer historic and scenic guided tours using Segway Human Transporters—you know, those cool electric scooter-type things you've seen on TV (and saw George W. Bush fall from). The friendly staffers here will have you up, riding, and comfortable (I swear) in a matter of minutes, with orientation, training, and as many practice runs as you need before you start off on your 5-mile, 2-hour 9am or 2pm tour of downtown Sarasota and the bayfront, including the vintage 1920s Towles Court Artist Colony.

200 S. Washington Blvd., no. 11 (on the corner of Adams Lane). ✆ **941/363-9330.** www.floridaever-glides.com. $85 per person; ask about summer specials. AE, DISC, MC, V. Daily 8am–5pm.

FSU Ringling Center for the Cultural Arts ★★★ By far the top attraction here, this 66-acre site is where showman and circus legend John Ringling and his wife, Mable, collected art and built a house on a grand scale. Now under the aegis of Florida State University, the **John and Mable Ringling Museum of Art** is the state's official art museum. It's filled with more than 500 years of European and American works, including one of the world's most important collections of 17th-century baroque paintings, collections of decorative arts, and traveling exhibits. The Old Masters collection includes five renowned tapestry cartoons by Peter Paul Rubens.

Built in 1924 and 1925 at a cost of $1.5 million and modeled after a Venetian palace, the Ringlings' 32-room palatial bayfront, four-story winter residence, **Ca'd'Zan** ("House of John" in the Venetian dialect), has been recently restored. An 8,000-square-foot terrace leads down to the dock at which Mable Ringling moored her Venetian gondola. Don't miss a tour of this house to see the period furniture and stunning architecture and artwork; in fact, I'd make it the first stop on your Ringling itinerary.

The **Ringling Museum of the Circus** is devoted to circus memorabilia (which is, in a way, more fascinating than the circus itself), including parade wagons, calliopes, costumes, and colorful posters. The grounds include a classical courtyard, a rose garden, a museum shop, and the historic **Asolo Theater,** a 19th-century Italian court playhouse, which the Ringlings moved here in the 1950s. It's now the centerpiece of the Florida State University Center for the Performing Arts. If you're hungry, check out the museum's on-site restaurant, **Treviso,** an elegant lunch-only spot serving fine Italian fare from 11am to 4pm. You can dine inside or, better yet, outside overlooking the Ringling's

Tips How to See the Ringling Museums

It's best to visit the FSU Ringling Center for the Cultural Arts on a weekday, when the center offers guided tours of the art museum, house, and circus museum (included in the price of admission). For tour times, call ahead or check at the information desk as soon as you arrive. While you're waiting for the next tour, explore the gardens or have lunch at Treviso (p. 413).

pristine grounds. A museum admission ticket isn't required to dine in the restaurant. You'll need most of a day to see everything here.

5401 Bay Shore Rd., at N. Tamiami Trail (U.S. 41). ✆ **941/359-5700** or 351-1660 for recorded information. www.ringling.org. Admission $19 adults, $16 seniors, $6 out-of-state students, free for Florida students and children 12 and under. Daily 10am–5:30pm. Closed New Year's Day, Thanksgiving, and Christmas. From downtown, take U.S. 41 N. to University Pkwy. and follow signs to the museum.

G. Wiz (Gulfcoast Wonder & Imagination Zone) This hands-on, state-of-the-art science center has two floors of fun exhibits that cover the physical, earth, and health sciences. The ExploraZone features rotating interactive exhibits from San Francisco's renowned Exploratorium. The 35 exhibits have themes ranging from sound and music to mathematics and motion, color and optics, sight and illusion, and more.

1001 Blvd. of the Arts (in the Blivas Science and Technology Center, 1 block west of U.S. 41). ✆ **941/906-1851.** www.gwiz.org. Admission $9 adults, $8 seniors, $6 kids 2 and over; free 5–8pm the 1st Wed of the month. Mon–Sat 10am–5pm; Sun noon–5pm.

Marie Selby Botanical Gardens ★★ A must-see for serious plant lovers and a should-see for those looking for good photo ops, this peaceful retreat on the bay, just south of downtown, is said to be the only botanical garden in the world specializing in the preservation, study, and research of epiphytes—that is, "air plants" such as orchids. It's home to more than 20,000 exotic plants, including more than 6,000 orchids, as well as a bamboo pavilion, a butterfly and hummingbird garden, a medicinal-plant garden, a waterfall garden, a cactus and succulent garden, a fernery, a hibiscus garden, a palm grove, two tropical-food gardens, and a native shore-plant community. Selby's home and the Payne Mansion (both on the National Registry) are also located here.

811 S. Palm Ave. (south of U.S. 41). ✆ **941/366-5731.** www.selby.org. Admission $17 adults, $6 children 6–11, free for children 5 and under accompanied by an adult. Daily 10am–5pm. Closed Christmas.

Sarasota Classic Car Museum In operation since 1953, this is now a nonprofit museum dedicated to preserving antique automobiles. But there's more to the place than its 90-plus classic and "muscle" autos, from Rolls-Royces and Pierce Arrows to the four cars used personally by circus czar John Ringling. Also here are more than 1,200 antique music boxes and several of Thomas Edison's early phonographs, including a 1909 diamond-tipped-needle model. Check out the Penny Arcade's antique games (with original prices), and grab a cone at the ice-cream and sandwich shop.

5500 N. Tamiami Trail (at University Pkwy.). ✆ **941/355-6228.** www.sarasotacarmuseum.org. Admission $8.50 adults, $7.65 seniors, $5.75 children 13–17, $4 children 6–12, free for children 5 and under. Daily 9am–6pm. Take U.S. 41 north of downtown; museum is 2 blocks west of the airport.

On St. Armands Key

Mote Aquarium ★★ Kids Kids get to touch such cool stuff as stingrays (minus the stinger, of course) and watch sharks in the shark tank at this excellent aquarium. Part of the noted Mote Marine Laboratory complex, it is more broad based than Tampa's Florida Aquarium, which concentrates primarily on local sea life. See manatees in the Marine Mammal Center, a block's walk from the aquarium, as well as many research-in-progress exhibits. Start by watching the aquarium's 12-minute film on the feeding habits of sharks; then allow at least 90 minutes to take in everything on land. Add another 2 hours for a narrated sea-life encounter cruise with the **Sarasota Bay Explorers** (✆ **727/388-4200;** www.sarasotabayexplorers.com). These fun and informative cruises visit a deserted island, and the guides throw out nets and bring up sea life for inspection. It's a good idea to make reservations a day in advance. This company has unusual kayaking adventures, too (p. 433).

1600 Ken Thompson Pkwy. (on City Island). ✆ **800/691-6683** or 941/388-2541. www.mote.org. Admission $17 adults, $16 seniors, $12 children 4–12, free for children 3 and under. Combination aquarium-cruise tickets $36 adults, $29 children. Daily 10am–5pm. Nature cruises daily 11am and 1:30 and 4pm. From St. Armands Circle, head north toward Longboat Key; turn right just before the Lido-Longboat bridge.

In & Near Bradenton

DeSoto National Memorial Nestled on the Manatee River, west of downtown, this park attracts history buffs by re-creating the look and atmosphere of the period when Spanish explorer Hernando de Soto landed here in 1539. It includes a restoration of de Soto's original campsite and a scenic .5-mile nature trail that circles a mangrove jungle and leads to the ruins of one of the first settlements in the area. Start by watching the 21-minute film about de Soto in America. From December to March, park employees dress in 16th-century costumes and portray the early settlers' way of life, including cooking and the firing of an arquebus, one of the world's earliest firearms.

DeSoto Memorial Hwy. (north end of 75th St. W.). ✆ **941/792-0458.** www.nps.gov/deso. Free admission. Daily 9am–5pm. Take Manatee Ave. (Fla. 64) west to 75th St. W. and turn right; follow the road to its end and the entrance to the park.

Gamble Plantation ★ Situated northeast of downtown Bradenton, this is the oldest structure on the southwestern coast of Florida, and a fine example of an antebellum plantation home—something that's quite rare in Florida. It was constructed during a 6-year period in the late 1840s by Maj. Robert Gamble, made primarily of "tabby mortar" (a mixture of oyster shells, sand, molasses, and water), with 10 rooms, verandas on three sides, 18 exterior columns, and eight fireplaces. Now maintained as a state historic site, it includes a fine collection of 19th-century furnishings. Entrance to the house is by tour only, although you can explore the grounds on your own.

3708 Patten Ave. (U.S. 301), Ellenton. ✆ **941/723-4536.** www.floridastateparks.org/gambleplantation. Free admission. Tour $5 adults, $3 children 6–12, free for children 5 and under. Thurs–Mon 9am–4:30pm; 30-min. guided house tour at 9:30 and 10:30am and at 1, 2, 3, and 4pm. Take U.S. 301 north of downtown to Ellenton; the site is on the left, just east of Ellenton-Gillette Rd. (Fla. 683).

Solomon's Castle ★★ This attraction gets the award in the Weirdest and Wackiest (and, boy, are there many) of Florida category. In 1974, Howard Solomon began building what has become a 60-foot-tall, 12,000-square-foot castle in a Manatee County swamp. Solomon, a metal and wood sculptor by trade, built the huge structure (where he now lives) out of 22×34-inch offset aluminum printing plates discarded by a local newspaper. He and the other tour guides (try to get the tour led by Solomon, or at least talk with him about his work) lead guests on a pun-filled tour of the castle, which is decked out with some of his smaller artistic creations, mostly made of other people's "trash," including a chair made out of 86 beer cans, an elephant pieced together with seven oil drums, a unicorn fashioned out of coat hangers, and about 80 stained-glass windows. Howard is continually building new things—you never know what you'll find. If that's not enough to tempt you, you can have lunch in the restaurant, which is in a Spanish galleon that Howard built in his spare time. If you're hungry, check out the Boat in the Moat restaurant, which is literally just that. You *have* to experience this to believe it. Seriously.

4533 Solomon Rd., Ona. ✆ **863/494-6007.** www.solomonscastle.com. Admission $10 adults, $4 kids 11 and under. Tours Oct–June Tues–Sun 11am–4pm. Closed July–Sept. Take Hwy. 64 east of I-75 29 miles to Hwy. 665, go south 9 miles, and turn left at the sign to the castle.

South Florida Museum and Parker Manatee Aquarium (Kids) The star at this downtown complex is Snooty, the oldest manatee born in captivity (1948) and Manatee County's official mascot. The South Florida Museum tells the story of Florida's history, from prehistoric times to the present; it includes a Native American collection with life-size dioramas, and a Spanish courtyard containing replicas of 16th-century buildings. The museum recently completed a $5-million renovation program.

201 10th St. W. (on the riverfront, at Barcarrota Blvd.). © **941/746-4131.** www.southfloridamuseum.org. Admission $16 adults, $14 seniors, $12 children 5–12, free for children 4 and under. Jan–Apr and July Mon–Sat 10am–5pm, Sun noon–5pm; rest of year Tues–Sat 10am–5pm, Sun noon–5pm. Closed New Year's Day, Thanksgiving, and Christmas. From U.S. 41, take Manatee Ave. west to 10th St. W. and turn right.

SHOPPING

Visitors come from all over the world to shop at **St. Armands Circle★★**, on St. Armands Key. Wander around this outdoor circle of more than 150 international boutiques, gift shops, galleries, restaurants, and nightspots, all surrounded by lush landscaping, patios, and antiques. Pick up a map at the Sarasota Convention and Visitors Bureau (p. 430). Many shops here are comparable to those in Palm Beach and on Naples's 3rd Avenue South, so check your credit card limits—or resort to some great window-shopping.

WHERE TO STAY

The beaches here are virtually lined with condominiums, many of which are actually all-condo projects operated as hotels. Among the rental agencies requiring stays of less than a month are **Argus Property Management,** 2477 Stickney Point Rd., Sarasota, FL 34231 (© **941/927-6464;** fax 941/927-6767; www.argusmgmt.com); and **Florida Vacation Accommodations,** 4030 Gulf of Mexico Dr., Longboat Key, FL 34228 (© **800/237-9505** or 941/364-9505; fax 941/364-1830; www.vacationinfl.com).

The hotels below are organized by geographic region: in downtown Sarasota, on Lido Key, on Longboat Key, and on Siesta Key. The high season is from January to April. The hotel tax here is 10%.

Downtown Sarasota

Most visitors stay out at the beaches, but cost-conscious travelers will find some good deals on the mainland, such as the **Best Western Midtown,** 1425 S. Tamiami Trail (U.S. 41) at Prospect Street (© **800/722-8227** or 941/955-9841; fax 941/954-8948; www.bwmidtown.com). This older but well-maintained motel is 2 miles in either direction from the main causeways leading to the keys. Winter rates are about $99 for a double room, dropping to about $69 during off-season.

Downtown's top hotel before the opening of the Ritz-Carlton (see below), the **Hyatt Sarasota,** 1000 Blvd. of the Arts (© **800/233-1234** or 941/953-1234; fax 941/952-1987; www.sarasota.hyatt.com), is adjacent to the Civic Center and the Van Wezel Performing Arts Hall, and within walking distance of downtown shops and restaurants.

Most other chain motels are near the airport, including **Quality Inn** (© **800/228-5151** or 941/355-7091), **Days Inn** (© **800/329-7466** or 941/355-9271), and **Comfort Inn** (© **800/521-2121** or 941/351-7734). All stand side by side on Tamiami Trail (U.S. 41) near the FSU Ringling Center for the Cultural Arts and the Asolo Center for the Performing Arts.

The Cypress ★★★ A throwback to the 1940s, the Cypress is a two-story, tin-roofed inn tucked amid giant mango trees and hovering palms. Best of all, it overlooks the bay.

You can't get accommodations much better than this, with its antiques, a grand piano, and guest rooms with private bathrooms, queen-size beds, hardwood floors, ceiling fans, and Oriental rugs. The best unit is the Essie Leigh Key West Room, which has its own side entrance, a front-porch view of the bay, a brass-and-pewter bed, an antique oak chest, and Spanish-pine side tables. Other rooms are distinctly "Victorian meets Ralph Lauren," some with French doors and others with neoclassical twists.

621 Gulfstream Ave. S., Sarasota, FL 34236. ✆ **941/955-4683.** www.cypressbb.com. 5 units. Winter $249–$279 double; off-season $170–$199 double. AE, DISC, MC, V. *In room:* A/C, TV, Wi-Fi.

The Ritz-Carlton Sarasota ★★★ Downtown's swankiest digs, just north of the Ringling Causeway and across a narrow creek from the Sarasota Quay shopping-and-dining complex (p. 448), the Ritz occupies the bottom eight floors of an 18-story Mediterranean-style building (the top floors are private residences). It sits perpendicular to the bay, so most of the spacious guest units have views looking across the water to the keys and the Gulf. The rooms are luxuriously appointed in typical Ritz-Carlton fashion, including marble bathrooms. The hotel's four restaurants are led by Vernona, while the Bay View Bar & Grill offers casual dining both indoors and out. The elegantly appointed lobby opens to a bayside courtyard with a heated pool. There is no beach on-site, but a shuttle will take you to the hotel's fabulous, private beach club on Lido Key. There's also a full-service spa and fitness center on-site.

1111 Ritz-Carlton Dr. (at Tamiami Trail/U.S. 41), Sarasota, FL 34236. ✆ **800/241-3333** or 941/309-2000. Fax 941/309-2100. www.ritzcarlton.com. 266 units. Winter $329–$695 double; off-season $299–$519 double. AE, DC, DISC, MC, V. **Amenities:** 3 restaurants (2 additional at off-site beach and golf club); 3 bars (2 additional at off-site beach and golf club); 2 outdoor pools (heated, including a children's pool); golf course; 3 tennis courts; health club; Jacuzzi; sauna; children's programs; concierge; activities desk; car-rental desk; business center; 24-hr. room service; massage; babysitting; laundry service; concierge-level rooms. *In room:* A/C, TV, dataport, minibar, hair dryer, iron, safe.

On Lido Key

The Helmsley Sandcastle ★ Set on 600 feet of private, white-sand beach on the Gulf of Mexico and only minutes from the upscale St. Armands Circle, this place has an incredibly friendly staff and a nice, resorty feel. The large guest rooms, updated in 2008, are decorated in the casually comfortable colors of Florida and most have great views of the water. Stay here if you want to relax in a fine location without dealing with the stuffiness of a fancier hotel.

1540 Ben Franklin Dr., Sarasota, FL 34236. ✆ **800/225-2181** or 941/388-2181. Fax 941/388-2655. www.helmsleysandcastle.com. 179 units. Winter $219–$339 double; off-season $159–$259 double. AE, DC, DISC, MC, V. **Amenities:** 3 restaurants; poolside bar; 2 outdoor heated pools; nearby golf and tennis; business center. *In room:* A/C, TV, fridge, coffeemaker, hair dryer, iron.

Holiday Inn Lido Beach Conveniently located at the north end of Lido, this modern seven-story hotel is within walking distance of St. Armands Circle. The beach is right across the street. The motel-style rooms have balconies that face the Gulf or the bay, and the rooftop restaurant and lounge offer panoramic views of the Gulf of Mexico.

233 Ben Franklin Dr. (at Thoreau Dr.), Sarasota, FL 34236. ✆ **800/465-4329,** 800/892-9174, or 941/388-5555. Fax 941/388-4321. 135 units. Winter $130–$250 double; off-season $120–$290 double. AE, DC, MC, V. **Amenities:** Restaurant; 2 bars; heated outdoor pool; access to nearby health club; exercise room; watersports equipment/rentals; bike rental; limited room service; babysitting; laundry service; coin-op washers/dryers; concierge-level rooms. *In room:* A/C, TV, dataport, fridge, coffeemaker, hair dryer, iron.

On Longboat Key

Colony Beach & Tennis Resort ★★ Sitting 3 miles north of St. Armands Circle, this beachside facility is consistently rated one of the nation's finest tennis resorts. The Colony Restaurant and pool date from 1952, when this was a beach club, but today's accommodations are in modern one- and two-bedroom condominium apartments that come complete with living room, dining area, fully equipped kitchenette, sun balcony, whirlpool tub, and steam shower. The choice units are the three private cottages right on the superb beach. The condominiums are built around a 21-court tennis center, where a staff of professionals conducts highly acclaimed programs for adults and children alike. The beachside Colony Restaurant offers fine Continental cuisine for lunch and dinner (jackets requested for men at dinner).

1620 Gulf of Mexico Dr., Longboat Key, FL 34228. ✆ **800/282-1138** or 941/383-6464. Fax 941/383-7549. www.colonybeachresort.com. 235 units. Winter $280–$1,150 suite; off-season $195–$975 suite. Packages available. AE, DC, DISC, MC, V. **Amenities:** 2 restaurants; 2 bars; heated outdoor pool; 21 clay and hard tennis courts; health club; Jacuzzi; sauna; watersports equipment/rentals; bike rental; children's programs; game room; concierge; activities desk; car-rental desk; business center; salon; limited room service; massage; babysitting; laundry service; coin-op washers/dryers. *In room:* A/C, TV, kitchen, coffeemaker, hair dryer, iron.

The Resort at Longboat Key Club ★★ Part of a 410-acre real-estate development at the southern end of Longboat Key, this award-winning condominium resort pampers the country-club set with upscale restaurants and a variety of recreational activities in a lush tropical setting. The spacious, newly renovated luxurious rooms and suites have private balconies overlooking the Gulf, a lagoon, or golf-course fairways. All have custom-designed furnishings and neoclassical decor, and all but 20 have full kitchens. Among several dining options here, the Sands Pointe Restaurant has the feel of an informal but elegant supper club, serving classical Italian cuisine in a romantic setting by the Gulf, while the adjacent lounge offers casual dining and live entertainment.

301 Gulf of Mexico Dr. (P.O. Box 15000), Longboat Key, FL 34228. ✆ **800/237-8821** or 941/383-8821. Fax 941/383-0359. www.longboatkeyclub.com. 232 units. Winter $229–$435 double, $575–$1,350 suite; off-season $179–$275 double, $225–$635 suite. Packages available. AE, DISC, MC, V. From St. Armands Key, take Gulf of Mexico Dr. north; take 1st left after bridge. **Amenities:** 4 restaurants; 2 bars; heated outdoor pool; 2 golf courses (45 holes); 38 tennis courts; fitness center; spa; Jacuzzi; sauna; watersports equipment/rentals; bicycles; children's programs; concierge; room service; massage; babysitting; laundry service. *In room:* A/C, flatscreen TV, high-speed Internet, kitchen, coffeemaker, hair dryer, iron, safe.

On Siesta Key

Captiva Beach Resort ★ Value Located about half a block from the beach in a tropical oasis with other small resorts, Captiva Beach Resort, Sarasota's first Green Lodging, eco-friendly resort, is very popular with longer-term guests during winter, Europeans during the summer. Every one of the comfortable, sparkling-clean units here has some form of cooking facility and five-star queen-size pillow-top beds, and some have separate living rooms with sleeper sofas. These are older buildings, so you'll find window air conditioners mounted through the walls; however, the property has been upgraded for all the modern conveniences, such as high-speed Internet connection and bottle-quality water at every faucet. Rooms also have personal barbecues, beach chairs, and umbrellas. You'll get fresh linens and towels daily except Sunday. Daily maid service is available for a small fee. Guests get complimentary use of sand toys. Several restaurants and shops are a short walk away.

6772 Sara Sea Circle, Siesta Key, FL 34242. ✆ 800/349-4131 or 941/349-4131. Fax 941/349-8141. www.captivabeachresort.com. 20 units. Winter $255–$285 double, $215–$370 bungalow and suite; off-season $115–$165 double, $115–$250 bungalow and suite. Weekly and monthly rates available. See website for packages. AE, DISC, MC, V. Amenities: Heated outdoor pool; watersports equipment/rentals; coin-op washers/dryers; outdoor gas grills. In room: A/C, satellite TV/VCR, high-speed Internet access, kitchen, coffeemaker, hair dryer.

Tropical Breeze Resort & Spa ★★ A family-owned beach resort on the Gulf side of Siesta Key Village, Tropical Breeze exudes romance and relaxation, with lush tropical gardens and private units located across the street from the beach with an ocean view. All the units are walking distance to the beach, shops, restaurants, and nightlife. Newly remodeled rooms are spacious—sizes ranging from a standard to a five-bedroom suite—and decorated in comfortable furniture, nothing fancy, but completely beachy and most with kitchens. Coffee and pastries are served in the morning. The Key Spa and Salon provides full services, from massages on the beach to aromatherapy treatments. Gas grills are available and the resort offers bike, beach lounger, and umbrella rentals.

153 Avenida Messina, Siesta Key, Sarasota, FL 34242. © **941/349-1125.** Fax 941/349-0057. www.tropicalbreezeinn.com. 67 units. Winter $105–$170 double, $149–$466 suite; off-season $99–$168 double, $149–$430 suite. Weekly and monthly rates available. AE, DISC, MC, V. Pets accepted for an extra charge. **Amenities:** Cafe; pool; spa. *In room:* A/C, TV/VCR, Wi-Fi, kitchen, coffeemaker, hair dryer, iron.

Turtle Beach Resort ★★★ On Siesta Key's south end, this intimate bayside charmer is one of Florida's most romantic retreats. Some units are close to a small bayside swimming pool, heavy tropical foliage provides a reasonable degree of privacy, and high wooden fences surround each unit's private outdoor hot tub. Sitting right on the bay, all units also have one-way privacy mirror windows. The cottages are done in various styles, such as Caribbean and Nantucket, and have at least one bedroom each. There's no restaurant on the grounds, but there are two waterfront restaurants and a pub right next door, and all units have kitchens. Guests can use bikes, fishing poles, kayaks, and canoes for free. Boaters especially love the property's 10 boat docks. Turtle Beach is only a 5-minute walk. Ten new studios and one-bedroom luxury units, called the **Inn at Turtle Beach,** have been added across the street on the Gulf side. All units have hot tubs with aromatherapy jets. Facilities include kitchenettes and bathrooms, two boat docks, fountains, and a heated pool.

9049 Midnight Pass Rd., Sarasota, FL 34242. © **941/349-4554.** Fax 941/312-9034. www.turtlebeachresort.com. 10 units. Winter $360–$450 cottage, $350–$450 Inn studios; off-season $235–$370 cottage, $235–$370 Inn studios. Weekly rates available. AE, DISC, MC, V. Pets accepted for an extra charge. **Amenities:** Outdoor pool; free use watersports equipment and bikes. *In room:* A/C, TV/DVD/VCR, free Wi-Fi, kitchen, coffeemaker, hair dryer, iron, hot tub.

WHERE TO DINE

The restaurants below are organized geographically: in downtown Sarasota, in Southside Village (the city's hottest new dining scene), on St. Armands Key (next to Lido Key), on Longboat Key, and on Siesta Key.

In Downtown Sarasota

Downtown's best breakfast spot is the local branch of **First Watch,** 1395 Main St., at Central and Pineapple avenues (© **941/954-1395**). Like its siblings in Naples (p. 374) and elsewhere, First Watch offers a wide variety of breakfast and lunch fare. It's open daily from 7:30am to 2:30pm. If the wait's too long, walk south along Central Avenue; this block has several coffeehouses and cafes with sidewalk seating.

Bijou Cafe ★★ INTERNATIONAL Chef Jean-Pierre Knaggs prepares award-winning cuisine from around the world in his cafe, a former gas station, in the heart of the theater district. Although the more casual Michael's on East (see below) bistro draws a

The Neglected Island

Most people are familiar with Longboat Key, but what they don't know is that it's actually part of Old Florida, collectively called Florida's Gulf Islands. In addition to Longboat, there's **Anna Maria Island,** a place where the streets are sand swept and the white beaches are dotted with pastel-colored cottages. It's the kind of community where the hottest spot in town is an ice-cream parlor. Hop on the Manatee Trolley, and you can explore the island at its highest speed limit—25 mph. Everything in Anna Maria is slow paced, which is just how the locals like it. There are no high-rises—the town won't allow anything to obstruct the million-dollar view of the Gulf. For peace and quiet, this is where it's at. No big hotels exist here, just mom-and-pop establishments such as the **Anna Maria Beach Cottages,** 12 Oak Ave. (✆ **941/778-1503**), owned by Britisher Nigel Brown and his wife. Here you can disappear into your own world, relax by the pool, walk the beach, or retreat into your cozy cottage. It's spectacular—none of it should be neglected by visitors ever again. **Palm Tree Villas,** 207 66th St. (✆ **941/778-0910;** www.palmtreevillas.com), is another great getaway featuring one- and two-bedroom villas just a shell's throw away from the beach.

For great ocean views, live music, cocktails, and chow, check out **Sandbar,** 100 Spring Ave. (✆ **941/778-0444**). Sandbar has two sister waterfront bar/restaurants in the area as well: **Beachhouse,** 200 Gulf Dr., Bradenton Beach (✆ **941/779-2222**), and **Mar Vista,** 760 Broadway St., North Longboat Key (✆ **941/383-2391**).

For more information on the Gulf Islands, check out www.flagulfislands.com. Anna Maria, Longboat, and Bradenton (on the "Mainland") are connected by bridges.

hefty after-theater crowd, this is the best place to dine within walking distance of the downtown entertainment venues. Jean-Pierre artfully presents the likes of chicken Louisville (with crushed pecans and bourbon-pear sauce), pan-seared crab cakes served under a rémoulade and over a bed of fresh greens, and gently simmered lamb shanks with rosemary and garlic. His outstanding wine list has won accolades from *Wine Spectator* magazine.

1287 1st St. (at Pineapple Ave.). ✆ **941/366-8111.** www.bijoucafe.net. Reservations recommended. Main courses $10–$17. AE, DC, MC, V. Mon–Sat 11:30am–2pm and 5–9:30pm; Sun 5–9:30pm. Closed Sun June–Dec. Free valet parking nightly in winter, on weekends off-season.

Island Time Grill ★★ SEAFOOD Although it's miles from the water, Island Time Grill does a good job convincing you that you're right on the surf with excellent seafood specialties such as coconut and curry lobster bisque made with Maine lobster and spiced with red curry and lemongrass; a sea bass crusted with wild mushrooms and topped with a tangy ginger broth; or grilled center-cut salmon with pine nuts, cranberries, and green onions. The wine list is equally divided between reasonably priced reds and whites, and the restaurant's wine cellar features a private dining area. Decor is very waterfront-oriented as well, with bay windows, teal walls, whitewashed shutters, and African mahogany hardwood floors. Service is equally splashy.

8225 Cooper Creek Blvd. ✆ **941/351-5128.** www.islandtimegrill.com. Reservations recommended. Main courses $11–$20. AE, DC, MC, V. Sun–Thurs 5–10pm; Fri–Sat 5–11pm.

Marina Jack's SEAFOOD/CONTINENTAL Overlooking the waterfront with a wraparound 270-degree view of Sarasota Bay and both Siesta and Lido keys, this establishment has spectacular vistas and a carefree "on vacation" attitude, especially on the open-air raw-bar deck, which is often packed all afternoon on weekends and at sunset every day. The food is good but not the best in town, so come here for a fun time. You may have to wait for a table or bar stool down on the portside patio bar, but be sure to make reservations if you want to have a meal in the upstairs dining room. Fresh local seafood is the star both upstairs and down—grilled grouper is your best bet. The downstairs piano lounge and raw bar also serves sandwiches and burgers.

In Island Park, Bayfront at Central Ave. ✆ **941/365-4232.** www.marinajacks.com. Reservations recommended in dining room. Dining room main courses $23–$43; lounge menu $6–$43, patio bar $9–$13; sandwiches and salads $8–$14. AE, DISC, MC, V. Daily 11:30am–2am. Closed Christmas.

Mattison's City Grille ★★ ITALIAN Downtown Sarasota's premier alfresco hot spot, Mattison's features Italian fare, including pretty good pizza as well as tapas, burgers, and salads, but the main draw here isn't the food, per se, it's the live jazz and blues bands that play nightly. Mattison's is also a hot spot for Saturday and Sunday brunch.

1 N. Lemon Ave. ✆ **941/330-0440.** www.mattisons.com. Reservations recommended. Tapas $9–$15; pizza $16–$20; main courses $18–$27. AE, DC, MC, V. Mon–Thurs 11am–11pm; Fri 11am–midnight; Sat 9am–midnight; Sun 11am–10pm.

Michael's on East ★★ INTERNATIONAL At the rear of the Midtown Plaza shopping center on U.S. 41 south of downtown, Michael Klauber's chic bistro is one of the top places here for fine dining—it's the locals' favorite after-theater haunt. Huge cut-glass walls create three intimate dining areas, one a piano bar for pre- or after-dinner drinks. Prepared with fresh ingredients and a creative flair, the offerings here will tempt your taste buds. House specialties are pan-roasted blue fin crab cakes, pan-braised striped black sea bass with spicy chili-glazed udon noodles, bok choy, and littleneck clams in *tom-ka* broth, and slow-roasted duck bourbon glazed, with silky collard greens, fire-roasted corn, and spoon bread.

1212 East Ave. S. (btw. Bahia and Prospect sts.). ✆ **941/366-0007.** www.michaelsoneast.com. Reservations recommended. Main courses $18–$36. AE, DC, DISC, MC, V. Mon–Fri 11:30am–2pm and 5:30–10pm; Sat–Sun 5:30–10pm. Free valet parking.

Morel ★★ NEW AMERICAN A warm, sophisticated, bistrolike ambience and innovative menu created by chef/owner Fredy Mayer has made Morel one of Sarasota's hottest and hautest restaurants. Of all the excellent fare, I recommend the potato-and-leek latkes with house-smoked salmon, the grilled veal chop in tomato-basil coulis, and the glazed Chilean sea bass. A $17 prix-fixe menu is also available from 4:30 to 5:30pm.

3809 S. Tuttle Ave. ✆ **941/927-8716.** www.morelrestaurant.com. Reservations recommended. Main courses $17–$26. AE, MC, V. Tues–Sat 4:30–9:30pm.

Patrick's AMERICAN/PUB FARE With a semicircular facade, this upscale, polished-oak and brass-rail sports bar offers wide-window views of downtown's main intersection. The menu offers very good pub fare: steaks and chops, burgers, seafood, pastas, small pizzas, salads, sandwiches, and omelets. Other entrees include Yankee pot roast, broiled salmon with dill-hollandaise sauce, sesame chicken, and veal done three ways—piccata, Française, or Marsala. There's a good happy hour here Monday through Friday between 5 and 7pm.

1400 Main St. (at Pineapple Ave.). ✆ **941/952-1170.** www.patricksrestaurant.net. Main courses $12–$17; sandwiches and burgers $7–$11. AE, DC, DISC, MC, V. Daily 11am–midnight; Sun brunch 11am–3pm. Closed Christmas.

Petrella Bros. Italian Tapas and Wine Bar ★★ ITALIAN This bustling Italian tapas and wine bar has been recognized by *Delta Sky Miles* magazine as one of the best Italian restaurants in America thanks to its fresh pastas, imported seafood, wood-fired pizzas, and steaks. The wine list is exceptional, thanks to a unique collection of quality Italian wines from various regions. Feel free to order a selection of small plates to share—Pinot Grigio shrimp, veal meatballs, salumi, calamari—or choose from an impressive list of main courses such as chicken Marsala. At the time of this writing, owner Mateo Fagin was about to host his own cooking show, so be prepared for a major wait!

6331 S. Tamiami Trail. ✆ **941/922-8466.** www.petrellabros.com. Main courses $16–$25; tapas $7–$10; pizzas $10–$13. AE, DC, DISC, MC, V. Sun–Thurs 5–10pm; Fri–Sat 5–11pm.

The Rustic Grill ★★★ SOUTHERN Located in Sarasota's revitalized Rosemary District, the Rustic Grill is a fabulous restaurant housed in a former 1920s motorcycle repair shop. With an interior reminiscent of a Spanish galleon, complete with exposed brick and wrought iron ornaments, Rustic Grill is a delicious departure from typical sunshiny Florida decor. The menu is even better, focusing on Southern-style comfort food with a modern twist, including Cornish game hen split roasted and finished with an orange Grand Marnier glaze; and, for dessert, baked peaches in pastry with goat cheese (!) ice cream. The wine list is equally exceptional.

400 N. Lemon Ave. ✆ **941/906-1111.** www.rusticgrillsarasota.com. Main courses $18–$26. AE, DC, DISC, MC, V. Tues–Sat 6–11pm.

Yoder's ★ Value AMISH/AMERICAN Just 3 miles east of downtown is an award-winning, value eatery operated by an Amish family (Sarasota and Bradenton have sizable Amish communities and several other Amish restaurants). Evoking the Pennsylvania Dutch country, the simple dining room displays handicrafts, photos, and paintings celebrating the Amish way. The menu emphasizes plain, made-from-scratch cooking such as home-style meatloaf, Southern fried chicken, country-smoked ham, and fried filet of flounder. Burgers, salads, soups, and sandwiches are also available. Leave room for Mrs. Yoder's traditional shoofly and other homemade pies, one of the restaurant's biggest draws. ***Note:*** Alcohol is neither served nor allowed here.

3434 Bahia Vista St. (west of Beneva Rd.). ✆ **941/955-7771.** www.yodersrestaurant.com. Main courses $7–$11; breakfast $3–$8; sandwiches, burgers, and salads $4–$9. No credit cards (ATM on premises). Mon–Sat 6am–8pm.

Zoria ★★★ ECLECTIC Sleek and stylish, Zoria is a trendsetter in terms of Sarasota's innovative cuisine scene, with such interesting menu items as pepper-crusted Broken Arrow Ranch antelope, with foie gras, rosemary poached pear, and onion jam; duck foie gras, fig jam, pear purée, and 8-year-old balsamic; and, my favorite—from the bar menu, which also happens to be exquisite and much cheaper—a ground-beef burger with rosemary, roasted garlic, and goat cheese on focaccia bread.

1991 Main St. ✆ **941/955-4457.** www.zoria.net. Reservations recommended. Main courses $18–$31. AE, DC, MC, V. Mon–Sat 5–10pm; Sun 5–9pm.

In Southside Village

Sarasota's hottest dining area is **Southside Village,** centered on South Osprey Avenue between Hyde Park and Hillview streets, about 15 blocks south of downtown. Here you'll find several hip restaurants, including Fred's and Pacific Rim (see below). The village landmark is **Morton's Gourmet Market** ★, 1924 S. Osprey Ave. (✆ **941/955-9856;** www.mortonsmarket.com), which offers a multitude of deli items, specialty sandwiches, a ton of fresh salads, freshly baked pastries and desserts, and cooked meals dispensed from a cafeteria-style steam table. You can dine picnic-fashion at sidewalk tables. Most ready-to-go items cost less than $10. The market is open Monday through Saturday from 8am to 8pm, Sunday from 10am to 5pm.

Hillview Grill ★ ECLECTIC A locals' favorite, Hillview Grill offers an unabridged menu of burgers, salads, small plates ranging from fish tacos to escargot, and large plates including salmon wrapped in cedar paper and drizzled with maple-soy, and grilled meatloaf with applewood bacon and mushroom gravy. A late-night bar scene Wednesday through Saturday nights brings in the hip cocktail set and features a late-night menu.

In Hillview Centre, 1920 Hillview St. (btw. Osprey Ave. and Laurent Place). ✆ **941/952-0045.** www.hillviewgrill.com. Main courses $6.25–$19. AE, DISC, MC, V. Mon–Fri 11am–1am and 5–9pm; Sat–Sun 4pm–midnight.

Pacific Rim ★ (Value) JAPANESE/THAI Sarasotans love this chic and very casual restaurant for exceptional cuisine at economical prices. Japanese influence is felt at the sushi bar along one side of the dining room, while Thai spices make a strong impact on the regular menu. The chargrilled shrimp with Thai curry and coconut-milk sauce is especially tasty, as is the combination of chicken and vegetables stir-fried in a wok. Here you can select your meat and vegetables separately from the sauce, and the chefs will combine them on the grill, in the wok, or in the bowl (as in rice dishes).

In Hillview Centre, 1859 Hillview St. (btw. Osprey Ave. and Laurent Place). ✆ **941/330-8071.** www.pacificrimsarasota.com. Main courses $13–$25. AE, DISC, MC, V. Mon–Thurs 11:30am–2pm and 5–9pm; Fri 11:30am–2pm and 5–10pm; Sat 5–10pm.

On St. Armands Key

While locals are hanging out in Southside Village, part-year residents and visitors flock to St. Armands Circle. Plan to spend at least one evening here: The nighttime scene is like a fair, with everyone strolling around the circle, poking heads into the few stores that stay open after dark, and window-shopping the others. It's fun and safe, so come early and plan to stay late.

The circle has a branch of Tampa's famous **Columbia** (p. 402), between John Ringling Boulevard and John Ringling Parkway (✆ **941/388-3987**). The Spanish food is excellent, there's outdoor seating, and the Patio Lounge is one of the liveliest spots here for evening entertainment Thursday through Sunday. Like its sibling in Naples (p. 373), the local edition of **Tommy Bahama's Tropical Cafe,** 300 John Ringling Blvd. (✆ **941/388-2446**), draws a lively crowd of young professionals for its moderately priced seafood. It's upstairs over the Tommy Bahama's clothing store.

At dinner, you may wish to forgo an expensive dessert and wander over to the local branch of **Kilwin's,** 312 John Ringling Blvd. (✆ **941/388-3200**), for some gourmet chocolate, Mackinac Island fudge, or ice cream or yogurt in a homemade waffle cone. Enjoy your sweets on one of the sidewalk park benches—everyone else does.

Blue Dolphin Cafe (Value) AMERICAN/DINER On the John Ringling Boulevard spoke of St. Armands Circle, this informal diner is the affluent area's best inexpensive place to have breakfast (served anytime). The owners, Jill and Rob Ball, are fonts of free information, too. They serve standard breakfast fare as well as fresh crab or lobster Benedict, raspberry pancakes, and pecan-peach waffles. Lunchtime highlights are the homemade soups and grouper sandwiches. The Blue Dolphin is open for dinner on Friday nights during the winter season, offering the likes of flaky-crust chicken potpie, slow-roasted prime rib, and spicy crab cakes.

470 John Ringling Blvd. (1 block off St. Armands Circle). ✆ **941/388-3566.** www.bluedolphincafe.com. Breakfast $6–$10; sandwiches, burgers, and salads $5–$10. AE, DC, DISC, MC, V. Daily 7am–3pm.

Café L'Europe ★★★ CONTINENTAL One of Sarasota's most lauded restaurants, Café L'Europe has been the recipient of countless awards and praise for its Continental fare that fuses French, Caribbean, and Spanish influences into what the chef prefers to call New European cuisine. An elegant ambience makes Café L'Europe the place to celebrate special occasions, whether over the classic Dover sole (served for two people) or an updated version of sweetbreads—with brandied demi glace and mushrooms. Sea bass—pan seared with truffle honey and a curry glaze—is a sublime choice as well, especially when matched with one of the restaurant's many vintages. Service, as to be expected in an establishment of this caliber, is outstanding.

431 St. Armands Circle (at John Ringling Blvd.). ✆ **941/388-4415.** www.cafeleurope.net. Reservations recommended. Main courses $27–$49. AE, DC, MC, V. Daily 11am–10:30pm.

Hemingway's ★ FLORIBBEAN For a casual spot with an eclectic Floribbean menu and a large bar with a friendly, laid-back Key West vibe, take the elevator or climb the winding stairs to this second-floor hideaway. Hemingway's is a charming and comfortable combination of good food and Old Florida tradition. You can dine inside or outside on the first- or second-floor balcony.

325 John Ringling Blvd. (½-block off St. Armands Circle). ✆ **941/388-3948.** www.hemingwaysretreat.com. Reservations recommended Sat–Sun. Main courses $16–$34. AE, DC, DISC, MC, V. Sun–Thurs 11:30am–10pm; Fri–Sat 11:30am–11pm.

On Longboat Key

Euphemia Haye/The Haye Loft ★★★ INTERNATIONAL This area's most extraordinary restaurant, the romantically lit Euphemia Haye is best known for Chef Raymond Arpke's crispy roast duckling filled with bread stuffing and accompanied by a tangy fruit sauce. His prime strip steak rolled in cracked peppercorns and served with an orange, brandy, and butter sauce is another winner, as is his shrimp in a delightful curry and coconut-cream sauce. If all this sounds sweet, wait until you go upstairs to the Haye Loft, his casual dessert bar and lounge with live entertainment. Up here, you can take your pick from fabulous pies topped with thick whipped cream or Ben & Jerry's ice cream. You can also sample the kitchen's offerings because the loft has its own light-fare menu, including soups, appetizers, small pizzas, and sandwiches. If you're lucky, the night's special sandwich will be steak topped with Raymond's peppercorn sauce, available for sale by the bottle if you like it.

5540 Gulf of Mexico Dr. (at Gulfbay Rd.). ✆ **941/383-3633.** www.euphemiahaye.com. Reservations recommended downstairs, not accepted in the Haye Loft. Main courses $22–$47; sandwiches, pizzas, and salads $7–$15. DC, DISC, MC, V. Restaurant Sun–Thurs 5–10pm; Fri–Sat 5–10:30pm. Haye Loft daily 6pm–midnight.

Moore's Stone Crab SEAFOOD Located in Longbeach, the old fishing village on the north end of Longboat Key, this popular bayfront restaurant began in 1967 as an offshoot of a family seafood business established 40 years earlier. From the outside, in fact, it still looks a little like a packing house, but the view of the bay dotted with mangrove islands makes a fine complement to stone crabs fresh from the family's own traps from October 15 to May 15. Otherwise, the menu offers an incredibly large variety of seafood, most of it fried or broiled. Sandwiches and salads are served all day.

800 Broadway (at Bayside Dr.). ✆ **941/383-1748.** Main courses $20–$30; stone crab market price (as much as $40–$45 in season, from mid-Oct to mid-May); sandwiches and salads $9–$15. AE, DISC, MC, V. Winter daily 11:30am–9:30pm; off-season Mon–Fri 4:30–9:30pm, Sat–Sun 11:30am–9:30pm.

Pattigeorge's ★★ SEAFOOD A bayside eatery with views of mangrove-covered islands, PG's, as its known by regulars, offers fantastic coastal cuisine, including a miso-glazed sea bass in a lobster consommé and crispy Bahamian lobster tails served with Asian slaw, red bliss potatoes, and honey-mustard sauce. Try the panko-crusted fried banana for dessert, or if you'd rather stay healthy—okay, *healthier*—check out the hashed Brussels sprouts, thinly shredded and sautéed with butter and poppy seeds.

4120 Gulf of Mexico Dr. ✆ **941/383-0102.** www.pattigeorges.com. Main courses $13–$38. AE, DISC, MC, V. Daily 6–11pm (bar from 5:30pm).

On Siesta Key

Ocean Boulevard, which runs through **Siesta Village,** the area's funky, laid-back beach hangout, is virtually lined with restaurants and pubs. Most have bars and outdoor seating, which attracts the beach crowd during the day. At night, rock-'n'-roll bands draw teenagers and college students to this lively scene.

Blasé Café ★★ (Finds) INTERNATIONAL Tongue-in-cheeky, to say the least, this restaurant doesn't take itself seriously, hence the ironic and oxymoronic name. One of Florida's most unusual restaurants, this supercasual establishment has tables indoors and a few under the cover of the Village Corner shopping center's walkway, but most are alfresco, on a wooden deck built around a palm tree in the center's asphalt parking lot. Never mind the cars pulling in and out virtually next to your chair: The food is so good that it draws droves of locals who don't mind waiting for a table. Dinner includes the likes of pan-seared, sushi-quality yellowfin tuna with brandy, shallots, demi glace, and cream. You can while away the rest of the evening in the martini bar, where the owners have installed the original bar from Don CeSar Beach Resort & Spa in St. Pete Beach. Live music is featured on weekends.

In Village Corner, 5263 Ocean Blvd. (at Calle Miramar), Siesta Village. ✆ **941/349-9822.** www.theblasecafe.com. Reservations recommended. Main courses $10–$30. MC, V. Mon–Thurs 6–9:30pm; Fri–Sat 6–10pm. Closed Mon June–Nov.

SKOB ★★ SEAFOOD Siesta Key Oyster Bar, or SKOB to the locals, features live music, daily drink specials, and, of course, oysters of all varieties, raw on the half shell, fried, or steamed. There are also a slew of sandwiches, salads, and a kids' menu, but what the place is known for is one of the best happy hours in town, daily from 3 to 6pm, when there are two-for-one appetizers, live bands, and drink specials.

5238 Ocean Blvd. ✆ **941/346-5443.** www.skob.com. Raw bar $5–$12; sandwiches, salads $10–$12; main courses $12–$17. AE, DISC, MC, V. Mon–Sat 11am–close; Sun 11:30am–close.

Turtles AMERICAN With tropical overtones and breathtaking water vistas across from Turtle Beach, this informal restaurant on Little Sarasota Bay has tables indoors and on an outdoor deck. Unique seafood offerings include snapper New Orleans and potato-encrusted mahimahi. You can't go wrong ordering grouper grilled, broiled, blackened, or fried. A selection of pastas is also available. The economical early-bird specials offer several choices, such as spicy Szechuan shrimp.

8875 Midnight Pass Rd. (at Turtle Beach Rd.). ✆ **941/346-2207.** www.turtlesrestaurant.com. Main courses $7–$22; salads and sandwiches $6–$10; early-bird specials $8–$12. AE, DISC, MC, V. Mon–Sat 11:30am–9:30pm; Sun 10am–9pm. Early-bird specials daily 4–6pm.

SARASOTA AFTER DARK

The cultural capital of Florida's west coast, Sarasota is home to a host of performing arts, especially during the winter season. To get the latest on what's happening anytime of year, call the city's 24-hour **Artsline** (✆ **941/365-2787**). Also check the "Ticket" section in Friday's *Herald-Tribune* (www.newscoast.com), the local daily newspaper; copies are usually available at the Sarasota Convention and Visitors Bureau (p. 430).

THE PERFORMING ARTS Located at the FSU Ringling Center for the Cultural Arts (p. 435), the Florida State University Center for the Performing Arts, 5555 N. Tamiami Trail (U.S. 41; ✆ **800/361-8388** or 941/351-8000; www.asolo.org), presents the winter-through-spring **Asolo Theatre Festival** ★★★. This annual program of ballet and Broadway-style musicals and drama is one of the state's finest. In addition to the Asolo Theatre, a 19th-century Italian court playhouse moved here from Asolo, Italy, in the 1950s by the Ringlings, the center uses the 487-seat Harold E. and Ethel M. Mertz Theatre, originally constructed in Scotland in 1900 and transferred piece by piece to Sarasota in 1987. The 161-seat Asolo Conservatory Theatre was later added as a smaller venue for experimental and alternative offerings. The complex is under the direction of Florida State University (FSU).

The city's other prime venue is the lavender, seashell-shaped **Van Wezel Performing Arts Hall** ★★★, 777 N. Tamiami Trail (U.S. 41), at 9th Street (✆ **800/826-9303** or 941/953-3368; www.vanwezel.org). Recently renovated, it offers excellent visual and acoustic conditions, and a wide range of year-round programming, including touring Broadway shows and visiting orchestras and dance troupes. It and the FSU Center host performances by the **Florida West Coast Symphony** (✆ **941/953-4252;** www.fwcs.org), the **Jazz Club of Sarasota** (✆ **941/366-1552** or 316-9207; www.jazzclubsarasota.com), the **Sarasota Pops** (✆ **941/795-7677**), and the **Sarasota Ballet** (✆ **800/361-8388** or 941/351-8000; www.sarasotaballet.org).

Downtown Sarasota's theater district is home to the **Florida Studio Theatre,** 1241 N. Palm Ave., at Cocoanut Avenue (✆ **941/366-9000;** www.fst2000.org), which has contemporary performances from December to August, including a New Play Festival in May. Built in 1926 as the Edwards Theater, the **Opera House,** 61 N. Pineapple Ave., between Main and 1st streets (✆ **941/366-8450;** www.sarasotaopera.org), presents classical operas (in their original languages) as well as highbrow concerts. Next door to the Opera House, the **Golden Apple Dinner Theatre,** 25 N. Pineapple Ave. (✆ **941/366-5454;** www.thegoldenapple.com), presents cocktails, dinner, and a professional Broadway-style show year-round. The non-Equity **Theatre Works,** 1247 1st St., at Cocoanut Avenue (✆ **941/952-9170**), presents musical revues and other works year-round.

THE CLUB & MUSIC SCENE You can find plenty of music to dance to on the mainland at **Sarasota Quay,** the downtown waterfront dining-shopping-entertainment complex on Tamiami Trail (U.S. 41), a block north of John Ringling Causeway. Just walk around this brick building and your ears will take you to the action. One of downtown's most popular places for a night out is **Mattison's City Grille,** 1 N. Lemon Ave. (✆ **941/330-0440;** www.mattisons.com). In Siesta Key Village, the **Old Salty Dog,** 5023 Ocean

Blvd. (✆ **941/349-0158;** www.theoldsaltydog.com), offers a fabulous selection of British ales and a lovely outdoor patio. Strolling St. Armands Circle provides for an entertaining night out, especially if you stop into some of the Circle's bustling bars and restaurants. Also on St. Armands Circle, the **Patio Lounge** in the Columbia restaurant (✆ **941/388-3987;** p. 402) is one of the liveliest spots along the beach strip, featuring live, high-energy dance music Tuesday through Sunday evenings. And on Siesta Key, the pubs and restaurants along Ocean Boulevard in Siesta Village have noisy rock-'n'-roll bands entertaining a mostly young crowd—**SKOB,** 5238 Ocean Blvd. (✆ **941/346-5443;** www.skob.com), is a major hot spot, featuring fabulous happy hours and live music nightly; or you can retire to the pleasant confines of the martini bar at **Blasé Café** (✆ **941/349-9822;** p. 447) for live jazz. On Longboat Key, it's the **Haye Loft** at **Euphemia Haye,** 5540 Gulf of Mexico Dr., at Gulfbay Rd. (✆ **941/383-3633;** www.euphemiahaye.com), command central for the cocktail set. Be sure to check out all the beach bars on Anna Maria Island and Bradenton Beach for some salty, sandy nights.

13

Walt Disney World & Orlando

by Laura Miller

When Walt Disney World first opened its gates to the public just shy of 40 years ago, I doubt anyone, even Walt himself, could have imagined the incredible transformation that followed in its wake. Orlando, once known only for its citrus groves and cattle ranches, has since evolved into a bustling international vacation destination. An extraordinary and diverse array of recreational activities, shopping and dining experiences, and world-class accommodations await those who visit, and the bonus is that it's all set amid the natural beauty of Central Florida.

Walt Disney World (WDW), practically a city unto itself at 47 square miles, is now home to four major theme parks; two water parks; an incredible shopping, dining, and entertainment complex; tens of thousands of hotel rooms; scores of restaurants; and, to top it all off—a cruise line all its own.

When **Universal Orlando** (consisting of two major theme parks; an entertainment, dining, and shopping complex; and three luxury resorts), **SeaWorld** (including Discovery Cove and Aquatica, SeaWorld's water park), and the handful of smaller players toss their wonders into Orlando's mix of diverse offerings, well, it can get quite overwhelming.

To save you from having to wade through the seemingly endless amount of information, we've included the lowdown on the area's best hotels, restaurants, and attractions throughout this chapter. You'll also find tips to help you plan and budget your vacation, making it not only easier to arrange, but we hope more affordable too.

Note: For a more in-depth look at WDW as well as Orlando's other offerings, check out Frommer's *Walt Disney World® & Orlando* as well as *Frommer's Walt Disney World® With Kids* (Wiley Publishing, Inc.).

1 ESSENTIALS

GETTING THERE

BY PLANE More than 50 scheduled airlines and several more charter companies serve more than 37 million Orlando-bound passengers who arrive at the **Orlando International Airport** (✆ **407/825-2001;** www.orlandoairports.net) each year. The best travel fares to Orlando are often available during the months of November, December, and January, excluding holidays (when fares go way up).

Southwest Airlines retains the lion's share of Orlando International's business with just over 21% of the flights in and out of the airport. **Airtran Airways** comes in a distant second with 11.5%, followed closely by **Delta** (which continues to operate individually even after its merger with Northwest) at roughly 11%. Additional carriers include **Air Canada, American, British Airways, Continental, JetBlue, Lufthansa, Northwest,**

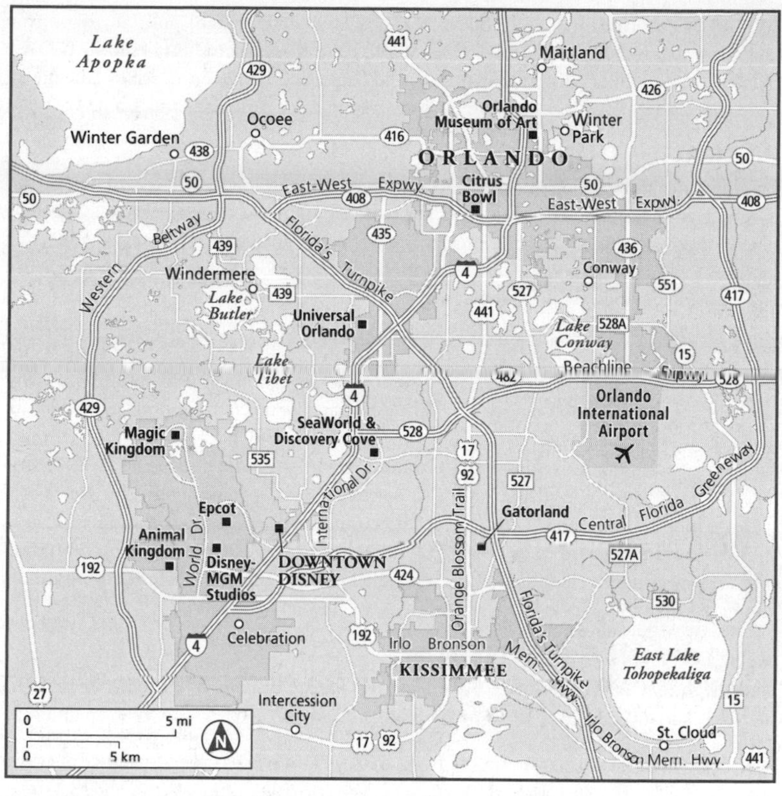

United Airlines, and **US Airways,** among many others. See "Appendix: Fast Facts, Toll-Free Numbers & Websites," p. 638, for airline contact information.

Located only 25 miles from Walt Disney World, Orlando International is a relatively easy drive from the area's most popular tourist destinations. If you're not renting a car, **Mears Transportation** (✆ **407/423-5566;** www.mearstransportation.com) provides town car and shuttle service to and from the airport; vans run 24 hours a day and depart every 15 to 25 minutes. Round-trip fares are $29 to $45 for adults and $23 to $36 for children ages 4 to 11 (actual price depends on your destination); children 3 and under ride free. **Quicksilver Tours and Transportation** (✆ **888/468-6939** or 407/299-1434; www.quicksilver-tours.com) provides town car, shuttle, and limo service along with such extras as meet and greet, luggage assistance, safety seats for the kids, and a 30-minute grocery stop included in the price. One-way shuttle fares run $75 to $80, round-trip $125 to $135, for up to 10 passengers. Rates vary depending on the destination and the type of vehicle.

BY CAR From Atlanta, take I-75 South to the Florida Turnpike to I-4 West. From the northeast, take I-95 South to I-4 West. From Chicago, take I-65 South to Nashville, then I-24 South to I-75, then south to the Florida Turnpike to I-4 West. From Dallas, take

I-20 East to I-49 South, then head south to I-10, east to I-75, and south to the Florida Turnpike to I-4 West.

BY TRAIN **Amtrak** trains (✆ **800/872-7245;** www.amtrak.com) pull into stations in both Downtown Orlando (23 miles from WDW) and Kissimmee (15 miles from WDW). Winter Park (10 miles north of downtown) and Sanford (23 miles northeast of Downtown Orlando) have stations as well; Sanford is the terminus for Amtrak's Auto Train.

PACKAGE TOURS

Finding a vacation package to Orlando is easy; it's picking the right one that can be difficult, given the assortment of services and options you have to choose from. Choosing wisely means you must determine exactly what you want ahead of time, whether that includes airline tickets, a rental car, accommodations, park tickets, dining arrangements, recreational activities, or all of the above.

If you plan to spend most of your time at Walt Disney World, contact **Walt Disney World Central Reservation Operations (CRO)** at ✆ **407/934-7675** for a wide assortment of packages. **AAA,** the American Automobile Association (✆ **800/222-6953;** www.aaa.com), is another good source for WDW packages. Another good place to look for packages is **www.mousesavers.com**—it's an "unofficial" site, but provides plenty of useful information and deals. **Universal Orlando** packages can be booked at ✆ **877/801-9720;** information is available online at **www.universalorlando.com**. For **SeaWorld** package information, call ✆ **800/557-4268** or go to **www.seaworldorlando.com**.

American Express Travel (✆ **800/732-1991;** http://travel.americanexpress.com/travel) offers packages that include special deals for their cardholders. Many of the major airlines also have Orlando packages.

VISITOR INFORMATION

The **Orlando/Orange County Convention & Visitors Bureau,** 8723 International Dr., Ste. 101, Orlando, FL 32819 (✆ **800/972-3304** or 407/363-5872; www.orlandoinfo.com), can answer questions and will send you an array of maps and brochures, including the *Official Vacation Guide* and a calendar of events. The packet takes a few weeks to arrive—be sure to request it far enough in advance—and includes the "Orlando Magicard," good for up to $500 in discounts on rooms, car rentals, attractions, and more. You can also order the guide by calling ✆ **800/643-9492.**

For information about **Walt Disney World**—including vacation brochures, CDs and DVDs—contact Walt Disney World, Box 10000, Lake Buena Vista, FL 32830-1000 (✆ **407/934-7639** or 939-6244; www.disneyworld.com). The website is an especially good bet; it's easy to navigate and provides detailed information and photos of the Disney parks, restaurants, and resorts. A very comprehensive unofficial website worth checking out is **www.allearsnet.com**. Another site filled with a wealth of information (covering not only Disney but the entire Orlando and central Florida area) is **www.travel-insights.com**.

For information about **Universal Orlando,** call ✆ **800/837-2273** or 407/363-8000; surf the Internet to **www.universalorlando.com**; or write to Universal Orlando, 1000 Universal Studios Plaza, Orlando, FL 32819.

You can obtain **SeaWorld** information online at **www.seaworld.com** or by calling ✆ **407/351-3600.**

CITY LAYOUT

Interstate 4 (I-4) will take you everywhere you want to go in and around Orlando, with several exits along the way to get you to Walt Disney World, SeaWorld, and Universal

Orlando, not to mention the areas of International Drive (or I-Dr.), Lake Buena Vista, and Kissimmee. ***Note:*** I-4 can often be jampacked with traffic—due in part to ongoing construction near the intersection of U.S. 192 near the Walt Disney World entrances. (When completed, the new roadways should alleviate much of the tourist traffic tie-ups currently plaguing the area.) Consult a detailed local map to find one of the many alternative routes best suited to your touring plans. If you must use the highway, it's least congested from late morning to midafternoon.

The Florida Turnpike crosses I-4 and links with I-75 to the north. U.S. 192, a major east–west highway, runs along Kissimmee's major motel area to U.S. 27, where it crosses I-4 near the Disney World entrance. The Beachline Expressway runs east from I-4 past Orlando International Airport to Cape Canaveral.

NEIGHBORHOODS IN BRIEF

Walt Disney World WDW is located just southwest of the actual city of Orlando. Encompassing more than 47 square miles, and practically a city unto itself, it includes within its boundaries four major theme parks, two smaller water parks, several themed resorts, and a plethora of restaurants and shops. It's also home of Downtown Disney (see below), Disney Quest, and the Wide World of Sports Complex.

Lake Buena Vista Lake Buena Vista encompasses all of WDW, and includes much of the area bordering the resort. Here you can find the "official" (but not Disney-owned) hotels set along Hotel Plaza Boulevard. The area along Highway 535, or Apopka-Vineland as it is also known, is home to many a resort and restaurant. Most, though not all, resorts, restaurants, and shops are set far off enough from the main thoroughfare to maintain a quieter atmosphere—making it one of the area's more popular places to stay.

Celebration This quaint 4,900-acre community of gingerbread trimmed houses, some with white picket fences and shade trees in the front yard, evokes Disney-esque perfection. It should come as no surprise that Disney had a hand in its creation—experts as they are at creating the perfect vision of almost anything. The Market Street area, filled with a charming collection of upscale shops, restaurants, even its own boutique hotel, is a throwback to a bygone era when a stroll around town was fashionable and fun.

Downtown Disney Though not actually a neighborhood, Downtown Disney is certainly large enough to be distinguished as such. It encompasses Disney's entertainment district (what remains of it following the demise of the Pleasure Island clubs) known as Disney's West Side, the shopping and dining district known as the Marketplace, and the newly "reimagined" Pleasure Island where upscale restaurants, new specialty shops, and unique attractions have begun to line the more tourist-friendly streetscape where nightclubs and bars once welcomed only those 21 and older. At Downtown Disney you can shop 'til you drop, tempt your taste buds, and take in a show all in a single stop.

Kissimmee Brought back to life by a multimillion-dollar "Rebeautivacation" project, U.S. 192, Kissimmee's main tourist area, sports extrawide sidewalks, colorful (and plentiful) streetlamps, landscaping, and location markers. Once home to mostly budget hotels, it now has a handful of moderate hotels, and even a few high-end luxury resorts, a myriad of eateries, and a handful of minor attractions. That said, U.S. 192 still remains frustratingly busy.

International Drive Area (Hwy. 536) This busy thoroughfare, better known as **I-Drive,** is home to more than 100 resorts and hotels, countless restaurants, attractions both big and small, and some of the best shopping around. It's even got its own transportation system—the I Ride Trolley. The endless array provides something for every taste and budget.

Downtown Orlando Actually located some 25 miles or so northeast of Walt Disney World on I-4, downtown Orlando has been revitalized by the addition of ultrachic eateries, trendy nightclubs, eclectic shops, and cultural venues (including theaters, museums, parks, and the visitor-friendly Orlando Science Center), and has reemerged as a center of new urbanism.

2 GETTING AROUND

In a city that thrives on tourism, getting from point A to point B is certainly easy enough, especially by car; it's the time it takes to get there that can wreak havoc on your schedule. What looks like a quick trip on a map, at times, can take what seems like forever. If you're traveling by highway, it's best to avoid the 7-day-a-week rush hour (7–9am and 4–6pm) whenever possible. Note that alternate routes can remain congested later into the evening thanks to the dinner rush.

Tip: Generally speaking, unless you will be confining your touring solely to Disney World or only to Universal Orlando (and staying at those parks' respective hotels), you're almost always better off renting a car in Orlando than using alternate methods of transportation. All the major rental chains have desks at or adjacent to the airport.

INTERNATIONAL DRIVE Traffic on I-Drive can be absolutely infuriating, compounded exponentially if you are visiting at one of the busier times of year (the 2 weeks surrounding both Easter and Christmas and during select conventions in the very early spring). Two of the best ways to conquer the traffic of I-Drive are to travel by foot (points of interest can be reasonably close together, but heavy traffic can be hazardous to pedestrians) or by the **I-Ride Trolley** (✆ **407/248-9590;** www.iridetrolley.com), which stops about every 2 blocks as it moves from one end of I-Drive to the other. The trolley runs from 8am to 10:30pm ($1.25 adults, 25¢ seniors, free for children 12 and under; *exact change is required*). Unlimited trolley passes covering between 1 and 14 days are available as well (the cost averages out to just over a dollar a day for the latter). It's a fun and easy way to get around that's often a timesaver when I-Drive is at a standstill.

BY THE DISNEY TRANSPORTATION SYSTEM If you plan to stay at WDW and spend most of your time there, an extensive, free transportation network runs throughout the WDW property. Disney resorts and official hotels offer unlimited free transportation via bus, monorail, ferry, or water taxi to all WDW properties throughout the day and, at times, well into the evening.

The free system saves you money on a rental car, insurance, and gas, as well as parking fees (though Disney resort guests get free parking). The drawback, however, is that you're at the mercy of the Disney departure schedules and routes, which can often be slow and sometimes *very* indirect (especially from Disney's cheaper resorts). Check Disney's official website (www.disneyworld.com), or ask your concierge to determine the best route available.

BY SHUTTLE **Mears Transportation** (✆ **407/423-5566;** www.mears transportation.com) operates town cars, vans, and buses that go to all of the theme parks, as well as the Kennedy Space Center and Busch Gardens Africa (yes, in Tampa), among others. **Quicksilver Tours and Transportation** (✆ **888/468-6939** or 407/299-1434; www.quicksilver-tours.com) offers similar services. Rates for both companies vary according to destination; call or check their websites for current prices.

BY TAXI Taxis gather at the major resorts, and smaller properties will be happy to call a cab for you. **Yellow Cab** (✆ **407/699-9999**) and **Ace Metro** (✆ **407/855-0564**) are both good choices, but keep in mind that taxis are expensive and charges may run as high as $3.25 for the first mile and $1.75 or more per mile thereafter.

Fast Facts Walt Disney World & Orlando

Babysitters Many Orlando hotels, including all of Disney's resorts, offer in-room babysitting services, usually from an outside service such as **Kids Night Out** (✆ **800/696/8105** or 407/828-0920; www.kidsniteout.com) or **All About Kids** (✆ **800/728-6506** or 407/812-9300; www.all-about-kids.com). Rates for in-room sitters usually run $13 to $16 per hour for the first child and another $2 to $3 per hour for each additional child. A premium fee of $2 per hour (not per child) is often added for services provided during unusually early or late hours. A transportation fee of approximately $10 to $12 is usually charged as well. Several resorts offer child-care facilities with counselor-supervised activity programs right on the premises, including, among others, select Disney resorts (for kids ages 4–12; ✆ **407/939-3463**). This type of child care usually costs between $10 and $15 per hour, per child. Reservations are highly recommended, and are often required for either type of service.

Business Hours Theme-park operating hours vary greatly depending on the time of year, even on the day of the week. While most open at 8 or 9am and close at 6 or 7pm, you should call or check a park's website for its most current schedule. Extended hours are usually in effect during summer and holiday periods. Other businesses are generally open from 9am to 5pm, Monday through Friday.

Doctors & Dentists There are basic first-aid centers in all of the theme parks. There's also a 24-hour, toll-free number for the **Poison Control Center** (✆ **800/282-3171**). To find a dentist, call **Dental Referral Service** at ✆ **800/235-4111** or go online to **www.dentalreferral.com**.

Doctors on Call Service (✆ **407/399-3627**) makes house and room calls in most of the Orlando area (including the Disney resorts). **Centra-Care** lists several walk-in clinics in the Yellow Pages, including locations on Turkey Lake Road near Universal (✆ **407/351-6682**), and Lake Buena Vista, near Disney (✆ **407/934-2273**). **East Coast Medical** (✆ **407/648-5252;** www.themedicalconcierge.com) offers similar services.

Emergencies Dial ✆ **911** for the police, the fire department, or an ambulance.

Hospitals **Sand Lake Hospital,** 9400 Turkey Lake Rd. (✆ **407/351-8500**), is about 2 miles south of Sand Lake Road. **Celebration Health** (✆ **407/303-4000**), located in the near-Disney town of Celebration, is at 400 Celebration Place.

Kennels The theme parks board pets during the day for $10 to $15 per day. WDW also offers overnight boarding ($15–$20 for the general public or $13–$18 for Disney resort guests—pets are not allowed to stay at the Disney resorts—the sole exception: select campsites at Disney's Fort Wilderness Resort & Campground) at each of its kennels. Universal Orlando's kennel is located in the parking garage ($10 per day, no overnight boarding). All of Universal Orlando's resorts welcome pets to stay with you right in your room. SeaWorld boards pets as well ($6 per day, no overnight boarding); the kennel is located near the park entrance.

Lost Children Every theme park has a designated spot where parents can reunite with lost children. Ask a park employee or check at guest services for details. Always instruct young children to talk to park personnel only if they get lost; children 6 and under should wear name tags on the *inside* of their clothing that have a contact phone number listed on them.

Pharmacies **Walgreens** (www.walgreens.com) operates a 24-hour drive-through pharmacy at 5935 W. Irlo Bronson Memorial Hwy. (U.S. 192; ✆ **407/396-2002**). It has another location at 12650 International Dr., in the Regency Shopping Center (✆ **407/238-5344**). Additional locations are listed in the Yellow Pages or on the website.

Post Office The post office most convenient to Universal is at 10450 Turkey Lake Rd. (✆ **800/275-8777**). It's open Monday through Friday from 9am to 4:30pm and Saturday from 9am to noon. A smaller branch, closer to Disney, is at 12133 Apopka-Vineland (S.R. 535) in Lake Buena Vista, just up the road from Hotel Plaza Boulevard (✆ **800/275-8777**).

Taxes In Florida, a 6% to 7.5% sales tax (depending on which local county you happen to be in) is charged on all goods, with the exception of most edible grocery-store items and medicines. Hotels add an additional 3% to 6% in resort taxes to your bill, so the total tax on accommodations can run up to 12%.

Telephone If you make a local call in Orlando, even to someone just across the street, *you must dial the 407 area code followed by the number you wish to call,* for a total of 10 digits.

Weather Call ✆ **321/255-0212** for the local weather forecast; or check out the Weather Channel at **www.weather.com** for the most up-to-date information.

3 WHERE TO STAY

There are more than 115,000 rooms in the Orlando area, with hundreds, sometimes thousands, added annually. Don't let that number fool you, however, as occupancy can be high much of the time. Even with the economy in a state of disarray, it's still a wise idea to book your room as far ahead as possible—especially if you're coming during peak season, generally around the holidays and in the summer. The lowest rates are usually available September through the first 2 weeks of December (excluding the week of Thanksgiving) and January through April (excluding the weeks of spring break).

WALT DISNEY WORLD CENTRAL RESERVATIONS OFFICE

To reserve a room or book packages at Disney's resorts, villas, campgrounds, and official hotels, contact **Central Reservation Operations (CRO),** P.O. Box 10000, Lake Buena Vista, FL 32830-1000 (✆ **407/934-7639** or 407/939-6244; www.disneyworld.com), or the **Walt Disney Travel Company** by calling ✆ **407/939-7675** for packages or 407/939-7429 for room-only reservations. They can recommend accommodations suited to your price range and specific needs, such as proximity to your favorite park or to those with supervised child-care centers. Though the people who answer the telephones can be very helpful and knowledgeable, they won't volunteer information about a better deal or a special, so be sure to ask.

DISNEY RESORTS

Very Expensive

Disney's BoardWalk Inn & Villas ★★★ Romantics and families alike will enjoy staying at this plush 1940s-style "seaside" resort. Here you will find an array of restaurants, shops, clubs, and carnival-style entertainment located along a quarter-mile boardwalk situated directly behind the resort, overlooking the water. The resort recaptures the spirit of Coney Island and Atlantic City back in their heydays. The BoardWalk's Cape Cod–style rooms comfortably sleep four, some featuring balconies. The priciest rooms overlook the boardwalk (most provide a good view of Epcot's nightly fireworks) and the pool; the less expensive rooms face the parking lot, but are sheltered from the activity and noise of the boardwalk below. Hang onto your swimsuit if you hit the pool's famous—or infamous, depending on how you look at it—200-foot "keister coaster" water slide. The BoardWalk's accommodations range from studios to grand villas that can comfortably sleep up to 12 people and have all of the comforts of home. All rooms are nonsmoking. Epcot and Hollywood Studios are only minutes away by walkway or water taxi.

2101 N. Epcot Resorts Blvd. (off Buena Vista Dr.; P.O. Box 10000), Lake Buena Vista, FL 32830-1000. ✆ **407/934-7639** or 939-5100. Fax 407/934-5150. www.disneyworld.com. 892 units, including 520 villas. $335–$825 double; $630–$2,715 suite; $335–$2,215 villa. Extra person $25. Children 17 and under stay free in parent's room. AE, DC, DISC, MC, V. Valet parking $10; self-parking free. Take I-4 to the Hwy. 536/Epcot Center Dr. exit and follow the signs. **Amenities:** 4 restaurants; grill; 2 lounges; 3 clubs; 2 outdoor heated pools; kids' pool; 2 lighted tennis courts; health club; Jacuzzi; bike and sporting equipment rentals; playground; arcade; concierge; WDW Transportation System; transportation to non-Disney parks for a fee; business center; limited Wi-Fi access (fee); shopping arcade; 24-hr. room service; babysitting; guest laundry; concierge-level rooms. *In room:* A/C, TV, dataport, high-speed Internet (fee), kitchen (in villas), fridge, hair dryer, iron, safe, washer/dryer (in villas), portable crib.

Disney's Contemporary Resort and Bay Lake Tower ★★ If location is one of your priorities, it's hard to beat this Disney resort, which is right beside the Magic Kingdom, and one of only three resorts **on the monorail system** (the Grand Floridian and Polynesian are the others). Both the Contemporary and the all new Bay Lake Tower offers great views of the Magic Kingdom as well as the Seven Seas Lagoon from its west side and Bay Lake from its east. The main resort, a 15-story concrete A-frame dates to WDW's infancy, though recent top-to-bottom renovations bring it into the modern era. Rooms now reflect an upscale Asian/retro look that should appeal to adults (the flatscreen TVs are fab and the color scheme very appealing—oh, and don't forget the in-room computers with free Internet and online concierge), and those with kids in tow will appreciate the rounded corners, kid-proof locks on the sliding doors (remember how high up you are here), and breakables placed high above a little one's reach. Notable

Walt Disney World & Buena Vista Accommodations

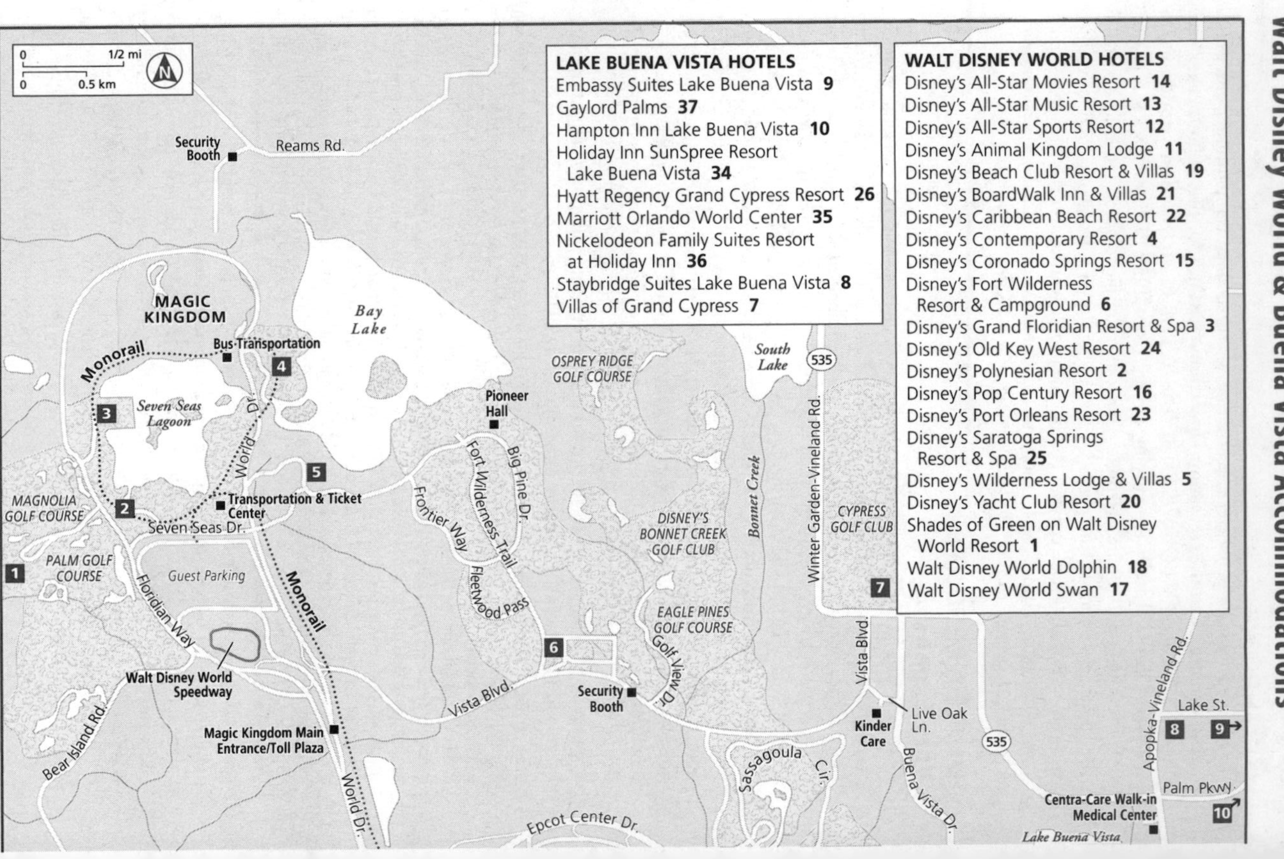

LAKE BUENA VISTA HOTELS
Embassy Suites Lake Buena Vista 9
Gaylord Palms 37
Hampton Inn Lake Buena Vista 10
Holiday Inn SunSpree Resort Lake Buena Vista 34
Hyatt Regency Grand Cypress Resort 26
Marriott Orlando World Center 35
Nickelodeon Family Suites Resort at Holiday Inn 36
Staybridge Suites Lake Buena Vista 8
Villas of Grand Cypress 7
WALT DISNEY WORLD HOTELS
Disney's All-Star Movies Resort 14
Disney's All-Star Music Resort 13
Disney's All-Star Sports Resort 12
Disney's Animal Kingdom Lodge 11
Disney's Beach Club Resort & Villas 19
Disney's BoardWalk Inn & Villas 21
Disney's Caribbean Beach Resort 22
Disney's Contemporary Resort 4
Disney's Coronado Springs Resort 15
Disney's Fort Wilderness Resort & Campground 6
Disney's Grand Floridian Resort & Spa 3
Disney's Old Key West Resort 24
Disney's Polynesian Resort 2
Disney's Pop Century Resort 16
Disney's Port Orleans Resort 23
Disney's Saratoga Springs Resort & Spa 25
Disney's Wilderness Lodge & Villas 5
Disney's Yacht Club Resort 20
Shades of Green on Walt Disney World Resort 1
Walt Disney World Dolphin 18
Walt Disney World Swan 17
0 1/2 mi
0 0.5 km
N
Security Booth
Reams Rd.
MAGIC KINGDOM
Monorail
Bus Transportation
Seven Seas Lagoon
World Dr.
Bay Lake
MAGNOLIA GOLF COURSE
Transportation & Ticket Center
Seven Seas Dr.
PALM GOLF COURSE
Guest Parking
Floridian Way
Walt Disney World Speedway
Bear Island Rd.
Magic Kingdom Main Entrance/Toll Plaza
OSPREY RIDGE GOLF COURSE
Pioneer Hall
Frontier Way
Fort Wilderness Trail
Big Pine Dr.
Fleetwood Pass
Vista Blvd.
DISNEY'S BONNET CREEK GOLF CLUB
Bonnet Creek
EAGLE PINES GOLF COURSE
Golf View Dr.
Security Booth
South Lake
535
Winter Garden-Vineland Rd.
CYPRESS GOLF CLUB
Vista Blvd.
Kinder Care
Live Oak Ln.
Sassagoula Cir.
Buena Vista Dr.
Epcot Center Dr.
Apopka-Vineland Rd.
Lake St.
Palm Pkwy.
Centra-Care Walk-in Medical Center
Lake Buena Vista

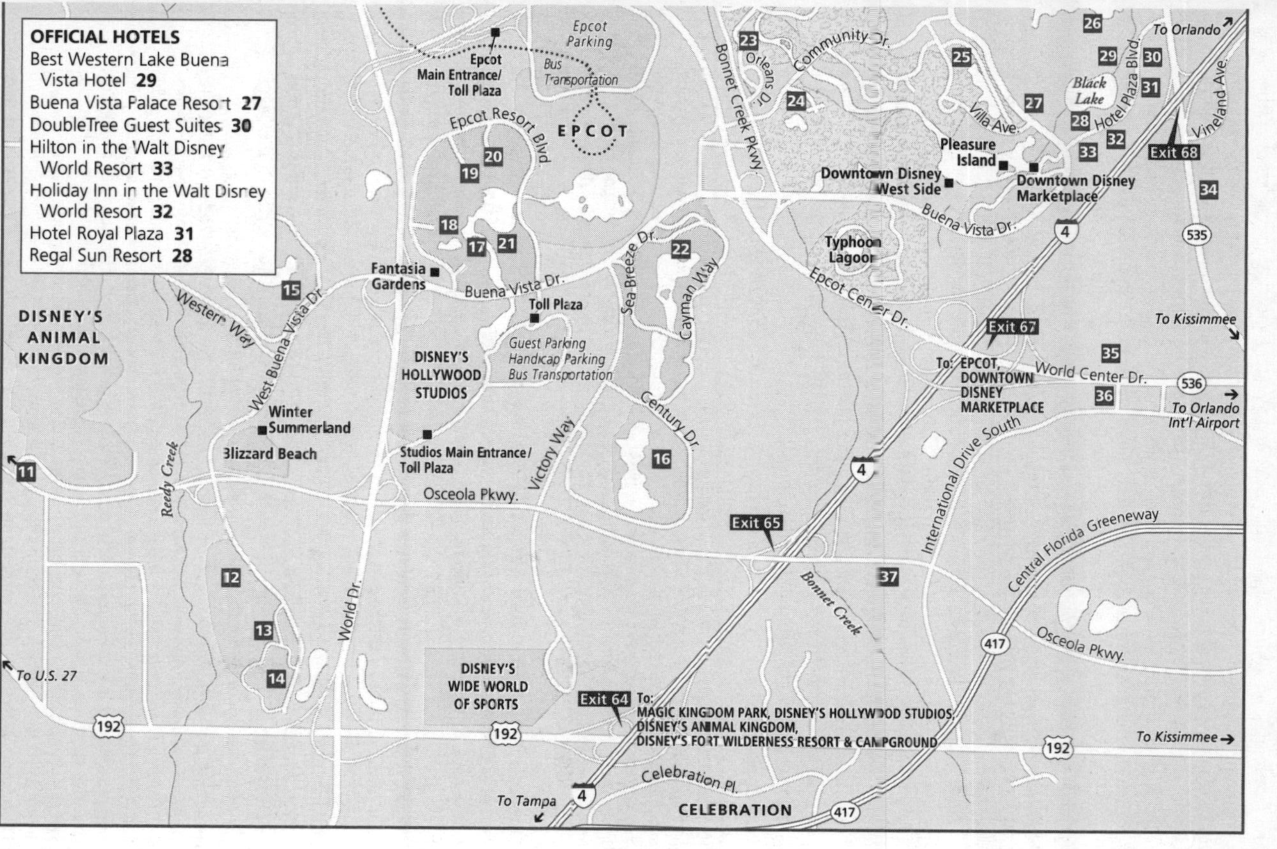
OFFICIAL HOTELS
Best Western Lake Buena Vista Hotel 29
Buena Vista Palace Resort 27
DoubleTree Guest Suites 30
Hilton in the Walt Disney World Resort 33
Holiday Inn in the Walt Disney World Resort 32
Hotel Royal Plaza 31
Regal Sun Resort 28
DISNEY'S ANIMAL KINGDOM
Epcot Parking
Bus Transportation
EPCOT
Epcot Main Entrance/ Toll Plaza
Epcot Resort Blvd.
Fantasia Gardens
Buena Vista Dr.
Toll Plaza
Guest Parking
Handicap Parking
Bus Transportation
DISNEY'S HOLLYWOOD STUDIOS
Studios Main Entrance/ Toll Plaza
Western Way
West Buena Vista Dr.
Winter Summerland
Blizzard Beach
Reedy Creek
World Dr.
Osceola Pkwy.
Victory Way
Sea Breeze Dr.
Cayman Way
Century Dr.
Bonnet Creek Pkwy.
Orleans Dr.
Community Dr.
Villa Ave.
Pleasure Island
Downtown Disney West Side
Downtown Disney Marketplace
Typhoon Lagoon
Epcot Center Dr.
Black Lake
Hotel Plaza Blvd.
Vineland Ave.
To Orlando
Exit 68
535
To Kissimmee
Exit 67
To: EPCOT, DOWNTOWN DISNEY MARKETPLACE
World Center Dr.
536
To Orlando Int'l Airport
International Drive South
Exit 65
Central Florida Greeneway
Bonnet Creek
417
Osceola Pkwy.
DISNEY'S WIDE WORLD OF SPORTS
Exit 64
To: MAGIC KINGDOM PARK, DISNEY'S HOLLYWOOD STUDIOS, DISNEY'S ANIMAL KINGDOM, DISNEY'S FORT WILDERNESS RESORT & CAMPGROUND
192
To Kissimmee
To U.S. 27
Celebration Pl.
To Tampa
4
CELEBRATION
11
12
13
14
15
16
17
18
19
20
21
22
23
24
25
26
27
28
29
30
31
32
33
34
35
36
37

changes to public areas include the addition of the Wave—a new full-service restaurant—and Contempo, an all new high-tech quick-service eatery sporting touch screens rather than menus. The pool, while far less spectacular than most, is large and has a wading pool for toddlers with a small beach area nearby. On the plus side, the rooms can fit up to five people instead of the usual four (though space will be tight). Kid-friendly facilities include a playground with a good-size sandbox and a decent arcade (which recently relocated to the main concourse). The best views are from the upper floors of the tower (ninth floor and up), where the rooms are a tad quieter than those on the lower floors, which are exposed to noisy public areas and the monorail (which runs right through the hotel). Come here for dinner at **Chef Mickey's** or the **California Grill** (p. 480), but if you have only very young kids, you may be better off checking into accommodations elsewhere.

Note: At press time construction was wrapping up on the resort's Bay Lake Tower—the newest member of the Disney Vacation Club resorts. Connected by a sky bridge to the existing resort (its restaurants, shops, and the monorail), the Tower sports a swanky rooftop lounge, a fireworks viewing deck, its own full-service restaurant (yet to be named), and lakeside zero-entry pool and water play area. Spacious public areas, accents of modern artwork, trendy suite-style rooms, and an innovative contemporary design add up to Disney chic from top to bottom.

4600 N. World Dr. (P.O. Box 10000), Lake Buena Vista, FL 32830-1000. ✆ **407/939-6244** or 407/824-1000. Fax 407/824-3539. www.disneyworld.com. 1,303 units. $280–$835 double; $910–$2,885 suite. Extra person $25. $375–$2,430 villa. Children 17 and younger stay free in parent's room. AE, DC, DISC, MC, V. Valet parking $10; self-parking free. **Amenities:** 3 restaurants; cafe; 2 lounges; 3 outdoor heated pools; kids' pool; fitness center; Jacuzzi; watersports equipment; arcade; concierge; WDW Transportation System; transportation to non-Disney parks for a fee; business center; limited Wi-Fi access (fee); salon; 24-hr. room service; babysitting; laundry service; concierge-level rooms; valet. *In room:* A/C, TV, dataport, high-speed Internet access (fee), kitchen (in villas), fridge, hair dryer, iron, safe, washer/dryer (in villas), portable crib.

Disney's Grand Floridian Resort & Spa ★★★ Finds As an orchestra plays in the background, the elegance of this turn-of-the-20th-century Victorian resort transports guests back in time to a bygone era. The crystal chandeliers that hang above the grand five-story domed lobby are just one example of the opulent touches you'll find throughout the resort. High tea is served in the afternoon. If you prefer, you can spend the day luxuriating at the spa, the best in WDW. The Grand Floridian is one of the most romantic resorts for couples, especially honeymooners, though families will appreciate the children's programs and extensive recreational facilities. The Victorian-style rooms sleep at least four; almost all overlook a garden, a pool, a courtyard, or the Seven Seas Lagoon. Located directly on the monorail system, the resort makes for a quick trip to the Magic Kingdom or Epcot. Note that all rooms are nonsmoking.

4401 Floridian Way (P.O. Box 10000), Lake Buena Vista, FL 32830-1000. ✆ **407/934-7639** or 824-3000. Fax 407/824-3186. www.disneyworld.com. 900 units. $399–$1,040 double; $1,050–$2,895 suite. Extra person $25. Children 17 and under stay free in parent's room. AE, DC, DISC, MC, V. Valet parking $10; self-parking free. Take I-4 to the Hwy. 536/Epcot Center Dr. exit and follow the signs. **Amenities:** 5 restaurants; grill; 3 lounges; character meals; heated outdoor pool; kids' pool; beach; 2 lighted tennis courts; health club; spa; watersports equipment; children's club; arcade; concierge; car-rental desk; WDW Transportation System; transportation to non-Disney parks for a fee; business center; limited Wi-Fi access (fee); shopping arcade; salon; 24-hr. room service; babysitting; guest laundry; concierge-level rooms; valet. *In room:* A/C, TV, dataport, high-speed Internet (fee), minibar, fridge, hair dryer, iron, safe, microwave (free upon request), portable crib (free upon request).

Disney's Polynesian Resort ★★ (Kids) One of only three resorts found on the Disney monorail line, the 25-acre Polynesian features extensive recreational areas, including a stretch of beach along a lagoon dotted with hammocks and palm trees, a volcano-themed swimming pool, and watercraft rentals. An on-site child-care facility makes it a good choice for those traveling with kids. Its landscaped and torch-lit walkways, along with its longhouse-style thatched-roof buildings, give the resort a South Pacific ambience. The entire resort recently underwent extensive renovations, and rooms now sport new, space-conscious furnishings, a muted earth-tone color scheme, and such upscale amenities as flatscreen TVs and refrigerators. Rooms can accommodate up to five people, and are all nonsmoking.

1600 Seven Seas Dr. (P.O. Box 10000), Lake Buena Vista, FL 32830-1000. ✆ **407/934-7639** or 824-2000. Fax 407/824-3174. www.disneyworld.com. 853 units. $355–$900 double; $610–$2,910 suite. Extra person $25. Children 17 and under stay free in parent's room. AE, DC, DISC, MC, V. Valet parking $10; self-parking free. Take I-4 to the Hwy. 536/Epcot Center Dr. exit and follow the signs. **Amenities:** Restaurant; cafe; 2 lounges; dinner show; character meals; 2 heated outdoor pools; kids' pool; watersports equipment; children's club; arcade; concierge; WDW Transportation System; transportation to non-Disney parks for a fee; shopping arcade; 24-hr. room service; babysitting; guest laundry; concierge-level rooms. *In room:* A/C, TV, dataport, high-speed Internet (fee), fridge, hair dryer, iron, safe, portable crib.

Disney's Yacht Club Resort ★★★ The posh, upscale, and nautically themed Yacht Club shares its extensive recreational facilities with its sister resort, the Beach Club, just next door. White sandy beaches and an immense, beautifully landscaped swimming area (with sand-bottom pools, water slides, and a life-size shipwreck to explore) line the lagoon side of the resort. The atmosphere is geared more toward adults and families with older children, although young kids are certainly catered to (this *is* Disney). The turn-of-the-20th-century New England theme can be felt throughout, as the public areas are filled with brass accents, nautical instruments, and a lighthouse to help you find your way home. Rooms have space for up to five people, and most have balconies. All rooms are nonsmoking. Epcot is just a short walk away.

1700 Epcot Resorts Blvd. (off Buena Vista Dr.; P.O. Box 10000), Lake Buena Vista, FL 32830-1000. ✆ **407/934-7639** or 934-7000. Fax 407/924 3450. www.disneyworld.com. 630 units. $335–$780 double; $610–$2,725 suite. Extra person $25. Children 17 and under stay free in parent's room. AE, DC, DISC, MC, V. Valet parking $10; self-parking free. Take I-4 to the Hwy. 536/Epcot Center Dr. exit and follow the signs. **Amenities:** 3 restaurants; grill; lounge; 2 heated outdoor pools; kids' pool; 2 lighted tennis courts; Jacuzzi; watersports equipment; children's club; arcade; concierge; WDW Transportation System; transportation to non-Disney parks for a fee; business center; limited Wi-Fi access (fee); shopping arcade; salon; 24-hr. room service; babysitting; guest laundry; concierge-level rooms. *In room:* A/C, TV, dataport, high-speed Internet (fee), minibar, fridge, coffeemaker, iron, safe, microwave, portable crib (free upon request).

Walt Disney World Dolphin ★★ If Antonio Gaudí and Dr. Seuss had teamed up on an architectural design, they might have created something like this Starwood resort (and it's adjacent sister, the Swan). The Dolphin centers on a 27-story pyramid with two 11-story wings crowned by 56-foot twin dolphin sculptures (the Swan has—no surprise—45-ft. swans). Not nearly as theme-intensive as the other Disney resorts, it's popular with business travelers and those who prefer their accommodations a bit less sugary. Rooms (all nonsmoking) feature a contemporary decor and the public areas are a bit more avant-garde, thanks in part to the dramatic lighting, an earth-tone color scheme, and upscale furnishings. Rooms comfortably sleep four (the Swan's are a tad smaller). The resort's grotto pool is lined by waterfalls, a water slide, and whirlpools; a small children's play area is close by. The Swan and Dolphin share a stretch of beach, a Body by Jake health club, a Mandara Spa, and a handful of restaurants including Todd English's bluezoo and Il Mulino New York Trattoria, as well as other trimmings. Epcot and Hollywood Studios are a water-taxi ride away. ***Tip:*** The beach next to the pool has a great view of Epcot's IllumiNations fireworks.

1500 Epcot Resorts Blvd. (off Buena Vista Dr.; P.O. Box 22653), Lake Buena Vista, FL 32830-2653. ✆ **800/227-1500** or 407/934-4000. Fax 407/934-4884. www.swandolphin.com. 1,509 units. $169–$579 double; $675–$4,300 suite. Extra person $25. Children 17 and under stay free in parent's room. Resort fee $10 per day. AE, DC, DISC, MC, V. Valet parking $16; self-parking $9. Take I-4 to the Hwy. 536/Epcot Center Dr. exit and follow the signs. **Amenities:** 4 restaurants; grill; 2 lounges; character meals; 4 heated outdoor pools; 4 lighted tennis courts; health club; spa; watersports equipment; children's club; 2 game rooms; concierge; car-rental desk; WDW Transportation System; transportation to non-Disney parks for a fee; business center; limited Wi-Fi access (fee); shopping arcade; salon; 24-hr. room service; massage; babysitting; guest laundry; concierge-level rooms. *In room:* A/C, TV, dataport, high-speed Internet (fee), minibar, fridge, hair dryer, iron, safe, portable crib (free upon request), Nintendo.

Expensive

Disney's Animal Kingdom Lodge & The Villas at Disney's Animal Kingdom ★★★ (Finds Enter this resort's grand lobby, with its thatched roof and ornate shield chandeliers, and you'll feel like you've stepped into a lodge in an African game preserve. The resorts kraal design (a semicircular layout), with many rooms overlooking a 33-acre savanna, allows guests an occasional view of the birds, giraffes, and other African animals that roam the savanna below. Families will appreciate the array of unique activities, including storytelling by the fire, sing-alongs, and more. Those in the mood for romance will appreciate the more remote and relaxed setting. Standard rooms are slightly smaller than at Disney's other "deluxe" resorts, but the distinctive theme and spectacular surroundings are unparalleled, making it well worth the slightly tighter squeeze. Vacation Club villas are available on the top floors of the Lodge for those needing additional room and homey amenities. In 2009, the Kidani Village opened it doors. Built adjacent to the existing lodge, the all new Vacation Club village features its own full-service restaurant (Sanaa, featuring African-inspired cuisine with an Indian touch), a themed pool and water-play area, and more. Boma (p. 480), one of Orlando's best and most unique restaurants, is a must, regardless of where you end up staying. The lodge and villas are adjacent to Animal Kingdom, but most everything else on WDW property is quite a distance away. Note that all rooms are nonsmoking.

2901 Osceola Pkwy., Bay Lake, FL 32830. ✆ **407/939-6244** or 938-3000. Fax 407/939-4799. www.disneyworld.com. 1211 units. $240–$555 double; $335–$2,215 villa. Extra person $25. Children 17 and under stay free in parent's room. AE, DC, DISC, MC, V. Valet parking $10; self-parking free. Take I-4 to the Hwy. 536/Epcot Center Dr. exit and follow the signs. **Amenities:** 4 restaurants; lounge; heated outdoor pool; kids' pool; health club; children's center; arcade; concierge; WDW Transportation System; transportation to non-Disney parks for a fee; shopping arcade; limited room service; babysitting; guest laundry; concierge-level rooms. *In room:* A/C, TV, dataport, fridge, hair dryer, iron, safe, portable crib (free upon request).

Disney's Saratoga Springs Resort and Spa and the Treehouse Villas at Disney's Saratoga Springs Resort and Spa ★★ The first phase of this Disney Vacation Club resort opened in May 2004, its final phase—or so we thought—in 2007. While lying idle and unoccupied for several years, Disney's Treehouse Villas were resurrected (and completely redesigned) in 2009—adding 60 new and very unique Vacation Club villas to the lineup. The main resort transports guests back in time to the heyday of upstate New York's 19th-century resorts. The resort town of Saratoga Springs is evoked through lavish gardens, Victorian architecture, and bubbling springs. The resort's main pool brings to mind its namesake's natural springs, with "healing" waters spilling over the rocky landscaping. The renowned spa provides an array of services and treatments meant to invoke the healing powers of Saratoga's springs themselves. Accommodations resemble those of the other Disney timeshare properties and range from studios that sleep four to grand villas that can sleep up to 12 people more than comfortably. The Treehouse Villas, unlike any other Vacation Club villa on-site, are elevated some 10 feet up off the ground by pedestals and beams, nestled amid the trees. Each three-bedroom "cabin casual" villa sleeps up to nine and features all the comforts of home along with such modern touches as cathedral ceilings, granite countertops, and flatscreen TVs. Downtown Disney is a short ferry ride across the lake, but getting to the parks will require a bit more effort.

1960 Broadway St., Lake Buena Vista, FL 32830. ✆ **407/827-1100** or 934-3400. Fax 407/827-1151. www.disneyworld.com. 888 units. $295–$425 studio; $390–$1,690 villa; $545–$900 treehouse villa. Children 17 and under stay free in parent's room. AE, DC, DISC, MC, V. Free parking. Take I-4 to exit 67; take Community Dr. to Broadway and follow the signs. **Amenities:** Restaurant; lounge; themed heated pool; kids' interactive pool area; golf; tennis; health club; spa; biking; boating; playground; arcade; free WDW transportation; limited room service; babysitting; guest laundry; barbecue areas; limited grocery delivery. *In room:* A/C, TV, VCR (in villas), dataport, high-speed Internet (fee), full kitchen (in villas), kitchenette (in studios), fridge, hair dryer, iron, safe, microwave, washer/dryer (in villas), portable crib.

Disney's Wilderness Lodge & Villas ★★★ The Wilderness Lodge is surrounded by a forest of towering pines, cypress, and oaks far away from the rest of Mickey's world. Beyond the "spring fed" pool, set amid the rocky landscape, a spouting geyser erupts periodically. The grand log-framed lobby is adorned by a mammoth stone hearth, two gigantic twin totem poles, and four massive tepee chandeliers, giving the resort an old-time national-park feel and making it a favorite of families and couples alike. Standard rooms at the lodge sleep four, while the villas just next door can accommodate up to 12. The decor is among Disney's best, and the restaurants have some of the most spectacular views in WDW. Though it's not that far from the Magic Kingdom, the bus ride to that park can be very long.

901 W. Timberline Dr. (on the southwest shore of Bay Lake just east of the Magic Kingdom; P.O. Box 10000), Lake Buena Vista, FL 32830-1000. ✆ **407/934-7639** or 938-4300. Fax 407/824-3232. www.disneyworld.com. 909 units. $240–$770 lodge; $835–$1,405 suite; $325–$1,155 villa. Extra person $25. Children 17 and under stay free in parent's room. AE, DC, DISC, MC, V. Valet parking $10; self-parking free. Take I-4 to the Hwy. 536/Epcot Center Dr. exit and follow the signs. **Amenities:** 2 restaurants; 2 lounges; heated outdoor pool; kids' pool; 2 Jacuzzis; watersports equipment; children's club; arcade; WDW Transportation System; transportation to non-Disney parks for a fee; limited room service; babysitting; guest laundry; nonsmoking rooms; concierge-level rooms. *In room:* A/C, TV, dataport, high-speed Internet (fee), full kitchen (in villas), kitchenette (in villa studios), fridge, hair dryer, iron, safe, microwave, washer/dryer (in villas), portable crib (free upon request).

Moderate

Disney's Port Orleans Resort ★ Value Made up of two separate sections, each with a distinctive Southern theme, Port Orleans has the best landscaping and coziest atmosphere of Disney's moderate resorts. The **French Quarter** reflects the charm of New Orleans at the turn of the 20th century, with obvious accents of Mardi Gras; **Riverside,** filled with grand mansions and back bayous, is reflective of the Old South. The dragon-themed Doubloon Lagoon pool, the Ol' Man Island swimming hole, and a nearby playground are a hit with kids. Guest rooms are large enough for four, but it'll be a tight fit. (Bayou Rooms have a trundle bed, offering room for an extra child.) Its central location is just east of Epcot and Disney's Hollywood Studios; there's boat service to Downtown Disney.

2201 Orleans Dr. (off Bonnet Creek Pkwy.; P.O. Box 10000), Lake Buena Vista, FL 32830-1000. ✆ **407/934-7639** or 934-5000. Fax 407/934-5353. www.disneyworld.com. 3,056 units. $149–$249 double. Extra person

$15. Children 17 and under stay free in parent's room. AE, DC, DISC, MC, V. Free parking. Take I-4 to the Hwy. 536/Epcot Center Dr. exit and follow the signs. **Amenities:** 2 restaurants; grill/food court; 2 lounges; 6 heated outdoor pools; 2 kids' pools; Jacuzzi; watersports equipment/rentals; playground; 2 arcades; WDW Transportation System; transportation to non-Disney parks for a fee; limited room service; babysitting; guest laundry; nonsmoking rooms. *In room:* A/C, TV, dataport, high-speed Internet access (fee), fridge, hair dryer, iron, safe, portable crib (free upon request), trundle bed (fee, upon request at the French Quarter).

Inexpensive

Disney's All-Star Music Resort (Value) Oversize instruments are scattered about the grounds—explained by the musical motif that runs throughout this resort. From calypso to country, you'll find it all here. As at all of the Disney value resorts, standard rooms are on the small side and lacking in frills. But thanks to a recent redesign, two-bedroom suites—ensuring that budget-conscious families with more than two kids can still stay at Disney without breaking the bank—are available too. It's these family suites that set this resort apart. The suites, which sleep up to six, feature upgraded amenities, including two full bathrooms, a separate master bedroom, flatscreen TVs, and a kitchenette with a small fridge and a microwave.

Note: Disney has two additional All-Star resorts—the All-Star Movies Resort and the All-Star Sports Resort—both identical to the Disney's All-Star Music Resort where it counts (like standard room size and layout—but no suites). The only real difference is the theme: One sports an athletic theme, the other features movies (of the Disney variety, of course). Any of the All-Star resorts are a good choice for the budget-conscious family who wants to stay on Disney property—but they're located out in the Disney boonies, so a car is almost a must. The closest park is Animal Kingdom.

1701 W. Buena Vista Dr. (at World Dr. and Osceola Pkwy.; P.O. Box 10000), Lake Buena Vista, FL 32830-1000. ✆ **407/939-6000.** Fax 407/939-7333. www.disneyworld.com. 1,706 units. $82–$160 double; $184–$327 suite. Extra person $10. Children 17 and under stay free in parent's room. AE, DC, DISC, MC, V. Free parking. Take I-4 to the Hwy. 536/Epcot Center Dr. exit and follow the signs. **Amenities:** Food court; lounge; 2 heated outdoor pools; kids' pool; arcade; WDW Transportation System; transportation to non-Disney parks for a fee; limited room service; babysitting; guest laundry; nonsmoking rooms. *In room:* A/C, TV, dataport, fridge (upon request for a fee in standard rooms; included in family suites), safe, portable crib (free upon request in standard rooms, included in family suites).

Disney's Pop Century Resort (Value) Gigantic memorabilia from decades past—remember the eight-track and Rubik's Cube?—mark the exteriors at Disney's newest value resort. While there might not be a lot of frills, the price is right for families on a budget who want to bunk with Mickey. The guest rooms and bathrooms—just like those at Disney's All-Star properties—are tiny, but will work for a family of four with a bit of concerted effort. The resort is closest to the Wide World of Sports Complex.

1050 Century Dr. (off Osceola Pkwy; P.O. Box 10000), Lake Buena Vista, FL 32830-1000. ✆ **407/938-4000** or 939-6000. Fax 407/938-4040. www.disneyworld.com. 2,880 units. $82–$160 double. Extra person $10. Children 17 and under stay free in parent's room. AE, DC, DISC, MC, V. Free parking. Take I-4 to exit 65, make a right on Victory Way followed by a right onto Century Dr., which takes you to the resort. **Amenities:** Food court; lounge; 2 heated outdoor pools; kids' pool; arcade; WDW Transportation System; transportation to non-Disney parks for a fee; limited room service; babysitting; guest laundry; nonsmoking rooms. *In room:* A/C, TV, dataport, fridge (upon request for a fee), safe, portable crib (free upon request).

Roughing It, Disney Style

Disney's Fort Wilderness Resort & Campground ★ Pine trees, cypress trees, and fish-filled lakes and streams surround this woodsy 780-acre camping resort. The closest park is the Magic Kingdom, which you can reach by boat. If you're a true outdoors

Check-In Made Easy

In an effort to make check-in a bit easier, Disney is now offering resort guests the option of checking in ahead of time—allowing them to skip the long lines often encountered upon arrival at Disney's various resorts. Simply go online within 10 days of your arrival date, enter the requested check-in information and advise the resort of your arrival time. You can also make room requests at this time should you have any (keeping in mind that requests are not guaranteed). You'll need to register the names of all the people in your party and provide a credit card to cover any WDW resort charges. Upon arrival at the resort, simply head to the special welcome area where you'll find your room keys and other registration material waiting for you.

type, you'll enjoy the breath of fresh air away from the hustle and bustle of the parks. There are 110- to 220-volt outlets, grills, and comfort stations with private showers and restrooms. Tents and RVs are welcome. The 409 cabins sleep up to six and have many of the comforts of home, with full kitchens and daily housekeeping service. The wide variety of outdoor recreational activities just adds to the appeal of this resort. Standouts include a Segway tour, the all new Archery Experience, nightly campfires, and movies under the stars. It is also home to the *Hoop De Doo Musical Review* dinner show (p. 510) and Mickey's Backyard Barbeque (offered seasonally).

Some sites are open to pets—at a cost of $5 per site, *not* per pet—which is cheaper than using the WDW overnight kennel, where you pay $13 to $18 per pet.

3520 N. Fort Wilderness Trail (P.O. Box 10000), Lake Buena Vista, FL 32830-1000. ✆ **407/934-7639** or 824-2900. Fax 407/824-3508. www.disneyworld.com. 784 campsites, 409 wilderness cabins. Campsite $43–$116 double; wilderness cabin $265–$410 double. Extra person $2 for campsite, $5 for cabin. Children 17 and under stay free in parent's room. AE, DC, DISC, MC, V. Free parking. Take I-4 to the Hwy. 536/ Epcot Center Dr. exit and follow the signs. Pets $13–$18 per night at the onsite kennel. **Amenities:** 2 restaurants; grill; lounge; 2 heated outdoor pools; kids' pool; 2 lighted tennis courts; watersports equipment/rentals; 2 game rooms; WDW Transportation System; transportation to non-Disney parks for a fee; limited Wi-Fi access (fee); babysitting; guest laundry; nonsmoking cabins; outdoor activities (fishing, horseback and hay rides, campfires). *In room:* A/C, TV/VCR, dataport (in cabins), kitchen, fridge, coffeemaker, hair dryer (in cabins), microwave, portable crib (free in cabins upon request), outdoor grill.

LAKE BUENA VISTA/OFFICIAL HOTELS

The "official" Disney hotels, though not owned and operated by Disney, line Hotel Plaza Boulevard, on the northeast side of Disney property and adjacent to Downtown Disney. Guests can enjoy some of the perks of staying in a WDW resort (free transportation to the Disney parks, among others) while staying in a location somewhat more central to the rest of Orlando's offerings. You can reserve a room through **Central Reservations Operations** (✆ **407/934-7639**), but it's best to call (or check online) the individual hotel or parent chain to check for special deals and packages.

Expensive

Buena Vista Palace ★★ The most upscale of the "official" properties, popular with business and leisure travelers alike, now sports a chic and trendy new look. Recently renovated guest rooms sleep at least four—corner rooms feature a bit of extra space. Many have balconies or patios; ask for one above the fifth floor with a "recreation view" facing the pools and Downtown Disney. Recreation Island is home to the resort's three pools (one partially indoors), game center, playground, tennis courts, beach volleyball, and the Island Suites. The resort is well known for its full-service, European-style Golden Door spa. Downtown Disney's numerous shopping, dining, and entertainment venues are just across the road.

1900 Buena Vista Dr. (just north of Hotel Plaza Blvd.; P.O. Box 22206), Lake Buena Vista, FL 32830. ✆ **866/397-6516** or 407/827-2727. Fax 407/827-6034. www.buenavistapalace.com or www.downtowndisneyhotels.com. 1,012 units. $99–$278 double; $219–$450 suite. Extra person $20. Children 17 and under stay free in parent's room. AE, DC, DISC, MC, V. Valet parking $16; self-parking free. From I-4, take the Hwy. 535/Apopka-Vineland Rd. exit north to Hotel Plaza Blvd. and go left. At 1st stoplight, turn right onto Buena Vista Dr. It's the 1st hotel on the right. **Amenities:** 3 restaurants; 3 lounges; character brunch; 3 heated outdoor pools; kids' pool; 1 tennis court; spa; Jacuzzi; sauna; arcade; playground; concierge; car-rental desk; complimentary bus service to WDW parks; transportation to non-Disney parks for a fee; business center; 24-hr. room service; massage; babysitting; guest laundry; nonsmoking rooms; valet. *In room:* A/C, TV w/pay movies, dataport, high-speed Internet access; limited Wi-Fi (fee), minibar, fridge, coffeemaker, hair dryer, iron, safe, game system.

Moderate

Note: Accommodations in this category are usually a step above the "moderate" resorts located inside WDW.

DoubleTree Guest Suites in the Walt Disney World Resort ★ (Kids) Children get their own check-in desk and a gift upon arrival at this hotel, which is the best of the official hotels for families traveling with little ones. All of the accommodations in this seven-story hotel are two-room suites, large by most standards (with space for up to six), and include all the comforts of home. Be sure to sample the cookies given to guests at check-in, a tasty tradition at the DoubleTree properties. It's the farthest "official" hotel from Downtown Disney, but a bus is available for those not quite up to the lengthy though pleasant walk.

2305 Hotel Plaza Blvd. (just west of Hwy. 535/Apopka-Vineland Rd.), Lake Buena Vista, FL 32830. ✆ **800/222-8733** or 407/934-1000. Fax 407/934-1011. www.downtowndisneyhotels.com or www.doubletreeguestsuites.com. 229 units. $110–$310 double. Extra person $20. Children 17 and under stay free in parent's room. AE, DC, DISC, MC, V. Free parking. From I-4, take the Hwy. 535/Apopka-Vineland Rd. exit north to Hotel Plaza Blvd. and go left. It's the 1st hotel on the left. **Amenities:** Restaurant; 2 lounges; heated outdoor pool; kids' pool; 2 lighted tennis courts; fitness center; playground; game room; arcade; concierge; car-rental desk; complimentary bus service to WDW parks; transportation to non-Disney parks for a fee; Disney gift shop; minimarket; limited room service; valet; guest laundry; nonsmoking rooms; theater; volleyball. *In room:* A/C, 2 TVs, dataport, fridge, coffeemaker, hair dryer, iron, safe, microwave, video games.

The Hilton in the Walt Disney World Resort ★★ This resort's major claim to fame: It's the only official resort on Hotel Plaza Boulevard to offer guests Disney's Extra Magic Hour option (see p. 486 for details). The hotel's vast array of guest services, numerous dining options, upscale yet friendly atmosphere, and prime location across from Downtown Disney, makes it one of best bets on the boulevard. The recently renovated rooms sport an upscale and contemporary Shaker-style decor; junior suites, featuring sleeper sofas, are more spacious and a better option for families. Rooms on the upper three floors (on the boulevard side—or front side of the resort) offer a glimpse of Disney's nightly fireworks displays as well as a good view of Downtown Disney.

1751 Hotel Plaza Blvd., Lake Buena Vista, FL 32830. ✆ **407/827-4000.** Fax 407/827-6369. www.hilton.com. 814 units. $99–$279 double. Extra person $20. Children 17 and under stay free in parent's room. AE, DC, DISC, MC, V. Valet parking $15; self-parking $8. From I-4 take exit 68, turn right onto S.R. 535, then left onto Hotel Plaza Blvd. Follow the boulevard, and the resort is near the end on the left. **Amenities:** 4

restaurants; 3 lounges; character breakfast; 2 outdoor heated pools; whirlpool; game room; concierge; car rental; complimentary bus service to WDW parks; transportation to non-Disney parks for a fee; business center; shops; minimarket; salon; 24-hr. room service; babysitting; valet; concierge-level rooms. *In room:* A/C, TV, dataport, high-speed Internet access (fee), Wi-Fi access (fee), minibar, fridge (fee), coffeemaker, hair dryer, iron, microwave (fee), video games.

Hotel Royal Plaza ★ The Royal Plaza is one of the boulevard's original hotels, but periodic renovations throughout its 25-year history (including a multimillion-dollar overhaul in 2006) have ensured it remains one of the best. A favorite with the budget-minded, its hallmark is a friendly staff, many of whom have been here since the hotel opened. The nicely decorated rooms, now sporting all new furnishings and decor (pull-out sofas and plasma TVs are now standard in every room) are of good size, with enough space for five. Poolside rooms have balconies and patios. Tower rooms have separate sitting areas, and some have whirlpool tubs in the bathrooms. If you want a view from up high, ask for a room facing west toward WDW.

1905 Hotel Plaza Blvd. (btw. Buena Vista Dr. and Hwy. 535/Apopka Vineland Rd.), Lake Buena Vista, FL 32830. ✆ **800/248-7890** or 407/828-2828. Fax 407/827-6338. www.downtowndisneyhotels.com or www.royalplaza.com. 394 units. $129–$209 double; $189–$269 suite. Children 17 and under stay free in parent's room. AE, DC, DISC, MC, V. Valet parking $16; self-parking free. From I-4, take the Hwy. 535/Apopka-Vineland Rd. exit north to Hotel Plaza Blvd. and go left. It's the 2nd hotel on the left. **Amenities:** Restaurant; lounge; heated outdoor pool; 2 lighted tennis courts; fitness center; whirlpool; children's activity program; guest-services desk; complimentary bus service to WDW parks; transportation to non-Disney parks for a fee; Disney gift shop; limited room service; babysitting; valet; guest laundry; nonsmoking rooms. *In room:* A/C, TV, dataport, high-speed Internet access (fee), Wi-Fi (fee), minibar, coffeemaker, hair dryer, iron, safe, video games.

OTHER LAKE BUENA VISTA HOTELS

The hotels in this section are within a few minutes' drive of the WDW parks, offering the location but not the privileges of a stay at an "official" hotel.

Very Expensive

Gaylord Palms ★★★ Finds It's the most extensively themed resort outside of Disney's not-so-little world. Practically a destination unto itself, the resort offers its own entertainment, fabulous themed dining, shops, recreational facilities, and a Canyon Ranch Spa Club for working out the kinks from the day's activities. The 4½-acre octagonal Grand Atrium, topped by an impressive glass dome, surrounds a replica of the Castillo de San Marcos, a Spanish fort located in St. Augustine. Waterfalls, lush foliage, live alligators, cobblestone walkways, and a rocky landscape complete the setting. The Emerald Bay, a 362-room hotel within the hotel, has the most elegant air about it, while other themed areas include Key West, St. Augustine, and the Everglades. The rooms are spacious, beautifully decorated, and well appointed, each with a balcony overlooking the interior Floridian landscapes. The service is impeccable, extremely friendly, and welcoming—not standoffish as at most other resorts of this class.

6000 Osceola Pkwy., Kissimmee, FL 34747. ✆ **877/677-9352** or 407/586-0000. Fax 407/239-4822. www.gaylordpalms.com. 1,406 units. $149–$269 double; $635–$2,700 suite. Daily resort fee $15. Extra adult $20. Kids 17 and under stay free in parent's room. AE, DC, DISC, MC, V. Valet parking $20; self-parking $12. Take the I-4 Osceola Pkwy. exit east to the hotel. **Amenities:** 3 restaurants; 4 lounges; 2 outdoor heated pools; fitness center; spa; children's center; concierge; tour desk; car-rental desk; free transportation to Disney parks; transportation to non-Disney parks for a fee; business center; shopping arcade; salon; 24-hr. room service; massage; babysitting; valet; guest laundry; nonsmoking rooms; concierge-level rooms; cabana rentals. *In room:* A/C, TV w/pay movies, dataport, high-speed Internet access, coffeemaker, hair dryer, iron, safe, PlayStation.

Hyatt Regency Grand Cypress Resort ★★★ Finds The guest list is multifaceted as this upscale resort appeals to honeymooners, families, and the business set alike. A redesigned lobby, slated for completion around the time this book hits the shelves, is more welcoming than ever thanks to a redesign of the front desk and the creation of unique and inviting seating areas (meant to encourage gatherings and get-togethers whether social or for business), including an all new Sushi Bar, where Chef Yoshi, a local celebrity of sorts, amazes onlookers and diners alike. The 18-story atrium has inner and outer glass elevators (ride the outer ones to the roof for a panoramic rush) and a recently redesigned skylight to top it all off. The rooms, large enough to sleep four, are also in the midst of major renovations, which, when completed, will sport an updated and trendy decor along with modernized amenities—some completely reconstructed from top to bottom. The addition of a full-service spa and all new dining options are also underway. The Hyatt shares a golf club and academy, racquet club, and equestrian center with its sister property, the Villas of Grand Cypress; both offer excellent packages aimed at the sports set. The Hyatt's half-acre, 800,000-gallon pool is one of the best in Orlando and features caves, grottoes, waterfalls, rope bridges, and a 45-foot water slide. ***Tip:*** Families in need of extra space can often get a great discount on a second room when booking connecting rooms.

1 N. Jacaranda (off Hwy. 535), Orlando, FL 32836. ✆ **800/233-1234** or 407/239-1234. Fax 407/239-3800. www.grandcypress.com. 750 units. $179–$509 double; $599–$5,750 suite. Optional daily resort fee $15. Extra person $25. Children 17 and under stay free in parent's room. AE, DC, DISC, MC, V. Valet parking $19; self-parking free. Take I-4 to the Hwy. 535/Apopka-Vineland Rd. exit and go north; then turn left at the 2nd light (after the ramp light) onto Hwy. 535. **Amenities:** 4 restaurants; 4 lounges; large heated outdoor pool; 3 golf courses; 12 tennis courts (5 lighted); health club; spa; watersports equipment; children's center; arcade; concierge; car-rental desk; free Disney shuttle; transportation to non-Disney parks for a fee; store; salon; 24-hr. room service; in-room massage; babysitting; valet; guest laundry; nonsmoking rooms; concierge-level rooms; equestrian center; 2 racquetball courts. *In room:* A/C, TV, dataport, high-speed Internet access (fee), Wi-Fi (fee), minibar, hair dryer, iron, safe.

Marriott's Orlando World Center ★★★ Golf, tennis, and spa lovers will find plenty to do at this 230-acre upscale resort, thanks to the wide array of recreational activities it offers (which also makes it good for families, though it welcomes a lot of business trade, too). The largest of its five pools has water slides and waterfalls surrounded by plenty of space to relax among the palm trees and tropical landscaping. The location, set back from the main thoroughfare, and only 2 miles from the Disney parks, is a fabulous plus. The large, comfortable, and beautifully decorated rooms sleep four, and the higher poolside floors have views of Disney. Discounts and special packages are often offered throughout the year, making this a more affordable option than at first glance.

8701 World Center Dr. (on Hwy. 536 btw. I-4 and Hwy. 535), Orlando, FL 32821. ✆ **800/621-0638** or 407/239-4200. Fax 407/238-8777. www.marriottworldcenter.com. 2,004 units. $349–$411 for up to 5; $750–$1,600 suite. Children 17 and under stay free in parent's room. AE, DC, DISC, MC, V. Valet parking $22; self-parking $13. Take I-4 to the Hwy. 535/Apopka-Vineland Rd. exit, go south 1 1/2 miles, proceed right/west on Hwy. 536, and continue 1/3 mile. **Amenities:** 4 restaurants; 2 lounges; 3 heated outdoor pools; heated indoor pool; kids' pool; 18-hole golf course; 8 lighted tennis courts; health club; spa; whirlpool; sauna; concierge; car-rental desk; transportation to all theme parks for a fee; business center; Wi-Fi (fee); salon; 24-hr. room service; massage; babysitting; guest laundry; nonsmoking rooms. *In room:* A/C, TV w/pay movies, dataport, high-speed Internet access (fee), minibar, coffeemaker, hair dryer, iron, safe, PlayStation.

Moderate

Nickelodeon Family Suites ★★ Finds Kids This all-suite property is the first-ever Nickelodeon-branded resort, and one of the best resorts in the Orlando area for families.

Its brightly colored Kid Suites feature a separate bedroom just for the kids (with either bunks or twin beds, TV, video game system, and more), minikitchens, and pullout sofas in the living areas. Three-bedroom suites (sporting a much trendier decor than smaller suites) include a second bathroom and a full kitchen. The lobby and mall area are filled with casual kid-friendly restaurants, an arcade, shops, and nightly entertainment venues (including Studio Nick and a new 4-D Theater). Kids love the Nickelodeon characters and color schemes (neon-Nick green and orange) that run throughout the resort. The resort's two pool areas are veritable water parks, with extensive multilevel water slides, flumes, climbing nets, and water jets. "Nick After Dark," an evening supervised activity program for kids ages 5 to 12, allows weary parents a night off on their own. Budget-minded parents will appreciate that up to four kids can eat for free per paying adult at the hotel's extensive breakfast buffet (not including the character breakfast).

14500 Continental Gateway (off Hwy. 536), Lake Buena Vista, FL 32821. ✆ **877/387-5437,** 407/387-5437, or 866/GO2-NICK (462-6425). Fax 407/387-1489. www.nickhotel.com. 789 units. $130–$1,050 suite. AE, DC, DISC, MC, V. Free parking. From I-4, take the Hwy. 536/International Dr. exit east 1 mile to the resort. **Amenities:** Restaurant; lounge; food court; character breakfast; 2 water-park pools; minigolf course; fitness center; kids' spa; 2 Jacuzzis; game room; complimentary recreation center for ages 4–12; tour desk; free shuttle to Disney, Universal Orlando, and SeaWorld parks; small business center; minimarket; coin-op washers/dryers; 3 outdoor Ping-Pong tables; 2 shuffleboard courts. *In room:* A/C, TV/VCR, dataport, high-speed Internet access (free), kitchen (in some suites), fridge, coffeemaker, hair dryer, iron, safe, microwave, Nintendo (in some rooms).

Staybridge Suites Lake Buena Vista ★ This member of the Staybridge Suites chain is located just off Apopka-Vineland, close to the action of Downtown Disney and the theme parks, as well as many restaurants, shops, and smaller recreational venues along Route 535. One- and two-bedroom suites come with full kitchens and all the comforts of home. The suites' separate living areas are larger and more comfortable than similar ones at other all-suite hotels. A nicely landscaped inner-courtyard is where you'll find the resort's pool—and plenty of space to soak up the sun.

8751 Suiteside Dr., Orlando FL 32836. ✆ **800/866-4549** or 407/238-0777. Fax 407/238-2640. www.sborlando.com. 150 units. $139–$299 2-bedroom suite (up to 8 people). Rates include continental breakfast. AE, DC, DISC, MC, V. Free parking. From I-4, take the 535 exit no. 68 and turn right. Follow the road to Vinings Way Rd. and turn right. The hotel is located on the left. **Amenities:** Outdoor heated pool; children's pool; exercise room; Jacuzzi; game room; guest services desk; high-speed Internet access; free shuttle to Disney parks; 24 hr. convenience store; 24-hr. guest laundry; nonsmoking rooms; suites for those w/limited mobility. *In room:* A/C, TV/VCR, high-speed Internet access, kitchen, hair dryer, iron/ironing board, safe, rollaway beds and cribs available (free)

ON U.S. 192/KISSIMMEE

This appealing, yet busy, stretch of highway within proximity of the Disney parks is lined with restaurants, shops, and smaller attractions. The hotels and restaurants here generally cater to the budget-conscious traveler. However, a few luxury resorts are beginning to sprout just a few miles to the south of the highway, making the mix a bit more diverse.

Expensive

Celebration Hotel ★★ This hotel is as picturesque as the town that surrounds it. Its three-story, wood-frame design is straight out of 1920s Florida, as is its very charming Old World interior. The hotel's public areas are filled with antiques and artwork, creating a warm and inviting, yet elegant atmosphere. Beautifully decorated rooms have views of either the lakefront or the Marketplace—both of which are postcard-perfect. The upscale ambience caters to adults, especially those seeking a romantic getaway. Free Wi-Fi is available in the lobby. The only drawback: You'll have to deal with the traffic on U.S. 192 to get almost anywhere.

700 Bloom St., Celebration, FL 34747. ✆ **888/499-3800** or 407/566-6000. Fax 407/566-6001. www.celebrationhotel.com. 115 units. $169–$369 for up to 4; $299–$469 suite. Daily resort fee $10. Extra person $20. AE, DC, DISC, MC, V. Valet parking $15; self-parking free. Take I-4 to the U.S. 192 exit, go east to the 2nd light, then go right on Celebration Ave. and follow the signs. **Amenities:** Restaurant; lounge; outdoor heated pool; 18-hole golf course; state-of-the-art health-and-fitness center; spa; concierge; free shuttle to Disney parks; transportation to non-Disney parks for a fee; nearby shopping district. *In room:* A/C, TV, dataport, high-speed Internet access, hair dryer, iron, safe, Nintendo.

The Omni at ChampionsGate ★★★ One of the latest luxury resorts to spring up just south of the Disney district in ChampionsGate, the Omni offers a comprehensive array of leisure facilities, including two championship golf courses designed by Greg Norman, a vast Grecian-style pool area with its very own lazy river, and a 10,000-square-foot European spa. The beautifully decorated rooms have 9-foot ceilings and plush amenities, including cozy bathrobes and free Wi-Fi access. Camp Omni is a program especially geared to youngsters (ages 3–14), so parents can get some relaxation time on their own.

8390 ChampionsGate Blvd., ChampionsGate, FL 33896. ✆ **888/444-6664** or 407/390-6664. Fax 321/677-6600. www.omnihotels.com. 730 units. $249–$329 standard; $450–$2,500 suite. Daily resort fee $16. AE, DC, DISC, MC, V. Valet parking $16; self-parking free. Take I-4 to exit 58, and bear right to the main entrance. Pets less than 25 lb. accepted ($50 fee). **Amenities:** 5 restaurants; grill; 3 lounges; 2 outdoor heated pools; 2 18-hole golf courses; 2 tennis courts; health and fitness center; spa; video arcade; Omni Kids Program; concierge; free shuttle to WDW parks; transportation to non-Disney parks for a fee; 24-hr. business center; shopping arcade; salon; 24-hr. room service; laundry service; valet; volleyball. *In room:* A/C, TV, Wi-Fi, minibar, hair dryer, iron/ironing board, safe, CD player, Nintendo, bathrobe.

Moderate

Comfort Suites Maingate East ★ Value Set back from the main drag, this welcoming hotel is one of the nicest in the area. The lobby and accommodations—consisting of studio and one-bedroom suites—are bright and inviting. The main pool and the children's pool, with an umbrella fountain to keep everyone cool, are open around the clock. Entertainment is a stone's throw away: Old Town (a small-scale shopping, dining, and entertainment complex) is just next door, and a great miniature-golf course is located in front of the property.

2775 Florida Plaza Blvd., Kissimmee, FL 34746. ✆ **888/782-9772** or 407/397-7848. Fax 407/396-7045. www.comfortsuitesfl.com. 198 units. $79–$250 double. Extra person $10. Rates include continental breakfast. Children 17 and under stay free in parent's room. AE, DC, DISC, MC, V. Free parking. From I-4 take the U.S. 192 E. exit; continue 1¾ miles, then turn right on Florida Plaza Blvd. **Amenities:** Outdoor heated pool; kids' pool; fitness center; game room; concierge; free shuttle to Disney, Universal, and SeaWorld; business center; guest laundry; nonsmoking rooms. *In room:* A/C, TV, dataport, free high-speed Internet access, fridge, coffeemaker, hair dryer, iron, safe, microwave.

INTERNATIONAL DRIVE AREA

The hotels and resorts listed here are 7 to 10 miles northeast of the Walt Disney World parks and 1 to 3 miles from Universal Orlando and SeaWorld, which makes this area the most centrally located for those who want to sample all that Orlando offers. The disadvantages: The northern end of International Drive is horribly congested (both on the road and off). The shops, motels, eateries, and attractions along this stretch can vary greatly in quality (some are decidedly tacky); as a general rule (with some exceptions), the closer you get to the convention center, the better the class of hotels and dining.

Very Expensive

Peabody Orlando ★★★ Finds The five mallards that march into a lobby fountain every morning at 11am and then back out at 5pm, accompanied by John Philip Sousa's *King Cotton March,* are just part of the appeal of this very upscale and service-oriented hotel. If your budget allows, you won't be disappointed with a stay here. Primarily a business and convention destination, the Peabody also appeals to adults looking for a classy hotel that provides top-of-the-line service, amenities, and atmosphere. Rooms sleep up to five, and are tastefully decorated and well-appointed. Those on the west side (sixth floor and higher) offer distant views of Disney and its fireworks displays. ***As a Note:*** As this guide went to print, a second tower was under construction and upon completion will add 870 additional guest rooms and suites, a full-service spa, a gourmet deli, a Napa Valley–wine-themed restaurant, a grotto-style pool, and a parking garage to the mix. Dux, the resort's signature restaurant, will remain closed during construction—it is, however, slated to reopen in January 2010 (prior to the Tower's opening in Nov).

9801 International Dr. (btw. Beachline Expwy. and Sand Lake Rd.), Orlando, FL 32819. ✆ **800/732-2639** or 407/352-4000. Fax 407/354-1424. www.peabodyorlando.com. 891 units. $297–$395 standard (up to 3 persons); $550–$1,775 suite. Extra person $25. Children 17 and under stay free in parent's room. AE, DC, DISC, MC, V. Valet parking $20. From I-4, take the Sand Lake Rd./Hwy. 482 exit east to International Dr., then go south. Hotel is on the left across from the Convention Center. **Amenities:** 4 restaurants; 3 lounges; outdoor heated pool; kids' pool; 4 lighted tennis courts; fitness center; spa; Jacuzzi; game room; concierge; shuttle to WDW and other parks for a fee; business center; shopping arcade; salon; 24-hr. room service; massage; valet; nonsmoking rooms; concierge-level rooms. *In room:* A/C, TV, dataport, high-speed Internet access (fee), minibar, hair dryer.

Renaissance Orlando Resort at SeaWorld ★★ A simple hotel exterior gives way to a beautiful and inviting interior at this resort, which is peppered with luxurious touches. A glass-covered atrium soars high above a stunning and chic indoor courtyard area filled with cascading waterfalls, a trendy lounge, and a sushi bar. The tastefully decorated rooms are oversize, providing plenty of space to spread out and relax. After extensive renovations to the pool area in 2006, the interior received a $20-million makeover that included the addition of a full-service spa in 2007. SeaWorld and Aquatica fans will appreciate the location—it's just across the street from both parks.

6677 Sea Harbour Dr., Orlando, FL 32821. ✆ **800/327-6677** or 407/351-5555. Fax 407/351-1991. www.renaissanceseaworld.com. 778 units. $195–$298 double. Children 17 and under stay free in parent's room. AE, DC, DISC, MC, V. Valet parking $16; self-parking $12. From I-4, take the Hwy. 528/Beachline Expwy. exit east to International Dr., then go south to Sea Harbor Dr. and turn right. **Amenities:** 3 restaurants; grill; 3 lounges; outdoor heated pool; kids' pool; golf privileges at nearby courses (fee); 4 lighted tennis courts; health club; spa; 2 Jacuzzis; sauna; arcade; playground; concierge; tour desk; car-rental desk; transportation to all the parks for a fee; business center; Wi-Fi (fee); shopping arcade; salon; 24-hr. room service; massage; babysitting; valet; guest laundry; nonsmoking rooms; basketball; volleyball. *In room:* A/C, TV, dataport, high-speed Internet access (fee), minibar, fridge (in some), hair dryer, safe, PlayStation.

Moderate

Hyatt Place ★ This modern and stylish property sports an inviting lobby—designed as the perfect spot for catching up on the news, surfing the Net on your laptop, or just grabbing a snack at the semi-self-service cafe. The chic and upscale decor carries through to the noticeably oversize rooms, where you'll find comfy bedding, a sleeper sofa, a mini-fridge, work desk, and 42-inch flat-panel TVs with plenty of space to spare. Self-service check-in and check-out kiosks offer an efficient alternative to standing in line at the front desk, and complimentary Wi-Fi (available throughout the hotel) keeps you connected without costing you a bundle. A free continental breakfast is part of the package, but for those with a heartier appetite, hot breakfast entrees are available (they'll cost you extra).

8741 International Dr., Orlando, FL 32819. ✆ **800/833-1516** or 407/370-4720. Fax 407/331-4721. www.amerisuites.com. 149 units. $99–$249 for up to 4. Rates include free full breakfast. Children 17 and younger stay free in parent's room. AE, DC, DISC, MC, V. Free parking. **Amenities:** Outdoor heated pool; exercise room; tour desk; laundry service. *In room:* A/C, TV, Wi-Fi, coffeemaker, hair dryer, iron, safe.

La Quinta Inn & Suites Convention Center This is one of a handful of upscale, moderately priced motels on Universal Boulevard, which runs parallel to (but isn't as congested as) International Drive. The hotel is aimed at business travelers, but families traveling with kids will find the accommodations comfortably equipped with all the necessary amenities. King rooms come with a fridge and microwave. A limited number of two-room suites provide separate living and sleeping areas.

8504 Universal Blvd., Orlando, FL 32819. ✆ **800/531-5900** or 407/345-1365. Fax 407/345-5586. www.laquinta.com. 184 units. $79–$159 double; $159–$179 suite. Extra person $10. Rates include continental breakfast. Children 18 and under stay free in parent's room. AE, DC, DISC, MC, V. Free parking. Take I-4 to the Sand Lake Rd./Hwy. 482 exit, go east toward Universal, then right. Small pets accepted. **Amenities:** Outdoor heated pool; exercise room; Jacuzzi; transportation to all theme parks for a fee; guest laundry; nonsmoking rooms. *In room:* A/C, TV, dataport, free high-speed Internet access, fridge (in king rooms), coffeemaker, hair dryer, iron, microwave (in king rooms), Nintendo.

Inexpensive

Fairfield Inn and Suites International Drive ★ Value If you're looking for I-Drive's best value, it's hard to beat the Fairfield. It has a quiet location off the main drag; earthly rates; and clean, comfortable motel rooms in one package. Some of the shops, restaurants, and smaller attractions that line I-Drive are within walking distance.

7495 Canada Ave. (off International Dr. near Sand Lake Rd.), Orlando, FL 32819. ✆ **407/351-7000.** Fax 407/351-0052. www.fairfieldinn.com. 200 units. $98–$106 for up to 4. Rates include continental breakfast. AE, DC, DISC, MC, V. Free parking. From I-4, take the Sand Lake Rd./Hwy. 482 exit east, then turn east onto Canada Ave. **Amenities:** Outdoor heated pool; game room; guest-services desk; transportation to the parks for a fee; valet; guest laundry; nonsmoking rooms. *In room:* A/C, TV, dataport, free high-speed Internet access, fridge (in some), hair dryer, iron/ironing board, safe, microwave (in some).

UNIVERSAL ORLANDO RESORTS

Universal Orlando has three unique and upscale themed properties of its own, all run by the Loews hotel group. Like the Disney resorts, Universal gives its resort guests additional privileges, including preferred access to the Universal parks' rides and attractions—show your room key and you will head right to the front of the line.

Portofino Bay Hotel ★★★ Universal's first hotel has the stature and magnificence of Disney's Grand Floridian. This romantic, upscale resort is designed to resemble the seaside village of Portofino, Italy, complete with a harbor and canals that lead you via water taxi to the theme parks. The stylish rooms sleep up to five. Ask for a view overlooking the piazza and "bay" area. For those with young children, a select number of Seuss-themed kids' suites were added in 2008. The Portofino doesn't just have swimming pools; its beach pool has a stone fort with a water slide, while the villa pool is lined with cabanas complete with laptop hookups, fridge, and TV for the perfect mix of business and pleasure. The resort's Mandara Spa includes a state-of-the-art fitness center and full-service spa. The drawbacks: There are stairs everywhere you turn, and the sheer size of the resort can make it difficult to find your way around.

5601 Universal Blvd., Orlando, FL 32819. ✆ **888/322-5541** or 407/503-1000. Fax 407/224-7118. www.loewshotels.com/hotels/Orlando or www.universalorlando.com. 750 units. $274–$559 double; $529–$2,500 suite and villa. Extra person $25. Children 17 and under stay free in parent's room. AE, DC, DISC, MC, V. Valet parking $22; self-parking $15. From I-4, take the Kirkman Rd./Hwy. 435 exit and follow the signs to Universal. Pets $25. **Amenities:** 4 restaurants; deli; 3 lounges; 3 outdoor heated pools (1 for concierge-level and suite guests only); kids' pool; fitness center; spa; watersports equipment; kids' club; playground; arcade; concierge; tour desk; free water taxi and bus transportation to Universal Studios, Islands of Adventure, and CityWalk; free shuttle to SeaWorld; transportation to WDW parks for a fee; business center; shopping arcade; salon; 24-hr. room service; babysitting; valet; guest laundry; nonsmoking rooms; concierge-level rooms. *In room:* A/C, TV/DVD, high-speed Internet access (fee), minibar, fridge, hair dryer, iron, safe, CD player, microwave (in suites), rollaway bed (fee), crib (free), video games (fee).

Expensive

Hard Rock Hotel ★★★ Kids You can't get any closer than this to Universal Studios Florida. Opened in 2001, this California mission–style resort sports a rock-'n'-roll theme with rates a shade less expensive than the Portofino's (above). The atmosphere is slightly more casual than those of its fellow Universal resorts, though with an air of chic sophistication. Public areas are filled with rock memorabilia, but it's the pool area that takes center stage—the large free-form pool's underwater sound system ensures that you won't miss a beat. Thanks to a recent multimillion-dollar renovation, the stylish and modern rooms now have flat-panel TVs, MP3 docking stations, and upgraded bedding. Unfortunately, though the units are fairly soundproof, a few notes seep through the walls, so ask for one away from the lobby area. If you're bringing school-age kids or teens, it's the best bet of the three Universal resorts. ***Tip:*** The Hard Rock is a cut above some of Disney's comparable properties.

5000 Universal Blvd., Orlando, FL 32819. ✆ **800/232-7827** or 407/503-2000. Fax 407/224-7118. www.loewshotels.com/hotels/Orlando or www.universalorlando.com. 650 units. $234–$519 double; $479–$2,020 suite. Extra person $25. Children 17 and under stay free in parent's room. AE, DC, DISC, MC, V. Valet parking $22; self-parking $15. From I-4, take the Kirkman Rd./Hwy. 435 exit and follow the signs to Universal. Pets $25. **Amenities:** 3 restaurants; grill; 2 lounges; outdoor heated pool; kids' pool; fitness center; kids' club; arcade; playground; concierge; free water taxi or bus transportation to Universal Studios, Islands of Adventure, and CityWalk; free shuttle to SeaWorld; transportation to WDW parks for a fee; shopping arcade; 24-hr. room service; babysitting; valet; guest laundry; nonsmoking rooms; concierge-level rooms. *In room:* A/C, TV, high-speed Internet access (fee), minibar, fridge, hair dryer, iron, safe, CD player, microwave (in suites), rollaway bed (fee), crib (free), video games (fee).

Royal Pacific Resort ★★★ Kids The third of Universal Orlando's three resorts features a spectacular beachfront lagoon-style pool. It's lined with palm trees, winding walkways, waterfalls, and an exquisite orchid garden, all giving it a remote island feel (apart from the screams emanating from the nearby Islands of Adventure). The rooms, smaller than those at other Universal resorts, are decorated with wooden carvings and accents, but are rather plain when compared to other Disney resorts. Recent renovations include the addition of Jurassic Park kids' suites—they feature a separate bedroom just for the kids complete with a flatscreen TV, twin beds, and a dino-themed decor. The public areas are quite impressive and well worth exploring. The addition of the Wantilan Luau Pavilion ensures the weekly luau is now held rain or shine. If you're traveling with young children, the Royal Pacific is the best choice at Universal.

6300 Hollywood Way, Orlando, FL 32819. ✆ **800/232-7827** or 407/503-3000. Fax 407/503-3202. www.loewshotels.com/hotels/Orlando or www.universalorlando.com. 1,000 units. $219–$459 double; $339–$1,950 suite. Extra person $25. Children 17 and under stay free in parent's room. AE, DC, DISC, MC, V. Valet parking $22; self-parking $15. From I-4, take exit 75B, Kirkman Rd./Hwy. 435 and follow the signs to Universal. Pets $25. **Amenities:** 2 restaurants; 3 lounges; outdoor heated pool; kids' pool; sauna; Jacuzzi; kids' club; arcade; concierge; free water taxi and bus transportation to Universal Studios, Islands of Adventure, and CityWalk; free shuttle to SeaWorld; transportation for a fee to WDW parks; babysitting; valet; nonsmoking rooms; concierge-level rooms. *In room:* A/C, TV, dataport, high-speed Internet access (fee), fridge, coffeemaker, hair dryer, iron, safe, microwave (in suites), rollaway bed (fee), crib (free).

4 WHERE TO DINE

From family-style restaurants to fast-food to five-star dining, Orlando has restaurants to please every palate and to bend to every budget. As most Orlando visitors spend the majority of their time at Disney, most of the dining options I list below can be found there, too. However, I do list plenty of other worthwhile restaurants, including some of the better places to eat at Universal and along International Drive.

ADVANCED RESERVATIONS AT DISNEY RESTAURANTS

"Advanced Reservations" *aren't* really reservations at all. They are simply a way of claiming the first table that becomes available (and can accommodate your party) close to the time of your choosing. You'll be given priority over any other diners who simply walked up in the hopes of getting a table without prior arrangements. There may still be a wait (usually 10–20 min.), but it will be significantly shorter than it would be if you simply walked in. If you don't make Advanced Reservations, especially for the most popular restaurants, you may miss out altogether, as they're usually booked well in advance, leaving little or no room at all for guests who decide to drop in. To make Advanced Reservations at any WDW restaurant (in the parks or at the resorts), call ✆ **407/939-3463.** You can book as far as 90 days (previously 180 days) in advance of your arrival for most restaurants (which may be necessary during the busier times of year, and is essential at the most popular restaurants).

Disney's **dinner shows** (by far, the most popular dining experiences at WDW) and Mickey's BBQ can also be booked 90 days in advance, but you must pay in full at the time of booking for these experiences.

If you're staying on Disney property and haven't made arrangements prior to coming, you can make Advanced Reservations at your resort. At Epcot, you can do it at Guest Relations near Innoventions East; at the Magic Kingdom, head to City Hall or the guest relations counter near the park entrance; and at Disney's Hollywood Studios head to Hollywood Junction for help. You can also go directly to the restaurant of your choice and make arrangements in person.

TIPS ON WALT DISNEY WORLD RESTAURANTS

All park restaurants (as well as all restaurants in Florida) are **nonsmoking.**

Magic Kingdom restaurants don't serve alcohol, but those at Animal Kingdom, Epcot, and Disney's Hollywood Studios do.

Sit-down restaurants in WDW take American Express, Diners Club, Discover, MasterCard, Visa, and the Disney Card.

Unless otherwise noted, *restaurants in the parks require park admission.* Unless you're using WDW transportation, there is a $12 parking fee.

Nearly all WDW restaurants with sit-down or counter service offer children's menus with items ranging from $5 to $9.

INSIDE THE WALT DISNEY WORLD THEME PARKS

For the most part, the food offered throughout the parks is fairly decent, though you won't find Disney's park restaurants winning accolades from *Food & Wine* or *Bon Appétit.* While portions are generally on the large side, so are prices. On the dining news front, children's entrees now include healthy options such as milk, veggies, and fruit (soda and fries are still available upon request). And all of WDW (theme parks and resorts) is transitioning to entirely trans-fat-free menu items. The following list includes Magic Kingdom,

Epcot, Disney's Hollywood Studios, and Animal Kingdom. You can get information on all Disney restaurants by calling ✆ **407/939-3463** or visiting **www.disneyworld.com**.

Epcot

World Showcase

The World Showcase has some of the best and most unique dining options inside the WDW theme parks, thanks to the cultural cuisine of its 11-nation pavilions. Although many consider a meal here an essential part of the park experience, I must point out that the food (as in all the parks) is priced higher than comparable fare in the free world, though of course you're paying for the atmosphere and architectural surroundings.

The restaurants below are arranged geographically, beginning at the Canada pavilion and proceeding counterclockwise around the World Showcase Lagoon. Note that the United States pavilion is not listed below; it's a burger-and-fries style counter service eatery. *Prices below are for entrees only.* For ratings of the pavilions' attractions, see "World Showcase," starting on p. 493.

CANADA **Le Cellier Steakhouse**'s vaulted archways, stone walls, and lanterns create a cozy and unique atmosphere much like that of a centuries-old wine cellar. While sandwiches and salads make for a meatier lunch than most, steaks are the main menu item at dinner, with a variety of cuts to choose from, including filet, porterhouse, and prime rib. Try one of the Canadian Ice Wines for a very sweet after-dinner treat. Lunch runs $12 to $31; dinner is $23 to $37.

UNITED KINGDOM The Tudor-beamed **Rose & Crown** is a cozy English pub where folk music and saucy servers entertain as you dine. The short menu has traditional British favorites, including fish and chips, bangers and mash, cottage pie, and warm bread pudding. Head over later in the evening for a pint of Bass ale or Guinness Stout, as the patio is one of the best places to see the IllumiNations fireworks display. Lunch is $13 to $19; dinner is $16 to $24.

FRANCE One of Disney's priciest park restaurants, **Les Chefs de France** has a glass exterior that's among the prettiest around. The interior, agleam with mirrors and brass chandeliers, is impressive as well. Three renowned French chefs can take credit for the menu, which includes such entrees as roasted perch with lobster mousse, potato scales on sautéed fennel with a lobster reduction, and grilled tenderloin of beef with a black pepper sauce, original potato gratin of Savoy, and green beans. Lunch is $12 to $20; dinner is $19 to $34.

MOROCCO Of all the Epcot restaurants, **Marrakesh** ★ best exemplifies the spirit of the park. However, guests often pass it by, worried the menu may be too exotic (it isn't). The setting is grand; the interior is filled with intricate tile mosaics, brilliantly colored carpets, and brass chandeliers. Belly dancers and Moroccan music often entertain guests as they feast on options such as roast lamb, marinated beef or chicken shish kabobs, as well as a host of seafood and salad choices. The combination appetizer (for two) is a great way to start off your meal—allowing you to sample a variety of unique Moroccan flavors all at once. Couscous accompanies most entrees. Lunch costs $18 to $26; dinner is $21 to $43.

JAPAN If you've been to any of the Japanese steakhouse chains, you know what to expect at **Teppan Edo:** Guests are seated around large grill tables while white-hatted chefs rapidly dice, slice, stir-fry, and launch the occasional shrimp onto your plate with amazing skill. The culinary acrobatics here are a sight to see; the cuisine, however, is average. Lunch and dinner range from $18 to $29. While the restaurant retains its original appeal, it now sports a more upscale decor. **Tokyo Dining** (replacing the Matsunoma Lounge and Tempura Kiku), now open with a far more trendy decor, features a menu of traditional Japanese cuisine with an emphasis on sushi. The adjoining **Yakitori House,** a rather small bamboo-roofed teahouse, features such fare as teriyaki chicken, beef simmered in a spicy curry sauce and served with vegetables and rice, sushi rolls, and tempura vegetables with shrimp. Meals here are generally less than $9.

ITALY **Tutto Italia** (replacing L'Originale Alfredo di Roma, albeit only temporarily) is set inside one of the most beautiful of the world pavilions, and is retaining its spot as one of Epcot's most popular restaurants even after recently changing hands. This elegant establishment features a menu filled with traditional pastas, fish, chicken, and pork. If you want a quieter setting, ask for a seat on the veranda overlooking the center courtyard. Lunch costs $15 to $28; dinner runs $24 to $36. A permanent restaurant is slated to replace Tutto Italia in late 2009; official details have yet to be released and signs of any type of refurbishment remained nonexistent at press time.

GERMANY The **Biergarten ★** feels like a Bavarian village at Oktoberfest. The lively mood is due in part to the Bavarian musicians who perform during the dinner hour, and quite possibly due to the beer—it's served in some rather tremendous steins. Diners are encouraged to join the fun by singing and dancing with the performers. The all-you-can-eat buffet is heaped with traditional Bavarian fare (assorted sausages, pork schnitzel, sauerbraten, seafood, roast chicken, spaetzle with gravy, sauerkraut, salads, and plenty of other trimmings). The lunch buffet is $20 for adults, $11 for kids 3 to 11; dinner is $29 for adults, $14 for kids.

CHINA The **Nine Dragons ★**, after months of renovations, now reflects a more modern motif with sleek and stylish furnishings, trendy dishware, and an updated decor complimented by colorful lanterns and silk hangings. The menu, while retaining its traditional flair, features a selection of familiar favorites—but don't overlook the light and very tasty Dioa Yu Tai Cucumber Salad or the shrimp summer rolls wrapped in rice paper and served with a rich and creamy peanut sauce—for those who can't decide, the samplers are a great option. Unlike most restaurants at Disney, appetizers and entrees (even the specialty drinks) are on the smaller side in size. Lunch runs $14 to $21; dinners $16 to $26.

NORWAY **Akershus** is a re-created 14th-century castle complete with tremendous iron chandeliers hanging high above the large banquet hall. An impressive smorgasbord of *smavarmt* (hot) and *koldtbord* (cold) dishes are on the menu here. While the Storybook breakfast features American fare, a variety of more traditional Norwegian fare, including cured salmon with spicy mustard, poached cod, braised lamb and cabbage, and venison stew are among the choices during the Storybook lunch and dinner. Kids can choose from grilled chicken, pasta, hot dogs, and turkey sandwiches. Several Disney princesses (excluding Cinderella) make their way around the hall, stopping at each table to say hello. Storybook Breakfast costs $29 for adults, $18 for kids 4 to 9; Storybook Lunch costs $31 for adults, $19 for kids; and Storybook Dinner costs $36 for adults, $20 for kids.

MEXICO It's always night at the **San Angel Inn ★**, where amid the marketplace, candlelit tables set a romantic mood under a faux star-lit sky. Reasonably authentic food, including the popular *mole poblano* (chicken simmered in spices, ground tortillas, and a hint of cocoa), is on the menu here. Lunch runs $15 to $22, and dinners around $24 to $34. The **Cantina de San Angel,** a cafeteria with outdoor seating at umbrella tables overlooking the lagoon, currently offers soft tacos, burritos, churros, and other items less than $9. Look for a new tequila bar to open (inside the pavilion) and a new menu at the Cantina (outside) in the summer of 2009—and just as this book goes to print.

Future World

Inside the Living Seas pavilion, the aptly named **Coral Reef** features tables scattered around a 5.6-million-gallon aquarium filled with tropical fish. From their tables, diners can observe Disney's denizens of the deep swim by; tiered seating ensures that everyone gets a decent view. The menu features mainly fresh seafood and shellfish with favorites such as mahimahi, tilapia, salmon, and ahi tuna (for landlubbers, prime rib and grilled chicken). Lunch is $13 to $28; dinner is $23 to $31.

The **Sunshine Season Food Faire,** an upscale food court located just inside the Land pavilion, consists of six separate eateries, each offering a small menu of items, including Asian dishes, a variety of salads, chicken, fish, and beef entrees, sandwiches, and desserts. The contemporary earthy decor continues the look and feel of the intricate mosaic leading to the entrance while variations in the carpet and carefully placed partitions separate the large open seating area into smaller sections. Open to the second story, and with no real walls, it retains an airy feel. Most items cost between $4 and $12.

In the Magic Kingdom

In addition to the restaurants listed below, there are plenty of fast-food outlets throughout the park, of which Pecos Bill Cafe, Cosmic Ray's Starlight Cafe, and the Columbia Harbour House are your best choices. That said, you may find that a quiet, sit down meal is an essential, if brief, getaway from the day's activities.

FANTASYLAND High atop the winding stone staircase inside Cinderella Castle awaits the medieval-themed **Cinderella's Royal Table** ★. Stained-glass windows line the stone walls, and servers treat you like a lord or lady while fetching you such entrees as pan-seared salmon, roast prime rib, and spice-rubbed roasted chicken as Disney princesses visit your table. Breakfast costs $24 to $35; lunch costs $25 to $38; dinner is $27 to $43. Advanced Reservations are a must if you plan on dining here.

The **Crystal Palace,** named for its beautiful glass exterior, is a favorite with families because of its all-you-can-eat character buffets (where kids and adults can choose from an ever-changing and decent variety of meats, veggies, and desserts). Breakfast costs $19 for adults and $11 for children ages 3 to 9. Lunch costs $21 for adults and $12 for children 3 to 9. Dinner runs $29 for adults and $14 for children 3 to 9. Advanced Reservations are strongly suggested.

At Disney's Hollywood Studios

There are more than a dozen unique places at which to refuel in this Hollywood-style theme park. Most of them feature more fun than fabulous food; the ones listed below are the best of the bunch. Again, Advanced Reservations are a must.

Modeled after the Los Angeles celebrity haunt where Louella Parsons and Hedda Hopper held court, the **Hollywood Brown Derby** re-creates the feel and atmosphere of a 1930s supper club. Caricatures of Hollywood's most famous celebrities line the walls. Highlights include the Cobb salad and spiced pan-roasted pork; the Derby's signature dessert, grapefruit cake with cream-cheese icing, is a perfect meal capper. Entrees go for $15 to $32 at lunch, $22 to $36 at dinner.

The **50's Prime Time Café** is like going home to Mom's for dinner—back in the 1950s. The atmosphere delivers, with black-and-white TV sets showing *My Little Margie* and servers threatening to withhold dessert if you don't eat all your veggies. There are no elbows on the table here! The mainstays are the meatloaf and pot roast, though they aren't quite as good as Mom used to make. Come here for the atmosphere, not necessarily the food. Kids will get a kick out of the neon ice cubes glowing in their drinks. Lunch costs $12 to $17; dinner costs $13 to $21. Advanced Reservations are a must to eat here.

The best bets at the casual **Mama Melrose's Ristorante Italiano** are the wood-fired and brick-baked specialties, including the flatbreads (grilled pepperoni, portobello mushroom, and four cheeses). The warm and welcoming atmosphere makes you feel like you're at your local mom-and-pop-run restaurant. Lunch costs $12 to $20; dinner costs $12 to $21.

Take the above review for the 50's Prime Time Café, give it a science-fiction spin, and welcome to the **Sci-Fi Dine-In Theater Restaurant.** Diners sit in colorful chrome-plated convertibles with the Hollywood Hills as a backdrop and are treated to newsreels, cartoons, and "B" horror flicks. Sandwiches, burgers, and salads make up the lunch menu; dinner features heartier fare such as steak, pasta, ribs, and chicken. Lunches run $12 to $19; dinners are $14 to $19. Eating here is a bit pricey for what you get (and adding a cosmic concoction or two can really blow your budget), but the incredibly unique atmosphere is worth it (at least once). Advanced Reservations are a must to dine here.

In the Animal Kingdom

You'll find only a few meal options in the Animal Kingdom, and most of those are of the grab-and-go style (of these, the Flame Tree BBQ is the best). Nevertheless, there are three spots where you can sit yourself down for a spell.

Expect California fare with an island spin at the **Rainforest Cafe.** Menu offerings tend to be tasty and somewhat creative, but the prices run on the high side for what you get—most people come for the junglelike tropical atmosphere. Lunch and dinner run anywhere from $9 to $40. ***Note:*** The restaurant is accessible from outside the park, so you don't have to pay park admission to eat here.

The thatched-roof **Tusker House,** in Harambe village, features a buffet with a bit of flair. The slightly shaded patio out back, with a view over the trees, allows you to relax and enjoy your meal tucked away from the crowds. Out front, the pavilion provides shade and, if timed right, a view of the live entertainment. Options include a variety of salads, vegetarian dishes, and meats ranging from Blatjang Chustneys with south African preserves, sambals tabbouleh, hummus, and baba ghanouj to vegetable couscous, root vegetables, and cabbage to salmon filets. Kids will likely find the PB&J, mac and cheese, or corn dog nuggets more to their liking. Lunch runs $11 for kids, $20 for adults, dinner $13 for kids, $27 for adults. A character meal is available at breakfast ($11 for kids, $19 for adults).

Yak & Yeti, the park's newest dining spot, opened in Asia (near Expedition Everest) in the fall of 2007. This Pan-Asian eatery offers both sit-down and counter service dining in a uniquely eclectic and meticulously detailed setting that blends seamlessly into the Himalayan village surrounding it. The menu inside features specialties including crispy wok-fried green beans (even the kids will love these); lettuce cups filled with minced chicken, chopped veggies, and a yummy maple tamarind sauce; seared miso salmon; crispy mahimahi; and maple tamarind chicken. Be sure to leave room for dessert—the mango pie and fried wontons (filled with cream cheese and served with skewers of fresh pineapple, vanilla ice cream, and a sweet honey vanilla drizzle) are simply delish. Kids will appreciate the miniburgers, veggie lo mein, egg rolls, and chicken bites. Entrees run between $17 and $25 (the same for lunch and dinner), while kids' meals cost just under $8.

IN THE WALT DISNEY WORLD RESORTS

Most of these restaurants continue the trend of being above market price, but the food generally is a few notches (or more in certain cases) higher than what you find in the theme parks. Advanced Reservations are a must for dinner, but these restaurants can be far less crowded at lunch and during off-hours, when most people are out pounding the pavement at the parks.

Very Expensive

Citricos ★ FRENCH ECLECTIC Eat here and you'll be treated to a fabulous view of the Seven Seas Lagoon; a warm, colorful Mediterranean atmosphere filled with orange and yellow hues; and a fine meal created by the fusion of French and Mediterranean cuisine with a Florida twist. The oft-changing menu might offer a citron rotisserie pork chop with creamy polenta, garlic-wilted red kale, and cilantro lime drizzle; or sautéed wild king salmon with oven-roasted leeks and an herb butter sauce.

4401 Floridian Way, in Disney's Grand Floridian Resort & Spa. ✆ **407/939-3463.** www.disneyworld.com. Advanced Reservations recommended. Main courses $22–$46. AE, DC, DISC, MC, V. Wed–Sun 5:30–10pm. Valet parking $10.

Victoria & Albert's ★★★ Finds INTERNATIONAL It's not often that dinner can be described as "an event," but Disney's most elegant restaurant earns that distinction. Dinner is next to perfect—if the portions seem small, it's simply so you can better enjoy all seven courses. The setting is exceptionally romantic; a violinist or harpist often plays softly in the background. The fare changes nightly, but you might find main events such as lamb seared with foie gras over brioche with imported Fuji apples; tamari-glazed bluefin tuna over bok choy stir-fry; or Colorado lamb with corn risotto. The intimate dining room is crowned by a domed, chapel-style ceiling; 20 exquisitely appointed tables are lit softly by Victorian lamps; and your waitstaff (always named Victoria and Albert) provide superb service.

4401 Floridian Way, in Disney's Grand Floridian Resort & Spa. ✆ **407/939-3463.** www.disneyworld.com. Reservations required. Jackets required for men. Not recommended for children. Prix fixe $125 per person, $185 with wine pairing; $185 Chef's Table, $245 with wine. AE, DC, DISC, MC, V. 2 dinner seatings daily Sept–June 5:45–6:30pm and 9–9:45pm; 1 seating July–Aug 6:45–8pm. Chef's Table 6pm only. Valet parking $10.

Yachtsman Steakhouse ★ SEAFOOD/STEAK Even by outside the park standards, this is a solid steakhouse with a cordial staff. In keeping with the resort, the atmosphere is nautical New England, with a slightly brighter decor than at most steakhouses. The exhibition kitchen provides a tantalizing peek at steaks, chops, and seafood being seared over oak and hickory. Options range from an 8-ounce filet to a 12-ounce strip to a belly-busting 24-ounce T-bone. The menu also has rack of lamb, salmon, and chicken.

1700 Epcot Resorts Blvd., in Disney's Yacht Club Resort. ✆ **407/939-3463.** Advanced Reservations recommended. Main courses $24–$47. AE, DC, DISC, MC, V. Daily 5:30–10pm. Free self- and valet parking.

Expensive

Artist Point ★★ Finds SEAFOOD/STEAK Enjoy a grand view of Disney's Wilderness Lodge in this rustically elegant establishment. Hand-painted murals of Southwestern scenery adorn the impressive raised center ceiling, and ornate lanterns hang from tremendous timber columns. Select from a seasonally changing menu that might include grilled buffalo sirloin with a sweet potato and hazelnut gratin, or cedar-plank roasted king salmon. ***Note:*** Artist Point has a more relaxed atmosphere than some of the busier WDW resort restaurants, but kids will have more fun at the very lively **Whispering Canyon Café** just next door.

901 W. Timberline Dr., in Disney's Wilderness Lodge. ✆ **407/939-3463** or 824-1081. www.disneyworld.com. Advanced Reservations recommended. Main courses $20–$42; fixed price $46. AE, DC, DISC, MC, V. Daily 5:30–10pm. Free valet and self-parking.

Boma ★★ INTERNATIONAL One of the Animal Kingdom Lodge's signature restaurants, Boma offers a diversion from the usual Disney fare, and a warm atmosphere in a setting that evokes an African marketplace. In front of the open exhibition kitchens lies an incredible buffet of international cuisine featuring authentic African dishes from more than 50 different countries alongside a few more familiar favorites—including dishes especially for kids. Chefs are close by to answer questions and make suggestions throughout the various stations. A specialty of the house is the very delicious watermelon rind. Everything is fresh and tasty. ***Note:*** An American buffet breakfast is served here daily.

2901 Osceola Pkwy., at Disney's Animal Kingdom Lodge. ✆ **407/938-3000.** www.disneyworld.com. Advanced Reservations recommended. All-you-can-eat buffet $17–$27 adults, $10–$13 children 3–9. AE, DC, DISC, MC, V. Daily 7:30–11am and 5:30–10pm.

California Grill ★★ CALIFORNIA Make your way to the 15th floor of the Contemporary Resort and enjoy views of the Magic Kingdom—and its fireworks—while your meal is prepared in an extraordinary exhibition kitchen. Headliners change often, but usually include brick-oven flatbreads, Atlantic salmon, and grilled pork tenderloin with creamy goat-cheese polenta, cremini mushrooms, and a zinfandel glaze. A vegetarian selection is available as well. The Grill also features a sushi and sashimi menu. This is one of the few spots in WDW that isn't particularly well suited to kids. The upbeat and charged atmosphere is enhanced by the contemporary yet colorfully artistic decor. Reservations are required to ride the elevator to the restaurant, so be sure to make arrangements well ahead of time—this is a tough spot to get a table.

4600 N. World Dr., at Disney's Contemporary Resort. ✆ **407/939-3463** or 824-1576. www.disneyworld.com. Reservations required. Main courses $22–$44; sushi and sashimi $19–$25. AE, DC, DISC, MC, V. Daily 5:30–10pm.

Todd English's bluezoo ★★★ SEAFOOD Here's the hippest, hottest place in town, with a contemporary and sophisticated marine-themed decor, an impressive exhibition kitchen, and an intimate lounge where live music is often featured. Internationally acclaimed chef Todd English has created an amazing menu of fresh seafood and coastal dishes that are served with creative flair. Don't miss the amazing "Olive's" *classico* flatbread. Entrees include lobster Bolognese and fresh grilled fish with a choice of three unique sauces. Portions are large, but note that side dishes will run you an extra $5 to $7. Dress is casual, but the upscale atmosphere is chic and adult (even though there's a children's menu . . . this is, after all, Disney).

1500 Epcot Resort Blvd., at the WDW Dolphin. ✆ **407/934-1111.** www.disneyworld.com. Advanced Reservations recommended. Main courses $27–$60. AE, DISC, MC, V. Daily 5–11pm. Validated valet and self-parking free.

Moderate

ESPN Club ★ AMERICAN If you are a sports enthusiast, this is *the* place for you. Upon entering, you will be surrounded by monitors showing every possible sporting event. The all-American fare includes such choices as "Boo-Yeah" chili, hot wings, and burgers. Sandwiches and salads are available as well. The service is impeccable—never have I had a waiter so quick on his feet. While the food is quite good, it's really the atmosphere that draws the crowds here.

2101 N. Epcot Resorts Blvd., at Disney's BoardWalk. ✆ **407/939-1177.** www.disneyworld.com. Advanced Reservations not available. Lunch and dinner $9–$15. AE, DC, MC, V. Mon–Thurs 11:30am–1am; Fri–Sat 11:30am–2am.

'Ohana ★ Kids PACIFIC RIM Its star is earned on the fun front, but the decibel level here may turn off those without children in tow. As your luau is prepared exhibition-style over an 18-foot-wide fire pit, the staff keeps you busy with coconut races, hula lessons, and other shenanigans. Servers come around the tables with 3-foot skewers of pork, turkey, steak, and vegetables, while starters and sides are all served family-style. More kid-friendly fare can be requested. ***Note:*** A daily character breakfast with Lilo, Stitch, Mickey, and Pluto is served up family-style too.

1600 Seven Seas Dr., at Disney's Polynesian Resort. ✆ **407/939-3463** or 824-2000. www.disneyworld.com. Advanced Reservations strongly encouraged. $19–$27 adults; $11–$13 children 3–11. AE, DC, DISC, MC, V. Daily 7:30–11am and 5–10pm.

DOWNTOWN DISNEY

Very Expensive

Fulton's Crab House ★★ SEAFOOD Oysters and stone-crab claws are the specialties of this upscale eatery, located in a replica of a 19th-century Mississippi riverboat. A casual yet elegant decor is accented by folk art and seafaring paraphernalia for a nautical though somewhat New England feel. Outdoor decks offer the best views of the lake and Downtown Disney. As it's one of the area's best seafood houses, you might want to bring along some extra cash. The menu changes often, at times even daily, but with more than 50 fresh seafood selections, you won't be disappointed. Though you may not see many of them, kids are welcome.

1670 Buena Vista Dr., aboard the riverboat docked at Downtown Disney. ✆ **407/934-2628.** www.levyrestaurants.com. Advanced Reservations recommended. Main courses $10–$18 lunch, $20–$52 dinner. AE, DC, DISC, MC, V. Daily 11:30am–4pm and 5–11pm. Valet parking $7.

Moderate

Rainforest Cafe Kids CALIFORNIA Don't arrive starving (or expecting a peaceful meal—the extensively themed jungle atmosphere entertains most kids, but can be distractingly noisy). Waits here average 2 hours if you fail to call ahead to make an Advanced Reservation. The menu can be tasty and creative, though somewhat overpriced. The choices seem endless, but a few of the more fun dishes include Mogambo Shrimp (sautéed in olive oil and served with penne pasta), Rumble in the Jungle Turkey Wrap (with romaine, tomatoes, and bacon), and Maya's Mixed Grill (ribs, chicken breast, and shrimp).

Downtown Disney Marketplace, near the smoking volcano. ✆ **407/827-8500.** www.rainforestcafe.com. Advanced Reservations strongly recommended. Main courses $11–$40 (most less than $25). AE, DISC, MC, V. Sun–Thurs 10:30am–11pm; Fri–Sat 10:30am–midnight.

T-Rex Kids CALIFORNIA A sibling of the Rainforest Cafe (see above) and Downtown Disney's latest addition, T-Rex adds yet another unique element to its lineup of family friendly dining options. Bubbling geysers, a fossil dig site, life-size animatronic dinosaurs, and themes of fire and ice run throughout this prehistoric eatery. Each distinctively themed room will surely entertain even the squirmiest kids, but be aware—it can be overload for those easily bothered by loud noises and flashing lights. Waits here average 2 hours if you fail to call ahead to make an Advanced Reservation. The menu can be tasty and creative, though like most Disney restaurants, somewhat overpriced. The choices seem endless but a few of the more fun dishes include Footprints Flatbread (cheddar, mozzarella, Parmesan, and goat cheese with rotisserie chicken, caramelized onions, and a balsamic glaze), Fire-Roasted Rotisserie Chicken (with a choice of yummy sides), and don't forget to save room for dessert—the Chocolate Extinction is fabulous (chocolate fudge cake with vanilla ice cream, whipped cream, chocolate, and caramel drizzle as well as Butterfinger crumbles—this one's big enough for two or more).

Downtown Disney Marketplace. ✆ **407/828-8739.** www.trexcafe.com. Advanced Reservations strongly recommended. Main courses $11–$40 (most less than $25). AE, DISC, MC, V. Sun–Thurs 11am–11pm; Fri–Sat 11am–midnight.

Wolfgang Puck Café ★★ CALIFORNIA The wait can be distressing, but the energized, upscale, and contemporary atmosphere, along with the eclectic mix of menu choices, make it worth the effort. An eye-catching exhibition kitchen in the more casual downstairs section allows you to watch as your food is prepared. A favorite stop is the sushi bar, an artistic copper-and-terrazzo masterpiece that delivers some of the best sushi in Orlando. The upstairs dining room has a more refined atmosphere with its very own menu to match. Puck's is noisy, making conversation difficult no matter which level you choose. ***Note:*** In a hurry? Try the Wolfgang Puck Express at either the West Side or Marketplace.

1482 Buena Vista Dr., at Disney's West Side. ✆ **407/938-9653.** www.wolfgangpuck.com or www.levyrestaurants.com. Reservations not accepted on lower level; Advanced Reservations recommended for upstairs dining room. Main courses upstairs $25–$43; main courses cafe $17–$27; pizza and sushi $12–$18; Express $10–$15. AE, DC, DISC, MC, V. Daily 11am–1am.

ELSEWHERE IN LAKE BUENA VISTA

Moderate

The Crab House SEAFOOD Decent seafood (as well as other options for landlubbers) at decent prices is what you get at this casual restaurant. The all-you-can-eat seafood-and-salad bar is a great way to sample all the tasty offerings. On the regular menu, you will find a variety of fish and shrimp dishes, Maine lobster, and, of course, crab—from Alaskan to King to Maryland Blue. The service is friendly and prompt however I suggest making reservations during peak travel times.

8496 Palm Pkwy. (just off Apopka-Vineland across and up from Hotel Plaza Blvd.). ✆ **407/239-1888.** www.landrysrestaurants.com. Reservations accepted. Main courses $9–$22 lunch, $14–$45 dinner. AE, DC, DISC, MC, V. Daily 11:30am–11pm. Take I-4 to exit 68 (Hwy. 535), turn right, follow the road past the Crossroads to Palm Pkwy., and turn right. The restaurant is back a bit on the right.

Inexpensive

Romano's Macaroni Grill ★ **Value** NORTHERN ITALIAN Though it's part of a multistate chain, Romano's has the down-to-earth cheerfulness and friendly service of a mom-and-pop joint. The laid-back atmosphere makes it a good place for families or those looking for a casual dinner. The menu offers thin-crust pizzas made in a wood-burning oven and topped with such items as barbecued chicken. The grilled chicken Portobello (simmering between smoked mozzarella and spinach orzo pasta) alone is worth the visit.

12148 Apopka-Vineland Rd. (just north of Hwy. 535/Palm Pkwy.). ✆ **407/239-6676.** www.macaronigrill.com. Main courses $6–$21 lunch, $9–$21 dinner (most less than $12). AE, DC, DISC, MC, V. Sun–Thurs 11am–10pm; Fri–Sat 11am–11pm. Take I-4 exit 68, Hwy. 535/Apopka-Vineland Rd. N., and continue straight when Hwy. 535 goes to the right. Romano's is about 2 blocks on the left.

UNIVERSAL ORLANDO

Universal Orlando's CityWalk and its resorts are home to a number of diverse dining spots—some of the best in Orlando.

Very Expensive

Emeril's ★★ NEW ORLEANS It's next to impossible to get short-term reservations for dinner here unless you're willing to take your chances with no-shows or visiting during the off-peak season. If you do get in, you'll find the dynamic, Creole-inspired cuisine worth the struggle. Best bets are the andouille-crusted Texas redfish (a moist white fish with roasted vegetable relish and Creole meunière sauce and toasted pecans) and the pan-seared filet mignon served with garlic creamed mashed potatoes, red wine reduction, horseradish-herb compound butter, asparagus, and yellow pea shoots. The back half of the building is a glass-walled, 12,000-bottle aboveground cellar. If you want a show, we recommend one of eight counter seats, where you can watch chefs work their magic; but to get one, reservations are required *excruciatingly* early (2–3 months, at least).

Note: Lunch costs about half what you'll spend on dinner, and the menu and portions are almost the same. It's also easier to get a midday reservation. No matter when you come, leave the kids at home—this restaurant caters to adults.

6000 Universal Studios Blvd., in CityWalk. ✆ **407/224-2424.** www.emerils.com/restaurants. Reservations recommended. Main courses $9–$15 lunch, $21–$44 dinner. Sun–Thurs 11:30am–2pm and 5:30–10pm; Fri–Sat 11:30am–2pm and 5:30–11pm. AE, DISC, MC, V. Self-parking $12 ($3 after 6pm). From I-4, take the Kirkman Rd./Hwy. 435 exit and follow the signs to Universal.

Expensive

Tchoup Chop ★★★ PACIFIC RIM Culinary perfection is pronounced "chop chop." Emeril Lagasse's second restaurant in Orlando is named for the location of his original restaurant, Tchoupitoulas Street in New Orleans. Think bluezoo (see above) with an Asian Pacific twist—very chic, contemporary, and impressive. The service is impeccable, and the relaxing atmosphere, stunning decor, and excellent food ensure that the experience is memorable and worth the price. Some of the tasty Polynesian- and Asian-influenced dishes include macadamia nut–crusted Atlantic salmon, Kiawe grilled New York strip steak, and Hawaiian-style rotisserie chicken.

6300 Hollywood Way, in Universal's Royal Pacific Hotel. ✆ **407/503-2467.** www.emerils.com/restaurants. Reservations strongly recommended. Main courses $18–$36. AE, DISC, MC, V. Sun–Thurs 11:30am–2pm and 5:30–10pm; Fri–Sat 11:30am–2pm and 5:30–11pm. Valet parking $5. From I-4, take the Kirkman Rd./Hwy. 435 exit, and follow the signs to Universal.

Moderate

Pastamore Ristorante SOUTHERN ITALIAN The *antipasto amore* here is a meal unto itself, and includes bruschetta, melon with prosciutto, grilled portobello mushrooms, sliced Italian meats, marinated olives, tomato caprese, and mozzarella. This casual family eatery has a menu of Italian classics, seafood, pastas, and grilled specialties. Options include veal Marsala, chicken piccata, shrimp scampi, fettuccine Alfredo, and pizza, among several others. An open kitchen allows diners a view of the chefs at work. You can also eat in a cafe where lighter fare—breakfast and sandwiches—is served from 8am to 2am.

1000 Universal Studios Plaza, in CityWalk. ✆ **407/363-8000.** www.universalorlando.com. Reservations accepted. Main courses $9–$20. AE, DISC, MC, V. Daily 5pm–midnight. Self-parking $12 ($3 after 6pm). From I-4, take the Kirkman Rd./Hwy. 435 exit and follow the signs to Universal.

Value Bring On the Barbecue

Bubbalou's Bodacious BBQ ★, 5818 Conroy Rd., Orlando (✆ **407/423-1212;** www.bubbalous.com), has finally opened a location not too far off the beaten path. Come here for the best barbecue in Florida. Go for the full pork platter that comes with a heaping helping and all the fixin's. The uninitiated should stay away from the "Killer" sauce if you value your taste buds; you might even taste-test the mild sauce before moving up to the hot. Sandwiches run $5 to $9, main courses run $10 to $15. Hours are Monday through Saturday from 10am to 9pm. To get here, take exit 75B off of I-4, follow Kirkman, then make a left onto Conroy and follow your nose; Bubbalou's is on the left.

THE INTERNATIONAL DRIVE AREA

International Drive has one of the area's larger collections of fast-food joints, but its midsection and southern reaches also have some of this region's better restaurants. International Drive is 10 minutes by car from the Disney parks.

Expensive

Ocean Prime SEAFOOD An elegant and sophisticated establishment that combines a menu of the freshest steaks and seafood with an extensive wine list, and an upbeat atmosphere that's reminiscent of a 1930s supper club (albeit chic and updated). Berries and bubbles (a unique cocktail served tableside) is an experience in itself and a great way to start off the evening. Follow with a filet—it will simply melt in your mouth as steaks are seasoned to perfection (though an array of sauces are available as an extra)—if seafood is more your style, the choices are almost endless (ginger salmon, Chilean sea bass, and blackened swordfish are among the specialties). Sides (the Maytag blue cheese whipped potatoes are simply sumptuous) are separate, the choices plentiful and unique. The incredibly knowledgeable and attentive staff top off the exceptional experience—without a doubt among the very best restaurants in all of Orlando!

7339 West Sand Lake Rd., in the Rialto Plaza. ✆ **407/363-4801.** www.ocean-prime.com. Reservations recommended. Main courses $16–$85 (most less than $25). AE, DC, DISC, MC, V. Mon–Thurs 4–10pm; Fri–Sat 4–11pm; Sun 4–9pm. From I-4, take the Sand Lake Rd./Hwy. 528 (exit 74A), turn left at the end of the exit, the restaurant is on the right.

Ran-Getsu of Tokyo JAPANESE Its authentic cuisine and sushi bar has made Ran-Getsu a popular haunt for moneyed Asian tourists, though some diners find the prices too high. The blend of its simple yet upscale interior and traditional outdoor gardens is inviting. *Tekka-don,* tender slices of tuna mild enough for first-timers, is a refreshing sushi choice. *Yosenabe* is a bouillabaisse with a savory twist—duck and chicken are added to the seafood mix. A traditional Japanese drum show is performed Thursday through Saturday evenings.

8400 International Dr., near Orlando Convention Center. ✆ **407/345-0044.** www.rangetsu.com. Reservations recommended. Main courses $16–$85 (most less than $25); sushi entrees $22–$29. AE, DC, DISC, MC, V. Daily 5–11:30pm. From I-4, take the Sand Lake Rd./Hwy. 528 exit east to International Dr., then head south. Restaurant is on the right.

Moderate

Ming Court ★★ CHINESE Its diverse menu and tasty dishes make this one of Orlando's most popular Chinese restaurants. The lightly battered, deep-fried chicken breast gets zip from a delicate lemon-tangerine sauce. If you're in the mood for beef, try the grilled filet mignon seasoned Szechuan-style. Portions are sufficient and the service is excellent. The 250-foot, ornately carved dragons that greet you at the entrance are a hint at what awaits inside. Kids get their own menu, featuring beef, shrimp, chicken, and pork served with an Asian flair.

9188 International Dr. (btw. Sand Lake Rd. and Beachline Expwy.). © **407/351-9988.** www.ming-court.com. Reservations recommended. Main courses $6–$28 lunch, $11–$43 dinner, $50–$60 dinner for 2; dim sum mostly $3–$8. AE, DC, DISC, MC, V. Daily 11am–2:30pm and 4:30–11:30pm. From I-4, take the Sand Lake Rd./Hwy. 528 exit east to International Dr., then south. Ming Court is on the right opposite Pointe Orlando.

ONLY IN ORLANDO: DINING WITH DISNEY CHARACTERS

Dining with Disney characters is a treat for almost any Disney fan, but it's a special one for those 9 and under. The characters will greet you, sign autographs, pose for photos, and interact with the entire family. These dining experiences are extremely popular, so make Advanced Reservations (© **407/939-3463**) as early as possible (up to 180 days in advance), and call for schedules. Prices vary, but generally expect breakfast (most serve it) to be $19 to $34 for adults, $11 to $23 for kids 3 to 9. Restaurants that serve dinner charge $28 to $43 for adults and $14 to $27 for kids.

Character meals are offered at **Cape May Café** (in Disney's Beach Club Resort), **Chef Mickey's** (at Disney's Contemporary Resort), **Cinderella's Royal Table** (in Cinderella Castle, Magic Kingdom), **Crystal Palace Buffet** (at the Crystal Palace, Magic Kingdom), **Donald's Safari Breakfast at the Tusker House** (in Africa, Animal Kingdom), **Garden Grill** (in the Land Pavilion, Epcot), **'Ohana** (at Disney's Polynesian Resort), **Akershus Royal Banquet Hall** (in Epcot's Norway Pavilion), **Hollywood & Vine** (at Disney–MGM Studios), **1900 Park Fare** (at Disney's Grand Floridian Resort & Spa), and the **Garden Grove Café** and **Gulliver's Grill** (at the WDW Swan).

5 TIPS FOR VISITING WALT DISNEY WORLD ATTRACTIONS

Walt Disney World, home to the four major theme parks of Magic Kingdom, Epcot, Disney's Hollywood Studios, and Animal Kingdom, welcomes around 50 million guests in a typical year.

Besides its larger theme parks, Disney has an assortment of other venues, including Downtown Disney (Cirque du Soleil, DisneyQuest, Pleasure Island, West Side, and the Marketplace), Blizzard Beach, and Typhoon Lagoon, just to name a few.

PARKING Cars, light trucks, and vans pay $12. Visitors with disabilities can park in special areas near the entrances; ask the parking-lot attendants or call © **407/824-4321.** *Don't forget* to write down where you parked (area and row number); after a long day at the parks, Minnie, Mickey, Goofy, and Donald all start to look and sound alike.

WHEN YOU ARRIVE Grab a printed park guide. It not only tells you where the fun is (including current ride-restriction and FASTPASS information), but when and where to eat and shop. Pick up a copy of the "Times Guide," too—it includes a schedule for the parks' daily shows and parades. Arrive early (usually about 20–30 min., depending on the season) to get a good seat.

BEST TIMES TO VISIT There isn't really an off-season in Orlando, but crowds are usually thinner from early January to mid-March and from mid-September until the week before Thanksgiving. The busiest days at all theme parks are generally Saturday and Sunday, when the locals visit. Major holidays attract scores of visitors: Christmas to New Year's is by far the busiest time of year; with the week preceding and following Easter a very close second. ***Note:*** Summer, though one of the least expensive times to visit, can also be the worst. The crowds are heavy with locals, and the heat and humidity can be intolerable.

OPERATING HOURS Park hours vary and are influenced by special events as well as the economy. Call ahead or go to **www.disneyworld.com** to check operating times; otherwise you could find yourself expecting to stay all night when in reality the park closes at 6pm. Not only will hours vary from park to park, but from week to week, and even day to day. Don't just assume that a park is open; check the schedule ahead of time or once you arrive.

Tip: If you are a WDW Resort guest (or are staying at the WDW Hilton, the WDW Swan, or the WDW Dolphin), you can take advantage of Disney's **Extra Magic Hour** program. This allows WDW Resort guests early entry (or extended evening hours) at select theme parks (including the water parks) on select days. The Extra Magic Hour schedule can change frequently, so it's best to check with your resort upon arrival for the most up-to-date information.

TICKETS Disney's ticketing structure (called Magic Your Way) gives visitors who stay here for a few days far better deals than those who come for just a day. The system allows guests to customize tickets by first purchasing a base ticket for a set fee, and then purchasing add-ons, including a Park-Hopper option, a no-expiration option, and the option to include admission to some of Disney's smaller venues, such as Pleasure Island, the water parks, and DisneyQuest (the Water Parks & More option).

Ticket durations can vary from a single day to 10 days (after 7 days, however, an annual pass becomes a wise purchase), and the more you stay, the less you pay per day. Do note, however, that unlike years past, unless you purchase a no-expiration add-on to your ticket, it will now expire within 14 days of the first day of use. (However, you don't have to use your tickets on consecutive days.)

The following prices don't include 6.5% sales tax unless noted. ***Note:*** Price hikes are frequent occurrences, so call (✆ **407/824-4321**) or visit WDW's website (www.disneyworld.com) for the most up-to-the-minute pricing.

One-day/one-park tickets, for admission to the Magic Kingdom, Epcot, Animal Kingdom, or Disney's Hollywood Studios, are $75 for adults, $63 for children 3 to 9. (Ouch!) **Multiday tickets** allow you to visit *one park per day.* A 7-day ticket costs $228 for adults (about $33 a day), $193 for kids (about $28 a day).

A **Park-Hopper** add-on ($50 *per ticket,* per person) allows visitors unlimited admission to the Magic Kingdom, Epcot, Animal Kingdom, and Disney's Hollywood Studios for the length of their ticket. A 1-day adult Park-Hopper ticket costs $125, while the 7-day version costs $278—making the latter a far better deal. Because the $50 fee applies per ticket and not per day, the longer you stay, the better the deal.

Water Park Fun & More tickets also allow visitors their choice of three to six admissions (the number depends on the length of your pass) to Typhoon Lagoon, Blizzard Beach, Pleasure Island, DisneyQuest, or Disney's Wide World of Sports. Prices range from an obscene $125 for a 1-day adult pass to $278 for a 7-day pass (a very good deal).

A **1-day ticket** to **Typhoon Lagoon** or **Blizzard Beach** is $45 for adults, $39 for children, while a 1-day ticket to **DisneyQuest** will cost $40 for adults and $34 for children.

Tips Advance Ticket Purchase Saves Money

Purchasing your Disney tickets ahead of time can result in substantial savings (depending on the ticket and the add-ons you purchase) via the Orlando Convention & Visitors Bureau or AAA. You can often save between $2 and $7 (sometimes more) by purchasing tickets in advance. This can add up to $28 (or more) in savings for a family of four.

If you're planning an extended stay or are going to visit Walt Disney World more than once during the year, **annual passes** ($469–$599 adults, $414–$528 children) are another great option.

6 THE MAGIC KINGDOM

The Magic Kingdom is by far the most enchanting of all the Disney parks. Taking center stage is Cinderella Castle, the best known and most recognized symbol of Disney. From the minute you look down Main Street U.S.A., you're transported to a world of fantasy, ostensibly free from all the cares and worries of the outside world. The park's **seven "lands"** surround the castle to form the most magical place on earth.

MAIN STREET, U.S.A.

The gateway to the Kingdom, Main Street resembles the perfect turn-of-the-20th-century American street (okay, so it leads to a 13th-c. European castle, but nobody complains). It has shops, restaurants, and outdoor entertainment. Main Street, however, is best left for the end of the day when you're heading back to your hotel.

As soon as you arrive at Main Street, you can board the **Walt Disney World Railroad,** an authentic 1928 steam-powered train, for a 20-minute trip around the perimeter of the park. It's a good way to travel if you're headed to one of its three stations—the park entrance, Frontierland, or Mickey's Toontown Fair—or if you want to go for a relaxing ride that has shorter lines.

ADVENTURELAND

Cross a bridge and stroll through an exotic jungle of foliage, thatched roofs, and totems. Amid dense vines and stands of bamboo, drums are beating and swashbuckling adventures are beginning.

On the 10-minute **Jungle Cruise,** you sail through an African veldt in the Congo, an Amazon rainforest, and the Nile River in Egypt, among other locales. Dozens of animatronic creatures inhabit the hanging vines, cascading waterfalls, and tropical foliage.

The **Magic Carpets of Aladdin** ★ delights wee ones and a few older kids, too. Its 16 four-passenger carpets circle a giant genie's bottle while the camels spit water at the passengers and passersby. The flying carpets spin gently around, move up, down, forward, and back.

In the classic **Pirates of the Caribbean** ★★, pillaging pirates wreak havoc upon a small Caribbean town as your boat passes by. Audio-animatronic figures include a rather seedy cast of yo-ho-ho-ing characters; spurred by the popularity of the movie *Pirates of the Caribbean: Curse of the Black Pearl* and its sequels, Jack Sparrow, Barbossa, and Davy

Jones have signed on as part of the crew. A tweak in the story line to better mirror the movies, and a mix of new, updated special effects have been added. Still, the ride may be scary for kids 4 and under due to the unexpected (but small) drops and moments of darkness. **Captain Jack's Pirate Tutorial** takes place nearby and allows pint-size pirates (pulled from the audience) to train alongside none other that Captain Jack himself—learning the art of sword play and swashbuckling silliness before being sworn in as honorary members of the crew.

The **Enchanted Tiki Room Under New Management** is a very upbeat and enchanting show featuring a slew of tropical birds singing and telling jokes. It is a bit loud on the decibel front, but is otherwise cute and entertaining.

FRONTIERLAND

From Adventureland, step into the wild and woolly past of the American frontier. The landscape is straight out of the Wild West, complete with log cabins and rustic saloons.

The low-key **Big Thunder Mountain Railroad** ★★ roller coaster, situated on a 200-foot-high red-stone mountain, has tight turns and dark descents rather than sudden, steep drops. Your train careens through caves and canyons, under thundering waterfalls, past geysers, bubbling mud pots, and over a bottomless volcanic pool. It's tailor-made for kids and grown-ups who want a thrill but aren't quite up to tackling the big coasters. ***Note:*** You must be 40 inches or taller to ride.

The **Country Bear Jamboree** ★ is a hoot. It's a 15-minute show featuring audio-animatronic bears belting out rollicking country tunes and crooning plaintive love songs. It's a great place to cool off, too.

Based on Disney's 1946 film *Song of the South,* **Splash Mountain** ★★★ takes you flume-style past 26 colorful scenes that include swamps, bayous, caves, and waterfalls. Riders are caught up in the schemes of Brer Fox and Brer Bear as they chase the ever-wily Brer Rabbit. Your hollow-log vehicle twists, turns, and splashes, sometimes plummeting in darkness, as the ride leads to a 52-foot-long, 40-mph splashdown in a briar-filled pond. ***Note:*** You must be at least 40 inches tall to ride.

LIBERTY SQUARE

Step back into 18th-century America. Thirteen lanterns, symbolizing the colonies, hang from the Liberty Tree, an immense live oak in the center of the courtyard. You may even encounter a fife-and-drum corps on the cobblestone streets.

Reopened after a lengthy refurbishment, every American president is represented by a lifelike audio-animatronic figure in the **Hall of Presidents** ★. Look closely, and you'll see them fidget and whisper. The show begins with a film, and then the curtain rises on America's leaders. Each president's costume reflects his period's fashion, fabrics, and tailoring techniques.

Once you're inside the **Haunted Mansion** ★★, darkness, spooky music, howling, and screams enhance the ambience. After a brief and somewhat ominous welcome, the slow-motion ride takes you past a host of bizarre scenes, including a ghostly banquet and ball. It's a classic that's more amusing than terrifying for anyone older than the age of 5. A recent refurbishment has further enhanced it's unearthly special effects and spectral silliness.

FANTASYLAND

The attractions in this happy land are themed after classics such as *Snow White, Peter Pan,* and *Dumbo.* If your kids are 8 and under, you may want to make this and Mickey's Toontown your primary stops in the Magic Kingdom.

Tips FASTPASS

Don't like standing in long lines? Take advantage of Disney's FASTPASS system. Here's the drill:

Hang onto your ticket stub when you enter, and head to the hottest ride of your choosing. If it's a FASTPASS attraction (they're noted in the park guide you get when you enter) and there's a line, feed your ticket stub into the FASTPASS ticket taker. Retrieve both your ticket stub and the FASTPASS stub that comes with it. Two times will be stamped on the FASTPASS—come back during that 1-hour window, bypass the regular line, and head straight for the FASTPASS entrance where you'll have little or almost no wait.

Note: Early in the day, your window may begin as close as only 40 minutes after you feed the FASTPASS machine, but later in the day it could be hours. Initially, Disney allowed you to do this on only one ride at a time; however, now you can get a pass for a second attraction 2 hours after you get your first FASTPASS stamp—a time frame that's subject to change). Note, however, that the passes go quickly at times and the system can max out, sometimes by noon, so be sure to head to the rides most important to you earliest in the day.

There's not a lot to do at **Cinderella Castle ★**, but its status as the Magic Kingdom's icon makes it a must (not that you can really miss it, as it stands 185 ft. tall). Mickey, along with a slew of Disney characters, appears daily on the castle forecourt stage in "Dream along with Mickey," while Cinderella's Royal Table restaurant and the Bibiddi Bobiddi Boutique are located inside.

The elaborate and beautiful **Cinderella's Golden Carousel ★★** was constructed by Italian carvers in 1917 and refurbished by Disney artists, who added 18 hand-painted scenes from the Cinderella story on a wooden canopy above the horses. Kids of all ages will enjoy this ride.

Dumbo the Flying Elephant ★ is a very tame kids' ride, in which the Dumbos go around in a circle, gently rising and dipping. If you can stand the lines (and they are usually quite long here), it's very exciting for wee ones.

Built for the 1964 New York World's Fair, **It's a Small World ★** takes you to countries inhabited by appropriately costumed audio-animatronic dolls singing "It's a small world after all," in tiny doll voices. Every adult who has ever ridden this in the past will remember the tune, as it can be difficult to get out of your head.

Mad Tea Party is a traditional amusement park ride with an *Alice in Wonderland* theme that's always a hit with the younger set. Riders sit in big pastel-hued teacups on saucers that careen around a circular platform at the same time that they, too, are spinning. Adults may want to ground themselves when they get off, as the kids tend to spin as fast as physically possible.

Mickey's PhilharMagic ★★★ is by far the most amazing 3-D film I've ever seen. Covering one of the largest screens ever made for a 3-D movie, the production's special and sensory effects are incredible. Many of Disney's most beloved characters make an appearance to help (or in some cases hinder) the attempts of Donald Duck to retrieve Mickey's magical sorcerer's hat. This is a must-see for everyone.

On **Peter Pan's Flight** ★ you'll ride in airborne versions of Captain Hook's ship, and take a calm flight over nighttime London to Never-Never Land. You will fly above the mermaids, the ticking crocodile, the Lost Boys, Princess Tiger Lilly, Tinker Bell, Hook, and Smee. This is a fun ride for younger kids and Peter Pan fans of all ages. Just be prepared for one of the longest waits in the park.

A bit too scary for kids 4 and under, **Snow White's Scary Adventure** is as scary as the name implies. The story line, while bright in spots, still plays up the movie's darker scenes—and the witch puts in an appearance or two. The title heroine, however, does appear in a few pleasant scenes as she rides off to live happily ever after.

MICKEY'S TOONTOWN FAIR

Where's Mickey? This 2-acre site is a great place for small children to find him and his pals. Toontown offers you and your kids a chance to meet Disney characters, including Mickey, Minnie, Donald, Goofy as well as Tinker Bell and her fellow fairies. You can even have your photo taken with them (if you can make it through the sometimes endless lines).

The **Barnstormer at Goofy's Wiseacre Farm** ★★ is a mini roller coaster likely inspired by Woody Woodpecker's Nuthouse Coaster at Universal Orlando (p. 503). It looks and feels like a crop duster that flies off-course and through Goofy's barn. The ride has very little in the dip-and-drop department, but a bit of zip on the spin-and-spiral front. The 60-second corkscrew ride has a 35-inch height minimum.

Donald's Boat (S.S. *Miss Daisy*) ★ offers a lot of interactive fun, and the "waters" around it feature fountains of water snakes and other wet fun things that earn squeals of joy (and relief on hot days). Bring extra clothes or a swimsuit for this one.

Mickey's & Minnie's Country Houses ★ are separate cottages that offer a lot of visual fun and some marginal interactive areas for youngsters. Mickey's place features garden and garage playgrounds. Minnie's lets kids play in her kitchen, where popcorn goes wild in a microwave and a cake comes to life in the oven as the utensils play melodies. If you want to see the Big Mouse himself, head behind his house and through the garden—you'll find Mickey available for photos and autographs throughout the day.

TOMORROWLAND

The reasonably cute **Stitch's Great Escape** debuted in September 2004, recruiting riders to help capture and contain the infamous "experiment 626," who is wreaking havoc on the galaxy. Disney animatronics bring the friendly characters to life, and sensory effects and overhead restraints help provide atmosphere. ***Tip:*** Younger kids who reach the 38-inch height restriction may not care for the long periods of darkness and silence.

On **Buzz Lightyear's Space Ranger Spin** ★★★, join Buzz and try to save the universe while flying your cruiser through a world you'll recognize from the original *Toy Story* movie. Kids enjoy using the dashboard-mounted laser cannons as they spin through the sky (filled with gigantic toys instead of stars). If they're good shots, they can set off sight and sound gags with their lasers. You may be riding this more than once if you have kids.

The cosmic coaster, **Space Mountain** ★ usually has *long* lines (if you don't use FASTPASS), even though it's years past its prime (at press time a refurbishment was slated for the second half of 2009). Once aboard the "rocket," you'll climb and dive through the inky, starlit blackness of outer space. The hairpin turns and plunges make it seem as if you're going at breakneck speed, but your car doesn't go any faster than 28 mph. ***Note:*** Riders must be at least 44 inches tall.

The immersive **Monsters, Inc. Laugh Floor** takes its cue from the hit Disney/Pixar flick *Monsters, Inc.,* as Mike, along with an entire cast of monster comedians, pokes fun at audience members in hopes of getting enough laughs to fill the gigantic laugh canister. This new immersive experience is live and unscripted, using real-time animation, digital projection, sophisticated voice-activated animation, and a tremendous cast of talented improv comedians.

Younger kids love **Tomorrowland Indy Speedway,** especially if their adult companion lets them drive (without a big person, there's a 52-in. height minimum for driving a lap). Teens and other fast starters find it just too slow—the cars go only 7 mph and are loosely locked into lanes.

PARADES, FIREWORKS & MORE

For up-to-the-moment information, see the entertainment schedule in the park guide map as well as the *Times Guide & New Information* card that you can (and should) pick up when entering the park.

The Magic Kingdom's first new fireworks display in a little more than 30 years, **Wishes** ★★★ debuted in October 2003 to lots of acclaim. Its precise mix of choreographed bursts, music, and story is just amazing and has to be experienced to be appreciated. This is absolutely the best way to end your day in the Magic Kingdom. The fireworks go off nightly during peak periods, but only on selected nights the rest of the year.

A 20-minute after-dark display, **SpectroMagic** ★★, combines fiber optics, holographic images, old-fashioned twinkling lights, and a soundtrack featuring classic Disney tunes. The parade runs on a *very limited basis.*

7 EPCOT

Epcot is an acronym for Experimental Prototype Community of Tomorrow, and it was Walt Disney's dream for a planned residential community. However, long after his death, it opened in 1982 as Central Florida's second Disney theme park.

The 260-acre park has two very distinct sections: **Future World** and **World Showcase.** It's so large that hiking World Showcase from tip to tip ($1^1/_3$ miles) can be exhausting. That's why some folks say Epcot really stands for "Every Person Comes Out Tired." Depending on how long you intend to linger at each of the 11 countries in World Showcase, this park can be seen in 1 day, but it's better to do it in 2 days to take it all in properly.

FUTURE WORLD

Future World is centered on Epcot's icon, a giant geosphere known as Spaceship Earth. Major corporations sponsor most themed areas, with a focus on discovery, scientific achievements, and tomorrow's technologies in areas running from energy to undersea exploration. Here are the headliners:

The fountains at the **Imagination** ★★ pavilion are magical—they fire "water snakes" that arch in the air and dare kids to avoid their "bite." The 3-D ***Honey, I Shrunk the Audience*** ★★ show shrinks you, then terrorizes you with giant mice, a cat, and a 5-year-old who gives you a sound shaking. **Journey into Your Imagination** ★ features a park favorite, Figment the dragon.

Innoventions ★ is divided into two sections (both constantly updated, so it's always worth stopping in). House of Innoventions in **Innoventions East** heralds Storm Struck, where guests can experience the effects of hurricane force winds; Don't Waste It, where educating guests on the importance of recycling is the main message; and a smart house, equipped with a refrigerator that can make your grocery list and a picture frame that can send photos to other smart frames. The exhibits in **Innoventions West** are led by Sega's Video Games of Tomorrow. Good luck getting the kids out.

The largest of Future World's pavilions, the **Land** ★ looks at human relationships with food and nature. **Living with the Land** ★ is a 13-minute boat ride through a rainforest, an African desert, and the windswept American plains. **Circle of Life** ★ blends spectacular live-action footage with animation in a 15-minute movie based on *The Lion King* and it delivers a cautionary environmental message. **Soarin'** ★★★ allows guests a bird's-eye view of the diverse California landscape. With feet freely dangling 40 feet above the ground, you'll soar above spectacular scenery projected onto the gigantic domed screen. Sensory elements and gentle winds add realism to the experience. There's a 40-inch height minimum to ride.

The **Seas with Nemo & Friends** ★ pavilion has been completely renovated, save the 5.7-million-gallon aquarium that holds a reef and more than 4,000 sea creatures, including, among other aquatic creatures, sharks, barracudas, parrotfish, rays, and dolphins. Also inside is a family-friendly "clamobile" ride that slowly moves you along several stunning undersea scenes in search of Nemo; using new animation technology, the characters seemingly swim right along with the live inhabitants in the aquarium. Kids will get a kick out of **Turtle Talk with Crush** ★★, as Crush, the turtle from *Finding Nemo,* engages them in a real-time conversation right from his movie-screen tank.

Get set to blast off to Mars on **Mission: SPACE** ★★★, Epcot's most intense attraction. Sophisticated simulator technology, developed in partnership with NASA and Hewlett-Packard, launches you on an amazing ride through space that feels like the real deal (so some NASA astronauts have claimed, anyway). The original, or orange, version is definitely not for the faint at heart—the green however, is far less intense, allowing astronauts-in-training (those not ready for G-forces and spinning simulators) a chance to experience space travel. ***Note:*** Riders must be at least 44 inches tall for both.

Spaceship Earth, Epcot's icon, is a large, silvery geosphere with an audiovisual adventure through time awaiting guests inside. Slow-moving cars take you on a 15-minute journey through the history of communications which, thanks to recent updates and enhancements, has improved (though not significantly). The addition of interactive touch screens enables guests to create their own idea of what the future will look like—and to see themselves in it. An all new interactive exhibit area, where guests can test their skills in the areas of medicine, transportation, and energy management through interactive games and displays, has been added as well.

Test Track ★★ is a marvel that combines GM engineering and Disney Imagineering. Once you're in your six-passenger convertible, the 5-minute ride follows what looks like a real highway and includes a brake test, climb, and tight S-curves. There's also a 12-second burst of speed that reaches 65 mph on the straightaway. ***Note:*** Riders must be at least 40 inches tall.

Sponsored by Exxon, the **Universe of Energy** ★★ pavilion is home to a 32-minute ride, **Ellen's Energy Adventure,** which features comedian Ellen DeGeneres being tutored by Bill Nye the Science Guy to be a *Jeopardy!* contestant. In the process, you learn about energy resources from fossil fuels and take a ride through the age of the dinosaurs.

Moments A Grand Nightcap

IllumiNations ★★ is a blend of fireworks, lasers, and fountains in a display that's signature Disney. The show is worth the crowds that flock to the parking lot when it's over—don't miss it! ***Tip:*** Stake your claim to the best viewing areas a half-hour before show time (listed in your *Times Guide*). The ones near Showcase Plaza have a head start for the exits. The Rose & Crown Pub in the U.K. pavilion (see earlier in this chapter), offers a great view of the proceedings.

WORLD SHOWCASE

Surrounding the nearly 40-acre lagoon at the north end of the park is this community of 11 miniaturized nations, each re-created with meticulous detail and featuring indigenous architecture, landscaping, restaurants, and shops. The nations' cultural facets are explored in art exhibits, dance and live performances, or innovative films. The cast members working at each pavilion are natives of that country, making the experience that much more authentic. The World Showcase opens at 11am and remains open generally up to 2 hours after Future World closes, so plan on heading there after Future World.

The architecture in **Canada ★★** ranges from a mansard-roofed replica of Ottawa's 19th-century, French-style Château Laurier (here called Hôtel du Canada) to a British-influenced stone building modeled after a landmark near Niagara Falls. But the highlight is ***O Canada!*** **★**, a 22-minute, 360-degree CircleVision film that shows Canada's scenic splendor, from a dog-sled race to the thundering flight of thousands of snow geese.

Bounded by a serpentine wall that wanders its perimeter, the **China ★★** pavilion is entered via a triple-arched ceremonial gate inspired by the Temple of Heaven in Beijing, a summer retreat for Chinese emperors. Passing through the gate, you'll see a half-size replica of this ornately embellished, red-and-gold circular temple, built in 1420 during the Ming dynasty. Inside, the CircleVision film, *Reflections of China,* shows off China's greatest cities. Gardens simulate those in Suzhou, with miniature waterfalls, fragrant lotus ponds, bamboo groves, corkscrew willows, and weeping mulberry trees. Outside, the amazing **Dragon Legend Acrobats** provide live thrills.

The **France** pavilion focuses on La Belle Epoque, a period from 1870 to 1910 during which French art, literature, and architecture flourished. It's entered via a replica of the Pont des Arts footbridge over the Seine and leads to a 1/10-scale model of the Eiffel Tower, constructed from Gustave Eiffel's original blueprints. The big attraction here is ***Impressions du France*** **★★**, a 20-minute film featuring the country's top sights and scenery set to the music of famous French composers.

Enclosed by castle walls and towers, the festive **Germany** pavilion is centered on a cobblestone square with pots of colorful flowers girding a fountain statue of St. George and the Dragon. The adjacent clock tower's glockenspiel figures herald each hour with quaint melodies. The 16th-century facades replicate a merchant's hall in the Black Forest and the town hall in Römerberg Square. Model-train enthusiasts and kids shouldn't miss the detailed **miniature German village ★**.

One of the prettiest World Showcase pavilions, **Italy ★**, lures visitors over an arched footbridge to a replica of Venice's pink-and-white Doge's Palace. Other highlights include an 83-foot-tall bell tower, Venetian bridges, and a central piazza enclosing a version of Bernini's Neptune Fountain.

At **Japan** ★★, a flaming-red *torii* (gate of honor) leads the way to the Goju No To pagoda, inspired by a shrine built at Nara in A.D. 700. In a traditional Japanese garden, cedars, yews, bamboos, willows, and flowering shrubs frame pebbled footpaths, rustic bridges, waterfalls, rock landscaping, and a pond of koi. The Yakitori House is based on the 16th-century Katsura Imperial Villa in Kyoto, considered the crowning achievement of Japanese architecture. Another highlight is the moated **White Heron Castle,** a replica of the Shirasagi-Jo, a 17th-century fortress overlooking the city of Himeji. The drums of **Matsuriza** ★★—one of the best performances in the World Showcase—entertain guests daily.

You'll hear marimbas and mariachi bands (including **Mariachi Cobre**) as you approach the festive **Mexico** ★ showcase, fronted by a towering Mayan pyramid modeled on the Aztec temple of Quetzalcoatl (God of Life) and surrounded by dense Yucatán jungle landscaping. Upon entering the pavilion, you'll find yourself in a museum of pre-Columbian art and artifacts. Down a ramp, after you have passed through the marketplace and its shops, the newly refurbished **Gran Fiesta Tour Starring the Three Caballeros** offers an 8-minute cruise through Mexico, with a new story line and an overlay of animation starring Donald Duck, Jose, and Carioca.

When you enter **Morocco** ★★, note the imperfections in the mosaic tile in the Koutoubia Minaret, the prayer tower of a 12th-century mosque in Marrakech. They were put there intentionally in accordance with the belief that only Allah is perfect. The **Medina (Old City),** entered via a replica of an arched gateway in Fez, leads to Fez House (a traditional Moroccan home) and the narrow, winding streets of the *souk,* a bustling marketplace where all manner of authentic handcrafted merchandise is on display. **Treasures of Morocco** is a daily, 35-minute guided tour that highlights this country's culture, architecture, and history.

Inside **Norway** ★, a *stavekirke* (stave church), styled after the 13th-century Gol Church of Hallingdal, features changing exhibits. A replica of Oslo's 14th-century **Akershus Castle,** next to a cascading woodland waterfall, is the setting for the pavilion's restaurant (p. 476). **Maelstrom** ★, a ride in a dragon-headed Viking vessel, traverses fiords before you crash through a gorge into the North Sea, where you're hit by a storm (albeit a relatively calm one). Passengers disembark at a 10th-century Viking village to view the 70-millimeter film *Norway,* which documents Norwegian history.

The **United Kingdom** ★ pavilion beckons you with **Britannia Square,** a formal London-style park, complete with copper-roofed gazebo bandstand, stereotypical red phone booth, and a statue of the Bard. Four centuries of architecture are represented along quaint cobblestone streets. ***Tip:*** Don't miss the **British Invasion** ★, a group that impersonates the Beatles daily except Sunday, and live entertainment at the pub most evenings.

Housed in a Georgian-style structure, the 29-minute **U.S.A.—The American Adventure** ★ is a dramatization of U.S. history using video, rousing music, and a cast of audio-animatronic figures, including narrators Mark Twain and Ben Franklin. You'll see Jefferson writing the Declaration of Independence, the attack on Pearl Harbor, and the *Eagle* heading for the moon, among other historic scenes. Entertainment includes the **Spirit of America Fife & Drum Corps** and **Voices of Liberty,** an a cappella group that sings patriotic songs.

8 DISNEY'S HOLLYWOOD STUDIOS

Disney bills this park as "the Hollywood that never was and always will be." Hollywood's golden era, around 1940 or so, and done up à la Disney, surrounds you with Art Deco–style buildings accented with pastel colors and neon lights. You'd be hard-pressed to miss Mickey's giant sorcerer's hat looming ahead on Hollywood Boulevard, or the Tower of Terror and the Earful Tower rising above the landscape. This park is home to two of Disney's most pulse-quickening rides, a variety of movie- and TV-themed shows, and uniquely themed restaurants that outshine most others in WDW.

MAJOR ATTRACTIONS & SHOWS

The 35-minute **Hollywood Studios Backlot Tour** ★ takes you behind the scenes via tram for a look at the vehicles, props, costumes, sets, and special effects used in movies and TV shows. But the real fun begins once you reach **Catastrophe Canyon,** where an earthquake causes canyon walls to rumble. A raging oil fire, massive explosions, torrents of rain, and flash floods threaten you and other riders before you're taken behind the scenes to see how filmmakers use special effects to make such disasters. Over at soundstage 4, on Mickey Avenue, the magical world of Narnia comes alive. With the release of *Prince Caspian* came a transformation of the attraction—rather than venturing through the wardrobe to the wintry white set, guests will be able to explore Aslan's stone table chamber, even meet Prince Caspian himself. Remaining in the small gallery just beyond the set are elaborate creatures, actual costumes, armory, artwork, and props used in the latest film.

Producers adapted the 30-minute show, ***Beauty and the Beast Live on Stage*** ★, from the movie of the same name. The sets and costumes are lavish, and the production numbers are pretty spectacular. Arrive early to get a good seat.

On the **Great Movie Ride,** film footage, audio-animatronic movie stars, and miniature movie sets re-create some of the most famous scenes in film, including clips from *Casablanca, Mary Poppins,* and *Alien.* The ride is longer than most at 22 minutes, but true movie buffs will find this ride down memory lane sheer bliss.

Peek into the world of movie stunts at the 30-minute **Indiana Jones Epic Stunt Spectacular** ★★★, which re-creates the most memorable scenes from the Indiana Jones films. Arrive early and sit near the stage for your shot at being an audience participant. Alas, this is a job for adults only.

Kermit and Miss Piggy star in ***Jim Henson's Muppet*Vision 3D*** ★★, a must-see film that marries Jim Henson's puppets with Disney audio-animatronics, special effects, 70-millimeter film, and 3-D technology. The coming-at-you action includes flying Muppets, cream pies, and cannonballs, as well as high winds, fiber-optic fireworks, bubble showers, even an actual spray of water. This comical 25-minute show runs continuously.

Younger kids will appreciate the nearby Honey, I Shrunk the Kids Movie Set Adventure, as they can crawl and climb their way through the larger-than-life set filled with 30-foot blades of grass and gigantic spider webs, among other features.

Moments A Nighttime Spectacle

The fireworks, laser lights, and choreography of **Fantasmic!** ★★★ make it a spectacular, 25-minute, end-of-day experience. The extravaganza features shooting stars, fireballs, animated fountains, a cast of 50, a giant dragon, a king cobra, and 1 million gallons of water. And everything is orchestrated by a familiar sorcerer mouse. Throughout, musical scores and characters from Disney classics will entrance you.

The **Magic of Disney Animation** begins with a theater presentation co-hosted by Mushu the dragon (from Disney's *Mulan*), who reveals the secrets behind the creation of Disney's animated characters. The Q&A session that follows allows guests a chance to ask questions before attempting to draw their own Disney characters while under the supervision of a working animator (the best part of the experience). You'll also get the chance to meet and greet a variety of Disney characters.

Younger audiences (ages 2–5) love the 20-minute ***Playhouse Disney—Live on Stage!*** where they meet characters from *Mickey Mouse Clubhouse, Little Einsteins, Handy Manny,* and others. It encourages preschoolers to dance, sing, and play along with the cast. It shows several times a day. Check your schedule.

Want the best thrill ride WDW has to offer? Then tackle the fast-and-furious **Rock 'n' Roller Coaster ★★★**. Sitting in a 24-passenger "stretch limo" with 120 speakers blaring Aerosmith tunes at 32,000 watts, you'll blast from 0 to 60 mph in 2.8 seconds, then fly into the first gut-tightening inversion at 5Gs. The wild ride continues on through a make-believe California freeway system in the semidarkness (to the tune of Aerosmith's hit, "Sweet Emotion"). ***Note:*** Riders must be at least 48 inches tall.

Cutting edge when it opened, **Star Tours,** based on the original *Star Wars* trilogy, is now a couple of rungs below the latest technology, but is still a fun ride. After boarding a 40-seat "spacecraft," you're off in a whoosh on a journey that takes you through some of the more famous *Star Wars* scenes, full of sudden drops, crashes, and oncoming laser blasts as you seemingly careen out of control. ***Note:*** Riders must be at least 40 inches tall. Just next door, pint-size padawan can train alongside Jedi masters at the all new interactive **Jedi Training Academy.**

The **Twilight Zone Tower of Terror ★★★** is one of the most exciting rides at WDW. As legend has it, during a violent storm on Halloween night 1939, lightning struck the Hollywood Tower Hotel, causing an entire wing and an elevator full of people to disappear—and you're about to meet them as you star in a special episode of *The Twilight Zone.* The ride features random drop sequences, allowing for a real sense of the unknown. New visual, audio, and olfactory effects have also been added to make the experience even more frightening. Because it offers a different experience every time you dare to ride, it's the best attraction of its kind. ***Note:*** You must be at least 40 inches tall to ride.

Hazy lighting and special effects create an underwater effect in a reef-walled theater, helping set the mood for the charming 17-minute musical, ***Voyage of the Little Mermaid*** **★★**, which combines live performers with puppets, film clips, and more. Many of the movie's most popular songs, including the theme, "Under the Sea," are featured.

Lights, Motors, Action! Extreme Stunt Show features high-flying high-speed movie stunts full of pyrotechnic effects and more. It's similar to the Indiana Jones Stunt Spectacular, but far faster paced and action packed.

Toy Story Mania made its debut in the summer of 2008. Donning 3-D glasses, guests shrink to the size of a toy, hop into fanciful vehicles, then travel and twist along a colorful midway-themed route. Think Buzz Lightyear's Space Ranger Spin (at the Magic Kingdom) but with a classic midway twist. Hidden targets lead to different levels of play ensuring that each experience is unique—just be prepared to wait in a lengthy line as it's quickly become one of the most popular rides in the park.

It's American Idol à la Disney at the American Idol Experience. Debuting in early 2009, this all new high-energy show follows in the footsteps of the hit TV show of the same name. Staged on a set that replicates the TV original, guests audition, compete—and are judged live and on stage. It's definitely the hottest ticket in the park.

Block Party Bash, an interactive dance party parade, takes to the streets each afternoon. Debuting in the spring of 2008 (replacing the Disney's Stars and Motor Cars Parade), this lively celebration has guests singing and dancing along as high-flying acrobats and fan-favorites from such Disney-Pixar flicks as Finding Nemo, Toy Story 2, Monster's Inc., The Incredibles, A Bug's Life, and others join in all the interactive fun.

9 ANIMAL KINGDOM

Disney's fourth major park combines the elaborate and impressive landscapes of Asia and Africa, including the exotic (and real!) creatures that inhabit these distant lands, with the prehistoric lands of the dinosaur. A conservation venue as much as an attraction ensures that you won't find the animals blatantly displayed throughout the 500-acre park; instead, naturalistic habitats blend seamlessly into the spectacular surroundings. This unfortunately means that, at times, you'll have to search a bit to find the inhabitants. Your experience here will be far different than at Disney's other parks because the focus is on the surroundings, meticulously re-created architecture, and intricate detailing, not so much on the attractions themselves. ***A bonus:*** The park is easily enjoyed in a single day, usually less, making it a good choice when you need to cut back and take it a bit slower and easier.

DISCOVERY ISLAND

Like Cinderella Castle in the Magic Kingdom, the 14-story **Tree of Life** ★★ is the Discovery Island's central landmark. The tree itself has 8,000 limbs, 103,000 leaves, and 325 mammals, reptiles, amphibians, bugs, birds, Mickeys, and dinosaurs carved into its trunk, limbs, and roots. Teams of WDW artisans worked for a year creating its sculptures, and it's worth a walk around its roots, especially on the way to see ***It's Tough to Be a Bug!*** ★★, a fun 3-D movie with impressive special effects. Grab your glasses and settle into a creepy-crawly seat. It's not a great choice for younger kids (it's dark and loud, with a few buzzing sensory effects) or bug haters, but for others, it's a fun, sometimes poignant look at life from a smaller perspective.

DINOLAND U.S.A.

Enter beneath "Olden Gate Bridge," a 40-foot Brachiosaurus reassembled from fossils. You'll also find a replica of "Sue," a 67-million-year-old Tyrannosaurus Rex skeleton that was worked on by paleontologists here before being shipped to her home at Chicago's Field Museum.

Kids love the chance to slip, slither, slide, and slink through the **Boneyard** ★★, a giant playground where they can discover and uncover the realistic-looking remains of Triceratops, T-Rex, and other vanished giants. It's also a great place for parents to take a break from the pavement pounding of a day in the park.

Dinosaur ★ hurls you through the darkness in a CTX Rover "time machine" to the time when dinosaurs ruled the earth. The expedition takes you past an array of snarling and particularly ferocious-looking dinosaurs, one of which thinks that you would make a great lunchtime treat. Young children may find the dinos and darkness a bit frightening and the ride a bit jarring. ***Note:*** You must be 40 inches or taller to climb aboard.

Primeval Whirl is a spinning, freestyle twin roller coaster, where you control the action through its wacky maze of curves, peaks, and dippity-do-dahs. This is a modern version of those old carnival roller coasters of the '50s and '60s. ***Note:*** It carries a 48-inch height minimum.

TriceraTop Spin is a minithrill for youngsters. Friendly-looking dinosaur "cars" circle a hub while moving up and down and all around, much like Dumbo and the Magic Carpets of Aladdin (p. 487) at the Magic Kingdom.

Finding Nemo–The Musical ★★★, Disney's new enchanting stage production, sees Nemo, Marlin, Dory, Crush, and Bruce (among others) come to life, as live actors in creatively designed, puppetlike costumes work together to re-create the undersea adventure made popular by the hit film. Stunning special effects and a moving musical score (created especially for the show) complete and complement the experience. Even the squirmiest toddler will sit mesmerized through this 30-minute show—it's a must for the entire family.

CAMP MINNIE-MICKEY

A character meet-and-greet zone and one of the best theme-park shows in town are the main attractions in this small area of Animal Kingdom.

If your kids are hooked on filling their autograph books, the **Character Greeting Trails** should be your first stop (though lines can get excruciatingly long). Various Disney characters have separate trails where you can meet and mingle, snap photos, and get those autographs.

Everyone in the audience comes alive when the music starts at the rousing, 28-minute ***Festival of the Lion King*** ★★★ in the Lion King Theater. The festival celebrates nature's diversity with a talented troupe of singers, dancers, and life-size critters. It's a sight-and-sound spectacular that shouldn't be missed. Make sure to arrive at least 20 minutes early.

AFRICA

Enter through Harambe, a re-creation of an African coastal village at the edge of the 21st century. A central marketplace is surrounded by structures built of coral stone, aged for an authentic look, and thatched with reed by African craftsman.

Animal Kingdom has expanded its collection of rides, but the **Kilimanjaro Safaris** ★★★ is still one of the most popular. As you bump along through a simulated African savanna in a large truck, you may spot black rhinos, hippos, crocodiles, antelopes, wildebeests, zebras, giraffes, and lions. The downside: If the animals aren't feeling cooperative at the time you're riding, you may not see much. They're scarce at midday most of the year (in cooler months you may get lucky), so *ride this one as close to the park's opening or closing as you can.*

Hippos, tapirs, ever-active mole rats, and other critters are often on the **Pangani Forest Exploration Trail** ★★ for your viewing, but the real prize is getting a look at the gorillas. Don't expect full cooperation, however, because in hot weather, they spend most of the day in shady areas and out of view. Those who come early, stay late, are patient, or make return visits should be rewarded with a close-up look.

ASIA

Disney's Imagineers did an amazing job of creating the mythical kingdom of **Anandapur.** The intricately painted artwork is just another example of the lengths to which Disney has gone to transport you from the everyday real world to the places of your imagination.

Kali River Rapids ★ is a good raft ride. Its churning waters and optical illusions will have you wondering if you're about to drop over the falls. Expedition Everest makes a brief but impressive appearance along the way. You *will* most likely get wet. ***Note:*** There's a 38-inch height minimum.

Impressively detailed surroundings and up-close views of the animals make **Maharajah Jungle Trek** ★★ an often-overlooked jewel. If you don't show up in the midday heat, you may see Bengal tigers through the thick glass, while nothing but air divides you from dozens of giant fruit bats (with wingspans up to 6 ft.) and other smaller inhabitants. Be sure to pick up one of the guides that list the many unusual and often rare inhabitants to look for along the way.

Expedition Everest ★★★, the newest and most impressive attraction in the park, transports guests to the small and meticulously detailed Himalayan village of Serka Zong. Guests board the Anadapur Rail Service bound for Mount Everest; after passing through bamboo forests and waterfalls, diving through fields of glaciers, and climbing to the snowcapped peaks, the train suddenly veers "out of control" sending riders careening down Mount Everest's rough and rugged terrain. You'll be thrust forward and backward, in and out of the darkness. And that's not the end . . . a close encounter with a legendary Yeti will have your hair standing on end before it's over.

10 OTHER WDW ATTRACTIONS

TYPHOON LAGOON ★★★

A storm-stranded fishing boat—*Miss Tilly*—teeters atop 95-foot-high Mount Mayday overlooking this tropically themed and seemingly typhoon-tossed Disney water park. Guests can be tossed about on a number of twisting and turning wild rides and slides here. There are more relaxing activities as well.

Castaway Creek's rafts and inner tubes glide along a 2,100-foot-long river that circles most of the park, passing through a rainforest, caves, and grottoes. At **Water Works,** jets of water spew from shipwrecked boats.

Ketchakiddie Creek is for the 2- to 5-year-old set. An innovative water playground, it has bubbling fountains in which to frolic, mini water slides, a pint-size "white-water" tubing run, spouting whales and squirting seals, rubbery crocodiles to climb on, grottoes to explore, and waterfalls to loll under.

At **Shark Reef,** guests get free equipment and receive a few instructions—and then you're off for a 15-minute swim through a very small snorkeling area that's home to a simulated reef and sunken shipwreck, and populated by parrotfish, rays, and small sharks.

The **Surf Pool** ★★, the park's 2.75-million-gallon wave pool, is one of the world's largest. Every 90 seconds, a foghorn sounds, warning you of the impending and crashing waves, just in case you want to head for cover. Young children will appreciate wading in the lagoon's more peaceful tidal pools of **Blustery Bay** and **Whitecap Cove;** the bigger, more powerful waves of the Surf Pool would most likely sweep them away.

Humunga Kowabunga consists of three 214-foot Mount Mayday slides that send you plummeting down the mountain on a serpentine route through waterfalls and bat caves and past nautical wreckage before depositing you into a bubbling catch pool. ***Note:*** You must be 48 inches or taller to ride this. **White-Water Rides** at Mount Mayday is the setting for three white-water rafting adventures—**Keelhaul Falls, Mayday Falls,** and **Gangplank Falls**—all offering steep and drenching drops coursing through caves and passing lush scenery.

The newest thrill to splash onto the scene is the **Crush 'n' Gusher,** a first-of-its-kind water coaster with three separate experiences to choose from: the **Banana Blaster, Coconut Crusher,** and **Pineapple Plunger,** each offering steep drops, twists, and turns of varying degrees.

Typhoon Lagoon is open from 10am to 5pm, with extended hours during holiday periods and summer (✆ **407/560-4141;** www.disneyworld.com). A 1-day ticket is $40 for adults, $34 for children 3 to 9.

BLIZZARD BEACH ★★★

Snowcapped mountaintops in the middle of sunny Orlando—who else but Disney could have created this 66-acre "ski resort," set in the midst of a tropical lagoon and centered on the 90-foot Mount Gushmore? ***Note:*** The majority of this park's attractions are geared to thrill-seekers, making it a better choice for families with kids at least 8 years of age.

The 2,900-foot-long **Cross Country Creek** is a lazy river ride that runs the perimeter of the park, but watch out for the brisk though refreshing melting "ice" as you pass through the Polar Caves. The waves of Melt-A-Way Bay offer yet another relaxing and less heart-pounding option. **Runoff Rapids,** however, will send you and your inner tube careening down one of three twisting, turning runs through semidarkness.

Ski-Patrol Training Camp, designed for 'tweens and teens, features a rope swing, a T-bar hanging over the water, the wet and slippery **Mogul Mania** slide, and an ice-floe walk along slippery floating icebergs.

Snow Stormers has three flumes descending from the top of Mount Gushmore, following a switchback course through slalom-type gates.

Summit Plummet ★★ is one of the most breath-defying adventures in any water park. Read every speed, motion, vertical-dip, wedgie, and hold-onto-your-breastplate warning before hopping on. This starts slow, with a lift ride to the 120-foot summit. But it finishes as the world's fastest body slide—a test of your courage and swimsuit—that virtually goes straight down and has you moving sans vehicle at 60 mph into the catch pool. ***Note:*** It has a 48-inch height minimum.

Teamboat Springs is the world's longest white-water raft ride, twisting down a 1,200-foot series of rushing waterfalls.

Tike's Peak is a kid-friendly version of Mount Gushmore. It has short water slides, animals to climb aboard, a snow castle, a squirting ice pond, and a fountain play area for young guests.

Blizzard Beach is open from 10am to 5pm, with extended hours during some holiday periods and summer (✆ **407/560-3400;** www.disneyworld.com). A 1-day ticket is $40 for adults, $34 for children 3 to 9.

MINIATURE GOLF ★

Hippos, ostriches, and alligators decorate the **Fantasia Gardens** course, a good bet for beginners and kids. Seasoned minigolfers will likely prefer the second 18-hole course, **Fantasia Fairways,** filled with sand traps, water hazards, and trickier putting greens. With holes ranging from 40 to 75 feet, and no whimsical characters in sight, this one is definitely not for novices—unless you appreciate frustration.

Santa Claus and his elves provide the theme for **Winter Summerland,** which has two additional 18-hole courses, appropriate for all ages and abilities. The summer course is pure Florida, from sand castles to surfboards; the other course offers a touch of the North Pole and a visit with Santa on the "Winternet."

Tickets are about $13 for adults and $10 for kids 3 to 9. The courses are open from 10am to 10 or 11pm daily. For information about Fantasia Gardens, call © **407/560-4582.** For information on Winter Summerland, call © **407/560-3000.** Find both on the Internet at **www.disneyworld.com**.

11 WHAT TO SEE & DO BEYOND DISNEY: UNIVERSAL ORLANDO & SEAWORLD

There are so many attractions in Orlando (more than 95) that it's impossible to see even half of them unless you're here for a month. The following should help you finish your must-see list.

UNIVERSAL STUDIOS IN FLORIDA

Lights, camera, and action, action, action. Universal is touted as the park where you can "Ride the Movies," and that boast isn't far off the mark. It's filled with fast-paced, high-intensity attractions such as Revenge of the Mummy, Jaws, and Men in Black Alien Attack. There's lots here for kids, too. As a plus, it's a working motion-picture and TV studio, so occasional filming takes place at the sound stages. There are also plenty of characters on hand to meet and greet visitors throughout the park.

TICKET PRICES A **1-day, one-park ticket** costs $75 for adults, $63 for children 3 to 9. A 2-day, two-park admission ticket runs $105 for adults, $95 for children. A two-park premier annual pass will run $290 (any age). The latter includes free parking, CityWalk club access, Universal Express Plus access after 4pm, and plenty of other perks. The two-park preferred annual pass is less expensive at $230 (any age) and includes free parking with no blackout dates; the two-park power pass is the least expensive at $150; however, most holidays and many weekends are blacked out, and parking is not included.

Like Disney, Universal offers savings on ticket purchases as well as additional multiday tickets if you purchase them before you leave home. Buy your 2-day, two-park unlimited admission tickets, good for 7 consecutive days, online and you'll save a bundle at $99 for adults and kids alike. You can pick up your tickets at the front gate of either park or have them sent (for a delivery charge) to your home.

THE FLEXTICKET The least expensive way to see Universal, SeaWorld, Aquatica, *and* Wet 'n Wild is with a **FlexTicket.** This pass lets you pay one price for unlimited admission to participating parks during a 14-day period. The Orlando Flex Ticket, which includes admission to Universal Studios Florida, Islands of Adventure, Wet 'n Wild, SeaWorld, and Aquatica, is $235 for adults and $215 for children 3 to 9. The Orlando Flex Ticket Plus, which adds Busch Gardens Africa in Tampa Bay (p. 387), is $280 for adults and $260 for kids. FlexTickets can be ordered through Universal (© **800/711-0080** or 407/363-8000; www.universalorlando.com) as well the other participating parks. Free shuttle service between all of the parks, even Busch Gardens Africa, is included in the ticket price.

PARKING Parking is $12 for cars, light trucks, and vans—after 6pm it's $3. Valet parking is $20.

Major Attractions

Set in a parklike theater-in-the-round, the 25-minute musical, ***A Day in the Park with Barney,*** stars that big purple dinosaur, Baby Bop, and BJ. It uses song, dance, interactive play, and unique special effects to entertain younger guests. It's a must for preschoolers, though parents will need strength to endure it.

Not long after you climb on a San Francisco BART train at **Disaster ★★**, there's an earthquake that's 8.3 on the Richter scale! As you sit helplessly trapped, concrete slabs collapse around you, a propane truck bursts into flames, a runaway train hurtles your way, and the station begins to flood with no way out.

Revenge of the Mummy ★★★ is a high-speed, twisting, turning, pulsating adventure through Egyptian tombs, with creepy skeletal warriors in hot pursuit. This one is packed full of amazing pyrotechnic effects, a state-of-the-art propulsion system, and hair-raising robotic creatures.

Soar with E.T. on a mission to save his ailing planet at **E.T. Adventure ★**; you'll pass through the dense forest and gently glide into space aboard a bicycle.

The $45-million **Jaws ★★** begins calmly enough, a seemingly leisurely boat ride through New England coastal waters, when suddenly a 3-ton, 32-foot-long great white shark is spotted lurking about. You can pretty much figure out what happens next. There are plenty of special effects, including a rather heated wall of flame that surrounds your boat as you chargrill the fish before landing safely back at the dock.

Buckle up for **Jimmy Neutron's Nicktoon Blast ★★**, as Jimmy's Rocket Pod hurtles you through hyperspace thanks to sophisticated computer graphics, state-of-the-art ride technology, animation, and programmable motion-based seats. The attraction also features other popular characters, including SpongeBob SquarePants and Rugrats.

In **Men in Black Alien Attack ★★★**, you board a six-passenger cruiser, buzz the streets of New York, and use your "zapper" to splatter up to 120 bug-eyed targets. You have to contend with return fire as well as light, noise, and clouds of liquid nitrogen (also known as fog) that can spin you out of control. Your laser tag–style gun fires infrared bullets. The 4-minute, $70-million ride relies on 360-degree spins rather than speed for its thrill factor. ***Note:*** Guests must be at least 42 inches tall for this ride.

Hollywood Rip Ride Rockit, Universal Studios newest (and Central Florida's tallest) coaster to date, made its debut just as this book was going to print. Located between Jimmy Neutron's Nicktoon Blast and the new AQUOS Theater (home to the Blue Man Group), on a track spilling out beyond the boundaries of the park, twisting high above Citywalk, riders will be sent careening through corkscrews, tight turns, and dramatic drops—oh, and did I mention the record-breaking loop? Check it out for yourself—head to www.hollywoodripriderockit.com.

Shrek 4-D ★, is a 20-minute show that can be seen, heard, felt, and smelled, thanks to motion-simulator technology, OgreVision glasses, and special sensory effects. I expected more from Universal in the seating-effects department, but the preshow and the movie are definitely worthwhile.

The **Simpsons Ride** recently replaced Back to the Future: the Ride. According to Universal, guests get rocketed along with the Simpson family on an amusing adventure through a side of Springfield that has yet to be explored.

James Cameron, who directed *Terminator 2,* supervised the $60-million ***Terminator 2: 3-D Battle Across Time*** **★★**, which features Arnie and other original cast members (on film). It combines three huge screens with technical effects and live action on stage, including a custom-built Harley and six 8-foot-tall cyberbots. The crisp 3-D effects are among the best in any Orlando park. ***Note:*** Universal has given this show a PG-13 rating.

Two million cubic feet of air per minute (enough to fill four full-size blimps) create a funnel cloud five stories tall at ***Twister . . . Ride It Out*** **★★**. The roar of a freight train, at rock-concert decibel level, fills the theater as cars, trucks, and a cow fly by, while the audience watches just 20 feet away. Crowds sometimes applaud when it's all over. ***Note:*** This show has a PG-13 rating—and at press time was open only seasonally.

Woody Woodpecker's Nuthouse Coaster ★★ is a kiddie coaster that will thrill some moms and dads, too. Although only 30 feet at its peak, it offers quick, banked turns. The ride lasts only about 60 seconds and the wait can be 30 minutes or more, but few kids will want to miss the experience. ***Note:*** The coaster has a 36-inch height minimum.

For a good dose of reality, reality TV that is, be sure to catch ***Fear Factor Live.*** Audience members can sign up to be the stars of the show, but be prepared—the stunts, while toned down, are similarly challenging (and just as disgusting), so be sure you're up for the task before volunteering. ***Note:*** At press time the show was being offered only seasonally.

The Blue Man Group, a visually exciting and wildly unique stage show, can be seen daily at the all-new redesigned AQUOS Theater (previously Nickelodeon Studios in Production Central). Show-only tickets start at $64 for adults, $54 for children ages 3 to 9, with combination theme park/show tickets starting at $144 for adults and kids alike.

ISLANDS OF ADVENTURE

Universal's second theme park is even more impressive architecturally than its big brother, Universal Studios Florida. Roller coasters roar above pedestrian walkways, and water rides make some rather big splashes throughout the park. It is, bar none, ***the*** Orlando theme park for thrill-ride junkies, and also offers some of the best, and most unique, dining around—theme park or otherwise.

A few words of caution: *Nine of the park's 14 major rides have height restrictions.* Many rides may not be suitable for those who are tall enough, but who are pregnant or have health problems—physical restrictions; heart, neck, or back problems; or a tendency toward motion sickness.

TICKET PRICES See the "Ticket Prices" information for Universal Studios Florida on p. 501.

THE FLEXTICKET See "The FlexTicket" information for Universal Studios Florida on p. 501.

PARKING Parking is $12 for cars, light trucks, and vans—$3 after 6pm. Valet parking is $20.

Major Attractions

Port of Entry

A towering lighthouse marks the entrance to this seemingly centuries-old marketplace, which serves as a gateway to the Islands of Adventure's five uniquely themed "islands." Guest Services can be found near the gates; the remaining area is filled with shops and restaurants.

Seuss Landing

You'll feel as if you have jumped right into the pages of a Dr. Seuss classic as you enter the whimsically colorful Seuss Landing. Main attractions here are aimed at youngsters, but anyone who loved the good doctor as a child will enjoy the nostalgic fun.

It's hard to miss the cat's candy-striped hat marking the entrance to the **Cat in the Hat** ★★, where guests follow the famous story from beginning to end. You'll pass through scenes right out of the famous tale of a day gone very much awry. This chaotic ride has a few swirls and whirls along the way, making it a bit spunkier than most, though that's part of the fun.

The High in the Sky Seuss Trolley Train Ride is a whimsical, kid-friendly ride that runs along two separate tracks suspended high above Seuss Landing. Traveling in individual "cars," you'll pass by classic Seussian scenes and colorful characters—with the occasional view of Seuss Landing below. Lines for this one can be excruciatingly long, but high-power fans will keep you cool while you wait.

One Fish, Two Fish, Red Fish, Blue Fish ★ is a family favorite similar to the Magic Carpets of Aladdin and Dumbo rides at WDW (including the ridiculously long lines). Here, controls let you move your funky fish up or down as you circle a central hub. Watch out for "squirt posts," which spray unsuspecting riders.

Forget tradition and hop on **Caro-Seuss-El** ★★★. The not-so-normal carousel gives you a chance to ride whimsical characters from Dr. Seuss, including Cowfish, elephant birds, and Mulligatawnies.

The outdoor interactive play area, **If I Ran the Zoo** ★, features flying water snakes and a chance to tickle the toes of a Seussian animal. Kids can also spin wheels, explore caves, fire water cannons, climb, slide, and otherwise burn off excited energy that most adults can't remember ever having. They're also bound to get wet, so be prepared with extra clothes or even a swimsuit.

Marvel Super Hero Island

Adrenaline junkies and thrill-seekers thrive on the twisting, turning, stomach-churning rides found on this island of larger-than-life comic superheroes and villains.

The original web master is the star of the exceptional, special effects–laden ride, the **Amazing Adventures of Spider-Man** ★★★. Passengers wearing 3-D glasses squeal as their 12-passenger cars twist and spin, plunge, and soar through a comic-book universe. A simulated 400-foot drop feels an awful lot like the real thing.

Look! Up in the sky! It's a bird, it's a plane . . . uh, it's you falling 150 feet, if you're courageous enough to climb aboard **Doctor Doom's Fearfall** ★. The screams that can be heard far from the ride's entrance add to the anticipation. You're fired to the top, with feet dangling, and dropped in intervals, leaving your stomach at several levels. The fall isn't quite up to Disney's Tower of Terror's (p. 496), but it's still frightening. ***Note:*** Minimum height is 52 inches.

On the **Incredible Hulk Coaster** ★★★, you're launched from a dark tunnel and hurtled into the lower ozone while accelerating from 0 to 40 mph in 2 seconds. You will spin upside down 128 feet from the ground, feel weightless, and careen through the center of the park. Coaster-lovers will be pleased to know that this ride, which lasts 2 minutes and 15 seconds, includes seven inversions and two deep drops. ***Note:*** Riders must be at least 54 inches tall.

Toon Lagoon

More than 150 life-size cartoon images let you know you've entered an island dedicated to your favorites from the Sunday funnies.

Dudley Do-Right's Ripsaw Falls ★★, which lies under Dudley's staid red hat, has a lot more speed and drop than onlookers think. Six-passenger logs launch you into a 75-foot dip at 50 mph. You *will* get wet on this ride. ***Note:*** Riders must be 44 inches or taller.

The three-story boat, ***Me Ship, The Olive*** ★, is family-friendly from bow to stern. Kids can toot whistles, clang bells, or play the organ. Sweet Pea's Playpen is fun for young guests. Adults and kids 6 and over love Cargo Crane, which lets you drench riders on Popeye & Bluto's Bilge-Rat Barges.

Popeye & Bluto's Bilge-Rat Barges ★★ are similar to the rafts at WDW's Kali River Rapids (p. 498), but they're faster and bouncier. Adding to the fun, you'll be squirted by water cannons fired from *Me Ship, The Olive* (see above). The rafts bump and dip 14 feet at one point, as you travel a *c-c-cold* white-water course. You will get *soaked!* Riders must be at least 42 inches tall.

Jurassic Park

All of the basics and some of the high-tech wizardry from Steven Spielberg's wildly successful films are incorporated in this lushly landscaped tropical locale that includes a replica of the visitor center from the *Jurassic Park* movie.

The **Camp Jurassic** ★★★ play area has everything from lava pits with dino bones to a rainforest. Watch out for the spitters that lurk in dark caves. The multilevel play area has plenty of places for kids to crawl through, explore, and spend energy on. But keep an eye on young ones: It's easy to get confused in the caverns.

Jurassic Park Discovery Center, a virtual replica of the lab from the movie set, is an amusing, somewhat educational pit stop that offers life-size dinosaur replicas and interactive games. The sequencer lets you combine your DNA with a dinosaur's. The highlight is watching a Velociraptor "hatch" in the nursery.

On the **Jurassic Park River Adventure** ★★, after a leisurely raft tour along a faux river, things go awry (don't they always?). An immense T-Rex thinks you look like a rather tasty morsel, with spitters launching "venom" your way just to add insult to injury. The only way out: an 85-foot, almost vertical plunge in your log-style life raft. It's steep and quick enough to lift your fanny out of the seat. Expect to get wet. ***Note:*** Guests must be at least 42 inches tall.

The Lost Continent

This island is a blend of the mysterious and the mythical, with components of Atlantis, Merlin, and Sinbad. The entrance, marked by an enormous stone griffin clad in iron, sets an appropriately mystic mood.

The biggest thrill here is **Dueling Dragons** ★★★, an intertwined set of two leg-dangling racing roller coasters that test your bravery as they send you soaring 125 feet, invert five times, and miss each other by a mere 12 inches. The ride is rougher on its riders, with quick and jerky banking turns, than the Hulk Coaster. There's a special (longer!) line for the front seat. ***Note:*** Riders must be at least 54 inches tall.

The **Flying Unicorn** ★★ is a smaller roller coaster that travels through a mythical forest with a fast, corkscrew run sure to earn squeals, but probably not at the risk of losing your lunch. Riders must be at least 36 inches tall. At press time, the ride was closed due to construction of the Wizarding World of Harry Potter—its status after the construction is unknown.

Those who notice it have fun at the **Mystic Fountain** ★, a "smart" fountain that especially delights kids. It can "see," "hear," and "talk," leading to a lot of kibitzing with those who stand before it and take the time to kibitz back. But be careful: It can squirt you.

One of the park's two shows, ***Poseidon's Fury*** ★, revolves around a battle between Poseidon, god of the sea, and Darkenon, an evil sorcerer. The most impressive effect occurs as you pass through a small vortex, where 17,500 gallons of water swirl around before you enter a room to experience the battle's pyrotechnic glories.

The **Wizarding World of Harry Potter** is slated to make its debut in 2010, though at press time, details, other than what was originally released almost 2 years ago, and a handful of artist renderings, had yet to be released.

SEAWORLD

This 200-acre marine-life park explores the mysteries of the deep by combining conservation awareness with entertainment (also known as edutainment). Through the years it has expanded, adding a handful of thrill rides (including Manta in the summer of 2009), a large shopping and dining area, additional entertainment venues, and more wildlife. While not as large as its neighbors (Universal and Disney), it won't leave you as thoroughly exhausted, or exasperated by crowds. The unique combination of its animal life, calmer atmosphere, beautifully landscaped grounds, shows, and sprinkling of rides makes it a must-see for anyone visiting the Orlando area.

TICKET PRICES A **1-day ticket** costs $75 for ages 10 and over, $65 for children 3 to 9, plus 6.5% sales tax. If you purchase tickets in advance online (at home only) at least 7 days in advance from the time of your visit, you can save $10 off the price of an adult ticket and in addition, each ticket holder (child or adult) will get a second day free (valid for one additional visit up to 7 days from when you first used your ticket).

MULTIPARK PASSES For information on the **FlexTicket,** see p. 503. The **Fun Card** is a 1-year pass good for unlimited visits to SeaWorld. Prices run $75 for adults and $65 for kids ages 3 to 9. Fun Cards are only available to Florida residents.

Multiday and multipark **Passports** are also available. These are essentially annual passes, good for either 1 or 2 years, and cover one, two, three, or four parks, depending on which you choose. The passes start at $100 and run to as much as $320. For more information, call ✆ **407/351-3600** or check **www.seaworld.com**.

PARKING Parking is $12 for cars, light trucks, and vans. For $15, you can park close to the entrance in a specially designated section.

Major Attractions

A lovable sea lion and otter, with a supporting cast of walruses and harbor seals as well as some quick-witted SeaWorld actors/trainers, appear in ***Clyde & Seamore Take Pirate Island*** ★★, a fish-breath comedy with a swashbuckling theme. It's corny, but a lot of fun. Watch out if you enter too close to show time; the mime entertaining the crowds ahead of time may target you for the audience's amusement.

Taking a cue from Disney Imagineers, SeaWorld created a story to go with its $30-million water coaster, **Journey to Atlantis** ★★. But what really matters is the drop—a wild plunge from 60 feet with lugelike curves. ***Note:*** Riders must be at least 42 inches tall, and pregnant women as well as those with heart, neck, or back problems should not ride.

Kraken ★★★, named for a mythological beast, is a floorless, open-sided coaster where 32-passenger trains place you on a pedestal, high above the track, your feet dangling. You'll climb 151 feet, only to fall 144 feet at speeds of up to 65 mph seconds later, passing underground a total of three times (spraying bystanders with water), and making seven loops before you finally touch ground again. It's actually higher and faster than any coaster at Universal, probably making it the longest 3 minutes and 39 seconds of your life. ***Note:*** Kraken has a 54-inch height minimum.

Note: At press time, **Manta,** SeaWorld's newest thrill-a-minute mega-coaster, was about to make its debut. Said to be an experience unlike any other, the Manta-inspired flying coaster will take riders soaring high into the sky and diving deep into the ocean depths at speeds of up to 60 mph past some of the largest underwater habitats in the park—all the while riding face-down, in a prone horizontal position. Riders will at times find themselves within inches of the sea—at others skimming the sky thanks to the tracks four inversions.

Tips Shuttle Service

SeaWorld and Busch Gardens Africa (p. 387), both owned by Anheuser-Busch, offer round-trip shuttle service ($10 per person) to get you from Orlando to Tampa and back. The 1½- to 2-hour one-way shuttle runs daily and has five pickup locations in Orlando, including at Universal and on International Drive (✆ **800/221-1339**). The schedule allows for about 7 hours at Busch Gardens Africa. The service is free if you hold a FlexTicket.

In **Manatee Rescue** ★, underwater viewing stations, innovative cinema techniques, and interactive displays combine for a tribute to these gentle marine mammals. While this isn't as good as seeing them in the wild, it's as close as most folks get.

You are transported by moving sidewalk through arctic and Antarctic displays at **Penguin Encounter.** You'll get a glimpse of penguins as they preen, socialize, and swim at bullet speed in their 22°F (–6°C) habitat. You'll also see puffins and murres in a similar, separate area. While it gives you a nice view of the penguins (and they are always a hit with the kids), the viewing area's surroundings are in need of a face-lift.

The 4-acre **Shamu's Happy Harbor** ★★ play area has a four-story net tower with a 35-foot-high crow's nest, water cannons, remote-controlled vehicles, nine slides, a submarine, a water maze, and six all-new kid-friendly rides, including a cool little coaster. Most kids relish the freedom of running, jumping, and climbing (and, of course, getting wet) after hearing "Don't wander too far away from us" all day long. It is easy to escape a parent's watchful eye here, so little ones are best accompanied by an adult.

Everyone comes to SeaWorld to see Shamu and his friends—the stars of the all-new, impressively choreographed show, ***Believe*** (replacing *The Shamu Adventure*). A new set, spectacular special effects, and an excellent musical score combine with a top-notch performance to produce a great show. Be sure to heed the warnings, as those sitting in the first 14 rows are sure to get soaked with icy water—and not just once, either. ***Blue Horizons*** ★★, the park's all-new dolphin show, features aerial acrobatics, exotic birds, and dolphins of course. It's a far cry from the ho-hum dolphin show it replaced. ***A'Lure—The Call of the Ocean,*** the park's newest production, replaces *Odyessa*. Like its predecessor, this all new high-energy show is visually exciting as acrobatics and spectacular undersea scenery simply entrance the audience.

SeaWorld has added 220 species to its **Shark Encounter** attraction. The pools out front contain small sharks and rays (feeding isn't allowed). The interior aquariums have big eels, poisonous lionfish, menacing barracudas, bug-eyed puffer fish, and even larger and more menacing sharks. The eerie music playing in the background adds to the ominous ambience.

Enveloping guests in the beauty, exhilaration, and danger of a polar expedition, **Wild Arctic** ★ combines a high-definition adventure film with flight-simulator technology to display breathtaking arctic panoramas. After a hazardous flight over the frozen north, visitors emerge into an exhibit where you can see a playful polar bear, beluga whales, and walruses. Kids and those prone to motion sickness may find the ride bumpy. There's a separate line if you want to skip the flight.

The **Waterfront,** SeaWorld's most recent expansion, is a wonderfully themed 5-acre Mediterranean seaport village with unique shops, a wide variety of restaurants (each offering a very different atmosphere and menu), and, for entertainment, formal shows and street performances.

Dining at SeaWorld

The park offers an array of entertaining dining experiences in addition to its newly expanded collection of Waterfront eateries. **Dine with Shamu** ($42 adults, $33 kids ages 3–9) gives visitors the experience of seeing Shamu up close (inside an area restricted to trainers during normal hours) while enjoying a buffet-style meal (breakfast, lunch or dinner). Younger kids will get a kick out of **Breakfast with Elmo & Friends** ($17 adults, $15 kids ages 3–9). Favorites from *Sesame Street* are on hand to meet, greet, and have photos taken with the family each and every morning at the SeaFire Inn. The **Makahiki Luau** serves up island-style entertainment as well as a luau-type meal. The cost is $46 adults, $29 kids ages 3 to 9 (park admission is *not* required). **Sharks Underwater Grill** is an upscale restaurant geared mostly to adults and allows up-close viewing of sharks through a gigantic wall of glass. Entrees are a bit pricey, averaging around $18 (and reaching upwards of $36), but the gourmet Floribbean fare is a few cuts above the usual park cuisine.

DISCOVERY COVE: A DOLPHIN ENCOUNTER

Anheuser-Busch spent $100 million building SeaWorld's sister park, which debuted in 2000. Prices vary seasonally but range from $289 to $359 per person (plus 6.5% sales tax) for ages 6 and up if you want to swim with the dolphins; and $189 to $259 if you forego the experience. Double-check prices when you make your reservations (required to enter the park).

The **dolphin encounter** ★★★ allows guests the opportunity to swim, touch, play, and interact with these amazingly intelligent creatures. They can even take a brief, albeit thrilling ride with one. The entire experience lasts 90 minutes, 35 to 40 minutes of which are spent in the lagoon with a dolphin. The rest is a classroom experience on these remarkable mammals.

Here's what you get for your money, with or without the dolphin encounter.

- A limit of *no more than 1,000 other guests a day.* (The average daily attendance at Disney's Magic Kingdom is 41,000.) This ensures that your experience will be more relaxing and private.
- A continental breakfast, lunch, all-day snacks and drinks, a towel, a locker, sunscreen, snorkeling gear including a flotation vest, a souvenir photo, and free self-parking are also part of the deal.
- Other 9am-to-5:30pm activities include a chance to swim near (but on the other side of the Plexiglas) **barracudas** and **blacktip sharks.** There are no barriers, however, between you and the gentle rays and brightly colored tropical fish swimming amid the 1.3-million-gallon coral reef. The 3,300-foot-long Tropical River is a great place to swim or float in a mild current—it goes through a cave, two waterfalls, and a 100-foot-long, 30-foot-high aviary where you can take a stroll, becoming a human perch. There are also beaches for tanning and relaxing.
- Seven consecutive days of **unlimited admission** to SeaWorld, Busch Gardens Africa, *or* Aquatica. For an additional $30 per person, you can upgrade this option to 14 days of unlimited admission to two additional parks (you can choose from SeaWorld, Busch Gardens Africa, and Aquatica); or, for an additional $50 per person, you can upgrade to include 14 days of unlimited admission to all three additional parks.

Other Area Attractions

Several smaller Orlando-area attractions are well worth noting. Most require less than a full day and don't cost a fortune to experience.

Gatorland (✆ **800/393-5297** or 407/855-5496; www.gatorland.com) is among the most notable. Founded in 1949 and one of Orlando's original attractions, Gatorland now houses thousands of alligators and crocodiles on its 70-acre spread. Headliners include ***Gator Wrestlin',*** where trainers defy death by sticking their heads in the mouths of gators—you can even be part of the show and get your photo sitting atop a gator (his mouth wrapped, of course); ***Gator Jumparoo,*** a fan favorite that features the park's largest reptilian inhabitants lunging 4 to 5 feet out of the water to snatch a hunk of meat right from a trainer's hand; ***Upclose Encounters,*** showcasing the park's toothy carnivores and slithery snakes; and ***Critters on the Go,*** a mobile show that allows younger kids a chance to interact with the park's cuddlier critters. A stop here makes for an entertaining afternoon away from the hustle and bustle of the major parks. The park is generally open from 9am to 5pm (closing time varies seasonally). Admission runs $23 for adults, $15 children 3 to 12 (plus tax).

Wet 'n Wild (✆ **800/992-9453** or 407/351-1800; www.wetnwild.com or www.universalorlando.com/wetnwild), Orlando's favorite non-Disney water park, offers 25 acres of fun, including: the **Flyer,** a six-story, four-passenger toboggan run through 450 feet of banked curves; the **Surge,** one of the longest (curves totaling 580 ft.) and fastest multipassenger tube rides in the Southeast; and **Black Hole,** a two-person, spaceship-style raft that makes a 500-foot, twisting, turning voyage through darkness (all three require that kids 36–48 in. tall be accompanied by an adult). You also can ride the all-new **Brain Wash,** a six-story extreme tube ride with an intense 53-foot vertical drop followed by a whirling swirling ride 'round the 65-foot domed funnel (48-In. height minimum); **Mach 5,** a trio of twisting, turning flumes; and Disco H20**,** an enclosed flume ride that sends riders flying through a '70s flashback complete with mirrored lights and disco music. The park also has a large kids' area with miniversions of the big rides. In addition to the admission prices below, Wet 'n Wild is part of the multiday **FlexTicket package** (see "The FlexTicket" on p. 501 for details and prices). Admission runs $46 for adults, $39 children 3 to 9; however, online specials feature multiday discounts. Hours vary seasonally, depending on weather. Tubes, towels, and lockers are available for a small rental fee.

Private cabanas overlooking dolphin lagoon, including a table, chairs, chaise longues, and towels among other amenities, are available for an additional fee.

Get more information on Discovery Cove by calling ✆ **877/434-7268,** or go to **www.discoverycove.com**. If you want to try it, make a reservation as far in advance as possible. Despite the price, it reaches its capacity almost every day.

AQUATICA: SEAWORLD'S WATER PARK

SeaWorld's latest adventure park made its debut just as this book went to print. The 59-acre eco-themed water park blends its signature up-close animal encounters with high-energy thrills (including racing tunnels and raft rides, slides, and more) with a plethora of pools, lagoons, winding rivers, and stretches of white sandy beaches.

For additional information, call © **888/800-5447** or go to www.aquaticabyseaworld.com. Admission runs $39 for adults, $33 for kids ages 3 to 9. As with all other SeaWorld parks, multiday and multipark passes are available.

12 WALT DISNEY WORLD & ORLANDO AFTER DARK

Central Florida has plenty for night owls to do. Parties last into the wee hours at **Downtown Disney, CityWalk,** and other hot spots.

DISNEY DINNER SHOWS

Disney's Spirit of Aloha Dinner Show (Moments) POLYNESIAN While not nearly as in demand as the *Hoop De Doo* (see below), the Polynesian Resort's delightful 2-hour luau is worth attending. It features Tahitian, Samoan, and Hawaiian singers, drummers, and dancers who entertain while you feast on tropical appetizers, Lanai roasted chicken, Polynesian wild rice, South Seas vegetables, dessert, wine, beer, and other beverages. The action takes place twice nightly, 5 nights a week, in an open-air theater (dress for nighttime weather).

1600 Seven Seas Dr. (at Disney's Polynesian Resort). © **407/939-3463.** www.disneyworld.com. Reservations required. $51–$60 adults, $26–$31 children 3–9 (depends on seating), including tax and gratuity. Holiday surcharge applies on select days. Free parking. Tues–Sat 5:15pm and 8pm.

Hoop De Doo Musical Review ★★★ (Kids) AMERICAN This entertaining, high-energy dinner show is fun for the entire family. Featuring singing and dancing sprinkled with comedy, this show is the most popular of the Disney dinner shows—and with good reason. Dinner consists of country-fried chicken served in a bucket, along with corn on the cob, biscuits, and dessert. And though the food is pretty good, you could almost forget to eat, thanks to all the action going on around you.

4510 N. Fort Wilderness Trail, at Disney's Fort Wilderness Resort and Campground. © **407/WDW-DINE** (939-3463). Reservations required. $51–$60 adults, $26–$31 children 3–11 (depends on seating). Including tax and gratuity. Holiday surcharge applies on select days. Free parking. Nightly 5, 7:15, and 9pm.

ENTERTAINMENT MECCAS

Downtown Disney West Side

House of Blues This club/restaurant's darkened atmosphere is perfect for the oft-featured bluesy sounds that raise its rafters every night. Right next door, however, is the place to go for some of the city's best live entertainment. The huge three-tier concert hall has been known to feature some of the best bands around—local and big names both—and the dance floor is big enough to boogie without doing the bump with a stranger. © **407/934-2583.** www.hob.com. Cover varies.

CityWalk

Located between Islands of Adventure and Universal Studios Florida, this 30-acre club-and-restaurant district (© **407/363-8000;** www.citywalk.com) is five times larger than Pleasure Island. After dark (and even a bit before), the alcohol flows rather freely (don't get too excited—you still have to pay for the drinks!), making this a hot spot for adults, but not a place for kids.

Moments Not Your Ordinary Circus

Cirque du Soleil, the famous no-animals circus in Downtown Disney West Side, seems to put all 64 performers onstage at once in the trampoline routine. The eye-popping ***La Nouba*** ★★★ (from the French for "to live it up"), set in a state-of-the-art theater, is a Fellini-style amalgam of live music, dance, theater, and acrobatics that will have your jaw dropping in no time at all.

But in a world of pricey attractions, this is one of the priciest. There are three ticket categories: prices range from $67 to $117 for adults and $54 to $94 for kids 3 to 9 (including tax). The 90-minute shows are at 6 and 9pm; days rotate. Call ✆ **407/939-7600** or check out **www.cirquedusoleil.com** for details.

You can walk the entire area for free, but select clubs charge a cover to enter their doors. CityWalk also offers two types of **party passes.** A pass that includes access to all the clubs costs $12 plus tax. For $15 plus tax, you get a club pass and a movie at Universal Cineplex (✆ **407/354-5998**). ***Note:*** Daytime parking in the Universal Orlando garages costs $12, $3 after 6pm.

Bob Marley—A Tribute to Freedom Clubbers can nibble on Jamaican and Caribbean food here as they're treated to live reggae music. More than 100 portraits of the original Rastaman, Bob Marley, decorate the walls. The club is open daily from 4pm to 2am; only those 21 and older are admitted after 9pm. ✆ **407/224-3663.** Cover $7 after 8pm, more on special nights.

the groove This oft-crowded multilevel club features a huge dance floor, a number of bars, and a handful of lounges for just hanging out. The high-tech sound system will blow your hair back; if you need a sound check, try the upper-level patio for a brief reprieve. A DJ plays tunes most nights, featuring the latest in hip-hop, retro hits, techno, and alternative music. It's open 9pm to 2am daily. ✆ **407/363-8000.** Cover $7. Must be 21 or older to enter.

Jimmy Buffett's Margaritaville Music by the maestro booms loudly through the building, with live tunes occasionally performed on a small indoor stage later in the evening. There are three themed bars—Volcano, Land Shark, and 12 Volt—each with tropical touches. It's a parrothead's paradise. The open-air deck off to the side offers the quietest place to roost. Open daily from 11:30am to 2am. ✆ **407/224-2155.** Cover $7, after 10pm.

Pat O'Brien's Just like the French Quarter, which is home to the original Patty O's, drinking, drinking, and more drinking are the highlights here. Down the big drink of the Big Easy, a Hurricane, though there are plenty of other concoctions to choose from. Open daily from 4pm to 2am. ✆ **407/363-8000.**

The Red Coconut Club CityWalk's swankiest nightclub serves up live music and DJs nightly. Small, intimate tables fill the lounge; if you prefer the outdoors, you can sit under the stars on the balcony. Martinis are the signature drink here. Dress code here is casual-chic. Open Sunday to Thursday from 8pm to 2am, Friday and Saturday 6pm to 2am. ✆ **407/224/3663.** Cover $7 after 9pm. Must be 21 or older to enter.

Rising Star Live music, a live audience—and the chance to be a star—that's what you'll find at CityWalk's newest karaoke club. The club is open nightly from 8pm to 2am. ✆ **407/224-2189.** Cover $7. Must be 21 or older to enter Fri–Tues; Thurs nights 18 and over.

14 Northeast Florida

When driving through the elongated state of Florida, many people make the grave mistake of gunning their engines and jetting through the Northeast without as much as a single stop beyond the Cracker Barrels, Denny's restaurants, and gas stations lining the highways. Thankfully, Juan Ponce de León made the *fortunate* mistake of playing accidental tourist and discovering just how magnificent the northeast part of the state truly is. You would do well to explore in his footsteps.

Northeast Florida traces its roots back to 1513, when the wandering León, who later undertook a misguided quest for the Fountain of Youth, sighted this coast and landed somewhere between present-day Jacksonville and Cape Canaveral. (He was a bit off course—he meant to land in what is now Bimini—but who can blame a guy who didn't have GPS?) Observing the land's lush foliage, he named it *La Florida,* or "the flowery land."

In 1565, the Spanish established a colony at St. Augustine, the country's oldest continuously inhabited European settlement. Not much, if anything at all, has changed in St. Augustine (in a wonderful way). The streets of the restored Old City look much as they did in Spanish times.

Not everything in Northeast Florida is antiquated, however. To the south, there's the "Space Coast," where rockets blast off from the Kennedy Space Center at Cape Canaveral. In nearby Cocoa Beach, you can watch surfers riding the rather sizable waves. In Daytona Beach, brace yourself for the deafening roar of the stock cars and motorbikes that make this beach town the "World Center of Racing." And don't blink, because you wouldn't want to miss Daytona's other pop-cultural phenomenon, known as the *MTV Spring Break* bikini crowd. In recent years, it has dwindled from a whopping 400,000 party-hearty kids down to a crowd so tame, the Daytona Beach Area Convention & Visitors Bureau no longer maintains student visitor estimates!

Going north along the coast, you'll come to a place that's a far cry from being populated with Spring Breakers on a budget: the moneyed haven of Ponte Vedra Beach, where golf definitely takes precedence over manual labor. In Jacksonville, Florida's largest metropolis and a thriving port city and naval base, you can get a taste of city life before retreating back to the beach.

Up near the state of Georgia border, cross a bridge to Amelia Island, where you'll discover exclusive resorts that take full advantage of 13 miles of beautiful beaches. Amelia's Victorian-era town, Fernandina Beach, is another throwback to the past, helping to further render the northeast region of Florida a fascinating juxtaposition of the old, the new, and somewhere in between. However you perceive it, do not make the mistake of missing northeast Florida. Ponce de León didn't blow off Bimini for nothing, you know.

1 KENNEDY SPACE CENTER & THE SPACE COAST ★

46 miles SE of Orlando; 186 miles N of Miami; 65 miles S of Daytona

The "Space Coast," the area around Cape Canaveral, was once a sleepy place where city dwellers escaped the exploding urban centers of Miami and Jacksonville. But then

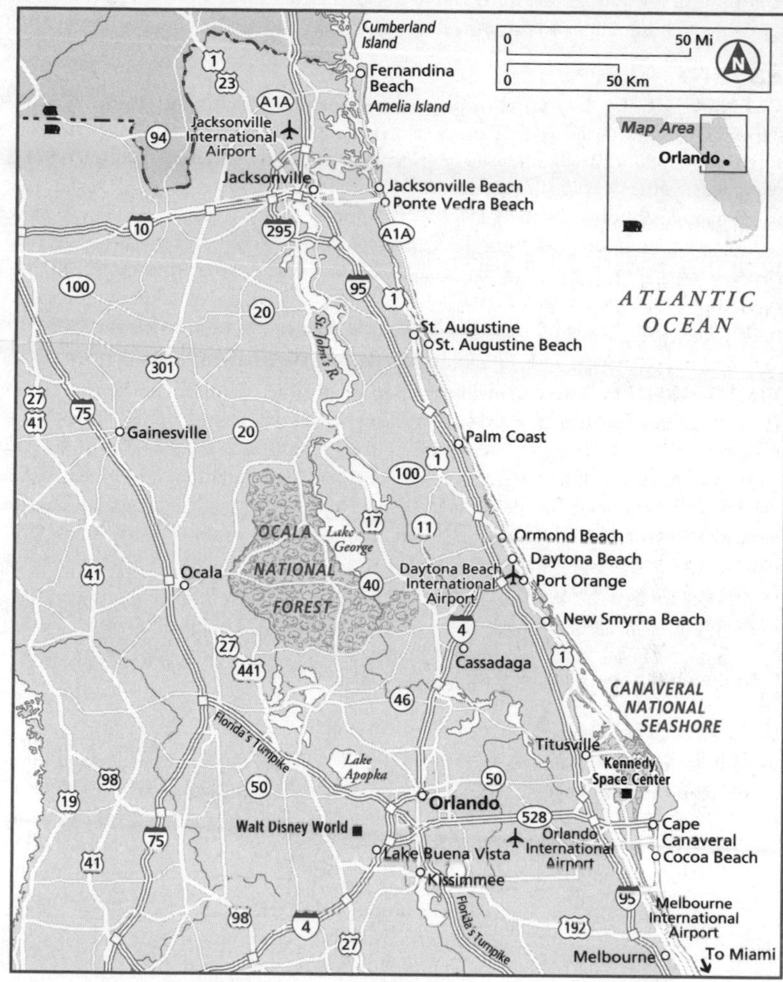

came the NASA space program. Today the region produces and accommodates its own crowds, particularly the hordes of tourists who come to visit the Kennedy Space Center and enjoy the area's 72 miles of beaches (this is, after all, the closest beach to Orlando's mega-attractions) as well as excellent fishing, surfing, and golfing.

Thanks to NASA, this is also a prime destination for nature lovers. The space agency originally took over much more land than it needed to launch rockets. Rather than sell off the unused portions, it turned them over to the Canaveral National Seashore and the Merritt Island National Wildlife Refuge (www.nbbd.com/godo/minwr), which have preserved these areas in their pristine natural states.

A handful of Caribbean-bound cruise ships also depart from Port Canaveral. The south side of the port is lined with seafood restaurants and marinas, which serve as home base for gambling ships and the area's deep-sea charter and group fishing boats.

ESSENTIALS

GETTING THERE The nearest airport is **Melbourne International Airport** (✆ **321/723-6227;** www.mlbair.com), 22 miles south of Cocoa Beach, which is served by **Continental** (✆ **800/525-0280;** www.continental.com) and **Delta** (✆ **800/221-1212;** www.delta.com). **Orlando International Airport** (p. 450), about 35 miles to the west, is a much larger hub with many more flight options and generally less expensive fares. It's an easy 45-minute drive from the Orlando Airport to the beaches via the Bee Line Expressway (Fla. 528, a toll road)—it can take almost that long from the Melbourne Airport, where **Avis, Budget, Hertz,** and **National** all have car-rental desks. The **Melbourne Airport Shuttle** (✆ **321/724-1600**) will take you from the Melbourne Airport to most local destinations for about $10 to $20 per person.

VISITOR INFORMATION For information on the area, contact the **Florida Space Coast Office of Tourism/Brevard County Tourist Development Council,** 8810 Astronaut Blvd., Ste. 102, Cape Canaveral, FL 32920 (✆ **800/872-1969** or 321/868-1126; www.space-coast.com). The office is in the Sheldon Cove building, on Florida A1A a block north of Central Boulevard, and is open Monday through Friday from 8am to 5pm. It also operates an information booth at the Kennedy Space Center Visitor Complex (p. 515).

GETTING AROUND A car is essential in this area. If you're not coming by car, you can rent one at the airport. **Space Coast Area Transit** (✆ **321/633-1878;** www.ridescat.com) operates buses ($1.25 adults, 60¢ seniors and students), but routes tend to be circuitous and, therefore, extremely time-consuming.

ATTRACTIONS

In addition to the two attractions below, Brevard College's **Astronaut Memorial Planetarium and Observatory,** 1519 Clearlake Rd., Cocoa Beach (✆ **321/634-3732;** www.brevardcc.edu/planet), south of Florida 528, has its own International Hall of Space Explorers, but its big attractions are sound-and-light shows in the planetarium. Call or check the website for schedules and prices.

Brevard Zoo ★★ Kids This delightful small-town zoo houses more than 500 animals, including white rhinos, red kangaroos, wallabies, crocodiles, howler monkeys, bald eagles, red wolves, and river otters. Enjoy a 10-minute train tour of the grounds ($2), a free-flight aviary, a cute and cuddly petting zoo, and alligator feedings usually 3 days a week. Check out the 10-acre Expedition Africa exhibit, where impala, gazelles, and scimitar-horned oryx chill out over the savanna. Don't miss the opportunity to kayak through the wetlands—this is the only zoo in the country that offers kayaking, and it's a bargain, at only $5 per person. For an up-close and personal view of the animals, take the behind-the-scenes tour with a zookeeper on Saturday and Sunday at 1pm. The zoo also offers eco-tours on the Indian River Lagoon (www.lagoonadventures.org). For $45 you get kayak rental, kayak instruction, snacks and drinks, a trained environmental educator guide, lunch on an island, and close viewing of manatees, dolphins, and wading birds. Plan to spend 1 to 4 hours here.

8225 N. Wickham Rd., Melbourne (just east of I-95 exit 73/Wickham Rd.). ✆ **321/254-9453.** www.brevardzoo.org. Admission $12 adults, $11 seniors, $8.50 children 3–12, free for children 2 and under. Daily 10am–5pm.

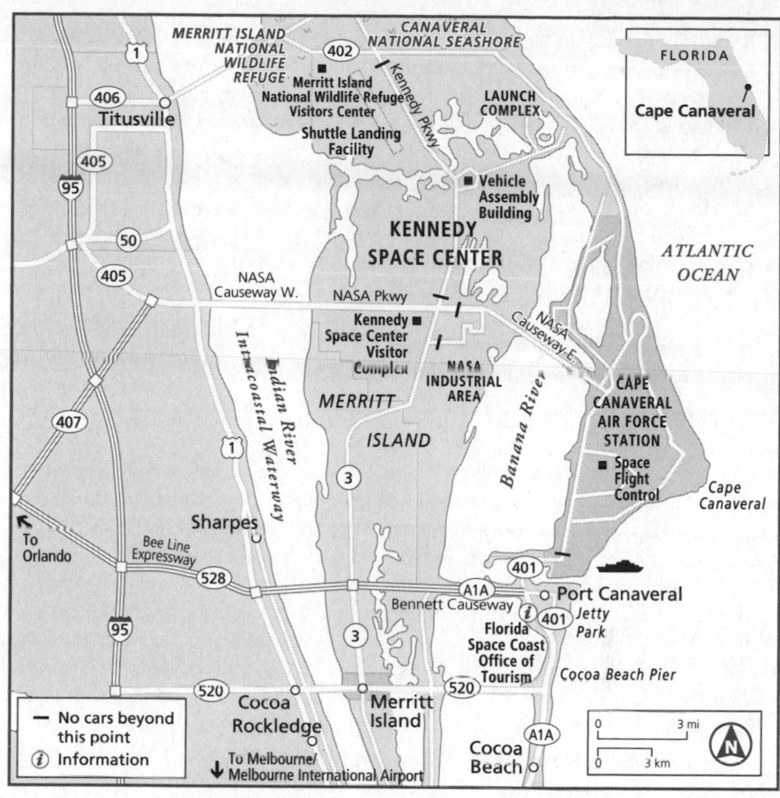

John F. Kennedy Space Center ★★★ Whether or not you're a space buff, you'll appreciate the sheer grandeur of the facilities and technological achievements displayed at NASA's primary space launch facility. Astronauts departed Earth at this site in 1969 en route to the most famous "small step" in history—the first moon walk—and today's space shuttles still regularly lift off from here on their latest missions.

Because all roads other than Florida 405 and Florida 3 are closed to the public in the Space Center, you must begin your visit at **Kennedy Space Center Visitor Complex.** A bit like an amusement theme park, this privately operated complex has received a renovation and expansion, so check beforehand to see if tours and exhibits have changed since press time. Call ahead to see what's happening on the day you intend to be here and arrive early. You'll need at least 2 hours to see the Space Center's highlights on the bus tour, up to 5 hours if you linger at the stops along the way, and a full day to see and do everything here. Buy a copy of the *Official Tour Book;* it's easier to use than the rental cassette tapes, and you can take it home as a colorful souvenir (though some readers think you probably don't need the extra information, as the bus tours are narrated and the exhibits have good descriptions).

The Visitor Complex has real NASA rockets and the actual Mercury Mission Control Room from the 1960s. Exhibits portray space exploration in its early days and where it's

Tips Out to Launch

If you'd like to see a shuttle launch at the **Kennedy Space Center,** first call ✆ **321/867-5000** or check NASA's official website (www.ksc.nasa.gov) for a schedule of upcoming takeoffs. You can buy launch tickets at the Kennedy Space Center Visitor Complex (✆ **321/449-4444**) or online at www.ksctickets.com. ***A word of caution:*** Shuttle launches are frequently delayed due to weather, equipment malfunctions, or other factors, so you might have to make multiple visits to see one. It is also possible the launch window may be delayed beyond your going-home date.

If you can't get into the space center, other good viewing spots are on the causeways leading to the islands and on U.S. 1 as it skirts the waterfront in Titusville. The **Clarion Inn Riverside–Kennedy Space Center,** on Washington Avenue (U.S. 1) in Titusville (✆ **800/465-4329** or 321/269-2121; www.choicehotels.com), has a clear view of the launchpads across the Indian River. Area motels raise their rates and often book up around the time a launch is scheduled.

going in the new millennium. There are hands-on activities for kids, a daily "Encounter" with a real astronaut, dining venues, and a shop selling space memorabilia. IMAX movies shown on five-and-a-half-story-high screens are both informative and entertaining.

Plan to spend about 2 hours here, or you could easily make a day of it.

New at the Visitor Complex is the *Shuttle Launch Experience,* an incredible journey of vertically launching into space and orbiting Earth aboard the space shuttle. Guest "crew members" strap in for this all-too-real simulation, which immerses visitors in the sights, sounds, and feelings of a space shuttle launch, designed under the guidance of NASA and veteran space shuttle astronauts. The Shuttle Launch Experience is included with regular admission to the Visitor Complex.

While you could spend an entire day at the Visitor Complex, you must take a **KSC Tour** to see the actual Space Center where rockets and shuttles are prepared and launched. Take the bus tour early in your visit, and be sure to hit the restrooms before boarding—there are only two on the tour. Buses depart every 15 minutes or so, and you can reboard as you wish. They stop at the LC-39 Observation Gantry, with a dramatic 360-degree view over launchpads where shuttles blast off; the International Space Station Center, where scientists and engineers prepare additions to the space station now in orbit; and the Apollo/Saturn V Center, which includes artifacts, photos, films, interactive exhibits, and the 363-foot-tall Saturn V, the most powerful rocket ever launched by the United States. Unfortunately, the bus tour was the low point of my recent visit. Though the commentary on the bus was interesting, the stops were relatively dull, and waiting to board and reboard buses was more than frustrating (though touching a moon rock at the Apollo/Saturn V Center was pretty cool). If you're short on time, I suggest sticking around the Visitor Complex.

Don't miss the Astronaut Memorial. Dedicated in 1991, the memorial honors the U.S. astronauts who gave their lives for space exploration. The 43-foot-high by 50-foot-wide "Space Mirror" brilliantly illuminates the names cut through the monument's black granite surface.

Launch days are great days to visit the Visitor Complex and watch history in the making. You may purchase a **combined ticket** that entitles you to admission to the Visitor

Complex plus transportation to the NASA Causeway to see the liftoff. Tickets to view launches from this viewing site are $58 per adult and $38 per child, and must be prepurchased, as they are very popular and sell out quickly. Launches can also be viewed from the main Visitor Complex with the regular admission price of $38 per adult and $28 per child.

For an out-of-this-world experience, do Lunch with an Astronaut, a once-in-a-lifetime opportunity available every day ($23 adults, $16 kids 3–11, in addition to Visitor Complex admission). Astronauts who have participated in the past include some of the greatest, such as, Jim Lovell, Walt Cunningham, Story Musgrave, and Jon McBride. Seating is limited; call ✆ **321/449-4400** to make a reservation.

New at Kennedy Space Center Visitor Complex is the repackaged **Astronaut Training Experience,** a thrilling combination of hands-on training and preparation for the rigors of spaceflight. You'll hear first-hand from veteran NASA astronauts as you progress through an authentic half-day of mission simulation and exploration and even get to check out a flight simulator. It's pricey, though, at $125 per person.

Note: Kennedy Space Center acquired many of the exhibits from the U.S. **Astronaut Hall of Fame** and added them as a separate attraction at the KSC Visitor Complex ($17 adults, $13 child 3–11; or $38 adults and $28 child for a 2-day admission ticket to the Visitor Complex and the Hall of Fame). The attraction includes exhibits and tributes to the heroes of the Mercury, Gemini, and Apollo space programs. There's also a collection of spacecraft, including a Mercury 7 capsule, a Gemini training capsule, and an Apollo 14 command module. In "Simulator Station," guests can experience four times the force of gravity, ride a rover across Mars, and land a space shuttle.

NASA Pkwy. (Fla. 405), 6 miles east of Titusville, 1/2 mile west of Fla. 3. ✆ **321/449-4444** for general information, or 449-4444 for guided bus tours and launch reservations. www.kennedyspacecenter.com. Admission $38 adults, $28 children 3–11. Annual passes $50 adults, $40 children 3–11. Audio guides $5 per person. All tours and movies free for children 2 and under. Open daily at 9am. Bus tours daily at 10am–2:15pm. Closed Christmas and certain launch days.

BEACHES & WILDLIFE REFUGEES

To the north of the Kennedy Space Center, **Canaveral National Seashore ★★★** is a protected 13-mile stretch of barrier-island beach backed by cabbage palms, sea grapes, palmettos, marshes, and Mosquito Lagoon. This is a great area for watching herons, egrets, ibises, willets, sanderlings, turnstones, terns, and other birds. You might also glimpse dolphins and manatees in Mosquito Lagoon. Canoeists can paddle along a marked trail through the marshes of Shipyard Island, and backcountry camping is possible November through April (permits required; see below).

The main **visitor center** is at 7611 S. Atlantic Ave., New Smyrna Beach, FL 32169 (✆ **321/867-4077**, or 867-0677 for recorded information; www.nps.gov/cana), on Apollo Beach, at the north end of the island. The southern access gate to the island is 8 miles east of Titusville on Florida 402, just east of Florida 3. A paved road leads from the gate to undeveloped **Playalinda Beach ★★★**, one of Florida's most beautiful. Though illegal, nude sunbathing has long been a tradition here (at least, for those willing to walk a few miles to the more deserted areas). The beach has toilets, but no running water or other amenities, so bring everything you'll need. The seashore is open daily from 6am to 8pm during daylight saving time, daily from 6am to 6pm during standard time. Entry fees are $3 per person but are expected to rise to $7 per person. National Park Service passports are accepted. Backcountry camping permits cost $10 for up to six people, $20 for seven or more, and must be obtained from the New Smyrna Beach visitor center. For advance information, contact the seashore headquarters at 308 Julia St., Titusville, FL 32796 (✆ **321/867-4077** or 321/267-1110; www.nps.gov/cana).

Canaveral National Seashore's neighbor to the south and west is the 140,000-acre **Merritt Island National Wildlife Refuge ★★**, home to hundreds of species of shorebirds, waterfowl, reptiles, alligators, and mammals, many of them endangered. Pick up a map and other information at the visitor center, on Florida 402 about 4 miles east of Titusville (it's on the way to Playalinda Beach). The center has a quarter-mile boardwalk along the edge of the marsh. Displays show the animals you may spot from 6-mile Black Point Wildlife Drive or from one of the nature trails through the hammocks and marshes. The visitor center is open Monday through Friday from 8am to 4:30pm, Saturday and Sunday from 9am to 5pm (closed Sun Apr–Oct). Entry is free. For more information and a schedule of programs, contact the refuge at P.O. Box 6504, Titusville, FL 32782 (✆ **321/861-0667;** www.nbbd.com/godo/minwr).

Note: Those parts of the national seashore near the Kennedy Space Center and all of the refuge close 4 days before a shuttle launch and usually reopen the day after a launch.

Another good beach area is **Lori Wilson Park,** on Atlantic Avenue at Antigua Drive in Cocoa Beach (✆ **321/868-1123**), which preserves a stretch of sand backed by a forest of live oaks. It's home to a small but interesting nature center, and restrooms are available. The park is open daily from sunrise to sunset; the nature center, Monday through Friday from 1 to 4pm.

The beach at **Cocoa Beach Pier,** on Meade Avenue east of Florida A1A (✆ **321/783-7549**), is a popular spot with surfers, who consider it the East Coast's surfing capital. The rustic pier was built in 1962 and has 842 feet of fishing, shopping, and dining overlooking a wide, sandy beach (see "Where to Dine," below). Because this is not a public park, there are no restrooms other than the ones in restaurants on the pier.

Jetty Park, 400 E. Jetty Rd., at the south entry to Port Canaveral (✆ **321/783-7111;** www.jettypark.org), has lifeguards, a fishing pier with bait shop, a playground, volleyball court, horseshoe pit, picnic tables, a snack bar, grocery store, restrooms, changing facilities, and the area's only campground. From here, you can watch the big cruise ships as they enter and leave the port's narrow passage. The park is open daily from 7am to 10pm; the pier is open 24 hours for fishing. Admission is $7 per car, $15 per RV. The 150 tent and RV campsites (some of them shady, most with hookups) cost $25 to $47 a night, depending on location and time of year. No pets are allowed.

OUTDOOR ACTIVITIES & SPECTATOR SPORTS

BASEBALL The **Washington Nationals** play spring-training games at **Space Coast Stadium,** 5800 Stadium Pkwy., Viera (✆ **321/633-4487**), located south of Cape Canaveral and north of Melbourne. Tickets are $5 to $20. The stadium also hosts minor-league action from the Brevard County Manatees, an affiliate of the Nationals.

ECO-TOURS **Funday Discovery Tours** (✆ **321/725-0796;** www.fundaytours.com) offers a variety of day trips, including dinner and sunset cruises, airboat and swamp-buggy rides, dolphin-watching cruises, bird-watching expeditions, and personalized tours of the Kennedy Space Center and Merritt Island National Wildlife Refuge. Reservations are required.

FISHING Head to Port Canaveral for catches such as snapper and grouper. **Jetty Park** (✆ **321/783-7111**), at the south entry to the port, has a fishing pier equipped with a bait shop (see "Beaches & Wildlife Refuges," above). The south bank of the port is lined with charter boats. Try deep-sea fishing on ***Miss Cape Canaveral*** (✆ **321/783-5274,** or

407/648-2211 in Orlando; www.misscape.com), one of the party boats based here. All-day voyages departing daily at 8am cost $70 adults, $65 seniors, $55 kids 11 to 17; or, if you want two cans of cold beer, bait, and tackle, it's $25 more.

GOLF You can read about Northeast Florida's best courses in the free *Golfer's Guide,* available at the tourist information offices and in many hotel lobbies. See p. 57 for information on ordering copies.

The municipal **Cocoa Beach Country Club,** 500 Tom Warringer Blvd. (✆ **321/868-3351;** www.golfcocoabeach.com), has 27 holes of golf and 10 lighted tennis courts set on acres of natural woodlands, rivers, and lakes. Greens fees (including cart) are about $53 in winter, dropping to about $46 in summer.

On Merritt Island south of the Kennedy Space Center, the **Savannahs at Sykes Creek,** 3915 Savannahs Trail (✆ **321/455-1377**), has 18 holes over 6,636 yards bordered by hardwood forests, lakes, and savannas inhabited by a host of wildlife. You'll have to hit over a lake to reach the 7th hole. Fees with a cart are about $50 in winter, lower in summer.

The best nearby course is the Gary Player–designed **Baytree National Golf Club,** 8010 N. Wickham Rd., a half-mile east of I-95 in Melbourne (✆ **321/259-9060;** www.baytreenational.com), where challenging marshy holes are flanked by towering palms. This par-72 course has 7,043 yards with a unique red-shale waste area. Fees are about $90 in winter, dropping to about $50 in summer, including cart.

For course information, go to www.golf.com or www.floridagolfing.com, or call the **Florida Sports Foundation** (✆ **850/488-8347**) or **Florida Golfing** (✆ **866/833-2663**).

SURFING Rip through some occasionally awesome waves (by Florida's standards, not California's or Hawaii's) at the **Cocoa Beach Pier** area or down south at **Sebastian Inlet.** Get outfitted at **Ron Jon Surf Shop,** 4151 N. Atlantic Ave. (✆ **321/799-8888;** www.ronjons.com), or learn how to hang five or ten with **Cocoa Beach Surfing School ★,** 150 E. Columbia Lane (✆ **321/868-1980;** www.cocoabeachsurfingschool.com). The school offers equipment and lessons for beginners and pros at area beaches. Be sure to bring along a towel, flip-flops, sunscreen, and a lot of nerve.

WHERE TO STAY

Most of the hotels listed below are in Cocoa Beach, the closest resort area to the Kennedy Space Center, about a 30-minute drive to the north. (For pop-culture junkies, Cocoa Beach was where the TV show *I Dream of Jeannie* took place.) Closest to the space center and Port Canaveral is the **Radisson Resort at the Port,** 8701 Astronaut Blvd. (Fla. A1A), in Cape Canaveral (✆ **800/333-3333** or 321/784-0000; www.radisson.com). It isn't on the beach, but you can relax in its landscaped courtyard, where a waterfall cascades over fake rocks into a heated pool. The hotel caters to business travelers and passengers waiting to board cruise ships (with free transportation to the port and free parking while you cruise); it offers complimentary breakfast.

The newer chain motels in this area are the **Hampton Inn Cocoa Beach,** 3425 Atlantic Blvd. (✆ **877/492-3224** or 321/799-4099; www.hamptoninncocoabeach.com), and **Courtyard by Marriott,** 3435 Atlantic Blvd. (✆ **800/321-2211** or 321/784-4800; www.courtyardcocoabeach.com). They stand side by side and access the beach via a pathway through a condominium complex.

The **Florida Space Coast Office of Tourism,** 8810 Astronaut Blvd., no. 102, Cape Canaveral, FL 32920 (✆ **800/93-OCEAN** [6-2326] or 321/868-1126; www.space-coast.com), publishes a booklet of the area's "Superior Small Lodgings."

The area has a plethora of rental condominiums and cottages. **King Rentals, Inc.,** 102 W. Central Blvd., Cape Canaveral, FL 32920 (© **888/295-0934** or 321/784-5046; www.kingrentals.com), has a wide selection in its inventory.

Given the proximity to Orlando, the generally warm weather year-round, and the business travelers visiting the space complex, there is little, if any, seasonal fluctuation in room rates here. They are highest on weekends, holidays, and during special events, such as space-shuttle launches.

Tent and RV camping are available at **Jetty Park,** in Port Canaveral (see "Beaches & Wildlife Refuges," above).

You'll pay a 5% hotel tax on top of the Florida 6% sales tax here.

DoubleTree Hotel Cocoa Beach Oceanfront ★ Although not as upscale as the Hilton Cocoa Beach Oceanfront (see below), this is the pick of the full-service beachside hotels. All newly renovated rooms have balconies with ocean views, and 10 suites have living rooms with sleeper sofas and separate bedrooms. A charming dining room serves decent Florida seafood and pizzas; it faces the beach and opens onto a brick patio where water cascades between two heated pools. Conference facilities draw groups.

2080 N. Atlantic Ave., Cocoa Beach, FL 32931. © **800/552-3224** or 321/783-9222. Fax 321/799-3234. www.cocoabeachdoubletree.com. 148 units. Winter $124–$184 double, $194–$224 suite; off-season $199–$249 double, $259–$299 suite. AE, DC, DISC, MC, V. **Amenities:** Restaurant; bar; 2 heated outdoor pools; exercise room; game room; limited room service; laundry service; coin-op washers/dryers; concierge-level rooms. *In room:* A/C, TV, dataport, coffeemaker, hair dryer, iron.

Hilton Cocoa Beach Oceanfront ★★ Damaged by Hurricane Frances, the Hilton Cocoa Beach Oceanfront reopened in early 2005 after a $21-million renovation to the guest rooms, pool area, restaurant, and lounge. The rooms at this seven-story Hilton lack balconies or patios; instead, they have small, sealed-shut windows, and only 16 of the rooms face the beach. These and other architectural features make this seem more like a downtown hotel transplanted to a beachside location. Nevertheless, it's one of the few upscale beachfront properties here. No doubt you'll run into a crew of name-tagged conventioneers, as it's especially popular with groups. Despite their lack of fresh air, the rooms are spacious and comfortable, especially since the renovations.

1550 N. Atlantic Ave., Cocoa Beach, FL 32931. © **800/445-8667** or 321/799-0003. Fax 321/799-0344. www.hiltoncocoabeach.com. 296 units. Winter $119–$149 double, $219 suite; off-season $149–$169 double, $249 suite. AE, DC, DISC, MC, V. **Amenities:** Restaurant; 2 bars; heated outdoor pool; exercise room; watersports equipment/rentals; game room; business center; limited room service; laundry service; coin-op washers/dryers; concierge-level rooms. *In room:* A/C, TV, dataport, coffeemaker, hair dryer, iron.

The Inn at Cocoa Beach ★★★ Despite having 50 units, this seaside inn has an intimate B&B ambience and is far and away the most romantic place in the area. Owner Karen Simpler, a skilled interior decorator, has furnished each unit with an elegant mix of pine, tropical, and French country pieces. Rooms in the three- and four-story buildings are much more spacious and have better sea views from their balconies than the "standard" units in the original two-story motel wing (all but six units here have balconies or patios). The older units open onto a courtyard with a pool tucked behind the dunes. Highest on the romance scale are the two rooms with Jacuzzi tubs and easy chairs. Guests are treated to continental breakfast, afternoon tea, and evening wine and cheese. There's also an honor bar, where you can pour your own drinks, and a library from which to feed your head.

4300 Ocean Blvd., Cocoa Beach, FL 32932. © **800/343-5307** or 321/799-3460. Fax 321/784-8632. www.theinnatcocoabeach.com. 50 units. $125–$325 double. Rates include continental breakfast and afternoon tea. AE, DISC, MC, V. No children 11 and under accepted. **Amenities:** Bar (guests only); heated outdoor pool; sauna; massage; laundry service. *In room:* A/C, TV, dataport.

Riverview Hotel ★★★ Right on the Intracoastal Waterway in New Smyrna Beach, the Riverview Hotel, a former fishing and hunting shack for sportsmen scoping the Indian River Lagoon, is a spectacularly restored hotel featuring a 5,000-square-foot spa complete with mineral pool. There's jazz on the deck every night and a fabulous restaurant (Grille at Riverview) to boot. Some rooms have private patios or porches; all are immaculate, charming, and stocked with modern amenities. If I had a choice, however, I'd go for the cottage or house with private pool, which are bargains at $200 to $250!

103 Flagler Ave., New Smyrna Beach, FL 32169. ✆ **800/945-7416** or 386/428-5858. Fax 321/423-8927. www.riverviewhotel.com. 18 units. $110–$125 double; $170 suite; $175 private cottage; $225 3-bedroom house for up to 4 people (extra person $20). Rates include expanded continental breakfast. AE, DISC, MC, V. **Amenities:** Restaurant; heated pool; spa; sauna; massage. *In room:* A/C, TV.

WHERE TO DINE

On the **Cocoa Beach Pier** (www.cocoabeachpier.com), at the beach end of Meade Avenue, you'll get a fine view down the coast to accompany the seafood offerings at **Atlantic Ocean Grill** (✆ **321/783-7549**) and the mediocre pub fare at adjacent **Marlins Good Times Bar & Grill** (same phone). The restaurants may not justify spending an entire evening on the pier, but the outdoor, tin-roofed **Mai Tiki Bar ★**, where live music plays most nights, is a prime spot to have a cold one while watching the surfers or a sunset.

Bernard's Surf/Fischer's Seafood Bar & Grill ★ SEAFOOD/STEAK Photos on the walls testify that many astronauts come to these adjoining establishments to celebrate their landings. It started as Bernard's Surf in 1948, serving standard steak-and-seafood fare in a nautical setting. The present Bernard's offers specials such as stone-crab claws, chargrilled red snapper, and a belly-busting platter of shrimp, scallops, grouper, crab cakes, lobster, and oysters. You can even get Russian beluga or sevruga caviar, if you so desire. The fresh seafood also finds its way into Fischer's Seafood Bar & Grill, a *Cheers*-like lounge popular with locals. The menu here features fried combo platters and mussels with a wine sauce over pasta, as well as burgers and other pub fare. It has the same 25¢ happy-hour oysters and spicy wings as a branch of **Rusty's Seafood & Oyster Bar** (see below), also part of this complex.

2 S. Atlantic Ave. (at Minuteman Causeway Rd.), Cocoa Beach. ✆ **321/783-2401.** www.geocities.com/bernardsseafood and www.geocities.com/fischersseafood. Reservations recommended in Bernard's, not accepted in Fischer's. Bernard's main courses $8–$40. Fischer's main courses $6–$20; sandwiches and salads $5–$15. AE, DC, DISC, MC, V. Bernard's Mon–Fri 4–10pm; Sat 4–11pm. Fischer's Mon–Fri 11am–10pm; Sat 11am–11pm. Closed Christmas.

The Mango Tree ★★ CONTINENTAL Gourmet seafood, pastas, and chicken are served in a plantation-home atmosphere with elegant furnishings in this stucco house, the finest dining venue around. Although the ambience borders on tourist-tacky, the restaurant is rather picturesque. Indoor goldfish ponds and an outdoor waterfall splashing into a koi pond in the gardens provide pleasing backdrops. Start with Indian River crab cakes, then go on to the chef's expert spin on roast Long Island duckling, beef tips with peppercorn-mushroom sauce, or other excellent dishes drawing inspiration from the Continent.

118 N. Atlantic Ave. (Fla. A1A, btw. N. 1st and N. 2nd sts.), Cocoa Beach. ✆ **321/799-0513.** www.themangotreerestaurant.com. Reservations recommended. Main courses $16–$38. AE, MC, V. Tues–Sun 6–10pm.

Rusty's Seafood & Oyster Bar Value SEAFOOD This lively sports bar beside Port Canaveral's man-made harbor serves inexpensive chow ranging from spicy seafood gumbo to a pot of seafood that will give two people their fill of steamed oysters, clams, shrimp, crab legs, potatoes, and corn on the cob. Raw or steamed fresh oysters and clams from the raw bar are first-rate and a good value, as is a weekday lunch buffet. Seating is indoors or out, but the inside tables have the best view of the fishing boats and cruise liners going in and out of the port. Daily happy hour from 3 to 6pm offers beers drafted at 60¢ a mug, and tons of raw or steamed oysters and spicy Buffalo wings go for 25¢ each. The joint is busy and sometimes noisy, especially on weekend afternoons, but the clientele tends to be older and better behaved than those at other pubs along the banks of Port Canaveral. There's another **Rusty's** in the Bernard's Surf/Fischer's Seafood Bar & Grill restaurant complex in Cocoa Beach (see above).

628 Glen Cheek Dr. (south side of the harbor), Port Canaveral. © **321/783-2033.** www.rustysseafood.com. Main courses $14–$30; sandwiches and salads $5–$12. AE, DC, DISC, MC, V. Sun–Thurs 11am–11:30pm; Fri–Sat 11am–12:30am (lunch buffet Mon–Fri 11am–2pm).

THE SPACE COAST AFTER DARK

For a rundown of current performances and exhibits, call the **Brevard Cultural Alliance's Arts Line** (© **321/690-6819**). For live music, walk out on the **Cocoa Beach Pier,** on Meade Avenue at the beach, where **Oh Shuck's Seafood Bar & Grill** (© **321/783-7549**), **Marlins Good Times Bar & Grill** (© **321/783-7549**), and the alfresco **Mai Tiki Bar** ★ (same phone as Marlins) feature bands on weekends, more often during the summer season. The Tiki Bar is a great place to hang out over a cold beer all afternoon and evening.

2 DAYTONA BEACH ★★

54 miles NE of Orlando; 251 miles N of Miami; 78 miles S of Jacksonville

Daytona Beach is a town with many personalities. It is at once the self-proclaimed "World's Most Famous Beach" and "World Center of Racing," a mecca for tattooed motorcyclists and pierced Spring Breakers (though it lost its Spring Break crown to Panama City Beach), *and* the home of a surprisingly good art museum. Though the city and developers spent millions of dollars to turn the somewhat seedy beachfront area (complete with the requisite T-shirt and souvenir shops) around the famous Main Street Pier into Ocean Walk Village, a redevelopment area of shops, entertainment, and resort facilities, there's still something bleak and seedy about Daytona's famous strip. Much of its '70s-style beachfront condos and hotels are still decrepit, run-down, and badly in need of a face-lift. In due time, we hope. Thank goodness for Ponce Inlet, a scenic fishing village that has seemingly remained impervious to development.

Racing fans, however, don't care what the place looks like. Daytona Beach has been a destination for racing enthusiasts since the early 1900s, when "horseless carriages" raced on the hard-packed sand beach. One thing is for sure: Daytonans still love their cars. Recent debate over the environmental impact of unrestricted driving on the beach caused an uproar from citizens who couldn't imagine it any other way. As it worked out, they can still drive on the sand, but not everywhere, and especially not in areas where sea turtles are nesting.

Today, hundreds of thousands of race enthusiasts come to the home of the National Association for Stock Car Auto Racing (NASCAR) for the Daytona 500, the Pepsi 400,

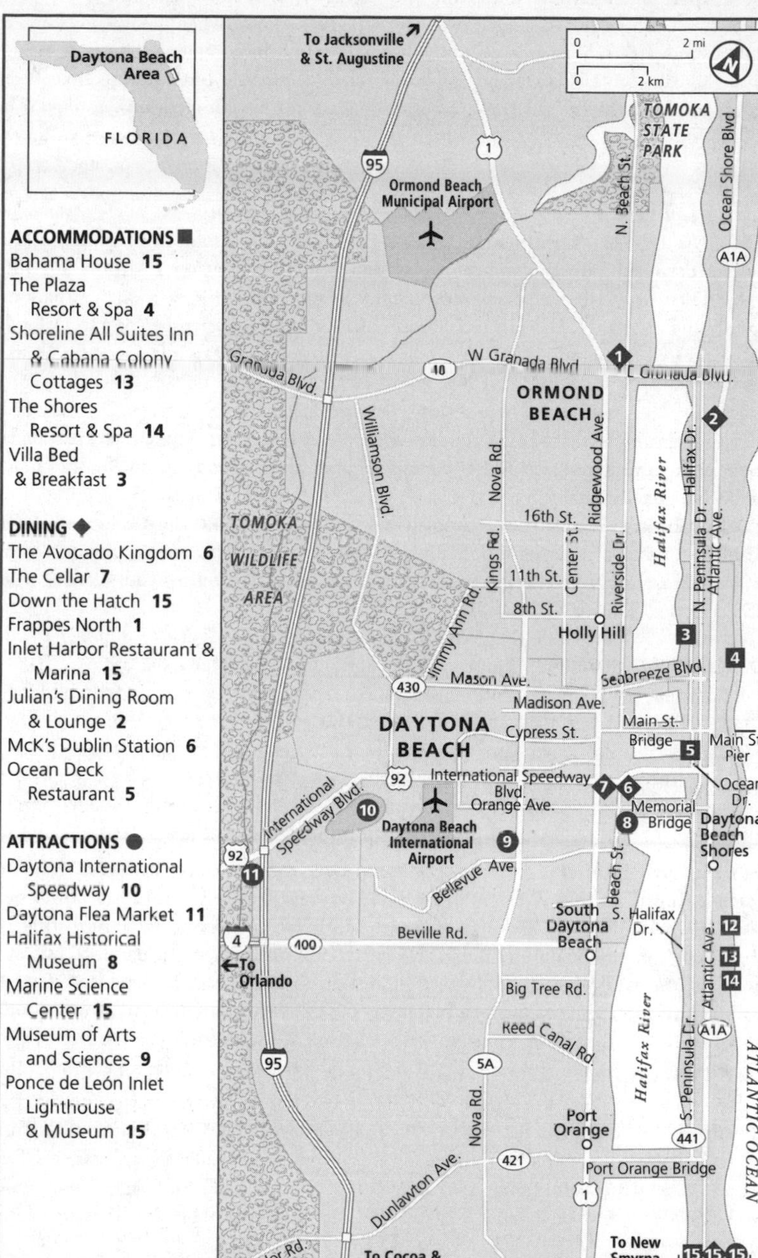
Daytona Beach Area
FLORIDA
ACCOMMODATIONS ■
Bahama House 15
The Plaza Resort & Spa 4
Shoreline All Suites Inn & Cabana Colony Cottages 13
The Shores Resort & Spa 14
Villa Bed & Breakfast 3
DINING ◆
The Avocado Kingdom 6
The Cellar 7
Down the Hatch 15
Frappes North 1
Inlet Harbor Restaurant & Marina 15
Julian's Dining Room & Lounge 2
McK's Dublin Station 6
Ocean Deck Restaurant 5
ATTRACTIONS ●
Daytona International Speedway 10
Daytona Flea Market 11
Halifax Historical Museum 8
Marine Science Center 15
Museum of Arts and Sciences 9
Ponce de León Inlet Lighthouse & Museum 15
To Jacksonville & St. Augustine
0 2 mi
0 2 km
N
TOMOKA STATE PARK
Ormond Beach Municipal Airport
N. Beach St.
Ocean Shore Blvd.
A1A
W Granada Blvd
E Granada Blvd.
Granada Blvd.
ORMOND BEACH
Williamson Blvd.
Nova Rd.
Ridgewood Ave.
Halifax River
Halifax Dr.
16th St.
N. Peninsula Dr.
Atlantic Ave.
TOMOKA WILDLIFE AREA
Kings Rd.
Center St.
Riverside Dr.
11th St.
8th St.
Jimmy Ann Rd.
Holly Hill
Mason Ave.
Seabreeze Blvd.
Madison Ave.
DAYTONA BEACH
Cypress St.
Main St. Bridge
Main St. Pier
International Speedway Blvd.
Ocean Dr.
Orange Ave.
Memorial Bridge
Daytona Beach Shores
Daytona Beach International Airport
Bellevue Ave.
Beach St.
South Daytona Beach
S. Halifax Dr.
Beville Rd.
To Orlando
Big Tree Rd.
Reed Canal Rd.
S. Peninsula Dr.
Port Orange
Dunlawton Ave.
Port Orange Bridge
ATLANTIC OCEAN
Taylor Rd.
To Cocoa & Ft. Pierce
To New Smyrna Beach

NORTHEAST FLORIDA 14 DAYTONA BEACH

and other races throughout the year. The speedway is also home to DAYTONA USA, a motor-sports entertainment attraction worth a visit even by non–race fans.

Be sure to check the "Calendar of Events" (p. 40) to know when the town belongs to college students on Spring Break (though not as many since Panama City took over as Spring Break Central), thousands of leather-clad motorcycle buffs during Bike Week (Mar) and Biketoberfest (Oct), or racing enthusiasts for big competitions. You won't be able to find a hotel room, drive the highways, or enjoy a peaceful vacation when they're in town.

ESSENTIALS

GETTING THERE **Continental** (© **800/525-0280**) and **Delta** (© **800/221-1212**) fly into the small, pleasant, and calm **Daytona Beach International Airport** (© **386/248-8030;** www.flydaytonafirst.com), 4 miles inland from the beach on International Speedway Boulevard (U.S. 92), but you can usually find less-expensive fares to **Orlando International Airport** (p. 450), about an hour's drive away. **Daytona-Orlando Transit Service (DOTS;** © **800/231-1965** or 386/257-5411; www.dots-daytonabeach.com) provides van transportation to and from Orlando International Airport. One-way fares are about $35 for adults, $18 for children ages 11 and under. The service takes passengers to the company's terminal at 1034 N. Nova Rd., between 3rd and 4th streets, or to beach hotels for an additional fee.

If you fly into the Daytona Airport, rates for the **Daytona Shuttle** (© **386/255-2294**) run up to $15 per person, $18 per couple, and $9 per person for parties of three or more. The ride from the airport to most beach hotels via **Yellow Cab Co.** (© **386/255-5555**) is between $10 and $20.

Alamo (© 800/327-9622), **Avis** (© 800/831-2847), **Budget** (© 800/527-0700), **Dollar** (© 800/800-4000), **Enterprise** (© 800/325-8007), **Hertz** (© 800/654-3131), and **National** (© 800/227-7368) have booths at the airport. Or why not rent a Harley? This is Daytona, after all. Contact **Daytona Harley-Davidson** (© 800/307-4464 or 386/258-0638; www.daytonahd.com). Rates are $135 to $155 daily, $600 to $640 weekly. A special sunset rate of $75 is available from 4pm to 9am.

Amtrak (© **800/872-7245;** www.amtrak.com) trains stop at Deland, about 15 miles southwest of Daytona Beach, with bus service from Deland to the beach.

VISITOR INFORMATION The **Daytona Beach Area Convention & Visitors Bureau,** 126 E. Orange Ave. (P.O. Box 910), Daytona Beach, FL 32115 (© **800/544-0415** or 386/255-0415; www.daytonabeach.com), can help you with information on attractions, accommodations, dining, and events. The office is on the mainland just west of the Memorial Bridge. The information area of the lobby is open daily from 9am to 5pm. The bureau also maintains a branch at DAYTONA USA, 1801 W. International Speedway Blvd. (daily 9am–7pm), as well as a kiosk at the airport.

GETTING AROUND Although Daytona is primarily a driver's town, Volusia County's public transit system, **VOTRAN** (© **386/761-7700;** www.votran.org), runs a **free shuttle** in the Main Street Pier/Ocean Walk Village area and a pay **trolley** along Atlantic Avenue on the beach, Monday through Saturday from noon to midnight. Fares are $1.25 for adults, 60¢ for seniors and children ages 6 to 17, and free for kids ages 5 and under who are riding with an adult. Votran also runs **buses** through downtown and the beaches.

For a taxi, call **Yellow Cab** (© **386/255-5555**) or **Southern Komfort Cab** (© **386/252-2222**).

A VISIT TO THE WORLD CENTER OF RACING

Daytona International Speedway/DAYTONA USA ★★ You don't have to be a racing fan to enjoy a visit to the **Daytona International Speedway,** 4 miles west of the beach. Opened in 1959 with the first Daytona 500, this 480-acre complex is one of the key reasons for the city's fame. The track presents about nine weekends of major racing events annually, featuring stock cars, sports cars, motorcycles, and go-karts, and is used for automobile and motorbike testing and other events many other days of the year. Its grandstands can accommodate more than 150,000 fans. Big events sell out months in advance—tickets to the Daytona 500 in February can be gone a year ahead of time—so buy yours and make hotel reservations as early as possible.

Start your visit at the **World Center of Racing Visitor Center,** in the NASCAR office complex at the east end of the speedway. Admission to the center is free, and you can walk out and see the track during non–race days (there's a small admission to the track during qualifying races leading up to the main events). Entertaining 30-minute guided tram tours of the facility (garage area, pit road, and so on) depart from the visitor center and are well worth taking.

The visitor center houses a large souvenir shop, a snack bar, and the phenomenally popular **DAYTONA 500 Experience,** a 60,000-square-foot, state-of-the-art interactive motor-sports attraction. Here you can learn about the history, color, and excitement of stock car, go-kart, and motorcycle racing in Daytona. In Daytona Dream Laps, you get the feel of what it's like to zoom around the track from a 32-seat motion simulator. If that doesn't get your stomach churning, hop inside your own 80%-scale NASCAR vehicle in Acceleration Alley, buckle up, and roar up to 200 mph in a spectacular simulator for the ultimate virtual reality–like racing experience ($5 per ride). On the milder side, you can participate in a pit stop on a NASCAR Winston Cup stock car, see an actual winning Daytona 500 car still covered in track dust, talk via video with favorite competitors, and play radio or television announcer by calling the finish of a race. An action-packed IMAX film will put you in the winner's seat of a Daytona 500 race.

To really experience what it's like, you can make (for $135) three laps around the track in a stock car from May to October with the **Richard Petty Driving Experience Ride-Along Program** (✆ **800/237-3889;** www.1800bepetty.com). Professional drivers (sorry, none is named Petty) are at the wheel as you see and feel what it's like to travel an average of 115 mph.

Allow at least 4 hours to see everything, and bring your video camera.

1801 W. International Speedway Blvd. (U.S. 92, at Bill France Blvd.). ✆ **386/253-7223** for race tickets, 253-7223 for information, or 386/947-6404 or 947-6800 for DAYTONA USA. www.daytonaintlspeedway.com and www.daytonausa.com. Admission to speedway free except on race days; tram rides $7.50; DAYTONA 500 Experience $24 adults, $19 seniors, $19 children 6–12, free for children 5 and under. Speedway daily 9am–7pm; trams depart every 30 min. 9:30am–5pm except during races and special events; DAYTONA 500 Experience daily 9am–7pm (later during race events). Closed Christmas.

HITTING THE WORLD'S MOST FAMOUS BEACH

The beautiful and hard-packed beach here runs for 24 miles along a skinny peninsula separated from the mainland by the Halifax River. The bustling hub of activity is at the end of Main Street, where you'll find the **Main Street Pier** (also known as the Daytona Beach Pier or Ocean Pier), the longest wooden pier on the East Coast. Out here you'll find a restaurant, bar, bait shop, beach-toy concessions, chairlift running its length, and views from the 180-foot-tall Space Needle. Admission as far out as the restaurant and bar is free (at about a third of the way, this is far enough for a good view down the beach), but you'll

Tips Driving on the Beach

You can drive and park directly on sections of the sand along 18 miles of the beach from 1 hour after sunrise to 1 hour before sunset. During sea turtle nesting season, May 1 to October 31, driving hours are set from 8am to 7pm. Traffic lanes and speed limits are clearly marked at low tide but watch for signs warning of nesting sea turtles. There's a $5-per-vehicle access fee and 10-mph speed limit. *Watch out for the tides.* If you park on an incoming tide and lose track of time, your vehicle may become an inadvertent rust bucket or artificial reef!

have to pay $1 to walk beyond that point, and more than that if you fish (see "Outdoor Activities," below). Beginning at the pier, the city's famous oceanside **Boardwalk** is lined with restaurants, bars, and T-shirt shops, as are the 4 blocks of Main Street nearest the beach. The city's $400-million **Ocean Walk Village** redevelopment project begins here and runs several blocks north, featuring a movie theater, boutiques, restaurants, and even a 175-room hotel/condo, the **Ocean Walk Resort** (✆ **877/845-WALK** [9255]).

There's another busy beach area at the end of **Seabreeze Boulevard,** which has a multitude of restaurants, bars, and shops.

Couples seeking greater privacy usually prefer the northern or southern extremities of the beach. **Ponce Inlet,** at the very southern tip of the peninsula, is especially peaceful, as there is little commerce or traffic there to disturb the silence. **Lighthouse Point Park** is the best beach there, consisting of 52 acres of pristine beaches on the northern end of Ponce Inlet. It features fishing, nature trails, an observation deck and tower, swimming, and picnicking. Admission is $3.50 per vehicle.

OUTDOOR ACTIVITIES

FISHING The easiest and least expensive way to fish offshore for cobia, sea bass, sharks, king mackerel, grouper, red snapper, and more is with the **Critter Fleet,** 4950 S. Peninsula Dr., just past the lighthouse in Ponce Inlet (✆ **800/338-0850** or 386/767-7676; www.critterfleet.com), which operates two party boats. One goes on all-day trips (about $80 for adults, $50 for kids 16 and under), while the other makes morning and afternoon voyages (about $50 for adults, $40 for kids 7 and over, 6 and under free). The fares include a rod, reel, and bait. Call for schedules, prices, and reservations.

Save the cost of a boat by fishing with the locals at **Main Street Pier,** at the ocean end of Main Street (✆ **386/253-1212**). Admission for anglers is $6 for adults, $4 for kids 11 and under. Bait and gear are available for $14, and no license is required.

GOLF There are more than 25 courses within 30 minutes of the beach, and most hotels can arrange starting times for you. **Golf Daytona Beach,** 126 E. Orange Ave., Daytona Beach, FL 32114 (✆ **800/881-7065** or 386/239-7065; fax 386/239-0064), publishes an annual brochure describing the major courses. It's available at the tourist information offices (see "Essentials," above).

For course information, go to www.golf.com or www.floridagolfing.com; or you can call the **Florida Sports Foundation** (✆ **850/488-8347**) or **Florida Golfing** (✆ **866/833-2663**).

Two of the nation's top-rated links for women golfers are at the **LPGA International ★★**, 1000 Championship Dr. (✆ **386/274-5742;** www.lpgainternational.com):

the Champions course, designed by Rees Jones, and the Legends course, designed by Arthur Hills. Each boasts 18 outstanding holes. LPGA International is a center offering workshops and teaching programs for professional and amateur women golfers, and the pro shop carries a great selection of ladies' equipment and clothing. Greens fees with a cart are usually about $100, lower in summer. *Pssst*—they let guys play here, too!

A Lloyd Clifton–designed course, the centrally located 18-hole, par-72 **Indigo Lakes Golf Course,** 2620 W. International Speedway Blvd. (✆ **386/254-3607**), has flat fairways and large bunkered Bermuda greens. Fees here are about $65 in winter (including a cart), lower in summer.

The semiprivate South Course at **Pelican Bay Country Club,** 550 Sea Duck Dr. (✆ **386/756-0034;** www.pelicanbaygolfclub.com), is one of the area's favorites, with fast greens to test your putting skills. Fees are about $50 with cart in winter, lower in summer (no walking allowed). The North Course is for members only.

The city's prime municipal course is the **Daytona Beach Golf Club,** 600 Wilder Blvd. (✆ **386/258-3119;** www.daytonabeachgc.com), which has 36 holes. Winter fees are about $20 to $25 to walk, $25 to $30 to share a cart. Rates drop in summer.

HORSEBACK RIDING **Shenandoah Stables,** 1759 Tomoka Farms Rd., off U.S. 92 (✆ **386/257-1444**), offers daily trail rides and lessons. Call for prices and schedules.

SPECTATOR SPORTS The **Daytona Cubs** (✆ **386/872-2827;** www.daytonacubs.com), a Class A minor-league affiliate of the Chicago Cubs, play April through August at Jackie Robinson Ballpark, on City Island downtown. A game here is a treat, as the park has been restored to its classic 1914 style by the designers of Baltimore's Camden Yards and Cleveland's Jacobs Field. Tickets are $6 to $12.

WATERSPORTS Watersports equipment, bicycles, beach buggies, and mopeds can be rented along the Boardwalk, at the ocean end of Main Street (see "Hitting the World's Most Famous Beach," above), and in front of major beachfront hotels.

MUSEUMS & ATTRACTIONS

Halifax Historical Museum ★ Located on Beach Street, Daytona's original riverfront commercial district on the mainland side of the Halifax River (see "Shopping," below), this local museum is worth a look just for the 1912 neoclassical architecture of its home, a former bank. A mural of Old Florida wildlife graces one wall, the stained glass ceiling reflects sunlight, and across the room is an original teller's window. The eclectic collection includes tools and household items from the Spanish and British periods, thousands of historic photographs, possessions of past residents (even a ball gown worn at Lincoln's inauguration), and, of course, model cars. A race exhibit opens annually in mid-January as a stage-setter for Race Week.

252 S. Beach St. (just north of Orange Ave.). ✆ **386/255-6976.** www.halifaxhistorical.org. Admission $5 adults, $1 children 11 and under; free Sat for children. Tues–Sat 10am–4pm.

Marine Science Center ★ Kids This marine museum has interior displays (with exhibits on mangroves, mosquitoes, shells, artificial reefs, dune habitats, and pollution solutions), a 5,000-gallon aquarium, and educational programs and activities. Though the exhibit area is rather small, there's more than enough information for a child to digest at one time. Perhaps the most interesting part of the center is the space reserved for the rehabilitation of endangered and threatened sea turtles and seabirds. You can watch them in any of seven turtle tanks—look for the ones that need life jackets to stay afloat!

 100 Lighthouse Dr., Ponce Inlet. ✆ **386/304-5545.** www.marinesciencecenter.com. Admission $5 adults, $4 seniors, $2 children 3–12, free for children 2 and under. Tues–Sat 10am–4pm; Sun noon–4pm. See directions for Ponce de León Inlet Lighthouse & Museum (below).

Museum of Arts and Sciences ★★ An exceptional institution for a town of Daytona's size and reputation (as culturally devoid beyond NASCAR), this hard-to-find museum is best known for its Cuba: A History of Art exhibit, with paintings acquired in 1956, when Cuban dictator Fulgencio Batista donated his private collection to the city. Among them is a portrait of Eva ("Evita") Perón, said to be the only existing painting completed while she was alive (it hangs near the lobby, not within the Cuban exhibit). The Dow Gallery displays American decorative arts, while the Bouchelle Study Center for the Decorative Arts contains American and European jewelry, furniture, mirrors, and more. Other rooms include the Schulte Gallery of Chinese Art; Africa: Life and Ritual, with the largest collection of Ashante gold ornaments in the U.S. (these are stunning); and the Center for Florida History, with the skeleton of a 13-foot-tall, 130,000-year-old giant ground sloth. Check out the unique collection of the late Chapman S. Root, a Daytona philanthropist and a founder of the Coca-Cola empire; among the memorabilia are the mold for the original Coke bottle and the Root family's two private railroad cars. The planetarium presents 30-minute shows of what the night sky will look like on the date of your visit. New to the museum in 2009, the **Charles and Linda Williams Children's Museum,** a world-class science center featuring over 9,000 square feet of hands-on science activities. The museum is located on a 90-acre nature preserve that features over 1/2 mile of boardwalk nature trails and learning stations. The museum displays new temporary exhibits bi-monthly.

352 S. Nova Rd. (btw. International Speedway Blvd. and Bellevue Ave.). ✆ **386/255-0285.** www.moas.org. Museum $13 adults, $11 seniors, $6.95 children and students with ID, free for children 5 and under. Planetarium shows included with paid admission. Mon–Sat 9am–5pm; Sun 11am–5pm. Closed Thanksgiving, Christmas Eve, and Christmas Day. Take International Speedway Blvd. west, make a left on Nova Rd. (Fla. 5A), and look for a sign on your right.

Ponce de León Inlet Lighthouse & Museum ★★ This National Historic Landmark is well worth a stop even if you're not a lighthouse enthusiast. The 175-foot brick-and-granite structure is the second-tallest lighthouse in the United States. Built in the 1880s, the lighthouse and the graceful Victorian brick buildings surrounding it have been restored. There are no guided tours, but you can walk through the 12 areas, which feature different exhibits (lighthouse lenses, historical artifacts, and a film of early car racing on the nearby beach), and stroll around the tugboat *F. D. Russell,* now sitting high and dry in the sand. Use common sense if you climb the 203 steps to the top of the lighthouse; it's a grinding ascent, but the view from up there is spectacular.

4931 S. Peninsula Dr., Ponce Inlet. ✆ **386/761-1821.** www.ponceinlet.org. Admission $5 adults, $1.50 children 11 and under. Memorial Day–Labor Day daily 10am–9pm; rest of year daily 10am–5pm. Follow Atlantic Ave. south, make a right on Beach St., and follow the signs.

SHOPPING

On the mainland, Daytona Beach's main riverside drag, **Beach Street,** is one of the few areas in town where people actually stroll. The street is wide and inviting, with palms down its median, and decorative wrought-iron archways and fancy brickwork overlooking a branch of the Halifax River. Today the stretch of Beach Street between Bay Street and Orange Avenue offers antiques and collectibles shops, galleries, clothiers, a magic shop, a historical museum (see "Museums & Attractions," above), and several good cafes. At 154 S. Beach St., you'll find the home of the **Angell & Phelps Chocolate Factory**

(✆ **386/252-6531;** www.angellandphelps.com), which has been making candy for more than 75 years. Watch the goodies being made (and get a free sample)!

"Hog" riders will find several shops to their liking along Beach Street, north of International Speedway Boulevard, including **Bruce Rossmeyer's Harley-Davidson Store,** 290 N. Beach St. (✆ **866/642-3464;** www.brucerossmeyer.com), a 20,000-square-foot retail outlet and diner serving breakfast and lunch. It's one of the nation's largest Harley dealerships. In addition to hundreds of gleaming new and used Hogs, you'll find as much fringed leather as you've ever seen in one place.

The **Daytona Flea and Farmers' Market,** on Tomoka Farms Road at the junction of I-95 and U.S. 92, a mile west of the speedway (✆ **386/253-3330;** www.daytonaflea market.com), is huge, with 1,000 covered outdoor booths plus 100 antiques and collectibles vendors in an air-conditioned building. Most of the booths feature new (though not necessarily first-rate) wares along the lines of socks, sunglasses, luggage, handbags, jewelry, tools, and the like. It's open year-round Friday through Sunday from 8am to 5pm. Admission and parking are free.

Ocean Walk Shoppes, at Ocean Walk Village, 250 N. Atlantic Ave. (✆ **386/257-5077;** www.oceanwalkvillage.com), is a collection of upscale boutiques and restaurants, along with a 10-screen movie theater.

WHERE TO STAY

Room rates here are among the most affordable in Florida. Some lodgings have several rate periods during the year, but generally they are somewhat higher from the beginning of the races in February all the way to Labor Day. They skyrocket during major events at the speedway, during bikers' gatherings, and during Spring Break (see the "Calendar of Events," beginning on p. 40), when hotels fill to the bursting point. Even if you can find a room then, there's often a minimum-stay requirement.

A slew of hotels and motels line Atlantic Avenue along the beach, many of them family owned and operated. The **Daytona Beach Area Convention & Visitors Bureau** (see "Essentials," earlier in this chapter) distributes a brochure that lists "Superior Small Lodgings" for Daytona Beach, Deland, and New Smyrna Beach. All of the small motels listed below are members.

If you're going to the races and don't care about staying on the beach, some upper-floor rooms at the **Hilton Garden Inn Daytona Beach Airport,** 189 Midway Ave. (✆ **877/944-4001** or 386/944-4000), overlook the international speedway track. Unlike most members of Hilton's Garden Inn chain, this one has a restaurant.

Thousands of rental condominiums line the beach. Among the most luxurious is the 175-unit condominium hotel **Wyndham Ocean Walk Resort,** 300 N. Atlantic Ave., Daytona Beach, FL 32118 (✆ **800/649-3566** or 386/323-4800; www.oceanwalk.com), which is part of the Ocean Walk Village redevelopment. Near the Main Street Pier, it's in the center of the action and has one-, two-, and three-bedroom apartments with full kitchens, washers and dryers, and all of the usual hotel amenities, plus a wondrous computer-golf simulator, a "lazy river" in one of the three outdoor pools (there are also two pools indoors), an island putting green, and much more—including one of the gaudiest lobbies I've ever seen. Rates are $129 to $799. One of the largest rental agents is **Peck Realty,** 2340 S. Atlantic Ave., Daytona Beach Shores, FL 32118 (✆ **800/447-3255** or 386/257-5000; www.peckrealty.com).

In addition to the 6% state sales tax, Volusia County levies a 6% tax on hotel bills.

Bahama House ★★ A Caribbean-chic boutique hotel, Bahama House is a family-owned, 10-story stay located on a quiet stretch of the Atlantic coastline. All rooms, each individually named after an area of the Caribbean, offer private balconies with fabulous ocean and Intracoastal Waterway views and tropical decor. In addition to complimentary deluxe continental breakfast served daily, there's also a nightly cocktail reception from 5:30 to 6:30pm that features free hors d'oeuvres, house wines, beer, and highballs. During the day, there are freshly baked cookies available in the lobby, giving this place more of a B&B feel than just a random resort. A heated pool; beach activities, including family surfing lessons; and a great selection of kids' activities make Bahama House an ideal place for families. All resort guests also have access to nearby tennis at the USTA Florida tennis complex.

2001 S. Atlantic Ave., Daytona Beach Shores, FL 32118. ✆ **800/571-2001** or 386/248-2001. Fax 386/248-0991. www.daytonabahamahouse.com. 87 units, including 74 efficiencies. $142–$192 double. Specials, packages, and discounts offered year-round. Rates include continental breakfast and evening cocktail reception. AE, DC, DISC, MC, V. Free parking. **Amenities:** 2-tiered heated pool/sun deck; Jacuzzi; seasonal activities desk; laundry facilities. *In room:* A/C, TV, Wi-Fi, kitchenette (in efficiencies), fridge, coffeemaker, hair dryer, iron, safe, microwave.

The Plaza Resort & Spa ★★ After $70 million in renovations, these elegant adjoining 7- and 13-story buildings hold some of Daytona Beach's best rooms (in a much more tasteful atmosphere than many of the neighboring hotels)—provided you don't need a large bathroom. The best units are the corner suites, each with a sitting area and two balconies overlooking the Atlantic; some even have a Jacuzzi. All units have balconies, plasma TVs, and microwaves. The full-service **Ocean Waters Spa ★★** (✆ **386/267-1660;** www.oceanwaterspa.com) has 16 treatment rooms and a soothing menu of facials, massages, and wraps.

600 N. Atlantic Ave. (at Seabreeze Ave.), Daytona Beach, FL 32118. ✆ **800/874-7420** or 386/255-4471. Fax 386/238-7984. www.plazaresortandspa.com. 323 units. $119–$199 double; $189–$449 suite. AE, DC, DISC, MC, V. **Amenities:** Restaurant; bar; heated outdoor pool; exercise room; spa; Jacuzzi; watersports equipment/rentals; game room; business center; limited room service; massage; babysitting; laundry service; coin-op washers/dryers; concierge-level rooms. *In room:* A/C, TV, dataport, fridge, coffeemaker, hair dryer, iron, microwave.

Shoreline All Suites Inn & Cabana Colony Cottages ★ Value The Shoreline All Suites Inn has one- and two-bedroom suites that occupy two buildings separated by a walkway leading to the beach. Most have small bathrooms with scant vanity space and—shall we say—intimate shower stalls. Every unit has a full kitchen, and there are barbecue grills on the premises. For a change of scenery, consider the Shoreline's sister property, the **Cabana Colony Cottages ★★**. All 12 of the cottages were built in 1927 but have since been upgraded. They aren't much bigger than a motel room with a kitchen, but they're light, airy, and attractively furnished. The cottages share a heated pool with the Shoreline.

2435 S. Atlantic Ave. (Fla. A1A, at Dundee Rd.), Daytona Beach Shores, FL 32118. ✆ **800/293-0653** or 386/252-1692. Fax 386/239-7068. www.daytonashoreline.com. 30 units, including 12 cottages. $69–$299 suite and cottage. Rates include continental breakfast. Golf packages available. AE, DISC, MC, V. **Amenities:** Heated outdoor pool; coin-op washers/dryers. *In room:* A/C, TV/VCR, kitchen, coffeemaker.

The Shores Resort & Spa ★★ Far enough south to escape the madding crowds of Main Street, and set in a residential area directly on the beach, this hotel is the most luxurious hotel here. It welcomes guests with an elegant terra-cotta-tiled lobby with a fountain and potted palms. The large guest rooms are grouped in pairs and can be joined to form suites; only one of each pair has a balcony. Oceanfront rooms are preferable; all have sea and/or river view. The restaurant, Azure, is one of Daytona's nicest, offering stellar seafood with a gourmet and regional twist; patio dining overlooking the ocean is a fine option. The spa offers an Indonesian-inspired menu of treatments.

2637 S. Atlantic Ave. (Fla. A1A, btw. Florida Shores Blvd. and Richard's Lane), Daytona Beach Shores, FL 32118. ✆ **866/934-SHORES** (7467) or 386/767-7350. Fax 386/760-3651. www.shoresresort.com. 212 units. Winter $249–$489 double, $549–$1,129 suite; off-season $169–$359 double, $509–$829 suite. AE, DC, DISC, MC, V. **Amenities:** Restaurant; bar; heated outdoor pool; exercise room; spa; salon; room service; babysitting; laundry service; dry cleaning. *In room:* A/C, TV, dataport, Wi-Fi, kitchen, coffeemaker, hair dryer, iron.

The Villa Bed & Breakfast ★★★ You'll think you're in Iberia upon entering this more-than-70-year-old Spanish mansion's great room with its fireplace, baby grand piano, and terra-cotta floors. A sunroom equipped with a TV and VCR, a formal dining room, and a breakfast nook are also located downstairs. The lush backyard surrounds a pool and a covered Jacuzzi. Upstairs, the nautically themed Christopher Columbus room has a vaulted ceiling and a small balcony overlooking the pool. The largest unit here is the King Carlos suite, once the original master bedroom, with a four-poster bed, entertainment system, fridge, rooftop deck, and bathroom equipped with a four-head shower. The Queen Isabella room has a portrait of the queen hanging above a queen-size bed, while the Marco Polo room features Chinese black-lacquer furniture and Oriental rugs. No children under 14 allowed.

801 N. Peninsula Dr. (at Riverview Blvd.), Daytona Beach, FL 32118. ✆/fax **386/248-2020.** www.thevillabb.com. 4 units. $100–$300 double. Rates include continental breakfast. AE, MC, V. No children 13 and under accepted. **Amenities:** Heated outdoor pool; Jacuzzi. *In room:* A/C, TV, hair dryer, no phone.

WHERE TO DINE

Daytona Beach has a few interesting dining venues, but not many are likely to leave an indelible memory. A profusion of fast-food joints line the major thoroughfares, especially along Atlantic Avenue on the beach and International Speedway Boulevard (U.S. 92) near the racetrack. Restaurants come and go in the Beach Street district on the mainland, and along Main Street and Seabreeze Boulevard on the beach. A casual restaurant out on the Main Street Pier serves burgers, chicken wings, and lots of suds.

Two chain restaurants are worth a special mention here. **Buca di Beppo,** 2514 W. International Speedway Blvd. (✆ **386/253-6523;** www.bucadibeppo.com), a boisterous restaurant serving family-style Southern Italian specialties, is open for dinner only. Expect to take home leftovers, as the portions are huge and the food surprisingly good, especially for a "theme" restaurant. **Stonewood Tavern & Grill,** 100 S. Atlantic Ave., in Ormond Beach (✆ **386/671-1200;** www.stonewoodgrill.com), is a casual upscale restaurant with a nice but dark mahogany interior, good American food, and excellent service. It's open only for dinner and usually packed; you won't be disappointed with its menu of steaks, seafood, and the like.

At the Beaches

Down the Hatch ★ (Value) SEAFOOD Occupying a 1940s fish camp on the Halifax River, Down the Hatch serves big portions of fresh fish and seafood (note its shrimp boat docked outside). Inexpensive burgers and sandwiches are available, too. The scenic views include boats and shorebirds visible through the picture windows. At night, arrive early to catch the sunset over the river, and also to beat the crowd to this very popular place. In summer, light fare is served on a covered deck.

4894 Front St., Ponce Inlet. ✆ **386/761-4831.** www.down-the-hatch-seafood.com. Call ahead for priority seating. Main courses $9–$25; breakfast $5–$8; burgers and sandwiches $7–$9. AE, MC, V. Daily 8am–10pm;

 early bird 11am–5pm. Closed 1st week in Dec. Take Atlantic Ave. south, make a right on Beach St., and follow the signs.

Inlet Harbor Restaurant and Marina ★ SEAFOOD For great waterfront views, outdoor and indoor dining, live music, and a scenic view of the Ponce Inlet Lighthouse, Inlet Harbor is one of those places that reminds you why you're here. In addition to the good sea-fare—peel-and-eat shrimp, pan-fried grouper, deep water lobster tails—there's also Florida fresh gator tail, fried and served with a honey mustard sauce. Try it—it tastes like chicken! The restaurant also has charter captains on-site to take you out boating; and, if you get lucky out there, the restaurant will even cook your catch for you. A new 65-passenger party boat also departs daily from the restaurant's dock, in case you haven't partied enough already.

133 Inlet Harbor Rd., Ponce Inlet. ✆ **386/757-5590.** www.inletharbor.com. Main courses $15–$26; sandwiches and burgers $5–$8. AE, MC, V. Daily 11am–midnight. Take A1A S.; make a right on Inlet Harbor Rd.

Julian's Dining Room & Lounge ★ AMERICAN This family-owned restaurant has catered to locals and tourists since 1967, providing a casual atmosphere and friendly service. Unlike most eateries in this area, it specializes in prime rib and prime Western beef (filet mignon, strip steak, and T-bone), but the seafood is far from second fiddle here. Good choices include broiled snapper, soft-shell crab, and king crab au gratin.

88 S. Atlantic Ave., Ormond Beach. ✆ **386/677-6767.** www.juliansrest.com. Reservations suggested. Main courses $10–$30. AE, DC, MC, V. Daily 4–11pm. From Daytona Beach, take Atlantic Ave./Fla. A1A N. and look for the large A-frame on the left, 2 blocks before Fla. 40.

Ocean Deck Restaurant & Beach Club (Value) SEAFOOD/PUB FARE Known by Spring Breakers, bikers, and other beachgoers as Daytona's best "beach pub" since 1940, the three-story Ocean Deck is also the best restaurant in the busy area around the Main Street Pier. The downstairs reggae bar is as sweaty and packed as ever (a band plays nightly 9pm–2:30am). The upstairs dining room can be noisy, too, but come here for good food, reasonable prices, and great ocean views. You can choose from a wide range of seafood, chicken, sandwiches, and the best burgers on the beach, but don't pass up the mahimahi (look for "trophy" on the menu), a bargain at $13. There's valet parking after dark, or you can park free at the lot behind the Ocean Deck's Reggae Republic surf shop, a block away on Atlantic Avenue.

127 S. Ocean Ave. (at Kemp St.). ✆ **386/253-5224.** www.oceandeck.com. Main courses $12–$16; salads and sandwiches $6–$10. AE, DISC, MC, V. Daily 11am–2am (bar to 3am).

On the Mainland

The Cellar ★★ ITALIAN This fine-dining classical Italian eatery occupies the basement of a 1907 Victorian built as President Warren G. Harding's winter home, and it is now listed on the National Register of Historic Places. Brick walls make for a cozy, un-Florida-like ambience. While the restaurant's history is authentically American, an all-Italian menu features some tempting options. Chef/owner Sam Moggio is a graduate of the Culinary Institute and, boy does it show! All pastas are homemade, and then there are the outstanding entrees. Among them: a snapper filet sautéed with artichokes, diced tomatoes, basil, saffron, and white wine; braised lamb shanks with vegetable risotto; and for dessert, a sinful, semisweet flourless chocolate torte.

220 Magnolia Ave. (btw. Palmetto and Ridgewood aves.). ✆ **386/258-0011.** www.thecellarrestaurant.com. Main courses $16–$26. AE, DISC, MC, V. Tues–Sun 5–10pm.

The Dancing Avocado Kingdom ★ VEGETARIAN A healthful place to start your day or to have lunch while touring downtown, this establishment purveys a number of vegetarian omelets, burritos, salads, pizzas, and sandwiches such as an avocado Reuben. A few chicken and turkey items are on the menu, but the only red-meat selection is a burger. You can dine outside or inside the store, which has brick walls and ceiling fans suspended from black rafters.

110 S. Beach St. (btw. Magnolia St. and International Speedway Blvd.). ✆ **386/947-2022.** Breakfast $3–$8; sandwiches, salads, and pizzas $5–$10. AE, DC, DISC, MC, V. Mon–Sat 8am–4pm.

Frappes North ★★ NEW AMERICAN It's worth the 6-mile drive north to Bobby and Meryl Frappier's sophisticated, hip establishment, which provides this area's most entertaining cuisine. Some like to call the food served here "organically groovy." We just call it great. Several chic dining rooms set the stage for an ever-changing "Menu of the Moment," fusing a multitude of styles. Ingredients are always fresh, and herbs come from the restaurant's garden. Bobby and Meryl offer at least one vegetarian main course. Lunch is a steal here and Sunday brunch features a stellar spinach, tomato, and cheddar cheese fritatta. The restaurant is in a storefront on the mainland stretch of Granada Boulevard, Ormond Beach's main drag.

123 W. Granada Blvd. (Fla. 40., btw. Ridgewood Ave. and Washington St.), Ormand Beach. ✆ **386/615-4888.** www.frappesnorth.com. Reservations recommended. Main courses $16–$33 dinner, $7–$14 lunch. AE, MC, V. Mon–Fri 11:30am–2:30pm and 5–10pm; Sat 5–10pm; Sun 10am–1:30pm and 5–8pm. From the beaches, drive 4 miles north on Fla. A1A and turn left on Granada Blvd. (Fla. 40); cross Halifax River to restaurant on right.

McK's Dublin Station AMERICAN/IRISH Worth knowing about because it serves food after midnight, this upscale Irish pub has an eclectic menu. The fare includes club sandwiches, burgers, mahimahi wraps, and a few main courses of steak, fish, and chicken. The food isn't exceptional, but it's perfectly acceptable after a few Bass ales. The service is sometimes rushed but usually pleasant.

218 S. Beach St. (btw. Magnolia St. and Ivy Lane). ✆ **386/238-3321.** Main courses $6–$15; salads and sandwiches $5–$10. AE, MC, V. Mon–Wed 11am–11:30pm; Thurs–Sat 11am–3am.

DAYTONA BEACH AFTER DARK

Check the Friday edition of the Daytona Beach *News-Journal* (www.n-jcenter.com) for its weekly "Go-Do," and the Sunday edition for the "Master Calendar" section, which lists upcoming events. Other good sources listing nighttime entertainment are *Happenings Magazine* and *Backstage Pass Magazine,* two tabloids available at the visitor center (see "Essentials," earlier in this chapter) and in many hotel lobbies.

Ghost tours are led by certified ghost hunters who merge legend with science. You're guaranteed to have a spooky time (at least, it's more interesting than most touristy ghost tours). A portion of all proceeds goes to cemetery preservation and restoration, so at least you can feel good about the fee. Tickets are $10 per person, free for children 5 and under. Contact **Haunts of Daytona** (✆ **386/253-6034;** www.hauntsofdaytona.com) for tours and times.

THE PERFORMING ARTS The city-operated **Peabody Auditorium,** 600 Auditorium Blvd., between Noble Street and Wild Olive Avenue (box office ✆ **386/254-4545** or 671-3460), is Daytona's major venue for serious art, including concerts by the local Symphony Society (✆ **386/253-2901**). Professional actors perform Broadway musicals during winter and summer at the **Seaside Music Theater,** 176 N. Beach St., downtown (✆ **800/854-5592** or 386/252-6200). The **Oceanfront Bandshell** (✆ **386/671-3400**),

Side Trip to Ocala

Just 78 miles west of Daytona Beach is **Ocala,** an entirely different world that is more Kentucky than central Florida. Known for its somewhat rolling hills, cow pastures, and Derby-caliber horse farms (www.horsecapitaldigest.com), Ocala is a nature lover's paradise and home to the stunning **Ocala National Forest** (© **877/HIKE-FLA** [445-3352]; www.floridatrail.org), with 600 lakes, 23 spring-fed streams, and two major rivers. Designated a National Scenic Trail in 1983, the forest's Florida Trail features the remains of homesteads made famous by Marjorie Kinnan Rawlings' classic *The Yearling.* If you want to spend the night, we suggest you do so at the **Seven Sisters Inn,** 820 SE Fort King St. (© **352/867-1170;** www.sevensistersinn.com), a Victorian landmark on the National Register of Historic Places with 13 rooms featuring fireplaces and Victorian soaking tubs or Jacuzzis. Some rooms have stone spa showers. Hand-pressed bed sheets and tea time are a few of its many charms. Rates range from $119 to $279. Just outside of Ocala is **Silver Springs,** 5656 E. Silver Springs Blvd. (© **352/236-2121;** www.silversprings.com), a 350-acre natural theme park whose main attraction is the country's largest collection of artisan springs. The park is listed on the National Register of Historic Landmarks and features wild animal displays, glass-bottom boat rides, a jungle cruise, and a jeep safari. Ocala, located in Marion County, which has been called the "Horse Capital of the World," also has a quaint, historic downtown district, with renovated Victorian homes and buildings, boutiques, antique shops, restaurants, and cafes. While Ocala isn't necessarily somewhere to spend a week, it is worth exploring what is known as the **Heart of Florida Scenic Trail** (www.floridaseden.org), which comprises the college town of Gainesville, the horse country of Ocala, Old Florida towns including the very Victorian McIntosh and Micanopy, and the scenic Rainbow River (www.therainbowriver.com), whose **Café on the River,** 19773 E. Pennsylvania Ave. (© **352/622-6763**), serves five-course gourmet dining alongside killer views. For more information on the area, contact the **Marion County Visitors and Convention Bureau,** 2102 SW 20th Place (© **888/356-2252;** www.ocalamarion.com).

on the Boardwalk, hosts a series of free big-name concerts every Sunday night from early June to Labor Day. Daytona also has a great relationship with the **London Symphony Orchestra,** which considers the city its official summer home, having performed more times in Daytona than any other city outside London. For more cultural affairs, check out www.daytonabeach.com/whattosee.cfm/mode/culturallydb.

THE CLUB & BAR SCENE **Main Street** and **Seabreeze Boulevard** on the beach are happening areas where dozens of bars (and a few topless shows) cater to leather-clad bikers.

The **Boot Hill Saloon,** 310 Main St. (© **386/258-9506;** www.boothillsaloon.com), is a bluesy, brewsy honky-tonk, especially popular during race and bike weeks.

A popular beachfront bar for more than 40 years, the **Ocean Deck Restaurant & Beach Club,** 127 S. Ocean Ave. (© **386/253-5224;** see "Where to Dine," above), is packed with a mix of locals and tourists, young and old, who come for live music and cheap drinks. Reggae or ska bands play daily and nightly. There's valet parking after dark, or leave your vehicle at Ocean Deck's Reggae Republic surf shop on Atlantic Avenue.

3 ST. AUGUSTINE: AMERICA'S FIRST CITY ★★

105 miles NE of Orlando; 302 miles N of Miami; 39 miles S of Jacksonville

With its 17th-century fort, old city gates, horse-drawn carriages clip-clopping along narrow streets, historic buildings, and reconstructed 18th-century Spanish Quarter, St. Augustine seems more like a picturesque European village than a modern Floridian city. This is, after all, the oldest permanent European settlement in the United States (no, it wasn't Jamestown in 1607 or the Pilgrims' settlement at Plymouth Rock in 1620). A group of French Huguenots settled in 1562 near the mouth of the St. Johns River, in present-day Jacksonville. Three years later, a Spanish force under Pedro Menéndez de Avilés arrived on the scene, wiped out the Huguenot men (de Avilés spared their women and children), and established a settlement he named St. Augustín.

The colony survived a succession of attacks by pirates, Indians, and the British over the next 2 centuries. The Treaty of Paris, ending the French and Indian War, ceded the town to Britain in 1763, but the British gave it back to Spain 20 years later. The United States took control when it acquired Florida from Spain in 1821.

Tourism is St. Augustine's main industry these days. However, despite the daily invasion (with good reason—there is a plethora of interesting attractions), it's an exceptionally charming town, with good restaurants, a small-town nightlife, and shopping bargains. Give yourself 2 days here to see the highlights, longer to savor this historic gem: St. Augustine is one of those places that actually lives up to most of the sickly sweet and sentimental promotional literature written about it.

ESSENTIALS

GETTING THERE The **Daytona Beach International Airport** (p. 524) is about an hour's drive south of St. Augustine, but service is more frequent—and fares usually lower—at **Jacksonville International Airport** (p. 552), about the same distance north. The nearest **Amtrak** train station is in Jacksonville (p. 552).

VISITOR INFORMATION Before you go, contact the **St. Augustine, Ponte Vedra & The Beaches Visitors and Convention Bureau,** 88 Riberia St., Ste. 400, St. Augustine, FL 32084 (✆ **800/653-2489** or 904/829-1711; www.visitoldcity.com). Request the *Visitor's Guide,* which details attractions, events, restaurants, accommodations, shopping, and more.

The **St. Augustine Visitor Information Center** is at 10 Castillo Dr., at San Marco Avenue, opposite the Castillo de San Marcos National Monument (✆ **904/825-1000**). There are numerous ways to see the city, depending on your interests and schedule; this makes a good first stop. For $1, you can watch *Struggle to Survive,* a 42-minute video about the town's difficult first 14 years. (History buffs will enjoy it; otherwise, it's a good way to kill an hour on a rainy day.) The free 22-minute orientation video is more helpful in planning a visit. Once you've looked through the extensive information and made plans, you can buy tickets for the sightseeing trains and trolleys, which include discounted admissions to the attractions (see "Getting Around," below). The center is open daily from 8:30am to 5:30pm.

Tips Where to Park in "St. Aug"

On-street parking is nonexistent in St. Augustine's historic district, and metered parking lots are not only difficult to find, but often full. Your best bet is to park in the brand-new, large, *free* **Historic Downtown Parking Facility** behind the visitor center on Castillo Drive. Plus, most of the top historic attractions are within walking distance of the center, as it is virtually across the street from the Old City Gates.

GETTING AROUND Once you've parked at the visitor center, you can walk or take one of the sightseeing trolleys, trains, or horse-drawn carriages around the historic district. The trolleys and trains follow 7-mile routes, stopping at the visitor center and at or near most attractions between 8:30am and 5pm daily. You can get off at any stop, visit the attraction, and step aboard the next vehicle that comes along about every 20 minutes. If you don't get off at any attractions, it takes about 1 hour and 10 minutes to complete the tour. The vehicles don't all go to the same sights, so speak with their agents at the visitor center in order to pick the right one for you. You can buy tickets, as well as discounted tickets to some attractions, at the visitor center or from the drivers.

Old Town Trolley Tours (© **800/213-2474;** www.historictours.com) takes you on an hour tour with more than 20 stops at the historic district and its most famous sites. Best of all, you can hop on and off at your leisure all day. Tickets include admission to the Florida Heritage Museum and the St. Augustine Beach Bus, which picks up and drops off passengers at various resorts and attractions around town. The tour costs $21 for adults, $8 for kids 6 to 12. Rates are cheaper online.

St. Augustine Sightseeing Trains (© **800/226-6545** or 904/824-1606; www.redtrains.com) cover all the main sights except the Authentic Old Jail and the Florida Heritage Museum at the Authentic Old Jail, but its red open-air trains, operated by Ripley's of Believe It or Not fame, are small enough to go down more of the narrow historic-district streets. Tickets are $21 for adults, $8 for kids 6 to 12, and are good for 3 consecutive days. The company also sells package tickets for your convenience, and rates are cheaper online.

You may want to see the sights by horse-drawn carriage. **St. Augustine Transfer Company** (© **904/829-2391;** www.staugustinetransfer.com) has been showing people around town since 1877. Its carriages line up on Avenida Menendez, south of Castillo de San Marcos National Monument. Slow-paced, entertaining, driver-narrated 45-minute to 1-hour rides past major landmarks and attractions are offered from 8am to midnight. Private tours and hotel and restaurant pickups are available for $85 per person. There is also a very cool, spooky ghost ride from 6pm until closing every night. Carriage tours cost $20 for adults, $10 for kids 5 to 11.

For more personalized group excursions, call **Tour Saint Augustine** (© **800/797-3778** or 904/825-0087; www.staugustinetours.com), which offers guided walking tours around the historic area. Rates vary based on the number of people in the group.

You can also search for old spirits with the nightly **Ghost Tours of St. Augustine** ★★ (© **888/461-1009** or 904/461-1009; www.ghosttoursofstaugustine.com), in which guides in period dress lead you through the historic district or to the St. Augustine Lighthouse. Tickets are $12 to $22 per person, depending on the tour you choose. Also offered are

1-hour ghost cruises on the river in a 72-foot-tall mast schooner. These cost $35 per person, including soft drinks and snacks. Call for schedules and reservations.

The **Sunshine Bus Company** (✆ **904/823-4816;** www.sunshinebus.net) operates public bus routes Monday through Saturday from 6am to 7pm. The line runs between the St. Augustine Airport on U.S. 1 and the historic district via San Marco Avenue and the Greyhound bus terminal on Malaga Street. Rides cost $1 per person. All day tickets are $3. Call for the schedule.

For a taxi, call **Yellow Cab** (✆ **904/824-6888**).

Solano Cycle, 61 San Marco Ave., at Locust Avenue, 2 blocks north of the visitor center (✆ **904/825-6766;** www.solanocycle.com), rents bicycles and scooters. Bikes cost $18 a day, while scooters are $75 for a single passenger and $80 for two. Open daily from 10am to 6pm.

SEEING THE TOP HISTORIC ATTRACTIONS

St. George Street, from King Street north to the Old City Gate (at Orange St.), is the heart of the historic district. Lined with restaurants and boutiques selling everything from T-shirts to antiques, these 4 blocks get the lion's share of the town's tourists. You'll have much less company if you poke around the narrow streets of the primarily residential neighborhood south of King Street. Most of the town's attractions do not have guided tours, but many do have docents on hand to answer questions.

Be sure to drive through the parking lot of the Howard Johnson Express Inn, at 137 San Marco Ave., to see a gorgeous and stately **live oak tree** ★★ that is at least 600 years old; then continue east to **Magnolia Avenue** ★★, a spectacularly beautiful street with a lovely canopy of old magnolia trees.

Castillo de San Marcos National Monument ★ As far as fortresses are concerned, this one's pretty cool. America's oldest and best-preserved masonry fortification took 23 years (1672–95) to build. It is stellar in design, with a double drawbridge entrance (the only way in or out) over a 40-foot dry moat. Diamond-shaped bastions in each corner, which enabled cannons to set up a deadly crossfire, contained sentry towers. The indestructible Castillo was never captured in battle, and its coquina (limestone made from broken seashells and corals) walls did not crumble when pounded by enemy artillery or violent storms throughout more than 300 years. Today the old bombproof storerooms surrounding the central plaza have exhibits about the history of the fort, a national monument since 1924. You can tour the vaulted powder magazine, a dank prison cell (supposedly haunted), the chapel, and guard rooms. Climb the stairs to get a great view of Matanzas Bay. A self-guided tour map and brochure are provided at the ticket booth. If available, the 20- to 30-minute ranger talks are well worth attending. Popular torchlight tours of the fort are offered in winter.

If you like forts, you should also check out **Fort Matanzas,** built on an island in the 1740s to warn St. Augustine of enemy attacks from the south (which were out of reach of Castillo de San Marcos). For information, call ✆ **904/471-0116** or visit www.nps.gov/foma. Fort Matanzas is open daily from 8:30am to 5:30pm, and admission and the ferry ride to the island are free, though donations are accepted.

1 E. Castillo Dr. (at San Marco Ave.). ✆ **904/829-6506.** www.nps.gov/casa. Admission $6 adults for 7-day pass, free for children 15 and under. Fort daily 8:45am–4:45pm; grounds daily 5:30am–midnight.

Colonial Spanish Quarter and Spanish Quarter Museum ★★ If H. G. Wells were alive, he'd get a load of this re-created colonial Spanish village—complete with costumed folks doing things they used to do back in the 1700s—and think he was witnessing living proof of a bona fide time-travel machine. Watch as the blacksmiths, carpenters, leatherworkers, and homemakers demonstrate their skills and show you what life was like before the Internet. All of the architecture and landscape have been re-created within this 2-square-block park which, in my opinion, is infinitely more fun than the museum itself. Do take a 20-minute guided tour of the **DeMesa-Sanchez House** (ca. 1740–60), the only authentic colonial-era structure in the compound (the others are reproductions). If you're into this re-created history, then don't miss the Old St. Augustine Village Museum, which covers even more history.

33 St. George St. (btw. Cuna and Orange sts.). ✆ **904/825-6830.** www.historicstaugustine.com. Admission $7 adults, $6 seniors, $4.25 students 6–18, free for children 5 and under, $13 per family. Daily 9am–5:30pm (last entry at 4:30pm).

Dow Museum of Historic Houses ★★ More time travel in St. Augustine is available at this awesome museum re-creating life back in the old days. Operated by Daytona Beach's excellent Museum of Arts and Sciences (p. 528), this museum brings to life each period of the city's history, from Spanish colonial times to the early 20th century. The eight restored homes here—built between 1790 and 1910—are on their original building sites. Some homes are decorated with period furniture and decor, while others serve as galleries. The reconstructed Star General Store sells preserves and other Victorian-era goods. You'll need 2 hours to see it all, including the 30-minute guided tour. Admission is good all day, so if you miss the start of a tour, you can leave and come back.

149 Cordova St. (entry on Bridge St. btw. St. George and Cordova sts.). ✆ **904/823-9722.** www.old-staugvillage.com. Admission $9 adults, $8 seniors, $7 children 11 and under. Mon–Sat 10am–4:30pm; Sun 11am–4:30pm. Guided tours on the hour 10am–3pm, except 1pm.

Lightner Museum ★★★ Now *this* is a museum. Henry Flagler's opulent Spanish Renaissance–style Alcazar Hotel, built in 1889, closed during the Depression and stayed vacant until Chicago publishing magnate Otto C. Lightner bought the building in 1948 to house his vast collection of Victoriana. The lobby of the museum is exactly as the hotel lobby was back in the 1800s. The building is an attraction in itself and makes a gorgeous museum, centering on a palm-planted courtyard with an arched stone bridge spanning a fishpond. The first floor houses a Victorian village, with shop fronts representing emporia selling period wares. The Victorian Science and Industry Room displays shells, rocks, and Native American artifacts in beautiful turn-of-the-20th-century cases. Other exhibits include stuffed birds, an Egyptian mummy, steam-engine models, and examples of Victorian glass blowing. (Yes, it's a strange amalgamation for a museum, but there's sure to be *something* you're interested in here.) Plan to spend about 90 minutes exploring, and be sure to be here at 11am or 2pm, when a room of automated musical instruments erupts into concerts of period music. Check out the cafe, too, housed in what used to be a stunning indoor pool.

The imposing building across King Street was Henry Flagler's rival resort, the Ponce de León Hotel. It now houses **Flagler College,** which runs not-to-be-missed 45-minute tours daily (at 10am and 2pm) of its magnificent Tiffany stained-glass windows, ornate Spanish Renaissance architecture, and gold-leafed Maynard murals ($6 adults, $5 kids 11 and under). Call ✆ **904/823-3378,** or visit www.flagler.edu for more information. Across Cordova Street stands another competitor of the day, the 1888-vintage **Casa Monica Hotel** (p. 546).

75 King St. (at Granada St.). ✆ **904/824-2874.** www.lightnermuseum.org. Admission $10 adults, $5 students with ID and children 12–18, free for children 11 and under. Daily 9am–5pm (last tour 4pm).

ACCOMMODATIONS ■
Alexander Homestead 12
Bayfront Westcott House Bed & Breakfast Inn 28
Best Western Spanish Quarter Inn 7
Carriage Way Bed & Breakfast 11
Casablanca Inn on the Bay 18
Casa de Solana 30
Casa Monica Hotel 22
Kenwood Inn 27
Monterey Inn 15
Pirate Haus Inn & Hostel 16
Victorian House 26

DINING ◆
A1A Ale Works 24
Antonio's Pizza 19
The Bunnery Bakery & Café 17
Collage 14
Gypsy Cab Co. 19
Opus 39 13
Raintree 5

ATTRACTIONS ●
Authentic Old Jail 2
Castillo de San Marcos National Monument 8
Colonial Spanish Quarter and Spanish Quarter Museum 10
Dolphin Conversation Center at Marineland 31
Florida Heritage Museum at the Authentic Old Jail 2
Fountain of Youth Archaeological Park 3
Lightner Museum 21
Mission of Nombre de Dios 4
The Oldest House 29
The Oldest Wooden Schoolhouse in the U.S.A. 9
Old Florida Museum 1
Old St. Augustine Village Museum 25
Ripley's Believe It Or Not! Museum 6
Spanish Military Hospital 23
St. Augustine Alligator Farm and Zoological Park 20
St. Augustine Lighthouse & Museum 20
World Golf Village 1

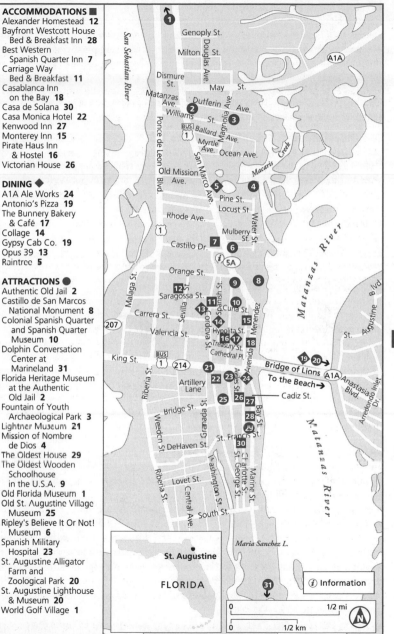

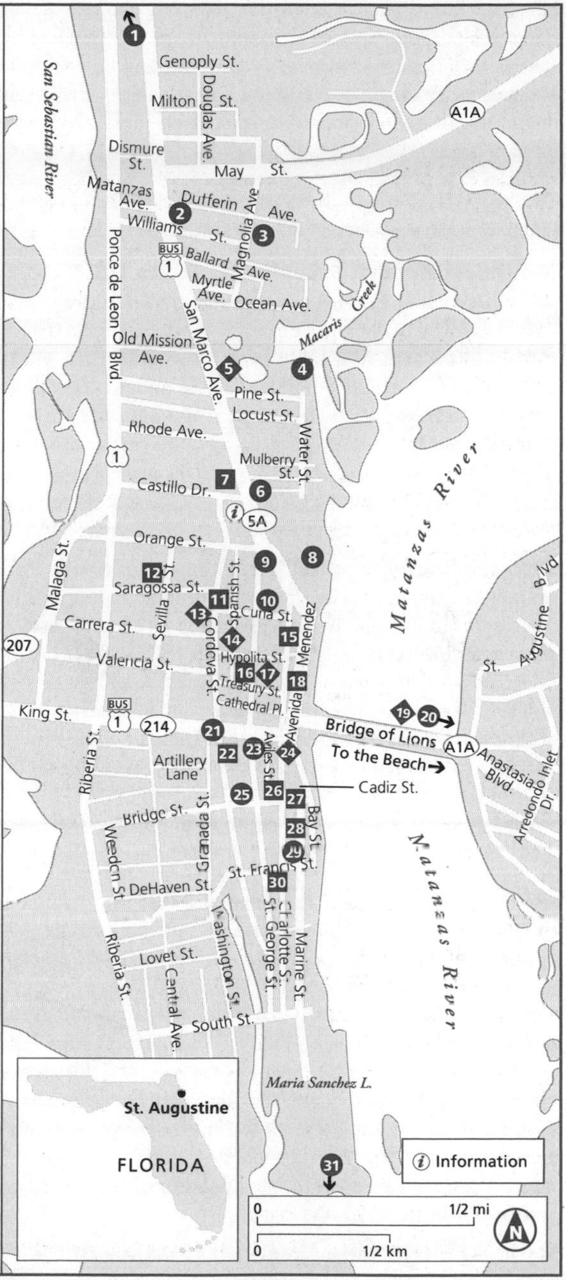

San Sebastian River
Genoply St.
Milton St.
Douglas Ave.
Dismure St.
May St.
Matanzas Ave.
Dufferin Ave.
Williams St.
Magnolia Ave.
Ballard Ave.
Myrtle Ave.
Ocean Ave.
Macaris Creek
Ponce de Leon Blvd.
San Marco Ave.
Old Mission Ave.
Pine St.
Locust St.
Rhode Ave.
Water St.
Mulberry St.
Castillo Dr.
5A
Orange St.
Malaga St.
Saragossa St.
Sevilla St.
Spanish St.
Cuna St.
Carrera St.
Cordova St.
Hypolita St.
Treasury St.
Cathedral Pl.
Avenida Menendez
Valencia St.
207
King St.
BUS 1
214
Bridge of Lions
A1A
To the Beach
Riberia St.
Artillery Lane
Aviles St.
Cadiz St.
Bay St.
Bridge St.
Granada St.
Weeden St.
DeHaven St.
St. Francis St.
Charlotte St.
St. George St.
Marine St.
Washington St.
Lovet St.
Central Ave.
Riberia St.
South St.
Maria Sanchez L.
Matanzas River
Anastasia Blvd.
Arredondo Inlet Dr.
Augustine Blvd.
St.
St. Augustine
FLORIDA
Information
0 1/2 mi
0 1/2 km
N

NORTHEAST FLORIDA 14 ST. AUGUSTINE: AMERICA'S FIRST CITY

The Oldest House ★★ Archaeological surveys indicate that a dwelling stood on this site as early as the beginning of the 17th century. What you see today, called the Gonzáles-Alvarez House (named for two of its prominent owners), evolved from a two-room coquina dwelling built between 1702 and 1727. The rooms are furnished to evoke various historical eras. Admission also entitles you to explore the adjacent **Manucy Museum of St. Augustine History,** where artifacts, maps, and photographs document the town's history from its origins through the Flagler era a century ago. Allow about 30 minutes here.

14 St. Francis St. (at Charlotte St.). ✆ **904/824-2872.** www.staugustinehistoricalsociety.org. Admission $8 adults, $7 seniors 55 and over, $4 students, free for children 6 and under, $18 per family. Daily 9am–5pm; tours depart every half-hour (last tour at 4:30pm).

The Oldest Wooden Schoolhouse in the U.S.A. ★ Kids Excellent photo ops abound at this old-fashioned schoolhouse. One of three structures here dating from the Spanish colonial period, this cedar-and-cypress structure is held together by wooden pegs and handmade nails, its hand-wrought beams still intact. The last class was held in 1864. Today the old-time classroom is re-created using cheesy animated pupils and a teacher, complete with a dunce and below-stairs "dungeon" for unruly children, which will make your kids count their lucky stars that they weren't in school back then.

14 St. George St. (btw. Orange and Cuna sts.). ✆ **904/824-0192.** www.oldestwoodenschoolhouse.com. Admission $3.50 adults, $2.50 children 6–12, free for children 5 and under. Daily 9am–5pm (later in summer).

Spanish Military Hospital Hypochondriacs, doctors, and fans of medicine in general will love this place—but if you're squeamish in hospitals, this one isn't an exception. The clapboard building is a reconstruction of part of a hospital that stood here during the second Spanish colonial period, from 1784 to 1821. A 20-minute guided tour will show you what the apothecary, administrative offices, patients' ward, and herbarium probably looked like in 1791. The ward and a collection of actual surgical instruments of the period will enhance your appreciation of modern medicine. They say it's haunted, and, as a result, there's a great ghost tour here every night at 8pm, with a 9:30pm tour on Saturdays for $12 a person.

3 Aviles St. (south of King St.). ✆ **904/827-0807.** www.spanishmilitaryhospital.com. Admission $5 adults, $4 seniors, $3 children. Mon–Sat 10am–5pm; Sun noon–5pm.

MORE HISTORIC ATTRACTIONS

Authentic Old Jail It's no Alcatraz, but in a sinister way, this old jail is kind of quaint. The compact prison, a mile north of the visitor center, may be authentic, but it's not particularly historic. It was built in 1890 and served as the county jail until 1953. The sheriff and his wife raised their children upstairs and used the same kitchen facilities to prepare the inmates' meals and their own. Among the "regular" cells, you can also see a maximum-security cell where murderers and horse thieves were confined, a cell housing prisoners condemned to hang (they could see the gallows being constructed from their window), and a grim solitary-confinement cell—with no windows or mattress. A restaurant here serves inexpensive lunch fare.

167 San Marco Ave. (at Williams St.). ✆ **904/829-3800.** Admission $9 adults, $5 children 6–12, free for children 5 and under. Daily 8:30am–5pm.

Florida Heritage Museum at the Authentic Old Jail Compared to the other museums in town, this one isn't so special. After you've seen the Authentic Old Jail, you can spend another 30 minutes wandering through this commercial museum documenting 400 years of Florida's past, focusing on the life of Henry Flagler, the Civil War, and the Seminole Wars. Highlights are a collection of toys and dolls, mostly from the 1870s to the 1920s, and a replica of a Spanish galleon filled with weapons, pottery, and treasures, along with display cases filled with actual gold, silver, and jewelry recovered by treasure hunters. A typical wattle-and-daub hut of a Timucuan Indian in a forest setting illustrates the lifestyle of St. Augustine's first residents.

167 San Marco Ave. (at Williams St.). ✆ **904/829-3800.** Admission $6 adults, $5 children 6–12, free for children 5 and under. Free admission with purchase of Old Town Trolley Tour. Daily 8:30am–5pm.

Fountain of Youth Archaeological Park (Overrated) Considering that Botox and plastic surgery are the real fountains of youth, why bother? Never mind that Juan Ponce de León never found the Fountain of Youth; this 25-acre archaeological park bills itself as North America's first historic site. Smithsonian Institution archaeological digs have established that a Timucuan Indian village existed here some 1,000 years ago, but there's no evidence that Ponce de León visited the spot during his 1513 voyage. You can wander the not-so-interesting grounds yourself, but you'll learn more on a 45-minute guided tour or at a planetarium show about 16th-century celestial navigation. ***Be warned:*** This place could be a secondary dictionary definition for the phrase *tourist trap* (not to mention that the fountain's water smells and tastes *awful*). Nevertheless, the grounds are lovely and the nonfountain exhibits are okay, which is good because people feel the need to visit even though it's basically a waste of time.

11 Magnolia Ave. (at Williams St.). ✆ **800/356-8222** or 904/829-3168. www.fountainofyouthflorida.com. Admission $7.50 adults, $6.50 seniors, $4.50 children 6–12, free for children 5 and under. Daily 9am–5pm.

Mission of Nombre de Dios This serene setting overlooking the Intracoastal Waterway is believed to be the site of the first permanent mission in the United States, founded in 1565. The mission is a popular destination of religious pilgrimages. Whatever your beliefs, it's a beautiful tree-shaded spot, ideal for quiet meditation.

27 Ocean Ave. (east of San Marco Ave.). ✆ **904/824-2809.** Free admission; donations appreciated. Daily 8am–5:30pm.

Old Florida Museum ★★ (Kids) For those who can't resist touching things in museums, it's okay to do so here and it's even encouraged! This mostly outdoors museum gives you the chance to experience historic Florida, with many hands-on activities (shelling and grinding corn, pumping water, writing with a quill pen) that kids may enjoy. Showcasing daily activities, everyday objects (games, weapons, tools, and more), and recreational pastimes, the museum demonstrates how three different eras of people in the area—the native Timucuan Indians, colonial Spaniards, and American pioneers—lived, worked, and played from the 16th to the early 20th century.

254-D San Marco Ave. ✆ **800/813-3208** or 904/824-8874. www.oldfloridamuseum.com. Admission $6 adults, $5 children 12 and under. Daily 10am–5pm.

St. Augustine Lighthouse & Museum ★ Photo-op alert! This 165-foot-tall structure, Florida's first official lighthouse, was built in 1875 to replace the old Spanish lighthouse that had stood at the inlet since 1565. The lightkeeper's cottage was destroyed by fire in 1970 but was meticulously restored to its Victorian splendor. The Victorian-style visitor center houses a museum explaining the history of the lighthouse and the area. You should be in good physical condition (children must be at least 7 years old *and* 4 ft.

tall) to climb the 219 steps to the top of the lighthouse. In 2007, the Sci Fi Network's popular show *Ghost Hunters* filmed an episode here and found that, after a thorough paranormal investigation, the lighthouse is, indeed, haunted!

81 Lighthouse Ave. (off Fla. A1A east of the Bridge of Lions). ✆ **904/829-0745.** www.staugustinelighthouse.com. Admission to museum and tower $9 adults, $8 seniors, $7 children 7–11, free for children 6 and under and all active-duty and retired military personnel. Admission to museum and grounds $7.50 adults, $6.50 seniors, and $5.50 children. Daily 9am–6pm. Follow Fla. A1A S. across the Bridge of Lions; take the last left before the turnoff to Anastasia State Park.

OTHER ENTERTAINMENT ATTRACTIONS

Dolphin Conservation Center at Marineland ★★ What once was a schlocky 7-acre beachfront tourist trap is now a world-class Dolphin Conservation Center. This, the world's first oceanarium (1938), is 15 minutes south of St. Augustine and is on the National Register of Historic Places. See dolphins, sea lions, penguins, and myriad ocean life here, or snorkel or scuba in the 450,000-gallon oceanarium with some of them, if you make reservations. ***Note:*** Swimming with dolphins has both its critics and its supporters. You may want to visit the Whale and Dolphin Conservation Society's website at www.wdcs.org. For more information about responsible travel in general, check out www.treadlightly.org and www.ecotourism.org.

9600 Ocean Shore Blvd. ✆ **904/460-1275.** www.marineland.net. Admission $6 adults, $3 children 12 and under. Dolphin Immersion $179–$189 (ages 5 and up, minimum height 50 in.). Wed–Mon 9:30am–4:30pm. South of St. Augustine on A1A.

Ripley's Believe It or Not! Museum (Kids) A total tourist trap, this is a place to go only if it's raining outside and you have absolutely nothing to do. This is the original Ripley's museum, housed in an architecturally interesting converted 1887 Moorish Revival residence—complete with battlements, massive chimneys, and rose windows. Like the Ripley's in a dozen other U.S. cities, the exhibits run the gamut from a Haitian voodoo doll owned by Papa Doc Duvalier to letters carved on a pencil with a chainsaw by Ray "Wild Mountain Man" Murphy.

19 San Marco Ave. (at Castillo Dr.). ✆ **904/824-1606.** www.staugustine-ripleys.com. Admission $15 adults, $12 seniors, $8 children 5–12, free for children 4 and under. June 8–Labor Day daily 9am–9pm; rest of year 9am–7pm.

St. Augustine Alligator Farm and Zoological Park ★★ (Kids) At the St. Augustine Alligator Farm and Zoological Park, gators and crocs are a dime a dozen. In fact, there are more than 2,700 of them—including some rare white ones—on display at this more-than-a-century-old attraction. It houses the world's only complete collection of all 22 species of crocodilians, a category that includes alligators, crocodiles, caimans, and gavials. There are also ponds and marshes filled with ducks, geese, swans, herons, egrets, ibises, and other native wading birds, as well as a petting zoo with pygmy goats, potbellied pigs, and miniature horses. Entertaining (and educational) 20-minute alligator and reptile shows take place hourly throughout the day, and you can often see narrated feedings from spring through fall. Don't miss Maximo, an Australian croc that weighs 1,250 pounds; is 15 feet, 3 inches long; and is the father to 17 baby crocs.

999 Anastasia Blvd. (Fla. A1A), east of Bridge of Lions at Old Quarry Rd. ✆ **904/824-3337.** www.alligatorfarm.com. Admission $22 adults, $18 seniors, $11 children 3–10, free for children 2 and under. Discounts available online. Daily 9am–5pm; summer 9am–6pm.

Where Golf Is King

Passionate golf fans can easily spend a day at the **World Golf Hall of Fame** ★ (✆ **904/940-4123;** www.wgv.com), a state-of-the-art museum honoring professional golf, its great players, and the sport's famous supporters (including comedian Bob Hope and singer Dinah Shore). It's the centerpiece of **World Golf Village,** a complex of hotels, shops, offices, and 18-hole golf courses (see "Outdoor Activities," below). There's an IMAX screen next door.

Museum admission is $20 for adults, $18 for seniors and students, and $9 for children 4 to 12 and includes an IMAX film and a round of golf on the putting green. IMAX tickets range from $8 to $12 for adults, $7 to $11 for seniors and students, and $5 to $10 for children. The museum is open daily from 10am to 6pm; IMAX movies run until 8pm Friday and Saturday.

You don't have to play the real courses because the village is built around a lake with a "challenge hole" sitting out in the middle, 132 feet from the shoreline. You can hit balls at it or play a round on the nearby putting course. Admission to the Hall of Fame includes a round on the putting course. The Walkway of Champions (whose signatures appear in pavement stones) circles the lake and passes a shopping complex where the main tenant is the two-story **Tour Stop** (✆ **904/940-0422**), a purveyor of pricey apparel and equipment.

If you'd like to stay overnight, contact the luxurious **World Golf Village Renaissance Resort,** 500 S. Legacy Trail, St. Augustine, FL 32092 (✆ **888/740-7020** or 904/940-8000; www.worldgolfrenaissance.com), which completed a $10-million renovation in 2008 to include remodeled rooms and suites, new technology, and a new restaurant.

The village is at exit 95A off I-95. For more information, contact World Golf Village, 21 World Golf Place, St. Augustine, FL 32092 (✆ **904/940-4000;** www.wgv.com).

HITTING THE BEACH

There are several places to find sand and sea: **Vilano Beach,** on the north side of St. Augustine Inlet; and **St. Augustine Beach,** on the south side (the inlet dumps the Matanzas and North rivers into the Atlantic). Be aware, however, that erosion has almost swallowed the beach from the inlet as far south as Old Beach Road in St. Augustine Beach. The U.S. Army Corps of Engineers is reclaiming the sand, but in the meantime, hotels and homes here have rock seawalls instead of sand bordering the sea.

Erosion has made a less noticeable impact on beautiful **Anastasia State Park** ★★, on Anastasia Boulevard (Fla. A1A) across the Bridge of Lions and just past the Alligator Farm, where the 4 miles of beach (on which you can drive and park) are still backed by picturesque dunes. On its riverside, the area faces a lagoon. Amenities include shaded picnic areas with grills, restrooms, windsurfing, sailing and canoeing (on a saltwater lagoon), a nature trail, and saltwater fishing (for bluefish, pompano, redfish, and flounder; a license is required for nonresidents). In summer, you can rent chairs, beach umbrellas, and surfboards. There's good bird-watching here, especially in spring and fall; pick up a brochure at the entrance. The 139 wooded campsites are in high demand year-round; they come with picnic tables, grills, and electricity. Admission to the park is $5 per vehicle, $1 per bicyclist or pedestrian. Campsites cost $25. For camping reservations, call © **800/326-3521** or go to www.reserveamerica.com. The day-use area is open daily from 8am to sunset. You can bring your pets. For information, contact Anastasia State Park, 1340A Fla. A1A S., St. Augustine, FL 32084 (© **904/461-2033;** www.floridastateparks.org/anastasia).

From Memorial Day to Labor Day, all St. Augustine beaches charge a fee of $3 per car at official access points; the rest of the year, you can park free, but there are no lifeguards on duty or restroom facilities on the beach.

OUTDOOR ACTIVITIES

For additional outdoor options, contact the St. Augustine, Ponte Vedra & The Beaches Visitors and Convention Bureau (p. 535) and request a copy of its *Outdoor Recreation Guide.*

CRUISES The Usina family has been running **St. Augustine Scenic Cruises** (© **904/824-1806;** www.scenic-cruise.com) on Matanzas Bay since the turn of the 20th century. They offer 75-minute narrated tours aboard the double-decker *Victory III,* departing from the Municipal Marina just south of the Bridge of Lions. You can sometimes spot dolphins, brown pelicans, cormorants, and kingfishers. Snacks, soft drinks, beer, and wine are sold onboard. Departures are usually at 11am, 1pm, 2:45pm, and 4:30pm daily except Christmas, with an additional tour at 6:15pm from April 1 to May 21 and from Labor Day to October 15. From May 22 to Labor Day, there are two additional tours, at 6:45 and 8:30pm. Call ahead—schedules can change during inclement weather. Fares are $16 for adults, $13 for seniors, $9.25 for youths ages 13 to 18, and $7.50 for children ages 4 to 12. If you're driving, allow time to find parking on the street.

You can also take the free ferry to Fort Matanzas on Rattlesnake Island. There are often dolphins in the water as you make the trip, and the fort is interesting. Ferries take off from 8635 Hwy. A1A (follow A1A S. out of St. Augustine for about 15 miles). Call © **904/471-0116,** or visit www.nps.gov/foma for more information.

FISHING You can fish to your heart's content at **Anastasia State Park** (see "Hitting the Beach," above). Or you can cast your line off **St. Johns County Fishing Pier,** at the north end of St. Augustine Beach (© **904/461-0119**). The pier is open 24 hours daily and has a bait shop with rental equipment that's open from 6am to 10pm. Admission is $2 ($1 children 11 and under) for fishing, 50¢ for sightseeing.

For full-day, half-day, and overnight **deep-sea fishing** excursions (for snapper, grouper, porgy, amberjack, sea bass, and other species), contact the **Sea Love Marina,** 250 Vilano Rd. (Fla. A1A N.), at the eastern end of the Vilano Beach Bridge (© **904/824-3328;** www.sealovefishing.com). Full-day trips on the party boat *Sea Love II* cost about $80; half-day trips $60. No license is required, and rod, reel, bait, and tackle are supplied. Bring your own food and drink.

GOLF The area's best golf resorts are in Ponte Vedra Beach—a half-hour's drive north on Florida A1A, closer to Jacksonville than St. Augustine (see p. 558 for details).

The **Tournament Players Club Sawgrass** (© **888/421-8555;** www.pgatourexperience.com) offers the Tour Player Experience, where duffers will be treated like a pro and have access to the exclusive wing of the 77,000-square-foot clubhouse where only actual pros, such as Vijay Singh and Jim Furyk, are allowed. You also get a personal caddy wearing a bib with your name on it. The experience also includes a stay at the Sawgrass Marriott Resort and Spa, dinner, spa services, instruction at the Tour Academy, and a golf gift bag that includes balls, marker, and shirt. From $1,295 per person, per night.

At World Golf Village, 12 miles north of St. Augustine, at exit 95A off I-95 (see the box "Where Golf Is King," above), the **Slammer & The Squire** and the **King & The Bear** (© **904/940-6088;** www.wgv.com) together offer 36 holes amid a wildlife preserve. Locals say they're not as challenging as their greens fees: about $139 in summer, $190 in winter, including cart. For those not schooled in golf history, the "Slammer" is in honor of Sam Sneed, the "Squire" is for Gene Sarazen, the "King" is Arnold Palmer, and the "Bear" is Jack Nicklaus. Palmer and Nicklaus collaborated in designing their course.

Nicklaus also had a hand in the stunning course at the **Ocean Hammock Golf Club** ★★ (© **386/477-4600;** www.oceanhammock.com), on Florida A1A, in Palm Coast, about halfway between St. Augustine and Daytona Beach. With 6 of its holes skirting the beach, it is the first truly oceanside course built in Florida since the 1920s.

There are only a few courses in St. Augustine, including **Ponce de León Hotel, Golf & Conference Resort,** 4000 U.S. 1 (© **904/829-5314**), with its rather flat 18; and the **St. Augustine Shores Golf Club,** 707 Shores Blvd., off U.S. 1 (© **904/794-4653**), a par-70, 18-hole course with lots of water, a lighted driving range and putting green, and a restaurant and lounge. Greens fees usually are less than $30, including cart.

For more course information, go to www.golf.com or www.floridagolfing.com; or call the **Florida Sports Foundation** (© **850/488-8347**) or **Florida Golfing** (© **866/833-2663**).

WATERSPORTS Jet skis and equipment for surfing and windsurfing can be rented at **Surf Station,** 1020 Anastasia Blvd. (Fla. A1A), a block south of the Alligator Farm (© **904/471-9463**); and at **Raging Water Sports,** at the Conch House Marina Resort, 57 Comares Ave. (© **904/829-5001**), off Anastasia Avenue (Fla. A1A) halfway between the Bridge of Lions and the Alligator Farm.

SHOPPING

The winding streets of the historic district are home to dozens of **antiques stores** and **galleries** stocked full of original paintings, sculptures, bric-a-brac, fine furnishings, china, and other treasures. Brick-lined **Aviles Street,** a block from the river, has an especially good mix of shops for browsing, as does **St. George Street** south of the visitor center, and the Uptown area on **San Marco Avenue** a few blocks north of the center. The **Alcazar Courtyard Shops,** at the Lightner Museum (© **904/824-2874;** p. 538), have a good selection of antiques. Check at the visitor center for lists of art galleries and antiques shops, or contact the **Antique Dealers Association of St. Augustine,** 60 Cuna St., St. Augustine, FL 32084 (no phone).

Experience chocolate heaven at **Whetstone Chocolates,** 2 Coke Rd. (Fla. 312), between U.S. 1 and the Mickler O'Connell Bridge (© **904/825-1700**). Free self-guided tours of the store and factory usually take place Monday through Saturday from 10am to 5pm, but call ahead to confirm the schedule. Whetstone has a retail outlet at 42 St. George St., in the historic district.

Outlet shoppers will find plenty of good hunting 7 miles northwest of downtown on Florida 16, on the west side of I-95, in the **St. Augustine Premium Outlets** (© **904/825-1555;** www.staugustineoutlets.com), the new in 2008 and swankier (Gucci, Cole Hahn, Kate Spade, Hugo Boss, and the like) **Prime Outlets** (© **904/826-1311;** www.primeoutlets.com), and at the **Belz Factory Outlet World,** on the east side of the interstate (© **904/826-1311;** www.belz.com). All three malls are open Monday through Saturday from 9am to 9pm, Sunday from 10am to 6pm.

WHERE TO STAY

There are plenty of moderate and inexpensive motels and hotels in St. Augustine. Most convenient to the historic district is the 40-room **Best Western Spanish Quarter Inn,** 6 Castillo Dr. (✆ **800/528-1234** or 904/824-4457; www.staugustinebestwestern.com), directly across from the visitor center. It's completely surrounded by an asphalt parking lot, but it does have a pool and hot tub.

Another nice spot directly on the beach is **La Fiesta Ocean Inn & Suites,** 810 A1A Beach Blvd. (✆ **800/852-6390** or 904/471-2220; www.lafiestainn.com). Each room or suite features a microwave and refrigerator. There's a large heated swimming pool and nice gardens. Best of all, guests enjoy a daily complimentary breakfast, delivered to your room, with fresh baked scones and muffins, bagels and cream cheese, yogurt, and fruit cup. Rates start at $129 in the winter and $150 in the summer.

If you're coming on a weekend, expect the higher end of the listed rates—almost all accommodations increase their prices on weekends, when the town is most crowded with visitors. St. Johns County charges a 9% tax on hotel bills. At press time there were talks of raising the current bed tax of 3% to 5%, but no decision has been made yet.

Hotels & Motels

Casa Monica Hotel ★★★ This Moorish Revival hotel is easily the best in town, with top-notch rooms and services. Most of the guest quarters are spacious, modern hotel rooms with Iberian-style armoires, wrought-iron headboards, and tapestry drapes. All units have big bathrooms equipped with high-end toiletries and either a large walk-in shower or a tub/shower combination. Much more interesting are the seven "signature suites" installed in the building's two tile-topped towers and fortresslike central turret. Each of these one- to four-bedroom units is unique. One in the turret has a half-round living room with gun-port windows overlooking the historic district, while a three-story town house in one of the towers has a huge whirlpool bathroom on its top floor. The 95 Cordova restaurant has an excellent wine list, great service, and beautiful decor.

95 Cordova St. (at King St.), St. Augustine, FL 32084. ✆ **800/648-1888** or 904/827-1888. Fax 904/819-6065. www.casamonica.com. 138 units. $159–$899 double. Packages available. AE, DC, DISC, MC, V. Valet parking $20; limited free self-parking 2 blocks from hotel. **Amenities:** Restaurant; European-style cafe; bar; oceanfront beach club; heated outdoor pool; access to nearby health club; exercise room; Jacuzzi; bike rental; concierge; business center; Wi-Fi; room service; babysitting. *In room:* A/C, TV, dataport, high-speed Internet access, fridge (in some rooms), coffeemaker, hair dryer, iron, safe.

Monterey Inn (Value) For the price, you can't find a better choice than this modest, wrought-iron-trimmed motel overlooking the Matanzas Bay and close to the attractions of the Old City. Three generations of the Six family have run this simple two-story motel, and they keep the 1960s building and grounds clean and functional. Rooms are not especially spacious, but they're good enough to sleep in after a day at the beach.

16 Avenida Menendez (btw. Cuna and Hypolita sts.), St. Augustine, FL 32084. ✆ **904/824-4482.** Fax 904/829-8854. www.themontereyinn.com. 59 units. $109–$199 double. AE, DC, DISC, MC, V. **Amenities:** Restaurant; heated outdoor pool. *In room:* A/C, TV, dataport, hair dryer.

Bed & Breakfasts

St. Augustine has more than two dozen bed-and-breakfasts in restored historic homes—and one boat! They all provide free parking, breakfast, 24-hour refreshments, and plenty of atmosphere, but most accept neither young children nor smokers (check before booking). Those listed below are in the historic district. For more choices, contact **St. Augustine**

Tips A Swashbuckling Hostel

International travelers on the cheap congregate at the **Pirate Haus Inn & Hostel,** 32 Treasury St., at Charlotte Street (✆ **904/808-1999;** www.piratehaus.com), smack in the middle of the historic district. Done up in a pirate theme, this Spanish-style building has a communal kitchen, living room, and rooftop terrace. The inn has five private rooms (three with their own bathrooms), each equipped with a queen-size or double bed, plus one or two bunk beds. Two other rooms have dormitory-style bunks. Rooms cost $50 to $75 a night (higher on some weekends), while dorm beds go for $19. MasterCard and Visa are accepted. Reservations are advised, especially on weekends. Rates include the hostel's famous all-you-can-eat pancake breakfast.

Historic Inns, P.O. Box 5268, St. Augustine, FL 33085-5268 (no phone; www.staugustineinns.com), for descriptions of its member properties.

Alexander Homestead ★★ This restored 1888 Victorian beauty is spectacular, not to mention romantic, and makes a popular place for weddings and honeymoons. One room has a Jacuzzi, two have fireplaces, and all have private porches, bathrooms, and antiques. Gourmet breakfasts include baked French toast with almond syrup; at night, you can enjoy a complimentary brandy along with your complimentary chocolate. Even better, coffee is delivered directly to your door in the morning, so there's no need to stir too much before your caffeine fix.

14 Sevilla St., St. Augustine, FL 32084. ✆ **888/292-4147** or 904/826-4147. www.alexanderhomestead.com. 4 units. $169–$229 double. Rates include full breakfast. AE, DISC, MC, V. *In room:* A/C, TV.

Bayfront Westcott House Bed & Breakfast Inn ★ Overlooking Matanzas Bay, this romantic, Key West–style wood-frame house offers rare opportunities for uncluttered views from the porch, the second-story veranda, and a shady courtyard. The rooms—some with bay windows, two-person whirlpool tubs, and working fireplaces—are immaculate and exquisitely furnished. Yours might have authentic Victorian furnishings and a brass bed made up with a white quilt and lace dust ruffle.

146 Avenida Menendez (btw. Bridge and Francis sts.), St. Augustine, FL 32084. ✆ **800/513-9814** or 904/824-4301. Fax 904/824-4301. www.westcotthouse.com. 15 units. $149–$269 double. Rates include full breakfast. AE, DISC, MC, V. **Amenities:** Access to nearby health club; Jacuzzi; free use of bicycles; massage. *In room:* A/C, TV, hair dryer.

Carriage Way Bed & Breakfast ★ Value Primarily occupying an 1883 Victorian wood-frame house fronted by roses and hibiscus, this B&B isn't fancy or formal, but it is comfortable and a good value. TV, books, and games are provided in a homey parlor. Guest rooms in the main house are furnished with simple reproductions, including many four-poster beds. One room retains its original fireplace. For more privacy, two more rooms are located down the street in the Cottage, a clapboard house built in 1885. The Cottage has a living room and kitchen, and both of its bedrooms have claw-foot tubs. The Miranda room also sports a two-person Jacuzzi, while the Ashton has a small back porch. Special packages provide nice little touches such as a gourmet picnic lunch, a horse-drawn carriage ride, and breakfast in bed.

70 Cuna St. (btw. Cordova and Spanish sts.), St. Augustine, FL 32084. ✆ **800/908-9832** or 904/829-2467. Fax 904/826-1461. www.carriageway.com. 11 units. $99–$199 double; $159–$269 Cottage rooms. Rates include full breakfast. AE, DISC, MC, V. **Amenities:** Free use of bikes. *In room:* A/C, dataport.

Casablanca Inn on the Bay ★ This 1914 Mediterranean-style white-stucco house, listed on the National Register of Historic Places, faces the bay, although only a few of the rooms have views. The most stunning are the second-floor suites with hammocks and private porches. The furnishings—a mix of turn-of-the-20th-century American oak, European, and Victorian pieces—are of a higher quality than those at many other inns. One modern convenience is a cassette player with a small selection of classical tapes. This may be appreciated, especially if you're in a ground-floor room that unfortunately suffers from the noise of the street and the next-door bar and grill. Breakfast is served alfresco on the porch or in a glass-enclosed conservatory. A porch with rocking chairs is an ideal spot to chill out, read a book, or sip a cocktail.

24 Avenida Menendez (btw. Hypolita and Treasury sts.), St. Augustine, FL 32084. ✆ **800/826-2626** or 904/829-0928. Fax 904/826-1892. www.casablancainn.com. 20 units. Season $99–$349 double; off-season $99–$279 double. Rates include full breakfast. AE, DISC, MC, V. **Amenities:** Access to nearby health club; free use of bikes. *In room:* A/C, TV (in 18 units), no phone (in 6 units).

Casa de Solana Bed and Breakfast ★★★ Recently purchased by an interior designer, this St. Augustine landmark has been beautifully restored with British colonial furnishings and accessories. Just 2 blocks from the marina, the B&B offers a delicious Southern breakfast buffet, evening cocktails in the inn's stunning garden courtyard, bikes, late-night desserts and coffee, and free parking. Eight out of the ten rooms have fireplaces and whirlpool tubs.

24 Aviles St., St. Augustine, FL 32084. ✆ **888/796-0980** or 904/824-3355. Fax 904/824-3316. www.casadesolana.com. 10 units. Season $109–$319 double; off-season $129–$269 double. Rates include full breakfast and complimentary social hour and desserts. AE, DISC, MC, V. **Amenities:** Free use of bikes; free Wi-Fi. *In room:* A/C, TV, DVD, CD player.

Kenwood Inn There's lots of pink here, but what makes this inn so unusual is its relatively large outdoor space, which includes a pool, a lushly landscaped sun deck, and a secluded garden courtyard (complete with a koi pond and flower bed under a sprawling pecan tree). The Victorian wood-frame house with graceful verandas has served as a boardinghouse or inn since the late 19th century. Everything from the carpeting to the linens to the china is first-class. Rooms are larger and more private than most other accommodations in converted single-family homes.

38 Marine St. (at Bridge St.), St. Augustine, FL 32084. ✆ **800/824-8151** or 904/824-2116. Fax 904/824-1689. www.thekenwoodinn.com. 14 units. $95–$250 double. Rates include continental breakfast. DISC, MC, V. **Amenities:** Outdoor pool; free use of bikes. *In room:* A/C, TV (in some), fax, dataport, kitchen, minibar, fridge, coffeemaker, hair dryer, iron, no phone (in some).

Victorian House (Kids) This 1897-vintage Victorian B&B has a wraparound porch and an adjoining old store, now dubbed the Carriage House. The latter is divided into four units, one of which has a kitchenette. What's unusual is that children can stay in the Carriage House units, all of which have TVs and private entrances, but the main house is adults only. Victorian antiques adorn all units.

11 Cadiz St. (btw. Aviles and Charlotte sts.), St. Augustine, FL 32084. ✆ **877/703-0432** or 904/824-5214. Fax 904/824-7990. www.victorianhousebnb.com. 10 units. $99–$199 double. Rates include full breakfast. AE, DISC, MC, V. **Amenities:** Wi-Fi. *In room:* A/C, TV (in 4 units), kitchen (in 1 unit), no phone.

WHERE TO DINE

In a town with as much tourist traffic as St. Augustine, there are, of course, a fair number of "tourist trap" restaurants. But on the whole, the food here, even at the popular eateries, is fairly priced and of good quality. But before you eat, check out a local winery, the **San Sebastian Winery,** 157 King St. (© **904/826-1594;** www.sansebastianwinery.com), located in one of Henry Flagler's old East Coast Railway buildings a few blocks from downtown St. Augustine. The winery offers free guided tours and free (!) tastings of wines produced on their vineyards in central Florida. Apparently Florida's muscadine grapes are high in fiber and antioxidants, so drink up! The third floor of the winery, the **Cellar Upstairs,** is a wine and jazz bar that serves appetizers, wines, and beer.

Fans of chilies and hot peppers will be thrilled to know that St. Augustine is the home of the Datil pepper, one of the hottest around. Lots of local restaurants have their own Datil pepper sauces and even "Datil Dust," which is used to heat up any dish. **Hot Stuff Mon,** located right in the historic shopping district at 34 Treasury St. (© **904/824-1944**), features an assortment of hard to find sauces and sauces made exclusively with Datils in St. Augustine. Also check out www.datildoit.com.

The historic district has a branch of Tampa's famous **Columbia,** 98 St. George St., at Hypolita Street (© **904/824-3341**). Like the original in Ybor City (p. 402), this one sports Spanish architecture, including intricate tile-work and courtyards with fountains.

Antonio's Pizza ★★ Value PIZZA New York–style pizza in St. Augustine? Indeed. In fact, it's better than some sliceries I've been to in Gotham! Good, old-fashioned greasy, cheesy pizza is what you'll find here, in addition to reasonably priced entrees such as lasagna, baked ziti, and chicken or eggplant Parmesan.

590 A1A Beach Blvd. © **904/471-5200.** Pizza $2 per slice or $8–$20 per pie; entrees $9. AE, MC, V. Daily 11am–11pm.

A1A Ale Works ★ SEAFOOD Anyone who has ever chugged from a beer bong, entered a beer-drinking contest, or just simply loves beer must visit this brewpub. You can't miss the two-story Victorian-style building, on the waterfront opposite the Bridge of Lions. One of the city's most popular watering holes, the downstairs bar offers nightly entertainment, which sometimes filters upstairs into the restaurant. Despite the noise potential, the kitchen turns out a surprisingly good blend of New World Floribbean, Cuban, Caribbean, and Latino styles, in a nice setting with big windows and outdoor seating. Most of the seafood is very fresh, and the sauces are made to order. The spicy ahi stick appetizer (sushi-grade tuna, pickled ginger, and sesame seeds wrapped in a wonton skin, cooked rare, and topped with a wasabi and *sriracha* aioli) is as good as it gets. Don't overlook nightly specials, either, especially the fresh fish. The house brew ranges from a very light lager to a nonalcoholic root beer.

1 King St. (at Avenida Menendez). © **904/829-2977.** www.a1aaleworks.com. Call for preferred seating. Main courses $13–$30; sandwiches $8–$11. AE, DC, DISC, MC, V. Sun–Thurs 11am–10:30pm; Fri–Sat 11am–11pm. Late-night menu served downstairs.

The Bunnery Bakery & Café ★ Value BAKERY/DELI If you suffer from a raging sweet tooth, get thee to the Bunnery. Alluring aromas waft from this bakery and cafe in the heart of the historic district. It's a lovely spot for breakfast or for a pastry and cappuccino anytime you need a break from sightseeing. At lunch, plop yourself into one of the colorful booths and indulge in the soups, salads, burgers, or panini—or perhaps a croissant stuffed with walnut-and-pineapple chicken salad. Order at the counter; the staff will call your number when it's ready.

121 St. George St. (btw. Treasury and Hypolita sts.). ✆ **904/829-6166.** Breakfast $3–$10; sandwiches and salads $4–$10. No credit cards. Daily 8am–6pm. Closed New Year's Day, Easter, Thanksgiving, Christmas Eve, and Christmas Day.

Collage ★★ INTERNATIONAL Somewhat of an accidental tourist in these parts, Collage (formerly La Parisienne) is a welcome respite from all the nearby Americana. The creative menu includes tasty dishes including the wild mushroom and crab cheesecake appetizer—a blend of cream cheese, Parmesan, and smoked Gouda with sautéed shitake mushrooms, crab, roasted peppers, and onions; and a fantastic Florida bouillabaisse. The restaurant also serves homemade ice cream and a sinful Bougainvillea Dessert of strawberries sautéed in butter and black pepper, homemade vanilla bean ice cream, and a cabernet vanilla sauce served in a leaf-shaped phyllo cup.

60 Hypolita St. (btw. Spanish and Cordova sts.). ✆ **904/829-0055.** www.collagestaug.com. Reservations recommended. Main courses $18–$34. AE, DISC, MC, V. Daily 5:30–9pm.

Gypsy Cab Co. ★★ **Value** NEW AMERICAN Billing itself as a temple of "urban cuisine," Ned Pollack's high-energy establishment, with gaudy neon stripes outside and art-filled dining rooms inside, is the town's most interesting culinary experience. Ned's creative menu changes daily, though black-bean soup is a constant winner. If it's available, try the veal with bacon-horseradish cream or the grouper in a tomato-basil sauce. As a capper, I recommend Amaretto cheesecake or Key lime pie. Also of note is the house salad dressing, which is so good they sell it by the bottle. Lunch is served (Mon–Fri 11am–4pm) in the **Gypsy Bar & Grill** (✆ **904/808-1305**) next door, which features live music Wednesday, Friday, and Saturday evenings. Taking the concept a little too far, there's a Gypsy Comedy Club right next door.

828 Anastasia Blvd. (Fla. A1A, at Ingram St., east of the Bridge of Lions). ✆ **904/824-8244.** www.gypsycab.com. Main courses $15–$22. AE, DC, DISC, MC, V. Mon–Thurs 4:30–10pm; Fri 4:30–11pm; Sat 11am–11pm; Sun 10:30am–10pm.

Opus 39 ★ NEW AMERICAN Executive Chef Michael McMillan likes to call his fantastic restaurant a food gallery, and we couldn't have said it better. McMillan's presentation transforms food into art, based on the chef's daily trips to organic farms and produce stands. The same recipe is never served twice, but whatever you happen to choose that night, you won't be disappointed. On one night, you may choose from white truffle–scented braised beef cheek or grilled grouper mushroom risotto and chive emulsion. A $65 three-course tasting menu is available and, in my opinion, your best bet, and lets you sample most of their fine organic vegetables, herbs, meats, and fishes. Desserts are also impressive and use fresh local ingredients. The chocolate mousse comes with organic tangerine glaze and toasted almonds. After dinner, you can peruse the restaurant's art gallery, where actual art, not food, is displayed amid an impressive selection of wines.

39 Cordova St. ✆ **904/824-0402.** www.opus39.com. Reservations recommended. Main courses $16–$30; tasting menu $65. AE, DC, MC, V. Tues–Sun 5–9pm.

Raintree ★ INTERNATIONAL Even if you don't have a full meal at this romantic 1879 Victorian house (about a half-mile north of the historic district), the tempting variety of crepes and an exemplary crème brûlée are worth a visit. Sweetness works its way onto the main menu, as in cashew-encrusted pork tenderloin mignonettes with a champagne and ruby raspberry sauce. More traditional choices include beef Wellington and rack of New Zealand lamb. The food is all very good, though not as modern as at Gypsy Cab Co. or as expertly prepared as at Collage (see above). The list of more than 300 vintages has won *Wine Spectator* awards. The Dessert Bar is heavenly, with choices such as a lace cookie basket, Granny Smith apple pie, or "Evil Chocolate Cake." Evil never tasted so good! Keep in mind that Raintree is a destination restaurant, which means hordes of people are constantly traipsing through and marveling at the lovely Old World ambience.

102 San Marco Ave. (at Bernard St.). ✆ **904/824-7211.** www.raintreerestaurant.com. Reservations recommended. Main courses $11–$28; dessert bar from $6. AE, DC, MC, V. Sun–Thurs 6–9:30pm; Fri–Sat 6–10pm. Courtesy car provides transportation from/to downtown hotels.

ST. AUGUSTINE AFTER DARK

Especially on weekends, the Old Town is full of strollers and partyers making the rounds of dozens of bars, clubs, and restaurants. For up-to-date details on what's happening in town, check the local daily, the *St. Augustine Record* (www.staugustine.com), or the irreverent *Folio Weekly* (www.folioweekly.com). Another nighttime activity is taking one of the many ghost tours.

The best-looking and rowdiest crowd in town can be found at the **A1A Ale Works** (p. 549). Twenty-something hipsters and middle-aged partyers mingle at this New Orleans–style microbrewery and restaurant. You'll find live music Thursday through Saturday at the bar—usually light rock and R&B tunes.

Ann O'Malley's, 23 Orange St., near the Old City Gate (✆ **904/825-4040**), is an Irish pub that's open until 1am. Besides the selection of ales, stouts, and drafts, this is one of the only spots in town where you can grab a late-night bite.

Also popular with locals, **Mill Top Tavern,** 19½ St. George St., at the Fort (✆ **904/829-2329**), is a warm and rustic tavern housed in a 19th-century mill building (the water wheel is still outside). Weather permitting, it's an open-air space. There's music here every day from 1pm to 1am.

At **Scarlett O'Hara's,** 70 Hypolita St., at Cordova Street (✆ **904/824-6535;** www.scarlettoharas.net), a catacomb of cozy rooms with working fireplaces in a rambling, 19th-century wood-frame house, is the setting for everything from DJs and karaoke to live music. Sporting events are aired on a large-screen TV; and, if you're hungry, check out the Southern fried chicken.

Across the river, the **Gypsy Bar & Grill,** part of the Gypsy Cab Co. restaurant (p. 550), 828 Anastasia Blvd. (✆ **904/824-8244**), often has live music, as well as a comedy club next door.

4 JACKSONVILLE

36 miles S of the Georgia border; 134 miles NE of Orlando; 340 miles N of Miami

Once infamous for its smelly paper mills, the sprawling metropolis of Jacksonville—residents call it "Jax," from its airport abbreviation—is now one of the South's insurance and banking capitals. Development was rampant throughout Duval County during the 1990s, with hotels, restaurants, attractions, and clubs springing up, especially in suburban areas near the interstate highways. Aside from that, there are 20 miles of Atlantic Ocean beaches upon which to sun and swim, championship golf courses, and an abundance of beautiful and historic national and state parks to roam.

Spanning the broad, curving St. Johns River, downtown Jacksonville is a vibrant center of activity during weekdays and on weekend afternoons and evenings, when many locals head to the restaurants and bars of Jacksonville Landing and Southbank Riverwalk. These two dining-and-entertainment complexes face each other across the river and have helped to revitalize the downtown area.

ESSENTIALS

GETTING THERE **Jacksonville International Airport,** on the city's north side, about 12 miles from downtown (✆ 904/741-2000; www.jaxairport.org), is served by **Air Canada** (✆ 888/247-2262), **AirTran** (✆ 800/247-8726), **American** (✆ 800/433-7300), **Continental** (✆ 800/525-0280), **Delta** (✆ 800/221-1212), **Midway** (✆ 800/446-4392), **Northwest** (✆ 800/225-2525), **Southwest** (✆ 800/435-9792), **United** (✆ 800/241-6522), and **Metro Jet** and **US Airways** (✆ 800/428-4322).

Alamo (✆ 800/327-9633), **Avis** (✆ 800/331-1212), **Budget** (✆ 800/527-0700), **Dollar** (✆ 800/800-4000), **Enterprise** (✆ 800/325-8007), **Hertz** (✆ 800/654-3131), and **National** (✆ 800/227-7368) have rental-car booths at the airport.

Gator City Taxi (✆ **904/741-0008** at the airport, or 355-8294 elsewhere) provides cab service. Fares for up to four persons are about $20 to downtown, $40 to $45 to beach hotels, $55 to $65 to St. Augustine, and $40 to Amelia Island. **Express Shuttle** (✆ **904/353-8880;** www.airportexpresspickup.com) provides van service to and from hotels and resorts throughout the area. Per-person fares are about $25 to downtown Jacksonville, $30 to $40 to the beaches, $60 to $70 to St. Augustine, and $50 to Amelia Island.

There's an **Amtrak** station in Jacksonville at 3570 Clifford Lane, off U.S. 1, just north of 45th Street (✆ **800/USA-RAIL** [872-7245]; www.amtrak.com).

VISITOR INFORMATION Contact the **Jacksonville and the Beaches Convention & Visitors Bureau,** 201 E. Adams St., Jacksonville, FL 32202 (✆ **800/733-2668** or 904/798-9111; fax 904/789-9103; www.jaxcvb.com), for maps, brochures, calendars, and advice. The bureau is open Monday through Friday from 8am to 5pm. It operates an information booth in the upstairs food court of **Jacksonville Landing** (p. 553), open Monday through Saturday from 10am to 7pm, and Sunday from 12:30 to 5:30pm, as well as a walk-in information office in **Jacksonville Beach,** at 403 Beach Blvd., between 3rd and 4th streets (✆ **904/242-0024**), open Monday through Saturday from 10am to 6pm.

GETTING AROUND In general, you're better off having a car if you want to explore this vast area. To get around downtown Jacksonville, you can take the **Skyway,** an elevated and completely automated train that runs down Hogan Street from Florida Community College's Jacksonville campus through downtown and across the river via the Acosta/Florida 13 bridge to the Southbank Riverwalk. The Skyway operates Monday through Friday from 6am to 11pm, Saturday from 10am to 11pm, and Sunday only for special events. The fare is 50¢. The **Trolley** connects with the Skyway and runs east–west through downtown, primarily along Bay Street. It's free and operates Monday through Friday from 6:30am to 7pm and Saturday from 8am to 6pm. Get maps and schedules from the visitors bureau or information booths (see above). Both the Skyway and the Trolley are operated by the **Jacksonville Transportation Authority** (✆ **904/630-3181;** www.jtaonthemove.com), which also provides local bus service.

You can hail a cab downtown if you spot one, though it's usually best to call **Gator City Taxi** (✆ **904/355-8294**) or **Yellow Cab** (✆ **904/260-1111**) for a pickup. Fares are around $2 when the flag drops and about $1.50 per additional mile thereafter.

Out at the beaches, the **St. Johns River Ferry** (✆ **904/241-9969;** www.stjohnsriverferry.com) shuttles vehicles across the river between Mayport, an Old Florida fishing

Fun Facts Once a Cow Town

Although Jacksonville claims to be the capital of Florida's historic "First Coast," the city dates its beginnings from an early-1800s settlement named Cowford because cattle crossed the St. Johns River here. It changed its name in 1822 to honor Gen. Andrew Jackson, who forced Spain to cede Florida to the United States 2 years earlier.

village on the south side, and Fort George, on the north shore. The boats run daily; times vary, so call for the current schedule. One-way fare is $5 per two-axle private vehicle, $1 per pedestrian or bicyclist. Even if you have to wait 30 minutes for the next ferry, the 5-minute ride greatly shortens the trip between the Jacksonville beaches and Amelia Island.

Bikers and hikers traveling along the 3,000-mile East Coast Greenway connecting major cities from Calais, Maine, to Key West can now take the "Blueway Bypass" thanks to the **Cumberland Sound Ferry Service** (✆ **877/264-9972;** www.ameliarivercruises.com), which runs a minimum of three round-trips per day from Amelia Island, Florida, to St. Marys, Georgia, on Thursday, Friday, and Saturday. The trip takes approximately 1 hour and features live narration of the region's history, natural features, and wildlife. You'll also get to explore each of the cities. Trip costs $15 per person.

EXPLORING THE AREA

Cummer Museum of Art & Gardens ★★ Built on the grounds of a private Tudor mansion, this modestly sized but impressive museum is worth a visit for anyone who appreciates the visual arts. The permanent collection encompasses works from 2000 B.C. to the present. It's especially rich in American Impressionist paintings, 18th-century porcelain, and 18th-century Japanese woodblock prints. Personally, I find the art here a bit boring and too focused on landscapes, but that's my taste. Frankly—and art snobs may gasp at this statement—the landscaping of the museum is infinitely more spectacular. Don't miss the stunning Italian and English gardens set on the scenic St. Johns River. The museum hosts temporary and traveling exhibits, and sponsors a multitude of activities during the year, so call ahead to see what's happening.

829 Riverside Ave. (btw. Post and Fisk sts.). ✆ **904/356-6857.** www.cummer.org. Admission $10 adults, $6 seniors 66 and over and military, $6 students and children 4 and under; free Tues after 4pm. Tues 10am–9pm; Wed–Sat 10am–4pm; Sun noon–5pm.

Jacksonville Landing Resembling New York City's South Street Seaport, Boston's Faneuil Hall, Miami's Bayside, and Baltimore's Inner Harbor, this glass-and-steel complex on the north bank of the river serves as the focus of downtown activity. Yes, you may see a mime or two occasionally, and there's a Hooters and a Starbucks, but there's also amazing local live music, good nonchain sushi, and Thai and Mexican restaurants. This complex is not just for tourists—it's command central for many locals looking for a lively day or night out. There are more than 65 stores here, but shopping is secondary to dining and entertainment. Choose from full-service restaurants, plus an inexpensive food court with indoor and outdoor seating overlooking the river. The Landing hosts numerous special events, from arts festivals to baseball-card shows, plus outdoor rock, blues, country, and jazz concerts on weekends. Call or check the website to find out what's going on during your stay.

2 Independent Dr. (btw. Main and Pearl sts.), on the St. Johns River. ✆ **904/353-1188.** www.jacksonvillelanding.com. Free admission. Mon–Thurs 10am–8pm; Fri–Sat 10am–9pm; Sun noon–5:30pm; bars and restaurants open later. From I-95, take exit 107 downtown to Main St., go over the Blue Bridge, and turn left at Bay St. Then go 2 blocks and make a left on Laura St., which dead-ends at the Landing. Park on east side of complex.

Jacksonville Zoo and Gardens ★ Kids Another city, another zoo. But this isn't just any zoo. Located between downtown and the airport, this environmentally sensitive zoo is well on its way to becoming one of the Southeast's best. While the zoo's Wild Florida area presents local wildlife—including black bears, red wolves, Florida panthers, and alligators—the main exhibits feature an extensive and growing collection of lions, rhinos, elephants, antelopes, cheetahs, western lowland gorillas, and other African wildlife. You'll enter the 120-acre park through an authentic thatched roof built in 1995 by 24 Zulu craftsmen. Whether you go on foot or by train, allow at least 3 hours to tour this vast zoo. Upon your arrival, ask about current animal shows and special events. Strollers and wheelchairs are available for rent. Range of the Jaguar focuses on a neotropical rainforest setting that can be found in Central or South America. Although this attraction spotlights the jaguar, you will also see other animals such as golden lion tamarins, tapirs, capybaras, giant river otters, anteaters, and a variety of bird, amphibian, fish, and reptile species, including the anaconda. New to the zoo is the Asian Bamboo, host to 111 plant species and varieties and 29 species and varieties of bamboo. The tallest bamboo in the garden includes the Parker's Hawaiian Giant which can grow to 70 plus feet. Kids will especially love the 2½-acre, $6.7-million Kids' Zone with mazes, a splash ground, treehouse, and rock-climbing area.

370 Zoo Pkwy. ✆ **904/757-4462** or 904/757-4463. www.jacksonvillezoo.org. Admission $13 adults, $11 seniors, $8 children 3–12, free for children 2 and under. Daily 9am–5pm. Closed Thanksgiving and Christmas. Take I-95 N. to Hecksher Dr. (exit 358A) and follow the signs.

MOCA Jacksonville ★★ Opened in 2003, this museum of contemporary art is one of the Southeast's largest, housed in the renovated Western Union Telegraph Building and featuring five changing exhibition galleries, an ArtExplorium Loft, children's interactive center, education studios, auditorium, cafe, and shop. Permanent works are impressive and include works by Ed Paschke, Hans Hoffmann, Joan Mitchell, and James Rosenquist.

333 N. Laura St. ✆ **904/366-6911.** www.mocajacksonville.org. Admission $8 adults, $5 seniors 66 and over and military, $5 students and children; free Wed after 4pm. Tues and Thurs–Sun 10am–4pm; Wed 10am–9pm.

Ritz Theatre & LaVilla Museum From 1921 to 1971, the Ritz Theatre was the center of cultural life in LaVilla, an African-American neighborhood so vibrant that it was known as the Harlem of the South. Many entertainers played the Ritz before moving on to the Apollo Theater in the real Harlem. Most of LaVilla's small clapboard "shotgun" houses (so called because you could fire a shotgun through the central hallway to the back room and not hit anything) have been torn down in anticipation of urban renewal, but the Ritz has been rebuilt and is once again a center of the city's cultural life. Only the northwest corner of the building, including the Ritz sign, is original, but the new 426-seat theater captures the spirit of vaudevillian times. Off the lobby, LaVilla Museum recounts local African-American history and exhibits the works of black artists.

829 N. Davis St. (btw. State and Union sts.). ✆ **904/632-5555.** www.ritzlavilla.org. Admission $6 adults, $3 seniors and children 17 and under. Tues–Fri 10am–6pm; Sat 10am–2pm; Sun 2–5pm. From downtown, take Main St. north, turn left (west) on State St. to theater and museum on Davis St.

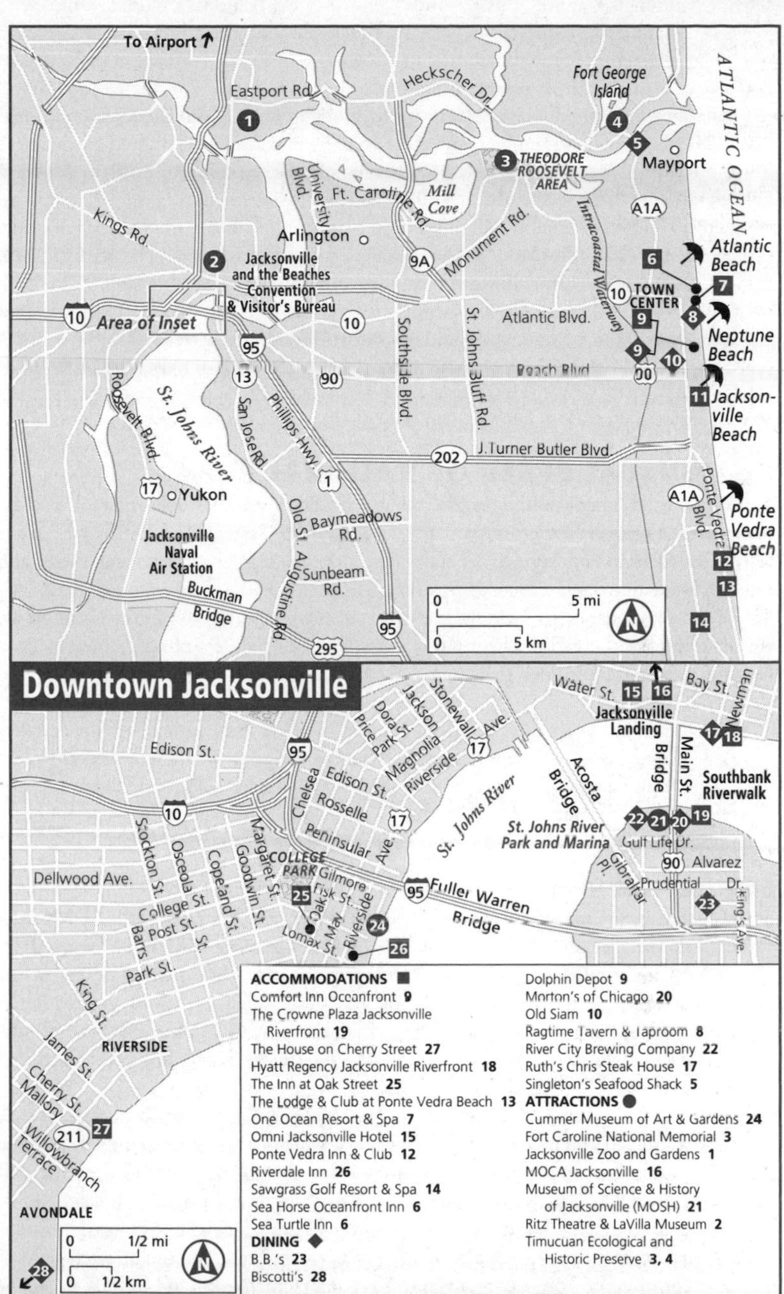
To Airport
Eastport Rd.
Heckscher Dr.
Fort George Island
Mayport
ATLANTIC OCEAN
THEODORE ROOSEVELT AREA
University Blvd.
Ft. Caroline Rd.
Mill Cove
Kings Rd.
Arlington
Monument Rd.
Intracoastal Waterway
Atlantic Beach
Jacksonville and the Beaches Convention & Visitor's Bureau
TOWN CENTER
Area of Inset
Atlantic Blvd.
Southside Blvd.
St. Johns Bluff Rd.
Neptune Beach
Beach Blvd.
Jacksonville Beach
Roosevelt Blvd.
St. Johns River
San Jose Rd.
Phillips Hwy.
J. Turner Butler Blvd.
Yukon
Ponte Vedra Blvd.
Ponte Vedra Beach
Old St. Augustine Rd.
Baymeadows Rd.
Jacksonville Naval Air Station
Sunbeam Rd.
Buckman Bridge
0 5 mi
0 5 km
Downtown Jacksonville
Water St.
Bay St.
Newnan
Stonewall
Jackson
Dora
Price
Park St.
Ave.
Jacksonville Landing
Edison St.
Magnolia
Riverside
Main St.
Bridge
Acosta Bridge
Southbank Riverwalk
Edison St.
Chelsea
Rosselle
St. Johns River
Peninsular Ave.
St. Johns River Park and Marina
Gulf Life Dr.
Stockton St.
Osceola
Margaret St.
Goodwin St.
Copeland St.
COLLEGE PARK
Gilmore
Fisk St.
Oak
May
Riverside
Gibraltar Pl.
Prudential Dr.
Alvarez
King's Ave.
Dellwood Ave.
College St.
Post St.
St.
Barrs
Lomax St.
Fuller Warren Bridge
Park St.
King St.
RIVERSIDE
James St.
Cherry St.
Mallory
Willowbranch Terrace
AVONDALE
0 1/2 mi
0 1/2 km
ACCOMMODATIONS
Comfort Inn Oceanfront 9
The Crowne Plaza Jacksonville Riverfront 19
The House on Cherry Street 27
Hyatt Regency Jacksonville Riverfront 18
The Inn at Oak Street 25
The Lodge & Club at Ponte Vedra Beach 13
One Ocean Resort & Spa 7
Omni Jacksonville Hotel 15
Ponte Vedra Inn & Club 12
Riverdale Inn 26
Sawgrass Golf Resort & Spa 14
Sea Horse Oceanfront Inn 6
Sea Turtle Inn 6
DINING
B.B.'s 23
Biscotti's 28
Dolphin Depot 9
Morton's of Chicago 20
Old Siam 10
Ragtime Tavern & Taproom 8
River City Brewing Company 22
Ruth's Chris Steak House 17
Singleton's Seafood Shack 5
ATTRACTIONS
Cummer Museum of Art & Gardens 24
Fort Caroline National Memorial 3
Jacksonville Zoo and Gardens 1
MOCA Jacksonville 16
Museum of Science & History of Jacksonville (MOSH) 21
Ritz Theatre & LaVilla Museum 2
Timucuan Ecological and Historic Preserve 3, 4

Southbank Riverwalk (Kids) Bordering the St. Johns River, directly opposite Jacksonville Landing (see above), this 1¼-mile wooden zigzag boardwalk is usually filled with joggers, tourists, folks sitting on benches, and lovers walking hand-in-hand, all of them watching the riverboats, the shorebirds, and downtown's skyline reflected in the water. At 200 feet in diameter, the **Friendship Fountain,** near the west end, is the nation's largest self-contained fountain; it's especially beautiful at night when illuminated by 265 colored lights. Nearby, you'll pass military memorials, a small museum dedicated to the city's history, and the **Museum of Science & History of Jacksonville (MOSH),** at Museum Circle and San Marco Boulevard (© **904/396-6674;** www.themosh.org). MOSH is an interactive children's museum focusing on the science and history of Northeast Florida. One of its stars is an Allosaurus dinosaur skeleton. It also has a small planetarium, with shows included in museum admission: $9 for adults, $7.50 for seniors, and $7 for children ages 3 to 12. The museum is open Monday through Friday from 10am to 5pm, Saturday from 10am to 6pm, and Sunday from 1 to 6pm. The Riverwalk is the scene of special MOSH programs, seafood fests, parties, parades, and arts-and-crafts festivals.

On the south bank of St. Johns River, flanking Main St. Bridge, btw. San Marco Blvd. and Ferry St. © **904/396-4900.** Take I-95 N. to Prudential Dr. exit, make a right, and follow the signs.

AN UNUSUAL BREED OF NATIONAL PARK

Named after the American Indians who inhabited Central and North Florida some 1,000 years before European settlers arrived, the **Timucuan Ecological and Historic Preserve** provides visitors an opportunity to explore untouched wilderness, historic buildings, and informative exhibits on the area's natural history. Unusual for a national park, this 46,000-acre preserve hasn't been hacked off from the rest of the community and drawn within arbitrary boundaries. The result is a vast, intriguing system of sites joined by rural roads alongside tumbledown fish camps, trailer parks, strip malls, condominiums, and stately old homes.

Entry to all park facilities is free (though donations are accepted). The visitor centers at Fort Caroline National Memorial and Zephaniah Kingsley Plantation (see below) are open daily from 9am to 5pm, except New Year's Day, Thanksgiving, and Christmas. The Theodore Roosevelt Area is open daily from 7am to 8pm during daylight saving time and daily from 7am to 5pm during standard time; closed for Christmas.

South of the River

The preserve's prime attractions are 14 miles northeast of downtown on the south bank of the St. Johns River. Your starting point is the **Fort Caroline National Memorial ★**, 12713 Ft. Caroline Rd. (© **904/641-7155;** www.nps.gov/timu), which serves as the preserve's visitor center. This was the site of the 16th-century French Huguenot settlement that was wiped out by the Spanish who landed at St. Augustine. This two-thirds-size replica shows you what the original was like. You can see archaeological artifacts and two well-produced half-hour videos highlighting the area as well.

The fort sits at the northwestern edge of the 600-acre **Theodore Roosevelt Area,** a beautiful woodland and marshland rich in history, which has been undisturbed since the Civil War. On a 2-mile hike along a centuries-old park trail, you'll see a wide variety of birds, wildflowers, and maritime hammock forest. Bring binoculars, because such birds as endangered wood storks, great and snowy egrets, ospreys, hawks, and painted buntings make their homes here in spring and summer. On the ground, you might catch sight of a gray fox or raccoon. You may also want to bring a picnic basket and blanket to spread beneath the ancient oak trees that shade the banks of the wide and winding St. Johns

Escaping Intolerance

Zephaniah Kingsley, the white man who, from 1817 to 1829, owned the plantation that is now part of the Timucuan Ecological and Historic Preserve, held some seemingly contradictory views on race. Although he owned more than 200 slaves, he believed that "the coloured race were superior to us, physically and morally." He married a Senegalese woman—one of his former slaves—and in 1837 moved his mixed-race family to what is now the Dominican Republic to escape what he called the "spirit of intolerant injustice" in Florida.

River. After the trail crosses Hammock Creek, you're in ancient Timucuan country, where their ancestors lived as far back as 500 B.C. Farther along is the site of a wilderness cabin that belonged to the reclusive brothers Willie and Saxon Browne, who lived without the modern conveniences of indoor plumbing or electricity until the last brother's death in 1960.

If you're here on a weekend, take the fascinating 1½-hour guided tour of the fort and Theodore Roosevelt Area, offered every Saturday and Sunday (when weather and staffing permit). Call the fort for details and schedules.

The **Ribault Monument,** on St. Johns Bluff about a half-mile east of the fort, was erected in 1924 to commemorate the arrival in 1562 of French Huguenot Jean Ribault, who died defending Fort Caroline from the Spanish. It's worth a stop for the dramatic view of the area.

To get here from downtown Jacksonville, take Atlantic Boulevard (Fla. 10) east, make a left on Monument Road, and turn right on Fort Caroline Road; the Theodore Roosevelt Area is entered from Mt. Pleasant Road, about 1 mile southeast of the fort (look for the trail-head parking sign and follow the narrow dirt road to the parking lot).

North of the River

On the north side of the river, history buffs will appreciate the **Zephaniah Kingsley Plantation** ★, at 11676 Palmetto Ave., on Fort George Island (© **904/251-3537**). A winding 2½-mile dirt road runs under a canopy of dense foliage to the remains of this 19th-century plantation. The National Park Service maintains the well-preserved two-story clapboard residence, kitchen house, barn/carriage house, and remnants of 23 slave cabins built of "tabby mortar"—oyster shell and sand. Exhibits in the main house and kitchen focus on slavery as it existed in the rice-growing areas of Northern Florida, Georgia, and South Carolina. You can see it all on your own, but 40-minute ranger-guided tours are much more informative. They're usually given at 1pm Monday through Friday, 1 and 3pm Saturday and Sunday; call to confirm. Allot time to explore the grounds. The well-stocked book-and-gift shop will keep you even longer. The plantation is open daily from 9am to 5pm, except Christmas Day.

To get here from I-95, take Heckscher Drive East (Fla. 105) and follow the signs. From Fort Caroline, take Florida 9A North over St. Johns River to Heckscher Drive East. The plantation is about 12 miles east of Florida 9A, on the left. From the beaches, take Florida A1A to the St. Johns River Ferry and ride it from Mayport to Fort George; the road to the plantation is a half-mile east of the ferry landing.

HITTING THE BEACH

You can fish, swim, snorkel, sail, sunbathe, or stroll on the sand dunes—at least from March to November, as winter can get downright chilly here. All of these activities are just a 20- to 30-minute drive east of downtown at Jacksonville's four beach communities.

Atlantic Boulevard (Fla. 10) will take you to **Atlantic Beach** and **Neptune Beach.** The boulevard divides the two towns, and where it meets the ocean, you'll come to **Town Center,** a quaint community with shops, restaurants, pubs, and a few inns.

Beach Boulevard (U.S. 90) dead-ends at **Jacksonville Beach,** where you'll find beach concessions, rental shops, and a fishing pier. This is also the most popular local surfing beach.

To the south, J. Turner Butler Boulevard (Fla. 202) leads from I-95 to the boundary between Jacksonville Beach and Ponte Vedra Beach. A right turn there will take you to **Ponte Vedra Beach** (pronounced here as Ponti *Vee*-dra). This ritzy, golf-oriented enclave is actually in St. Johns County (St. Augustine), but it's so much closer to Jacksonville that it's included in this section.

OUTDOOR ACTIVITIES & SPECTATOR SPORTS

CRUISES **Jacksonville River Cruises** (**© 904/396-2333;** www.jaxrivercruises.com) operates sightseeing, dinner, and dancing cruises on the stern-wheel paddle boats, the *Lady St. Johns* and the *Annabelle Lee.* They usually dock at the Radisson Riverwalk Hotel on the Southbank Riverwalk. Cost is $40 to $45; schedules vary greatly by season, so call ahead or check the website.

FISHING The least expensive way to fish for red snapper, grouper, sea bass, small sharks, amberjack, and more, 15 to 30 miles offshore in the Atlantic Ocean, is aboard the ***Majesty,*** a brand-new 65-foot, air-conditioned deep-sea party boat that has a galley offering hot meals. The full-day trips depart at 7:30am daily from Monty's Marina, 4378 Ocean St. (Fla. A1A), a half-mile south of the Mayport Ferry landing (**© 904/246-7575;** www.kingneptunefishing.com); they return at 4:30pm. The price is $75 per adult, $60 per child 6 to 14, including bait and tackle. You don't need a license, but reservations are required.

GOLF The Jacksonville area has a great variety of golf courses, some of which are ranked among the top in the country. In Ponte Vedra Beach, the Sawgrass Marriott Resort sits on the most famous course, the Players Stadium Course at **TPC at Sawgrass ★★★**, home of the Players Championship in March. Ranked among the nation's top courses, its island hole is one of the most photographed in the world. Nearby are the Ocean and Lagoon courses at the Ponte Vedra Inn & Club. See "Where to Stay," below, for information on the resorts.

Top courses open to the public include the **Golf Club of Jacksonville,** 10440 Tournament Lane (**© 904/779-0800;** www.golfbentcreek.com), which is managed by the PGA Tour. It's a great bargain, with greens fees between $39 and $49. The semiprivate **Cimarrone,** 2690 Cimarrone Blvd. (**© 904/287-2000;** www.cimarronegolf.com), is a fast and watery course with greens fees ranging from $30 to $65.

Be on the lookout for the free *Golfer's Guide* in visitor centers and hotel lobbies (see p. 57 for information on how to order a copy).

For course information, go to www.golf.com or www.floridagolfing.com; or call the **Florida Sports Foundation** (**© 850/488-8347**) or **Florida Golfing** (**© 866/833-2663**).

HORSEBACK RIDING For lessons or a scenic ride along the dunes, try **Sawgrass Stables,** 23900 Marsh Landing Pkwy., off Florida A1A in Ponte Vedra Beach (**© 904/285-3791**). Call for rates and reservations.

SPECTATOR SPORTS The 73,000-seat **Jacksonville Municipal Stadium,** 1 Stadium Place, at East Duval and Haines streets (✆ **904/633-6100** for tickets), hosts the annual Florida-Georgia football game every October, and other college football games September through December. It's also the home field of the National Football League's **Jacksonville Jaguars** (✆ **877/452-4784,** or 904/633-2000 for ticket information; www.jaguars.com). One of the stadium's biggest draws is the **Konica Minolta Gator Bowl,** usually held on New Year's Day.

The 16,000-seat **Jacksonville Veterans Memorial Arena,** 300 A. Phillip Randolph Blvd. (✆ **904/630-3900** for information, or 353-3309 for tickets), hosts National Hockey League exhibition games, college basketball games, ice-skating exhibitions, wrestling matches, and family shows.

SHOPPING

Jacksonville has plenty of shopping opportunities, including the upscale **Avenues Mall,** south of town at 10300 Southside Blvd., as well as a number of flea markets. At **Beach Boulevard Flea and Farmers' Market,** on Beach Boulevard/Florida 90 (✆ **904/645-5961**), more than 600 vendors show up Saturday and Sunday from 9am to 5pm to sell their wares in the partially covered facility. Some booths are open other days of the week as well.

San Marco Square, at San Marco and Atlantic boulevards, south of the river, is a quaint shopping district in the middle of a stunning residential area. Shops housed in meticulously refashioned Mediterranean Revival buildings sell antiques and home furnishings, in addition to clothing, books, and records.

Another worthwhile neighborhood to explore is the **Avondale/Riverside** historic district, southwest of downtown on St. Johns Avenue between Talbot Avenue and Boone Park, on the north bank of the river. More than 60 boutiques, antiques stores, art galleries, and cafes line the wide, tree-lined avenue.

Nearby, the younger set hangs out at **Five Points,** on Park Street at Avondale Avenue, where used-record stores, vintage clothiers, coffee shops, and funky galleries stay open late.

Like St. Augustine, Jacksonville is a mecca for chocoholics. If you've never tried chocolate-covered popcorn or pretzels, **Peterbrooke Chocolatier Production Center,** 1470 San Marco Blvd., on San Marco Square (✆ **904/398-2489;** www.peterbrooke.com), is the place, if you're up for the experience. It's open Monday through Friday from 10am to 5pm. Peterbrooke also has a retail shop on St. Johns Avenue in Avondale.

WHERE TO STAY

Because Jacksonville hasn't yet made it onto the hip list, there are no boutique hotels in the city—yet. Instead, you have a choice of either a large chain hotel, à la Hilton or Omni, or a much cozier, more charming bed-and-breakfast.

The accommodations listed below are arranged geographically, in and around downtown first, followed by the beach scene. The suburbs have dozens more options to choose from, especially along I-95. Many are clustered south of downtown in the **Southpoint** (exit 101, Turner Butler Blvd./Fla. 202) and **Baymeadows** (exit 101, Baymeadows Rd./Fla. 152) areas. These locales have a multitude of chain restaurants, and you can hop on the highways and zoom to the beach or downtown.

Rates in the downtown hotels are higher midweek, when rooms are in demand by business travelers. Beach accommodations are somewhat less expensive in the colder months from December to March.

Note: Hotel taxes in the area tack on an additional 12% to 14%!

Prudential Drive in the Southbank Riverwalk area is home to the **Wyndham Jacksonville Riverwalk Hotel** (✆ **800/996-3426** or 904/396-5100), the **Hampton Inn Central** (✆ **800/426-7866** or 904/396-7770), and the all-suites **Extended Stay America Downtown** (✆ **800/398-7829** or 904/396-1777; www.extendedstay.com).

The Crowne Plaza Jacksonville Riverfront ★ Set on the Southbank Riverwalk, this 10-story tower was famous for its Elvis Presley Suite, where the King purportedly stayed half a dozen times between 1955 and 1976 when this establishment was known as the Jacksonville Hotel. Funny, but it still looks as if it's steeped in the 1970s, even though the hotel was renovated in 2006. Units have dark-wood furniture, Tempur-Pedic mattresses, and smallish marble bathrooms. Riverfront rooms have balconies (those on the west end catch traffic noise from the Main St. Bridge). A branch of Ruth's Chris Steak House offers extraordinarily tender beef.

1201 Riverplace Blvd. (at Main St. on Southbank Riverwalk), Jacksonville, FL 32207. ✆ **877/2-CROWNE** (227-6963) or 904/398-8800. Fax 904/398-9170. www.cpjacksonville.com. 292 units. $145–$300 double; $280–$405 suite. AE, DC, DISC, MC, V. Valet parking $14; self-parking $10. **Amenities:** 2 restaurants; 2 bars; heated outdoor pool; exercise room; Jacuzzi; concierge; business center; limited room service; laundry service; concierge-level rooms. *In room:* A/C, TV, dataport, coffeemaker, hair dryer, iron.

The House on Cherry Street ★★ This colonial-style wood-frame house, on the St. Johns River in the Historic District, is ideal for a romantic getaway. French doors open onto a delightful screened-in porch furnished with rocking chairs; it overlooks an expanse of tree-shaded lawn (where guests play croquet) leading through the organic garden to the river (where guests can watch ospreys and sunrises). You might go for the Riverside Room or the Duck Room, each with a canopied four-poster bed and river view. Florida artists are rather a theme here, with original art in each room. All units have adjacent sitting rooms, private bathrooms, ceiling fans, and fresh flowers. No smoking is permitted inside. This place gets booked up fast, so make reservations as early as possible.

1844 Cherry St. (on St. Johns River), Jacksonville, FL 32205. ✆ **904/384-1999.** Fax 904/384-5013. www.houseoncherry.com. 4 units. $95–$165 double. Rates include full breakfast. AE, MC, V. No small children accepted. **Amenities:** Free architectural walk of the neighborhood. *In room:* A/C, TV, hair dryer, no phone.

Hyatt Regency Jacksonville Riverfront ★★ After $15 million in renovations, this Hyatt is now one of the city's most elegant lodgings. In the heart of the downtown business district, it's popular with the suit-and-tie crowd, but also with those who want to be within walking distance of Jacksonville Landing and all its nocturnal offerings. Renovations to the hotel included extensive changes to guest rooms, restaurants, bars, and the rooftop pool area. All 966 units now sport the Hyatt Grand Bed, 250-thread-count triple sheeting, down comforters, and very plush pillows. Bathrooms also received a much-needed makeover, with new tiles, paint, and marble countertops. The hotel features a YogaAway program offering guests a free 11-minute On-Demand yoga session with an option to extend it for a fee.

225 E. Coast Line Dr., Jacksonville, FL 32202. ✆ **904/588-1234.** Fax 904/634-4554. www.jacksonvillehyatt.com. 966 units. $179–$299 double; $309–$399 suite. AE, DC, MC, V. **Amenities:** 4 restaurants; rooftop pool; fitness center; concierge; room service. *In room:* A/C, TV, high-speed Internet access, coffeemaker, hair dryer, iron.

The Inn at Oak Street ★★★ A luxury B&B in the historic Riverside area, the Inn at Oak Street is just 2 miles from downtown Jax, but worlds away. The Inn's 6,000-square-foot main house has an eclectic, upscale ambience—no tchotchkes or clutter are found here. Instead, it just has peace, quiet, and a bit of chic, too, with chandeliers and silk, linen and bamboo window treatments, and touches of exposed brick. Guest rooms are spacious, with a funky mix of antiques and reproductions fused with modern comforts such as fine linens, a wine fridge, and flatscreen TVs with DVD players. Three units have balconies, and one (the Boudoir) has a gas fireplace. Wi-Fi is available throughout the house—even on the 70-foot wraparound front porch. Private bathrooms have whirlpool spa tubs, Italian fixtures, and fantastic Gilchrist & Soames bath products. Every night in the Parlor, guests can enjoy wine hour, or just chill out in the tranquil spa room.

3114 Oak St., Jacksonville, FL 32205. ✆ **904/379-5525.** www.innatoakstreet.com. 6 units. $135–$180 suite. Rates include full breakfast. AE, MC, V. No small children accepted. **Amenities:** Coffee bar; spa. *In room:* A/C, TV/DVD, Wi-Fi, wine fridge, hair dryer.

Omni Jacksonville Hotel ★ Directly across the street from the Times-Union Center for the Performing Arts (p. 566) and a block west of Jacksonville Landing, the Omni enjoys a more convenient location than the Crowne Plaza across the river. It caters primarily to a corporate clientele who fill the meeting facilities during the week. Most rooms are of moderate size, with the pick of the litter being the Florida suites, which have sitting areas with river or city views. Room 1433 in particular offers the best views of Main Street Bridge stretching over the St. Johns River. The pool is on the roof overlooking the river. Reasonably priced Juliette's Bistro has a locally famous pasta bar.

245 Water St. (btw. Pearl and Hogan sts.), Jacksonville, FL 32202. ✆ **800/843-6664** or 904/355-6664. Fax 904/791-4809. www.omnihotels.com. 354 units. $149–$249 double. Discounts available. AE, DC, DISC, MC, V. Valet parking $18. Pets accepted ($50 fee). **Amenities:** Restaurant; bar; heated outdoor pool; small exercise room; Jacuzzi; concierge; business center; limited room service; laundry service; concierge-level rooms. *In room:* A/C, TV, dataport, minibar, coffeemaker, hair dryer, iron.

Riverdale Inn ★★ In turn-of-the-20th-century Jacksonville, more than 50 mansions lined Riverside Avenue in an area known as "the Row." Today, sadly, only two of these legendary Victorian-style homes remain. Riverdale Inn is one of them, and thank goodness for preservation. Ten period guest rooms are available with antique rugs and furniture, some featuring canopy and four-poster beds and fireplaces, and all with free Wi-Fi connection for those who insist on the true retro-modern experience. Plush robes are found in all the bathrooms. Best of all, there's an on-site restaurant, the Row (www.rowrestaurant.com), serving dinner that's heavy on fresh, organic greens and overall exquisite cuisine. For a nightcap, there's the Gum Bunch Pub, a cozy brick-walled bar serving all sorts of spirits.

1521 Riverside Ave., Jacksonville, FL 32204. ✆ **866/808-3400** or 904/354-5080. Fax 904/354-6859. www.riverdaleinn.com. 10 units. $109–$189 double; $260–$495 combination suites. Rates include full breakfast. AE, DISC, MC, V. **Amenities:** Restaurant; bar; laundry services. *In room:* A/C, TV, Wi-Fi, hair dryer, iron.

At the Beaches

A dozen modest hotels line Jacksonville Beach's First Street, along the Atlantic. Completely renovated in 1998, the **Comfort Inn Oceanfront,** 1515 N. First St., 2 blocks east of Florida A1A (✆ **800/654-8776** or 904/241-2311; fax 904/249-3830; www.comfortinnjaxbeach.com), is one of the better values. Its rooms have balconies or screened patios, and guests can enjoy a large pool with four rock waterfalls and a palm-fringed deck, a secluded grotto whirlpool, an exercise room, a gift/sundries shop, and a multicourt sand volleyball park.

If you'd like to rent an old-fashioned cottage or a luxurious condominium in the affluent enclave of Ponte Vedra, contact **Ponte Vedra Club Realty,** 280 Ponte Vedra Blvd.,

 Ponte Vedra Beach, FL 32082 (✆ **800/278-8171** or 904/285-6927; fax 904/285-5218; www.pvclubrealty.com). The company has more than 100 properties in its rental inventory, about 75% of them on the ocean. Its renters get a discount on use of facilities at the Lodge & Club at Ponte Vedra Beach, and at the Ponte Vedra Inn & Club (see below).

The Lodge & Club at Ponte Vedra Beach ★★★ This gorgeous two-story Mediterranean-style building is right on the beach. A stunning lobby is decked out in stone floors and hand-carved Tommy Bahama furniture. All 66 rooms are the epitome of high-end luxury, with gorgeous artwork, two-person settees recessed in front of windows looking onto the beach, and huge bathrooms with two-person tubs and separate showers. The "preferred" rooms and all of the suites also have gas fireplaces; ceiling fans hang from vaulted ceilings in the upstairs units. Some suites have marble-faced fireplaces and French doors. The beach has a couples-only pool and hot tub. Guests here have access to all the facilities at Ponte Vedra Inn & Club (see below). The Innlet Dining Room has gorgeous views, plus afternoon tea daily in the lounge, where a pianist performs by the fireplace at night. ***Note:*** There is a nightly gratuity charge of $15 per double room for the bellman, doorman, chambermaid, and valet-parking staff, so *don't double tip.*

607 Ponte Vedra Blvd. (at Corona Rd.), Ponte Vedra Beach, FL 32082. ✆ **800/243-4304** or 904/273-9500. Fax 904/273-0210. www.pvresorts.com. 66 units. Winter $260–$290 double, $340–$420 suite; summer $310–$340 double, $380–$632 suite. Packages available. AE, DC, DISC, MC, V. **Amenities:** 2 restaurants; 2 bars; 3 heated outdoor pools; health club (w/lap pool); access to nearby spa; Jacuzzi; sauna; watersports equipment/rentals; bike rental; concierge; business center; 24-hr. room service; babysitting; laundry service. *In room:* A/C, TV, fax, dataport, kitchen (in suites), minibar, coffeemaker, hair dryer, iron, safe.

One Ocean Resort & Spa ★★★ This hyperluxe eight-story beachfront hotel, formerly known as the Sea Turtle Inn, has received a major multimillion-dollar makeover and is incomparable in terms of service, style, and amenities. Need help unpacking or just aren't in the mood to do so at all? Let them do it for you. All rooms and suites feature ocean views and are soothingly decorated in shades of azure, sand, and pear, outfitted with custom-designed, plush One Ocean mattresses, plasma screen TVs, and fantastic mood lighting. A world-class spa and gourmet restaurant, Azurea, which uses locally produced food and ingredients, not to mention a pristine stretch of sand and a great kids' club, make for a fantastic, luxurious beach vacation.

1 Ocean Blvd. (at beach end of Atlantic Blvd.), Atlantic Beach, FL 32233. ✆ **800/874-6000** or 904/247-0305. Fax 904/247-0308. www.oneoceanresort.com. 193 units. $199–$349 double. AE, DC, DISC, MC, V. **Amenities:** Restaurant; 2 bars; outdoor pool; spa; watersports equipment/rentals; 24-hr. room service; babysitting; laundry service. *In room:* A/C, TV/DVD, fax, dataport, minibar, fridge, coffeemaker, hair dryer, iron.

Ponte Vedra Inn & Club ★★ This luxurious 300-acre country club and spa is a great place to pamper yourself between rounds of golf or games of tennis. The brand-new 28,000-square-foot spa provides fabulous treatments. A new three-story building in front of the original 1937 clubhouse contains spacious, upscale guest rooms. Across the road are condominiums in two-story beachfront buildings. All have patios or balconies; some have four-poster or sleigh beds. In addition to the inn's two 18-hole golf courses, its excellent tennis center, and its fully equipped gym with six-lane Olympic pool, guests can use the three beachside pools and facilities at the nearby Lodge & Club at Ponte Vedra Beach (see above). The Island House has 28 luxurious rooms and suites, all overlooking the famous Island 9th golf hole and blue lagoons. ***Note:*** There is a nightly gratuity charge of $15 per double room for the bellman, doorman, chambermaid, and valet-parking staff, so *don't double tip.*

200 Ponte Vedra Blvd. (off Fla. A1A), Ponte Vedra Beach, FL 32082. ✆ **800/234-7842** or 904/285-1111. Fax 904/285-2111. www.pvresorts.com. 250 units. Winter $190–$290 double, $340–$510 suite; summer $220–$440 double, $380–$660 suite. Packages available. AE, DC, DISC, MC, V. **Amenities:** 3 restaurants; 3 bars; indoor pool; 2 golf courses; 15 tennis courts; health club; spa; watersports equipment/rentals; bike rental; children's programs (summer only); concierge; business center; 24-hr. room service; massage; babysitting; laundry service; coin-op washers/dryers. *In room:* A/C, TV, dataport, kitchen (in some), minibar, coffeemaker, hair dryer, iron.

Sawgrass Golf Resort & Spa ★★★ One of the nation's largest golf resorts, this luxury destination in prestigious Ponte Vedra Beach, Florida, is virtually surrounded by golf, including the Pete Dye–designed THE PLAYERS Stadium Course at TPC Sawgrass, home of the annual THE PLAYERS Championship in May. In fact, the resort was ranked the best golf resort in Florida and ninth best in the country by *Travel + Leisure Golf* magazine in 2008. Overlooking the picturesque 13th hole, the seven-story hotel sits beside one of the lakes that make the course so challenging. The view augments the gourmet fusion cuisine served in the resort's restaurants, including Augustine Grille, 619 Ocean View, and V. Kelly's. The guest rooms in the hotel are exceptional and have recently been refurbished with new furniture and decor. Fully equipped one- and two-bedroom "villa suites" (condominium apartments) on or near the golf course have large patios. A complimentary shuttle takes guests to the oceanside Cabana Beach Club for a day at the beach.

1000 PGA Tour Blvd. (off Fla. A1A, btw. U.S. 210 and J. Turner Butler Blvd.), Ponte Vedra Beach, FL 32082. ✆ **800/228-9290** or 904/285-7777. Fax 904/285-0906. www.sawgrassmarriott.com. 508 units. $109–$179 double; $179–$769 suite. Golf packages available. AE, DC, DISC, MC, V. Valet parking $20; self-parking free. **Amenities:** 7 restaurants; 4 bars; 4 outdoor pools (2 heated); 8 golf courses; 2 health clubs; Jacuzzi; watersports equipment/rentals; bike rental; children's programs; game room; concierge; activities desk; business center; limited room service; babysitting; laundry service; coin-op washers/dryers; concierge-level rooms. *In room:* A/C, TV, dataport, kitchen (in condos), minibar, coffeemaker, hair dryer, iron.

Sea Horse Oceanfront Inn (Value) This old-school beachfront motel provides clean, spacious rooms with ocean views from its balconies and patios. Families will appreciate the six units with kitchenettes, not to mention the big beachfront lawn with pool. Others will enjoy proximity to some of Jacksonville's top nightspots. The pool itself boasts a happening watering hole, the Lemon Bar. If you have a large family or group, consider the vast and lovely, recently remodeled third-floor penthouse—it has a big living room and dining area, full-size fridge, microwave, sink area, and separate bedroom; the huge balcony is furnished with a dining table. There's also an adjoining room with a queen bed, small fridge, microwave, and coffeemaker. They also both have Jacuzzi tubs. Town Center's restaurants and bars are across the street.

120 Atlantic Blvd. (at beach end of Atlantic Blvd.), Neptune Beach, FL 32266. ✆ **800/881 2330** or 904/246-2175. Fax 904/246-4256. www.seahorseoceanfrontinn.com. 39 units. $99–$149 double; $179–$199 penthouse suite for up to 6 (adjoining room to penthouse $139–$159). AE, DC, DISC, MC, V. **Amenities:** Bar; pool. *In room:* A/C, TV, Wi-Fi, fridge, coffeemaker.

WHERE TO DINE

The **Jacksonville and the Beaches Convention & Visitors Bureau** (p. 552) puts out an annual guide that contains a complete list of restaurants. For more choices, check listings in the "Shorelines" and "Go" sections of Friday's *Florida Times-Union* (www.jacksonville.com) and in *Folio Weekly* (www.folioweekly.com), the free local alternative paper available at restaurants, hotels, and nightspots all over town. I've concentrated here on restaurants in downtown Jacksonville and at the beaches.

In Downtown Jacksonville

Southbank Riverwalk is the city's up-and-coming mecca for eating out. In addition to B.B.'s and the River City Brewing Company, both reviewed below, the area has riverfront branches of **Ruth's Chris Steak House,** in the Crowne Plaza Jacksonville Riverfront, 1201 Riverplace Blvd. (© **904/396-6200**); **Morton's of Chicago,** 1510 Riverplace Blvd. (© **904/399-3933**); and the **Wine Cellar,** 1314 Prudential Dr. (© **904/398-8989**), which offers very good Continental fare and has a wine list to justify its name.

You'll also find a plethora of good cafes and restaurants in the San Marco Square and Avondale neighborhoods, perfect for breaking up your shopping excursions.

Don't forget that on the north side of the river, **Jacksonville Landing** (p. 553) has several full-service restaurants and an inexpensive food court with outdoor seating.

B.B.'s ★★ NEW AMERICAN South of the Southbank Riverwalk, this bistro son of Biscotti's (see below) is one of the city's hottest restaurants. You'll find local yuppies congregating at the big marble-top bar on one side of the sometimes noisy Art Deco dining room, especially during weekday "wine-downs," featuring beer and wine specials and discounted appetizers (the mozzarella bruschetta is a big hit), from 4 to 7pm. A small but inventive selection of sandwiches, salads, and pizzas is available all day. The nightly specials feature local seafood and run the gamut from sea bass with ratatouille vegetables, smoked tomato butter, and black truffle oil to the black pepper–goat cheese ravioli tossed with rock shrimp in a lobster cream sauce. Save room for the famous desserts. Saturday brunch sees the likes of yummy Benedict-style crab cakes and flaming bananas Foster.

1019 Hendricks Ave. (btw. Prudential Dr. and Home St.). © **904/306-0100.** Call for priority seating. Main courses $15–$30; sandwiches and salads $5–$10; pizzas $7–$10. AE, DC, DISC, MC, V. Mon–Thurs 11am–10:30pm; Fri 11am–midnight; Sat 10am–midnight (Sat brunch 10am–2pm).

Biscotti's ★★ Value NEW AMERICAN/MEDITERRANEAN This brick-walled gem in the trendy Avondale neighborhood might easily have come out of New York's East Village. Start your day here (except on Mon) with a pastry and cup of joe. At lunch and dinner, daily specials, such as pan-seared tuna or pork loin, are always fresh and beautifully presented. The Parmesan-crusted rainbow trout with short rib ragout, shitake mushroom risotto, and wilted spinach is divine. But if that's too heavy for you, the huge and inventive salads are especially good: Try the Asian version, with chicken breast, orange slices, roasted peppers, and creamy sesame dressing. Pizzas, too, are served with wonderfully exotic and delicious toppings—ever try balsamic duck confit on your slice? And by all means, don't leave without sampling the wonderful desserts. On warm days, choose a tiny sidewalk table for great people-watching. ***Note:*** If the wait's too long here, other choices line these 2 blocks of St. Johns Avenue, ranging from a neighborhood diner to expensive haute cuisine.

3556 St. Johns Ave. (btw. Talbot and Ingleside aves.), Avondale. © **904/387-2060.** www.biscottis.net. Main courses $10–$22; sandwiches and salads $5–$9; pizzas $7–$9. AE, DC, DISC, MC, V. Mon 11am–10pm; Tues–Thurs 7am–10pm; Fri 7am–midnight; Sat 8am–midnight; Sun 8am–3pm.

River City Brewing Company ★★ NEW AMERICAN/CAJUN Occupying a prime location on the Southbank Riverwalk, this gorgeous restaurant and microbrewery has dramatic waterfront and skyline views. For an even better vantage point, sit outside on the enormous covered deck. The quality of the cuisine very nearly lives up to the vista, especially the coconut shrimp with a sweet mandarin-orange sauce. For a main course, try the pork chops grilled with a raspberry chipotle glaze. While you could easily drop a bundle in the main dining room, you can also devise an inexpensive, simpler meal (burgers, beer cheese soup, and such) in the Brew Haus, a large sports bar that opens onto the deck and the riverbank. Bands play here on weekend evenings. Sunday brunch brings incredible buffets with decadent desserts.

835 Museum Circle (on Southbank Riverwalk). ✆ **904/398-2299.** www.rivercitybrew.com. Main courses $19–$33; sandwiches and salads $5–$11; Sun brunch buffet $22 adults, $21 seniors, $15 children 3–12. AE, DC, DISC, MC, V. Dining room Sun–Thurs 11am–3pm and 5–10pm; Fri–Sat 11am–3pm and 5–11pm; Sun 10:30am–2:30pm and 5–10pm. Pub and deck (light fare) Sun–Thurs 3–10pm (bar until midnight); Fri–Sat 3–11pm (bar until 2am). Closed Christmas. Valet parking $3, available Sat–Sun.

At the Beaches

In addition to the Ragtime Tavern & Taproom (see below), you'll find several dining (and drinking) choices in the brick storefronts of **Town Center,** the old-time beach village at the end of Atlantic Boulevard.

Dolphin Depot ★ LOW-COUNTRY CUISINE When it comes to ambience and food, this place is usually off the charts. Housed in a former gas station, the very rustic, antiques-filled Dolphin Depot provides a Low Country high, with such dishes as shrimp and grits, she-crab soup, blackened scallops, and five fresh fish choices daily. Check out the blackboard, where there are usually 25 to 50 (!) daily specials. Only adding to the restaurant's allure, the staff is Southern-style friendly, and the setting resplendent. Unfortunately, recent reviews from readers have pointed out overcooked and overpriced food lately, so we guess when it comes to a great catch here, it's hit or miss.

704 1st St. N. ✆ **904/270-1424.** Reservations recommended. Main courses $12–$30. AE, DC, DISC, MC, V. Mon–Thurs 5:30–10pm; Fri–Sat 5:30pm–midnight; Sun 5:30–9pm.

Old Siam ★★ THAI The best of several Thai restaurants here, this sophisticated little cafe serves fine cuisine and a good selection of wines to match the fare's spicy yet subtle flavors. The signature dish is a seafood special: shrimp, sea scallops, mussels, squid, and crab claws in a red-chili sauce accented with sweet basil. The "number three" spice level (out of six) touches the tongue but won't overwhelm the other seasonings. Standard favorites, such as pad Thai, are perfectly balanced with sweet and slightly sour fish sauce.

1716 N. 3rd St. (Fla. A1A, in Holiday Plaza shopping center, btw. 16th and 17th aves. N.), Jacksonville Beach. ✆ **904/247-7763.** Main courses $10–$27. AE, DISC, MC, V. Mon–Thurs 5–10pm; Fri–Sat 5–11pm; Sun 5–9:30pm.

Ragtime Tavern & Taproom ★★ SEAFOOD/CAJUN In the heart of Town Center, this lively sister of St. Augustine's A1A Ale Works (p. 549) offers six hand-crafted brews, including a refreshing pilsner known as Dolphin's Breath. You can imbibe at one of two bars on either end of the building. In between, a rabbit warren of dining rooms provides fine enough fare to keep it filled with local professionals, right through the cool winter months. Try the barbecued oysters or the Louisiana crawfish as an appetizer. For a main course, choose from blackened Cajun snapper or several other treatments of fish, shrimp, chicken, and pasta. Save room for New Orleans–style beignets for dessert. Also from the Big Easy, po' boy sandwiches are served at all hours. Good local bands play here Thursday through Sunday evenings.

207 Atlantic Blvd. (at 1st Ave.), Atlantic Beach. ✆ **904/241-7877.** www.ragtimetavern.com. Call ahead for priority seating. Main courses $13–$29; sandwiches and salads $6–$11. AE, DC, DISC, MC, V. Sun–Thurs 11am–10:30pm; Fri–Sat 11am–11pm (bar open later).

Singleton's Seafood Shack ★★ (Value) SEAFOOD This rustic fish camp has been serving every imaginable kind of fresh-off-the-boat seafood since 1969. And rustic it is, constructed primarily of unpainted, well-weathered plywood nailed to two-by-fours. Unlike most other fish camps that tend to overwork the deep-fryer, here the fried standbys, such as conch fritters, shrimp, clam strips, oysters, and squid, retain their seafood taste! Singleton's also offers other preparations such as blackened mahimahi and Cajun shrimp. Best bets at lunch are the fried shrimp or oyster po' boy sandwiches covered in crispy onion rings. At dinner, your Styrofoam plate will come stacked with a choice of sides such as black beans and rice, marvelous horseradishy coleslaw, fries, and hush puppies. There's a selection of chicken dishes, too, but stick to the seafood.

4728 Ocean St. (Fla. A1A, at St. Johns River Ferry landing), Mayport. ✆ **904/246-4442.** Main courses $10–$20; sandwiches $5–$10. AE, DISC, MC, V. Sun–Thurs 10am–9pm; Fri–Sat 10am–10pm.

JACKSONVILLE AFTER DARK

In addition to the spots recommended below, check the listings in the "Shorelines" and "Go" sections of Friday's *Florida Times-Union* (www.jacksonville.com) and *Folio Weekly* (www.folioweekly.com), the free local alternative paper available all over town. Another source is **www.jaxevents.com**.

THE PERFORMING ARTS Jacksonville has plenty of seats for concerts, touring Broadway shows, dance companies, and big-name performers at the 73,000-seat **Jacksonville Municipal Stadium,** at East Duval and Haines streets (✆ **904/630-3900**); the 16,000-seat **Jacksonville Veterans Memorial Arena,** 300 A. Phillip Randolph Blvd. (✆ **904/630-3900** for information, or 353-3309 for tickets); the 4,400-seat **Times-Union Center for the Performing Arts,** 300 Water St., between Hogan and Pearl streets (✆ **904/630-3900**); and the revitalized **Ritz Theatre** (✆ **904/632-5555;** p. 554). A good website of event listings is www.jaxevents.com. Call or check the sources above for what's playing.

THE BAR SCENE You will find several libation options downtown at **Jacksonville Landing** (p. 553), including, if you must, a lively waterfront **Hooters** (✆ **904/356-5400**), plus free outdoor rock, blues, country, and jazz concerts every Friday and Saturday night, except during winter. There's also live music on weekends, across the river at the **River City Brewing Company** (p. 564).

Out at Town Center, at the ocean end of Atlantic Boulevard, one of several popular spots is **Ragtime Tavern & Taproom** (p. 565), where local groups play live jazz and blues Wednesday through Sunday nights. On weekends, especially, the place is really jumping and the crowd is young, but it's lively rather than rowdy. Across the street is the **Sun Dog,** 207 Atlantic Blvd. (✆ **904/241-8221;** www.sundogjax.com), with nightly acoustic music and decent diner food. If these don't fit your mood, walk around Town Center until you find something you like.

Freebird Live, 200 N. 1st St. (✆ **904/246-2473;** www.freebirdlive.com), is a two-story homage to native Jacksonville band Lynyrd Skynyrd, run by late lead singer Ronnie Van Zant's widow and his daughter, and featuring live music 6 nights a week.

5 AMELIA ISLAND ★★

32 miles NE of Jacksonville; 192 miles NE of Orlando; 372 miles N of Miami

Alas, paradise is found on the northernmost barrier island of Florida. With 13 beautiful miles of beach and a quaint Victorian town, Amelia Island is a charming getaway about a 45-minute drive northeast of downtown Jacksonville. Overall, this skinny barrier island, 18 miles long by 3 miles wide, has more in common with the Low Country of Georgia (across Cumberland Sound from here) and South Carolina. In fact, it's more like St. Simons Island in Georgia or Hilton Head Island in South Carolina than other beach resorts in Florida.

Amelia has five distinct personalities. First is its southern end, an exclusive real-estate development built in a forest of twisted, moss-laden live oaks. Here you'll find world-class tennis and golfing at two of Florida's most luxurious resorts. Second is modest **American Beach,** founded in the 1930s so that African Americans would have access to the ocean in this then-segregated part of the country. Today it's a modest, predominantly black community tucked away among all that south-end wealth. Third is the island's middle, a traditional beach community with a mix of affordable motels, cottages, condominiums, and a seaside inn. Fourth is the historic bayside town of **Fernandina Beach ★★★**, which boasts a 50-square-block area of gorgeous Victorian, Queen Anne, and Italianate homes listed on the National Register of Historic Places. And fifth is lovely **Fort Clinch State Park,** which keeps developers from turning the island's northern end into more ritzy resorts.

The town of Fernandina Beach dates from the post–Civil War period, when Union soldiers who had occupied Fort Clinch began returning to the island. In the late 19th century, Amelia's timber, phosphate, and naval-stores industries boomed. Back then, the town was an active seaport, with 14 foreign consuls in residence. You'll see (and occasionally smell) the paper mills that still stand near the small seaport here. The island experienced another economic explosion in the 1970s and 1980s, when real-estate developers built condominiums, cottages, and two big resorts on the island's southern end. In recent years, Fernandina Beach has seen another big boom, this time in bed-and-breakfast establishments.

ESSENTIALS

GETTING THERE The island is served by **Jacksonville International Airport** (p. 552), 12 miles north of Jacksonville's downtown and 43 miles from the island. Skirting the Atlantic in places, the scenic drive here from downtown Jacksonville is via Florida A1A and the St. Johns River Ferry. The fast, four-lane way is via I-95 North and the Buccaneer Trail East (Fla. A1A).

VISITOR INFORMATION For advance information, contact the **Amelia Island–Fernandina Beach–Yulee Chamber of Commerce,** 102 Centre St. (P.O. Box 472), Fernandina Beach, FL 32035 (✆ **800/226-3542** or 904/277-0717; fax 904/261-6997; www.ameliaisland.org). The chamber's visitor center, in the rustic train station at the bay end of Centre Street, is open Monday through Friday from 9am to 5pm, and Saturday from 10am to 2pm.

GETTING AROUND There's no public transportation on this 13-mile-long island, so you'll need a vehicle. An informative and entertaining way to tour the historic district is a 30-minute ride with **Old Towne Carriage Company** (✆ **904/277-1555;** www.amelia carriagetours.com), whose horse-drawn carriages leave from the waterfront on Centre Street between 6:30 and 9pm. Advance reservations are essential. Rides cost $15 for adults and $7.50 for kids 12 and under; private 30-minute tours are the same but with a minimum of $60 per ride, 1-hour tours with a minimum of $120 per ride. The carriage company closes from November to April, when the horses get a much-deserved rest.

Another excellent way to see the town is on a walking tour sponsored by the Amelia Island Museum of History (p. 570).

Thanks to a reclamation project, the widest beaches here are at the exclusive enclave on the island's southern third. Even if you aren't staying at one of the swanky resorts here, you can enjoy this section of beach at **Peters Point Beach Front Park,** on Florida A1A, north of the Ritz-Carlton. The park has picnic shelters and restrooms. North of the resort, the beach has public-access points with free parking every quarter-mile or so. The center of activity is **Main Beach,** at the ocean end of Atlantic Avenue (Fla. A1A), with good swimming, restrooms, picnic shelters, showers, a food concession, a playground, and lots of free parking. This area is popular with families.

The beach at **Fort Clinch State Park** ★★, which wraps around the island's heavily forested northern end, is backed by rolling dunes and is filled with shells and driftwood. A jetty and pier jutting into Cumberland Sound are popular with anglers. There are showers and changing rooms at the pier. Elsewhere in the park, you might see an alligator—and certainly some of the 170 species of birds that live here—by hiking the Willow Pond nature trail. Rangers lead nature tours on the trail, usually beginning at 10:30am on Saturday. There are also 6 miles of off-road bike trails here. Construction on the remarkably well-preserved **Fort Clinch** began in 1847 on the northern tip of the island and was still underway when Union troops occupied it in 1862. The fort was abandoned shortly after the Civil War, except for a brief reactivation in 1898 during the Spanish-American War. Reenactors gather the first full weekend of each month to re-create how the Union soldiers lived in the fort in 1864 (including wearing their wool underwear, even in summer!). Rangers are on duty at the fort year-round, and they lead candlelight tours ($3 per person) on Friday and Saturday evenings during summer, beginning about an hour after sunset. You can arrange guided tours at other times for an extra fee. The park entrance is on Atlantic Avenue near the beach. Entrance fees are $5 per vehicle with up to eight occupants, $1 per pedestrian or bicyclist. Admission to the fort costs $2, free for children 4 and under. The park is open daily from 8am to sunset; the fort, daily from 9am to 5pm. For a schedule of tours and events, contact the park at 2601 Atlantic Ave., Fernandina Beach, FL 32034 (✆ **904/277-7274;** www.floridastateparks.org/fortclinch).

The park also has 62 **campsites**—some behind the dunes at the beach (no shade out there), most in a forest along the sound side. They cost $22 per night, including tax. Pets are an extra $2 per night. You can reserve a site up to 11 months in advance (a very good idea in summer) by calling ✆ **800/326-3521** or going to www.reserveamerica.com.

Pets on leashes are allowed on all of the island's public beaches and in Fort Clinch State Park.

OUTDOOR ACTIVITIES

BOATING, FISHING, SAILING & KAYAKING The **Amelia Island Charter Boat Association** (✆ **800/229-1682** or 904/261-2870), at Tiger Point Marina on 14th Street, north of the historic district (though the boats dock at Centre St.), can help arrange deep-sea fishing charters, party-boat excursions, and dolphin-watching and sightseeing cruises. Other charter boats also dock at Fernandina Harbor Marina, downtown at the foot of Centre Street.

Windward Sailing School, based at Fernandina Harbor Marina, 3977 First Ave. (✆ **904/261-9125;** www.windwardsailing.com), will teach you to skipper your boat; it also has charters and boat rentals. Call for details and reservations.

You have to be careful in the currents, but the backwaters here are great for kayaking, whether you're a beginner or a pro. However, you'll have to travel just off the island to do it. Ray and Jody Hetchka's **Kayak Amelia** ★★ (✆ **888/305-2925** or 904/251-0016;

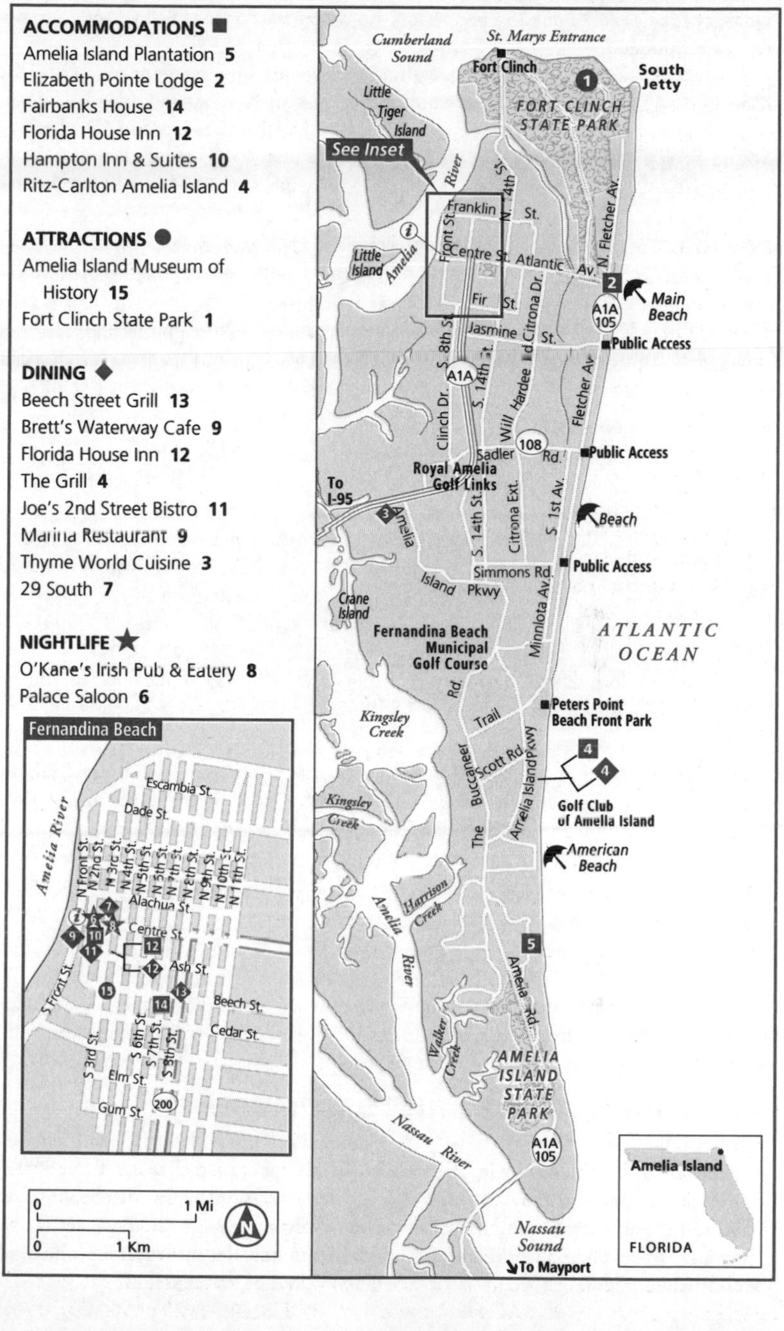

ACCOMMODATIONS ■
Amelia Island Plantation **5**
Elizabeth Pointe Lodge **2**
Fairbanks House **14**
Florida House Inn **12**
Hampton Inn & Suites **10**
Ritz-Carlton Amelia Island **4**

ATTRACTIONS ●
Amelia Island Museum of History **15**
Fort Clinch State Park **1**

DINING ◆
Beech Street Grill **13**
Brett's Waterway Cafe **9**
Florida House Inn **12**
The Grill **4**
Joe's 2nd Street Bistro **11**
Marina Restaurant **9**
Thyme World Cuisine **3**
29 South **7**

NIGHTLIFE ★
O'Kane's Irish Pub & Eatery **8**
Palace Saloon **6**

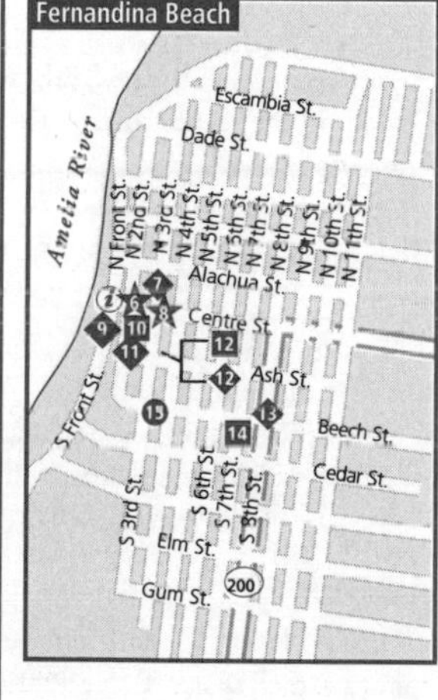

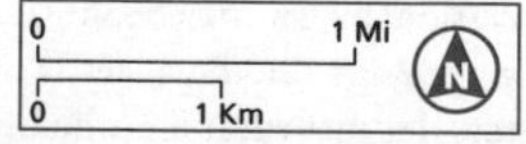

Cumberland Sound
St. Marys Entrance
Fort Clinch
South Jetty
FORT CLINCH STATE PARK
Little Tiger Island
See Inset
Amelia River
Little Island
Franklin St.
Centre St.
Atlantic Av.
Fir St.
Jasmine St.
Front St.
S. 8th St.
N. 14th St.
S. 14th St.
Citrona Dr.
Will Hardee Rd.
N. Fletcher Av.
Fletcher Av.
Main Beach
Public Access
A1A
105
108
Clinch Dr.
Sadler Rd.
Royal Amelia Golf Links
To I-95
Amelia Island Pkwy
S. 14th St.
Citrona Ext.
S. 1st Av.
Public Access
Beach
Simmons Rd.
Public Access
Crane Island
Fernandina Beach Municipal Golf Course
Minnlota Av.
ATLANTIC OCEAN
Kingsley Creek
Peters Point Beach Front Park
Trail
Scott Rd.
The Buccaneer
Amelia Island Pkwy
Golf Club of Amelia Island
American Beach
Harrison Creek
Amelia River
Amelia Rd.
Walker Creek
AMELIA ISLAND STATE PARK
Nassau River
Nassau Sound
To Mayport
Amelia Island
FLORIDA

www.kayakamelia.com) is based near Talbot Island State Park (technically in Jacksonville) and offers beginner and advanced-level trips on back bays, creeks, and marshes. Half-day trips go for about $55 per person. Kayak rentals go from $30 to $60. Reservations are required.

A fabulous company that takes you along the salt marshes, wilderness beaches, and historic river banks of Amelia, Fernandina Beach, and Cumberland Island, Georgia, where wild horses roam the unfettered beaches, **Amelia River Cruises and Cumberland Sound Ferry** (© **877/264-9972;** www.ameliarivercruises.com), offers all sorts of tours ranging from $20 to $26 for adults, $18 to $24 for seniors, and $14 to $20 for children 12 and under.

ECO-TOURS **EcoMotion Tours** (© **904/251-9477;** www.ecomotiontours.com) provide Segway excursions through Florida's state park trails on Fort George Island and Little Talbot Island. The guided tour will take you through the sandy paths of these two protected islands and through the lush vegetation where you'll see butterflies, tortoises, dunes, and waterside bluffs. Tours are $55 to $85 per person and highly recommended.

GOLF If you're not staying in a resort with a golf course (see "Where to Stay," below, and note that these courses can be extremely expensive), try the 18-hole **Amelia River** (© **904/491-8500;** www.aipfl.com/golf/golf.htm) at Amelia Island Plantation for $140 a person ($100 after 1pm). **Amelia River** is open to the public and located just 3 miles from the resort's main entrance; this course is renowned as one of the best conditioned courses in the area, designed by Tom Jackson, with championship golf that all skill levels describe as "very playable." The **Long Point** ★★ course, a mind-blowingly beautiful Tom Fazio–designed 18-holer, has two par-3s in a row bordering the ocean. Or play the older and less expensive 27-hole **Fernandina Municipal Golf Course** (© **904/277-7370;** www.fernandinabeachgolfclub.com), where prices are $19 to $49.

For course information, go to www.golf.com or www.floridagolfing.com; or you can call the **Florida Sports Foundation** (© **850/488-8347**) or **Florida Golfing** (© **866/833-2663**).

HORSEBACK RIDING You can go riding on the beach with the **Kelly Seahorse Ranch** (© **904/491-5166;** www.kellyranchinc.com), located on the southernmost tip of Amelia Island within the Amelia Island State Park. The cost is $60 per person for a 1-hour ride; the ranch is open daily from 8am to 6pm. Reservations are required. ***Note:*** Riders must be 13 or older, at least 4½ feet tall, and weigh less than 230 pounds. No experience is necessary.

TENNIS Ranked among the nation's top 50 by *Tennis* magazine, Amelia Island Plantation's **Racquet Park** (© **904/261-6161;** www.aipfl.com/Tennis/tennis.htm), with 23 Har-Tru tennis courts (naturally shaded by a canopy of gorgeous trees), hosts many professional tournaments, including the annual Bausch & Lomb Championships, and is home to the renowned Gunterman Tennis School.

AN OLD JAIL TURNED HISTORIC MUSEUM

Amelia Island Museum of History ★ Housed in the old Nassau County jail, built of brick in 1878, this award-winning local museum explains Amelia Island's fascinating history, from Timucuan Indian times through its possession by France, Spain, Great Britain, the United States, and the Confederacy. Only an upstairs photo gallery is open for casual inspection, so plan to take the 1-hour, 15-minute docent-led tour of the newly remodeled ground floor if you want to get the most out of this museum.

The museum also offers excellent **walking tours** of historic Centre Street on Thursday and Friday from September through June. These depart at 3pm from the chamber of commerce (p. 567) and cost $10 for adults, $5 for students. You can't make a reservation; just show up. Longer tours of the entire 50-square-block historic district can be arranged with 24-hour notice; these cost $10 per person with a minimum of four persons required.

233 S. 3rd St. (btw. Beech and Cedar sts.). © **904/261-7378.** www.ameliamuseum.org. Admission $7 adults, $4 students. Tours $10 adults, $5 students. Mon–Sat 10am–4pm. Tours Mon–Sat 11am and 2pm.

WHERE TO STAY

More than two dozen of the town's charming Victorian and Queen Anne houses have been restored and turned into B&Bs. For a complete list, contact the chamber of commerce (p. 571) or the **Amelia Island Bed & Breakfast Association** (© **888/277-0218;** www.ameliaislandinns.com). You can tour all the B&Bs during an island-wide open house the first weekend in December.

Your best camping option here is **Fort Clinch State Park** (p. 568).

Note: Rates are subject to a 9% hotel tax.

Amelia Island Plantation ★★ An immense state-designated Green Lodging property (nontoxic pest control, clean and green housekeeping, resort-wide recycling, smart HVAC in the Inn that shuts off when sliding glass doors open and returns to a preset temperature when the guest leaves the room for an extended period of time) that could easily host several plantations, this resort occupies 1,350 lush beachfront acres of manicured golf greens, bike trails, and a breathtaking coastal wilderness of marshes and lagoons. The resort is so spread out that a free tram runs around the grounds every 15 minutes. The Plantation is known for its outstanding sports offerings (see "Golf" and "Tennis" above) and all golf courses are Audobon International Certified sanctuaries. A 25-room, all-natural spa also features a meditation garden, plus nontoxic, paraben-free products and services. The eight-story, Mediterranean-style **Amelia Inn & Beach Club** is the resort's focal point, with 249 spacious, upscale rooms. Traditionally furnished, the rooms boast oceanview patios or balconies. Other accommodations here are one- to three-bedroom privately owned condominium apartments (or "villas," in Florida speak). All but a few have balconies or patios. All have fully equipped kitchens. The Ocean Grill restaurant serves exceptional and expensive contemporary regional cuisine, accompanied by stunning ocean views. Other restaurants and nightspots are also on the property. ***Note:*** You can Segway your way around the massive resort. Prices for Segway transportation devices range from $40 for a 30-minute kids' excursion to $80 for a 1½-hour safari tour of the property. All tours include orientation, coaching, and tour guides.

6800 First Coast Hwy., Amelia Island, FL 32035-3000. © **888/261-6161** or 904/261-6161. Fax 904/277 5945. www.aipfl.com. 610 units, including 300 1-, 2-, and 3-bedroom villas. $197–$429 double; $229–$993 villa. Packages available. AE, DC, DISC, MC, V. Valet parking $15; self-parking free. **Amenities:** 10 restaurants; 5 bars; heated indoor pool; 20 outdoor pools (1 heated); 4 golf courses; 23 tennis courts; health club; spa; Jacuzzi; sauna; bike rental; Island Hopper (golf cart–like cars to drive around the property) rental; age-specific youth programs; nature programs; game room; concierge; business center; shopping arcade; salon; 24-hr. room service; massage; babysitting; laundry service. *In room:* A/C, TV, dataport, Wi-Fi Internet access, kitchen (in condos), minibar (in Amelia Inn only), coffeemaker, hair dryer, iron, safe.

Elizabeth Pointe Lodge ★★ You'd swear that this three-story, Nantucket-style shingled beauty sitting right on the beach is a lovingly maintained Victorian home—but you'd be wrong. Built in 1991 by David and Susan Caples, it has big-paned windows that look out from the comfy library (with stone fireplace) and a dining room to an expansive front porch and the surf beyond. Antiques and reproductions, handmade quilts, and other touches lend the 20 rooms in the main building a turn-of-the-20th-century cottage ambience. All have oversize tubs. Four other rooms are located in the Harris Lodge next door, and the two-bedroom, two-bathroom Miller Cottage is also available.

98 S. Fletcher Ave. (just south of Atlantic Ave.), Fernandina Beach, FL 32034. ✆ **800/772-3359** or 904/277-4851. Fax 904/277-6500. www.elizabethpointelodge.com. 25 units, including 1 cottage. $185–$345 double; $450 cottage. Rates include full seaside buffet breakfast and morning newspaper. Packages available. AE, DISC, MC, V. **Amenities:** Light fare lunch/dinner, beverage service; access to nearby health club; complimentary beach equipment; bike rental; high-speed Internet access; Wi-Fi; 24-hr. room service; laundry service. *In room:* A/C, TV, dataport, hair dryer, iron, Jacuzzi (some rooms).

Fairbanks House ★★ Boasting all the amenities and almost as much privacy as a first-class hotel, this superbly refurbished, romantic 1885 Italianate home is a top B&B choice in the historic district. As gorgeous as it is, it used to be known as "Fairbanks' Folly," because of its pronounced decor. Many rooms and all of the cottages offer private entrances for guests who prefer not to walk through the main house. Room no. 3 is one of the finest units, with a private entrance, sitting room, plush king-size bed, period antiques, and fresh flowers. The two-bedroom Tower Suite, occupying the entire top floor, has plenty of room to spread out, plus 360-degree views and its own whirlpool tub. Five other units here have whirlpool tubs as well. The Fairbanks also has a great pool. No smoking is permitted, indoors or out.

227 S. 7th St. (btw. Beech and Cedar sts.), Fernandina Beach, Amelia Island, FL 32034. ✆ **888/891-9882** or 904/277-0500. www.fairbankshouse.com. 12 units, including 3 cottages. $175–$265 double; $265–$365 cottage; $395 tower suite. Rates include full breakfast and evening social hour (beverages and hors d'oeuvres). Packages available. AE, DISC, MC, V. No children 11 and under. **Amenities:** Outdoor pool; free use of bikes; free use of beach equipment. *In room:* A/C, TV, Wi-Fi, kitchen (in some rooms and cottage), fridge, coffeemaker, hair dryer, iron, bathrobes.

Florida House Inn ★ Value Built in 1857 by one of Florida's founding fathers, David Yulee, this clapboard Victorian building is Florida's oldest operating hotel. Ulysses S. Grant stayed here, as did Cuban revolutionary José Martí. Rockefellers and Carnegies broke bread at the boardinghouse-style dining room that still provides family-style traditional Southern fare, live music, and old school Carolina shag dancing! You can rock away on the two gingerbread-trimmed front verandas or on a back porch overlooking a brick courtyard shaded by a huge oak tree. The 18 rooms in the original building, all mostly up to modern standards, are loaded with antiques. Most have working fireplaces; some have claw-foot tubs. One of these has log-cabin walls, the others are done in country or Victorian style. Some have fireplaces and Jacuzzi tubs. The 10-room Carriage House has a variety of bedrooms, including a pair of two-bedroom efficiency apartments.

22 S. 3rd St. (btw. Centre and Ash sts.), Fernandina Beach, FL 32034. ✆ **800/258-3301** or 904/261-3300. Fax 904/277-3831. www.floridahouseinn.com. 28 units. $99–$249 double; $299–$349 carriage house. Rates include full breakfast. AE, DISC, MC, V. Pets accepted ($15–$25 nightly fee). **Amenities:** Restaurant; bar. *In room:* A/C, TV, hair dryer, iron.

Hampton Inn & Suites ★★ A Hampton Inn that garners two stars, you ask? Believe it or not, it's true. One of the most unusual Hampton Inns I've ever seen, although there's only one building, the exterior looks like a row of different structures, all in the styles and sherbet hues of the Victorian storefronts lining Centre Street. Wooden floors taken from an old Jacksonville church, slatted door panels evocative of 19th-century schooners, and many other touches add to the Victorian ambience inside.

About half of the guest rooms are near the top of the romance scale, with king-size beds, gas fireplaces, and two-person whirlpool tubs. The standard suites are large enough for families, and the other rooms are adequately equipped for business travelers. About a third of the units have balconies. Those higher up on the west side have fine views over the river and marshes. The only drawback: Trains slowly rumble by the west side a few times a day.

19 S. 2nd St. (btw. Centre and Ash sts.), Fernandina Beach, FL 32034. ✆ **800/426-7866** or 904/491-4911. Fax 904/491-4910. www.hamptoninnandsuites.net. 122 units. $129–$209 double. Rates include extensive breakfast buffet. AE, DC, DISC, MC, V. **Amenities:** Outdoor pool; exercise room; Jacuzzi; business center; babysitting; laundry service; coin-op washers/dryers. *In room:* A/C, TV, dataport, fridge, coffeemaker, hair dryer, iron.

Ritz-Carlton Amelia Island ★★★ Kids Sprawling over 13 acres of stunning beachfront, the Ritz offers slightly glitzier accommodations than its neighbor, the Amelia Island Plantation. While some may like the fact that it's perfectly acceptable to walk through the lobby of this Ritz in shorts (it's downright relaxed in this way), others may find the service and surroundings not as polished as they have experienced in other Ritz-Carltons. The kids' program makes well-heeled families feel just as much at home as the conventioneers who flock here to meet and make use of the extensive recreational facilities, including a beautiful 18-hole championship golf course. The spacious guest rooms—all with oceanfront or oceanview balconies or patios—have many amenities, such as scales, cosmetic mirrors, and phones in their marble bathrooms. The playfully gourmet **Salt ★★★**, the longest-running AAA Five Diamond restaurant in Florida, leads the hotel's restaurants, with an ocean view that accompanies exceptional seafood and seasonal dishes by Chef Richard Gras; the restaurant is named after the 30-plus international salts the kitchen collects. You could easily plan your stay around one of their fantastic, hands-on cooking classes. Check the website for dates. The state-of-the-art spa opened in 2007.

4750 Amelia Island Pkwy., Amelia Island, FL 32034. ✆ **800/241-3333** or 904/277-1100. Fax 904/277-1145. www.ritzcarlton.com. 444 units. $199–$439 coastal view double; $409–$629 oceanview suite. Golf, tennis, and other packages available. AE, DC, DISC, MC, V. Valet parking only $17. **Amenities:** 5 restaurants; 3 bars; heated indoor and outdoor pools; golf course; 9 tennis courts; fitness center; spa, watersports equipment/rentals; bike rental; children's programs; game room; concierge; business center; salon; 24-hr. room service; massage; babysitting; laundry service; concierge-level rooms. *In room:* A/C, TV, dataport, minibar, coffeemaker, hair dryer, iron, safe.

WHERE TO DINE

You'll find several restaurants, pubs, and snack shops along Centre Street, between the bay and 8th Street (Fla. A1A), in Fernandina Beach's old town. Two good dining options stand opposite the Hampton Inn & Suites on South 2nd Street, between Centre and Ash streets: the hip **Joe's 2nd Street Bistro** (✆ **904/321-2558**) and the more formal but still relaxed **Le Clos** (✆ **904/261-8100;** www.leclos.com). Joe's serves fine international fare in an old store, while Le Clos provides provincial French fare in a charming old house. Both are open for dinner only; reservations are recommended. Drop by during the day for a look at the menus posted outside each.

And don't forget **Salt** at the Ritz-Carlton Amelia Island (see above); a world-class seven-course "Chef's Adventure" menu is worth the $125 per-person price tag ($175 per person paired with wines).

Lastly, the **Florida House Inn's Frisky Mermaid** (p. 572; www.floridahouseinn.com) serves everything from all-you-can-eat fried chicken and fried pork chops to pizzas and Thai food. The restaurant also features live blues, bluegrass, and local singers every night.

Beech Street Grill ★★ REGIONAL NEW AMERICAN On par with the Grill in the Ritz-Carlton, the cosmopolitan-chic Beech Street Grill pleases all palates with a rich menu of fish, chicken, and meat choices, including seasonal game dishes such as roasted venison loin in a black-currant sauce with sweet-potato-and-onion hash. Nightly fish specialties are always exceptional. I also loved the low-country gumbo over dirty rice with blackened shrimp. Housed in a century-old landmark home and in a newer wing to one side, the five dining rooms have a lively atmosphere. The upstairs section features a pianist.

801 Beech St. (at 8th St./Fla. A1A), Fernandina Beach. ✆ **904/277-3662.** www.beechstreetgrill.com. Reservations strongly recommended. Main courses $17–$30. AE, DC, DISC, MC, V. Daily 6–10pm.

Brett's Waterway Cafe SEAFOOD/STEAK You'll pay for the view, but this friendly waterfront cafe at the foot of Centre Street is the only place in town to dine while watching the boats coming and going on the river—and to sip a drink (try one of the excellent martinis) while watching the sun setting over the marshes between here and the mainland. In fine weather, grab a table out by the docks. One of the best dishes is broiled shrimp with a sun-dried-tomato/cream sauce. The nightly fresh-fish specials are well prepared. Steaks and chops are also served.

1 S. Front St. (at Centre St., on the water), Fernandina Beach. ✆ **904/261-2660.** Main courses $15–$28. AE, MC, V. Mon–Sat 11:30am–2:30pm and 5:30–9:30pm; Sun 5:30–9:30pm.

Joe's 2nd Street Bistro ★★★ NEW AMERICAN In the heart of the Fernandina Beach historic district is this diminutive restored 1900s home that's filled with flavor. The island-inspired dining room features a brick fireplace, and upstairs is a private dining room, but I suggest grabbing a table out on the covered porch. A meal here is almost like eating in a chef's home, a quaint and delectable experience, to say the least. Try the grilled leg of lamb rubbed with black pepper, garlic, and herbs and served with tomato mint salsa, potatoes, and "cotton fried onions." Yowza! For dessert, the apple bread pudding kicks that part of your body where perhaps the calories will end up. It rocks. Joe's rocks. Don't miss it. Eat at Joe's.

14 S 2nd St. (at Front St.), Fernandina Beach. ✆ **904/321-2558.** www.joesbistro.com. Reservations recommended. Main courses $14–$32. AE, DC, MC, V. Daily 6–9:30pm.

Marina Restaurant (Value) AMERICAN Occupying a brick store built in the 1880s, this quintessential small-town restaurant has been feeding low-country fare to locals since 1965. A lot of the seafood here is fried and broiled, but you can order grouper topped with scallops and a garlicky wine sauce. Budgeters love the $10-and-under list of Southern favorites, such as country-fried steak and breaded veal cutlet. Meatloaf with tomato-and-basil gravy, stuffed peppers with a Greek-style tomato sauce, and other lunch specials come with three fresh country-style vegetables, which are themselves worth the price of the meal. Hearty breakfasts feature eggs, omelets, French toast, and hot cakes.

101 Centre St. (at Front St.), Fernandina Beach. ✆ **904/261-5310.** Main courses $10–$28; sandwiches $5–$10; breakfast $3–$10. DC, MC, V. Daily 7–10am and 11:30am–9pm.

Thyme World Cuisine ★★ FUSION ITALIAN Intracoastal Waterway views compete with colorful and creative martinis at this Amelia Island Italian-influenced hot spot. This is not the chianti and checkered tablecloth Italian restaurant Billy Joel sings about either. Instead of just a bottle of red or white, consider funky martinis, such as Italian Wedding Cake or Mozzarella—don't ask us, they won't give away the recipes. As for the food, it ranges from traditional—spaghetti and meatballs—to offbeat—Pancetta Strudel, stuffed with Italian bacon and sauerkraut with a walnut cream sauce. Although we haven't had it, we hear the Fig Plate is particularly exceptional, with black mission figs, Gorgonzola mousse, *soppressata* salami, spring greens, strawberry-fig vinaigrette, and grilled flatbread.

960062 Gateway Blvd., Fernandina Beach ✆ **904/261-3827.** Reservations strongly suggested. Main courses $18–$30. AE, MC, V. Daily 5–10pm.

29 South ★★ NEW AMERICAN Chef Scotty Schwartz presides over this chic neighborhood bistro where nothing is ordinary. Signature items include lobster corn dogs with spicy horseradish ketchup spiked with Ketel One vodka, sweet tea–brined DelKat Family Farm pork chop on macaroni gratin with warm blackberry preserves, and grilled heart of romaine salad with Maytag blue vinaigrette with bacon and toasted walnuts. You get the idea. Best of all, it's not a trendy snobby spot but a casual eatery that manages to turn everything into something extraordinary. Even coffee and doughnuts are served here—as glazed doughnut bread pudding with butterscotch drizzle and mocha ice cream.

29 S. 3rd St. Fernandina Beach. ✆ **904/277-7919.** www.29southrestaurant.com. Reservations strongly suggested. Main courses $18–$30; sandwiches $5–$14. AE, MC, V. Sunday 10am–2pm; Tues–Sat 11:30am–2:30pm; Mon–Thurs 5:30pm–9:30pm; Fri–Sat 5:30pm–10pm.

15

Northwest Florida: The Panhandle

The Florida Panhandle is to the state as Jan Brady of TV's *The Brady Bunch* is to her family. Cindy, the cute younger sister, could represent Orlando and Tampa, with their amusements and attractions. South and Southwest Florida could be Marcia, the gorgeous older sister whom everyone fawns over and talks about. Then there's the misunderstood, underestimated, middle sister Jan—in this case, Northwest Florida, also known as the Panhandle—always getting the shaft, even though she has some great qualities all her own, if only people took the time to discover them. For the Panhandle, this is a particular shame, as it is a dynamic, uncommonly beautiful part of Florida.

If you like beaches, you'll love the Panhandle, the land of the two-way sun, which runs east to west along the Gulf of Mexico and, therefore, has sunrises *and* sunsets. It was once known—and sometimes erroneously still is known—as the Redneck Riviera (thanks to a steady crowd from Georgia, Alabama, and Louisiana), a refreshing change from the glitz and glamour oozing from South Florida. The Panhandle, while still rugged in a sexy, Marlboro Man kind of way, has slowly shed that reputation with the emergence of upscale residential developments and boutique hotels.

Three other reasons to love this zone: water as turquoise as colored contact lenses, smaller crowds than at other Florida beaches, and ghost-white sand so talcumlike that it squeaks when you walk on it. The sand in these parts is brilliantly white because, over thousands of years, quartz particles were washed downstream from the eroding Appalachian Mountains and pummeled into grains as fine and soft as baby powder before finally landing at their final resting place: under the towels of the three million sunbathers who flock here every year. Speaking of walking, you can, because some 100 miles of these incomparable sands are protected in state parks and the gorgeous Gulf Islands National Seashore.

Pensacola, Destin, Fort Walton Beach, and Panama City Beach are summertime meccas for families, couples, and singles from the aforementioned adjoining states—a geographic proximity that lends this area the languid charm of the Deep South. Indeed, Southern specialties such as collard greens and cheese grits (in the South, "grits" is a two-syllable word, pronounced *gree*-its) appear frequently on menus here.

But there's more to the northwestern Panhandle than beaches and Southern charm. Record catches of grouper, amberjack, snapper, mackerel, cobia, sailfish, wahoo, tuna, and blue marlin have made Destin one of the world's fishing capitals. In the interior, near Pensacola, the Blackwater, Shoal, and Yellow rivers teem with bass, bream, and catfish and also allow for some of Florida's best canoeing and kayaking adventures.

The area is steeped in history as well. Rivaling St. Augustine as Florida's oldest town, picturesque Pensacola preserves a heritage derived from Spanish, French, English, and American conquests. Famous for its oysters, Apalachicola saw the invention of the air conditioner, a moment of great historic note for Florida. Tallahassee, seat of state government since 1824, has a host of 19th-century buildings, including the majestic Old State Capitol, not to mention a cool little town named, yes, Havana, which is one of the largest antiques centers in the Southeast U.S.

One note to those traveling the entire state: While "season" in South Florida tends to fall in the winter months, due to the Panhandle's geographic location and tendency to get chilly or downright cold during the winter, its "season" is during the summer, so hotel rates will be higher during that time, while it's the opposite down south.

EXPLORING NORTHWEST FLORIDA BY CAR

Both I-10 and U.S. 98 link Tallahassee and Pensacola, some 200 miles apart. The fastest route is I-10, but all you'll see is a huge pine forest divided by two strips of concrete. Plan to take U.S. 98 instead, a scenic excursion in itself. Although it can be traffic clogged in the beach towns during summer, U.S. 98 has some beautiful stretches out in the country, particularly as it literally skirts the bay east of Apalachicola and the Gulf west of Port St. Joe. It's also lovely along skinny Okaloosa Island and across the high-rise bridge between Fort Walton Beach and Destin. From the bridge, you'll see the brilliant hue of the Gulf and immediately understand why this is called the Emerald Coast. If you turn off U.S. 98 onto 30A, a 20-mile drive along the coastline, you will immediately be transported back in time to the pre-Golden-Arches-lined highways of Florida. Along this scenic stretch, you'll see not only sand and surf but also, believe it or not, pine forests, saw palmettos, the Choctawhatchee Bay, and Hogtown Bayou, a magnet for fiery sunsets.

1 PENSACOLA ★★

191 miles W of Tallahassee; 354 miles W of Jacksonville

A charming blend of Old Spanish brickwork, colonial French balconies reminiscent of New Orleans, and magnificent Victorian mansions built by British and American lumber barons, Pensacola is definitely worthy of its motto, "City of Five Flags." However, it's much more than just pretty buildings and a nice vibe. Thanks to the Pensacola Downtown Improvement Board, work has continued to progress on the revitalization of downtown, promoting the full occupancy of once-abandoned 125-year-old buildings and the emergence of downtown businesses, stores, historic theaters, restaurants, bars, and events such as the Florida Springfest, a 3-day music festival that lures such big names as Cheap Trick, the Black Crowes, Bonnie Raitt, Trace Adkins, the Allman Brothers, and Jethro Tull, with coverage by VH-1.

West of town, the excellent National Museum of Naval Aviation at the U.S. Naval Air Station celebrates the storied past of U.S. Navy and Marine Corps pilots who trained at Pensacola. The Blue Angels are based here, and they demonstrate the high-tech present with thrilling exhibitions of precision flying in the navy's fastest fighters.

Also on the naval station, historic Fort Barrancas looks across the bay to Perdido Key and Santa Rosa Island, which reach out like narrow pincers to form the harbor. Out here, powdery white-sand beaches beckon sun-and-surf lovers to the spectacular Gulf shores, which include Pensacola Beach, a small family-oriented resort, and most of Florida's share of Gulf Islands National Seashore, home of historic Fort Pickens.

A Friendly Feud

Native Americans left pottery shards and artifacts in the coastal dunes in Pensacola centuries before Tristan de Luna arrived with a band of Spanish colonists in 1559. Although his settlement lasted only 2 years, modern Pensacolans claim that their town is the oldest in North America. Pensacola actually dates its permanence from a Spanish colony established here in 1698, however, so St. Augustine wins this friendly feud, having been continuously settled since 1565. France, Great Britain, the United States, and the Confederacy subsequently captured (and, in one case, recaptured) this strategically important deepwater port.

ESSENTIALS

See "Appendix: Fast Facts, Toll-Free Numbers & Websites," p. 638, for the contact information of airlines and car services.

GETTING THERE **Pensacola Regional Airport,** 12th Avenue, at Airport Road (✆ 850/436-5005; www.flypensacola.com), is served by **AirTran, Continental, Delta, Northwest,** and **US Airways.**

Alamo, Avis, Budget, Dollar, Enterprise, Hertz, and **National** have rental-car operations here.

Taxis wait outside the modern terminal. Fares are $2 at flag drop and $2.25 for each additional mile.

The **Amtrak** (✆ **800/872-7245;** www.amtrak.com) transcontinental *Sunset Limited* stops in Pensacola at 980 E. Heinberg St.

VISITOR INFORMATION The **Pensacola Visitor Information Center,** 1401 E. Gregory St., Pensacola, FL 32501 (✆ **800/874-1234** or 850/434-1234; fax 850/432-8211; www.visitpensacola.com), gives away helpful information about the Greater Pensacola area, including maps of self-guided tours of the historic districts, and sells a detailed street map of the area. The office is at the mainland end of the Pensacola Bay Bridge and is open daily from 8am to 5pm (until 4pm Sat–Sun Oct–Mar).

For information specific to the beach, contact the **Pensacola Beach Chamber of Commerce,** 735 Pensacola Beach Blvd. (P.O. Box 1174), Pensacola Beach, FL 32561 (✆ **800/635-4803** or 850/932-1500; fax 850/932-1551; www.visitpensacolabeach.com). The chamber's offices and visitor center are on the right as you drive onto Santa Rosa Island across the Bob Sikes Bridge. It's open daily from 9am to 5pm.

GETTING AROUND For a trolley tour around town, check out **Beach Bum Trolley** (✆ **850/941-2876;** www.beachbumtrolley.com), which operates one to eight tours of all the historic sights. Prices range from as low as $18 per person for a 50-minute narrated tour of downtown Pensacola, to $150 per person for a 7-hour trolley tour and a full-day of deep-sea fishing. To see the historic sights in town during the warmer months, take the **ECAT Trolley** (✆ **850/595-3228;** www.goecat.com), which leaves every 30 minutes from Portofino Boardwalk and runs to Fort Pickens Gate on the west side of the island, and to Portofino Island Resort & Spa on the east side. The trolley is free from Memorial Day weekend to Labor Day weekend, Friday 5pm to midnight, Saturday noon to midnight, and Sunday 5 to 10pm. ECAT also runs public buses around town Monday through Saturday ($1.75 adults, 85¢ seniors)—but not to the beach. Call for schedules.

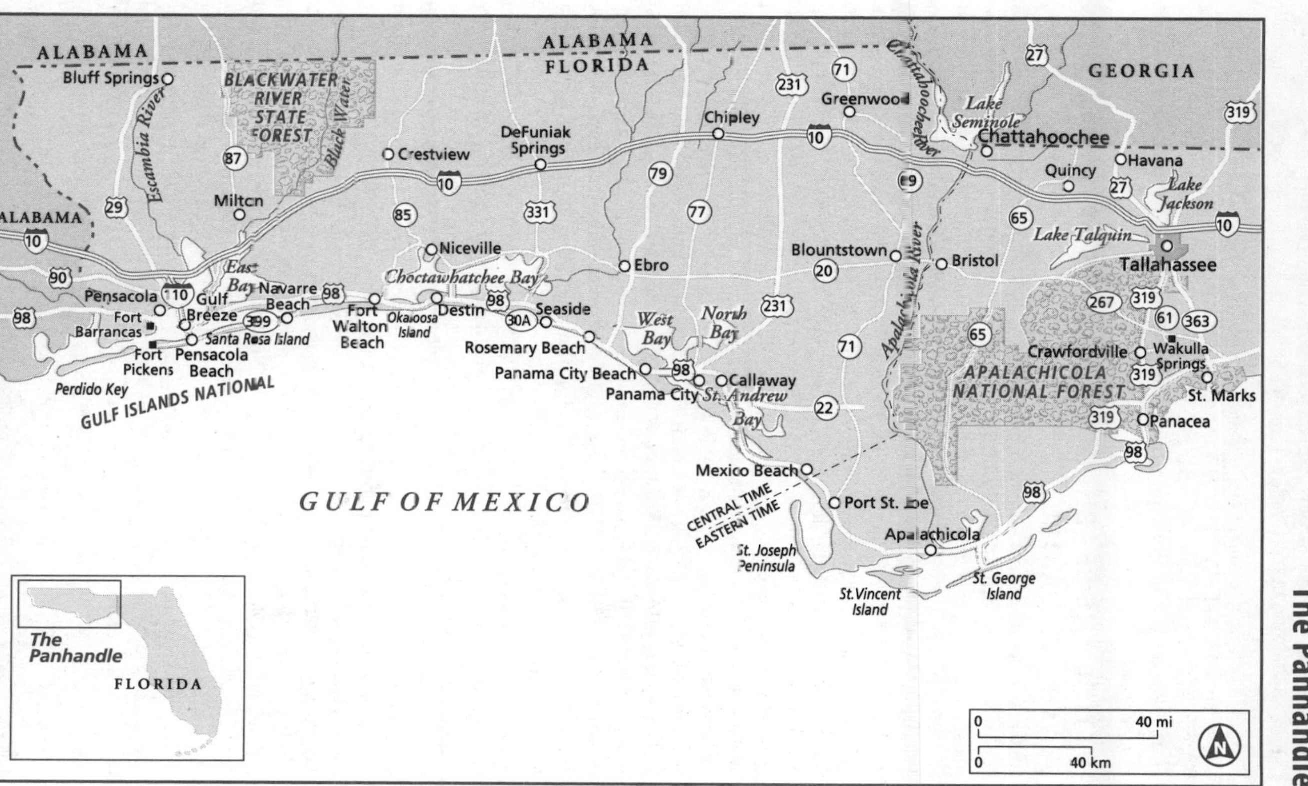
ALABAMA
Bluff Springs
BLACKWATER RIVER STATE FOREST
Black Water
Escambia River
ALABAMA
FLORIDA
GEORGIA
Greenwood
Chipley
DeFuniak Springs
Crestview
Milton
Lake Seminole
Chattahoochee River
Chattahoochee
Quincy
Havana
Lake Jackson
Lake Talquin
Tallahassee
Blountstown
Bristol
Ebro
Niceville
Choctawhatchee Bay
East Bay
Navarre Beach
Pensacola
Gulf Breeze
Fort Barrancas
Santa Rosa Island
Fort Pickens
Pensacola Beach
Perdido Key
GULF ISLANDS NATIONAL
Fort Walton Beach
Okaloosa Island
Destin
Seaside
Rosemary Beach
Panama City Beach
Panama City
West Bay
North Bay
Callaway
St. Andrew Bay
Apalachicola River
APALACHICOLA NATIONAL FOREST
Crawfordville
Wakulla Springs
St. Marks
Panacea
Mexico Beach
CENTRAL TIME
EASTERN TIME
Port St. Joe
St. Joseph Peninsula
Apalachicola
St. Vincent Island
St. George Island
GULF OF MEXICO
The Panhandle
FLORIDA
0 40 mi
0 40 km

If you need a cab, call **Airport Express Taxi/City Cab** (✆ **850/478-4477**), **Orange Cab** (✆ **850/478-0222**), or **Yellow Cab** (✆ **850/433-3333**). Fares are $2 at flag fall, plus $2.25 a mile.

You can rent bikes from **Eco-Beach,** 8460 Gulf Blvd. (✆ **850/936-SAND** [7263]; www.eco-beach.com). Rentals are $10 per day.

TIME Pensacola is in the Central Time zone, 1 hour behind Miami, Orlando, and Tallahassee.

HITTING THE BEACH: GULF ISLANDS NATIONAL SEASHORE & MORE

Stretching eastward 47 miles, from the entrance to Pensacola Bay to Fort Walton Beach, skinny Santa Rosa Island is home to the resorts, condominiums, cottages, restaurants, and shops of **Pensacola Beach,** the area's prime vacation spot. This relatively small and low-key resort began life a century ago as the site of a beach pavilion, or "casino," as such facilities were called back then; and the heart of town—at the intersection of Pensacola Beach Boulevard, Via de Luna, and Fort Pickens Road—is still known as Casino Beach. This lively area at the base of the town's water tank has restaurants, snack bars, an arcade, a miniature golf course, public restrooms, walk-up beach bars with live bands blaring away, an indoor sports bar, and an outdoor concert pavilion with summertime entertainment. The shops, restaurants, and bars of Quietwater Boardwalk are just across the road on the bay side of the island. If you want an active beach vacation, it's all here in one compact zone.

One reason Pensacola Beach is so small is that most of Santa Rosa Island is included in the **Gulf Islands National Seashore** ★★★. Jumping from island to island from Mississippi to Florida, this magnificent preserve, possibly the best beach in the entire state, includes 150 miles of undeveloped and federally protected white-sand beach and rolling dunes covered with sea grass and sea oats. Established in 1971, the national seashore is a protected environment for more than 280 species of birds.

The most interesting part of the seashore is **Fort Pickens** (✆ **850/934-2635;** www.nps.gov/guis), on the western end of Santa Rosa Island, about 7 miles west of Pensacola Beach. Built in the 1830s to team with Fort Barrancas in guarding Pensacola's harbor entrance, this huge brick structure saw combat during the Civil War, but it's best known as the prison home of Apache medicine man Geronimo from 1886 to 1888. The visitor center has a small museum featuring displays about Geronimo, coastal defenses, and the seashore's ecology. Plan to be here at 2pm, when rangers lead 45-minute tours of the fort (the schedule can change, so call the fort to make sure). Seven-day admission permits (that's the minimum you can get) to the Fort Pickens area are $8 per vehicle, $3 per pedestrian or bicyclist, and free for holders of National Park Service passes. The fort and museum are open March through October daily from 9:30am to 5pm, November through February daily from 8:30am to 4pm. Both are closed Christmas Day.

The Fort Pickens area had 200 **campsites** (135 with electricity) in a pine forest on the bay side of Santa Rosa Island. Nature trails led the camp through Blackbird Marsh and to the beach. Unfortunately at the time of this writing, the campsites there were closed indefinitely, due to previous hurricane damage. Call ✆ **800/365-2267** for reservations (enter code GUL) or 850/934-2623 for recorded information.

The national seashore's headquarters are in the 1,378-acre **Naval Live Oaks Area,** on U.S. 98, a mile east of Gulf Breeze (✆ **850/934-2600**). This former federal tree plantation is a place of primitive beauty, with nature trails leading through the oaks and pines

to picnic areas and a beach. Pick up a map at the headquarters building, which has a small museum and a gorgeous view through the pines to Santa Rosa Sound. Picnic areas and trails are open from 8am to sunset year-round, except Christmas. Admission is free. The visitor center is open daily from 8am to 5:30pm.

The national seashore maintains historic **Fort Barrancas,** on the U.S. Naval Air Station west of town. See "Pensacola's Other Fort" (p. 585) for details.

OUTDOOR ACTIVITIES

FISHING Red snapper, grouper, mackerel, tuna, and billfish are abundant off the Panhandle. The easiest way to drop a line into the Gulf is off the new **Pensacola Beach Gulf Fishing Pier,** on Fort Pickens Road in Pensacola Beach (© **850/934-7200;**

Florida's Canoe Capital

The little town of Milton, the official "Canoe Capital of Florida" (by an act of the state legislature, no less), is about 20 miles northeast of Pensacola via U.S. 90. Its title is well earned, as the nearby Blackwater River, Coldwater River, Sweetwater Creek, and Juniper Creek are perfect for canoeing, kayaking, tubing, rafting, and paddle boating.

The Blackwater is considered one of the world's purest sand-bottom rivers. It has remained a primordial backwoods beauty, thanks chiefly to Florida's largest state forest (183,000 acres of oak, pine, and juniper) and **Blackwater River State Park ★★**, 7720 Deaton Bridge Rd., Holt, FL 32564 (✆ **850/983-5363;** www.floridastateparks.org/blackwaterriver), where you can closely observe plant life and wildlife along nature trails. The park has facilities for fishing, picnicking, and camping. Admission is $3 per day per vehicle with driver, $1 per extra vehicle passenger, $1 per pedestrian or bicyclist. Campsites cost $12, plus $2 per pet with tags and vaccination papers. For camping reservations, call ✆ **800/326-3521** or go to www.reserveamerica.com.

Adventures Unlimited, 8974 Tomahawk Landing Road Milton, FL 32570 (✆ **800/239-6864** or 850/623-6197; fax 850/626-3124; www.adventuresunlimited.com) is a year-round resort with canoeing, kayaking, and tubing trips. Canoe trips start at $25 per person with a two-person minimum charge per canoe. Kayaking adventures from $30. Tubes start at $16. There are also 12 furnished cabins, including five riverfront cabins, three creek-front cabins, and several bungalows nestled in the woods. Cabin prices range from $99 to $189 a night. Some cabins have fireplaces and tubs. Two-night minimum stays are required, 3 nights on holidays and from Memorial Day to Labor Day. Rustic cabins range in price from $39 to $59 per night and do not have indoor kitchens or bathrooms. There's also the School House Inn (eight rooms, all with private bathroom) whose rooms range in price from $89 to $109 per night. Campsites are priced from $20 per night. Call for reservations.

Blackwater Canoe Rental, 10274 Pond Rd. in Milton (✆ **800/967-6789** or 850/623-0235; www.blackwatercanoe.com), also rents canoes, kayaks, floats, tubes, and camping equipment. It has two kinds of camping trips by canoe or kayak: a day trip, ranging from $21 to $28 per person, and an overnight excursion, ranging from $30 to $40 per person. Tents, sleeping bags, and coolers are all available for rent.

www.fishpensacolabeachpier.com). At 1,471 feet, it's the longest fishing pier on the Gulf Coast. The pier is open 24 hours a day, year-round. Fees for fishing are $6.50 per day for adults, $5.50 for seniors, and $3.50 for children 6 to 12. Bait and equipment cost extra. Observers can watch for $1 per person.

Fishing-charter services are offered at Pensacola by the **Beach Marina Fishing Fleet** (✆ **877/650-3474** or 850/932-0304), and at Pensacola Beach by **Reel Eazy Charters** (✆ **877/733-5329** or 850/932-8824; www.reeleazy.com). Expect to pay between $425 and $2,600 for 1 to 10 passengers, depending on the length of your trip. You may be able to save by driving to Destin, where party boats charge less per person (p. 595). Sightseeing and evening cruises here go for $50 to $200 per person.

GOLF The Pensacola area has its share of Northwest Florida's numerous championship golf courses. Look for free copies of *South Coast Golf Guide,* an annual directory describing all of them, at the visitor center and in many hotel lobbies (see p. 56 for information on ordering copies). Reasonably priced golf packages can be arranged through many local hotels and motels.

For course information, go to www.golf.com or www.floridagolfing.com; or call the **Florida Sports Foundation** (✆ **850/488-8347**) or **Florida Golfing** (✆ **866/833-2663**).

Among this region's best courses is **Marcus Pointe,** on Marcus Pointe Boulevard, off North W Street (✆ **800/362-7287** or 850/484-9770; www.marcus-pointe.com), which has hosted the Nike Tour, the American Amateur Classic, and the Pensacola Open. *Golf Digest* described this 18-hole course as a "great value," and that's not far off: Greens fees with cart are about $25 to $50, depending on the season.

The **Moors,** on Avalon Boulevard north of I-10 (✆ **800/727-1010** or 850/995-4653), has also greeted the Nike Tour and is home to the Emerald Coast Classic, a PGA Seniors event. Pot bunkers here make you think you're playing in Scotland. Greens fees are also about $25 5o $50. The Moors also has a lodge with eight luxury rooms.

Other courses worth considering are the **Lost Key Golf Club,** on Perdido Key (✆ **888/256-7853** or 850/492-1300), one of the area's more difficult courses; **Scenic Hills,** on U.S. 90 northwest of town (✆ **850/476-9611**), with rolling fairways that are unique for this mostly flat area; the 36-hole **Tiger Point,** 1255 Country Club Rd., east of Gulf Breeze by Santa Rosa Sound (✆ **850/932-1330**), overlooking the water (the 5th-hole green of the East Course actually sits on an island); **Hidden Creek,** 3070 PGA Blvd., in Navarre, between Gulf Breeze and Fort Walton Beach (✆ **850/939-4604**); **Creekside Golf Course,** 2355 W. Michigan Ave. (✆ **850/944-7969**); and **Osceola Municipal Golf Course,** 300 Tonawanda, off Mobile Highway (✆ **850/456-2761**).

In addition, the renovated **Perdido Bay Golf Club,** 1 Doug Ford Dr. (✆ **866/319-2471** or 850/492-1223; www.perdidobaygolf.com), on the mainland north of Perdido Key, has accommodations available for visiting golfers. It was the home of the PGA Pensacola Open from 1978 to 1987. Greens fees here range from $39 to $79.

WATERSPORTS Visibility in the waters around Pensacola can range from 30 to 50 feet deep inshore, to 100 feet deep 25 miles offshore. Although the bottom is sandy and the area is too far north for coral, the battleship USS *Massachusetts,* submerged in 30 feet of water 3 miles offshore, is one of some 35 artificial reefs where you can spot loggerhead turtles and other creatures. There are also good snorkeling sites just off the beach; get a map from the Gulf Islands National Seashore (see "Hitting the Beach: Gulf Islands National Seashore & More," above).

Scuba Shack, 711 S. Palafox St. (✆ **850/433-4319**), offers sales, rentals, classes, and diving and fishing charters on the *Wet Dream,* moored behind the office. **Divers Den,** 512 N. 9th Ave. (✆ **850/438-0650**), also provides trips, equipment rental, and PADI (Professional Association of Diving Instructors) training instruction. **MBT Divers** (✆ **850/455-7702;** www.mbtdivers.com) has rentals, instruction, and trips to several sites, including the habitats of sea turtles, manta rays, and nurse sharks.

Key Sailing Center, 500 Quietwater Beach Rd., on the Quietwater Beach Boardwalk (✆ **877/932-7272** or 850/932-5520; www.keysailing.com), and **Radical Rides,** 444 Pensacola Beach Blvd., near the Bob Sikes Bridge (✆ **850/934-9743**), rent Hobie Cats, pontoon boats, WaveRunners, jet skis, and windsurfing boards.

Adjacent to the Historic Pensacola Village, the city's **Vietnam Memorial,** on Bayfront Parkway at 9th Avenue, is known as the "Wall South," as it is a three-quarter-size replica of the national Vietnam Veterans' Memorial in Washington, D.C. Look for the "Huey" helicopter atop the wall.

Civil War Soldiers Museum ★ Founded by Dr. Norman Haines, Jr., a local physician who started collecting Civil War relics when he was growing up in Sharpsburg, Maryland, this 4,200-square-foot museum in the heart of the Palafox Street business district emphasizes how ordinary soldiers lived during that bloody conflict. The doctor's collection of military medical equipment and treatment methods is especially informative. A 23-minute video tells of Pensacola's role during the Civil War. The museum's bookstore carries more than 600 titles about the war.

108 S. Palafox St. (south of Romana St.). ✆ **850/469-1900.** www.cwmuseum.org. Admission $6 adults, $5 seniors, $2.50 children 6–12. Tues–Sat 10am–4:30pm. Closed New Year's Day, Thanksgiving, Christmas Eve, and Christmas Day.

Historic Pensacola Village ★★★ History buffs, as well as those who appreciate delightful architecture, will *love* this retro-fabulous old-school village, comparable to Long Island's Old Bethpage Village Restoration or Virginia's Colonial Williamsburg. Bounded by Church, Zaragoza, Jefferson, Tarragona, and Adams streets, this original part of Pensacola resembles a shady English colonial town—albeit with Spanish street names—complete with town green and its own Christ Church, built in 1832 and resembling Bruton Parish in Williamsburg, Virginia. Some of Florida's oldest homes, now owned and preserved by the state, are here, and the village is located in the heart of the broader historic district, home to charming boutiques and interesting restaurants as well.

Start your visit by buying tickets at **Tivoli High House,** 205 E. Zaragoza St., just east of Tarragona Street and one street above the Port of Pensacola, where you can get free maps and brochures. Try to take one of the 90-minute guided walking tours of the village, which will lead you through buildings not otherwise open to the public, the French Creole–style 1805 Charles Lavalle House, the elegant Victorian 1871 Dorr House, Old Christ Church, and the 1890 Lear-Rocheblave House.

Among the landmarks you can self-guide through with your ticket are the Museum of Industry, the Museum of Commerce, and the Manuel Barrios Cottage, all interpreting Pensacola from the late 1800s through the Roaring '20s. The 1805 Julee Cottage displays an African-American heritage exhibit, telling the story of the African-American experience in Pensacola from Spanish exploration to the reconstruction periods.

Don't miss the T. **T. Wentworth, Jr., Florida State Museum,** 330 S. Jefferson St. (✆ **850/595-5985**), a 1907 elaborate Renaissance Revival building originally built on Plaza Ferdinand as the city hall. It is now open to the public for free as a local history museum, displaying exhibits of regional interest and Pensacola history. The third floor houses the Discovery Gallery, a hands-on children's exhibit, appropriate for children of preschool age through second grade.

205 E. Zaragoza St. (east of Tarragona St.). ✆ **850/595-5985.** www.historicpensacola.org. Admission $6 adults, $5 seniors, $3 children 4–16. Mon–Sat 10am–4pm; 90-min. guided tours 11am, 1pm, and 2:30pm. Closed New Year's Day, Thanksgiving, Christmas Eve, Christmas Day, and all other state holidays. It may be closed for further hours during holiday season, please call in advance.

National Museum of Naval Aviation ★★ Given the present world circumstances, this museum should be required attendance for everyone. Yes, it's fascinating, but

Pensacola's Other Fort

Standing on Taylor Road near the National Museum of Naval Aviation, **Fort Barrancas** ★★ (✆ **850/455-5167**) is definitely worth a visit while you're at the naval station. This imposing brick structure sits on a bluff overlooking the deepwater pass into Pensacola Bay. The Spanish built the water battery in 1797. Linked to it by a tunnel, the incredibly intricate brickwork of the fort's upper section was constructed by American troops between 1839 and 1844. Entry is by means of a drawbridge across a dry moat, and an interior scarp gallery goes all the way around the inside of the fort. Meticulously restored and operated by the National Park Service as part of Gulf Islands National Seashore, the fort is open March through October daily from 9:30am to 4:45pm, November through February daily from 8:30am to 3:45pm. Ranger-led, 1-hour guided tours are well worth taking. The schedule changes seasonally, so call for the latest information. Admission and tours are free.

The **Pensacola Lighthouse,** opposite the museum entrance on Radford Boulevard, has guided ships to the harbor entrance since 1825. Except for occasional guided tours (call the Pensacola visitor center (p. 578) for a schedule), the lighthouse is not open to the public, but you can drive right up to it. The nearby **Lighthouse Point Restaurant** (✆ **850/452-3251**) offers bountiful, all-you-can eat luncheon buffets and magnificent bay views for about $8 per person Monday through Friday. It's open Monday through Friday from 10:30am to 2pm, and reservations are not required.

it also gives you a look into just how much blood, sweat, and tears go into defending this country. The U.S. Navy and Marine Corps have trained at the sprawling U.S. Naval Air Station since they began flying planes early in the 20th century. Celebrating their heroics, this remarkable museum has more than 100 aircraft dating from the 1920s to the space age, plus interesting exhibits on subjects such as POWs. There's even a torpedo bomber flown by former U.S. president George H. W Bush during World War II. Children and adults alike can sit at the controls of a jet trainer, and the mock-ups of aircraft-carrier conning towers and hangar decks are realistic. You can almost feel the tug of gravity while watching the Blue Angels and other naval aviators soaring about the skies in the stunning *Magic of Flight,* one of two IMAX films shown at the museum. If the movie doesn't get your stomach churning, then a 15-minute ride in the flight-motion simulator will. Using high-tech video and real motion, it simulates a high-speed, low-level mission in the navy's F-18 Hornet jet fighter. A ride on a Top Gun Air Combat Simulator is $25 per person and memorable to say the least! All guides are retired naval and Marine Corps aviators, which adds a personal touch to the hour-long museum tours. Allow at least half a day here, and save 20 minutes for a Flight Line bus tour of more than 40 aircraft parked outside the museum's restoration hangar.

Radford Blvd., U.S. Naval Air Station. ✆ **850/452-3604.** www.naval-air.org. Free admission. IMAX movies $8 adults; $7.50 seniors, military, and children 5–13. Add $4 for 2nd movie. Flight-motion simulator rides $5 per person or $11 for a ride on both a Blue Angels and Desert Storm simulator. Daily 9am–5pm. Guided tours daily at 9:30 and 11am, 1 and 2:30pm. Flight Line bus tours daily every 30 min. 10am–noon and 1–4pm. IMAX movies on the hour daily 10am–4pm. Flight-motion simulator every 15 min. 9am–4:45pm. Closed New Year's Day, Thanksgiving, and Christmas. Enter naval station either at the Main Gate at the south end of Navy Blvd. (Fla. 295) or at the Back Gate on Blue Angel Pkwy. (Fla. 173) and follow the signs. No passes required.

Pensacola Historical Museum To learn more about Pensacola's diverse, five-flag history, spend 30 to 60 minutes at this local museum in the Arbona Building, a commercial structure built around 1882. An archaeological dig of the Spanish commanding officer's compound across Zaragosa Street has a boardwalk with explanatory signposts. The museum is operated by the Pensacola Historical Society, which has a resource center and library at 117 E. Government St. (© **850/434-5455**).

115 E. Zaragosa St. (btw. Tarragona and Jefferson sts.). © **850/433-1559.** www.pensacolahistory.org. Free admission. Mon–Sat 10am–4:30pm.

Pensacola Museum of Art ★ Housed in what was the city jail from 1906 to 1954, this museum showcases an impressive collection of decorative glass, some African tribal art, and sometimes minor works by Salvador Dalí, John Marin, Ansel Adams, Thomas Hart Benton, Milton Avery, Alexander Calder, and Andy Warhol, among others, all displayed in the former cell blocks. It also sponsors cool events such as Art After Dark, in which you are invited to use the walls of the museum as your personal canvas for personal, artistic expression. Call before going to see what's on.

407 S. Jefferson St. (at Main St.). © **850/432-6247.** www.pensacolamuseumofart.org. Admission $5 adults, $2 students and active-duty military, free for children 5 and under; free to all Tues. Tues–Fri 10am–5pm; Sat–Sun noon–5pm.

Historic Districts

In addition to Historic Pensacola Village (see above) in the Seville Historic District, the city has two other preservation areas worth a stroll. The Pensacola visitor center (p. 578) provides free walking-tour maps, if you're interested.

PALAFOX HISTORIC DISTRICT ★★ Running up Palafox Street from the water to Wright Street, the Palafox Historic District is also the downtown business district. Beautiful Spanish Renaissance and Mediterranean-style buildings, including the ornate Saenger Theatre, still stand from the early days. In 1821, Gen. Andrew Jackson formally accepted Florida into the United States during a ceremony in Plaza Ferdinand VII, now a National Historic Landmark. His statue commemorates the event.

For architecture buffs, this district is a theme park, with the 1902 Theisen Building and its vivid displays of Beaux Arts details, as well as the 1925 Saenger Theatre, with its terra-cotta ornamentation and grillwork on the front facade, showcasing it as an elegant gem of the Spanish baroque style.

The Palafox District is home to the **Pensacola Historical Museum,** the **Pensacola Museum of Art,** in the old city jail, and the **T. T. Wentworth, Jr., Florida State Museum** (see "Exploring Historic Pensacola," above, for all three).

For boozehounds, the **Palace Oyster Bar,** 130 E. Government St. (© **850/434-6211**), has a bar from the old Palace Hotel, where Florida's first liquor license was issued.

NORTH HILL PRESERVATION DISTRICT ★ Another entry in the National Register of Historic Places, the North Hill Preservation District covers the 50 square blocks north of the Palafox Historic District bounded by Wright, Blount, Palafox, and Reus streets. Descendants of Spanish nobility, timber barons, British merchants, French Creoles, buccaneers, and Civil War soldiers still live in some of the more than 500 homes. They are not open to the public, but are a bonanza for anyone interested in architecture. In 1863,

Union troops erected a fort in Lee Square, at Palafox and Gadsden streets. It later was dedicated to the Confederacy, complete with a 50-foot-high obelisk and sculpture based on John Elder's painting *After Appomattox.*

A NEARBY ZOO

The Northwest Florida Zoological Park and Botanical Gardens Kids Situated in a 50-acre forest 15 miles east of Pensacola, this zoo, formerly known as, well "The Zoo," has more than 700 exotic animals—including tigers, lions, rhinos, and lowland gorillas—living in landscaped habitats. Japanese gardens, a giraffe-feeding tower, and a petting farm make for a fun visit. A Safari Line train chugs through a 30-acre wildlife preserve with free-ranging herds. The 2003 birth of a Pygmy hippo and a sable antelope here garnered national attention for the zoo on the Animal Planet cable channel. Set aside 3 to 4 hours to cover the entire park. Part of the zoo family is a 110-pound, 6½-foot Komodo dragon named Ivan who resides in the new Dragon World exhibit. In 2006, the zoo saw the births of a baby common waterbuck, and Honeysuckle, a precious baby spider monkey; and new in 2008, an 18-foot-tall giraffe named Colby, 3-inch-tall twin baby golden-headed lion tamarins, and a baby siamang all made their first appearances.

5701 Gulf Breeze Pkwy. (U.S. 98), Gulf Breeze. ✆ **850/932-2229.** www.thezoonorthwestflorida.org. Admission $12 adults, $11 seniors, $8.25 children 3–11. Train rides $3 per person. Carousel rides $2 per person. Daily 9am–5pm. Closed New Year's Eve, Thanksgiving, Christmas Eve, and Christmas Day.

SHOPPING

Sightseeing and shopping can be combined in Pensacola's Palafox and Seville historic districts, where many shops are housed in renovated centuries-old buildings. The **Quayside Art Gallery,** Plaza Ferdinand, at Zaragosa and Jefferson streets (✆ **850/438-2363;** www.quaysidegallery.com), is the largest cooperative gallery in the Southeast. More than 100 artists display their works here. The friendly staff will direct you to other nearby galleries as well.

The **Blue Moon Antique Mall,** 3721 W. Navy Blvd. (✆ **850/455-7377;** www.antiqueguide.biz/bluemoon.htm), is the oldest and largest antiques mall in Pensacola. Open Tuesday to Saturday 10am to 5pm and Sunday noon to 5pm, it has over 65 shops selling antiques and collectibles at reasonable prices.

Browsers will enjoy poking through the 400-dealer space at the **Flea Market,** on U.S. 98 opposite the Zoo, 15 miles east of Pensacola (✆ **850/934-1971**). It's open on Saturday and Sunday from 9am to 5pm. Admission is free.

WHERE TO STAY

The Pensacola visitor center (p. 578) publishes a complete list of rental condominiums and cottages. Among the leading rental agents are **JME Management,** 22-A Via de Luna, Pensacola Beach (✆ **800/554-3695;** www.jmevacations.com), and **Tristan Realty,** 1020 Fort Pickens Rd., Pensacola Beach (✆ **800/445-9931** or 850/932-7363; fax 850/932-8361).

The **Fort Pickens Area** of Gulf Islands National Seashore is your best bet for camping (p. 580).

Escambia County adds a 17% tax to all hotel and campground bills.

The accommodations listed below are arranged by geographic area: downtown Pensacola and Pensacola Beach. Bear in mind that Pensacola Beach is at least a 15-minute drive from downtown.

Tips When Room Rates Are Lowest

Room rates at all Panhandle beaches are highest from mid-May to mid-August, and premiums are charged at Easter, Memorial Day, July 4, and Labor Day. Hotel or motel reservations are essential during these periods. There's another high-priced peak in March, when thousands of raucous college students invade during Spring Break. Economical times to visit are April (except Easter) and September—the weather is warm, most establishments are open, and room rates are significantly lower than during summer. The lowest rates are available during winter, but many attractions and some restaurants may be closed then.

Downtown Pensacola

The University Mall complex at I-10 and Davis Highway, about 5 miles north of downtown, has a host of chain motels, and there's an ample supply of inexpensive restaurants on Plantation Road and in the adjacent mall. Another good bet is the **Hampton Inn Airport,** 2187 Airport Blvd. (✆ **800/426-7866** or 850/478-1123; fax 850/478-8519), in an area that's not as congested as that around University Mall; there's a free shuttle to nearby Cordova Mall and its adjacent chain restaurants.

Several of the town's Victorian homes have been turned into luxurious bed-and-breakfasts. Among the best is **Springhill Guesthouse,** 903 N. Spring St. (✆ **800/475-1956** or 850/438-6887; www.bbonline.com/fl/springhill).

New in 2009 in downtown Pensacola: Solé Inn and Suites, opened on Palafox Street, in the heart of downtown Pensacola (✆ **850/470-9298;** www.soleinnandsuites.com). Rates at the 1950s-style, retro hotel start at $89 and include breakfast and complimentary cocktails from 5 to 7pm.

Crowne Plaza Pensacola Grand ★ Opposite the Civic Center in the Seville Historic District near the southern end of I-110, this unique hotel has turned the historic L&N Railroad Depot into a grand lobby with a bar, restaurants, lounges, and a cozy library. You'll see such turn-of-the-20th-century accouterments as an ornate railroad clock, oak stair rails, imported marble, mosaic-tile floors, and old-fashioned carved furniture. A 15-story glass-and-steel tower behind the depot holds the rooms and suites, which are popular primarily with business travelers and groups.

200 E. Gregory St. (at Alcaniz St.), Pensacola, FL 32501. ✆ **850/433-3336.** Fax 850/432-7572. www.pensacolagrandhotel.com. 210 units. $149–$199 double; $350–$450 suites available. AE, DC, DISC, MC, V. **Amenities:** Restaurant; bar; outdoor pool; exercise room; business center; room service; laundry service. *In room:* A/C, TV, dataport, Wi-Fi, fridge, coffeemaker, hair dryer, iron, safe.

New World Inn ★ Near the scenic bay and in the historic district, this urban, boutiquey version of a comfortable country inn (it looks more like a concrete fortress) is part of a meeting facility known as New World Landing. Inside, however, is an entirely different—and much more pleasing to the eye—story. From the colonial-style lobby, a grand staircase leads to high-ceilinged, spacious rooms. The Inn was renovated in 2007, adding a fresh, contemporary twist to the rooms, including new beds and a sleek decor. Also new at the Inn: 600 South, a wine and martini bar.

600 S. Palafox St. (at Pine St.), Pensacola, FL 32501. ✆ **850/432-4111.** Fax 850/432-6836. www.newworldlanding.com. 16 units. $129 double; $169 suite. Rates include continental breakfast. AE, MC, V. **Amenities:** Access to nearby health club; laundry service. *In room:* A/C, TV, dataport.

Days Inn Pensacola Beachfront This modest hotel has a better view than some fancier hotels could ever dream of, right on the Gulf, and it's notable for its bright, clean, and extra-spacious accommodations that were renovated in 2006. Outside corridors lead to all rooms. Although none of the units have a private balcony, those facing the beach do have great views (and higher prices). Two pools and a playground are on the beach; restaurants are within walking distance.

16 Via de Luna Dr., Pensacola Beach, FL 32561. ✆ **800/934-3301** or 850/934-3300. Fax 850/934-4366. www.pensacolabeachresort.net. 123 units. Summer $159–$199 double; off-season $79–$149 double. Rates include continental breakfast. Golf packages available. AE, DC, DISC, MC, V. **Amenities:** 2 outdoor pools; watersports equipment/rental; game room. *In room:* A/C, TV, dataport, fridge, coffeemaker, hair dryer, iron, microwave.

Hampton Inn Pensacola Beach ★ Kids This pastel, four-story hotel sits on a sliver of land—600 feet, specifically—between Santa Rosa Sound and the Gulf, next to the action on Casino Beach. The bright lobby opens to a sun deck with beachside pools on either side (one is heated). Half of the oversize rooms—recipients of a $6.5-million renovation in 2007—have balconies overlooking the Gulf; these are more expensive than rooms on the bay side, which have nice views but no outside sitting areas. A Tiki bar is directly on the beach, making it a fun place to spend some time. Camp Hampton is an excellent children's program with supervised activities; it costs $20 for the first child and $10 for each additional child, and includes a meal.

2 Via de Luna, Pensacola Beach, FL 32561. ✆ **800/320-8108** or 850/932-6800. Fax 850/932-6833. www.hamptonbeachresort.com. 181 units. Summer $169–$199 double, $299 suite; off-season $109–$149 double, $399 suite. Rates include continental breakfast. AE, DC, DISC, MC, V. **Amenities:** Bar; 2 outdoor pools; access to nearby health club; exercise room; watersports equipment/rental; laundry service; coin-op washers/dryers. *In room:* A/C, TV, dataport, fridge, coffeemaker, hair dryer, iron.

Portofino Island Resort and Spa ★★★ Kids The only luxe spot in the area, the Portofino is a stunning, Mediterranean-style, 28-acre condominium resort at the quieter east end of Pensacola Beach adjacent to the pristine beaches of the Gulf Islands National Seashore. In 2007, the resort completed its fifth tower and now offers more than 300 sky homes. Designed as tower residences, its richly decorated suites are spectacular and feel very much like luxury apartments, with panoramic views of the Gulf and Santa Rosa Bay. The resort boasts an indoor Olympic-size pool and seven heated pools; whirlpool spas, saunas, and steam rooms; a spa offering many treatments; indoor and outdoor dining restaurant; and a complimentary water shuttle to the Pensacola Boardwalk for shopping and entertainment and tram service to Tiger Point, a 36-hole championship golf course. Guests who book direct enjoy lush spa towels upon arrival, beach chair set for two, tennis court time, access to the 40,000-square-foot Lifestyle Center with state-of-the-art fitness center, and unlimited DVD rentals. Guests also enjoy one round of golf per day on any of the four Emerald Coast Golf Trail courses as well as a deep-sea fishing excursion (per party).

10 Portofino Dr., Pensacola Beach, FL 32561. ✆ **866/478-3400** or 850/916-5000. Fax 850/916-5010. www.portofinoisland.com. 315 units. Summer $388–$529 2- or 3-bedroom apt; off-season $250–$309 2- or 3-bedroom apt. AE, DC, DISC, MC, V. **Amenities:** 2 restaurants; bar; 8 pools; 5 Rubico tennis courts; fitness center; watersports equipment/rentals; children's program. *In room:* A/C, TV, high-speed Internet access, gourmet kitchen, coffeemaker, hair dryer, iron, washer/dryer.

Pensacola

Dharma Blue ★★★ CAFE Occupying a restored Victorian home overlooking Seville Square in Historic Pensacola Village, Dharma Blue is a cozy cafe with an expansive menu featuring everything from sushi to an excellent pork tenderloin with molasses-braised collard greens over roasted red potatoes with whole grain mustard beurre blanc. For lunch, try the prime rib po' boy, with shaved prime rib on gambino bread, crunchy cabbage, tomato, onion, and horseradish-cracked black pepper mayonnaise.

300 S. Alcaniz St. ✆ **850/433-1275.** www.dharmablue.com. Reservations recommended. Main courses $16–$28. AE, DISC, MC, V. Mon–Sat 11am–4pm; Mon–Thurs 5–10pm; Fri–Sat 5–11pm; Sun 5–9pm.

Marina Oyster Barn ★ Value SEAFOOD Exuding the ambience of the quickly vanishing Old Florida fish camps, this plain but clean restaurant at the Johnson-Rooks Marina is a local legend. It's been a local favorite since 1969, for both its view and its down-home seafood. Freshly shucked oysters, served raw, steamed, fried, or Rockefeller style, are the main feature; but the seafood salad is also first-rate, and the fish, shrimp, and oysters are breaded with cornmeal in true Southern fashion. The daily luncheon specials give you a light meal at a bargain price.

505 Bayou Blvd. (on Bayou Texar). ✆ **850/433-0511.** www.marinaoysterbarn.com. Main courses $8–$16; sandwiches $5–$7; lunch specials $5–$7. AE, DISC, MC, V. Tues–Sat 11am–9pm (lunch specials 11am–2pm). Go east on Cervantes St. (U.S. 90) across the Bayou Texar Bridge, then take 1st left on Stanley Ave., and turn left again to the end of Strong St.

McGuire's Irish Pub ★ STEAKS/SEAFOOD Every day is St. Patrick's Day at this bustling pub with the motto "Feasting, Imbibery, and Debauchery." The menu is delectably Irish, complete with Irish stew and corned beef and cabbage. Supersize steaks are the best offerings, however, as are hickory-smoked ribs and chicken. You can also order seafood, including a hearty bouillabaisse with shrimp, red snapper, clams, mussels, and oysters. The big burgers come with a choice of more than 20 toppings, from smoked Gouda cheese to sautéed Vidalia onions. You can watch your ale being brewed in copper kettles and dine in a cellarlike room where 8,000 bottles of wine are on display. Live music is offered most nights. There's another McGuire's on Destin Beach, 33 Hwy. 98 (✆ **850/650-0000**).

600 E. Gregory St. (btw. 11th and 12th aves.). ✆ **850/433-6789.** www.mcguiresirishpub.com. Main courses $18–$30; snacks, burgers, and sandwiches $8–$12. AE, DC, DISC, MC, V. Daily 11am–midnight, later on weekends.

Skopelos on the Bay ★ SEAFOOD/STEAK/GREEK If you didn't know any better—or drank too much ouzo—you'd think you were in Santorini. Perched on a bluff overlooking the bay, this family-owned restaurant has been famous hereabouts since 1959 for its great views and creative seafood dishes, such as the scamp Cervantes (scamp is a deepwater fish with white, flaky meat) and the Mediterranean-style grouper prepared with tomato and roasted eggplant. The menu also features chargrilled steaks and, befitting the owner's Greek heritage, roast lamb served with moussaka, dolmades, *tiropita,* and spanakopita. In warm weather, opt for an outside table with a bay view.

670 Scenic Hwy. (U.S. 90 E., at E. Cervantes St.). ✆ **850/432-6565.** www.myskopelos.com. Reservations recommended. Main courses $16–$30. AE, DISC, MC, V. Tues–Thurs and Sat 5–10:30pm; Fri 11:30am–2:30pm and 5–10:30pm.

Pensacola Beach

Flounder's Chowder & Ale House ★★ SEAFOOD Floundering around for a place where you can get fresh fish cooked any way, accompanied by live reggae almost nightly? Then you need to be at Flounder's Chowder & Ale House, on the boardwalk overlooking the Santa Rosa Sound, where you'll find great food for breakfast, brunch, lunch, dinner, or late-night snacks. The best of the offerings include the Maine lobster and the chargrilled tuna, grouper, and mahimahi. If you're lucky, a big smoker grill outside will be producing more fish and exceptional ribs. Burgers, salads, and sandwiches are offered all day. The dining room is cool and not at all what you'd expect from a fish house; its bookshelves, confessional booth walls straight from a New Orleans church, and stained-glass windows imported from a convent, of all places, contribute to a cozy, Nantucket-in-the-winter kind of feel. But when the weather's warm, you'll definitely want to be outdoors.

800 Quietwater Beach Rd. (at Via de Luna and Fort Pickens Rd.). ✆ **850/932-2003.** www.flounderschowderhouse.com. Main courses $15–$21; burgers and sandwiches $8–$10. AE, DC, DISC, MC, V. Sun–Thurs 11am–midnight (to 11pm in winter); Fri–Sat 11am–2am (to 11pm in winter).

PENSACOLA AFTER DARK

For what's hip and happening when the sun goes down, pick up the daily *Pensacola News Journal* (www.pensacolanewsjournal.com), especially its Friday entertainment section. Another good source for nightly events is the *Pensacola Downtown Crowd* (www.downtownpensacola.com), a free publication available at the visitor center (p. 578).

THE PERFORMING ARTS Pensacola has a surprisingly sophisticated array of entertainment choices for such a relatively small city. For a schedule of events, get a copy of *Vision,* a bimonthly newsletter published by the Arts Council of Northwest Florida (✆ **850/432-9906;** www.artsnwfl.org). Also pick up **Sneak Preview,** a calendar of events at the Pensacola Civic Center and the Saenger Theatre. Both publications are available at the visitor center (p. 578). Tickets for all major performances can be purchased from **Ticketmaster** (✆ **800/488-5252** or 850/433-6311; www.ticketmaster.com).

The highlight venue here is the ornate **Saenger Theatre** ★, 118 S. Palafox St., near Romana Street (✆ **850/444-7686;** www.pensacolasaenger.com), a painstakingly restored

Fun Facts The Last Great Road House

Sitting precisely on the Florida-Alabama state line on Perdido Key, about 15 miles west of downtown Pensacola, the **Flora-Bama Lounge,** 17401 Perdido Key Dr. (✆ **850/492-0611;** www.florabama.com), is almost a shrine to country music. Billing itself as the "Last Great American Road House," this Gulf-side pub is famous for its Saturday and Sunday jam sessions from noon until way past midnight. Flora-Bama is the prime sponsor and a key venue for the Frank Brown International Songwriters' Festival, held during the first week of November. But the wackiest shindig held here has to be the Interstate Mullet Toss and Beach Party (the last weekend in Apr), which defies more in-depth description. The raw oyster bar is popular all the time. Granted, the joint can get a bit rough from time to time, but you won't soon forget the great Gulf views while sipping a cold one at the Deck Bar. The Flora-Bama is open daily from 8:30am to 2:30am.

masterpiece of Spanish baroque architecture. Presentations feature the local opera company and symphony orchestra, Broadway musicals, and touring performers. The 10,000-seat **Pensacola Civic Center,** 201 E. Gregory St., at Alcaniz Street (✆ **850/432-0800;** www.pensacolaciviccenter.com), hosts a variety of concerts, exhibitions, sports events, and conventions. Call ahead for the current schedule.

THE CLUB & BAR SCENE Pensacola's downtown nighttime entertainment center is **Seville Quarter,** 130 E. Government St., at Jefferson Street (✆ **850/434-6211;** www.rosies.com), in the Seville Historic District. This restored antique-brick complex with New Orleans–style wrought-iron balconies is actually a collection of pubs and restaurants whose names capture the ambience: Rosie O'Grady's Goodtime Emporium, Palace Oyster Bar (see earlier in this chapter), Lili Marlene's Aviator's Pub, Apple Annie's Courtyard, End o' the Alley Bar, Phineas Phogg's Balloon Works (a dance hall, not a balloon shop), and Fast Eddie's Billiard Parlor (which has electronic games, too). The pubs serve up libations, food, and live entertainment from Dixieland jazz to country and western. Get a monthly calendar at the information booth next to Rosie O'Grady's. Seville Quarter is open daily from 11am to 2am.

Every night is party time at **McGuire's Irish Pub,** the city's popular Irish pub, brewery, and eatery (p. 590). Irish bands appear nightly during summer, and on Saturday and Sunday the rest of the year.

Beach nightlife centers on **Quietwater Boardwalk,** Via de Luna at Fort Pickens Road (no phone), a shopping-and-dining complex on Santa Rosa Sound. With the lively beach-and-reggae bar at **Flounder's Chowder & Ale House** (p. 591) just a few steps away, it's easy to barhop until you find a band to your liking. Across Via de Luna, at Casino Beach, is the **Dock** (✆ **850/934-3314**), which has live bands nightly in summer, and on weekends off-season. Finally, **Sidelines Sports Bar & Restaurant** (✆ **850/934-3660;** www.sidelinessportsbarandrestaurant.com) has a great game lineup.

2 DESTIN & FORT WALTON BEACH ★★

40 miles E of Pensacola; 160 miles W of Tallahassee

Sitting on a round harbor off East Pass, which lets broad and beautiful Choctawhatchee Bay flow into the Gulf of Mexico, Destin, along with Fort Walton Beach and Okaloosa Island, comprises the Emerald Coast. It's justly famous for its fishing fleet, the largest in the state. It's also Northwest Florida's fastest-growing and most upscale vacation destination, with a multitude of high-rise condominiums, the huge Sandestin resort, several golf courses, and some of the Panhandle's best restaurants and lively nightspots. By and large, Destin attracts a more affluent crowd than Fort Walton Beach, its more down-to-earth neighbor.

Although Fort Walton Beach has its own strip of white sand on Okaloosa Island, the city's economy is supported less by tourism than by the sprawling Eglin Air Force Base. Covering more than 700 square miles, Eglin is the world's largest air base and is home to the U.S. Air Force's Armament Museum and the 33rd Tactical Fighter Wing, the "Top Guns" of Operation Desert Storm in 1991.

To the east of Destin, development is picking up steam along the beaches of southern Walton County. Still, this picturesque area has mostly cottages nestled among rolling sand dunes covered with sea oats. Here you'll find Grayton Beach State Park, which sports one of America's finest beaches, and the quaint, albeit Stepford-esque planned village of **Seaside** ★★, which served as the set for Jim Carrey's movie *The Truman Show.* Seaside was built on a lovely stretch of beach in the 1980s, but with Victorian architecture that makes it look a century older. The village's Gulf-side honeymoon cottages are some of Florida's most romantic retreats. Seaside also has interesting shops and galleries; a stamp-size, Greek Revival–style post office; and a resident population of artists, writers, and other creative folks, who permit only their own cars in their relatively expensive little enclave. Don't worry, there are parking spaces for tourists on the one main road through Seaside, but you can't drive into the village itself unless you live there. Although I appreciate Seaside for what it is, the secret had gotten out by the last time I was there, and the village was slowly falling under the weight of commercialism and tourism.

ESSENTIALS

GETTING THERE Flights arriving at and departing from **Okaloosa Regional Airport** (**© 850/651-7160;** www.flyvps.com) actually use the enormous strips at Eglin Air Force Base. The terminal is on Florida 85, north of Fort Walton Beach, and is served by **Delta** (**© 800/221-1212**), **Northwest** (**© 800/225-2525**), and **US Airways** (**© 800/428-4322**).

Avis (**© 800/331-1212**), **Budget** (**© 800/527-0700**), **Hertz** (**© 800/654-3131**), and **National** (**© 800/CAR-RENT** [227-7368]) have rental cars at the airport, while **Enterprise** (**© 800/325-8007**) is located in town.

Bayside Shuttle (**© 850/581-1505;** www.baysideshuttle.com) provides 24-hour van transportation to and from the airport. Fares are based on a three-person minimum: $24 to Fort Walton Beach, $40 to Destin, $18 to Sandestin, and $75 to southern Walton County.

The **Amtrak** (**© 800/872-7245;** www.amtrak.com) *Sunset Limited* transcontinental service stops at Crestview, 26 miles north of Fort Walton Beach.

VISITOR INFORMATION For advance information on both Fort Walton Beach and Destin, contact the **Emerald Coast Convention and Visitors Bureau,** P.O. Box 609, Fort Walton Beach, FL 32549 (**© 800/322-3319** or 850/651-7122; fax 850/651-7149; www.destin-fwb.com). The bureau shares quarters with the **Okaloosa County Visitors Welcome Center** in a tin-roofed, beachside building on Miracle Strip Parkway (U.S. 98), on Okaloosa Island at the eastern edge of Fort Walton Beach. Stop here for brochures, maps, and other information. This visitor center is open Monday through Friday from 8am to 5pm, Saturday and Sunday from 10am to 4pm.

The **Destin Area Chamber of Commerce,** 4484 Legendary Dr., Destin, FL 32541 (**© 850/837-6241;** fax 850/654-5612; www.destinchamber.com), gives away brochures and sells maps of the area. The chamber is in an office complex at the entry to Regatta Bay Golf & Country Club, on U.S. 98, a half-mile east of the Mid-Bay Bridge. It's open Monday through Friday from 9am to 5pm; closed holidays.

For information on the beaches of South Walton, contact the **South Walton Tourist Development Council,** P.O. Box 1248, Santa Rosa Beach, FL 32459 (**© 800/822-6877** or 850/267-1216; fax 850/267-3943; www.beachesofsouthwalton.com). Its visitor center is at the intersection of U.S. 98 and U.S. 331, in Santa Rosa Beach (**© 850/267-3511**); open daily from 8:30am to 5:30pm.

GETTING AROUND The **Okaloosa County Tourist Development Council** (**© 850/651-7131;** www.destin-fwb.com) operates a free **Island Shuttle** trolley during the summer months along the entire length of Santa Rosa Boulevard on Okaloosa Island. The two trolleys run every 30 minutes Sunday through Thursday from 7am to 10pm,

How to Find a Street Address

Don't worry about getting lost, as most of what you'll want to see and do in Destin and Fort Walton Beach is either on, or no more than a few blocks from, U.S. 98, the area's main east–west drag. Finding a street address is another matter, however, because even many local residents don't fully comprehend the post office's bizarre naming and numbering system along U.S. 98.

In Fort Walton Beach, U.S. 98 is known as "Miracle Strip Parkway," with "southwest" and "southeast" addresses on the mainland and "east" addresses on Okaloosa Island.

In Destin, U.S. 98 is officially known as "Highway 98 East" from the Destin Bridge east to Airport Road, and street numbers get progressively higher as you head east from the bridge. East of Airport Road, however, the post office calls U.S. 98 the "Emerald Coast Parkway"—although locals still say a place is on "98 East." The highway is also known as the Emerald Coast Parkway in Walton County, but the street-numbering system changes completely once you pass the county line.

Adding to the confusion in Destin, "Old Highway 98 East" is a short spur from Airport Road to the western side of Henderson Beach State Park, and "Scenic Highway 98 East" parallels the real U.S. 98 along the beach from the eastern side of Henderson Beach to Sandestin.

In other words, call and ask for directions if you're not sure how to find an establishment here.

and Friday and Saturday from 7am to 1am. They also connect the island to the uptown bus station, on Eglin Parkway Northeast, on the Fort Walton Beach mainland.

For a cab in Fort Walton Beach, call **Black and Gold Taxi** (✆ **850/244-7303**) or **Yellow Cab** (✆ **850/244-3600**). In Destin, call **Destin Taxi** (✆ **850/654-5700**). Fares are usually $2.25 at flag fall and $2.25 each additional mile.

TIME The area is in the Central time zone, 1 hour behind Miami, Orlando, and Jacksonville.

HITTING THE BEACH

DESTIN Like an oasis in the middle of Destin's rapid development, the 208-acre **Henderson Beach State Park** ★★, east of Destin Harbor on U.S. 98, allows easy access to swimming, sunning, surf fishing, picnicking, and seabird-watching along its 1½ miles of beach. There are restrooms, outdoor showers, and surf chairs for people with disabilities. The area is open daily from 8am to sunset. Admission is $4 per vehicle with up to eight occupants, $1 per pedestrian or cyclist. Several good restaurants are just outside the park's western boundary. Pets on leashes are allowed in the park, including the beach and campground. Campers will find 60 sites in a wooded setting here; they cost $21, including electricity, and can be reserved up to 11 months in advance. For camping reservations, call ✆ **800/326-3521** or go to www.reserveamerica.com. For more information, contact the park at 1700 Emerald Coast Pkwy., Destin, FL 32541 (✆ **850/837-7550;** www.floridastateparks.org/hendersonbeach).

The **James W. Lee Park,** between Destin and Sandestin, on Scenic Hwy. 98, has a long white-sand beach and overlooking it are covered picnic tables, an ice-cream parlor, and a moderately priced seafood restaurant with great views.

FORT WALTON BEACH Do your loafing on the white sands of **Okaloosa Island,** joined to the mainland by the high-rise Brooks Bridge over Santa Rosa Sound. Most resort hotels and amusement parks are grouped around the Gulfarium marine park on U.S. 98, east of the bridge. Here you'll find the **Boardwalk,** a collection of tin-roofed beachside buildings that have an arcade for the kids, a saloon for adults, covered picnic areas, a summertime snack bar, and a seafood restaurant. Just to the east, you can use the restrooms, cold-water showers, and other free facilities at **Beasley Park,** home of the Okaloosa County Visitor Welcome Center.

Across U.S. 98, the Okaloosa portion of the **Gulf Islands National Seashore** has picnic areas and sailboats for rent on Choctawhatchee Bay, plus access to the Gulf. Admission to this part of the national seashore is free.

SOUTHERN WALTON COUNTY Sporting the finest stretch of white sand on the Gulf, **Grayton Beach State Park★★★**, on C.R. 30A, also has 356 acres of pine forests surrounding scenic Western Lake. There's a boat ramp and a campground with electric hookups on the lake. Get a leaflet at the main gate for a self-guided tour of the nature trail. Pets are not allowed anywhere in the recreation area. The park is open daily from 8am to sunset. Admission is $4 per vehicle with up to eight occupants, $1 per pedestrian or bicyclist. Campsites cost $19, including electricity. For camping reservations, call ✆ **800/326-3521** or go to www.reserveamerica.com. For general information, contact the park at 357 Main Park Rd., Santa Rosa Beach, FL 32459 (✆ **850/231-4210;** www.floridastateparks.org/graytonbeach).

Seaside has free parking along C.R. 30A and is a good spot for a day at the beach, a stroll or bike ride around the quaint village, and a tasty meal at one of its restaurants. The same goes for **Seagrove Beach,** which has some charming eateries.

OUTDOOR ACTIVITIES

BOATING Pontoon boats are highly popular for use on the back bays and for Sunday-afternoon floating parties in East Pass. Several companies rent them, including **Gilligan's Watersports** (✆ **850/650-9000;** www.destinadventure.com) and **Brooks Bridge Bait and Tackle** (✆ **850/243-5721;** www.destin-ation.com). Expect to pay about $80 for a half-day, $125 for a full day.

FISHING Billing itself as the "World's Luckiest Fishing Village," Destin has Florida's largest charter-boat fleet, with more than 140 vessels based at the marinas lining the north shore of Destin Harbor, on U.S. 98, east of the Destin Bridge. Arranging a trip is as easy as walking along the Destin Harbor waterfront, where you'll find the booking booths of several agents, the best being **Harborwalk Charters** (✆ **800/242-2824** or 850/837-2343; www.harborwalkfishing.com). Rates for private charters range from about $100 per person to $300 per person, depending on the length of the voyage.

For additional information on small- and large-group charters, check out **FishDestin.com** (✆ **850/837-9401** or 850/585-0049; www.fishdestin.com). If you're a die-hard angler, consider coming in October for the **Destin Fishing Rodeo** (✆ **850/837-6734;** www.destinfishingrodeo.org), a month-long fishing extravaganza.

You don't have to go to sea to fish from the catwalk of the 3,000-foot **Destin Bridge,** over East Pass. The marinas and bait shops at Destin Harbor can provide gear, bait, and fishing licenses. In Fort Walton Beach, you can cast a line off **Okaloosa Island Fishing**

 Pier, 1030 Miracle Strip Pkwy. E./U.S. 98 (✆ **850/244-1023;** www.okaloosaislandpier.com), open 24 hours a day. Adults pay $7 to fish, seniors $6; children 12 and under pay $4. Observers pay $1. Bait and equipment rentals are available.

GOLF For advance information on area courses, contact the **Emerald Coast Golf Association,** P.O. Box 304, Destin, FL 32540. Also look for *South Coast Golf Guide,* the free annual directory published in Pensacola; see p. 57 for details. Be sure to ask whether your choice of accommodations offers golf packages, which can mean significant savings.

For course information, go to www.golf.com or www.floridagolfing.com; or call the **Florida Sports Foundation** (✆ **850/488-8347**) or **Florida Golfing** (✆ **866/833-2663**).

On the mainland, nonresidents are welcome to play at the city-owned **Fort Walton Beach Golf Club,** on Lewis Turner Boulevard (C.R. 189) north of town (✆ **850/833-9530**). The club has two 18-hole courses—the **Pines** and the **Oaks** (✆ **850/833-9528**)—plus a pro shop. Greens fees at both courses are about $18 to $27 year-round, including cart.

In Destin, scenic **Indian Bayou Golf and Country Club,** off Airport Road (✆ **850/837-6191;** www.indianbayougolf.com), has three 9-hole courses with large greens and wide fairways. They look easy, but watch out for water hazards and strategically placed hidden bunkers! Greens fees, including cart, are about $50 to $75.

Sandestin Golf and Beach Resort (p. 601), on U.S. 98 East, in southern Walton County (✆ **850/267-8211** for tee times; www.sandestin.com), is the largest facility here. Its 72 holes are spread over three outstanding championship courses. The Baytowne and Links courses overlook Choctawhatchee Bay. Fees for 18 holes are $69 to $115 for resort guests, $89 to $155 for nonguests.

Some of the 18 championship holes at **Emerald Bay Golf Club,** 2 miles east of the Mid-Bay Bridge on U.S. 98 (✆ **850/837-5197;** www.emeraldbaygolfclub.com), run along Choctawhatchee Bay; the water adds both beauty and challenges to the otherwise wide and forgiving fairways. Greens fees are about $95 with cart, $75 in winter.

In southern Walton County, the semiprivate **Santa Rosa Golf & Beach Club,** off C.R. 30A in Dune Allen Beach (✆ **850/267-2229;** www.santarosaclub.com), offers a challenging 18-hole course through tall pines looking out to vistas of the Gulf. The club has a pro shop, a beachside restaurant, a lounge, and tennis courts. Fees are about $29 to $55 for nonmembers, or "social guests."

In Niceville, a 20-minute drive north via the Mid-Bay Bridge, nonguests may play golf (four 9-hole courses; $43 to $75) or tennis (21 courts; $10/hr.) at the **Bluewater Bay Resort** (✆ **850/897-3241;** www.bwbresort.com), which also has condominiums for rent.

Call ahead for reservations and current fees at all these clubs; also ask about afternoon and early-evening specials.

SAILING **Sailing South,** on U.S. 98 at Destin Harbor (✆ **850/837-7245**), has half-day cruises aboard the 72-foot schooner *Daniel Webster Clements.* The 2½-hour afternoon cruises stop for swimming and snorkeling virtually under the Destin Bridge; these cost $40 for adults and $25 for kids 11 and under. It also offers 2½-hour sunset cruises for the same price. The 54-foot schooner ***Nathaniel Bowditch*** (✆ **850/650-8787;** www.bowditchsailing.com) will take you on sunset cruises, $35 per person, and half-day shelling excursions, $40 per person.

SCUBA DIVING & SNORKELING At least a dozen dive shops are located along the beaches. Considered one of the best, **Scuba Tech Diving Charters** has two locations in Destin: at 301 U.S. 98 E. (© **850/837-2822;** www.scubatechnwfl.com) and at 10004 U.S. 98 E. (© **850/837-1933**), about a half-mile west of the Sandestin Beach Resort.

WATERSPORTS Hobie Cats, WaveRunners, jet boats, jet skis, and parasailing are available all along the beach. The largest selection of operators is at the marina just east of the Destin Bridge, behind the Hooters and Fat Tuesday's pubs. These include **Boogies** (© **850/654-4497;** www.boogieswatersports.com) and **Gilligan's of Destin** (© **850/650-9000;** www.gilligansofdestin.com).

If surfing the wild surf is a bit too adventurous for you, check out **YOLO Boarding,** 820 N. County Hwy. 393, in Santa Rosa Beach (© **850/496-7286**), a new kind of "surfing" that suits those who love the water but not the wave action. YOLO (an acronym for You Only Live Once) involves standing up and paddling on a big, safe, comfortable long-board, offering a whole new point of view—from paddling with dolphins or sneaking up on blue crabs to dropping in at your favorite surf-break or just enjoying the view towards the beach. YOLO-ing, or stand-up paddling, has evolved from its surfing roots to a far more gentle way to enjoy time on the water from a new perspective—anywhere—anytime.

EXPLORING THE AREA

Eden Gardens State Park Evoking images from *Gone With the Wind,* these 115 acres house the magnificent 1895 Greek Revival–style Wesley Mansion, which has been lovingly restored and richly furnished with period antiques. The second-largest collection of Louis XVI furniture in the country is here, along with a Chippendale nightstand worth about $1 million. The mansion overlooks scenic Choctawhatchee Bay and is surrounded by immense Spanish moss–draped oak trees. The house is particularly stunning during Christmastime, when it is draped in lights and decoration. The Eden Gardens are resplendent with camellias and azaleas. Your visit won't be complete without a guided tour of the house, so avoid coming here on a Tuesday or Wednesday. Picnicking is allowed on the plantation grounds.

181 Eden Gardens Rd. (off C.R. 395), Point Washington. © **850/231-4214.** www.floridastateparks.org/edengardens. Grounds and gardens $3 per vehicle, $1 per pedestrian or bicyclist. Mansion tours $3 adults, $1.50 children 12 and under. Gardens and grounds daily 8am–sunset. 45-min. mansion tours on the hour Thurs–Mon 10am–3pm. Take C.R. 395 north from Hwy. 98. Proceed for a mile; park entrance is on the left.

Florida's Gulfarium Kids The country's second-oldest marine park (it opened in 1955) presents ongoing 25-minute shows with dolphins, sea lions, Peruvian penguins, loggerhead turtles, sharks, stingrays, moray eels, and alligators. Fascinating exhibits include the Living Sea, with special windows for viewing undersea life. During one of the shows, a scuba diver explains the sea life while swimming among the various creatures. The Spotted Dolphin Encounter is a terrific program in which brave participants receive an up-close-and-personal hand-to-flipper encounter with two of the dolphins, Kiwi and Daphne. A trainer will guide you through the 40-minute interactive session. If you're not satisfied with just seeing a few dolphins and leaving, expect to spend about 3 hours here between all the shows and exhibits. (Be aware that swimming with dolphins has both its critics and supporters. You may want to visit the Whale and Dolphin Conservation Society's website at www.wdcs.org. For more information about responsible travel in general, check out www.treadlightly.org and www.ecotourism.org.)

1010 Miracle Strip Pkwy. (U.S. 98), on Okaloosa Island. ✆ **850/244-5169.** www.gulfarium.com. Admission $19 adults, $17 seniors, $11 children 4–11; Dolphin Encounter $150. Mid-May to Labor Day daily 9am–8pm (last entry at 6pm); Labor Day to mid-May daily 9am–6pm (last entry at 4pm).

Indian Temple Mound and Museum This ceremonial mound, one of the largest ever discovered, dates from A.D. 1200. The museum showcases some of its 6,000 ceramic artifacts from southeastern American Indian tribes, the nation's largest such collection. Exhibits depict the lifestyles of the four tribes that lived in the Choctawhatchee Bay region for 12,000 years.

139 Miracle Strip Pkwy. SE, on the mainland. ✆ **850/833-9595.** Park admission free; museum $5 adults, $4.50 seniors, $3 children 4–17. Park daily dawn–dusk. Museum Sept–May Mon–Fri 11am–4pm, Sat 9am–4pm; June–Aug Mon–Sat 9am–4:30pm, Sun 12:30–4:30pm.

U.S. Air Force Armament Museum ★ Although this fascinating museum is not on a par with Pensacola's National Museum of Naval Aviation (p. 584), you'll love it if you're into warplanes. Located on the world's largest air base, it traces military developments from World War II to Operation Desert Storm. Reconnaissance, fighter, and bomber planes, including the SR-71 Blackbird spy plane, are on display.

100 Museum Dr., off Eglin Pkwy. (Fla. 85) at Eglin Air Force Base, 5 miles north of downtown. ✆ **850/882-4062.** www.afarmamentmuseum.com. Free admission. Daily 9:30am–4:30pm. Closed federal holidays.

SHOPPING

Silver Sands Factory Stores ★★, on U.S. 98 between Destin and Sandestin (✆ **800/510-6255** or 850/864-9771; www.silversandsoutlet.com), has more than 120 upscale stores, such as Liz Claiborne, DKNY, J. Crew, Brooks Brothers, Coach, Bose, and so on. Shops are open Monday through Saturday from 10am to 9pm (to 7pm Jan–Feb), Sunday from 10am to 6pm (noon–6pm Jan–Feb). There are also electronic games for kids and a sports bar for adults.

Over at the Sandestin Beach Resort on U.S. 98, you can window-shop in the **Market at Sandestin,** where boutiques sell expensive clothing, gifts, and Godiva chocolates.

WHERE TO STAY

The area has a vast supply of condominiums and cottages for rent. One good-value example is Venus by the Sea, listed below. The visitor information offices (p. 593) will provide lists of others. The largest rental agent is **Resort Quest,** 3500 Emerald Coast Pkwy., Destin (✆ **888/909-6807;** fax 850/654-2937; www.abbott-resorts.com), which publishes a magazine-size annual brochure picturing and describing its many properties throughout the area.

The **Flamingo Cottage,** on Santa Rosa Beach (✆ **832/309-5866;** www.flamingocottage.com), is perfect for families or groups (it can sleep up to 16), with fabulous features such as stone tiles, 9-foot bead-board ceilings, crown moldings, an oak staircase, and a master suite with Jacuzzi and private covered balcony. In addition to a large den and kitchen, laundry room, and outdoor gas grill, the cottage has four bedrooms and three bathrooms. Rates are $250 to $340 nightly, or $1,475 to $3,200 per week, depending on the season.

There are several commercial campgrounds here, but the best camping is at **Henderson Beach State Park,** in Destin, and at **Grayton Beach State Park,** in south Walton County (p. 594 and 595).

State and local governments add 11% tax to all hotel and campground bills.

xpensive units, in the adjacent building, overlook a parking lot. Though the and, the hotel's views make up for that. On-site dining options include a bar-ck out in the tropical forest. The Boardwalk beach pavilion and restaurants are r.

iracle Strip Pkwy. (U.S. 98), Fort Walton Beach, FL 32548. ✆ **800/874-8962** or 850/243-9161. 243-2391. www.ramadafwb.com. 335 units. Summer $176–$279 double; off-season $79–$99 AE, DC, DISC, MC, V. **Amenities:** 3 restaurants; 3 bars; 2 outdoor pools (1 heated); exercise room; watersports equipment/rental; children's programs; game room; limited room service; coin-op s/dryers. *In room:* A/C, TV, dataport, fridge, coffeemaker, hair dryer, iron, safe.

us by the Sea ★ (Value) Offering considerably more space than a hotel normally ld at these rates, this pleasant three-story enclave on western Okaloosa Island was t in the 1970s and has been well maintained ever since, though the decor is still stuck that era (think retirement home) and should be updated. Each of the one-, two-, and ree-bedroom units has a long living/dining/kitchen area, with a rear door leading to a alcony or a patio that opens onto a grassy courtyard. The beach is a short walk across he dunes, and you can stroll along the undeveloped beach at an Eglin Air Force Base auxiliary facility about 600 feet away. The same management operates the new and much more luxurious **Sea Crest Condominiums** (see above), and Venus guests can use the indoor/outdoor pool there.

885 Santa Rosa Blvd., Fort Walton Beach, FL 32548. ✆ **800/476-1885** or 850/301-9600. Fax 850/301-9205. www.venuscondos.com. 45 units. Summer $140–$205 apt; off-season $115–$180 apt. Weekly and monthly rates available. Ask about off-season specials. MC, V. **Amenities:** Outdoor pool; tennis court; coin-op washers/dryers. *In room:* A/C, TV/VCR, kitchen, coffeemaker, iron.

Southern Walton County

If you want to stay near the Sandestin Golf and Beach Resort (see below) without paying its prices, there's a modern **Sleep Inn,** 5000 Emerald Coast Pkwy./U.S. 98 (✆ **800/627-5337** or 850/654-7022), just a mile west. Opened in 2007, **Emerald Grande** (✆ **866/755-7824;** www.legendaryresorts.com) is a luxury condo/hotel situated on 15 acres in Destin Harbor. While most units are owned by individuals, some are available for nightly (minimum 3-night stay) and weekly rental. Amenities include a recreational sun deck resting 63 feet above sea level, with luxurious swimming pools, the new location of beloved waterfront eatery Harry T's (see "Where to Dine," below), a full-service spa and fitness center, a 24-hour concierge, and more.

Hilton Sandestin Beach & Golf Resort ★★ (Kids) This all-inclusive, all-suites beachside resort, housed in two adjacent towers, is the top full-service hotel here. It's nicely situated on the grounds of Sandestin Golf and Beach Resort (see the next listing) and shares its golf and tennis facilities. Enjoy a casual meal overlooking the Gulf at Barefoots Beachside Bar & Grill, or dine at the hotel's AAA Four-Diamond award-winning Seagar's Prime Steaks and Seafood Restaurant. For ultimate pampering and relaxation, visit their Serenity by the Sea spa and fitness center, which includes separate men's and women's locker areas with steam room, sauna, and cascading whirlpool. Executive suites in one wing are equipped primarily for business travelers and conventioneers (lots of meeting space here), while the spacious junior suites in the old wing are geared toward families, with a special area for children's bunk beds. Parents can send the kids off to a supervised summertime program while pampering themselves at the full-service spa. Miniature golf, three pools, 15 tennis courts, four championship golf courses, and the stunning private beach make for a very enticing stay. The resort offers a convenient tram

Destin and Destin Beach

The local **Motel 6,** 405 U.S. 98 E. (✆ **800/466-83**... 5325; www.motel6.com), across the highway from the... ally larger than those at other members of this cut-rat... pool on the premises.

Henderson Park Inn ★★★ Overlooking 6,000 feet ... decidedly Nantucket-style bed-and-breakfast is nestled at th... eastern edge of the Henderson State Park. Featuring Victor... large veranda, and private terraces overlooking the Gulf of Mex... is a stellar option for couples looking to rekindle the romance... provided in your room upon arrival, a nightly wine reception ... whirlpools, and even some with fireplaces. Best of all, it's an adults-... lunches are ideal to take to a picnic on the beach; and, for those wit... community fridge is stocked with candy bars.

2700 Scenic Hwy. 98, Destin, FL 32541. ✆ **866/398-4432** or 850/269-8646. Fax ... forhendersonparkinn.com. 35 units. Summer $259–$539 double; off-season $169–$... include continental breakfast, gourmet boxed lunches, unlimited beer and wine at ha... bars and sodas, wine/grapes/flowers in room upon arrival. AE, DISC, MC, V. **Amenities:** ... door pools; exercise room; Jacuzzi; free use of kayaks; free use of bikes; business center; coi... dryers; beach service. *In room:* A/C, TV, dataport, fridge, coffeemaker, hair dryer.

SummerPlace Inn Just a block from the beach, this four-story, Spanish-mo... is a refreshing change from its cookie-cutter chain siblings. It offers innlike room... rated with wildlife prints. A few suites have hot tubs in their living rooms. The... expensive Gulf-side units have balconies (those facing the bay do not). Doors open ... an indoor pool, whirlpool, and exercise room to an outdoor pool, but you'll have... negotiate your way across busy U.S. 98 to reach the Gulf.

14047 Emerald Coast Pkwy. (U.S. 98, at Airport Rd.), Destin, FL 32541. ✆ **888/232-2499** or 850/650-8003. Fax 850/650-8004. www.summerplaceinn.com. 72 units. Summer $143–$209 double; off-season $69–$99 double. Rates include continental breakfast. AE, DISC, MC, V. **Amenities:** Indoor and outdoor pools; exercise room; Jacuzzi; business center; coin-op washers/dryers. *In room:* A/C, TV, dataport, fridge, coffeemaker, hair dryer.

Fort Walton Beach

The managers of Venus by the Sea (see below) also run the **Sea Crest Condominiums,** next door at 895 Santa Rosa Blvd. (✆ **800/476-1885** or 850/301-9600; fax 850/301-9205; www.seacrestcondos.com). The 112 units in this seven-story building aren't as spacious as those in Venus, but they're considerably more luxurious, and those on the higher floors have great views toward the west. The complex has indoor and outdoor pools (actually one pool—you can swim under a glass partition between them), and it sits next to a county park with a boardwalk leading over the dunes to the beach.

Among the chain motels here is the **Hampton Inn Fort Walton Beach,** 1112 Santa Rosa Blvd. (✆ **800/426-7866** or 850/301-0906; http://hamptoninn1.hilton.com).

Ramada Plaza Beach Resort ★ This big resort boasts the prettiest outdoor areas in the region, with waterfalls cascading over lofty rocks and a romantic grotto bar, all surrounded by thick foliage. Although the resort has another pool, sun deck, and bar out by the beach, its gorgeous courtyard would have even more charm if it weren't cut off from the Gulf by a six-story block of hotel rooms. The rooms and suites in this beachfront building are the resort's best, with Gulf or courtyard views from balconies or patios.

Tips Luxurious Cottages & Luscious Surroundings

Rosemary Beach, at the east end of C.R. 30A, just 8 miles east of Seaside (✆ **888/855-1551;** www.rosemarybeach.com), a newer, smaller, and, I think, better, seaside-style community, has a collection of about 300 luxurious Pan-Caribbean-style cottages and carriage houses (from studios to six bedrooms) for rent, all of which are nonsmoking. This is another pedestrian-friendly community—almost everything on the 107 acres is within a 5-minute walk of the town center—and most of the homes are owned by people who live here part-time and lease to vacationers the rest of the year. The white-sand (and soft as talcum-powder) beach here is ridiculously gorgeous, though guests can also choose from among four pools. Nothing on the architecturally stunning and strikingly planted property here is higher than four stories, and all the homes telescope in from the beach, so everyone can have a view (or partial view) of the Gulf. Other amenities include a health club, bike rental, racquet club, 2.3-mile fitness trail, spa, shops, town hall, post office, and a few very good restaurants, including the delightful Onano Neighborhood Café. Cottages are individually decorated, so check online to see pictures of the properties before deciding. Though all come with a full kitchen, washer/dryer, and TV/VCR, some have added amenities such as a Jacuzzi or private pool. There is also an inn, the **Pensione** (✆ **850/453-8396**), on the premises and the town is building a full-service hotel. The inn's daily rates are $200 to $215 spring and fall, from $215 in summer, and $150 in winter. Opening sometime this century, **Hotel Saba** (✆ **800/310-5768**) is a 53-room boutique hotel in Rosemary Beach's Town Center.

service to take guests to and from nearby shopping, dining, and entertainment complexes. ***Note:*** The hotel is 100% smoke free.

4000 Sandestin Blvd. S., Destin, FL 32541. ✆ **800/367-1271** or 850/267-9500. Fax 850/267-3076. www.HiltonSandestinBeach.com. 598 units. Summer $289–$459 suite; off-season $109–$229 suite. Golf and tennis packages available. AE, DC, DISC, MC, V. Valet parking $20, self-parking $10. **Amenities:** 5 restaurants; 2 bars; indoor and outdoor pools; golf course; tennis courts; health club; spa; Jacuzzi; watersports equipment/rental; children's programs; game room; concierge; activities desk; car-rental desk; 24-hr. business center; shopping arcade; salon; room service; massage; babysitting; laundry service; coin-op washers/dryers. *In room:* A/C, TV, minibar, coffeemaker, hair dryer, iron.

Sandestin Golf and Beach Resort ★★★ Kids Sprawling over 2,400 acres with a spectacular beach 5 miles west of Destin and a marina, this resort is notable for its 72 holes of championship golf, a tennis center, spa, and much more. An array of luxury accommodations overlooking the Gulf, Choctawhatchee Bay, the fairways, lagoons, or a nature preserve. The hotel rooms and suites are in the Bayside Inn; all have kitchenettes and balconies. Private condominiums are individually decorated and each has a full kitchen and a patio or balcony; many have a washer and dryer. Grand Boulevard, a 28-acre pedestrian village overlooking the Choctawhatchee Bay, has a unique collection of more than two dozen specialty merchants ranging from quaint boutiques and charming eateries to lively bars and nightclubs. It also features hotel rooms and one-, two-, and

Tips Picture Perfect

Designed by renowned architect David Rockwell, the **WaterColor Inn,** 34 Goldenrod Circle (✆ **866/426-2656** or 850/534-5000; www.watercolorresort.com), is a stunning 499-acre beachfront boutique hotel. With just 60 rooms, it feels more like a private beach house than a hotel. A ground-floor library with club chairs and a cocktail lounge opening onto the pool deck drive home that feeling even more. Guest rooms feature a walk-in shower with views to the beach, and Adirondack chairs on the balcony. Six ground-floor bungalows have outdoor showers enclosed by striped tents, lending a very French Riviera feel, à la F. Scott Fitzgerald's *Tender Is the Night.* Rotunda guest rooms in the center tower provide stunning 180-degree views from massive balconies. Access to WaterColor community facilities, such as the Tom Fazio–designed Camp Creek Golf Club, 6 miles east, and Greg Norman–designed Shark's Tooth Golf Club, 13 miles east, are also bonuses. Five Har-Tru tennis courts are also available. A Gulf-front beach club (complete with pool deck, children's pool, and beach services), a lakefront boathouse (with canoes, kayaks, and fishing), as well as Camp WaterColor, with supervised kids' activities, will keep you from ever wanting to leave this fabulous piece of paradise. Rates range from $295 to $595 for a king room, $745 to $910 for a suite. In addition to the 60 rooms at the Inn, WaterColor offers a large selection of rental homes, ranging from one to seven bedrooms. The rental homes are very popular with families and groups of friends traveling together. Rental guests can use all of the resort's facilities, and just as for Inn guests, kayaks, canoes, and fishing gear are complimentary.

three-bedroom luxury accommodations surrounding the bay, with rates ranging from $100 to $479 in the off-season to $165 to $719 in the summer.

9300 Emerald Coast Pkwy. W. (U.S. 98), Destin, FL 32541. ✆ **800/277-0800** or 850/267-8000 in the U.S., or 800/933-7846 in Canada. Fax 850/267-8222. www.sandestin.com. 1,600 units, including 1,425 condo apts. Summer $165–$719 double, $165–$719 condo apt; off-season $100–$479 double, $100–$479 condo apt. Packages and weekly/monthly rates available. AE, DC, DISC, MC, V. **Amenities:** 22 restaurants; 8 bars; 19 heated outdoor pools; 4 golf courses; 15 tennis courts; health club; spa; Jacuzzis; watersports equipment/rentals; free use of bikes; children's programs; game room; concierge; shopping arcade; salon; limited room service (hotel only); massage; babysitting; laundry service; coin-op washers/dryers. *In room:* A/C, TV, dataport, kitchen, coffeemaker, hair dryer, iron.

Seaside

Mayberry meets *Metropolitan Home* in this pastel-hued community, where life is a dreamlike state of mind. If you decide to rent a home or a **romantic honeymoon cottage ★★** in this quaint village, contact the **Seaside Cottage Rental Agency,** P.O. Box 4730, Seaside, FL 32459 (✆ **800/277-8696** or 850/231-1320; fax 850/231-2293; www.seasidefl.com). The agency has several hundred cottages in its rental inventory, from one to six bedrooms. The beachside cottages are one of Florida's best getaways for newlyweds or anyone else looking for a romantic escape, though if you want a little more privacy and less action, you might choose Rosemary Beach (see above) instead.

Inn by the Sea by Vera Bradley ★★★ With its large Tuscan columns reminiscent of a Virginia mansion, the inn formerly known as Josephine's French Country Inn has been redesigned completely by lifestyle guru Vera Bradley. Straight out of a country-style home-decor magazine, it has fresh bright colors and styling throughout. Each of the nine bedrooms feature flatscreen TVs and, even better, a distinctive VB-quilted tote filled with bottled water and other gifts. Every room is a different style. Every guest has full privileges at the private swim, tennis, and fitness club in Seaside. Two rooms are located in the carriage house and feature king-size beds, private sitting room, and kitchenette. The dining room offers a Southern menu and serves breakfast, lunch, and afternoon tea.

38 Seaside Ave., Seaside, FL 32459. ✆ **800/358-8696.** Fax 850/231-2373. www.innbytheseavb.com. 9 units. $250–$550 double. Rates include gourmet breakfast. AE, DISC, MC, V. **Amenities:** Restaurant; Swim, Tennis & Fitness Club; beach access. *In room:* A/C, TV, Wi-Fi, kitchen (in some), fridge, coffeemaker, hair dryer, iron.

WHERE TO DINE

Except for the strip on Okaloosa Island, a plethora of fast-food and family chain restaurants line U.S. 98.

Destin

If you didn't catch a fish to be grilled at Fisherman's Wharf (see below), you can buy one to brag about at **Sexton's Seafood,** 602 Hwy. 98 E., opposite Destin Harbor (✆ **850/837-3040**). It's the best market here.

AJ's Seafood & Oyster Bar ★★ SEAFOOD Jimmy Buffett tunes set the tone at this fun, Tiki-topped establishment on the picturesque Destin Harbor docks, where fishing boats unload their daily catches right into the kitchen. The best items here are grilled or fried fish, but raw or steamed Apalachicola oysters also headline the menu. You can sample a bit of everything with a "run of the kitchen" seafood platter. AJ's is most famous for its topside bar, Club Bimini, open nightly and featuring live bands (you should have dinner elsewhere if you're not in a partying mood). At lunch, picnic tables on the covered dock make a fine place to eat with a view across the harbor. Locals love this place and you will, too.

116 Hwy. 98 E., Destin Harbor. ✆ **850/837-1913.** www.ajs-destin.com. Main courses $11–$30; sandwiches and salads $6–$12. AE, DISC, MC, V. Apr–Sept Sun–Thurs 11am–10pm, Fri–Sat 11am–midnight (bar until 4am); off-season daily 11am–9pm.

Back Porch ★ SEAFOOD This cedar-shingled seafood shack has glorious beach and Gulf views from its long porch. The popular casual restaurant originated chargrilled amberjack, which you'll now see on menus throughout Florida. Other fish and seafood, as well as chicken and juicy hamburgers, also come from the coals. Come early, order a rum-laden Key lime freeze, and enjoy the sunset. The Back Porch sits with a number of other restaurants near the western boundary of the Henderson Beach State Park and is a popular hangout for Frisbee players and sunbathers.

1740 Old Hwy. 98 E. ✆ **850/837-2022.** www.theback-porch.com. Main courses $15–$25; sandwiches, burgers, and pastas $9–$13. AE, DC, DISC, MC, V. Apr–Sept daily 11am–11pm; off-season daily 11am–10pm. From U.S. 98, turn toward the beach at the Hampton Inn.

Callahan's Island Restaurant & Deli ★ (Value) AMERICAN/DELI The best place in the area for picnic fare, this family-operated deli serves burgers, excellent Reubens, and other made-to-order sandwiches, pastas, and nightly specials such as chargrilled chicken and grilled pork chops. A long refrigerator case holds a variety of top-grade cheeses, deli meats, steaks, and chops (choose your own cut, and the chef will chargrill it to order). Tables and booths are set up garden-fashion, adding an outdoorsy ambience to this pleasant storefront establishment. Locals like to have lunch here. Breakfast is served only on Saturday morning.

950 Gulf Shore Dr. (2 blocks south of U.S. 98). ✆ **850/837-6328.** Main courses $10–$20; sandwiches, burgers, and salads $5–$10. DISC, MC, V. Mon–Fri 10am–9pm; Sat 8am–9pm.

Copper Grill ★★ STEAK An upscale restaurant lit by gas torches, the Copper Grill is a delicious dichotomy of swank and kitsch—check out the zebra prints inside the dining room. Each table has its own DVD player, TV screen, and coffeemaker, and, to add to the distraction, there's an open-pit grill in the middle of the action. The Angus beef is top-notch, but order the African lobster tails with scampi sauce—it's absolutely to die for.

11225 Hwy. 98, Destin. ✆ **850/654-6900.** www.coppergrill.com. Reservations recommended. Main courses $25–$52. AE, DISC, MC, V. Sun–Thurs 5:30–9:30pm; Fri–Sat 5:30–11pm.

Donut Hole ★ SOUTHERN Available around the clock, breakfasts at this popular spot include eggs Benedict, fluffy biscuits under sausage gravy, Belgian waffles, and freshly baked doughnuts. Lunch choices are deli sandwiches, half-pound burgers, and big salads. Daily specials are a bargain. The rough-hewn building has booth and counter seating. Be prepared to wait out on the deck, especially on weekends. There's another Donut Hole in southern Walton County, on U.S. 98 E. 2½ miles east of the Sandestin Beach Resort (✆ **850/267-3239**); it's open daily from 6am to 10pm.

635 U.S. 98 E., Destin. ✆ **850/837-8824.** Main courses $7–$10; breakfast items, sandwiches, salads, and burgers $5–$9. No credit cards. Daily 24 hr. Closed 2 weeks before Christmas.

Fisherman's Wharf Seafood House ★★ SEAFOOD Go fishing, bring your catch here, and then have the chef chargrill it at this atmospheric restaurant next to a charter-fleet marina. (The restaurant hosts most of Destin's fishing competitions.) If you struck out fishing and didn't stop by Sexton's Seafood (see above) on the way here, you can select from the restaurant's fresh-off-the-boat catch for grilling, broiling, frying, or blackening. Chargrilling is the house specialty—the triggerfish filet comes white and flaky but still moist. All main courses include a trip to the salad bar, rice pilaf, baked potato, or roasted vegetables. Although this building dates from 1996, it reminds me of an Old Florida fish camp, with rough-hewn wood walls and double-hung windows looking onto a large harborside deck, a venue during the warmer months for two bars, an oyster bar, live music, and great sunsets.

210D Hwy. 98 E., Destin Harbor. ✆ **850/654-4766.** www.fishermanswharfdestin.com. Main courses $16–$25; sandwiches and burgers $8–$11. AE, DC, DISC, MC, V. Summer daily 11am–11pm (deck bar open later); off-season daily 11am–9pm.

Fudpucker's Beachside Bar & Grill ★ AMERICAN A sprawling 26,000-square-foot complex, Fudpucker's is a beachside burger-and-beer joint with a twist—or, rather, many twists. For one, there's also a sushi bar. The decor is funky, with antique beer cans, mirrors, and what they call "Fud Junk." The Fudburger is the menu's most popular, but an unabridged selection of everything from fried crab to Puckeroni Pizza is available for the taking. Eight different dining rooms, a playground, and game rooms are nothing compared to Fudpucker's Gator Beach, the restaurant's very own alligator collection in the pond underneath the building. Live music and a new addition, Club Key West, make this place one of the area's most popular nightspots. **Fudpucker's on the Island,** 108 Santa Rosa Blvd., Fort Walton Beach (✆ **850/243-3833**), is the original, located on Okaloosa Island.

20001 Emerald Coast Pkwy., Destin. ✆ **850/654-4200.** www.fudpuckers.com. Main courses $15–$54. AE, DC, DISC, MC, V. Mon–Wed 11am–10pm; Thurs–Sat 11am–4am.

Harbor Docks SEAFOOD/JAPANESE The harbor views are spectacular from indoors or outdoors at this casual, somewhat rustic establishment. You can order your fill of fried fish, but such specialties as the daily catch sautéed with artichoke hearts are far more enjoyable. Asian influences include a sushi bar and hibachi table, which are open for dinner, and a few Thai specialties that grace the lunch menu. The bar here is popular with charter-boat skippers, and frequent live entertainment keeps the action going on the outdoor deck at night.

538 U.S. 98 E., Destin Harbor. ✆ **850/837-2506.** www.harbordocks.com. Reservations accepted only for hibachi table. Main courses $12–$29; sushi $8–$15. AE, DC, DISC, MC, V. Feb–Oct daily 5:30–10:30am and 11am–11pm; Nov–Jan daily 11am–11pm. Sushi bar daily 5–10pm.

Harry T's Boat House ★ Kids AMERICAN To honor the memory of trapeze artist "Flying Harry T" Baben, his family opened this lively spot on the ground floor of Destin Harbor's tallest building. Standing guard is the stuffed Stretch, Harry's beloved giraffe. The decor includes circus memorabilia and relics from the luxury cruise ship *Thracia,* which sank off the Emerald Coast in 1927; Harry T was presented with the ship's salvaged furnishings and fixtures for personally leading the heroic rescue of its 2,000 passengers. In 2007, Harry's moved into the lighthouse building along the harborfront in a 13,000-square-foot space in the new HarborWalk Village at Emerald Grande. Luckily the kitsch—and the giraffe—remain. The menu offers traditional seafood, steak, chicken, and pasta dishes. The house specialty is smokehouse ribs, juicy and full of flavor. Call for information on Kids' Night, which features clowns, face painting, and balloon animals.

46 Harbour Blvd., Destin Harbor. ✆ **850/654-4800.** www.harryts.com. Main courses $15–$30; soups and salads $5–$15. Menu cheaper during winter months. AE, DISC, MC, V. Summer Mon–Sat 11am–2am, Sun 10am–2am; off-season Mon–Sat 11am–9pm, Sun 10am–9pm. Bar open later. Sun brunch year-round 10am–3pm.

Marina Cafe ★★★ NEW AMERICAN Destin's finest restaurant provides a classy atmosphere with soft candlelight, subdued music, and walls of glass overlooking the harbor. The changing menu offers nouveau preparations of seafood, such as almond-crusted mahimahi. Pizzas are topped with the likes of cayenne rock shrimp, roasted corn, and onion marmalade, while pastas might feature fusilli with roasted chicken, sun-dried tomatoes, goat cheese, broccoli, and pine nuts. Try the sautéed lump blue crab cakes with grainy mustard caper rémoulade in a cucumber habanero relish. Weather permitting, enjoy the outdoor deck for drinks and appetizers. There's also a sushi bar, and, in spring 2008, the owners of this restaurant opened **Destin Chops 30A,** a steak, seafood, and sushi house in Rosemary Beach. Call Marina Cafe for more information.

404 Hwy. 98 E., Destin Harbor. ✆ **850/837-7960.** www.marinacafe.com. Reservations recommended. Main courses $25–$45; pizza and pasta $11–$20. AE, DC, DISC, MC, V. Daily 5–11pm. Closed 1st 3 weeks in Jan.

McGuire's Irish Pub & Brewery STEAK/SEAFOOD Like Pensacola's original McGuire's (p. 590), this younger sibling sports thousands of dollar bills stuck on the ceilings and walls, plus Notre Dame football schedules, a prominent logo of the Boston Celtics, and other Irish-American memorabilia. This is Destin's most popular hangout, and local professionals congregate at the big oak bar for live entertainment Tuesday through Sunday from 9pm. Opt for a table on either side of the bar or on a rooftop deck. Dining here is almost secondary to the see-and-be-seen scene, although the tender char-grilled steaks and giant burgers are worthy antidotes to a big appetite.

33 Hwy. 98 E., Destin Harbor (in Harborwalk Center, near Destin Bridge). ✆ **850/654-0567.** www.mcguiresirishpub.com. Main courses $18–$35; snacks, burgers, and sandwiches $8–$12. AE, DC, DISC, MC, V. Mon–Sat 11am–midnight; open later Fri–Sat.

Rutherford's 465 ★★ NEW AMERICAN An elegant lunch-and-brunch-only restaurant overlooking Lake Regatta, Rutherford's 465 is an eclectic dining experience, thanks to Chef Todd Misener's New American cuisine. Dishes such as the panko grilled Gulf shrimp with red chili sauce, and the pan-fried local triggerfish in a sunflower-seed crust with blackened jumbo shrimp and golden-pineapple butter sauce are outstanding. Breakfast and brunch items are also excellent, with $2 Bloody Marys or mimosas.

465 Regatta Bay Blvd. (inside the Regatta Bay community), Destin. ✆ **850/337-8888.** www.rutherfords465.com. Main courses $7–$15. AE, DC, DISC, MC, V. Tues–Sat 11am–2pm; Sun 10am–2:30pm.

Fort Walton Beach

Big City American Bistro ★★★ AMERICAN BISTRO For a caffeine fix, an inexpensive breakfast, brunch or lunch, or afternoon tea, head to Tina and Jim Ivanchukov's bright cafe on the mainland near the Brooks Bridge. The owners make great salads—such as herb-roasted chicken with apples, walnuts, and tarragon dressing (sold by the pound)—and sandwiches served on homemade focaccia. Don't miss the sweet-potato fries either. Dinner entrees are also tempting—the cowboy-style flame-grilled skirt steak is served with a coffee-and-black-pepper crust that's sure to awaken both you and your taste buds!

201 Miracle Strip Pkwy. SE (U.S. 98). ✆ **850/664-0664.** Main courses $11–$25; sandwiches and salads $7–$10. MC, V. Mon–Fri 7am–7pm; Sat 8am–5pm; Sun 10:30am–2:30pm.

Café Tango ★★ AMERICAN Despite the name, this restaurant has nothing to do with Argentina. Housed in a 50-something-year-old vine-covered red cottage, Café Tango is best known for its seafood, steaks, and pastas. With only eight tables, the restaurant is so romantic that you'll want to do some sort of after-dinner tango.

14 Vicki St., Santa Rosa Beach. ✆ **850/267-0054.** Reservations recommended. Main courses $15–$30. AE, MC, V. Summer 5–10pm; off-season, call for hours.

Caffè Italia ★★ NORTHERN ITALIAN Nada Eckhardt is from Croatia, but she met her American husband, Jim, while working at a restaurant named Caffè Italia in Italy. The Eckhardts duplicated that establishment in this 1925 Sears Roebuck mail-order house tucked away on the waterfront. You can dine on the patio, with a view of the sound through sprawling live oak trees (one table is set romantically under a gazebo), or sit inside, where Nada has installed floral tablecloths and photos from the old country. A limited but fine menu includes excellent pizzas; pasta dishes, such as lobster ravioli, risotto with asparagus, or smoked salmon; and meat and seafood dishes to fit the season. The cappuccino is absolutely first-rate, as are the genuine Italian desserts.

189 Brooks St., on the mainland in the block west of Brooks Bridge. ✆ **850/664-0035.** www.acaffeitalia.com. Reservations recommended. Main courses $19–$28; pizza and pasta $12–$19. AE, DC, DISC, MC, V. Sun and Tues–Fri 11am–10pm; Sat 5–11pm. Closed Thanksgiving and Christmas.

Pandora's Restaurant & Lounge ★ STEAK/SEAFOOD The front of this unusual restaurant is a beached yacht now housing the main-deck lounge. Below is a dining room with ceiling beams and aglow with lights from copper chandeliers. Try for the private Bob Hope Booth, where you can dine beneath two of the great comedian's golf clubs (he used to come here to raise money for a local Air Force widows' home). Anything from the charcoal grill is excellent, including the wonderful appetizer of bacon-wrapped scallops. Several varieties of freshly caught fish are among the main-course choices, but oak-grilled steaks and prime rib keep the locals coming back for more. The tender beef is cut on the premises and grilled to perfection. The delicious breads and pies are homemade. ***Note:*** Service has been known to be spotty here. There's another Pandora's in Grayton Beach, at the corner of Florida 283 and C.R. 30A (✆ **850/231-4102**).

1120B Santa Rosa Blvd. ✆ **850/244-8669.** www.pandorassteakhouse.com. Reservations recommended. Main courses $21–$33. AE, DISC, MC, V. Sun–Thurs 5–10pm; Fri–Sat 5–10:30pm.

Staff's Seafood Restaurant SEAFOOD/STEAK Considered the first Emerald Coast restaurant, Staff's started as a hotel in 1913 and moved to this barnlike building in 1931. Among the memorabilia on display are an old-fashioned phonograph lamp and a 1914 cash register. Staff's tangy seafood gumbo has gained fame for this casual, historic restaurant. One of the most popular main dishes is the chargrilled amberjack served with gazpacho salsa. Main courses are served with baskets of hot, home-baked wheat bread from a secret 70-year-old recipe, plus salad and dessert. A pianist plays at dinnertime year-round.

24 SW Miracle Strip Pkwy. (U.S. 98), on the mainland. ✆ **850/243-3526.** www.staffrestaurant.com. Main courses $19–$28. AE, DISC, MC, V. Summer daily 5–11pm, off-season Mon–Thurs 5–9pm, Fri–Sat 5–10pm.

Southern Walton County

Café Thirty-A ★★★ SEAFOOD/AMERICAN Only 1½ miles east of Seaside, along Scenic Hwy. 30A, this comfortable yet classy restaurant prepares exquisite seafood, steaks, and wood-oven pizzas. It's mostly a vacationing white-collar crowd here, but that shouldn't stop anyone from enjoying the remarkable offerings (including drinks from the creative martini menu and wine from the extensive, award-winning list), served up by a friendly and efficient staff. The menu changes daily, but usually available is the fantastic grilled Georgia quail served with creamy grits and sage fritters. For entrees, you can't miss with any of the seafood dishes, such as the wood-oven-roasted snapper with andouille jambalaya and blackened green beans, or the cumin-dusted grouper. If you're feeling more turf than surf, the filet mignon served with roasted-garlic whipped potatoes and a balsamic reduction is excellent. Leave room for such desserts as the luscious molten chocolate torte or the heavenly banana beignets.

3899 E. Scenic Hwy. 30A, Seagrove Beach. ✆ **800/231-2166.** www.cafethirtya.com. Reservations highly recommended. Main courses $26–$38; wood-oven pizzas $14–$15. AE, DC, DISC, MC, V. Summer daily 6–10pm; off-season Mon–Fri 5:30–9pm, Sat–Sun 5:30–9:30pm.

The Red Bar & Picolo's ★★★ SEAFOOD Housed in a former general store, this funky Grayton Beach spot is best known for its bric-a-brac and chalkboard menu featuring excellent low-country-esque entrees, such as sautéed shrimp and crawfish. There's live jazz nightly and a buzzing cocktail scene. Celebrities from Sheryl Crow to Jim Carrey have been spotted sipping a few drinks with the locals who call this place their home away from home. New in 2008: breakfast, featuring all sorts of omelets and delicious egg dishes.

70 Hotz Ave., Grayton Beach. ✆ **850/231-1008.** www.theredbar.com. Main courses $13–$21; breakfast $4–$11. No credit cards. Daily 7am–10:30am, 11am–3pm, and 5pm "until late."

Fun Facts Building Fences

Seaside's Urban Code requires that all homes sport white-painted wood picket fences at the street-front and path-front property lines, and that no two fences be the same on any one avenue. Explore all the fences, which range from subdued to downright wacky.

Several cafes and sandwich shops in Seaside's Gulf-side shopping complex sell inexpensive snacks to beachgoers.

Bud & Alley's ★★ SEAFOOD/STEAK/MEDITERRANEAN In this cracked-crab-and-champagne-loving village, Bud & Alley's (named for a dog and a cat) has spectacular sunset views from the rooftop bar and a menu that changes frequently, but always has savory surprises. The menu offers an infusion of Basque, Italian, Louisiana, and Floridian dishes that might include seafood stew or sautéed head-on shrimp with garlic, shallots, and cracked pepper. You can dine indoors or out, on the screened porch or under an open-air gazebo where you'll hear waves splashing against the white sand. Jazz is usually in the spotlight on weekends. There's even a taco bar where you can toss back a few tacos or burritos for just $3 to $8. The roof-deck bar overlooking the water is always hopping and features its own impressive menu of frozen cocktails, martinis, and wines. On New Year's Eve, everyone from miles around celebrates at Bud & Alley's. Call ahead to see whether a noted guest chef is cooking or a special wine-tasting dinner is scheduled.

C.R. 30A, in the beachside shops. ✆ **850/231-5900.** www.budandalleys.com. Reservations recommended. Main courses $31–$36; lunch $8–$11. MC, V. Apr–Sept daily 11:30am–3pm and 5:30–9:30pm (Fri–Sat until 10pm); Oct–Mar Wed–Mon 5:30–9pm (Fri–Sat until 9:30pm).

DESTIN & FORT WALTON BEACH AFTER DARK

In summer, there's live entertainment at most resorts, including the Ramada Plaza Beach Resort, in Fort Walton Beach; the Hilton Sandestin Beach & Golf Resort; and Sandestin Golf and Beach Resort, in southern Walton County (see "Where to Stay," earlier in this chapter). Call ahead to find out what's scheduled, especially during the slow season between October and February.

For other ideas and listings of what's happening, pick up a copy of the weekly *Walton Sun* newspaper.

DESTIN Several Destin restaurants provide entertainment nightly in summer, and on weekends in the off-season. See "Where to Dine," earlier in this chapter, for details about restaurants. The dockside **AJ's Club Bimini,** 116 U.S. 98 E. (✆ **850/837-1913**), has live reggae under a big thatched-roofed deck. A somewhat older, if not more sober, crowd gathers for entertainment at the big harborside deck at **Fisherman's Wharf,** on U.S. 98 E. (✆ **850/654-4766;** www.fishermanswharfdestin.com), and the **Deck,** on U.S. 98 E. at the Harbor Docks restaurant, overlooking the harbor (✆ **850/837-2506**). For Irish tunes nightly year-round, head for **McGuire's Irish Pub & Brewery,** in the Harborwalk Shops, U.S. 98 just east of the Destin Bridge (✆ **850/650-0567**). The **Sky Bar,** above Gratzi Italian Restaurant, 1771 Old Hwy. 98 (✆ **850/837-7475;** www.skybar.net), draws the after-dinner crowd from the Back Porch and other adjacent restaurants. But it's the **Red Bar** (✆ **850/231-1008**) that sees the funkiest crowd, from rowdy locals to bona fide celebrities. As the night goes on, the place gets crazier. Brace yourselves.

Twenty-somethings are attracted to the dance club, rowdy saloon, Jimmy Buffett–style reggae bar, and sports TV and billiards parlor all under one roof at the acclaimed **Nightown,** 140 Palmetto St. (✆ **850/837-6448;** www.nightown.com), near the harbor on the inland side of U.S. 98 E. One admission covers it all. There's live music Friday and Saturday nights, and amateur boxing on Tuesday. Nearby, **Hogs Breath Destin,** 541 Hwy. 98 E. (✆ **850/837-5991;** www.hogsbreath.com), is another lively pub from Key West with bands playing rock, blues, and jazz.

Out toward Sandestin, **Fudpucker's Beachside Bar & Grill** (p. 604), opposite the Henderson Beach State Park, offers double the fun with two summertime stages. There's another Fudpucker's at 108 Santa Rosa Blvd., on Okaloosa Island in Fort Walton Beach (© **850/243-3833**).

FORT WALTON BEACH Country music and dancing fans will find a home at the **High Tide Oyster Bar,** at Okaloosa Island off the Brooks Bridge (© **850/244-2624**). **Papa Joe's Hideaway,** 104 S. Perry Ave. (© **850/244-5599**), is a great locals hangout for live music—everything from country and blues to experimental jazz—and, on Thursdays and Saturdays at 6:30pm, final table poker.

3 PANAMA CITY BEACH

100 miles E of Pensacola; 100 miles SW of Tallahassee

Panama City Beach, a Spring Break mecca once erroneously featured as a bleak, desolate wasteland of sun and strip malls in the Ashley Judd film *Ruby in Paradise,* has long been known as the "Redneck Riviera." Millions flock here from the bordering states of Georgia, Alabama, Mississippi, and Louisiana. It still has a seemingly unending strip of bars, amusement parks, and old-fashioned motels, but this lively and crowded destination (in season) also has luxury resorts and condominiums to go along with its 20-plus miles of sandy beaches, golf courses, fishing, boating, and fresh seafood.

Panama City Beach is the most seasonal resort in Northwest Florida, as many restaurants, attractions, and some hotels close between October and March. Spring Break is a big deal here; MTV sets up shop in Panama City Beach for its annual beach-party broadcasts.

ESSENTIALS

GETTING THERE The commuter arms of **Delta** (© **800/221-1212**), **Northwest** (© **800/225-2525**), and **US Airways** (© **800/428-4322**) fly into **Panama City/Bay County International Airport,** on Lisenby Avenue, north of St. Andrews Boulevard, in Panama City (© **850/763-6751**; www.pcairport.com).

Alamo (© 800/327-9633), **Avis** (© 800/331-1212), **Budget** (© 800/527-0700), **Enterprise** (© 800/325-8007), **Hertz** (© 800/654-3131), and **National** (© 800/CAR-RENT [227-7368]) have rental-car offices here.

Taxi fares to the beach are about $25 to $30.

The **Amtrak** (© **800/USA-RAIL** [872-7245]; www.amtrak.com) transcontinental *Sunset Limited* service stops at Chipley, 45 miles north of Panama City.

VISITOR INFORMATION For advance information, contact the **Panama City Beach Convention & Visitors Bureau,** P.O. Box 9473, Panama City Beach, FL 32417 (© **800/722-3224** in the U.S., 800/553-1330 in Canada, or 850/233-6503; fax 850/233-5072; www.800pcbeach.com). It operates a visitor center in the City Hall complex, 17001 Panama City Beach Pkwy. (U.S. 98), at Florida 79. The center is open daily from 8am to 5pm; closed New Year's Day, Thanksgiving, and Christmas.

GETTING AROUND The **Bay Town Trolley** (© **850/769-0557**; www.baytowntrolley.org) runs along Thomas Drive and on Front Beach Road as far west as Florida 79; it operates year-round Monday through Friday five times a day. Rides cost $1.25 for adults and 60¢ for seniors. Children 5 and younger ride free. Call for the schedule.

For a taxi, call **Yellow Cab** (✆ **850/763-4691**). Fares at the beach are approximately $3.25 to climb aboard and $2 per mile, or $5 to $10 for rides within Panama City Beach.

TIME The Panama City area is in the Central time zone, 1 hour behind Miami, Orlando, and Tallahassee.

HITTING THE BEACH: ST. ANDREWS STATE PARK

A nearly unbroken strand of fine white sand fronts all 22 miles of Panama City Beach, but the highlight for many is **St. Andrews State Park** ★★★, at the east end. With more than 1,000 acres of dazzling white sand and dunes, this preserved wilderness demonstrates what the area looked like before motels and condominiums lined the beach. Lacy, golden sea oats sway in the refreshing Gulf breezes, and fragrant rosemary grows wild. Picnic areas (on the Gulf beach and the Grand Lagoon), restrooms, and open-air showers are available for beachgoers. Anglers will find jetties and a boat ramp. A nature trail reveals wading birds and perhaps an alligator or two. Drive carefully here because the area is home to foxes, coyotes, and a herd of deer. A historic turpentine fir tree still on display was formerly used by lumbermen to make turpentine and rosin, both important for caulking old wooden ships.

The park's 176 RV and tent **campsites** are among the state's most beautiful, especially the 40 situated in a pine forest right on the shores of Grand Lagoon. They are very popular, so reservations are highly recommended—and absolutely essential in summer. Call ✆ **800/326-3521** or go to www.reserveamerica.com. Sites cost $24 year-round.

Park admission is $5 per car, and $1 per pedestrian or cyclist. The area is open daily from 8am to sunset. Pets are not allowed in the park. For more information, contact the park at 4607 State Park Lane, Panama City, FL 32408 (✆ **850/233-5140;** www.floridastateparks.org/standrews).

Pristine **Shell Island** ★★, a 7½-mile-long, 1-mile-wide barrier island accessible only by boat, sits a few hundred yards across an inlet from St. Andrews State Park. This uninhabited natural preserve is great for shelling and also fun for swimming, sun-tanning, or just relaxing. Visitors can bring chairs, beach gear, coolers, food, and beverages. The best way to get here is on the park's **Shell Island Shuttle** (✆ **800/227-0132** or 850/234-7245; www.shellislandshuttle.com), which runs every 30 minutes—in summer, daily from 9am to 5pm; in spring and fall, Saturday and Sunday from 10am to 3pm. Fares are $15 for adults and $6.50 for children 11 and under, plus the admission fees to the state park (see above). A special snorkeling package costs $22 for adults and $17 for kids 12 and under, which includes the shuttle ride and equipment. Kayak rentals are $45 a day for a single-seat boat, $55 for a double-seater.

Several cruise boats go to Shell Island, including the glass-bottomed ***Captain Anderson III,*** which departs from Captain Anderson's Marina, 5500 N. Lagoon Dr., at Thomas Drive (✆ **850/234-3435;** www.captandersonsmarina.com). It charges $18 for adults, $10 for kids ages 2 to 11 (Mar–Oct).

OUTDOOR ACTIVITIES

BOATING A variety of rental boats are available at the marinas near the Thomas Drive bridge over Grand Lagoon. These include the **Captain Davis Queen Fleet,** based at Captain Anderson's Marina, 5500 N. Lagoon Dr. (✆ **800/874-2415** or 850/234-3435); the **Lighthouse Marina,** 5325 N. Lagoon Dr. (✆ **850/234-5609**); the **Pirates Cove Marina,** 3901 Thomas Dr. (✆ **850/234-3939**); and the **Treasure Island Marina,** 3605 Thomas Dr. (✆ **850/234-6533**).

Many resorts and hotels provide beach toys for their guests' use. WaveRunners, jet boats, inflatables, and other equipment can also be rented from **Lagoon Rentals** (✆ **850/234-7245**).

FISHING The least expensive way to try your luck is with **Captain Anderson's Deep Sea Fishing,** at Captain Anderson's Marina, Thomas Drive at Grand Lagoon (✆ **800/874-2415** or 850/234-5940; www.captandersonsmarina.com). The captain's party-boat trips last 5 to 6 hours, with prices ranging from $50 to $75 per person, including bait and tackle. Observers can go along for $25.

The more expensive charter-fishing boats depart daily from March to November from the marinas mentioned in "Boating," above.

You definitely won't get seasick casting your line from the **M. B. Miller County Pier,** 12213 Front Beach Rd. (✆ **850/233-3039**), or the **Dan Russell Municipal Pier,** 16101 Front Beach Rd. (✆ **850/233-5080**).

GOLF At Marriott's Bay Point Resort (p. 613), the **Bay Point Yacht and Country Club,** 3900 Marriott Dr., off Jan Cooley Road (✆ **850/235-6950;** www.baypointgolf.com), offers 36 holes of championship play, including the Bruce Devlin–designed course **Lagoon Legends ★★**, rated one of the country's most difficult. Both it and the Club Meadows course have clubhouses, putting greens, driving ranges, clinics, and private instruction. Greens fees with cart start at about $109 in summer and $69 in winter, depending on the day of the week.

The **Edgewater Beach Resort,** 11212 U.S. 98A (✆ **850/235-4044**), also has a 9-hole resort course, and its guests have access to the **Hombre,** 120 Coyote Pass, 3 miles west of the Hathaway Bridge off Panama City Beach Parkway/U.S. 98 (✆ **850/234-3573;** www.hombregolfclub.com), a par-72 championship course that is home to the Nike Panama City Beach Classic. Also, 15 of its 18 holes have water hazards (the unforgiving 7th hole sits on an island). Greens fees are about $50 to $89 with cart.

The course at the semiprivate **Holiday Golf Club,** 100 Fairway Blvd. (✆ **850/234-1800;** www.holidaygolfclub.com), sports lake-lined fairways and elevated greens. Greens fees with cart are about $35 to $65. You can play at night on a lighted 9-hole, par-29 executive course.

The cheapest place to play here is the flat and forgiving **Signal Hill,** 9516 N. Thomas Dr. (✆ **850/234-3218;** www.signalhillgolfcourse.com), where you'll pay about $35 to walk 18 holes in summer, $30 in winter. Add about $8 per person for a cart.

For course information, go to www.golf.com or www.floridagolfing.com; or call the **Florida Sports Foundation** (✆ **850/488-8347**) or **Florida Golfing** (✆ **866/833-2663**).

SCUBA DIVING & SNORKELING Although the area is too far north for extensive coral formations, more than 50 artificial reefs and shipwrecks in the Gulf waters off Panama City attract a wide variety of sea life. The largest local operator is **Hydrospace Dive Shop,** 6422 W. Hwy. 98 (✆ **850/234-3063**). Others include **Panama City Dive Center,** 4823 Thomas Dr. (✆ **850/235-3390;** www.pcdivecenter.com), and **Emerald Coast Divers,** 5121 Thomas Dr. (✆ **800/945-DIVE** [3483] or 850/233-3355; www.divedestin.com). These companies lead dives, teach courses, and take snorkelers to the grass flats off Shell Island.

EXPLORING THE AREA

Gulf World Marine Park (Kids) This landscaped tropical garden and marine attraction has shows with talented dolphins, sea lions, penguins, and more. Not to be upstaged, parrots perform daily, too. Scuba demonstrations, shark feedings, and underwater shows keep the crowds entertained. The park has special interactive programs, including a trainer-for-a-day program ($199 per person) and a dolphin encounter ($150). Allow about 3½ hours to see it all, more if you do one of the encounters. ***Note:*** Swimming with dolphins has both its critics and its supporters. You may want to visit the Whale and Dolphin Conservation Society's website at www.wdcs.org. For more information about responsible travel in general, check out www.treadlightly.org and www.ecotourism.org.

15412 Front Beach Rd. (at Hill Ave.), Panama City Beach. ✆ **850/234-5271.** www.gulfworldmarinepark.com. Admission $24 adults, $15 children 5–11. Summer daily 9am–4pm; off-season daily 9am–2pm.

Museum of Man in the Sea Owned by the Institute of Diving, this small museum exhibits relics from the first days of scuba diving, historic displays of the underwater world dating from 1500, and treasures recovered from sunken ships. Hands-on exhibits explain water and air pressure, light refraction, and why diving bells work. Both kids and adults can climb through a submarine and see live sea animals in a pool. Videos and aquariums explain the sea life found in St. Andrews Bay.

17314 Panama City Beach Pkwy. (at Heather Dr., west of Fla. 79), Panama City Beach. ✆ **850/235-4101.** Admission $5 adults, children 5 and under free. Daily 10am–4pm. Closed New Year's Day, Thanksgiving, and Christmas.

ZooWorld Zoological & Botanical Park ★ Kids Situated in a pine forest, this educational and entertaining zoo is an active participant in the Species Survival Plan, which helps protect endangered species by employing specific breeding and housing programs. Among the 350 guests here are orangutans and other primates; lions, tigers, and leopards; and alligators and other reptiles. The zoo's most precious attraction is the Tilghman Infant Care Facility, a nursery facility that allows you to closely view the baby animals born at ZooWorld.

9008 Front Beach Rd. (near Moylan Dr.), Panama City Beach. ✆ **850/230-4839.** www.zooworldpcb.net. Admission $17 adults, $13 children 5–11. Daily 9am–5:30pm (to 4:30pm in winter).

Amusement Parks

For that Panama City–meets–Coney Island vibe, there's one amusement park good for killing some time. A 105-foot-high roller coaster is just one of the 30 rides at the **Shipwreck Island Water Park,** 12000 Front Beach Rd., at Alf Coleman Road (✆ **850/234-5810;** www.shipwreckisland.com; $32 adults, $21 seniors, $27 kids 35–50 in. tall). Little ones will love the traditional carousel. The park is lots of fun, with continuing live entertainment and tons of junk food. There's also a variety of water amusements, including the 1,600-foot-long winding Lazy River for tubing and a daring 35-mph Speed Slide. The Tad Pole Hole is exclusively for young kids. Lounge chairs, umbrellas, and inner tubes are free, and lifeguards are on duty. Open Saturday and Sunday from mid-March to Memorial Day, then daily until mid-August, and back to weekends from then to Labor Day weekend.

WHERE TO STAY

There are scores of motels along the beach here, ranging from small mom-and-pop operations to sizable members of national chains. The annual guide distributed by the Panama City Beach Convention & Visitors Bureau (p. 609) has a complete list.

The **Hampton Inn,** 2909 Thomas Dr. (✆ **850/236-8988**), is just a mile away from the beach and offers reasonably priced, clean rooms. The **Hilton Garden Inn,** 1101 U.S.

Hwy. 231 (✆ **850/392-1093**), is a nice choice, but in the business district and a bit of a way from the beach.

Panama City Beach abounds with condominium complexes, such as the Edgewater Beach Resort, listed below. Among the many rental agents are **Coldwell Banker Beach Rental,** 726 Thomas Dr., Panama City Beach (✆ **800/621-2462** or 850/235-4075; fax 850/233-2833; www.panamabeachrentals.com), and **Condo World,** 8815A Thomas Dr. (P.O. Box 9456), Panama City Beach (✆ **800/232-6636** in the U.S., 800/824-5411 in Canada, or 850/234-5564; fax 850/233-6725; www.condoworld.com).

The best camping is at the lovely sites in **St. Andrews State Park** (p. 610), one of this area's major attractions.

Rates at even the most expensive properties here drop precipitously during winter, when the town rolls up the sidewalks. Bay County adds 3.5% tax to all hotel and campground bills, bringing the total add-on tax (with the county's 6% sales tax) to 9.5%.

Bay Point Marriott Golf Resort & Spa ★★ Value Ranked among the nation's top golf and tennis resorts, Bay Point Marriott is a great value, not to mention the centerpiece of a manicured development sprawling over 1,100 acres on a wildlife sanctuary bordered by St. Andrews Bay and the Grand Lagoon. Situated beside the lagoon, the vivid coral stucco hotel is surrounded by beautiful gardens. From the glamorous three-story lobby, window walls look out to scenic water views and two pools (one in its own glass-enclosed building). Guest rooms are spacious and luxurious, some with balconies or patios. The recently renovated Golf Villas at Bay Point Marriott is a group of seven buildings situated next to the only Nicklaus Golf Course in Northwest Florida. Watersports are available at the resort's Grand Lagoon Beach. There's also a free water shuttle to beautiful Shell Island on the Gulf of Mexico. The 11,000-square-foot Serenity Spa at Bay Point opened in 2007.

4200 Marriott Dr., Panama City Beach, FL 32408. ✆ **800/874-7105** or 850/236-6000. Fax 850/236-6158. www.marriottbaypoint.com. 319 units. Summer $179–$519 double; off-season $99–$309 double. Packages available. AE, DC, DISC, MC, V. From Thomas Dr., take Magnolia Beach Rd. and bear right on Dellwood Rd. to resort complex. **Amenities:** 2 restaurants; 3 bars; 3 heated outdoor pools; indoor pool; 2 golf courses; 5 tennis courts; health club; Jacuzzi; watersports equipment/rentals; concierge; business center; room service; massage; babysitting; laundry service; free washers/dryers. *In room:* A/C, TV, dataport, fridge, coffeemaker, hair dryer, iron.

Beachcomber by the Sea ★ Watercolors by local artist Paul Brent grace every unit in this eight-story, all-suites resort, at the junction of Front Beach Road and Florida 79. All units also have balconies overlooking a Gulf-side pool and hot tub bordered by a concrete deck accented by palm trees. The well-equipped suites come in two sizes. Each of the larger ones has a living room with sleeper sofa, kitchenette, bathroom, and bedroom with either one king-size or two double beds. The suites are similar to those at the Flamingo Motel & Tower (see below), except here they have air conditioners in both the living room and the bedroom. The smaller units are more like motel rooms, but do contain microwaves; two have whirlpool tubs as well. A new restaurant opened in 2007, the Barefoot Beach Club, and complimentary continental breakfast is available in the lobby each morning.

17101 Front Beach Rd., Panama City Beach, FL 32413. ✆ **888/886-8916** or 850/233-3600. Fax 850/233-3622. www.beachcomberbythesea.com. 96 units. Summer $109–$250 double; off-season $59–$129 double. Rates include continental breakfast. Packages available. AE, DISC, MC, V. **Amenities:** Restaurant; heated outdoor pool; access to nearby health club; Jacuzzi; game room; coin-op washers/dryers. *In room:* A/C, TV, dataport, kitchen, fridge, coffeemaker, hair dryer, iron.

Edgewater Beach Resort ★★ (Kids) One of the Panhandle's largest condominium resorts, this sports-oriented, privately gated facility enjoys a beautiful beachfront location and 110 landscaped acres. Units in five Gulf-side towers have commanding views of the emerald waters and gorgeous sunsets from their private balconies. A pedestrian overpass leads across Front Beach Road to low-rise apartments and town homes fringing the ponds and fairways of the resort's 9-hole golf course. A daytime shuttle runs around the resort to pools, whirlpools, tennis center, and golf course. (Guests also get privileges at the 18-hole Hombre Golf Club, a quarter-mile north.) The Shoppes at Edgewater restaurants are across the road. Last but not least, the gorgeous 11,000-square-foot, Polynesian-style pool has waterfalls, islands, and a deck with live entertainment daily from 11am to 4pm.

11212 Front Beach Rd., Panama City Beach, FL 32407. ✆ **800/874-8686** or 850/235-4044. Fax 850/235-6899. www.edgewaterbeachresort.com. 525 units. Summer $174–$595 condo; off-season $93–$190 condo. Weekly rates and maid service available for a fee. AE, DC, DISC, MC, V. **Amenities:** 3 restaurants; 2 bars; 11 outdoor pools; 9-hole executive golf course; 11 Plexicushion tennis courts; health club; spa services; 4 Jacuzzis; watersports equipment/rentals; children's programs; guest services; limited room service. *In room:* A/C, TV, dataport, Wi-Fi, full kitchen, coffeemaker, iron, washer/dryer.

Flamingo Motel & Tower ★ (Value) This well-maintained motel features a gorgeous tropical garden surrounding a heated pool and a sun deck overlooking the Gulf. The brightly decorated rooms have either full kitchens or fridges and microwaves. Kitchenette rooms in a two-story motel block across the road are less appealing, but will accommodate six to eight. Budget-conscious families can opt for the lower-priced rooms, accommodating two to four. Next door, the seven-story Flamingo Tower contains 49 suites, all with living rooms that have sofa beds and dining tables, balconies overlooking the Gulf, and a beachside pool and hot tub. These suites have new air-conditioning units. Some older units have shower-only bathrooms.

15525 Front Beach Rd., Panama City Beach, FL 32413. ✆ **800/828-0400** or 850/234-2232. Fax 850/234-1292. www.flamingomotel.com. 117 units. Summer $94–$159 double; off-season $39–$139 double. AE, DISC, MC, V. **Amenities:** 2 heated outdoor pools; access to nearby health club; Jacuzzi; watersports equipment/rentals; coin-op washers/dryers. *In room:* A/C, TV, kitchen, fridge, coffeemaker.

Holiday Inn SunSpree Resort ★ One building removed from the Edgewater Beach Resort and across the road from the Shoppes at Edgewater, this 15-story establishment is the top full-service Gulf-front hotel here. It's designed in an arch, with all rooms' balconies looking directly down on the beach, where a heated, lagoon-style pool and sun deck are separated from the sand by a row of palms and Polynesian torches. The hotel has won architectural awards for its dramatic lobby with a waterfall and the Fountain of Wishes (the coins go to charity). Each attractive, spacious guest room has a full-size refrigerator, microwave, and two spacious vanity areas. Decor is dramatically different from that found in your typical Holiday Inn—it's more reminiscent of a resort in, say, the Caribbean, with its pastel colors and tile floors.

11127 Front Beach Rd., Panama City Beach, FL 32407. ✆ **800/633-0266** or 850/234-1111. Fax 850/235-1907. www.holidayinnsunspree.com. 340 units. Summer $185–$259 double; off-season $89–$139 double. AE, DC, DISC, MC, V. **Amenities:** 2 restaurants; bar; heated outdoor pool; exercise room; Jacuzzi; watersports equipment/rentals; game room; concierge; limited room service; babysitting; laundry service; concierge-level rooms. *In room:* A/C, TV, dataport, fridge, coffeemaker, hair dryer, iron, safe.

Sunset Inn This well-maintained establishment, near the east end of the beach, is right on the Gulf but away from the crowds. The spacious beachside rooms accommodate families in one- and two-bedroom apartments, while refurbished efficiencies and a new building with tropically furnished, one- and two-bedroom condominiums are across the street. The condominiums are the most expensive units here, but the units with patios or balconies right on the beach will better suit sun-and-sand lovers. The best part about this motel is the quiet beach—it offers a sense of peace not necessarily found elsewhere along the strip.

8109 Surf Dr., Panama City Beach, FL 32408. ✆ **850/234-7370.** Fax 850/234-7370, ext. 303. www.sunsetinnfl.com. 62 units. Spring Break and summer $65–$145 rooms and efficiencies, $150–$175 condos (4–6 people); spring $55–$100 rooms and efficiencies, $110–$125 condos; fall and winter $45–$85 rooms and efficiencies, $80–$100 condos. Weekly and monthly rates available. AE, DISC, MC, V. **Amenities:** Heated outdoor pool; coin-op washers/dryers. *In room:* A/C, TV, kitchen, fridge, coffeemaker.

WHERE TO DINE

Except for fast-food joints, there aren't many national-chain family restaurants in Panama City Beach (you'll find those along 15th and 23rd sts. over in Panama City). One local chain worth trying is the **Montego Bay Seafood House** (www.montegobaypcb.com), which offers a wide range of fairly inexpensive sandwiches, burgers, and seafood main courses. Branches are at the "curve" at 4920 Thomas Dr. (✆ **850/234-8686**) and in the Shoppes at Edgewater, 473 Beckrich Rd. at Front Beach Drive (✆ **850/233-6033**).

Pay attention to the restaurant hours here, as some places are closed in winter. Even if they're open, many will close early when business is slow; call ahead to make sure.

Billy's Oyster Bar and Crab House (Value) SEAFOOD More a lively raw bar than a restaurant, Billy and Eloise Poole's casual spot has been serving the best crabs in town since 1982. These are hard-shell blue crabs prepared Maryland-style: steamed with spicy Old Bay seasoning. Unlike crab houses in Baltimore, however, Billy and Eloise remove the crab's top shell, clean out the "mustard" (intestines), and cut the crabs in two for you; all you have to do is "pick" out the meat. Don't worry, they'll show you how. Other steamed morsels include shrimp, oysters, crabs, and lobster served with corn on the cob and garlic bread. Order anything from the briny deep here, but pass over other items.

3000 Thomas Dr. (btw. Grand Lagoon and Magnolia Beach Rd.). ✆ **850/235-2349.** Main courses $6–$20; sandwiches $5–$10. AE, DISC, MC, V. Daily 11am–9pm.

Boar's Head Restaurant ★ STEAK/SEAFOOD An institution since 1978, this shingle-roofed establishment appears from the road to be a South Seas resort. Inside, its impressive beamed ceiling, stone walls, and fireplaces create a warm, tavernlike atmosphere suited to the house specialties: tender, marbled prime rib of beef and perfectly cooked steaks. Beef eaters don't have the Boar's Head to themselves, however, as the coals are also used to give a charred flavor to salmon, grouper, and yellowfin tuna. Other temptations include scallops in a cream sauce over angel-hair pasta. Venison, quail, and other game dishes also find their way here in winter. The extensive wine list has won awards. Try the fried lobster if you're in the mood to really indulge. A cozy tavern to one side features live music, usually Wednesday through Saturday evenings.

17290 Front Beach Rd. (just west of Fla. 79). ✆ **850/234-6628.** www.boarsheadrestaurant.com. Main courses $17–$29. AE, DC, DISC, MC, V. Summer daily 4:30–10pm; off-season Sun–Thurs 4:30–9pm, Fri–Sat 4:30–10pm.

Captain Anderson's Restaurant & Waterfront Seafood Market ★ SEAFOOD Since 1953, this famous restaurant has been attracting early diners, who come to watch the fishing fleet unload the catch of the day at the busy marina on Grand Lagoon. It's so popular, in fact, that you may have to wait 2 hours for a table during the peak summer months; the three bars help you pass the time. The Captain's menu is noted

Fun Facts "We Shuck 'Em, You Suck 'Em"

That's the motto at **Shuckums Oyster Pub & Seafood Grill,** 15614 Front Beach Rd., at Powell Adams Drive (✆ **850/235-3214;** www.shuckums.com). Comedian Martin Short made this noisy, lively, and smoky pub famous when he tried unsuccessfully to shuck oysters at its bar during the making of an MTV Spring Break special. The original bar where Short tried to shuck is virtually papered over with dollar bills signed by old and young patrons who have been flocking here since 1967. The obvious specialty is fresh Apalachicola oysters, served raw, steamed, or baked with a variety of toppings. Otherwise, the menu consists of pub fare and mediocre seafood main courses. In summer, Shuckums is open daily from 11am to 2am. During the off-season, it closes at 9pm Monday through Friday, at midnight Saturday and Sunday.

for grilled local fish (grouper, amberjack, and yellowfin tuna), crab-stuffed jumbo shrimp, and a seafood platter that's heaped high.

5551 N. Lagoon Dr. (at Thomas Dr.). ✆ **850/234-2225.** www.captanderson.com. Main courses $14–$44. AE, DC, DISC, MC, V. Summer Mon–Sat 4–10pm; off-season Mon–Sat 4:30–10pm. Closed Nov–Jan.

Firefly ★★ INTERNATIONAL The Firefly is a very stylish, New York–style, global cuisine restaurant, but it's not too New Yorky. You can still dine outdoors under a grand old oak tree! The menu changes monthly, but hope you're there the night they are serving tempura-fried Apalachicola oysters. Other selections could include salmon and cream leek pizza with truffle oil; sushi-quality yellowfin tuna in a sherry-soy sauce; a "trio" of tuna, salmon, and grouper with a citrus-butter sauce served with mandarin-orange salsa and Vidalia-onion mashed potatoes; and sautéed grouper with lump crabmeat in a sherry-butter sauce. Forget the crab cakes. Landlubbers can partake of award-winning beef, veal, lamb, pork, and game dishes. White-chocolate mousse is among several wonderful sweet endings.

535 Beckrich Rd. (in Shoppes at Edgewater), Panama City. ✆ **850/872-8444.** www.fireflypcb.com. Reservations recommended. Main courses $18–$42. AE, DC, DISC, MC, V. Daily 5–10pm.

Special Dining Experiences

You've got to see the **Treasure Ship,** at Treasure Island Marina, 3605 S. Thomas Dr. at Grand Lagoon (✆ **850/234-8881;** www.thetreasureship.com), to believe it. This amazing 2 acres of ship space is claimed to be the world's largest land-based Spanish galleon and a reputed replica of the three-masted sailing ship that carried loot back to Spain in the 16th and 17th centuries. You can get anything from an ice-cream cone or peel-it-yourself shrimp to a sophisticated dinner in the restaurant and bar here, which are open daily from 4:30 to 10pm (and sometimes later); closed during the winter months. Call to make sure it's open when you want to go.

Dinner-dance cruises on the ***Lady Anderson*** are a romantic evening escape; they're available March through October. This modern, three-deck ship boards at Captain Anderson's Marina, 5550 N. Lagoon Dr. (✆ **800/360-0510** or 850/234-5940; www.ladyanderson.com), Monday through Saturday evenings, with the cruises lasting from 7 to 10pm. Buffet dinners are followed by live music for dancing on Monday, Wednesday, Friday, and Saturday nights; gospel music on Tuesday and Thursday. Dinner-dance tickets cost $45 for adults, $40 for seniors, $23 for children 6 to 11, and $15 for children 2 to 5. Gospel-music cruises go for $35 adults, $32 seniors, $23 children 6 to 11, and $15 children 2 to 5. Tips are included. Summertime reservations should be made well in advance.

PANAMA CITY & PANAMA CITY BEACH AFTER DARK

The Bar & Club Scene

The Breakers, 12627 Front Beach Rd. (© **850/234-6060;** www.breakerspcb.com), is the area's premier supper club, with unsurpassed Gulf views and music for dining and dancing. The beachfront **Harpoon Harry's Waterfront Cafe** is part of the same complex.

Romantic lounges with live entertainment can be found at the **Treasure Ship** (p. 616), at 3605 S. Thomas Dr. (© **850/234-8881**), where, during summer, the comedian-hypnotist Mike Harvey performs in the top-floor Captain's Quarters and at the **Boar's Head** (p. 615), at 17290 Front Beach Rd. (© **850/234-6628**).

The 20-something crowd likes to boogie all night at such beach clubs as **Schooners,** 5121 Gulf Dr. (© **850/235-3555;** www.schooners.com), where every table has a Gulf view, and **Club La Vela,** also on the beach at 8813 Thomas Dr. (© **850/234-3866;** www.clublavela.com), a bikini-contest kind of place and one of Florida's largest nightclubs. The clubs often stay open until 4am in summer. **Pineapple Willy's Lounge,** beachside at 9900 S. Thomas Dr. (© **850/235-0928;** www.pineapplewillys.com), is open from 11am until 2am, serving ribs basted with Jack Daniel's and spotlighting live entertainment during summer and a host of sports on TVs year-round.

4 APALACHICOLA ★★

65 miles E of Panama City; 80 miles W of Tallahassee

Sometimes called Florida's Last Frontier (a claim that overlooks the Everglades) or the Forgotten Coast, Apalachicola makes a fascinating day trip from Panama City Beach or Tallahassee, as well as a destination in its own right. The long, gorgeous beaches on St. George Island, 7 miles from town, are among America's best. Justifiably famous for Apalachicola oysters, the bays and estuaries are great for fishing and boating. If you love nature, the area is rich in wildlife preserves.

The charming little town of Apalachicola (pop. 2,600) was a major seaport each autumn from 1827 to 1861, when plantations in Alabama and Georgia shipped tons of cotton down the Apalachicola River to the Gulf. The town had a racetrack, an opera house, and a civic center that hosted balls, socials, and gambling. The population shrank during the mosquito-infested summer months, however, when yellow fever and malaria epidemics struck. It was during one of these outbreaks that Dr. John Gorrie of Apalachicola tried to develop a method of cooling his patients' rooms. In doing so, he invented the forerunner of the air conditioner, a device that made Florida tourism possible and life a whole lot more bearable for locals.

Apalachicola has traditionally made its living primarily from the Gulf and the lagoon-like bay protected by a chain of offshore barrier islands. Today this area produces the bulk of Florida's oyster crop, and shrimping and fishing are major industries, too. The town has also been discovered by a number of urban expatriates, who have moved here, restored old homes, and opened interesting antiques and gift shops (there aren't many towns this size where you can buy Crabtree & Evelyn products).

ESSENTIALS

GETTING THERE The nearest airport is 65 miles to the west at Panama City Beach (p. 609). From there, you'll have to rent a car or take an expensive taxi ride. The Tallahassee Regional Airport (p. 622) is about 85 miles to the northeast.

The scenic way to drive here is via the Gulf-hugging U.S. 98 from Panama City Beach, or via U.S. 319 and U.S. 98 from Tallahassee. From I-10, take exit 142 at Marianna, then follow Florida 71 south to Port St. Joe; from there, take U.S. 98 East to Apalachicola.

VISITOR INFORMATION The **Apalachicola Bay Chamber of Commerce,** 99 Market St., Apalachicola, FL 32320 (✆ **850/653-9419;** fax 850/653-8219; www.apalachicolabay.org), supplies information about the area from its office on Market Street (U.S. 98) between Avenue D and Avenue E. The chamber is open Monday through Friday from 9:30am to 5pm.

TIME The town is in the Eastern time zone, like Orlando, Miami, and Tallahassee (1 hr. ahead of Panama City Beach and the rest of the Panhandle). ***Note:*** Many shops are closed on Wednesday afternoon, when Apalachicolans go fishing.

BEACHES, PARKS & WILDLIFE REFUGES

Some experts consider the 9 miles of beaches in the **Dr. Julian G. Bruce St. George Island State Park ★★★** among America's best. This pristine nature preserve occupies the eastern end of St. George Island, about 15 miles east of Apalachicola. A 4-mile-long paved road leads through the dunes to picnic areas, restrooms, showers, and a boat launch. An unpaved trail leads another 5 miles to the island's eastern end, but be careful: It's easy to get stuck in the soft sand, even in a four-wheel-drive SUV. From a hiking trail leading from the campground out to a narrow peninsula on the bay side, you can see countless terns, snowy plovers, black skimmers, and other birds. Entry costs $5 per vehicle with up to eight occupants, and $1 per pedestrian or bicyclist. East End access costs $6 per person. Campsites go for $19. The park is open daily from 8am to sunset. Pets are allowed. For more information, contact the park at 1900 E. Gulf Beach Dr., St. George Island, FL 32328 (✆ **850/927-2111;** www.floridastateparks.org/stgeorgeisland). If you'd rather stay on St. George Island in the cushier confines of one of 270 privately owned rental homes, from luxe six-bedroom beach homes to old-fashioned Florida cottages, call **Collins Vacation Rentals** (✆ **800/423-7418;** www.collinsvacationrentals.com). In addition to the state park, the island offers restaurants, bars, and some of the best fishing in the state.

There are no facilities whatsoever at the **St. Vincent National Wildlife Refuge,** southwest of Apalachicola and accessible only by boat. The U.S. Fish & Wildlife Service has left this 12,358-acre barrier island in its natural state, but visitors are welcome to walk through its pine forests, marshlands, ponds, dunes, and beaches. In addition to native species, such as bald eagles and alligators, the island is home to a small herd of sambar deer from Southeast Asia. Red wolves are bred here for relocation in other wildlife areas. **St. Vincents Island Shuttle Service** (✆ **850/229-1065;** www.stvincentisland.com), at Indian Pass, 21 miles west of Apalachicola via U.S. 98 and C.R.s 30A and 30B, will take you to the island in a pontoon boat. If you bring your bike, the boat will drop you at one end of the island and pick you up later at the other. Call for prices and reservations, which are required. The refuge headquarters, at the north end of Market Street in town, has exhibits of wetland flora and fauna; it's open Monday through Friday from 8am to 4:30pm. Admission is free. For more information, contact the refuge at P.O. Box 447, Apalachicola, FL 32329 (✆ **850/653-8808**).

The huge **Apalachicola National Forest** (p. 634) begins a few miles northeast of town. It has a host of facilities, including canoeing and mountain-bike trails.

OUTDOOR ACTIVITIES

CRUISES Jeanni McMillan of **Journeys of St. George Island ★** (✆ **850/927-3259;** www.sgislandjourneys.com) takes guests on narrated nature cruises to the barrier islands, and on canoe and kayak trips in the creeks and streams of the Apalachicola River basin. She also leads night hikes with blue-crab netting, shelling excursions, and fishing and scalloping trips, plus excursions tailored exclusively for children. Prices range from $250 to $400 per person. Reservations are required, so call to find out what she's offering when you'll be in town. Jeanni also rents canoes, kayaks, sailboats, and sailboards. Closed January and February.

A less adventurous way to see the marshes, swamps, and shallow-water rivers is via a nature cruise with **EcoVentures, Inc.** (✆ **850/653-2593;** www.apalachicolatours.com). It uses the *Osprey,* a 40-foot, all-weather boat that can carry up to 32 passengers. Fares are $25 per person. Private charters cost $75 an hour with a 2-hour minimum. Call for schedule and reservations.

You can go afternoon or sunset sailing on the bay on Capt. Jerry Weber's 40-foot sloop ***Wind Catcher*** (✆ **850/653-3881**). The 2½-hour voyages on Apalachicola Bay cost $35 for adults and $30 for children 15 and under, including snacks and soft drinks. Reservations are essential.

FISHING You can't go oystering, but fishing is excellent in these waters, where trout, redfish, flounder, tarpon, shark, and drum abound. The chamber of commerce (p. 618) can help arrange charters on the local boats, many of which dock at the Rainbow Inn on Water Street. For guides, contact **Robinson Brothers Guide Service** (✆ **850/653-8896;** www.flaredfish.com). Rates run about $375 for a half-day and $400 to $550 for a full day for up to four anglers.

EXPLORING THE TOWN

Start your visit by picking up a map and a self-guided tour brochure from the chamber of commerce (p. 618), and then stroll around Apalachicola's waterfront, business district, and Victorian-era homes.

Along Water Street, several tin warehouses date back to the town's seafaring days of the late 1800s, as does the 1840s-era **Sponge Exchange,** at Commerce Street and Avenue E. A highlight of the residential area, centered on Gorrie Square at Avenue D and Sixth Street, is the Greek Revival–style **Trinity Episcopal Church,** built in New York and shipped here in 1837. **Battery Park,** at the water end of Sixth Street, has a children's playground. A number of excellent art galleries and gift shops are grouped on Market Street, Avenue D, and Commerce Street.

The showpiece at the **John Gorrie Museum State Park ★**, Avenue D, at Sixth Street (✆ **850/653-9347;** www.floridastateparks.org/johngorriemuseum), is a replica of Dr. Gorrie's cooling machine, a prototype of today's air conditioner: It really works! The park is open Thursday through Monday from 9am to 5pm; closed New Year's Day, Thanksgiving, and Christmas. Admission is $1 (free for children 6 and under).

The renovated **Dixie Theatre,** 21 Ave. E (✆ **850/653-3200;** www.dixietheatre.com), a 1912 movie house, hosts live theater productions. It has maintained its original ticket booth and restored its facades to their original glory.

The **Estuarine Walk,** at the north end of Market Street, on the grounds of the Apalachicola National Estuarine Research Reserve (✆ **850/653-8063**), contains aquariums full of fish and turtles, along with displays of other estuarine life. It's open Monday through Friday from 8am to 5pm. Admission is free.

WHERE TO STAY

Built in 1997, the 42-room **Best Western Apalach Inn,** 249 Hwy. 98 W. (✆ **800/528-1234** or 850/653-9131; fax 850/653-9136; www.bwapalachinn.com), a mile west of downtown, is the only national chain hotel here.

Apalachicola River Inn ★ The town's only waterfront lodging, this two-story motel has rough-hewn exterior timbers that make it look like one of the neighboring warehouses. Units in the main building all have views across a marina to Apalachicola Bay. Those on the second floor are larger and have balconies, making them preferable to the smaller downstairs units, with doors opening directly onto the marina's boardwalk. All accommodations have been renovated, and they have new carpeting, windows, and French doors. Most of the upstairs rooms have shower-only bathrooms; however, there are whirlpool tubs in two of the units, as well as in a two-bedroom apartment in a building next door. The redone lobby now features the Frog Level Oyster Bar, a casual bar serving—what else?—oysters. There's also Boss Oyster, the inn's popular riverfront restaurant; Caroline's; and the Roseate Spoonbill Lounge—*the* local watering hole, with a grand view and music on an outdoor deck on weekends.

123 Water St., Apalachicola, FL 32320. ✆ **850/653-8139.** Fax 850/653-2018. www.apalachicolariverinn.com. 26 units. $95–$115 double; $125–$150 Jacuzzi suite; $200–$400 2-bedroom suite. AE, DC, DISC, MC, V. Pets accepted in smoking rooms ($10 nightly fee). **Amenities:** Restaurant; 2 bars and lounges. *In room:* A/C, TV.

Coombs House Inn ★★★ The most luxurious place around, this large B&B occupies two Victorian homes. The main house was built in 1905 by a lumber baron, and it shows: Polished black-cypress paneling lines the entire central hall and parlor. Each of the 10 guest rooms here is tastefully decorated, with lots of Victorian reproductions. The Coombs Suite (with bay windows, sofa, four-poster bed, and whirlpool tub) is outstanding. The Love Bungalow has its own private entrance. Less grand, but still impressive, are eight rooms in another restored Victorian, known as Coombs House East, half a block away. One of these rooms has a whirlpool tub and bidet. A major truck route, U.S. 98, runs along the north side of both houses; request a south room to escape the periodic road noise. Guests are treated to complimentary wine receptions on weekends. The breakfast is not just Danish and coffee, but a home-cooked extravaganza. All rooms are nonsmoking.

80 6th St., Apalachicola, FL 32320. ✆ **850/653-9199.** Fax 850/653-2785. www.coombshouseinn.com. 18 units. $89–$225 double. Rates include full breakfast. DISC, MC, V. **Amenities:** Access to nearby health club; free use of mountain bikes. *In room:* A/C, TV, dataport, hair dryer.

Gibson Inn ★★★ Built in 1907 as a seamen's hotel and gorgeously restored, this cupola-topped inn is such a brilliant example of Victorian architecture that it's listed on the National Register of Historic Inns. No two guest rooms are alike (some still have the original sinks in the sleeping areas), but all are richly furnished with period reproductions. Nonguests are welcome to wander upstairs and peek into unoccupied rooms (whose doors are left open). Reservations are advised during summer and on spring and fall weekends, and as much as 5 years in advance for the seafood festival in November. Grab a drink from the bar and relax in one of the high-backed rockers on the old-fashioned veranda. The dining room serves excellent seafood and is open to all comers, so don't expect this to be private like a B&B; instead, you'll find yourself in a reborn, absolutely charming, turn-of-the-20th-century hotel—one, albeit, with Wi-Fi Internet access!

51 Ave. C, Apalachicola, FL 32320. ✆ **850/653-2191.** Fax 850/653-3521. www.gibsoninn.com. 31 units. $105–$155 double; $175–$250 suite. AE, MC, V. **Amenities:** Restaurant; bar; Wi-Fi. *In room:* A/C, TV.

WHERE TO DINE

Townsfolk still plop down on the round stools at the marble-topped counter to order Coca-Colas and milkshakes at the **Old Time Soda Fountain & Luncheonette,** 93 Market St. (✆ **850/653-2606**). This 1950s relic was once the town drugstore. It's open Monday through Saturday from 10am to 5pm.

The Boss Oyster ★ SEAFOOD You've heard about the aphrodisiac properties of Apalachicola oysters. Well, you can see if those properties are real at this rustic dockside eatery, whose motto is "Shut Up and Shuck." This is one of the best places in Florida to try the bivalves raw, steamed, or under a dozen toppings, ranging from capers to crabmeat. Steamed shrimp are also on offer, as are delicious po' boy sandwiches. Most main courses come from the fryer, so consider this joint a great local experience, not fine dining. Sit at the picnic tables inside, on a screened porch, or out on the dock.

At the Apalachicola River Inn, 125 Water St. (btw. aves. C and D). ✆ **850/653-9364.** Main courses $17–$25; oysters $4.50–$16; sandwiches and baskets $7–$10. AE, DC, DISC, MC, V. Apr–Sept Sun–Thurs 11:30am–10pm, Fri–Sat 11:30am–11pm; Oct–Mar Sun–Thurs 11:30am–9pm, Fri–Sat 11:30am–10pm.

Chef Eddie's Magnolia Grill ★★★ CONTINENTAL/CAJUN One of the top places to dine in Northwest Florida, Boston-bred chef-owner Eddie Cass's pleasant, homey restaurant offers nightly specials ranging from classic French rack of lamb and beef Wellington to fresh local seafood with New Orleans–style sauces. You will long remember Eddie's mahimahi Pontchartrain with cream and artichoke hearts. Start with a bowl of spicy seafood gumbo, a consistent hit during the Florida Seafood Festival.

99 11th St. (btw. aves. E and F). ✆ **850/653-8000.** www.chefeddiesmagnoliagrill.com. Reservations recommended. Main courses $12–$24. MC, V. Mon–Sat 6–9:30pm.

The Owl Cafe ★★ SEAFOOD Ensconced on the first floor of a two-story clapboard building in the heart of downtown, this sophisticated restaurant ranks only behind Chef Eddie's Magnolia Grill as having the best cuisine in town. Go for the nightly seafood specials or opt for the terrific black grouper filet with garlic, capers, and artichokes. Now paneled in rich wood, the walls are adorned with the works of noted local photographer Richard Bickel.

15 Ave. D (at Commerce St.). ✆ **850/653-9888.** www.owlcafeflorida.com. Reservations recommended. Main courses $12–$25. MC, V. Mon–Sat 11:30am–3pm and 5:30–10pm.

Tamara's Cafe Floridita FLORIBBEAN/LATIN AMERICAN Tamara Suarez's storefront cafe offers a change of pace and, sadly, since she handed the restaurant over to her daughter and son-in-law, a change from a once-fabulous experience to a somewhat disappointing one. The black-bean soup may still have zing, but the service is spotty and not nearly as attentive as it used to be. You'll also find Latino spices accentuating Floribbean fare, such as a creamy jalapeño sauce putting a little fire into pecan-encrusted grouper. The paella is still a winner, but be forewarned—it ain't what it used to be.

17 Ave. E. (at Commerce St.). ✆ **850/653-4111.** www.tamarascafe.com. Reservations recommended. Main courses $12–$24. MC, V. Daily 11am–10pm.

5 TALLAHASSEE

163 miles W of Jacksonville; 191 miles E of Pensacola; 250 miles NW of Orlando

As a University of Miami alumna, I was practically taught to hate Tallahassee, just because it's the home of the Miami Hurricanes' biggest rivals—Florida State University's Seminoles (or 'Noles, as locals refer to them). Because I couldn't care less about football, I just chalked up Tallahassee as the state capital and, later in life, as command central for that pesky 2000 election bug known as the chad. Boy, was I wrong. It's not just about football and hanging chads here. There's a ton of charm and other history here, too.

Tallahassee was selected as Florida's capital in 1823 because it was halfway between St. Augustine and Pensacola, then the state's major cities. That location puts it almost in Georgia—and, in fact, Tallahassee has more in common with Macon than with Miami. There's as much Old South ambience here as anywhere else in Florida. You'll find lovingly restored, 19th-century homes and buildings, including the 1845 Old Capitol. They all sit among so many towering pines and sprawling live oaks that you'll think you're in an enormous forest. The trees form virtual tunnels along Tallahassee's five official Canopy Roads, which are lined with historic plantations, ancient Native American settlement sites and mounds, gorgeous gardens, quiet parks with picnic areas, and beautiful lakes and streams. The nearby Apalachicola National Forest is a virtual gold mine of outdoor pursuits.

While tradition and history are important here, you'll also encounter the modern era, beginning with the New Capitol Building towering 22 stories over downtown. Usually sleepy Tallahassee takes on a very lively persona when the legislature is in session and when the football teams of Florida State University and Florida A&M University take to the gridiron.

If you're inclined to give your credit cards a workout, the nearby town of Havana is Florida's antiques capital.

ESSENTIALS

GETTING THERE **AirTran, Delta, Northwest,** and **US Airways** serve **Tallahassee Regional Airport** (✆ **850/891-7802;** www.talgov.com/airport), 10 miles southwest of downtown on Southeast Capital Circle.

Alamo, Avis, Budget, Hertz, and **National** have airport sites; **Dollar, Enterprise,** and **Thrifty** are nearby. See "Appendix: Fast Facts, Toll-Free Numbers & Websites," p. 638, for the contact information of airlines and car services.

You can take a **taxi** downtown for about $20.

The **Amtrak** (✆ **800/872-7245;** www.amtrak.com) transcontinental *Sunset Limited* train stops in Tallahassee at 918½ Railroad Ave.

VISITOR INFORMATION For advance information, contact the **Tallahassee Area Convention and Visitors Bureau,** 200 W. College Ave. (P.O. Box 1369), Tallahassee, FL 32302 (✆ **800/628-2866** or 850/413-9200; fax 850/487-4621; www.seetallahassee.com). The bureau's excellent quarterly visitors guide has descriptions (including hours and admission fees) of just about everything going on here.

Go to the **Tallahassee Area Visitor Information Center,** 106 E. Jefferson St., across from the capitol (✆ **850/413-9200**), for free street and public-transportation maps, brochures, and pamphlets outlining tours of the historic districts and the Canopy Roads. It's open Monday through Friday from 8am to 5pm, Saturday from 9am to noon.

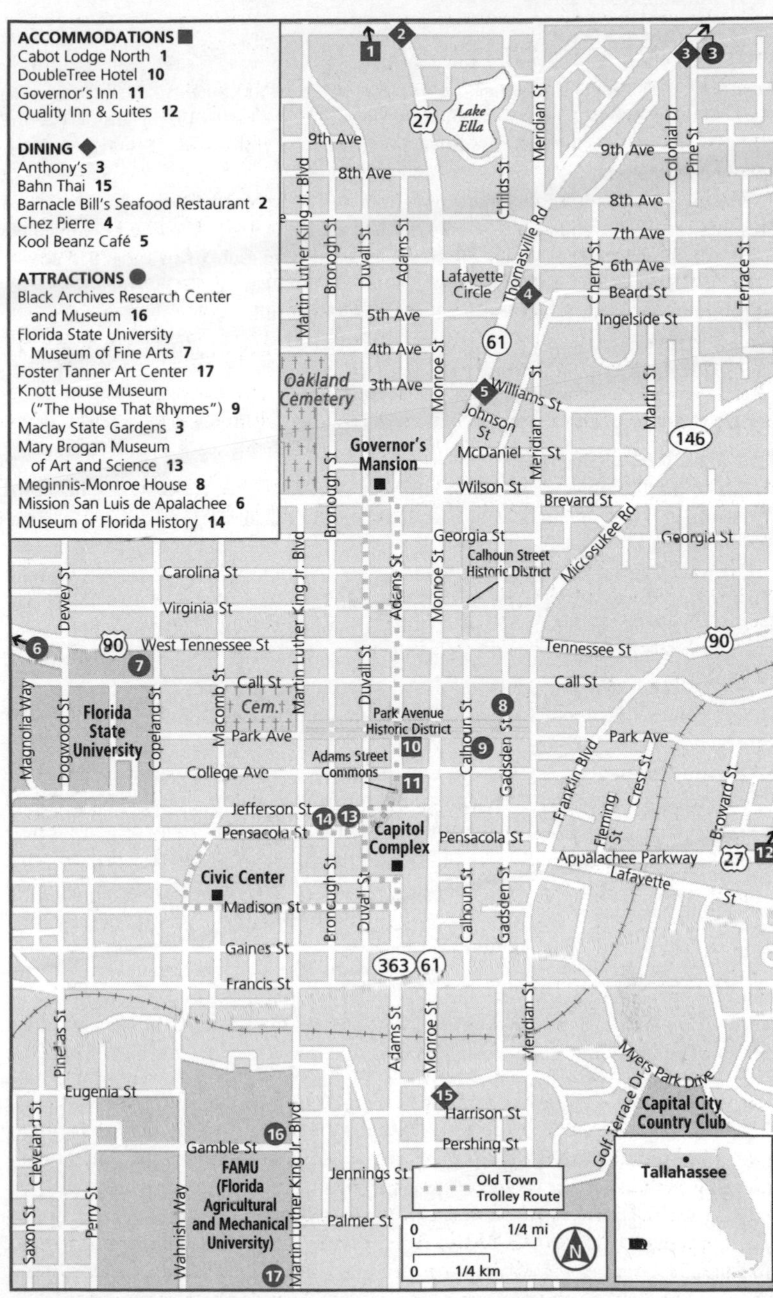
ACCOMMODATIONS
Cabot Lodge North 1
DoubleTree Hotel 10
Governor's Inn 11
Quality Inn & Suites 12
DINING
Anthony's 3
Bahn Thai 15
Barnacle Bill's Seafood Restaurant 2
Chez Pierre 4
Kool Beanz Café 5
ATTRACTIONS
Black Archives Research Center and Museum 16
Florida State University Museum of Fine Arts 7
Foster Tanner Art Center 17
Knott House Museum ("The House That Rhymes") 9
Maclay State Gardens 3
Mary Brogan Museum of Art and Science 13
Meginnis-Monroe House 8
Mission San Luis de Apalachee 6
Museum of Florida History 14
Lake Ella
Oakland Cemetery
Governor's Mansion
Calhoun Street Historic District
Florida State University
Park Avenue Historic District
Adams Street Commons
Capitol Complex
Civic Center
FAMU (Florida Agricultural and Mechanical University)
Capital City Country Club
Old Town Trolley Route
Tallahassee

For statewide information, a **Florida Welcome Center** is in the west foyer of the New Capitol Building (see below).

GETTING AROUND The city's public-transportation agency, **TALTRAN** (**© 850/891-5200**), operates the free **Old Town Trolley,** the best way to see the sights of historic downtown Tallahassee. You can get on or off at any point between Adams Street Commons, at the corner of Jefferson and Adams streets, and the Governor's Mansion (see the exact route on the "Downtown Tallahassee" map). The trolley runs Monday through Friday, every 20 minutes between 7am and 6:30pm.

TALTRAN also provides city **bus** service from its downtown terminal, at Tennessee and Adams streets ($1.25 adults, 60¢ seniors and kids 12 and under). The ticket booths there and at the Tallahassee Area Visitor Information Center have route maps and schedules.

For taxi service, call **Yellow Cab** (**© 850/580-8080**) or **City Taxi** (**© 850/562-4222**). Fares are about $2.50 at flag fall, plus $2.25 per mile.

TIME Tallahassee is in the Eastern time zone, like Orlando, Miami, and Apalachicola. It's 1 hour ahead of the rest of the Panhandle.

EXPLORING THE CITY

The Capitol Complex

Florida's capitol complex, on South Monroe Street, at Apalachee Parkway, dominates the downtown area and should be your first stop after the Tallahassee Area Visitor Information Center, just across Jefferson Street.

The **New Capitol Building** (**© 850/488-6167**), a $43-million skyscraper, was built in 1977 to replace the 1845-vintage Old Capitol. State legislators meet here for at least 60 days, usually beginning in March. The house and senate chambers have public viewing galleries. For a spectacular view, take the elevators to the 22nd-floor **observatory,** where, on a clear day, you can see all the way to the Gulf of Mexico. You can also view works by Florida artists while up here. The New Capitol is open Monday through Friday from 8am to 5pm.

Directly in front of the skyscraper is the strikingly white **Old Capitol ★** (**© 850/487-1902;** www.inusa.com/tour/fl/tallahas/capitol.htm). With its majestic dome, this "Pearl of Capitol Hill" has been restored to its original beauty. An eight-room exhibit portrays Florida's political history. Turn-of-the-20th-century furnishings, cotton gins, and other artifacts are also of interest. The Old Capitol is open Monday through Friday from 9am to 4:30pm, Saturday from 10am to 4:30pm, and Sunday and holidays from noon to 4:30pm. Admission is free to both the old and new capitols.

The twin granite towers of the **Vietnam Veterans Memorial,** honoring Florida's Vietnam vets, are across Monroe Street from the Old Capitol. Next to it, facing Apalachee Parkway, the **Union Bank Museum** (**© 850/561-2603**) is housed in Florida's oldest surviving bank building. For a while, it was the Freedman's Savings and Trust Company, which served emancipated slaves. Now part of Florida Agricultural and Mechanical University's Black Archives Research Center, it houses a small but interesting collection of artifacts and documents reflecting black history and culture and is definitely worth a brief visit. The museum is open Monday through Friday from 9am to 4pm; admission is free.

The Old Town Trolley will take you north of the capitol to the lovely Georgian-style **Governor's Mansion,** at Adams and Brevard streets (**© 850/488-4661**). Enhanced by a portico patterned after Andrew Jackson's columned antebellum home in Tennessee, the Hermitage, and surrounded by giant magnolia trees and landscaped lawns, the mansion is furnished with 18th- and 19th-century antiques and collectibles. Tours are given when the legislature is in session, usually beginning in March. Call for schedules and reservations.

Adjacent to the Governor's Mansion, the **Grove** was home to Ellen Call Long, known as "The Tallahassee Girl," the first child born after Tallahassee was settled.

Historic Districts

Although modern buildings have made inroads into the downtown area, Tallahassee has made an ongoing effort to preserve its historic homes and buildings. Many of them are concentrated in three historic districts within an easy walk north of the capitol complex. The information center in the New Capitol distributes free brochures of walking tours that cover the three areas. Taken together, the tours are about 4 miles long and should take half a day. Most interesting is the Park Avenue Historic District, 3 blocks north of the capitol complex, which you can see in about 1 hour.

ADAMS STREET COMMONS This block-long, winding brick street and landscaped area along Adams Street begins on the north side of the capitol complex (btw. Jefferson St. and College Ave.) and retains an old-fashioned town-square atmosphere. Restored buildings include the Governor's Club, a 1900s Masonic lodge, and Gallie's Hall, where Florida's first five African-American college students received their Florida A&M University diplomas in 1892. Restaurants, shops, and Gallie Alley are also here. Adams Street crosses Park Avenue 3 blocks north of the capitol complex. This is a good place for lunch; choose from one of the several cafes that cater to downtown office workers.

PARK AVENUE HISTORIC DISTRICT The 7 blocks of Park Avenue between Martin Luther King, Jr., Boulevard and North Meridian Street are a lovely promenade of beautiful trees, gardens, and outstanding old mansions. This broad avenue, with a shady median strip lined with moss-bearded live oaks, was originally named 200 Foot Street and then McCarty Street, but was later renamed Park Avenue to satisfy a snobbish Anglophile society matron who didn't want an Irish name imprinted on her son's wedding invitations.

Several Park Avenue historic homes are open to the public, including the **Knott House Museum,** at Calhoun Street (see "Museums, Galleries & Archaeological Sites," below). The **Columns,** at Duval Street, was built in the 1830s and is the city's oldest surviving building (it's now the home of the Tallahassee Chamber of Commerce). The **First Presbyterian Church,** at Adams Street, built in 1838, is the city's oldest church and has been an important African-American historic site since slaves were welcome to worship here without their masters' consent. The **Walker Library,** between Monroe and Calhoun streets, was one of Florida's first libraries, dating from 1903 (it's home to Springtime Tallahassee, which is the city's top special event). Just north of Park Avenue on Gadsden Street, the **Meginnis-Monroe House** contains the Lemoyne Art Gallery (see "Museums, Galleries & Archaeological Sites," below).

At Martin Luther King, Jr., Boulevard, the adjacent **Old City Cemetery** and **Episcopal Cemetery** contain the graves of Prince Achille Murat, Napoleon's nephew, an Princess Catherine Murat, the prince's wife and George Washington's grandniece. Also buried here are two governors and numerous Confederate and Union soldiers who died at the Battle of Natural Bridge during the Civil War. The cemeteries are important to African-American history, as a number of slaves and the first black Florida A&M graduates are interred here. The visitor center in the New Capitol provides a cemetery walking-tour brochure.

CALHOUN STREET HISTORIC DISTRICT The 3 blocks of Calhoun Street between Tennessee and Georgia streets, and running east on Virginia Street to Leon High School, sport elaborate homes built by prominent citizens between 1830 and 1880. A highlight here is the **Brokaw-McDougall House,** built in 1856, located in front of Leon High School at the eastern end of Virginia Street.

Museums, Galleries & Archaeological Sites

Black Archives Research Center and Museum ★ Housed in the columned library built by Andrew Carnegie in 1908, and set on the grounds of the Florida Agricultural and Mechanical University (FAMU), this fascinating research center and museum displays one of the nation's most extensive collections of African-American artifacts, as well as such treasures as a 500-piece Ethiopian cross collection. The archives contain one of the world's largest collections on African-American history. Visitors can listen to tapes of gospel music and of elderly people reminiscing about the past. FAMU was founded in 1887, primarily as a black institution. Today it's acclaimed for its business, engineering, and pharmacy schools.

Martin Luther King, Jr., Blvd. and Gamble St., on the Florida A&M University campus. ✆ **850/599-3020.** www.famu.edu. Free admission. Mon–Fri 9am–4pm. Closed major holidays. Parking lot next to building.

Florida State University Museum of Fine Arts ★ This permanent, 4,000-piece collection includes 16th-century Dutch paintings, 20th-century American paintings, Japanese prints, pre-Columbian artifacts, and much more. Touring exhibits are displayed every few weeks.

250 Fine Arts Building, Copeland and Call sts. (on the FSU campus). ✆ **850/644-6836.** www.mofa.fsu.edu. Free admission. May–Aug Mon–Fri 9am–4pm; Sept–Apr Mon–Fri 9am–4pm, Sat–Sun 1–4pm. Closed holidays and weekends May–Aug.

Foster Tanner Art Center This gallery focuses on works by local, national, and international African-American artists, with a wide variety of paintings, sculptures, and more.

Florida A&M University (btw. Osceola and Gamble sts., off Martin Luther King, Jr., Blvd.). ✆ **850/599-3161.** www.famu.edu. Free admission. Mon–Fri 9am–5pm.

Knott House Museum ★★ Adorned by a columned portico, this stately mansion was constructed in 1843, probably by a free black builder named George Proctor. Florida's first reading of the Emancipation Proclamation took place here in 1865. In 1928, it was purchased by politician William Knott, whose wife Louella wrote eccentric (read: kooky) rhymes about the house and its elegant Victorian furnishings (including the nation's largest collection of 19th-c. gilt-framed mirrors). She also wrote about social, economic, and political events of the era. Attached by satin ribbons to tables, chairs, and lamps, her poems are the museum's most unusual feature. The house is in the Park Avenue Historic District and is listed on the National Register of Historic Places. It's preserved as it looked in 1928, when the Knott family left it and all of its contents to the city (it's now administered by the Museum of Florida History). The gift shop carries Victorian greeting cards, paper dolls, tin toy replicas, reprints of historic newspapers, and other nostalgic items.

301 E. Park Ave. (at Calhoun St.). ✆ **850/922-2459.** www.taltrust.org/knott.htm. Free admission. Wed–Fri 1–4pm; Sat 10am–4pm. 1-hr. tours depart on the hour.

Mary Brogan Museum of Art and Science (Kids) This museum's mission, "to stimulate interest in and understanding of the visual arts, sciences, mathematics, and technology through experiences that educate and inspire," pretty much says it all. Associated with the Smithsonian Institution, the Mary Brogan Museum has changing exhibitions, educational programs, and lectures, as well as permanent science museum–type exhibits.

350 S. Duval St. (at Pensacola St.). ✆ **850/513-0700.** www.thebrogan.org. Admission $6 adults; $3.50 seniors 60 and over, college students, military with ID, and children 3–17. Mon–Sat 10am–5pm; Sun 1–5pm.

Meginnis-Monroe House ★★ This restored 1852 antebellum home, listed on the National Register of Historic Places, is a lovely setting for fine art. The home's **Lemoyne Art Gallery** is named in honor of Jacques LeMoyne, a member of a French expedition to Florida in 1564. Commissioned to depict the natives' dwellings and to map the seacoast, LeMoyne was the first European artist known to have visited North America. Exhibits here include permanent displays by local artists, sculpture, pottery, and photography—everything from the traditional to the avant-garde. The gardens, with an old-fashioned gazebo, are spectacular during the Christmas holiday season. Programs of classical music are combined with visual arts during the year; check in advance for the current schedule.

125 N. Gadsden St. (btw. Park Ave. and Call St.). ✆ **850/222-8800.** www.lemoyne.org. Admission $1 adults, free for children 12 and under; free to all Sun. Tues–Sat 10am–5pm; Sun 1–5pm. Closed holidays.

Mission San Luís de Apalachee ★ A Spanish Franciscan mission named San Luís was set up in 1656 on this hilltop, already a principal village of the Apalachee Indians. From then until 1704, it served as the capital of a chain of Spanish missions in Northwest Florida. The mission complex included a tribal council house, a Franciscan church, a Spanish fort, and residential areas. Based on extensive archaeological and historical research, the council house and the 10×50-foot thatched-roofed church have been reconstructed. They are both open to the public. Interpretive markers are found across the 60-acre site, and self-guided tour brochures are available at the visitor center. Call for a schedule of ranger-led guided tours on weekends.

2021 Mission Rd. (btw. W. Tennessee and Tharpe sts.). ✆ **850/487-3711.** www.taltrust.org/san_luis.htm. Free admission. Tues–Sun 10am–4pm. Closed Thanksgiving and Christmas. From downtown, take Tennessee St. (U.S. 90 W.) to entrance on right past Ocala St.

Museum of Florida History ★ An 11-foot-tall mastodon greets you at this state history museum, where you can look back 12,000 years to the first Native Americans to live in Florida (mastodons were very much alive back then). Ancient artifacts from Native American tribes are exhibited, along with such relics from Florida's past as a reconstructed steamboat and treasures from 16th- and 17th-century sunken Spanish galleons. Inquire about guided tours and special exhibits.

Lower level of R. A. Gray Building, 500 S. Bronough St. (at Pensacola St.). ✆ **850/245-6400.** http://dhr.dos.state.fl.us/museum. Free admission. Mon–Fri 9am–4:30pm; Sat 10am–4:30pm; Sun and holidays noon–4:30pm. Closed Thanksgiving and Christmas. Parking available in garage around the corner on St. Augustine St., btw. Bronough and Duvall sts.

PARKS & NATURE PRESERVES

Maclay State Gardens ★★ In 1923, New York financier Alfred B. Maclay and his wife Louise began planting the floral wonderland that surrounded their winter home on Lake Hall, on Tallahassee's northeastern outskirts. After her husband's death in 1944, Louise continued his dream of an ornamental garden to delight the public. In 1953, the land was bequeathed to the state of Florida. On more than 300 acres, there are at least 200 varieties of flowers; 28 acres are devoted exclusively to azaleas and camellias. The surrounding park provides nature trails, canoe rentals, boating, picnicking, swimming, and fishing. The high blooming season is January through April, with the peak about mid-March. Beyond the house and gardens, the state park includes Lake Overstreet, around which wind 5.5 miles of hiking, biking, and horseback-riding trails, making this a major venue for those outdoor activities.

3540 Thomasville Rd. (U.S. 319, north of I-10). ✆ **850/487-4556.** www.floridastateparks.org/maclaygardens. Admission to park $4 per vehicle with up to 8 passengers, $1 per pedestrian or cyclist. May–Dec free admission to gardens; Jan–Apr $4 adults, $2 children 11 and under. Park daily 8am–sunset. Gardens daily 9am–5pm. Maclay House Jan–Apr daily 9am–5pm; closed May–Dec.

TRAVELING THE CANOPY ROADS

Graced by canopies of live oaks draped with Spanish moss, the St. Augustine, Miccousukee, Meridian, Old Bainbridge, and Centerville roads are the five official Canopy Roads leading out of Tallahassee. Driving is slow on these winding, two-lane country roads (the locals reluctantly are turning limited sections of them into four-lane highways); some of them are canopied for as long as 20 miles. Take along a picnic lunch, since there are few places to buy a meal along these tranquil byways. The visitor center in the New Capitol (p. 624) provides a useful driving-guide map of the Canopy Roads and Leon County's country lanes.

If you have time for only one, take **Old Bainbridge Road,** which leads to the Lake Jackson Mounds State Archaeological Site in the northwest suburbs and then on to Havana, Florida's antiquing capital (see "Shopping," below).

SHOPPING

Antiques hounds flock to the little village of **Havana ★★**, 12 miles northwest of I-10 on U.S. 27. Havana used to make its living growing shade tobacco (the outer wrapper on cigars). When that industry fizzled in the 1960s, the town went with it. Things turned around 20 years later, however, when Havana began opening art galleries and shops featuring antiques, handicrafts, and collectibles. Today these are housed in lovingly restored, turn-of-the-20th-century brick buildings along Havana's commercial streets. Just drive into town on Main Street (U.S. 27), turn left on 7th Avenue, find a parking place, and start browsing. You'll have plenty of company on weekends.

Bradley's Country Store, about 8 miles north of I-10 on Centerville Road (✆ **850/893-1647;** www.bradleyscountrystore.com), sells more than 80,000 pounds of homemade country smoked sausage a year, both over-the-counter and by mail order. You can also buy coarse-ground grits, country-milled cornmeal, hogshead cheese, liver pudding, cracklings, and specially cured hams. This friendly store, which is on the National Register of Historic Places, is also a sightseeing attraction with self-guided tours. It's open Monday through Friday from 8am to 6pm, Saturday from 8am to 5pm.

OUTDOOR ACTIVITIES & SPECTATOR SPORTS

BIKING & IN-LINE SKATING The 16-mile **Tallahassee–St. Marks Historic Railroad Trail State Park** (✆ **850/922-6007;** www.dep.state.fl.us/gwt/guide/regions/panhandleeast/trails/tallahassee_stmarks.htm) is the city's most popular bike route. Constructed with the financial assistance of wealthy Panhandle cotton-plantation owners and merchants, this was Florida's oldest railroad, functioning from 1837 to 1984. Cotton and other products were transported from Tallahassee to St. Marks for shipment to other cities. In recent years, the tracks were removed and 16 miles of the historic trail improved for joggers, hikers, bicyclists, and horseback riders. A paved parking lot is at the north entrance, on Woodville Highway (Fla. 363), just south of Southeast Capital Circle. See "Side Trips from Tallahassee," beginning on p. 632, for more information on what you can see in the St. Marks area.

The **Apalachicola National Forest** (p. 634) also has extensive mountain-biking trails, and there are 5.5 miles of trails at **Maclay State Gardens** (p. 627).

GOLF Play golf at outstanding Hilaman Park, 2737 Blair Stone Rd., where the **Hilaman Park Municipal Golf Course** (✆ **850/891-3935** for information and fees) features 18 holes (par 72), a driving range, racquetball and squash courts, and a pool. Rental equipment is available at the club, and there's a restaurant, too. Compared with most courses in Florida, greens fees are a steal: about $27 on weekdays and $38 on weekends, including cart. The park also includes the **Jake Gaither Municipal Golf Course,** at Bragg and Pasco streets (✆ **850/891-3942**), with a 9-hole, par-35 fairway and a pro shop. Call for fees.

The leading golf course is at the **Killearn Country Club and Inn** (✆ **800/476-4101** or 850/893-2186), which once hosted the Sprint Classic. Moss-draped oaks enhance the beautiful 27-hole championship course, which is for members with reciprocal privileges only. Call for fees.

For course information, go to www.golf.com or www.floridagolfing.com; or call the **Florida Sports Foundation** (✆ **850/488-8347**) or **Teebone Golfing** (✆ **866/833-2663**).

SPECTATOR SPORTS Tallahassee succumbs to football frenzy whenever the perennially powerful Seminoles of **Florida State University (FSU)** take to the gridiron. Call ✆ **888/378-6653** or 850/644-1830, or go to www.seminoles.com, well in advance, for tickets. Even when the Seminoles play on the road, everything except Tallahassee's many sports bars comes to a stop while fans watch the games on TV.

The **Florida A&M University (FAMU)** Rattlers are cheered on by the school's high-stepping, world-famous Marching 100 Band. Call ✆ **850/599-3230** or check http://thefamurattlers.cstv.com for FAMU schedules and tickets.

Both FSU and FAMU have seasonal basketball, baseball, tennis, and track schedules. Call the numbers above for information.

WHERE TO STAY

There is no high or low season here, but every hotel and motel for miles around is completely booked during FSU and FAMU football weekends from September to November, at graduation in May, and, to a far lesser degree, weekdays during the 60-day legislative session that begins in March. Reserve well in advance—or you may have to stay 60 miles or more from the city. For the game schedules, call FSU or FAMU (see "Spectator Sports," above).

Most hotels are concentrated in three areas: in downtown Tallahassee; north of downtown, along North Monroe Street, at exit 199 off I-10 (where you'll find most chains); and along Apalachee Parkway, east of downtown.

Tax on all hotel and campground bills is 4% in Leon County.

Cabot Lodge North (Value) It looks like a random motel, really, but look closer: There's charm to be found here. A clapboard plantation-style house with a tin roof and a wraparound porch provides Southern country charm that distinguishes this friendly motel from its nearby competitors. Guests can relax in rockers on the porch or on comfy sofas by the fireplace in the living room. Although the guest rooms in the two-story buildings out back don't hold up their end of the atmosphere factor, they're still quite satisfactory at these rates, and they give quick access to the outdoor pool. Guests can also enjoy a complimentary continental breakfast buffet and evening cocktails.

2735 N. Monroe St., Tallahassee, FL 32303. ✆ **800/223-1964** or 850/386-8880. Fax 850/386-4254. www.cabotlodgenorthmonroe.com. 160 units. $73–$84 double. Rates include continental breakfast and evening reception. AE, DC, DISC, MC, V. **Amenities:** Outdoor pool; access to nearby health club; free Wi-Fi; laundry service. *In room:* A/C, TV, dataport, coffeemaker, hair dryer, iron, free local calls.

DoubleTree Hotel Most of the media reporters covering the Bush-Gore 2000 election case before the Florida Supreme Court stayed at this 16-story hotel, one of the tallest buildings in town. The best thing about it is the location, just 2 blocks north of the Capitol Building at Park Avenue, as well as the views from the spacious rooms, especially those on the upper floors. It's usually booked solid by politicians and lobbyists during legislative sessions from March to May.

101 S. Adams St., Tallahassee, FL 32301. ✆ **800/222-8733** or 850/224-5000. Fax 850/513-9516. 243 units. Winter $159–$179 double; summer $189–$319 double. AE, DC, DISC, MC, V. **Amenities:** Restaurant; bar; outdoor pool; exercise room; limited room service; laundry service; concierge-level rooms. *In room:* A/C, TV, dataport, coffeemaker, hair dryer, iron.

Governor's Inn ★★ Legislators, lobbyists, groupies, and Southern gentry stay at this elegantly furnished inn, just half a block north of the Old Capitol in the Adams Street Commons historic district. It's very old-school Washington, D.C. The building was once a livery stable, and part of its original architecture has been preserved, including the impressive beams. The guest rooms are distinctive, with four-poster beds, black-oak writing desks, rock-maple armoires, and antique accouterments. Of the suites, each one named for a Florida governor, one has a whirlpool tub; another has a loft bedroom with wood-burning fireplace. Complimentary continental breakfast and afternoon cocktails are served in the pine-paneled Florida Room, and a restaurant across the street provides limited room service. Hang out in the bar area and eavesdrop on amusing political banter. The staff here is superfriendly and helpful. Note that all the rooms are nonsmoking.

209 S. Adams St., Tallahassee, FL 32301. ✆ **800/342-7717** or 850/681-6855. Fax 850/222-3105. www.thegovinn.com. 41 units. $169–$189 double; $229–$319 suite. Rates include continental breakfast and evening cocktails. AE, DC, DISC, MC, V. Free valet parking. **Amenities:** Complimentary access to nearby health club; free Wi-Fi; limited room service; laundry service. *In room:* A/C, flatscreen TV, dataport, minifridge.

Quality Inn & Suites (Value) In contrast to most Quality Inns, this property loses some of the motel-chain-gang feel in favor of a classy, marble-lined lobby and guest rooms furnished with sofas and reclining wing chairs. A complimentary continental breakfast is served in a lounge with views of the inn's pool, and guests can partake of a free wine bar Monday through Thursday evenings. A nearby restaurant will deliver food, and several fast-food and family-style eateries are within a short walk.

2020 Apalachee Pkwy., Tallahassee, FL 32301. ✆ **800/228-5151** or 850/877-4437. Fax 850/878-9964. www.qualityinn.com. 100 units. $100–$159 double; $169–$189 suite. Rates include full breakfast and evening drinks. AE, DC, DISC, MC, V. **Amenities:** Outdoor pool; access to nearby health club; Jacuzzi; business center; limited room service; laundry service. *In room:* A/C, TV, dataport, fridge, coffeemaker, hair dryer, iron, safe.

WHERE TO DINE

Anthony's ★ SOUTHERN ITALIAN Locals flock to Dick Anthony's elegantly relaxed trattoria, which supplies the city's best Italian cuisine. Among his specialties is *pesce Venezia,* spinach fettuccine tossed in a cream sauce with scallops, crab, and fish.

Chicken piccata and chicken San Marino are also favorites, and Dick's thick, juicy steaks are always popular with beef eaters. A wall-size wine cupboard has choices from Italy and the United States by the bottle or the glass. Espresso pie leads the dessert menu.

1950 Thomasville Rd., at Bradford Rd., in the Betton Place Shops. ✆ **850/224-1447.** www.anthonysitalianrestaurant.net. Reservations recommended. Main courses $14–$34. AE, DC, DISC, MC, V. Daily 5–9pm.

Bahn Thai THAI/CANTONESE Lamoi (Sue) Snyder and progeny have been serving the spicy cuisine of her native Thailand at this storefront since 1979. In deference to local Southerners, who may never have sampled anything spicier than cheese grits, much of her menu is devoted to mild Cantonese-style Chinese dishes. More adventurous diners, however, flock here to order such authentic tongue-burners as *yon voon-sen,* a combination of shrimp, chicken, bean threads, onions, lemongrass, ground peanuts, and the obligatory chili peppers. Sue's specialty is a deliciously sweet, slightly gingered version of Penang curry. You can ask her to turn down the heat in her other Thai dishes. Come at lunch and sample everything from the all-you-can-eat buffet—a real bargain.

1319 S. Monroe St. (btw. Oakland Ave. and Harrison St.). ✆ **850/224-4765.** Main courses $6–$15; lunch buffet $7.50. DISC, MC, V. Mon–Thurs 11am–2:30pm and 5–10pm; Fri 11am–2:30pm and 5–10:30pm; Sat 5–10:30pm.

Barnacle Bill's Seafood Restaurant SEAFOOD There's always plenty of action at this noisy, casual spot, a favorite of the downtown crowd, including journalists, bureaucrats, and politicians. Freshly shucked Apalachicola oysters are the stars at the enormous raw bar, but the menu also offers a mélange of seafood. The cooking is simple and usually done by Florida State University students working part-time jobs. Best bets are chargrilled mahimahi, tuna, amberjack, and grouper. For a smoked sensation, try the mahimahi and amberjack cured on the premises. A downstairs bar serves the regular seafood items, plus sushi, deli sandwiches, and salads.

1830 N. Monroe St. (north of Tharpe St.). ✆ **850/385-8734.** www.barnaclebills.com. Main courses $8–$18; sandwiches and salads $5–$10. AE, DC, DISC, MC, V. Sun–Thurs 11am–11pm; Fri–Sat 11am–midnight.

Chez Pierre ★★ TRADITIONAL FRENCH You become an instant Francophile in Florida at this chic restaurant, situated in a beautifully restored 1920s brick home. French-born chef Eric Favier and his American wife and partner, Karen Cooley, serve traditional French cuisine either inside the house or out on a large deck partly shaded by live oaks draped with Spanish moss. Opening onto the deck, a bistro-style bar provides a light-fare menu between lunch and dinner. Among the winning daily specials are rack of lamb, a version of Provençal-style ratatouille, Kobe beef with black truffle butter, and crab cakes with a luscious mustard-and-thyme demi glace. French table wines are moderately priced, and California house wines are also served. Live music regularly accompanies dining. Smoking is permitted on the front porch, where you can enjoy stogies and brandy while lounging in wicker chairs. Book as early as possible for Bastille Day (July 14), which sees a grand fete here.

1215 Thomasville Rd. (at 6th Ave.). ✆ **850/222-0936.** www.chezpierre.com. Reservations recommended. Main courses $16–$29. AE, DC, DISC, MC, V. Mon–Sat 11am–10pm; Sun 11am–2:30pm and 6–9pm.

Kool Beanz Cafe ★★ CARIBBEAN The coolest cafe in town, this noisy emporium of trendy cooking draws lots of patrons in their late 20s and early 30s, who appreciate the exciting blends of flavors. The joint is dimly lit but painted in bright pastels from the

Caribbean. You'll find many island-style items on the constantly changing menu, including Jamaican jerk grouper served with black beans, rice, and a sweet tropical-fruit relish. You may want to get here early: The more inventive items, such as the seared rare tuna crusted with spice and served with a terrific roasted-peanut sauce, will sell out early, as will the curried lamb shank and the pork tenderloin marinated with orange molasses.

921 Thomasville Rd. (at Williams St.). © **850/224-2466.** www.koolbeanz-cafe.com. Main courses $15–$29. AE, DISC, MC, V. Mon–Fri 11am–2:30pm and 5:30–10pm; Sat 5:30–10pm.

TALLAHASSEE AFTER DARK

Check the "Limelight" section of Friday's *Tallahassee Democrat* (www.tallahasseedemocrat.com) for weekend entertainment listings.

As a college town, Tallahassee has numerous pubs and clubs with live dance music, not to mention a multitude of sports bars. Pick up a copy of *Break* and other entertainment tabloids at **Barnacle Bill's Seafood Restaurant** (see above) or other venues.

West Tennessee Street is where you'll find most of the happening bars in town. One of the best bars in Tallahassee is **Bullwinkle's Saloon,** 620 W. Tennessee St. (© **850/224-0651;** www.bullwinklessaloon.net), a capital institution with a laid-back vibe and even a Thirsty Moose Club, in which members never pay a cover and drink free every Wednesday and Friday. For live music, **Floyd's Music Store,** 666 W. Tennessee St. (© **850/222-3506;** www.floydsmusicstore.com), features local and national bands and, for the daring, a mosh pit that fills up quickly, so get here early.

The major performing-arts venue is the **Tallahassee–Leon County Civic Center,** 505 W. Pensacola St. (© **800/322-3602** or 850/222-0400; www.tlccc.org), which features a Broadway series, concerts, and sporting events including Florida State University (FSU) collegiate basketball games. Special concerts are presented by the **Tallahassee Symphony Orchestra** (www.tsolive.org) at FSU Ruby Diamond Auditorium, at College Avenue and Copeland Street (© **850/224-0461**). The **FSU Mainstage/School of Theatre,** at the Fine Arts Building, Call and Copeland streets (© **850/644-6500**), presents excellent productions, from classic dramas to comedies.

SIDE TRIPS FROM TALLAHASSEE

The following excursions are generally on the way to Apalachicola, so if you're headed that way, plan to make a detour or two.

Wakulla Springs ★★

The world's largest and deepest freshwater spring is 15 miles south of Tallahassee in the 2,860-acre **Edward W. Ball Wakulla Springs State Park ★★**, on Florida 267 just east of its junction with Florida 61. Ball, a financier who administered the du Pont estate, turned the springs and the moss-draped surrounding forest into a preservation area. Divers have mapped an underwater cave system extending more than 6,000 feet back from the spring's mouth. Wakulla has been known to dispense an amazing 14,325 gallons per second of water at certain times. Mastodon bones, including those of Herman, now in Tallahassee's Museum of Florida History, were found in the caves. The 1930s Tarzan movies, starring Johnny Weissmuller, were also filmed here.

A free 10-minute orientation movie is shown in the park's theater at the waterfront. You can hike or bike along the nature trails, and swimming is allowed in designated areas. ***Note:*** It's important to observe swimming rules as alligators are present here.

If the spring water is clear enough, 30-minute glass-bottom-boat sightseeing trips depart every 45 minutes daily, from 9:45am to 5pm during daylight saving time, and from 9:15am to 4:30pm the rest of the year. Even if the water is murky, you're likely to see alligators, birds, and other wildlife on 30-minute riverboat cruises, which operate during these same hours. Either boat ride costs $6 for adults, $4 for children 12 and under.

Entrance fees to the park are $4 per vehicle with up to eight passengers, $1 per pedestrian or bicyclist. The park is open daily from 8am to dusk. For more information, contact the park at 550 Wakulla Springs Dr., Wakulla Springs, FL 32305 (✆ **850/224-5950;** www.floridastateparks.org/wakullasprings).

Where to Stay & Dine

Wakulla Springs Lodge ★ On the shores of Wakulla Springs, this dated but charming lodge is distinctive for its magnificent Spanish architecture and ornate Old World furnishings, such as rare Spanish tiles, black-granite tables, marble floors, and ceiling beams painted with Florida scenes by a German artist (supposedly Kaiser Wilhelm's court painter). The guest rooms are simple by today's standards (you'll get a marble bathroom and phone, but no TV). By all means, ask for a room in the front so you'll have a lake view. You don't have to be a lodge guest to enjoy the warm, smoky ambience of the great lobby, with its huge stone fireplace and arched windows looking onto the springs, or to enjoy reasonably priced meals featuring Southern cuisine in the lovely Ball Room (reservations recommended). The fountain (a 60-ft.-long marble drugstore-style counter for old-fashioned ice-cream sodas) provides snacks and sandwiches. The only things missing here are taxidermic specimens—no boar, deer, or bear heads perched high on the walls.

550 Wakulla Park Dr, Wakulla Springs, FL 32305. ✆ **850/224-5950.** Fax 850/561-7251. www.wakullacounty.org/wakulla-24.htm. 27 units. $85–$105 double. AE, DISC, MC, V. **Amenities:** Restaurant. *In room:* A/C.

The St. Marks Area

Rich history lives in the area around the little village of **St. Marks,** 18 miles south of the capital at the end of both Florida 363 and the Tallahassee–St. Marks Historic Railroad Trail State Park (p. 628).

After marching overland from Tampa Bay in 1528, the Spanish conquistador Panfilo de Narvaez and 300 men arrived at this strategic point at the confluence of the St. Marks and Wakulla rivers near the Gulf of Mexico. Because their only avenue back to Spain was by sea, they built and launched the first ships made by Europeans in the New World. Some 11 years later, Hernando de Soto and his 600 men arrived here after following Narvaez's route from Tampa. They marked the harbor entrance by hanging banners in the trees, then moved inland. Two wooden forts were built here, one in 1679 and one in 1718, and a stone version was begun in 1739. The fort shifted among Spanish, British, and Native American hands until Gen. Andrew Jackson took it away from the Spanish in 1819.

Parts of the old Spanish bastion wall and Confederate earthworks built during the Civil War are in the **San Marcos de Apalachee Historic State Park,** reached by turning right at the end of Florida 363 in St. Marks and following the paved road. A museum built on the foundation of the old marine hospital contains exhibits and artifacts covering the area's history. The site is open Thursday through Monday from 9am to 5pm (closed New Year's Day, Thanksgiving, and Christmas). Entrance to the site is free; admission to the museum costs $1 (free for children 6 and under). For more information, contact the site at 1022 DeSoto Park Dr., Tallahassee, FL 32301 (✆ **850/922-6007;** www.florida stateparks.org/sanmarcos).

De Soto's men marked the harbor entrance in what is now the **St. Marks Lighthouse and National Wildlife Refuge** ★, P.O. Box 68, St. Marks, FL 32355 (✆ **850/925-6121**). Operated by the U.S. Fish and Wildlife Service, this 65,000-acre preserve occupies much of the coast from the Aucilla River east of St. Marks to the Ochlockonee River west of Panacea; it's home to more species of birds than anyplace else in Florida except the Everglades. The visitor center is 3½ miles south of U.S. 98 on Lighthouse Road (Fla. 59); turn south off U.S. 98 at Newport, about 2 miles east of St. Marks. Stop at the center for self-guided tour maps of the roads and hiking trails, some built atop levees running through the marshland.

Apalachicola National Forest

The largest of Florida's three national forests, this huge preserve encompasses 600,000 acres stretching from Tallahassee's outskirts southward to the Gulf Coast and westward some 70 miles to the Apalachicola River. Included is a variety of woodlands, rivers, streams, lakes, and caves populated by a host of wildlife. There are picnic areas with sheltered tables and grills, canoe and mountain-bike trails, campgrounds with tent and RV sites, and a number of other facilities, some of them especially designed for visitors with disabilities.

The **Leon Sinks Area** is closest to Tallahassee, 5½ miles south of Southeast Capital Circle on U.S. 319 near the Leon-Wakulla county line. Nature trails and boardwalks lead from one sinkhole (a lake formed when water erodes the underlying limestone) to another. The trails are open daily from 8am to 8pm.

A necessary stop before heading into this wilderness is the visitor center at the **Wakulla Area Ranger District,** 57 Taft Dr., Crawfordville, FL 32327 (✆ **850/926-3561;** fax 850/926-1904), which provides information and sells topographical and canoe trail maps. The station is off U.S. 319, about 20 miles south of Tallahassee and 2 miles north of Crawfordville. It's open Monday through Thursday from 8am to 4:30pm, Friday from 8am to 4pm.

Appendix: Fast Facts, Toll-Free Numbers & Websites

1 FAST FACTS: FLORIDA

AMERICAN EXPRESS There are a number of American Express offices in Florida. Call ✆ **800/528-4800** or go to www.americanexpress.com for the location nearest you.

ATM NETWORKS ATMs are as ubiquitous in Florida as palm trees. They're found at nearly every street corner, main shopping area, and, in most cases, supermarkets and even convenience stores. See "Money & Costs," p. 48.

CURRENCY The most common bills are the $1 (a "buck"), $5, $10, and $20 denominations. There are also $2 bills (seldom encountered), $50 bills, and $100 bills (the last two are usually not welcome as payment for small purchases).

Coins come in seven denominations: 1¢ (1 cent, or a penny); 5¢ (5 cents, or a nickel); 10¢ (10 cents, or a dime); 25¢ (25 cents, or a quarter); 50¢ (50 cents, or a half dollar); the gold-colored Sacagawea coin, worth $1; the $1 presidential coins that debuted in 2007; and the rare silver dollar.

For additional information see "Money & Costs," p. 48.

ELECTRICITY Like Canada, the United States uses 110 to 120 volts AC (60 cycles), compared to 220 to 240 volts AC (50 cycles) in most of Europe, Australia, and New Zealand. Downward converters that change 220 to 240 volts to 110 to 120 volts are difficult to find in the United States, so bring one with you.

EMBASSIES & CONSULATES All embassies are located in the nation's capital, Washington, D.C. Some consulates are located in major U.S. cities, and most nations have a mission to the United Nations in New York City. If your country isn't listed below, call for directory information in Washington, D.C. (✆ **202/555-1212**), or log on to **www.embassy.org/embassies**.

The embassy of **Australia** is at 1601 Massachusetts Ave. NW, Washington, DC 20036 (✆ **202/797-3000;** www.austemb.org). There are consulates in New York, Honolulu, Houston, Los Angeles, and San Francisco.

The embassy of **Canada** is at 501 Pennsylvania Ave. NW, Washington, DC 20001 (✆ **202/682-1740;** www.canadianembassy.org). Other Canadian consulates are in Buffalo (New York), Detroit, Los Angeles, New York, and Seattle.

The embassy of **Ireland** is at 2234 Massachusetts Ave. NW, Washington, DC 20008 (✆ **202/462-3939;** www.irelandemb.org). Irish consulates are in Boston, Chicago, New York, San Francisco, and other cities. See their website for a complete listing.

The embassy of **New Zealand** is at 37 Observatory Circle NW, Washington, DC 20008 (✆ **202/328-4800;** www.nzemb.org). New Zealand consulates are in Los Angeles, Salt Lake City, San Francisco, and Seattle.

The embassy of the **United Kingdom** is at 3100 Massachusetts Ave. NW, Washington, DC 20008 (✆ **202/588-7800;** www.britainusa.com). Other British consulates are in Atlanta, Boston, Chicago, Cleveland, Houston, Los Angeles, New York, San Francisco, and Seattle.

EMERGENCIES To reach the police, ambulance, or fire department, dial ✆ **911** from any phone. No coins are needed.

HOLIDAYS Banks, government offices, post offices, and many stores, restaurants, and museums are closed on the following legal national holidays: January 1 (New Year's Day), the third Monday in January (Martin Luther King Day), the third Monday in February (Presidents' Day), the last Monday in May (Memorial Day), July 4 (Independence Day), the first Monday in September (Labor Day), the second Monday in October (Columbus Day), November 11 (Veterans Day/Armistice Day), the fourth Thursday in November (Thanksgiving Day), and December 25 (Christmas Day). The Tuesday after the first Monday in November is Election Day, a federal government holiday in presidential-election years (held every 4 years, and next in 2012).

For more information on holidays see "Calendar of Events" in chapter 3.

MAIL Domestic postage rates are 28¢ for a postcard and 44¢ for a letter. For international mail, a first-class letter of up to 1 ounce and a first-class postcard each cost 90¢ (69¢ to Canada and Mexico). For more information go to **www.usps.com** and click on "Calculate Postage."

If you aren't sure what your address will be in the United States, mail can be sent to you, in your name, c/o General Delivery at the main post office of the city or region where you expect to be. (Call ✆ **800/275-8777** for information on the nearest post office.) The addressee must pick up mail in person and must produce proof of identity (driver's license, passport, and so on). Most post offices will hold your mail for as long as 1 month and are open Monday to Friday from 8am to 6pm and Saturday from 9am to 3pm.

Always include zip codes when mailing items in the U.S. If you don't know your zip code, visit www.usps.com/zip4.

PASSPORTS **For Residents of Australia:** You can pick up an application from your local post office or any branch of Passports Australia, but you must schedule an interview at the passport office to present your application materials. Call the **Australian Passport Information Service** at ✆ **131-232,** or visit the government website at www.passports.gov.au.

For Residents of Canada: Passport applications are available at travel agencies throughout Canada or from the central **Passport Office,** Department of Foreign Affairs and International Trade, Ottawa, ON K1A 0G3 (✆ **800/567-6868;** www.ppt.gc.ca). ***Note:*** Canadian children who travel must have their own passport. However, if you hold a valid Canadian passport issued before December 11, 2001, that bears the name of your child, the passport remains valid for you and your child until it expires.

For Residents of Ireland: You can apply for a 10-year passport at the **Passport Office,** Setanta Centre, Molesworth Street, Dublin 2 (✆ **01/671-1633;** www.irlgov.ie/iveagh). Those under age 18 and over 65 must apply for a 3-year passport. You can also apply at 1A South Mall, Cork (✆ **021/272-525**), or at most main post offices.

For Residents of New Zealand: You can pick up a passport application at any New Zealand Passports Office or download it from their website. Contact the

Passports Office at ✆ **0800/225-050** in New Zealand, or 04/474-8100; or log on to www.passports.govt.nz.

For Residents of the United Kingdom: To pick up an application for a standard 10-year passport (5-year passport for children under 16), visit your nearest passport office, major post office, or travel agency, or contact the **United Kingdom Passport Service** at ✆ **0870/521-0410;** or search its website at www.ukpa.gov.uk.

POLICE To reach the police, dial ✆ **911** from any phone. No coins are needed.

TAXES The United States has no value-added tax (VAT) or other indirect tax at the national level. Every state, county, and city may levy its own local tax on all purchases, including hotel and restaurant checks and airline tickets. These taxes will not appear on price tags. The Florida state sales tax is 6%. Many municipalities add 1% or more to that, and most levy a special tax on hotel and restaurant bills. In general, expect at least 9% to be added to your final hotel bill. There are also hefty taxes on rental cars here (see "Getting There & Getting Around," in chapter 3).

TIME The Florida peninsula observes Eastern Standard Time, but most of the Panhandle, west of the Apalachicola River, is on Central Standard Time, 1 hour behind the rest of the state.

Daylight saving time is in effect from 1am on the second Sunday in March to 1am on the first Sunday in November, except in Arizona, Hawaii, the U.S. Virgin Islands, and Puerto Rico. Daylight saving time moves the clock 1 hour ahead of standard time.

TIPPING Tips are a very important part of certain workers' income, and gratuities are the standard way of showing appreciation for services provided. (Tipping is certainly not compulsory if the service is poor!) In hotels, tip **bellhops** at least $1 per bag ($2–$3 if you have a lot of luggage) and tip the **chamber staff** $1 to $2 per day (more if you've left a disaster area for him or her to clean up). Tip the **doorman** or **concierge** only if he or she has provided you with some specific service (for example, calling a cab for you or obtaining difficult-to-get theater tickets). Tip the **valet-parking attendant** $1 every time you get your car.

In restaurants, bars, and nightclubs, tip **service staff** 15% to 20% of the check, tip **bartenders** 10% to 15%, tip **checkroom attendants** $1 per garment, and tip **valet-parking attendants** $1 when you retrieve your vehicle.

As for other service personnel, tip **cab drivers** 15% of the fare; tip **skycaps** at airports at least $1 per bag ($2–$3 if you have a lot of luggage); and tip **hairdressers** and **barbers** 15% to 20%.

TOILETS You won't find public toilets or "restrooms" on the streets in most U.S. cities but they can be found in hotel lobbies, bars, restaurants, museums, department stores, railway and bus stations, and service stations. Large hotels and fast-food restaurants are often the best bet for clean facilities. If possible, avoid the toilets at parks and beaches, which tend to be dirty; some may be unsafe. Restaurants and bars in resorts or heavily visited areas may reserve their restrooms for patrons.

USEFUL PHONE NUMBERS U.S. Department of State Travel Advisory: ✆ **202/647-5225** (manned 24 hr.)

U.S. Passport Agency: ✆ **202/647-0518**

U.S. Centers for Disease Control International Traveler's Hotline: ✆ **404/332-4559**

VISAS For information about U.S. visas go to **http://travel.state.gov** and click on "Visas," or go to one of the following websites:

Australian citizens can obtain up-to-date visa information from the **U.S. Embassy Canberra,** Moonah Place, Yarralumla, ACT 2600 (✆ **02/6214-5600**) or by checking the U.S. Diplomatic Mission's website at **http://usembassy-australia.state.gov/consular**.

British subjects can obtain up-to-date visa information by calling the **U.S. Embassy Visa Information Line** (✆ **0891/200-290**) or by visiting the "Visas to the U.S." section of the American Embassy London's website at **www.usembassy.org.uk**.

Irish citizens can obtain up-to-date visa information through the **Embassy of the USA Dublin,** 42 Elgin Rd., Dublin 4, Ireland (✆ **353/1-668-8777**), or by checking the "Visas to the U.S." section of the website at **http://dublin.usembassy.gov**.

Citizens of **New Zealand** can obtain up-to-date visa information by contacting the **U.S. Embassy New Zealand,** 29 Fitzherbert Terrace, Thorndon, Wellington (✆ **644/472-2068**), or get the information directly from the website at **http://wellington.usembassy.gov**.

WEATHER Hurricane season runs June through November. For an up-to-date recording of current weather conditions and forecasts, call ✆ **305/229-4522.** Online, you can check www.intellicast.com or www.weather.com.

2 TOLL-FREE NUMBERS & WEBSITES

MAJOR U.S. AIRLINES

(*flies internationally as well)

Alaska Airlines/Horizon Air
✆ 800/252-7522
www.alaskaair.com

American Airlines*
✆ 800/433-7300 (in U.S. or Canada)
✆ 020/7365-0777 (in U.K.)
www.aa.com

Cape Air
✆ 800/352-0714
www.flycapeair.com

Collins Aviation
✆ 305/743-4222
www.flyparadiseair.com

Continental Airlines*
✆ 800/523-3273 (in U.S. or Canada)
✆ 084/5607-6760 (in U.K.)
www.continental.com

Delta Air Lines*
✆ 800/221-1212 (in U.S. or Canada)
✆ 084/5600-0950 (in U.K.)
www.delta.com

Frontier Airlines
✆ 800/432-1359
www.frontierairlines.com

Hawaiian Airlines*
✆ 800/367-5320 (in U.S. and Canada)
www.hawaiianair.com

JetBlue
✆ 800/538-2583 (in U.S.)
✆ 080/1365-2525 (in U.K. or Canada)
www.jetblue.com

Midwest Airlines
✆ 800/452-2022
www.midwestairlines.com

Nantucket Airlines
✆ 800/635-8787
www.nantucketairlines.com

North American Airlines*
✆ 800/371-6297
www.flynaa.com

Northwest Airlines
✆ 800/225-2525 (in U.S.)
✆ 870/0507-4074 (in U.K.)
www.flynaa.com

PenAir
✆ 800/448-4226 (in U.S.)
www.penair.com

United Airlines*
✆ 800/864-8331 (in U.S. and Canada)
✆ 084/5844-4777 in U.K.
www.united.com

US Airways*
✆ 800/428-4322 (in U.S. and Canada)
✆ 084/5600-3300 (in U.K.)
www.usairways.com

Virgin America*
✆ 877/359-8474
www.virginamerica.com

MAJOR INTERNATIONAL AIRLINES

Air France
✆ 800/237-2747 (in U.S.)
✆ 800/375-8723 (in U.S. and Canada)
✆ 087/0142-4343 (in U.K.)
www.airfrance.com

Air New Zealand
✆ 800/262-1234 (in U.S.)
✆ 800/663-5494 (in Canada)
✆ 0800/028-4149 (in U.K.)
www.airnewzealand.com

Alitalia
✆ 800/223-5730 (in U.S.)
✆ 087/0608-6003 (in U.K.)
✆ 800/361-8336 (in Canada)
www.alitalia.com

British Airways
✆ 800/247-9297 (in U.S. and Canada)
✆ 087/0850-9850 (in U.K.)
www.british-airways.com

Caribbean Airlines (formerly BWIA)
✆ 800/920-4225 (in U.S. and Canada)
✆ 084/5362 4225 (in U.K.)
www.caribbean-airlines.com

Cubana
✆ 020/7538-5933 (in U.K.)
✆ 888/667-1222 (in Canada)
www.cubana.cu

Iberia Airlines
✆ 800/722-4642 (in U.S. and Canada)
✆ 087/0609-0500 (in U.K.)
www.iberia.com

Japan Airlines
✆ 012/025-5931 (international)
www.jal.co.jp

Korean Air
✆ 800/438-5000 (in U.S. and Canada)
✆ 0800/413-000 (in U.K.)
www.koreanair.com

LAN Airlines
✆ 866/435-9526 (in U.S.)
✆ 305/670-9999 (in other countries)
www.lan.com

Lufthansa
✆ 800/399-5838 (in U.S.)
✆ 800/563-5954 (in Canada)
✆ 087/0837-7747 (in U.K.)
www.lufthansa.com

Philippine Airlines
✆ 800/I-Fly-Pal (800/435-9725; in U.S. and Canada)
✆ 632/855-8888 (in Philippines)
www.philippineairlines.com

Qantas Airways
✆ 800/227-4500 (in U.S.)
✆ 084/5774-7767 (in Canada or U.K.)
✆ 13-13-13 (in Australia)
www.qantas.com

South African Airways
✆ 271/1978-5313 (international)
✆ 086/1-FLYSAA (086/135-9122; in South Africa)
www.flysaa.com

Swiss Air
✆ 877/359-7947 (in U.S. and Canada)
✆ 084/5601-0956 (in U.K.)
www.swiss.com

TACA
✆ 800/535-8780 (in U.S.)
✆ 800/722-TACA (722-8222; in Canada)
✆ 087/0241-0340 (in U.K.)
✆ 503/2267-8222 (in El Salvador)

BUDGET AIRLINES

Aegean Airlines
© 210/626-1000 (in U.S., Canada, and U.K.)
www.aegeanair.com

Aer Lingus
© 800/474-7424 (in U.S. and Canada)
© 087/0876-5000 (in U.K.)
www.aerlingus.com

Aero California
© 800/237-6225 (in U.S. and Mexico)
www.aerocalifornia.com.mx

Air Berlin
© 087/1500-0737 (in U.K.)
© 018/0573-7800 (in Germany)
© 180/573-7800 (all others)
www.airberlin.com

AirTran Airways
© 800/247-8726
www.airtran.com

Avolar
© 888/3-AVOLAR (888/326-8527; in U.S.)
© 086/6370-4065 (in U.K.)
© 800/21-AVOLAR (800/326-8527; in Mexico)
www.avolar.com.mx

BMI Baby
© 870/126-6726 (in U.S.)
© 087/1224-0224 (in U.K.)
www.bmibaby.com

Click Mexicana
© 800/11-CLICK (800/112-5425; international)
© 800/112-5425 (in Mexico)
www.clickmx.com

easyJet
© 870/600-0000 (in U.S.)
© 090/5560-7777 (in U.K.)
www.easyjet.com

Frontier Airlines
© 800/432-1359
www.frontierairlines.com

go! (Hawaii based)
© 888/435-9462
www.iflygo.com

Interjet
© 800/101-2345
www.interjet.com.mx

JetBlue
© 800/538-2583 (in U.S.)
© 801/365-2525 (in U.K. and Canada)
www.jetblue.com

Jetstar Airways (Australia)
© 866/397-8170
www.jetstar.com

Ryanair
© 353/1248-0856 (for U.S.)
© 087/1246-0000 (in U.K.)
© 081/830-3030 (in Ireland)
www.ryanair.com

Southwest Airlines
© 800/435-9792 (in U.S., U.K., and Canada)
www.southwest.com

Spirit Airlines
© 800/772-7117
www.spiritair.com

Volaris
© 866/988-3527
© 800/7-VOLARIS (800/786-5274; in Mexico)
www.volaris.com.mx

WestJet
© 800/538-5696 (in U.S. and Canada)
www.westjet.com

CAR-RENTAL AGENCIES

Alamo
© 800/GO-ALAMO (800/462-5266)
www.alamo.com

Avis
© 800/331-1212 (in U.S. and Canada)
© 084/4581-8181 (in U.K.)
www.avis.com

Budget
✆ 800/527-0700 (in U.S.)
✆ 087/0156-5656 (in U.K.)
✆ 800/268-8900 (in Canada)
www.budget.com

Dollar
✆ 800/800-4000 (in U.S.)
✆ 080/8234-7524 (in U.K.)
✆ 800/848-8268 (in Canada)
www.dollar.com

Hertz
✆ 800/645-3131
✆ 800/654-3001 (international)
www.hertz.com

National
✆ 800/CAR-RENT (800/227-7368)
www.nationalcar.com

Payless
✆ 800/PAYLESS (800/729-5377)
www.paylesscarrental.com

Thrifty
✆ 800/367-2277
✆ 918/669-2168 (international)
www.thrifty.com

MAJOR HOTEL & MOTEL CHAINS

Best Western International
✆ 800/780-7234 (in U.S. and Canada)
✆ 0800/393-130 (in U.K.)
www.bestwestern.com

Clarion Hotels
✆ 800/CLARION (252-7466) or 877/424-6423 (in U.S. and Canada)
✆ 0800/444-444 (in U.K.)
www.clarionhotel.com

Comfort Inns & Suites
✆ 800/228-5150
✆ 0800/444-444 (in U.K.)
www.comfortinn.com

Courtyard by Marriott
✆ 888/236-2427 (in U.S.)
✆ 0800/221-222 (in U.K.)
www.marriott.com/courtyard

Crowne Plaza Hotels
✆ 888/303-1746
www.crowneplaza.com

DoubleTree Hotels
✆ 800/222-TREE (800/222-8733; in U.S. and Canada)
✆ 087/0590-9090 (in U.K.)
www.doubletree.hilton.com

Four Seasons Hotels & Resorts
✆ 800/819-5053 (in U.S. and Canada)
✆ 0800/6488-6488 (in U.K.)
www.fourseasons.com

Hampton Inn Hotels
✆ 800/HAMPTON (800/426-4766)
www.hamptoninn.hilton.com

Hilton Hotels
✆ 800/HILTONS (800/445-8667; in U.S. and Canada)
✆ 087/0590-9090 (in U.K.)
www.hilton.com

Holiday Inn
✆ 800/315-2621 (in U.S. and Canada)
✆ 0800/405-060 (in U.K.)
www.holidayinn.com

Hyatt Hotels & Resorts
✆ 888/591-1234 (in U.S. and Canada)
✆ 084/5888-1234 (in U.K.)
www.hyatt.com

InterContinental Hotels & Resorts
✆ 800/424-6835 (in U.S. and Canada)
✆ 0800/1800-1800 (in U.K.)
www.intercontinental.com

Marriott Hotels
✆ 877/236-2427 (in U.S. and Canada)
✆ 0800/221-222 (in U.K.)
www.marriott.com

Quality Inn Hotels
✆ 877/424-6423 (in U.S. and Canada)
✆ 0800/444-444 (in U.K.)
www.qualityinn.com

Radisson Hotels & Resorts
✆ 888/201-1718 (in U.S. and Canada)
✆ 0800/374-411 (in U.K.)
www.radisson.com

Ramada
✆ 888/2-RAMADA (272-6232; in U.S. and Canada)
✆ 080/8100-0783 (in U.K.)
www.ramada.com

Residence Inn by Marriott
✆ 800/331-3131
✆ 800/221-222 (in U.K.)
www.marriott.com/residenceinn

Westin Hotels & Resorts
✆ 800/937-8461 (in U.S. and Canada)
✆ 0800/3259-5959 (in U.K.)
www.westin.com

INDEX

C

NOTES